English Law

English Law

Kenneth Smith

MSc(Econ), BCom, PhD, ACCS, FSS
of Lincoln's Inn, Barrister-at-Law
Late Head of the Department of Commerce and Management
Mid-Essex Technical College and School of Art

Denis J Keenan

LLB(Hons), FCIS, DMA, CertEd
of the Middle Temple, Barrister-at-Law
Formerly Head of Department of Business Studies and Law
Mid-Essex Technical College and School of Art

Sixth Edition by Denis J Keenan

Pitman

PITMAN PUBLISHING LIMITED
39 Parker Street, London WC2B 5PB

Associated Companies
Copp Clark Ltd, Toronto
Fearon–Pitman Publishers Inc, Belmont, California
Pitman Publishing New Zealand Ltd, Wellington
Pitman Publishing Pty Ltd, Melbourne

© Kenneth Smith and Denis J Keenan, 1963, 1966
© Denis J Keenan and Mrs K Smith, 1969, 1973, 1975, 1979

Sixth Edition 1979

Text set in 10/12 pt VIP Times
printed by photolithography and bound in Great Britain
at The Pitman Press, Bath

ISBN 0 273 01196 0

Contents

courts—Arbitration—The legal profession—Some important judicial officers.

Preface to sixth edition

This edition has been substantially rewritten and updated following the advice of many lecturers who have recommended the book for use by students over the years. The changes reflect the movement away from external examinations in the subject in favour of foundation courses in Law where the selection of material, both for the course and the examination, is more commonly under the control of the lecturers involved.

On the basis of advice received the chapters on Trusts and Succession have been omitted and a short chapter on general principles of Criminal Law included. It was also felt that the old chapter on the Courts of Law was too detailed and the new one confines itself to more basic material. Chapter 3 gives a different approach to criminal and civil procedure and attempts to set matters such as legal aid and the use of a jury into the context of a criminal and civil trial.

A section on the contract of employment has been included and there is additional material relating to the EEC appropriate, it is hoped, for students at foundation level. The rewriting has enabled the publishers to reset the book in a more open and readable style.

My thanks are due to the many lecturers who took the time and trouble to complete the publisher's questionnaires on suggestions for change and it is hoped that this edition is a reasonable response to the advice received.

There are a number of matters on which changes have been made since the typescript of this edition was submitted. The more important are as follows—

(*a*) the right of cross-examination at a public inquiry was upheld in *Nicholson* v. *Secretary of State for the Environment*, *The Times*, 6 August, 1977 on the basis that the denial of that right was a breach of natural justice (see p. 80).

(*b*) As regards the 'judicial review' referred to on page 83, the necessary procedural reforms have now been made to implement the Law Commission's proposals.

(*c*) The Lord Chancellor has exercised his power in regard to rights of audience in the County Court by legal executives. The County Courts (Right of Audience) Direction, 1978 allows Fellows of the Institute the right of audience in regard to an unopposed application for an adjournment and an application for judgment by consent where there is no question as to the applicant's entitlement to the judgment or its terms. (See p. 92.)

(*d*) The High Court in *First National Securities Ltd* v. *Jones*, *The Times*, 9 November, 1977 decided that a deed could still be valid even though in fact it was not sealed. (See p. 170.)

(*e*) The reader should also note that references to the ability of an occupier of land to exclude his liability for negligence referred to at pp 357, 358 and 359 must now be read in the light of the Unfair Contract Terms Act of 1977 which, in spite of its name, is not restricted to exclusion clauses in contracts but deals also with exclusion clauses in notices.

In the preparation of this edition the publishers and I have received the invaluable assistance of my wife in terms of the preparation and editing of the typescript, indexes and proofs, together with the general organization of sources of new material since the last edition.

I must also express my thanks to the staff of the University and College Department at Pitman Publishing and also Pitman Press for their assistance in processing the typescript and the proofs.

In conclusion, mention should be made of the contribution of my students; our discussions have helped me and, one hopes, them, to clarify some of the intricacies of the law.

For the errors and omissions I am, of course, solely responsible.

May 1978   D. J. Keenan

1 The development of English Law

Our present legal system began, for all practical purposes, in the reign of Henry II (1154–1189). When he came to the throne justice was for the most part administered in local courts, i.e. by local lords to their tenants in the feudal courts, and by the County Sheriffs, often sitting with the Earl and the Bishop, in the courts of the Shires and Hundreds. They administered the law in their respective areas and decided the cases which came before them on the basis of local custom. Many of these customary rules of law were the same or similar in all parts of the country, but there were some differences. For instance, primogeniture, the right of the eldest son to inherit the whole of his father's land where there was no will, applied almost universally throughout England; but in Kent there existed a system of landholding called gavelkind tenure whereby all the sons inherited equally; while in Nottingham and Bristol, under the custom of Borough-English, the property passed to the youngest son. These customs were finally abolished by the Administration of Estates Act, 1925.

The Curia Regis existed as a central royal court but was the feudal court for those high-ranking persons who were tenants-in-chief of the king, and not a general court open to all. Henry II took steps to ensure that royal justice would be open to all. In the Assizes of Clarendon (1166) and Northampton (1176) he provided in relation to the Criminal Law that there should be 12 men in every county to be responsible for presenting to the sheriff those suspected of serious crimes. The accused were brought before certain royal officials who travelled the country from time to time looking after the king's affairs, a system known as the General Eyre (see below). As regards the Civil Law a new civil remedy called 'The Assize of Novel Disseisin' was offered to persons who complained that their land had been wrongly seized. From this remedy grew a range of civil actions and in this way the General Eyre came to have a criminal and civil jurisdiction. Thus royal and more uniform justice began to come to the country as a whole.

THE COMMON LAW

The administrative ability of the Normans began the process destined to lead to a unified system of law which was nevertheless evolutionary in its development. The Normans were not concerned to change English customary law entirely by imposing Norman law on England. Indeed, many charters of William I giving English boroughs the right to hold courts stated that the laws dispensed in those courts should be laws of Edward the Confessor, which meant that English customary law was to be applied.

Attempts were made to ensure a greater uniformity in English law and the chief means by which this was achieved was the introduction of the General Eyre whereby representatives of the King were sent from Westminster on a tour of the Shires for the purpose of checking on the local administration. During the period of their visit they would sit in the local court and hear cases, and gradually they came to have a judicial rather than an administrative function. The judges for the General Eyre were selected from the Court of Common Pleas which normally sat at Westminster but which closed down while the judges were on circuit.

The General Eyre disappeared in the reign of Richard II (1377–99), but a system of circuit judges from the King's Bench took its place, the first circuit commission being granted in the reign of Edward III (1327–77). By selecting the best customary rulings and applying these outside their county of origin, the circuit judges gradually moulded existing local customary laws into one uniform law 'common' to the whole kingdom. Thus, customs originally local ultimately applied throughout the whole of the realm. Even so, there was no absolute unification even as late as 1389, and in a case in the Common Pleas in that year, a custom of Selby in Yorkshire was admitted to show that a husband was not in that area liable for his wife's trading debts, though the common law elsewhere regarded him as liable. However, many new rules were created and applied by the royal judges as they went on circuit and these were added to local customary law to make one uniform body of law called 'common law'.

Thus the identity between custom and the common law is not historically true, since much of the common law in early times was created by the judges, who justified their rulings by asserting that they were derived from the 'general custom of the Realm'. Thus, in *Beaulieu* v. *Finglass*, (1401), Y.B. 2 Hen. 4, f. 18, pl. 6, it was said that a man who by negligence failed to control a fire so that it spread to his neighbour's house was liable in damages according to 'the law and custom of the realm', though it is not easy to see which customary rule the court based its decision on.

The circuit judges from King's Bench derived their authority *in criminal matters* from Royal Commissions, the granting of which marked the real beginning of the assize system. The Commissions were—

Commission of oyer and terminer.   This commission, which dates from 1329, directed the judges to 'hear and determine' all complaints of grave crime within the jurisdiction of the circuit.

General gaol delivery.   This commission, which dates from 1299, gave the judges power to clear the local gaols and try all prisoners within the jurisdiction of the circuit.

Other criminal cases were heard by Justices of the Peace either summarily or sitting in quarter sessions and the circuit judges were also made Justices of the Peace so as to increase their jurisdiction.

Civil actions were usually heard at Westminster but under the Statute of Westminster II the circuit judges heard *civil cases* under provisions known as *nisi prius* which required the local sheriff to send a jury to London *unless before* the appointed time the royal justices came to hear the case locally, which in practice they always did. Thus civil cases were opened in London, tried by circuit judge and jury in the locality and the verdict recorded in London. This lasted until the nineteenth century when a Commission of Assize for Civil Actions was granted.

The system, which lasted for many years, was brought to an end by the Courts Act, 1971, Sect. 1(2) of which provides that all courts of assize are abolished and commissions to hold any court of assize shall not be issued. (See p. 26.)

Many of the itinerant justices were clerics, initially perhaps because they could read and write. However, it seems likely that the real reason for appointing them to livings in the church was to provide them with an income, a practice followed with other servants of the Crown, the church being rich and the King often poor. In general they had no priestly duties. From the middle of the thirteenth century the number of lay judges gradually increased.

When not on circuit the justices sat in the Royal Courts at Westminster, and it was probably at Westminster that they discussed the differences in the customary law on the various circuits, selecting the best rulings and applying them both at Westminster and on circuit.

The Royal Courts of Westminster developed out of the *Curia Regis* (or King's Council) which was originally a body of noblemen advising the King. The Court of Exchequer was the first court to emerge from the *Curia Regis* and dealt initially with disputes connected with royal revenues; later it dealt with many common law actions not necessarily connected with revenue. The Court of Common Pleas was set up in the time of Henry II to hear disputes between the King's subjects. The Court of King's Bench was the last to emerge from the *Curia Regis* and initially was closely associated with the King himself. This association enabled the Court of King's Bench to exercise a supervisory jurisdiction over the other courts by the use of prerogative writs (now orders). (See pp. 73–83.)

The system was held together by the doctrine of *stare decisis,* or standing by previous decisions. Thus when a judge decided a new problem in a case brought before him, this became a new rule of law and was followed by subsequent judges. In later times this practice crystallized into the form which is known as the binding force of judicial precedent, and the judges felt bound to follow previous decisions instead of merely looking to them for guidance. By these means the common law earned the status of a system. Indeed it was possible for Bracton, Dean of Exeter and a Justice Itinerant of Henry III, to write the first exposition of the common law before the end of the thirteenth century—*A Treatise on the Laws and Customs of England.* There was also an earlier treatise ascribed to Ranulph de Glanvill in 1187, but this was not so comprehensive as the work of Bracton. Nevertheless, the number of writs which Bracton describes as being available in the Royal Courts is much in excess of those described by Glanvill and shows the rapid growth of the system in its first 100 years.

To sum up, the common law is a judge-made system of law, originating in ancient cutsoms, which were clarified, *much* extended and universalized by the judges, although that part of the common law which concerned the ownership of land was derived mainly from the system of feudal tenures introduced from Europe after the Norman Conquest. It is perhaps also worth noting that the term 'common law' is used in four distinct senses, i.e. as opposed to (*a*) local law; (*b*) Equity; (*c*) statute law; and (*d*) any foreign system of law.

EQUITY

The growth of the common law was rapid in the thirteenth century but in the fourteenth century it ceased to have the momentum of earlier years. As a legal profession came into existence the judges came to be chosen exclusively from that profession instead of from a wider variety of royal officials as had been the case in the thirteenth century. The common law courts became more self-conscious about what they were doing and attempted to become more systematic. There was much talk about the proper way of doing things, of not being able to do this or that and much clever reasoning. Reports of cases in the Year Books, the nearest we have to law reports at this time, show a considerable concern with procedural points and niceties, a reluctance to depart from what had become established, a close attention to the observance of proper forms and much less concern with what the circumstances of a particular case demanded if it was to be settled in an appropriate way.

DEFECTS OF THE COMMON LAW

As a result of this hardening up of the system complaints were made by large numbers of people about the inadequacy of the service provided by the courts and the defects of the common law. The main defects were as follows—

(i) *The writ system.* Writs were issued by the clerks in the Chancellor's office, the Chancellor being in those days a clergyman of high rank who was also the King's Chaplain and Head of Parliament. In order to bring an action in one of the King's courts, the aggrieved party had to obtain from the Chancery a writ for which he had to pay. A writ was a sealed letter issued in the name of the King, and it ordered some person, Lord of the

Manor Sheriff of the County or the defendant, to do whatever the writ specified.

The old common law writs began with a statement of the plaintiff's claim, which was largely in common form, and was prepared in the Royal Chancery and not by the plaintiff's advisers as is the statement of claim today. Any writ which was novel, because the plaintiff or his advisers had tried to draft it to suit the plaintiff's case, might be abated, i.e. thrown out by the court. Thus, writs could only be issued in a limited number of cases, and if the complaint could not be fitted within the four corners of one of the existing writs, no action could be brought. Moreover, writs were expensive, and their very cost might deprive a party of justice.

However, a practice grew up under which the clerks in Chancery framed new writs even though the complaint was not quite covered by an existing writ, thus extending the law by extending the scope of the writ system. This appeared to Parliament to be a usurpation of its powers as the supreme lawgiver. Further, it took much work away from the local courts, diminishing the income of the local barons who persuaded Parliament to pass a statute called the Provisions of Oxford in 1258, forbidding in effect the practice of creating new writs to fit new cases. This proved so inconvenient that an attempt to remedy the situation was made by the Statute of Westminster II in 1285 which empowered the clerks in Chancery to issue new writs *in consimili casu* (in similar cases), thus adapting existing writs to fit new circumstances. The common law began to expand again, but it was still by no means certain that a writ would be forthcoming to fit a particular case, because the clerks in Chancery used the Statute with caution at first.

(ii) *Procedure.* Other difficulties arose over the procedure in the common law courts, because even the most trivial error in a writ would avoid the action. If X complained of the trespass of Y's mare, and in his writ by error described the mare as a stallion, his action could not proceed and he would have to start again. Furthermore, some common law actions were tried by a system called 'wager of law', and the plaintiff might fail on what was really a good claim if a defendant could bring more, or more powerful, people to say that the claim was false than the plaintiff could muster to support it.

(iii) *Defences and corruption.* In common law actions the defendant could plead certain standard defences known as *essoins* which would greatly delay the plaintiff's claim. For example, the defendant might say that he was cut off by floods or a broken bridge, or that he was off on a Crusade. He might also plead the defence of sickness which could delay the action for a year and a day. In early times these defences were verified by sending four knights to see the defendant, but at a later stage there was no verification and the defences were used merely to delay what were often good claims. There were also complaints about the bribery, corruption or oppression of juries, the partiality of sheriffs and the inability of a litigant to enforce a judgment or recover property from his more powerful neighbour.

(iv) *Remedies.*   The common law was also defective in the matter of remedies. The only remedy the common law had to offer for a civil wrong inflicted on a plaintiff was damages, i.e. a payment of money, which is not in all cases an adequate compensation. The common law could not compel a person to perform his obligations or cease to carry on a wrong, though it is not true to say that the common law was entirely devoid of equitable principles, and even in early times there were signs of some equitable development; but generally the rigidity of the forms of action tended to stifle justice.

(v) *Trust and mortgages.*   Furthermore, the common law did not recognize 'the concept of the trust or use' and there was no way of compelling the trustee to carry out his obligations under the trust. Thus if S conveyed property to T on trust for B, T could treat the property as his own and the common law would ignore the claims of B. In addition, the main right of a borrower (or mortgagor) is the right to redeem (or recover) the land he has used as a security for the loan. Originally at common law the land became the property of the lender (or mortgagee) as soon as the date decided upon for repayment had passed, unless during that time the loan had been repaid. However, Equity regarded a mortgage as essentially a security, and gave the mortgagor the right to redeem the land at any time on payment of the principal sum, plus interest due to the date of payment. What is more important, this rule applied even though the common law date for repayment had passed. This rule, which still exists, is called the Equity of Redemption.

Many people, therefore, unable to gain access to the King's courts, either because they could not obtain a writ, or because the writ was defective when they got it, or because they were caught in some procedural difficulty, or could not obtain an appropriate remedy, began to address their complaints to the King in Council. For a time the Council itself considered such petitions, and where a petition was addressed to the King in person, he referred it to the Council for trial. Later the Council delegated this function to the Chancellor, and eventually petitions were addressed to the Chancellor alone.

The Chancellor appears to have been chosen because he was already involved in legal matters. His clerks were engaged in the issue of common law writs and so it was convenient to delegate this new function to him. His jurisdiction had nothing to do with his supposed position of Keeper of the King's Conscience, i.e. the person to whom the King confessed his sins. In fact a compilation of the King's Confessors reveals that not one of them was Chancellor, though it is true that the early Chancellors were clerics.

The Chancellor began to judge such cases in the light of conscience and fair dealing. He was not bound by the remedies of the common law and began to devise remedies of his own. For example, the Chancellor could compel a person to perform his obligations by issuing a decree of *specific performance* or could stop him from carrying on a wrong by the issue of an *injunction*. The Chancellor also recognized interests in property which were unknown to the common law, in particular the concept of the *use*, under which persons might be made the legal owners of property for the use or benefit of another or others. As we have seen, the common law did not recognize the interests of the beneficiaries under a trust, but allowed the legal owner to deal with the property as if no other interests existed. Equity, however, enforced the beneficial interests. In order to bring persons before him the Chancellor issued a form of summons, called a *subpoena*. Equity was thus not cramped by anything analogous to the writ system. Eventually as new Chancellors took over, and Vice-Chancellors were appointed to cope with the increasing volume of work, uncertainty crept into the system, conflicting decisions abounded, and it was said that 'Equity varies with the Chancellor's foot'.

At this stage in its development Equity began to follow the practice of *stare decisis* which had proved so powerful a force in unifying the diverse systems of local custom under the common law. This was precipitated by the Reformation and by the appointment in 1530 of Sir Thomas More as Chancellor. More was a common lawyer and not a cleric. From then on non-clerical Chancellors were drawn from the ranks of the common lawyers and naturally followed the system of precedent which they had seen used in the common law courts. Lord Ellesmere (1596–1617) began to apply the same principles in all cases of the same type, and later, under Lord Nottingham (1673–1682), Lord Hardwicke (1736–1756) and Lord Eldon (1801–1827), Equity developed in scope and certainty.

Relationship of Law and Equity.

Although Law and Equity eventually operated alongside each other with mutual tolerance, there was a period of conflict between them. This arose out of the practice of the Court of Chancery which issued 'common injunctions' forbidding a person on pain of imprisonment from bringing an action in the common law courts, or forbidding the enforcement of a common law judgment if such a judgment had been obtained.

Thus, if X by some unconscionable conduct, such as undue influence, had obtained an agreement with Y, whereby Y was to sell X certain land at much below its real value, then, if Y refused to convey the land, X would have his remedy in damages at common law despite his unconscionable conduct. However, if Y appealed to the Chancellor, the latter might issue a common injunction which would prevent X from bringing his action at common law unless he wished to suffer punishment for defiance of the Chancellor's injunction. Similarly, if X had already obtained a judgment at common law, the Chancellor would prevent its enforcement by ordering X, on pain of imprisonment, not to execute judgment on Y's property.

However, the common law courts retaliated by waiting for the Chancellor to imprison the common law litigant for defiance of the injunction, and then the common law would release him by the process of *habeas corpus*.

This period of rivalry culminated in the *Earl of Oxford's* case in 1615,[1] when Lord Coke offered a direct challenge to the Court of Chancery's jurisdiction. The challenge was taken up and James I, on the advice of Lord Bacon, then his Attorney-General and later Lord Chancellor, gave a firm decision that where common law and equity were in conflict Equity should prevail. Thereafter the two systems settled down and carved out separate and complementary jurisdictions. Equity filled in the gaps left by the common law, and became a system of case law governed by the binding force of precedent. By the same token, it lost much of its earlier freedom and elasticity. It is certainly no longer a court of conscience.

Many reforms were still to come. Equitable and legal remedies had to be sought in different courts, but this in due course was rectified by the Judicature Acts, 1873–1875, which brought about an amalgamation of the English Courts. Since then both common law and equitable remedies have been available to a litigant under the same action and in the same court.

Before leaving the topic, a final characteristic of Equity should be noted which is that Equity never says the common law is wrong but merely provides alternative solutions to legal problems. It is thus a gloss upon the common law and this is illustrated by certain cases in the Law of Contract. For example, the decisions in *Central London Property Trust Ltd* v *High Trees House Ltd.*, 1947[159] and *Solle* v. *Butcher,* 1950[209] show how modern Equity sometimes adopts a different solution to that provided by the common law.

LEGISLATION

In early times there were few statutes and the bulk of law was case law, though legislation in one form or another dates from A.D. 600. The earliest Norman legislation was by means of Royal Charter, but the first great outburst of legislation came in the reign of Henry II (1154–1189). This legislation was called by various names: there were Assizes, Constitutions, and Provisions, as well as Charters. Legislation at this time was generally made by the King in Council, but sometimes by a kind of Parliament which consisted in the main of a meeting of nobles and clergy summoned from the shires.

In the fourteenth century parliamentary legislation became more general. Parliament at first requested or prayed the King to legislate, but later it presented a bill in its own wording. The Tudor period saw the development of modern procedure, in particular the practice of giving three readings to a bill; and this was also the age of the *Preamble,* which was a kind of preface to the enactment, describing often at great length the reasons for passing it and generally justifying the measure.

From the Tudor period onwards Parliament became more and more independent and the practice of law making by statute increased. Nevertheless statutes did not become an important source of law until the last two centuries, and even now, although the bulk of legislation is large, statutes form a comparatively small part of the law as a whole. The basis of our law remains the common law, and if all the statutes were repealed we should still have a legal system, even if it were inadequate; whereas our statutes alone would not provide a system of law but merely a set of disjointed rules.

Parliament's increasing incursions into economic and social affairs increased the need for statutes. Some aspects of law are so complicated or so novel that they can only be laid down in this form; they would not be likely to come into existence through the submission of cases in court. A statute is the ultimate source of law, and, even if a statue is in conflict with the common law or Equity, the statute must prevail. It is such an important source that it has been said—'A statute can do anything except change man to woman,' although in a purely legal sense even this could be achieved. No court or other body can question the validity of an Act of Parliament. (*Cheney* v. *Conn*, 1968.)[2]

Statute law can be used to abolish common law rules which have outlived their usefulness, or to amend the common law to cope with the changing circumstances and values of society. Once enacted, statutes, even if obsolete, do not cease to have the force of law, but common sense usually prevents most obsolete laws from being invoked. In addition, statutes which are no longer of practical utility are repealed from time to time by Statute Law Repeal Acts. Nevertheless, a statute stands as law until it is specifically repealed by Parliament. (*Prince of Hanover* v. *Attorney General*, 1956.)[3]

However, a new method of correcting Acts of Parliament when errors have been made inadvertently appears in the Acts of Parliament (Correction of Mistakes) Bill, 1977. Under the provisions of the Bill when a mistake made in the course of the passage of a bill is not discovered until it has become an Act, the Clerk of the Parliaments lays a statement before Parliament setting out the relevant facts.

At a later stage the minister of the department concerned with the legislation, after consulting such persons as appear to him appropriate, lays an order in council before Parliament making such changes in the Act (and any consequential changes in any other enactment affected) 'in order to bring the law into conformity with what, in his opinion, it would be had the mistake not been made'.

The order must be approved by a resolution of both Houses and the Queen makes an order in the terms of the draft.

An Act of Parliament is absolutely binding on everyone within the sphere of its jurisdiction, but all Acts of Parliament can be repealed by the same or subsequent Parliaments; and this is the only exception to the rule of the absolute sovereignty of Parliament—it cannot bind itself or its successors. (*Vauxhall Estates Ltd* v. *Liverpool Corporation*, 1932.)[4]

The obligation of the British Parliament on entry to the European Economic Community was to ensure that Community law was paramount. However, many authorities on constitutional law see this obligation as a dilemma in the sense that Community law cannot be paramount when like the rest of our law it is at the mercy of any future Act of Parliament which must, under the fundamental rule of our constitution, prevail over any pre-existing law whatsoever. Nevertheless, Parliament has a new role in relation to legislation emanating from the institutions of the Community and now has the right to send representatives to the European Parliament. (See also p. 103.)

DELEGATED LEGISLATION

Many modern statutes require much detailed work to implement and operate them, and such details are not normally contained in the statute itself, but are filled in from some other source. For example, much of our Social Security legislation gives only the general provisions of a complex scheme of social benefits, and an immense number of detailed regulations have had to be made by civil servants in the name of, and under the authority of, the appropriate Minister. These regulations, when made in the approved manner, are just as much law as the parent statute itself. This form of law is known as delegated or subordinate legislation.

CUSTOM

In early times custom was taken by the judges and turned into the common law of England, and it is still possible, even today, to argue the existence of a local (*Beckett* v. *Lyons,* 1967)[5] or trade (*Hutton* v. *Warren,* 1836)[272] custom before the courts. As a present-day source of law, however, it is of little importance.

THE LAW MERCHANT

Mercantile Law, or *Lex Mercatoria,* is based upon mercantile customs and usages, and was developed separately from the common law. The Royal Courts did not have a monopoly of the administration of justice and certain local courts continued to hear cases long after the Royal Courts were established. One notable area was that involving mercantile and maritime disputes. Disputes between merchants, local and foreign, which arose at the fairs where most important commercial business was transacted in the fourteenth century, were tried in the courts of the fair or borough, and were known as 'Courts of Pie Powder' (*pieds poudrés*) after the dusty feet of the traders who used them. These courts were presided over by the mayor or his deputy or, if the fair was held as part of a private franchise, the steward appointed by the franchise holder. The rules applied were the rules of the European law merchant developed over the years from the customary practices of merchants and the jury was often made up of merchants. The fair or borough courts were supplemented for a time by 'Staple Courts' which sat in the staple towns. These towns, which were designated by Edward III (1327–1377) as the exclusive centres of trade for such commodities as wine, wool, leather and tin, were required to hold courts to decide the trading disputes of merchants and again the customary practices of merchants were used.

Maritime disputes were heard by maritime courts sitting in major ports such as Bristol. These, too, applied a special European customary law developed from the customary practices of seamen.

The common law courts were slow to show an interest in dealing with commercial matters. In part this was due to the idea that their jurisdiction had a geographical limit and was restricted to matters which had arisen in England between English citizens. Foreign matters, and many of these commercial disputes did involve either a foreign merchant or a contract made or to be performed abroad, were left to some other body, especially if it could raise questions about the relations between the King and foreign sovereigns where the King's Council might be a more appropriate body. To some extent also it was due to the fact that the common law courts and the common law had come into existence at a time when land was the most important commodity and the procedures and concerns of the common law courts were adapted to problems arising from disputes about the possession and ownership of land. They were formal and slow and ill-adapted to the needs of merchants who required a speedier justice administered according to rules with which they were familiar.

When the Court of Admiralty developed, it took over much of the work of the merchants' courts, but from the seventeenth century onwards the common law courts began to acquire the commercial work, and many rules of the Law Merchant were incorporated into the common law. This was achieved partly by fiction. For example, to get over the fact that technically it still lacked jurisdiction over matters arising abroad the Court accepted allegations that something that had occurred abroad had in fact occurred in England within its jurisdiction, e.g. by using the fiction that Bordeaux was in Cheapside. Lord Mansfield and Lord Holt played a great part in this development, in particular by recognizing the main mercantile customs in the common law courts without requiring proof of them on every occasion. Perhaps the most important mercantile customs recognized were that a bill of exchange was negotiable and that mere agreements should be binding as contracts. In this way the custom of merchants relating to negotiable instruments and contracts including the sale of goods became part of the common law, and later, by codification, of statute law in the Bills of Exchange Act, 1882, and the Sale of Goods Act, 1893.

CANON LAW

Before the Norman Conquest the then existing courts heard all suits, both lay and ecclesiastical, and the Bishop and the Earl sat as joint judges. These joint courts were disliked by the Papacy because of the quarrels which took place between the lay and ecclesiastical members of the various tribunals. Prior to his conquest of England, William I had promised to set up separate ecclesiastical courts in this country, in return for the Pope's blessing of his proposed campaign. After the Conquest, William carried out his promise and removed suits 'which belong to the government of souls' from lay to ecclesiastical courts, and thus began the separation of the two.

The ecclesiastical courts dealt not only with offences against doctrine and morality, but also with secular matters, e.g. matrimonial causes, legitimacy, and testamentary succession. Many of their rules were derived from Roman Law, and were inherited by the civil courts, to which the jurisdiction was transferred in 1857.

The Matrimonial Causes Act, 1857, transferred matrimonial causes to a new civil court called the Divorce Court. The Court of Probate Act, 1857, transferred suits concerning wills to a new court called the Probate Court. The Judicature Act, 1873, incorporated the Probate and Divorce Courts into a newly created Supreme Court of Judicature as part of the Probate, Divorce and Admiralty Division, which under Sect. 1 of the Administration of Justice Act, 1970, became the Family Division (see p. 27), and the legal principles evolved over the centuries were expressly incorporated in the laws of England.

The present position is that the Church Courts remain to deal with disciplinary and moral offences committed by the Clergy and certain of the Laity, e.g. parish clerks and churchwardens, of the Church of England, and certain other matters, e.g. decoration, alteration and use of churches.

The court of first instance is that of the diocesan chancellor, who must be a member of the Church of England and is usually a practising barrister. Appeal lies from him to the Court of Arches in the province of Canterbury, and to the Chancery Court of York in the northern province. On matters concerning conduct, there is a further appeal to the Judicial Committee of the Privy Council and on other matters there may be an appeal to the Court of Ecclesiastical Cases Reserved. The church courts are not courts of common law and the prerogative orders (see p. 78)—which operate as a valuable check on the abuse of power by other courts and tribunals—do not apply to them.

LEGAL TREATISES

One last source remains to be considered, namely legal treatises. Throughout the centuries great English jurists have written books, some in the nature of legal text-books, which have helped to shape the law and inform the legal profession.

We have already mentioned *Bracton* whose *Treatise on the Laws and Customs of England* was written in the thirteenth century and was probably based on the decisions of Martin de Pateshull, who was Archdeacon of Norfolk, Dean of St. Pauls and an Itinerant Justice from 1217 to 1229, and on those of William de Raleigh who was the Rector of Bratton Fleming in Devon and an Itinerant Justice from 1228 to 1250.

Coke's is a celebrated name and his *Institutes* covered many aspects of law. For example, his First Institute, published in 1628, was concerned with land law. His Second Institute, published in 1642, was concerned with the principal statutes. The Third Institute, published in 1644, dealt with Criminal Law, while the Fourth Institute, also published in 1644, was concerned with the Jurisdiction and History of the Courts, this work containing bitter attacks on the Court of Chancery. During his lifetime Coke occupied the offices of Recorder of London, Solicitor-General, Speaker of the House of Commons, Attorney-General, and finally Chief Justice of Common Pleas.

Sir William Blackstone published his *Commentaries* in 1765. These are concerned with various aspects of law and are based on his lectures at Oxford. He was a Judge of the Common Pleas and was also the first Professor of English Law to be appointed in any English University.

In addition to older treatises such as those mentioned above, the works of modern writers, sufficiently eminent in the profession, are sometimes quoted when novel points of law are being argued in the Courts. (*Boys* v. *Blenkinsop,* 1968.)[6]

2 The courts of law

The Royal Courts of Westminster developed out of the *Curia Regis* (or the King's Council). The Court of Exchequer was the first court to emerge from the Curia Regis and dealt initially with disputes connected with royal revenues. The Court of Common Pleas was set up in the time of Henry II to hear disputes between the King's subjects. The Court of King's Bench was last to emerge and initially was closely associated with the King himself, hearing disputes between subjects and the King.

As the system developed the Court of Chancery was added and there was also a Court of Admiralty. The Court of Probate and the Divorce Court developed from the old ecclesiastical courts which formerly dealt with these matters. Each of these courts had its own jurisdiction, sometimes overlapping and sometimes conflicting. This was particularly true with regard to the common law courts and the Court of Chancery. For example, in *Knight* v. *Marquis of Waterford,* (1844) 11 Cl. & Fin. 653, the appellant was told by the House of Lords after 14 years of litigation in Equity, that he had a good case but must begin his action again in a common law court. This was how the English legal system entered the nineteenth century and it was this inheritance that the Victorians set out to rationalize into the form with which we are familiar.

THE SUPREME COURT OF JUDICATURE

In order to rationalize the system the Supreme Court of Judicature was established. Under the Judicature Acts, 1873–1875 the High Court was divided into five divisions: Queen's Bench, Common Pleas, Exchequer, Chancery, and Probate, Divorce and Admiralty, the number being reduced to three by an Order in Council in 1881 when the Common Pleas and Exchequer Divisions were merged into the Queen's Bench Division. The Court of Appeal was given jurisdiction over appeals.

The House of Lords

The House of Lords was not included in the Supreme Court of Judicature by the judicature Acts because of Parliament's opposition to its hereditary character. Its jurisdiction as a final court of appeal was established by the Appellate Jurisdiction Act, 1876 which also provided the House with trained judges, i.e. Life Peers with legal training. The Judicature Acts, 1873–1875 were consolidated in the Supreme Court of Judicature (Consolidation) Act, 1925.

THE COURTS TODAY

In recent times far-reaching changes have been made in the structure and jurisdiction of the Civil and Criminal courts by various reforming statutes. The present system of courts exercising both civil and criminal jurisdiction is set out on pp. 16 and 17.

Magistrates' Courts

Although, as we shall see, the Crown Court tries the most serious criminal cases (all those in fact which are tried on indictment with a jury), the great bulk of the criminal work of the country is performed in the Magistrates' Courts.

Types of Magistrates.   Magistrates may be of several kinds as follows —

(a) *Lay magistrates.* These are appointed by the Queen on the advice of the Lord Chancellor who is in turn advised by a local advisory committee.

(b) *Stipendiary magistrates.* These are full-time magistrates who sit in certain commission areas which have applied for a stipendiary. They are appointed by the Queen on the recommendation of the Lord Chancellor and must be barristers or solicitors of at least seven years' standing. At the present time there are 11 stipendiary magistrates in the provinces, appointments having been made, e.g. in Birmingham, Greater Manchester, and Liverpool. Metropolitan stipendiary magistrates are the counterpart in London of the Stipendiary Magistrates in the provinces and are appointed in the same way. Currently there are 41 such magistrates working, for example, in courts such as Bow Street and Tower Bridge.

(c) *Ex-officio magistrates.* Persons can become magistrates by holding another office. This is now confined to High Court judges and the Lord Mayor and aldermen of the City of London.

The Clerk.   Each bench of lay magistrates has a salaried clerk, who is usually employed whole time. He assists the magistrates on questions of procedure and law and is responsible for the administration of the court. Certain functions of the magistrates may be delegated to him. For example, Sect. 5 of the Justices of the Peace Act, 1968, gives power to make rules delegating to the clerk the functions of a single justice. This could include pre-trial work such as committals and the issue of warrants. The clerk is appointed by the Magistrates' Courts Committee for the relevant area from barristers or solicitors of not less than five years' standing.

SYSTEM OF COURTS EXERCISING CIVIL JURISDICTION
(EXCLUDING INDUSTRIAL TRIBUNALS)

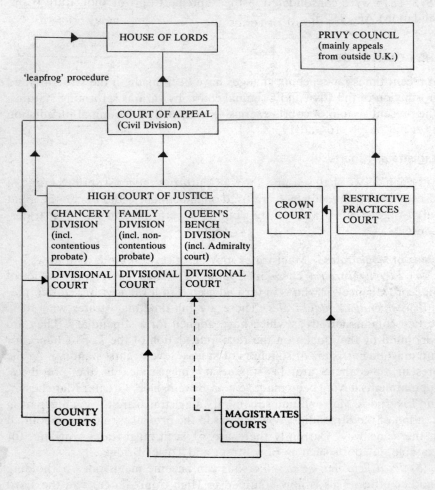

Appeals are indicated thus ———————————
Appeals by way of 'case stated,' thus – – – – – – – –

SYSTEM OF COURTS EXERCISING CRIMINAL JURISDICTION

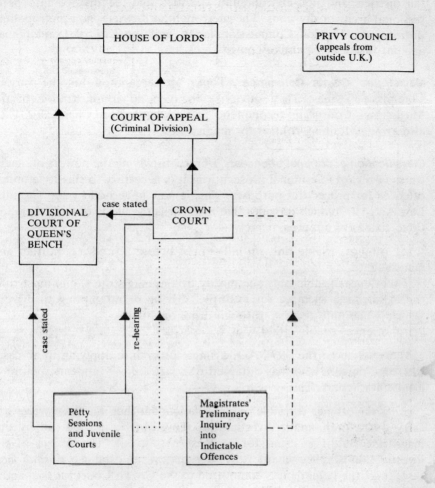

Appeals are indicated thus —————————
Committed for trial, thus — — — — — — — — —
Committed for sentence, thus ....

Commission Areas.   The Commission Areas for which magistrates sit are metropolitan districts metropolitan counties, non-metropolitan counties, London Commission Areas and the City of London. Of these, metropolitan districts and non-metropolitan counties may be divided into petty sessional areas or divisions. The metropolitan districts, non-metropolitan districts, the London Commission areas, and the City of London may appoint full-time stipendiary magistrates.

Magistrates' Courts Committee.   These are appointed for the various Commission Areas. They supervise the general administration of the Magistrates' Courts and recommend changes to the Lord Chancellor. They also arrange training courses for magistrates.

Classification of criminal offences.   Before discussing the powers of magistrates in regard to criminal prosecutions it is necessary to classify criminal offences for procedural purposes. This is now governed by the Criminal Law Act, 1977 which provides that as regards the mode of trial, there are three classes of offences, namely —

(a) offences triable only on indictment before a jury, e.g. murder and manslaughter;

(b) offences triable only summarily by the magistrates, e.g. most road traffic offences, such as, for example, driving or attempting to drive a vehicle when unfit to drive through drink or drugs;

(c) offences triable either way, e.g. perjury.

There is, under the 1977 Act, a single procedure applying to all cases where a person who has attained the age of 17 appears before a magistrates' court. This is as follows —

(a) if the offence is triable only on indictment then the magistrates will carry out a preliminary investigation. This can be carried out by one magistrate but it is usual for at least two to sit. The object of the investigation is to see whether the prosecution can establish a *prima facie* case. If so, the defendant is committed to the Crown Court for trial and if not, the case is dismissed, though such dismissals are extremely rare.

(b) If the offence is triable only summarily the magistrates will actually try the offence and not merely investigate the prosecutor's case.

(c) Where the offence is triable either way the procedure is as follows —

(i) the magistrates must begin by considering whether the offence is more suitable for summary trial or for trial on indictment;

(ii) if the magistrates consider that the offence is more suitable for summary trial the accused must be asked whether he consents to be tried summarily or wishes to be tried by a jury. If he consents to be tried summarily the court proceeds with summary trial; if he does not so consent the court proceeds as examining justices.

(iii) If the court considers that the offence is more suitable for trial on indictment the accused must be given an opportunity to make representation that he should be tried summarily and the court is then to decide whether to proceed to summary trial or as examining justices.

(iv) Where the magistrates have begun to try a case summarily and the offence in question is triable either way the court may at any time before the conclusion of the prosecution evidence change from summary trial to committal proceedings. Similarly, if the court has begun to inquire into the information as examining justices, it may (but only with the accused's consent unless he is under 17) change to summary trial.

Sentencing.   The maximum penalty which the magistrates may impose for any offence is in most cases six months' imprisonment. The maximum fine for any one offence may now be as much as £1000. In addition the magistrates can make compensation orders requiring a defendant to compensate the victim of his crime. There are also restitution orders under which the defendant can be required to return stolen property and, in addition, the magistrates may make supervision orders which operate to some extent like probation, and community service orders under which the defendant may be required to carry out some useful service within the community. In addition, it should be noted that if the magistrates are trying an indictable offence summarily and feel that the circumstances are such that the defendant should be given a greater sentence than can be given in a Magistrates' Court, they may commit the defendant to the Crown Court for sentence.

Civil Jurisdiction.   The magistrates also have a civil jurisdiction which includes the making of affiliation orders and domestic proceedings under which applications for matrimonial relief such as separation and maintenance orders may be made, by women who do not initially on breakdown of marriage opt for divorce. They can also deal with questions concerning the custody and adoption of children and matters relating to licensing and the enforcement of rates.

Appeals.   Appeals from the magistrates in domestic proceedings are to the Divisional Court of the Family Division. As regards criminal offences, appeal may be to the Crown Court or to the Divisional Court of Queen's Bench as follows —

(*a*) *Crown Court.*   An appeal to the Crown Court may be made by the accused only. The appeal may be against conviction or sentence on law or fact and no permission is required. The appeal takes the form of rehearing in the Crown Court and although the Crown Court may give greater punishment than the magistrates in fact gave, it is limited to a prison sentence of not more than six months or a fine of not more than £1000.

(*b*) *Divisional Court of Queen's Bench.*   An appeal to the Divisional Court of Queen's Bench may be made by either the accused or the prosecution by means of *case stated.* This means that the magistrates must set out in writing the reasons for their decision. The appeal is on law only and it is in fact the only form of appeal for an accused who pleaded guilty before the magistrates. If the Divisional Court or the House of Lords gives leave, there may be a further appeal to the House of Lords but the Divisional Court must certify that the case raises a matter of law of public importance.

The juvenile court. The magistrates also have a part to play in regard to children under 14 and young persons between 14 and 17 whose behaviour or circumstances require some form of official action. For this purpose the magistrates sit as a juvenile court. This court must sit in a different building or room from that in which other courts are held or else must sit on a different day. The magistrates are drawn from a special panel of persons under 65 years of age and it is usual for one or more female magistrates to be present. As regards the way in which the court treats young offenders, the Children and Young Persons Act, 1969, is relevant. Section 4 prohibits criminal proceedings for offences committed by children under 14. Section 5 restricts criminal proceedings for offences committed by young persons under 17 and Sect. 7 raises the minimum age qualification for a Borstal sentence from 15 to 17 and plans the phasing out of detention centres and attendance centres. However, differences between the political parties in Parliament have resulted in these sections of the Act remaining unimplemented.

Nevertheless, proceedings against young persons in a juvenile court need not necessarily be criminal by nature. What is known as care proceedings on the commission of an offence are possible and in such proceedings the primary choice open to the magistrates is a supervision order by which the child or young person will be placed under the supervision of a probation officer, local authority, or other person, and a care order, by which the juvenile will be removed from his home environment and committed to the care of a local authority for residential treatment. However, in practice such proceedings are rare and the traditional 'punitive' sentences which were to be abolished by Sect. 7 are increasingly used. During the period 1969–1973 sentences to detention centres rose by 67%, Borstal sentences for 15–17-year-olds doubled, and attendance centre orders rose by 20%.

The County Court

The Magistrates' Courts deal with most of the less serious criminal matters in this country. At something like the same level, but dealing exclusively with civil cases, is the County Court. County Courts were created by the County Courts Act, 1846, to operate as the chief lower courts for the trial of civil disputes, and a large number of cases are heard in these courts annually. A County Court is presided over by a circuit judge appointed by the Crown on the advice of the Lord Chancellor. (See p. 26.) In addition, the Courts Act, 1971 provides that every judge of the Court of Appeal and of the High Court and every Recorder may sit as a judge in a County Court if he consents and the Lord Chancellor thinks that it is desirable. The judge usually sits alone, though there is provision for a trial by a jury of eight persons in some cases, e.g. where fraud is alleged. Appeal lies direct to the Court of Appeal (Civil Division). The judge is assisted by a Registrar who is appointed by the Lord Chancellor from solicitors of at least seven years' standing. The Registrar acts as Clerk of the Court, and may try certain cases where the amount involved does not exceed £200 and no objection is raised by any of the parties. If the parties agree, his jurisdiction extends to any action or matter within the general jurisdiction of the court. The Lord Chancellor may appoint a solicitor of at least seven years' standing to be a Deputy County Court Registrar as a temporary measure to dispose of business in the County Court. (Administration of Justice Act, 1973, Sect. 16(2) and (3).) The appointment of the Deputy formerly had to be made by the Registrar, who had himself to be in a position where he was prevented from performing his office, or, if that was impossible, by the judge.

Regarding the jurisdiction of the court, there are limitations as to place, and as to the nature and amount of the claim. The general rule is that the plaintiff must bring his action in the court of the district where the defendant dwells or carries on business. Where land is involved, the action is generally brought in the court of the district in which the land is situated. The Administration of Justice Act, 1977 gives the County Court the same jurisdiction as the High Court to grant an injunction or a declaratory judgment setting out the rights of the parties, in respect of, or relating to, any land or the possession, occupation, use or enjoyment of any land. This jurisdiction applies only where the net annual value for rating of the relevant land does not exceed the county court limit on jurisdiction (currently £1000).

The general jurisdiction of County Courts and the procedure therein are governed by the County Courts Act, 1959 (as amended in particular by the Administration of Justice Acts, 1969, 1973 and 1977), and the County Court Rules. The latter are in the form of delegated legislation and are set out in an annual volume known as the County Court Practice. In general terms, the extent of the jurisdiction is as follows—

(i) *Actions founded on contract and tort* with a limit of £2000 unless the parties agree to waive the limit. For certain torts (i.e. libel and slander) the court has no jurisdiction unless both parties agree.

(ii) *Equity matters,* e.g. mortgages and trusts where the amount involved does not exceed £15,000, unless the parties agree to waive the limit.

(iii) *Actions concerning title to land, and actions for recovery of possession of land,* where the rateable value of the land does not exceed £1000. There is unlimited jurisdiction in cases within the Rent Acts or by agreement between the parties.

(iv) *Bankruptcies.* Here there is unlimited jurisdiction, but not all county courts have bankruptcy jurisdiction. (Bankruptcy Act, 1914.) Bankruptcy cases in the Metropolitan Area are heard in the Bankruptcy Court of the High Court.

(v) *Company winding up,* where the paid-up share capital of the company does not exceed £120,000, if the court has a bankruptcy jurisdiction.

(vi) *Probate proceedings,* where the value of the deceased's estate is estimated to be £15,000 or less. (Administration of Justice Act, 1977.)

(vii) *Admiralty matters.* Some County Courts in coastal areas have Admiralty jurisdiction which is limited to £5000 except in salvage cases where the limit is £15,000. The parties may by agreement waive these limits. (Administration of Justice Act, 1977.)

(viii) *Matrimonial causes.* The Matrimonial Causes Act, 1967, confers jurisdiction on County Courts in certain matrimonial proceedings.

A County Court designated by the Lord Chancellor as a 'divorce county court' has jurisdiction in certain matters relating to any undefended matrimonial cause, but may *try* such a cause only if further designated as a court of trial (Sect. 1(1)). Every matrimonial cause must be commenced in a divorce county court, though under rules of court defended cases *will* be transferred to the High Court and even undefended cases *may* be so transferred (Sect. 1(3)). There is also provision for the transfer from the High Court to a divorce county court of a matrimonial cause which becomes undefended (Sect. 1(4)).

Divorce county courts may make orders for ancillary relief and the protection of children and may deal with wilful neglect to maintain and the variation of maintenance agreements (Sect. 2). They may also hear applications made before presentation of the petition which relate to arrangements made between parties (Sect. 3). The jurisdiction of divorce county courts may be exercised in the principal probate registry (Sect. 4). The Lord Chancellor may assign particular Circuit judges to matrimonial proceedings (Sect. 5).

(ix) *Arbitration.* In order to strengthen the County Court as a tribunal for the determination of small claims, Sect. 7 of the Administration of Justice Act, 1973 together with new County Court rules give the Registrar power to refer any County Court proceedings to arbitration if the sum involved does not exceed £100 or if both parties agree. In other cases an order of the judge is necessary. The Administration of Justice Act, 1977 provides that county court rules will now prescribe cases in which proceedings are (without any order of the court) to be referred to arbitration and will prescribe the manner in which and the terms on which cases are to be so referred.

Usually the arbitrator will be the Registrar, but in cases involving larger sums of money, where the parties have agreed to arbitrate, the judge may act as arbitrator. However, if both parties agree, someone else other than the judge or Registrar may be appointed. If a charge of fraud is being made against a party to the proceedings, they will not be referred to arbitration except with that party's consent. The arbitration arrangements are not confined to any particular class of case but are likely to be especially appropriate in consumer disputes.

A major advantage of arbitration is that the proceedings are heard in private and the Registrar or judge is unrobed. Thus no litigant present in person need feel deterred by having to appear in public in strange surroundings when he brings or defends an action. The precise terms on which the arbitration is to take place are settled by the court according to the circumstances of the individual case. In general the strict rules of evidence are dispensed with and, if the parties agree, the arbitrator can be authorized to decide the case on the basis of statements and documents submitted by the parties. Either party may ask for arbitration and, except in the cases mentioned above, the court may order it whether or not the other party agrees. The plaintiff can include in his particulars of claim a request for arbitration if the defendant contests the case and the form supplied to the defendant with the summons enables him to say, if he does not admit the claim, whether he wishes the case to be arbitrated. It is also open to a party to ask for arbitration at a later stage, e.g. at a pre-trial review (see below).

The award of the arbitrator is entered as the judgment in the proceedings. There is no appeal as such although as in other cases of arbitration it will be possible to have the award set aside on the exceptional grounds justifying such a course, for example, where the award is uncertain. (See *Stonehewer* v. *Farrar*, 1845.)[7]

County Court rules also extend the power to refer questions to experts for enquiry and report. The Registrar can order this in cases of up to £100 or with the consent of the parties. Consumer cases often depend on an expert opion about a piece of equipment alleged to be faulty. To enable such reports to be more easily obtained the Government has invited the co-operation of competent bodies such as trade associations and the Weights and Measures Inspectorate with a view to ensuring that the services of suitable experts are available at a reasonable fee.

When a case is referred to arbitration the court will indicate how the costs are to be dealt with but in general terms they will be left to the discretion of the arbitrator. However, where a claim does not exceed £100 no costs other than those of issuing the summons are normally recoverable unless a difficult question of law or a question of fact of exceptional complexity is involved. However, if the court considers that costs have been incurred through the unreasonable conduct of the opposite party, it may order them to be paid to a successful litigant. These provisions in County Court rules do not exclude legal representation where the claim does not exceed £100, either in ordinary County Court proceedings or in cases referred to arbitration. However, in such cases the employment of solicitors and barristers is likely to be discouraged unless there is a special reason for it. In arbitration proceedings a litigant in person will usually be allowed to take a friend or relative along with him to help him present his case. The action in a small claim can be commenced by using special and simple forms and not by writ.

(x) *Pre-trial review.*   It should also be noted that a *pre-trial review* by the Registrar is now a regular feature of ordinary actions in the County Court and also in default actions, i.e. cases in which a fixed sum of money, such as a debt, is claimed. A major advantage of the pre-trial review is that the parties may compromise the claim and settle, thus saving time and money involved in going to trial. However, if there is no compromise then at the conclusion of the review the date of trial is fixed or the action is adjourned for the hearing to be fixed at a later date.

(xi) *Miscellaneous matters.*   The County Court derives an important part of its jurisdiction from social legislation, e.g. adoption of children, guardianship of infants, legitimacy, race relations, and the enforcement of legislation concerning landlord and tenant.

Although in many matters the County Court has concurrent jurisdiction with the High Court, there are certain matters over which the County Courts have *exclusive* jurisdiction so that actions concerning them cannot be commenced in the High Court, e.g. regulated consumer credit agreements or hire agreements where the fixed sum credit does not exceed £5000 or, in a running account, the credit limit does not exceed £5000, though the court's jurisdiction in proceedings relating to extortionate credit agreements under Sect. 139 of the Consumer Credit, Act, 1974, is limited to £2000. Furthermore, where the lender on mortgage is seeking to take possession of land and the mortgage includes a dwelling house and no part of the land is in Greater London, the county court has exclusive jurisdiction provided the rateable value does not exceed £1000. (Administration of Justice Act, 1970, Sect. 37.) In addition, the Attachment of Earnings Act, 1971, Sect. 1 gives the County Court alone the power to order attachment of earnings for ordinary civil debt.

A *plaintiff* may ask for an action to be transferred to the High Court. The following examples are based upon an action in contract or tort. Under Sect. 43 of the County Courts Act, 1959, an order transferring the action will be made if the plaintiff can establish that there are reasonable grounds for believing that the damages will exceed £2000 if the action is transferred to the High Court. (*Stiffel* v. *Industrial Dwellings Society Ltd.*, 1973.)[8]

Provision is also made for actions to be transferred to the High Court where the sum involved is over £350 if the *defendant* objects to the case being tried in the County Court, provided that the judge certifies that in his opinion some important question of law or fact is likely to arise, and the defendant gives security for the amount claimed and the costs of the trial in the High Court (County Courts Act, 1959, Sect. 44). Similarly if an action is begun in the High Court for a sum of not more than £2000 the defendant may apply to have the case transferred to a County Court and it will be transferred if the judge of master who hears the application thinks fit (County Courts Act, 1959, Sect. 45). If in an action brought in the High Court a sum of less than £350 is recovered, the plaintiff will not be entitled to costs (Administration of Justice Act, 1969, Sect. 4). If he recovers less than £1200 he will only be awarded costs on the County Court scale unless it appears to the judge or master 'that there was reasonable ground for supposing that he would recover more than he could have claimed in the County Court or if they are satisfied that there was sufficient reason for bringing the action in the High Court or, of course, if the defendant objected to the case being transferred to a County Court (County Courts Act, 1959, Sect. 47).

Appeal from a decision of a county court judge lies direct to the Court of Appeal (Civil Division) on a point of *law* so long as the claim exceeds £20 and, provided in general terms that at least £200 is in dispute, appeal also lies on a question of *fact*.

Small claims courts

Arrangements other than those in County Court exist for settling small claims. For example, the Westminster Small Claims Court (now called the London Small Claims Court) was established by the City of Westminster Law Society with the assistance of a grant from the Nuffield Foundation. Its object is to provide a quick and cheap means of settling small claims by arbitration in an informal atmosphere. A court fee of between £5 and £10, depending on the size of the claim, is paid by the Claimant and may be recovered from an unsuccessful Respondent. No other costs are allowed nor indeed is legal representation. The Adjudicator, who is an experienced practising solicitor barrister or magistrate, asks questions of the parties in order to unravel the facts and reach a conclusion. Thus the procedure is inquisitorial. The great difficulty about such schemes is that they depend on the willingness of both parties to submit to arbitration, and it will be interesting to see what effect the provisions for compulsory arbitration in the County Court will have upon their operation. However, the less formal atmosphere and wider financial jurisdiction (the London Court has an upper limit of £250) may encourage its growth especially where no complicated questions of law are involved.

The claims heard in 1975/76 involve consumer cases, in particular shoes, clothes, carpets, cars and furnishing materials, motor accident and personal injury claims, disputes about employment and problems concerning landlord and tenant. There were also some cases involving debts and travel disputes. If a judgment is not complied with the successful party can enforce it through the County Court where he need not prove his case again but simply issue default proceedings and prove his judgment as his opponent is in breach of the Arbitration Agreement.

The Crown Court

Section 4(1) of the Courts Act, 1971 establishes the Crown Court for England and Wales and states that this court is a superior court of record.

The Crown Court system replaced Courts of Assize and Quarter Sessions. The Crown Court deals in the main with criminal work, though all the domestic, betting and gaming, and licensing jurisdiction of the old Quarter sessions was transferred to the Crown Court.

Constitution

The jurisdiction and powers of the Crown Court are exercised by the following—

(a) *High Court judges.*   Certain cases are not appropriate for trial in a Crown Court by a circuit judge or recorder but are reserved for trial in that court by a High Court judge. All offences have been divided for the purpose of trial into four classes and, for example, Class 1 offences must be tried by a High Court judge. These include murder and treason. On the other hand, offences such as wounding or causing grievous bodily harm would normally be tried by a circuit judge or recorder.

(b) *Circuit judge.*   Circuit judges are appointed by the Queen on the recommendation of the Lord Chancellor from barristers of at least ten years' standing, or from recorders who have been in post for at least three years.

(c) *Recorder.*   This is a part-time appointment made by the Queen on the recommendation of the Lord Chancellor from barristers or solicitors of at least ten years' standing. Since a solicitor may be appointed as a recorder, he may after three years in post become a circuit judge, and a number of appointments of solicitors to the position of circuit judge have been made.

(d) *Magistrates.*   When the Crown Court is hearing an appeal or a committal for sentence from the Magistrates' Court between two and four justices sit with the judge or recorder. Although the magistrates are in this situation judges of the Crown Court, and play a full part in its decisions, where a decision of the court involves a question of law the judge or recorder alone must give a ruling on the law and the court must then come to a decision on the basis of that ruling. (*R.* v. *Orpin,* [1974] 2 All E.R. 1121.)

Jurisdiction

All indictable offences are triable in the Crown Court. The Court also hears appeals from magistrates and committals for sentence from the magistrates. It also hears appeals from juvenile courts and for this purpose forms a juvenile appeals court. This consists of a circuit judge plus two magistrates drawn from the juvenile court panel.

Central Criminal Court

Before leaving the subject of the Crown Court special mention should be made of the Central Criminal Court, otherwise referred to as the 'Old Bailey'. This court continues as a Crown Court sitting in the City of London, though its constitution is slightly different in that the Lord Mayor and any alderman of the City may sit with the judge.

The High Court

The High Court is staffed by a maximum of 70 judges known as *puisne* judges (pronounced 'puny'). The number of puisne judges may be increased by order in Council. Appointment is by the Queen on the advice of the Lord Chancellor and the qualification is being barrister of at least ten years' standing.

The Queen's Bench Division has the largest staff, of 44 *puisne* judges. The Court is presided over by the Lord Chief Justice. As regards jurisdiction, every type of common law civil action, e.g. contract and tort, can be heard by the Queen's Bench Division at the Royal Courts of Justice in the Strand. In addition, the judges of this division staff the Crown Court and sit in the Court of Appeal (Criminal Division) as well as the Divisional Court of Queen's Bench and the Central Criminal Court. Admiralty business is now assigned to a separate court called the Admiralty Court within the Queen's Bench Division. The same is true of commercial business which is heard by a separate court called the Commercial Court within the Queen's Bench Division. The Commercial Court also provides an arbitration service. (See below.)

The Chancery Division has 11 *puisne* judges and is presided over by the Lord Chancellor. However, he is nominal head only and does not try cases. A Vice-Chancellor is now appointed to perform organizational and administrative functions as deputy to the Lord Chancellor. The Vice-Chancellor also hears cases. Company business is assigned to a separate court called the Companies Court within the Chancery Division. The work of the Companies Court is divided into company liquidation proceedings and other company matters. Apart from company work the Chancery Division deals with partnership matters, mortgages, trusts, revenue matters, rectification of deeds and documents, the administration of estates of deceased persons and contentious probate. The bulk of the bankruptcy work of the Chancery Division is performed by Registrars in Bankruptcy who deal with cases arising in the London area, provincial bankruptcies being dealt with by the local County Court.

The Family Division has 16 *puisne* judges and is presided over by the President of the Division. The Court deals with all business which concerns marriage, family property and children, including adoption and wardship.

Divisional courts. Each of the three divisions of the High Court has divisional courts. These are constituted by two or more judges from the division. However, under the Administration of Justice Act, 1977 rules can be made to allow a single judge of the High Court, instead of a Divisional Court, to hear appeals from inferior tribunals.

(a) *Divisional Court of Queen's Bench.*   This hears appeals on points of law on cases stated by magistrates and the Crown Court. It also has a supervisory jurisdiction under which it exercises the power of the High Court to discipline inferior courts and to put right their mistakes by means of the orders of *mandamus, certiorari,* and *prohibition.* It can also deal with the writ of *habeas corpus* and *election petitions.*

(b) *Divisional Court of the Chancery Division.*   This court hears appeals in bankruptcy cases from county courts outside London, the Bankruptcy Court of the Chancery Division hearing bankruptcy appeals from London.

(c) *The Divisional Court of the Family Division.* This court hears appeals from magistrates' courts in matrimonial cases.

The Commercial Court

Section 3 of the Administration of Justice Act, 1970 constitutes, as part of the Queen's Bench Division, a Commercial Court for the trial of causes of a commercial nature, e.g. insurance matters. By Sect. 3 (*ibid.*) the judges of the Commercial Court are such High Court Judges as the Lord Chancellor may from time to time nominate to be Commercial Judges. There are at the present time three judges so nominated. They combine the general work of a Queen's Bench Judge with priority for commercial cases. The Act merely gives formal independence to the Commercial Court. Commercial litigation has since 1895 been dealt with in the Queen's Bench Division on a simplified procedure and before a specialist judge, the intention being to overcome the reluctance of commercial men, who prefer the privacy of arbitration, to resort to the machinery of the courts.

Two specific steps were proposed in the Administration of Justice Bill to attract such customers: first a power was to be taken to allow the court to sit in private and to receive evidence which would not normally be admissible in an ordinary court, and secondly High Court judges were to be allowed to sit as arbitrators. The first of these proposals was rejected by the House of Commons at the Report Stage but the second was passed into law and Sect. 4 of the 1970 Act enables a judge of the Commercial Court to take arbitrations. Before doing so he must obtain clearance from the Lord Chief Justice that the pressure of work in the High Court and Crown Court will enable him to be made available for this purpose, but in practice this is unlikely to cause difficulty.

Thus, although in theory the Court has no wider power than other courts of the Queen's Bench Division, there is, in practice, a general discretion for departures in procedure and admission of evidence where the parties consent or where the interests of justice demand it or where it is necessary to expedite business. The power to hold hearings in private is restricted but Sect. 12 of the Administration of Justice Act, 1960, gives a power which could be used if, for example, trade secrets were involved. Commercial cases may be tried by a judge alone, or by a judge and a jury. It was once a special jury in that it consisted of persons who had knowledge of commercial matters. An ordinary jury would now be used since Sect. 40 of the Courts Act, 1971, abolishes special juries. All actions in the Commercial Court are tried in the City of London.

The work of the Commercial Court now probably consists of a greater number of cases which arise in some way out of arbitrations than cases which are taken direct to the Court. An arbitrator can be required to state a 'special case' on an issue of law for consideration by the Commercial Court. There may then be an appeal to the Court of Appeal and the House of Lords. Where a judge of the Commercial Court is used as an arbitrator he may be required by the parties or the Court of Appeal to state a 'special case' but if he does so, then any 'special case' goes straight from him into the Court of Appeal. This has three great advantages as follows—

(*a*) where an arbitration involves substantial points of law—and it is in particular in such cases that a Commercial Judge is likely to accept appointment as arbitrator or umpire—the number of requests for 'special cases' should be substantially reduced because the parties and their lawyers may well be willing to accept a decision from a Commercial Judge without appeal more readily than from an arbitrator or umpire;

(*b*) the awkward feature of a split between one tribunal deciding the facts (i.e. the arbitrator) and a High Court judge then deciding the law on these facts is eliminated;

(*c*) there is an obvious advantage if the 'special case' warrants an appeal, because then one stage of the appellate process drops out.

Where a judge of the Commercial Court is acting as an arbitrator he sits in private and in any place convenient to the parties. There is no requirement for such arbitrations to take place in the Law Courts. The conduct of the hearing should be as informal as any other arbitration. In addition, the award is made privately to the parties and not published like a judgment.

The Companies' Court

This is really a court of the Chancery Division where company matters are tried before a single judge whose special concern is with company work. The work of the court is divided into company liquidation proceedings, and other company matters.

The Bankruptcy Court

The bulk of the bankruptcy work of the Chancery Division is performed by Registrars in Bankruptcy who deal with cases arising in the London area, provincial bankruptcies being dealt with by the local county court.

The Restrictive Practices Court

This superior court of record was set up by the Restrictive Trade Practices

Act, 1956. Following a consolidation of restrictive trade practices legislation the registration and judicial investigation of restrictive trading agreements is now covered by the Restrictive Practices Court Act, 1976, the
Restrictive Trade Practices Act, 1976 and the Resale Prices Act, 1976.
These Acts, which are further discussed in the chapter on the law of
contract (see p. 250), are designed to prevent manufacturers entering into
agreements which restrict free competition and tend to fix prices in regard
to *goods*. The court investigates agreements which may be of this nature to
see whether they are contrary to the public interest. The court has power to
enforce its ruling by injunction, but in practice business men do not try to
implement an agreement which the court has not sanctioned. The court
also deals with the question of resale price maintenance agreements under
the Resale Prices Act, 1976 (see page 250) and acquired an additional
jurisdiction under the Fair Trading Act, 1973 (see now Restrictive Trade
Practices Act, 1976) to consider restrictive agreements in regard to *services*
(see p. 250). In addition, now that we have become a member of the EEC
the competition rules laid down in the Treaty of Rome are as from the 1st
January 1973 part of our own law. Two Articles of the Treaty of Rome
provide for common rules of competition (Articles 85 and 86) and the
Court may be required to consider these from time to time. Under Sect. 5
of the Restrictive Trade Practices Act, 1976 the Restrictive Practices Court
may postpone or defer taking certain decisions under the provisions of the
Restrictive Trade Practices Act, 1976, where this would conflict with
Community law. In addition, under Sect. 34 of the Restrictive Trade
Practices Act, 1976, an agreement is exempt from registration so long as
there is in force in relation to that agreement an authorization given for the
purpose of any provision in the European Coal and Steel Community
Treaty relating to restrictive trade practices.

The Court consists of the following judges—one of whom is appointed
by the Lord Chancellor to be President of the Court; three *puisne* judges of
the High Court nominated by the Lord Chancellor; one judge of the Court
of Session of Scotland nominated by the President of that Court; one judge
of the Supreme Court of Northern Ireland nominated by the Lord Chief
Justice of Northern Ireland. The judges, are assisted by up to ten laymen
appointed by the Queen on the recommendation of the Lord Chancellor,
as being persons with knowledge of, or experience in industry, commerce
or public affairs. The court may sit in divisions, each division being
constituted by one judge and two laymen. The judges decide matters of law
but matters of fact are decided by a majority of the members of the court.
Where the proceedings involve only issues of law the court may consist of a
single member, that member being a judge.

The Court of Appeal

The Court of Appeal consists of two divisions—

(*a*) the *Civil Division* which exercises the jurisdiction formerly exercised
by the former Court of Appeal, and

(*b*) the *Criminal Division* which exercises the jurisdiction formerly exercised by the Court of Criminal Appeal.

Civil Division.   The work of the Civil Division is carried out by up to 16 Lords Justices of Appeal. This number may be increased by Order in Council. The Court is presided over by the Master of the Rolls. A normal court consists of three judges but there may on occasion be a full court of five or seven. The qualification for a Lord Justice of Appeal is 15 years' standing as a barrister or having been a *puisne* judge. They are appointed by the Queen on the advice of the Prime Minister and the Master of the Rolls. It should be noted that also included in the judiciary in the Civil Division are the Lord Chancellor, ex-Lord Chancellors, Law Lords, the Lord Chief Justice, and the President of the Family Division. The Lord Chancellor may also request judges of the High Court to sit.

As regards jurisdiction, the Civil Division hears appeals from any division of the High Court and from the County Court and from orders of Judges in Chambers or Masters in Chambers regarding pre-trial matters. The Court may on appeal uphold or reverse the lower court or substitute a new judgment. Exceptionally, it may order a new trial as where evidence has been improperly admitted or rejected.

Criminal Division.   The work of the Criminal Division is carried out by the Lord Chief Justice and the 16 Lords Justices of Appeal who also sit in the Civil Division. It should also be noted that the Lord Chief Justice may ask any judge of the High Court to sit in the Criminal Division. The normal court consists of three judges but sometimes a full court of five or seven will sit if the case is a difficult one.

As regards jurisdiction, the Criminal Division hears appeals from the Crown Court against conviction and sentence and may dismiss or allow the appeal but cannot increase a sentence. In addition the Home Secretary may refer a case to the Criminal Division so that, for example, a sentence might be reviewed. Furthermore, the Attorney General may refer for an opinion a point of law arising from a charge which resulted in an acquittal. The Court may order a new trial under Sect. 7 of the Criminal Appeal Act, 1968. However, this power can only be used in cases where there is fresh and credible evidence and the Court considers that it is in the interests of justice to receive it even though it was available and admissible at the trial. There is also a power to order a new trial at common law where there has been a fundamental defect in the trial so that it was a nullity. Thus, in *R. v. Ishmael,* [1970] Crim. LR. 399 the accused had been sentenced to life imprisonment having pleaded guilty at his trial to an offence under Sect. 3 of the Malicious Damage Act, 1861 (arson of buildings, punishable by life imprisonment) thinking he was charged with an offence under Sect. 7 of the 1861 Act (arson of goods, punishable by 14 years' imprisonment). The Court of Appeal held that he must be tried again.

House of Lords

Constitution.   The Court is constituted by the Lord Chancellor and up to 11 Lords of Appeal in Ordinary (or Law Lords). The Law Lords are life peers and each of them is appointed by the Queen on the Prime Minister's advice from among barristers of at least 15 years' standing or from *puisne* judges who have held office for at least two years. Normally the appointments are made from among the Lords Justices of Appeal. Three judges normally constitute a court.

Jurisdiction.   (*a*) *Civil.* On the civil side the House of Lords hears appeals from the Court of Appeal (Civil Division), the Court of Session in Scotland, when one or two Scottish Law Lords sit, and the Supreme Court of Northern Ireland when a Law Lord from Northern Ireland sits. In all cases the lower court must certify that a point of law of general public importance is involved and either the lower court or the Appeal Committee of the House of Lords consisting of three Law Lords must give leave. In addition, there is a direct appeal from the High Court or Divisional Court to the House of Lords by what is referred to as the 'leapfrogging method'. This phrase is used because the appeal goes straight to the House of Lords and not through the Court of Appeal. All parties must consent and the appeal must raise a point of law of public importance relating wholly or mainly to a statute or statutory instrument. The trial judge must certify the importance of the case and the House of Lords must give leave. This 'leapfrogging' procedure is most likely to be used in revenue appeals and patent matters where construction of statutes is often very involved.

(*b*) *Criminal.*   On the criminal side the Court hears appeals from the Court of Appeal (Criminal Division) and the Divisional Court of Queen's Bench. In both cases the lower court must certify that a point of law of general public importance is involved and either the lower court or the Appeal Committee of the House of Lords must give leave.

The Judicial Committee of the Privy Council

The Privy Council is a lineal descendant of the ancient King's Council, and was originally a sort of cabinet advising the Crown. The Judicial Committee, which is not part of the Supreme Court, is a final court of appeal in civil and criminal matters from the courts of some Commonwealth and Colonial territories, but the changes which have taken place in the Commonwealth have restricted the number of cases coming before it, many Commonwealth countries preferring to hear appeals within their own judicial systems. However, some aspects of this jurisdiction survive. The court is still the final court of appeal from the Channel Islands and the Isle of Man, and also from those islands and colonies, such as Gibraltar, Hong Kong and Belize, whose independence is not a viable proposition. There is strictly speaking no right of appeal, but it is customary to petition the Crown for leave to appeal. It is also the final court of appeal from English ecclesiastical courts, and here it is assisted by the Archbishops of Canterbury and York who, as assessors, advise on ecclesiastical matters. In wartime it hears appeals from the Admiralty Court on matters concerning prize. The Judicial Committe is comprised of the Lord Chancellor, the Lords of Appeal in Ordinary, and all Privy Councillors who have held high judicial office in the United Kingdom, together with Commonwealth judges who have been appointed members of the Privy Council. It does not actually decide cases, but advises the Crown which implements the advice by an Order in Council. This advice used to be unanimous, but since March, 1966, dissenting members of the Privy Council who were present at the hearing of the appeal may express their dissent, giving reasons therefor. The Court is not bound by its own previous decisions.

The European Court of Justice

This Court, which sits in Luxembourg, is charged with ensuring that Community law is observed in regard to the interpretation and implementation of the Treaties. Its decisions must be accepted by the courts of member states and there is no right of appeal. Matters before the Court are disposed of in front of all the judges, though some preliminary (or interlocutory) matters can be dealt with by a division of three judges.

Each member state appoints one judge so that there are nine and the judges themselves elect the President of the Court. There is no requirement of professional law practice and the Court consists of professional judges, academic lawyers and public servants. A judge may be removed only by unanimous decision of the other judges.

Procedure. There is more emphasis upon submissions in writing (pleadings) rather than oral argument. The proceedings are more inquisitorial and the judges play a more active role in terms of asking questions during hearings.

There are three advocates-general to assist the court and they give an independent view of the proceedings *at the end of the case.*

The Court gives a single judgment and no dissenting views are given. Enforcement of judgments is through the national courts of member states. The language in which the case is heard is a matter for the plaintiff, except where the defendant is a member state when it will be in the language of that state.

Role of the European Court at Luxembourg. It was decided by the Court of Appeal in *Bulmer* v. *Bollinger,* [1974] 2 All E.R. 1226 that the High Court and the Court of Appeal have a jurisdiction to interpret Community Law and that they are not obliged to grant a right of appeal to the European Court of Justice. However, if the case goes to the House of Lords on appeal, the House of Lords is bound to refer the matter to the European Court of Justice if either or both of the parties wishes this. The decision in

Bulmer was based upon an interpretation of Article 177 of the Treaty. In the case Bulmers had marketed products for many years under the name of 'Champagne Cider' and 'Champagne Perry'. Bollingers claimed that this was contrary to an EEC regulation which restricted the use of the word 'champagne' to wine produced from grapes grown in the Champagne district of France. The Court of Appeal decided that since cider was made from apples and perry was made from pears, there was no infringement of the regulation. The Court also refused to refer the matter to the European Court.

In the course of his judgment Lord Denning, M.R., laid down certain guidelines to assist judges in deciding whether to refer a case to the European Court or not. The main guidelines are as follows—

(i) *The time to get a ruling.* The length of time which may elapse before a ruling can be obtained from the European Court should always be borne in mind. The average length of time at present seems to be between six and nine months. It is important to prevent undue protraction of proceedings.

(ii) *The European Court must not be overloaded.* In this connection it should be borne in mind that the European Court consists of nine judges. All nine must sit on a reference from a national court and they cannot split up into divisions of three or five judges. Thus, if there are too many references, the Court would not be able to get through its work.

(iii) *The reference must be on a question of interpretation only of the Treaty.* It is a matter for the national courts to find the facts and apply the Treaty, though the way in which the national court has interpreted the Treaty can then be a matter for reference.

3　Criminal and civil procedure

Having described the system of major civil and criminal courts existing in England and Wales, we shall before looking at other courts and tribunals, consider the procedure in those major courts which leads to a prosecution for crime or to an action for, say, damages at civil law.

CRIMINAL PROCEDURE

The system of trial in this country is accusatorial in that a trial is a contest between two persons. As regards crime, these persons are normally the Queen (on behalf of the community) and the person accused of the crime.

Barristers (called counsel) representing the prosecution and the defence each put forward evidence to the court so that a decision may be made on the question before the court which is, did the accused commit the offence with which he is charged?

It should also be noted in particular that a person accused of crime is presumed innocent until proved guilty and is given certain protections in regard to the proof of his guilt as follows—

(a) the Judges' Rules which ensure that a person cannot be trapped by questioning into an admission of guilt. The main safeguard of the Rules is that once an investigating police officer has evidence which gives reasonable grounds for suspecting that the person being questioned has committed an offence, questioning can continue, but only after the suspect has been 'cautioned'. This involves telling the suspect that he need not say anything but that, if he does, what he says may be written down and used at his trial. At any subsequent trial anything said by the person while a suspect may be used for or against his case.

(b) Once in court the prosecution must prove its case beyond all reasonable doubt.

The prosecutor

A prosecution is usually started by the police acting on behalf of the community but a private individual can ask the court to issue a summons.

The police are usually advised whether or not to bring a prosecution in terms, for example, of the evidence available, by prosecuting solicitors who are employed also to conduct prosecutions for the police authority.

Government departments, such as the Inland Revenue, also employ a staff of prosecutors to bring prosecutions for offences in connection with the department's activities, for example fraudulent tax evasion.

The Director of Public Prosecutions. The Director of Public Prosecutions may also become involved. The office of Director of Public Prosecutions was created by the Prosecution of Offences Act, 1879. He is appointed by the Home Secretary from among barristers or solicitors of not less than ten years' standing but acts under the superintendance of the Attorney-General. The Director prosecutes through his own staff and on some occasions through Treasury Counsel.

Sometimes an offence *must* be referred to the Director before prosecution. For example, under Sect. 25 of the Companies Act, 1976, a company whose shares are quoted on the Stock Exchange is required to inform the Stock Exchange of the purchase of shares in the company by its own directors. Failure to give such information can lead to the prosecution of the company and its directors but such a prosecution can only be brought with the consent of either the Secretary of State for Trade or the Director of Public Prosecutions.

Even if the offence is not one which must be referred to the Director, his advice is often sought by police authorities where, for example, the authority concerned is not sure whether there is sufficient evidence to warrant the institution of criminal proceedings in a particular case.

If there is sufficient evidence the Director may decide to undertake the prosecution and where this is so a member of the Director's staff will deal with the hearing before the magistrates. However, once the case is committed for trial to a Crown Court the Director applies to the Attorney-General for a barrister practising on the relevant circuit to take the case. If the case is committed to the Central Criminal Court (the Old Bailey) the Director will himself nominate one or two Treasury Counsel to prosecute. Treasury Counsel are barristers who have been nominated by the Attorney-General to receive briefs from the Director of Public Prosecutions in respect of prosecutions at the Central Criminal Court.

The prosecutions usually undertaken by the Director are—

(*a*) those of a serious nature, such as the prosecution of terrorists;

(*b*) those where the standing of the accused in the community is such as to cause embarrassment to a local police force as where, for example, a Lord Mayor is accused of driving while under the influence of drink;

(*c*) those involving corruption and false reporting, as where a local councillor has accepted bribes from a property developer in return for the granting of planning permission, and where a hoaxer has wasted police time by deliberately giving false information in regard, for example, to the planting of a bomb.

Involvement of Attorney-General. In some cases the consent of the Attorney-General is required before prosecution. This applies, for example, in the case of prosecutions under the Official Secrets Acts.

Getting the person accused into court

All persons accused of crime appear first in the Magistrates' Court. The appearance of the person accused is obtained by a summons or warrant. To get a summons the prosecutor, usually a police officer, must give a short account of the alleged offence in writing or orally to the magistrates or their clerk (a process called laying an information). A summons setting out the offence is then issued and served upon the person accused either in person or through Recorded Delivery or Registered post.

If the accused is not likely to attend court voluntarily in answer to the summons, or if the police do not know where he is, then they may apply for a warrant for his arrest. This involves the person laying the information referred to above being required to swear an oath that it is true.

In addition, an accused person may be brought before the court without a summons or warrant since a police officer has powers of arrest without a warrant. For example, if he suspects that an arrestable offence has been, is being, or is about to be committed, he may arrest without warrant anyone whom he reasonably suspects to be guilty of committing or about to commit that offence. Most crimes of theft under the Theft Act, 1968, are arrestable offences because they fit the definition of such offences being punishable with five years' imprisonment or more.

When a person is arrested he must be charged as soon as possible and should appear before the magistrates within 24 hours. When he appears the prosecution or defence can ask the court to adjourn the proceedings in order for example, that witnesses may be found, and that the case for and against the accused person may be put together. In these circumstances the question of giving bail to the defendant arises.

Bail

The granting of bail is now covered by the Bail Act, 1976. Section 4 of the Act contains a new statutory presumption in favour of granting bail. Under the section a person accused of crime must be granted bail unless—

(*a*) he is charged with, or convicted of, an offence which is punishable with imprisonment and the court is satisfied there are good grounds for believing that, if released on bail, he would fail to appear at a subsequent hearing or commit an offence while on bail or obstruct the course of justice by intimidating witnesses; or

(*b*) the court is satisfied that he ought to remain in custody for his own protection, or if he is a juvenile, for his own welfare; or

(*c*) there has not been enough time to obtain information about the defendant for the court to reach a decision; or (*d*) the defendant has been convicted of an imprisonable offence and remanded for enquiries or, say, a medical report, and it seems to the court that it is not practical to complete the enquiries or make the report unless the defendant is kept in custody.

Where the defendant is charged with, or convicted of, an offence which is not punishable with imprisonment, the grounds for refusing bail are much more restricted. However, such a person can be refused bail if he has previously failed to answer bail and if the court believes, in view of that failure, that he will again fail to surrender to custody if released on bail.

Section 3 abolishes the old system under which persons, including the defendant, were asked to agree to pay a sum of money if the defendant absconded and did not attend at court as required. In its place the section imposes a duty upon a person granted bail to surrender to custody. This duty is enforceable by the creation of the new offence of absconding in Sect. 6. Security for surrender to custody and sureties may not be required nor conditions imposed on the grant of bail except as provided by the section. Thus security may be required only of a defendant if it appears likely that he will leave Great Britain. The court may ask for sureties to provide an additional guarantee to secure the defendant's surrender to custody. As regards conditions, the section makes it plain that these are only to be imposed to ensure the defendant's surrender to custody, that he does not commit a further offence while on bail, that he does not interfere with the course of justice, as by intimidating witnesses, and that he makes himself available for the purposes of enabling enquiries or a report to be made. The section also provides for the parent or guardian of a juvenile to stand as surety in a sum not exceeding £50 to ensure that the juvenile complies with the requirements attached to the grant of bail.

Section 6 creates the new offence of failing, without reasonable cause, to surrender at the time and place appointed. The offence is punishable in a magistrates' court by a maximum of three months' imprisonment and/or a fine, and in a superior court, such as a Crown Court, with 12 months' imprisonment and/or a fine. Section 7 provides for the arrest of a defendant who fails to surrender himself to custody at the appointed time and place or who breaches any of the conditions attached to the grant of bail.

If the court requires sureties under Sect. 3, then Sect. 8 provides for the first time in statutory form some matters which should be taken into account in deciding the suitability of sureties. The list, which is neither mandatory nor exhaustive, relates to the financial resources, character (including previous convictions) and proximity to the defendant (in terms of blood relationship, dwelling, or otherwise) of the proposed surety. In addition, the section enables a person who is not accepted as a surety to apply to a court to have the matter reconsidered. Section 9 creates the new offence of agreeing at any time and regardless of whether or not a person becomes in fact a surety, to indemnify that person against his liability as a surety. Thus, if A asks B to stand as a surety for C and tells B that he (A) will pay to B any sum which B has to pay into court because C absconds, then A commits this new offence. The penalties for this offence are the same as those for the offence of absconding. No proceedings may be instituted under this section without the consent of the Director of Public Prosecutions. Section 10 extends the power of Coroners to grant bail where a coroner's inquisition charges a person with an offence so that it covers the offences of murder, manslaughter, or infanticide. The section also applies the main provisions of the Act to bail granted by coroners.

Section 11 provides for the granting of legal aid on a wider basis than before for defendants who wish to be represented in actions relating to whether they are entitled to bail or not.

The two major weaknesses of the Act are as follows—

(*a*) it does not place any duty on the court to find out the defendant's personal circumstances so that there continues to be the risk that the court will hear only the police view on the bail/custody issue.

(*b*) The Act does not deal with the duration of remands in custody. Remands in custody are frequently made because of a police objection to bail on the basis that there are further police enquiries to be made. There are those who think that this should not stand as a distinct ground for refusing bail and that the court should question the police more closely when they object to bail on these grounds. However, the Act makes no reference to this problem.

Before leaving the subject of bail, the provision of bail hostels is worthy of consideration. These hostels, which are provided by the probation service, are growing in number and provide an accused person with an address so that he need not necessarily be remanded in custody because he has no fixed abode which is still a ground under Sect. 24(1)(b) of the Criminal Justice Act, 1967, though persons of no fixed abode are not bound to be refused bail. The Secretary of State is given power to approve bail hostels and to provide a system of inspection under sections 49 and 50 of the Powers of Criminal Courts Act, 1973. Before this statutory measure there were only a limited number of such hostels provided by voluntary organizations.

Summary trial before magistrates (other than juvenile offenders)

Since the majority of summary trials before magistrates relate to motoring offences, such an offence has been chosen as an example of the form summary trial.

The alleged offence.   Let us suppose that on 29 March, 1978, Freda Jones was driving her sports car along George Road, Barchester and that her attention was distracted by road works so that she ran into the back of a stationary delivery van which was parked at the kerbside in an area where no parking restrictions were in force.

The summons.   The police are intending to bring a prosecution against Freda under the Road Traffic Act, 1972, for careless driving. Freda will receive a summons as follows.

'IN THE COUNTY OF BARCHESTERSHIRE
PETTY SESSIONAL DIVISIONAL OF BARCHESTER

To Freda Jones
  Acacia Avenue, Barchester, Barchestershire.

INFORMATION has this day been laid before me, the undersigned by PETER GREEN of the Barchestershire Constabulary that you on the 29th day of March, 1978 at Barchester in the said County, unlawfully did drive a motor car on a road called George Road without due care and attention.
Contrary to Sect. 3 of the Road Traffic Act, 1972.

YOU ARE THEREFORE HEREBY SUMMONED TO APPEAR on Monday the 9th day of July, 1978 at the hour of ten in the forenoon, before the Magistrates' Court sitting at Church Road, Barchester in the said County to answer to the said information.
Dated the 30th Day of May, 1978

(signed) J. Bloggs
Clerk of the Magistrates' Court sitting at Barchester.'

Freda will be asked to send her driving licence to the court before the hearing or produce it at the hearing. She will also be advised that her attendance at the hearing, either personally or by a solicitor on her behalf, is essential. It is usual to take guilty pleas on the day fixed in the summons which will tell Freda this. If she pleads guilty she must inform the Barchester Police; otherwise a new date is fixed for the trial of pleas of not guilty.

The trial.   On the assumption that Freda is to plead not guilty, the procedure is as set out below.
The charge.   Freda appears in answer to the summons and the first thing that happens is that the Clerk to the Magistrates reads out the offence with which she is charged.
Election to trial by jury.   This does not arise in Freda's case because the offence of careless driving under Sect. 3 of the Road Traffic Act, 1972, cannot be tried on indictment before a jury. If, however, the police had decided to charge her with reckless driving under Sect. 2 of the Road Traffic Act, 1972 (as amended by Sect. 50 of the Criminal Law Act, 1977) the question of trial on indictment would have arisen because the offence is triable either way.
Freda's plea.   Since Freda's case will be dealt with summarily by the magistrates, the next step is that the clerk will ask her whether she pleads

guilty or not guilty. If Freda pleads guilty the magistrates have the power to convict her without hearing evidence, though they also have the power to decide that even on a guilty plea it is desirable in the circumstances to hear evidence on oath.

The prosecution's case.   Since we know that Freda will plead not guilty, the prosecution will have to prove its case. The prosecutor, usually a police officer or a solicitor acting for the police, will give a summary of the evidence which he proposes to call and of the effect of that evidence on the charge. He will then call his witnesses and ask questions of them (called examination in chief). It is then open to Freda or her solicitor to cross-examine the witnesses for the prosecution.

The defence.   When the case for the prosecution has been presented the defence may—

(*a*) submit that there is no case to answer; or

(*b*) proceed to open the case for the defence.

The choice in (*a*) above could be taken where, for example, the witnesses for the prosecution had broken down under cross-examination and changed or partly changed their evidence, or contradicted each other. Freda's solicitor may support his submission of no case to answer by a speech in which he may draw the attention of the court to inconsistencies and omissions in the prosecution's case.

The court will then consider the submission and may retire in order to do so. Should the court accept the submission the case is dismissed. If they find that there is a case to answer the the defence proceeds. On the assumption that the court does not accept the submission of no case to answer, oral evidence is given by witnesses for the defence and by the defendant and there may be a speech by or on behalf of the defendant, either before or after the evidence is heard, or if the court permits, both before and after and the prosecution may call witnesses in reply. If there are two speeches by or on behalf of the defendant the prosecution has a right to make a speech in reply. Should there be no witnesses for the defence other than the defendant there may be a speech by or on behalf of the defendant, either before or after the defendant has given evidence.

Otherwise the prosecution has no right to address the court in reply unless a point of law is raised in which case the prosecution can present arguments in relation to the law.

Decision and sentence.   When the case for the defence is closed and after hearing witnesses for the prosecution who may have been called in reply, the court must consider whether to convict the defendant or dismiss the information. If it decides to convict it will then enquire whether the accused has any previous convictions recorded against him and may hear both the prosecution and the defence as to his character. The defence may also address the court in what is called mitigation. This could consist, for example, of an address outlining the defendant's domestic stress, perhaps in Freda's case, that her boyfriend had recently been severely injured in a road accident. The court will then decide upon the sentence and announce it. Once the court has done this, or has dismissed the summons, it will not normally change its decision. However, magistrates' courts are given the power to re-open a case to rectify a mistake in any order they have made within 14 days. The court on the second occasion must be constituted in the same way as it was on the first occasion or with a majority of the same justices. This procedure could be used, for example, where the magistrates had omitted to order the endorsement of a defendant's driving licence.

If Freda's defence has failed, the magistrates can fine her or, in the case of a second or subsequent conviction, may sentence her to imprisonment for three months or fine her, or both. They have a discretion as to whether to disqualify her from driving, though an endorsement of her licence is obligatory.

Trial in a juvenile court

Those over the age of ten and under 17 *who are charged with a criminal offence* appear before a juvenile court as either a child (if aged ten to 14) or a young person (if over 14 and under 17). Minors under ten years of age are by presumption of law incapable of any crime. However, it is thought that children under ten, if caught in the act of damaging property, could be restrained by the police under their common law power to protect property or detained under Sect. 28(2) of the Children and Young Persons Act, 1969, on the grounds that they were beyond the control of their parents or guardians.

In addition to criminal proceedings, there are *care proceedings* which may be brought by the officers of a local authority, the police or other persons, for example, an inspector of the National Society for the Prevention of Cruelty to Children.

Care proceedings.   These may be brought because a minor of any age up to 17 is thought to be in some sort of trouble short of the commission of crime, as where he is not attending school or is beyond the control of parents or guardians.

However, care proceedings can be used even where an offence has been committed and so far as children and young persons are concerned, criminal proceedings are usually brought only as a last resort.

In order to illustrate the procedure in care proceedings we shall take the case of Philip Green, aged 14, who has had a history of not attending school for periods of time and of violence within the school involving attacks on other pupils and, more recently, on a teacher. Philip's father is dead and his mother finds difficulty in preventing this sort of conduct. Let us assume that all of this has resulted in the county council making application for a care order.

When Philip arrives at the court accompanied by his mother (parents are asked to be present and if they do not attend the court may adjourn the hearing until one of them does) he will find that there are no formalities. The bench in juvenile courts consists of not more than three persons of whom one must be a woman and one a man. The hearing is whenever possible held in an ordinary room and not in a court room.

Before the case starts Philip and his mother will be invited to enter the room and sit on chairs facing the magistrates' table.

The clerk will explain that the county council allege that Philip is beyond the control of his mother and that his proper development will be prevented unless a care order is made. Philip and his mother will then be asked if they understand the county council's allegations.

Counsel for the county council will then go through the details of Philip's difficult behaviour and may call witnesses, e.g. Philip's headmaster. Philip will be invited to ask questions of the witnesses and in any case Philip's own lawyer will cross-examine the witnesses. In addition to evidence as to the facts evidence will also be given by experts, e.g. those employed by child guidance clinics who would normally have seen Philip over the period of his difficult behaviour and have formed a view as to the best method of dealing with the problem.

When all the witnesses have been examined and cross-examined Philip will be asked to make a statement which is mainly designed to see whether he disagrees with what has been said about him. Philip's mother will also be asked to make a statement.

After this the magistrates retire and let us assume that they find that the county council has proved its case. If so, and the court feels that there is no alternative, it will put Philip into the care of the county council, which means that he will live, for example, in a community home, until he is 18, though if he responds well the county council may go back to the juvenile court and ask that the order be revoked before he reaches 18.

Criminal proceedings.   Where children or young persons are found guilty of a criminal offence in a juvenile court the magistrates may still make a care order, even though the proceedings are not care proceedings. However, there are other possibilities open to them. In the main these are fines and also the following—

(a) *supervision orders.*   These have replaced probation orders and when such an order has been made the child continues to live at home under the supervision of the local authority social services department, though in the case of persons of 14 years and over, the Probation Service carries out the supervision.

(b) *Borstal treatment.*   This is in the main intended for young offenders who are over 17. However, where the person of, say, 16 is found guilty of an offence which is punishable by imprisonment and his previous record is bad, the magistrates can recommend Borstal treatment and commit the offender to the Crown Court which alone can make the decision whether to send the offender to Borstal on the magistrates' recommendation.

A criminal trial in the juvenile court proceeds in the usual way with the prosecution opening its case and witnesses being examined in chief and cross-examined. Then the case for the defence is presented and the magistrates retire to make a decision. If they decide that the young person is guilty his previous convictions, if any, are made known to the court. There is often a report by a probation officer and after considering this sentence is passed.

Section 36 of the Criminal Law Act, 1977 empowers magistrates courts to enforce fines imposed on juveniles by making an attendance centre order on the juvenile if he does not pay or by binding over the juvenile's parents or legal guardian, or by transferring the fine to the parent or legal guardian.

Juveniles in adult courts

Sometimes a person under 17 may appear in an adult court. The circumstances are as follows—

(*a*) when the young person is charged jointly with a person over 17 and the magistrates think they should be tried together, as where they are members of a gang;

(*b*) when a child or young person is charged, for example, with murder or some other serious offence, he will be sent for trial to the Crown Court.

Trial on indictment in the Crown Court

Persons appearing in the Crown Court for trial on indictment have committed rather serious offences. They will have appeared before a magistrates' court and been committed for trial by that court after a preliminary hearing in which the prosecution has made out a *prima facie* case against the person accused. That is, the prosecution has shown that there is sufficient evidence against the accused to make a full trial necessary.

Before the preliminary hearing the accused will no doubt have appeared before the magistrates and may have been remanded. Issues of bail or no bail will have been decided and the accused will have been instructed how to apply for legal aid and given the necessary form.

Legal aid. The Legal Aid Act, 1974, Sects 28–40 consolidate the law relating to legal aid in criminal proceedings. Aid is given only to those charged with offences and is not available to persons wishing to bring a prosecution.

Application for legal aid in criminal cases is made either orally or in writing to the Clerk of the Court. The applicant must complete a written statement as to his means and the clerk or the court itself must be satisfied that it is desirable in the interests of justice that legal aid should be given and that the applicant's means are such that he needs assistance in meeting the costs of his case. The applicant may be required to make a contribution towards his costs.

The Act covers most criminal proceedings ranging from those in magistrates' courts to appeals to the House of Lords. However, appeals to the Divisional Court of Queen's Bench and from that court to the House of Lords are dealt with under the civil legal aid scheme.

When legal aid is granted the defendant will normally receive the services of a solicitor in those courts such as the magistrates' courts where solicitors have a right of audience. In those courts where solicitors may not appear as advocates the defendant is given a solicitor and counsel. In serious cases such as murder the legal aid certificate will be for two counsel, i.e. a leader and a junior. (See p. 90.)

The cost of legal aid which is given in magistrates' courts is provided from the legal aid fund maintained under the civil legal aid system. In cases in all other courts it is met by the Home Secretary.

There is also the custom of 'Dock Briefs' under which an accused person can for a small fee choose any counsel who is robed and in court to defend him. Counsel so chosen is bound to defend the accused.

Reporting of committal proceedings.   In general, the only evidence given at committal proceedings is by the prosecution, the accused merely reserving his defence for the actual trial. If full reporting of committal proceedings was allowed, the accused could be prejudiced because by the time his trial occurred the general public, including probably the jury, would have read only one side of the case and might have reached the conclusion that the accused was guilty. However, this need not happen because under Sect. 3 of the Criminal Justice Act, 1967, newspaper, television, and radio reports of committal proceedings are restricted to the following matters—

(a) the name of the court and the names of the justices;

(b) the names, addresses, ages and occupations of the prosecutor, defendants, and witnesses;

(c) the offences under consideration;

(d) the names of the advocates;

(e) the decision of the court;

(f) where a committal is ordered, the charges involved;

(g) the name of the higher court to which the committal is ordered;

(h) in the case of an adjournment, the date and place to which the hearing is adjourned;

(i) any order as to bail and whether or not legal aid was granted.

On conviction for an offence against the above provisions, editors and publishers of newspapers and periodicals, together with their counterparts in the field of broadcasting, are liable to a maximum fine not exceeding £500. (Criminal Justice Act, 1967, Sect. 3(5)(c).)

If a defendant, or one of a number of co-defendants, applies to the court for unrestricted reports, the court must so order. The order applies to the totality of the committal proceedings, unless they are severed as between defendants, so that full reports can be made of the evidence against all the defendants whether they have agreed or not. (*R.* v. *Russell, ex parte Beaverbrook Newspapers,* [1968] 3 All E.R. 695.)

This provision was included for the benefit of a defendant who believed that full reporting was, on balance, beneficial to him because the publicity might, for example, induce witnesses to come forward in his defence. It is regrettable, however, that the provision was so worded as to require the court to lift the restrictions entirely whenever one defendant makes an application and regardless of the wishes of other defendants who are being proceeded against at the same hearing; it would have been better to have so worded the provision that the court was only required to lift the restriction insofar as it applied to matters relevant to the proceedings against the defendant making the application.

There is no restriction on reporting if the magistrates decide not to commit for trial. After the trial of the defendant (or the last if there is more than one defendant) reporters can mention in detail matters raised in committal proceedings.

When a preliminary hearing changes into a summary trial reporters can report fully the committal proceedings which took place before the summary trial.

Liability may be incurred under the 1967 Act where a report of committal proceedings contains *any* details other than those permitted by Sect. 3 and quite irrespective of whether or not the details are potentially prejudicial in nature. (*The Eastbourne Herald Case,* 1973.)[9] This distinguishes the statutory offence from the common law offence of contempt of court. If there is to be a contempt, the material published must be likely to be prejudicial to a fair trial.

Alibi. Section 11 of the Criminal Justice Act, 1967, is designed to prevent the use of 'sprung' or late alibis which were once so widespread in criminal trials. The section provides that, in general, notice of alibi must be given in advance of a trial on indictment. This is not required in summary trials because of the ease with which the prosecution can ask for an adjournment where the defendant 'springs' an alibi on the prosecution at the last moment.

The following warning (or one similar to it) must be given during the course of committal proceedings.

'You will be committed for trial by jury, but I must warn you that at that trial you may not be permitted to give evidence of an alibi or to call witnesses in support of an alibi unless you have earlier given particulars of the alibi and of the witnesses. You may give those particulars now to this court or at any time in the next seven days to the solicitor for the prosecution, who is . . . (name and address of solicitor).'

Although this warning need not be given if it seems unecessary having regard to the nature of the offence charged, it should as a general rule be given where there is any doubt, because the Act provides that failure to give it will allow the defendant to introduce a last-minute alibi at his trial. Where an unrepresented defendant does not appear to understand what is meant by 'alibi', the word must be explained to him.

There is a discretion in the trial judge to allow alibi evidence to be heard even though particulars of it were not given within seven days, provided the prosecution has been given time to investigate the alibi before the trial started. (*R. v. Sullivan,* [1970] 2 All E.R. 681.) Notice is also required when the only evidence to be given in regard to alibi is that of the accused himself. (*R. v. Jackson and Robertson,* [1973] Crim. L.R. 356.)

Place and time of trial.   Under Sect. 7(1) of the Courts Act, 1971, a magistrates' court committing a person to trial on indictment to the Crown Court has to specify the Crown Court centre at which he is to be tried and in selecting that centre must have regard to—

(*a*) the convenience of the defence, the prosecution and the witnesses;

(*b*) the expediting of the trial;

(*c*) any directions regarding the distribution of Crown Court business given by the Lord Chief Justice or by an officer of the Crown Court with the concurrence of the Lord Chancellor under Sect. 4(5) of the Act.

Under Sect. 7(2) the Crown Court may alter the place of any trial on indictment by varying the decision of the magistrates or a previous decision on the matter made by the Crown Court. Under Sect. 7(3) the defendant or the prosecutor, if dissatisfied with the place of trial as fixed by the magistrates or by the Crown Court, may apply to the Crown Court to vary the place of trial. The Crown Court may deal with the application as it sees fit. An application under Sect. 7(3) must be heard in open court by a High Court judge.

The above provisions are designed to bring an accused person to trial as quickly as possible. However, the prosecutor and the accused and his advisers must be given time in which to prepare the case properly. Accordingly, Sect. 7(4) provides for the laying down under Crown Court Rules of minimum and maximum periods from the date of committal when the trial shall commence. These minimum periods cannot be *shortened* without the consent of the accused and the prosecutor or *lengthened* without an order of the Crown Court.

The offence and indictment.   Let us suppose that Jim Green has recently and successfully objected to the granting of planning permission to Fred Brown, his neighbour, which has prevented Fred from using part of his land for car-breaking. Let us also suppose that on the evening of 25th February, 1978, Jim left home for work and shortly afterwards in a lane not far from his home he was attacked by Fred who was wearing a black balaclava over his head. Fred hit Jim over the head with a spanner and medical evidence showed that Jim sustained a laceration on top of his head which required several stitches. Jim was detained in hospital for several days.

Fred is now to be tried on indictment for the offence. An indictment is a printed accusation of crime made at the suit of the Queen and read out to the accused at the trial. In Fred's case the main contents of the indictment will state the court of trial and set out the following—

Fred Brown is charged with the following offence—

Statement of Offence—WOUNDING contrary to Sect. 20 of the Offences Against the Person Act, 1861.
Particulars of Offence—Fred Brown on the 25th February, 1978, in the County of Barchestershire, maliciously wounded Jim Green.

In this case there is only one offence but if there had been more each would have appeared in a separate paragraph. Each paragraph is referred to as 'count'.

Arraignment. When the day of Fred's trial arrives the clerk of the court will read out the indictment and ask Fred whether he pleads guilty or not guilty. This is called the arraignment.

If Fred pleads guilty counsel for the prosecution will give the court a summary of the evidence together with details of Fred's background and record. The defence will put in a plea for mitigation of sentence and sentence will then be passed.

We will assume that Fred pleads not guilty and in this case a jury must be sworn in.

Membership of the jury. There used to be two juries in criminal cases; the Grand Jury which considered the bill of indictment and, if satisfied that a *prima facie* case had been made out against the accused, certified it as a 'true bill'. The jury which actually tried the accused was known as the Petty Jury. The Grand Jury was abolished by the Criminal Justice Act, 1948. A preliminary hearing before magistrates now takes the place of a hearing before the Grand Jury. All indictable offences are triable before a jury of 12 persons which derives from the Petty Jury.

Under the Juries Act, 1974, a person is eligible for jury service if he or she is between the ages of 18 and 65, is included on the Register of Electors for parliamentary and local government elections, and has been resident in the United Kingdom, the Channel Islands, or the Isle of Man for at least five years since the age of 13. As regards exemptions and disqualifications, these include members of the judiciary, those concerned with the administration of justice, such as barristers and solicitors, the clergy, and persons receiving treatment for mental illness. The 1974 Act makes it an offence for anyone in these categories to serve as a juror. In addition, penalties are imposed upon persons who are eligible and have been duly summoned but fail to attend or are unfit through drink or drugs.

Those sentenced to life, or five years or more imprisonment, and anyone who has served a sentence of three months or more in prison or a Borstal institution during the previous ten years are disqualified.

Certain persons, although not ineligible for jury service, can if asked to serve, claim to be excused 'as of right'. These include members of Parliament, full-time serving members of H.M. Forces, and those in medical or similar professions. In addition, the 1974 Act provides that a person summoned for jury service may be excused for good reasons whether he is in one of the special classes or not. The Act also provides for exemptions to be granted administratively for previous jury service; before only the trial judge could grant exemption.

As regards summoning and excusal, each summons for jury service is accompanied by details of the provisions for eligibility, disqualifications, and excusals as of right. A person receiving a summons will be asked to complete a form telling the court whether he or she is qualified for jury service and, if so, whether it is the person's wish to be excused either 'as of right' or for any other reason.

As regards disabilities, the 1974 Act provides that the court may also exclude anyone from jury service because physical disability or insufficient understanding of English makes his ability to act effectively as a juror doubtful. However, Sect. 18 provides that no judgment after verdict should be reversed by reason, amongst other things, that any juror was unqualified or unfit to serve. Thus in *R*. v. *Chapman*, (1976) 63 Cr. App.R. 75 where, after a trial at which both defendants had been found guilty by a unanimous verdict, it was discovered that one juror had been deaf so that he was unable to follow the proceedings, it was held that that did not make the verdict unsafe or unsatisfactory and was a situation covered by the Juries Act, 1974, Sect. 18.

Under Sect. 3 of the 1974 Act the responsibility for summoning jurors is placed upon the Lord Chancellor, though the court's administration at each centre acts as summoning officer. Juries are paid travelling and subsistence allowances and are compensated for loss of earnings and other expenses.

Advantages and disadvantages of jury trial.   Some take the view that the verdict of a jury is more acceptable to the public than the verdict of a judge, and certainly the jury system gives ordinary persons a part to play in the administration of justice. It is perhaps better that lay men and women should decide matters of fact and the credibility of witnesses. The jury system also tends to clarify the law, in that the judge has to explain the more important points arising at the trail in clear and simple terms, so that the jury may arrive at a proper verdict.

On the other hand, juries may be too easily swayed by experienced counsel and the random method of selection sometimes produces a jury which is not as competent in intellectual terms as it might be in weighing the evidence and following the arguments presented. It has been suggested that trial by (say) three judges would be better, particularly where difficult issues are involved.

Challenge.   The names of the jury are called out and each person goes into the witness box. At this point the defence may challenge up to three of them, without giving reasons, and they must be replaced. After that a challenge must be supported by reasons. A man may, for example, challenge the inclusion of a woman juror where his case involves wife-assault on the grounds that she will be less tolerant of that sort of conduct. The prosecution can also challenge jurors but must always give reasons.

The oath.   The jury are sworn by each holding a Bible in his right hand and reading the following oath—

'I swear by almighty God that I will faithfully try the several issues joined between our Sovereign Lady the Queen and the defendant and give a true verdict according to the evidence.'

The jury is then addressed by the clerk who explains the charges and tells them that having heard the evidence they must decide whether the defendant is guilty or not.

The judge.   Criminal offences are divided into four classes for the purpose of trial in a Crown Court. The full list is published in a Practice Note [1971] 3 All E.R. 829 but in broad terms the position is that *Class 1* offences, e.g. murder and offences under the Official Secrets Act, are tried by a High Court judge. *Class 2* offences, e.g. manslaughter, abortion, rape, sexual intercourse or incest with a girl under 13, are tried by a High Court judge unless a particular case is released as suitable for a circuit judge by or on the authority of the Circuit Presiding Judge (see p. 96) as where the circumstances of the offence are not of unusual gravity. *Class 3* offences, i.e. all indictable offences other than those in Classes 1, 2 and 4, e.g. sexual intercourse with a girl between the ages of 13 and 16, may be tried by a High Court judge or a Circuit judge or Recorder. *Class 4* offences are all offences which are triable summarily or on indictment, e.g. reckless driving, plus certain others, e.g. causing death by reckless driving. These may be tried by a High Court judge but will normally be listed for trial by a circuit judge or Recorder.

Thus it is likely that Fred will be tried by a Circuit judge or Recorder.

Trial and evidence.   The barrister appearing for the prosecution will outline his case to the Court and will call witnesses to confirm the facts. During the examination in chief, counsel for the prosecution must not lead his witnesses, i.e. must not suggest a particular answer to his question. Thus counsel for the prosecution cannot ask one of his witnesses, say, a police officer, 'did the defendant punch you when you arrested him?' He must instead say 'what happened when you arrested the defendant?'.

In addition hearsay evidence is not admissible. A witness must give evidence only as to what he himself saw or heard. Thus evidence given by a witness either for the prosecution or the defence in the form 'Alice told me that she saw Bill in the pub on Wednesday' would be inadmissible.

After counsel for the prosecution has carried out his examination in chief of a witness counsel for the defence can cross-examine the witness. In this situation he can lead and say, for example, 'my client was upset by the circumstances of his arrest, wasn't he? There was no need to have called him a lying swine, was there?'

When the prosecution has called all its witnesses the defence will present its case and call witnesses to support it. These witnesses are examined in chief, cross-examined, and sometimes re-examined.

The defendant may give evidence on oath or by affirmation on his own behalf or, alternatively, may make a statement, not on oath, without going into the witness box. If he gives evidence on oath in the ordinary way he may be cross-examined but there can be no cross-examination where a mere statement is made, though the making of a statement in this way often leads to the suggestion that the defendant has something to hide.

After the defence witnesses have been heard the prosecution makes its final speech, followed by the defence.

Summing up.   The judge will then explain his role to the jury. He will say that he will tell them what the law is and that the law is a matter for him but that they are the only judges of the facts in the case. The judge will then sum up the evidence on both sides and will explain that the verdict of the jury must be unanimous (but see below). The judge will then leave the court and the jury, escorted by a bailiff, will retire to a jury room where they must stay until they reach a verdict.

If the jury is unanimous in finding Fred guilty they will return to the court and the one count on the indictment will be put to the foreman of the jury who will give the verdict.

At this stage Fred's previous convictions, if any, will be handed to the judge who may refer to some of them openly in court. Counsel for the defence will then normally put in a plea in mitigation, saying, perhaps, that Fred has not been in trouble before or at least not for some time, according to his record, in the hope that this plea will lead to a lighter sentence.

The judge will then address the defendant and pass sentence, which, in view of the violence involved in Fred's case, is likely to be a term of imprisonment.

Majority verdicts.   The Juries Act, 1974, provides for majority verdicts of juries in criminal proceedings. Section 17 provides that the verdict of the jury in criminal proceedings need not be unanimous if—

(*a*) in a case where there are not less than *eleven* jurors, *ten* of them agree on the verdict; and (*b*) in a case where there are *ten* jurors, *nine* of them agree on the verdict.

A court must not accept a majority verdict of guilty unless the foreman of the jury has stated in open court the number of jurors who respectively agreed to and dissented from the verdict. No such statement is required if the verdict is one of not guilty so that it will not be known that a verdict of not guilty was by a majority.

Furthermore, a court must not accept a majority verdict unless it appears to the court that the jury have had not less than two hours' deliberation or such longer period as the court thinks reasonable, having regard to the nature and complexity of the case.

Nevertheless, the judge must encourage the jury in the first instance to try to arrive at a unanimous decision. He cannot accept a majority verdict after less than two hours' deliberation and if the jury is not unanimous after two hours he should send them back, at least once more, to try to reach unanimity. If they still cannot he should send them back to see if they can reach a decision by the necessary majority, having directed them on the law relating to majority verdicts.

When the jury returns to the courtroom the judge will ask whether the required majority has agreed on a verdict. If they have, the verdict is accepted *provided,* according to a Practice Direction made on 11 May 1970, that at least two hours and *ten minutes* have elapsed between the time at which the last juror left the jury box to go to the jury room and the time when the judge asked whether the jury had reached a verdict by the required majority.

Before the judge asks whether the jury has reached a majority verdict the senior officer of the court present must announce the deliberation time which the jury has had. The extra ten minutes was added in order to reduce the number of appeals made to the Court of Appeal on the ground that majority verdicts had been accepted although the deliberation time had been less than two hours, as for example, where the jury had returned to put a question to the court during the deliberation period.

The majority provision is, of course, a controversial one because the principle of the unanimous decision was an old and much-respected feature of English law. The main reason for the change was the growing problem of deliberate corruption or intimidation of jurors to secure an acquittal. The majority of ten to two was chosen because it was felt that it would be difficult to find more than one or two who were susceptible to bribery or intimidation, particularly in view of the fact that those with criminal records are excluded from jury service under the Juries Act, 1974.

Alternative verdicts. The common law, as re-stated by Sect. 6(3) and (4) of the Criminal Law Act, 1967, provides for alternative verdicts, which means that a jury can convict an accused of an offence other than the one with which he is charged. Although the wording of Sect. 6 appears wider that the common law rule, subsequent cases seem to indicate that a jury cannot convict of an offence different in *character* from the offence charged. The power is limited to a conviction for an offence involving *the same criminal act* but with a lesser degree of aggravation. For example, in Fred's case it would have been possible for the jury to bring in a verdict of common assault, although the charge was of unlawful wounding.

Number of jurors.   The number of jurors will normally be 12 unless the number has been reduced in accordance with Sect. 16 of the Juries Act, 1974. The section provides for the continuation of criminal trials where a juror dies or is discharged by the court, whether through illness or for any other reason.

If the number of members of the jury is not reduced below nine, the trial may proceed and the verdict may be given accordingly.

However, on a trial for murder or for any offence punishable with death, e.g. treason, this rule only applies if assent in writing is given by or on behalf of both the prosecution and the accused, or each of the accused if there is more than one.

Moreover, the court has discretion in any criminal trial to discharge the jury if it sees fit to do so when its numbers are depleted. If a trial has continued under the above provisions with nine jurors, Sect. 17 of the Juries Act, 1974, does not apply and the verdict must be unanimous.

Committal to Crown Court for sentence.

As we have seen, there are times when the Crown Court sits to sentence persons convicted of offences before the magistrates. This happens where the magistrates have found a particular defendant guilty and then have had access to his previous convictions showing, shall we say, a very bad record, and feel that the defendant should receive a greater sentence than they can give. In such a situation they will commit the defendant to the Crown Court for sentence.

The Crown Court may sit solely for the purpose of sentencing and if so consists of a judge (either a High Court judge or Circuit judge or Recorder) and not less than two nor more than four magistrates. The decision as regards the sentence is by a majority and if there is an equality of voting the judge has a casting vote.

Appeals in criminal cases

A person who has been convicted and sentenced by a criminal court has rights of appeal. These have already been considered in chapter 2 (and see p. 17).

Sentencing.

Before considering the range of sentences a criminal court can now give it may be advantageous to state in broad terms the purposes which are, or were, behind certain types of sentence. These are as follows—

(a) *the philosophy of retribution.* This is based on the idea of atonement. Retribution emphasizes the position of the social group against which the criminal offends rather than that of the criminal himself. By imposing punishment society exacts retribution. The science of criminal law has gradually moved away from this philosophy.

(b) *The philosophy of deterrence.* This emphasizes the social objective. Punishment must be designed so as to deter, as far as possible, the commission of similar defences in terms both of deterring an actual offender and other members of society who have not yet committed crimes. This philosophy still prevails in modern criminology.

(c) *The philosophy of reformation.* This involves the use of, for example, educational methods, either in addition to, or in substitution for, punishment proper. In general terms the increasing attempt to understand the social and psychological causes of crime has led to a growing emphasis on this philosophy.

Underlying all of the above philosophies is, of course, the need to protect society from the criminal and this leads on occasions to sentences which are *preventive* in aim such as, for example, long prison sentences and disqualification from driving.

Types of sentence. The death penalty is still available for treason but the Murder (Abolition of Death Penalty) Act, 1965, abolished the death penalty for murder. The sentence is now life imprisonment but the trial judge may recommend a minimum period for which the convicted person should be detained. In addition, there is no power to administer corporal punishment upon an offender. Sentences which are available are set out below.

(a) *Custodial sentences.* The punishment for most crimes is laid down by Acts of Parliament. The usual provision lays down a maximum fine and/or imprisonment, leaving the court to decide what sentence to give up to that maximum.

Persons who are serving life imprisonment may be released on licence by the Home Secretary at any time. Others are entitled to a reduction of sentence of up to one-third for good behaviour. In addition, those who have served one-third of their sentences may be released on licence or parole. The sentences available to the magistrates in juvenile courts have already been considered (see p. 42).

The Powers of Criminal Courts Act, 1973, provides for the system of suspended sentences. The essential features of the system are as follows—

(i) any court which passes a sentence of imprisonment for a term of not more than two years *may* order the sentence as a suspended sentence and announce the *operational period,* i.e. the length of the term of suspension. The maximum operational period is two years and the minimum one year (Sect. 22(1));

(ii) a sentence of imprisonment must be appropriate in the circumstances of the case even though the defendant will not in fact go to prison unless he offends again. (Sect. 22(2).) The court is now required to consider other forms of sentence before passing a suspended sentence of imprisonment.

(b) *Fines.* Any criminal court may order the payment of a sum of money by an offender, in general up to a maximum laid down by statute. Failure to pay can lead to imprisonment but the court will first enquire into the offender's ability to pay.

The fine is a most appropriate sentence to give against a corporation and company legislation often provides for default fines on registered companies, e.g. failure to file returns with the Registrar of Companies.

(c) *Probation.* An offender may be placed under the supervision of a probation officer for a period not exceeding three years.

(d) *Absolute and conditional discharge.* A court may give an absolute discharge where no punishment is required or a conditional discharge which means that the court will not pass sentence on the offender unless he commits another offence within the next 12 months.

(e) *Community Service Orders.* With the offender's consent the court may make a 'Community Service Order' to be performed at given times but not interfering with educational or work routines. A probation report must be considered. The total number of hours is between 40 and 240 to be served within a year. The service is prescribed by the Home Secretary and consists of such things as building playgrounds, gardening, or helping elderly or disabled people. The Community Service Order may be made for breach of probation or instead of committal to prison for failure to pay a fine. (Section 6 and Sects 14–17 of the Powers of Criminal Courts Act, 1973, and Sect. 49(1) of the Criminal Justice Act, 1972.) Proceedings for breach of a Community Service Order may be initiated by probation officers through the supervising court either by summons or warrant.

(f) *Miscellaneous sentences.* These include binding over to keep the peace with the sanction that a sum of money will be forfeited if there is a breach; endorsement of driving licence and disqualification from driving.

The following provisions relating to sentencing are also of interest—

(1) any person of 20 years of age or over shall not be sentenced to imprisonment if he has not been sentenced to imprisonment previously unless no other method of dealing with him appears appropriate. A suspended sentence which has not been activated does not count as a previous imprisonment (Powers of Criminal Courts Act, 1973, Sect. 20);

(2) if the accused is a 'first offender' in the above sense and is not legally represented at a summary trial, he must not be sentenced to imprisonment, Borstal or detention, unless either he failed in his application for legal aid

on the ground that he had sufficient means, or he refused or failed to apply for legal aid (Powers of Criminal Courts Act, 1973, Sect. 21);

(3) Crown Courts and magistrates' courts are given power to defer sentence for six months to see how the offender behaves after conviction, e.g. whether he has made any reparation for his offence. The consent of the offender is required before sentence can be deferred (Powers of Criminal Courts Act, 1973, Sect. 1);

(4) The court has power to order forfeiture of *any* property in the offender's possession which was used or intended for use for the purpose of committing or facilitating the commission of *any* offence, provided the offender has been convicted of an offence punishable on indictment by two years or more imprisonment. (Section 43, Powers of Criminal Courts Act, 1973.) This section is intended to cover property such as motor vehicles and radio equipment as well as the traditional tools of the criminal's trade.

(5) On a conviction similar to that set out in (4) above the court may order the offender to be disqualified from driving if a vehicle was used for the purpose of committing or facilitating the commission of an offence. (Powers of Criminal Courts Act, 1973, Sect. 44.) The person disqualified need not have been the driver.

Compensatory awards. In order to avoid the need for a victim of crime to bring an action in a civil court for compensation there is some power in criminal courts to give small amounts of compensation. Sections 35 to 38 of the Powers of Criminal Courts Act, 1973, provide for reparation by the offender. *Compensation orders* are available for any 'personal injury, loss or damage resulting from' an offence of which the offender is convicted or which he asks to have taken into consideration in sentence. Compensation is not available to dependants of a person killed as result of a crime, nor is it for 'loss or damage due to an accident arising out of the presence of a motor vehicle on a road'. Where property which is the object of an offence under the Theft Act, 1968 is damaged the offender may be ordered to pay compensation however and by whomsoever the damage was caused.

Magistrates' courts are limited to a total of £400 in respect of one conviction, i.e. the offence of which the person is convicted and any other offences which he asks to have taken into consideration. In making an order the court must consider the offender's means. These compensation orders operate alongside the scheme for compensation for criminal injuries out of public funds (see below).

The compensation order can be appealed against (Sect. 36) or reviewed by the magistrates' court having the function of enforcing it (Sect. 37). It can be reviewed if the property to which it relates has been recovered or if civil damages have been awarded which are less than the amount of the order but there is no provision for the person compensated to pay the excess in either case.

Section 38 provides that in civil proceedings no account shall be taken of the compensation order in assessment of damages, but the civil judgment cannot be enforced in respect of the amount paid under the order. Leave of the court must be obtained to enforce the outstanding amount of the civil judgment which corresponds to the outstanding amount of the order. It should be noted that compensation orders can be made by the court without application by the person aggrieved.

Restitution orders may also be made in regard to property which is the object of an offence under Sect. 28(1)(c) or (3) of the Theft Act, 1968 under Sect. 6 of the Criminal Justice Act, 1972. Restitution orders may also be made in respect of an offence which the accused asks to have taken into consideration. A restitution order and a compensation order may be made in respect of the same goods if recovered in a damaged condition.

The Crown Court is also involved in *criminal bankruptcy.* An order bankrupting a criminal will be available where a person is found guilty of offences (and/or asks to have them taken into consideration) which have caused loss or damage in excess of £15,000. (Section 39, Powers of Criminal Courts Act, 1973.) The Criminal Bankruptcy Order acts as an act of bankruptcy (Sched. 2, Powers of Criminal Courts Act, 1973) and the Director of Public Prosecutions in his capacity as Official Petitioner (Sect. 41, *ibid.*) decides whether it would be in the public interest to present a petition. Thereafter the bankruptcy proceedings follow the normal course.

The compensatory awards set out above are ineffective if the offender is never caught or if when caught he has no money or property with which to pay compensation. In consequence there is a scheme of state compensation operated by the Criminal Injuries Compensation Board.

The Board may make discretionary payments to those suffering personal injury which is attributable to a criminal offence, which offence has been reported to the police as soon as possible. In order to discourage minor claims the applicant must show that three weeks' loss of earnings was involved or that the injury was one for which compensation of at least £150 should be awarded. This figure, which was £50, was raised in February, 1977 (Parliamentary Reply of the Home Secretary, 15th February, 1977) to take into account the falling value of money since 1964 when the figure was fixed. Police and magistrates' courts were advised that this would mean that quite a few injuries would no longer be compensatable, for example, victims of assault who are not detained in hospital or absent from work and that their only chance of compensation would be a compensation order made under Sect. 35 of the Powers of Criminal Courts Act, 1973. In addition, it should be noted that motoring offences, except where the vehicle has been used as a means of injury, and offences committed against members of the offender's family are excluded.

Rehabilitation of Offenders Act, 1974. The provisions of this Act are an attempt to give effect to the principle that when a person convicted of crime has been successful in living down that conviction and has avoided further criminal activities, common justice demands that his efforts should not be prejudiced by the unwarranted disclosure of that earlier conviction.

All sentences are subject to rehabilitation except—

(a) imprisonment for life;

(b) imprisonment or corrective training for a term exceeding 30 months;

(c) preventive detention and sentences of detention passed under Sect. 53 of the Children and Young Persons Act, 1933 if the detention was to be during Her Majesty's pleasure or for a term exceeding 30 months.

Corrective training and preventive training were abolished in England and Wales by Sect. 27(1) of the Criminal Justice Act, 1967, but it is necessary to provide for them in relation to living persons who have served such sentences. Furthermore, the Children and Young Persons Act, 1933, Sect. 53 (as amended by the Criminal Justice Act, 1961) provides for the detention during Her Majesty's pleasure of persons convicted of murder who appear to have been under 18 at the time of commission of the offence and for the detention at the discretion of the Secretary of State of children and young persons convicted of offences carrying more than four years' imprisonment.

Subject to what is said above, the rehabilitation period for other sentences depends upon the particular sentence imposed. Thus by Table A the rehabilitation period, if it was a sentence of imprisonment or corrective training for a term exceeding six months but not exceeding 30 months, is ten years, if it was for a term not exceeding six months, it is seven years, or, if the sentence was a fine, it is five years. Moreover in these cases if the person convicted was at the date of the conviction under 17 the rehabilitation periods are half of those stated.

Table B covers the rehabilitation periods for certain sentences on younger offenders. For example, for Borstal training it is seven years, for detention at a detention centre it is three years. In addition to Tables A and B various other rehabilitation periods are also covered by Sect. 5 of the Act. For example, the rehabilitation period for an absolute discharge is six months and for a conditional discharge or probation it is one year or the end of the period when the order ceases to have effect, whichever is the longer. If more than one sentence is imposed in respect of a person, the rehabilitation period applicable is the longest for any of the sentences imposed.

So far as the employment of persons with previous convictions is concerned, it should be noted that any questions seeking information as to a person's previous convictions shall be treated as not relating to spent convictions and any obligation on any person to disclose matters shall not require him to disclose a spent conviction and a spent conviction or failure to disclose a spent conviction is not a proper ground for dismissing or excluding a person from or prejudicing him in any occupation or employment. It should be noted that the above provisions do not affect the admission of evidence relating to a person's previous convictions in any criminal proceedings or in proceedings relating, for example, to adoption, guardianship, custody or care and control of any minor. A person may, moreover, consent to the admission of evidence of his own spent convictions.

The provisions of the Act apply to convictions, whether by courts in Great Britain or outside, and they also apply to persons dealt with in service disciplinary proceedings.

The Act also covers actions for libel or slander begun after the commencement of the Act by a rehabilitated person. If the defendant imputed, for example, in a reference, that the plaintiff had a conviction and that conviction was at the time of publication a spent conviction, the defendant may still successfully plead justification, i.e. the truth of his statement, unless the plaintiff can prove malice.

CIVIL PROCEDURE

We shall consider the way in which a civil action is brought and concluded in the High Court.

For the purposes of our High Court action we shall deal with a case of breach of contract under which John, a miller operating as a sole trader, was to sell to Nature Foods Ltd 100 tons of special stone-ground flour in accordance with a sample shown to an agent of Nature Foods at the time, the price being £25 per ton. John claims that flour in accordance with the sample was delivered and that he has not been paid.

Bringing a civil action to trial

John's claim is too high in monetary terms to be brought in the County Court, either before a judge or in arbitration, unless Nature Foods agree which we shall assume they will not. Therefore John's action must be brought in the High Court. If John is wealthy no problems arise in terms of his ability to pay for the service of lawyers. If he is not wealthy then his position is much more difficult. If the claim against Nature Foods proceeds to trial and John is successful then he will receive most of his costs from Nature Foods. However, if he fails in his claim he may have to pay his own and most of Nature Foods' costs.

Legal aid. It is unlikely that John will be able to claim legal aid because legal aid in civil proceedings is only for persons of very limited means. Even old-age pensioners' with savings in excess of £340 may be currently excluded.

However, the provisions are useful to persons of very limited means in some instances, say employment disputes, since legal aid is available, for example, for proceedings before the Employment Appeal Tribunal.

However, in civil proceedings a person of very limited means can get two kinds of legal aid: advice and assistance from a solicitor and legal aid for civil court proceedings.

(a) *Advice and assistance.* Where there is a chance of settling a claim out of court, the Legal Aid Act, 1974 provides for a scheme of legal advice and assistance. The following is a summary of the scheme.

(i) The Act makes provision for what is known as the Green Form Scheme under which a practising solicitor can provide £25 worth of his services, without any prior authority, for anyone who is eligible.

(ii) The scheme is available to persons with disposable capital of up to £340 who are either in receipt of Supplementary Benefit or Family Income Supplement, or have 'disposable weekly incomes of £48 or less'. 'Disposable' means after deductions such as Income Tax and National Insurance and allowances, for example, for dependants. Assessment of disposable capital and income is carried out by the solicitor.

(iii) Advice and assistance is free to those in receipt of Supplementary Benefit and Family Income Supplement and to those with disposable incomes of £23 per week or less. No contribution is payable out of disposable capital. Persons with disposable incomes over £23 per week are required to pay a contribution towards their costs on a scale. These sums may be collected in instalments.

(iv) The solicitor can give advice or assistance on any legal subject. He can write letters, draft documents, negotiate or obtain counsel's opinion. However, assistance does not extend (except as set out below) to taking proceedings in court (for which legal aid may be available) or directly for representation before a tribunal (but see p. 75).

(v) An exception to the rule against taking proceedings in court is that in a County Court or Magistrates' Court the court can request a solicitor within the precincts of the court to act on behalf of a party to either civil or criminal proceedings who has not got legal aid. A solicitor can also propose to the court that he should act and may do so if the court approves. This arrangement, which applies to *solicitors* is not dissimilar to the 'dock brief' arrangement which applies to *barristers*.

(vi) If the advice or assistance needed is estimated to cost more than £25 the solicitor concerned can apply to a committee of the Law Society for authority to spend the additional sum.

(vii) Where money or property is recovered or preserved for the client the cost of the advice and assistance will normally be deducted from it. However, there are many exceptions to this rule, for example, maintenance and social payments. In addition, where to enforce the rule would cause grave hardship or distress or it would be difficult to enforce it because of the nature of the property recovered, e.g. household furniture, the solicitor may apply for the rule to be relaxed.

(viii) Where the solicitor's charges and counsel's fees (if any) are more than any contribution and the value of anything recovered or preserved from which costs are to be deducted, the solicitor renders a bill to a committee of the Law Society who pay what they assess to be a fair and reasonable amount. The solicitor or barrister may appeal against the assessment to the Law Society. These charges are met out of public funds through the Legal Aid Fund.

The Act of 1974 also provides for the establishment of legal centres, staffed by salaried solicitors employed by the Law Society at public expense. These centres will be able to provide all the services a solicitor in ordinary practice can provide, including legal aid for the purpose of bringing an action in court. The Act also provides for the employment of solicitors to act as liaison officers in promoting contacts between such agencies as Citizens' Advice Bureaux and solicitors acting in the area concerned. They will also help those agencies with legal assistance and by giving oral legal advice to those who attend at agencies and whose problems can be resolved in this way.

The provisions set out above will not be brought into force until experience has been gained of the operation of the '£25 scheme' and the Legal Aid Advisory Committee will consider what the timing should be. The Legal Aid Advisory Committee advises the Lord Chancellor on questions relating to legal aid and comments on the Law Society's annual reports on the scheme. Its functions have been extended to cover the legal advice and assistance scheme. As regards the provision of legal centres, this has been hit by the recent recession and implementation may not be seen for some time. However, since it has now been decided that no legal aid will be given in regard to divorce or judicial separation unless the case is defended or there is physical or mental incapacity in the applicant, this should save money since in recent times over 90 per cent of civil legal aid has gone on divorce. Any money saved could be used to set up some legal centres.

(b) *Court proceedings.* The Law Society administers the legal aid scheme for civil proceedings. If court proceedings are thought necessary the solicitor will advise his client to apply for a legal aid certificate. The system is administered by the Law Society through area committees consisting of solicitors and barristers. These committees are under the general control of the Lord Chancellor. The scheme is financed by the Treasury through the Legal Aid Fund. There is a means test which the applicant for legal aid must undergo, and this is conducted by the Supplementary Benefit Commission. Eligibility for legal aid depends upon the applicant's disposable income and his capital. The figures involved change from time to time but the number of people eligible for legal aid in civil proceedings is falling rapidly. For example, the proportion of married couples with children eligible for legal aid on income grounds was 64 per cent in 1954 but had declined to 23 per cent by 1974 and is probably still declining in spite of some increases in the limit.

An applicant may be required to make some contribution to his own costs and, where his action or defence fails, he may also be required to make a contribution towards his opponent's costs, depending upon what the court thinks is reasonable for him to pay.

The Legal Aid Committee must be satisfied that the applicant's claim or defence is a reasonable one.

Attempt to settle. On the assumption that John has sufficient funds to proceed and has duly consulted a solicitor, the next step is to attempt a settlement, and the solicitors of each party will correspond on this. If this fails then John's solicitor must consider going to court (or litigation) and whether or not an action by John would be successful.

On this issue John's solicitor may rely on his own view but in a difficult case will usually consult counsel. Counsel will give a written opinion and on the assumption that this is favourable, proceedings are commenced.

The writ. The first step is to issue a writ which is drafted by John's counsel and filed in the court office where it is also sealed and returned to the plaintiff. The writ is then served on the defendant, or his solicitors, but in the case of Nature Foods, which is a corporation, service will be at its registered office or solicitors.

The writ tells the defendants, Nature Foods, that the plaintiff, John, has a claim against them and sets out briefly its nature.

Entering appearance. On the assumption that Nature Foods wish to contest John's case, their solicitor will inform the court that this is so. This is called 'entering an appearance'; strictly speaking this should be done within eight days of service of writ and failure to do so may theoretically result in the hearing taking place and judgment being given against the defendant in his absence.

In practice, however, the time limits imposed by the Rules of Supreme Court are not followed strictly. It would be difficult for a busy firm of solicitors consulting with counsel, who are also often overworked, to keep to the times imposed and each party will, in practice, make concessions in terms of the times laid down, provided that there is no undue delay.

Statement of claim. If Nature Foods enter an appearance then John, through his lawyers, must deliver a 'statement of claim'. This may have been done with the writ but if not, it is delivered separately.

The statement sets out in detail the facts which John alleges support his claim and the defendant receives a copy. All material facts must be set out and John will not be allowed at the trial to introduce material of which Nature Foods have not been given notice.

The evidence supporting John's claim need not be stated and there need be no mention that the facts set out reveal a breach of contract because this is obvious, both to the court and Nature Foods' lawyers.

The facts must be given in sufficient *detail* to enable the defendants to prepare a defence. Places and dates must be given so that the defendant may try to show that the event did not happen or, if it did, to give a different version of it.

Striking out.   If a statement of claim is too vague or so full of irrelevant matter as to prejudice a proper defence at the trial, the defendant can apply to a Master (see p. 95) to have it 'struck out'. If the application is successful the plaintiff must deliver a new statement of claim.

Further and better particulars.   A statement of claim which merely fails to give sufficient detail will not be struck out but the defence may ask for 'further and better particular', and the plaintiff must then supply the details required of the allegations he has made. He may not allege totally new matters.

The request for particulars is made initially by letter but if the plaintiff fails to give the necessary details, either properly or at all, the defendant may apply to a Master who may order the plaintiff to comply with the request.

The defence.   When the defence is satisfied that it understands the allegations in the statement of claim and the detail given in the particulars, then it must put forward its version of the dispute. The document in which this is done is called a 'defence'.

The defence sets out the facts as the defendant sees them and the allegations he makes. If an allegation in the statement of claim is denied, the defence must say so. If it is not denied the court will assume that it is admitted.

A defence which is vague or irrelevant may be struck out, and one which does not give sufficient detail gives the right to the plaintiff to ask for further and better particulars of it.

Reply.   If the plaintiff merely wishes to deny the defendant's allegations he need do nothing more. If, however, he wants to raise further allegations in order to answer a point in the defence, he pleads these in a further document called a 'reply'. This process may continue, replies being exchanged, until each party has raised every point which is considered relevant.

Counterclaim.   In many cases only a statement of claim and a defence are necessary. However, sometimes the defendant says that not only is the plaintiff's claim unfounded, but that it is he who has a claim against the plaintiff. Where this is so the defendant sets out his claim in a separate part of his defence, called a 'counterclaim'. This is, in effect, a reverse statement of claim to which the plaintiff will deliver a reply containing a 'defence to counterclaim'.

The Pleadings.   Thus, in our case the statement of claim may allege that on a given date the parties signed a written contract under which John was to supply 100 tons of flour in accordance with sample at a price of £25 per ton; that the flour was duly delivered but the price has not been paid.

Nature Foods may admit the contract and the non-payment but deny that the full quantity of flour was delivered, saying that only 20 tons was delivered which was rejected because it did not conform with the sample. In addition, because of John's failure to perform the contract properly, Nature Foods were unable to bake sufficient bread to fulfil all their contracts with health food shops. Nature Foods, having become liable to pay damages to their customers counterclaims for those damages plus compensation for loss of goodwill. John then delivers a reply denying the allegations made in the defence and saying that he offered an alternative supply of flour which did conform with the agreed sample.

The various documents are referred to as 'pleadings' and when the plaintiff and the defendant do not wish to plead any additional facts, the pleadings are said to be closed.

The precise matters now in dispute are clear to both sides so that they can now prepare their evidence accordingly. In addition, a judge will see clearly from the pleadings the matters which he is called upon to decide.

Drafting the pleadings.   All the documents forming the pleadings are usually drafted by counsel so that papers, e.g. letters, must be sent to counsel and returned after drafting and delivery to the other party. All of this takes time and leads to the delays which occur before trial.

Discovery.   Although every fact relied upon by a party must be disclosed to the other, the evidence which will be used to prove those facts in court need not be disclosed until it confronts the other party at the trial.

To this there is a major exception which is that each party can be required to disclose to the other the *documentary evidence* which he has whether it *assists or impedes his case.* The opponent may take copies of the documents which may include any kind of writing, however informal, e.g. bills and rent books. The method of exchanging documents after close of pleading is called 'discovery'.

Advice on evidence.   The next step is to ask counsel to use his ability and experience to decide how to use the rules of procedure before trial to get John into the best possible position and what evidence should be called at the trial.

This stage is most important because cases are often won or lost by the way in which the evidence is prepared and presented.

Interrogatories.   If a fact essential to success cannot be proved by a party because those facts are peculiarly within the knowledge of his opponent, the problem may be overcome by the use of 'interrogatories'.

These are questions which one side may require the other to *answer on oath.* The answer may then be read at the trial. Whether a particular question may or may not be asked is a matter to be decided by a Master.

Remember that particulars are designed to make clear the opponent's allegations which, if he fails to prove, will lose him his case. Discovery and interrogatories are concerned with evidence. If they fail to provide the evidence required then other methods of proof may be used. However, each party is tied to the pleadings and if he cannot establish the facts there set out no other facts will do, unless, of course, in his pleadings he sets out two fact situations on which he may rely.

Thus, Nature Foods may be asked for particulars as to why the delivery of flour failed to conform with the sample, but not whether there is any record in, say, a stock book. That should have been dealt with on discovery. Nor may Nature Foods be asked for particulars relating to whether they told one of their customers by telephone prior to delivery of the flour that they did not want it. Such a question might be asked as an interrogatory.

Notice to admit.   A party faced on the pleadings with the problem of proving a particular fact, e.g. that a letter was in fact written by the person whose signature it appears to bear, may serve a notice on his opponent requiring him to admit that fact in order to save the expense of producing the necessary evidence.

If the other party refuses to admit then, when costs are being considered, the party asking for the admission may try to convince the judge or Master that refusal to admit was unreasonable and that his opponent must pay the cost of proving that point, whatever the result of the case.

Notice to produce a document.   It either party wishes at the trial to refer to a document which is in his opponent's possession he must serve on his opponent a Notice to Produce the Document. This notice does not make the opponent produce it at the trial but it gives him warning that its contents may be brought into question so that he has a reasonable opportunity of bringing the document to the trial in order to prove his own version of what it contains.

Setting down for trial.   The case may now be 'set down' to wait a time for hearing.

There is much criticism of the time taken to get a case into court and reforms may be desirable. However, the procedure outlined above is important because the most costly part of any civil action is the actual proceedings in court so that it is vital that the pre-trial procedure should ensure that the precise issues at stake are clear and that no time in court will be wasted on irrelevant matters. Also, it would be most unjust if pre-trial procedure did not ensure that both parties had fair warning of the case which each has to meet and of the facts and documents which will be put in question.

The trial

The parties and their witnesses will assemble for the trial. If a witness refuses to appear a 'subpoena' may be issued. This is a summons to appear and give evidence on condition that reasonable expenses are offered by the party calling the witness. Those who ignore a *subpoena* are in contempt of court and may be punished by fine or imprisonment.

Often the case will not be heard at the time stated in the list. The court must not be kept waiting and so cases are listed in such a way as to cope, for example, with actions which are settled out of court at the last moment. If this does not happen, however, there is a trial and others are kept waiting.

When the action is 'called on' counsel for the plaintiff begins. He explains the matters in dispute to the judge, goes through the pleadings and outlines the plaintiff's case, indicating how it will be supported by evidence. Then he calls his witnesses.

The court requires that evidence be given on oath (or affirmation by a person who objects to swearing on the Bible). Documentary evidence such as a letter is not normally admissible and the writer must be called and give evidence on oath unless it is difficult or impossible to call him.

As in a criminal trial counsel for the plaintiff cannot ask his own witnesses 'leading questions' nor is hearsay evidence admissible. After the examination in chief the witnesses for the plaintiff may be cross-examined by counsel for the defence, the object being to discredit their evidence. After cross-examination counsel for the plaintiff may re-examine a witness.

Sometimes a witness will give an account of events which is totally different from that which he told to the plaintiff's solicitors; counsel for the plaintiff is not allowed to discredit his own witness unless the judge gives leave as he may do if he feels that the witness is prejudiced against the person who called him. Such a witness is called a hostile witness and his examination in chief is more like a cross-examination since it is designed to discredit his evidence.

At the end of the plaintiff's case it is the turn of counsel for the defence to produce evidence to refute it. The plaintiff does not have to prove his case beyond a reasonable doubt, as the prosecution in a criminal trial does but must show that what he alleges is probably the right version.

The defence need not necessarily produce evidence. If the plaintiff's case is weak the defence may submit to the judge that there is no case to answer. If the judge agrees the action is finished and judgment is given for the defence. However, if the judge does not accept the submission of no case to answer he will immediately give judgment for the plaintiff, so counsel for the defendant will not easily take this course of action.

If there is no submission of no case to answer the defence will call its witnesses who will be examined, cross-examined and re-examined.

Counsel for the defence then makes a speech showing in his view how the plaintiff's case has failed. The plaintiff's counsel then presents his view.

The judge will have remained largely silent during the trial, though he may have asked for an obscure point to be clarified. However, during the closing speeches he will indicate to counsel what he regards as the weaknesses in their respective cases so that they can answer the judge on them.

After the closing speeches the judge considers the evidence and will then give judgment stating the grounds on which it is based, though if a judge requires more time to consider the case he may reserve judgment and give it at a later date.

Civil jury. The Administration of Justice (Miscellaneous Provisions) Act, 1933 gives the court discretion with regard to juries in civil cases, though a jury must be empanelled at the request of the defendant where fraud is alleged, or at the request of either party in cases of libel, slander, malicious prosecution and false imprisonment. If the trial is likely to involve long and detailed examination of documents or accounts or scientific evidence, the court has the discretion to refuse a jury trial even in these cases.

However, libel actions involving issues or persons of national importance should be tried with a jury, even if complex documents are involved. (*Rothermere* v. *Times Newspapers,* [1973] 1 All E.R. 1013.) The percentage of jury trials in civil actions is very small.

Juries are not used in Admiralty cases but there is a power to summon a jury in the Chancery Division. This power is, in practice, neglected. Juries are sometimes applied for in defended divorce petitions, and where a will is contested.

A civil jury consists of 12 persons, though the parties may, in a particular case, agree to proceed with less. There is a right to ask for a jury of eight persons in a county court, where the case is an appropriate one. These rights are rarely exercised. In addition, a coroner must summon a jury of seven to eleven persons in some cases and may accept the verdict of the majority if the dissentients are not more than two. Where there is no jury the judge determines the facts as well as the law.

Apart from a coroner's jury a civil jury had formerly to be unanimous. However, under the Courts Act, 1971, Sect. 39, the verdict of the jury in civil proceedings in the High Court need not be unanimous if—

(*a*) where there are not less than eleven jurors, ten of them agree on the verdict; and

(*b*) where there are ten jurors, nine of them agree on the verdict.

The verdict of a jury of eight persons in a county court need not be unanimous if seven of them agree on the verdict. The two hours deliberation necessary for a jury before a majority verdict is permissible is not required for a civil jury. It is enough if it appears to the court that the jury had such period of time for deliberation as the court thinks reasonable, having regard to the nature and complexity of the case. Majority verdicts are possible in civil cases without the consent of both of the parties.

Appeals

Consideration has already been given in chapter 2 to the rights of appeal in civil cases (and see p. 16).

Enforcing a Judgment

Let us assume that the judge has accepted John's version of the facts as being correct and has awarded damages against Nature Foods for non-acceptance of the flour, which was in accordance with the contractual requirements. John has accordingly been given judgment for a sum of money, but suppose Nature Foods refuse to pay? How can John get his money? Some of the more important methods are set out below.

(a) *The writ of fi fa.* A plaintiff can ask the High Court for this writ which orders the sheriff through bailiffs to seize the defendant's goods and sell them if necessary in order to pay the plaintiff. In the County Court there is a similar procedure but it is based upon a warrant of execution.

(b) *The charging order.* The court may make such an order over, say, the defendant's land or other property such as shares. If the money is not paid the plaintiff can have the property sold and recover his damages from the proceeds of sale.

(c) *The garnishee order.* The court may grant this order under which money which is owed to the defendant by someone else is paid direct to the plaintiff. Thus a garnishee order issued to a bank would cause the bank to pay to the plaintiff the required sum of money from the defendant's bank account if it was in credit.

(d) *Receiver.* The court may appoint a receiver where, for example, the defendant owns property. The receiver can take over income such as rent and apply it in order to pay the plaintiff.

(e) *Attachment of earnings.* Where the defendant is in employment the plaintiff can obtain an attachment of earnings order through the county court. Under such an order the defendant's employer is required to deduct a specified sum from the defendant's wages or salary and pay the money into court for the plaintiff.

What is said above refers, of course, to money judgments. The enforcement of a non-money judgment, such as an injunction, is by means of the offence of contempt of court. If a defendant fails to obey an injunction he is in contempt of court and the court may, if the plaintiff applies, punish him. It may make, for example, an order for committal under which if the defendant still refuses to comply with the injunction, he may be imprisoned. Alternatively, the court may issue a writ of sequestration. This writ, which is directed by the court to commissioners, usually four in number, commands them to enter the lands and take the rents and profits and seize the goods of the person against whom it is directed. Thus the court can in effect take control of the defendant's property until the plaintiff has been paid.

4 Other courts and tribunals and the legal profession

All of the famous writers on constitutional theory have drawn attention to the dangers of any system which takes away from the citizen, in his dealings with government and other officials, the protection of the law functioning in its traditional setting, i.e. the courts of law, which were considered in the previous chapter.

However, one of the most significant developments of this century is the considerable increase in what might be called broadly administrative justice dispensed in special courts outside of the ordinary system.

This has arisen from the great extension in the functions of goverment which has taken place, particularly in the last twenty years, For example, the government pays pensions to various classes of persons, it pays sickness benefit and industrial injuries benefit, family allowances and the like. In order to further schemes of social welfare, it is often necessary for a public body to acquire land by compulsory purchase, and it has also been necessary to establish a system of controlling the rents of dwellings, so that the free operation of the laws of supply and demand might be restricted.

Obviously disputes arise between individuals and the State. A person may claim a benefit which the State suggests he is not entitled to, and landowners are often aggrieved by the compulsory purchase of their land and the compensation offered for it. The settlement of such disputes might have been given over to the ordinary courts of law, but instead, increasing use has been made of an administrative court of one kind or another.

Lord Denning, in *Freedom under the Law,* has said of these tribunals—

> They are a separate set of courts dealing with a separate set of rights and duties. Just as in the old days there were ecclesiastical courts dealing with matrimonial cases and the administration of estates and just as there was the Chancellor dealing with the enforcement and administration of trusts so in our day there are the new tribunals dealing with the rights and duties between man and the State.

It should not be assumed, however, that all administrative tribunals are concerned with disputes between man and the State. Some deal with disputes between individuals. The Rent Assessment Committees set up under rent control legislation are an example of a situation in which the Government has provided a specialized court to deal with certain disputes between landlord and tenant rather than give the particular jurisdiction to the ordinary courts of law.

Furthermore, administrative justice is not always meted out in an independent tribunal. For example, in the field of housing and town and country planning there is in general no right to appeal from a decision of the Government or local authority to an independent tribunal. Instead there is an opportunity to put a case against the decision to a public local enquiry conducted by an inspector—usually an official of the appropriate Ministry. The inspector reports to the Minister, whose decision is final.

In addition, there are some cases in which no machinery is provided for appeal to a tribunal or a local enquiry. For example, there is no appeal against withdrawal of a passport by the Foreign Office.

We shall now consider in more detail the way in which certain of these tribunals work.

Administrative tribunals

It is not appropriate in a book of this nature to deal with all the tribunals in this field but consideration will be given to some important ones as examples.

(a) *Social security tribunals.* Where a person wishes to make a claim for benefit under the Social Security Act, 1975, e.g. sickness or unemployment benefit, the claim must in the first instance be made to a local insurance officer who may authorize payment, or refuse payment, or refer the claim to a local tribunal.

If payment is simply refused, the person claiming can appeal to a local tribunal which has three members, two non-lawyers, one drawn from a panel of persons representing employers and the self-employed, and one drawn from a panel of persons representing employees. The third member is usually a lawyer, for example a local solicitor appointed by the Secretary of State to be chairman.

If the tribunal allows the appeal the insurance officer may appeal against that decision to a National Insurance Commissioner. The same right of appeal is given to the person making the claim where the tribunal does not decide in his favour.

National Insurance Commissioners are appointed by the Crown from amongst barristers and solicitors of not less than ten years' standing. Anyone who wishes to change a commissioner's decision on a matter of law in the High Court can do so on the basis that there is an error of law on the record. (See p. 81.)

(b) *Valuation and use of land tribunals.* Another important tribunal is the *Lands Tribunal* which deals with disputes arising over the valuation and compensation payable on compulsory acquisition of land by public authorities under a variety of statutes, together with appeals from local valuation courts on the value of property for rating purposes. The tribunal has a President, who is either a person who has held high judicial office or a barrister of at least seven years' standing, and other members, who must be solicitors or barristers of like standing, or persons experienced in the valuation of land. The jurisdiction of the tribunal may be exercised by any one or more of its members. Procedure is governed by rules made by the Lord Chancellor, and these are published by Statutory Instrument. The tribunal ordinarily sits in public and travels round the country, and there is a right of audience and legal representation. The decisions of the tribunal are written and reasoned, and appeal lies to the Court of Appeal on points of law. Either party can require the tribunal to state a case for consideration by the Court of Appeal. Legal aid, and by implication legal representation, is available in respect of proceedings in the Lands Tribunal. There are also *Rent Tribunals* set up to assess rents for certain types of *furnished* dwellings, though the County Courts administer the Rent Restriction Acts which govern the rents of *unfurnished* accommodation.

(c) *Conciliation and employment tribunals.*

(i) *Conciliation.*   The Advisory, Conciliation and Arbitration Service (ACAS) is, under the Employment Protection Act, 1975, given a role in settling matters which are, or could be, the subject of proceedings before an industrial tribunal.

When a complaint or claim is presented to an industrial tribunal, say for equal pay or sex discrimination, a copy is sent to the conciliation officer. It is his duty to try to settle the dispute so that it need not go to an industrial tribunal. He can do this if asked to by the person making the complaint or the person against whom it is made, or even on his own initiative where he thinks there is a good chance of a settlement.

During the course of conciliation the parties can speak freely with the conciliation officer because anything which is said to the conciliation officer during the course of an attempted settlement is not admissible in evidence if the matter goes to an industrial tribunal unless the person who made the statement agrees.

(ii) *Industrial tribunals.*   The jurisdiction of these tribunals includes, for example, disputes arising out of the contract of employment or unfair dismissal, redundancy, equal pay and sex discrimination.

The chairman of each tribunal is a barrister or solicitor of not less than seven years' standing, appointed by the Lord Chancellor and he sits with two other members selected by the President of Industrial Tribunals who is himself appointed by the Lord Chancellor. The selection is made from a panel of persons compiled by the Secretary of State for Employment on the basis of knowledge or experience of employment problems in industry or commerce. The tribunals sit at suitable centres throughout the United Kingdom.

If a sum of money awarded by a tribunal is not paid over to the claimant he can apply to the county court for a warrant of execution. (See p. 68.)

Legal aid is not available for a lawyer to represent a claimant before a tribunal but legal advice may be given under the 'Green Form Scheme' in respect of employment matters. This can include the drafting of documents in relation to the proceedings and assistance with the way in which the case is to be presented to the tribunal.

Written applications for the case to be heard by an industrial tribunal can be made on forms available from local offices of the Department of Employment but these are not essential. The person against whom the claim is made will receive a copy of the application from the tribunal secretariat and should enter an appearance through the secretariat within 14 days of receiving it.

Industrial tribunals have power to request the parties to give each other further particulars of the grounds which are relied upon and to grant discovery of documents.

Hearings before industrial tribunals normally take place in public though there may be a private hearing where, in the opinion of the tribunal, this would be appropriate, as where evidence is to be presented which relates to national security.

As regards costs, an industrial tribunal does not make an award but may do so where in its opinion a party to any proceedings has acted frivolously or vexatiously, as where, for example, an employer refuses to take any part in the proceedings.

The decision is made by a majority and is given orally at the meeting or, if necessary, reserved and given at a later date. In any case it is recorded in a document which is signed by the chairman and contains reasons for the decision. The parties each receive a copy. It should also be noted that where an employee has died tribunal proceedings may be started or continued by his personal representatives.

An industrial tribunal can review and change its decision afterwards where, for example, new evidence has become available which could not have been known of or foreseen at the original hearing.

(iii) *The Employment Appeal Tribunal.* Appeal from an industrial tribunal lies only on questions of law. The determination of the facts by an industrial tribunal cannot be challenged on appeal and it is therefore most important that the facts are properly presented to the tribunal at the hearing.

The Employment Appeal Tribunal is a superior court of record with an official seal. Although the central office of the tribunal is in London, it may sit at any time and in any place in Great Britain. It may also sit in one or more divisions.

Appeals are usually heard by a judge of the High Court or a judge of the Court of Appeal and either two or four appointed members who do not belong to the judiciary but have special knowledge or experience of industrial relations, either as representatives of employers or workers. The reason why the judge will sit with either two or four appointed members is so that in either case there are an equal number of persons whose experience is as representatives of employers and of workers. Exceptionally, if the parties to the proceedings consent a case may be heard by a judge and one appointed member.

Appeals to the Employment Appeal Tribunal are commenced by serving on the tribunal within 42 days of the date on which the document recording the decision or order appealed against was sent to the person appealing, a notice of appeal. The appropriate form is set out in the Employment Appeal Tribunal Rules.

The hearing will normally take place in public but the tribunal may sit in private to hear evidence where, for example, it relates to national security or could cause substantial injury to an organization appearing before it, as where a company's trade secrets might be revealed. Legal aid is available for proceedings in the Employment Appeal Tribunal.

The Employment Appeal Tribunal may review and change any order made by it on a similar basis to the provisions already mentioned in regard to industrial tribunals. Appeal lies on any question of law, decision, or order of the Employment Appeal Tribunal, either with leave of the Tribunal or of the Court of Appeal to the Court of Appeal. Legal aid would be available on such appeal according to the usual rules. There may then be a further appeal to the House of Lords under the usual rules.

Administrative inquiries

As we have seen in some areas of administrative action, e.g. housing and town and country planning, there is in general no right of appeal from the initial decision of the Government or a local authority to an independent tribunal. The relevant Acts of Parliament normally provide for an opportunity to put a case against the decision at a public inquiry conducted before an inspector who is normally a Ministry official. The inspector makes a report to the Ministry concerned and the final decision is made by the Minister himself or a senior civil servant on his behalf. Sometimes the inspector makes the final decision.

Advantages of tribunals

As a method of deciding disputes, administrative tribunals and inquiries have advantages. For example, the tribunals and inquiries generally specialize in a particular field, and can thus acquire a detailed knowledge of disputes in that field. The procedure of tribunals is simple and informal, and it is often suggested that this puts those appearing before them at ease so that they are better able to present their case. Certainly administrative justice is cheaper, and, there are in general no court fees and costs, though if the assistance of a lawyer is required he will have to be paid and there is as yet no legal aid in this field except in the Lands Tribunal and the Employment Appeal Tribunal.

However, appellants who are not represented by lawyers may take full advantage of the rights of appeal given, though sometimes this results in references to tribunals which are frivolous by nature. Generally speaking, administrative tribunals and inquiries give quick decisions, and appellants are not subjected to the delays which are sometimes met with in ordinary courts of law. Tribunals and inquiries are usually local by nature; they are therefore able to acquaint themselves with local conditions, and can carry out inspections of property and sites where this would assist them in their decision.

Disadvantages of tribunals

The disadvantages attaching to the use of administrative tribunals and inquiries lie in the lack of publicity which attaches to their findings. Furthermore, in some cases, the party whose dispute is being heard does not appear in person before the court, and the public are sometimes excluded from the hearing. Even when the tribunal or inquiry publishes its decision, it does not always give a reasoned judgment, so that it may be impossible to ascertain why it decided as it did.

There is the possibility of political interference, since the members of tribunals and inspectors are often appointed by the Minister or are employed by the government; and since one party in a dispute is generally a governmental authority, there may be bias, though there is no evidence that this exists. Often there is no appeal from a tribunal or a Minister after an inquiry but a reason must be given for rejecting an Inspector's finding of facts at the inquiry. (*Coleen Propts Ltd.* v. *Min. of Hsg & L. Govt.*, [1971] 1 All E.R. 1049.)

The Tribunals and Inquiries Acts

Some of these difficulties have been overcome by Tribunals and Inquiries Acts passed since 1958.

The 1958 Act was passed to put into effect certain of the recommendations of the Franks Committee on Administrative Tribunals which reported in 1957. The Acts set up a Council on Tribunals, the function of which is to keep under consideration the personnel and working of the tribunals set out in the Act, and to report to the Lord Chancellor on any other matters relevant to administrative tribunals which he may refer to them. The Lord Chancellor nominates the members of the Council, and the dismissal of a member of a tribunal must be approved by him, thus giving the members of the various tribunals increased independence. A right of appeal to the High Court is given on points of law in many cases, even if an existing statute prevents or limits the right, and there are no restictions whatever on the supervisory jurisdiction of the High Court by means of the prerogative orders (see p. 78), where these are appropriate. An attempt has also been made to institute public hearings, legal representation, and reasoned decisions, and the reports of inspectors who have conducted inquiries are made available.

The 1966 Act extended the provisions of the 1958 Act by giving the Council on Tribunals wider powers over local enquiries, providing, for example, that a member of the Council on Tribunals can attend an inquiry.

These Acts, which are now consolidated in the Tribunals and Inquiries Act, 1971, may answer the criticisms made of tribunals and inquiries if their provisions are fully utilized. Unfortunately, Governments have often set up new tribunals without proper consultation with the Council on Tribunals to see whether an existing tribunal might take on the work. This has resulted in a proliferation of tribunals with a bewildering multiplicity of separate jurisdictions.

Legal Aid

Legal aid in tribunals has been reviewed from time to time by the Legal Aid Advisory Committee which has felt it appropriate to recommend that legal aid should be extended to the Lands Tribunals only, though more recently it has been extended to proceedings before the Employment Appeal Tribunal. Many still regard the present position as unreasonable.

In particular it is felt that legal aid is appropriate in cases heard before rent assessment committees, the Supplementary Benefits Appeal Tribunal, the National Insurance Commissioners, the mental health review tribunals, and valuation courts. In addition there is no reason why legal aid should not be extended to some of the domestic tribunals, e.g. in respect of hearings before the Disciplinary Committee of the Law Society and the General Nursing Council.

It is interesting to note that the Legal Aid Advisory Committee has recently suggested that a solicitor may be able to claim costs for attendance at a tribunal hearing with a client for whom he has prepared a written case for the tribunal. The Advisory Committee's view is based on a combination of Sect. 2(1) of the Legal Aid Act, 1974 which enables a solicitor to claim remuneration for *assisting* a party to take steps *on his own behalf* in proceedings and the case of *McKenzie* v. *McKenzie*, [1970] 3 All E.R. 1034 where the Court of Appeal held that a party to an action could be assisted in court by 'a friend' who could take notes and make suggestions, for example, as to what to ask in cross-examination. It is clear that the friend could be a solicitor who may recover his charges for so assisting.

There is also the Free Representation Unit run by Bar students with the approval of the Bar Council, under which Bar students represent people before Social Security Tribunals. Most of the cases are referred to the Unit by Citizens' Advice Bureaux through the College of Law, Chancery Lane. The Unit deals with a substantial number of cases each year.

Domestic tribunals

Another area in which persons or groups of persons or other public agencies exercise judicial or quasi-judicial functions over others is to be found in the system of domestic tribunals. These are, in general, disciplinary committees concerned with the regulation of certain professions and trades, some having been set up by statute and others merely by contract between members and the association concerned. Examples of tribunals regulating professions are the General Medical Council, Architects' Registration Council, The Law Society, the General Nursing Council, and the Inns of Court.

Discipline over barristers is exercised by a Senate of the four Inns of Court. The Senate is assisted in the matter of control of professional standards by the Professional Conduct Committee of the Bar Council which can inquire into the professional conduct of a barrister. Appeal from the Senate lies to a committee of judges appointed by the Lord Chancellor.

When there is a complaint about a solicitor to the Law Society the Society makes investigation through its Professional Purposes Committee. This is referred to as the investigatory stage. Section 45 of the Solicitors Act, 1974, provides that the Lord Chancellor may appoint one or more lay observers to examine the manner in which the Law Society carries out its investigations (see p. 92).

One step which the Law Society may take is to refer the complaint to the Disciplinary Tribunal, and at this adjudicatory stage the non-lawyer has also been introduced since the Tribunal is not properly constituted unless one lay member is present. Thus while the appointment of a lay observer is discretionary, a lay member is an essential element of the Tribunal. However, solicitor members must be in a majority on the Tribunal and members of the Tribunal, both lay and solicitor members, are appointed by the Master of the Rolls; any practising solicitor of not less than ten years' standing may be appointed a solicitor member.

Appeal from the Tribunal is to the Master of the Rolls in certain matters, e.g. refusal to restore to the roll a former solicitor who has been struck off, and on other matters, e.g. an order to strike off, to the High Court.

There are also certain trade organizations which are corporate bodies set up under statute. They represent the producers and distributors of particular commodities, and they control the production and sale of those commodities mainly by fixing prices. They are able to enforce their instructions by levying fines on members or excluding them from the scheme, and are mainly concerned with agriculture. Each Board has a Disciplinary Committee which has a chairman who is generally a lawyer. The parties are normally entitled to an oral hearing in public, and the Committee may subpoena witnesses and take evidence on oath. One of the most important Boards is the Milk Marketing Board.

The supervisory jurisdiction of the High Court is exercisable over these tribunals by means of remedies similar to those available against administrative tribunals (see below).

JUDICIAL CONTROL OVER INFERIOR COURTS AND TRIBUNALS

We must now consider what *control* the ordinary courts of law have over administrative action as expressed in the decisions of tribunals and inquiries and what *methods* are used to exercise that control.

Control by the judiciary is exercised as follows—

(a) by statutory rights of appeal from the tribunal;
(b) by application of the doctrine of *ultra vires*;
(c) by the use of prerogative orders;
(d) by injunctions and declaratory judgments.

These methods of control will now be considered in more detail.

Statutory Right of Appeal

Where, as in the case of the Lands Tribunal, the Act of Parliament setting up or controlling the tribunal gives a right of appeal to the ordinary courts of law, the courts are entitled to re-hear the whole case and are not limited to a consideration of the reasons given by the tribunal for its decision. The court can consider the whole matter afresh, and can substitute a new decision for that of the tribunal.

Ultra vires

No public authority may lawfully make a decision and take action on it unless it is authorized by law to do so or the act is construed as being reasonably incidental to its authorized activities. An act which does not conform with the above is treated by the courts as void under the doctrine of *ultra vires* (beyond the powers of).

The doctrine applies to bodies and individuals such as Ministers (see p. 84) exercising judicial, quasi-judicial, legislative or administrative functions, including local authorities, tribunals, Government departments and other public authorities, though Parliament's legislative powers are unlimited. (See p. 9.) The topic is a difficult one but the main principles are given below

(a) *Decision taken unauthorized by law.*   A number of cases have been brought before the courts to challenge actions of local authorities on the ground that they were unauthorized by law (*A.G.* v. *Fulham Corporation,* 1921,[10] but see *A.G.* v. *Smethwick Corporation, 1932*).[11]

(b) *Decision taken on wrong facts.*   For example, it is a condition precedent to the exercise by the Home Secretary of his discretionary powers to deport aliens that the person concerned is in fact an alien (*Eshugbaye Eleko* v. *Government of Nigeria,* [1931] A.C. 662).

(c) *Action taken by wrong person or body.*   A statute, in giving a power, will usually state who is to exercise it. Purported exercise of the power by anyone else will be *ultra vires* and void (*Allingham* v. *Ministry of Agriculture and Fisheries, 1948*).[12]

(d) *Action taken by a body improperly appointed or constituted.*   The way in which the body or tribunal exercising the statutory powers is to be appointed and constituted is generally laid down in the relevant statute or in regulations made under it. Thus, if a duly constituted tribunal is to consist of a chairman and two members then a decision made by a tribunal consisting of a chairman and one member will be *ultra vires* and void (*Woollett* v. *Ministry of Agriculture and Fisheries,* [1955] 1 Q.B. 103).

(e) *Action taken without following correct procedure.*   Where statute requires, e.g. that a certain period or type of notice be given before action is taken, then failure to comply with the provisions relating to notice will render the act *ultra vires* and void (*Bradbury* v. *London Borough of Enfield,* 1967).[13]

(f) *Action within powers but for improper purpose.*   The action of an authority which is within its powers will nevertheless be *ultra vires* and void if it is taken for an improper purpose, e.g., one not intended by the Act giving the power (*Sydney Municipal Council* v. *Campbell,* 1925).[14]

(g) *Action within powers but extraneous and irrelevant matters taken into account.*   An authority will abuse its powers if it exercises them after extraneous matters have been taken into account (*Roberts* v. *Hopwood,* 1925).[15]

(h) *Unreasonableness.*   It would seem that only in extreme cases is it possible to challenge administrative action in the courts merely on the grounds of unreasonableness. In most cases the challenge will have to be brought within (a) to (g) above. However, a local authority bye-law can be challenged on the grounds of unreasonableness but only in extreme cases will the courts invalidate it (*Kruse* v. *Johnson,* [1898] 2 Q.B. 91).

Prerogative Orders

Where no right of appeal is given it may be possible to challenge the decision of an inferior court or tribunal by having recourse to the supervisory jurisdiction of the High Court.

This jurisdiction is exercised by the Queen's Bench Division of the High Court by means of the prerogative orders known as *certiorari, prohibition,* and *mandamus.* These orders, which are not available as of right but at the discretion of the court (*R.* v. *Aston University Senate, ex parte Roffey,* 1969),[16] were formerly prerogative writs, which a subject might obtain by petitioning the Crown.

The Sovereign has no such power today, the control being exercised by the Queen's Bench Division, the former writs being now called orders. (Administration of Justice (Miscellaneous Provisions) Act, 1938.)

Before a person can invoke the supervisory jurisdiction of the High Court, he must in general have exhausted all other remedies and rights of appeal (*R.* v. *Brighton Justices ex parte Robinson* 1973).[17]

Certiorari lies to have the record of the proceedings of an inferior court

removed into the High Court for review on certain limited grounds, i.e.
want or excess of jurisdiction, denial of natural justice and error of law on
the face of the record.

The High Court may quash the decision, if it is bad, but cannot substitute
its own decision as it could on an ordinary appeal. What is an inferior court
for this purpose is a matter for the High Court to decide. Certainly the
order of *certiorari* (and *prohibition*) has for very many years applied only in
relation to a body which has a duty to act judicially. However, in *R*. v.
*Liverpool Corporation, ex parte Liverpool Taxi Fleet Operators' Associa-
tion*, [1972] 2 Q.B. 299 the Court of Appeal affirmed an order of
prohibition made to prevent the Corporation issuing additional taxicab
licences although the issue of such licences has always been regarded as an
administrative function. Although the point was not discussed, it seems
that, since the Court made an order of prohibition the requirement of
'acting judicially' is no longer applied to the prerogative orders. If this view
is correct then *certiorari* appears to be emerging as a general judicial
remedy, which was the view taken by the court in *R*. v. *Hillingdon London
Borough Council, ex parte Royco Homes Ltd.*, 1974.[18]

In addition, the exercise by educational institutions of the power to
discipline their members has usually been purely a domestic affair and not
of a judicial or quasi-judicial character, thus excluding any intervention by
the courts. However, this view has been challenged with the result that the
courts may, where appropriate, be prepared to review such matters
especially on the grounds of natural justice. (*R*. v. *Aston University Senate,
ex parte Roffey*, 1969[16] but see *Herring* v. *Templeman*, 1973.)[19]

Certiorari has been held to lie against the Patents Appeal Tribunal, a
legal aid committee, a local valuation court, rent tribunals, a coroner and
the decision of a Minister or a local authority in a planning matter (*R*. v.
Hillingdon London Borough Council, ex parte Royco Homes Ltd, 1974.)[18]

Grounds on which certiorari lies.

The only grounds on which *certiorari* lies (*R*. v. *West Sussex Quarter
Sessions, ex parte Albert and Maud Johnson Trust Ltd*, 1972[20] are as
follows—

(i) *Want or excess of jurisdiction.*   This exists where the inferior court or
body has adjudicated on a matter which it had no power to decide, i.e.
where it is acting beyond its powers (*ultra vires*) (*R*. v. *London County
Council, ex parte Entertainments Protection Association*, 1931.)[21]

As we have already seen, the *ultra vires* rule is a major method of control
of inferior courts and bodies of decision makers. The remedy of *certiorari* is
only one of many which may be used to contol *ultra vires* acts. Note, for
example, the use of an injunction in the *ultra vires* situation seen in *A.G.* v.
Fulham Corporation, 1921,[10] *Bradbury* v. *London Borough of Enfield*,
1967[13] and *Sydney Municipal Council* v. *Campbell*, 1925.[14]

(ii) *Denial of natural justice.*   The principle is that although an administrative tribunal should not be required to conform to judicial standards, but

should be free to work out its own procedures, nevertheless it must observe the rules of natural justice, i.e. there must be no bias and both sides should be heard.

A mere general interest will not constitute bias (such as that of a Minister or local authority in a planning enquiry); there must be some direct connection with the subject matter (*R.* v. *Deal Justices, ex parte Curling,* 1881.)[22] A pecuniary interest, however slight, will disqualify (*Dimes* v. *Grand Junction Canal,* 1852);[23] as also will other forms of bias (*R.* v. *Bingham Justices, ex parte Jowitt,* 1974[24] and *R.* v. *Altringham Justices, ex parte Pennington,* 1974.[25]

Both sides should be heard, but there is no inherent right to an oral hearing; written evidence may be acceptable. The right to be heard (*audi alteram partem*) implies that *notice* of the hearing or other method of stating one's case must be given together with notice of the case which is to be met. Furthermore no tribunal should take into account any particular evidence or reasoning unless the parties concerned have had an opportunity to deal with it (*R.* v. *Paddington Rent Tribunal, ex parte Bell Properties Ltd,* 1949,[26] and *R.* v. *Stratford-on-Avon Justices, ex parte Edmunds,* 1973).[27] Though, of course, until it is made clear to what extent the rules of natural justice apply to bodies exercising administrative rather than judicial functions, there will be cases in which the right to be heard is denied. (*R.* v. *Metropolitan Police Commissioner, ex parte Parker,* 1953.)[28]

The law relating to the right to cross-examine witnesses is also in a somewhat confused state. In *Ceylon University* v. *Fernando,* [1960] 1 All E.R. 631, the Judicial Committee of the Privy Council held that the rules of natural justice did not require that a party should have the right to cross-examine. This decision was applied in *Brighton Corporation* v. *Parry* 1972.[29] However, Diplock, L. J. (as he then was) in *Wednesbury Corporation* v. *Ministry of Housing and Local Government* (No. 2), [1965] 3 All E.R. 571, said that a reasonable opportunity to cross-examine was required at an inquiry. (See preface.)

With regard to legal representation, two recent cases—*Pett* v. *The Greyhound Racing Association Ltd,* 1968,[30] and *Enderby Town Football Club Ltd* v. *The Football Association Ltd,* 1971[31]—have laid down some general principles. These principles appear to be as follows—

(*a*) There is no inherent right to legal representation, though if the case involves difficult points of law legal representation should be allowed. A rule forbidding legal representation absolutely and in any circumstances is probably invalid;

(*b*) Cases involving difficult points of law should not in general be decided by domestic tribunals. The parties should ask the ordinary courts for a declaratory judgment setting out their rights. The ordinary courts are better-equipped to deal with cases of legal difficulty and to follow the arguments of lawyers.

However, it seems that in *disciplinary cases* it might well be appropriate to refuse legal representation. Thus, in *Fraser* v. *Mudge,* [1975] 3 All E.R.

78, the Court of Appeal held that natural justice did not require that a prisoner should be represented by a lawyer at the hearing of a prison disciplinary offence involving an assault on a prison officer. The decision in *Fraser* was applied in *Maynard* v. *Osmond,* [1977] 1 All E.R. 64, where the Court of Appeal held again that natural justice did not require that a police constable should have legal representation at a hearing before the chief constable on a disciplinary matter involving an allegation that a sergeant had falsely stated that P.C. Maynard had been asleep while on duty.

Effect of failure to comply with rules.   It is not certain in the present state of the law whether failure to comply with the rules of natural justice makes the decision of a tribunal void or voidable. In *R.* v. *University of Oxford, ex parte Bolchover* (1970), *The Times,* 7 October, and *Glynn* v. *University of Keele,* [1971] 2 All E.R. 89, the Court took the view that its decision was voidable and that it had, therefore, a discretion whether to upset it or not. This involves the Court in a decision as to the merits of the course of action taken by the tribunal, which is a matter of opinion not law. The better view is that denial of natural justice should always render the tribunal's decision void, which was the position taken in *Ridge* v. *Baldwin,* 1964.[32]

The present position.   The position in modern law would appear to be as follows—

(*a*) where the decision is judicial or quasi-judicial the formal rules of natural justice apply so that there must be no bias, all parties must be heard and may be legally represented;

(*b*) where the decision is administrative or disciplinary by nature the formal rules of natural justice do not necessarily apply but the decision must be reached in a 'fair' way. Fairness may, in some situations, involve a strict application of all the rules of natural justice. In other cases the court may be satisfied that no injustice was done even though the formal principles of natural justice were ignored. Each case will, it seems, depend upon its own facts;

(*c*) whether a decision is judicial, quasi-judicial or administrative, or disciplinary, the rules of natural justice need not necessarily be applied if national security is involved (*R.* v. *Secretary of State for Home Department, ex parte Hosenball,* 1977.)[33]

(iii) Error of law on the face of the record.   *Certiorari* lies to quash a decision the record of which discloses an error of law. According to Lord Denning in *R.* v. *Northumberland Compensation Appeal Tribunal, ex parte Shaw,* [1952] 1 All E.R. 122, the record consists of 'the document which initiates the proceedings, the pleadings (if any), and the adjudication, but not the evidence or the reasons unless the tribunal chooses to incorporate them.' As we have seen, *certiorari* can go to control a local planning authority's jurisdiction in granting planning permission where, for example, the permission in question is liable to be upset because on the face of it there is an error of law (*R.* v. *Hillingdon London Borough Council, ex parte Royco Homes Ltd,* 1974).[18] As we have seen, the Tribunals and Inquiries Act, 1971, Sect. 12, requires reasoned decisions in cases coming

before tribunals and inquiries so that there should now normally be a record giving reasons which will assist the High Court in exercising its supervisory jurisdiction. In addition, if a reasoned decision is required by the 1971 Act the order of *mandamus* lies to compel the tribunal or inquiry to give one.

However, the above provisions do not apply to magistrates' courts. If an order of a magistrates' court does not contain reasons for the making of the order, then, provided the magistrates have stayed within their jurisdiction and observed the rules of natural justice, *certiorari* does not lie on the order under this heading.

Whether affidavits made, e.g. by the chairman of the magistrates after the order has been made, form part of the record so that if the affidavits reveal an error the order can be quashed, is not yet settled. The Court of Appeal in *R.* v. *Southampton Justices, ex parte Green,* [1975] 2 All E.R. 1073, where the chairman and the clerk had submitted affidavits, said that the affidavits were part of the record but the Divisional Court of Queen's Bench in *R.* v. *Southampton Justices, ex parte Corker,* The Times 12 February 1976 expressed doubt on the matter of the inclusion of affidavits as part of the record and in addition said that if the magistrates did not give affidavits willingly they could not be forced to do so.

Prohibition lies to prevent an inferior tribunal from exceeding its jurisdiction, or infringing the rules of natural justice. It is governed by similar principles to *certiorari,* except that is does not lie when once a final decision has been given (*certiorari* is then the appropriate order). The object of prohibition is to prevent an inferior tribunal from hearing and deciding a matter which is beyond its jurisdiction. Prohibition and *certiorari* are available against the Crown but not against private persons or bodies, e.g. committees of clubs.

Applications for *certiorari* and *prohibition* are often brought together, e.g. to quash a decision already made by a tribunal, and to prevent it from continuing to exceed or abuse its jurisdiction.

The order of mandamus may be issued to any person or body (not necessarily an inferior court, since it might be issued to a local authority). It commands him or them to carry out some public duty.

It might be used to compel an administrative tribunal to hear an appeal which it is refusing to hear, or to compel a local authority to carry out a duty lying upon it, e.g. to produce its accounts for inspection by a ratepayer. (*R.* v. *Bedwellty U.D.C.,* [1943] 1 K.B. 333.) *Mandamus* lies to compel the exercise of a duty and of a discretionary power, though in the case of the latter not in a particular way (*R.* v. *Commissioner of Police of the Metropolis, ex parte Blackburn* 1973).[34]

It is not available against the Crown itself; but it may issue against Ministers (*R.* v. *Secretary of State for Social Services, ex parte Grabasky,* 1972)[35] or other Crown servants to enforce a personal statutory duty. Thus in *Padfield* v. *Minister of Agriculture, Fisheries and Food,* [1968] 1 All E.R. 694, the House of Lords decided that an order of *mandamus* should issue to the Minister of Agriculture requiring him to refer a complaint by milk producers against the working of a Milk Marketing Board scheme to a committee of investigation in the exercise of a discretionary power conferred on him by Sect. 19 of the Agricultural Marketing Act, 1958.

The divisional court has power to issue prerogative orders under Sect. 10(5) of the Courts Act, 1971 in respect of all decisions of the Crown Court, with the exception of matters relating to trial on indictment, where such orders are normally appropriate, e.g. where an error of law appears on the face of the record in, say, a licensing decision. (*R.* v. *Exeter Crown Court, ex parte Beattie,* [1974] 1 All E.R. 1183.) Appeals from trials on indictment are to the Court of Appeal, Criminal Division.

Injunction and declaratory judgment

The High Court can also exercise control over the decisions of inferior tribunals by granting, at its discretion, an injunction to prevent, for example, the implementation of a decision made by an inferior tribunal which does not observe the rules of natural justice. The remedy is not available against the Crown. Defiance of an injunction ammounts to contempt of court.

A *declaratory judgment* may be asked for by a person aggrieved by the decision of an inferior tribunal so that the High Court can state the legal position of the parties. Defiance of a declaratory judgment is not a contempt of court but parties usually observe it. It is particularly useful in respect of complaints against the actions of Government departments (*Laker Airways* v. *Department of Trade,* 1977)[36] and ministers (*Congreve* v. *Home Office,* 1976).[37]

Before leaving the topic of judicial control of certain areas of decision making, reference should be made to the Law Commission's Report on Remedies in Administrative Law (Cmnd 6407) which was presented to Parliament in 1976. It recommends in particular one form of procedure 'an application for judicial review' (ASR) under which an applicant could apply to the Divisional Court for any of the prerogative orders or, if appropriate, an injunction or declaration.

Additionally, the Divisional Court would be able (i) to send the case back to the deciding tribunal or authority for reconsideration of the decision instead of merely quashing the decision which is its only power at present, and (ii) to award damages where the power to make such an award exists in the law. Claims for damages cannot at present be joined with applications for prerogative orders. (See preface.)

OTHER CONTROLS ON DECISION MAKING

Ministers of the Crown

Sometimes an Act of Parliament places a minister in a supervisory role over, for example, the decisions of local authorities, and where this is so he must act judicially and not administratively in respect of that supervisory role. If he does not exercise the supervisory role in the way envisaged by the Act which gave it to him, the Minister's directions are themselves subject to review by the court. (*Secretary of State for Education and Science* v. *Thameside Metropolitan Borough Council,* 1976.)[38]

The Parliamentary Commissioner for Administration

A further check on abuse of power by government departments was created by the appointment of the Parliamentary Commissioner for Administration (or 'Ombudsman') under the provisions of the Parliamentary Commissioner Act, 1967. The Commissioner is appointed by the Crown and has the same security of tenure as a judge of the Supreme Court. He is also a member of the Council on Tribunals. His function is to investigate complaints relating to the exercise of administrative functions. However, investigation of Central Government departments is made only at the request of a Member of Parliament and a citizen who wishes to have a complaint investigated must first bring it to the notice of an M.P.

Unfortunately, the Commissioner is very often limited to a consideration of the *administrative procedures* followed and is powerless to act if the correct procedure has been followed even though the decision is bad. Nevertheless, each year sees a steady rise in the number of complaints referred to him, though the Commissioner and his functions are still not well enough known and he is at the present time less effective than his counterparts in other countries. Most of the complaints involve Government departments in constant contact with the public, more complaints being levied against the Department of Health and Social Security, followed by the Inland Revenue, than any other department. The Commissioner's jurisdiction under the Act of 1967 is limited to certain aspects of Central Government administration but legislation has now been introduced to create similar offices in different fields.

Under Sect. 31 of the National Health Service Reorganisation Act, 1973 there is now a Health Service Commissioner for England and Wales to investigate complaints about certain aspects of the National Health Service. The first Commissioner under the 1973 Act is the present Parliamentary Commissioner who therefore combines the two offices.

In addition, Part III of the Local Government Act, 1974 makes provision for two Commissions for Local Administration in England and Wales each consisting of Local Commissioners appointed by the Secretary of State plus the Parliamentary Commissioner. A Local Commissioner may investigate a written complaint made by a member of the public who claims to have sustained injustice in consequence of maladministration in connection with action taken by or on behalf of a local authority, joint board, police authority or water authority, being action taken in the exercise of administrative functions. The complaint will normally be made in writing and initially to a member of the authority concerned and referred by him to a Local Commissioner. Furthermore it must be made within a time limit of 12 months. Any one of the Local Commissioners has the same powers as the High Court to require the attendance of witnesses and production of documents when he is conducting an investigation. He must report the results of any investigation to the person who referred the complaint to him, to the complainant and to the authority concerned which must make copies available for public inspection. If he finds that injustice has been caused, the authority concerned must consider his report and notify him of what action they have taken. The greatest number of complaints relates to activities of local planning authorities. Certain matters listed in Schedule 5 of the Act, such as the conduct of legal proceedings, action taken to prevent crime, or action concerning the giving of instruction or discipline in schools, are excluded from the jurisdiction of a Local Commissioner.

Under the Act of 1967 the Parliamentary Commissioner is given discretion whether to investigate a complaint or not. In consequence, the order of *mandamus* will not issue to him since he has no duty to hear a complaint (*re Fletcher's Application*, [1970] 2 All E.R. 527).

Council on tribunals

The control exercised by this body has already been considered (see p. 74).

CORONER'S COURTS

These courts are perhaps the oldest English courts still in existence. Their chief function is to inquire into cases of sudden death, or death by violence, or death in suspicious circumstances. They also inquire into deaths in prison and deaths by hanging—which is still a possible punishment, for example, for the crime of treason. The procedure is that of an inquest or inquiry; it is not a trial. The object is to find out the identity of the deceased, the cause of his death, and where the death took place.

In cases such as suspected murder or death in prison, the coroner may summon a jury of from seven to eleven persons, and he may accept the verdict of the majority so long as there are not more than two dissentients. The coroner can require a *post mortem,* and the attendance of medical and other witnesses who may be examined on oath.

If the court finds that a death was a result of murder, manslaughter or infanticide, this does not operate to convict the person said to be responsible, and a coroner can in no case charge a person with those offences.

If on an inquest regarding a death the coroner, before the conclusion of the inquest—

(a) is told by the clerk of a magistrates' court that some person has been charged before a magistrates' court with the murder, manslaughter or infanticide of the deceased, or with an offence under Sect. 1 of the Road Traffic Act, 1972, committed by causing the death of the deceased, or with an offence under Sect. 2(1) of the Suicide Act, 1961 consisting of aiding, abetting, counselling, or procuring the suicide of the deceased; or

(b) is informed by the Director of Public Prosecutions that some person has been charged before examining justices with an offence not mentioned in (a) above but alleged to have been committed in circumstances connected with the death of the deceased, and is requested by the Director to adjourn the inquest,

then, the coroner must adjourn the inquest until after the conclusion of the relevant criminal proceedings and if he has summoned a jury he may, if he thinks fit, discharge them.

After the conclusion of the relevant criminal proceedings the coroner may resume the adjourned inquest if, in his opinion, there is sufficient cause to do so. If he does resume an inquest then the finding of the inquest as to the cause of death must not be inconsistent with the outcome of the relevant proceedings. (Criminal Law Act, 1977, Sched. 10.)

Under Sect. 220 of the Local Government Act, 1972 the appointment of coroners falls to county councils, the Greater London Council and the Common Council of the City of London (in respect of appointments in the City and the Temples). They are barristers, solicitors or medical practitioners having five years' standing in their profession. The appointment is generally part-time and a coroner can be dismissed for inability or misbehaviour. The Lord Chief Justice and the judges of the High Court are coroners *ex officio*.

The coroner also retains jurisdiction in treasure trove. Treasure trove is money, coin, manufactured gold, silver plate or bullion deliberately hidden in the earth or other private place, the owner being unknown. Such property belongs to the Crown. The coroner is concerned to establish that the property was deliberately hidden because, if it was not, but merely lost, the finder, not the Crown, acquires a good title to it, except as against the true owner. However, if the finder makes prompt report of his discovery of treasure trove, the present practice of the Crown is to restore the article to him, or if it is required for a museum, to pay him its value.

ARBITRATION

(a) *Arising from contract.* Not uncommonly commercial contracts, for example contracts of insurance, contain a provision under which the parties agree to submit disputes arising under the contract to an arbitrator who need not be a lawyer but might in, say, a building dispute, be a surveyor who has knowledge and experience of the subject matter of the dispute.

Arbitration proceedings are in some ways better than court proceedings, being in many cases cheaper, quicker, and private in the sense that there need be no publicity in terms, for example, of a law report.

Arbitration proceedings are governed by the Arbitration Act, 1950 and the award of an arbitrator, if properly arrived at, will be enforced if a judge of the High Court gives leave in the same way as a judgment (see p. 68).

Where an arbitration involves a difficult point of law the arbitrator may state a case for decision by the High Court and either party to the dispute can ask the High Court to make an arbitrator state a case. Thus even in arbitration the High Court has a supervisory role.

(b) *Arbitration in the High Court and County Court.*   This has already been considered on pages 22 and 29.

THE LEGAL PROFESSION

The legal profession in England has two branches. There are barristers and solicitors. Each profession has developed independently, and each has its own controlling body. No person may practise in both capacities at the same time.

Barristers

Barristers conduct cases in court, and generally draft the pleadings which outline the manner in which the case is to be conducted. They also give opinions on difficult legal problems. Barristers have an exclusive right to be heard in the House of Lords, the Judicial Committee of the Privy Council, the Court of Appeal, the three divisions of the High Court, except in the exercise of the High Court's bankruptcy jurisdiction where solicitors may also appear. Solicitors and legal executives can appear in chambers in a High Court action in connection with the interlocutory matters that precede a trial.

Only barristers can appear in the Crown Court except in those cases which have come to it by way of appeal from a Magistrates' Court or where the accused has been committed to the Crown Court for sentence.

Both barristers and solicitors may appear in the County Courts but solicitors may only appear in cases which they themselves are conducting. Thus they cannot be 'briefed' by another solicitor. Both barristers and solicitors may appear in Magistrates' Courts. No other persons may appear there, although the accused is entitled to have someone to assist him in framing questions to witnesses.

There is, of course, nothing to stop a party presenting his own case, though when it comes to an appeal to the House of Lords, unless leave has been granted by the Court of Appeal, it is necessary for two Queen's Counsel to certify that it is reasonable to bring the case to appeal.

Call to the English Bar, is the prerogative of the four Inns of Court—Lincoln's Inn, Gray's Inn, the Inner Temple and the Middle Temple. The Inns of Court are unincorporated societies governed by Masters of the Bench, who are judges or senior barristers, and Call to the Bar is by the Benchers. Disciplinary powers are exercised by a disciplinary tribunal of the Senate of the Inns of Court and the Bar. Appeal is to a domestic tribunal consisting of the Lord Chancellor and judges of the High Court.

The Bar Council.   Another important body in relation to barristers is the Bar Council which represents the interests of the Bar. The Council is not a trade union. It is also responsible for interpreting the rules of etiquette and setting the standards of what is and what is not professional and unprofessional conduct. The behaviour of barristers is partly regulated by these rulings, and by the ordinary law of the land and by the Consolidated Regulations published by the four Inns of Court.

As far as conduct in court is concerned, it is the judge who is responsible for seeing that the proceedings are properly conducted and that the usual courtesies are observed. In extreme cases the judge can back up his authority with his power to punish for contempt of court and report to his Inn any barrister (or to the Law Society any solicitor) whom he thinks has been guilty of professional misconduct. The Bar Council consists of the Chairman, Vice-Chairman and Treasurer, the Attorney General, the Solicitor-General, the Leader of each Circuit, and the 39 persons elected to the General Council. Twelve more barristers may be co-opted. As we have seen the main functions of the Bar Council are to maintain the standards, honour and independence of the Bar, to promote, preserve, and improve the services and functions of the Bar, and to represent it in its relations with other organizations and in all matters affecting the administration of justice. It is concerned with participation in the Legal Aid Scheme, with relations with the solicitors' branch of the profession, other professions, and with lawyers in other countries. It carries out its functions through a number of committees dealing for example with overseas relations, young barristers, fees and legal aid.

Council of Legal Education.   The Council of Legal Education is responsible for the education and examination of students at later stages, and holds lectures which are conducted by leading academic and practising lawyers.

Those wishing to become barristers must apply to become a student at one of the Inns and then satisfy the requirements of the Council in terms of the Academic Stage of legal education. This is followed by a Vocational Stage of legal training leading to the Part II examination.

It is also a requirement that before being called to the Bar the student has 'kept terms' by dining in the hall of his Inn a set number of times.

Once a student has passed the examination he must (if he wishes to practise), either before or after call to the Bar, become the pupil of a senior barrister, often referred to as a pupil master, or attend an approved Practical Training Course. A barrister must in any case find chambers from which to practise and some fail to do so and forsake the Bar for careers in industry and commerce.

Senate of the Inns of Court and the Bar.   An important body in relation to barristers is the General Council of the Inns of Court and the Bar.

The Council consists of 90 members. The Attorney-General, the Solicitor-General and the Chairman of the Council of Legal Education are members ex officio. Six members are appointed by the Bench of each of the four Inns of Court (Lincoln's Inn, Inner Temple, Middle Temple, Gray's Inn), and three members are elected by the Hall of each Inn (that is, all members of the Inn who are not Benchers). Thirty-nine members are elected by the Bar, of whom at least 18 must be practising junior barristers (as opposed to Queen's Counsel) including at least six of under seven years seniority. Six of the 39 Bar representatives are elected from persons nominated by associations of non-practising barristers. The Council may appoint twelve additional members, one half being Benchers of the Inns.

The Council lays down, and where necessary implements, general policy for the Inns of Court and the Bar on a wide variety of topics affecting the profession, including all matters relating to the recruitment, training, and deployment of barristers, on qualifications for admission to the profession and on legal education for barristers, the location and use of barristers' chambers and the provision of accommodation for barristers in London and in the provinces and policy for law libraries in London and elsewhere. The Council raises the funds necessary for its purposes by contribution from the Inns of Court and by subscription from individual barristers.

The whole Council meets four times a year immediately before each legal term, but its committees meet at regular intervals during the terms. These committees include: Executive, Finance, Accommodation, Library, Professional Conduct, Planning, and Law Reform and Procedure. The Council also appoints when necessary a disciplinary tribunal to hear and determine any charge of professional misconduct against a barrister. The Council of Legal Education continues to be responsible for the Bar examinations and for the Inns of Court School of Law in Gray's Inn.

Within the framework of the new constitution, the Bar Council is an autonomous body for the purpose of its separate powers and functions, in the performance of which it is not subject to any directions from the General Council.

Circuits.   After call, a barrister intending to practise will join a circuit and he will then practise within that circuit though he may take cases on others. At one time, these circuits broadly followed the Assize circuits of England and Wales. Now under the Courts Act, 1971, the link is with the new High Court and Crown Court Centres. In addition, since these new centres operate as continuous or semi-continuous courts, barristers tend to practise in one centre only.

There are no partnerships at the Bar, and one barrister cannot employ another, but it is usual for counsel to group together in chambers and employ a clerk who is responsible for the administration of the chambers, fees, appointments and instructions.

Queen's Counsel.   Experienced barristers may apply to the Lord Chancellor to 'take silk,' i.e. to become Queen's Counsel, and the Lord Chancellor recommends suitable applicants to the Queen who makes the appointment. After appointment as Queen's Counsel a barrister will not in general appear without a junior, i.e. another barrister who is not a Q.C., and his practise henceforth tends to be restricted to the more important cases requiring two counsel, i.e. a junior to deal with less difficult but time-consuming procedural matters and the drafting of pleadings, leaving the Q.C. to concentrate on advocacy.

However, it should be noted that following complaints in regard to the cost of the two-counsel rule, the Report of the Monopolies and Mergers Commission on Barristers' Services, a Report on the supply by Her Majesty's Counsel alone of their services, recommends that the two-counsel rule should be terminated so that Q.C.s can appear in court without a junior. This recommendation has now been accepted by the Bar Council.

Briefing and negligence.   A barrister will not normally deal directly with a client but must be briefed by a solicitor, and he cannot sue for his fees, though a solicitor who fails to pay over to counsel fees received from a client is liable to disciplinary action.

A barrister is not liable to his client for professional negligence in regard to his advice on and conduct and management of litigation whether in court or at an earlier stage. (*Saif Ali* v. *Sydney Mitchell & Co.*, 1977.)[39] However, this immunity may not extend to work of a non-litigious nature, though the matter is not decided. (*Rondel* v. *Worsley* 1967.)[40]

Etiquette.   In matters of etiquette, counsel is under an obligatory duty to conduct his case in a proper manner. He must inform the court of all the relevant statutes and precedents, and, where a legal authority is against his argument, he must not suppress it, though he may attempt to distinguish or criticize it. He must also ensure that his client has a fair hearing. If a prosecuting counsel in a criminal case is aware of facts which support the case for the accused, or lessen the gravity of the offence, he must state them. Counsel may not plead guilty for a client, but may persuade him to do so if it is in the client's interest.

The Bar and the Bench.   So far as claims to sit on the bench are concerned, Lords of Appeal in Ordinary are chosen only from barristers as are Lords

Justices of Appeal and High Court Judges. Circuit judges are chosen from barristers or from those who have held the office of Recorder for three years and Recorders from barristers and solicitors of at least ten years' standing. Thus a solicitor can now become a Circuit judge if he has previously been a Recorder.

Stipendiary magistrates are chosen from barristers and solicitors. Masters of the Queen's Bench Division must be barristers, though Masters of other divisions can also be solicitors. The National Insurance Commissioner and the National Insurance (Industrial Injuries) Commissioner are barristers as is the President of the Lands Tribunal.

Solicitors

The profession of solicitor is derived from three former branches of the legal profession. The early stages of litigation in the King's Bench and Common Pleas was conducted by *attorneys*; in the Court of Chancery by *solicitors* and in the Ecclesiastical Courts and Admiralty by *proctors*. These three branches fused in 1831 to form the Law Society, which is responsible for enrolling solicitors, for prescribing the qualifications and setting the examinations, issuing practising certificates and preserving minimum standards of behaviour. It also runs a compensation fund for those who have suffered from the wrongful acts and defaults of solicitors, and supervises the charges made by solicitors for their work.

Today a solicitor is in some respects a business man who advises his clients on legal, financial and other matters. His work is not all of a legal nature, but most of it requires legal training. Much of the work of a solicitor is concerned with property. He investigates title to land, prepares contracts of sale, conveyances and wills, and often acts as executor and trustee. He also assists promoters in company formation. There is a Practice Rule forbidding a solicitor from acting for both parties to a transaction. Solicitors are commissioners for oaths and any person who is required to sign a document and swear as to the truth of the statements in it may go to a solicitor so that the latter can declare that he has witnessed the taking of the oath. Some documents, particularly those required for use abroad such as dishonoured bills of exchange, must be sworn before a solicitor who is also a 'notary public.'

The distinction between solicitors and barristers is quite marked in the matter of litigation. The solicitor's function is to prepare the case, ascertain the facts, and arrange for the presence of the necessary witnesses and any documents which may be required. He also conducts any disputes over costs which have been awarded after judgment. Regarding advocacy, a solicitor has a right to be heard in county courts and magistrates' courts. He may also be heard in bankruptcy matters in the High Court and Divisional Court, and in interlocutory proceedings in the House of Lords, the Court of Appeal and the High Court. The Lord Chancellor may under Sect. 12 of the Courts Act, 1971, issue directions regarding the right of audience of solicitors in the Crown Court. Directions have been made under which a solicitor may appear, conduct, defend and address the Court in criminal or in civil appeals or committals where he or his partner or employee appeared for the defendant in the magistrates' court. As we have seen, it is also possible under the Courts Act, 1971, for solicitors to be eligible for appointment to the circuit bench. (See pp. 26 and 91.)

In order to qualify as a solicitor it is necessary to complete the academic stage of training and thereafter to complete a professional stage. The academic stage can be completed either by graduating with an approved law degree or by passing the Common Professional Examination. The professional stage comprises—(i) a period of service under articles; (ii) attendance at a recognized course of 36 weeks' duration; (iii) passing a final examination based on that course. After this application must be made to The Law Society for admission as a solicitor, and admission must be approved by the Master of the Rolls, since a solicitor is an officer of the court. A person may then practise alone, or as a member of a partnership, though every practising solicitor must take out an annual practising certificate. A number of solicitors are employed in local and central government departments and by commercial firms.

As we have seen, the Solicitors Act, 1974, provides for the appointment of Lay Observers to receive complaints from the public of the handling by the Law Society of complaints against solicitors. The Lord Chancellor appointed a Lay Observer in 1975 with offices in the Royal Courts of Justice in the Strand. His first annual report, which covered the period until February 1976, listed 437 complaints in the first year of operation. This declined to 305 in 1976–77.

Section 82 of the Criminal Justice Act, 1967, gives the Lord Chancellor power to set up a tribunal to hear complaints against barristers and solicitors, and if necessary exclude from acting for legally assisted persons, either permanently or temporarily, any barrister or solicitor against whom a complaint is proved.

Legal Executives

The Institute of Legal Executives which was established in 1963 gives professional status to the unadmitted staff employed in solicitors' offices. There are two examinations, the first leads to Associate membership of the Institute and the second, which is of higher standard, leads to Fellowship. Senior unadmitted employees are known as managing clerks and they frequently carry heavy responsibilities in connection with the business of the firm. The Administration of Justice Act, 1977, enables the Lord Chancellor to confer on legal executives and other solicitors' employees limited rights of audience in the County Court. (See preface.)

Reform

It has often been suggested that members of the public would be able to obtain cheaper legal services if the two branches of the profession were to merge. This is to some extent true in that only one person would be employed throughout the case doing both the pre-trial work and acting as advocate in court.

However, there are disadvantages involved in an amalgamation some of which are as follows—

(a) *Independence.* Since a barrister is not involved to a great extent or at all with the client in pre-trial work, he is better able to treat the case when it gets to court with detachment as regards, for example, the personality and social background of the client. He sees the case as a legal problem requiring solution and this attitude of detachment is regarded by many as necessary if the Court is to reach sound and unemotional decisions.

(b) *Availability.* At the present time the services of a barrister who is an expert in a particular branch of law are available to the clients of all solicitors, subject only to the ability to pay. Fusion of the profession would be likely to lead to larger firms of lawyers, some specializing in pre-trial work, and some in advocacy and opinions in special areas. The services of these specialists would unfortunately tend to be available, in the main, to clients of the particular firm and not to others.

(c) *Relationship of Bench and Bar.* Since the judiciary is for the most part selected from members of the Bar a special relationship of trust exists between judge and advocate. This can and does result in the speeding up of trials since the judge can accept more readily the method of dealing with the case which the advocates on both sides have agreed upon. This may mean, for example, that certain witnesses are not heard on the ground that the point which their evidence would make is accepted by both sides.

Some fusion of the education and training of the two branches of the profession will be achieved as a result of the Report of the Committee on Legal Education—the Ormerod Report (Cmnd. 4595). In the developed future the first stage of education and training in both branches of the profession will be completed by obtaining an approved law degree or the taking of Diploma in Law (barristers) or Common Professional Examination (solicitors). Those taking the Diploma will be exempt from the Common Professional Examination and *vice versa.*

At the present time a Royal Commission on Legal Services is hearing evidence on the supply of legal services. It has issued one interim report on progress to mid-April 1977. The report merely outlines work to date and does not contain even provisional conclusions on the evidence so far received.

SOME IMPORTANT JUDICIAL OFFICERS

The Lord Chancellor

The Lord Chancellor is the Speaker of the House of Lords and the ultimate head of the Judiciary in that he is the chief judge in the country, and controls the administration of the courts of law. He is also the Chairman of the Judicial Committee of the Privy Council. He advises the Crown on the appointment of High Court Judges, and Circuit Judges. He is responsible for the appointment of Justices of the Peace, and advises on the appointment of Recorders, Stipendiary Magistrates and Metropolitan Police Magistrates. He is the custodian of the Great Seal, which represents the signature of the Crown in its corporate capacity, and all writs of summons in the High Court are witnessed in his name. Unlike the Speaker of the House of Commons, he may take part in debates and may vote in all divisions, but has no casting vote. The office is political, and the holder is a Cabinet Minister. His position serves to support the contention that there is no separation of judicial, legislative and executive powers in the British Constitution.

The Attorney-General and the Solicitor-General

The Attorney-General and the Solicitor-General are know as the Law Officers. The appointments are political and change with the Government. As a rule the Law Officers are not members of the Cabinet.

The Attorney-General is appointed by Letters Patent under the Great Seal, and is usually a member of the House of Commons. He represents the Crown in civil matters and prosecutes in important criminal cases. He is the Head of the English Bar, and points of professional etiquette are referred to him. He also advises government departments on legal matters, and advises the court on matters of parliamentary privilege. He can institute litigation on behalf of the public, e.g. to stop a public nuisance or the commission of a crime and to enforce or regulate public charitable trusts, because he acts on behalf of the public as a whole. Individuals do not have sufficient interest (or *locus standi*) to bring actions in these cases.

Where a person does not have sufficient *locus standi* to initiate proceedings himself, he may ask the Attorney-General to take proceedings. If the Attorney-General does act at the relation of a private individual, the action is known as a 'relator action' and the relator is responsible for the costs incurred. If the Attorney-General refuses to act no court can compel him to do so. However, a member of the public, even without a special interest, may claim a declaration that an apprehended action will be unlawful and, pending final determination of such an application, the court may grant an interim injunction. A final injunction, however, cannot be granted to such a plaintiff. (*Gouriet* v. *Union of Post Office Workers,* 1977.)[41]

The Solicitor-General is the subordinate of the Attorney-General, and sometimes gives a joint opinion with him when asked by government departments. In spite of his title he is a barrister, and he need not, strictly speaking, be in the House of Commons. His duties are similar to those of the Attorney-General and he is in many ways his deputy. Both Law

Officers are precluded from private practice. The Law Officers Act, 1944, provides that any functions authorized or required to be discharged by the Attorney-General may be discharged by the Solicitor-General, if the office of Attorney-General is vacant, or if the Attorney-General is unable to act because of absence or illness, or where the Attorney-General authorizes the Solicitor-General to act in any particular matter.

Masters

Many matters arise for decision between the time of issue of the writ and the trial of the action, e.g. what documents must be shown by one side to the other; what time should be allowed for putting in statements of claim and defences; what is the most convenient and proper place for the trial to be held. These will usually be dealt with by a master, but sometimes by a judge.

Queen's Bench Masters are salaried officials of the High Court appointed from among barristers of not less than ten years' standing. They have some judicial functions and deal with matters leading to the trial of cases in the Queen's Bench Division.

Chancery Masters are salaried officials of the High Court appointed from among solicitors of not less than ten years' standing. They also have certain judicial functions, e.g. appointment of trustees and deal with matters leading to the trial of cases in the Chancery Division.

District Registrars. In most important provincial towns there is a District Registry under the supervision of a District Registrar, who performs the same functions as a master in London.

Taxing Masters are salaried officials of the Supreme Court concerned with the levying of costs. They fix the amount which one party to an action is directed to pay to the other party by way of costs. They are solicitors of at least ten years' standing, and are appointed by the Lord Chancellor with the agreement of the Treasury.

The Director of Public Prosecutions and Treasury Counsel

The roles of the Director of Public Prosecutions and Treasury Counsel were fully considered on p. 36.

Official Referee's Business

Cases which involve detailed examination of books and documents, e.g. accounts, are referred separately for trial, and are known as Official Referee's Business. Two Circuit Judges are available to deal with Official

Referee's Business on each Circuit other than the South Eastern Circuit. On that Circuit functions conferred on Official Referees are carried out by the three Circuit Judges who were Official Referees immediately before the coming into force of the Courts Act, 1971.

The Official Solicitor

The Official Solicitor is an officer of the Supreme Court who acts in litigation to protect the interests of persons suffering under mental disability. He is also concerned to protect the interests of children in adoption matters and those of persons imprisoned for contempt of court.

Circuit administrators

The Royal Commission on Assizes and Quarter Sessions (Beeching Commission) recommended the appointment of a Circuit administrator in each of the six Circuits into which England and Wales was divided. A legal qualification is not essential, but if the applicant is legally qualified he must be a barrister or solicitor of at least 10 years' standing during which time he or she must have been in practice or had substantial experience in the courts. Their function is to a large extent managerial and they took over from Clerks of Assize, Clerks of the Peace, and other officers of the numerous different courts who previously had to try to provide the public and the legal profession with a court service. There is now one person at each High Court and Crown Court Centre to whom all involved can turn in respect of administrative problems.

Circuit administrators must as far as possible ensure prompt hearings for civil and criminal cases at their centres. Six appointments were made and Circuit administrators are now based in London, Bristol, Birmingham, Cardiff, Leeds and Manchester. Their function in the new High Court and Crown Court Centres is to decide whether cases should be heard by High Court Judges or Circuit Judges.

Presiding Judges

Two High Court Judges known as Presiding Judges are assigned to each of the six Circuits in England and Wales. They take it in turn to spend substantial periods of time in the area and have general responsibility for the local High Court and Crown Court Centre. They see to the convenient and efficient distribution of judges in the area, acting on the advice of the Circuit Administrator. There are three Presiding Judges on the South Eastern region, one of whom is the Lord Chief Justice.

5 Law in Action

The work 'source' has various meanings when applied to law. One may treat the word 'source' as referring to the *historical or ultimate origins of law* and trace the *development* of the common law, equity, legislation, delegated legislation, custom, the law merchant, canon law and legal treatises, as we have done in Chapter 1. But on the other hand one may treat the word 'source' as referring to the *methods by which laws are made or brought into existence,* and consider the current processes of legislation, delegated legislation, judicial precedent and, to a limited extent, custom. In this chapter we shall be concerned with the *methods by which laws are made,* i.e. the *active* or *legal* sources of law.

LEGISLATION

It is common knowledge that much of our law is contained in Acts of Parliament. Parliament consists of two chambers—the House of Commons and the House of Lords. The House of Commons contains 635 members, each of whom represents a geographical area in the country called his constituency. Members of Parliament are elected *en bloc* at general elections. Casual vacancies, occurring through the death or withdrawal of a member, are filled separately at by-elections. The House of Lords, on the other hand, consists in the main of hereditary peers, though under the provisions of the Life Peerages Act, 1958, there has been added a number of distinguished people from various walks of life who hold life peerages, but whose descendants will have no right to a seat when the life peers are dead.

An Act of Parliament begins as a Bill, which is the draft of a proposed Act.

Types of Bills

A Session of Parliament normally lasts for one year commencing in October or November. During that time, a large number of Bills become law most of which are *Government Bills*. The Government is formed by the parliamentary party having an overall majority, or at least the greatest number, of members in the House of Commons, or more rarely by a formal coalition of, or more informal arrangement between two or more parties who between them can command such a majority. The Government is led by a Prime Minister who appoints a variety of other Ministers such as the Chancellor of the Exchequer, the Home Secretary, the Foreign Secretary, and others to manage various departments of State. A small group of these Ministers, called the Cabinet, meets frequently under the chairmanship of the Prime Minister and formulates the policy of the Government, and an important part of this policy consists of presenting Bills to Parliament with a view to their becoming law in due course. Such Bills are usually presented by the Minister of the department concerned with their contents.

The legislative intentions of the Government are given in outline to Parliament at the commencement of each session in the Queen's Speech. This is read by the Queen but is prepared by the Government of the day. Most Government Bills are introduced in the House of Commons, going later to the House of Lords and finally for the Royal Assent. However, some of the less controversial Government Bills are introduced in the House of Lords, going later to the Commons and then for the Royal Assent.

Members of either House whether Government supporters or not have a somewhat restricted opportunity to introduce *Private Members' Bills*. Such Bills are not likely to become law unless the Government provides the necessary Parliamentary time for debate. Some, however, survive to become law, for example, the Murder (Abolition of Death Penalty) Act, 1965. Those that are lost usually fail to be debated fully because influential and anonymous objectors work behind the scenes to ensure that they are taken towards the end of the session when Parliamentary time is at a premium. In addition, the severe restriction of debating time for private members' bills makes such time as is available an ideal stamping ground for the determined filibuster who wishes to talk the bill out. Two reforms are required. In the first place, objectors should be named and recorded in *Hansard* and, when the Government is the objector, as a matter of courtesy, it should give a brief explanation of its objections to the bill. Secondly, more time should be allocated for private members' bills and since there are many M.P.s who would be prepared to take these measures outside the usual sitting hours, they are ideal material for the revival of an experiment in morning sittings of Parliament.

A session of Parliament is brought to an end by prorogation and a Bill which does not complete the necessary stages and receive the Royal Assent in one Sesssion will lapse. It can be introduced in a subsequent Session but must complete all the necessary stages again. Bills also lapse when Parliament is dissolved prior to a General Election. The above provisions do not apply to *private bills* (see below) which because of the costs involved in promotion can complete their remaining stages in a new session.

Bills are also divided into *Public* and *Private* Bills. *Public Bills,* which may be Government or Private Members' Bills, alter the law throughout England and Wales and extend also to Scotland and Northern Ireland unless there is a provision to the contrary. A *Private Bill* does not alter the general law but confers special local powers. These Bills are often promoted by local authorities, where local development requires compulsory purchase of land for which a statutory power is needed. Enactment of these Bills is by a different Parliamentary procedure.

Enactment of Bills

A Public Bill and a Private Members' Bill follow the same procedure in Parliament. These Bills may be introduced in either House; though a money Bill, which is a public Bill certified by the Speaker as one containing only provisions relating to taxation or loans, must be introduced in the Commons by a Minister and not a Private member. The following procedure relates to a Public or Private Members' Bill introduced in the Commons.

On its introduction the Bill receives a purely formal first reading, at which it is not read at all. This stage is used to tell members that the Bill exists and that they can now get printed copies. Later is given a second reading, at which point its general merits may be debated, but no amendments are proposed to the various clauses it contains. In 1965 a special procedure was introduced under which the House need not debate the Bill, the second reading being merely formal. This procedure does not apply if twenty members rise to object.

Having survived the second reading may be as a result of a division in the House, the Bill passes to the Committee stage. Here details are discussed by a Standing Committee of fifteen to twenty members chosen in proportion to the strength of the parties in the House of Commons. Amendments to the clauses are proposed, and, if not accepted by the Government, are voted on, after which the Bill returns to the House at the Report stage. The Committee mentioned may be a Committee of the Whole House, if the legislation is sufficiently important. At the Report stage the amendments may be debated, and the Bill may in some cases be referred back for further consideration. It is then read for the third time, when only verbal alterations are permissible.

After passing the third reading, the Bill is sent to the House of Lords where it goes through a similar procedure. If the Lords propose amendments, the Bill is returned to the Commons for approval. At one time the House of Lords had the power to reject Bills sent up by the Commons. Now, under the provisions of the Parliament Acts, 1911 and 1949, this power amounts to no more than an ability to delay a Public Bill (other than a money Bill) for a period of one year; a money Bill may be delayed for one month only. The supremacy of the Commons stems from the fact that it is an elected assembly, responsible to its electors and coming periodically at intervals of not more than five years before the public for re-election.

The main difference between the enactment of a *Private Bill* and a *Public Bill* is that the committee stage of a Private Bill is judicial. For example, in the case of a Bill promoted by a local authority seeking to provide a yacht marina, and requiring perhaps powers of compulsory purchase of land, the local authority and those who object may brief counsel or appear themselves to state their case. Witnesses may be called and cross-examined. Since this is a somewhat lengthy procedure, some statutes allow ministers to grant special powers to local authorities by what is called a Provisional Order. Such an order does not take effect unless and until it is embodied (usually along with others) in a Provisional Order Confirmation Bill which is passed by Parliament and given the Royal Assent.

When a Bill has passed through both the Commons and the Lords, it is transmitted to the Queen for the Royal Assent, which in practice is given by a committee of three peers, including the Lord Chancellor. The Royal Assent Act, 1967, provides that an Act is duly enacted and becomes law if the Royal Assent is notified to each House of Parliament, sitting separately, by the Speaker of that House or acting Speaker. The former Bill is then referred to as an Act or a Statute, and may be regarded as a *literary* as well as a *legal* source of law. However, an Act may specify a future date for its coming into operation, or it may be brought into operation piecemeal by ministerial order. The courts have no power to disregard an Act of Parliament, whether public or private, nor have they any power to examine proceedings in Parliament in order to determine whether the passing of an Act has been obtained by means of any irregularity or fraud. (*British Railways Board* v. *Pickin,* 1974.)[42]

It should be noted that, as well as having a title setting out what its objects are, each Act has, under the provisions of the Short Titles Act, 1896, a short title to enable easy reference to be made. Each Act has also an official reference. The Companies Act, 1948, is the short title of an Act whose official reference is 11 & 12 Geo. 6, c. 38, which means that the Companies Act, 1948, was the thirty-eighth statute passed in the eleventh and twelfth years of the reign of George the Sixth.

The Acts of Parliament Numbering and Citation Act, 1962, provides that chapter numbers assigned to Acts of Parliament passed in 1963 and after shall be assigned by reference to the calendar year and not the session in which they are passed. For example, the official reference of the Companies Act, 1976, is 1976, c. 69.

Statute law and case law distinguished

The essential differences between statute law and case law are apparent from the definition of a statute. It is—

an express and formal laying down of a rule or rules of conduct to be observed in the future by the persons to whom the statute is expressly or by implication made applicable.

Thus a statute openly creates new law, whereas a judge would disclaim any attempt to do so. Judges are, they say, bound by precedent and merely select existing rules which they apply to new cases. (But see p. 115.) A statute lays down general rules for the guidance of future conduct; a judgment merely applies an existing rule to a particular set of circumstances. A judgment gives reasons and may be argumentative; a statute gives no reasons and is imperative.

Devolution

At the time of writing attempts are being made to give some variable degree of self-government to Scotland and Wales while retaining the concept of the United Kingdom. In spite of the fact that the Government has published two White Papers and a Bill, it is still proving difficult to get agreement as to the terms of any form of devolution and it is not possible to predict what sort of legislation, if any, might prove acceptable.

Parliament and the European Community

Now that Britain is a member of the European Economic Community, Parliament will have to adapt to a new role in regard to legislation emanating from the institutions of the Community. There are three principal types of Community legislation. *Regulations* which are of general application in the nine member countries and, under Art. 189 of the Treaty of Rome in theory, become part of domestic law without Parliament needing to take cognizance of them. In practice, however, some may give rise to consequential subordinate legislation or require the repeal or amendment of existing Acts. *Decisions* are of more particular application, and are also immediately operative. Decisions may be addressed to a state or to an individual or a corporation and an example of a decision would be a Commission ruling that a company was adopting restrictive practices in its operations within the Market contrary to Arts 85/86 of the Treaty. (See p. 251.) Such a decision could also impose a fine. *Directives* are under Art. 189 binding in principle, but it is left to the member countries to decide upon the means of giving them legal and administrative effect usually within a given time scale. In Britain this is dealt with by Sect. 2 of the European Communities Act, 1972, and the most common method of incorporating directives into British law will be by statutory instruments, subject to annulment by 'negative' resolution of Parliament. (See p. 106.) However, the UK's response to the First Directive on Company Law was included in Sect. 9 of the European Communities Act, 1972. (See p. 206.) Nevertheless, fundamental obligations in a directive, such as free movement of workers, which are not subject to any exception or conditions may have immediate effect without the need for legislation in the UK. (*Van Duyn* v. *The Home Office*, 1974.)[43]

As regards the provisions of the Treaty of Rome itself, these are enforceable in the High Court under Sect. 2 of the European Communities Act, 1972, provided the High Court can ascertain from the words of the Treaty itself what right has been infringed. If this is not possible, as where a person claims relief against sex discrimination generally on the basis of an article of the Treaty which deals merely with discrimination on the grounds of pay, no 'enforceable Community right' is created. (*Amies* v. *I.L.E.A.*, 1977.)[44] There is also the additional problem that many articles of the Treaty are expressed in general terms making it difficult to judge precisely what rights are conferred, so that in many cases the Treaty provides only the bones of suggested rights and is not enforceable in the absence of a UK Act of Parliament which expresses clearly the *detailed* rights conferred in the UK as a response to the *general* requirements of the Treaty. In any case an industrial tribunal cannot take into acount an 'enforceable Community right' since it was set up by a UK Act of Parliament to administer only UK Acts of Parliament dealing with specific industrial matters. (*Amies* v. *ILEA*, 1977.)[44]

The Treaties

There are three Treaties setting up three European Communities as follows—

(a) *The European Coal and Steel Community, (ECSC),*   established by the Treaty of Paris 1951 with the object of managing a common market in coal and steel;

(b) *The European Atomic Energy Community,(Euratom),*   established by the second Treaty of Rome 1957 to develop a common market in nuclear energy and the distribution of power produced thereby;

(c) *The European Economic Community,(EEC),*   established by the first Treaty of Rome 1957. The EEC has broader objectives. An immediate aim is economic integration of the member states and, in the longer term, political integration.

The institutions

There are four main institutions dealing with the functions of the communities as set out below.

The Commission.   This consists of 13 Commissioners, France, Germany, Italy and Britain appointing two each and other countries one each. A president is appointed from the commissioners and there are five vice-presidents.

The term of office of a commissioner is five years, though they may resign or be compulsorily retired for misconduct by the Court of Justice before that period expires. In addition, a vote of censure carried by a two-thirds majority in the European Parliament (or Assembly) results in the compulsory retirement of the whole Commission. Commissioners must not take instructions from their national governments but must act independently in the interests of the communities. Individual commissioners have special responsibilities, e.g. for agriculture and transport.

The Commission initiates most Community legislation and places it before the Council of Ministers for enactment. In some areas, e.g. agriculture, the Commission can enact legislation itself because the Council has delegated power to the Commisssion to do so.

The Commission can bring any member state or commercial undertaking before the Court of Justice where it feels community obligations are not being carried out and in the case of breach of restrictive practices and anti-monopoly provisions, the Commission operates quasi-judicially and, as we have seen, can issue a decision on the matter and impose a fine.

Council of ministers   The council is composed of one representative from each of the member states. The representative is usually the Foreign Secretary but others may attend where a matter of importance in a particular field is involved, e.g. if agriculture, the Minister of Agriculture.

There is a Committee of Permanent Representatives consisting of the various ambassadors to the member states which assists the Council in preliminary discussions designed to clarify issues before they reach the Council.

The Council enacts legislation on proposals from the Commission. The representatives of the larger countries have more votes than others and in most cases more than a simple majority is required. Thus for the admission of a new member state the Council must approve unanimously.

European Parliament (or Assembly).   This represents the peoples of the member states. Seats are allocated to member states on the basis of population. The members, who tend to act in political rather than national groups, are at the present time nominated by the various parliaments of member states but the aim is the total adoption of direct elections—a matter which is now before the UK Parliament.

The Parliament does not legislate, but advises. It provides a place where community problems can be discussed and questions put to the Council and Commission. As we have seen, an important power is to remove the Commission by a vote of censure passed by a majority of two-thirds.

Introduction of Community law

As we have seen, Sect. 2 of the European Communities Act, 1972, provides that the Treaties and all secondary legislation, such as regulations, intended to take effect in member states shall become part of our law. This includes legislation made before and after our entry into the community and gives what are referred to as 'enforceable Community rights'. Directives must be implemented by legislation in the member states.

The Act also requires our courts to take account of principles laid down by the Court of Justice where they have relevance to proceedings here. Furthermore, all acts of Parliament are to be interpreted on the assumption that Community law is part of UK law *and superior to it.* Thus Parliamentary sovereignty in the UK has been abandoned so far as matters relating to the Community are concerned. Parliament could, of course, repeal the Act of 1972 though this would involve renouncing membership of the Communities.

Control over Community Law

The bulk of Community law (some 90 per cent) is made by the European Commission in its day-to-day administration of the common agricultural policy. Much of this law is trivial and is not published in draft so that such scrutiny as is both necessary and feasible falls within the responsibility of the European Parliament to which Britain sends representatives.

The more substantial kinds of Community law come from the Council of Ministers acting usually on proposals put forward by the Commission and published in draft months or sometimes years before the final decision is taken. Such legislative proposals must be referred to the European Parliament before the Council takes the final decision, though the Council is in no way bound by opinions of the Parliament.

Thus all important legislative proposals are published in draft at an early stage, and this gives the legislatures of member countries a chance to exert influence at the formative stages of law making. Of course, in the case particularly of directives there is a second opportunity when the appropriate instrument or Bill comes before the domestic Parliament for endorsement. There is clearly a considerable potential for effective scrutiny, perhaps even for control, but whether that potential is realized in practice depends upon a number of factors. In the first place the willingness of governments to make information available and to accept responsibility for Community decisions. In the second place the enthusiasm of parliamentarians, already operating under some strain, to work in unfamiliar territory, and finally, the provision of adequate parliamentary machinery to assist them in their new tasks.

There is little doubt that Parliament finds it difficult to give proper scrutiny to European legislation in its formative stages and needs a select committee of some kind to assist it. It has been suggested that a Joint Committee on European Affairs be formed for this purpose. The Committee would examine proposals for legislation and report to Parliament on matters requiring attention.

Certainly there are those who feel that unless the British Parliament gives more time to debating Community legislation, the ultimate thrust of legislative authority within the British constitution could shift from Westminster to Strasbourg.

LAW REFORM

It should be noted that a number of official bodies exist to consider and make proposals for *law reform,* and the work of these bodies can have a considerable influence on the development of statute law. The most important of these bodies is the Law Commission, which was set up by the Law Commission Act, 1965. Section 1 of the Act establishes the Commission to promote the reform of English Law and deals with the constitution of the Commission. The Lord Chancellor appoints the members of the Commission, on a full-time basis, from among persons holding judicial office, experienced barristers and solicitors and university teachers of law. Section 3 states the duty of the Commission to be to keep under review the whole of the English law with a view to its systematic development and reform, including the codification of such law, the elimination of anomalies, the repeal of obsolete enactments and generally the simplification and modernization of the law. The present programme of the Law Commission includes the codification of the law of contract. The Criminal Law Act, 1967, which abolished the distinction between felonies and misdemeanors and certain obsolete crimes, resulted from proposals made by the Commission.

In arriving at its programme the Commission consults with the chairmen of the Criminal Law Revision Committee and the Law Reform Committee, which are bodies set up on a part-time basis by the Home Secretary to consider specific matters of law reform which he may refer to them in the fields of criminal and civil law respectively. The work of the Commission and the Committees may be regarded as a source of law in that it is an *historical source* of the law contained in the statute which implements its proposals. Thus the proposals of the Law Commission may be regarded as an historical source of the Criminal Law Act, 1967.

In connection with reform, it is interesting to note proposals by the Statute Law Committee for the publication of a new official edition of the Statute Book. Although the Committee has made no recommendations as to the method of printing, it has been suggested that computer typesetting be used. This would enable the text to be analysed and searched by computer and would assist research into methods of drafting and interpretation.

DELEGATED LEGISLATION

Modern statutes may require much detailed work to implement and operate them. In such a case the Act is drafted so as to provide a broad framework, the details being filled in by ministers by means of delegated legislation. For example, much of our Social Security legislation gives only the general provisions of a complex scheme of social benefits and an immense number of detailed regulations have had to be made by civil servants in the name of and under the authority of the appropriate minister. These regulations when made in the approved manner are just as much law as the parent statute itself. This form of law is known as *delegated* or *subordinate* legislation.

Advantages

A number of advantages are claimed for delegated legislation as follows.

(a) *It saves Parliamentary time* in that ministers are left to make the detailed rules. Parliament concerning itself solely with the broad framework of the legislation.

(b) *Speed.* The Parliamentary procedure for enacting bills is slow whereas rules and orders can be put more rapidly into law, particularly in a time of national emergency.

(c) *Parliament cannot foresee all the problems* which may arise after an Act has become law. Delegated legislation can deal with these if and when they arise.

(d) *Delegated legislation is less rigid* in that it can be withdrawn quickly if it proves impracticable by another statutory instrument.

(e) *The aptitude of the legislature is limited* and experts in the Departments of State can better advise a minister on the technicalities of a certain branch of law. It would be difficult to give this kind of advice to the Lords or Commons as a whole.

Disadvantages

However, there are disadvantages as follows.

(a) *Parliamentary control over legislation is undoubtedly reduced.* However, statutory instruments are laid before the House for a period of time and if the House resolves against the instrument it does not become law. This is a somewhat negative approach but certain instruments do require positive approval of the House before they become law which means that the House must resolve in favour of them otherwise they do not pass into law. There are also other controls both by the judiciary and by Parliament itself. (See below.)

(b) *It is said that there is too much delegated legislation* so that it is difficult to know what the law is, particularly in view of the fact that little publicity is given to statutory instruments whereas most important Acts of Parliament are referred to at one time or another in the Press. The difficulty is that a defendant's *ignorance of the law is no excuse,* though Sect. 3(2) of the Statutory Instruments Act of 1946 protects a person in respect of a crime contained in a statutory instrument *if the instrument has not been published.* The section does not protect if the instrument has been published by a particular defendant does not know of its existence.

(c) *The dangers of sub-delegation are on occasions quite real.* One can find in some cases a predigree of five generations of instruments emanating from a statute as follows—

(i) regulations made under the statute;
(ii) orders made under the regulations;
(iii) directions made under the orders;
(iv) licences issued under the directions

When this happens it does reduce very seriously the control by Parliament of the making of new laws since Parliament would only see the parent statute and the first set of regulations.

Types of delegated legislation.

A great variety, indeed confusion, of nomenclature can be found in Acts of Parliament. The terms *regulations, rules, orders,* and *minutes* are used and in the case of local authorities, the expression bye-laws is adopted. However, in modern statutes delegated powers are exercisable by three main vehicles as follows—

(a) *Statutory instruments.* Most powers conferred on ministers in modern statutes are exercisable by statutory instrument.

(b) *Orders in Council.* Powers of special importance relating to constitutional issues, e.g. emergency powers, are conferred on the Queen in Council. These powers are in fact exercised by the Cabinet who are all Privy Councillors by means of an Order in Council which is thereafter referred to as a Statutory Instrument.

(c) *Bye-laws of Local Authorities.* These are made by local authorities under powers given to them in Acts of Parliament and require the approval of the appropriate Minister.

Judicial control

The courts cannot declare an Act of Parliament *ultra vires,* i.e. beyond the powers of Parliament but they can and do declare the exercise of delegated powers invalid under the *ultra vires* rule. There are two approaches to the *ultra vires* rule as regards statutory instruments as follows—

(a) *Substantive ultra vires.* This means that the Minister has exceeded the powers given to him in the parent statute. If a minister is authorized to make regulations as to road traffic, clearly if he purports to make regulations under the same parent statute concerning rail traffic, they would be held by the courts to be *ultra vires* and invalid. (See *Hotel and Catering Industry Training Board* v. *Automobile Proprietary Ltd,* (1969).)[45]

(b) *Procedural ultra vires.* This means that the instrument is invalid because the minister has failed to follow some mandatory procedural requirement specified in the parent act. For example, much Social Security legislation requires the minister to consult various advisory bodies before making rules and orders. If a rule or order was made without the necessary consultation, then it would be *ultra vires* in procedural terms and invalid.

It should be noted that the courts will not examine the internal proceedings of Parliament in order to invalidate delegated legislation. (*R. v. Immigration Appeal Tribunal, ex parte Joyles*, 1972.)[46]

Henry VIII Clauses

Sometimes a section of an act will give a minister or the Queen in Council very wide powers so that it is difficult to say that any instrument made under it is *ultra vires*. These are referred to as 'Henry VIII Clauses' after the way in which that monarch used to legislate in arbitrary fashion by a proclamation. For example, the Southern Rhodesia Act of 1965 gives Her Majesty in Council power 'to make such provision in relation to Southern Rhodesia . . . as appears to her to be necessary or expedient.' It would be hard indeed for any court to declare an order made under the above provision *ultra vires* and judicial review is virtually excluded.

Parliamentary control

As regards Parliamentary control there is a Joint Committee on Statutory Instruments between the House of Commons and the House of Lords. The predecessors of this Joint Committee were the Lords' Special Orders Committee and the Commons' Statutory Instruments Committee. The Joint Committee has been appointed to consider—

(1) Every instrument which is laid before each House of Parliament; being:

(*a*) a statutory instrument or a draft thereof or scheme requiring approval by statutory instrument;

(*b*) any other instrument (whether or not in draft), where the proceedings in pursuance of an Act of Parliament are proceedings by way of an affirmative resolution; or

(*c*) an order subject to special Parliamentary procedure.

(2) Every general statutory instrument not within the above classes and not required to be laid before or to be subject to proceedings in the House of Commons only, with a view to determining whether the special attention of the Houses should be drawn to the legislation on various grounds not impinging on merits or policy. The grounds, briefly, are as follows; that the legislation—

(i) imposes a tax on the public;

(ii) is made in pursuance of an enactment containing specific provisions excluding it from challenge in the courts;

(iii) purports to have retrospective effect where there is no express authority in the enabling statute;

(iv) has been unduly delayed in publication or laying before Parliament;

(v) has come into operation before being laid before Parliament and there has been unjustifiable delay in informing the Speaker of the delay under Sect. 4(1) of the Statutory Instruments Act, 1946;

(vi) is of doubtful *vires* or makes some unusual or unexpected use of the powers conferred by the enabling statute;

(vii) calls for any special reason of form or purport for elucidation;

(viii) is defective in its drafting.

The House of Commons Select Committee on Statutory Instruments remains to consider legislation which is to be laid before and subject to proceedings in the House of Commons *only*. In addition, there is a Standing Committee of the House of Commons to consider statutory instruments and draft statutory instruments referred to them on the question of merits. The setting up of this Committee was recommended by the Brooke Committee and should serve a useful function in debating issues touching upon policy which for so long have remained outside the jurisdiction of Parliamentary scrutiny committees.

Reference has already been made to the possibility of setting up a Scrutiny Committee in respect of legislative instruments emanating from the European Community (see p. 104).

Bye-laws of Local Authorities

These must be *intra vires*; i.e. within the powers given to the local authority in the enabling statute and also reasonable. Thus, in *Kruse* v. *Johnson* [1898] 2 Q.B. 91 a local authority bye-law making it an offence to sing within 50 yards of a dwelling house was upheld but the court decided that unreasonableness could be a ground for invalidating bye-laws. This can occur where the bye-law is partial and unequal in its operation as between different classes or if it involves oppressive and gratuitous interference with the rights of persons subject to it so that it cannot be justified in the minds of reasonable men. (And see *Denithorne* v. *Davies*, 1967.)[47]

CASE LAW OR JUDICIAL PRECEDENT

Case Law provides the bulk of the law of the country. Some case law enunciates the law itself, and some is concerned with the interpretation of statutes. We will examine first the case law which is law in its own right. Case law is built up out of precedents, and a precedent is a previous decision of a court which may, in certain circumstances, be binding on another court in deciding a similar case. This practice of following previous decisions is derived from custom, but it is a practice which is generally observed. As Park, C.J., said in *Mirehouse* v. *Rennell* (1833), 1 Cl. & Fin. 527, 'Precedent must be adhered to for the sake of developing the law as a science.' Even in early times the itinerant judges adopted the doctrine of *stare decisis,* and this doctrine has been developed in modern times so that it means that a precedent binds, and must be followed in similar cases, subject to the power to distinguish cases in certain circumstances.

The modern doctrine of the binding force of judicial precedent only fully emerged when there was (a) good law reporting; and (b) a settled judicial hierarchy. By the middle of the nineteenth century law reporting was much more efficient, and the Judicature Acts, 1873–75, created a proper pyramid of authority which was completed when the Appellate Jurisdiction Act, 1876, made the House of Lords the final Court of Appeal. Judicial precedents may be divided into two kinds—

(1) Binding Precedents
(2) Persuasive Precedents

but before we elucidate the precise meaning of these terms, we have still to ascertain where these precedents are to be found. The answer is in the law reports; and as we have seen the doctrine of judicial precedent depends upon an accurate record being kept of previous decisions.

Law Reports

Bracton was the first person to compile cases (some two thousand of them) in his Notebook which appeared before the Year Books. The latter were gossipy and fragmentary notes of cases, written in Anglo-Norman, and covering a period of two and a half centuries from the reign of Edward I to that of Henry VIII—that is from the thirteenth century to about the middle of the sixteenth. The Year Books are little used by the modern practitioner because of their many inaccuracies, because of the language in which they are written, and because they do not always report the *ratio decidendi* of the case, but they were studied by the law apprentices in the Inns of Court.

Access to court records was only allowed to lawyers acting on behalf of the Crown. Hence we get the private reports, one of the first sets being Dyer's Collection, 1513–1581. Like the Year Books, many early private reports are of doubtful quality being inaccurate and gossipy. For example, it was said of Barnardiston who was a King's Bench reporter from 1726 to 1734 'that he was accustomed to slumber over his notebook and the wags in the rear took the opportunity of scribbling nonsense in it.' The following are among the most notable and accurate early collections: Plowden's Reports, Coke's Reports, and Burrow's Reports. The last-named runs from 1756–72, and is the first attempt to report in the modern sense of the word, an effort being made to report arguments and judgments. Other good collections are those of Barnewell & Cresswell, and Meeson & Welsby.

Since 1865 law reports have been published under the control of what is now called the Incorporated Council of Law Reporting, which is a joint committee of the Inns of Court, The Law Society, and the Bar Council. They are known simply as the Law Reports, and they have priority in the courts because the judge who heard the case sees and revises the report before publication. Nevertheless private reports still exist, and of these the All England Reports, published weekly and started in 1936, are the only *general* reports existing in the private sector. These reports are now revised by the judge concerned with the case, though this was not always so and differences do appear between the version of a case in the official reports and that in the unrevised All England Reports. In addition, there is some judicial editing of the transcript of the trial prior to publication in the reports. This has extended beyond minor textual amendments and in some cases the report states rules of law which were not in fact laid down in the judgment given at the trial. In 1953 the Incorporated Council began to publish reports on a weekly basis and these are known as the Weekly Law Reports. *The Times* newspaper publishes summarized reports of certain cases of importance and interest on the day following the hearing and there are also certain specialized series of reports covering, for example, the fields of taxation and shipping. It is not absolutely essential that a case should have been reported in order that it may be cited as a precedent, and occasionally oral evidence of the decision by a barrister who was in court when the judgment was delivered may be brought.

Decided cases are usually referred to as follows: *Smith* v. *Jones, 1959.* This means that, in a court of first instance, Smith was the plaintiff, Jones the defendant, and that the case was published in the set of reports of 1959, though it may have been heard at the end of 1958. This is called the Short Citation. A longer citation is required if the report is to be referred to, and might read as follows: *Smith* v. *Jones,* [1959] 1 Q.B. 67 at p. 76. The additional information means that the case is to be found in the First Volume of the Reports of the Queen's Bench Division, the report commencing on page 67, the number 76 being used to indicate the page on which an important statement is to be found. Where the date is cited in square brackets it means that the date is an essential part of the reference, and without the date it is very difficult to find the report in question. For many years now the Incorporated Council's reports have been written up in a certain number of volumes each year. It will be seen that a mere reference to Vol. 1 of the Queen's Bench Division will not be sufficient unless the year is also quoted.

The early reports by the Incorporated Council and other collections did not use the year as a basic item of the citation, but continued to extend the number of volumes regardless of the year. So a case may be cited as follows: *Smith* v. *Jones,* 17 Ch. D. 230. It can be found by referring to Vol. 17 of the Chancery Division reports, and it is not necessary to know the year in which the report was published, though this will be ascertained when the report is referred to. Where the date is not an essential part of the citation, the date is quoted in round brackets. The abbreviations used for the various divisions are: Q.B. for Queen's Bench; Ch. for Chancery; P. for Probate, etc.; Fam. for Family; and A.C. for the House of Lords and Privy Council (Appeal Cases). The reports of decisions of the Court of Appeal appear under the reference of the division in which they were first heard. As regards the case title petitions for leave to appeal and appeals to the Court of Appeal carry the same title as that which obtained in the court of first instance. This results in the plaintiff being shown first in the title whether he or she be the petitioner/appellant or respondent in the Court of Appeal. This is now true of the House of Lords so that appeals to the House of Lords now carry the same title as that which obtained in the court of first instance, though the reference A.C. is still used in House of Lords and Privy Council cases.

Precedents

We are now in a position to refer to a decided case but we still have to ascertain where the precedent is to be found, since the whole of the case is reported, and the judge may have said things which are not strictly relevant to the final judgment. We must know what to take as precedent, and what to ignore, so that we can find what is called the *ratio decidendi*. This is the principle on which the case was decided. In this connection it is worth noting the remarks of Sir George Jessel in *Osborne* v. *Rowlett* (1880), 13 Ch. D. 774, that 'the only thing in a judge's decision binding as an authority upon a subsequent judge is the principle upon which the case was decided.'

The *ratio decidendi* of a decision is ascertained by a subsequent judge before whom the case is cited as an authority. Thus the eventual and accepted *ratio decidendi* of a case may not be the *ratio decidendi* that the judge who decided the case would himself have chosen, but the one which has been approved by subsequent judges. This is inevitable; because a judge, when deciding a case, does not usually distinguish in his remarks between what we have called the *ratio decidendi* and what are called *obiter dicta*. The latter are things said in passing, and they do not have binding force. Such statements of legal principle are, however, of some persuasive power, particularly the *dicta* of cases heard in the House of Lords.

The reason why *obiter dicta* are merely persuasive is because the prerogative of judges is not to make the law by formulating it and declaring it (this is for the legislature) but to make the law by applying it to cases coming before them. A judicial decision, unaccompanied by judicial application, is not of binding authority. A judge does sometimes indicate which of his statements are *obiter dicta*. For example he may say: 'If it were necessary to decide the further point, I should be inclined to say that. . . .' What follows is said in passing.

It may therefore be said that the *ratio decidendi* of any given case is an abstraction of the principle from the facts and arguments of the case, and, of course, the higher the level of abstraction, the more circumstances the *ratio decidendi* will fit. Let us take the following fact situation—'At 12 noon on a Saturday A, a woman aged 30, drove a car through the centre of Manchester at 80 mph. She mounted the pavement and injured B, an old man of 90. B. sued A and the judge found that she was liable.' If a subsequent judge feels that the principle in *B* v. *A* should be restricted he will tend to retain many of the facts of the case in the *ratio*. If he feels that the principle should be extended he will drop out many of the facts of the situation to produce a broad principle of wide application. Thus, a very narrow *ratio* would be as follows 'If a woman aged 30 by the negligent driving of a car injures an old man of 90, she is liable to compensate him in damages.' However, the law of Negligence is a much wider principle and the ratio is—'If A, by negligence injures B, A is liable to compensate B in damages.'

The same principles of abstraction apply when a judge chooses to follow *obiter dicta*. This is well illustrated by the way in which the decision of the House of Lords in *Donoghue* v. *Stevenson,* 1932[468] was developed to produce the doctrine of professional negligence in *Hedley Byrne* v. *Heller and Partners,* 1963[248] which eventually became the *ratio* of *Esso Petroleum Co.* v. *Mardon,* 1976.[658]

Binding Force

It is now necessary to examine which precedents are binding, and this depends upon the level of the court in which the decision was reached.

House of Lords.   Starting with the highest authority, the House of Lords, we find that this body was bound by its own decisions (*London Street Tramways* v. *London County Council,* [1898] A.C. 375), except, for example, where the previous decision had been made *per incuriam,* i.e. where an important case or statute was not brought to the attention of the court when the previous decision was made. However, in July, 1966, the House of Lords abolished the rule that their own decisions on points of law were absolutely binding upon themselves. The Lord Chancellor announced the change on behalf of himself and the Lords of Appeal in Ordinary in the following statement—

Their Lordships regard the use of precedent as an indispensable foundation upon which to decide what is the law and its application to individual cases. It provides at least some degree of certainty upon which individuals can rely in the conduct of their affairs, as well as a basis for orderly development of legal rules.

Their Lordships nevertheless recognize that too rigid adherence to precedent may lead to injustice in a particular case and also unduly restrict the proper development of the law. They propose therefore to modify their present practice and, while treating former decisions of this House as normally binding, to depart from a previous decision when it appears right to do so.

In this connexion they will bear in mind the danger of disturbing retrospectively the basis on which contracts, settlements of property and fiscal arrangements have been entered into and also the especial need for certainty as to the criminal law.

This announcement is not intended to affect the use of precedent elsewhere than in this House.

A practice direction issued in March, 1971, by the Appeal Committee of the House of Lords requires lawyers concerned with the preparation of cases of appeal to state clearly in a separate paragraph of the case any intention to invite the House to depart from one of its own decisions.

The use by the House of Lords of the declaration of 1966 is illustrated by *Schorsch Meier Gmbh* v. *Hennin,* 1975[48] and *Miliangos* v. *George Frank (Textiles) Ltd,* 1975[49].

Appeal Courts.   On the next rung of the hierarchy there is the Court of Appeal (Civil Division), and this court is bound by its own previous decisions, and those of its predecessors of co-ordinate jurisdiction as well as by those of the House of Lords. (*Young* v. *Bristol Aeroplane Co.,* [1944] 2 All E.R. 293). The Court of Appeal is not bound by a previous decision, if that decision cannot stand with a decision of the House of Lords, or the Judicial Committee of the Privy Council. Thus *Re. Polemis,* 1921,[540] which was a decision of the Court of Appeal, was disapproved of the Judicial Committee of the Privy Council in *The Wagon Mound,* 1961[542] and *Re Polemis*[540] was not followed by the Court of Appeal in *Doughty* v. *Turner Manufacturing Co.,* 1964.[546]

On the criminal side, the Court of Appeal (Criminal Division) is bound by the decisions of the House of Lords and normally by its own decisions and those of the former Court of Criminal Appeal and the earlier Court for Crown Cases Reserved. However, an ordinary court of three judges in the Criminal Division may deviate from previous decisions more easily than the Civil Division because different considerations apply in a criminal appeal where the liberty of the accused is at stake (*R.* v. *Gould,* 1968),[50] and in any case a full court of the Criminal Division can overrule its own previous decisions. A full court generally consists of five judges instead of three as is usual in an ordinary sitting. A decision of the Civil Division is not binding on the Criminal Division and vice versa.

Divisional Courts.   Divisional Courts are, in civil cases, bound by the decisions of the House of Lords, the Court of Appeal (Civil Division) and by their own previous decisions. In criminal cases there is, under the Administration of Justice Act, 1960, an appeal from the Divisional Court of the Queen's Bench Division straight to the House of Lords, and the Divisional Court is not bound by the decisions of the Criminal Division of the Court of Appeal and those of its predecessors of co-ordinate jurisdiction.

High Court.   At the next lower stage, a High Court judge, although bound by the decisions of the Court of Appeal and the House of Lords is not bound by the decisions of another High Court judge sitting at first instance. (*Huddersfield Police Authority* v. *Watson,* [1947] 2 All E.R. 193.) Nevertheless such a judge will treat previous decisions as of strong persuasive authority. The present High Court is not bound by the decisions of the old courts of Common Pleas, Queen's Bench or Exchequer. It was stated by Lord Goddard, C.J., in *Huddersfield Police Authority* v. *Watson,* [1947] 2 All E.R. 193 that a High Court judge is bound to follow 'the decisions of the Court of Appeal, the House of Lords and Divisional Courts'. It is, however, sometimes disputed whether decisions of Divisional Courts are binding on High Court judges. It appears that a Divisional Court cannot overrule the decision of a High Court judge; and that a High Court judge may properly prefer a decision of one of his brethren to that of a Divisional Court. On the other hand, the Divisional Court professes to be bound by its own decisions (see *Huddersfield Police Authority* v. *Watson* above) and it is therefore odd if such decisions are binding on two or more judges sitting in a Divisional Court but not on one judge sitting alone.

Crown Court. A judge sitting in a Crown Court, the jurisdiction of which is confined to criminal cases, is bound by decisions made in criminal matters by the House of Lords and Court of Appeal (Criminal Division) but not apparently by decisions of the Divisional Court of the Queen's Bench Division. (*R.* v. *Colyer,* [1974] Crim. L.R. 243.) The Crown Court is a branch of the Supreme Court, having equal status with the High Court. A judge sitting in a Crown Court and exercising a civil jurisdiction, e.g. licensing, is bound by the decisions of the House of Lords, Court of Appeal and the High Court.

Employment Appeal Tribunal. As regards this Tribunal only the decisions of the Court of Appeal and the House of Lords on matters of law are binding, though, the decisions of the Industrial Relations Court and the High Court in England are of great persuasive authority and the Tribunal would not lightly differ from the principles which are to be found in those decisions. (per Bristow, J. in *Portec (UK) Ltd* v. *Mogensen,* [1976] 3 All E.R. 565 at p. 568.)

Judicial Committee of the Privy Council. The decisions of the Judicial Committee of the Privy Council are not binding, either on the Committee itself or on other English courts save the Ecclesiastical and Prize Courts. Its decisions are technically only of persuasive authority in English law, and this derives from the fact that the Judicial Committee hears appeals from overseas territories. Thus, when it hears an appeal from Hong Kong, it may not apply a rule of law used (say) in a previous appeal from Australia.

Exceptions to the rule of binding precedent

Having examined the relationship of the above courts with regard to the doctrine of binding precedent, it should be noted that a court is not always bound to follow a precedent which according to the rules outlined above ought to be binding on it. It is by avoiding the following of precedents that judges can, and do, make law.

Thus, when the court in question is invited to follow a binding precedent, it may refuse to do so—

(i) by *distinguishing* the case now before it from the previous case *on the facts* (compare *Phillips* v. *Brooks*, 1919[217] with *Ingram* v. *Little*, 1961[218] and *Lewis* v. *Averay*, 1971[219]);

(ii) by refusing to follow the previous case because its *ratio* is *obscure* (see *Harper* v. *NCB*, [1974] 2 All E.R. 441);

(iii) by declaring the previous case to be in *conflict with a fundamental principle of law*, as where, for example, the court in the previous case has not applied the doctrine of privity of contract;

(iv) by finding the previous decision to be *per incuriam*, i.e. where an important case or statute was not brought to the attention of the court (see view of Bristow, J. in *Miliangos*[49]) when the previous decision was made;

(v) by declaring the principle or *ratio* of the previous decision to be *too wide*, and regarding some of it as *obiter* and therefore not binding. The views of the judiciary as regards the true *ratio* of *Donoghue* v. *Stevenson*, 1932[468] have varied according to whether the plaintiff or the defendant was thought entitled to succeed. (See *Candler* v. *Crane, Christmas*, 1951[655] and *Hedley Byrne & Co. Ltd* v. *Heller and Partners Ltd*, 1963[248].);

(vi) because the previous decision is one of several *conflicting decisions* at the same level. (*Tiverton Estates Ltd* v. *Wearwell Ltd*, 1974)[51];

(vii) because the *previous decision* had been *overruled by statute*.

Cases heard in the county court and in the magistrates' courts are not generally reported, and do not create binding precedents. It would not be desirable to report such cases, for English law already possesses such a large number of reported cases that decisions are sometimes made in which relevant precedents are not cited or considered, and may therefor be *per incuriam*. Moreover decisions on civil matters in the former assize courts are sometimes criticized and not regarded as binding, since time did not always allow for full consideration of the points involved.

Persuasive precedents

These, then, consist of decisions made in lower courts, and in the Judicial Committee of the Privy Council of *obiter dicta* at all levels and also decisions of Irish, Scottish, Dominion, and United States courts, the reason being that these nations also base their law on the common law of England, though some parts of the law of Scotland are derived from Roman Law. Cases coming to the House of Lords from Scotland do not bind English courts. They are only persuasive unless the legal principles involved are the same in both systems of law. The House of Lords normally gives a directive as to the binding nature of such decisions; for example, *Donoghue* v. *Stevenson*, 1932,[468] which is a most important case on the law of negligence, is binding in both jurisdictions, although it was an appeal from the Scottish Court of Session.

In the absence of any persuasive authority from the above sources the court may turn to text-books and sometimes to Roman law. The weight which a court will give to persuasive authority may depend upon the standing of the judge whose decision or dictum it was and whether it was a reserved judgment, i.e. a case in which the court took time to consider the judgment. Reserved judgments are highly regarded. Undefended cases in which the issues have not been fully argued on both sides do not carry great weight.

Declaratory and original precedents

One further classification of precedents must be noted. They may be either 'declaratory' or 'original'—

A declaratory precedent is one which is merely the application of an existing rule of law.

An original precedent is one which creates and applies a new rule. Original precedents alone develop the law; declaratory precedents are merely further evidence of it. Thus, if a judge says: 'The matter before us is not covered by authority and we must decide it on principle. . . .' an original precedent is indicated.

Reversing, overruling and *res judicata*

It often happens that when a case has been decided in (say) the High Court, a decision is taken to appeal to an appellate court, in this case the Court of Appeal. The Court of Appeal will re-examine the case and, if it comes to a different conclusion from the judge in the High Court, it reverses his decision. Reversal, therefore, applies to a decision of an appellate court in the same case. Sometimes, however, the case which comes before the appellate court has been decided by following a previously decided case, the judge having followed precedent. In this case, if the appellate court decides to differ from the decision reached in the lower court, it is said to overrule the case which formed the basis of the precedent. *Reversal affects the parties,* who are bound by the decision of the appellate court, and it affects precedent because lower courts will in future be bound to follow the decision. *Overruling affects precedent,* but does not reach back to affect the parties in the original case, now regarded as wrongly decided, and it is not necessary, for example, for a successful plaintiff to return his damages. Furthermore, the case could not be tried again because the doctrine of *res judicata* would apply. So the doctrine of *res judicata* (a matter which has been adjudicated on) protects defendants against a multiplicity of actions in regard to the same issues.

If a judge of the High Court refuses to follow a previous decision on a similar point of law, the case books will contain two decisions by judges of equal authority, and the cases will remain in conflict until the same point of law is taken to an appeal before a higher tribunal whose decision will then resolve the position.

Distinguishing

A case is *distinguished* when the court considers that there are points of difference between the case now before it and a previous decision which it is being invited to follow. As Lord Halsbury said in *Quinn* v. *Leathem,* [1901] A.C. 495—

> Every judgment must be read as applicable to the particular facts proved, or assumed to be proved, since the generality of the expressions which may be found there are not intended to be expositions of the whole law but govern and are qualified by the particular facts of the case in which such expressions are found.

As we have seen, this process of narrowing down the implications of the *ratio decidendi* of a previous case by 'distinguishing' is a device often used by a court which does not wish to follow an earlier decision which would otherwise be binding on it.

If a court feels that an earlier case was wrongly decided but cannot overrule it because the *ratio decidendi* of the case now before it does not cover all the matters raised in the earlier case, it may, by way of *obiter dictum, disapprove* the earlier case which is then to some extend affected as a precedent.

Advantages and drawbacks of case law

The system of judicial precedent has several advantages. Up to a point it can claim the advantage of certainty, since it is possible to predict the ruling of a court because judicial decisions tend to be consistent. Nevertheless judges have a habit of distinguishing cases on the facts, or of limiting the application of a principle which had formerly been thought to be of wider scope, and *vice versa.* This means that the claim to certainty has to be taken with reservations. Another claim put forward in favour of case law is its power of flexibility and growth. New decisions are constantly being added as new cases come before the courts. In this way the law tends to keep pace with the times and can adapt itself to changing circumstances. Judicial precedent covers a wealth of detail. There is a case in point for every rule, and there is a practical character to judicial rulings. Legal rules are made only as the need arises, and the law is not made in advance on the basis of theory. When a case arises, a decision is taken and the ruling is usually recorded, so that when a similar case arises again the law will be there to be applied.

Case law has certain drawbacks. These drawbacks are in some cases merely the converse aspects of the advantages. For example, Jeremy Bentham criticized the principle of the 'law following the event,' and applied the epithet 'dog's law' to the system. 'It is,' he says, 'the judges that make the common law. Do you know how they make it? Just as a man makes laws for his dog. When your dog does something you want to break him of, you wait till he does it and then beat him. This is the way you make laws for your dog: this is the way the judges make law for you and me'.

A further criticism is that *the binding force of precedent limits judicial discretion*. It has been said that judges are engaged in 'forging fetters for their own feet.' This can be illustrated by the doctrine of common employment, which was laid down by the House of Lords in *Priestley* v. *Fowler* (1837), 3 M. & W. 1. This doctrine said that if an employee was injured by a fellow employee whilst both were acting within the scope of their employment, their employer was not liable vicariously for that negligence. The rule operated in a most unjust fashion during the period of great industrial development, but it continued to bind judges for over a century until it was finally abolished by the Law Reform (Personal Injuries) Act, 1948. All the judges could do in the meantime was to try to limit its scope.

Limiting the scope of a decision may lead to the court's making *illogical distinctions*. Judges and counsel pay attention to differences in cases which are fundamentally similar, in order to uphold the doctrine of precedent and still not feel bound to follow an inconvenient rule. Often these distinctions have real substance, but occasionally they are illogical and serve to complicate the law.

Difficulties of the kind outlined above may not now arise in such an acute form because, as we have seen, the House of Lords is no longer bound by its own decisions, though this tends to detract from the element of certainty.

A further criticism must be noted— that of *bulk and complexity*. The number of reported cases is so large that the law can be ascertained only by searching through a large number of reports. This search has been eased somewhat where case law has been codified by statute in order to produce a rational arrangement. The Bills of Exchange Act, 1882, the Sale of Goods Act, 1893, and the Law of Property Act, 1925, have to a large extent produced order in what might have been called chaos, but case law still tends to develop even around a codifying statute, and its sections soon have to be read in the light of interpretative cases.

Finally, it is a major criticism of our system of case law that only the House of Lords gives the ultimate authoritative judicial ruling on a matter. However, whether this happens depends upon the litigants footing the bill to get to the House of Lords or the Legal Aid Fund doing so. It would be an improvement if we had a system under which the High Court or Court of Appeal could refer a question of law to the House of Lords at public expense, rather on the lines of Art. 177 of the EEC Treaty which allows reference to the Court of Justice by domestic courts on matters involving Community Law.

Case Law in the European Court. In line with the normal Continental approach, there is no doctrine of binding precedent, though the body of decisions which the court is making in the interpretation of the Treaty are having strong persuasive influence. These decisions are cited before the court in argument and are also quoted in judgments.

INTERPRETATION OF STATUTES

The main body of the law is to be found in statutes, together with the relevant statutory instruments, and in case law as enunciated by judges in the courts. But the judges not only have the duty of declaring the common law, they are also frequently called upon to settle disputes as to the meaning of words or clauses in a statute.

Parliament is the supreme lawgiver, and the judges must follow statutes. Nevertheless there is a considerable amount of case law which gathers round important Acts of Parliament, since the wording sometimes turns out to be obscure. Statutes were at one time drafted by practising lawyers who were experts in the particular branch of law of which the statute was to be a part. Today, however, statutes are drafted by parliamentary counsel to the Treasury, and, although such persons are skilled in the law, the volume of legislation means that statutes are often obscure and cases continue to come before the courts in which the rights of the parties depend upon the exact meaning of a section of a statute. When such a case comes before a judge, he must decide the meaning of the section in question. Thus even statute law is not free from judicial influence.

The judges have certain recognized *aids to interpretation,* and these are set out below.

Statutory Aids

Judges may get some guidance from statute law.

(*a*) The Interpretation Act, 1889, which is itself a statute, defines terms commonly used in Acts of Parliament. (*Hutton* v. *Esher U.D.C.,* 1973.)[52]

(*b*) A complex statute will normally contain an interpretation section, defining the terms used in the particular Act, e.g. Sect. 455 of the Companies Act, 1948 defines, among other things, 'accounts' and 'director', and the judges have recourse to this.

(*c*) Every Act of Parliament used to have what was known as a preamble, which set out at the beginning the general purpose and scope of the Act. The preamble was often quite lengthy and assisted the judge in ascertaining the meaning of the statute. Modern Public Acts do not have this type of preamble, but have instead a long title which is not of so much assistance in interpretation. All Private Acts must have a preamble setting out the objects of the legislation, and this preamble must be proved by the promoters at the Committee stage in the House of Lords. So far as private acts are concerned the preamble may be of considerable assistance.

General rules of interpretation evolved by judges

There are a number of generally recognized rules or canons of interpretation, and some of the more important ones are now given.

The mischief rule.   This was propounded in *Heydon's* case, (1584), 3 Co. Rep. 7a. Under this rule the judge will look at the Act to see what was its purpose and what mischief in the common law it was designed to prevent. As was said in *Heydon's* case—

> Four things are to be discussed and considered: (i) What was the common law before the making of the Act? (ii) What was the mischief and defect for which the common law did not provide? (iii) What remedy hath Parliament resolved and appointed to cure the disease of the commonwealth? (iv) What is the true reason for the remedy? Judges shall . . . make such construction as shall suppress the mischief and advance the remedy.

Broadly speaking, the rule means that where a statute has been passed to remedy a weakness in the law the interpretation which will correct that weakness is the one to be adopted.

An example of the use of the rule can be seen in *Gardiner* v. *Sevenoaks R.D.C., 1950.*[53]

The literal rule.   According to this rule, the working of the Act must be construed according to its literal and grammatical meaning whatever the result may be. The same word must normally be construed thoughout the Act in the same sense, and in the case of old statutes regard must be had to its contemporary meaning if there has been a change with the passage of time.

The Law Commission, in an instructive and provocative report on the subject of interpretation (Law Com. 21), said of this rule that 'to place undue emphasis on the literal meaning of the words of a provision is to assume an unattainable perfection in draftsmanship.'

The Golden Rule.   This rule is to some extent an exception to the literal rule and under it the words of a statute will as far as possible be construed according to their ordinary plain and natural meaning, unless this leads to an absurd result. (*Prince of Hanover* v. *Attorney-General, 1956.*)[3] It is used by the Courts where a statutory provision is capable of more than one literal meaning or where a study of the statute as a whole reveals that the conclusion reached by applying the literal rules is contrary to the intentions of Parliament.

The classic example is perhaps Sect. 105 of the Law of Property Act, 1925, which provides as follows—

> Where a mortgagee [*the Act is here describing a lender*] sells land to recover the amount of a loan advanced on the security of the land and

the land realises more than the balance of the mortgage the balance after sale shall go to the person entitled to the mortgaged property.

By applying the Literal Rule to the last six words the purchaser from the mortgagee would be entitled. Thus if, say, a building society, sold A's house for £20,000 to B because A could not pay his mortgage of £10,000, the building society should under the section give the balance of £10,000, after deducting the costs of sale, to B. Since this would be a absurd result, the words have been taken in *Young* v. *Clarey,* [1948] 1 All E.R. 197 and subsequent cases, to refer to the mortgagor (or borrower), i.e. A.

The ejusdem generis rule.   This is a rule covering things of the same genus, species or type. Under it, where general words follow particular words, the general words are construed as being limited to persons or things within the class outlined by the particular words. So in a reference to 'dogs, cats, and other animals,' the last three words would be limited in their application to animals of the domestic type, and would not be extended to cover animals such as lions and tigers. (*Evans* v. *Cross,* 1938,[54] and *Lane* v. *London Electricity Board,* 1955.)[55]

Expressio unius est exclusio alterius.   (The expression of one thing implies the exclusion of another.) Under this rule, where specific words are used and are not followed by general words, the Act applies only to the instances mentioned. For example, where a statute contains an express statement that certain statutes are repealed, there is a presumption that other relevant statutes not mentioned are not repealed.

Noscitur a sociis.   (The meaning of a word can be gathered from its context.) Under this rule words of doubtful meaning may be better understood from the nature of the words and phrases with which they are associated. (*Muir* v. *Keay,* 1875.)[56]

Other considerations and presumptions

In addition to the major rules of interpretation, there are also several other considerations which the judge will have in mind. He will concern himself only with the wording of the Act, and will not go to *Hansard* to look up reports of the debates during the passage of the Act. Nor will he take notice of the statements of Ministers, or the recommendations of committees which may have led to the legislation. An Act of Parliament comes into being as a result of many recommendations, and is modified in the course of debate, and it would be impracticable to refer to such miscellaneous sources with any degree of certainty as to their value.

There is here some conflict with the Mischief Rule, since it might be thought that there is no better way to ascertain what mischief the Act was designed to prevent than by reference to the debates. Nevertheless, the

Law Commission decided against the use of Hansard since they doubted the reliability of statements made in Parliamentary debates.

As regards the reports of Committees on which the Act was based, Lord Denning, M.R. said in *Letang* v. *Cooper,* 1964[570] that the court could look at the Report to get the facts and surrounding circumstances in order to see the background against which the Act was passed, but not in order to interpret the words of the statute so that it agreed with the Committee's recommendations which Parliament may not necessarily have accepted in that form. This is so, according to the House of Lords in *Black-Clawson International Ltd* v. *Papierwerke Waldhof-Aschaffenburg AG,* [1975] 1 All E.R. 810, even where the Act is almost exactly the same as a draft Bill which the Committee included in its Report.

A statute is presumed not to alter the existing law unless it expressly states that it does. There is also a presumption against the repeal of other statutes and that is why statutes which are repealed are repealed by specific reference.

In *DPP.* v. *Schildkamp,* [1969] 3 All E.R. 1640, the House of Lords considered, *inter alia,* the extent to which marginal notes and punctuation might be used to clarify the meaning of a particular section or paragraph. In the course of his judgment Lord Reid said 'So, if the Authorities are equivocal and one is free to deal with the whole matter, I would not object to taking all these matters into account provided that we realize that they cannot have equal weight with the words of the Act. Punctuation can be of some assistance in construction. A cross-heading ought to indicate the scope of the sections which follow it but there is always a possibility that the scope of one of the sections may have been widened by amendment. But a side-note is a poor guide to the scope of a section for it can do no more than indicate the main subject with which the section deals.'

When a statute deprives a person of property, there is a presumption that compensation will be paid. Unless so stated it is presumed that an Act does not interfere with rights over private property. Acts are presumed not to have retrospective effect, and there is a presumption against alteration of the common law. Any Act which presumes to restrict private liberty will be very strictly interpreted, though the strictness may be tempered in times of emergency. It is presumed that an Act does not bind the Crown on the ground that the law, made by the Crown on the advice of the Lords and Commons, is made for subjects and not for the Crown. Furthermore, as we have seen, the courts lack the power to examine proceedings in Parliament in order to determine whether the passing of an Act has been obtained by means of any irregularity or fraud. (*British Railways Board* v. *Pickin,* 1974.)[42]

It must be noted that the courts do not appear to favour what is known as a Social Policy Rule, or the interpretation of Acts in the direction of the social policy behind them by filling in gaps and omissions. Denning, L.J. (as he then was) said in *Magor and St. Mellons R.D.C.* v. *Newport Corporation,* [1951] 2 All E.R. 839,: 'Having discovered the intention of Parliament the judge may achieve it by filling in gaps in the Statute if such appear.' On appeal to the House of Lords, Lord Simonds said: 'There is no such rule; if a gap is disclosed the remedy lies in an amending Act.'

However, the Law Commissioners recommended that more emphasis should be placed on the importance of interpreting a statute in the light of the general purposes behind it and although this recommendation has not been enacted there are signs that some members of the judiciary are prepared to take into account the intentions of Parliament. Thus in *Fletcher* v. *Budgen*, [1974] 2 All E.R. 1243 the Divisional Court of Queen's Bench decided that under the Trade Descriptions Act, 1968, a buyer of goods, in this case a car dealer, could be guilty of the offence of falsely describing goods when he told a private seller that his car was almost worthless, bought it, repaired it and sold it at a considerable profit. Lord Widgery, C.J. said that although he had never thought of the Act as applying to buyers of goods, it was necessary in the public interest that it should, at least in the case of expert buyers, and that in his view such decision '. . . is not in any sense illogical and is not likely to run counter to any intention which Parliament may have had.'

Rules of interpretation tend to some extent to cancel each other. Thus by using one or other of these rules judges can be narrow, reformist, or conservative. In fact Pollock, in his *Essays in Jurisprudence and Ethics,* suggests—

> English judges have often tended to interpret statutes on the theory that Parliament generally changes the law for the worse and that the business of the judges is to keep the mischief of its interference within the narrowest possible bounds.

It must be said that this comment applies particularly to judicial interpretation of welfare law where they have been reluctant to fill in gaps in order to make the law work, whereas if the Act is in the field of 'lawyers' law then they have been prepared to fill in gaps in order, for example, to convict a guilty person of crime. This is, however, not surprising since judges are the product of a legalistic training and are clearly ill-equipped to fill in gaps in welfare law, whereas in crime, for example, they are dealing with rules which they better understand so that they feel less reluctant to fill in gaps.

Interpretation of European Treaties and instruments

English courts are now likely to face on an increasing basis problems in connection with the interpretation of Community Treaties and instruments. In this connection Sect. 3(1) of the European Communities Act, 1972, makes any question of interpretation of Community Treaties or instruments a matter of law which, if not referred to the European Court, is for interpretation in accordance with principles laid down by any relevant decision of the European Court. Article 177 of the EEC Treaty provides for reference to the European Court for a preliminary ruling on any matter of interpretation of the Treaties or instruments in order to ensure uniform interpretation. Thus an English court faced with a problem of interpretation of a treaty or instrument can dispose of it by a reference to the European Court. However, this does of course carry with it the problem of costs and could lead to delays. (See *Bulmer* v. *Bollinger,* [1974] 2 All E.R. 126, p. 34.)

Interpretation of enactments by the European Court

In terms of the interpretation of legislation, the European Court has much broader powers than those which English courts have. There is no question of being restricted, for example, to the words of the Treaty or regulations. The Court may consider the reasons for enactment and the general objectives and policy of the Communities. It can have regard to *travaux préparatoires,* i.e. statements and publications made prior to enactment and *doctrine,* i.e. views of learned writers as to what the law should be.

6 Law of persons and fundamental concepts

NATURAL AND LEGAL PERSONS

A *person* in law possesses certain rights and owes certain duties. There are two categories of persons as follows—

(*a*) *Natural persons.*   These are human beings who are referred to as natural persons. An adult human being has in general terms a full range of rights and duties. However, even in regard to human beings, the law distinguishes between certain classes and ascribes to them a *status* which may carry with it a more limited set of right and duties than are aseribed to the normal adult. These classes are minors, persons of unsound mind, bankrupts and aliens, and the significance of belonging to these categories will be more fully examined in connection with the chapters on substantive law, such as Contract and Tort. Non-human creatures are not legal persons and do not have the full range of rights and duties which a human being acquires at birth. However, animals may be protected by the law for certain purposes, e.g. conservation.

(*b*) *Juristic persons.*   Legal personality is not restricted to human beings. In fact various bodies and associations of persons can, by forming a corporation to carry out their functions, create an organization with a range of rights and duties not dissimilar to many of those possessed by human beings. In English law such corporations are formed either by charter, statute or registration under the Companies Acts; there is also the common law concept of the Corporation Sole.

NATURAL PERSONS

We can divide this section, for the purpose of exposition, into two parts, i.e. general legal concepts applicable to all natural persons and legal rules designed to deal with nationality and immigration and prevent discrimination on the grounds, e.g. of sex and race.

General legal concepts

These are set out below.

Domicil. The basis of jurisdiction and the law to be applied in many matters coming before English courts, e.g. wills, matrimonial causes and taxation, may depend on the domicil of the parties. (See, e.g. *IRC* v. *Bullock,* 1976.)[57] A person's domicil is the country which he regards as his permanent home, and thus contains a dual element of actual residence in a country and the intention of remaining there. Where a country has within its national boundaries several jurisdictions, the person's domicil must be determined with reference to a particular jurisdiction, e.g. there is no such thing as domicil in the United States of America, though a person may be domiciled in a particular State. England and Wales, Scotland, Northern Ireland, the Channel Islands, and the Isle of Man are distinct jurisdictions within the British Isles. A person must always have a domicil, and he can only have one domicil at a time. It should be noted that the concepts of domicil and nationality are, as appropriate, applied to corporate bodies.

Domicil of origin. The domicil of origin of a child is that of its father at the date of the child's birth if the father is alive at that date and is married to the child's mother, i.e. if the child is legitimate (for example, the Nova Scotia domicil of Mr. Bullock in *IRC* v. *Bullock*, 1976)[57]. If the child is illegitimate or, though legitimate, the father is not alive when it is born, it takes its domicil of origin from that of its mother at the date of the child's birth. Foundlings take their domicil of origin from the place where they were found.

Dependent domicil. The concept of dependent domicil applies as follows—

(a) *Minors,* i.e. persons under the age of 18 years

(i) *at common law.* The domicil of a legitimate, legitimated or adopted child is dependent on, and changes with that of its father or adoptive father, and after the father's death with that of its mother or adoptive mother. The domicil of an illegitimate child depends on, and changes with, that of its mother.

(ii) *under statute.* Sections 3 and 4 of the Domicile and Matrimonial Proceedings Act, 1973 are concerned with the domicil of minors. Where previously the domicil of a minor had to follow that of his father until the age of majority, a minor can under the Act acquire an independent domicil at the age of 16, or under that age if he marries before then. This latter principle cannot of course apply to any marriages in this country, but it may apply to those in this country, e.g. Nigerians, who may be married under 16 according to their domiciliary law. The provision referred to above, which is in Sect. 3 of the Act, avoids the previous possibility of a father leaving this country and establishing a domicil elsewhere, thus changing the domicil of his minor son who has remained in this country. Furthermore, it had always been uncertain whether, after the divorce of the parents, a child's domicil continued to follow his father's or followed that of his mother with whom the child was living. Now Sect. 4(2) of the 1973 Act provides that the child's domicil where he is under 16 or has not set up an independent domicil and his father and mother are alive but living apart shall be that of his mother if—

(a) he then has his home with her and has no home with his father; or

(b) he has at any time had her domicil by virtue of (a) above and has not since had a home with his father.

The section also deals with other possible situations, for example where the mother is dead and the child has not returned to his father, he will keep the domicil he acquired under Sect. 4(2).

(b) Married women

(i) *At common law.* A wife could not acquire a domicil separate from that of her husband at common law whilst the marriage lasted wherever the parties lived and even if, for example, the husband had deserted his wife and was living far from England. As the English courts base their jurisdiction in divorce and related matters upon the domicil of both parties in England, a deserted wife could often not bring proceedings in England at all. However, there was a statutory provision under which a wife who had resided in England for three years before presenting a petition could claim jurisdiction on that ground alone.

(ii) *Under statute.* By Sect. 1 of the Domicile and Matrimonial Proceedings Act, 1973, the domicil of a married woman is not bound to be determined by that of her husband. She is now capable of acquiring a separate domicil in exactly the same manner as her husband. By Sect. 1(2) of the 1973 Act a married woman is treated as retaining the domicil of her husband (as a domicil of choice if it is not one of origin) at the coming into force of the Act unless and until it is changed in accordance with common law rules for determining such change.

Certain consequences regarding jurisdiction in divorce proceedings follow from the general principles enacted by the above section.

As a wife can now acquire a separate domicil from that of her husband, jurisdication is now based upon the domicil of either party in England and Wales at the time of the proceedings or on the ground that either party was habitually resident in those countries for one year prior thereto. Similar rules apply to proceedings for nullity and presumption of death. As a corollary to these new principles, the court has power to stay proceedings where courts in two countries have jurisdiction. This would prevent, for example, divorce proceedings being taken in an English court and a Scottish court contemporaneously as where the husband had an English domicil but his wife had acquired one in Scotland.

Domicil of choice. A person, other than a minor under 16, can change his domicil of his own volition. To do so he must be in the new country, and have 'fixed and settled intention' to abandon his domicil of origin or

Nick Pearson

choice, and to settle instead in the new country.

A person retains his domicil of origin until he acquires a domicil of choice, and since a person must always have a domicil, there can be no abandonment of the domicil of origin unless a domicil of choice is acquired instead. However, having acquired a domicil of choice, a person who abandons it without acquiring a fresh domicil of choice, reverts to his domicil of origin. (*Tee* v. *Tee,* 1973.)[58]

The country in which a person resides is on the face of it the country of his domicil. Where it is claimed that a domicil of origin has been changed for one of choice, the onus of proof is on the party claiming that such a change has taken place. Examples of evidence which suggest a change of domicil are oral or written declarations to this effect, letters, wills (*IRC* v. *Bullock,* 1976)[57], the adoption of a new name, as where a German living in England changes his name to Richmond from Reichman, an application for naturalization (*Steiner* v. *IRC,* 1973)[59], the purchase of land, or a grave, or of a home or a business (*Steiner*)[59] in the new country.

Residence.   The residence of a person is important for certain purposes, e.g. liability for Income Tax. Furthermore the jurisdiction of magistrates in matrimonial matters is based on the residence of the parties and not their domicil, as is the right to vote in a particular constituency at an election. On the other hand the jurisdiction of the High Court in matrimonial proceedings is based either on domicil or habitual residence for one year. (Section 5, Domicile and Matrimonial Proceedings Act, 1973.) Domicil must, therefore, be distinguished from residence.

The term residence imports a certain degree of permanence, and must not be casual or merely undertaken as a traveller. In *Fox* v. *Stirk,* [1970] 3 All E.R. 7, the Court of Appeal decided that two undergraduates were resident at their universities and entitled to have their names on the electoral register for that constituency although their parental homes were elsewhere. On the other hand in *Scott* v. *Phillips,* 1973 S.L.T. (Notes) 75 it was held that the plaintiff who lived mainly at his house in Inveresk but had a cottage on lease in Berwickshire in which he spent $3\frac{1}{2}$ months each year, was not resident in Berwickshire and therefore not entitled to have his name included on the electoral roll for that county. Obviously, residence can be changed at any time by moving to a new home. Temporary absences abroad while on holiday or on business do not create a gap in the period of residence, which is determined on the facts of the case.

Husband and wife.   Although marriage is in essence a form of contract, it has special features in that it alters the status of the parties. Persons under the age of sixteen cannot be married nor can persons who are too closely related. Until recently, the contract of marriage could not be discharged by mutual consent. However, under the Matrimonial Causes Act, 1973, a divorce decree may be granted where the parties have been separated by consent for a continuous period of at least two years immediately preceding the presentation of a petition for divorce by one of them and the other consents to a decree being granted. (Sect. 1(2)(a).)

In addition, divorce without consent of both parties is possible provided that they have lived apart for a continuous period of at least five years preceding the presentation of the petition. (Sect. 1(2)(e).) This is the most controversial provision of the Act in that it permits an 'innocent' party to be divorced against his or her will.

Regarding property, the status of married woman was low during the nineteenth and early twentieth centuries and in particular all the wife's personal property passed to the husband on marriage. However, their emancipation was brought about by a series of statutes culminating in the Law Reform (Married Women and Tortfeasors) Act, 1935, so that today their status is the same as that of a *feme sole* (single woman).

In addition there have been a number of important developments in regard to distribution of matrimonial property on breakdown of marriage. These are beyond the scope of a general book.

The following aspects of the legal position of husband and wife are worthy of note here.

(i) The husband has a duty to maintain his wife and children and where a husband is destitute his wife must maintain him if her income allows;

(ii) there is a duty to cohabit;

(iii) husband and wife have special rights with regard to succession on death.

Since the Law Reform (Husband and Wife) Act, 1962, husband and wife have been able to sue each other in tort. (See p. 301.)

Parents and legitimate children.   At common law a child is legitimate only if his parents are lawfully married to each other at the time of his conception or birth or at any intervening time between the two, though, where the marriage is void, e.g. in the case of a bigamous marriage, the child will be legitimate only if at the time of its conception or, if later at the time of celebration of the 'marriage', both or either parent reasonably believed that the marriage was valid. (Section 1(1), Legitimacy Act, 1976.) Section 1(1) only applies where the father of the child was domiciled in England and Wales at the time of the birth or, if he died before the birth, was so domiciled immediately before his death.

Under Sect. 1 of the Guardianship Act, 1973, a mother and father are given equal powers in relation to the child. This applies to the child's custody and upbringing and to his property. Some powers must be exercised jointly, for example, consent to marriage, but otherwise the Act gives the mother all the necessary powers whether or not she is living with the father. Thus, where living apart, whichever parent has *de facto* custody can take decisions without referring either to the other parent or to the Court. *Equality* does not end with rights, however, and the mother may be ordered to pay maintenance for the child if he or she is not living with her.

A legitimate child has a right to succeed to the property of his father and mother where they die without having made a will (i.e. intestate).

Illegitimate children. . A child which cannot satisfy the tests of legitimacy outlined above is illegitimate. Where the mother is unmarried the child must be illegitimate, subject of course to the provisions of Sect. 1 of the Legitimacy Act, 1976, which relate to void marriages (see above). If the mother is married, then a presumption that her husband is the father of the child arises. This is a presumption of legitimacy and must be rebutted if illegitimacy is to be established. In the past the standard of proof offered in rebuttal had to be very strong; generally speaking, proof beyond a reasonable doubt. However, Sect. 26 of the Family Law Reform Act, 1969, now provides that the presumption of legitimacy may be rebutted on a balance of probabilities. Three main types of evidence are relevant—

(*a*) *Evidence of Non-access,* which means that the husband could not or did not have sexual intercourse with the wife at the time when the child was conceived, as where he was serving in the Forces overseas.

(*b*) *Blood tests,* which have become more popular in recent times because of improved medical techniques. Such a test can exclude the possibility of a particular man being the father of the child but cannot prove that he is, though it may show that he could be. Part III of the Family Law Reform Act, 1969, contains the following important provisions relating to blood tests—

(i) any court can in any civil proceedings in which a person's legitimacy is in question give directions for the use of blood tests (Sect. 20);

(ii) the court cannot order a party to submit to a test, the following consents being necessary—in the case of an adult or of a child who has reached the age of 16, his own consent; in the case of a child under 16, the consent of the person having care and control of him (Sect. 21);

(iii) if a person does not consent, the court can draw such inference as seems proper in the circumstances (Sect. 23(1))—thus refusal may be some evidence against what a party says; if refusal is by a party claiming relief and relying on a presumption of legitimacy, the court may adjourn the case to enable him to comply and if he does not do so within a reasonable time may dismiss the claim (Sect. 23(2)). This could apply to a mother claiming maintenance for a child but refusing to submit herself or the child for a test.

(*c*) *Previous affiliation proceedings.* By Sect. 12 of the Civil Evidence Act, 1968, the fact that a man has been adjudged to be the father of a child in affiliation proceedings in any court in the U.K. is *prima facie* (not conclusive) evidence of his paternity in other civil proceedings. This Section reverses for this purpose the rule in *Hollington* v. *Hewthorn,* [1943] K.B. 587 which provided that the fact that one court had been satisfied as to a particular matter was not admissible in evidence in another trial.

Rights of the illegitimate child. These are as follows—

(*a*) *Matrimonial proceedings.* The Matrimonial Causes Act, 1973, Sect. 27, increases the rights of illegitimate children by providing that the court can in matrimonial proceedings make provision for any 'child of the family'. There is no reference to parentage so that the expression will include a child of either party, including illegitimate children and for example an orphaned child who had been brought up as one of the family. Under the Act, either a husband or wife can be ordered to make periodical payments or pay a lump sum or transfer property for the benefit of a child of the family. Payments cease at eighteen unless the child is receiving instruction at an educational institution or undergoing training for a trade or profession. Section 25(3) of the Act does, however, provide that in making an order for payments to a child which is not his the court may take into account how far the husband has accepted responsibility for it and whether acceptance of his responsibility was with the knowledge that the child was not his together with the liability of any other person to maintain the child.

Matrimonial proceedings before magistrates continue to be governed by the Matrimonial Proceedings (Magistrates' Courts) Act, 1960. Under Sect. 16 of that Act, maintenance can be ordered for a 'child of the family'. The expression has a more restricted meaning, however, and includes illegitimate children only if they are children of both parties or of one party accepted as a member of the family by the other.

(*b*) *Affiliation Orders.* These orders, under which the father of an illegitimate child is required to make payments, are made in favour of the mother but are of indirect benefit to the illegitimate child which is the intention.

(*c*) *Fatal Accidents Act.* The Fatal Accidents Act, 1976, gives the dependents of a person who is killed as a result of a tort, a right of action against the tortfeasor. (See p. 304.) Dependents include an illegitimate child. (1976 Act, Sect. 1(4)(b).)

(*d*) *Social Security.* An illegitimate child is eligible for family allowances (Family Allowances Act, 1965, Sect. 17(5)) and supplementary benefits.

(*e*) *Succession.* The Family Law Reform Act, 1969, Sect. 14, has given extended rights of succession to an illegitimate child. On the death intestate (without a will) of either of his parents an illegitimate child, or if he is dead his issue, take the same interest as he would have taken had he been legitimate. Furthermore, if an illegitimate person dies intestate both his parents take the same interest as they would have taken had he been legitimate. Section 15 of the Act of 1969 also provides that a gift in a will or other instrument to a child or other relation includes illegitimate persons. In addition, Sect. 18 of the 1969 Act brings illegitimate dependents within the scope of the Inheritance (Provision for Family and Dependents) Act, 1975. These Acts apply where a deceased person has not made reasonable provision by his will or on intestacy for those who were dependent upon him during his lifetime.

Legitimation.   A person may be legitimated *by and from* the date of the subsequent marriage of his or her parents provided the father is domiciled in England and Wales (Sect. 2, Legitimacy Act, 1976), and this is so whether or not the birth arose out of adultery, as where either or both of the parents were married to another person.

Effect of legitimation.   Once a person has been legitimated he has the same rights (in respect of settlements made and death occurring on or after 1 January, 1976) as if he had been born legitimate. Thus if a testator dies in 1975 leaving property to 'the lawful children of A born before or after my death who attain 21' a child of A who is legitimated by his parents' marriage in 1977 will not qualify. However, if the testator were to die in 1976 such a child would qualify. In practice the change is not of great practical importance. Since 1970 legitimated children have had the right to claim as former illegitimate children under the new rule contained in Sect. 15(4) of the Family Law Reform Act, 1969. The change will only benefit legitimated persons claiming, for example, under a settlement made before the date of legitimation which is so expressed that illegitimate persons cannot claim. For example, a testator leaves property to the lawful children of A living at A's death. Two years after the testator's death A marries the mother of his child. If the testator died in 1975 that child could not take any of the property but if the testator dies in 1976 the child would qualify. (Legitimacy Act, 1976, Sects 5 and 6.)

Section 5(6) of the Legitimacy Act, 1976 reverses the rule that a person cannot be legitimated unless he is living at the date of his parents' marriage, in respect of settlements and deaths occurring on or after 1 January, 1976. For example, if a testator dies in 1975 leaving property to the legitimate issue of A living 21 years after his death, a child of A whose parents marry after his death would not be legitimated with the result that his own children could not take any of the property. However, if the testator dies in 1976 such children will qualify.

Application for a declaration of legitimacy may be made to the High Court or in some circumstances to the County Court, and persons who may be affected, e.g. in matters of succession, may oppose the application.

Adoption.   Adoption was not possible in England until the passing of the Adoption of Children Act, 1926. The rules relating to adoption are now governed by the Adoption Act, 1976, to which section refrerences relate, and adoption may be effected by order of a magistrates' court, a county court or the High Court (Sect. 62), though different procedures are involved. A court order is essential. A mere agreement by a parent to transfer his or her rights and duties to someone else is ineffective. (Section 1(2), Guardianship Act, 1973.)

So far as persons domiciled in the United Kingdom, the Channel Islands or the Isle of Man are concerned, the position in regard to adoption is set out below.

Adoptions by married couples. Under Sect. 36 an adoption order may be made on the application of a married couple where each has attained the age of 21 years.

Adoption by one person. Under Sect. 15 an adoption order may be made on the application of one person where that person has attained the age of 21 years and is not married, or is married and the court is satisfied that the spouse cannot be found or the spouses have separated and are living apart and the separation is likely to be permanent, or the spouse is, by reason of ill-health, whether physical or mental, incapable of making an application for an adoption order. An adoption order will not be made on the application of the mother or father of the child alone unless the court is satisfied that the other natural parent is dead or cannot be found or there is some other reason justifying the exclusion of the other natural parent.

Parental agreement. Under Sect. 16 an adoption order will not be made unless in the case of each parent or guardian of the child the court is satisfied that he or she freely and with full understanding of what is involved, agrees unconditionally to the making of an adoption order (whether or not he or she knows the identity of the applicants), or his or her agreement to the making of the adoption order should be dispensed with on the grounds that the parent or guardian concerned—

(*a*) cannot be found or is incapable of giving agreement;
(*b*) is withholding agreement unreasonably;
(*c*) has persistently failed without reasonable cause to discharge the parental duties in relation to the child;
(*d*) has abandoned or neglected the child;
(*e*) has persistently illtreated the child;
(*f*) has seriously illtreated the child and the rehabilitation of the child within the home of the parent or guardian is unlikely.

Freeing for adoption. Sections 18–21 set up a new freeing procedure whereby parental rights and duties may be transferred to an adoption agency and not to particular adoptive parents. This requires parents' and guardians' consents but they may be dispensed with. Unless a parent has declared that he or she prefers not to be involved in future questions concerning the child's adoption, the adoption agency must give progress reports to the parents. If no adoption order is made and the child is not placed with prospective adopters a parent may apply for a revocation of the freeing order at any time after it has been in force for 12 months.

Living with adopter. Section 13 provides that unless the child is related to the adopters or has been placed with them by an adoption agency, an adoption order shall not be made unless the child has had his or her home at all times with the applicants or one of them for at least 12 months.

Effect of adoption. An adopted child qualifies as a child of the adoptive parents' marriage. (Sect. 39.) This principle applies in interpreting wills, settlements made during lifetime and intestacies which take effect on or after 1 January, 1976. Where questions of seniority arise Sect. 42 provides that the adopted child is deemed to have been born on the date of the adoption and if adoptive parents adopt two or more children on the same day they are regarded as born on that day in the order of the actual dates of their births. For example, we may take a gift in the will of a testator 'to the eldest son of X'. Suppose that X had a natural child (A) in 1965 and in 1966 adopted a child (B) then aged 10, it appears that the natural child (A) takes the gift although B is biologically the elder.

However, the above rules do not affect a document where there is reference to the age of a child. (Sect. 42(2)(b).)

Thus if a testator gave his estate 'to the children of X at 25' it is clear that an adopted child would take the gift when he in fact attained that age and not 25 years after his adoption. It also seems that a gift to 'the first son of X to attain 25' would go to an adoptive child if he attained 25 before X's natural born children, although, as we have seen, he would not take as X's 'eldest son' in the example given above.

Adoptions in other countries. The Adoption Act, 1976, Sect. 72(2) enables adoptions authorized in other countries to be effective in the UK by giving legal recognition to adoption orders made in certain countries outside the UK

Custodianship. Section 33 of the Children Act, 1975, provides that, on the application of any qualified person who is not the mother or father of the child, the court may make a custodianship order vesting legal custody of the child in the applicant. A person is qualified when he is, for example, a relative or step-parent and he has the consent of the person currently having custody and the child has had his home with him for the three months preceding the application. Custodianship is an alternative to adoption for relatives and others looking after children on a long-term basis. Custodianship is a new concept. A custodian is in a similar position to a parent having custody of the child but the Children Act deliberately refrains from giving him the title of 'guardian'. Custodianship is in fact a new form of guardianship, though giving less rights and powers than guardianship. Under Sect. 35 of the Children Act, 1975, custodianship orders may be revoked and varied by the court. The powers of a custodian are not clear, though it appears that they can consent to medical matters and can decide where a child goes to school. They can also give permission for a passport and consent to marriage. They also appear to be free to punish the child. A custodian, however, does not determine the nationality or domicil of the child.

Minors. The Family Law Reform Act, 1969, Sect. 1(1) reduced the age of majority from twenty-one to eighteen years. There is also a provision in the Act which states that a person attains a particular age, i.e. not merely the age of majority, at the first moment of the relevant birthday, though this rule is subject to any contrary provision in any instrument (i.e. a deed) or statute. (Sect. 9.)

Section 1 (2) provides that the age of eighteen is to be substituted for twenty-one wherever there is a reference to 'full age', 'infant', 'infancy', 'minor', 'minority' in—

(a) any statutory provision made *before or after* 1 January, 1970;

(b) any deed, will or other instrument made *on or after* that date.

This subsection draws a distinction between *statutory provisions* and *private dispositions*. In the case of the former the new age of eighteen is substituted. Thus, in the Infants' Relief Act, 1874, references to 'infants' will be construed as applying to persons under eighteen years of age. However, in the case of private dispositions such as deeds, wills and settlements the Act does not apply retrospectively. Accordingly, if in a deed made before 1 January, 1970, a person X is to take property 'on attaining his majority,' he will take it at age twenty-one years. If the deed was made on or after 1 January, 1970, he would take it at eighteen years. The reason for this rule is that where persons in the past have arranged their affairs in reliance on the law as it stood, it would be unjust to interfere.

The law has always regarded minors as being in need or protection, and consequently they enjoy certain immunities and are subject to certain disabilities at law. We have dealt with the legal position of minors with regard to domicil and nationality (see p. 127), and we shall be giving fuller consideration to their legal position in contract, tort, and property, in the chapters which follow. However, certain general matters may be considered at this point.

(i) A minor cannot contract a valid marriage under the age of sixteen years and requires the consent of his parents (or on failure that of a magistrates' court) to marry under eighteen years of age.

(ii) A person under eighteen years cannot vote at elections and must be 21 before he can sit in Parliament or be a member of the council of local authority.

(iii) With regard to civil litigation, a minor sues through a 'next friend', i.e. an adult who is liable for the costs (if any) awarded against the minor in the action, though the minor must indemnify him. A minor defends an action through a 'guardian *ad litem*' who is not liable for costs. The minor's father usually acts as 'next friend' or 'guardian *ad litem*'.

In criminal matters the minor himself is the person prosecuted and may defend himself or be represented by a solicitor or counsel.

(iv) For the purposes of criminal liability minors are divided into three classes—

(a) *Those under ten years.* It is presumed that minors under ten years of age are incapable of any crime, and the presumption is irrebuttable. (Children and Young Persons Act, 1963, Sect. 16.) However, it is thought that children under 10 who are caught in the act of damaging property could be restrained by the police under their common law powers to protect property, or detained under Sect. 28(2) of the Children and Young Persons Act, 1969, on the grounds that they were beyond the control of their parents or guardians.

(*b*) *Those between ten and fourteen years.*   The presumption which is wholly dependent on the common law is that a minor is incapable of forming a guilty intent, but this can be rebutted by proving 'mischievous discretion', i.e. knowledge that what was done was morally wrong.

(*c*) *Minors of fourteen years and over* are fully liable for crimes, but there are certain differences as to procedure and punishment, e.g. a person who is a minor at the time of the commission of a murder is not sentenced to life imprisonment but is detained during Her Majesty's pleasure under the Children and Young Persons Act, 1933, Sect. 53(1). The Twelfth Report of the Criminal Law Revision Committee recommends that where a person under 18 is convicted of murder the form of sentence should be detention in such place and for such period and subject to such conditions of release as the Home Secretary may direct in place of the existing form of detention during Her Majesty's pleasure.

The Government intends to raise the minimum age for prosecution to twelve but only when it is satisfied that local authorities have enough care facilities to cope with the change.

In the meantime, children from ten upwards will remain liable for criminal proceedings though new provisions under the Children and Young Persons Act, 1969, relating to care proceedings are in force (see p. 20).

The following additional matters relating to minors are of interest—

(*a*) A person of sixteen or over can give valid consent to medical treatment and it is not necessary as before to obtain the consent of a parent or guardian. (Family Law Reform Act, 1969 (Sect. 8).)

(*b*) The Tattooing of Minors Act, 1969, makes it an offence for a person other than a duly qualified medical practitioner to tattoo a person under that age of eighteen (£50 on first conviction, £100 subsequently). The person charged with the offence will have a defence if he can show that at the time he had reasonable cause to believe that the person tattooed was eighteen years of age or over.

Persons suffering from mental disorder.   We shall be giving fuller consideration to the position of mentally disordered persons in contract, tort and succession in the chapters which follow. However, the position in criminal law is worth noting at this point and is to some extent governed by the following rules which arise from the case of *R.* v. *M'Naghten* (1843), 10 Cl. & Fin. 200.

(i) Every defendant is presumed to be sane until the contrary is proved.

(ii) To establish a defence on the ground of insanity, it must be clearly proved that, at the time of the committing of the act, the party accused was labouring under such a defect of reason, from disease of mind (*R.* v. *Kemp,* 1957),[60] as not to know the nature and quality of the acts he was doing; or, if he did know it, that he did not know he was doing what was wrong. It is a question of the party's knowledge of right and wrong in respect of the very act with which he is charged.

(iii) If the accused labours under a partial delusion only, he must be considered in the same situation as to responsibility as if the facts with respect to which the delusion exists were real.

If a man suffering from a delusion supposes another man to be in the act of killing him, and he kills this man, as he supposes, in self-defence, he would be exempt from punishment. If the delusion was that the victim had inflicted a serious injury to his character and fortune, and the accused killed him in revenge for such a supposed injury, he would be liable to punishment.

If the defence of insanity is successful, the verdict is 'Not guilty by reason of insanity', and if not the accused has a right of appeal on the same conditions applicable to criminal appeals generally.

Diminished responsibility. By virtue of Sect. 2 of the Homicide Act, 1957, this defence is now available in respect of a murder charge only. The burden of proof is on the defence, and if the defence is successfully established, it reduces the conviction for murder to one of manslaughter.

The defence must show that the accused 'was suffering from such abnormality of mind (whether arising from a condition of arrested or retarded development of mind, or any inherent causes, or induced by disease or injury) as substantially impaired his mental responsibility for his acts and omissions in doing, or being a party to, the killing'.

It should be noted that the Mental Health Act of 1959 now gives a comprehensive and more enlightened definition of mental disorder which is as follows—

Mental illness, arrested or incomplete development of mind, psychopathic disorder, and any other disorder or disability of the mind.

A killing arising from drink or drugs is not covered, because the condition is self-induced, and jealousy, hate and rage are not covered because they are ordinary human frailties which the defendant is expected to control. The merit of diminished responsibility for the offender before 1965 was that it enabled him to escape the death penalty. Since 1965 it has enabled him in many cases to escape the fixed life imprisonment (the only sentence for murder) or indefinite detention following an insanity verdict.

The accused's sanity or mental disorder is also relevant—

(a) *When he is put up for trial.* Although there may be no doubt that the accused was sane when he did the act with which he is charged, he may be too insane to stand trial or as it is usually put—'unfit to plead'. If this is found to be so by a jury, he will be detained during the Queen's pleasure until he recovers. He could then be tried but in practice never is.

(b) *On conviction.* Here the accused's mental condition is relevant to punishment. Under the Mental Health Act, 1959, the court can make a variety of hospital and guardianship orders though not in the case of murder.

(c) *After sentence.*   If the accused is found to be suffering from mental disorder after receiving a sentence of imprisonment he may be transferred to a mental hospital under the Mental Health Act, 1959.

If a person suffering from mental disorder goes through a ceremony of marriage but cannot understand the nature of marriage, i.e. the responsibilities and change of status involved, the marriage will be void.

In connection with mental disorder, it is of interest to note the existence of the Court of Protection which is concerned with proper management of a mental patient's property. The Court operates through receivers who are, in many cases, close relatives of the patient.

Nationality, immigration, and discrimination

Nationality.   The main importance of nationality today is in the realms of public law, since aliens and nationals are treated similarly in most matters of civil law. However, matters such as allegiance, the right to vote at elections and sit in Parliament are governed by the nationality of the person concerned. A person may have a dual or multiple nationality or may be stateless, as where he has been deprived of the nationality of one country without having acquired the nationality of another. British Nationality is now governed by the British Nationality Act, 1948 (as amended), and the 1948 Act creates the status of citizenship. Every person who under the Act is a citizen of the United Kingdom and Her Colonies, or is a citizen of certain other countries, often referred to as 'sub-section (3)' countries, e.g. Canada, Australia, New Zealand, India, Ceylon, Ghana, Nigeria, Sierra Leone, and Bangladesh, among others, has, by virtue of that citizenship, the status of a British subject.

In the United Kingdom there are now three main classes of persons—
  (i) Citizens of the United Kingdom and Colonies,
  (ii) Citizens of other Commonwealth countries, i.e. Commonwealth citizens, and
  (iii) Aliens.
The first two classes constitute British subjects.

Citizenship of the United Kingdom and Colonies, which does not necessarily identify those who belong to this country and have the right to enter and live here, may be acquired in the following ways—
By birth.   Citizenship is acquired by a person born within the United Kingdom or Colonies, unless his father (not being himself a citizen of the UK or Colonies) possesses diplomatic immunity, or unless the birth was in a place then occupied by an enemy, and the father is an enemy alien.
By descent.   Citizenship is acquired by descent by a person whose father is a citizen of the United Kingdom and Colonies, irrespective of the place of birth, but the birth, must be registered at a United Kingdom consulate within one year, or, with the permission of the Home Secretary, at any time.

By registration. A citizen of a sub-section (3) country, or of Eire, who is of full age and capacity, amy register as a citizen of the UK and Colonies if he can satisfy the Home Secretary that—

(i) he is a patrial within the meaning of the Immigration Act, 1971 (see p. 142);

(ii) he is ordinarily resident in or is in the Crown Service of the UK, or partly one and partly the other; and

(iii) he has remained so throughout the preceding five years.

(iv) he is of good character and has a sufficient knowledge of the English or Welsh language;

(v) he intends in the event of his being registered to reside in the United Kingdom or a colony or protectorate or to enter into or continue in relevant employment, e.g. with the Crown.

The Immigration Act, 1971, removed the right of registration as a citizen of the UK and Colonies formerly possessed by a Commonwealth citizen after he had been here for five years except in the case of patrials (see p. 142). Registration under the Act of 1971 is at the discretion of the Home Secretary and there is no right of appeal against refusal of citizenship. However, Commonwealth citizens who were resident in the UK on 31 July, 1971, retain their entitlement to registration on completing five years' ordinary residence. (See p. 143.)

By reason of the South Africa Act, 1962, South African citizens cannot apply for registration.

A woman (whether or not of full age) who is married to a citizen of the UK and Colonies after 1 January, 1949 may register, but if she is an alien she must take an oath of allegiance. However, a man from overseas who marries a woman from this country has no such rights. A person who has been deprived of citizenship of the UK and Colonies, or has renounced it, may register if the Home Secretary gives permission. A minor child of a citizen of the UK and Colonies may be registered upon application by his parent or guardian.

By naturalization. Citizenship by naturalization is acquired at the Home Secretary's discretion by an alien of full age (18 years) and capacity who can show, that—

(i) throughout the year preceding his application he has resided in the UK or been in the service of the Crown; and

(ii) for four of the seven years immediately preceding such year he has either resided in the UK or any colony, or has been in the service of the Crown, and

(iii) he is of good character, and

(iv) he has a sufficient knowledge of the English or Welsh language, and

(v) he intends, if a certificate is granted, either to reside in the UK or any colony, or to enter or continue in Crown service under the UK government, or in the service of an international organization of which the UK government is a member.

The wife of a naturalized alien may acquire citizenship by registration.

By incorporation of territory.   Section 11 of the British Nationality Act, 1948, provides—

If any territory becomes a part of the United Kingdom and Colonies, His Majesty may, by Order in Council, specify the persons who shall be citizens of the UK and Colonies by reason of their connection with that territory: and those persons shall be citizens of the UK and Colonies as from a date to be specified in the Order.

The Act provides for loss of United Kingdom citizenship by renunciation and deprivation as follows—

(*a*) A citizen of the UK and Colonies of full age, who is also a citizen of a sub-section (3) country or of Eire or who is a foreign national, can renounce citizenship by declaration. In time of war the Home Secretary may withhold registration of the declaration.

(*b*) A citizen of the UK and Colonies by registration or by naturaliza-tion can be deprived of citizenship, if the Home Secretary is satisfied that registration or naturalization was obtained by fraud, false representation, or concealment of a material fact.

(*c*) A naturalized person can be deprived of citizenship if the Home Secretary is satisfied that he has—

(i) shown himself by act or speech to be disloyal or disaffected towards Her Majesty, or

(ii) in time of war traded with the enemy, or

(iii) within five years after becoming naturalized been sentenced in any country to not less than 12 months' imprisonment, or

(iv) continuously resided in a foreign country for seven years, and during that period has neither at any time been in the service of the Crown or of certain international organizations, nor registered annually at a UK consulate his intention to retain citizenship.

Under these provisions the Home Secretary must also be satisfied that it is not conducive to the public good that such a person should continue to be a citizen of the UK and Colonies.

(*d*) Where a naturalized person is deprived of citizenship of a sub-section (3) country or of Eire, the Home Secretary may also deprive him of citizenship of the UK and Colonies.

Aliens.   An alien cannot acquire property in a British ship, save as a member of limited liability company if the company itself is British, nor can he become the master of a British ship. Aliens cannot vote at elections or become members of Parliament. They also require work permits if they wish to take up employment here and may be deported if convicted of certain crimes. Citizens of the Republic of Ireland are not treated as aliens and may vote at elections and become members of Parliament.

Immigration.   The Immigration Act, 1971, replaced the Aliens Restriction Act, 1914, the Commonwealth Immigrants Acts, 1962 and 1968, and the Immigration Appeals Act, 1969, with 'a single code of permanent legislation on immigration control'.

Control of immigration.   The Act provides a single system for control of entry to Britain for Commonwealth citizens and aliens. Commonwealth citizens coming to Britain for work no longer have an automatic right to settle unless they are patrials (see below). They require a work permit issued for a specific job in a specific place for a fixed initial period, usually twelve months. The work permit must be obtained by the prospective employer from the Department of Employment before the employee's arrival in Britain. After arrival, employment may be changed only with the approval of the Department, and registration with the police is required. At the end of a year a Commonwealth citizen may apply for an extension of stay in approved employment. After four more years of permitted stay the above conditions are cancelled unless there are grounds for keeping them. Thus, there will be no time limit on his stay and he may change his employment at will. Furthermore, his obligation to register with the police ends. Wives and children of those coming to work will be admitted but must register as the head of the family does. In addition the head of the family must show that he is able to provide accommodation as well as financial support. Commonwealth citizens already *lawfully settled* in the UK on 31 July, 1971, are entitled to bring dependents to the UK. 'Settled' means being here without conditions on length of stay in the country.

The UK, the Irish Republic, the Channel Islands and the Isle of Man remain a common travel area and in consequence Irish citizens will continue to be admitted for employment and other purposes without work permits or other restrictions.

Commonwealth doctors or dentists taking up professional appointments may enter without work permits. This also applies to aliens in the above categories. If these persons do not have pre-arranged appointments they may stay for six months without a permit provided they have a place in the attachment scheme run by the Department of Health and Social Security.

Students may enter as before, i.e. subject to an initial limitation of not more than one year. Extensions are granted in appropriate circumstances, e.g. to continue studies. Visitors and tourists are not affected and Commonwealth and alien girls may enter as 'au pair' to learn English. For this purpose they may live for a reasonable time as a member of a resident English-speaking family. Representatives of overseas firms, ministers of religion and certain seasonal workers may enter without work permits or employment vouchers.

Right of abode (patrial).   The Act sets out certain categories of people who have a 'right of abode' in the UK and are free of immigration control. They are persons having direct personal or ancestral connection with the UK and are as follows—

(*a*) all persons who are citizens of the UK and Colonies by being born here or who become citizens of this country by adoption, registration or naturalization in the UK or who have a parent who was born here or acquired citizenship by adoption, registration or naturalization;

(*b*) citizens of the United Kingdom and Colonies who have come from overseas and been accepted for permanent residence and since that acceptance have resided here for five years;

(*c*) Commonwealth citizens who have a parent born in the United Kingdom.

Persons in the above category are described by the Act as 'patrials'.

Immigration control for those who, while holding UK passports are not patrials, continues. They are required to have special vouchers before they are admitted for settlement, and can also apply for work permits in the same way as Commonwealth citizens.

Right of appeal.   All persons subject to immigration control have a right of appeal against refusal of admission to an independent adjudicator and then to a tribunal. Both the adjudicator and the tribunal are within the scope of the Tribunals and Inquiries Act, 1971. A person who is refused entry on arrival because he has not got a work permit, entry certificate or visa will first have to return to his country and make appeal from there in the same way as he would if he had been refused an entry certificate or visa before departure. He is not allowed to stay here until the appeal is pending because of the difficulties this would cause to the immigration authorities at sea and airports.

Decisions taken by the Home Secretary personally on the ground that entry or continued presence here *is not conducive to the public good* are not subject to appeal. Thus the special appeal procedure for security and political cases which caused criticism in the Dutschke case is abolished.

Deportation.   The Act extends to Commonwealth citizens the Home Secretary's power to deport an alien if he considers his presence is not conducive to the public good. As we have seen, such a decision is not subject to a right of appeal although in *Hosenball*[33] representations to an independent advisory panel were allowed. There are also powers under which the dependents of a deported person may themselves be deported. Patrials are exempt from deportation so that a Commonwealth citizen or alien may obtain exemption after five years' residence by acquiring citizenship by registration or naturalization. The Act re-states the main grounds for deportation as follows—

(*a*) conviction of an offence punishable with imprisonment where the court has recommended deportation, and

(*b*) breach of the conditions imposed on a stay in this country.

The Act also creates a new offence of assisting illegal entry and empowers immigration officers to require persons admitted for a limited time to register with the police. Aliens who are here for more than six months are *required* in any case to register with the police.

Retrospective effect.   Before 1962 any Commonwealth citizen could come to Britain as of right without the leave of anyone and stay as long as he or she liked. Thereafter there were a number of Acts setting up immigration controls and creating offences for illegal immigration. A number of people came in during this period of time without satisfying immigration requirements. Under the Immigration Act of 1971 'settled' persons are treated as having been given indefinite leave to enter or remain here. They cannot therefore be removed. A person is not, however, 'settled' if he or she is here in breach of the immigration laws. When cases came before the courts, therefore, there was a choice which the court could have made. In the first place they could have regarded clandestine entrants as 'settled' and therefore irremovable, secondly the courts could treat the Act as having retrospective effect and thus enable the executive to seize and deport a Commonwealth citizen, a long resident in this country because of an immigration offence committed since 1962. In *R.* v. *Governor of Pentonville Prison, ex parte Azam,* [1973] 2 All E.R. 765 the House of Lords opted for retrospectivity, as regards deportation but in *Waddington* v. *Miah,* [1974] 2 All E.R. 377 decided that other penal provisions, e.g. possessing a false passport, were not retrospective.

In summary therefore, there are seven categories of persons in the United Kingdom at the present time as follows—

(*a*) *United Kingdom Citizens.*   These are, for example, people who were born in the United Kingdom. Such persons are free to re-enter the UK and can move freely within the EEC. They can take UK jobs without a work permit and cannot be deported. They are able to vote in local and central government elections.

(*b*) *Patrial Commonwealth Citizens,* e.g. Australians, Canadians and New Zealanders with a UK-born Parent. They can enter the UK but cannot move freely within the EEC. They can take UK jobs and vote. They cannot be deported.

(*c*) *Non-Patrial Commonwealth Citizens.*   These are Commonwealth citizens with a UK grandparent. They are in the main UK descended Australians, Canadians and New Zealanders. They can only enter the UK on production of entry clearance which is freely given by the immigration authorities. They cannot move freely within the EEC, but can take UK jobs and vote. They can be deported.

(*d*) *Citizens of the Irish Republic.*   They can enter the UK and move freely within the EEC. They can also take jobs and vote. They can be deported.

(*e*) *Non-Patrials who are EEC Nationals.*   These are citizens of EEC countries such as France and Holland. They have no right under UK law to enter and stay in the UK because they are not patrials. (But see *Van Duyn* v. *The Home Office,* 1974.)[43] However, they are admitted freely in order to work and can move freely within the EEC. They can take UK jobs but must report to the police. They cannot vote and may be deported subject to EEC directives on this matter.

(f) *Non-Patrial Commonwealth Citizens (Without a UK Grand-parent).* These are citizens of Commonwealth countries who are not UK descended and include East African Asians who hold UK passports and Gibraltarians. They have no right to enter and stay in the UK, nor can they move freely within the EEC except for UK citizens from Gibraltar. They must have a work permit before they can take work here. They have a right to vote but can be deported.

(g) *Others.* These are citizens of independent non-Commonwealth and non-EEC countries. They have no right to enter and stay in the UK nor can they move freely within the EEC. They cannot take UK jobs without a work permit and must report regularly to the police. They have no right to vote and can be deported.

Racial discrimination. The Race Relations Act, 1976 is designed to deal with discrimination on racial grounds and with relations between different racial groups.

Discrimination to which the Act applies. Section 1 provides that it is *direct* discrimination to treat a person less favourably on racial grounds and *indirect* discrimination where there is some requirement or condition, e.g. of employment, which, although it applies to all potential employees, is discriminatory since a smaller proportion (or none) of black applicants can comply with it than can white. Thus a rule insisting that bus conductors wear company caps could be *indirect* discrimination against Sikh applicants.

Section 2 deals with discrimination by way of victimization of a person who has, for example, brought or given evidence in proceedings under the Act against a discriminator or alleged discriminator. Thus if A brings proceedings against his employer, B, for alleged discrimination and as a consequence A's landlord will not allow A to use a goods lift provided for common use in the block of flats where A lives, then C could be guilty of victimization under Sect. 2. Under Sect. 3 'racial grounds' means colour, race, nationality, or ethnic or national origins, and 'racial group' means a group of persons defined by reference to colour, race, nationality, or ethnic or national origin. The Act still permits discrimination on grounds of religious belief unless that constitutes racial discrimination, as it would if the religion was Jewish but not if it is Catholic or Protestant since the last two named are not matters of race.

Discrimination in employment. The provisions of the Act which relate to discrimination in employment are set out below.

(i) *Offers of Employment.* Under Sect. 4(1) it is unlawful for a person in relation to employment by him at an establishment in Great Britain (other than a private house) to discriminate against another person on the grounds of colour, race, nationality, or ethnic or national orgins; (i) in the arrangements he makes for the purpose for deciding who should be offered the job; or (ii) in the terms on which the job is offered; or (iii) by refusing or deliberately omitting to offer him the job.

'Arrangements' is a wide expression covering a range of recruitment techniques, e.g. asking an employment agency to send only white applicants. Discriminatory advertisements are unlawful (Sect. 29) as is discrimination by employment agencies (Sect. 14).

(ii) *Terms of the Contract of Employment.* Section 4(2) makes it unlawful to discriminate against an employee (other than those employed in a private household) in terms of the employent which is given to him or in terms of access to opportunites for promotion, transfer or training, or to any other benefits, facilities or services, or by dismissing him or subjecting him to any other detriment. Section 4(4) makes unlawful discrimination in regard to matters such as privileged loans and mortgages by banks and building societies and discounts on holidays given to employees of travel firms.

(iii) *Exceptions*

(a) *Genuine Occupational Qualifications.*   Section 5 gives a list of circumstances in which it is lawful to discriminate because it is a genuine occupational qualification (GOQ) for the job that the person appointed belongs to a particular racial group, e.g. employment of a West Indian social worker or probation officer to deal with problems relating to young West Indians. Other instances are dramatic performances or other entertainment, artists' or photographic models, and employment in places serving food or drink to be purchased *and consumed* on the premises by the public. Thus, being Chinese is a GOQ for employment in a Chinese restaurant but not in a 'take-away'.

(b) *Training.* Section 6 allows discrimination in regard to the training in this country of persons from overseas. Thus if a person allocates a number of employment-for-training places on the basis of nationality, there is clearly discrimination against other people who might do the job. However, Sect. 6 protects an employer against an action for discrimination in this situation.

(iv) *Contract workers.*   Previous legislation did not apply to contract workers but Sect. 7 plugs this gap. The discrimination provisions now apply to workers supplied by a third party so that temporary staff supplied by an agency are covered.

Partnerships.   Section 10 extends protection against discrimination to partnerships as regards failure to offer a partnership or the terms on which it is offered, including benefits, facilities and services, except where a GOQ applies. The section applies only to firms of six or more partners, though there is a power in Sect. 73 to reduce this number. The provision as it stands will allow discrimination in the majority of medical practices. The section also covers discrimination in cases where persons are preparing to form themselves into a partnership.

Trade unions.   Section 11 renders unlawful discriminatory practices by trade unions, employers' associations and professional trade bodies. Surprisingly, individual discriminatory action by shop stewards is not covered by the Act. Thus if a shop steward discriminates with the authority of his union, the union will be liable, but if he acts without authority, no-one is liable. This appears to be a defect in the Act since it is well-known that white organized labour has in several areas of the country held back black development in employment.

Qualifying bodies.   Section 12 provides that it is unlawful for an authority or body which can confer an authority or qualification which is needed for, or facilitates employment in, a particular trade or profession to discriminate against a person in terms of conferring that authorization or qualification.

Miscellaneous.   The Act does not apply to those whose work is wholly or mainly outside Great Britain (Sect. 8) and discrimination is allowed against foreign seamen recruited abroad (Sect. 9) since the *immediate* abolition of the right to employ seamen recruited overseas at lower rates of pay than those applicable in the UK would cause serious difficulties for the UK shipping industry. However, shipowners are required to make early and visible progress towards eliminating the practice of paying lower wages to foreign (mainly Asian) seamen, otherwise the Government will intervene. Sections 13 and 15 apply the Act to vocational training bodies such as industrial training boards and to the Manpower Services Commission, the Employment Service Agency and the Training Services Agency. Section 16 covers discrimination in terms of employment in the police force.

Victimization.   This may arise in the employment situation because, as we have seen, Sect. 2 provides that it is unlawful to victimize a person, i.e. treat him less favourably than others, because he has, for example, exercised or proposed to exercise his rights under the Act.

Discrimination in education.   Sections 17–19 make it unlawful for responsible bodies, e.g. governing bodies of educational establishments including both State and private schools, to discriminate on racial grounds as regards, for example, allocation of places.

Discrimination in provision of goods, facilities or services.   Under Sect. 20 discrimination by, for example, shops, hotels, boarding houses and banks is outlawed as is discrimination in clubs which have 25 or more members. When membership of a club reaches 25 or more a licence to serve intoxicating liquor must be sought. Clubs with membership of less than 25 members are excluded and may discriminate.

Discrimination in the disposal or management of premises.   Section 21 states that discrimination on racial grounds by a seller of property in terms of the buyer or by, say, a brewery in terms of who shall manage a public house, is unlawful. The section does not apply to owner-occupiers of houses who sell the property without employing an estate agent or advertising it for sale. (Sect. 21(3).) There is also an exemption for the letting of accommodation in premises where the occupier or a near relative of his resides and intends to continue to reside on the premises which are 'small premises' under Sect. 22(2), e.g. where there is not room for more than six persons in addition to the occupier and members of his household. Section 23 provides for exemptions allowing discrimination where a person takes into his home and treats as a member of his family a child, an elderly person or a person requiring a special degree of care and attention. Thus discrimination on racial grounds in the choice of foster children is not unlawful. Section 24 provides that where a tenant requires the licence or consent of the landlord to assign or sublet to another person it is unlawful for that licence or consent to be withheld in a discriminatory was, as where a landlord will not allow a tenant to assign to a black tenant.

As we have seen, discrimination in clubs with 25 or more members is unlawful but Sect. 26 provides an exemption for organizations whose main object is to confer benefits on ethnic or national groups and does not exclude others. Thus the London Welsh Club is still a lawful association but must not exclude black Welshmen.

By Sect. 27 the Act applies only to benefits, facilities and services in Great Britain. However, it does extend outside Great Britain in some cases. For example, discrimination in Great Britain in regard to the provision of facilities for travel is unlawful even though the facilities are to be supplied outside Great Britain.

Discriminatory practices. Under Sect. 28 there may be a discriminatory practice, even where there is no victim. Thus a factory which has discriminatory recruiting procedures may be regarded as discriminating even during a recession when there has been no recruitment for some time. However, proceedings under Sect. 28 can be brought only by the Commission for Racial Equality.

Advertisements. Section 29 makes discriminatory advertisements unlawful unless, as in an employment advertisement, there is, for example, a GOQ.

Instructions or pressure to discriminate. Under Sects 30 and 31 it is unlawful to instruct a person to discriminate or to put pressure on a person to discriminate. However, the act must be unlawful so instructions by a landlord to his tenant not to take black foster children would not be unlawful. Under Sect. 32 an employer is vicariously liable (see p. 307) together with the offending employee for any act done by the employee in course of employment, whether the act was done with the knowledge or approval of the employer or not. Similarly, principals will be liable for the *authorized* acts of their agents but in neither case does vicarious liability extend to criminal proceedings. An employer (not a principal) is given a defence if he can show that he took such steps as were reasonably practicable to prevent his employee doing discriminatory acts. Under Sect. 33 those who assist others to do unlawful acts are also liable.

Charities. Section 34 makes it clear that any provision in an existing or future charitable instrument, e.g. a trust, which confers benefits on persons of a different colour is void. Further, it is unlawful to do any act in Great Britain to give effect to such a provision.

General exceptions. Certain general exceptions from liability are set out in Part IV of the Act. Under Sect. 35 acts done to meet the special needs of racial groups with regard, for example, to education, training and welfare, such as special language training for groups whose first language is not English, are not unlawful; there is some overlap here with Sect. 6. Sections 37 and 38 allow positive discrimination in favour of particular racial groups by training bodies, employers and trade unions, employers' associations, and professional and trade associations, by encouraging members of those groups to take work by giving special talks and guided tours of factories and premises. Under Sect. 39 the selection of sports teams on the basis of nationality, place of birth, and length of residence is exempted from the provisions of the Act. Thus a county cricket club may, if that is a rule, continue to select teams from among those born in the county but cannot refuse to select a person otherwise willing and able, who was born in the county of, say, Pakistani parents.

The Commission for Racial Equality.   Section 43 sets up the Commision (CRE) which is to work towards the elimination of discrimination; to promote equality of opportunity; good relations between different racial groups and to keep under review the working of the Act. Under Sect. 47 the CRE has the power to issue codes of practice giving guidance on ways of achieving equality of opportunity and eliminating discrimination in the employment field. Sections 48–52 give the CRE power to conduct formal investigations, for example, into alleged discriminatory employment practices in order to carry out its duties.

Enforcement.   The enforcement provisions which are set out in Part VIII are of two types—

(*a*) *Complaints by an individual* who is the subject of unlawful conduct other than 'discriminatory practices', advertising or pressures or instructions to discriminate. In employment cases the complaint goes to an industrial tribunal (Sect. 54) (see below). Complaints of discrimination in education and in the provision of goods, facilities and services and in housing may be made to the county court. (Sect. 57.) Complaints that a responsible body in an educational establishment has discriminated must be notified to the Secretary of State for Education who must be given a maximum of two months to consider the matter before court proceedings can be commenced. (Sect. 57(5).) It should be noted that individual is given direct access to courts and tribunals for the first time in race relations matters; under previous legislation only the Race Relations Board (now abolished) could institute proceedings.

(*b*) *Enforcement by the CRE.*   This involves—(i) the issuing of a non-discrimination notice (Sect. 58); (ii) proceedings in the county court or industrial tribunal where there are discriminatory practices advertisements or pressures or instructions to discriminate (Sect. 63); (iii) proceedings in the county court for an injunction where there has been persistent discrimination (Sect. 62); (iv) assisting individual complainants in certain matters of principle or complexity or other special considerations (Sect. 66).

It should be noted that a non-discrimination notice will require a person not to commit any further discriminatory acts and, where in order to comply with this it is necessary to change practices or arrangements, to inform the CRE that the changes have been effected and bring these changes to the attention of other persons concerned. There is a right of appeal within six weeks against such a notice to an industrial tribunal which may modify or quash the notice (Sect. 59). If an appeal against a notice is dismissed, the notice becomes final and is entered on the CRE's Register of Notices (Sect. 61).

(c) *Enforcement in the employment field.*   Section 55 provides for conciliation by the Advisory, Conciliation and Arbitration Service to try to help the parties to settle the matter without going to a tribunal.

That failing, complaints in the employment field are, with the exception of those relating to discrimination by certain qualifying bodies under Sect. 12 (see below), heard by industrial tribunals. (Sect. 54.) The complaint must be brought within three months of the occurrence of the act complained of (Sect. 68(1)). There is no legal aid but the CRE may arrange for legal advice or assistance (Sect. 66) and the Green Form Scheme, under which a solicitor can provide £25 worth of his services free to those whose incomes and disposable capital make them eligible, also applies.

Where a person is refused a qualification he may take the matter to an industrial tribunal unless there is already another statutory right of appeal. Thus appeals against the Law Society will continue to be to the Court of Appeal and doctors will appeal, as before, to the Privy Council.

(d) *Remedies in employment field.*   Under Sect. 56 a tribunal may make—

(i) an order declaring the rights of the parties with the intention that this should be observed; (ii) an order to pay compensation for loss of earnings and other losses, including prospective loss of earnings and injured feelings (Sect. 57(4)), up to a maximum of £5200; (iii) a recommendation that the person discriminating take action for the purpose of obviating or reducing the adverse effect on the person complaining of the act of discrimination. If the person discriminating fails to comply with the recommendation the tribunal may increase the amount of compensation or make an order for compensation if such an order could have been made but was not.

Sex discrimination.   The two main Acts of Parliament involved here are the Sex Discrimination Act, 1975 and the Equal Pay Act, 1970.

Sex Discrimination Act, 1975.   The form of drafting used in the Race Relations Act, 1976, was based on the Sex Discrimination Act, 1975, and the reader will recognize many similar features.

Under the Act of 1975 it is unlawful to treat anyone, on the grounds of sex, less favourably than a person of the opposite sex is or would be treated in the same circumstances.

Sex discrimination defined.   There are two kinds of discrimination as follows—

(a) *Direct* discrimination which involves, for example, treating a woman less favourably than a man because she is a woman;

(b) *Indirect* discrimination which occurs where conditions are applied which favour, quite unjustifiably, one sex more than the other, as where a firm advertises for clerical workers who must be six feet tall.

It should be noted that although the Act is written in terms of discrimination against women, it applies equally to discrimination against men.

Areas of discrimination.   These are exactly the same as those covered by the Race Relations Act, 1976, as follows—

(a) *Employment.*   Employers may not discriminate because of sex in their recruitment of employees or in the treatment of them once in employment. This also applies to promotion and training.

Except in rare situations employers may not label jobs as being 'for men' or 'for women', though there are a number of exceptions. For example, in employment in a private household; in jobs where a person's sex is a genuine occupational qualification, as in acting; or where there are not more than five people on the staff. In employment it is also unlawful to discriminate because a person is married. Again, such discrimination may be *direct*, as where a person is treated, on the grounds that he or she is married, less favourably than a single person of the same sex; or *indirect* where there is a condition or requirement which fewer married people than single people of the same sex can comply with, e.g. a refusal by an employer to promote employees with children.

(b) *Education.*   Co-educational schools, colleges, and universities may not discriminate in the provision of facilities or in their admissions. Thus it would be unlawful to refuse a girl admission to a metalwork class because she is a girl. In addition, the Careers Service must not discriminate in the advice and assistance offered to girls and boys, though single-sex schools are still permissible.

(c) *Housing, goods, facilities and services.*   In general, no-one providing housing, goods, facilities or services to the public may discriminate because of sex. There are some exceptions where discrimination will not be unlawful; these include, for example, situations where it is necessary to preserve decency and privacy, e.g. public lavatories.

Discrimination must not be used in the buying or renting of accommodation and an hotel, boarding house or restaurant may not refuse accommodation or refreshment on the grounds of sex.

In addition, a bank, building society, or finance house must offer credit, a mortgage or loan on the same terms that it would offer the facilities to someone of the opposite sex.

(d) *Advertising.*   Advertisements with job description such as 'salesgirl, waiter, stewardess, postman' are deemed to discriminate unless they contain an indication that both men and women are elegible, though it should be noted that only the Equal Opportunities Commission (EOC) can bring proceedings in matters to do with advertising.

Victimization. The provisions here are the same as those set out in the Race Relations Act, 1976, so that the law will protect a person if they are victimized for bringing a complaint under the Sex Discrimination Act, 1975.

The Equal Opportunities Commission. The Equal Opportunities Commission was set up to ensure effective enforcement of the Sex Discrimination Act and the Equal Pay Act (see below) and to promote equal opportunity between the sexes. The Commission has power to hold formal investigations, and if satisfied that practices are unlawful, can issue non-discrimination notices requiring that they cease. When holding a formal investigation, either on its own initiative or because it has been asked to do so by the Secretary of State the Commission has power to require any person to furnish information and to attend hearings to give evidence.

The Commission has power to help individuals in the preparation and conduct of complaints in both courts and tribunals and as well as investigating areas of inequality between the sexes, the Commission has a duty to make recommendations to the Government about the operation of existing law. It is also empowered to undertake or assist others to undertake research and educational work and generally to advise people as to their rights.

The Race Relations Act, 1976, makes minor amendments in the Sex Discrimination Act. In particular, the EOC is given power to issue codes of practice giving practical guidance on equality of opportunity and the elimination of discrimination in the employment field between men and women, i.e. powers matching those given to the CRE. This is achieved by adding Sect. 56A to the Sex Discrimination Act.

Enforcement. The provisions, which are similar to those of the Race Relations Act, 1976, are as follows—

(*a*) *Individuals' rights.* Complaints in the employment field may be made to industrial tribunals in exactly the same way as complaints in relation to race. Again, a conciliation officer of ACAS has a duty to help the parties to reach a settlement without the need for a tribunal hearing. If there is a hearing before a tribunal the remedies are exactly the same as those available for discrimination on the grounds of race (see p. 149).

Complaints in all other fields may be made to a county court and if the court finds in favour of the complainant it may award—(i) an order declaring the rights of the parties; (ii) an injunction; or (iii) damages which may include loss of earnings and also compensation for injured feelings.

(*b*) *The Equal Opportunities Commission.* The functions of the EOC in regard to enforcement are as follows—

(i) the Commission may conduct formal investigations into any matter in order to carry out its duties and where it discovers conduct which contravenes the Sex Discrimination Act or the Equal Pay Act it is empowered to issue a non-discrimination notice. The result of issuing such a notice is the same as that under the Race Relations Act, 1976 (see p. 149);

(ii) the Commission can institute legal proceedings in respect of persistent discrimination;

(iii) the Commission has the sole right to institute legal proceedings in respect of discriminatory practices in advertisements, and instructions and pressure to discriminate;

(iv) the Commission has power to assist individual complainants in preparing their case on, e.g. difficult aspects of the law.

(*c*) *Qualifying bodies.*   Where a qualifying body is required by law to satisfy itself as to the good character of an applicant for the authorization or qualification it can confer, it must have regard, in deciding whether or not to issue, renew, or extend the authorization or qualification, to any evidence tending to show that the applicant, or any of his past or present employees or agents has practised unlawful discrimination in, or in connection with, the carrying on of any profession or trade. Discrimination by persons who require such authorizations or qualifications to carry on their profession or trade may therefore be drawn to the attention of the appropriate qualifying body, e.g. the Law Society. An additional example would be an allegation against a person in the consumer credit or hire business, for which a licence from the Director-General of Fair Trading is required. Such an allegation may be referred to the Director-General who is required to have regard to evidence of discrimination when considering the fitness of a person to hold a licence under the Consumer Credit Act, 1974.

Equal pay.   This Act seeks to elininate discriminatory treatment between men and women in pay and other terms and conditions of employment The Act applies to all kinds of work, both manual and non-manual, full-time or part-time, whether in factories, offices, shops, or anywhere else.

If a person is doing the same or broadly similar work as another and both are working for the same employer they are entitled to the same rate of pay and other terms of employment. In addition, if a person's job has been given the same value as another person's job under a job evaluation scheme, they are both entitled to the same rate of pay and other terms of employment. The work being done need not be exactly the same but may be classed as broadly similar if, although there are differences between the things that each employee does, they are not of practical importance. What is of practical importance is for an industrial tribunal to decide.

By the 'same terms of employment' is meant basic rates of pay and other forms of additional payment, e.g. for overtime, bonus, output and piecework and other conditions of work such as normal working hours, holiday, sick leave entitlement, and so on. However, there is no right to claim equal treatment under the Act for any terms and conditions of employment which relate to retirement, marriage or death.

It is not necessary that the person making the comparison should work at the same establishment. Those who work at different establishments for the same or an associated employer can claim equal pay provided that both establishments have the same terms and conditions of employment.

Equal pay may also be denied where there is a genuine reason for treating a person differently. For example, an employer may pay all workers (both men and women) extra remuneration after a number of years' qualifying service. In these circumstances, therefore, there could be no complaint by, say, a woman who had just joined the firm that her pay was not as high as that of a man who had been with the firm for a number of years.

Where pay is based on an agreement between employers and trade unions which specifies different rates for men and women or where the employer has a pay structure which specifies different rates for men and women, the Industrial Arbitration Board can be asked to amend the agreement or pay structure so as to remove the discrimination. The approach to the Board will normally be made by employers or trade unions where the agreement is, as it will usually be, a collective one, though the Secretary of State for Employment has an independent power to refer a collective agreement to the Board. A non-collective agreement can be referred to the Board by the employer concerned or on behalf of the employees by the Secretary of State for employment.

Enforcement. As regards enforcement, an employee can raise the matter of equal pay with his employer or a trade union and if agreement cannot be reached at that level the employee can go to an industrial tribunal for a decision. Employment Offices, Job Centres and Unemployment Benefit Offices give advice on how to register a complaint. In addition, advice can be obtained from the Advisory, Conciliation and Arbitration Service, either from the head office in London or regional offices.

JURISTIC PERSONS

As we have seen, the concept of personality is not restricted to human beings and we shall now consider corporate personality in terms of the nature and types of corporations.

The Joint Stock Company

The enormous increase in industrial activity during the industrial revolution made necessary and inevitable the emergence of the joint stock company and the concept of limited liability. For the first time it was possible for the small investor to contribute to the capital of a business enterprise with the assurance that, in the event of its failure, he could lose no more than the amount he had contributed or agreed to contribute. The principles of 'legal entity' and 'perpetual succession' apply, whereby the joint stock company is deemed to be a distinct legal person, able to hold property and carry on business in its own name, irrespective of the particular persons who may happen to be the owners of its shares from time to time. (*Salomon* v. *Salomon,* 1897.)[61]

The concept of corporate personality is capable of abuse and where, for example, the concept has been used to evade legal obligations, the courts have been prepared to investigate sharp practice by individuals who are trying to hide behind a company front. Thus in *Gilford Motor Co.* v. *Horne,* [1933] Ch. 935 a former employee bound by a restraint of trade set up a company in order to evade its provisions, claiming that he as a person might be bound by the restraint but the company, being a separate entity, could not be. An injunction was granted against both him and his company which the court described as 'a device, a stratagem . . . a mere cloak or sham'.

Joint Stock Companies are formed by registration under the Companies Act, 1948 or previous Acts. The current controlling statutes are the Companies Acts, 1948, 1967 and 1976. The Acts provide for two types of registered companies: the Public Company and the Private Company. A registered company is fully liable for its debts but the liability of the members may be limited either to the amount unpaid on their shares, i.e. *a company limited by shares,* or to the amount they have agreed to pay if the company is brought to an end (wound up), i.e. *a company limited by guarantee.* Some companies are *unlimited* and the members are fully liable for the unpaid debts of the company.

The capital of a public company is usually raised by the public subscribing for its shares, which are issued with varying rights as to dividends, voting powers, and degrees of risk. Shares are freely transferable and are almost invariably quoted on the Stock Exchange. When making a public issue of shares, the company is under a statutory obligation to publish full particulars of the history, capital structure, loans, profit record, directors, and many other matters calculated to assist the intending shareholder to assess the possibilities of the company. Such a document is called a Prospectus, and the directors are liable to penalties for fraud, misrepresentation or failure to disclose the material information as required by the Fourth Schedule to the Companies Act, 1948.

The minimum number of members is seven, but there is no upper limit. Incorporation is achieved by lodging with the Registrar of Companies certain documents of which the following are the most important—

(*a*) *The Memorandum of Association* is a document which defines the constitution of the company, and sets out in the Objects Clause the powers of the company. This clause governs the activities into which the company can legally enter (but see Sect. 9, European Communities Act, 1972, p. 206) and it may be said that the Memorandum governs the company's relations with the outside world. In the Memorandum one also finds the company's name; together with a statement that the liability of the members is limited (where this is the case); the situation of its Registered Office, i.e. England or Wales or Scotland (this governs the company's nationality and domicile); the amount of its Authorized Capital; and an

Association Clause in which the subscribers ask for incorporation and agree to take at least one share.

(b) *The Articles of Association* contain the regulations governing the relationship between the company and its members, and thus cover the internal or domestic affairs of the company. Such matters as alteration of shareholders' rights, powers of directors, conduct of meetings, and resolutions, are contained in the Articles.

The directors of a public company stand in the fiduciary position of agents towards the company whose money they control, and many of the provisions of the Companies Acts, 1948, 1967, and 1976 are so framed as to ensure the maximum possible degree of disclosure by the directors of information calculated to keep the members acquainted with the affairs of the company.

The Memorandum and Articles of Association are public documents which must be deposited with the Registrar of Companies, and are open to public inspection along with other records relating to charges on the company's property, and copies of important resolutions. Each year the company's Annual Return, giving particulars of share capital, debentures, mortgages and charges, list of members, particulars of directors and secretary, must be filed with the Registrar. In addition, the company's accounts and the directors' and auditors' reports must be laid before a general meeting of the company and filed with the Registrar within ten months (private company) and seven months (public company) of the end of the accounting period to which they relate. Any person may inspect the Register of Members at the Registered Office of the company.

The private company with a minimum of two members and in general a maximum of fifty is now a firmly established feature of the present day business world. The private company is barred from going to the general public for subscriptions for its shares and must restrict in some manner the right of share transfer and the number of its members to 50, excluding employees and ex-employees.

Dissolution of a registered company usually takes place by the company being put into liquidation, as a result of the process of winding up.

Other types of corporation

Incorporation may also be achieved by a *Royal Charter* granted by the Crown. The procedure is for the organization desiring incorporation to address a petition to the Privy Council, asking for the grant of a charter and outlining the powers required. If the Privy Council consider that the organization is an appropriate one, the Crown will be advised to grant a charter. Charter companies were formerly used to further the development of new countries, e.g. the East India Company and the Hudson Bay Company, but now they are usually confined to non-commercial corporations, e.g. the Institute of Chartered Accountants in England and Wales and the Institute of Chartered Secretaries and Administrators. Universities are also incorporated in this way. It is possible for the liability of members to be limited, and a chartered company, sometimes known as a 'Common Law Corporation,' has the same powers as an individual person in spite of limitations in its charter. However, it is said that the Crown may forfeit the charter if the company pursues *ultra vires* activites, and certainly a member can ask the court to grant an injuction preventing the company from carrying out *ultra vires* activities. (*Jenkin* v. *Pharmaceutical Society,* 1921.)[62]

Companies may be created by special Act of Parliament, and are governed by their special Acts and also by Acts which apply to statutory companies generally, which are known as 'Clauses Acts.' These Acts together define and limit their activities. The purpose of statutory companies is to promote undertakings of the nature of public utility services, e.g. water supply, where monopolistic powers and compulsory acquisition are essential to proper functioning. The liability of members may be limited. Many of the former statutory public utility companies have now been nationalized by other statutes and are operated on a national basis, e.g. the National Coal Board.

All the forms of incorporation which we have discussed have one feature in common, i.e. they produce corporations aggregate having more than one member. However, English law recognizes the concept of the *Corporation Sole,* i.e. a corporation having only one member. A number of such corporations were created by the common lawyers because they were concerned that land did not always have an owner, and that there could be a break, however slight, in ownership. Church lands for example were vested in the vicar of the particular living, and at higher levels in other church dignitaries, such as the bishop of the diocese. When such persons died, the land had no legal owner until a successor was appointed, so the common lawyers created the concept of the corporation sole whereby the office of Vicar or Bishop was a corporation, and the present incumbent the sole member of that corporation. The death of the incumbent had thereafter no effect on the corporation, which never dies, and each successive occupant of the office carries on exactly where his predecessor left off. The Bishop of London is a corporation sole, and the present holder of the office is the sole member of the corporation. The Crown is also a corporation sole.

It does not seem likely that any further corporations sole will be created by the common law, but they may still be created by statute. For example, the Public Trustee Act, 1906, sets up the office of Public Trustee as a corporation sole. The Public Trustee is prepared to act as executor or trustee, when asked to do so, and much property is vested in him from time to time in the above capacities. It would be most inconvenient to transfer this property to the new holder of the office on death of retirement, and so the person who holds the office of Public Trustee is the sole member of a corporation called the Public Trustee, and the property over which he has control is vested in the corporation, and not in the individual who is the holder of the office.

UNINCORPORATED ASSOCIATIONS

Having considered juristic personality, we will now turn to organizations which have no personality separate and distinct from the members. Many groups of people and institutions exist which carry on their affairs in much the same way as incorporated associations, but which are in fact non-charitable unincorporated associations. Examples are cricket clubs, tennis clubs, and societies of like kind. Such associations have no independent legal personality, and their property is treated as the joint property of all the members. The main areas of legal difficulty arising in regard to these associations are as follows—

Liability of members in contract. This rests on the principles of the law of agency. Thus a member who purports to make a contract on behalf of his club is usually personally liable. The other members will only be liable as co-principals if they had authorized the making of the contract. This would be the case if, for example, the rules of the club so provided. Alternatively, the members may ratify the contract after it is made. However, it appears that no member has authority to make a *purchase on credit (Flemyng* v. *Hector* (1836), 2 M & W 172) unless he is specifically authorized to do so. Membership of a club usually involves payment of an annual subscription and nothing more. Consequently it is expected that everything needed by the club will be paid for from existing funds. If more money is needed a meeting of members should be called so that subscriptions might be raised rather than pledge the credit of the members.

Liability of members in tort. A person is liable if he committed the tort and in addition may be liable vicariously for the tort of his servant (see p. 307). These principles have been applied to clubs in two main types of case, viz.—

(*a*) Where a person has been injured as a result of the dangerous condition of the club premises. The tendency here is to hold all the members liable as 'occupiers' and not merely the club's officers or a committee or trustees. (*Campbell* v. *Thompson,* [1953] 1 Q.B. 445.)

(*b*) Where a person has been injured as a result of the negligence of a servant of the club. The tendency here is to find that the servant is employed by the officer or committee or trustees who appointed him. (*Bradley Egg Farm Ltd* v. *Clifford,* [1943] 2 All E.R. 378.)

Rights of members in the assets of the association. While a club is functioning the individual members have no separate rights in its property. They do, however, acquire realizable rights when the club is dissolved. On dissolution the general rule is that the assets are sold and after liabilities have been discharged any surplus is divided equally among those persons who are members *at the time the assets are distributed (Brown* v. *Dale* (1879), 8 Ch. D. 78), subject, of course, to any contrary provision in the rules of the club. It should be noted that a club is not dissolved simply because it changes its name and constitution with the express or implied consent of the members. (*Abbatt* v. *Treasury Solicitor,* [1969] 3 All E.R. 1175.)

Rights of members under the rules.   The rules of an unincorporated association constitute a contract between the members of the association and the court will grant an injuction to a member who is denied a right given under the rules, e.g. the right to vote at meetings (*Woodford* v. *Smith,* [1970] 1 All E.R. 1091), or if he is expelled either where there is no power of expulsion under the rules, or if the power exists it has not been exercised properly as where the principles of natural justice have not been observed.

Procedure.   If only a few of the members are liable no problems arise since they can all be sued personally. If, however, it is intended to allege that all the members are liable this procedure is impracticable since all would have the right to be individually defended and represented. In this sort of case a representative action is available. Under the Rules of Supreme Court and the County Court rules the plaintiff may ask for a *representative order* to be made against certain members of the association and sue them. If he is successful these members will be liable to pay the damages but may also be entitled to an indemnity from the funds of the association, and in this way the plaintiff is in effect paid from the association's funds. Similarly some members of an unincorporated association can sue for wrongs done to the association by means of the representative order procedure.

Trade unions

As regards the status of trade unions, Sect. 2(1) of the Trade Union and Labour Relations Act, 1974, provides that a trade union shall not be treated as if it were a body corporate but it is capable of making contracts; the property of the trade union is vested in trustees on trust for the union; it is capable of suing and being sued in its own name, whether in proceedings relating to property or founded on contract or tort (though liability in tort is restricted (see p. 302) or any other cause of action whatsoever; proceedings for any offence alleged to have been committed by it or on its behalf may be brought against it in its own name and any judgment made in proceedings of any description brought against a trade union are enforceable, e.g. by way of execution against the property held in trust for the union as if the union were a body corporate.

Section 3(1) of the 1974 Act extends the identical provisions to an employers' association where it is unincorporated. However, an employers' association may be a body corporate.

The present law relating to the immunity of trade unions (and employers' associations) is to be found in Sect. 14 of the 1974 Act. (See p. 303.) Contracts made by a trade union are normally enforceable in accordance with the general principles of the law of contract. However, under Sect. 18 of the Trade Union and Labour Relations Act, 1974 collective agreements, i.e. with an employer in regard to wages, hours and conditions of work of a group of workers, are presumed *not* to be intended to be legally enforceable *unless* they are in writing and contain a provision to that effect.

The partnership

A partnership is defined in Sect. 1 of the Partnership Act, 1890, as 'the relationship which subsists between persons carrying on a business in common with a view of profit'. It will be noted that there must be a business; that it must be carried on in common by the members (whether by all of them, or by one or more of them acting for the others, will depend on the agreement subsisting between them); and that there must be the intention to earn profits. An association of persons formed for the purpose (say) of promoting some educational or recreational object to which the whole of the funds of the association shall be devoted, and from which no advantage in the nature of a distribution of a profit shall accrue to the members, is not a partnership.

Participation in the profits of a business may be regarded as *prima facie* evidence of a partnership, but it is not conclusive—the intention of the parties must be examined. Thus, an employee whose remuneration is based on a share of profits, or the widow or child of a deceased partner receiving an annuity in the form of a share of profits, would not legally be deemed to be partners. Neither does the common ownership of property constitute a partnership, nor the lending of money in consideration of an agreement to pay the interest, or to repay the capital, out of profits as they accrue. (But in such a case the lender should take the precaution of having the agreement embodied in writing, signed by all the parties, and setting out clearly the fact that he is not to be considered a partner.)

The question of citation as a partner is of great importance because the existence of a partnership, if such is proved, will involve all parties cited as partners in unlimited liability for the debts of the firm. Partners are agents for the firm, and can bind the other partners in contracts concerning the business of the firm.

Two or more persons can combine to form a partnership, which can be brought into existence in a highly formal or a very casual manner. *No legal formalities are essential,* but it is desirable and usual for the rights and liabilities of the partners to be defined in a a formal Deed of Partnership, or at least in a written Partnership Agreement. On the other hand, a mere oral agreement is equally binding, and in extreme cases a relationship of partnership may be inferred from the conduct of the parties. The partners are at liberty to vary the arrangements made between them, and where the conduct of the parties has for a lengthy period been inconsistent with the terms as originally agreed, it will be presumed that they intend that the new arrangements shall be binding on them. The Partnership Act makes provisions as to contribution of capital, division of profits, rights of partners to participate in active management, and so on, but these only apply in so far as they are not varied by agreement between the partners.

Section 434 of the Companies Act, 1948, prohibits the formation of a partnership consisting of more than twenty persons for the purpose of carrying on any business for gain. However, certain partnerships of solicitors, accountants and members of stock exchanges were exempted from this prohibition by Sect. 120 of the Companies Act, 1967. Regulations made by the Department of Trade since 1967 exempt from the prohibition in Sect. 434 of the Act of 1948 certain other partnerships, e.g. patent agents and also certain partnerships of surveyors, auctioneers, valuers and estate agents.

There is no limitation on the activities of partners provided these are legal; nor is there any limit to the liability of the individual partners for the debts of the firm, each partner being liable to the full extent of his personal estate for any deficiencies of the partnership. However, provision is made for the introduction of limited partners whose liability is limited to the amount of capital they have introduced, though there must always be at least one general partner who is fully liable for the debts of the firm. Such a partnership must be registered as a limited partnership under the Limited Partnerships Act, 1907.

The partnership was the normal form of business organization for operations on a fairly large scale before the advent of the joint stock company, but it is now largely restricted to the type of enterprise requiring intimate personal collaboration between the members, or where incorporation is not possible or desirable, as among doctors, solicitors and accountants. However, this type of business organization has become more popular since Corporation Tax was introduced for companies by the Finance Act, 1965.

One of the defects of the partnership is its lack of continuity. The death of a partner automatically dissolves the partnership, and the continuing partners must account to his personal representatives for the amount of his interest in the firm. This difficulty may be met to some extent by providing funds out of the proceeds of an insurance policy on the deceased partner's life, or by arranging for the balance of his capital account to be left in the business as a loan, but failing these measures the sudden withdrawal of a large amount of capital may well cause serious dislocation of the business, or even end its operations. The most serious defect of a partnership, however, is the difficulty of providing additional funds for expansion, and this may induce partners to admit new members for the sake of their capital, regardless of their fitness for taking an active part in controlling the business.

A partnership firm is not a persona *at law;* a partnership is an aggregate of its members. In the matter of procedure the Rules of Supreme Court make it possible for the firm to sue and be sued in its own name, but this does not confer upon it a legal personality as is possessed by a corporation.

THE CROWN

The Crown is the executive head in the United Kingdom and Commonwealth, and government departments and civil servants act on behalf of the Crown.

Until 1947 the Crown was not liable for the tortious acts of its servants, and was liable only to a limited extent in contract, though the actual tortfeasor could be sued and the Crown often stood behind him and paid the damages awarded against him. Actions in contract could only be started by a cumbrous procedure known as a Petition of Right, with the consent of the Crown given on the advice of the Attorney-General.

The rather anomalous position at common law which has been outlined above arose out of the ancient maxim, 'The King can do no wrong,' which was extended to cover the activities of the Departments of State and their servants. The Crown Proceedings Act, 1947, and the Rules of the Supreme Court (Crown Proceedings) Act, 1947, which were required to support the Act in the matter of procedure, came into force together on 1 January, 1948, to rectify the matter.

The general effect of this legislation is to abolish the rule that the Crown is immune from legal process, and to place the Crown as regards civil proceedings in the same position as a subject. Proceedings by Petition of Right are abolished, and all claims which might before the Act have been enforced by Petition of Right can be brought by ordinary action in accordance with the Act.

The Crown is now liable in contract where a Petition of Right could have been brought before, and also in tort. Regarding contractual claims, there are some limitations upon the rights of the other party, viz.—

(a) Executive necessity.   In *Rederiaktiebolaget Amphitrite* v. *R.*, [1921] 3 K.B. 500, a neutral shipowner's vessel was detained in England although the British Legation in Stockholm had given an undertaking that it would not be. The basis of Rowlatt's, J., decision for the Crown was that the Government cannot by contract hamper its freedom of action in matters which concern the welfare of the State.

This statement has been regarded as much too wide and is probably of very limited application.

(b) Parliamentary funds.   In *Churchward* v. *R.* (1865), 1 Q.B. 173, a contract to carry mail for eleven years was terminated by the Crown in the fourth year. Shee, J., in deciding for the Crown, held that it was a condition precedent of the contract that Parliament would allocate funds and if they chose not to there was no claim. This view came under criticism in subsequent cases and the better view is that the decision is limited to cases where Parliament has *expressly* refused to grant the necessary funds.

(c) Freedom to legislate.   In *Reilly* v. *R.*, [1934] A.C. 176, a barrister who was employed by the Canadian Government had his contract terminated by legislation. The Privy Council found for the Crown on the ground that the Crown cannot by contract restrict its right to legislate

(d) Contracts of employment. Here the position is as follows—

(i) *Military personnel.* Military employees cannot successfully claim against the Crown for breach of contract (*Dickson* v. *Combermere* (1863), 3 F. & F. 527) nor can they claim arrears of pay. (*Leaman* v. R., [1920] 3 K.B. 663.)

(ii) *Civil Servants.* At common law civil servants are dismissible at pleasure (*Shenton* v. *Smith,* [1895] A.C. 229) but can claim arrears of pay. (*Kodeeswaran* v. *A.G. of Ceylon,* [1970] 2 W.L.R. 456.) Furthermore, *dicta* in *Reilly* v. *R.,* [1934] A.C. 176 suggest that even at common law an express promise to employ for a definite period, the contract to be determinable only 'for cause', e.g. misconduct, overrides the implied term relating to dismissal at pleasure. However, the provisions of the Trade Union and Labour Relations Act, 1974 which protect employees against unfair dismissal apply to civil servants but not to military personnel.

Actions in tort will lie against the Crown for the torts of its servants or agents committed in the course of their employment; for breach of duty owed at common law by an employer to his servants; for breach of the duties attaching to the ownership, occupation, possession or control of property; and for breach of statutory duties, e.g. breaches of the duty of fencing dangerous machines under factory legislation. No proceedings lie in tort against Her Majesty in her private capacity.

The law as to indemnity and contribution under the Law Reform (Married Women and Tortfeasors) Act, 1935, applies to Crown cases, so if the Crown is a joint tortfeasor, it can claim a contribution from fellow wrongdoers, and where the Crown is led into publishing a libel, it may claim an indemnity against the party responsible. The Law Reform (Contributory Negligence) Act, 1945, also applies to Crown cases.

No action lies in tort against the Crown or the individual Crown servant for anything done or omitted to be done in relation to any postal packet or telephone communication, except that an action will lie for damages for loss of a registered inland postal packet, not being a telegram. Such action must be brought within twelve months of the date of posting of the packet. (Law Reform (Limitation of Actions, etc.) Act, 1954.) It should be noted that the Post Office Act, 1969, established the Post Office as a public authority which is not an agent of the Crown and does not enjoy the immunities and privileges of the Crown. Nevertheless, the immunities outlined above still apply being contained in Sections 29 and 30 of the Act of 1969, and were raised in *Harold Stephen & Co. Ltd* v. *Post Office, The Times,* 18 July, 1977 where the Court of Appeal refused to grant an injuction against the Post Office to companies in the Cricklewood area of London whose business was in jeopardy because they were receiving no mail through the Post Office's action in closing the local sorting office and suspending Post Office workers refusing to handle mail in support of workers employed in the private sector (Grunwick). The Court said that the Act of 1969 put the Post Office in a privileged position by making it immune against actions in contract and tort except for registered letters. Both the Crown and any member of the Armed Forces are immune from liability in tort in respect of the death of, or personal injury to another member of the Armed Forces on duty, provided that the death or injury arises out of service which ranks for the purpose of pension.

Actions under the Act may be brought in the High Court or a county court, and the Treasury is required to publish a list of authorized government departments for the purposes of the Act, and of their solicitors. Actions by the Crown will be brought by the authorized department in its own name, or by the Attorney-General. Actions against the Crown are to be brought against the appropriate department, or, where there is doubt as to the department responsible or appropriate, against the Attorney-General.

In any civil proceedings by or against the Crown, the court can make such orders as it can make in proceedings between subjects, except that no injunction or order for specific performance can be granted against the Crown. The court can, in lieu thereof, make an order declaratory of the rights of the parties in the hope that the Crown will abide by it. No order for the recovery of land, or delivery up of property, can be made against the Crown, but the court may instead make an order that the plaintiff is entitled as against the Crown to land or to other property or to possession thereof. No execution or attachment will issue to enforce payment by the Crown of any money or costs. The procedure is for the successful party to apply for a certificate in the prescribed form giving particulars of the order. This is served on the solicitor for the department concerned, which is then required to pay the sum due with interest if any. The above exceptions show that, in spite of the Act, the rights of the subject against the Crown are still somewhat imperfect.

Crown Privilege in Civil Proceedings. As we have seen, either party to a civil action can, amongst other things, ask the Court to order the other party to produce any relevant documents for inspection. (See p. 65.) Under Sect. 28 of the Crown Proceedings Act, 1947, this right lies against the Crown though the Crown could refuse to obey the order if production of the document(s) would be injurious to the public interest. It had been felt for some time that Ministers whose departments were involved in civil litigation had abused this right. Undoubtedly, some plaintiffs failed in an action against the Crown because even the judge could not obtain access to documents necessary to support the claim. As a result of a number of cases of this kind, the House of Lords decided in *Conway* v. *Rimmer*, [1968] 1 All E.R. 874, that even though a Minister certifies that production of a particular document would be against the public interest the judge may nevertheless see it and decide whether the Minister's view is correct. If the judge cannot accept the Minister's decision he may overrule him and order disclosure of the document to the party concerned. Thus the decision of the Minister is no longer conclusive though it is unlikely that a judge would order disclosure if there was a danger of real prejudice to the national interest.

However, despite dicta in *Conway* v. *Rimmer* that claims to privilege on grounds of confidentiality could not expect sympathetic treatment, the courts vary in their interpretation of this view. (*Norwich Pharmacal Co.* v. *Commissioners of Customs and Excise,* 1973;[63] *Alfred Crompton Amusement Machines* v. *Customs and Excise Commissioners,* 1973.)[64]

In the *Alfred Crompton* case the House of Lords was of opinion that 'Crown privilege' was not the best phrase to use in this context and that the phrase 'privilege on the ground of public interest' was more appropriate. That this is so is illustrated by the fact that privilege extends beyond cases against the Crown. Thus in *D* v. *NSPCC,* [1977] 1 All E.R. 589 the House of Lords held that the NSPCC or a local authority is entitled to privilege from disclosing the names of its informants in relation to child neglect or ill-treatment.

SOME FUNDAMENTAL LEGAL CONCEPTS

Before entering into a more detailed study of the various branches of substantive law we must first of all examine certain fundamental legal concepts and classifications.

Private and Public Law

Private law is concerned with the legal relationships of ordinary persons in everyday transactions. It is also concerned with the legal position of corporate bodies and associations of persons the first of which are endowed with a special form of legal personality. Private law includes contract and commercial law, the law of tort, family law, e.g. divorce adoption and guardianship, trusts and the law of property which involves a consideration of the rights which can exist in property and how property can be transferred.

Public law is concerned with the constitution and functions of the many different kinds of governmental organisations, including local authorities, such as county and district councils, and their legal relationship with the citizen and each other. These relationships form the subject matter of constitutional and administrative law. Public law is also concerned with crime which involves the state's relationship with the power of control over the individual.

There is also a division into *criminal and civil law.* Criminal law is concerned with legal rules which provide that certain forms of conduct shall attract punishment by the state, e.g. homicide and theft. Civil law embraces the whole of private law and all divisions of public law except criminal law.

In order to understand the various branches of substantive private law which are considered in detail later, it is necessary to be able in particular to distinguish the following—

Contract. A contract is an agreement made between two or more persons which is intended to have legal consequences. Thus, if there is a breach of contract, the parties can go to court and obtain a remedy. We shall see in the appropriate chapter which agreements the courts will enforce, under what conditions they are enforceable, and what remedies are available to injured parties. It should be noted that the parties to a contract enter voluntarily into their obligations; the function of the law is merely to enforce or adjudicate on such agreements.

Tort. A tort on the other hand, is a civil wrong independent of contract. It arises out of a duty imposed by law, and a person who commits a tortious act does not voluntarily undertake the liabilities which the law imposes on him. There are many kinds of tort with a common characteristic; injury of some kind inflicted by one person on another. Nuisance, trespass, slander and libel are well-known civil wrongs. The typical remedy in this branch of the law is an action for damages by the injured party against the person responsible for the injury. Such damages are designed not to punish the wrongdoer but to compensate the injured party.

Crime. A crime is in a different category. It is difficult to define a crime, but it is a public offence against the State, and, while an individual may be injured, the object of a criminal charge is to punish the offender, not to compensate the victim though under the provisions of the Powers of Criminal Courts Act, 1973, compensation orders can now be made. (See p. 56.) Criminals are prosecuted, usually by the police, and if found guilty receive the appropriate punishment.

Trusts. A trust arises where one person holds property for the benefit of another. Suppose a man wishes to provide for his children when he dies; he may leave them some of his property on trust, particularly if they are minors, i.e. under age 18 years. He will appoint trustees in whom the property will be vested, but they will not benefit from the proceeds, since the income arising from the trust property will have to be devoted to the purposes of the trust; in this case for the benefit of the children, who are called the beneficiaries or the *cestuis que trust* (pronounced 'setty que trust'). Trusts may also be set up by living persons. The characteristics of a trust are that the trustees own the property but the *cestuis que trust* get the benefits.

It must not be assumed that all acts fall into these tidy categories. Certain breaches of trust are also criminal offences. Some activities may be both torts and crimes, and an act which is a breach of contract is often a tort. Thus, if a taxi-driver drives dangerously and injures a passenger, he is liable to that passenger for breach of contract and negligence. He may also have committed the crime of dangerous driving for which he may be prosecuted.

Some Common Legal Relationships

The law recognizes and defines certain common relationships. The following, in particular, have relevance to the various branches of substantive law dealt with in later chapters.

Agency. It is quite common to find parties having the relationship of principal and agent. Sometimes a person (the principal) wishes to have certain tasks carried out—he may wish to sell a house or buy shares in a company. He therefore employs an estate agent or a stockbroker to carry out his purposes. Sometimes an agent is a specialist who carries out a limited range of duties, e.g. an auctioneer who sells a wardrobe put into an auction. Sometimes he has wider powers, and may even be able to bind the principal in all the ways the principal could bind himself, as where the agent has a power of attorney.

An agent may be specifically appointed as such, but in some cases an agent acquires his status without specific authority being given to him, and such an agent may bind his principal by what is called usual authority. If P appoints A to be the manager of an hotel, A may be able to bind P in a contract although he had no actual authority to make it, for the law is not solely concerned with the actual authority of an agent but regards him as having the usual powers of an agent of his class. It follows that the usual powers of an hotel manager will be relevant in deciding the sort of agreement which A can make on behalf of P. The doctrine of usual authority does not apply where the third party knows that the agent has no authority to make the contract.

An agent's powers may also be extended in an emergency. If A is a carrier of perishable goods for P, he may be able to sell them on behalf of P if the goods are deteriorating and he cannot get P's instructions with regard to disposal. A becomes an agent of necessity for the purpose of sale, though his actual authority is to carry the goods. Agency may also arise out of conduct resulting in apparent authority. If a husband pays the debts which his wife incurs with a local dressmaker, he may be liable to pay for an expensive article of clothing which she buys without his consent, because the husband has, by his conduct, led the dressmaker to believe that the wife has power to bind her husband in contracts of this nature. This type of agency is not peculiar to the relationship of husband and wife and could arise wherever P holds out A as having authority to make contracts on P's behalf. It is also possible in certain circumstances for a principal to ratify, i.e. adopt, the contracts of his agent, even though the agent had no actual authority when making the contract.

Bailment.   A bailment arises when one person (the bailor) hands over his property to the care of another (the bailee). The reasons for such a situation are many. The bailee may have the custody of the property by way of loan or for carriage. The article may be pledged, or left with another to be repaired or altered. Sometimes the bailee has the mere custody of the goods; sometimes he may use the property, as when he 'purchases' a radio set under a hire-purchase (or consumer credit) agreement or borrows a lawn mower. In all cases of bailment, the property or ownership remains with the bailor; the possession with the bailee.

A bailment is an independent legal transaction and need not necessarily originate in a contract. When X hands his goods to Y under a bailment Y has certain duties in regard to the care of the goods even though the bailment is not accompanied by a contract. Thus Y may be held liable for negligent damage to the goods even though he had not been promised any money or other benefit for looking after them. Bailment is considered in more detail on p. 379.

Lien.   A lien is a right over the property of another which arises by operation of law and can be independent of any contract. In its simplest form it gives a creditor, such as a shoe repairer, the right to retain possession of a debtor's property, in this case his shoes, until he has paid or settled the debt, incurred in this case as a result of repairing the shoes. Lien is considered in more detail on p. 416.

7 The Law of Contract

A contract may be defined as an *agreement,* enforceable by the law, between two or more persons to do or abstain from doing some act or acts their intention being to create *legal relations* and not merely to exchange mutual promises, both having given something, or having promised to give something of *value as consideration* for any benefit derived from the agreement.

The definition can be criticized in that some contracts turn out to be unenforceable and, in addition, not all legally binding agreements are true contracts. For example, a transaction by deed under seal derives its legally binding quality from the special way in which it is made rather than from the operation of the laws of contract, e.g. a deed is enforceable even in the absence of valuable consideration. In consequence, transactions under seal are not true contracts at all. Nevertheless, the definition at least emphasizes the fact that the basic elements of contracts are (i) an agreement, (ii) an intention to create legal relations, and (iii) valuable consideration.

THE ESSENTIALS OF A VALID CONTRACT

The essential elements of the formation of a valid and enforceable contract can be summarized under the following headings—

(i) There must be an offer and acceptance, which is in effect the agreement.

(ii) There must be an intention to create legal relations.

(iii) There is a requirement of written formalities in some cases.

(iv) There must be consideration (unless the agreement is under seal).

(v) The parties must have capacity to contract.

(vi) There must be genuineness of consent by the parties to the terms of the contract.

(vii) The contract must not be contrary to public policy.

In the absence of one or more of these essentials, the contract may be void, voidable, or unenforceable.

CLASSIFICATION OF CONTRACTS

Before proceeding to examine the meaning and significance of the points enumerated above the following distinctions should be noted.

Void, voidable and unenforceable contracts

A *void* contract has no binding effect at all and in reality the expression is a contradiction in terms. However, it has been used by lawyers for a long time in order to describe particular situations in the law of contract and its usage is now a matter of convenience. A *voidable* contract is binding but one party has the right, at his option, to set it aside. An *unenforceable* contract is valid in all respects except that it cannot be enforced in a court of law by one or both of the parties should the other refuse to carry out his obligations under it.

Executed and Executory Contracts

A contract is said to be *executed* when one or both of the parties have done all that the contract requires. A contract is said to be *executory* when the obligations of one or both of the parties remain to be carried out. For example, if A and B agree to exchange A's scooter for B's motor cycle and do it immediately, the *possession* of the goods and the *right* to the goods are transferred *together* and the contract is *executed*. If they agree to exchange the following week the *right* to the goods is transferred but not the *possession* and the contract is *executory*. Thus an *executed* contract conveys a *chose in possession* (see p. 375), while an *executory* contracts conveys a *chose in action* (see p. 375).

Specialty and Simple Contracts and Contracts of Record

Specialty contracts are also called contracts under seal, or deeds. All the terms of such contracts are reduced to writing and then the contract is signed, sealed and delivered. The signature is usually attested, i.e. witnessed. A deed operates from the date of delivery, though a deed is presumed to have been delivered on the day of the date of the deed, unless this can be rebutted by evidence to the contrary. Delivery may be (*a*) *actual,* where the deed is handed over to the other party, or (*b*) *constructive,* where the party delivering the deed touches the seal with his finger and says: 'I deliver this my act and deed!' This is then construed as delivery and the deed becomes operative. In many cases, however, there is no delivery, actual or constructive, and once a deed has been signed by the parties, it will be extremely difficult for either of them to show that the deed was not delivered. (*Per* Danckwerts, J., in *Stromdale and Ball Ltd* v. *Burden,* [1952] 1 All E.R. 59.)

The general law of contract *requires* a deed in the case of a lease of more than three years, which must be under seal if it is to create a legal estate. In addition a transfer of property, e.g. a conveyance, which imposes covenants (or agreements) in regard, for example, to the use of the land, is a contract and must also be by deed.

Sometimes a deed is delivered subject to a condition, e.g. that it is not effective until the purchase money has been paid; or is delivered now, but is not to become operative until some future time. In these cases, the deed is not operative until the condition is carried out or the stipulated time has elapsed and such a deed has the special name of 'escrow'. (*Vincent* v. *Premo Enterprises (Voucher Sales) Ltd*, 1969.)[65]

There are two forms of escrow—

(i) Where the deed is delivered to a third party who delivers to the other party when the condition is fulfilled.

(ii) Where the deed is delivered to the other party directly, but is not operative until the condition is fulfilled.

An escrow is useful where a person is selling property but will be abroad before completion. He may sign and deliver an escrow before leaving the country so that the deal can be completed if the conditions are carried out.

A deed has certain characteristics which serve to distinguish it from a simple contract—

(a) Merger   If a simple contract is afterwards embodied in a deed made between the same parties, the simple contract merges into, or is swallowed up by the deed, for the deed is the superior document. But if the deed is only intended to cover part of the terms of the previous simple contract, there is no merger of that part of the simple contract not covered by the deed.

(b) *Limitation of Actions.*   The right of action under a specialty contract is barred unless it is brought withing twelve years from the date when the cause of action arises on it, i.e. when the deed could first have been sued upon. Time does not run from the date of making the deed. A similar right of action is barred under a simple contract after only six years. (Limitation Act, 1939.)

(c) **Consideration is not essential** to support a deed, though specific performance will not be granted if the promise is gratuitous (see p. 276). Simple contracts must be supported by consideration.

(d) *Estoppel.*   Statements in a deed tend to be conclusive against the party making them, and although he might be able to prove they were not true, the rule of evidence called 'estoppel' will prevent this by excluding the very evidence which would be needed. In modern law, however, a deed does not operate as an estoppel where one of the parties wishes to bring evidence to show fraud, duress, mistake, lack of capacity, illegality, or that the deed is an escrow. In addition, where a deed is rectifiable (see p. 213) the doctrine of estoppel by deed does not bind the parties to it.(*Wilson* v. *Wilson*, 1969.)[66]

Simple contracts form the great majority of contracts, and are sometimes referred to as parol contracts. This class includes all contracts not under seal, and for their enforcement they require consideration. Simple contracts may be made orally or in writing, or they may be inferred from the conduct of the parties; but no simple contract can exist which does not arise from a valid offer and a valid acceptance supported by some consideration. When these elements exist, the contract is valid in the absence of some vitiating element such as lack of capacity of one of the parties, lack of reality of consent, or illegality or impossibility of performance.

THE FORMATION OF CONTRACT

In order to decide whether a contract has come into being it is necessary to establish that there has been an *agreement* between the parties. In consequence it must be shown that an *offer* was made by one party (called the offeror) which was *accepted* by the other party (called the offeree) and that *legal relations* were intended.

OFFER AND ACCEPTANCE

A contract is an agreement and comes into existence when one party makes an offer which the other accepts. The person making the offer is called offeror, and the person to whom it is made is called the offeree. An offer may be express or implied. Suppose X says to Y—'I will sell you this watch for £5,' and Y says—'I agree.' An express offer and acceptance have been made; X is the offeror and Y the offeree. Alternatively Y may say to X—'I will give you £5 for that watch.' If X says—'I agree,' then another express offer has been made, but Y is the offeror and X is the offeree. In both cases, the acceptance brings a contract into being. In order to find out who makes the offer and who the acceptance, it is necessary to examine the way in which the contract is negotiated.

Offer

An offer is an undertaking by the offeror that he will be bound in contract by the offer if there is a proper acceptance of it. An offer may be made to a specific person or to any member of a group of persons, or to the world at large (*Carlill* v. *Carbolic Smoke Ball Co.*, 1893),[67] though sometimes what looks like an offer may be no more than an invitation to make an offer, or as it is sometimes called an *invitation to treat*. If I expose in my shop window a coat priced £15, this is not an offer to sell. It is not possible for a person to enter the shop and say: 'I accept your offer; here is the £15.' It is the would-be-buyer who makes the offer when tendering the money. (*Pharmaceutical Society of Great Britain* v. *Boots Cash Chemists Ltd*, 1953.)[68] If by chance the coat has been wrongly priced, I shall be entitled to say: 'I am sorry; the price is £50,' and refuse to sell.

The same principles have been applied to prices set out in price lists, catalogues and circulars, (*Spencer* v. *Harding,* 1870,[69] and *Partridge* v. *Crittenden*, 1968)[70] and a prospectus issued by a company in order to invite the public to subscribe for its shares is an invitation to treat so that members of the public make an offer to buy the shares when they make application for them and the company is the acceptor insofar as shares are allotted to a subscriber. In other cases, such as automatic vending machines, the position is doubtful, and it may be that such machines are invitations to treat or represent an implied offer which is accepted when a coin is put into the machine. However, it does seem that if a bus travels along a certain route, there is an *implied offer* on the part of its owners to carry passengers at the published fares for the various stages, and it would appear that when a passenger puts himself either on the platform or inside the bus, he makes an *implied acceptance* of the offer, agreeing to be bound by the company's conditions and to pay the appropriate fare. Per Lord Greene *obiter* in *Wilkie* v. *London Passenger Transport Board*, [1947] 1 All E.R. 258. With regard to negotiations for the sale of land, the same principles are again applied with perhaps this difference, that in a case involving the sale of land where *specific performance is a possible remedy* the court may be reluctant to grant that remedy unless the intention to contract is very clear. (*Harvey* v. *Facey,* 1893,[71] and *Clifton* v. *Palumbo,* 1944,[72] but see *Bigg* v. *Boyd Gibbins Ltd,* 1971.)[73]

Problems relating to contractual offers have risen in the case of *auction sales* but the position is now largely resolved. An advertisement of an auction is not an offer to hold it. (*Harris* v. *Nickerson,* 1873.)[74] At an auction the bid is the offer; the auctioneer's request for bids is merely an invitation to treat. (*British Car Actions* v. *Wright,* 1972.)[75] The sale is complete when the hammer falls, and until that time any bid may be withdrawn. (*Payne* v. *Cave* (1789), 3 Term Rep. 148.)

The position when the auction is without reserve is not absolutely certain because it has never been clearly decided whether an advertisement to sell articles by auction without any reserve price constitutes an offer to sell to the highest bidder. It is at any rate clear that Sect. 58(2) of the Sale of Goods Act, 1893 prevents any *contract of sale* coming into existence if the auctioneer refuses to accept the highest bid. There remains the possibility once the auction of an item has began that the auctioneer may be liable in damages on the basis of a breach of warranty that he has authority is sell, and will sell, the goods to the highest bidder. This device appears to be sanctioned by the decision of the Court of Exchequer Chamber in *Warlow* v. *Harrison,* (1859), 1 E & E 309.

Acceptance

Once the existence of an offer has been proved, the Court must be satisfied that the offeree has accepted the offer, otherwise there is no contract. An agreement may nevertheless be inferred from the conduct of the parties. (*Brogden* v. *Metropolitan Railway*, 1877.)[76]

The person who accepts an offer must be aware that the offer has been made. Thus if B has found A's lost dog and, not having seen an advertisement by A offering a reward for its return, returns it out of goodness of heart, B will not be able to claim the reward. He cannot be held to accept an offer of which he is unaware. However, as long as the acceptor *is aware* of the making of the offer, his motive in accepting it is immaterial. (*Williams* v. *Carwardine*, 1833.)[77]

Conditional Assent.   An acceptance must be absolute and unconditional. One form of conditional assent is an acceptance 'subject to contract.' The law has placed a special significance on these words, and they are always construed as meaning that the parties do not intend to be bound until a formal contract is prepared. (*Winn* v. *Bull*, 1877[78] and *Tiverton Estates Ltd* v. *Wearwell Ltd*, 1974.)[51] However, if the statement is qualified and the terms of a proposed contract can be identified, the court will enforce it. (*Filby* v. *Hounsell*, 1896[79] and *Michael Richards Properties* v. *Corporation of Wardens of St. Saviour's Parish Southwalk*, 1975.)[80] A potential purchaser can generally recover an deposit paid if he does not continue with a 'subject to contract' purchase. (*Chillingworth* v. *Esche*, 1923.)[81] Additionally, it should be noted that if A employs B, an estate agent, to sell a property, then unless A actually authorizes B to receive a deposit from a puchaser, C, on his (A's) behalf, then A will not be liable to repay it to C if B receives it and misappropriates it. (*Sorrel* v. *Finch*, 1972.)[82] Furthermore, it was held in *Potters* v. *Loppert*, [1973] 1 All E.R. 658 that unless otherwise agreed, a deposit paid to an agent as stake-holder on exchange of contracts is not paid to him as a trustee, but on a contractual or quasi-contractual basis. Consequently, he is not liable to account for any profit, e.g. interest which he may have earned on the money.

In other cases of conditional assent the attitude of the court is not so predictable, but it would seem that if the court decides that the further agreement of the parties is not a condition precedent to the formation of the contract, but is merely part of the performance of an already binding agreement, the court will enforce the contract. (*Branca* v. *Cobarro*, 1947.)[83] The effect of the use of the words 'without prejudice' in letters forming the basis of negotiations between parties to a contract was considered by the court in *Tomlin* v. *Standard Telephone and Cables Ltd*, 1969.[84] It was decided that the words meant 'without prejudice to the position of the writer of it if the terms which he proposed therein were not accepted.' If the terms were accepted a binding contract was established.

Incomplete (or Inchoate) Agreements.   While considering the matter of conditional assent, it is convenient to deal briefly with an additional problem which may face a court in certain of these cases.

A contract will not be enforced unless the parties have expressed themselves with reasonable clarity on the matter of essential terms. A situation may therefore exist in which there is sufficient assent to satisfy the basic requirements of offer and acceptance yet the contract is unenforceable because it is incomplete (or inchoate) as to certain of its terms.

In such a case it may be possible for the court to complete the contract by reference to a *trade practice* or *course of dealing* between the parties. (*Hillas* v. *Arcos*, 1932.)[85] Sometimes the agreement itself may provide a method of completion. (*Foley* v. *Classique Coaches Ltd*, 1934[86] and *Brown* v. *Gould*, 1971.)[87] However, if the court cannot obtain assistance from these sources, it will not usually complete the contract for the parties, and the contract, being *inchoate*, cannot be enforced. (*Scammell* v. *Ouston*, 1941.)[88] However, a covenant in a conveyance that the purchaser should be given 'the first option of purchasing . . . at a price to be agreed upon' certain adjoining land imposes an obligation on the vendor at least to offer the land at a price at which he is willing to sell. (*Smith* v. *Morgan*, [1971] 2 All E.R. 1500.)

However, it is necessary to distinguish between a term which has yet to be agreed by the parties and a term on which they have agreed but is in the event meaningless or ambiguous. In the first case, no contract exists unless the deficiency can be made good by the methods outlined above. In the second case, it may be possible to ignore the term and enforce the contract without it. (*Nicolene* v. *Simmonds*, 1953.)[89] However, if, as in *Scammell* v. *Ouston*, 1941,[88] the term is still being negotiated the contract will be inchoate and unenforceable. In addition, the term must be *clearly* severable from the rest of the contract, i.e. it must be possible to enforce the contract without it, which was the case in *Nicolene*[89] but not in *Scammel.*[88]

Oounter offer. A counter-offer is a rejection of the original offer and in some cases has the effect of cancelling it. Where the counter-offer *introduces a new term*, the original offer is cancelled (*Hyde* v. *Wrench*, 1840,[90] *Neale* v. *Merrett*, 1930,[91] and *Northland Airlines Ltd* v. *Dennis Ferranti Meters Ltd*, 1970[92]), though the counter-offer may be accepted either expressly or by implication as in *Butler Machine Tool Co.* v. *Ex-cell-O Corp.* (*England*), 1977.[93] However, a simple request for information where the offeree merely *tries to induce a new term* may not amount to an actual counter-offer. (*Stevenson* v. *McLean*, 1880.)[94]

Retrospective acceptance. Acceptance may be retrospective, i.e. the parties may carry out certain acts on the assumption that a contract will eventually be made. When the acceptance is eventually made, it is capable of operating retrospectively, thus giving legal effect to everything that has been done before. That the contract is to operate retrospectively may be provided for by an express term in the contract or may be inferred from conduct as in *Trollope and Colls Ltd* v. *Atomic Power Construction Ltd*, 1962.[95]

Acceptance in the case of tenders. It is common enough in business for companies wishing to buy goods to invite suppliers to submit tenders giving details of the price for which the goods may be bought. It is essential to understand precisely what is meant by 'accepting' a tender, since different legal results are obtained according to the wording of the invitation to tender. If the invitation by its wording implies that the potential buyer *will* require the goods, acceptance of a tender sent in response to such an invitation results in a binding contract under which the buyer undertakes to buy all the goods specified in the tender from the person who has submitted it. On the other hand, if the invitation by its wording suggests that the potential buyer *may* require the goods, the vagueness in the requirements of the purchaser prevents a contract for the whole goods coming into being. Acceptance of such a tender results in a standing offer by the supplier to supply the goods set out in the tender as and when required by the person accepting it. Each time the buyer orders a quantity, there is a contract confined to that quantity; but if the buyer does not order any of the goods set out in the tender, or a smaller number than the supplier quoted for, there is no breach of contract. Conversely, if the person submitting the tender wishes to revoke his standing offer, he may do so, except in so far as the buyer has already ordered goods under the tender. These must be supplied or the tenderer is in breach of contract. (*Great Northern Railway* v. *Witham*, 1873.)[96]

Methods of acceptance

An acceptance may be made in various ways. It may be made in writing or orally, or at an auction by the fall of the hammer, but it must in general be communicated and communication must be made by a person authorized to make it. (*Powell* v. *Lee*, 1908.)[97] Silence cannot amount to acceptance, except perhaps in the case of prior consent by the offeree. Thus if P says to Q: 'If I do not hear from you before noon tomorrow, I shall assume you accept my offer,' he will find he is unable, at least without Q's consent to this method of making a contract, to bind Q in this way, and Q need take no action at all. (*Felthouse* v. *Bindley*, 1862.)[98] This rule of the common law goes some way towards preventing inertia selling, though protection is now given by the Unsolicited Goods and Services Act, 1971 (as amended by the Unsolicited Goods and Services (Amendment) Act, 1975) and see *Fairline Shipping Corpn* v. *Adamson*, 1974.[99] The Act provides for fines to be made on persons making demands for payment for goods which they know are unsolicited. If the demand is accompanied by threats a higher scale of fines applies. Furthermore, unsolicited goods may be kept by the recipient without payment *after a period of 30 days* provided the recipient gives notice to the sender asking that they be collected, or *after six months* even if no such notice has been given.

There are some cases in which the offeror is deemed to have waived communication of the acceptance. This occurs in the case of *unilateral contracts* such as promise to pay money in return for some act to be carried out by the offeree. Performance of the act operates as an acceptance, and no communication is required. (*Carlill* v. *Carbolic Smoke Ball Co.*, 1893.)[67]

The offeror may stipulate a method of acceptance and where this is done it would seem that, if the offeror makes it clear that one method only will suffice, then there is no contract unless the offeree accepts by the method prescribed. Nevertheless, in such a case the offeror could waive his right to have the acceptance communicated in a given way and agree to the substituted method. Apart from the case of *Eliason* v. *Henshaw,* 1819[100], which takes a rather strict view of the method of communication, it seems that if the offeror has stipulated a method of acceptance *but does not make it clear that only one method will suffice,* then a quicker or equally expeditious method will be effective, since there is no prejudice to the offeror if he learns that the offer has been accepted sooner than, or at the same time as he would have known had the offeree used the prescribed method. (*Manchester Diocesan Council for Education* v. *Commercial and General Investments Ltd,* 1969[101] and *Yates Building Co.* v. *R. J. Pulleyn & Sons (York),* 1975.)[102] Certainly an offer by telegram is good evidence of the offeror's desire for a quick reply so that a reply by letter would probably be ineffective.

If the offeror has not stipulated a method of acceptance, the offeree may choose his own method, though where acceptance is by word of mouth it is not enough that it be spoken, it must actually be heard by the offeror. In this connection an interesting development occurs with the use of the telephone and teleprinter. Since these are methods of instantaneous communication, it is held that the contract is not complete unless the apparent communication takes place. (*Entores Ltd* v. *Miles Far East Corporation,* 1955.)[103]

Use of Post

The general rule is that acceptance must be communicated to the offeror and that the contract is made *when* and *where* the acceptance is received by the offeror. (*Entores Ltd.* v. *Miles Far East Corporation,* 1955.)[103]

However, if the Post is the proper method of communication between the parties then acceptance is deemed complete immediately the letter of acceptance is posted, even if it is delayed or is lost or destroyed in the post so that it never reaches the offeror. (*Household Fire Insurance Co.* v. *Grant,* 1879.)[104] Nevertheless, the letter of acceptance must be properly addressed and properly posted (*Re London and Northern Bank, ex parte Jones,* 1900),[105] and the court must be satisfied that it was within the contemplation of the parties that the post might be used as method of communicating acceptance. Thus in *Henthorn* v. *Fraser,* [1892] 2 Ch. 27 the fact that the post was the proper method of accepting an offer handed to the offeree was that the parties lived in different towns. It is not certain whether the exchange of contracts for the sale of land falls within the post rule and whether posting or delivery is the vital time. However, where the sale is governed by the Law Society's Conditions posting is regarded as the time of exchange. The rule relating to acceptance by post is in practice kept within narrow confines. If the statements of the parties or the provisions of a statute appear to exclude the rule then the court will not apply it. (*Holwell Securities Ltd* v. *Hughes,* 1974.)[106] Where there is a misdirection of the letter containing the offer, then the offer is made when it actually reaches the offeree, and not when it would have reached him in the ordinary course of post. (*Adams* v. *Lindsell,* 1818.)[107] In contrast with the rule regarding acceptance by post, a letter of revocation is not effective until it actually reaches the offeree, whereas a letter of acceptance is effective when it is posted. (*Byrne* v. *Van Tienhoven*, 1880.)[108] A telegram is effective as an acceptance when it is handed in at the post office. (*Cowan* v. *O'Connor*, (1880) 20 QBD 640.)

The better view is that, in English law, an acceptance cannot be recalled once it has been posted even though it has not reached the offeror. Thus, if X posted a letter accepting Y's offer to sell goods, X could not withdraw the acceptance by telephoning Y and asking him to ignore the letter of acceptance when it arrived, and Y could hold X bound by the contract if he wished to do so. This is obvious, the rules being what they are, since otherwise Y would be bound when the letter was posted, and X would be reserving the right to withdraw his acceptance during the transit of the letter even though Y was still bound. However, by Scots law the affect of an acceptance can be altered after posting. (*Dunmore (Countess)* v. *Alexander,* 1839.)[109]

There is some controversy as to whether agreement can result from *cross-offers*. For example, suppose X by letter offers to sell his bicycle to Y for £50, and Y, by means of a second letter, which crosses X's letter in the post, offers to buy X's bicycle for £50. Can there be a contract? The matter was discussed by an English court in *Tinn* v. *Hoffman* (1873), 29 L.T. 271, and the court's conclusion was that no contract could arise, though this is regarded as too strict a view of the position. However, the matter is still undecided by the judges and it is possible to hold the view that today a contract would come into being where it appears that the parties have intended to create a legally binding agreement on the same footing.

Revocation of offer

The general rule is that *an offer may be revoked at any time before* it is accepted (*Payne* v. *Cave,* (1789) 3 Term Rep. 148) though sometimes there is what is known as an option attached to the offer, and time is given in which to make the decision whether to accept or not. If the offeror says it is a provision of the offer which he sends to the offeree that he agrees to give seven days, then the offeree may accept the offer at any time within seven days, or he need not accept at all. However, the offeror need not keep the offer open for seven days but can revoke it (*Routledge* v. *Grant*, (1828)[110], unless the offeree has given some consideration for the option. The consideration need not be adequate. (See *Mountford* v. *Scott*, 1974.)[453] The option is really a separate contract to allow time to decide whether to accept the original offer or not. It was thought at one time that, where the option to buy property was not supported by consideration, the offer could be revoked by its sale to another, but in modern law it is necessary for the offeror to communicate the revocation to the offeree either himself, or by means of some reliable person. (*Stevenson* v. *McLean*, 1880.)[94]

Before leaving the topic of options, it should be noted that the Law Commission in Working Paper No. 60 entitled 'Firm Offers' and published in 1975 criticized the present position under which a promise to keep an offer open will not be binding on the offeror unless consideration for the promise is given by the offeree (though of course this is not necessary where the option is made in a deed), on the grounds that it is contrary to business practice and also contrary to the law of most foreign countries. The Law Commission make a provisional recommendation that 'an offeror who has promised that he will not revoke his offer for a definite time should be bound by the terms of that promise provided that the promise has been made in the course of business'.

Revocation, to be effective, must be communicated to the offeree before he has accepted the offer. The word 'communication' merely implies that the revocation must have come to the knowledge of the offeree. (*Byrne* v. *Van Tienhoven*, 1880.)[108]

Presumably the offeree cannot ignore facts suggesting an attempt to communicate a revocation. If A offers B a car and before B accepts A posts a letter of revocation which B receives but, recognizing A's handwriting, does not open until he has written and posted a letter of acceptance, it would seem unfair to regard A as bound in contract and he would probably not be.

Communication may be made directly by the offeror or may reach the offeree through some other reliable source. Suppose X offers to sell a car to Y and gives Y a few days to think the matter over without actually giving him a valid option. If, before Y has accepted, X sells the car to Z and Y hears from P that X has in fact sold the car, it will be of no avail for Y to purport to accept and try to enforce the contract against X. (*Dickinson* v. *Dodds*, 1876.)[111]

Where the offer consists of a promise in return for an act, as where a reward is offered for the return of lost property, the offer, although made to the whole world, can be revoked as any other offer can. It is thought to be enough that the same publicity be given to the revocation as was given to the offer, even though the revocation may not be seen by all the persons who saw the offer.

A more difficult problem arises when an offer which requires a certain act to be carried out is revoked after some person has begun to perform the act but before he has completed it. If, for example, X offers £1000 to anyone who can successfully swim the Channel, and Y, deciding he will try to obtain the money, starts his swim from Dover, can X revoke his offer when Y is half-way across the Channel? One view is that he cannot on the grounds that an offer of the kind made by X is two offers in one, namely (i) to pay £1000 to a successful swimmer and (ii) something in the nature of an option to hold the offer open for a reasonable time once performance has been embarked upon, so that the person trying to complete the task has a reasonable time in which to do so.

Other lawyers reach the same conclusion by distinguishing between the acceptance of the offer and the consideration necessary to support it. As regards the latter, the completion of the act involved is necessary before the offeror can be required to pay any money because until the act is completed the necessary consideration has not been supplied. However, acceptance may be assumed as soon as the offeree has made a beginning on the performance of the contract and proof of the fact that he has made a beginning makes revocation impossible. The problem could have arisen in *Carlill's* case[67] if the company had tried to revoke its offer after Mrs. Carlill had started to perform the contract by using the Smokeball.

Lapse of time

If a time for acceptance has been stipulated, then the offer lapses when the time has expired. If no time has been stipulated, then the acceptance must be within a reasonable time. What is reasonable is determined by the court from the circumstances of the case. (*Ramsgate Victoria Hotel Co.* v. *Montefiore*, 1866,[112] *Manchester Diocesan Council for Education* v. *Commercial and General Investments Ltd*, 1969.)[101] However where the offer is made by telegram, it is likely to lapse very quickly.

Conditional offers

An offer may terminate on the happening of a given event if it is made subject to a condition that it will do so, e.g. that the offer is to terminate if the goods offered for sale are damaged before acceptance. Such a condition may be made expressly, but may also be implied from the circumstances. (*Financings Ltd,* v. *Stimson,* 1962.)[113]

Effect of death of a party

The effect of death would appear to vary according to the type of contract in question, whether the death is that of the offeror or offeree, and whether death takes place before or after acceptance.

(a) *Death of offeror before acceptance.* It would seem that if the contract envisaged by the offer is not one involving the personality of the offeror, the death of the offeror may not, until notified to the offeree, prevent acceptance. (*Bradbury* v. *Morgan,* 1862.)[114] However, there is a contrary point of view based on the judgment of Mellish, L. J. in *Dickinson* v. *Dodds,* 1876[111] where he said 'it is admitted law that, if a man who makes an offer dies, the offer cannot be accepted after he is dead . . . .'. If the contract envisaged by the offer does involve a personal relationship, such as an offer to act as agent, then the death of the offeror certainly prevents acceptance.

(b) Death of offeree before acceptance. Once the offeree is dead, there is no offer which can be accepted. His executors cannot, therefore, accept the offer in his stead. The offer being made to a living person can only be accepted by that person and assumes his continued existence. The rule would seem to apply *whether the proposed contract involves a personality relationship or not. (Re Cheshire Banking Co., Duff's Executors' Case,* 1886.)[115]

(c) Death of parties after acceptance. Death after acceptance has normally no effect unless the contract is for personal services, when the liability under the contract ceases. Thus, if X sells his car to Y and before the car is delivered X dies, it would be possible for Y to sue X's personal representatives for breach of contract if they were to refuse to deliver the car. But if X agrees to play the piano at a concert and dies two days before the performance, one could hardly expect his personal representatives to play the piano in his stead.

Collateral contracts

Before leaving the topic of offer and acceptance it should be noted that the courts may from time to time infer the existence of a contract from the words and acts of the parties in a situation where there has been *no offer and acceptance.* Such contracts are referred to as collateral contracts because they derive from another main contract, and for purposes of illustration reference should be made to *Clarke* v. *Dunraven,* 1897[116] where the main contract was with the yacht club, and *Rayfield* v. *Hands,* 1958[117] where the main contract was with the company through the memorandum and articles.

INTENTION TO CREATE LEGAL RELATIONS

The law will not necessarily recognize the existence of a contract simply because of the presence of mutual promises. Some agreements are not intended to be the subject of legal actions, and if the parties expressly declare, or clearly indicate in their agreement, that they do not intend to assume contractual obligations, then the law accepts and implements their intention. There are many promises made which are of such a nature that no reasonable person could imagine that there was any intention to create legal relations. If P invites Q to dinner, he does not also invite an action for damages if he fails to keep the appointment.

In deciding the question of intention the courts have regard to two main presumptions: (i) that domestic agreements are unenforceable without proof of intention to create legal relations and (ii) that commercial agreements are enforceable in the absence of clear proof that legal relations were not intended.

The subject can be considered under four headings—

(i) Cases where the parties have not expressly denied their intention to create legal relations

(a) Advertisements.   It is commonplace in business to advertise goods by making extravagant claims as to their efficacy, often supported by promises or guarantees of a vague character if the goods do not live up to expectations. The construction placed by the courts on such statements depends on the circumstances, but where a company deposits money in the bank against possible claims, then the court is likely to hold that legal relations were contemplated. (*Carlill* v. *Carbolic Smoke Ball Co.*, 1893.)[67] But not all advertisements are treated as serious offers, and advertising 'puffs' are often treated as mere sales talk; otherwise the courts would be perpetually passing judgment on the merits or demerits of a host of products. In addition, of course, advertisements are generally regarded as invitations to treat and not offers unless the advertment can result in a unilateral contract when it may be regarded as an offer. (See *Carlill's* case.)[67]

(b) Family agreements.   Many of these cannot be imagined to be the subject of litigation, but some may be. The question is basically one of construction, and the court looks at the words and the surrounding circumstances. With regard to agreements between husband and wife, it is difficult to draw precise conclusions from the decided cases. However, it seems that the courts will not enforce these agreements where—

   (i) the husband and wife were living together even though the relationship was strained when the agreement was made—on the ground perhaps that in the view of the court it would be unseemly and distressing to use legal proceedings for settling marital differences (*Balfour* v. *Balfour*, 1919,[118] and *Spellman* v. *Spellman*, 1961)[119]; however, where husband and wife were not living together when the agreement was made the court may enforce it. (*Merritt* v. *Merritt*, 1969);[120]

   (ii) the words used by the parties were uncertain—on the ground perhaps that uncertainty in deciding upon important terms of the agreement leads to the conclusion that there was no intention to create legal relations (*Gould* v. *Gould*, 1969).[121]

An agreement between husband and wife is much more likely to be enforced if it is clear and unequivocal. This might be achieved if the parties made an agreement supported by a simple note or memorandum setting out the terms and preferably prepared by a solicitor.

It should be noted that agreements of a non-domestic nature made between husband and wife may be enforceable, e.g. a husband may be his wife's tenant.

In family agreements other than those between husband and wife, the court will more readily reach the conclusion that legal relations can be inferred and the injured party may be given a remedy. (*Simpkins* v. *Pays,* 1955[122] and *Snelling* v. *John G. Snelling Ltd,* 1972.)[123] This is particularly true where one of the parties has altered his position to his detriment in reliance on the promises of the other (*Parker* v. *Clark,* 1960),[124] or where the family relationship has been destroyed by disagreements. (*Snelling* v. *John G. Snelling Ltd,* 1972.)[123] However, the terms must be certain otherwise the court will conclude that there was no contractual intent. (*Jones* v. *Padavatton,* 1969.)[125]

(iii) *Other cases.*   In other situations whether there is an intention to create legal relations must be deduced by the court from the circumstances of the case. (See, for example, *Peck* v. *Lateu,* 1973.)[126] However, in the case of clubs and societies, many of the relationships which exist and promises which are made are enforceable only as moral obligations. Thus, if a man competes for a prize in a local golf competition and is the winner, he may not be able to sue for the prize he has won if it is not otherwise forthcoming.

(ii) Cases where the parties expressly deny any intention to create legal relations

Some types of agreement, which would normally be the subject of a contract, are expressly taken outside the scope of the law by the parties' agreeing to rely on each other's honour. (*Jones* v. *Vernon's Pools Ltd,* 1938.)[127] In such cases there is a standardized agreement and the advantage of excluding legal action appears to be predominantly in favour of one of the parties. However, as the judges appear to recognize, the pools companies are particularly susceptible to fraud by those who would try to conceal late entries made after the games had finished and it is probably for this reason that the courts accept honour clauses which the pools companies can invoke where they suspect that an investor is fraudulent, rather than to go to court over the matter. It has been pleaded, but without success, that standardized agreements which exclude the possibility of legal redress are against public policy, and clearly if such procedures become widespread Parliament may have to intervene.

There is no such objection where business men reach agreements at arm's length, and if the parties expressly declare or clearly indicate that they do not wish to assume contractual obligations, then the law accepts and implements their decision, though the agreement is enforceable so far as it has been acted upon. (See *Rose and Frank Co.* v. *Crompton and Brothers Ltd,* 1925.)[128]

(iii) Statutory provisions

Sometimes an act of Parliament renders an agreement unenforceable. Thus under Sect. 1 of the Law Reform (Miscellaneous Provisions) Act, 1970, a contract of engagement which is, in effect, an agreement to marry, is not enforceable at law since there is a statutory presumption that there was no intention to create legal relations. Thus actions for breach of promise are no longer possible.

Furthermore, under the Post Office Act, 1969, the acceptance of letters and packets for transmission does not give rise to a contract between the Post Office and the sender (see p. 163).

Finally, under Sect. 18 of the Trade Union and Labour Relations Act, 1974, collective agreements between trade unions and employers (or employers' associations) concerning industrial conditions (hours, wages, holidays, procedures in disputes, and so on) are presumed *not* to be intended to be legally enforceable *unless* they are in writing and contain a provision to that effect.

CONSIDERATION

Definition and related matters.   Consideration, which is essential to the formation of any contract not made under seal, was defined in *Currie* v. *Misa,* (1875), L.R. 10 Ex 153 as—

> Some right, interest, profit or benefit accruing to the party, or some forbearance, detriment, loss or responsibility given, suffered or undertaken by the other.

Paying (or promising to pay) money in return for the supply of goods or services constitutes the most common form of consideration.

Consideration may be *executory,* where the parties exchange promises to perform acts in the future, e.g. C promises to deliver goods to D and D promises to pay for the goods; or it may be *executed,* where one party promises to do something in return for the act of another, rather than for the mere promise of future performance of an act. Here the performance of the act is required before there is any liability on the promise. Where X offers a reward for the return of his lost dog, X is buying the act of the finder, and will not be liable until the dog is found and returned.

The definition in *Currie* v. *Misa* suggests that consideration always refers to the type called executed consideration since it talks of 'benefit' and 'detriment', whereas in modern law executory contracts are enforceable. Perhaps the definition given by Sir Frederick Pollock is to be preferred—

An act of forbearance of one party, *or the promise thereof,* is the price for which *the promise* of the other is bought, and *the promise* thus given for value is enforceable.

This definition which was adopted by the House of Lords in *Dunlop* v. *Selfridge*, 1915,[129] fits executory consideration as well as executed.

CONSIDERATION IN RELATION TO FORMATION OF CONTRACT

There are a number of general rules governing consideration in terms of the *formation* of a contract—

(a) *Simple contracts must be supported by consideration.* This has a long history, and we can note only the following points.

Towards the end of the eighteenth century, Lord Mansfield attacked the doctrine of consideration in two ways. In *Pillans* v. *Van Mierop* (1765), 3 Burr. 1663, he said that where a contract was reduced to writing no consideration was necessary, thus reducing consideration to an aspect of evidence. It may be that this is why consideration is not necessary in a deed, for a deed is good evidence, being written and sealed, and entered into with due solemnity. In France and Scotland, gratuitous promises are enforced, but the court normally requires some good evidence, and often asks for writing. However, Lord Mansfield's attempt to dispense with consideration was shortlived, and his ruling was rejected in *Rann* v. *Hughes* (1778), 7 Term Rep. 350 n. Lord Mansfield also desired the recognition of pre-existing moral obligations as consideration, e.g. a promise to pay a statute-barred debt (see p. 265), or a promise after attaining majority to pay a debt contracted during infancy (see p. 203), but this view was finally rejected in *Eastwood* v. *Kenyon* (1840), 11 Ad. & El. 438. Some of these matters are now dealt with by statute, e.g. a written acknowledgment of a statute-barred debt is binding, even though not supported by consideration. (Limitation Act, 1939, Sect. 23.) Nevertheless, a promise to pay a debt incurred during minority is not enforceable. (Infants' Relief Act, 1874, Sect. 2.)

(b) *Consideration need not be adequate, but must have some value, however slight.* The courts do not exist to repair bad bargains, and though consideration must be present, the parties themselves must attend to its value. (*Thomas* v. *Thomas*, 1842[130] and *Mountford* v. *Scott*, 1974.)[453] However, where the consideration for a transaction is woefully inadequate, it may raise a suspicion of fraud, duress or undue influence on the part of the person gaining the advantage. However, what is offered by way of consideration must be capable of expression in terms of value. Thus a parent who makes a promise to induce his son to refrain from boring him with complaints cannot be sued upon it since the essential elements of a bargain are lacking. (*White* v. *Bluett*, 1853.)[131] That apart, acts or omissions even of a trivial nature may be sufficient to support a contract. (*Chappell* v. *Nestle*, 1959.)[132]

Although there were once arguments to the contrary, it is now accepted that forbearance to sue may be adequate consideration. It is not necessary to show that the action would have succeeded but merely that if it had been brought to trial it might have done (see *Horton* v. *Horton*, 1961).[133] Thus the court would be unlikely to accept that a bookmaker could supply consideration by forgoing a claim against a client for stake money. Such an action, being based on an illegal transaction, could have no hope of success.

A self-seeking act in itself may not suffice, and in the case of *Carlill* v. *Carbolic Smoke Ball Co.*, 1893,[67] the consideration was provided not by using the smoke ball to cure influenza, but by the unpleasant method of its use. A gift promised conditionally may be binding, if the performance of the condition causes the promisee trouble or inconvenience, e.g. 'I will give you my old car if you will tow it away.' So too may a gift of property with onerous obligations attached to it, e.g. a promise to give away a lease would be binding, if the donee promised to perform the covenants to repair and pay rent. A promise to give away shares which were partly paid up would be good, if the donee promised to pay the outstanding calls.

The concept of *bailment* gives rise to problems because a person may be held liable for negligent damage to or loss of goods in his care, although he received no money or other consideration for looking after them. (*Coggs* v. *Bernard*, 1703,[134] and *Gilchrist Watt and Sanderson Pty.* v. *York Products Pty.*, 1970.)[135] However, confusion can best be avoided by regarding bailment as an independent transaction, which has characteristics of contract and tort but is neither. It seems that when X hands his goods to Y under a bailment Y has certain duties in regard to the care of the goods, whether the bailment is accompanied by a contract or not.

(c) Consideration must be sufficient. Sufficiency of consideration is not the same thing as adequacy of consideration. The concept of sufficiency arises in the course of deciding whether the acts in question *amount to consideration at all*. This situation arises where the consideration offered by the promisor is an act which he is already bound to carry out. Thus, the discharge of a *public duty* imposed by law is not consideration. (*Collins* v.' *Godefroy*, 1831);[136] nor is the performance of a *contractual duty* already owed to the defendant (*Vanbergen* v. *St Edmund's Properties Ltd*, 1933;[137] *Stilk* v. *Myrick*, 1809).[138] However, where the contractual duty is not precisely coincident with the public duty but is in excess of it, performance of the contractual duty may provide consideration (*Glasbrook Bros Ltd* v. *Glamorgan County Council*, 1925[139] and *Ward* v. *Byham*, 1956)[140] and the actual performance of an outstanding contractual obligation may be sufficient to support a promise of a further payment by a third party. (*Shadwell* v. *Shadwell*, 1860.)[141]

(d) Consideration must be legal. An illegal consideration makes the whole contract invalid. (See further p. 238.)

(e) Consideration must not be past. Sometimes the act which one party to a contract puts forward as consideration was performed before any promise of reward was made by the other. Where this is so, the act in question may be regarded as *past consideration* and will not support a contractual claim. This somewhat technical rule seems to be based on the idea that the act of one party to an alleged contract can only be regarded as consideration if it was carried out in response to some promise of the other. Where this is not so, the act is regarded as gratuitous, being carried out before any promise of reward was made. (*Roscorla* v. *Thomas*, 1842,[142] and *Re McArdle*, 1951.)[143]

However, there are exceptions to this rule—

(i) Where services are rendered at the express or implied request of the promisor in circumstances which raise an implication of a promise to pay. (*Re Casey's Patents, Stewart* v. *Casey*, 1892.)[144] This exception is not entirely a genuine one since the promisor is assumed to have given an implied undertaking to pay at the time of the request, his subsequent promise being regarded as deciding merely *the actual amount to be paid*. In this situation the act, which follows the request but precedes the settling of the reward, is more in the nature of *executed consideration* which, as we have seen, will support a contract.

(ii) Where a debt is barred by the Limitation Act, 1939, since this can be revived by a subsequent acknowledgement in writing. Such an acknowledgement is effective if it indicates that a debt is due even if it does not state the amount. (*Dungate* v. *Dungate*, 1965.)[145] Again, this exception is not wholly genuine since the Limitation Act, 1939, does not provide that past consideration will support the subsequent acknowledgement of debt. The Act simply states that *no consideration of any kind* need be sought.

(iii) Section 27 of the Bills of Exchange Act, 1882, provides that past consideration will support a bill of exchange. (See p. 426.) This genuine exception was probably based on a pre-existing commercial custom.

(f) *Consideration must move from the promisee*, i.e. the person to whom the promise is made (the promisee) must give some consideration for it to the promisor. From this arises the doctrine of privity of contract which is considered below.

Privity of contract

This means that in general third parties cannot sue for the carrying out of promises made by the parties to a contract. Thus, if a contract between A and B requires B to benefit C, the privity rule prevents C from suing B. However, A may sue B if B breaks the contract, and the court may award C damages (*Jackson* v. *Horizon Holidays*, 1975)[146] or may grant a decree of specific performance under which B must perform the contract for the benefit of C. (*Beswick* v. *Beswick*, 1967.)[147] If A and C are, in fact, both parties to the contract with B then C still cannot sue B unless he has provided some consideration. Merely being a party to the contract is not enough. Even though C may be named in the document, if any, which records and constitutes the contract between A and B, or may be a party to their oral deliberations, if he does not undertake anything in return for a promise from A or indeed from B, then he is not participating in a bargain with A and/or B and is no party to the contract. This view is based upon the belief that the 'privity' rule is merely an aspect of the rule that 'consideration must move from the promisee'. The application of the rule is illustrated by *Tweddle* v. *Atkinson*, 1861,[148] *Dunlop* v. *Selfridge*, 1915,[129] and *Dunlop* v. *New Garage and Motor Co. Ltd*, 1915.[149]

However, there are cases in which a person is allowed to sue upon a contract to which he is not a party—

(*a*) A principal, even if undisclosed, may sue on a contract made by an agent. This exception is perhaps more apparent than real, because in fact the principal is the contracting party who has merely acted through the instrumentality of the agent.

(*b*) Attempts have been made to modify the rule of privity by invoking the equitable doctrine of the constructive trust. Thus, if A and B agree to confer a benefit on C, it may be possible to regard B as a constructive trustee for C of the benefit of the contract. C would then have an action against B if the latter had received the benefit and would not pass it on to C, or against A. However, if A were sued, B would be joined in the action. The application of this principle has always been uncertain and limited, and the courts do not seem eager to extend it. However, one aspect of this equitable doctrine has been established in the commercial world, and was recognized by the House of Lords in *Les Affréteurs Réunis Société Anonyme* v. *Walford,* 1919.[150]

(*c*) In other cases, where a fund is created in the hands of one of the contracting parties in favour of a third party, it may be possible to give the latter a remedy in quasi-contract on the grounds that to allow the contracting party to keep the fund would be to allow unjust enrichment. (*Shamia* v. *Joory*, 1958.)[151]

(*d*) The assignee of a debt or chose in action may, if the assignment is a legal assignment, sue the original debtor. (See p. 419.)

(*e*) The holder for value of a bill of exchange can sue prior parties and the acceptor. (See p. 426.)

(*f*) Under the Resale Prices Act, 1976, Sect. 26, the supplier of goods is given a statutory cause of action, so that he may enforce against a person not a party to the contract of sale a condition as to re-sale price. However, the re-sale price agreement must have been approved under the provisions of the Resale Prices Act, 1976, otherwise there can be no enforcement of it. (See p. 250.) Books are one of the few items approved for this purpose. (See *Net Book Agreement,* 1957, [1962] 3 All E.R. 751.)

(*g*) Certain other exceptions are to be found in statute, e.g. Sect. 11 of the Married Women's Property Act, 1882, provides that if a man insures his life for the benefit of his wife and/or children, or a woman insures her life for the benefit of her husband and/or children, a trust is created in favour of the objects of the policy, who, although they are not parties to the contract with the insurance company, can sue upon it. In addition the policy moneys are not liable for the deceased's debts. However, since a trust arises under the policy Capital Transfer Tax is payable according to the rules relating to trusts. Thus Capital Transfer Tax would be payable on the distribution of the policy monies to children but not on a distribution to a wife/husband.

(*h*) The position in land law is that benefits and liabilities attached to of imposed on land may in certain circumstances follow the land into the hands of other owners. (*Smith and Snipes Hall Farm* v. *River Douglas Catchment Board,* 1949,[152] and *Tulk* v. *Moxhay,* 1848.)[153]

(*i*) Bankers' Commercial Credits also present problems in the field or privity. It is common commercial practice for an exporter, E, to ask the buyer of the goods, B, to open, with his banker, a credit in favour of E, the credit to remain irrevocable for a specified time. B agrees with his banker that the credit should be opened and, in return, promises to repay the banker, and usually gives him a lien over the shipping documents. The banker will also require a commission for his services. B's banker then notifies E that a credit has been opened in his favour, and E can draw upon it on presentation of the shipping documents.

However, if B's banker refuses to pay E on presentation of the documents, E could sue B on the original contract of sale, but would be unable to sue B's banker if the rule of privity were applied. The credit arises out of an agreement between B and his banker, and E is a stranger to it.

However, if an exporter had to sue the buyer's banker on a commercial credit the court would allow the action as an exception to the rule of privity on the grounds that a commercial practice in favour of third party rights exists. (See *Malas* (*Hamzeh*) v. *British Imex,* [1958] 1 All E.R. 262.) There are also similar developments in the field of performance bonds. These are illustrated by *Edward Owen Engineering Ltd* v. *Barclays Bank International Ltd,* 1977.[154]

(*j*) Attempts have also been made to modify the rule of privity by an *appropriate interpretation of Section* 56(1) *of the Law of Property Act,* 1925.

The subsection provides that 'a person may take an immediate or other interest in land or other property, or the benefit of any condition, right of entry, covenant or agreement over or respecting land or other property, although he may not be named as a party to the conveyance or other instrument.'

Section 205(1) of the 1925 Act provides that 'unless the context otherwise requires, the following expressions have the meanings hereby assigned to them . . . (xx) 'property' includes any thing in action and any interest in real or personal property.'

Section 56(1) certainly applies to provisions in covenants concerning land. Thus, if X derives his title to real property under a conveyance of, say, 1977, he can enforce a restrictive covenant regarding the use of the land made in an earlier conveyance between other parties. However, some judges, including Lord Denning, have been of the opinion that the word 'property' in Section 56(1) should be interpreted as covering all things in action, even contractual rights in a contract not concerned with land. This interpretation would open the door to claims formerly barred by the rule of privity, and would do away with the rule in *Tweddle* v. *Atkinson*, 1861,[148] and similar cases.

The matter came before the House of Lords in *Beswick* v. *Beswick*, 1967,[147] and their Lordships could not accept the wider interpretation of Section 56(1) advocated by Lord Denning and others in previous cases, but regarded the subsection as being limited to cases concerning real property.

(*k*) As a result of the decision in *Snelling* v. *John G. Snelling Ltd*, 1972[123] it would appear that if A makes a contract with B for the benefit of C, as where C is A's employee and A has included an exemption clause in a contract with B which excludes the liability of A and C, then if there is an action between B and C, say, for C's negligence, C will not be able to claim the benefit of the contract as such by way of defence but A can apply for an injunction to prevent the action between B and C coming to trial, or if it has come to trial, apply for a stay of proceedings under Sect. 41 of the Supreme Court of Judicature (Consolidation) Act, 1925. In either case if all parties are before the court and B's case would, if pursued, fail, then the court may dismiss the claim and not merely stop the action.

CONSIDERATION VIEWED IN RELATION TO THE DISCHARGE OF A CONTRACT

All that has so far been said in regard to consideration relates to the *formation* of a contract. As we have seen there must be offer, acceptance, consideration and intention to create legal relations in order to bring a contract into existence. The rules are rather different where a contract is to be *discharged*. There are a number of ways in which a contract may be discharged, all of which will be dealt with later. However, the one with which we are now concerned is *discharge by agreement* under which contract A is to be discharged by a new contract, B, the question being to what extent does contract B require consideration? The attitude of the common law is different from that of equity, as we shall see.

Common law—the doctrine of accord and satisfaction

At common law if A owes B £10 and wishes to discharge that obligation by paying B £9 he must—

(i) obtain the agreement (accord) of B; and

(ii) provide B with some consideration (satisfaction) for giving up his right to £10 unless the release is under seal.

This is the common law doctrine of accord and satisfaction. The doctrine is an ancient one and an early example of it is to be found in the judgment of Brian, C.J. in *Pinnel's Case*, (1602), 5 Co. Rep., 117a. Pinnel sued Cole in debt for what would now be £8.50 which was due on a bond on 11 November 1600. Cole's defence was that at Pinnel's request he had paid him £5.12½ on 1 October and that Pinnel had accepted this payment in full satisfaction of the original debt. Although the court found for Pinnel on a technical point of pleading, it was said that—

(*a*) payment of a lesser sum on the due day in satisfaction of a greater sum cannot be any satisfaction for the whole; but

(*b*) payment of a smaller sum at the creditor's request before the due day is good consideration for a promise to forego the balance for it is a benefit to the creditor to be paid before he was entitled to payment and a corresponding detriment to the debtor to pay early.

The first branch of the rule in *Pinnel's Case* was much critized but was approved by the House of Lords in *Foakes* v. *Beer,* 1884[155] and the doctrine then hardened because of the system of binding precedent. However, the practical effect of the rule is considerably reduced under common law by the following—

(i) Where there is a dispute as to the sum owed. If the creditor accepts less than he thinks is owed to him the debt will be discharged.

(ii) Where the creditor agrees to take something different in kind, e.g. a chattel, the debt is discharged by substituted performance. Thus, if A gives B a watch worth £5 and B is agreeable to taking it, then the debt of £10 will be discharged. In this connection it should be noted that a cheque for a smaller sum no longer constitutes substituted performance. (*D. & C. Builders Ltd* v. *Rees*, 1965.)[156]

(iii) The payment of a smaller sum before the larger is due gives the debtor a good discharge. This is the second branch of the rule in *Pinnel's Case.*

(iv) If a debtor makes an arrangement with his creditors to compound his debts, e.g. by paying them 85p. in the £1, he is satisfying a debt for a larger sum by the payment of a smaller sum. Nevertheless, it is a good discharge, the consideration being the agreement by the creditors with each other and with the debtor not to insist on their full rights. (*Good* v. *Cheesman*, 1831.)[157]

(v) Payment of a smaller sum by a third party operates as a good discharge. (*Welby* v. *Drake*, 1825.)[158]

It should be noted that the situations outlined in (iv) and (v) above are based not so much on the law of Contract but in Tort in the sense that once an agreement of this kind has been made it would be a fraud on the other creditors for one of their number to sue the debtor separately and equally on the third party, should the creditor return again to sue the original debtor.

Equity—the doctrine of promissory estoppel

There has always been some dissatisfaction with the common law rule of accord and satisfaction. After all, if A owes B £10 and B agrees to take £9, as he must before there can be any question of discharging the obligation of A to pay £10, why should B be allowed afterwards to break his promise to take £9 and succeed in an action against A simply because A gave him no consideration?

It was to deal with this sort of situation that the equitable doctrine of promissory estoppel was propounded, first by Lord Cairns in *Hughes* v. *Metropolitan Railway,* (1877), 2 App. Cas. 439 and later by Denning, J. (as he then was) in the *High Trees Case*, 1947[159] and later by the House of Lords in *Tool Metal Manufacturing Co. Ltd* v. *Tungsten Electric Co. Ltd,* 1955.[160]

The doctrine of estoppel is basically a rule of evidence under which the court, suprisingly enough, is not prepared to listen to the truth.

It occurs at common law out of physical conduct. Suppose A and B go into a wholesaler's premises and A asks for goods on credit. The wholesaler, who knows that B is credit-worthy, but has no knowledge of A, is not prepared to give credit until A says 'do not worry, you will be paid, B is my partner.' If B says nothing and A receives the goods on credit and does not pay, then B could be sued for the price, even though he can produce evidence that he was not in fact A' s partner. This evidence will not be admitted because the wholesaler relied on a situation of partnership created by B's conduct.

Promissory estoppel in equity is very little different except that the estoppel arises from a *promise,* not *conduct.* The common law does not recognize an estoppel arising out of a promise.

As a result of the above decisions and others (as indicated below) the doctrine of promissory estoppel has the following ingredients—

(*a*) It arises from a promise made with the intention that it should acted upon.

(*b*) It was once thought that the person who had received the promise must do something to show that he had relied on it. If A, a landlord, said B could pay only half his usual rent while he was unemployed, it was thought that B would have to show, for example, that he had spent what should have been the rent money on travelling expenses to find work in the district. (See *Ajayi* v. *Briscoe (Nigeria) Ltd,* 1964.)[161] Reliance upon the promise in this way is not, it would appear, a necessary requirement. (*Alan* v. *El Nasr,* 1972.)[162]

(*c*) It relates only to variation or discharge of contract by agreement and does not affect the requirement of consideration on formation of contract. (*Combe* v. *Combe,* 1951.)[163]

(*d*) So far as the rule has been developed in cases, it merely *suspends* rights but does not totally preclude enforcement of the original contract after reasonable notice has been given. (*Tool Metal Manufacturing Co. Ltd.* v. *Tungsten Electric Co. Ltd,* 1955.)[160]

(*e*) The promise must be freely given and not extorted by threats. (*D. & C. Builders Ltd* v. *Rees,* 1965.)[156]

(*f*) Of considerable importance is a *dictum* by Lord Denning in *D. & C. Builders* v. *Rees,* 1965[156] that the rule could be developed to the point at which it operated, not merely to suspend rights, but to preclude enforcement of them. If this point is reached, then if A owes B £10 and B agrees to take £9, A will be discharged from his obligation to pay £10 without the need for consideration.

Such a situation would involve a virtual over-ruling of *Foakes* v. *Beer,* 1884[155] and would put an end to the first branch of the rule in *Pinnel's Case* which is that payment of a lesser sum on the due day in satisfaction of a greater sum cannot be any satisfaction for the whole. Although in the past a number of *dicta* by Lord Denning have been incorporated into the *ratio* of subsequent decisions, the position outlined in (*f*) above has not as yet been reached.

The rule of equitable estoppel has relevance in discharge of a contract by performance. (See p. 257.) Although the agreed date of delivery must usually be complied with in a contract of sale, the buyer may waive the condition relating to the date of delivery and accept a later date. Such a waiver may be binding on him whether made with or without consideration. It was held by Lord Denning in *Charles Rickards Ltd* v. *Oppenheim,* 1950[393] that the binding nature of a waiver without consideration might be based on the *High Trees Case*[159] (i.e. a promissory estoppel to accept a later delivery date). Alternatively, the seller may rely on Sect. 11(1)(*a*) of the Sale of Goods Act, 1893, which states: 'Where a contract of sale is subject to any condition to be fulfilled by the seller, the buyer may waive that condition.'

Equitable estoppel—other applications

The principle of equity on which promissory estoppel is based is one of general application and may be applied whenever the court feels it is necessary in the interests of justice to do so. For examples of its use in situations not concerned with discharge of contract see *Durham Fancy Goods* v. *Michael Jackson* (*Fancy Goods*) *Ltd*, 1968[164] and *Crabb* v. *Arun District Council,* 1975.[165]

FORMALITIES

We have already discussed the main differences between contracts under seal and simple or 'parol' contracts. In most cases, it does not matter which of the various forms of simple contract is used and a contract made orally or by conduct will usually be just as effective as a written one. Exceptionally, however, written formalities are required.

Contracts which must be made by Deed

A lease of more than three years should be made by deed otherwise no legal estate is created. There is, however, an equitable interest in the land but unfortunately this could be ignored by a person who purchased the freehold for value from the landlord and without notice of the lease.

However, it is possible to register the equitable interest at the Land Registry and where this has been done all purchasers of a freehold are deemed to have notice. Thus where the equitable interest is registered, the practical effect of not having a deed is not serious.

Contracts which must be in writing

The following simple contracts are required by statute to be in writing otherwise they are *void*—
  (a) cheques, other bills of exchange and promissory notes (see p. 423);
  (b) contracts of marine insurance (Marine Insurance Act, 1906, Sect. 22);
  (c) acknowledgments of statute-barred debts (see p. 265).

Consumer credit transactions, including hire-purchase and money-lending, must be in writing and properly executed. Where this is not so the agreement is *unenforceable* against the debtor or the hirer except on an order of the court. (Consumer Credit Act, 1974, Sects 61 and 189(4).)

Contracts which must be evidenced in writing

In two cases writing, though not essential to the formation of a contract, is needed for evidential purposes, and in its absence the courts will not enforce the agreement. These two special cases are—

  (i) contracts of guarantee, and
  (ii) contracts for the sale or other disposition of land or any interest in land.

The Statute of Frauds, 1677, originally set out six classes of contracts which required this evidential writing. The provision concerning land was embodied in Sect. 40 of the Law of Property Act, 1925, as part of the consolidation of the law of property. The provision regarding guarantees remained after the Statute of Frauds was largely repealed by the Law Reform (Enforcement of Contracts) Act, 1954, which, having served its purpose, was itself repeated by the Statute Law (Repeals) Act, 1974.

Even in these cases the writing need not be in the form of a contract, but may be the exchange of letters or other memoranda; and where one party has partly performed his side of the contract, the courts may dispense with the need for written evidence. Further, the absence of a memorandum must be specially pleaded by the party seeking to rely on its absence, otherwise the court will hear oral evidence to prove the contract.

These rules apply to contracts of guarantee but they do not apply to contracts of indemnity. It is necessary, therefore, to distinguish between these two. In a contract of indemnity, the person giving the indemnity makes himself primarily liable by using such words as, 'I will see that you are paid.' In a contract of guarantee, the guarantor expects the person he has guaranteed to carry out his obligations, and the substance of the wording would be, 'If he does not pay you, I will.' An indemnity does not require writing because it did not come within the Statute of Frauds; a guarantee requires a memorandum. (*Mountstephen* v. *Lakeman*, 1871.)[166]

In this connection it should be noted that it is an essential feature of a guarantee that the person giving it is totally unconnected with the contract he guarantees except by reason of his promise to pay the debt. Thus, a *del credere* agent who for an extra commission promises to make good losses incurred by his principal in respect of the unpaid debts of third parties introduced by the agent, gives an indemnity and not a guarantee because his undertaking to reimburse his principal is part of a wider transaction, i.e. agency.

Difficulties have arisen in the application of the provisions concerning land in cases dealing with the sale of crops. A distinction must be made between *fructus naturales* (natural products of the soil, or the products of things which do not have to be sown each year) and *fructus industriales* (crops produced annually by man). Thus, an agreement to sell growing timber or grass must be evidenced in writing, but an agreement to sell growing potatoes need not be. (*Parker* v. *Staniland* (1809), 11 East, 362.) However, if the *fructus naturales* are to be cut at once by either party and therefore *no further benefit is to be derived from the soil* the contract is regarded as one for the sale of goods and no memorandum is required. (*Marshall* v. *Green* (1875), 1 C.P.D., 35.)

The memorandum.

The memorandum in writing, to satisfy the courts in the two cases where it is now required, need not be made when the contract is made, but must exist before the action is brought. There are four requirements—

(i) *It must contain the names or a sufficient description of the parties.*   It must state which is the buyer and which is the seller, and it is not sufficient to call the seller the vendor, since the court wishes to ascertain the owner and not the person who purports to sell. It is sufficient if they are described so as to be capable of identification, even if this involves the admission of some oral evidence (*Carr* v. *Lynch*, 1900)[167] and the fact that one of the parties is misnamed will not prevent the contract being enforced if he can be identified by reference to characteristics other than his name. (*F. Goldsmith (Sicklesmere) Ltd* v. *Baxter*, 1969.)[168]

(ii) *The subject matter of the contract must be described so that it can be identified, and all the material terms of the contract must be stated.*   However, the subject matter may be sufficiently described without going into great detail, e.g. a memorandum recording the sale of '24 acres of land at Totmanslow', was held sufficient on proof that the seller had no other land there. (*Plant* v. *Bourne* [1897], 2 Ch. 281.) The absence of a material term may make the memorandum ineffective (*Tweddell* v. *Henderson*, 1975),[169] though not if it is beneficial to only one party and the other party agrees to carry it out or the party to benefit agrees to waive it. (*Hawkins* v. *Price*, 1947,[170] and *Scott* v. *Bradley*, 1971.)[171]

(iii) The consideration must appear, except in contracts of guarantee. In the latter case Sect. 3 of the Mercantile Law Amendment Act, 1856, dispenses with the necessity for setting out the consideration, but it must exist. The consideration for a guarantee is usually the extension of credit. It follows that the guarantee must be given before the credit was extended, otherwise it is for past consideration, and is unenforceable unless made under seal.

(iv) The memorandum must contain the signature of the party to be charged or his agent properly authorized to sign. This means in effect that there may be cases where one party has a sufficient memorandum to found an action, whereas the other may lack the necessary signature. The rule is made less rigid by a somewhat free interpretation of the word signature, and it may take any form so long as it was intended to be a signature. (*Caton* v. *Caton*, 1867.)[172] It may be printed, typed, or stamped, and mere initials or an identifying mark will suffice. It need not be at the end of the document, but may be in the middle or at the beginning. In the case of an auction sale, the auctioneer or his clerk signs for both buyer and seller.

(v) The memorandum must not be made 'subject to contract'. It was at one time thought that a memorandum was not defective merely because it contained the words 'subject to contract' provided that there was evidence to show that the parties had waived the provision. (*Griffiths* v. *Young*, 1970[173] and *Law* v. *Jones*, [1973] 2 All E.R. 437.) However, in *Tiverton Estates* v. *Wearwell Ltd*, 1974[51] it was held that this was not so. As a result of this case it would now appear that any writing which denies that there was any contract; does not admit that there was any contract; says that the parties are in negotiation; or says that there was an agreement 'subject to contract' does not satisfy Sect. 40 of the Law of Property Act, 1925, because none of them contains any recognition or admission of the existence of a contract.

The rigidity of these rules is mitigated by the fact that the memorandum need not be a single document, but may consist of a number of connected documents. Oral evidence will be admitted to connect them if (*a*) one refers to the other; or (*b*) the documents are *prima facie* connected, since in the latter case proof of connection in not entirely oral. (*Pearce* v. *Gardner*, 1897,[174] and *Timmins* v. *Moreland Street Property Ltd*, 1958.)[175] In addition, an interesting development is contained in the decision in *Hardy* v. *Elphick*, 1973[176] in regard to the possibility of statements made in pleadings (see p. 63) being acceptable as part of a written memorandum for the purposes of Sect. 40 of the Law of Property Act, 1925.

Effect of Absence of Memorandum

In the absence of a memorandum the contract is not void at common law but is unenforceable, although it may sometimes be relied upon as a defence. Thus, if X orally agrees to let Y dig for gravel on X's land, Y would not commit a trespass if he entered on the land to dig. If, however, X asks him to leave and Y refuses, then he may become a trespasser in spite of the contract, since it was at best a licence which has now been withdrawn. It follows that if the contract is not void, money paid or property transferred under it cannot be recovered, unless there is a total lack of consideration. (*Monnickendam* v. *Leanse*, 1923.)[177]

Although the common law requires a written memorandum, there may still be equitable remedies, and equity will grant specific performance in suitable cases where the plaintiff has partly performed his agreement. This remedy is particularly appropriate in contracts for the sale or other disposition of land. The basis of this equitable jurisdiction probably stems from the maxim: 'Equity will not allow a statute to be used as an engine of fraud.'

The following conditions must exist before the doctrine can operate—

(a) The contract must be one of which specific performance will be granted. Specific performance is a discretionary remedy and it follows that; 'He who comes to Equity must come with clean hands.' It will not be granted where the court thinks damages are an adequate remedy, and never in the case of contracts with minors. (See p. 202.) This seems in the context of written memoranda to confine the remedy to contracts concerning land, because Equity will not specifically enforce a guarantee.

(b) Relationship of the act(s) of part performance to the alleged contract. In *Chaproniere* v. *Lambert*, [1917] 2 Ch. 356, Warrington, L.J., laid down in the Court of Appeal the doctrine that the acts of part performance relied on must be not only referable to a contract such as that alleged but referable to no other, and this rule was applied in some subsequent cases. Thus in *Rawlinson* v. *Ames*, 1925[178] and *Broughton* v. *Snook*, 1938[179] we find the court requiring acts of part performance which are unequivocal to a high degree. However, strict adherence to this doctrine could produce hardship and in some circumstances run contrary to the overriding principle that a Court of Equity will not allow a statute to be used as an engine of fraud, i.e. if the party seeking to enforce the contract can show that on the faith of that contract and in performance of his obligations under it, he has so altered his position that unless the other party is bound by it there will be an injustice of a kind which the statute cannot be thought to have had in contemplation. (*Daniels* v. *Trefusis*, 1914.)[180]

Accordingly, in *Kingswood Estate Co. Ltd* v. *Anderson*, [1962] 3 All E.R. 593, the Court of Appeal refused to follow *Chaproniere* v. *Lambert* and stated that the plaintiff's part performance need not be unequivocally or exclusively referable to the contract alleged. It was sufficient if it proved the existence of some contract and was consistent with the contract which the plaintiff claimed existed. This principle was applied by Stamp, J., in *Wakeham* v. *Mackenzie*, 1968[181] and by the Court of Appeal in *Steadman* v. *Steadman*, 1973.[182]

However, acts of part performance may still be ineffective if they are explainable on grounds other than the existence of a contract. (*Maddison* v. *Alderson*, 1883[183] and *Re Gonin (deceased)*, 1977.)[184]

(c) There must be adequate oral evidence of the terms of the contract, and the act of part performance must be the act of the plaintiff.   It is said that a mere payment of money is not a sufficient act of part performance, because money has no exclusive nature; such a payment raises no equity except the right to recover the money. This is certainly true of the payment of purchase money in a sale of land. In other situations a payment of money may be enough (see *Steadman* v. *Steadman,* 1973).[182] Occupation of property is usually considered a sufficient act of part performance.

CAPACITY TO CONTRACT

Adult citizens have full capacity to enter into any kind of contract, but certain groups of persons, and corporations or unincorporated groups, have certain disabilities in this connection.

Aliens

They normally have full capacity to contract, but they cannot acquire property in a British ship (Merchant Shipping Act, 1894, Sect. 1), save as a member of a limited liability company if the company itself is British. However, contracts with *enemy aliens* during the period of hostilities are illegal and void. The term 'enemy alien' includes not only aliens, but British subjects voluntarily resident or carrying on business in the enemy's country or in a country occupied or controlled by the enemy. The test is not nationality, but the place where the person resides or carries on business.

An enemy alien who is in England during the period of hostilities *may be sued* in the English courts but he cannot himself *bring an action* in those courts. (*Porter* v. *Freudenberg,* [1951] 1 K.B. 857.) However, an enemy alien present in England by licence of the Crown, as where he is registered under relevant legislation such as the Aliens Restriction Acts, may sue and be sued in the English courts and may make valid contracts even during hostilities.

Contracts made during peace with persons who later become enemy aliens by reason of outbreak of war and which require continuous business relations or are prejudicial to this country, e.g. armaments contracts, are treated as follows—

(a) The contract gives no rights after the oubreak of war.   It is thus cut short and enforcement of the contract will relate only the part which was *executed* before the war, the *executory* rights and duties being cancelled. Thus, if A and B enter into a contract under which A charters a ship from B for ten years, then if after two years B becomes an enemy alien, the contract will be cut in effect to two years and the parties released from all obligations arising under the charter after the outbreak of war. This is so even though hostilities may cease before the eight years remaining under the charter have elapsed.

(b) The rights and duties outstanding in respect of performance before the

outbreak of war are not destroyed though they cannot be enforced until hostilities cease. Thus a debt due under a contract before the outbreak of war would survive the hostilities and be enforceable on the return of peace. (*Arab Bank Ltd,* v. *Barclays Bank,* [1954] A.C. 495.) Where the contract does not involve commercial intercourse with the enemy alien or prejudice to this country, the rights and duties are merely suspended and not destroyed. Thus, in a separation agreement made between husband and wife before the outbreak of hostilities the husband would be liable after the war to pay to the wife sums falling due by way of maintenance during the period of hostilities even though the wife became an enemy alien for that period. (*Bevan* v. *Bevan,* [1955] 2 Q. B. 227.)

Foreign sovereigns and diplomats are in a privileged position, since they cannot be sued at civil law or prosecuted in this country unless they submit to the jurisdiction of our courts. (*Mighell* v. *Sultan of Johore,* 1894.)[184]

The law relating to the privileges and immunities of diplomatic representatives in the United Kingdom is now laid down by the Diplomatic Privileges Act, 1964.

The Act gives effect to most of the provisions of the Vienna Convention of Diplomatic Relations, 1961, and replaces the Diplomatic Privileges Act, 1708. The Act divides the members of a diplomatic mission into three classes—

(*a*) Members of the diplomatic staff who have full personal immunity, civil and criminal, with three exceptions where they can be sued;

(i) a real action relating to private immovable property situated in the territory of the receiving State, unless the diplomatic agent holds it on behalf of the sending State for the purposes of the mission;

(ii) an action relating to succession in which the diplomatic agent is involved as an executor, administrator, heir or legatee as a private person and not on behalf of the sending State;

(iii) an action relating to any professional or commercial activity exercised by the diplomatic agent in the receiving State outside his official functions.

(*b*) Members of the administrative and technical staff, who enjoy full immunity for official acts, but who are liable civilly, though not criminally, for acts performed outside the course of their duties.

(*c*) Members of the service staff, who enjoy immunity for official acts, but are liable civilly and criminally for acts performed outside the course of their duties.

It follows from the above provisions of the Act that the courts have power to determine whether an act committed by a member of a diplomatic mission was performed in the course of his duties.

Privileges and immunities may be withdrawn by Her Majesty by Order in Council from any State granting fewer privileges and immunities to British missions. The certificate of the Foreign Secretary is conclusive as to the entitlement of a person to any privilege or immunity, though as we have seen, the courts have the power to decide whether the act was performed in the course of his duties.

The privileges and immunities set out in the Diplomatic Privileges Act, 1964, are extended to the following persons among others—

(i) The chief representatives of the Republic of Ireland and Commonwealth countries, e.g. High Commissioners, their staffs, families and servants (Diplomatic and other Privileges Act, 1971).

(ii) Persons concerned with International Organizations of appropriate status, immunity being derived from the International Organizations Act, 1968. Such organizations are defined from time to time by Orders in Council made in pursuance of the Act, and include such bodies as the United Nations Organization and the International Court of Justice.

Immunity is not normally conferred on persons of quasi-diplomatic character, such as consular officials, but an exception may be made where the diplomatic and consular functions are carried out by the same person. However, some immunities, e.g. in respect of rates and taxes, are given to consular officers by orders made under the Consular Relations Act, 1968, and Diplomatic and other Privileges Act, 1971, Sect. 4.

Diplomatic privilege may be waived, though in the case of an ambassador or other head of a mission, waiver must be with the consent of his Sovereign. In other cases waiver must be by the head of the mission.

It should be noted that a foreign state's unilateral action in appointing a diplomatic agent does not confer immunity on him. Until this country has accepted and received him, i.e. until he has been officially accredited to the Court of St. James, he is not immune from proceedings in the English courts. (*R. v. Pentonville Prison Governor, ex parte Teja*, [1971] 2 W.L.R. 816.) Foreign state corporations may also be immune from suit in the English courts (*Mellenger v. New Brunswick Development Corporation*, [1971] 1 W.L.R. 604) though not in commercial transactions as is generally recognized by international law. Thus in *Trendex Trading Corpn v. Central Bank of Nigeria*, [1977] 2 W.L.R. 356 the Court of Appeal held that the Central Bank of Nigeria (created by statute and modelled upon the Bank of England) could not plead immunity in respect of an irrevocable letter of credit given to the plaintiffs since it was not regarded by Lord Denning, M.R. and Shaw, L.J. as a part of the State of Nigeria and in any event (per Stephenson, L.J.) sovereign immunity should not apply to commercial transactions. Private corporations, e.g. an independent bank, are not immune. (*Swiss-Israel Trade Bank v. Government of Salta*, [1972] 1 Lloyd's Rep. 514.)[497]

Furthermore, the trend of the modern law is against absolute sovereign state immunity. It is allowed as regards actions *in personam* (against the person) for money, i.e. debt or damages, but not where the action is *in rem* (against a thing). Thus in *The Philippine Admiral*, [1976] 1 All E.R. 78 repairers of a ship belonging to the Republic of the Philippines who had not been paid wished to impound the ship. The Privy Council decided that they could do so and that sovereign state immunity pleaded by the Republic of the Philippines did not apply because the action was *in rem* and not *in personam* and set in a commercial context.

Minors

The Family Law Reform Act, 1969, Sect. 1(1) reduces the age of majority from 21 to 18 years. This provision operates from 1 January, 1970. There is also a provision in the Act which states that a person attains a particular age, i.e. not merely the age of majority, at the first moment of the relevant birthday, though this rule is subject to any contrary provision in any instrument (i.e. a deed) or statute. (Sect. 9.) However, the common law rule that the age is attained at the first moment of the day preceding the birthday is at least repealed.

Section 1(2) provides that the age of 18 is to be substituted for 21 wherever there is a reference to 'full age', 'infant', 'infancy', 'minor', 'minority' in—

(*a*) any statutory provision made *before or after* 1 January, 1970;

(*b*) any deed, will or other instrument made *on or after* that date.

This subsection draws a distinction between *statutory provisions* and *private dispositions*. In the case of the former the new age of 18 is substituted. Thus, in the Infants' Relief Act, 1874, references to 'infants' will be construed as applying to persons under 18 years of age. However, in the case of private dispositions such as deeds, wills and settlements the Act does not apply retrospectively. Accordingly, if in a deed made before 1 January, 1970, a person X is to take property 'on attaining his majority', he will take at age 21 years. If the deed was made on or after 1 January, 1970, he would take at 18 years. The reason for this rule is that where persons in the past have arranged their affairs in reliance on the law as it stood, it would be unjust to interfere.

With regard to procedure, a minor sues through a 'next friend', i.e. an adult who is liable for the costs (if any) awarded against the minor in the action, though the minor must indemnify him. A minor defends an action through a 'guardian *ad litem*', who is not liable for costs. It should be noted that a parent is not liable for his child's debts unless the child is an agent of the parent in respect of the transaction concerned. (*Mortimer* v. *Wright* (1860), 6 M. & W. 482.)

A minor's contracts may be void, valid, voidable or unenforceable.

Void contracts.   These are as follows—

(a) *Those under the Infants' Relief Act, 1874, Sect. 1—*

(i) Contracts for the repayment of money lent or to be lent. (*Coutts & Co.* v. *Browne-Lecky,* 1947.)[185]

(ii) Contracts for goods supplied, or to be supplied, other than necessaries.

(iii) All accounts stated with minors, e.g. I.O.U.'s, and other statements of indebtedness.

(b) Those under the Betting and Loans (Infants) Act, 1892. This Act renders void any agreement made by a person after he comes of age to pay a loan contracted during minority.

A minor cannot be held liable on a bill of exchange (e.g. a cheque) even though given in payment of a debt incurred for necessaries supplied and delivered. (Bills of Exchange Act, 1882, Sect. 22.) So far as the actual supplier is concerned there would be an action in quasi-contract on the consideration, i.e. for a reasonable price, not necessarily the contract price, but third parties, to whom the bill had been negotiated, would have no claim whatever on the minor.

It appears that despite the use of the words 'absolutely void' in Sect. 1 of the Infants' Relief Act, 1874, a minor can sue on the void contract, except as against another minor, because an adult party cannot use the other's minority as a defence to an action.

This would not seem to apply to equitable remedies such as specific performance because equity requires mutuality as regards remedies. (See further p. 276.) Furthermore, it will be seen that the minor cannot recover money paid or goods transferred under a void contract unless there has been total failure of consideration. In addition, the minor seems to obtain property in the goods and can give a good title to third parties.

Valid contracts.   These are as follows—

(a) Executed contracts for necessaries.   Necessaries are defined in the Sale of Goods Act, 1893, Sect. 2, as 'goods suitable to the condition in life of the infant and to his actual requirements at the time of sale and delivery'.

If the goods are deemed necessaries, the minor may be compelled to pay a reasonable price which is not necessarily the contract price. The minor is not liable if the goods, though necessaries, have not been delivered. This illustrates that a minor's liability for necessaries is only quasi-contractual.

The general test of necessaries is that of utility, and in this connection the minor's condition of life, together with the supply of such goods which he already has, becomes relevant. (*Nash* v. *Inman,* 1908.)[186] Thus food, clothes, lodging and the like are obviously necessary; but educational books, medical attention, burial of the minor's wife or children, and legal advice, and in some cases even articles of apparent luxury are classed as necessaries. (*Elkington* v. *Amery,* 1936.)[187] Necessaries for a married minor's family are judged by the same standards as necessaries for himself. The rule regarding necessaries applies not merely to the purchase of goods but also to necessary services. Thus a contract to hire a car may be a necessary contract for a salesman who is a minor.

(b) Contracts for the minor's benefit.   A minor may make valid contracts if they are for his benefit, but these have generally been contracts of

apprenticeship, contracts of service, contracts for education, or something analogous thereto. (*Roberts* v. *Gray*, 1913.)[188] Nevertheless, a contract which is in general for the minor's benefit will not be enforced if its terms are onerous, although the court will look at the whole not merely at isolated terms, and will arrive at its decision on the total effect of the agreement. (*De Francesco* v. *Barnum*, 1890,[189] and *Clements* v. *L. and N. W. Railway Co.*, 1894.)[190] Trading contracts of minors are not enforceable, no matter how beneficial they may be to the minor's trade or business. (*Mercantile Union Guarantee Corporation Ltd* v. *Ball*, 1937.)[191] A trading contract for this purpose is one in which the minor's capital is at risk. Where capital is not at risk a trading contract will be binding on a minor particularly where it is possible to regard the contract as analogous to a contract of service. (*Chaplin* v. *Leslie Frewin (Publishers)*, 1965[192] and *Denmark Productions* v. *Boscobel Productions*, 1967.)[193]

Voidable contracts.   These are usually contracts by which the minor acquires an interest of a permanent nature in the subject matter of the contract, e.g. a lease of premises, a partnership contract, or the holding of shares in a company. Such contracts bind the minor unless he takes active steps to avoid them either during his minority (*Steinberg* v. *Scala*, 1923),[194] or within a reasonable time thereafter. (*Davies* v. *Beynon-Harris*, 1931,[195] and *Goode* v. *Harrison*, 1821.)[196]

Unenforceable contracts.   Section 2 of the Infants' Relief Act, 1874, applies and is concerned with the effect of the minor's ratification after full age of a contract made during minority and with fresh promises made by the minor after reaching full age in respect of transactions which took place during minority.

Before the effect of Sect. 2 can be appreciated it is necessary to look at the common law position before the Act of 1874 was passed. The common law classified contracts as follows—

(i) *Contracts for necessaries,* where the seller had a quasi-contractual claim and there could be no ratification after full age.

(ii) *Contracts of a continuing nature,* e.g. leases and partnerships. Such contracts were voidable during infancy or within a reasonable time thereafter, so that the minor could and still can ratify a contract of this nature.

(iii) *Loans.* These were void at common law and there could be no ratification by the minor after age, but a fresh promise plus new consideration, e.g. a fresh advance, might bind the minor.

(iv) *Contracts of a beneficial nature.* These were and are still binding on the minor.

All other contracts made by minors were voidable at common law, and consequently were capable of ratification after full age. The most important contracts in this residuary class were (*a*) the minor's contract of engagement, which was capable of ratification after full age; and (b) debts incurred under contracts for non-necessary goods, which debts could also be ratified after full age. Section 2 provides—

No action shall be brought whereby to charge any person upon any promise made after full age to pay any debt contracted during infancy or upon any ratification made after full age of any promise or contract made during infancy whether there shall or shall not be any new consideration for such promise or ratification after full age.

Since under the Law Reform (Miscellaneous Provisions) Act, 1970, Sect. 1, engagements to marry are not enforceable at law, the only effect of Sect. 2 of the 1874 Act now is to prevent ratification after full age of debts for non-necessaries incurred during minority.

Section 2 of the Infants' Relief Act, 1874, was not entirely effective in the case of loans. It rendered certain promises unenforceable against the minor but, although the promise to repay the loan was unenforceable, the lender could sell any security the minor had used to secure the loan, because here he was pursuing a real remedy against the security and was not suing the minor on his promise.

The Betting and Loans (Infants) Act, 1892, was therefore passed rendering loans as distinct from debts void, so that any security taken is also void, and the lender can neither enforce the minor's promise, nor proceed against any security the minor may have given to secure the loan.

Consequences of the Contracts of Minors

When a minor has paid money under a void or voidable contract although he can repudiate the contract and disclaim all future liability, he cannot recover money paid unless he can prove a total failure of consideration, i.e. that he has received no benefit at all under the contract. It would seem that the court is reluctant to find that no benefit has been received (*Pearce* v. *Brain*, 1929,[197] and *Steinberg* v. *Scala*, 1923),[194] though if there has been no consideration at all the minor will be able to recover his money. (*Corpe* v. *Overton*, 1833.)[198]

Although the Infants' Relief Act, 1874, states that contracts for goods other than necessaries are absolutely void, the minor can give a good title to a third party who acquires goods which have been bought by the minor, provided the third party takes *bona fide* and for value. (*Stocks* v. *Wilson*, 1913.)[199] The tradesman who sold the goods to the minor cannot recover them from the third party; whether he can recover money paid to the minor for the goods is doubtful, but the better view is that he cannot. (*Stocks* v. *Wilson*, 1913,[199] and *Leslie* (*R*) *Ltd* v. *Sheill*, 1914.)[200]

Where a minor has committed a fraud, e.g. overstated his age, then the equitable doctrine of restitution of the goods is available to the tradesman, assuming the goods are non-necessaries and that no action for a reasonable price is available. The remedy of restitution exists so long as the minor still has the goods in his possession and they can be identified. It is well established that a person cannot sue the minor on the tort of deceit, as this would amount to using the law of torts to circumvent the Infants' Relief Act, nor can quasi-contractual remedies be used. (*Leslie* v. *Sheill*, 1914).[200] As regards torts, a minor is, apart from circumstances involving contract, fully liable in tort even though he is under 18. (*Burnard* v. *Haggis*, 1863.)[201] (And see further p. 299.)

The doctrine of estoppel, which is a rule of evidence rather than a rule of law, means that a person is sometimes prevented from denying in court the truth of a statement which he has made where another person has relied on that statement to his detriment. This doctrine might have prevented a fraudulent minor from proving his real age when defending an action for the price of goods delivered to him, but the court is so concerned that the 1874 Act should not be circumvented that this doctrine has been held not to apply to a minor so as to prevent him from setting up his real age as a defence.

Married Women

A married woman has the same contractual capacity as an unmarried woman (*feme sole*) or a man. However, a husband is not liable for his wife's contracts unless she is his agent for the particular transaction and she can no longer be an agent of necessity in respect of domestic transactions. (See p. 167.)

Corporations

Corporations are another special case of capacity to contract. A corporation aggregate may be a body incorporated by Royal Charter, a corporation formed by a special Act of Parliament, or a company registered under the Companies Act, 1948–1976, or previous Acts.

The contractual capacity of a corporation is limited—

(*a*) *By natural impossibility,* which arises from the fact that it is an *artificial* and not a *natural* person. Thus it can only make contracts through an agent and in consequence cannot fulfil contractual obligations of a *personal nature*. It is obviously impossible for a corporation to marry and it cannot act as a solicitor, doctor or accountant, nor can it act as the treasurer of a friendly society. (*Re West of England and South Wales District Bank* (1879), 11 Ch. D. 768.)

(*b*) *By legal impossibility,* since corporations are subject to what is called the *ultra vires* rule, which limits what they can legally do. A corporation can only act within its powers, and actions outside this scope are called *ultra vires*, or beyond its powers.

Parliamentary approach to ultra vires. Limited protection for persons dealing in good faith with a registered company is given by the European Communities Act, 1972. Section 9 of the Act is the United Kingdom's response to the first directive issued by the Council of Ministers of the European Communities for the harmonization of company law in the member states. Section 9(1) provides that in favour of a person dealing in good faith with a company any transaction decided on by its directors shall be deemed to be within the capacity of the company to enter into validly, and the other party to the transaction shall not be bound to enquire about the capacity of the company to engage in it and shall be presumed to have acted in good faith unless the contrary is proved.

The *ultra vires* rule is not abolished because the sub-section merely allows the other party to an *ultra vires* transaction with a company to enforce it against the company if the necessary conditions are fulfilled.

Thus the sub-section does not—

(*a*) prevent a member of the company from obtaining an injunction to restrain the company and its directors from entering into an *ultra vires* transaction; or

(*b*) absolve the directors from liability for any loss they cause the company by carrying out such a transaction, though of course there may be no loss since the *ultra vires* contract may be very profitable to the company; or

(*c*) make the transaction enforceable by the company but only against it; thus the other party can raise the defence of *ultra vires* if sued by the company. However, if the other party sues the company it could plead defences and make counter-claims, e.g. if the company was sued for the value of goods supplied under an *ultra vires* contract, the company could plead, in order to reduce the claim, that they were defective. Furthermore, if the other party accepts benefits under the transaction or allows the company to incur expense in connection with it he may be estopped from denying the validity of the transaction.

Unfortunately Sect. 9(1) applies only if the transaction has been 'decided on by the directors'. Few transactions of public companies are formally resolved upon at board meetings and the sub-section would seem to apply only where the transaction has been authorized, effected, or ratified by a resolution of a board meeting or by all the directors assenting to it. It does not seem to extend to transactions entered into by one director acting under broad delegated powers because the precise nature of the transaction is not a matter upon which the directors decide. However, if the board has decided, say, that A, a director, shall negotiate for a lease in the City of London for 99 years at a named price, so that A is merely left to negotiate minor details, the lease may be regarded as a transaction 'decided on by the directors' and enforceable by the landlord if the lease happened to be beyond the company's powers.

Thus although the section has still to be interpreted by the courts it seems that very few *ultra vires* transactions of public companies will be validated by Sect. 9(1). Most will remain invalid and be covered by the common law rules set out below. For the time being, therefore, plaintiffs will probably re-inforce actions for breach of *ultra vires* contracts by asking in the alternative for one or more of the secondary remedies, e.g. subrogation and tracing, in case they cannot rely on the Act of 1972, and the usual contractual remedies are therefore denied to them.

Section 9 would seem to validate a large number of *ultra vires* contracts made by *private* companies. So many of these are 'one man' companies in which everything is decided by the one man in his capacity as sole director.

It is interesting to note that the Conservative Government's Companies Bill of 1973 provided in Clause 5 that a transaction between a company and another party shall not be repudiated by the company on the ground that it was beyond the capacity of the company or the powers of the directors unless the other party had actual notice of that fact. Such a provision would have been much more effective in validating *ultra vires* transactions with both types of registered companies.

Charter and statutory companies and the ultra vires rule. Charter corporations may contract as an ordinary person can, and even though the Charter may impose limitations on the corporation's contractual capacity, any contracts which it makes beyond those limitations are nevertheless good. (*Baroness Wenlock* v. *River Dee Co.* (1887), 36 Ch. D. 674.) The Crown may in such a case forfeit the Charter, or a member of the corporation may ask the court to restrain the corporation by injunction by from doing acts which are *ultra vires*. (*Jenkin* v. *Pharmaceutical Society*, 1921.)[62]

Statutory corporations have powers contained in the statute setting them up, and these powers are sometimes increased by subsequent statutes or by delegated legislation. Any acts beyond these powers are *ultra vires* and void.

Registered companies and the ultra vires rule. Registered companies possess powers determined by the Objects Clause of their Memorandum of Association, and an act in excess of the powers given in this Memorandum is *ultra vires* and void. Thus an *ultra vires* contract is unenforceable against the company unless it is one which was 'decided on by the directors' (see above). (*Ashbury Railway Carriage and Iron Co.* v. *Riche*, 1875,[202] and *Re Jon Beauforte*, 1953.)[203] Corporations may carry out acts 'fairly incidental' to the specified objects (*Deuchar* v. *Gas, Light and Coke Co.*, 1925)[204] though whether an activity was fairly incidental has hitherto been a matter for the court to decide. However, the rule has been so uncertain in its operation that it has become customary for legal draftsmen to draft objects clauses which are extremely wide in scope and, in addition, include a provision that each specified object or power should be considered separate and distinct and in no way ancilliary to, or dependent upon, any other object (*Cotman* v. *Brougham*, 1918).[205] In this way, the severe limitations placed on a company's business by the *ultra vires* rule have been mitigated, provided that each paragraph of the objects clause can genuinely be regarded as separate and distinct. (*Re Introductions Ltd,* 1969.)[206] However, in 1966 the Court of Appeal, anticipating in a sense the passing of the European Communities Act, 1972, made a decision which may, in effect, allow the decisions of the directors of a company to usurp the courts in deciding what is reasonably incidental to the company's stated objects, and even allow them to bind the company even to an activity which cannot conveniently be combined with the existing objects, and ought therefore to be regarded as *ultra vires.* (*Bell Houses Ltd* v. *City Wall Properties Ltd,* 1966.)[207]

Contracts of companies—formalities. At common law contracts made by corporations had to be under seal. The requirement of sealing would have been extremely onerous but for the exceptions allowed, e.g. contracts of trifling importance or daily necessity were not required to bear the company's seal.

The above rules have been amended by statute. The Companies Act, 1948, provides in Sect. 32 that a registered company need not contract under seal except where an ordinary person would have to do so, and the Corporate Bodies' Contracts Act, 1960, extends this privilege to all companies, no matter how formed.

Unincorporated Bodies

In addition to corporations there are certain types of unincorporated bodies, such as tennis clubs and other societies. These bodies contract through agents, and the persons authorizing these agents are personally liable, since the association has no separate existence in law, being only an aggregate of its members, though the rules of the Supreme Court allow unincorporated groups of persons to sue or to be sued collectively. The liability of the members in contract has already been considered (see p. 158).

Persons Suffering from Mental Disorder

Contracts made by a person of unsound mind are valid, but if the other party knew that he was contracting with a person who, by reason of the unsoundness of his mind, *could not understand the nature of the contract,* then the contract is voidable at the option of the insane party. The person of unsound mind must prove (*a*) the unsoundness of mind at the time of the contract, and (*b*) that the other party knew of it. (*Imperial Loan Co.* v. *Stone,* [1892] 1 Q.B. 599.) If necessaries are supplied to a person of unsound mind he, like a minor, is bound to pay a reasonable price under Sect. 2 of the Sale of Goods Act, 1893.

A person of unsound mind can make a valid contract during a lucid interval, even though the other party knew that he was of unsound mind at times. Further, a contract made during a period of unsoundness of mind can be ratified during a lucid interval.

There seems to be no reason why persons suffering from some forms of mental disorder should not make valid contracts for non-necessary goods and services even where the other party knows of the disorder. Provided the person concerned understands the *nature* of the transaction a contract resulting from it could be binding. For example, a person who suffers under an insane delusion that he is Napoleon may nevertheless understand the nature of a commercial transaction such as the purchase of a watch. Where this is so he may be bound by a contract to buy the watch even though the seller knew of the delusion. (*Birkin* v. *Wing* (1890), 63 L.T. 80.) Nevertheless, it is likely that the court would regard the contract as voidable if there was evidence to show that the person suffering from the delusion had been overreached as where the price asked for the watch was extortionate.

The above rules of law relating to persons of unsound mind must now be read in the light of the provisions of the Mental Health Act, 1959. This Act, which came into operation fully on 1 November, 1960, introduced a completely new code and system for the care, treatment, and detention, of persons suffering from mental disorder. 'Mental disorder' is now a statutory term embracing all forms of unsoundness of mind and in particular a person of unsound mind whose property is subject to the control of the Court under Sect. 149(2) of the Act cannot personally make a valid contract, though the court can make a contract for him or order the carrying out of a contract already made by him (*ibid* Sect. 103(1)(g)). However, persons of unsound mind whose property is not subject to the control of the court are governed in contractual matters by the common law rules given above.

Drunkards

Similar rules apply to contracts made by drunkards. The contract is voidable at the option of the party who was drunk at the time it was made, if he can show (i) that he was drunk, and (ii) that the other party knew this. (*Gore* v. *Gibson* (1845), 14 L.J. Ex. 151.) A contract made by a person when drunk can be ratified by him when he is sober. (*Matthews* v. *Baxter* (1873), L.R. 8 Ex. 132.) Drunken persons have a quasi-contractual liability to pay a reasonable price for necessaries supplied to them. (Sale of Goods Act, 1893, Sect. 2.)

REALITY OF CONSENT

A contract which is regular in all other respects may still fail because there is no real consent to it by one or both of the parties. There is no *consensus ad idem* or meeting of the minds. Consent may be rendered unreal by mistake, fraud, misrepresentation, duress and undue influence.

MISTAKE

Mistake may affect the validity of a contract, and a mistake which has this effect is called an operative mistake, and must be one of fact and not of law. (*Sharp Bros. and Knight* v. *Chant,* 1917.)[208] An operative mistake renders the contract void.

The concept of mistake has a somewhat technical meaning, and what would be considered a mistake by the layman will not always amount to an operative mistake. For example, errors of judgment are not operative mistakes. So if A buys an article thinking it is worth £100 when in fact it is worth only £50, the contract is good and A must bear the loss if there has been no misrepresentation by the seller. This is what is meant by the maxim '*caveat emptor*' (let the buyer beware). A mistake by one party as to his power to perform the contract is not an operative mistake. Where X agrees to build a house by 1 July, and finds he cannot complete the job before 1 September, he will be liable to an action for damages.

Operative mistake

Operative mistakes may be classified into the following categories—
  (1) Documents mistakenly signed.
  (2) Unilateral mistake, i.e. a mistake made by one party only.
  (3) Bilateral mistake, i.e. where both parties make a mistake, and subdivided into (*a*) Common Mistake; (*b*) Mutual Mistake.

These categories are helpful, but students find considerable difficulty in distinguishing between common and mutual mistake because the words are frequently confused, or used synonymously, even in law reports. This can be illustrated by the case of *Solle* v. *Butcher*.[209] Bucknill, L.J., in the course of his judgment is reported in the *All England Reports,* [1949] 2 All E.R. at page 1116 as saying: 'In my opinion, therefore, there was a *mutual* mistake of fact on a matter of fundamental importance.'

In the *Law Reports,* [1950] 1 K.B. at page 686 this is rendered as: 'In my opinion, therefore, there was a *common* mistake of fact on a matter of fundamental importance.'

In *Cooper* v. *Phibbs* (1867),[210] at page 170, Lord Westbury says: '. . . but if the parties contract under a *mutual* mistake and misapprehension as to their relative and respective rights, the result is, that that agreement is liable to be set aside as having proceeded upon a *common* mistake.' (And see also *Amalgamated Investment and Property Co. Ltd* v. *John Walker & Sons Ltd,* 1976.)[221]

We therefore propose to use words more self-identifying than common or mutual in order to assist the reader to understand and remember the categories. Common mistake occurs where *both* parties have made the *same* mistake and will be called, alternatively, *identical bilateral* mistake. Mutual mistake occurs where *both* parties make a *different* mistake and will be called *non-identical bilateral* mistake. These will then be clearly differentiated between themselves and contrasted with *unilateral* mistake.

Documents mistakenly signed

If a person signs a contract in the mistaken belief that he is signing a document of a totally different nature, there will be a mistake which avoids the contract, and he will be able to plead *non est factum*. However, as a result of the decision of the House of Lords in *Saunders* v. *Anglia Building Society,* 1970[211] the plea of mistake is available in such circumstances only if the person signing under a mistake can show that he was not negligent in so doing as in *Foster* v. *Mackinnon,* 1869.[212]

As between the immediate parties to what is always in effect a fraud, there is, of course, no difficulty in avoiding the contract or transaction mistakenly entered into. The rules set out above are relevant only where the contract or transaction mistakenly entered into has affected a third party, as where he has, as in *Saunders*[211] lent money on an interest in land obtained by fraudulent assignment under circumstances of mistake.

The principles set out in *Saunders*[211] apply also to those who sign blank forms as well as to those who sign completed documents without reading them. Thus if as in *United Dominions Trust Ltd* v. *Western, The Times,* 28 October, 1975 A takes a car from B, a dealer, on hire purchase and signs a finance company's blank form of proposal leaving the dealer to fill it in for him, then if the dealer fills in the price of the car as greater than it was A cannot avoid paying the finance company the additional sum on the grounds of *non est factum*.

Unilateral mistake

Unilateral mistake occurs when one of the parties to a contract, X, is mistaken as to some fundamental fact concerning the contract and *the other party Y, knows or ought to know this.* (*Legal and General Assurance Society Ltd* v. *General Metal Agencies Ltd,* 1969.)[213] This latter requirement is important because if Y does not know that X is mistaken, the contract is good. (*Higgins* v. *Northampton Corporation,* 1927.)[214]

Effect of unilateral mistake at common law.   The cases are mainly concerned with mistake by one party as to the *identity* of the other party. Thus, a contract may be void if X makes a contract with Y, thinking that Y is another person, Z, and if Y knows that X is under that misapprehension. Proof of Y's knowledge is essential, but since in most cases Y is a fraudulent person, the point does not present great difficulties. (*Cundy* v. *Lindsay,* 1878.)[215]

It is also essential that there should exist in the mind of the party who has been misled some other person (or entity) with whom the contract could have been made, as in *Cundy* v. *Lindsay,* 1878.[215] If Jones contracts with Brown by leading Brown to believe that he (Jones) is Green, the contract *will not be void* for mistake if Brown has never heard before of either Jones or Green. It *may be voidable* for fraud but the difference may vitally effect the interests of third parties. (*King's Norton Metal Co. Ltd* v. *Edridge,*

Merrett & Co. Ltd, 1897.)[216] However, even where there are two entities, the court may still find, *on the facts of the case,* that the contract is not void for mistake. (*Phillips* v. *Brooks,* 1919,[217] *Ingram* v. *Little,* 1961[218] and *Lewis* v. *Averay,* 1971.)[219]

Effect of unilateral mistake in Equity.   If the plaintiff is asking for an equitable remedy, such as rescission of the contract or specific performance of it, then equitable principles will apply. As far as unilateral mistake is concerned Equity follows the law and regards a contract affected by unilateral mistake as void, and will rescind it or refuse specific performance of it. (*Webster* v. *Cecil,* 1861.)[220]

Bilateral mistake

A bilateral mistake arises when both parties to a contract are mistaken. They may have made a *common* or *identical* mistake; or a *mutual* or *non-identical* mistake.

(A) Common or identical mistake.   This occurs when the two parties have reached agreement but both have made an identical mistake as to some fundamental fact concerning the contract. Suppose, for example, that X sells a particular drawing to Y for £5000 and all the usual elements of agreement are present including offer and acceptance and consideration, and the agreement concerns an identified article. Nevertheless, if both X and Y think that the drawing is by Rembrandt, when it is in fact only a copy worth £25, then the agreement is rendered imperfect by the *identical* or *common* mistake. The mistake must exist at the time the contract is made. (*Amalgamated Investment & Property Co. Ltd* v. *John Walker & Sons Ltd,* 1976.)[221]

Effect of indentical bilateral mistake at common law.   At common law a mistake of the kind outlined above has no effect on the contract, and the parties would be bound in the absence of fraud or misrepresentation. There are only two cases in which the common law appears to regard an *identical bilateral* mistake as a vitiating element, and even these cases are probably examples of precedent impossibility rather than mistake. The two categories of case are—

(a) *Cases of Res Extincta*
   (i) *Identical bilateral mistake as to the existence of the thing contracted for.*   If X agrees to sell his car to Y, and unknown to them both the car had at the time of the sale been destroyed by fire, then the contract will be void because X has innocently undertaken an obligation which he cannot possibly fulfil. (*Couturier* v. *Hastie,* 1856.)[222] There are, however, cases in which the court may assume from the circumstances that the seller is warranting the existence of the goods. (*McRae* v. *Commonwealth Disposals Commission,* 1951.)[223]

If the goods are lost after the sale takes place then the contract is good, and the loss lies with the buyer if the property in the goods has passed to him; if not the loss lies with the seller. The goods must also be specific or ascertained, otherwise the property will not normally pass, and the seller must supply similar goods or be liable in breach on contract.

(ii) *Identical bilateral mistake as to the existence of a state of affairs forming the basis of the contract.* If A and B, believing themselves to be married, enter into a separation agreement and later learn that they are not validly married, the agreement is void.

(*b*) *Cases of Res Sua.* These occur where a person makes a contract to buy something which already belongs to him. Such a contract is, at any rate in Equity, void though the remarks of Knight Bruce, L.J. in *Cochrane* v. *Willis,* 1865[224] suggest that the common law view is the same.

Apart from cases of *res extincta* and *res sua* the common law does not seem to recognize an *identical* bilateral mistake as having any effect on a contract. (*Bell* v. *Lever Bros Ltd,* 1932,[225] and *Leaf* v. *International Galleries,* 1950.)[226]

Effect of indentical bilateral mistake in Equity. Where an equitable remedy is sought the position is as follows—

(*a*) *Cases of Res Extincta and Res Sua.* Equity treats these in the same way as the common law, regarding the agreement as void. Consequently Equity will not grant specific performance of such an agreement (*Jones* v. *Clifford,* 1876)[227] and will rescind it. (*Cooper* v. *Phibbs,* 1867.)[210]

(*b*) *Other Cases.* Equity will apparently regard an agreement affected by *identical* bilateral mistakes as *voidable* even though the case is not one of *res extincta* or *res sua.* (*Solle* v. *Butcher,* 1950,[209] and *Magee* v. *Pennine Insurance Co. Ltd,* 1969.)[228] This remedy is a discretionary one and the party seeking it may be put on terms, i.e. since the remedy is a discretionary one the parties seeking it may be required to accept other solutions to the problem which the court puts forward. (*Solle* v. *Butcher,* 1950,[209] *Grist* v. *Bailey,* 1966.)[229]

(*c*) *Rectification.* Equity has power to rectify agreements affected by *identical bilateral* or common mistake.

If the parties are agreed on the terms of their contract, but by mistake write them down incorrectly, the court may order equitable rectification of the contract. In order to obtain rectification it must be proved—

(i) that there was agreement in the contractual sense on all the terms of the contract or at least some outward expression of agreement between the parties *on the term in question,* even though that agreement was not in fact a contract. (*Joscelyne* v. *Nissen,* 1970.)[230]

(ii) that the agreement continued unchanged until it was reduced into writing (for if the parties disputed the terms of the agreement, then the written contract will be taken to represent their final agreement); and

(iii) that the writing does not express what the parties had agreed. (*Rose* v. *Pim,* 1953.)[231]

The power of the court to rectify agreements is generally confined to identical bilateral and not to unilateral mistake. (*Higgins (W.) Ltd* v. *Northampton Corporation*, 1927.)[214] In the case of unilateral mistake, rectification will only be granted in cases of fraud or misrepresentation.

(B) Mutual or non-identical mistake. This occurs where the parties are both mistaken as to a fundamental fact concerning the contract but each party has made a *different* mistake. Thus if X offers to sell Car A, and Y agrees to buy thinking X means Car B, there is a bilateral mistake which is *non-identical*. This may prevent a contract coming into being between the parties because of *defective offer and acceptance,* and may result from the negligence of a third party. (*Henkel* v. *Pape,* 1870.)[232] It will be remembered that in the previous category the mistake was bilateral but both parties had made an *identical* mistake.

Effect of non-identical bilateral mistake at common law.   The contract is not necessarily void because the court will try to find the 'sense of the promise', i.e. the sort of bargain which the reasonable man looking at the dealings of the parties would have thought had been made.

In many cases of *non-identical mistake* the court has been able to ascertain the 'sense of the promise' and has decided that an enforceable contract has been made *on the terms understood by one of the parties.* (*Wood* v. *Scarth,* 1858.)[233] If the circumstances are such that the court cannot find the 'sense of the promise', then the contract is void not so much because of mistake as because of uncertainty. (*Raffles* v. *Wichelhaus,* 1864,[234] and *Scriven Brothers & Co.* v. *Hindley & Co.,* 1913.)[235]

Effect of non-identical bilateral mistake in Equity.   Equity also tries to find the 'sense of the promise', thus following the law in this respect. (*Tamplin* v. *James,* 1880.)[236] However, equitable remedies are discretionary, and even where the 'sense of the promise' can be ascertained. Equity will not necessarily insist on performance, particularly if this would cause hardship to the defendant. (*Wood* v. *Scarth,* 1858.)[233]

MISREPRESENTATION

Representation—meaning of

A representation is an inducement only and its effect is generally to lead the other party merely to make the contract. A representation must be a statement of some *specific existing* and *verifiable* fact or *past event* and in consequence the following are excluded.

(*a*) *Statements of law.*

(*b*) *Statements as to future conduct or intention.*   In some cases, however, a statement of intention may, in effect, be a representation of existing fact. (*Edgington* v. *Fitzmaurice,* 1885.)[237]

(*c*) *Statements of opinion.*   However, if it can be shown that the person making the statement had no such opinion, it may be considered in law to be a misstatement of existing fact. (*Smith* v. *Land and House Property Co.*, 1884.)[238]

(*d*) *Mere 'puffing', as in advertising or sales talk.*   Not all statements amount to representations. Some of them are obviously of the nature of sales talk and cannot be relied upon. If a salesman says: 'This polish is as good as Snook's Polish,' this is a mere statement of opinion. If he says: 'This is the finest polish in the world,' this is mere sales talk. However, if he says: 'This polish has as much wax in it as Snook's Wax Polish,' he is making a statement of specific verifiable fact. The first two of these statements have no effect on the contract whether true or untrue; the third if untrue will amount to a misrepresentation.

(*e*) *Silence.*   Silence or non-disclosure by one or both of the parties does not normally affect the contract. However, it may do so—

(i) *where the statement is a half-truth*—if the statement made is true but *partial* so that a false impression is created it may be regarded as an actionable misrepresentation (*Curtis* v. *Chemical Cleaning and Dyeing Co.*, 1951);[239]

(ii) *where the statement was true when made but became false before the contract was concluded*—where a statement is made in the course of negotiating a contract and that statement, though true when it was made, becomes false because of a change in circumstances, there is a duty on the party making the statement to disclose the change, otherwise the contract may be rescinded (*With* v. *O'Flanagan*, 1936);[240]

(iii) *where the contract is uberrimae fidei* (of utmost good faith) such as a contract of insurance (see p. 235);

(iv) *where there is a fiduciary or confidential relationship between the parties*—the equitable doctrine of *constructive fraud* may be applied whenever the relationship between the parties to a contract is such that one of them has a special influence over the other.

In such a case, the person having the special influence cannot hold the other to the contract unless he can satisfy the court that it was advantageous to the other and that there was full disclosure of all material facts.

This branch of the law is closely akin to undue influence (see p. 237) which occurs, for example in certain relationships such as parent and child. However, the doctrine of constructive fraud is wider and according to Lord Chelmsford in *Tate* v. *Williamson*, 1866[241] may be applied—

Whenever two persons stand in such a relation that, while it continues, confidence is necessarily reposed by one, and the influence which naturally grows out of that confidence is possessed by the other, and this confidence is abused, or the influence is exerted to obtain an advantage at the expense of the confiding party, the person so availing himself of his position will not be permitted to retain the advantage, although the transaction could not have been impeached if no such confidential relation had existed.

Thus it may be that while undue influence is the proper term to use of influence between certain established and accepted relationships, such as parent and child, trustee and beneficiary, when the influence is shown to exist outside of these relationships the true basis of the action is probably constructive fraud.

Inducement—meaning of

In order to operate as an inducement the representation must—

(a) be made with the intention that it should be acted upon by the person misled (*Peek* v. *Gurney,* 1873,[242] and *Gross* v. *Lewis Hillman Ltd,* 1969),[243]

(b) induce the contract so that the person making the claim to have been misled must not have relied on his own skill and judgment (*Redgrave* v. *Hurd,* 1881),[244]

(c) be material in the sense that it affected the plaintiff's judgment (*Smith* v. *Chadwick* 1884);[245]

(d) be known to the plaintiff. The plaintiff must always be prepared to prove that an alleged misrepresentation had an effect on his mind, a task which he certainly cannot fulfil if he was never aware that it had been made. (*Horsfall* v. *Thomas,* 1863.)[246]

Types of actionable misrepresentation

In cases which have come before the courts judges speak of two types of misrepresentation only: innocent misrepresentation, by which they mean innocent of fraud, and fraudulent misrepresentation, which involves dishonesty. Innocent misrepresentation is then further sub-divided into innocent statements made negligently, i.e. without reasonable grounds for believing them to be true.

However, for purposes of exposition we discuss three types of misrepresentation, i.e. innocent, negligent, and fraudulent. This should not cause any practical difficulty provided the above paragraph is understood. Thus an *innocent misrepresentation* is a false statement made by a person *who had reasonable grounds* to believe that the statement was true not only when he made it but also at the time the contract was entered into.

A *negligent misrepresentation* is a false statement made without dishonesty by a person *who had no reasonable grounds* for believing the statement to be true. A *fraudulent misrepresentation* is a false representation of a material fact made dishonestly knowing it to be false, or believing it to be false, or recklessly, not caring whether it be true or false. (*Derry* v. *Peek,* 1889.)[247]

Agent's breach of warranty of authority.   Under the law of agency, where an agent represents himself as having authority he does not possess, the third party may sue the agent for breach of warranty of authority if he suffers loss by not obtaining a contract with the principal, the action being based on quasi-contract. (See p. 278.)

Compensation under Companies Act, 1948   Under Sect. 43 of the Companies Act, 1948, company promoters and directors are liable for negligent misstatements in prospectuses though they have certain defences (see p. 222).

Negligence at common law.   The House of Lords has ruled in *Hedley Byrne* v. *Heller and Partners*[248] that where there is a sufficient 'special relationship' between the maker of the statement and the person who is to rely on it, the former owes tha latter a duty of reasonable care in making the statement and may be liable in damages in tort for negligence to the recipient if the statement contains false information given negligently rather than intentionally.

The remedy in negligence is useful where the parties concerned were *not* in a pre-contractual relationship when the statement was made because if they were not Sect. 2(1) of the Misrepresentation Act, 1967, will not apply.

However, in *Esso Petroleum* v. *Mardon,* [1976] 2 All E.R. 5 the Court of Appeal held that the principle in *Hedley Byrne*[248] could apply even where the parties concerned were in a pre-contractual relationship and in addition that the person who had made the statement need not necessarily be in business to give advice, as had once been thought. Mr. Mardon was awarded damages for a negligent misstatement by a senior sales representative of Esso in regard to the amount of petrol he could expect to sell per year from a petrol station in Southport which he was leasing from Esso. The facts of *Mardon* pre-dated the 1967 Act and the court could not use it. The decision is obviously important but where the facts have occurred since 1967 the Misrepresentation Act is likely to prove more popular with plaintiffs since they can ask the representor to show he was not negligent. In *Hedley Byrne*[248] claims the burden of proof is on the plaintiff to prove negligence.

REMEDIES

There are the following possible remedies for misrepresentation—

(*a*) Rescission of the contract is a possible remedy in all cases of misrepresentation whether fraudulent, negligent or innocent.

(*b*) The refusal of the injured party to perform his part of the contract if he has not already done so. He can then raise the misrepresentation as a defence to an action for specific performance, debt or damages.

(*c*) An action for damages in the case of fraud. In this case the plaintiff sues not on the contract but on the tort of deceit.

The object of damages in fraud is to compensate the plaintiff for *all the loss* he has incurred as a result of the fraudulent inducement (*Doyle* v. *Olby*

(*Ironmongers*) *Ltd,* 1969)[249] although it has not been finally decided whether an award of exemplary damages may be made. (*Mafo* v. *Adams,* 1970.)[250] This contrasts, for example, with damages for breach of a term of the contract where only damage which was in the contemplation of the parties is recoverable. This is not necessarily all of the plaintiff's loss. (See further p. 268.)

(*d*) Where the misrepresentation is negligent the person making the false statement is liable in damages and the onus of proving that the statement was not made negligently, but that there were reasonable grounds for believing it to be true, is on the maker of the statement (or representor). (Misrepresentation Act, 1967, Sect. 2(1).) The manner in which damages for negligent misrepresentation are assessed is discussed at p. 221.

In addition a principal can be affected by his agent's negligent misstatement of which he, the principal, is wholly unaware. (*Gosling* v. *Anderson,* 1972.)[251] (Compare fraudulent misrepresentation and *Armstrong* v. *Strain,* 1952.)[252]

(*e*) A purely innocent misrepresentation may be remedied by an award of damages but these cannot be claimed as such. The person seeking relief must ask for rescission of the contract and the court may, in its discretion, award damages instead. (Misrepresentation Act, 1967, Sect. 2(2).)

Rescission

This remedy is available to a party misled by innocent, negligent, or fraudulent misrepresentation. It restores the *status quo,* i.e. it puts the parties back in the position they were in before the contract was made. Rescission dates from the time when the party misled notifies his repudiation of the contract to the other party, or does any other act indicating repudiation. (*Car & Universal Finance Co.* v. *Caldwell,* 1963.)[253] A contract induced by fraud or misrepresentation (innocent or negligent) is voidable at the option of the party misled. The ways in which an injured party may lose the right of rescission are set out below.

(i) *If the injured party affirms the contract, he cannot rescind.* He will affirm the contract if, with full knowledge of the misrepresentation, he *expressly* affirms it by stating that he intends to go on with it, or if he does some act from which an implied intention may properly be deduced. (*Long* v. *Lloyd,* 1958.)[254]

Lapse of time, or delay in asking for the remedy, is evidence of affirmation and can defeat an action for rescission. This is sometimes known as the doctrine of *laches,* and it is based on the maxim: 'Delay defeats equities.' (*Leaf* v. *International Galleries,* 1950.)[226] Lapse of time has no effect on rescission where fraud is alleged as long as the action is brought within six years of the time when the fraud was, or with reasonable diligence could have been, discovered. (Limitation Act, 1939, Sect. 26.)

(*Applegate* v. *Moss*, 1970[422] and *King* v. *Parsons*, 1973[423] and p. 266.)

(ii) *Rescission is impossible if the parties cannot be restored to their original positions.* (*Clarke* v. *Dickson*, 1858.)[255]

(iii) *It cannot be obtained where third party rights have accrued.* Rescission of a contract to take shares in a company cannot be obtained if the company has gone into liquidation because creditor's rights are paramount. Further, if X obtains goods from Y by fraud and pawns them with Z, Y cannot rescind the contract on learning of the fraud in order to recover the goods from Z, nor can he sue Z in conversion. (*Phillips* v. *Brooks Ltd*, 1919,[217] and *Lewis* v. *Averay*, 1971.)[219]

(iv) There were two further rules which had a serious effect on the remedy—

(*a*) Where a representation had been sufficiently important to be incorporated in the contract, the party to whom it was made could not claim rescission of the contract in equity but had to pursue the common law remedies for breach of a term. These remedies depended upon the status of the term. If a condition was broken the aggrieved party could repudiate the contract, but for breach of warranty the only remedy was a claim for damages.

Now the equitable right of rescission is preserved even where the representation has been incorporated in the contract. (Misrepresentation Act, 1967, Sect. 1(a).) Although the Section says 'Where . . . the misrepresentation has become a *term* of the contract,' it is not thought that there is a right to rescind for breach of warranty but only for a representation *incorporated in* the contract. If this is so, the availability of a remedy as drastic as rescission for a misrepresentation of minor importance when mere damages are available for a more serious breach of warranty is anomalous. Possibly, if the court is asked to rescind a contract for misrepresentation of minor importance, it will exercise its discretion under Sect. 2(2) of the 1967 Act to award damages in lieu of rescission.

(*b*) Where the contract had been performed, rescission could not be obtained if the misrepresentation was non-fraudulent. Now a person is not prevented from asking for rescission merely because the contract has been performed. (Misrepresentation Act, 1967, Sect. 1(b).)

Certain problems are raised by the provisions of this section which are illustrated by the following example. A buys a drawing from B having been told by B, in innocence, that it is by Constable though it is in fact a fake. This assertion is then written in the subsequent contract as a condition of sale. If A wishes to reject the goods, he must do so within a reasonable time otherwise conditions become warranties for the purposes of remedies and A will have only an action for damages for the breach of condition. However, it seems that under Sect. 1(b) of the 1967 Act, A may ask for rescission for the innocent misrepresentation made by B. It would seem illogical to allow a person to rescind for innocent misrepresentation when his right to reject for breach of condition is barred. The problem may be solved by treating performance of the contract as *evidence* of the plaintiff's intention to treat the contract as subsisting, leaving him with an action for damages for the misrepresentation.

Damages for non-fraudulent misrepresentation

Damages are obtainable for non-fraudulent misrepresentation in the following cases—

(1) Innocent misrepresentation

(*a*) Section 2(2) of the Misrepresentation Act, 1967, provides that—

Where a person has entered into a contract after a misrepresentation has been made to him otherwise than fraudulently, and he would be *entitled,* by reason of the misrepresentation, to rescind the contract, then, if it is claimed, in any proceedings arising out of the contract, that the contract *ought to be* or has been rescinded, the court or arbitrator may declare the contract subsisting and award damages in lieu of rescission, if of opinion that it would be equitable to do so, having regard to the nature of the misrepresentation and the loss that would be caused by it if the contract were upheld, as well as to the loss that rescission would cause to the other party.

This subsection seems to be designed to give the court discretion to treat a contract as subsisting and award damages to the injured party in those cases where the misrepresentation is of a minor nature. However, damages cannot be awarded unless the party seeking them would have been *entitled* to rescind. Presumably, therefore, if a bar to rescission exists, e.g. delay, then damages cannot be awarded either. However, the subsection also uses the words 'ought to be . . . rescinded' and this may give the court a discretion to award damages even when a bar to rescission exists. For example, A sells a car to B, innocently representing that it is a 1975 model whereas it is a 1973 model. Six months later B discovers this fact and asks for rescission. Presumably, B is not *entitled* to rescind on grounds of delay, but whether he can obtain damages or not will depend upon which of the two constructions outlined above is adopted by the court.

(*b*) Agency.   Where an agent in good faith represents himself as having authority he does not possess, as where his principal is, unknown to the agent, dead, the third party may sue the agent for breach of warranty of authority if he suffers loss by not obtaining a contract with the principal, the action being based on quasi-contract.

(2) Negligent misrepresentation

(*a*) Section 2(1) of the Misrepresentation Act, 1967, provides that—

Where a person has entered into a contract after a misrepresentation has been made to to him by another party thereto and as a result thereof he has suffered loss, then, if the person making the misrepresentation would be liable to damages in respect thereof had the misrepresentation been made fraudulently, that person shall be so liable notwithstanding that the misrepresentation was not made fraudulently, unless he proves that he had reasonable ground to believe and did believe up to the time the contract was made that the facts represented were true.

Presumably, the representor must have reasonable grounds for believing the statement to be true when he made it and right up to the time the contract was made. Thus, if a person makes a representation honestly and reasonably believing it to be true, and before contract receives additional information, which makes his belief unreasonable, he may be liable for negligent misrepresentation if he does nothing to correct his statement.

It is still not decided whether damages under Sect.2(1) are to be assessed as for fraud or as for negligence or as for breach of contract. The matter is of some importance because if the measure of damages is as for fraud then the plaintiff will recover *all his loss*. (*Doyle* v. *Olby*, 1969.)[249] If the measure is as for breach of contract the damages awarded will be designed to put the plaintiff in the position he would have been in if the representation had been true. Thus in *Jarvis* v. *Swans Tours*, 1973[256] the Court of Appeal took the view that the measure was contractual as did the judge in *Davies & Co. (Wines) Ltd* v. *Afa-Minerva (EMI) Ltd*, 1974.[257] If the measure is to be based on negligence then the court must try to put the plaintiff in the position he would have been in had the representation not been made. Thus in *Davies*[257] if the measure in tort had been applied, i.e. what position would the plaintiffs have been in if the representation had not been made, the court would probably have taken the view that they would not have contracted for the installation of the alarm and would therefore not be entitled to damages for loss of stock. There are also cases in which the courts have decided that the measure is as in fraud, e.g. *Watts* v. *Spence*, [1975] All E.R. 528 and *E & B Entertainments Ltd* v. *Leisure Enterprises Ltd, Estates Gazette,* 6 November, 1976, and until the courts deal with the matter in a reasoned and detailed fashion there will be doubt and confusion. Certainly, the contractual approach appears the most popular being at the basis of the decisions in *Jarvis*[256], *Davies*[257] and to some extent also *Gosling* v. *Anderson,* 1972.[251]

The sub-section recognizes only a claim for damages and says nothing as to rescission. However, in *Mapes* v. *Jones,* (1974) 232 E.G. 717, a property dealer contracted to lease a grocer's shop to the plaintiff for 21 years but did not in fact have sufficient interest in the property himself to grant such a lease, the maximum period available to him being 18 years. Despite constant requests no lease was supplied as originally promised and the plaintiff shut the shop and elected to treat the contract as repudiated. Willis, J. held that the plaintiff was entitled to rescission for the misrepresentation under Sect. 2(1) of the 1967 Act. He also found that the defendant's delay in completion was a breach of condition allowing the plaintiffs to repudiate the contract.

(b) Under Sect. 43 of the Companies Act, 1948, where the directors publish a prospectus containing false statements made innocently, the directors will have to pay what is called compensation unless—

(i) the directors had reasonable grounds for believing the statement to be true;

(ii) the statements were made on the authority of an expert who was thought to be competent; or

(iii) the statements were a copy of an official document;

(iv) they were not responsible for the prospectus, as where they withdrew consent to act as directors before it was issued, or being directors did not consent to the issue of the prospectus, or having consented to its issue withdrew that consent before the shares issued under the prospectus were allotted.

Experts, such as accountants, are also liable under the section for false statements in their reports which are included in the prospectus. Again, the defence of lack of responsibility is available as where the expert has not consented to the inclusion of his report in the prospectus. However, given that he accepts responsibility for the inclusion of his report, he has a defence if he can show that he had reasonable grounds for believing his statement to be true. Presumably, he could sustain this defence by showing, amongst other things, that the false statement came from an official document.

(c) Negligence at Common Law. As we have seen, where the parties concerned were not in a pre-contractual relationship when the statement was made Sect. 2(1) of the Misrepresentation Act, 1967, will not apply. However, an action for damages for negligence will lie in tort provided the false statement is made negligently and a special relationship exists between the parties. (*Hedley Byrne & Co. Ltd* v. *Heller and Partners Ltd,* 1963.)[248] (See p. 353.)

(3) *Misrepresentation may raise an estoppel.*   If a person has relied on a misstatement and has altered his previous position because of it, he may be able to base an action for damages on estoppel. (*Henderson* v. *Williams,* 1895.)[258]

It is also possible to recover a monetary indemnity for some losses caused by misrepresentation. This remedy can be asked for along with rescission where the court decides it will not award damages. Sect. 2(2) of the Misrepresentation Act, 1967, gives the court power to award damages instead of rescission but it cannot award both. Thus, if the court decides to grant rescission it is limited in its monetary award to that amount of loss for which Equity would give an indemnity. (*Whittington* v. *Seale-Hayne,* 1900.)[259]

Criminal penalties

In addition to the civil law remedies set out above the Trade Descriptions Act, 1968, makes it a criminal offence for a person to falsely or misleadingly describe goods. Furthermore, under the Trade Descriptions Act, 1972, it is an offence not to give an indication of origin where goods bearing a UK name or make have been produced or made outside the UK.

THE CONTENTS OF THE CONTRACT

Even where it is clear that a valid contract has been made, it is still necessary to decide precisely what it is the parties have undertaken to do in order to be able to say whether each has performed or not performed his part of the agreement.

In order to decide upon the terms of the contract it is necessary to find out what was said or written by the parties. Furthermore, having ascertained what the parties said or wrote, it is necessary to decide whether the statements were mere inducements (or representations) or terms of the contract itself, i.e. part of its actual contents.

EXPRESS TERMS

The Statements of the Parties

As we have seen in order to decide upon the *express terms* of the contract, it is necessary to find out what was said or written by the parties.

Where the contract is wholly oral this is a matter of fact to be decided by the court from the evidence presented to it and may give rise to problems where the evidence is conflicting and difficult to substantiate.

In the case of a written contract it is usually obvious what the parties have written down though there may be problems of interpretation arising, for example, from ambiguity, which the court may have to resolve. In addition it should be noted that where the terms of a contract have been written down the court may refuse to allow oral evidence to be admitted if it has the effect of adding to, varying or contradicting the written agreement. This rule is, however, subject to the following exceptions—

(*a*) *Oral evidence may be admitted to prove a trade custom or usage.* This will usually have the effect of adding a term or terms to the agreement.

(*b*) *Oral evidence may be admitted to show that the contract has not yet become effective.* This is not truly an exception since the contract is not varied, added to or contradicted. (*Pym* v. *Campbell*, 1856.)[260]

(*c*) *Oral evidence may be admitted where the court is of the opinion that the written document contains part only of the agreement.* This device is quite frequently used by the courts and represents a major exception to the rule relating to the admission of oral evidence. (*Quickmaid Rental Services* v. *Reece*, 1970.)[261]

Representation and terms

Having ascertained what the parties said or wrote it is necessary to decide whether the statements are representations or terms. Representations are statements which merely induce a contract whereas terms are part of the contract itself and make up its contents. The distinction is, of course, less important than it was since before the Misrepresentation Act, 1967, there was often no remedy for a misrepresentation which was not fraudulent and in such a case the plaintiff's only hope of obtaining a remedy was to convince the court that the defendant's statement was not a mere inducement but a term of the contract of which the defendant was in breach. As we have seen, the Misrepresentation Act, 1967, has broadened the scope of the remedies available for non-fraudulent misrepresentation.

Certain tests may be applied in order to decide whether a statement is a representation or a term of the contract—

(i) The court is always concerned to implement the *intentions of the parties* as they appear from statements made by them. Where, in a written contract, the parties have by their words indicated that a particular provision is to be considered as a term of the contract, then the court will normally follow that intention. Where the statement is an oral one, the court will decide the question by trying to ascertain the intentions of the parties and may come to the conclusion that the circumstances suggest that the statement was intended to be a term

(ii) A statement is likely to be an inducement rather than a term if the person making the statement asks the other party to check or verify it, e.g. 'The car is sound, but I should get an engineer's report on it.'

(iii) A statement is likely to be a term if it is made with the intention of preventing the other party from finding any defects, and succeeds in doing this, e.g. 'The car is sound; you need not look it over.'

(iv) If the statement is such that the aggrieved party would not have made the contract without it, then the statement will be a term of the contract. (*Bannerman* v. *White,* 1861.)[262]

(v) A statement made during *preliminary negotiations* tends to be an inducement. Where the interval between the making of the statement and the making of the contract is distinct, then the statement is almost certain to be an inducement. However, the interval is not always so well marked, and in such cases there is difficulty in deciding whether the statement is an inducement or a term. However, a college prospectus containing an outline of the syllabus of a course of study may form part of a contract between the college and a student who enters the college intending to follow that course. (*D'Mello* v. *Loughborough College of Technology,* 1970.)[263.]

If the statement was oral and the contract was afterwards reduced to writing then the terms of the contract tend to be contained in the writing, and all oral statements tend to be pre-contractual inducements.

(vi) Where one of the parties has *special knowledge or skill* with regard to the subject-matter of the contract, then such a party can more easily give warranties to the other, and will find it difficult to convince the court that warranties have been given to him. (*Oscar Chess Ltd* v. *Williams,* 1957.)[264]

Conditions and warranties

Having decided that a particular statement is a term of the contract and not a mere inducement, the court must then consider the importance of that statement in the context of the contract as a whole. Not all of the obligations created by a contract are of equal importance and this is recognized by the law which has applied a special terminology to contractual terms in order to distinguish the vital or fundamental obligations from the less vital, the expression *condition* being applied to the former and the expression *warranty* to the latter.

A *condition* is a vital term which goes to the root of the contract. It is an obligation which goes directly to the substance of the contract, or is so essential to its very nature that its non-performance may be considered by the other party as a substantial failure to perform the contract at all.

A *warranty,* on the other hand, is subsidiary to the main purpose. A warranty has been variously defined, but it may be said to be an obligation which, though it must be performed, is not so vital that a failure to perform it goes to the substance of the contract.

The distinction is important in terms of remedies. A breach of condition is called a repudiatory breach and the injured party may elect either to repudiate the contract or claim damages and go on with the contract. The plaintiff must go on with the contract and sue for damages if he has affirmed the contract after knowledge of a breach of condition. He may do this expressly, as where he uses the goods, or by lapse of time as where he simply fails to take any steps to complain about the breach for what in the court's view is an unreasonable period of time. A breach of warranty is not repudiatory and the plaintiff must go on with the contract and sue for damages. An interesting contrast is provided in *Poussard* v. *Spiers & Pond,* 1876[265] and *Bettini* v. *Gye,* 1876.[266]

Whether a term is a condition or a warranty is a question of the intention of the parties, and this is deduced from the circumstances of the case. Furthermore, the words used by the parties, while not conclusive may be followed. They may have called a particular term a condition or a warranty, or even have used less specific terms whose intention is clear. In some cases where the parties state the effect of a breach, it becomes clear whether a condition or warranty was intended. (*Harling* v. *Eddy,* 1951.)[267] If there is no such indication, the court must decide the legal result of the breach, e.g. by addressing itself to the commercial importance of the term. (*Behn* v. *Burness,* 1863.)[268] However, the mere fact that a commercial contract describes one of its terms as a 'condition' does not compel the court to hold that that term is a condition in the strict sense; the question must be decided by construing the contract as a whole. (*L. Schuler A.G.* v. *Wickham Machine Tool Sales,* 1973.)[269]

Before leaving the topic of conditions and warranties, the concept of the *intermediate term* should be noted. There are terms called intermediate terms which the parties may have called conditions or warranties. The effect of these on the contract depends upon how serious the breach has turned out to be *in fact*. If the breach has turned out to be serious the court will then treat the term as a condition so that the contract can be repudiated. If *in fact* the breach has not had a serious effect on the contract the court will treat it as a breach of warranty so that the parties must proceed with the contract, though the injured party will have an action for damages. (*Cehave NV* v. *Bremer Handelsgesellschaft,* mbH, 1975.)[270]

Waiver of Express Terms

A person who is trying to enforce a contract may waive terms which have not been carried out but only if they are for his own exclusive benefit. This will rarely be the case. (*Heron Garage Properties Ltd* v. *Moss,* 1974.)[271]

IMPLIED TERMS

In addition to the *express* terms inserted by the parties and referred to above a contract may contain and be subject to *implied* terms. Such terms are derived from custom or statute. Furthermore, a term may be implied by the court where it is necessary in order to achieve the result which the parties obviously intended the contract to have.

Customary Implied Terms

A contract may be subject to customary terms not specifically mentioned by the parties. (*Hutton* v. *Warren,* 1836.)[272] However, customary terms will not be implied if the express terms of the contract reveal that the parties had a contrary intention.

Statutory Implied Terms

In a contract for the sale of goods the Sale of Goods Act, 1893, as amended by the Supply of Goods (Implied Terms) Act, 1973, and in the case of a contract of hire purchase, the Consumer Credit Act, 1974, settle the matter of implied terms. These terms, which are now identical in both types of contract are as follows—

Title. There is a condition that the seller has the right to sell the goods (which in the case of hire purchase means at the end of the hiring period when the property is to pass) plus two warranties relating to the fact that the goods are free from encumbrances and that the buyer/hirer will have quiet possession of the goods. (*Rowland* v. *Divall,* 1923[273] and *Microbeads A.C.* v. *Vinhurst Road Markings,* 1975.)[274]

A seller who is not sure of his title may take advantage of a provision inserted into the Sale of Goods Act, 1893 by the 1973 Act under which the sale of a limited interest is possible. Where the parties intend only to transfer such a title as the seller may have, there is an implied warranty that all charges or encumbrances known to the seller and not known to the buyer have been disclosed to the buyer before the contract was made. There is an action by the buyer for breach of that warranty if this has not been done. Furthermore, the seller is not able to contract out of this liability.

Description.   There is an implied condition that the goods shall correspond with the description. (*Beale* v. *Taylor*, 1967.)[275]

Fitness for the purpose.   There is an implied condition that the goods shall be reasonably fit for the purpose for which they are required.

Merchantable quality.   There is an implied condition that the goods shall be of merchantable quality. (*Godley* v. *Perry*, 1960.)[276]

Sale by sample.   There are three implied conditions in a transaction by sample—
(*a*) the bulk must correspond with the sample in quality, (*b*) the buyer shall have a reasonable opportunity of comparing the bulk with the sample, (*c*) the goods shall be free from any defect rendering them unmerchantable which would not be apparent on reasonable examination of the sample. (*Godley* v. *Perry*, 1960.)[276]

The exclusion of Statutory Implied Terms

Before the passing of the Supply of Goods (Implied Terms) Act, 1973, it was possible for a seller to exclude these implied terms from a particular contract. The same was true of hire purchase contracts though certain terms which were implied under hire purchase legislation could not be excluded. (See now p. 232.)

Caveat emptor

It should be noted that the above provisions relating to implied terms only applied to sales or hirings 'in the course of business'. The Unfair Contract Terms Act, 1977 prohibits the use of exclusion clauses in *private* sales and hire purchase deals between those who are *not* in business.

Judicial Implied Terms

The court may imply a term into a contract which is not inchoate but complete and enforceable without the implied term, whenever it is necessary to do so in order that the express terms decided upon by the parties shall have the effect which was presumably intended by them. This is often expressed as the giving of 'business efficacy' to the contract, the judge regarding himself as doing merely what the parties themselves would have done in order to cover the situation if they had addressed themselves to it. The operation of the doctrine is illustrated by *The Moorcock,* 1889,[277] and *Lister* v. *Romford Ice and Cold Storage Co. Ltd,* 1957.[278] It should be noted that the court will not improve a contract which the parties have made, however desirable the improvement might be. If the express terms are perfectly clear and free from ambiguity, and there is no choice to be made between different possible meanings, the clear terms must be applied. (*Trollope & Colls Ltd,* v. *North West Metropolitan Regional Hospital Board,* 1973.)[279]

EXCLUSION CLAUSES

A contract may contain express terms under which one or both of the parties excludes or limits liability for breach of contract or negligence. Although such express terms are permissible, both the courts and Parliament have been reluctant to allow exclusion clauses where they have been imposed on a weaker party, such as an ordinary consumer, by a stronger party, such as a person or corporation in business to supply goods or services.

The attitude of the courts

The judges have protected consumers of goods and services against the effect of exclusion clauses in two main ways, i.e. by deciding that the exclusion clause never became part of the contract and by construing (or interpreting) the contract in such a way as to prevent the application of the clause.

1. Was the clause part of the contract? The court will require the person wishing to rely on an exclusion clause to show that the other party agreed to it at or before the time when the contract was made, otherwise it will not form part of the agreement. In this connection—

(*a*) Where a contract is made by signing a written document the signer will in general be bound by everything which the document contains, even if he has not read it (*L'Estrange* v. *Graucob,* 1934),[280] unless the signature was induced by misrepresentation as to the effect of the document. (*Curtis* v. *Chemical Cleaning and Dyeing Co.,* 1951.)[239]

(*b*) Where the terms are contained in an unsigned document, the person seeking to rely on an exclusion clause must show that the document was a integral part of the contract which could be expected to contain term (*Chapelton* v. *Barry U.D.C.,* 1940.)[281] However, if the document contractual in the sense outlined above the clause will apply even thou the plaintiff did not actually know about the exclusion clause in the sense that he had not read it. Communication may be constructive so long as the document adequately draws the attention of a reasonable person to the existence of terms and conditions. (*Thompson* v. *L.M.S. Railway,* 1930[282] and *Richardson Steamship Co. Ltd* v. *Rowntree,* 1894.)[283]

(*c*) Where the defendant has not given the plaintiff a copy of conditions or drawn his attention to them when making a particular contract, constructive notice will not apply, at least in consumer transactions, to enable the defendant to rely on previous communications in previous dealings. (*McCutcheon* v. *David MacBrayne,* 1964[284] and *Hollier* v. *Rambler Motors,* 1972.)[285] For non-consumer transactions see *British Crane,* etc. 1974.[286]

(*d*) Any attempt to introduce an exclusion clause *after* the contract has been made is ineffective because the consideration for the clause is then past. (*Olley* v. *Marlborough Court Ltd,* 1949[287] and *Thornton* v. *Shoe Lane Parking Ltd,* 1971.)[288]

(*e*) The doctrine of privity of contract may also prevent the application of an exclusion clause. Thus, if A, the owner of a bus company, excludes his own and his employees' liability for damage to property of passengers by a properly communicated clause, an employee who causes damage to property will be liable, although his employer will not be, because the employee is not a party to the contract which is between his employer and the passenger. (But see *Snelling* v. *J. G. Snelling,* 1972[123] and *The New Zealand Shipping Co. Ltd* v. *A. M. Satterthwaite & Co. Ltd,* 1974.)[289]

It should be noted that where there is no contract between the parties there can be no contractual assent to damage inflicted. In such a case the defendant can only hope to show that the plaintiff has voluntarily assumed risk, i.e. plead the defence of *volenti non fit injuria* (see p. 318) (*Burnett* v. *British Waterways Board,* 1973.)[290]

2. Construction of exclusion clauses. Rules of construction (i.e. interpretation) of contract may, when applied, prevent the application of an exclusion clause. The major rules of construction are as follows—

(a) *The contra proferentem rule.* Under this rule if there is any ambiguity or room for doubt as to the meaning of an exclusion clause the courts will construe it in a way unfavourable to the person who put it into the contract. An example of the application of this rule is to be seen in *Hollier* v. *Rambler Motors,* 1972[285] because the Court of Appeal, having decided that previous dealings were not incorporated, went on to use the rule by saying that the wording in the form was not sufficiently plain to exclude negligence. That ambiguity had therefore to be construed against the defendants who put it into the contract. (And see also *Akerib* v. *Booth,* 1961.)[291]

(b) *The repugnancy rule.* This rule says in effect that the exemption clause is in direct contradiction to another term of the contract and is therefore repugnant to it. Where such repugnancy exists the exemption clause can be struck out. Thus, to take an extreme case, if A makes a contract to supply oranges to B but includes a clause which allows him to supply any sort of fruit, the clause is repugnant to the main purpose of the contract and could be struck out. Thus, A would be liable in breach of contract if he supplied B with apples and could not rely on the clause to excuse his breach of contract. (See *Pollock* v. *Macrae*, 1922.)[292]

The rule also applies to the construction of a main contract with a collateral one as *Mendelssohn* v. *Normand Ltd*, 1969[293] and *Evans* v. *Merzario*, 1976[294] illustrate.

(c) *The four corners rule.*   Under this rule exemption clauses only protect a party when he is acting within the four corners of the contract. Thus he is liable for damage which occurs while he is deviating from the contract and he would not be protected by any exclusion clause. (See *Thomas National Transport (Melbourne) Pty Ltd and Pay* v. *May and Baker*, 1966.)[295]

3. The doctrine of fundamental breach.   This doctrine was usually invoked where a plaintiff sought a remedy on a contract containing exemption clauses which had been adequately communicated. The doctrine said, in effect, that where one party had fundamentally broken his contract, that is, done something fundamentally different from what he contracted to do, an exclusion clause could not, as a matter of *law* and not of *construction* protect him. Examples of the application of the doctrine are to be found in *Karsales (Harrow) Ltd* v. *Wallis*, 1956[296] and *Alexander* v. *The Railway Executive*, 1951.)[297]

Difficulties arose over the meaning of a fundamental breach and attempts where made to distinguish it from a condition (or repudiatory breach) so that an exemption clause excluding liability for breach of condition would be ineffective to exclude liability for fundamental breach.

As a result of the decision of the House of Lords in the *Suisse Case* 1966[298] and subsequent cases, the position is as follows—

(i) there is no breach of contract more fundamental than a breach of condition. In the *Suisse Case*[298] the House of Lords defined a fundamental breach as a breach by one party entitling the other to treat the contract as terminated. This definition equates fundamental breach with repudiatory breach of condition.

(ii) The effect of a breach of condition on an exclusion clause would appear to be as follows—

(*a*) If on breach of condition the innocent party *elects* to repudiate and bring the contract to an end the clause falls with the contract and does not exclude liability for the breach of condition giving rise to the right to repudiate. (*Suisse Case*, 1966.)[298] Thus, if A supplies goods to B which are in breach of a condition as in the case of a car which is in such a poor state that it cannot be driven, the buyer may refuse to take delivery and repudiate the contract. In such a case any exemption clauses are repudiated with the main contract itself and would not excuse the seller for delivering a vehicle in such a poor state.

(*b*) The position is the same where the defendant's breach of condition brings the contract to an end automatically without the innocent party being in a position to elect as where it is impossible for him to go on with the contract. (*Harbutt's Plasticine Ltd* v. *Wayne Tank and Pump Co Ltd,* 1970.)[299]

(*c*) If a breach of condition is established by the innocent party with knowledge of the breach proceeds to treat the contract as continuing and then sues for damages, the exclusion clause may survive and be raised as a defence. Whether it will be effective to exclude or modify the defendant's liability will depend upon the relevant rules of construction of contracts. These are as follows—

(1) Under the *contra proferentem* rule exclusion clauses are read strictly against those wishing to rely on them. The application of this rule would provide an alternative way of arriving at the decision in *Alexander* v. *Railway Executive,* 1951.[297]

(2) A court will strike out or modify an exemption clause which is repugnant to the main purpose of the contract. The application of this rule would provide an alternative way of arriving at the decision in *Karsales (Harrow) Ltd* v. *Wallis,* 1956.[296]

(3) Exemption clauses will protect a party only when he is acting within the four corners of the contract. Thus, if a party deviates from the contract an exemption clause will not protect him in respect of breaches committed during the period of deviation. (*Thomas National Transport (Melbourne) Pty Ltd and Pay* v. *May and Baker,* 1966.)[295]

(4) In addition the courts may reject as a matter of construction even the widest exemption clause if it '. . . would lead to an absurdity or because it would defeat the main object of the contract or perhaps for other reasons. And where some limit must be read into a clause it is generally reasonable to draw the line at fundamental breaches.' (per Lord Reid in the *Suisse*[298] case adopted by Lord Denning in *Harbutt's Case.*)

This general rule of construction that normally an exception or exclusion clause or similar provision in a contract should be construed as not applying to a situation created by a fundamental breach of contract was applied by the Court of Appeal in *Farnworth Finance Facilities Ltd* v. *Attryde,* 1970.[300]

Although it is expressed as a rule of construction it appears in practical terms to go back almost to the old doctrine of fundamental breach.

As to what is a fundamental breach, Donaldson, J. in *Kenyon, Son & Craven Ltd* v. *Baxter Hoare Ltd,* 1971[301] said that on his understanding of the *Suisse*[298] case a fundamental breach would normally occur only when the method of performance was *totally different* from that contemplated by the contract, though this does not seem to have been a necessary requirement in subsequent cases, the Court of Appeal in particular being satisfied to strike down an exemption clause even though performance was not totally different (see *Farnworth*[300] and *Wathes (Western)* v. *Austins (Menswear) Ltd,* 1976).[302] This is in part a result of the attitude of the Court of Appeal towards exemption clauses. Some judges in the Court of Appeal, particularly Lord Denning, appear to be moving away from the rules of construction approach of *Suisse*[298] to what might be called a policy approach. For example, Lord Denning's judgment in *Evans* v. *Merzario,* 1976[294] rejects exemption clauses—at least in standard from—as being sharp practice, so that they can never exclude liability for fundamental breach. If the policy rule prevails no exclusion clause would ever be able to excuse a fundamental breach. Finally it should be noted that in a contract of bailment other than carriage when a bailee seeks to escape liability on the ground that he is excused by an exclusion clause and the owner of the goods pleads a fundamental breach of the bailment, the burden of proof is on the bailee to disprove fundamental breach by showing what happened to the goods while they were in his possession. (*Hunt and Winterbotham (West of England) Ltd* v. *B.R.S. (Parcels) Ltd,* 1962[303] and *Levison* v. *Patent Steam Carpet Cleaning Co. Ltd,* 1977.)[304]

The approach of Parliament

Legislation affecting exclusion clauses is as follows—

Sale of Goods.   The terms implied into a contract for sale of goods by the Sale of Goods Act, 1893 as amended by the Supply of Goods (Implied Terms) Act, 1973, cannot in some circumstances be excluded.

There is a distinction between *consumer sales* and other sales. A consumer sale is one where the seller *in the course of business* sells goods which are ordinarily bought for private use or consumption to a buyer who intends to use them for his own private purposes.

If the sale is a consumer one Sects 12 to 15 of the Sale of Goods Act which imply terms relating to title, description, fitness for purpose, merchantability and sales by sample, cannot be excluded. If the sale is not a consumer one as, for example, if it is a sale by a wholesaler to a retailer or by one business to another, the above Sections can be excluded if the court thinks in a subsequent action that it is fair and reasonable to allow the seller to use an exclusion clause.

Credit agreements.   By the Consumer Credit Act, 1974, the implied obligations imposed on the owner of goods who lets them out on a credit agreement which are the same as those in the Sale of Goods Act cannot be excluded in consumer transactions. They may be excluded in non-consumer transactions if the courts thinks that it is fair and reasonable to allow the owner to rely on an exclusion clause.

As regards what is fair and reasonable in the case of sale of goods and credit agreements, the Acts of 1973 and 1974 set out certain criteria to assist the court, as follows—

(a) Strength of the bargaining position of the parties. Thus if one party is in a strong position and the other in a weaker in terms of bargaining power, the stronger party may not be allowed to retain an exclusion clause in the contract.

(b) Availability of other supplies. Again, if a seller is in a monopolistic position so that it is not possible for the buyer to find the goods readily elsewhere, the court may decide that an exclusion clause in the contract of a monopolistic seller shall not apply.

(c) Inducements to agree to the clause. If the goods have been offered for sale at £10 without an exemption clause but at £8 with the inclusion of the clause, the court may see fit to allow the clause to apply at the lower price because there has been a concession by the seller in terms of the price.

(d) Buyer's knowledge of the extent of the clause. If the clause has been pointed out to the buyer and he is fully aware that it reduces the liability of the seller, then this will be relevant in deciding whether the seller should be allowed to rely on the clause. If a buyer is reasonably fully informed and aware of the seller's intentions as regards exclusion of liability, then the buyer may have to accept the clause.

(e) Customs of trade and previous dealings. If, for example, exclusion clauses are usual in the trade or have been used by the parties in previous dealings, then the court may decide that an exclusion clause should apply. It should be noted that previous dealings do not seem relevant in consumer transactions but they are in this area where one is considering a non-consumer situation.

(f) Whether the goods have been made, processed or adapted to the order of the buyer. Obviously if the seller has been required by the buyer to produce goods in a certain way, then it may well be fair and reasonable for the seller to exclude his liability in respect of faults arising out of, for example, the buyer's design which he insisted was used.

Misrepresentation.   By Sect. 3 of the Misrepresentation Act, 1967, any term which excludes liability for misrepresentation is void unless the court allows reliance on it as being fair and reasonable in the circumstances of the case. It should be noted that there are no statutory criteria in the 1967 Act to assist the court in deciding what is fair and reasonable. (But see p. 235.) However, in *Overbrook Estates Ltd* v. *Glencombe Properties Ltd*, [1974] 3 All E.R. 511 the conditions of sale contained in an auction catalogue stated that neither the auctioneers nor any person in their employ, had any authority to make or give any representations or warranty in relation to any particular property. Brightman, J. held that this clause did not fall within Sect. 3. The section prevents a person excluding liability for statements amounting to misrepresentation made by his duly author-ized agent in circumstances where the agent has authority to make the statement. It does not prevent persons from cutting down the authority of their agents to make statements at all. Thus, if the agent has authority to make the statement and it is false, liability cannot be excluded by reason of Sect. 3. If, however, the agent has no authority to make the statement at all Sect. 3 does not apply and the principal will not be liable for what he says to a person who knew the agent had no authority to make the statement or had no reasonable grounds to believe that he had authority.

Passenger transport—roads. Under Sect. 151 of the Road Traffic Act, 1960, a person providing public passenger transport by road cannot exclude his liability for death or personal injury

Passenger transport—rail. Under Sect. 43(7) of the Transport Act, 1962, British Rail cannot exclude its liability for death or personal injury. This legislation would, of course, have affected the decision in *Thompson* v. *L.M.S. Railway,* 1930[282] though the case is still good in terms of what it has to say about constructive notice. (See now p. 235.)

Fair Trading Act, 1973. Under Sects 13 and 17 of this Act the Director-General of Fair Trading can in the course of investigating consumer trade practices deal in particular with 'terms and conditions on which or subject to which goods or services are supplied'. This, of course, concerns exemption clauses being used in consumer transactions. If after investigation the Director-General feels that a particular practice in terms of exemption clauses should cease he will make a report to the Minister who may pass a statutory instrument to stop the practice. For example, the Consumer Transactions (Restrictions on Statements) Order, 1976 (No. 1813) prohibits persons who, in the court of business, sell goods to consumers or supply them under hire purchase or trading stamp agreements from purporting by means, amongst other things, of notices in shops to apply terms which are void by reason of the Sale of Goods Act, 1893, or the Supply of Goods (Implied Terms) Act, 1973, and from supplying statements about the consumer's rights against the supplier relating to quality and fitness without at the same time notifying the consumer that his statutory rights are not affected.

Unfair Contract Terms Act, 1977. This legislation, which derives from the report of the Law Commission (No. 69), will have a profound effect on the use of all exclusion clauses, including those in guarantees. In broad terms the provisions of the Sale of Goods Act, 1893, Sects 13–15 relating to implied terms and the provisions of the Supply of Goods (Implied Terms) Act, 1973, relating to exclusion clauses are extended to contracts of hire and exchange and contracts for work and materials, e.g. car repairs. No exclusion of liability for breach (including non-performance) of other contracts is allowed in consumer deals and deals on standard terms; nor is it possible to exclude liability for a performance of the contract which is substantially different from that reasonably expected. In other situations an exclusion clause will only be effective if the court thinks it is reasonable.

As regards harm caused intentionally or by negligence by a person *in the course of a business* (including duties arising under the Occupiers Liability Act, 1957) there can be no exclusion of liability for death or personal injury. Liability for other loss or damage can only be excluded if reasonable. Furthermore the fact that a person is aware of the existence of an exclusion clause is not evidence of *volenti*, i.e. that he is willing to assume the risk (see p. 318).

The tests of reasonableness in the Supply of Goods (Implied Terms) Act, 1973, are applied to Sect. 3 of the Misrepresentation Act, 1967.

CONTRACTS *UBERRIMAE FIDEI*

There is generally no obligation on a contracting party to enlighten the other party even where he knows or suspects there is a misapprehension. For example, X offers to sell a watch to Y, and Y, thinking it is a gold watch, offers £100 for it. X, knowing the watch is not gold, accepts Y's offer without enlightening him. The contract is binding provided X made no representation in the matter. The essential maxim in such cases is *caveat emptor* (Let the buyer beware). This rather harsh rule is modified in certain circumstances, e.g. in the case of sales by persons privately or in a business the Sale of Goods Act, 1893 (as amended by the Supply of Goods (Implied Terms) Act, 1973) imports into all contracts for the sale of goods certain implied conditions and warranties, which cannot be excluded in consumer sales but may be if it is fair and reasonable to do so in non-consumer sales.

However, there are certain contracts in which disclosure of material facts is required by law. They are called contracts *uberrimae fidei* or contracts of the utmost good faith. Here silence can amount to misrepresentation, in the sense that non-disclosure of some material fact by one of the parties to the contract will give rise to a remedy in the injured party. The following contracts are of this type—

(i) *Contracts of insurance.*   There is a duty on the person insured to disclose to the insurer all facts which might affect the premium. Failure to do so renders the contract voidable at the option of the insurer.

In addition, most proposals for insurance require the proposer to sign a declaration in which he warrants that the statements he has made are true and agrees that they be incorporated into the contract as terms. Where this is so any false statement which the proposer makes will be a ground for avoidance of the contract by the insurance company even though the statement was not material in terms of the premium. (See *Dawsons* v. *Bonnin*, 1922.)[305]

(ii) *Contracts to take shares in a company under a prospectus.*   There is a duty on the company or its promoters to disclose the various matters set out in the Fourth Schedule to the Companies Act, 1948. Failure to do so may render those responsible liable in damages, unless the omission resulted from an honest mistake of fact or the omission was immaterial or ought reasonably to be excused. It is settled that a subscriber cannot rescind an allotment of securites which he has been induced to take by a prospectus which omits information required to be disclosed by the Fouth Schedule. (*Re Wimbledon Olympia Ltd,* [1910] 1 Ch. 630.)

(iii) *Family arrangements.* In contracts and dealings between members of a family, each member must disclose all material facts within his knowledge. (*Gordon* v. *Gordon,* 1819.)[306]

(iv) *Contracts for the sale of land.* The vendor is under a duty to disclose all defects in his title if they are known to him, and also the extent of any restrictive covenants affecting the land.

(v) *Suretyship and partnership contracts.* There is a duty on partners to disclose all matters within their knowledge which affect or may affect the business. However, this duty arises only when the partners are partners so that disclosure is not required during the negotiations leading to the admission of a partner. Similarly there is some duty of disclosure between a creditor and the person who guarantees the debt due from the principal debtor.

Probably, contracts of insurance are the only true contracts *uberrimae fidei.* The others are analogous thereto, but are based more on the equitable concept of fiduciary relationship. The question of disclosure in the case of company prospectuses is, of course, statutory, the courts having consistently refused to declare that a contract to take shares from a company was of the class *uberrimae fidei.* A contract of service does not give rise to duties of disclosure. (*Bell* v. *Lever Bros Ltd,* 1932.)[225]

DURESS

Duress will affect all contracts and gifts procured by its use. Duress, which is a common law concept, means actual violence or threats of violence to the person of the contracting party or those near and dear to him. (*Welch* v. *Cheesman*, 1974.)[307] The threats must be calculated to produce fear of loss of life or bodily harm.

A contract will seldom be procurred by actual violence but threats of violence are more probable. The threat must be illegal in that it must be a threat to commit a crime or tort. Thus to threaten an imprisonment, which would be unlawful if enforced, constitutes duress (*Cumming* v. *Ince,* 1847).[308] but not, it is said, if the imprisonment would be lawful. However, the courts are unlikely to look with favour on a contract obtained by threatening to prosecute a criminal. A contract procured by a threat to sue for an act which was not a crime, e.g. trespass, would not be affected by duress.

The concept is not applicable to threats to property. Thus in *Skeate* v. *Beale,* (1840), 11 Ad. & El. 983, a tenant owed what would now be

£19.50p and agreed to pay £3.37½p immediately and the remaining £16·12½p within a month if his landlord would withdraw a writ of distress under which he was threatening to sell the tenant's goods. The tenant later disputed what he owed and the landlord tried to set up the agreement and sued for the remaining £16.12½p. It was held that the landlord was entitled to £16.12½p under the agreement which was not affected by duress since the threat was to sell the tenant's goods.

Duress probably renders contract *voidable* This, at least, is the view of Cheshire, though other writers have argued that the effect of duress is to render a contract void. The issue is an important one for third parties since if B procures goods from A by duress and sells the goods to C, who has no knowledge of the duress, A will be able to recover the goods from C if the contract is void, but will not be able to do so if it is voidable. There is support for the view that a contract affected by duress is voidable in the judgments of the Privy Council in *Barton* v. *Armstrong*, [1975] 2 All E.R. 465 where it is said that a disposition made under duress or undue influence is to be regarded in the same way as a disposition made as a result of a fraudulent misrepresentation. It is well known, of course, that the latter renders a contract voidable and therefore presumably so does duress. It was always known that undue influence rendered a contract voidable. (See below.)

UNDUE INFLUENCE

The doctrine of undue influence was developed by equity. The concept of undue influence is designed to deal with contracts or gifts obtained without free consent by the influence of one mind over another.

If there is no special relationship between the parties undue influence may exist, but must be proved by the person seeking to avoid the contract. (*Williams* v. *Bayley*, 1866.)[309]

Where a confidential or fiduciary relationship exists between the parties, the party in whom the confidence was reposed must show that undue influence was not used, i.e. that the contract was the act of free and independent mind. It is desirable, though not essential that independent advice should have been given.

There are several confidential relationships known to the law, viz. parent and child, solicitor and client, trustee and beneficiary, guardian and ward and religious adviser and disciple (*Allcard* v. *Skinner*, 1887[310] and see also *Mustafa* v. *Hudaverdi*, 1972).[311] There is no presumption of such relationship between husband and wife. The fiduciary relationship between parent and child ends usually, but not necessarily, on reaching 18 or on getting married (but see *Lancashire Loans Ltd* v. *Black*, 1934).[312] However there may be a presumption of undue influence even though the relationship between the parties is not in the established categories outlined above. In *re Craig Dec'd*, [1970] 2 W.L.R. 1219, Ungoed Thomas, J. ruled that a presumption of undue influence arose on proof—

(*a*) of a gift so substantial or of such a nature that it could not on the face of it be accounted for on the grounds of the ordinary motives on which ordinary men acted; and

(*b*) of a relationship of trust and confidence such that the recipient of the gift was in a position to exercise undue influence over the person making it. This principle was applied in *Hodgson* v. *Marks,* 1970.[313]

The concept has been used in situations of inequality of bargaining power between the parties to a contract, and this is a considerable widening of the concept. Thus in *Clifford Davis Management* v. *W.E.A. Records,* [1975] 1 All E.R. 237 a manager skilled in business and finance made each member of a pop group sign a contract which included an assignment of the copyright in all their compositions to the plaintiffs for a period of up to ten years. The Court of Appeal held that the plaintiffs could not enforce that assignment because there was inequality of bargaining power as between themselves and the pop group leading to a situation of undue influence in which the group should have had independent advice. In this context the case of *Lloyds Bank* v. *Bundy,* 1974[314] is also of interest.

Effect on the contract

Undue influence renders the contract voidable so that it may be rescinded. However, since rescission is an equitable remedy, there must be no delay in claiming relief after the influence has ceased to have effect. Delay in claiming relief in these circumstances may bar the claim since delay is evidence of affirmation. (*Allcard* v. *Skinner,* 1887.)[310]

Effect on third parties

A contract procured by undue influence cannot be avoided by rescission against third parties who acquire rights for value without notice of the facts, but it may be avoided against third parties for value with notice of the facts and also against volunteers (i.e. persons who have given no consideration) even though they were unaware of the facts.

CONTRACTS AND PUBLIC POLICY

Freedom of contract must always be subject to overriding considerations of public policy. In all actions brought in England the contract is subject to English rules of public policy even though the proper law of the contract is not English law. (*Kaufman* v. *Gerson,* 1904.)[315] Furthermore, restrictive covenants are construed strictly so as not to create a wider obligation than is imputed by the actual words. (*Rother* v. *Colchester Coporation,* 1969.)[316]

Public policy has been ascertained as follows—

(i) At common law by the judiciary. At one time the judiciary had wide powers of discretion in the matter of creating new categories of public policy but this view is now unacceptable. In *Fender* v. *Mildmay*, [1938] A.C.1. The House of Lords declared against the extension of the heads of public policy, at least by the judiciary. However, up to 1938 the judiciary had created a number of categories of public policy. These fell into two areas as follows—

(*a*) Illegal contracts. These involve some degree of moral wrong and contracts to commit crimes or to defraud the revenue fall into this category.

(*b*) Void Contracts. In these cases there is not in any strict sense blameworthy conduct; the contracts are rendered void because if enforced by the courts they could produce unsatisfactory results on society. Examples are contracts in restraint of trade, e.g. an agreement under which an employee covenants with his employer that on the termination of his contract he will not work for a rival firm or start a competing business, and contracts prejudicial to marriage, e.g. a contract under which a person promises not to marry at all.

(ii) By Parliament. Parliament expresses its view as to what is public policy by Acts of Parliament and rules and orders made by ministers under Acts of Parliament. Again, statute law in this area falls into two categories as follows—

(*a*) The creation of illegal contracts. This happens where the Act of Parliament actually makes the contract *unlawful.* Thus Sect. 1 of the Resale Prices Act, 1976, declares unlawful all *collective* agreements between suppliers of goods to 'blacklist' retailers who sell below the minimum resale price agreed by the suppliers.

(*b*) The creation of void contracts. Here there is no suggestion that the contract is unlawful in the strict sense or that moral blame attaches. There are two main areas as follows—

(1) Wagering contracts, which will be dealt with later, and

(2) The prevention of restrictive practices. Thus agreements by suppliers to fix prices or restrict supplies are void under the Restrictive Trade Practices Act, 1976, unless the parties can prove to the Restrictive Practices Court that their agreement is beneficial and in the public interest.

Public policy—the contribution of the judiciary

Illegal contracts. These contracts involve some form of moral weakness which society in general seeks to control. They are as follows—

(a) Contracts to commit crimes (see *Dann* v. *Curzon*, 1911)[317] **or civil wrongs.** Thus a contract between an agent and his client whereby the agent was to receive a double commission would be illegal because it has as its object the commission of a fraud on the principal, since if the agent takes a double commission there is a conflict of interest.

(b) Contracts involving sexual immorality. Agreements for future illicit cohabitation are void, because the promise of payment might encourage immoral conduct in a person who otherwise would not have participated. However, a contract under which a person promises to pay another money in return for past illicit cohabitation is not illegal because it does not necessarily encourage future immorality between the parties. Such a contract will, however, be unenforceable unless made under seal because it is for past consideration. Furthermore, contracts which are on the face of it legal may be affected if *knowingly* made to further an immoral purpose. (*Pearce* v. *Brooks,* 1866.)[318]

(c) Contracts affecting public safety. At common law all contracts made with a person (regardless of nationality) living in enemy territory in time of war are illegal unless made with licence of the Crown. This category also includes contracts to carry out acts which are illegal by the law of a foreign and friendly country, since to enforce such contracts would encourage disputes. (See *Foster* v. *Driscoll,* 1929[319] and *Regazzoni* v. *K. C. Sethia Ltd,* 1958.)[320]

(d) Contracts prejudicial to the administration of justice. Thus, a contract tending to defeat the bankruptcy laws is illegal at common law. (See *John* v. *Mendoza,* 1939.)[321]

(e) Contracts tending to corruption in public life. A contract to procure a title or honour is illegal under this head. (See *Parkinson* v. *College of Ambulance,* 1952.)[322]

(f) Contracts to defraud the Revenue. This applies whether the fraud is in connection with local rates or national taxes. (See *Alexander* v. *Rayson,* 1936[323] and *Napier* v. *National Business Agency Ltd,* 1951.)[324]

Consequences

The consequences of illegality in the above cases depends upon whether the contract was unlawful on the face of it, i.e. there was no way in which lawful performance could be achieved or whether the contract was lawful on the face of it, i.e. it could have been performed in a lawful manner.

(i) Contract unlawful on face of it. This includes all the categories mentioned above except some contracts involving sexual immorality. The consequences in this case are as follows—

(a) The contract is void and there is no action by either party for debt (*Dann* v. *Curzon,* 1911),[317] damages, specific performance or injunction.

(b) Money paid or property transferred to the other party under the contract is irrecoverable. (*Parkinson* v. *College of Ambulance,* 1925.)[322] Unless—

(1) The plaintiff is relying on rights other than those which are contained in the contract. Thus if A leases property to B for five years and A knows that B intends to use the property as a brothel, then A cannot recover rent or require any covenant to be performed without pleading the illegal lease. However, at the end of the term A can bring an action for the return of his property as *owner* and not as a landlord under an illegal lease (and see *Bowmakers Ltd* v. *Barnet Instruments Ltd,* 1944.)[325] In addition, if the action is to redress a wrong which, although in a sense connected with the contract, can really be considered independent of it, the law will allow the action. (*Edler* v. *Auerbach,* 1950.)[326]

(2) The plaintiff is not in *pari delicto* (equal wrong). Where the contract is unlawful on the face of it, equal guilt is presumed but this presumption may be rebutted if the plaintiff can show that the defendant was guilty of fraud, oppression or undue influence. (See *Hughes* v. *Liverpool Victoria Legal Friendly Society,* 1916[327] and *Atkinson* v. *Denby,* 1862.)[328]

(3) The plaintiff repents provided that the repentance is genuine (*Bigos* v. *Bousted,* 1951.)[329] and performance is *partial* (*Taylor* v. *Bowers,* 1876)[330] and not *substantial*. (*Kearley* v. *Thomson,* 1890.)[331]

It should be noted that collateral transactions *between the same parties* are void. (*Fisher* v. *Bridges,* 1854.)[332] Where *a third party* enters into a collateral contract with one or both of the parties to the original transaction his rights will depend upon whether he knew or not that the original transaction was illegal. (*Southern Industrial Trust* v. *Brooke House Motors,* 1968[333] and *Spector* v. *Ageda,* 1971.)[334]

(ii) **Contract lawful of face of it.** The result here is as follows—

(*a*) Where both parties intended the illegal purpose. There is no action by either party for debt, damages, specific performance or injunction (*Pearce* v. *Brooks,* 1866)[318] or to recover money paid or property transferred under the contract.

(*b*) Where one party was without knowledge of the illegal purpose. The innocent party's rights are unaffected and he may sue for debt, damages specific performance, or injunction, (See *Clay* v. *Yates,* 1856[235] and *Fielding and Platt Ltd* v. *Najjar,* 1969.)[336] or to recover money paid or property transferred.

(*c*) The party who would have performed the contract in an unlawful manner has no action on it (*Cowan* v. *Milbourn,* 1867[337] and *Ashmore, Benson, Pease* v. *A. V. Dawson Ltd,* 1973)[338] nor can he recover property delivered to the other party under the contract. (*Berg* v. *Sadler and Moore,* 1937.)[339] However, it is necessary to show that the plaintiff had knowledge of the illegal transaction and participated therein, though such knowledge may be imputed to the plaintiff even if he remains inactive as in *Ashmore, Benson, Pease.*[338]

Public policy and the judiciary—void contracts

These contracts do not involve any type of moral weakness but are against public policy because they are inexpedient rather than unprincipled. The contracts concerned are contracts to oust the jurisdiction of the courts, contracts prejudicial to the status of marriage, and contracts in restraint of trade. These are dealt with individually below.

Contracts to oust the jurisdiction of the courts

A contract which has the effect of taking away the right of one or both of the parties to bring an action before a court of law is void. (*Goodinson* v. *Goodinson*, 1954[340] and *Re Davstone Estates, Ltd*, 1969.)[341] This rule does not make void honourable pledge clauses because in such cases the parties do not intend to be bound by the contract at all. If the contract is to be binding, however, then the parties cannot exclude it from the jurisdiction of the courts. Furthermore, arbitration clauses are not affected. Many commercial contracts contain an arbitration clause, the object being to provide a cheaper or more convenient remedy than a court action. An arbitration clause in a contract is not void if the effect of it is that the parties are to go to arbitration *first* before going to court. An arbitration clause which denies the parties access to the courts completely is, or course, invalid.

Contracts prejudicial to the status of marriage

A contract in absolute restraint of marriage, i.e. one in which a person promises not to marry at all, is void. Partial restraints, if reasonable, are said to be valid, e.g. a contract not to marry a person of certain religious faith, or not to marry for a short period of time. However, there are no recent cases and it may be that even a partial restraint would be regarded as void today. Marriage brokage contracts, i.e. contracts to introduce men and women with a view to their subsequent marriage, are also void on the grounds that third parties should not be free to reap financial profit by bringing about matrimonial unions.

As regards separation agreements, these are invalid if made for the future, as where a husband promises that he will make provision for his wife if she should ever live apart from him, unless the agreement is made as part of a reconciliation arrangement. In this case the agreement is valid, although it may make provision for a renewed future separation. If the parties are not living in amity or are actually separated, then a separation agreement is valid. Once it is apparent that the parties cannot live together in amity it is desirable that a separation which has become inevitable should be concluded upon reasonable terms.

Contracts in restraint of trade

Such contracts are *prima facie* void and will only be binding if reasonable. Thus the contract must be reasonable between the parties which means that it must be no wider than is necessary to protect the interest involved in terms of the area and time of its operation. Mere competition is not an interest entitled to protection in this way. (*Morris* v. *Saxelby*, 1916.)[342] It must also be reasonable as regards the public interest. (See *Wyatt* v. *Kreglinger and Fernau*, 1933.)[343] Finally, the issue of reasonableness is a matter of law for the judge on the evidence presented to him which would include, for example, such matters as trade practices and customs.

Voluntary contractual restraints

There are four categories of voluntary contractual restraints as follows—

(a) Restraints imposed upon employees. In this connection it should be noted that there are only *two* things an employer can protect—

(i) Trade secrets. A restraint against competition is justifiable if its object is to prevent the exploitation of trade secrets learned by the employee in the course of his employment. (See *Forster & Sons Ltd* v. *Suggett*, 1918.)[344]

In this connection it should be noted that the area of the restraint must not be excessive. Thus in *Empire Meat Co. Ltd* v. *Patrick*, [1939] 2 All E.R. 85 a restraint concerning a retail butcher's business was held to be invalid because, amongst other things, the area within which the employee agreed not to carry on or be employed in the business of butcher, although it was only five miles from the place where the employer carried on business, was too wide in view of the limited area of the employers' trade.

In *Financial Collection Agencies (UK)* v. *Batey, The Times* 3 May, 1973 the Court of Appeal decided that restrictive covenants in the contracts of debt collectors in Birmingham restraining them for a period of six months after the termination of their employment from soliciting business for clients in Birmingham, Glasgow, Leeds, Liverpool, London and Manchester were too wide and unenforceable because on the evidence the employees had no contract with clients outside Birmingham.

Furthermore, a restraint may be invalid because its duration is excessive. The burden on the employer increases as the duration of the restraint is extended, though in rare situations a restraint for life may be valid. (*Fitch* v. *Dewes*, 1921.)[345]

The restraint must be restricted to the sphere of activity in which the employee has been engaged. (*Commercial Plastics Ltd* v. *Vincent*, 1965.)[346]

However, much depends on the influence over customers and clients which an employee may have acquired and in *S. W. Strange* v. *Mann*, [1965] 1 All E.R. 1096, Stamp, J. drew a distinction between a credit business and a cash business. In a cash business the names of the customers are known only to the employees and are not recorded in the books of the firm. For this reason the employees in a cash business are more likely to have influence over the customers of the firm and the court may be more sympathetic towards a wider restraint in respect of them, provided it does not exceed the area of the employer's trade.

(ii) Business connection. Sometimes an employer may use a covenant against *solicitation* of persons with whom the employer does business. No problem of area arises in this type of covenant, though its duration must be reasonable. (*Home Counties Dairies* v. *Skilton*, 1970.)[347] In order to enforce a covenant in restraint of solicitation it is normally necessary to show that the business has recurring customers. (*Scorer* v. *Seymour Jones*, 1966.)[348]

As regards the enforcement of post-employment restraints, Denning, L. J. (as he then was) said in *M. & S. Drapers* v. *Reynolds*, [1956] 3 All E.R. 814 at 820: 'During the last 40 years the courts have shown a reluctance to enforce covenants of this sort. They realise that a servant has often very little choice in the matter . . . he is very much at the mercy of his employer.' However, three more recent decisions of the Court of Appeal show a change of attitude which may result in employer/employee restraints being more readily enforceable by the employer. (See *Home Counties Dairies* v. *Skilton*, 1970[347] *White (Marion) Ltd* v. *Francis*, 1972[349] and *Lucas* v. *Mitchell*, 1972.)[350]

It must also be remembered that a covenant in restraint of trade is merely part of a larger contract of employment so that if the employer unjustifiably terminates the contract, as by wrongfully dismissing his employee, or the employee is, in the circumstances, justified in terminating his employment, the restraint will be unenforceable. (*General Billposting Co.* v. *Atkinson*, 1909.)[351]

Furthermore, an employer cannot enforce a contract restraining his employee from entering a particular field of business activity on the ground that the employer *may at a later date* wish to set up business in that field. (*Bromley* v. *Smith*, 1909.)[352] It should also be noted that a restraint may be applied even where an employee forms a limited company to carry on business in defiance of a restraint. Corporate status cannot be used for such a purpose. Thus in *Gilford Motor Co.* v. *Horne*, [1933] Ch. 935 a former employee bound by a restraint of trade set up a company in order to evade its provisions, claiming that he as a person might be bound by the restraint but the company, being a separate entity, could not. An injunction was granted against both him and his company which the court described as 'a device, a stratagem . . . a mere cloak or sham'.

In addition, where entering into a pension scheme is a term of a contract of service, a term in the scheme is that the pension be forfeited if the employee works for a competitor is void as an unreasonable restraint of trade. (*Bull* v. *Pitney Bowes*, 1966.)[353]

The *duty of fidelity* of employees is also of interest, since it is possible to prevent an employee from using trade secrets or business connections without any specific contract in restraint of trade. Certain activities by employees are regarded by the law as breaches of the duty of faithful service which an employee owes to his employer. Breaches of the duty of fidelity will sometimes be prevented by the court, so a person who retains secret processes in his memory can be restrained from using them to his employer's disadvantage. However, the employee's knowledge of trade secrets must be readily separable and not merely part of the total experience gained from employment. (*Printers and Finishers Ltd* v. *Holloway*, 1964[354] and *United Sterling Corporation* v. *Felton and Mannion*, 1973.)[355]

An employee who copies names and addresses of his employer's customers for use after leaving his employment can be restrained from using the lists without any express restriction in his contract. (*Robb* v. *Green*, 1895.)[356] In connection with the duty of fidelity, it should be noted that it does not matter who initiates the infidelity and, although in most cases the employee approaches the customer, the rule still applies even where the customers approach the employee. (*Sanders* v. *Parry*, 1967.)[357] The case of *Hivac Ltd.* v. *Park Royal Scientific Instruments Ltd,* 1946[358] is also of interest since it shows that skilled men with access to their employer's secrets may not be able to work for a rival firm *even in their spare time.*

Finally, a servant is under no implied obligation not to disclose information concerning his employer's misconduct if it ought in the public interest to be disclosed to a person having a proper interest to receive it. (*Initial Services* v. *Putterill,* 1967.)[359]

(b) Exclusive service contracts. There have been very few cases dealing with the extent of a restraint of an employee during the currency of his employment. However, it is now clear that an agreement between employer and employee can be declared an unreasonable restraint of trade even during the existence of the employment but in normal circumstances this appears to be unlikely. It is probable that the courts would be reluctant to interfere with such agreements in the absence of special circumstances, such as where the contract is contrary to normal trade practise or where it is totally one-sided. (*A. Schroeder Music Publishing Co. Ltd* v. *Macauley,* 1974.)[360] However, even if the restraint is not invalid the employer would still face difficulties in regard to a suitable remedy. The employer can, of course, always dismiss the employee but it is doubtful how far he can go to prevent the employee from working for a third person. The appropriate remedy in such a case is an injunction. However, there are a number of limitations on the availability of that remedy in respect of service contracts, for instance the restriction must be worded negatively. (*Warner Bros.* v. *Nelson,* 1937.)[449] In addition, the current trend seems to be against enforcing covenants of exclusive service either on the ground of restraint of trade or on the ground of the unavailability of an injunction.

(c) Agreements between partners. Clauses restricting an outgoing or retiring partner from practising within a defined area are frequently found in partnership agreements between professional men. Such clauses will not be enforceable if they are wider than is reasonably necessary for the protection of the practice. However, protection *against competition* as such is to some extent allowed and this distinguishes professional practice restraint from employer and employer restraint, though the test of reasonableness still applies. (*Lyne-Pirkis* v. *Jones,* 1969.)[361]

(d) Restraints imposed on the vendor of a business. Such a restraint will be void unless it is required to protect the business sold and not to stifle competition. (*British Concrete Co.* v. *Schelff,* 1921.)[362]

It should be noted, however, that the protection of the business sold may in rare situations involve a world-wide restraint. (*Nordenfelt* v. *Maxim Nordenfelt Guns and Ammunition Co.,* 1894.)[363]

(e) Restraints arising from agreements between manufacturers and traders. This branch of law is now largely regulated by statute, i.e. the Restrictive Trade Practices Act, 1976. Nevertheless, it is necessary to consider the common law position because not all restrictive agreements are covered by the above legislation and where it does not apply, the common law on the topic may be invoked. For example, the restrictive agreement which was at the root of *Kores Manufacturing Co.* v. *Kolok Manufacturing Co. Ltd,* 1959[364] was not covered by the Act which is not concerned with agreements between traders in regard to their employees and was decided on common law principles. These principles are that the agreement must be reasonable between the parties and reasonable in the public interest. Both of these points arose in *Kores,* the Court of Appeal holding that the agreement was unreasonable as between the parties and also that it was contrary to the public interest though the ratio is based on the fact that the agreement was unreasonable as between the parties.

(f) Restrictions accepted by distributors of merchandise. A manufacturer or wholesaler may refuse to make merchandise available for distribution to the public unless the distributor accepts certain conditions restricting his liberty of trading. This is the main purpose of the solus agreement used by petrol companies. Such agreements are void unless reasonable. (See *Esso Petroleum Co. Ltd* v. *Harper's Garage (Stourport) Ltd,* 1967.)[365] It should be noted that there is a distinction as regards the duration of the restraint between a garage proprietor who is already in possession of the land before he ties himself to the oil companies and a man who is out of possession and is let in by the oil company. A longer period of restraint may be allowed against a garage proprietor who is let into possession by the oil company. (*Cleveland Petroleum Co. Ltd* v. *Dartstone Ltd,* 1969.)[366]

Involuntary restraints

We have so far considered restrictions against trading contained in contracts. However, the doctrine is not confirmed to these voluntary restraints. It extends to involuntary restraints imposed by trade associations or professional bodies upon their members. Such restraints are void unless reasonable. *Pharmaceutical Society of Great Britain* v. *Dickson*, 1968.)[367]

Contracts restraining the liberty of the individual other than contracts of service

These also may be illegal (see *Horwood* v. *Millar's Timber Co.*, 1917)[368] though such restrictions may be valid for certain purposes. (*Denny's Trustee* v. *Denny*, 1919.)[369] Contracts which seek to stifle comment on public affairs are void either under this heading or as in restraint of trade. (*Neville* v. *Dominion of Canada News Co. Ltd*, 1915.)[370]

Consequences

Where a contract is rendered void by the judiciary it is unenforceable only in so far as it contravenes public policy. Thus—

(a) Money paid or property transferred is recoverable. (*Hermann* v. *Charlesworth*, 1905);[371] and

(b) lawful promises may be severed and enforced. Thus a contract of service which contains a void restraint is not wholly invalid and the court will sever and enforce those aspects of it which do not offend against public policy. Thus an employee who has entered into a contract of service which contains a restraint which is too wide can recover his wages or salary. (*Wallis* v. *Day*, 1837[372] and see also *Goodinson* v. *Goodinson*, 1954.)[340]

The court will not add to a contract or in any way redraft it but will merely strike out the offending words. What is left must make sense without further additions otherwise the court will not sever the void part in order to enforce what is good. (*Attwood* v. *Lamont*, 1920.)[373]

It should be noted that, even where severance is possible, the court is not bound to sever and the court will not sever a contract unless the provisions left leave the contract substantially what is was before. Severance will not be allowed if it alters the nature of the contract. (*Kenyon* v. *Darwin Cotton Manufacturing Co.*, 1936.)[374]

Illegal contracts—the contribution of Parliament

Some contracts are prohibited by statute in terms that they are illegal, the word 'unlawful' being used in the statute concerned. In this context 'statute' includes the orders, rules and regulations that ministers of the Crown and other persons are authorized by Parliament to issue.

The statutory prohibitions with which we are concerned may be express or implied.

(a) Implied prohibition.   In these cases the statute itself does not say expressly that contracts contravening its provisions are necessarily illegal. The statute may affect the formation of a particular contract as where a trader does business without taking out a licence. In some cases the statute may affect the manner of performance of the contract as where a trader is required to deliver to a purchaser a written statement such as an invoice containing, for example, details of the chemical composition of the goods.

In either case whether failure to comply with a statutory provision renders the contract illegal is a matter of construction of the statute and is for the judge to decide.

If, in the opinion of the judge, the Act was designed to protect the public then the contract will be illegal. Thus in *Cope* v. *Rowlands*, (1836) 2 M. & W. 149 an unlicensed broker in the City of London was held not to be entitled to sue for his fees because the purpose of the licencing requirements was to protect the public against shady dealers. Furthermore, in *Anderson Ltd* v. *Daniel*, [1924] 1 K.B. 138 a seller of artificial fertilizers was held unable to recover the price of goods which he had delivered because he had failed to state in an invoice the chemical composition of the fertilizers which was required by Act of Parliament. (And see *Ashmore, Benson, Pease & Co. Ltd* v. *A. V. Dawson Ltd*, 1973.)[338]

On the other hand, if in the opinion of the judge the purpose of the legislation was mainly to raise revenue or help in the administration of trade, contracts will not be affected. Thus, in *Smith* v. *Mawhood*, (1845) 14 M. & W. 452 it was held that a tobacconist could recover the price of tobacco sold by him even though he did not have a licence to sell it and had not painted his name on his place of business. The purpose of the statute involved was not to affect the contract of sale but to impose a fine on offenders for the purpose of revenue (and see *Shaw* v. *Groom*, 1970.)[375] In addition, in *Archbolds (Freightage) Ltd* v. *Spanglett Ltd*, [1961] 1 Q.B. 374 a contract by an unlicensed carrier to carry goods by road was held valid because the legislation involved was only designed to help in the administration of road transport.

In the case of statutory illegality, it may be that the object of the statute is to protect a class of person and the plaintiff is within that class. If so, the plaintiff may be able to recover money or property transferred under the contract, for he is not deemed to be in *pari delicto*. (*Kiriri Cotton Co. Ltd* v. *Dawani*, 1960.)[376]

(b) Express prohibition.   In a book of this nature it would be inappropriate to deal in detail with all statutes which render contracts illegal but a modern example is found in the Resale Prices Act, 1976, Sect. 1. One particular type of agreement, namely an agreement for the collective enforcement of conditions regulating the price at which goods may be sold is prohibited and made unlawful.

Such agreements were not usually regarded as illegal at common law but the doctrine of privity of contract prevented enforcement of the resale price agreement by a manufacturer against a retailer. Consequently, manufacturers not having access to the ordinary courts of law often brought the retailer before a secret and possibly unjust trade association tribunal which might put the retailer quite unreasonably on a stop list so that he was denied supplies.

Under Part I of the Resale Prices Act, 1976, *collective* agreements by two or more persons regulating the price at which goods may be resold are unlawful. There is no criminal penalty but the Crown may institute civil proceedings in the High Court and obtain, for example, an injunction to prevent the practice.

It is important to note that *individual* agreements between one manufacturer and his retailers are sanctioned by Sect. 26 of the Resale Prices Act, 1976, so that such a manufacturer now has access to the ordinary courts of law to enforce his agreement. The action may be for damages or an injunction, though it is important to note that Sect. 26 only applies if the resale price agreement has been approved by the Restrictive Practices Court under the Resale Prices Act, 1976. In fact very few such agreements have been approved although an example is the *Net Book Agreement*, (1964) L.R. 4 R.P. 484, under which publishers can enforce resale price maintenance agreements in respect of books.

Void contracts—the contribution of Parliament

There are certain classes of contracts which are expressly declared by statute to be void. It would not be appropriate in a book of this nature to deal with all of them and therefore only those with a commercial connotation are described.

Wagering contracts

In essence for a wager to exist it must be possible for one party to win and one party to lose and there must be two persons or two groups opposed to each other in their views as to a future event. Thus, where X, Y and Z each put £5 into a fund to be given to the party whose selected horse wins a given race, there is no wager. (And see *Peck* v. *Lateu*, 1973.)[126] The only commercial importance of the concept of wagering and the only reason why it is introduced in a book of this nature relates to insurance. A contract is not a wager if the person to whom the money is promised on the occurrence of the event has an interest in the non-occurrence of that event, e.g. where a person has paid a premium to insure his house against destruction by fire. Such an interest is called an *insurable interest* and is not a wager. However, to insure someone else's property would be a wager and not a valid contract of insurance.

The Gaming Act of 1845 renders wagering contracts void so that there is no action for the bet or for the winnings. However, it should be noted that if the bet or the winnings have actually been paid over they cannot be recovered. Payment operates as waiver of the Act and the payment over of money confers a good title to that money upon the person to whom it is paid.

Contracts affected by the Restrictive Trade Practices Act, 1976

Under the Act of 1976 collective agreements between two or more persons designed to fix prices and/or regulate supplies of *goods* must be registered with the Director General of Fair Trading. They are then presumed void unless the parties can prove to the Restrictive Trade Practices Court that the agreement is in the public interest. This might be done, for example, where the parties can show that the agreement is designed to maintain the export trade. If the parties attempt to operate the agreement in spite of the fact that it has not been approved by the Restrictive Practices Court, the Director General of Fair Trading may ask for an injunction to prevent the operation of the agreement. However, it is rare that such action has to be taken because in most cases the firms concerned have not attempted to operate an agreement if it has been rejected by the Court. However, in *Re Galvanized Tank Manufacturers' Association's Agreement*, [1965] 1 W.L.R. 1074, the court imposed fines amounting to £102,000 on eight members of the Association for contempt of court in breaking their undertakings to the court that they would not enforce or give effect to restrictions in a price fixing agreement which the court had declared to be contrary to the public interest six years before.

This Act also allows the Director General of Fair Trading to investigate restrictive practices in regard to services. If necessary the matter can be brought before the Restrictive Trade Practices Court which now has a jurisdiction in respect of restrictive agreements relating to *services*. (*Ravenseft Properties Ltd* v. *Director-General of Fair Trading*, 1977.)[377]

The Resale Prices Act, 1976

Resale price maintenance agreements are presumed void under the 1976 Act unless the supplier can prove to the Restrictive Practices Court that the restriction is in the public interest. This might be done, for example, by showing that after sales service would be reduced or non-existent unless the resale price maintenance agreement was enforced. (And see *re Chocolate and Sugar Confectionary Reference*, 1967.)[378] Except as regards agreements which have been approved, a supplier cannot legally withhold supplies to outlets selling at below a recommended price. However, if the supplier has other reasons for withholding supplies, as where the dealer owes him money, then the supplier will not be treated as withholding supplies of goods for the purposes of the Act. In *Oxford Printing Ltd* v.

Letraset, [1970] 2 All E.R. 815, when Letraset were sued by the plaintiffs for an injunction to prevent withholding of supplies, it was held by Plowman, J. that the defendants had a good defence when they showed that their reason for withholding supplies was that the plaintiffs were, in addition to cutting the price, also using the defendants' products to promote the sales of a rival firm. The injunction was refused.

We have already seen that if a resale price maintenance agreement is approved by the Restrictive Practices Court it can be enforced regardless of the doctrine of Privity of Contract under the Resale Prices Act, 1976, Sect. 26.

European Community

Under Articles 85 and 86 of the Treaty of Rome all agreements between firms which operate to prevent or restrict competition in the Market are void. Under Sect. 5 of the Restrictive Trade Practices Act, 1976, the Director General of Fair Trading and the Restrictive Practices Court and other courts as necessary are to take Articles 85 and 86 into account—

(*a*) on the issue of registration of a particular agreement, and

(*b*) if the agreement comes before the Court for adjudication. In this connection the case of *Esso Petroleum Co.* v. *Kingswood Motors (Addlestone) Ltd,* 1973[379] is of interest.

RESTRICTIVE TRADING AGREEMENTS AND THE TREATY OF ROME

We have considered above the position under English domestic law in regard to restrictive trading agreements. Some consideration must now be given to the position under Community Law.

Policy and source of law

The provisions of the Treaty, which have been part of our law since January, 1973, are based, as UK law is, on the protection of the public interest. The basis of the competition policy is to be found in articles 85 and 86 of the Treaty. These ban practices which distort competition between members of the Community (Art. 85) (see generally *Re German Ceramic Tiles Discount Agreement,* 1971,)[380] and prohibit the abuse of a monopolistic position by an organization within the market (Art. 86). There is an additional aim of raising living standards.

The result of a breach of the Treaty is that the agreement or decision concerned becomes automatically void whether or not there has been a ruling of the Commission in Brussels or the European Court of Justice in Luxembourg, or a national court. Additionally, the Commission may impose fines.

The development of the objectives of the Treaty can best be appreciated by looking at some of the major decisions which have been made under articles 85 and 86.

Article 85

(a) Use of trade marks to restrict competition.   One of the most famous decisions is that of *Consten and Grundig,* [1966] C.M.L.R. 418. Grundig set up a network of exclusive distributors for its products throughout the Community and appointed a French firm, Consten, to be its exclusive distributor in France. Consten, in common with all other Grundig distributors was not permitted to sell either directly or indirectly outside France, and to make certain that none of the other distributors violated Consten's exclusive territorial rights, Consten was permitted to register the trade mark G.I.N.T. (which stands for Grundig International) as its French trade mark. A third party imported Grundig products into France and Consten brought an action against the importer for infringement of trademark. The case went to the European Court of Justice and it was held that the purpose of the trade mark agreement between Grundig and Consten was to guarantee complete territorial protection to Consten in the sale of Grundig products in France. That agreement was prohibited by Art. 85 as its purpose was to hamper the importing into France of Grundig products by other firms and in these circumstances the agreement was void.

(b) Cartel arrangements.   A classic illustration of cartel arrangements is to be seen in the *Quinine* cartel [1969] C.M.L.R. D.41. In that case an agreement had been made between the six manufacturing companies holding a dominant position on European and world markets by which they agreed to charge the same prices for quinine and a drug extracted from quinine and also set up export quotas in respect of imports from other Member countries. The companies involved had received legal advice to the effect that their arrangement infringed Art. 85 but nevertheless they continued to apply it and took precautions to keep it secret, instructing their members to destroy any compromising documents. However, mainly as a result of an investigation by the U.S. Senate Anti-Trust Monopolies Sub-Committee, the European Commission opened its investigations of the companies' headquarters in the Community and this led them to impose fines ranging from $10,000 up to $210,000, the fines being set in relation to each company's market position and its responsibility for the arrangements.

In the *Dyestuffs* cartel [1969] C.M.L.R. D.23, the Commission's investigations were commenced on the basis of information which they received from trade organizations of industrial users. The investigations revealed that the ten major manufacturers of dyestuffs had made uniform, and for all practical purposes, simultaneous price increases between 1964 and 1967 on the sale of their goods. This price-fixing agreement led to the imposition of fines of $50,000 on the companies involved.

(c) The use of patent rights to restrict competition.   An illustration of the attitude of the European Court on this issue is to be found in *Parke-Davis*

v. *Probel*, [1968] C.M.L.R. 47. The Parke-Davis company, based on Detroit, held certain Dutch patents for an antibiotic. Another company imported the drug into Holland without the permission of the patent holder, Parke-Davis, and they brought an action against the other company for breach of the patent. It appeared that the defendant company had purchased the drug in Italy, where there was no patent protection in medicines, and had then imported it into Holland. Thus Parke-Davis had been unable to take out patents in Italy in order to protect their rights because there was a gap in Italian law as regards patents. In these circumstances Parke-Davis took the only action they could by suing the defendant company. The defendant company pleaded that the action was in breach of competition rules and the Dutch court referred the matter to the European Court of Justice. The European Court recognized the existence of the patent rights and that the exercise of those rights to prevent goods being imported into Holland from a country where such patent rights did not exist was a wholly proper action and did not constitute a restriction on competition. However, if the goods had been imported from another country where patent rights were in existence, an attempt to prevent their importation would probably have constituted an infringement of Art. 85.

Article 86

In order that Article 86 shall be applicable it must be shown firstly that a dominant position is held by some undertaking, and that secondly there has been an abuse of that domination and thirdly, that the abuse has had an effect on trade between member states. The attitude of the Commission and the European Court to the abuse of Article 86 is illustrated by the *Continental Can Case*, [1972] C.M.L.R. D.11. The Continental Can Company was an American company producing packing materials, e.g. meat tins, fish tins, and metal lids for glass jars. In 1969, through a Belgian subsidiary, it took control of the largest German producer of packaging and in 1970 followed this up by acquiring a majority holding in a Dutch company which was the leading manufacturer of packing materials in the Benelux countries. In the opinion of the Commission the situation arising from this concentration within the market of light packings in the North-West region of the Common Market constituted the necessary conditions for an abuse of the dominant position within Article 86. The finding of the Commission was set aside by the European Court on a technical ground that the Commission had failed to define which market was abused, whether it was that of meat tins, fish tins, metal lids for glass jars or all three. However, the Court stressed that Article 86 would have been infringed on a definition of the market abused so that mergers would have been void.

Relationship with UK law

National legislation on restrictive trade practices and monopolies applies alongside Community law unless it conflicts with Community law as interpreted by the Commission or the European Court of Justice Therefore, if a restrictive agreement or merger threat affects only the UK market, the matter will remain subject exclusively to UK legislation. If such agreement affects trade between two or more Member States then to that extent national law is excluded by Community law. Furthermore, if there is an overlap between Community and national law, Community law predominates. Therefore, once an agreement with inter-Market effect has been exempted by the Commission under Article 85, it will from then on be immune from attack under United Kingdom restrictive practices or resale prices legislation. If the agreement has already been regarded as invalid under that legislation the invalidation will cease to be effective if the Commission exempts it under Article 85. Additionally, if the restrictive practice has been approved by a UK court its approval will lapse if the agreement turns out infringe the provisions of Article 85. This is why it is important for UK restrictive practices courts to decline or postpone exercising jurisdiction where the Treaty applies and the Commission has already initiated proceedings. The reader will recall that this is provided for in the Restrictive Trade Practices Act, 1976.

Procedure for notification of potentially restrictive agreements

If an agreement is thought to infringe Article 85, the contracting parties may take one of three courses of action.

(i) The agreement may be amended by the deletion of the offending provisions thereby taking it outside the provisions of the Article altogether.

(ii) The parties may leave the agreement as it stands and run the risk of the practice coming to the notice of the Commission with the possible imposition of a fine.

(iii) The parties may register or notify the agreement to the Head of the Competition Department of the Commission in Brussels. Once registered the agreement may obtain provisional validity at civil law though there is doubt about this. (*Brasserie de Haecht* v. *Wilkin (2)(E.C.J.)*, [1973], C.M.L.R.287.) However, there is protection from fines until such time as the Commission declares it to be unlawful.

There is no need for notification of an agreement when all the parties are from one Member State and the agreement does not relate either to import or export between member states.

There is no need to notify agreements in which only two enterprises participate, regardless of the Member States to which they belong, provided the agreements are only concerned to fix prices or conditions of trading in the resale of goods which have been acquired from the other party to the contract; or where the restrictions are concerned with a licence to use industrial property rights or restrictions in terms of manufacturing processes or knowledge.

In addition, two enterprise agreements which are concerned, for example, with joint research and development, need not be notified.

There is nothing to stop the parties in case of doubt from notifying agreements in order to satisfy their own minds as to their legality and to cover the possible risk of misinterpretation of the agreement.

MONOPOLIES AND MERGERS

Parts IV and V of the Fair Trading Act, 1973, re-enact, with certain modifications, previous legislation relating to monopolies and mergers contained in the Monopolies and Restrictive Practices Act, 1948 and the Monopolies and Mergers Act, 1966. In addition, the Act of 1973 gives certain functions to the Director of Fair Trading and the Monopolies and Mergers Commission in relation to monopoly situations and competitive practices. The detail of these provisions is beyond the scope of a book of this nature but the Fair Trading Act, 1973, extends the previous legislation in a number of respects, perhaps the most important of which is that the proportion of the market required for a monopoly is defined as 'control of one-quarter of the sales in a marker' and not one-third as formerly. It should be noted, however, that the goods and services under consideration are still to be supplied in the United Kingdom or a substantial part of the United Kingdom.

DISCHARGE OF A CONTRACT

A contract is discharged when the obligation created by it ceases to be binding on the promisor, who is then no longer under a duty to perform his part of the agreement. Discharge may take place in various ways.

Discharge by agreement

A contract is made by agreement; and it is also possible to end it by a subsequent agreement if there is new consideration for the discharge, or if it is under seal. Where the contract is executory, i.e. a promise for a promise, and there has been no performance, the mutual release of the parties provides the consideration and is called bilateral discharge. But where the contract is executed, i.e. where it has been performed or partly performed by one party, then the party to be released must provide consideration, unless the agreement to abandon the contract is under seal. In other words, there must be *accord and satisfaction,* the agreement to discharge being the accord and the new consideration being the satisfaction. This method of discharge is called unilateral discharge. Where the discharge by agreement takes the form of the substitution of a new contract, the substitution is called a novation.

Sometimes a contract makes provision for its own discharge. It may make the completion of the contract subject to the fulfilment of a *condition precedent or warranty*. Thus, if I say I will buy your car if you fit new tyres to it, I shall incur no liability unless the tyres are so fitted. Similarly a contract to purchase land subject to planning permission being obtained can be rescinded if planning permission is refused. (*Hargreaves Transport Ltd* v. *Lynch*, [1969] 1 All E.R. 455.) Furthermore, in a contact of sale of land the payment of a deposit by the purchaser may be treated as a condition precedent of the contract of sale so that payment by cheque, which is later dishonoured, entitles the vendor to withdraw. (*Myton Ltd* v. *Schwab-Morris*, [1974] 1 All E.R. 326.)

A contract may provide that it shall be discharged by a *condition subsequent,* i.e. upon the occurrence of a certain subsequent event. An example of this is found in pre-incorporation contracts which company promoters make on behalf of a company in process of formation. The law does not allow them to act as agents for the company which, until incorporation, is a non-existent principal. Further, the company is not allowed to ratify the contract after incorporation, but must enter into a new contract or novation if it is to become liable. In addition, promoters incur personal liability under Sect. 9 of the European Communities Act, 1972. In order to avoid this, promoters' contracts may provide that they shall be discharged if the company is not incorporated at all, or within a reasonable time, or if the company when formed does not accept the contract by novation.

Contracts of employment usually provide for their own discharge in this way but it should be noted that the Employment Protection Act, 1975, provides for certain minimum periods of notice which must be given by employees and to employees whose contracts may be brought to an end by notice. The minimum notice to be given by an employee is one week, regardless of length of service. As regards employers, they must give one week's notice after four weeks' service, two weeks after two years' service and an additional week for each year of service up to 12 weeks after 12 years' service.

Longer periods of notice can, of course, be provided for expressly in particular contracts.

With regard to the form of discharge, a contract which is made in writing may be rescinded or varied by an oral agreement. A contract under seal may be rescinded or varied by a simple contract. However, while a contract required by statute to be evidenced in writing can be totally discharged by an oral agreement (*Moore* v. *Marrable*, 1866),[381] a partial discharge or variation must be in writing. (*Goss* v. *Nugent*, 1833.)[382]

It is also possible to discharge a contract by release. At any time before a contract is due to be performed, or after a breach of contract has taken place, a release of the obligations under the contract may be granted by deed. Such a deed dissolves the contract and is binding, whether or not it is based on consideration. No new contract is made; the old obligations are simply released.

Discharge by performance

A contract may be discharged by performance, the discharge taking place when both parties have performed the obligations which the contract places upon them. The court may construe a contract in such a way that the manner of performance must comply exactly with the terms of the contract. (*Moore & Co.* v. *Landauer & Co.,* 1921.)[383] the strict application of this rule would mean that all contracts would be *entire* so that no payment could be obtained for partial performance. The law assumes a contract between X and Y to be entire when it appears on construction of the contract that X has undertaken his obligations on the express or implied condition that he will not be obliged to perform those obligations unless Y completes or is willing to complete his obligations fully and exactly. (*Cutter* v. *Powell,* 1795)[384] and see *Heywood* v. *Wellers,* 1976.)[385]

However, there are *certain exceptions* to the rule of precise performance—

(i) *Where the contract is divisible.*   Although there is a presumption in favour of entire contracts, the court may sometimes find that a contract is a divisible one, a usual instance being the contract between landlord and tenant. This means that the tenant cannot refuse to pay the rent even though the landlord is not carrying out the covenants of the lease, e.g. a covenant to repair. The tenant can sue the landlord for breach of covenant but must continue to pay.

(ii) *Where a partial performance has been accepted.*   Where one of the parties to the contract has only partially carried out his obligations under the contract but the other party appears from his conduct to have accepted the benefit of the partial performance, the court may infer a promise to pay for the benefit received, and allow an action on a *quantum meruit* to the party who has partly performed the contract. If, for example, S agrees to deliver 3 dozen bottles of brandy to B and delivers 2 dozen bottles only, then B may exercise his right to reject the whole consignment. But if he has accepted delivery of the 2 dozen bottles he must pay a reasonable price for the bottles retained, and S's *quantum meruit* will normally be the agreed contract price per bottle.

However, the mere conferring of a benefit on one party by another is not enough; there must be evidence of the acceptance of that benefit by the party upon whom it was conferred. (*Sumpter* v. *Hedges,* 1898[386] and *IBMAC* v. *Marshall* (*Homes*), 1968.)[387]

(iii) *Where performance is prevented by one party.*   Here the party who cannot further perform his part of the contract may bring an action on a *quantum meruit* against the party in default for the value of work done up to the time when further performance was prevented. (*De Barnardy* v. *Harding,* 1853.)[388]

(iv) *Where there has been substantial performance.*   The doctrine of substantial performance is based on the notion that precise performance of every term of the contract by one party is not required in order to make the other party liable to some extent on it. If the court, as a matter of construction, decides that there has been substantial performance, the plaintiff may recover for work done under the contract, though the defendant can, of course, counter-claim for any defects in performance. (*Hoenig* v. *Isaacs,* 1952[389] and *Bolton* v. *Mahadeva,* 1972.)[390]

In this connection it should be noted that where a contractor is employed under the Royal Institution of British Architects' standard form of contract, an architect's final certificate that the work has been carried out properly is conclusive evidence in any proceedings. (*Hosier & Dickinson* v. *P. & M. Kaye*, [1972] 1 All E.R. 121.

In construing a contract to see whether a particular term must be fully performed or whether substantial performance is enough, the distinction between conditions and warranties is relevant. A condition must be wholly performed, whereas substantial performance of a warranty is enough. (*Poussard* v. *Spiers & Pond,* 1876,[265] and *Bettini* v. *Gye,* 1876.)[266]

A contract may provide for optional methods of performance. (*Narbeth* v. *James. The Lady Tahilla,* 1967.)[391]

Times of performance.   The time for performance may in some cases be *of the essence of the contract* and in others it may not. At common law, where the parties have fixed a time for performance, time is the essence of the contract, even though the parties have not expressly said so in the contract. The rule may be applied even where performance is earlier than the contract specifies. (*Bowes* v. *Shand,* 1877.)[392]

However, Equity took a different view, and where the plaintiff was asking for an equitable remedy, e.g. for specific performance of a contract to sell land, the failure of either the vendor or the purchaser to complete exactly to time did not prevent a claim for specific performance so long as no injustice was done to either party. *Time was of the essence even in Equity:* (*a*) where the parties has stipulated a time for performance in the contract and had in addition indicated that this time was in the nature of a condition; (*b*) where time was not originally of the essence but had been made so by the aggrieved party giving notice to this effect (*Rickards* (*Charles*) *Ltd* v. *Oppenheim,* 1950);[393] or (*c*) where from the circumstances of the case it appeared that the contract should be performed at the agreed time.

The sale of a reversionary interest would come into this last category. Suppose property is left by will to X for life with remainder to Y, then if Y sells his remainder, as he may do, it is obvious that the contract of sale should be completed at the agreed date, for delay will mean that the life tenant T is growing older and the value of the reversion is therefore increasing. Similarly in the sale of a business, Equity will generally take the view that the contract should be completed on time so that uncertainties regarding a change of owner should not be so prolonged as to affect adversely the goodwill of the business. Further, it was held in *Hare* v. *Nichol*, [1966] 1 All E.R. 285, that time is the essence of the contract where the property concerned is shares of a highly speculative nature. In addition, there is a presumption that time is of the essence of all mercantile contracts unless the circumstances show otherwise. (*Elmdore Ltd* v. *Keech,* 1969.)[394]

Where the contract is capable of specific performance, the equitable rule still applies, even though the plaintiff may in fact be asking for damages. In other cases, the common law rule that time is of the essence of the contract prevails. (Section 41, Law of Property Act, 1925.)

Tender.   With regard to the manner of performance, the question of what is good tender arises. *Tender is an offer of performance which complies with the terms of the contract.* If goods are tendered by the seller and refused by the buyer, the seller is freed from liability, given that the goods are in accordance with the contract as to quantity and quality. A tender of money which is refused does not discharge the tenderer, but if he pays the money into court without delay he will have a good defence to an action brought against him, and the debt will not bear interest. In a tender of money, the exact amount must be tendered without request for change. In England and Wales the notes of the Bank of England are legal tender to any amount. Decimal bronze coins are legal tender for amounts up to 20p. Silver or cupro-nickel coins up to and including the 10p piece are legal tender for amounts up to £5. The 50p coin is legal tender up to £10. Tender by cheque or other negotiable instrument is not good tender unless the creditor does not object; and the debt is discharged when the instrument is honoured, not when it is received. If the instrument is dishonoured, the creditor may sue for his money under either the contract or on the instrument. The tender must be unconditional, and must comply with the terms of the contract as to time, place and mode of performance. A payment of the amount due under a contract is a discharge, but the payment of a smaller sum is no discharge unless made earlier than it is due or by a third party. (See p. 191.)

Receipts.   A receipt may be given on payment, but a receipt is only *prima facie* and not conclusive evidence of payment. A payment may be proved by parol in cases where a receipt is lost or no receipt is given. At common law there is no right to demand a receipt, but under the Stamp Act, 1891, a receipt of £2 and upwards had to be stamped with a twopenny stamp, and if a creditor for such an amount refused to give a receipt when asked or did not stamp a receipt, he was liable to a penalty of £10. There were certain exceptions to this rule, e.g. a receipt for the payment of wages need not be stamped.

The Finance Act, 1970, abolished the old 2d. duty on bills of exchange and receipts as from 1 February, 1971 but the right to demand a receipt for amounts of £2 and upwards under the Act of 1891 remains, though there is now no need for such a receipt to be stamped.

If money is sent by post it is not good payment if the letter is lost in the post unless the creditor requested payment in this way. Even a request to pay through the post does not absolve the debtor from paying in a reasonable manner and according to business practice, e.g. by registered cash. Where there is such a request, payment is established by proof of posting, even though the letter is lost in transit, and delay in the post excuses late payment.

It is important to consider the *rules governing appropriation of payments.* Certain debts are barred by the Limitation Act 1939, and money which has been owed for six years under simple contracts or twelve years under specialty contracts, without acknowledgment, may not be recoverable by an action in the courts. Where a debtor owes several debts to the same creditor and makes a payment which does not cover them all, there are rules governing how the money should be appropriated—

(*a*) The debtor can appropriate the payment expressly, as where he says which debt he is paying, or by implication. If he owes two debts, one of £50 and one of £25, and sends a cheque for £25, there is an implied appropriation to the second debt.

(*b*) If there is no appropriation by the debtor, the creditor can appropriate the payment to any of the debts at any time, even to a statute-barred debt, since such a debt has not been extinguished; only the right of action in court has been lost. However, if the statute-barred debt is, say, £50 and the creditor appropriates a payment of £25 to it, the balance of the debt is not revived and cannot be sued for. (*Mills* v. *Fowkes,* (1839) 5 Bing. N.C.455.)

(*c*) Where there is what is called a current account, appropriation follows the rule in *Clayton's* case (1816), 1 Mer. 572. Bank current accounts provide a good example of accounts to which this rule applies. *Clayton's* case says that, in the absence of a contrary intention, the money first paid in is to be regarded as the money which is first withdrawn (*Deeley* v. *Lloyds Bank Ltd,* 1912)[395] or that the first item on the debit side of the account is discharged or reduced by the first item on the credit side.

Discharge by breach

A breach does not of itself discharge a contract, but it may in some circumstances give the innocent party the right to treat it as discharged if he so wishes.

There are several forms of breach of contract—

(*a*) Failure to perform the contract is the most usual form, as where a seller fails to deliver goods by the appointed time, or where they are not up to standard as to quality or quantity.

(*b*) Express repudiation arises where one party states that he will not perform his part of the contract. (*Hochster* v. *De La Tour,* 1853[396] and *Gorse* v. *Durham County Council,* 1971.)[397]

(*c*) Some action by one party which makes performance impossible. (See *Omnium D'Entreprises* v. *Sutherland,* 1919.)[398]

Any breach which takes place before the time for performance has arrived is called an anticipatory breach.

The remedies where a contract has been discharged by breach are an action for damages if any have been suffered, or, if the parties have stipulated the damages to be payable on breach, an action for that sum which is called liquidated damages. Not every breach entitles the innocent party to treat the contract as discharged. It must be shown that the breach affects a vital part of the contract, i.e. that it is a breach of condition rather than a breach of warranty (*Poussard* v. *Spiers and Pond,* 1896[265] and *Bettini* v. *Gye,* 1876),[266] or that the other party has become wholly and finally disabled from performing the contract or has no intention of doing so. (*The Angelica,* 1973[399] and *Decro-Wall International S.A.* v. *Practitioners in Marketing,* 1971.)[400] In the case of anticipatory breach, the innocent party may treat the contract as discharged at once and sue for damages, though the Court may have regard to whether the contract could have been carried out by the plaintiff at the time scheduled for performance. (*The Mihalis Angelos,* 1969.)[401] Alternatively he may ignore the breach and wait until the time for performance arrives. It may be dangerous to wait since the contract may later become impossible of performance, so providing the party who was in breach with a good defence to an action. (*Avery* v. *Bowden,* 1855.)[402]

Where one party to a contract wrongfully repudiates it and the other party refuses to accept the repudiation, it seems that the contract survives and the rights of the innocent party are preserved. He may, if it is within his power, perform his part of the contract and recover on that basis, for there is no duty on him to vary the contract at the request of the other party so as to deprive himself of its benefit. (*White and Carter (Councils) Ltd* v. *McGregor,* 1961.)[403]

It should also be noted that where a person is entitled to repudiate his liability under a contract by reason of the other party's breach his delay in so doing will not operate against him unless other parties are prejudiced or the delay is so long as to indicate to the court that he has accepted liability. (*Allen* v. *Robles (Compagnie Parisienne de Garantie, Third Party),* 1969.)[404]

Regarding leases it appears that since a lease conveys an estate in land it does not necessarily come to an end by repudiation and acceptance of repudiation as an ordinary contract would. (*Total Oil Great Britain Ltd* v. *Thompson Garages (Biggin Hill) Ltd,* 1971.)[405]

Discharge by subsequent impossibility (or frustration)

If an agreement is impossible of performance from the outset, it is no contract. Sometimes, however, parties may make a contract which at the time is possible of performance but subsequently becomes impossible to carry out in whole or in part. The view of the early common law judges was that such eventualities should be provided for in the contract, and if this was not done the party liable for the performance of an impossible undertaking would be obliged to pay damages to the other party for such non-performance.

This rule was gradually modified and made less rigorous, but even now the courts are not anxious to give remedies for eventualities which could have been foreseen, e.g. if a strike prevents performance this could have been provided for in the contract. (And see *Davis Contractors Ltd* v. *Fareham U.D.C.*, 1956.)[406]

The present doctrine is that if performance was possible when the contract was made, subsequent impossibility may discharge it in the following cases—

(a) If the impossibility is due to changes in law or operation of law, the contract is discharged. (*Re Shipton, Anderson & Co. and Harrison Brothers' Arbitration*, 1915.)[407]

(b) If the contract is for personal services, it becomes discharged by the death or incapacity of the person who has to perform it. Temporary illness or other incapacity will not in most cases discharge a contract (*Storey* v. *Fulham Steel Works*, 1907,[408] *Mount* v. *Oldham Corporation*, 1973,[409] and *Hare* v. *Murphy*, 1975)[410] but if the illness or other incapacity goes right to the root of the contract, it will (*Poussard* v. *Spiers and Pond*, 1876).[265]

(c) If the performance depends upon the existence of a certain thing, or a state of affairs which ceases to exist, the contract is discharged. (*Taylor* v. *Caldwell*, 1863,[411] and *Krell* v. *Henry*, 1903.)[412] But it must be shown that the contract will be substantially affected by the new circumstaces. (*Herne Bay Steam Boat Co.* v. *Hutton*, 1903.[413]

(d) A contract is also discharged when its commercial purpose is frustrated, often because its completion would be so delayed as to make the performance, when it occurred, of little or no value. (*Joseph Constantine Steamship Line Ltd* v. *Imperial Smelting Corporation Ltd*, 1942,[414] and *Jackson* v. *Union Marine Insurance Co. Ltd*, 1874.)[415] In terms of frustration, increased cost is rarely sufficient reason for invoking the defence. (*The Angelia*, 1973.)[399]

The doctrine will not apply—

(i) where the parties have made express provision for the event which has occurred. In such a case, the provisions inserted into the contract by the parties will apply;

(ii) where the frustrating event is self-induced (*Maritime National Fish Ltd* v. *Ocean Trawlers Ltd*, 1935);[416]

(iii) probably to a lease, because a lease creates an estate which survives any frustrating event, and not a mere contract. The same rule may also apply to an agreement for a lease and a contract for the sale of land. (*Cricklewood Property and Investment Trust Ltd* v. *Leightons Investment Trust Ltd*, 1945;[417] *Hillingdon Estates Co.* v. *Stonefield Estates Ltd*, 1952[418] and see also *Total Oil Great Britain Ltd* v. *Thompson Garages*

(*Biggin Hill*) *Ltd,* 1971[405] but see *Amalgamated Investment & Property Co. Ltd* v. *John Walker & Sons Ltd,* 1976.)[221]

The Law Reform (Frustrated Contracts) Act, 1943. An important modern statute has laid down the conditions which will govern the rights and duties of the parties when certain contracts are frustrated. This measure is the Law Reform (Frustrated Contracts) Act, 1943. Before this Act it was the law that when subsequence impossibility discharged a contract, it did not discharge it *ab initio* (from the beginning), but only from the time when the event making the contract impossible of performance actually occurred. Thus any loss lay where it fell. Money not due at the time could not be claimed. Money due and not paid could be claimed. Money paid under the contract before it became impossible could not be recovered. (*Chandler* v. *Webster,* 1904.)[419] However, money paid was recoverable if there was a total failure of consideration. (*The Fibrosa Case,* 1943.)[420]

The statute has amended the common law and provides what shall happen if the contract becomes discharged by frustration—

(i) All money paid before discharge is recoverable.

(ii) Money which was payable ceases to be payable.

(iii) The court will allow the parties to recover sums of money paid out on expenses incurred in connection with the contract, or to retain such sums from money already received under the contract.

(iv) It is also possible to recover, on a *quantum meruit,* a reasonable sum of money as compensation where one of the parties has carried out acts of part performance before frustration, i.e. where one party has received what the Act calls 'a valuable benefit' under the contract other than a money payment. There are difficulties in regard to the expression 'valuable benefit', particularly where the work is destroyed since the Act is not clear as to whether a sum can be recovered by the person conferring the benefit where there has been destruction of his work. There are no English cases on the point but in *Parsons Bros.* v. *Shea,* (1965) 53 D.L.R. (2d) 86, a Newfoundland court held that the carrying out of modifications to a heating system in an hotel subsequently destroyed by fire could not be regarded as conferring 'benefits' upon the owner. Of course, on the facts of *Cutter* v. *Powell,* 1795,[384] Mrs Cutter (or Mr Cutter if he had been alive) would have been able to recover under the 1943 Act because Mr Cutter did confer a benefit by reason of his work up to the time of his death.

The Act does not apply to contracts for the carriage of goods by sea or to contracts of insurance. If X insures against sickness on 1 January, and dies on 1 February, his executors cannot recover eleven-twelfths of the premium paid, even though the contract is now impossible of performance.

The Act also excepts from its provisions certain *sales* of *specific* goods which have *perished* the effect of which is, broadly speaking, as follows—

(a) *The goods must be specific and not unascertained.* Section 62 of the Sale of Goods Act, 1893, states that specific goods are goods identified and agreed upon at the time the contract of sale is made. Thus a contract to sell 'my 1977 Mini' is a contract to sell specific goods, whereas a contract to sell 'one of my two cars' would be a contract for the sale of unascertained goods since it is not certain which of the two cars will be sold.

(b) The goods must have perished. Goods are regarded as having perished—

(i) where they have been physically destroyed, say by fire; or

(ii) where although they physically exist they are so damaged that they cannot reasonably be regarded as the goods actually purchased, e.g. apples contaminated by sewage.

(c) The contract must be a sale and not an agreement to sell. A *contract of sale* is one in which the property (normally ownership) in the goods is transferred to the buyer at the time when the contract is made. In an *agreement to sell,* ownership is transferred to the buyer at a future date after the making of the contract. It should be noted that in English Law the transfer of ownership does not depend upon *delivery* of the goods. Where the goods are specific and in the absence of any contrary intention, the property in the goods passes to the buyer when he accepts the seller's offer, even though the seller physically retains the goods.

The application of these concepts may be illustrated by the following examples—

(1) If A offers to sell the only car he has, which is at his home, to B for £800 and B accepts the offer, the contract will be for the sale of specific goods and ownership (and normally risk) will pass to B when he accepts A's offer regardless of actual delivery of the vehicle. Ordinarily A will deliver the car to B and all will be well; but let us suppose that the car is destroyed by fire before delivery, so that A cannot perform the contract. In such circumstances the legal position would appear to be as follows—

(*a*) If the car was destroyed *before* B accepted A's offer the contract is rendered *void* by Sect. 6 of the Sale of Goods Act, 1893. Thus A need not pay damages for non-performance nor is B obliged to pay for the car. Furthermore, if B had made a payment to A it could be recovered.

(*b*) If the car was destroyed *after* B accepted A's offer B would have become owner of the car and would have to pay A £800 for it even though the car could never be delivered.

(*c*) If in the course of selling the car to A it was agreed that ownership should not pass for one week, then if the car was destroyed before the week had elapsed the position would be a follows—

(i) A would have to bear the loss of the car; and

(ii) the contract would be avoided by Sect. 7 of the Sale of Goods Act, 1893, so that A would not be liable in damages for failure to perform the contract—B would not be required to pay for it and could recover any money paid to A.

(2) If the goods were *unascertained,* as where A sold to B 'one of my two cars,' then if one or both of the cars were destroyed before ascertain-

ment the Act of 1943 would apply and the rules laid down therein would come into force, though B could of course accept the remaining car if he wished. B would probably not be compelled to accept the remaining car unless perhaps it was in all respects the same as the one destroyed. This is unlikely in the case of a car but might apply where the goods were, say, sugar or wheat.

(3) If the goods were *specific* but had *not perished* as where A's only car was requisitioned by the Crown in an emergency, then the Act of 1943 and the rules thereunder would also apply.

Before leaving the topic of frustration, it should be noted that the Act of 1943 does not apply to contracts governed by foreign law.

Discharge by lapse of time

Contracts entered into for a specified time are discharged when that period of time has elapsed. In other cases time is of no effect as regards discharge, but lapse of time may render contracts unenforceable in a court of law.

The Limitation Act, 1939, provides that actions on simple contracts are barred after six years from the date upon which the plaintiff could first have brought his action. Actions on specialty contracts are barred after twelve years from the cause of action. However, if the time expires on a day when the Court offices are not open the period is extended to the next working day. (*Pritam Kaur* v. *S. Russell & Sons Ltd*, [1973] 2 W.L.R. 147.) The Act does not truly discharge a contract, it merely makes it unenforceable in a court of law. It can, therefore, be made actionable again by the debtor, or his duly authorized agent, making a written acknowledgement of the debt to the creditor or his agent. Such an acknowledgement need not have been written for the purpose and is effective if it indicates that a debt is due even if it does not state the amount. (*Dungate* v. *Dungate*, 1965.)[145] Thus, a statement of liabilities to 'sundry creditors' in a company balance sheet was held to be enough. *Jones* v. *Bellgrove Properties Ltd*, [1949] 2 K.B. 700. The acknowledgment of the debt is as at the date on which the balance sheet was made up even though the date on which it was signed was later. (*Re Gee & Co. (Woolwich) Ltd*, [1974] 1 All E.R. 1149.) It should, however, be noted that a person cannot be forced to acknowledge a statute barred debt (*Lovell* v. *Lovell,* 1970.)[464] and also that a debtor does not acknowledge a claim by denying liability and alleging that he has a set-off or cross-claim against the creditor. (*Surrendra Overseas* v. *Government of Sri Lanka,* [1977] 2 All E.R. 481.) A right of action 'accrues' from the moment when the breach occurs, not from the date when the contract was made. Thus if money is lent today for four years under a simple contract the creditor's right to recover it will not expire until ten years from today.

Where the plaintiff is a minor or person of unsound mind, the period of limitation does not run against him until his contractual disability ends, i.e.

at eighteen or on becoming sane. But once time has started to run, any subsequent incapacity will not stop it running.

The defendant's fraud may also prevent his pleading the Statutes of Limitation. Section 26(b) of the Limitation Act, 1939, provides that where a right of action is concealed by the fraud of the defendant or his agent, the period of limitation shall not begin to run until the plaintiff has discovered the fraud or could with reasonable diligence have discovered it. (*Lynn* v. *Bamber,* 1930.)[421] In this connection it should be noted that 'fraud' is not used in the common law sense. It is used in the equitable sense to denote conduct by the defendant or his agent such that it would be 'against conscience' for him to avail himself of the lapse of time. (*Applegate* v. *Moss,* 1970[422] and *King* v. *Victor Parsons & Co.,* 1973.)[423]

Where the plaintiff's claims include a claim for damages in respect of personal injuries the limitation period is three years. However, a person may suffer personal injury the extent of which only comes to light more than three years after the breach of contract which caused it. For example, A is a passenger on B's coach and B's careless driving causes an accident as a result of which A suffers injury consisting of bruising of the face. Four years later A goes blind as a result of the accident. Under the Limitation Act, 1975, A has three years from his knowledge of his blindness to sue B and the court's permission is not required. The court may extend this period at its discretion, though in this case application must be made to the court for the extension. The implications of the Limitation Act, 1975, are dealt with in greater detail on p. 330.

Discharge by operation of law

This may occur in certain cases—

(a) Merger.   A simple contract is swallowed up, or merged into, a subsequent deed covering the same subject matter, and in such circumstances an action lies only on the deed. Similarly a judgment, which is a contract of record, merges the contract debt on which the action was brought, so that all future actions are based on the judgment.

(b) Material alteration.   An alteration of a material part of a deed or written contract, made by one party intentionally and without the consent of the other party, will discharge the contract. The alteration must alter the legal effect of the contract, and the mere alteration of a misdescription of one of the parties, or the insertion of the true date, will not operate as a discharge.

(c) Death.   Death will discharge a contract for personal services. Other contractual rights and liabilities survive for the benefit, or otherwise, of the estate.

(d) Bankruptcy. A right of action for breach of contract possessed by a debtor, which relates to his property and which if brought will increase his assets, will pass to his trustee in bankruptcy, e.g. a contract with a third party to deliver goods or to pay money to the debtor. The right to sue for injury to the debtor's character or reputation does not pass to the trustee, even though it arises from a breach of a contract. (*Wilson* v. *United Counties Bank,* 1920.)[424]

With regard to contracts for personal services, it depends upon the date of the breach whether the debtor's right to sue remains with him or passes to his trustee. If the breach occurs before the commencement of the bankruptcy, the right of action passes to the trustee; if it occurs after this date, the debtor may sue, but the trustee may intervene and deduct from the sum recovered such sums as are not required for the reasonable maintenance of the bankrupt and his family. A trustee cannot force the debtor to carry out contracts involving personal service by him.

REMEDIES FOR BREACH OF CONTRACT

When there is a breach of contract the following remedies may be available—

(i) A right of action for damages at common law (the most common remedy).

(ii) A right of action on a *quantum meruit.*

(iii) A right to sue for specific performance or for an injunction.

(iv) A right to ask for rescission of the contract.

(v) A refusal of any further performance by the injured party.

(vi) A right at common law when paying the contract price to deduct damages due in respect of breaches committed by the other party and, if sued, to set up against the plaintiff such breaches of contract in diminution or extinction of the price. This right can be expressly excluded by the terms of a particular contract. However, there is a presumption that parties to contracts do not intend to abandon any remedies for breach of contract arising by operation of law and clear express words must be used in order to rebut this presumption. (*Gilbert-Ash (Northern) Ltd* v. *Modern Engineering (Bristol) Ltd,* [1973] 3 All E.R. 195.)

Damages
Assessment of Damages. Damages are the common law remedy consisting of a payment of money and are intended as compensation for the plaintiff's loss and not as punishment for the defendant. The aim is to put the injured party in the same financial position as he would have been if the contract had been performed according to its terms. (*B. Sunley & Co. Ltd* v. *Cunard White Star Ltd,* 1940.)[425] This may involve taking into account the plaintiff's liability to taxation. (*Beach* v. *Reed Corrugated Cases Ltd,* 1956.)[426] Expenses incurred prior to the date of contract may be recovered

if they were within the contemplation of the parties as a likely result of the breach. In *Anglia Television Ltd* v. *Reed,* [1971] 3 All E.R. 690, A Ltd. engaged R to act in a film having previously spent £2750 in employing a director and designer. R repudiated the contract and A Ltd. recovered £2750 from him.

It was at one time thought that damages could not be recovered for inconvenience or injured feelings. In *Hobbs* v. *London & South Western Railway Co.,* (1875) L.R. 10 Q.B. 111, Mellor, J. said 'For the mere inconvenience, such as annoyance and loss of temper, or vexation, or for being disappointed in a particular thing which you have set your mind upon, without real physical inconvenience resulting, you cannot recover damages . . .' Later in *Addis* v. *Gramophone Co. Ltd,* [1909] A. C. 488, the House of Lords held that a wrongfully dismissed employee could not recover damages in respect of injured feelings. However, in *Jarvis* v. *Swans Tours Ltd,* 1973[256] it was held that the damages awarded should be increased to take account of the plaintiff's disappointment and mental distress resulting from the defendants' breach of contract, in a non-employment situation. Later in *Jackson* v. *Horizon Holidays Ltd,* 1975[146] the court again applied the principle and Lord Denning went further by riding roughshod over the doctrine of privity of contract. *Jarvis*[256] and *Jackson*[146] made new law but only in the context of contracts for holidays or entertainment so that *Addis* was not relevant being a case concerned with wrongful dismissal. However, in *Cox* v. *Philips Industries Ltd,* 1976[427] Lawson, J. applied *Jarvis* and *Jackson* to a contract of employment, though not in a situation of wrongful dismissal. Thus it would seem that if the action is for wrongful dismissal *Addis* applies but in other cases the court is free to apply the principle in *Jarvis* and *Jackson*.

On rare occasions punitive damages were awarded, i.e. damages in excess of the actual loss, and these might by appropriate in cases of breach of promise of marriage, particularly if there had been a seduction. Under the Law Reform (Miscellaneous Provisions) Act, 1970, Sect. 1, engagements to marry are not enforceable at law. They are relegated to the same position as any simple domestic agreement made between husband and wife, which the law regards as unenforceable since it is presumed that there was no intention to create a legal relationship with legal consequences. Compensation for pregnancy where this has occurred must now be pursued in affiliation proceedings in a Magistrates' Court. Generally, however, the aim of damages is one of simple compensation for actual loss. Difficulty in assessing damages is not necessarily a bar to a claim. (*Chaplin* v. *Hicks,* 1911.)[428]

Remoteness of damage. Apart from the question of assessment, the question of *remoteness of damage* arises. The consequences of a breach of contract may be far reaching, and the law must draw the line somewhere and say that damages incurred beyond a certain limit are too remote to be recovered. Damages in contract must therefore be proximate. The modern law regarding remoteness of damage in contract is founded upon the case of *Hadley* v. *Baxendale*, 1854[429] as further explained in *The Heron II*, 1967.[430] These cases are authority for the statement that damages in contract will be too remote to be recovered unless they are such that the defendant, as a reasonable man, would have had them in contemplation as likely to result, according to the usual course of things or because of special facts made known to him. Damage which is unlikely to occur in the ordinary course of events may be recovered only if the defendant was made aware of the possibility of such damage (*Horne* v. *Midland Railway Co.*, 1873),[431] though notice of possible loss can be constructive as well as actual. (*Pinnock Bros.* v. *Lewis and Peat Ltd*, 1923.)[432]

Having set out the above general principles we must now look at the decision of the Court of Appeal in *H. Parsons Ltd* v. *Uttley Ingham & Co. Ltd*, 1977.[433]

Regarding changes in the relative value of currencies, these are irrelevant in assessing damages and in the payments of debts if—

(i) they occur *after* the date on which damages are assessed or the debt became due—thus a revaluation of sterling after a case has been decided and the judge has awarded damages, or after the date on which a debt should have been paid, must be ignored and the defendant will pay at the rate of exchange prevailing when the award of damages was made or the debt became due;

(ii) they occur *on* or *before* the date on which damages were assessed or the debt became due *unless* the loss caused by revaluation can be shown to have been within the assumed contemplation of the parties or the contract expressly provides for variations in price if prevailing rates of exchange vary; otherwise the court will not increase the sterling value of the damages or the debt in order to give the plaintiff the same amount of money under the new rate of exchange as he would have received under the old. (*Aruna Mills* v. *Dhanrajmal Gobindram*, [1958] 1 All E.R. 113, and *The Teh Hu* [1969] 3 All E.R. 1200.)

As regards judgments given in foreign currency, it has for some time, in view of the devaluation of the Pound Sterling, been of little advantage to a foreign creditor to make a claim in an English court, since it was until recently a fundamental principle of English Law that an English court could not give judgment for an amount in foreign currency, and that a debt which was expressed and damages which were calculated in a foreign currency had to be converted into Sterling for the purposes of litigation in England, irrespective of the place in which they were payable and the law governing the substance of the obligation. However, there have been moves in the recent past towards changing the law to enable our courts to keep in step with commercial needs. The culmination of these moves was the case of *Miliangos* v. *George Frank (Textiles) Ltd*, 1975[49] in which, as we have seen, the House of Lords overruled its previous decision in *Re United Railways of Havana*, [1961] A.C. 1007 which was the decision which had established the judgment in Pound Sterling rule. This establishes a new principle, at least in so far as judgments for payments of a debt in foreign currency are concerned, and provides the opportunity for an extension of that principle to other forms of judgment.

Mitigation of loss.   It must be understood that, when a breach occurs, the party suffering from the breach must do all he can to reduce his loss, and he cannot recover damages which have resulted from his *unreasonable* failure to do so. (*Brace* v. *Calder,* 1895[434] and *Moore* v. *D.E.R. Ltd,* 1971.)[435] Thus if a person cancels an hotel booking, the hotel proprietor must try to relet the rooms and if a seller refuses to deliver goods, the buyer must attempt to obtain supplies elsewhere. In the latter case, where there is an available market, the damages might amount to no more than the difference between the contract price and the market price on the day appointed for delivery, together with incidental expenses. Useful examples of how these rules operate in practice may be drawn from three cases concerning motor car sales. If the plaintiff is a car dealer and has been able to find someone else to buy at the same price or a higher price the same car as has been wrongfully rejected by the defendant, he will not normally be entitled to damages other than, perhaps, nominal damages. The argument that he might have been able to sell a *different* car to that other purchaser was rejected by the Court of Appeal in *Charter* v. *Sullivan,* 1957[436] (in regard to a new car) and more recently in *Lazenby Garages Ltd* v. *Wright,* 1976[437] (in regard to a used car). However, in *Thompson* v. *Robinson (Gunmakers) Ltd,* 1955[438] the argument that it might have been possible to sell a different car to the other purchaser was accepted though in rather special circumstances. In the course of mitigating his loss a person may actually aggravate the damages and yet recover them (see *Hoffberger* v. *Ascot International Bloodstock Bureau,* 1976).[439] The principle of mitigation also applies in the law of tort. (*Luker* v. *Chapman,* 1970.)[440]

As regards anticipatory breach it seems that there is no duty on the part of the plaintiff to mitigate his damages before there has been any breach which he has accepted as a breach. (*White and Carter (Councils) Ltd* v. *McGregor,* 1961.)[403] It should be noted, however, that doubt was cast on the principle of *White and Carter* by the recent decision of the Court of Appeal in the *Attica Sea Carriers case, The Times,* 25 November, 1975. The facts of the case are somewhat complex but in essence the issue which the Court of Appeal had to decide was whether the owner of a ship hired to another could disregard that other's repudiation, refuse to take back the ship and continue to claim the hire charges during the whole term of the contract. The Court of Appeal held he was not entitled to do so. He could not rely on the *White and Carter* principle as a means of obtaining specific performance in circumstances where he ought to have been reasonable and accepted the other party's repudiation and sued for damages.

Classification of damages.   It is possible to classify damages under a number of headings, and this classification applies to both contract and tort.

(a) Ordinary damages. These are damages assessed by the court for losses arising naturally from the breach of contract; and in tort for losses which cannot be positively proved or ascertained, and depend upon the court's view of the nature of the plaintiff's injury. For example, the court may have to decide what to award for the loss of an eye, there being no scale of payments; and this is so whether the action be in tort or for breach of contract.

(b) Special damages. These are awarded in tort for losses which can be positively proved or ascertained, e.g. damage to clothing; garage bills, where a vehicle has been damaged; doctor's fees; and so on. However, where it is difficult to determine the exact proportions of a claim for special damages, e.g. loss of profit not supported by accurate figures the court must do its best to arrive at a fair valuation. (*Dixons Ltd* v. *J. L. Cooper Ltd* (1970), 114 S.J. 319.) In contract, the term covers losses which do not arise naturally from the breach, so that they will not be recoverable unless within the contemplation of the parties as described above.

(c) Exemplary and aggravated damages. The usual object of damages both in contract and tort is to compensate the plaintiff for loss which he has incurred arising form the defendant's conduct. The object of *exemplary damages* is to punish the defendant, and to deter him and others from similar conduct in the future. Thus, it was at one time thought that, if the court had arrived at a sum of money which would sufficiently compensate the plaintiff, it could award a further sum, not as compensation for the plaintiff, but as a punishment to the defendant, the exemplary damages being in the nature of a fine. An award of exemplary damages had always confused the functions of the civil and criminal law, and it would appear that since the judgment of Lord Devlin in *Rookes* v. *Barnard*, 1964, an award of exemplary damages should only be made in certain special cases. (See below.)

Aggravated damages, on the other hand, can be awarded (generally only in tort) where the defendant's conduct is such that the plaintiff requires more than the usual amount of damages to *compensate him* for the unpleasant method in which the tort was committed against him. However, an award of aggravated damages is still *compensatory*.

The state of the law after *Rookes* v. *Barnard*, 1964,[675] may perhaps be illustrated by taking a hypothetical case. Suppose a tenant T is evicted from his flat by the landlord L before T's term has expired, and that in order to evict T the landlord uses excessive violence. The court may decide that in an ordinary case of trespass and assault T would be adequately compensated by an award of damages of (say) £500. However, if the court considers that L used particularly violent and unpleasant methods to achieve this eviction, it may award a further sum (say) £100 as aggravated damages because, on the facts of the case, this is necessary to compensate T. It would appear that the court cannot now go on and make a further award to T in order to punish and deter L. (And see *Ansell* v. *Thomas,* 1973.)[441]

Exemplary or punitive damages were sometimes awarded in contract for breach of promise of marriage, particularly where a female plaintiff had allowed the defendant to have sexual intercourse with her on the promise of marriage. This action is now abolished by the Law Reform (Miscellaneous Provisions) Act, 1970, Sect. 1 and examples of exemplary damages would seem in the main to be confined to actions in tort. However, an action may lie where a promise to marry is made by a man *who is already married* on the grounds of breach by the man of an implied warranty that he is in a position to marry. That such an implied warranty exists in the circumstances was decided by the Court of Appeal in *Shaw* v. *Shaw*, [1954] 2 Q.B. 424. Damages for breach of such a warranty could be, and possibly still can be, exemplary.

Subject to what has been said above and as a result of Lord Devlin's judgment in *Rookes* v. *Barnard*, 1964 exemplary damages can be awarded only—

(i) *Where there is arbitrary or unconstitutional action by servants of the State*, e.g. an unreasonable false imprisonment or detention by State authorities.

(ii) *Where the defendant's conduct has been calculated by him to make a profit for himself which may well exceed the compensation payable to the plaintiff.* Thus a newspaper may decide that the increased sales of the paper containing a libel will more than compensate for any damages which may have to be paid to the person libelled. In such a case exemplary damages may be awarded to the plaintiff, though the intention to profit must be proved. It is not enough that the newspaper has been sold and some profit necessarily made. An example of the application of this head is to be seen in *Cassell & Co. Ltd* v. *Broome*, [1972] 1 All E.R. 801 where the House of Lords upheld an award of £25,000 exemplary damages against defendants who published a book containing defamatory passages where the right circumstances appeared to exist and a defence if raised, would have failed.

(iii) *Where exemplary damages are expressly authorized by statute.*

Having apparently restricted the number of situations in which exemplary damages might be awarded, Lord Devlin said at one point in his judgment in *Rookes* v. *Barnard*, 1964[675] that 'Exemplary damages can properly be awarded whenever it is necessary to teach a wrongdoer that tort does not pay.' The ramifications of this statement, which could have the effect of extending the power to award exemplary damages to torts such as deceit or negligence where exemplary damages have not previously been awarded, were considered in regard to the tort of deceit in *Mafo* v. *Adams*, 1969.[250] The House of Lords in *Cassell & Co. Ltd* v. *Broome*,

[1972] 1 All E.R. 801 held that *Rookes* v. *Barnard,* 1964 had correctly formulated the principles of law governing the circumstances in which exemplary damages might be awarded to a plaintiff in the case of certain torts. However, Lord Hailsham and Lord Diplock were of the opinion that the decision in *Rookes* v. *Barnard,* 1964 did not have the effect of extending the power to award exemplary damages to torts such as deceit or negligence where exemplary damages could not have previously been awarded and to this extent disapproved the dictum of Lord Widgery, L.J. in *Mafo* v. *Adams,* 1969.[250]

(d) Nominal damages. Sometimes a small sum (say £2) is awarded where the plaintiff proves a breach of contract, or the infringement of a right, but has suffered no actual loss.

(e) Contemptuous damages. A farthing was sometimes awarded to mark the court's disapproval of the plaintiff's conduct in bringing the action. Such damages have been awarded to male plaintiffs in breach of promise of marriage actions, and where the plaintiff has sued for defamation of character in spite of the fact that he has engaged in defamatory activities against the defendant. Since farthings are no longer legal tender, the new decimal halfpenny is now used.

(f) Liquidated damages. These are damages agreed upon by the parties to the contract, and only a breach of contract need be proved; no proof of loss is required. Damages in tort are not liquidated.

(g) Unliquidated damages. Where no damages are fixed by the contract it is left to the court to decide their amount. In such a case the plaintiff must produce evidence of the loss he has suffered, as is normal in the case of tort.

Liquidated damages must appear to be a genuine pre-estimate of loss, not a *penalty* inserted to make it an ill bargain for the defendant not to carry out his part of the contract. The court will not enforce a penalty, but will award damages on normal principles. It will be seen, therefore, that the term 'penalty clause' is a misnomer in that a clause which is truly penal will not be enforced. Nevertheless, this terminology is often used in commercial contracts but such a clause is unenforceable unless it defines a method of calculating liquidated damages.

Certain tests are applied in order to decide whether or not the provision is a penalty. Obviously extravagant sums are generally in the nature of penalties. Where the contractual obligation lying on the defendant is to pay money, then any provision in the contract which requires the payment of a larger sum on default of payment is a penalty, because the damage can be accurately assessed. Where the sum provided for in the contract is payable on the occurrence of any one of several events, it is probably a penalty; for it is unlikely that each event can produce the same loss (*Ford Motor Co.*

(England) Ltd v. *Armstrong,* 1915),[442] though the rule is only a presumption and is not always applied. (*Dunlop* v. *New Garage and Motor Co. Ltd,* 1915.)[149] If a sum is agreed by the parties as liquidated damages, it will be enforced as agreed, even though the actual loss is greater or smaller. (*Cellulose Acetate Silk Co. Ltd* v. *Widnes Foundry Ltd,* 1933.)[443]

Quantum meruit

This remedy means that the plaintiff will be awarded as much as is earned or deserved. In the event of a breach of contract, the injured party may have a claim other than the one for damages. He may have carried out the work or performed services and for such he may be entitled to claim on a *quantum meruit.* He will be awarded what the court thinks the work or services are worth. This action is quite distinct from an action for breach of contract and is in the nature of restitution for work done. The remedy can be used contractually or quasi-contractually, and, although the topic cannot be treated fully, examples of the use of the remedy are given below—

(a) Contractually. Here it may be used to recover a reasonable price or remuneration where there is a contract for the supply of goods or services, but the contract does not fix any precise sum to be paid. It may also be used where the original contract has been replaced by a new one, and a payment is required under the new agreement, e.g. X orders 20 bottles of brandy from Y at a certain price, and Y sends 18 bottles of brandy and 2 bottles of whisky. X is not, of course, bound to take delivery, but if he does he must pay a reasonable price for the whisky on a *quantum meruit.*

(b) Quasi-contractually. Here the remedy may be used to recover a sum of money for work done under a contract discharged by the defendant's breach. This is really an alternative to a claim for damages for breach of contract, but it does enable the court to award whatever it thinks the plaintiff has earned by his work, and this may be greater than the contract price. The remedy is also available when a contract is void, since for breach of a void contract no damages can be awarded (*Craven-Ellis* v. *Canons Ltd,* 1936);[444] and sometimes where the contract is frustrated. (*Davis Contractors Ltd* v. *Fareham U.D.C.,* 1956.)[406] The remedy is also available where there never was a contract. However, if a plaintiff has made an agreement to work for the defendant in return for a specified fee and then sued on a *quantum meruit* for extra work done, he must be in a position to show the court that the original agreement has been discharged. He must have finished with the old contract before he can start a new one. (*Gilbert and Partners* v. *Knight,* 1968.)[445]

Specific performance and injunction

These are equitable remedies and are not available as of right, as is the case with damages, but at the discretion of the court. Formerly these remedies would have had to be sought in the courts of Equity, but since the Judicature Acts, 1873–75 these remedies, as well as damages, are available in any court.

A decree of *specific performance* is an order of the court, and constitutes an express instruction to a party to a contract to perform the actual obligation which he undertook under its terms. It is often granted in contracts connected with land, and under Sect. 92 of the Companies Act, 1948, a contract to take debentures in a company can be specifically enforced, though normally specific performance of a loan would not be granted. However, the remedy is available in appropriate circumstances to enforce a payment of money. (See *Beswick* v. *Beswick,* 1967.)[147] In the case of contracts for the sale of goods, specific performance is not usually given, unless the goods are unique and cannot be purchased easily in the market, or where their value is difficult to assess, or in any other case where damages would not be an adequate remedy. See *Sky Petroleum Ltd* v. *VIP Petroleum Ltd,* 1974,[446] in which an injunction was granted in circumstances where it would operate like specific performance.

An *injunction* is an order of the court whereby an individual is required to refrain from the further doing of the act complained of. It may be used to prevent many wrongful acts, e.g. torts, but in the context of contract the remedy will be granted to enforce a negative stipulation in a contract in a case where it would be unjust to confine the plaintiff to an action for damages. 'The standard question in relation to the grant of an injunction, are damages an adequate remedy? might perhaps, in the light of the authorities of recent years, be re-written: is it just, in all the circumstances, that a plaintiff should be confined to his remedy in damages?' per Sachs, L.J. in *Evans Marshall* v. *Bertola SA,* [1973] 1 All E.R. 992 at p. 1005. Its application may be extended to contracts where there is no actual negative stipulation but where one may be inferred. (*Metropolitan Electric Supply Co.* v. *Ginder,* 1901.)[447] In a proper case an injunction may be used as an indirect method of enforcing a contract for personal services, but in that case a *clear* negative stipulation is required. (*Whitwood Chemical Co.* v. *Hardman,* 1891,[448] and *Warner Bros Pictures Incorporated* v. *Nelson,* 1937.)[449] However, the breach of contract which it is sought to redress by injunction must have resulted in a continuing wrong; the proper remedy to put right past wrongs being damages. (*Desk Advertising Co. Ltd* v. *Société Civile De Participations Du Group S.T. Dupont and Others,* 1973.)[450] Furthermore, the obligation to be enforced must be certain. (*Bower* v. *Bantam Investments Ltd,* 1972.)[451]

Injunctions may be (*a*) Interlocutory, (*b*) Perpetual, (*c*) Prohibitory, (*d*) Mandatory. An *interlocutory injunction* is granted before the hearing of the action, the plaintiff undertaking to be responsible for any damage caused to the defendant if in the subsequent action the plaintiff does not succeed. The decision of the House of Lords in *American Cyanamid* v. *Ethicon,* [1975] 1 All E.R. 504 puts forward the following legal propositions in regard to interlocutory injunctions: (i) an applicant for an interlocutory injunction need no longer show that he has a *prima facie* case, but rather the court should consider the balance of convenience unless the material before the court fails to disclose that the plaintiff had any real prospect of succeeding at the full trial; (ii) that in deciding the balance of convenience the court should consider—(*a*) whether, if no injunction were awarded and the plaintiff succeeded at the full trial, damages would adequately compensate him for loss suffered in the meantime, and (*b*) whether, if the injunction were granted, the plaintiff's undertakings as to damages would be sufficient to compensate the defendant for loss suffered in the meantime if the defendant finally won. There is a form of interlocutory injunction called *quia timet* (because he fears). This may be granted, though rarely, even though the injury has not taken place but is merely threatened. (*Hooper* v. *Rogers*, 1974.)[452] A *perpetual injunction* is granted after a trial, and when the point at issue has been finally determined. A *prohibitory injunction* orders that a certain act shall not be done; a *mandatory injunction* orders that a certain positive act shall be done, e.g. an order to pull down a wall erected in breach of covenant.

Since specific performance is an equitable remedy, it will be granted only when certain conditions apply—

(i) Consideration must exist, since 'Equity will not assist a volunteer.' (But see *Mountford* v. *Scott*, 1974.)[453]

(ii) The court must be able to supervise the performance. Specific performance will not be granted if constant supervision is necessary to ensure that the defendant complies with the decree. (*Ryan* v. *Mutual Tontine Westminster Chambers Association*, 1893.)[454]

(iii) It must be just and equitable that the remedy be granted. If the court considers that damages are an adequate remedy, it will not grant an equitable one.

(iv) Both parties must be able to obtain the remedy. The courts will not grant equitable remedies to a minor because his contracts cannot be enforced against him, and Equity requires equality or mutuality.

(v) The plaintiff must show that he was in a position to carry out his part of the bargain at the time fixed for performance.

(vi) The plaintiff's own conduct in the matter must be above reproach: for it is said that 'He who comes into Equity must come with clean hands.'

A contract for personal services will not be specifically enforced because—

(a) it would be undesirable to force persons to work together if they did not wish to do so; and

(b) it would be impossible to ensure that the contract was properly carried out unless the defendant was under the constant supervision of the court. The decision of the Court of Appeal in *Hill* v. *Parsons*, 1971[445] suggests to the contrary but the decision is now regarded (even by Lord Denning himself in *Chappell* v. *Times Newspapers Ltd*, [1975] 2 All E.R. 233) as so unusual as to constitute no real precedent.

However, as we have seen, the court may *encourage* but not *compel* performance of a contract of personal service by means of an injunction. (*Whitwood Chemical Co.* v. *Hardman*, 1891,[448] and *Warner Bros Pictures Incorporated* v. *Nelson*, 1937.)[449] If the effect of an injunction would be to *compel* performance it will not be granted. (*Page One Records Ltd* v. *Britton*, 1967.)[456]

The court will not, however, grant an equitable remedy where to do so would lead to further litigation, (*Wroth* v. *Tyler*, 1973),[457] or in a breach of another obligation. (*Warmington* v. *Miller*, 1973.)[458]

Defiance of the court's order granting an equitable remedy constitutes contempt of court, which is punishable by fine or imprisonment. The court's order is, therefore, likely to be obeyed. Some equitable remedies must be asked for within a given time by statute, but otherwise they must be asked for within a reasonable time, since 'Delay defeats Equities'. What is a reasonable time is determined by the court from the circumstances.

Rescission

This is a further equitable remedy for breach of contract. The rule is the same when the remedy is used for breach as it is when it is used for misrepresentation. If the contract cannot be completely rescinded, it cannot be rescinded at all; it must be possible to restore the *status quo*. All part payments must be returned on rescission and cannot be retained as security against future damages, but there are circumstances where part payment is regarded as a guarantee for the due performance of the payer's obligations, and, if this is so, it will be forfeited if he does not go on with the contract, although Equity will sometimes grant relief against forfeiture of deposits. A plaintiff cannot combine a claim for rescission with a claim for damages. (*Horsler* v. *Zorro*, 1975.)[459]

Refusal of further performance

It the person suffering from the breach desires merely to be quit of his obligations under the contract, he may refuse any further performance on his own part and set up the breach as a defence if the party who has committed the breach attempts to enforce the contract against him. Even so, he may, if he wishes, reinforce his position by bringing an action for rescission.

The recovery of interest

The rules governing the recovery of interest are as follows—

(a) It is payable where the parties have so agreed in the contract.

(b) The dealings between the parties may show that an agreement to pay interest may be implied.

(c) Overdue bills of exchange and promissory notes bear interest.

(d) Under the Law Reform (Miscellaneous Provisions) Act, 1934, the court may *at its discretion* allow interest at such a rate as it thinks fit on all claims for debt or special damages from the date when the claim arose to judgment.

It should be noted, however, that under Sect. 22 of the Administration of Justice Act, 1969, as from 1 January, 1970, judges are *directed* in personal injury cases to award interest on damages exceeding £200, though the rate of interest, the portion of the judgment on which it is to be calculated, and the particular period during which interest is to be paid, is left to the discretion of the court. However, since the Court of Appeal laid down guidelines in *Jefford* v. *Gee,* [1970] 1 All E.R. 1202, there has been uniformity in the application of the discretion by the courts. However, the Law Commission's Working Paper on Interest (No. 86) published in 1976 makes proposals for extending the general principle that a plaintiff should be compensated for being kept out of his money.

Once a judgment has been made the rate of interest on the judgment debt under Sect. 17 of the Judgments Act, 1838, is ten per cent per annum. (Judgment Debts (Rate of Interest) Order, 1977, S.I. 141.) Interest payable on the judgment debt under Sect. 17 of the Judgments Act, 1838, runs from the date of the pronouncement of the judgment. (See *Parsons* v. *Mather & Platt,* [1977] 2 All E.R. 715.)

QUASI-CONTRACTUAL RIGHTS AND REMEDIES

Before moving on to the law of tort, it is necessary to consider an area of law referred to as quasi-contract. Quasi-contract is based on the idea that a person should not obtain a benefit or an unjust enrichment as against another merely because there is no obligation in contract or another established branch of law which will operate to make him account for it. The law may in these circumstances provide a remedy by implying *a fictitious promise* to account for the benefit or enrichment. This promise can then form the basis of an action in quasi-contract. (*Greenwood* v. *Bennett,* 1972.)[460] The main areas in which quasi-contractual remedies have been used are as follows—

Actions for money paid

Where A has a secondary and B has a primary *legal liability* to a third person and A has paid over money which B was in the ultimate liable to pay, an action will lie in quasi-contract to enable A to recover from B. (*Brook's Wharf and Bull Wharf Ltd* v. *Goodman Bros*, 1936.)[461]

It is essential to the claim that B should have been under a *common and legal obligation* to pay. (*Metropolitan Police District Receiver* v. *Croydon Corporation*, 1957.)[462]

Actions for money had and received

An action for money had and received by the defendant to the use of the plaintiff lies in the following circumstances—

(a) *Total failure of consideration.* The plaintiff must prove that there has been a *total* and not a *partial* failure of consideration. A partial failure of consideration may result in an action for damages. A *total* failure will result in recovery of all that was paid. A common reason for total failure of consideration arises where A, who has no title, sells goods to B and B has to give up the goods to the true owner. (*Rowland* v. *Divall*, 1923.)[273]

In addition the action is based on *failure* of consideration not its *absence*. Thus, money paid by way of a gift cannot be recovered in quasi-contract.

(b) *Mistake of fact.* Where there is a fundamental and material mistake of fact which results in a payment of money, there may be an action in quasi-contract to recover the sums so paid either in whole or in part according to the effect of the mistake. (*Cox* v. *Prentice*, 1815.)[463]

(c) *Mistake of law.* Money paid as a result of a mistake of law cannot generally be recovered since ignorance of the law is no excuse. However, as we have seen, it is not easy to distinguish a mistake of law from a mistake of fact, and legislation relating to rents and security of tenure has produced some interesting cases showing the different results obtainable according to the category into which the mistake is put. (See *Sharp Bros and Knight* v. *Chant*, 1917,[208] *Solle* v. *Butcher*, 1950,[209] and *Grist* v. *Bailey*, 1966.)[229] It appears that a mistake as to a person's legal rights can be construed, at least in equity, as a mistake of fact thus giving rise to a remedy. (*Cooper* v. *Phibbs*, 1867.)[210]

There may be another ground for recovering money paid in circumstances of mistake of law, e.g. as in the case of an oppressed party to an illegal contract not *in pari delicto* with the other. Where this is so, the plaintiff will not be prevented from succeeding simply because he has made a mistake of law. (*Kiriri Cotton Co.* v. *Dawani*, 1960.)[376]

(d) *Duress and extortion.* Money paid under threats of physical violence or undue influence, i.e. moral duress, is not paid voluntarily and may be recovered in quasi-contract.

(e) Money received from a third person. An application of this aspect of quasi-contract is to be found in insurance. If an insurance company pays out a sum of money to A (the insured) in respect of loss or damage to himself or his property and A later recovers additional money in respect of the loss from another, e.g. the person causing the loss, the insurance company may sue A in quasi-contract to recover the sums received from the third person. (*Darrell* v. *Tibbitts* (1880), 5 Q.B.D. 560.)

In addition, where A has received money from B with instructions to pay it to C, then C may sue A in quasi-contract if A refuses to pay the money over. (*Shamia* v. *Joory*, 1958.)[151]

(f) Waiver of Tort. If A steals B's car which is valued at £500 and sells it to a dealer C for £550, then B may sue A or C for wrongful interference with goods but can if he wishes waive his right to sue in tort and recover the money in quasi-contract. The action in quasi-contract has some advantages over the action in tort, e.g. A may prove in a winding-up or bankruptcy for the sum of £550 which he cannot do if his claim is in tort and has not reached judgment.

Claims on a quantum meruit

Where a plaintiff has done work for the defendant but no specific sum is owing, the plaintiff can recover a reasonable sum of money on a *quantum meruit*. This aspect of quasi-contract is dealt with on page 274.

Accounts stated

If A gives B an IOU for £10, the IOU operates as an admission of the debt and gives a separate cause of action in quasi-contract. An IOU is not conclusive and A may prove the debt is void for want of consideration or illegal or that he gave the IOU under circumstances of mistake. Nevertheless, A has the burden of proving these matters and, if he cannot, B will succeed on the IOU.

Furthermore, if A (a debtor) and B (a creditor) have an account recording a number of transactions and agree to strike a balance at an agreed figure, this operates as an account stated and B can sue in quasi-contract for the amount. This is a separate source of action and would enable B to recover even in respect of debts which were formerly statute barred.

LEGISLATION RELATING TO THE CONTRACT OF EMPLOYMENT

An ever-increasing feature of contract law is the way in which particular contracts are controlled by legislation to which the general principles of contract law yield; nowhere is this more obvious than in the contract of employment. Accordingly, the main features of this legislation, which are so important in all walks of business life are given below. The statutes concerned are abbreviated for convenience so that the Employment Protection Act, 1975 becomes the EPA; the Sex Discrimination Act, 1974 the SDA; the Race Relations Act, 1976 the RRA; the Trade Union and Labour Relations Act, 1974 the TULRA and the Health and Safety at Work Act, 1974 the HASAWA.

Recruitment and selection of employees

Here the employer must take account of race relations and sex discrimination legislation. The Race Relations Act establishes a Commission for Racial Equality with a duty to work towards the elimination of discrimination on the grounds of race. Its powers are much the same as those of the Equal Opportunities Commission set up under the SDA. It is unlawful for an employer to discriminate between applicants for jobs on the grounds of colour, race, nationality, or ethnic or national origins. It is also unlawful to publish an advertisement which could be interpreted as discriminatory.

Under the SDA it is unlawful for a person to discriminate against another on grounds of sex or marital status when determining who will be offered a job and in regard to the terms and conditions of the job. There are exceptions where the sex or marital status of the person required is a genuine occupational qualification (goq), e.g. for reasons of physiology (as in the employment of a model) or for reasons of decency or privacy (as in the case of single-sex establishments such as schools and prisons) or where the job is one of two held by a married couple.

It should be noted that it is unlawful for a firm of six or more partners to discriminate in regard to the selection of new partners and benefits facilities, or services given to partners, unless a goq applies.

As regards enforcement, those who believe they have been discriminated against may complain to an industrial tribunal within three months of the date of the act complained of. A conciliation officer of the Advisory Conciliation and Arbitration Service must try to settle the complaint without the need for a tribunal hearing. If this is not possible and the matter goes to a tribunal the tribunal may make an order declaring the rights of the parties in relation to the complaint. In addition, it may make an order for compensation which could cover loss of prospective earnings and injured feelings. It may also recommend that the employer take, within a specified period, action which appears to the tribunal to be practicable for the purpose of obviating or reducing the adverse effect of any act of discrimination on which the complaint is based. Proceedings (relating for example to discriminatory advertisements and instructions to discriminate) may only be instituted by the Commission for Racial Equality or the Equal Opportunities Commission, as the case may be.

During employment

The contract of employment. The EPA provides that an employee is entitled to one week's notice after four weeks' service. After two years' service, the minimum notice is increased to two weeks, and for each year of service afterwards it is increased by one week, to a maximum of 12 weeks after 12 years' service.

In addition, an employer must give his employee written information about the terms of employment not later than 13 weeks after the employment has commenced. This statement must contain the names of the employer and the employee; the dates when the employment began; whether employment with a previous employer is to be counted as part of the employee's 'continuous period of employment' and, where this is so, the date on which it began (this is important to the employee, for example, in terms of redundancy payments); the title of the job; the scale or rate of remuneration or the method of calculating remuneration; the intervals at which remuneration is paid; any terms and conditions relating to the hours worked, entitlement to holidays and holiday pay, sickness or injury and sick pay, pensions and length of notice; there must also be a note specifying any disciplinary rules, the name of a person to whom the employee can apply in case of any disciplinary decision or grievance; and the disciplinary and grievance procedures, where these are laid down. The rules for calculating continuous employment, normal hours and a week's pay are in the EPA.

An employee who does not receive written particulars or who wants to dispute their accuracy or sufficiency may refer the matter to an industrial tribunal. The tribunal may then make a declaration that the employee has a right to a statement and what particulars should be included in it or amended within it. The statement approved by the tribunal is then deemed to have been given by the employer to the employee and will form the basis of his rights.

Pay. Under the EPA, an employee is entitled to an itemized pay statement, containing the gross amount for wages or salary; the amounts of any variable and fixed deductions and the reasons for them; and the net amount of wages or salary payable. As only gross and net amounts and deductions are required, it is apparently unnecessary for workers to be informed as to details of their basic rates, overtime payments or shift premiums. The fixed deductions can be aggregated so long as the employee is issued with a statement of fixed deductions which is re-issued every 12 months, and he is notified of any alterations when they are made. If an employee does not receive a pay statement or if he receives one that is inadequate, he may refer the matter to an industrial tribunal. The industrial tribunal will make a declaration which will include answers to questions relating to the employer's failure to give particulars or his failure to give accurate amounts. The declaration then determines these matters. Where there have been unnotified deductions for pay during the previous

13 weeks, the tribunal may order the employer to pay to the employee a sum not exceeding the total unnotified deductions.

Equal treatment in terms and conditions of employemt as between men and women in the same employment.   The Equal Pay Act 1970, as amended by the SDA, implies a term into women's contracts of employment which requires equal treatment in terms of pay, holidays, sick pay, and hours of work.

A woman who believes she is not being treated equally may complain to an industrial tribunal, which may award arrears of remuneration or damages.

Discrimination in the treatment of employees.   Under the SDA and RRA, it is unlawful to discriminate against a person on grounds of race, sex or marital status as regards opportunities for promotion, training or transfer, or in the provision of benefits, facilities or services or by dismissal or any other disadvantages. However, the EPA allows women to receive special treatment when they are pregnant, and employers may provide different pension arrangements and retiring ages based on sex. There is no discrimination where the sex or marital status of the employee is a genuine occupational qualification.

If an unlawful act of discrimination is committed by an employee, such as a personnel officer, the employer is held responsible for the act along with the employee unless the employer can show that he took all reasonable steps to prevent the employee from discriminating. If he can do this, only the employee is responsible. As regards enforcement by employees, those who believe that they have been discriminated against may make a complaint to an industrial tribunal within three months of the date of the act complained of. It is then the duty of a conciliation officer to see whether the complaint can be settled without going to a tribunal. If, however, a tribunal hears the complaint, it may make an order declaring the rights of the employee and employer in regard to the complaint, the intention being that both parties will abide by the order for the future. The tribunal may also give the employee compensation up to a maximum amount of £5200, and may additionally recommend that the employer take, within a specified period, action appearing to the tribunal to be practicable for the purpose of obviating or reducing discrimination.

Disclosure of information.   The EPA requires employers to disclose information necessary for the purposes of collective bargaining and for purposes of good industrial relations to representatives of trade unions. The Advisory Conciliation and Arbitration Service has published a code of practice indicating the sort of information that should be disclosed.

If a union representative asks for information for collective bargaining purposes and the employer fails to disclose it, a complaint may be made to the Central Arbitration Committee. Conciliation may be attempted at this stage. If it fails, or is not attempted, the Committee will hear the complaint and may make a declaration upholding it and pass on the necessary information obtained from the employer to the union representative. If the employer continues to fail to disclose information, a further complaint may be lodged, and if this is upheld after another hearing, it allows the Committee to force arbitration on an employer if the union presents a claim.

Guarantee payments. Employees with not less than four weeks' continuous service are entitled to a guarantee payment, currently £6.60 per day, if they are not provided with work on a normal working day (EPA). This guarantee is limited to five days in any calendar quarter starting on the first days of February, May, August and November, i.e. an absolute maximum of 20 days per year. The provisions do not apply if the failure to provide work is due to a trade dispute, or if the employee has been offered suitable alternative work but has refused it.

An employee may present a complaint to an industrial tribunal that his employer has failed to pay the whole or any part of a guarantee payment to which the employee is entitled. The industrial tribunal may make an order to pay the employee the amount of guarantee payment which it finds is due to him.

Suspension from work on medical grounds. An employee with not less than four weeks' continuous service who is suspended from work under the provisions of an Act of Parliament (e.g. the HASAWA) or a code of practice, not because he is ill but because he may become ill if he continues at work, is entitled to be paid normal wages while suspended for up to 26 weeks (EPA). A replacement employee whose health is not potentially affected may be engaged, and so long as this employee is informed in writing that his employment will end when the suspended employee resumes his work, he will be regarded as justifiably dismissed.

An employee may present a complaint to an industrial tribunal that his employer has failed to pay the whole or any part of remuneration to which he is entitled on suspension, and the tribunal may order the employer to pay the employee the remuneration due to him.

Terms and conditions of employment. Under the EPA, a trade union or employers' association can inform the Advisory Conciliation and Arbitration Service that an employer is not observing recognized minimum terms and conditions negotiated for workers in comparable employment. If no recognized terms exist, comparison may be made with similar employments within the district. Where an industry is under a wages council, e.g. catering, a trade union may claim to the Advisory Conciliation and Arbitration Service that a member is being paid less than the usual rate for comparable work provided the union concerned is a party to a collective agreement which covers a significant number of establishments in that industry.

Maternity. There are four areas to consider under the EPA; these are:

(1) *Dismissal of pregnant employee.* A woman who is dismissed because she is pregnant will be treated as having been unfairly dismissed unless certain circumstances apply, e.g. she is unable to do her job and cannot be offered or has refused suitable alternative work. Even if fairly dismissed, the woman is still entitled to maternity pay and reinstatement after confinement.

(2) *Maternity pay.* Women who are absent because of pregnancy are, if they have completed two years' service and been at work up to the eleventh week before the expected week of confinement, entitled to maternity pay from their employers. The maternity pay is paid for the first six weeks of absence and is in each week nine-tenths of a week's pay, less the amount of the standard rate of maternity allowance even if the particular employee is not in receipt of this. The employee must, at least three weeks beforehand or as soon as possible thereafter tell her employer that she will be absent, and he may require her to produce a medical certificate showing the expected week of confinement. Employers may claim a rebate for the full amount of maternity pay from a Maternity Pay Fund financed by an addition of 0.05% to employers' Social Security contributions.

(3) *Return to work.* If a woman returns to her job within 29 weeks after her baby is born, she must be given back her old job or a suitable alternative. However, she must have informed her employer (in writing, if he requires) of her intention to return at the time she notified him that she was going to be absent to have a baby. She must notify her employer at least one week before she intends to return, and the employer may postpone her return by up to four weeks, as may the employee if she provides a medical certificate giving reasons. Temporary replacements must be told at the start that the job is temporary, and there is no unfair dismissal of the temporary on the return of the original employee if the method of dismissal is reasonable.

(4) *Failure to pay maternity pay.* An employee may present a complaint to an industrial tribunal that her employer has failed to pay the whole or any part of maternity pay due, and may question its amount. The tribunal may order the employer to pay the employee the amount of maternity pay which the tribunal finds is due to her. If she cannot recover payment, as where the employer will not pay or is insolvent, the employee may apply to the Secretary of State, who will pay her what is due out of the Maternity Fund. The Secretary of State may then recover an appropriate amount from the employer. Where an employer will not take back a woman after absence for maternity leave, she will be treated as dismissed from the notified date of return. Then she may be treated as redundant or unfairly dismissed, and may pursue remedies on that basis.

Time off. Time off with pay must be granted by employers to trade union officials to carry out their trade union duties and to receive training both on and off the premises (EPA). Employees are also entitled to unpaid time off to take part in union activities (other than industrial action). The Advisory Conciliation and Arbitration Service has issued a Code of Practice as to what is reasonable. Reasonable unpaid time off must also be given to employees who hold certain public offices, e.g. as JPs or local councillors. Redundant employees must be given reasonable paid time off to look for work or arrange training for a job.

Insolvency of employer. An employee whose employer becomes insolvent is entitled to obtain payment of certain debts which are owed to him through the Redundancy Fund (EPA). The legal rights and remedies in respect of the debts covered are transferred to the Secretary of State for Employment so that he can try and recover from the assets of the insolvent employer the cost of any payments made. Employees must apply for payment to the employer's representative, e.g. receiver or liquidator, who will submit the application to the Secretary of State for payment from the Redundancy Fund. Debts included are arrears of pay up to £80 per week for a period not exceeding eight weeks; holiday pay up to £80 per week with a limit of six weeks in the last 12 months of employment; payment in lieu of notice for the minimum statutory period, up to £80 per week; any outstanding payment in regard to an award by an industrial tribunal of compensation for unfair dismissal; re-imbursement of the fees of an apprentice or articled clerk.

The administrators of an occupational pension scheme can apply to the Secretary of State for financial assistance where the insolvent employer has not been able to pay the contributions.

Health and safety at work. The HASAWA lays down certain general duties of employers to their employees in the field of health and safety. There is a general duty on employers to ensure as far as is reasonably practicable the health, safety and welfare of all employees while at work. However, in particular, the employer must provide and maintain plant and equipment and safe systems of work; avoid risks to safety and health in handling, storing and transporting articles and substances; provide and maintain safe premises and safe means of entering and leaving them; provide and maintain adequate welfare facilities and arrangements; provide information, training and supervision as required in order to ensure the safety and health of employees; prepare and/or revise policy statements on the safety and health of employees and give proper publicity to these; consult in these matters with safety representatives appointed by trade unions; establish safety committees where union representatives ask for this.

An employer must also conduct his undertaking in such a way that so far as is reasonably practicable those who are not his employees are not exposed to risk. Additionally, an employer must ensure so far as is reasonably practicable that premises which are open to others not employed by him are safe. There is also a duty to use the best practical methods to prevent noxious or offensive substances going into the atmosphere.

Directors are required to set out in their annual reports what their companies are doing in safety and health matters, and regulations will be issued specifying the classes of company that will have to comply with this provision and the kind of information which should be included.

Employees must take reasonable care of their own and other people's health and safety and co-operate with the employer in the carrying out of his duties. The Act also states that no person shall intentionally or recklessly interfere with or misuse anything which is provided in the interests of health, safety and welfare, e.g. safety equipment, and no employer may charge any employee for anything done or provided to comply with the employer's statutory duties.

Finally, those who design, manufacture, import, or supply equipment, machinery and plant must ensure that the design and construction is safe.

Enforcement is in the hands of the inspectorate of the Health and Safety Executive set up by the Act. Inspectors may issue a prohibition notice if there is a risk of serious personal injury. This operates to stop the activity concerned until remedial action specified in the notice has been taken. They may also issue an improvement notice if there is a contravention of any of the relevant statutory provisions, under which the employer must remedy the fault within a specified time. They may prosecute any person contravening the relevant statutory provision instead of or in addition to serving a notice. Failure to comply with a prohibition notice could lead to imprisonment, though there is an appeal to an industrial tribunal.

Pensions. The Social Security Pensions Act, 1975, requires employers to consult employees and trade unions in regard to 'contracting out' of occupational pension schemes, and also to provide equal access to membership of these schemes.

Trade unions and trade disputes. An employee must not be victimized by his employer for joining or trying to join a trade union or for playing a part in its activities at appropriate times.

Individuals cannot be sued at civil law for threatening or inducing a breach of employment or a commercial contract, as where employees prevent or induce an outside contractor to refuse to supply raw materials to the employer's organization, provided these steps are taken in furtherance of a trade dispute. In addition, no action may be taken against a trade union or its members or officials in respect of these matters. Picketing is lawful if peaceful, other than at a person's home.

Unfair dismissal

Under the TULRA, as amended by the EPA employees with 26 weeks or more of continuous service have a right not to be unfairly dismissed. The following matters should be noted;

(1) What is dismissal? `A dismissal means the termination of an employee's contract of service by the employer. Constructive dismissal is included, as where the employee is forced to terminate the contract because the employer breaks, or proposes to break, the contract, e.g. by changing, or proposing to change, the nature of the employment, the place of employment, or important terms of the contract, such as pay.

In fixed-term contracts, as where a person is employed for, say, five years, there is a dismissal if the contract is not renewed when the fixed term ends, though this is not so where the fixed term is two years or more and the employee has agreed not to complain of unfair dismissal.

(2) Reasons justifying dismissal. Dismissal may be justified if an employee is dismissed because of—

(a) *Lack of capability.* This would usually arise at the beginning of employment, where it becomes clear at an early stage that the employee cannot do the job in terms of lack of skill or mental or physical health. The longer a person is in employment, the more difficult it is to establish lack of capability.

(b) *Conduct.* This is aways a difficult matter to deal with, and much will depend upon the circumstances of the case. However, incompetence and neglect are relevant, as are disobedience and misconduct, e.g. by assaulting fellow employees. Immorality and habitual drunkenness could also be brought under this head.

(c) *Redundancy.* Where a person is redundant, his employer cannot be expected to continue the employment, although there are safeguards in the matter of unfair selection for redundancy (see below).

In addition, where there is a union membership agreement, it is fair to dismiss an employee who will not join or threatens to resign from an appropriate union, except where his reasons for so doing are based on religious beliefs.

(d) *Other grounds.* Apart from the specific grounds mentioned above, whether the dismissal is fair depends in the last analysis on whether the employer can satisfy an industrial tribunal that it was reasonable to dismiss the employee in all the circumstances of the case. It is difficult to generalize from the cases, most of which depend upon their own facts. For example, the dismissal of an employee absent through sickness may be regarded as unfair in most situations, but has been held to be fair where the employee concerned was the sole driver of a business operating deliveries with only one van.

(3) Unacceptable reasons for dismissal. These are as follows—

(a) *Trade union membership.* The dismissal of an employee, regardless of his length of service, because he is a member of, or intends to join, a trade union, or has taken or proposes to take part in its activities, or because he has refused to join a trade union on the grounds of religious belief, is unfair.

(b) *Unfair selection for redundancy.* Even an employee dismissed for redundancy may complain that he has been unfairly dismissed if he is of the opinion that he has been unfairly selected for redundancy, as where the employer has disregarded redundancy selection arrangements, e.g. 'last in, first out'. Ideally, all employers should have proper redundancy agreements on the lines set out in the Department of Employment booklet, 'Dealing With Redundancies'.

However, even though there is in existence an agreed redundancy procedure, the employer may defend himself by showing a 'special reason' for departing from that procedure, e.g. because the person selected for redundancy lacks the skill and versatility of a junior employee who is retained.

(c) *Lock-outs and strikes.* If an employee is dismissed during a lock-out or a strike, that dismissal will not be regarded as unfair unless other employees involved were not dismissed or, if dismissed, were afterwards offered re-engagement.

(d) *Pressure on employer to dismiss unfairly.* It is no defence for an employer to say that pressure was put upon him to dismiss an employee unfairly. Thus, if other workers put pressure on an employer to dismiss a non-union member so as, for example, to achieve a closed shop, the employer will have no defence to a claim for compensation for the dismissal if he yields to that pressure.

(4) Complaints of unfair dismissal. Employees may make a complaint of unfair dismissal to an industrial tribunal at any time from the date on which they receive notice until three months after the date of dismissal.

(a) *Conciliation.* An industrial tribunal will not hear a complaint until a conciliation officer has had a chance to see whether he can help. A copy of the complaint made to the industrial tribunal is sent to the conciliation officer, and if he is unable to settle the complaint, nothing said by employer or employee during the process of conciliation will be admissible in evidence before the tribunal.

(b) *Hearing by tribunal.* Where an industrial tribunal hears the case, the procedure is as follows—

(i) it must be established that the employee has been dismissed and is eligible to complain, e.g. on the grounds of continuous service;

(ii) the employer must then attempt to justify the reason for dismissal, i.e. that the circumstances were reasonable, and the way in which it was done was reasonable.

(*c*) *Remedies.* If a complaint of unfair dismissal is upheld, there are the following possibilities—

(i) *Reinstatement or re-engagement.* The employee must be told of his right to reinstatement or re-engagement, and asked whether he wishes such an order to be made. If he does, the tribunal must consider whether it would be practicable and reasonable in all the circumstances to make such an order. If such an order is made, the employer who does not comply with it when it is practical for him to do so, may find that the tribunal will increase the amount of compensation payable by an amount equal to between 13 and 26 weeks of the employee's pay; or where the dismissal involved racial or sexual discrimination, or was because of trade union activities, to between 26 and 52 weeks' pay.

(ii) *Compensation.* If the tribunal does not make an order of re-instatement or re-engagement, or makes one which the employer does not comply with, although it would have been practicable and reasonable for him to do so, the tribunal must make a basic award of compensation and may make, in addition, a compensatory award. The basic award is calculated according to the formula for redundancy payments, i.e. for each year of service up to a maximum of 20 years a number of weeks' pay up to a maximum of £80 per week as follows—

Ages 41 to 65 (60, women), $1\frac{1}{2}$ weeks' pay.

Ages 22 to 40, 1 week's pay.

Ages 15 to 21, half a week's pay.

There is a maximum payment of £2400 and a minimum of two weeks' pay. There may also be a compensatory award based on financial loss as a result of dismissal, the maximum compensatory award being £5200.

(iii) *Dismissal for union membership or activities.* An employee who is of the opinion that he has been unfairly dismissed for a reason connected with his trade union membership or activities may apply to an industrial tribunal for an order for reinstatement or re-engagement on an interim basis, or for his contract of employment to be revised, until a decision has been made on his complaint. The application must be made within seven days of dismissal, and has to be supported by a signed certificate from an official of the relevant trade union.

Redundancy

The EPA gives an employee a right to compensation by way of a redundancy payment if he is dismissed because of redundancy.

(1) Meaning of redundancy. Redundancy occurs where the services of employees are dispensed with because the employer ceases, or intends to cease, carrying on business, or does not require so many employees to do work of a certain kind. Employees who have been laid off or kept on short time without pay for four consecutive weeks (or for six weeks in a period of

13 weeks) are entitled to a redundancy payment if there is no reasonable prospect that normal working will be resumed.

(2) Eligibility. Employees who have completed two years continuous service are eligible for a redundancy payment. Additionally, they must work 16 hours or more per week (or eight hours or more where the employment has been for five years or more).

An employee who accepts an offer of suitable alternative employment with his employer is not entitled to a redundancy payment. Where a new offer is made, there is a trial period of four weeks following the making of the offer, during which the employer or the employee may end the contract while retaining all rights and liabilities under redundancy legislation.

(3) Amount of redundancy payment. As we have seen, those aged 41 to 65 (60, women) receive $1\frac{1}{2}$ weeks' pay (up to a maximum of £80 per week) for each year of service up to a maximum of 20 years. In other age groups, the above provisions apply except that the week's pay changes, i.e. for those aged 22 to 40, it is one week's pay, and for those aged 15 to 21, it is a half-week's pay.

Employees over 64 (59, women) have their redundancy payment reduced progressively, so that for each complete month by which the age exceeds 64 (or 59) on the Saturday of the week in which the contract ends, the normal entitlement is reduced by one-twelfth. Complaints by employees in respect of the right to a redundancy payment, or questions as to its amount, may be made to an industrial tribunal which will make a declaration as to the employee's right which forms the basis on which payment can be recovered from the employer.

(4) Rebates for employers. Employers who have made a redundancy payment may claim a rebate of 50% from the Redundancy Fund. To obtain the rebate, the employer must notify the local office of the Department of Employment that the intends to make a claim, three weeks or more before the expected date of dismissal if 10 or more employees are involved, or two weeks or more in the case of redundancies involving less than 10 employees. If the employer fails to give adequate prior notice of his intention to claim a rebate, the Secretary of State may reduce that rebate by up to 10%.

(5) Procedure for handling redundancies. This is as follows:

(a) *Notification.* Employers must notify the Department of Employment of redundancies being planned which would involve the dismissal of more than 10 employees in a period of one month. The minimum notification period is 60 days. This notification is different from the one referred in (4) above. If the employer fails to notify the Secretary of State of proposed redundancies, the Secretary of State may reduce the redundancy payments rebate to 10% or a magistrates' court may impose a fine not exceeding £400.

(*b*) *Consultation.* Employers are required to consult with trade union representatives as soon as possible which (in line with EEC requirements) if 100 or more employees are affected is not less than 90 days before the redundancies take effect, or 60 days if 10 or more employees are affected. Consultation involves the employer in telling the unions the reason for the proposals, together with number and type of employees to be dismissed, the total number of employees of that type at the establishment involved, the proposed method of selection and of carrying out the dismissals.

Representations made by the unions must be received and replied to. If this is not done, an industrial tribunal may, on the complaint of a trade union (or in a multi-union situation, by any one of them) make a declaration of the tribunal's findings, and the tribunal may make a 'protective award' under which the employees will be kept in employment and paid for not more than a period corresponding to the minimum time required for prior consultation, i.e. 90 or 60 days the case may be. If an employee is not paid during all or part of the period for which the protective award applies, he may apply to an industrial tribunal, which will issue an order to the employer to pay the amount of remuneration due to the employee.

(*c*) *Collective agreements on redundancy.* The Secretary of State may, on the application of the employer and unions involved, make an order modifying the requirements of redundancy pay legislation if he is satisfied that there is a collective agreement which makes satisfactory alternative arrangements for dealing with redundancies. The provisions of the agreement must be 'on the whole at least as favourable' as the statutory provisions, and must include, in particular, arrangements allowing an employee to go to independent arbitration or to make a complaint to an industrial tribunal.

Minimum period of notice

Under the EPA, an employee is entitled to one week's notice after four weeks' service; after two years' service the minimum entitlement is increased to two weeks, and for each year of service after that it is increased by one week up to a maximum of 12 weeks' notice after 12 years' service. An employee who is engaged for a specific job on a 12-week or shorter contract is not entitled to any notice unless in the event the contract is extended or he is retained for a period longer than 12 weeks.

Three matters should be noted. Firstly, the legislation does not affect the common law right of an employer to dismiss an employee summarily without notice for misconduct, e.g. disobedience, neglect or drunkenness. Secondly, the legislation does not prevent employer and employee from agreeing to longer periods of notice to be given by the employer. Thirdly, such longer periods of notice may be implied by law or custom, and an industrial tribunal will not necessarily consider the minimum period of notice laid down by legislation as sufficient. Consideration will be given to the employee's length of service, his age, and the possibility of his finding alternative employment.

Breach of the provisions relating to minimum period of notice do not involve an employer in any penalty, but the rights conferred by the Act will be taken into account in assessing the employer's liability for breach of contract. Thus an employer who has dismissed his employee without due notice is generally liable for the wages due to the employee for the appropriate period of notice at the contract rate.

Offences by corporations

The EPA provides that where an offence under that Act is committed by a body corporate, and it is proved that the offence was committed with the consent or connivance of, or neglect by, any director, manager, secretary or similar officer of the body corporate, or any person who was purporting to act in such capacity, that person as well as the body corporate shall be equally guilty of the offence and may be punished accordingly.

Some illustrative cases

It would not be appropriate in a book at this level to go into the very many cases on the above legislation which have come before industrial tribunals and the Employment Appeal Tribunal in the last few years. However, some illustrative cases appear below.

Sex discrimination and equal pay. In *McLean* v. *Paris Travel Service* [1976] I.R.L.R. 202, M was employed by P as a reservation ticketing clerk. She was dismissed when her employers were told that she intended to marry one of their assistant managers, it being against company policy to employ married couples. It was held by an industrial tribunal that it was unfair to dismiss M because of her intended marriage. By doing so, P had contravened s 1(1)(a) of the Sex Discrimination Act, 1975, in that on the ground of M's sex, they had treated her less favourably than they treated or would treat a man. M was entitled to £117 compensation and an additional £200 for injured feelings.

So far as those in business are concerned, the case bears upon a common practice of refusing to employ married couples in that such employment could facilitate fraud by the collusion of one with the other, e.g. in the falsification of records kept by one to facilitate the frauds of the other. Such a practice is, no doubt, sound in terms of the prevention of fraud, but it would seem from the above decision that it could lead to a claim against the employer for unfair dismissal.

Also of interest is *Meeks* v. *National Union of Agricultural and Allied Workers* [1976] I.R.L.R. 198. Meeks was employed as a part-time clerical assistant performing secretarial functions. She worked for 23 hours each week, and was paid 91p per hour. Secretarial workers employed full-time and doing similar work for 35 hours per week received 110p per hour. All the secretarial workers in the Norwich office, where Meeks worked, were women. Meeks claimed that the union's practice contravened the Sex Discrimination and Equal Pay Acts.

It was held by an industrial tribunal that although the union had committed an act of indirect discrimination on the grounds of sex in paying Meeks a lower rate per hour because she was part-time, this discrimination did not fall within the Sex Discrimination Act. Her alternative claim under the Equal Pay Act failed because there were no men employed on like work as defined in s 1(4) of that Act.

It would seem, therefore, that the payment of lower hourly rates to part-time workers does not necessarily lead to a claim under the Sex Discrimination or Equal Pay Acts, at least where the employees concerned are of one sex. However, the tribunal's decision leaves open the question as to whether a claim might be made under either or both of these Acts where the workers concerned are men and women.

Conduct justifying dismissal. In *Bates Farms and Dairy* v. *Scott* [1976] I.R.L.R. 214, S was dismissed from his job as a milk roundsman for dishonesty. An industrial tribunal found that he had been unfairly dismissed and that the company had failed to show a reason, because the evidence did not substantiate accusations of dishonesty that were made.

On an appeal by the company to the Employment Appeal Tribunal, it was held that neither the tribunal nor the employer need to dissect the reasons for dismissal in excessive analytical detail. Although the tribunal had held that it had not been established that the employee had acted dishonestly, the tribunal had found in various parts of their decision that S was inefficient, incompetent, unsuited to the work, and that he operated the milk round in a way that gave cause for dissatisfaction. Thus the tribunal was wrong in paying too much attention to the allegations of dishonesty and insufficient attention to other factors. In these circumstances, the company's appeal was upheld, and S was not regarded as having been unfaily dismissed.

Again, in *Trust Houses Forte Leisure* v. *Aquilar* [1976] I.R.L.R. 251, A, a waiter, was dismissed after a complaint that he had overcharged a customer and a management investigation indicated that he had overcharged others. An industrial tribunal found that he had been unfairly dismissed, but on appeal by the employers to the Employment Appeal Tribunal it was held that had the tribunal applied the proper test it would have found the dismissal fair.

The test was not whether the tribunal was satisfied that A was guilty of the misconduct alleged against him; there was adequate material and evidence upon which the management could reasonably dismiss A in terms of his general conduct. The test was not whether the tribunal would have dismissed A had they been his employers, and dismissal is not necessarily unfair simply because the tribunal would have acted otherwise. Such an attitude is subjective, whereas the real test is an objective one, i.e. whether the employer in all the circumstances had grounds on which he could reasonably have dismissed the employee.

The cases illustrate that those in business must consider all the circumstances of the case when seeking to justify a dismissal. There is a tendency in business to give stress to failure to account for funds. Such allegations may be difficult to prove, and it may even be the case that tribunals are not primarily concerned with whether such matters are proved or not, being more concerned with the general unsuitability of the employee across the range of his duties, rather than with isolated incidents of misconduct in the financial sense.

Unpaid overtime. Over the years, those in business have regarded it as to some extent a requirement of the job that from time to time they will be required to work a reasonable amount of unpaid overtime. In this connection, *Gilbert* v. *Goldstone* [1976] I.R.L.R. 257 is of interest.

Gilbert, a staff employee who was expected to work overtime without extra pay, refused to work some nine hours overtime a week (when the rest of the work-force was doing so owing to an increased workload) unless he was paid for that overtime. Gilbert resigned because, since the others were working overtime, there was no-one to take him home after his work had finished. He lived some 17 miles away from the place of his employment. He maintained that although he had resigned, he had in effect been forced to do so, and that therefore he had been dismissed constructively and unfairly by his employers.

It was held by the Employment Appeal Tribunal that he had not been dismissed. Although the EAT felt that nine hours unpaid overtime was unreasonable, the company had not been in breach of contract. It was necessary to consider the terms of Gilbert's employment, under which he was expected to work some overtime without extra pay, and his employers had listened to and given some consideration to his complaints. Gilbert had been too hasty in resigning and he should have waited to see how matters worked out.

It would seem, therefore, that the employee must establish a course of conduct by the employer under which unreasonable amounts of overtime are required without pay or, alternatively, that the employer is not prepared to listen to complaints or give them due consideration.

8 The law of torts

It is difficult to give a satisfactory definition of a tort. According to Professor Winfield 'tortious liability arises from a duty primarily fixed by law: this duty is towards persons generally and its breach is redressible by an action for unliquidated damages'.

THE NATURE OF A TORT

It is a matter of dispute whether there should be a law of tort or a law of torts: there are two schools of thought. One maintains that there should be a law of tort, i.e. that all harm should be actionable in the absence of just cause or excuse. If there was merely a law of specific torts, then no new torts could be created by the courts and the categories of tortious liability would be closed. It is urged that under the flexibility of case law new torts have come into being, and in no case has an action been refused simply because it was novel. This is called the *general principle of liability theory*. The other view is that there should be a law of torts—that there should be only specific torts and unless the damage suffered can be brought under a known or recognized head of liability, there should be no remedy. This view is supported by modern cases where an attempt has been made, unsuccessfully, to establish a purported tort of eviction (*Perera* v. *Vandiyar*, 1953),[465] and a tort of perjury. (*Hargreaves* v. *Bretherton,* 1958[466] and *Roy* v. *Prior,* 1969.)[467] Thus the courts have refused to create new torts even when given the opportunity. This is particularly unfortunate in the case of perjury. Perjury is not merely an offence against the state, as it has been traditionally regarded by the courts. It can cause an individual great loss or hardship and many feel that the victim should have a remedy.

In addition, there is a danger in modern society of a serious invasion of privacy resulting from the increasing availability and use of electronic and other devices as a means of surreptitious surveillance and the accumulation of personal information about individuals in data banks, computers and credit registers. Apart from e.g. the law of defamation which protects against the publication of falsehoods, the law of tort does not appear to be capable of extending to a remedy for invasion of privacy as such and legislation has been recommended.

Hence we may conclude that at the present there is no general principle of liability in tort. Nevertheless, if judges have not created new torts, they have applied old cases to new situations. This has resulted in an extension of the old torts and there is a tendency to expand the area of liability, particularly in the field of negligence. (See p. 347.) If this continues, the law may reach a stage approximating to a general liability for wrongful acts, for, as Lord Macmillan said in *Donoghue* v. *Stevenson,* 1932,[468] 'the categories of negligence are never closed'.

DAMAGE AND LIABILITY

The law distinguishes between two concepts—(1) *Damnum,* which means the damage suffered, and (2) *Injuria,* which is an injury having legal consequences. Sometimes, but not always, these two go together. For instance, if I negligently drive a car and injure a person, he suffers *damnum* (the hurt) and *injuria* (because he has a right of action to be compensated). There are, however, cases of *damnum sine injura* (damage suffered without the violation of a legal right), and *injuria sine damno* (the violation of a legal right without damage).

The mere fact that a person has suffered damage does not entitle him to maintain an action in tort. Before an action can succeed, the harm suffered must be caused by an act which is a violation of a right which the law vests in the plaintiff or injured party. (*Best* v. *Samuel Fox & Co. Ltd,* 1952.)[469] Damage suffered in the absence of the violation of such legal right is known as *damnum sine injuria*. Furthermore a person who suffers *damnum* cannot receive compensation on the basis of *injuria* suffered by another. (*Electrochrome Ltd* v. *Welsh Plastics Ltd,* 1968.)[470] The concept of *damnum sine injuria* is not the same as that concerning whether there is a law of tort or a law of torts because under the concept of *damnum sine injuria* a person may suffer harm and have no claim even though the harm was suffered *as a result of a known tort*.

The fact that the defendant acts with malice, i.e. with the intention of injuring his neighbour, does not give rise to a cause of action unless a legal right of the plaintiff is infringed. (*Bradford Corporation* v. *Pickles,* 1895,[471] and *Langbrook Properties* v. *Surrey County Council,* 1969.)[472] On the other hand, whenever there is an invasion of a legal right, the person in whom the right is vested may bring an action and recover damages (though these may be nominal) or, what may be more important, obtain an injunction, although he has suffered no actual harm. For example, an action will lie for an unlawful entry on the land of another (trespass) although no actual damage is done. Furthermore, in *Ashby* v. *White* (1703), 2 Ld. Raym. 938, it was held that an elector had a right of action, for a form of nuisance or disturbance of rights, when his vote was wrongly rejected by the returning officer although the candidate for whom he tried to vote was elected. This is know as *injuria sine damno*.

Motive

It is important to be clear on the mental element or the question of malice in tort. The law or torts is concerned more with the effects of injurious conduct than the motives which inspired it. Hence, just as a bad intention will not necessarily make the infliction of damage actionable (*Bradford Corporation* v. *Pickles*, 1895),[471] so an innocent intention is usually no defence. (*Wilkinson* v. *Downton*, 1897.)[473] However, there are circumstances in which malice is important. The publication of a libel is in law presumed to be malicious, and where a person puts in motion the criminal law against another, this is actionable if malice is shown to be present and is known as the tort of malicious prosecution. Furthermore the question of malice may be raised when certain *defences* are pleaded. Thus in the law of defamation the defences of qualified privilege and fair comment are allowed only where the defendant has not been malicious.

PARTIES IN THE LAW OF TORTS

It is now necessary to consider certain categories of persons whose capacity in connection with tortious acts is limited.

Minors

A minor can sue in tort as a plaintiff in the ordinary way except that, as in contract, he must sue through an adult as next friend. He cannot compromise his action except by leave of the court, unlike an adult, who does not require such permission.

At common law there was a doubt as to whether a child had a cause of action for personal injuries caused before its birth. The matter is now covered by the Congenital Disabilities (Civil Liability) Act, 1976. Section 1 establishes civil liability where a child is born disabled in consequence of the intentional act or the negligence or the breach of statutory duty of some person before the child's birth. There can be no liability unless the child is born alive, though if it is stillborn the parents might have an action, e.g. for nervous shock. Causation must be proved which may be difficult in the case of pre-natal injuries. A mother cannot be liable under Sect. 1 for causing injury to the child by her own negligence. Barristers and judges, among others, have been strongly opposed to children being given a cause of action against their mothers, recognizing the danger of inter-family disputes, and their view has prevailed in this Act. The liability of a father is not, however, excluded and he can be liable to his child for injuries caused by his own negligence. The section also distinguishes between matters arising *before* conception (where the injury can be to *either* parent) and matters arising when the child's mother is pregnant or during the actual process of childbirth (where the injury can *only* be to the mother). Thus the injury could result, for example, from irradiation which damages the progenitive capacity of the father. It also covers physical damage to the child during childbirth as by the negligent handling of instruments by those attending the mother. The injuries must be caused during the pregnancy and there could be problems in dating the beginning of this in some cases. The defendant is presumed to take the mother as he finds her and thus cannot say that he did not know she was pregnant nor that the damage to her child was not foreseeable.

The common law defence of *volenti non fit injuria* is applicable and in this sense if the mother is *volenti* so is the child. It is recognized that this may penalize the child but it was thought that any other solution would prejudice the position of women in society because organizations worried that a woman might be pregnant may refuse to enter into a wide variety of contracts with her. Incidentally, so far as the consent which the child is deemed to give results from an exemption clause in a contract made by the mother, Sect. 1 creates a new exception to the doctrine of privity of contract. Section 1 also provides that the child's damages awarded against the defendant are to be reduced by any contributory negligence of the mother. Finally, Sect. 1 provides that professional persons, such as doctors, are under no liability for treatment or advice given according to prevailing professional standards of care. This codifies the common law rule in *Roe* v. *Minister of Health,* 1954.[646]

As we have seen, Sect. 1 is so expressed that a woman cannot be liable to her own child. However, Sect. 2 creates an exception to that rule in the case of a disabled birth arising from the mother's negligent driving of a motor vehicle for which she would be liable. It would appear that the dangers of inter-family disputes are less when the claim is one which in practice is always against an insurance company and not really against the mother at all.

Section 3 clarifies the compensation provisions of the Nuclear Installations Act, 1965, where damage results from a nuclear incident and provides for compensation under the Act in the case of a child born subsequently with disabilities attributable to the incident.

Finally, it should be noted that the Act is not retrospective but applies to births after 22 July, 1976.

A minor is liable as defendant for all his torts except in a limited number of instances. Where the tort alleged requires a mental ingredient, the age of the minor (in cases of extreme infancy) may show an inability to form the necessary intent. In cases of negligence, a very young child cannot be expected to show the same standard of care as an older person, though in *Williams* v. *Humphrey,* 1975[474] a boy of nearly 16 was held liable in negligence. Nor can a minor be made liable on contracts which do not bind him by the device of suing him in tort. (*Jennings* v. *Rundall,* 1799[475] and *Leslie* v. *Sheill,* 1914.)[200] However, if the act complained of is associated with a contract but is independent of it, then the minor can be made liable. (*Burnard* v. *Haggis,* 1863.)[201]

A minor is not liable for the tort of deceit where he has by a fraudulent misrepresentation induced another party to contract with him and where there would otherwise be no contract, as in a loan of money. But where a minor obtains an advantage by falsely stating himself to be of full age, Equity requires him to restore his ill-gotten gains, but not if to do so would be to enforce a contract against the infant. 'Restitution ends where repayment begins.' This maxim means that, if there is no possibility of restoring the very thing obtained by fraud, the minor cannot be made liable to pay an equivalent sum, since this would amount to enforcing a void contract. (*Leslie* v. *Sheill*, 1914.)[200]

A minor is liable for wrongful interference if he hires goods and fails to return them. (*Ballett* v. *Mingay*, 1943.)[476]

Basically children are, therefore, liable for their own torts, but a father may be liable vicariously, if the relationship of employer and employee exists between him and the child or if there is the relationship of principal and agent. Simply as a father he is not liable unless the injury is caused by his negligent control of the child (*Donaldson* v. *McNiven*, 1952),[477] and so when he is liable, it is really for his own tort, i.e. negligence in looking after the child. (*Bebee* v. *Sales*, 1916.)[478] Such a liability may extend to other persons (not being parents) who have control of children, e.g. teachers and education authorities, and, if such persons or authorities act negligently, they may be held responsible for the harm caused by children under their care or control. Nevertheless, the basis of the action is negligent control or supervision. (*Carmarthenshire C.C.* v. *Lewis*, 1955,[479] and *Butt* v. *Cambridgeshire and Isle of Ely County Council*, 1969.)[480]

Persons suffering from mental disorder

In criminal law a person of unsound mind has considerable exemption from criminal liability (see p. 137), but these rules have never been applied to civil injuries. This is understandable if it is borne in mind that the aim of the law of torts is to compensate the injured party, not to punish the offender. In the light of this, any exemptions accorded to a person of unsound mind should be narrow, and he should be liable unless his state of mind prevents his having the necessary intent (where a mental ingredient is part of the tort) and in extreme cases where no voluntary act is possible. (*Morriss* v. *Marsden*, 1952.)[481]

Husband and wife

The rule used to be that a married woman was liable for her torts only to the extent of her separate property and that beyond this the husband was fully liable. Since the Law Reform (Married Women and Tortfeasors) Act, 1935, the wife is fully liable for her torts and the husband as such is no longer held responsible, unless, as in the case of a minor, there is a relationship of employer and employee or principal and agent.

The old common law rule whereby one spouse could not sue the other in tort has now been altered. The Law Reform (Husband and Wife) Act, 1962, provides that each of the parties to a marriage shall have the like right of action in tort against the other as if they were not married, but where the action is brought by one of the parties to the marriage against the other during the subsistence of the marriage, the court may stay the action if it appears—

(*a*) that no substantial benefit would accrue to either party from the continuation of the proceedings; or

(*b*) that the question or questions in issue could more conveniently be disposed of on an application made under Sect. 17 of the Married Women's Property Act, 1882. (This provides for the determination of questions between husband and wife regarding title to or possession of property by a summary procedure.)

It should also be noted that a husband has a right of action against a person who by a tortious act deprives him of the society and services of his wife, i.e. loss of consortium. A wife has no such right in respect of loss of consortium. (*Best* v. *Samuel Fox & Co. Ltd*, 1952.)[469]

The Crown and its Servants

Prior to 1947 the Crown had considerable immunity in the law of tort and contract stemming from the common law maxim: 'The King can do no wrong.' We have already seen that, by the Crown Proceedings Act, 1947, the Crown is, in general, now liable in the same way as a subject.

The Crown is not liable for torts committed by the police nor is the local authority which appoints and pays them. However, the Police Act, 1964, Sect 48(1), provides that the chief officer of police for any police area is liable for the torts of police officers, e.g. wrongful arrest. The Act also provides that any damages and costs awarded against the chief officer shall be payable out of police funds.

Judicial immunity

A judge has absolute immunity for acts in his judicial capacity, and this probably applies to justices of the peace when acting within their jurisdiction. (*Law* v. *Llewellyn*, 1906.)[482] Counsel and witnesses have immunity in respect of all matters relating to the cases in which they are concerned. This is mainly of importance in connection with possible actions for slander.

Foreign sovereigns and ambassadorial staffs

This heading includes all the categories of persons already enumerated in the chapter on Contract as having diplomatic immunity, and their liability is outlined on p. 199. However, it should be noted that if persons with immunity remain after finishing their duties, they may become liable even if the tort was committed before. They may, of course, voluntarily submit to the jurisdiction of our courts, since immunity is from suit and not from liability. (*Dickinson* v. *Del Solar*, 1929.)[483]

Aliens

Enemy aliens, including British subjects who voluntarily reside or carry on business in an enemy state, cannot bring an action in tort, although they themselves can be sued. Other aliens have neither disability nor immunity.

Corporations

A corporation can, as a plaintiff, sue for all torts committed against it. Obviously certain torts, such as assault, cannot by their nature be committed against corporations, but a corporation can maintain an action for injury to its business. (*D and L Caterers Ltd* v. *D'Anjou*, 1945.)[484] The European Communities Act, 1972 does not apply to tortious activities and in cases where the corporation is the defendant we must consider separately tortious acts which are *intra vires* (within its powers) and *ultra vires* (outside its powers).

(a) Intra vires activities.   Where a servant or agent of the corporation commits a tort while acting in the course of his employment in an *intra vires* activity, then the corporation is liable. Although it has been said that any tort committed on behalf of a corporation must be *ultra vires* (since Parliament does not authorize corporations to commit torts) this view is fallacious, since a corporation can have legal liability without legal capacity. A corporation is liable under the principles of vicarious liability for the torts of its employees or agents committed on *intra vires* activities.

(b) Ultra vires activities.   Here we have to distinguish between express and non-express authority. A corporation will not be liable if a servant engages in an *ultra vires* activity without express authority. Thus, if a corporation has not got authority and has not given it, you cannot infer it. (*Poulton* v. *L. & S.W. Railway*, 1867.)[485] On the other hand, where a tortious action is *ultra vires* but has been expressly authorized, the courts have taken the view that the *ultra vires* doctrine is irrelevant, and the corporation is liable for it. (*Campbell* v. *Paddington Borough Council*, 1911.)[486]

Unincorporated associations

These have already been considered in chapter 6 and their position in tort is set out on p. 158.

Trade unions

Trade unions, which are unincorporated associations, have certain immunity in the law of tort. The present law relating to the immunity of trade unions (and employers' associations) is to be found in Sect. 14 of the Trade Union and Labour Relations Act, 1974. Section 14(1) provides that no action in tort shall lie in respect of any act done by or on behalf of a trade union or so threatened or intended to be done. This gives immunity to the union and its officials in respect of torts. However, it must be read with Sect. 14(2) which says that immunity from any negligence, nuisance or breach of duty resulting in any personal injury to any person, or from breach of any duty imposed in connection with the ownership, occupation, possession, control or use of property arises only if the breaches arose from acts done in contemplation or furtherance of a trade dispute. Thus if a person was injured by the negligent driving of a trade union official's chauffeur whilst on official business, then the union would be liable because that is a tort which does not arise in the course or furtherance of a trade dispute.

Joint tortfeasors

Formerly there was no right of contribution between joint tortfeasors, but under the Law Reform (Married Women and Tortfeasors) Act, 1935, it is laid down that, if one joint tortfeasor is sued and pays damages, he can claim a contribution from fellow wrongdoers. Thus, if damages is caused by two or more persons *jointly,* e.g. employer and employee (*Lister* v. *Romford Ice and Cold Storage Co.,* 1957),[278] or *severally,* but at the same time, as where the negligent driving of A *and* B causes injury to C, one tortfeaser has a right of contribution against the other or others. However, there can be no contribution where the person claiming it is liable to *indemnify* the person from whom it is claimed. For example, an auctioneer is entitled to be indemnified by a client who has instructed him to sell goods to which, as it subsequently appears, the client does not have a title. (*Adamson* v. *Jarvis,* (1827) 4 Bing. 66.) Therefore if the true owner sues the client for wrongful interference and the client pays the damages, he has no right to a contribution against the auctioneer although the auctioneer is also liable for wrongful interference because the auctioneer is a person whom the client would have had to indemnify if the true owner had chosen to sue the actioneer. The amount of the contribution is settled by the court on the basis of the responsibility of each party for the injury and may be the full amount of the damages originally awarded against the person claiming the contribution.

In connection with the right of contribution the Law Reform (Husband and Wife) Act, 1962, has an important effect. Where a spouse A is injured by the joint negligence of the other spouse B and of a third party C, e.g. in a car accident, if C is sued by A, he can now claim a contribution from the negligent spouse B, since B is now a person liable for the purposes of the Act of 1935.

Executors and administrators

The common law maxim was *actio personalis moritur cum persona* (a personal action dies with the person). Consequently at common law an executor could only sue for torts to property, and not for torts against the person of the deceased. Now by the Law Reform (Miscellaneous Provisions) Act, 1934, all causes of action in tort subsisting at the time of a person's death survive for or against his estate. Nevertheless, there is one exception where there can be no action after death. This is in the case of defamation unless there is damage to the deceased's property.

Under the Proceedings Against Estates Act, 1970, all actions against the personal representative of a deceased person, whether founded in contract or tort, are now subject to the normal three-year or six-year limitation period.

Damages recoverable in an action by the representatives of the deceased shall not include exemplary damages, and the damages are calculated without reference to any loss or gain to the estate caused by the death (e.g. benefits under insurance policies), although funeral expenses can be awarded. Damages are recoverable in respect of loss of expectation of life though the sums awarded are not large because of the difficulty of assessment. This arises from *Benham* v. *Gambling,* [1941] A.C. 157 where the House of Lords held that amount recoverable is not to be affected by the wealth of the deceased, nor his prospects of future earnings, nor his views as to his future happiness, but by the happiness he might in fact enjoy. Their Lordships awarded £200 in this case, but in more recent cases the court has taken into account the fall in the value of money and higher awards have been made. Even so, in *Dodds* v. *Dodds, The Times,* 29 July, 1977 Balcombe, J. in considering the death of Mr. Dodds by reason of the negligence of another, awarded only £913 under the 1934 Act but some £17,168 to a a dependent son aged 12 under the Fatal Accidents Act (see below).

Fatal accidents As we have seen by the Law Reform (Miscellaneous Provisions) Act, 1934, all causes of action subsisting at the time of a person's death survive for the benefit of his *estate.* However, under the provisions of the Fatal Accidents Act, 1976, the person whose wrongful act caused the death may have an *additional* liability to certain relatives of the deceased who have suffered financial loss because of the death, though damages recoverable under the Fatal Accidents Act will be reduced by any sums awarded to the deceased's estate under the Act of 1934 if the estate devolves on the dependants either under a will or on intestacy. If before the accident finally kills the victim he manages to bring an action for damages, these are deducted from the Fatal Accidents Act claim except in so far as they are compensation for loss of earnings prior to death. Such a sum does not represent a benefit to the dependents arising from the death of the deceased but would have accrued to them during his lifetime if he had been able to work. (See *Murray* v. *Shuter,* [1975] 3 All E.R. 597.)

The relatives covered. The following persons are entitled to claim under the Fatal Accidents Act; husband, wife (but not a divorced wife: *Payne-Collins* v. *Taylor Woodrow Ltd,* [1975] 1 All E.R. 898, or the so-called common-law wife: *K.* v. *J.M.P. Co. Ltd,* [1975] 1 All E.R. 1030), children, grandchildren, parents, grandparents, brothers, sisters, aunts and uncles and their issue; the relationship may be traced through step relatives, adoption or illegitimacy, and relatives by marriage have the same rights as the deceased's own relatives. However, in *Harrison* v. *London and North Western Railway Co.* (1885), C. & E. 540, it was *held* that a husband living apart from his wife had no claim under the Acts. A husband living with his wife at the time of her death can recover damages for her death in respect of the loss of the pecuniary value of her domestic services, and the law interprets the term 'services' broadly—a wife and mother does not normally work set hours (see *Regan* v. *Williamson,* [1976] 2 All E.R. 241). In *Stimpson* v. *Wood* (1888), 57 L.J.Q.B. 484, it was *held* that a woman separated from, and not maintained by, her husband could not recover under the Act in respect of his death. It seems, however, that there could be a claim where there is a reasonable probability or expectation of a reconciliation. In the absence of such a probability there is no dependency under the Act. Where a plaintiff is able to satisfy this test of reconciliation the court will reflect the degree of probability in the amount of damages awarded. (*Davies* v. *Taylor,* [1972] 3 All E.R. 836.) Furthermore, it is submitted that a claim could be made where the separated widow was being maintained by her husband or was taking legal action to obtain maintenance. It was decided in *Burns* v. *Edman,* [1970] 1 All E.R. 886, that if a man who has lived on the proceeds of crime is killed by the negligence of the defendant, his widow and children who he has supported cannot claim damages under the Fatal Accidents Act. It would be contrary to public policy to award compensation for the loss of an income dishonestly acquired. The cost of the funeral was, however, recoverable.

In the *George and Richard* (1871), 24 L.T. 717, it was decided that a child *en ventre sa mère* (i.e. conceived but not yet born) could claim.

A single action must be brought on behalf of all the eligible dependants and the total damages apportioned according to their dependancy. The action may be brought by the personal representatives of the deceased, but if there are none, or if they fail to bring the action within six months from the death, the dependants may bring it. The action is barred if it is not brought within three years of the death which is the subject of the claim.

It should be noted that the infliction of death is not, in itself, a tort against the person killed and relatives who have suffered financial loss have no right of action unless the deceased would have had one had he merely been injured. Furthermore, if the deceased was guilty of contributory negligence or was a volunteer (see p. 318) the damages awarded to dependants will be reduced or extinguished according to the degree to which the deceased was at fault or was a volunteer.

To sustain an action under the Acts, the plaintiff must show reasonable probability of pecuniary loss by reason of the death, a mere possibility is not enough, and damages are not recoverable for mental suffering or loss of companionship, for if this were so young children, persons of unsound mind and posthumous children would be excluded. Funeral and mourning expenses are recoverable, though expenses in connection with monuments are not.

The probability of pecuniary loss is a matter for the plaintiff to prove, and the court to decide as a matter of fact. However, it should be noted that the object of the Fatal Accidents Act is to provide *maintenance* for relatives who have been deprived of maintenance by the death. Therefore, if the relative seeking to claim is already adequately provided for from some other source, he will not be able to claim under these provisions. Damages awarded are not, however, to be reduced on account of any insurance money, National Insurance or Friendly Society or Trade Union benefit, pension, or gratuity accruing to a relative, even though the pecuniary loss is thereby reduced. In addition, under Sect. 4(1) of the Law Reform (Miscellaneous Provisions) Act, 1971, prospects of remarriage are disregarded in the case of a widow's damages but not where children's damages are concerned. (*Thompson* v. *Price,* [1973] 2 All E.R. 846.) The Law Commission in a recent report (No. 56) has suggested amendments to Sect. 4(1) so that the prospects of remarriage are disregarded also in the case of children's damages. In addition, the Commission now proposes that in no circumstances should there be taken into account the remarriage or prospects of remarriage of a widow or *widower.*

In *Franklin* v. *South East Railway* (1858), 3 H. & N. 211, an old infirm father was *held* entitled to damages on his son's death since the son assisted his father with the latter's work. Probable earnings may be taken into account and in *Duckworth* v. *Johnson* (1859), 29 L.J. Ex. 25, the father of a boy of fourteen years who had earned 70p per week was awarded damages when the boy was killed, although he was unemployed at the time. Further, in *Taff Vale Railway Co.* v. *Jenkins,* [1913] A.C. 1, damages were recovered in respect of a girl who at her death was merely an apprentice dressmaker. Damages may include the cost of replacing services normally rendered free by a deceased relative, and in *Berry* v. *Humm,* [1915] 1 K.B. 627, it was *held* that a husband might claim in respect of his deceased wife where he was compelled to employ a housekeeper consequent upon his wife's death. Estate duty (now Capital Transfer Tax) is also recoverable as damages. Thus in *Davies* v. *Whiteways Cyder Co.,* [1974] 3 All E.R. 168, the deceased had made gifts to his wife and child with a view to mitigating the eventual impact of estate duty which would have been the case if he had lived for seven years or more after making the gifts. As a result of the defendants' negligence he was killed before the necessary seven years had elapsed, and as a result £17,000 in estate duty had to be paid by the donees. It was held that on their claim under the Fatal Accidents Acts they were entitled to recover this sum with a small deduction for the chance that the deceased might not in any event have survived for the necessary period.

With regard to inflation, the House of Lords decided in *Mallett* v. *McNonagle*, [1969] 2 All E.R. 178, that in assessing damages under the Fatal Accidents Acts the only practical course to adopt was to leave out of account the risk of further inflation and the high interest rates which reflect the fear of it and capital appreciation of property and equities which are a consequence of it. The Law Commission in a recent report (No. 56) has suggested the greater use of actuarial evidence so that allowance might be made for the effect of inflation.

There is no limitation in regard to the application of the Act as to the place of the wrong or of the death, or as to the nationality or domicil of the parties. (See *The Esso Malaysia*, [1974] 2 All E.R. 705.)

Partners, Principals and agents generally

Partners are liable for the torts of other partners committed in the ordinary course of business. A principal is liable for the torts of his agent committed within the scope of his authority, whether by prior authority or subsequent ratification.

VICARIOUS LIABILITY

While the person who is actually responsible for the commission of a tort is always liable, sometimes another person may be liable although he has not actually committed it. In such a case both are liable as joint tortfeasors. This is the doctrine of vicarious liability, and the greatest area of this type of liability is that of master and servant. A master is liable for the torts of his servant committed in the course of his employment, and so wide is the risk that it is commonly insured against. Under the Employers' Liability (Compulsory Insurance) Act, 1969, an employer *must* insure himself in respect of vicarious liability for injuries caused by his employees to their colleagues. Insurance is not compulsory in respect of injuries to persons other than employees.

Who is a servant?

According to Salmond on Torts, a servant may be defined as 'any person employed by another to do work for him on the terms that he, the servant, is to be subject to the control and direction of his employer in respect of the manner in which his work is to be done.' This definition was approved by the court in *Hewitt* v. *Bonvin*, [1940] 1 K.B. 188. In most cases the relationship is established by the existence of a *contract of service*, which may be express or implied and is usually evidenced by such matters as, for example, the power to appoint, the power of dismissal, the method of payment, the payment of National Insurance by the employer, the deduction of tax under PAYE, and membership of pension schemes (if any).

However, in deciding whether the relationship of employer and employee exists, the courts have not restricted themselves to cases in which there is an ordinary contract of service but have often stated that the right of *control* is the ultimate test. In *Performing Right Society Ltd* v. *Mitchel and Booker (Palais de Danse) Ltd,* [1924] 1 K.B. 762 at p. 767, McCardie, J., said—

> The nature of the task undertaken, the freedom of action given, the magnitude of the contract amount, the manner in which it is paid, the powers of dismissal, and the circumstances under which payment of the reward may be withheld, all these bear on the solution of the question. But it seems clear that a more guiding test must be secured . . . It seems . . . reasonably clear that the final test, if there be a final test, and certainly the test to be generally applied, lies in the nature and degree of detailed control over the person alleged to be a servant. This circumstance is, of course, one only of several to be considered by it is usually of vital importance.

The learned judge then went on to decide that the defendants, who employed a dance band under a written contract for one year, were liable for breaches of copyright, which occurred when members of the band played a piece of music without the consent of the holder of the copyright, because the agreement gave the defendants 'the right of continuous, dominant and detailed control on every point, including the nature of the music to be played'.

The existence of the control test means that where an employer (X) lends out his employee (Y) to another employer (Z), then Z may be liable for the wrongs of Y even though there is no contract of service between Y and Z, though such liability is rare.

An employer also owes certain duties to his employees, e.g. to provide proper plant, equipment and premises, and this is a further reason for deciding whether Z has become the master by virtue of the control test. (*Garrard* v. *Southey,* 1952.)[487] There is a presumption that control remains with X and the onus is upon him to prove that control has passed to Z. The burden is a heavy one and the temporary employer will not often become liable. (*Mersey Docks and Harbour Board* v. *Coggins and Griffiths (Liverpool) Ltd,* 1947.)[488] Nevertheless, transfer of control may be more readily inferred where a man is lent on his own without equipment (*Garrard* v. *Southey,* 1952),[487] or where he is unskilled.

Transfer of control is often a convenient method of making the temporary employer liable to, and for, the employee and does not affect the contract of service. A contract of service is a highly personal one and it cannot be transferred from one employer to another without the consent of the employee. However, where there is a contract for hire of plant and the loan of an employee to operate it, the contract of hiring may provide that the hirer shall indemnify the owners for claims arising in connection with the operation of the plant by the employee. (*Wright* v. *Tyne Improvement Commissioners,* 1968.)[489]

The control test was an appropriate one in the days when a master could be expected to be superior to his servant in knowledge, skill and experience. However, in modern times it is unreal to say that all employers of skilled labour can tell employees *how* to do their work. Accordingly the test has been modified in recent cases, the court tending to look for the power to control in incidental or collateral matters, e.g. hours of work and place of work. The existence of this sort of control enables the court to decide whether a person is part of the *organization* of another, and it might be called a *'when and where'* test (*Cassidy* v. *Minister of Health,* 1951[490] and see also *Ferguson* v. *John Dawson & Partners (Contractors),* 1976.)[491]

The control test also gives rise to difficulties in the case of the employees of companies. Subordinate employees are controlled by superior employees and some control is obviously present if the management is regarded as 'the company'. However, when one considers the position of directors and top management it is difficult to see how the company, being inanimate, can exercise control. In the case of 'one-man' companies, where the managing director is also virtually the sole shareholder, the reality of the situation is that the servant controls the company and not vice versa. Nevertheless, directors of companies, even 'one-man' companies, are regarded as employees, presumably because the usual incidents of a contract of service are present and despite the absence of genuine control. (*Lee* v. *Lee's Air Farming Ltd*, 1961.)[492]

Although control is the ultimate test in establishing the relationship of master and servant, it is also necessary to deal briefly with other circumstances which may be taken as evidence of the existence of the relationship. In *Short* v. *J. W. Henderson Ltd* (1946), 62 T.L.R. 427, Lord Thankerton regarded the power to select or appoint, the power to dismiss, and the payment of wages, as relevant in establishing the existence, or otherwise, of a contract of service.

The power to select or appoint. The absence of a power to select or appoint may prevent the relationship of employer and employee arising. Thus, in *Cassidy* v. *Minister of Health,* 1951[490] Denning, L.J., as he then was, made it clear that a hospital authority is not liable for the negligence of a doctor or surgeon who is *selected* and *employed* by the patient himself. The employer need not make the appointment himself, and an appointee may be an employee even though the employer *delegated* the power of selection to another employee, or even an independent contractor, such as a firm of management consultants, or was *required by law to accept* the employee, e.g. Ministers of State often have power to appoint members of statutory bodies who become the employees of those bodies.

The power to dismiss. An express power of dismissal is strong evidence that the contract is one of services. Many public bodies have a restricted power of dismissal in the sense that rights of appeal are often provided for, but such rights do not prevent a contract of service from arising, nor does the fact that these authorities cannot dismiss certain of their employees without the approval of the Crown or a Minister.

Payment of wages or salary.   A contract of service must be supported by consideration which usually consists of a promise to pay wages, or a salary. Where the amount of remuneration or the rate of pay is not fixed in advance, this suggests that the contract is not one of service, but is for services. The employer usually pays his employees directly, but in *Pauley* v. *Kenaldo Ltd,* [1953] 1 All E.R. 226, at p. 226, Birkett, L.J., said, '. . . . a person may be none the less a servant by reason of the fact that his remuneration consists solely of tips.'

An employee may be employed on terms that his remuneration is to consist wholly or partly of commission which the employer pays directly, the commission being a method of assessment of the amount of the remuneration.

Salaries are paid to people who are certainly not employees, e.g. Members of Parliament, whereas payment of wages generally indicates a contract of service. However, little, if anything, turns on the distinction between wages and salaries, and we may conclude that the terms used to describe the way in which a person is paid have little bearing on the relationship between himself and the person who pays him.

In addition to the above indications of a contract of service the following matters have also been regarded as relevant in deciding difficult cases of relationship.

Delegation.   In the normal contract of service the employee performs the work himself, and *power to delegate performance of the whole contract* to another is some indication that there is no contract of service. However, the fact that delegation is forbidden does not show *conclusively* that the contract is one of service, for agreements with independent contractors may forbid delegation.

Exclusive service.   The fact that an employer can demand the *exclusive services of another* is a material factor leading to the inference of a contract of service and in some cases it has been the deciding factor. However, in the absence of an express contractual provision an employer cannot usually require the exclusive services of his employee, and cannot complain if the employee works for someone else in his spare time, though *Hivac Ltd* v. *Park Royal Scientific Instruments Ltd,* 1946,[358] is an exceptional case. This being so, an employee and independent contractor are usually both able to work for more than one person, and the exclusive service test may not help in deciding difficult cases of relationship. However, it is true to say that the typical employee works for one person, and the typical independent contractor works for many.

Place of work.   If the services are always rendered on the *employer's* *premises* this is some evidence of the existence of a contract of service, though it is not conclusive. Similarly, the fact that a person works at this home or other premises is some evidence of a contract for services.

It may also be a material factor whether the services are rendered by a person having a *recognized trade or profession,* e.g. a surveyor, or a consulting engineer, which he is exercising in a business because such persons tend to be independent contractors rather than employees and persons not exercising a particular calling may more easily be regarded as the employees of those who employ them.

Plant and equipment. *Provision of large-scale plant and equipment* by the employer is an indication of the existence of a contract of service and a person who supplies his own large-scale plant and equipment is often an independent contractor. However, provision of minor equipment, such as tools, carries little weight as a test of relationship, for many employees provide their own tools.

Obligation to work. A contract of service and one for services usually *impose an obligation to do the work concerned* and an obligation to work is not helpful in the matter of relationships. However, persons such as salesmen, who are paid entirely by commission, and who are not obliged to work at all are probably not working under a contract of service.

Hours of work and holidays. The right to control the *hours of work and the taking of holidays* is also regarded as evidence of the existence of a contract of service. Further an independent contractor is usually engaged for a specific job, whereas an employee is usually employed for an indefinite time.

Employees and independent contractors. An employee is a person whose work is at least *integrated* into the employer's business organization, whereas an independent contractor merely *works for* the business but is *not integrated* into it. Thus, firms of builders, architects, and estate agents are usually regarded as independent contractors, while factory and office workers are usually regarded as employees.

An employee works under a contract of service, whereas an independent contractor's contract is said to be one 'for services' under which he is to carry out a particular task or tasks. Although he may be sued for breach of contract if he fails to carry out his contract properly, the purchaser of his services has no other control over the manner of his work.

Nature of vicarious liability

The doctrine seems at first sight unfair because it runs contrary to two major principles of liability in tort, viz.—

(*a*) that a person should be liable only for loss or damage caused by his *own acts or omissions*; and

(*b*) that a person should only be liable where he was at *fault*.

The doctrine of vicarious liability is a convenient one in the sense that employers are, generally speaking, wealthier than their employees and are better able to pay damages, though the doctrine is often justified on the grounds that an employer *controls* his employee. However, it should be noted that control is not in itself a ground for imposing vicarious liability, e.g. parents are not vicariously liable for the torts of their children. It is also said that vicarious liability is just because the employer profits from the employee's work and should therefore bear losses caused by the employee's torts. Again, the employer *chooses* his employee and there are those who say that if he chooses a careless employee he ought to compensate the victims of the careless employee's torts. Further, employer and employee are often identified in the sense that the act of the employee is regarded as the act of his employer and this theory that an employer and his employee are part of a *group* in much the same way as other associations of persons, e.g. companies, is expressed in the often quoted maxim *qui facit per alium facit per se* (he who does a thing through another does it himself). However, in practice the employer does not really suffer loss because he commonly insures against the possibility of vicarious liability and usually the cost of this insurance is put on to the goods or services which he sells. This has the effect of spreading the loss over a large section of the community in much the same way as welfare state benefits.

Course of employment

In order to establish vicarious liability it is necessary to show that the relationship between the defendant and the wrongdoer is that of employer and employee, and that when the employee committed the wrong he was in the *course of his employment*. It is sometimes difficult to decide whether a particular act was done during the course of employment, but the following matters are relevent.

Acts personal to the employee.   Some acts done by an employee while at work are so personal to him that they cannot be regarded as being within the scope of employment. Employees do not generally have authority to use violence against third parties, and the use of such violence will usually be beyond the scope of employment, and the employer will not be liable. Thus in *Warren* v. *Henlys Ltd,* [1948] 2 All E.R. 935, the employer of a petrol pump attendant was held not liable for the latter's assault on a customer committed as a result of an argument over payment for petrol. However, where such authority exists, e.g. in the case of door-keepers at dance halls, the master will be liable if the servant ejects a troublemaker but uses excessive force.

Improper performance of acts within scope of employment. The employer may be liable where the tort committed by the employee is not a personal or independent act but is merely an improper way of performing an act which is within the scope of employment. (*Century Insurance Co.* v. *Northern Ireland Road Transport Board,* 1942.)[493]

The tortious acts for which an employer may be liable must arise out of the employee's employment, but the employer may be liable in such circumstances even if the act is one which he has expressly forbidden his employee to do, since the courts will not allow the employer to evade his responsibilities by secret instructions to his employees. (*Limpus* v. *London General Omnibus Co.,* 1862.)[494] The point has arisen in cases in which employees have given lifts to third parties in the employer's vehicle. In *Twine* v. *Bean's Express Ltd,* [1946] 1 All E.R. 202, a driver employed by the defendants gave a lift to a third person who was killed by reason of the employee's negligent driving. Instructions that employees were not to give lifts were displayed in the van. The court held that the employers were not liable because in giving a lift to a third person the driver went *beyond the scope of his employment* and that the *passenger was a trespasser.* Therefore, by analogy with trespass to land, it could be said that the defendants owed no duty to a trespasser unless they knew he was there and even then their duty would only have been not to injure him wilfully or recklessly. (But see now *British Railways Board* v. *Herrington,* 1972[665] which raises the duty to a trespasser to a higher level.) In *Conway* v. *Geo. Wimpey & Co.,* [1951] 1 All E.R. 363, the facts were similar although lifts were frequently given but this was unknown to the employers, and again they were not liable, the same line of argument being followed. The reasoning in these cases has been subjected to criticism because it is difficult to regard the plaintiff as a trespasser when the employee has invited him into the vehicle and in both of the cases the employee did inflict the injury on the passenger while in the course of his employment because in driving the vehicle he was doing what he was employed to do.

It is clear that the employee in such cases has a duty of care towards the passenger, but in *Twine* and *Conway* the court seems also to have regarded the employer as having a similar duty of care. This has led to unreal arguments regarding scope of employment and a sounder solution to the problem may be found by regarding the employee, but not the employer, as having a duty of care towards the passenger. This would avoid straining the concept of scope of employment, for it can then be said that the breach of the duty of care arises out of the employment, but the duty does not. This would make the employee liable but not the employer, and the employee could be regarded as having imposed a duty of care upon himself, but not his employer, by giving the lift to a third person, though of course the plaintiff would lose his right to an action against a wealthier defendant, i.e. the employer. It is thought also that, since the employer's instructions in the two cases were not secret but displayed, the employer should have had the defence of *volenti non fit injuria* even if it was decided that he owed a duty of care, which it is suggested he does not. However, where the passenger is a fellow employee riding in the vehicle with the consent of the driver and a superior employee, the employer will be liable, because it seems from the decision in *Young* v. *Edward Box & Co. Ltd*, [1951] 1 T.L.R. 789, to be within the ostensible authority of a superior employee, and possibly of the driver, to sanction lifts for fellow employees but not strangers. That the matter is far from settled is illustrated by *Rose* v. *Plenty*, 1976.[495]

The position where a company provides a vehicle or the petrol for employees to come and go from work was considered in *Vandyke* v. *Fender*, 1970,[496] and *Elleanor* v. *Cavendish Woodhouse Ltd*, 1972.[498] In *Nottingham* v. *Aldridge*, 1971,[497] the Court was concerned with a situation in which the employee was using his father's vehicle to transport himself and a fellow-worker for which he was paid a mileage allowance for himself and his passenger.

Emergencies.   Where the employee takes emergency measures with the intention of benefiting his employer in cases where the latter's property appears to be in danger, the employer will tend to be liable even though the acts of the employee are excessive. Thus in *Poland* v. *John Parr & Sons*, [1927] 1 K.B. 236, a boy was injured by a carter who knocked the boy off the back of his cart to protect his employer's property from theft. It was held that the carter's action was within his implied authority and his employers were liable. If, however, the employee's act is not merely *excessive* but *outrageous* as in *Warren* v. *Henlys Ltd*, [1948] 2 All E.R. 935, the employer will not be liable.

Employee mixing employer's business with his own.   The cases under this heading have arisen largely out of the use of motor vehicles, and since it is clear that there can be no vicarious liability if the employee's wrong is not the result of his carrying out his contract of service, the employer will not be liable if he lends his vehicle to his employee entirely for the employee's own purpose. (*Britt* v. *Galmoye*, 1928.)[499]

However, a more difficult situation arises where the activity is basically an authorized one but the employee deviates from it in order to execute some business of his own. The mere fact of deviation will not prevent the employer being liable and this was made clear in the judgment of Cockburn, C.J., in *Storey* v. *Ashton* (1869), L.R. 4 Q.B. 476, when he said—

> I am very far from saying that, if the servant when going on his master's business took a somewhat longer road, that, owing to this deviation he would cease to be in the employment of the master so as to divest the latter of all liability; in such cases it is a question of degree as to how far the deviation could be considered a separate journey. Such a consideration is not applicable to the present case, because here the

carman started on an entirely new and independent journey which had nothing to do with his employment.

However, if the journey is unauthorized the employee does not render his employer liable merely by performing some small act for his employer's benefit during the course of it. Thus in *Rayner* v. *Mitchell* (1877), 2 C.P.D. 257, a brewer's vanman, without permission, took a van from his employer's stables for personal reasons, namely to deliver a coffin to a relative's house. On the way back he picked up some empty beer barrels and then was involved in an accident injuring the plaintiff. It was held that the brewer was not liable.

Employee using his own property on employer's business. The mere fact that an employee is using his own property in carrying out his employer's business will not prevent the employer from being liable for torts arising out of the use of the employee's property. The decided cases are largely concerned with methods of travel, and in *McKean* v. *Rayner Bros Ltd (Nottingham)*, [1942] 2 All E.R. 650, an employee who was told to deliver a message by using the firm's lorry was held to be in the course of his employment when he performed the task by driving his own car, contrary to his instructions. However, if the employee's act is unreasonable, as where an employee who is authorized to travel by car charters an aeroplane and flies it himself, then the act will be unauthorized and the employer will not be liable if the employee, or a third party, is injured.

Effect of contractual exceptions clauses. Cases may arise in which the employer has attempted to exempt himself for the wrongs of his employee by means of an exemption clause in a contract with a third person who is injured. Such clauses may be effective to exempt the employer from liability if they are properly communicated to the third person. However, they will not protect the employee against his personal liability at common law because he has not usually given any consideration to the third person and is not in privity of contract with him. Statute may extend the protection of an exemption clause in the employer's contract to his employees. (*Alder* v. *Dickson*, 1955[500] and see also *New Zealand Shipping Co.* v. *A. M. Satterthwaite & Co.*, 1974.[289]

Fraudulent and criminal acts. In early law the courts would not accept the principle of vicarious liability in fraud but gradually the concept was extended, first to cases in which the employee's fraud was committed for his employer's benefit, and later even to cases where the fraud was committed by the employee entirely for his own ends. (*Lloyd* v. *Grace, Smith & Co.*, [1912] A.C. 716.)

A more difficult situation arises where the employee makes a representation which he believes to be true but which the employer knows to be false. Suppose the employer, a landowner, knows that the drains of one of his farm cottages are faulty but has not told his employee, and the employee, in the course of his employment, represents to a potential purchaser that the drains are sound, believing this to be true. It might be thought that, in this sort of situation, the untrue statement of the employee could be added to the knowledge of the employer so as to make the employer liable in deceit, but in *Armstrong* v. *Strain,* 1952,[252] the Court of Appeal rejected this idea and stated, in effect, that an employer would not be liable in deceit unless it could be established that he kept his employee in ignorance of the truth in the *expectation* and *hope* that he would make some false statement in connection with the transaction.

However, it is almost certain that on the facts of *Armstrong* v. *Strain,*[252] liability in damages for negligence would now be imposed on the employer because English Law now recognizes that there may be liability for negligent mis-statements (*Hedley Byrne & Co. Ltd* v. *Heller & Partners Ltd,* 1964),[248] and the Misrepresentation Act, 1967, also provides for the payment of damages for negligent mis-statements which induce a contract. (See *Gosling* v. *Anderson,* 1972.)[251] It is probable that for the purpose of both jurisdictions, negligence could be inferred from the fact that an employee makes a statement in the course of his employment which another employee or the employer knows is untrue because the employee who makes the statement had the opportunity to check it.

Criminal conduct on the part of an employee may be regarded as being in the course of his employment so that the employer will be liable at civil law for any loss or damage caused to a third person by the employer's criminal act. (*Morris* v. *C.W. Martin and Sons Ltd,* 1966.)[501]

Casual delegation.   If Y lends his car to X for X's own purposes, then Y is not liable, even if in a general way X is his employee. (*Britt* v. *Galmoye,* 1928.)[499] Nevertheless, if Y has a purpose and X also has a purpose, and X is driving a car of Y's partly for his own and partly for Y's purposes, they Y would apparently be liable if X committed a tort. (*Ormrod* v. *Crossville Motor Services,* 1953.)[502] This is known as a case of casual delegation of authority. In these cases of casual delegation, the courts are guided by the doctrine of the *de facto* employee, and by using this doctrine they have extended the vicarious liability of the employer into the area of principal and agent. In fact the person actually committing the wrong is often called the agent. The result is to extend the area of operation of the doctrine of vicarious liability since it is easier to find the relationship of principal and agent than it is to establish the relationship of employer and employee.

However, merely giving permission to use the vehicle is not enough to make the owner liable (*Morgans* v. *Launchbury,* 1972),[503] nor is he liable merely because he is the owner (*Rambarran* v. *Gurrucharran,* 1970),[504] and there will, of course, be no vicarious liability in the owner where he did not consent to the taking of the vehicle. (*Klein* v. *Calnori,* 1971.)[505]

LIABILITY FOR TORTS OF INDEPENDENT CONTRACTORS

An independent contractor is by definition a person whose methods and modes of work are not controlled by the person who employs him, and this being so it would be unfair to give an employer general liability for the torts of such a contractor. However, there are circumstances in which a person may be liable for the torts of an independent contractor employed by him and these are as follows—

(a) *Where the employer authorizes or ratifies the torts of the contractor.* If, for example, an employer authorizes, or afterwards, with knowledge, approves the conduct of an independent contractor in tipping the employer's industrial waste material on another's land, both the employer and the contractor will be liable in trespass as joint tortfeasors.

(b) *Where the employer is negligent himself,* as where he selects an independent contractor without taking care to see, as far as he can, that he is competent to do the work required, or gives a competent contractor imperfect instructions or information, as where, for example, he knows that his land is liable to subsidence and fails to tell a contractor who erects something on the land which slips and causes damage to another.

(c) *Where liability for the tort is strict, so that responsibility cannot be delegated.* Thus, an employer is liable for injuries to workmen resulting from failure to securely fence dangerous machinery. This duty is laid down by safety legislation, and it is no defence that the employer has delegated the task of fencing to an independent contractor who has failed to do the job properly. Moreover, liability under the rule in *Rylands* v. *Fletcher,* 1868 (see p. 372), cannot be avoided by employing an independent contractor. It seems also that liability is strict where there is interference with an easement of support. Thus in *Bower* v. *Peate,* 1876,[506] the employer was held liable where he asked an independent contractor to pull down his house and excavate foundations for a new one and the contractor failed to support the house next door so that it was damaged.

(d) Finally there is a miscellaneous group of cases in which an employer has been held liable for the torts of an independent contractor and the principle which seems to run through them all is that the work which the employer has instructed the independent contractor to undertake is extra hazardous. Thus, work *on or under* the highway is attended with some risk if due precautions are not taken though, work *near* the highway is not for that treason alone regarded as extra hazardous. (*Salsbury* v. *Woodland,* 1969.)[507] In *Pickard* v. *Smith* (1861), 10 C.B., N.S. 470, the defendant who was the tenant of a refreshment room at a railway station was held liable when a coal merchant's servant left the coal cellar flap open while delivering coal to the defendant and a passenger on railway premises fell into the cellar and was injured. Again in *Honeywill & Stein Ltd* v. *Larkin Bros Ltd,* [1934] 1 K.B. 191, the plaintiffs had received permission from the theatre owner to take photographs in a theatre on which the plaintiffs had recently done work. A firm of photographers was employed by the plaintiffs and in order to take indoor photographs had, in those days, to use magnesium flares with the result that the theatre curtains caught fire and much damage was caused. The plaintiffs paid for the damage, and sued the photographers for an indemnity to which the court said they were entitled. It also emerged that the plaintiffs would have been liable if they had been sued by the theatre owner.

Where an employer is held liable to a third person for the torts of an independent contractor he will, in most cases, be able to claim an indemnity from the contractor. It should also be noted that an employer is not liable for what are called the *collateral* wrongs of his contractor, but only for wrongs which necessarily arise in the course of the contractor's employment. Thus, if A employs B, an independent contractor, to do some excavation work on his land, A will be liable if, say, his neighbour's greenhouse is damaged by the excavations but A will not be liable for loss caused by B's servants making off with the plants. (*Padbury* v. *Holliday*, 1912.)[508]

GENERAL DEFENCES

Some torts have special defences which can be raised in a particular action, but there are certain general defences which can be raised in any action in tort if they seem to be appropriate—

Volenti non fit injuria

(To one who is willing no harm is done.) This is alternatively called the doctrine of the assumption of risk. There are two main aspects of this defence—

(*a*) Deliberate harm.
(*b*) Accidental harm.

In the first case the plaintiff's assent may prevent his complaining of some deliberate conduct or the defendant which would normally be actionable. If A takes part in a game of Rugby football, he must be presumed to accept the rough tactics which are a characteristic and *normal* part of the game, and any damage caused would not give rise to an action (*Simms* v. *Leigh Rugby Football Club*, 1969),[509] although if the same tactics were employed in the street, an action could be sustained. Similarly, although to stick a knife into a person would normally be actionable, if a surgeon does it with the consent of the patient it is not so.

The plaintiff may *impliedly* consent to run the risk of accidental harm being inflicted upon him. Thus one of the risks incidental to watching an ice-hockey match is that the puck may strike and injure you (*Murray* v. *Harringay Arena Ltd*, 1951)[510] or in attendance at a motor race, that cars may run off the track for various reasons, injuring spectators. (*Hall* v.

Brooklands Auto Racing Club, 1933.)[511] These are possible hazards and the maxim *volenti non fit injuria* would apply. In addition, the plaintiff may be *expressly* put on notice that he undertakes a particular activity at his own risk. However, it is essential for the defendant to show as a matter of fact that the plaintiff agreed to *accept* the risk. This means, for one thing, that he must have had a choice and if a contract, e.g. of employment, forces him to accept the risk, there is no true assent. (*Burnett* v. *British Waterways Board,* 1973.)[290] A plea of *volenti* is open to a defendant against a plaintiff who is a minor. (*Murray* v. *Harringay Arena Ltd,* 1951.)[510]

If a person's assent to harm being inflicted upon him is purely contractual, it can only operate within the limits allowed by the law of contract; the doctrine of privity of contract applies, (*Adler* v. *Dickson,* 1955)[500] though sometimes a non-contractual agreement excluding liability for negligence has been upheld. (*White* v. *Blackmore,* 1972.)[512] The defendant must show that the plaintiff knew of the risk. (*White* v. *Blackmore,* 1972.)[512] He must then go on to show that the plaintiff agreed to accept the risk. It does not follow that because a person has knowledge of a potential danger he assents to it. The rule applies equally to cases of *implied volenti (Baker* v. *James,* 1921,[513] *Dann* v. *Hamilton,* 1939[514] and *Smith* v. *Baker,* 1891)[515] and to cases of *express volenti. (Burnett* v. *British Waterways Board,* 1973.)[290] This principle, i.e. that knowledge is not assent, is most often exemplified in the employer and employee cases and in the rescue cases, and has restricted the application of the defence.

Where the danger is inherent in the job, as in the case of a test pilot, the maxim applies; but where the danger is not inherent, then the defence will rarely succeed. (*Smith* v. *Baker,* 1891.)[515] In instances where an employee expressly assumes a risk, and is even paid extra for doing so, the harm resulting will hardly ever be laid at the door of the master, unless there is evidence that the master was negligent and created a risk which was not normally present even in a job inherently dangerous.

The doctrine of *volenti non fit injuria* cannot be pleaded by an employer in an action for damages based on breach of a statutory duty, e.g. to fence machinery under safety legislation. The reason is that the object of the statute, to protect workmen, cannot be defeated by a private agreement between employer and employee.

However, where an employee is in breach of a statutory duty and the employer is not, then if the party injured by the breach of statutory duty seeks to make the employer vicariously liable for the tort of the employee, the employer can plead the defence if the circumstances are appropriate. (*I.C.I. Ltd* v. *Shatwell,* 1964.)[516]

The rescue cases. A different situation arises in what are known as the *rescue cases.* In these the plaintiff is injured while intervening to save life or property put in danger by the defendant's negligence. If the intervention is a reasonable thing to do for the saving of life or property, than this does not constitute the assumption of risk, nor does the defence of contributory negligence apply (*Haynes* v. *Harwood,* 1935,[517] and *Baker* v. *Hopkins,* 1959);[518] but if it is not reasonable then the defences of *volenti* and contributory negligence could apply. (*Cutler* v. *United Dairies,* 1933.)[519] A person may take greater risks in protecting or rescuing life than in the mere protection of property, though even in protecting property reasonable risks may be taken. (*Hyett* v. *G.W. Railway,* 1948.)[520]

We reach the conclusion, therefore, that the operation of the maxim *volenti non fit injuria* is excluded when a person of ordinary courage would feel bound to intervene, though, as we have seen, even where knowledge of a risk does not bar the claim, it may reduce damages under the doctrine of contributory negligence. (See p. 351.) (*Videan* v. *B.T.C.,* 1963.)[521]

The duty of care owed to a rescuer is an original one and is not derived from or secondary to any duty owed to the rescued person by another. Thus a rescuer may recover damages even though no duty was owed to the person rescued.

Furthermore, it is important to remember that the question whether the plaintiff has assented to the possibility of harm being inflicted upon him does not arise until is has been shown that the defendant has committed a tort against the plaintiff. If the harm is not tortious the defence is irrelevant. (*Wooldridge* v. *Summer,* 1962[522] and *Wilks* v. *Cheltenham Home Guard Motor Cycle and Light Car Club,* 1971.)[523]

·Finally, Parliament has in Sect. 148(3) of the Road Traffic Act, 1972 legislated to prevent exclusion of liability to passengers in motor vehicles on the basis of *volenti.* This certainly covers cases of express *volenti* where a person is given a lift in a car in which there is a notice saying that passengers are at their own risk. Whether it covers cases of implied *volenti* such as *Dann* v. *Hamilton,* 1939[514] is more doubtful. A passenger who knows that a driver is under the influence of drink or drugs may, if he is injured, be barred from recovering damages on the grounds of *public policy* since he is aiding and abetting a criminal offence. 'There may in such cases sometimes be an element of aiding and abetting a criminal offence; or, if the facts fall short of aiding and abetting, the passenger's mere assent to benefit from the commission of a criminal offence may involve questions of *turpis causa.*' per Megaw, L.J. in *Nettleship* v. *Weston,* 1971.[524] For this reason there is doubt as to the correctness of the decision in *Dann* v. *Hamilton,* 1939 where the public policy principle was not considered.

Inevitable accident

The mere fact that the damage caused is accidental cannot itself be a defence if there is a duty to avert the particular consequences, but there are occasions where the defence of inevitable accident can be raised. Such an accident would be one which was not avoidable by any precautions a reasonable man could have been expected to take. (*Stanley* v. *Powell,* 1891[525] and *National Coal Board* v. *Evans,* 1951.)[526] It should be noted, however, that most so-called accidents have a cause, and this defence is of comparatively rare occurrence.

Act of God

This is something which occurs in the course of nature, which was beyond human foresight, and against which human prudence could not have been expected to provide. It is something in the course of nature so unexpected in its consequences that the damage caused must be regarded as too remote to form a basis for legal liability. (*Nichols* v. *Marsland*, 1876.)[527]

Necessity

This defence is put forward when damage has been intentionally caused, either to prevent a greater evil or in defence of the realm. Such damage is justifiable if the act was reasonable. (*Cresswell* v. *Sirl*, 1948.)[528] Thus where a whole area is threatened by fire, the destruction of property not yet alight with a view to stopping the spread of the flames would be damage intentionally done but reasonable in the circumstances. (*Cope* v. *Sharpe*, 1912.)[529] Furthermore, in *Leigh* v. *Gladstone*, (1909) 26 P.L.R. 139 the forcible feeding of a suffragette in prison was held justified by the necessity of preserving her life. This decision, which has been much criticized, means that it is not an assault for prison officials to take reasonable steps to preserve the health and life of those in custody.

However, duress does not appear to be a defence and in *Gilbert* v. *Stone* (1647), Aleyn 35, the defendant was held liable for trespass although he entered the plaintiff's house only because twelve armed men had threatened to kill him if he did not do so.

Mistake

It is normally no defence in tort to say that the wrongful act was done by mistake. Even if the consequences of an act were not fully appreciated, everyone is presumed to intend the probable consequences of his acts. A mistake of law is no excuse, and this is usually true of a mistake of fact, unless it is reasonable in the circumstances, e.g. in a case of wrongful arrest. (*Beckwith* v. *Philby*, 1827.)[530]

Act of state

Sometimes the state finds it necessary to protect persons from actions in tort when they have caused damage whilst carrying out their duties. (*Buron* v. *Denman*, 1848.)[531] This defence cannot be raised in respect of damage done anywhere to British subjects (*Nissan* v. *Att. Gen.*, 1969)[532] or where the court holds that damage has been done to a friendly alien. (*Johnstone* v. *Pedlar*, 1921.)[533]

Statutory authority

The acts of public authorities, e.g. Local Authority Councils, are often carried out under the provisions of a statute. This statutory authority to act may give the public authority concerned a good defence if an action in tort arises as a result. However, much depends upon the wording of the relevant statute. *Statutory authority may be absolute* in which case the public authority concerned has a *duty* to act. Alternatively, *statutory authority may be conditional,* in which case the public authority concerned has the *power* to act but is not bound to do so.

If the authority given is *absolute,* then the body concerned is not liable for damage resulting from the exercise of that authority provided it has acted reasonably and there is no alternative way of performing the act. (*Vaughan* v. *Taff Vale Railway,* 1860.)[534]

On the other hand, if the authority given is *conditional,* the body concerned may carry out the relevant act only if there is no interference with the rights of others. (*Penny* v. *Wimbledon, U.D.C.,* 1899.)[535]

Whether statutory authority is *absolute* or *conditional* is a matter of construction of the statute concerned, though statutory powers are usually conferred in *conditional* or permissive form. The basic rules of construction in these cases appear to be as follows—

(i) Is the authorized act of such public importance as to over-ride private interests?

(ii) If it is not, statutory powers are probably conferred subject to common law rights.

In addition, the matter of statutory compensation may be relevant. If the statute provides for compensation for loss resulting from an authorized act there may be no other claim even though the maximum compensation allowed by the statute is less than the actual loss. (*Marriage* v. *East Norfolk River Catchment Board*, 1950.)[536] On the other hand, if there is no provision for compensation in the statute there is a presumption that private rights remain and that an action in respect of any infringement of these rights may be brought.

It should be noted that the above principles also apply where the act done is authorized by delegated legislation.

Justification or self defence

Where a person commits a tort in defence of himself or his property, he will not be liable provided the act done in such defence is reasonable or proportionate to the harm threatened, though no provocation by words can justify a blow. (*Lane* v. *Holloway,* [1967] 3 All E.R. 129.) The defence extends to acts in defence of the members of one's family and probably to acts in defence of persons generally.

REMEDIES

The remedies available to a person who has suffered injury or loss by reason of the tort of another are *damages*, the granting of an *injunction*, and in some cases an order for *specific restitution* of land or chattels of which the plaintiff has been dispossessed.

Damages

As we have seen in the chapter on the law of contract damages may be nominal, contemptuous, punitive (or exemplary), aggravated or compensatory (which includes special damages).

Usually the damages awarded are *compensatory* and the underlying principle is that of *restitutio in integrum*, i.e. the damages awarded are designed to put the plaintiff in the position he would have been in if he had not suffered the wrong.

In the case of *personal injuries*, e.g. loss of a limb, damages obviously cannot restore the plaintiff to his previous position and, in order to establish some uniformity in damages awarded for personal injuries the Court of Appeal ruled in *Ward* v. *James*, [1965] 1 All E.R. 563, that juries should not normally be used in trials concerning personal injuries, and they very rarely are.

Damages for personal injuries may be awarded under the following heads—

   (i) pain and suffering;
   (ii) loss of enjoyment of life, or of amenity, as where brain damage causes permanent unconsciousness;
   (iii) loss of expectation of life;
   (iv) loss of earnings, both actual and prospective.

Deductions—tax. The House of Lords decided in *British Transport Commission* v. *Gourley* [1955] 3 All E.R. 796, that the fact that the plaintiff would have paid tax on his earnings must be taken into account so as to reduce the damages awarded in regard to earnings. The money is not paid to the Revenue so it is a benefit either to the defendant or his insurance company. However the rule has some logic on the grounds that damages are *compensatory,* and gross salary must be reduced to net salary to achieve true compensation.

Deductions—collateral benefits. Under the Law Reform (Personal Injuries) Act, 1948, Sect. 2, one-half of the value of any sickness benefit industrial injuries benefit and industrial disablement benefit received by the plaintiff must be deducted, though if the plaintiff did not know that he had a right to a particular form of national insurance benefit, e.g. disablement benefit, and had not acted unreasonably in failing to claim it, the sum which he might have received will not be deducted from the damages awarded. (*Eley* v. *Bradford,* [1971] 3 All E.R. 285.)

In general the policy is one of non-deduction and sums received from other forms of insurance are not taken into account, nor is a disability or state retirement pension (*Parry* v. *Cleaver*, 1969[537] and *Hewson* v. *Downes*, 1969.)[538] No deductions are to be made for an *ex gratia* payment equal to a pension made by a former employer (*Cunningham* v. *Harrison*, [1973] 3 All E.R. 463) nor are deductions to be made for gifts. Supplementary Benefit is not deducted (*Foxley* v. *Olton*, [1965] 2 Q.B. 306) but unemployment benefit is deducted in full. (*Cheeseman* v. *Bowaters*, [1971] 3 All E.R. 513.)

Remoteness of damage

The consequences of a defendant's wrongful act or omission may be endless. Even so a plaintiff who has established that the defendant's wrong caused his loss may be unable to recover damages because his loss is not sufficiently connected with the defendant's wrong to make the latter liable. In other words, the loss is too remote a consequence to be recoverable. The principles which determined at what point damage became too remote used to be as follows—

(a) Regarding culpability or responsibility for the harm. All that the law required was that the reasonable man would have foreseen that his act would have caused the plaintiff *some* harm.

(b) Regarding liability to compensate the plaintiff. Given that the dependant would, as a reasonable man, have foreseen some harm as likely to result from his act, he became liable for all the *direct* consequences of the act even though such consequences could not possibly have been foreseen.

This test can be seen in operation in *Smith* v. *London and South Western Railway*, 1870,[539] and in *Re Polemis and Furness Withy & Co.*, 1921.[540]

This method of establishing liability was rather hard on the defendant because he was often made liable for damage which he could not possibly have foreseen, and certain inroads into the doctrine were made (see for example *Liesbosch* v. *Edison*, 1933),[541] though the general principles of *Re Polemis*[540] were never over-ruled. However, the decision of the Judical Committee of the Privy Council in *Overseas Tankship (UK) Ltd* v. *Morts Dock and Engineering Co. Ltd*, 1961[542] (generally referred to as *The Wagon Mound*), lays down a new test for remoteness of damage in tort which is as follows—

(a) Regarding culpability or responsibility for the harm. The test is still an objective test rather than a subjective one, because the law substitutes for the defendant a hypothetical reasonable man, and then proceeds to make the defendant only responsible for the damage which the reasonable man would have foreseen as a likely consequence of his act.

(b) Regarding liability to compensate the plaintiff. The law now requires the defendant to compensate the plaintiff only for the foreseeable result of

his act. The defendant is no longer liable for all the direct consequences of his act, but only for those which, as a reasonable man, he should have foreseen. However, it appears from more recent decisions that the *precise* nature of the injury suffered need not be foreseeable: it is enough if the injury was of a *kind* that was foreseeable even though the form it took was unusual. (*Hughes* v. *Lord Advocate,* 1963,[543] *Bradford* v. *Robinson Rentals,* 1967[544] and *Weiland* v. *Cyril Lord Carpets Ltd,* 1969.)[545] Nevertheless difficulties still exist in regard to the application of the principles laid down in *Hughes*[543] and *Bradford*[544]. These difficulties are illustrated by the decisions reached in *Doughty* v. *Turner Manufacturing Co. Ltd,* 1964,[546] and *Tremain* v. *Pike,* 1969.[547]

Status of The Wagon Mound.   Certain problems were raised by the decision in *The Wagon Mound.*

(1) Being a decision of the Judicial Committee of the Privy Council, it was not binding on English courts but was persuasive only. The decision in *Re Polemis* was made by the Court of Appeal which is bound by its own decisions, and ought therefore to have followed the decision in *Re Polemis* in future similar cases, rather than the decision in *The Wagon Mound.* However, it did seem likely that the House of Lords would over-rule *Re Polemis* if a similar case came before it, and the Court of Appeal would, it was thought, be reluctant to make an award of damages under *Re Polemis* knowing that almost certainly the House of Lords would reverse the decision on appeal. It was thought also that the Court of Appeal might refuse to follow its own previous decision in *Re Polemis* on the grounds that the House of Lords had on a number of occasions suggested that *Re Polemis* was wrongly decided without actually over-ruling it.

In the event the Court of Appeal in *Doughty* v. *Turner Manufacturing Co. Ltd,* 1964,[546] and the House of Lords in *Hughes* v. *Lord Advocate,* 1963,[543] treated the decision in *The Wagon Mound* as a correct statement of the law, subject in *Hughes'* case to an additional principle that the precise chain of circumstances need not be envisaged if the consequence turns out to be within the general sphere of contemplation and not of an entirely different kind which no one can anticipate. In addition the High Court has expressly stated in *Smith* v. *Leech Braine & Co. Ltd,* 1962[548] that *Polemis* is no longer law and that *The Wagon Mound* is the governing authority.

(2) It remains to be seen how far *The Wagon Mound* has affected what is generally called 'the unusual plaintiff' rule. For example, if X strikes Y a puny blow which might be expected merely to bruise him, but in fact Y has a thin skull and dies from the blow, the law has regarded X as liable for Y's death. The same rule has been applied where the plaintiff is a haemophilic, i.e. a person with a constitutional tendency to severe bleeding. This rule squares with *Re Polemis* but cannot be reconciled with the decision in *The Wagon Mound.*

However, it is likely that the 'unusual plaintiff' rule will survive the decision in *The Wagon Mound* and be regarded as an exception to it. (*Smith* v. *Leech Braine & Co. Ltd*, 1962.)[548] The rule that a victim is to be taken as he is found was not necessarily valid where the loss was economic rather than physical. (*Liesbosch* v. *Edison*, 1933.)[541] However, a more recent decision suggests that loss caused by impecuniosity is not necessarily too remote. (*Martindale* v. *Duncan*, 1973.)[549] Furthermore, the 'unusual plaintiff' rule seems to apply only to disabilities existing before the accident and not to disabilities arising afterwards. (*Morgan* v. *T. Wallis*, 1974.)[550]

The test of remoteness of damage in tort as laid down in *The Wagon Mound* relies upon the foreseeability of a reasonable man both in respect of culpability and liability to compensate. It is therefore much the same as the test laid down in *Hadley* v. *Baxendale*, 1854,[429] which is used to decide questions of remoteness in contract. (See p. 268.) This can be regarded as an improvement in the law. Claims for personal injuries are often actionable as breaches of contract and as torts. It can only be confusing for the court to apply two tests in deciding liability for the same act. (But see now *The Heron II*, 1967[430] which has tended to narrow down damages for breach of contract by requiring them to be 'in contemplation' rather than 'foreseeable'.)

Finally, it is perhaps worth noting that *damage which is intended* is never too remote and in this connection there is an inference that a man intends the natural consequences of his acts. (*Scott* v. *Shepherd*, 1773.)[551]

Novus actus interveniens. (A new act intervening.) A loss may be too remote a consequence to be recoverable if the chain of causation is broken by an extraneous act. The scope of this concept is as follows—

(*a*) When the act of a third person intervenes between the original act or omission and the damage, the original act or omission is still the direct cause of the damage if the act of the third person might have been expected in the circumstances (*Scott* v. *Shepherd*, 1773)[551] or did not materially cause or contribute to the injury. (*Barnett* v. *Chelsea and Kensington Hospital Management Committee*, 1968[552] and *Robinson* v. *The Post Office*, 1973.)[553] There is a duty to guard against a *novus actus interveniens*. (*Davies* v. *Liverpool Corporation*, 1949.)[554]

(*b*) If the act of the third person is such as would not be anticipated by a reasonable man, the chain of causation is broken, and the third party's act and not the initial act or omission will be treated as the cause of the damage. (*Cobb* v. *Great Western Rly*, 1894.)[555]

(*c*) The *novus actus* may be the act of the plaintiff and in these cases liability will turn on the precise facts. (*Sayers* v. *Harlow U.D.C.*, 1958,[556] and *McKew* v. *Holland and Hannan, and Cubitts (Scotland) Ltd*, 1969.)[557]

(*d*) In order to establish the liability of the intervenor, it is essential to show that he consciously intended to carry out the act. (*Philco Radio Corporation* v. *Spurling*, 1949.)[558]

Nervous shock. Damages for illness brought on by nervous shock are not necessarily too remote and may be recoverable where the nervous shock causes physical illness and—

(a) the defendant *intended* the shock (*Wilkinson* v. *Downton,* 1897)[473], or

(b) where the shock arises from negligence the plaintiff was 'foreseeable'. A plaintiff will be foreseeable if the defendant's negligent act puts the plaintiff in fear of his or her safety (*Dulieu* v. *White,* 1901)[559] or if it threatens or actually injures some person who has a relationship with the plaintiff such as a family relationship (*Hambrook* v. *Stokes,* 1925[560] and *Hinz* v. *Berry,* 1970)[561] including the relationship of rescuer and rescued. (*Chadwick* v. *British Railways Board,* 1967.)[562]

Protection may even be given to a person who has witnessed some awful spectacle even though neither the life nor limb of any third party has been imperilled. (*Owens* v. *Liverpool Corporation,* 1939.)[563]

However, damages will not be recoverable unless—

(a) the defendant *owed a duty of care* to the plaintiff (*Bourhill* v. *Young,* 1943);[564]

(b) the shock was caused by *actually witnessing or hearing the accident* and not by *the account of others after the event* (*Hambrook* v. *Stokes,* 1925).[560]

The above rules have been developed because of the following problems inherent in actions for nervous shock—

(a) the difficulty of proving the degree of suffering involved and the possibility of fraudulent claims; thus, only where a known physical or mental condition is manifest are damages awarded;

(b) the difficulty which might arise if the number of possible claims, e.g. from relatives not present at the accident, was not limited; thus, the rule of foreseeability requires that the person claiming should at least have seen or heard the accident or witnessed its aftermath, as in *Chadwick* v. *British Railways Board,* 1967.[562]

Damage after successive accidents. Difficult legal problems arise when different tortfeasors *successively* injure the same plaintiff. In *Baker* v. *Willoughby,* 1969,[565] the House of Lords held that a tortfeasor is liable even though a later event causes the same or even greater damage to the plaintiff. A defendant who injures a plaintiff *who has already* been injured will be liable only in so far as his tortious act increases or exacerbates the pre-existing injury. (*Performance Cars Ltd* v. *Abraham,* 1961,[566] and *Cutler* v. *Vauxhall Motors Ltd,* 1970.)[567]

Injunction

An injunction may be granted to prevent the commission, continuance or repetition of an injury, and there is a form of interlocutory injunction called *quia timet* (because he fears) which may be granted, though rarely, even though the injury has not taken place but is merely threatened. As we have seen, injunctions are discretionary remedies and cannot be obtained as of right. Furthermore, an injuction will not be granted where damages would be an adequate remedy. However, it is no defence to say that it will be costly to comply with the injunction, though the court may, as in *Pride of Derby and Derbyshire Angling Association Ltd* v. *British Celanese Ltd,* [1953] 1 All E.R. 179, where expensive alterations to sewage plant were required to prevent the pollution of a river, grant an injunction and suspend its operation for such time as may seem necessary to enable the defendant to comply with the order.

Other remedies

The court may order *specific restitution* of land or goods where the plaintiff has been deprived of possession and a plaintiff may be given an order for an *account* of profits received as a result of a wrongful act. Thus where a company or other business organization carries on business under a name calculated to deceive the public by confusion with the name of an existing concern, it commits the tort of *passing off* and can be restrained by injunction from doing so. In addition, the existing concern may be given an order for an *account* of profits received by the offending concern as a result of the deception.

CESSATION OF LIABILITY

Liability in tort may be terminated by *death* (see p. 304), and also by *judgment, waiver, accord, satisfaction* and *lapse of time.*

Judgment

Successive actions cannot be brought by the same person on the same facts and if a competent court gives a final judgment in respect of a right of action that right of action is *merged* into the judgment. However, there are certain exceptional cases, for example, where two separate rights have been infringed. Thus in *Brunsden* v. *Humphrey* (1884), 14 Q.B.D. 141, the Court of Appeal held that a cab driver who had brought a successful action for damage to his cab caused by the defendant's negligence was able to bring a further action for personal injuries.

Waiver

The same conduct by the defendant may sometimes represent two separate and distinct torts or causes of action. If the plaintiff obtains judgment and satisfaction by electing to sue on tort A rather than tort B he cannot later sue in respect of tort B. However, the mere bringing of the action will not operate as an election: there must be judgment and satisfaction. (*United Australia Ltd* v. *Barclays Bank Ltd,* 1941.)[568] Furthermore *adoption* of the transaction giving rise to the tort operates as a waiver. (*Verschures Creameries Ltd* v. *Hull and Netherlands S.S. Co. Ltd,* 1921.)[569]

Accord and satisfaction

A person may surrender a right of action in tort by deed or an agreement for consideration.

Lapse of time

Under the provisions of Sect. 2(1)(a) of the Limitation Act, 1939 the general period of limitation is tort is six years from from the date on which the *cause of action accrues,* i.e. the date on which the plaintiff could first have brought his action. Where the action is in respect of personal injuries, including trespass to the person (*Letang* v. *Cooper,* 1964),[570] the period is three years from the date on which the cause of action accrued. (Law Reform (Limitation of Actions etc.) Act, 1954, Sect. 2(1).) As we have seen, if the time expires on a day when the court offices are not open the period is extended to the next working day. In addition, when completing the three-year period for personal injuries the day of the accident should be excluded. (*Pritam Kaur* v. *S. Russell & Sons Ltd,* [1973] 1 All E.R. 617.)

Where the tort is actionable without proof of damage, as in the case of trespass, time usually begins to run when the tort is committed, even if the aggrieved party is ignorant of the fact of its commission, provided that there is no fraudulent concealment of the tort by the defendant. However, if the tort is actionable only on proof of damage, as in the case of negligence, time begins to run under the Limitation Act, 1939, from the date on which the damage is caused. Thus it was decided in *Sparham-Souter* v. *Town and Country Developments (Essex),* [1976] 2 All E.R. 665, that the limitation period in respect of a cause of action for negligent building work, i.e. inadequate foundations, does not begin to run until the plaintiff discovers that damage has resulted or ought reasonably to have so discovered, as where he ignores the appearance of cracks without further investigation. This rule created hardship where the plaintiff had suffered personal injuries. For example, if X had been run down by Y's negligent driving, and unknown to X the injuries inflicted on him at the time of the accident caused him to go blind (say) four years after the accident, then X's cause of action in respect of his blindness was barred before he knew it existed, since it was formerly held that once damage had occurred the cause of action accrued and that time began to run against the plaintiff even though he was unaware or mistaken as to the consequences of the damage.

The matter is now covered by the Limitation Act, 1975. The act applies only to claims for personal injury arising out of negligence, breach of contract or breach of statutory duty. The basic limitation period of three years is retained but time runs from the date of accrual of the cause of action or the 'date of the plaintiff's knowledge if later'. As regards knowledge the Act says that it means—

(i) that the plaintiff knew that the injury was a significant one. 'Significant' means whether the plaintiff would have considered it sufficiently serious to justify suing a solvent defendant who did not dispute liability. Most injuries will therefore be significant and only the most trivial would fail to come within the definition, and

(ii) that the plaintiff knew that the injury resulted wholly or in part from the defendants act or omission, and

(iii) that the plaintiff knew the identity of the defendant.

The above provisions could, of course, extend the three-year rule since in some cases time will run from the date of the plaintiff's knowledge. Even beyond this, however, the court has a discretion to override time limits and can ignore either the basic three-year period or even any extended period which has arisen under the provisions set out above. However, the court must consider the prejudice to the plaintiff which would be caused by adhering to the limits and the prejudice any extension might cause to the defendant. The court must consider all the circumstances and in particular—

(i) the period of and reasons for the delay;

(ii) the difficulties that will be caused for witnesses being asked to recall evidence though obviously the more written documents that exist the less prejudice is likely to be caused under this head;

(iii) the conduct of the defendant after the cause of action arose, e.g. was he obstructive and trying to evade liability by refusing to give the plaintiff proper information;

(iv) the length of time any harm suffered by the plaintiff has lasted;

(v) how far the plaintiff acted promptly when he knew that he might be able to sue;

(vi) to what extent the plaintiff took professional advice, e.g. legal or medical, and the nature of the advice he received.

Two recent cases will serve to illustrate ways in which the courts discretion to override time limits has been used. In *Buck* v. *English Electric Co.,* [1977] 1 W.L.R. 806, Kilner Brown, J. held that a delay of more than five or six years in instituting proceedings was not prejudicial to the defendants because during the period of delay the defendants had been involved in a number of similar claims from the deceased plaintiff's fellow employees so that there was no lack of any cogency of evidence in regard to the way in which the plaintiff had contracted pneumoconiosis. However, in *Davies* v. *British Insulated Callender's Cables, The Times,* 15 February, 1977, the plaintiff claimed that his back injury was partly attributable to a fall at work in 1970. He issued a writ in 1976 and it was held—by Thesiger, J.—that leave for the action to proceed should be refused under the Limitation Act, 1975 since it appeared that the plaintiff was aware of the possibility of making a claim long before he issued his writ and the nature of the claim made an early trial imperative if prejudice to the defendants was to be avoided.

An action under the 1975 Act may be brought by dependents or on behalf of the estate of a deceased person.

Thus actions may be brought within three years of the date of death or of the date on which the personal representatives or dependents, as the case may be, acquired a knowledge of the relevant facts.

If the tort is of a continuing nature, as in the case of nuisance or possibly trespass, an independent cause of action arises on each day during which the tort is committed, and the aggrieved party can recover for such proportion of the injury as lies within the limitation period, even though the wrong was first committed outside the period.

Where the plaintiff is a minor or person suffering from mental disorder, the period of limitation does not run against him until his disability ends, i.e. on becoming eighteen or on becoming sane or on death. But once time has started to run, any subsequent disability will not stop it running.

However, a minor was only regarded as being under a disability if he was not in the custody of a parent when the cause of action accrued. If he was in the custody of a parent within the meaning of Sect. 22(2) of the Limitation Act, 1939, the parent was expected to commence an action within the limitation period and if he did not the minor's action would be statute barred. The Act of 1975, Sect. 2, abolishes that rule so that periods of limitation do not run against a minor whether he is in the custody of a parent or not.

Special periods of limitation.   The periods of limitation in respect of actions against the estate of a deceased tortfeasor have already been considered on page 304. However, it should be noted that the Limitation Act, 1975, does not operate to extend the time within which an action must be brought against a deceased tortfeasor's estate. So far as the death of an injured party is concerned, the ordinary six or three-year periods apply. They run from the accrual of the cause of action as if no death had occurred. As we have seen, personal representatives or dependents may ask for an extension of time under the provisions of the Limitation Act, 1975.

Other special periods of limitation are as follows—

(i) Actions arising out of collisions at sea; two years, subject to extension by the Court. (Maritime Conventions Act, 1911, Sect. 8.)

(ii) Proceedings against air-carriers; two years. (Carriage by Air Act, 1961, Sect. 5(1).)

(iii) A joint tortfeasor who wishes to recover a contribution must bring the action within two years from the date on which he admitted liability or judgment was entered against him. (Limitation Act, 1975, Sect. 2.)

(iv) Actions in respect of damage arising from nuclear incidents; thirty years. (Nuclear Installations Act, 1965, Sect. 15.)

Public authorities and their officers have no special position and actions against them are governed by the same rules as any other action in tort.

It should also be noted that by Sect. 26 of the Limitation Act, 1939, the defendant's *fraud* or *negligent concealment* may prevent his pleading the Statutes of Limitation. (*Beaman* v. *A.R.T.S.*, 1949,[571] *Eddis* v. *Chichester Constable*, 1969.)[572]

Assignment

It is against the rules of public policy to allow the assignment of rights of action in tort, since actions for damages should not become a marketable commodity. However, such rights may pass to others by operation of law in the following circumstances—

(i) *Death.* Rights and liabilities in tort survive for the benefit or otherwise of the estate, except actions for defamation unless damage to the deceased's estate has resulted.

(ii) *Bankruptcy.* Rights of action in tort possessed by a debtor which relate to his *property* and which if brought will increase his assets will pass to his trustee in bankruptcy. Actions for *personal torts,* e.g. defamation, remain with the bankrupt.

(iii) *Subrogation.* An insurance company which compensates an insured person under a policy of insurance can step into his shoes and sue in respect of the injury.

SPECIFIC TORTS

We shall next examine certain specific torts, beginning with those affecting the person.

TORTS AFFECTING THE PERSON

Trespass to the person

This has several aspects

(a) Assault. An assault is an attempt or offer to apply unlawful force to the person of another. There must be an apparent present ability to carry out the threat, the basis of the wrong being that a person is put in present fear of violence. On general principles, pointing even an unloaded weapon or a model gun at another, who does not know that it is unloaded or a model, would amount to an assault. It is often said that mere words cannot constitute an assault but this is a doubtful proposition. In *Ansell* v. *Thomas*, 1974[441] the assault seems to have consisted in the words threatening forcible ejectment if the plaintiff did not leave voluntarily. A threat to use force at some time in the future is not an assault, but it seems that it is enough if the threat is to use force if the person addressed does not immediately do some act. In *Read* v. *Cocker*, (1853) 138 E.R. 1437, it was held that an assault was committed where the defendants threatened to break the plaintiff's neck if he did not leave the premises. Words, however, may prevent an assault coming into being. (*Turbervell* v. *Savage*, 1669.)[573] In general there will be some active conduct constituting the assault. However, in *Fagan* v. *Metropolitan Police Commissioner*, 1968[574] the court appears to have accepted that an assault can arise from an omission.

As regards the unauthorized taking of a photograph, the position is somewhat complicated. It may be that where a flash is used the simple taking of the photograph without more is unlawful, since it is probably a battery to project light onto another person in such a manner as to cause personal discomfort. Where no flash is used, it is hard to see how, by itself, the taking of a photograph can amount to a battery, an assault or any other trespass.

(b) Battery. Intentionally to bring any material object into contract with the person of another is enough application of force to give rise to a battery. Thus to throw water on a person (*Pursell* v. *Horn*, (1838) 8 And. 602), or to apply a 'tone-rinse' to the scalp of a customer which was not ordered and causes damage is enough. (*Nash* v. *Sheen, The Times*, 13 March, 1953.) Substantial damages will be awarded when the battery is an affront to personal dignity, e.g. the wrongful taking of a finger-print. The mere jostling which occurs in a crowd does not constitute battery, because there is presumed consent. It should be noted that there may be a battery without an assault, as where a person is attacked from behind.

Defences. There are certain defences to an action for trespass to the person—

(i) *Self-defence*. This is not merely the defence of oneself but also of those whom one has a legal or moral obligation to protect. It also applies to the protection of property, but no more than reasonable force must be used.

(ii) *Parental or similar authority*. Moderate chastisement inflicted on children by parents, and school masters by way of delegation of the parent's authority, is not actionable.

(iii) *Volenti non fit injuria*. As in the case of the players in a rugby match. (*Simms* v. *Leigh Rugby Football Club*, 1969.)[509]

(iv) *Judicial authority.* This includes the right to inflict proper punishment and to make lawful arrests.

(v) *Necessity.* This is not favoured as a defence but may be allowed if the defendant can prove that he committed the battery in order to prevent the happening of a greater harm. Thus in *Leigh* v. *Gladstone* (1909), 26 T.L.R. 139, the forcible feeding of a suffragette in prison was held justified by the necessity of preserving her life.

(vi) *Prosecution in a magistrates' court.* Assault and battery is a crime as well as a civil wrong. If the wrongdoer is prosecuted, and *summary* proceedings are taken and the accused is convicted and punished, or the case is dismissed and the magistrates award a certificate of dismissal, no further action or civil proceedings may be taken in respect of the particular wrong. (Offences against the Person Act, 1861, Sects 44–45.)

It is now clear that trespass to the person is not actionable in itself; the plaintiff must prove intention or negligence (*Fowler* v. *Lanning*, 1959)[575] though he need not prove damage. It is also settled that where the interference is *unintentional* the plaintiff's only cause of action lies in negligence. (*Letang* v. *Cooper*, 1964.)[570]

(c) False imprisonment. This is the infliction of unauthorized bodily restraint without lawful justification. It is not necessarily a matter of bars and bolts, but any form of unlawful restraint might turn out to be false imprisonment. The imprisonment must be total, and if certain ways of exit are barred to a prisoner, but he is free to go off in another way, then there is no false imprisonment. (*Bird* v. *Jones*, 1845.)[576] If a person is on premises and is not given facilities to leave, then this does constitute false imprisonment, unless the refusal is merely the insistence on a reasonable condition. (*Herd* v. *Weardale Colliery*, 1915.)[577] It is not even essential that the plaintiff should be aware of the fact of his imprisonment, provided it is a fact. (*Meering* v. *Grahame White Aviation Co.*, 1919.)[578] *Volenti non fit injuria* is a defence to false imprisonment, as where a prison visitor agrees to be locked in a cell with the prisoner.

Powers of arrest

The old distinction between felonies and misdemeanours was abolished by Sect. 1 of the Criminal Law Act, 1967, as from 1 January, 1968. The Act created a new class of 'arrestable offence', i.e. offences for which the sentence is fixed by law, or for which a person (not previously convicted) may be sent to prison for five years, and attempts to commit such offences.

A private person may arrest without a warrant anyone who is, or whom he, with reasonable cause, suspects to be, *in the act* of committing an arrestable offence. (Criminal Law Act, 1967, Sect. 2(2).) Where an arrestable offence *has been committed,* any person may arrest without warrant anyone who is, or whom he, with reasonable cause, suspects to be, guilty of the offence. (Criminal Law Act, 1967, Sect. 2(3).) Thus it will be seen that the legality of the arrest depends not on the presence or otherwise of reasonable cause in the mind of the citizen when he carries out the arrest but on the outcome of the eventual prosecution, for which he is not responsible and cannot control. A prosecution may break down for a number of reasons and on this may depend the liability of an honest arrestor to pay damages, possibly running into hundreds of pounds.

A police constable is protected in respect of arrests made under the authority of a warrant. He may arrest without a warrant in the situations mentioned above. Furthermore he may arrest someone who is or is suspected, on reasonable grounds, to be *about to commit* an arrestable offence, and someone whom he suspects, on reasonable grounds, to be guilty of an arrestable offence even though the offence has *not* been committed. (Criminal Law Act, 1967, Sects 2(4) and (5).)

A police constable may also arrest without warrant for certain other offences by reason of special statutory powers. These include absconding while on bail or breaking the conditions of bail, reckless, dangerous or careless driving (where the driver will not give evidence of identity) and offences under the Firearms Act, 1968. Furthermore, under the Public Service Vehicles (Arrest of Offenders) Act, 1975, Sect. 1, a constable with reasonable cause to suspect a person of contravening regulations concerning the conduct of passengers in public service vehicles, may arrest that person without a warrant if he fails to answer certain questions, e.g. refuse to give his name and address.

At the time when an arrest is made the person arrested must be told the reason for his arrest, unless the reason is obvious, e.g. if he is caught in the act. (*Christie* v. *Leachinsky,* 1947,[579] *R.* v. *Kulynycz,* 1970,[580] and *Wheatley* v. *Lodge,* 1971.)[581] Furthermore, if arrested without warrant, he must be taken before a magistrate or police officer as soon as practicable. (Magistrates' Courts Act, 1952, Sect. 38(4).) If it is not practical to bring him before a Magistrates' Court within 24 hours, the police must release him on bail unless the offence appears to be a serious one. (*Ibid*, Sect. 38(1).) However, in practice, persons are sometimes kept for quite long periods without being arrested or charged where the offence is serious and this in spite of Article 5 of the European Convention on Human Rights, to which this country is a signatory, which stipulates that a person arrested or detained must be brought promptly before a judge or other officer authorized by law to exercise judicial power. Arrest may be by words (*Alderson* v. *Booth,* 1969).[582] Not every loss of liberty is arrest (*R* v. *Brown,* 1977).[583] Breath tests apart (*Squires* v. *Botwright,* 1973), detention without arrest is unlawful.

The *remedies* available against false imprisonment are self-help, i.e. breaking away, the writ of habeas corpus and an action for damages. This prerogative writ is designed to provide a person, who is kept in confinement without legal justification, with a means of obtaining his release. If he can show a *prima facie* case that he might be unlawfully detained, he will usually apply to a divisional court of the Queen's Bench Division, but application may be made to any judge of the High Court during vacation times. The person detained applies, through counsel, for the writ to be issued, the facts alleging unlawful detention being set out on an affidavit supporting the application. If the writ is issued the person detained must be released.

TORTS AFFECTING PROPERTY

Trespass to land

Trespass to land is interference with the possession of land. It is not enough that the plaintiff is the owner; he must also have possession. So where land is leased for a term of years, the lessee is the person entitled to sue in trespass, though the lessor may bring an action if the damage is such as to affect his reversion when the lease ends. However, when a person signs a contract for the purchase of land, he becomes entitled to possession of it, and if a trespass takes place before he actually takes possession, then he can sue in respect of that trespass when he does. His right to sue relates back to the date on which he became entitled to the land under the contract.

Interference with the possession of land may take many forms but it must be direct. (*Southport Corporation* v. *Esso Petroleum Co.*, 1954.)[584] For example, an unauthorized entry on land is a trespass. It is a trespass to place things on land, e.g. leaving a dead cat in a neighbour's garden. To remain on land after one's authority is terminated constitutes a trespass. So, if a friend invites you into his house for a meal, tires of your company and asks you to leave, then if you refuse you are a trespasser. If you abuse the purpose for which you are allowed to be on land you become a trespasser. In *Hickman* v. *Maisey*, [1900] 1 Q.B. 752, where the highway was used for making notes of the form of racehorses being tried out on adjoining land, this constituted a trespass, since the proper use of a highway is for passing and re-passing.

While trespass usually takes place above the surface, it may be underneath by means of tunnelling or mining. With regard to trespass in the air-space above land, the position is doubtful, since there is no good authority. It is probably only a trespass if it is either within the area of ordinary user, or if it involves danger or inconvenience. (*Kelson* v. *Imperial Tobacco Co.*, 1957,[585] and *Woollerton and Wilson Ltd* v. *Richard Costain (Midlands) Ltd*, 1969.)[586]

The Civil Aviation Act, 1949, Sect. 40(1), gives all aircraft, irrespective of nationality and including state aircraft, immunity in trespass, and nuisance in respect of the flight of aircraft at a reasonable height, but requires owners of aircraft to comply with extensive conditions regarding their operation and makes them liable strictly for any damage caused. (*Bernstein* v. *Skyviews & General*, 1977.)[587]

There was in this branch of law a somewhat technical rule called trespass *ab initio* (from the beginning). The rule said that, where a person entered on land by virtue of a legal right and abused the authority given to him, his original entry became an unlawful trespass. The abuse had to take the form of a positive act, i.e. misfeasance, and could not be a failure to act or an omission, i.e. mere non-feasance. (*The Six Carpenters Case,* 1610.)[588] Further the right of entry had to be conferred by law and not for example by contract. It was also necessary that the act was one which took away all justification for entry. (*Elias* v. *Pasmore,* 1934.)[589] However, the Court of Appeal threw doubt on the existence of the rules of trespass *ab initio* in modern law. (*Chic Fashions (West Wales)* v. *Jones,* 1968.)[590] Cases similar to *Elias* and *Chic Fashions* continue to come before the courts but the doctrine of trespass *ab initio* is not the real basis of them. Instead the law is developing a series of rules relating to the power under the constitution of the police and other public officials to enter and search premises and seize chattels found thereon. These powers have been extended to the point where the police have largely unfettered powers. The extension of these powers appears to be based on public policy. As Lord Denning has pointed out: 'In these present times, with the ever-increasing wickedness there is about, honest citizens must help the police and not hinder them in their efforts to track down criminals.' (*Chic Fashions (West Wales) Ltd* v. *Jones,* 1968.)[590] The present state of the law is contained in the judgment of Ackner, J. in *Garfinkel* v. *Metropolitan Police Commissioner,* (1971) (unreported), where he said: 'It is accepted that the law on this subject can be stated quite shortly. Where police officers enter a man's house by virtue of a warrant then, if in the course of their search they come upon any goods which show him to be implicated in some crime other than the crime at which the warrant was directed, they may take them provided they act reasonably and detain them no longer than is necessary, see *Ghani* v. *Jones,* [1970] 1 Q.B. 693 per Lord Denning, M.R. p. 706b.' This statement, taken from a transcript, gives the police very wide powers indeed and some reform by means of statute law is probably required. Certainly, it was thought to be too wide in *Jeffrey* v. *Black,* 1977.[591]

Problems have arisen where a plaintiff has entered the premises by virtue of a licence, contractual or otherwise, because at one time it was not certain whether this licence could be revoked so as to make the plaintiff a trespasser and permit his ejection.

The common law view was that, where a person paid for admission to premises, his licence to be on those premises could be revoked at any time, in spite of valuable consideration, so that he could then be ejected as a trespasser, the defendant being liable for breach of contract, but not for assault. (*Wood* v. *Leadbitter,* 1845.)[592]

On the other hand, Equity took the view that, if there was an enforceable contract not to revoke, express or implied, as where valuable consideration had been given, the licence could not be revoked so that if the plaintiff had been ejected he could sue for assault; he could not be made a trespasser by a mere attempt at revocation. (*Hurst* v. *Picture Theatres,* 1915.)[593]

The equitable view gave rise to certain problems because it seemed to confuse rights over land with mere contracts, but the matter may now be regarded as settled. In *Winter Garden Theatre* v. *Millenium Productions Ltd,* 1948,[594] it was held by the House of Lords that, although a licence for value is contractual in its nature and cannot create a right over land itself (or a right *in rem* which will run with the land and affect third parties), yet, as between the parties to the contract if may be implied, even if it is not expressed, that the licence cannot unreasonably be revoked during the period for which the parties intended it to continue. This rule was applied in *Hounslow London Borough* v. *Twickenham Garden Development,* 1970.[595]

There are certain extra-judicial remedies available to a person injured by a trespass. For example, *distress damage feasant* is the right to seize chattels which have done damage on land. There is no right to use or sell the chattels but merely to detain until the owner offers compensation. The remedy does not lie against Crown property, and the right to sue in trespass is postponed until the chattel is returned. Livestock may be detained subject to notice to the owner and police for compensation supported by a right of sale. (Animals Act, 1971.)

There is further extra-judicial remedy, often referred to as *self-help,* whereby the person in possession of the land may eject the trespasser, using such force as is reasonably necessary. The trespasser must be asked to depart peacefully and given time in which to quit the land. (*Hemmings* v. *Stoke Poges Golf Club,* 1920.)[596] A trespasser who enters by *force* may be removed immediately and without a previous request to depart.

Trespass to land is actionable *per se* (in itself) and it is not necessary for the plaintiff to show actual damage in order to commence his action, although the damages would be nominal in the absence of real loss. Nevertheless it is possible to obtain an injunction without proof of loss. Trespass upon property is not normally a criminal offence. The law does penalize by statute a trespass on particular property, e.g. railway property and also the law punishes trespass on property for the purpose of committing, e.g. theft or rape. Apart from these statutory exceptions the criminal law dealt with entering or remaining on property by means of the Statutes of Forcible Entry which were a confusing and archaic set of laws. The fact that trespass is not a criminal offence has led to difficulties, particularly in times of acute housing shortage where the civil law is not adequate to deal with the growing activities of 'squatters'. The Criminal Law Act, 1977, Sect. 6, now creates the offence of using or threatening violence to secure entry to premises on which there is another person who opposes entry. The offence can be committed by a person, notwithstanding he has some interest or right in the premises as where he is a landlord, but the offence cannot be committed by a displaced residential occupier, i.e. a person whose residential occupation of the premises has been interrupted by the occupation of the premises by a trespasser, or someone acting for a displaced residential occupier. Section 7 makes it a summary offence for a trespasser to fail to leave premises when required to do so by a displaced residential occupier. Section 8 makes it an offence for a person who is a trespasser on any premises which he has entered as a trespasser to have with him a weapon of offence. Section 9 makes it an offence to enter or be upon as a trespasser diplomatic or consular premises or the premises or residence of any body or person having diplomatic immunity in respect of its or his premises or residence. Section 10 creates a summary offence of resisting or intentionally obstructing a court officer seeking to execute an order for possession of premises, while Sect. 11 gives to a constable a power of entry and search for the purpose of exercising a power of arrest under that part of the Act which relates to offences of entering and remaining on property (i.e. Part II). Section 13 abolishes the common law offences of forcible entry and detainer and repeals related statutes.

Wrongful interference with goods

We propose to discuss the tort of wrongful interference by outlining the basic features of it, i.e. the relationship between the plaintiff and the goods, the conduct of the defendant which the plaintiff must prove, and the principle of liability, bearing in mind that the Torts (Interference with Goods) Act, 1977 defines, in Sect. 1, wrongful interference with goods as including conversion of goods, trespass to goods, negligence or any other tort so far as it results in damage to goods or to an interest in goods.

(a) Wrongful Interference by trespass to goods

(i) *The relationship between the plaintiff and the goods.* Wrongful interference by trespass to goods is a wrong against the possession of goods. Possession in English law is a difficult concept which is considered more fully on p. 376. For the moment it will suffice to say that a person possesses goods when he has some form of *control* over them and has the *intention to exclude* others from possession and to hold the goods on his own behalf.

Possession must exist at the moment when the wrongful interference is alleged to have been committed. Thus a bailee of goods can sue for a wrongful interference to them, but a bailor cannot because, although he is the owner of the goods, he does not possess them at the time. Where there is a *bailment at will,* i.e. one which can be determined at any time, both bailee and bailor have possession so that either can sue for a wrongful interference to the goods. Possession does not necessarily involve an actual grasp of the goods; often a lesser degree of control will suffice. (*The Tubantia,* 1924.)[597]

Difficulties have arisen over the requirement of the intention to exclude others as a necessary ingredient of possession. In regard to things found under or on land, it would appear that a person can have control of goods and the intention to exclude others sufficient to give him possession even when he does not know that the goods exist. (*Bridges* v. *Hawkesworth,*

1851,[598] *Elwes* v. *Brigg Gas Co.*, 1886,[599] *South Staffordshire Water Co.* v. *Sharman,* 1896,[600] *Corporation of London* v. *Appleyard* , 1963,[601] and *Hannah* v. *Peel,* 1945.)[602]

Although the plaintiff relies on possession and not on ownership or title, the defendant can set up the *jus tertii* (right of a third party), under Sect. 8(1) of the Torts (Interference with Goods) Act, 1977. Under that section the defendant is entitled to show in accordance with rules of court that a third party has a better right than the plaintiff as respects all or any part of the interest claimed by the plaintiff and any rule of law (sometimes and formerly called *jus tertii*) to the contrary is abolished. Under Sect. 8(2) rules of court relating to proceedings for wrongful interference require the plaintiff to give particulars of his title; to identify any person who to his knowledge has or claims any interest in the goods; authorize the defendant to apply for directions as to whether any person should be joined in the action with a view to establishing whether he has a better right than the plaintiff, or has a claim as a result of which the defendant might be doubly liable. If a party refuses to be joined the court may deprive him of any right of action against the defendant for the wrong, either unconditionally or subject to such terms or conditions as the court may specify.

(ii) *The conduct of the defendant which the plaintiff must prove.* In wrongful interference by trespass there must be a *direct* interference with the goods, and this may consist of moving a chattel or the throwing of something at it. A person who writes with his finger in the dust on the back of a car commits wrongful interference, as does a person who beats another's animals or administers poison to them.

(iii) *The principle of liability.* In wrongful interference by trespass to goods the liability would not now appear to be strict. The defence of inevitable accident would presumably be available to a defendant and it is possible that, since *Letang* v. *Cooper,* 1964,[570] the interference with the possession of goods must be intentional. Mere negligence may not suffice. This would follow a similar development in the tort of trespass to the person which began with the decision in *Fowler* v. *Lanning,* 1959.[575]

(b) Wrongful interference by conversion

(i) *The relationship between the plaintiff and the goods.* It is often said that the right to sue for wrongful interference by conversion depends on ownership, but this is not really true. To be able to sue for wrongful interference the plaintiff must have had either possession or the immediate right to possess at the time the wrong was committed. Mere ownership without one of the above rights is not enough. Nor is the mere right to possess unless it is coupled with ownership. (*Jarvis* v. *Williams,* 1955.)[603]

As in wrongful interference by trespass to goods so in wrongful interference by conversion, the defendant can set up the right of a third party and Sect. 8(1) and (2) of the 1977 Act apply.

(ii) *The conduct of the defendant which the plaintiff must prove.* In wrongful interference by conversion the defendant must do something which is a complete denial of, or is inconsistent with, the plaintiff's title to the goods; a mere interference with possession is not enough. (*Fouldes* v. *Willoughby,* 1841.)[604] Furthermore, wrongful interference by conversion need not be a trespass. (*Oakley* v. *Lyster,* 1931.)[605]

Generally the conduct of the defendant must be an act rather than a failure to act. Thus, although the plaintiff may base his case on a demand for the goods followed by a refusal, he must still show a denial of title in the defendant. If, therefore,the defendant can show that he was retaining the goods in the exercise of a lien for (say) repair charges unpaid, the plaintiff will fail in his action. A defendant may also refuse temporarily to give up the goods while he takes steps to check the title of the plaintiff.

(iii) *The principle of liability.* In general liability in wrongful interference by conversion is strict and it is not necessary for the plaintiff to prove that the defendant had a wrong intention. Neither is it a defence for the defendant to say that he acted honestly. (*Elvin and Powell* v. *Plummer Roddis Ltd,* 1933.)[606] However where the defendant has lost the goods by *negligence* there was no wrongful interference by conversion but the plaintiff may now sue under the provisions of the Torts (Interference with Goods) Act, 1977 for damage to goods caused by negligence.

Detention of goods.   Section 2(1) of the Torts (Interference with Goods) Act, 1977, abolishes the old tort of dentinue which was a tort relating to detention of goods. The Act substitutes statutory provisions. Under Sect. 2(2) the tort of wrongful interference by conversion is substituted for the old action of detinue. As regards the form of judgment where goods are detained, Sect. 3 provides that in proceedings for wrongful interference against a person who is in possession or in control of the goods relief may be given if appropriate in accordance with Sect. 3(2). Under Sect. 3(2) the relief is—

(*a*) an order for delivery of the goods, and for payment of any consequential damages, or

(*b*) an order for delivery of the goods, giving the defendant the alternative of paying damages by reference to the value of the goods, together in either alternative with payment of any consequential damages, or

(*c*) damages.

Section 3(2) provides that subject to rules of court relief should be given under only one of paragraphs (*a*), (*b*) and (*c*) above and relief under paragraph (*a*) is at the discretion of the court though the claimant may choose between the others. If it is shown to the satisfaction of the court that an order under (*a*) above has not been complied with the court may revoke the order or the relevant part of it and make an order for payment of damages by reference to the value of the goods. Where an order is made under (*b*) above the defendant may satisfy the order by returning the goods

at any time before execution of judgment, but without prejudice to liability
to pay any consequential damages. An order for delivery of the goods
under (*a*) or (*b*) may impose such conditions as may be determined by the
court or pursuant to rules of court and in particular where damages by
reference to the goods would not be the whole of the value of the
goods, may require an allowance to be made by the claimant to reflect the
difference. For example, a bailor's action against the bailee may be one in
which the measure of damages is not the full value of the goods, and then
the court may order delivery of the goods, but require the bailor to pay the
bailee a sum reflecting the difference. Under Sect. 3(7) the court may
make an allowance in respect of any improvements made to the goods by
the defendant whilst they were in his possession.

Remedies. Reference has already been made to the form of judgment
where goods are detained. So far as wrongful interference by trespass and
by conversion are concerned, the remedy is damages and this is covered by
the Torts (Interference with Goods) Act, 1977. Under Sect. 5(1) where
damages for wrongful interference are, or would fall to be, assessed on the
footing that the claimant is being compensated—

(*a*) for the whole of the interest in the goods, or
(*b*) for the whole of the interest in the goods subject to reduction for
contributory negligence,
payment of the assessed damages (under all heads) or, as the case may
be, settlement of a claim for damages for the wrong (under all heads)
extinguishes the claimant's title to that interest. Under Sect. 5(2) the
reference in sub-section to the settlement of a claim includes—

(*a*) where a claim is made in court proceedings, and the defendant has
paid a sum into court to meet the whole claim, the taking of that sum by the
claimant, and
(*b*) where the claim is made in court proceedings, and the proceedings
are settled or compromised, the payment of what is due in accordance with
the settlement or comprise, and
(*c*) where the claim is made out of court and is settled or compromised,
the payment of what is due in accordance with the settlement or compromise. Section 5 has effect, subject to any agreement which the parties have
made varying their rights.

Under Sect. 6 an allowance is available for an improvement in the goods.
For example, where a person in good faith buys a stolen car and improves it
he is entitled to an allowance for that improvement, and where a person in
good faith buys the car from the improver and is sued in conversion by the
true owner, the damages may be reduced to reflect the improvement.
Section 7 deals with double liability, providing in particular that where as
the result of enforcement of a double liability a claimant is unjustly
enriched to any extent he shall be liable to reimburse the wrongdoer to that

extent. For example, if a converter of goods pays damages first to a finder of the goods and then to the true owner, the finder is unjustly enriched unless he accounts over to the true owner, which he is required to do, and then the true owner is unjustly enriched and becomes liable to reimburse the converter of the goods.

Recaption. A person who is entitled to the possession of goods of which he has been wrongfully deprived may retake them but must not use more than reasonable force. It is not clear whether he may enter upon the land of an innocent third party in order to recover the goods.

Replevin. Goods which have been taken by what is alleged to be unlawful distress may be recovered by the owner giving security to the registrar of the county court that he will immediately bring an action to determine the legality of the distress.

NUISANCE

The tort of nuisance is of two types—public and private.

Public nuisance

This is some unlawful act or omission endangering or interfering with the lives, comfort, property, or common rights of the public, e.g. the obstruction of a highway (*AG* v. *Gastonia Coaches,* 1976)[607], or the keeping of dangerous premises near a highway. A public nuisance is a crime for which the remedy is criminal proceedings brought by the Attorney-General. But it is actionable as a tort at the suit of a private individual if he has suffered peculiar damage over and above that suffered by the public as a whole. (*Campbell* v. *Paddington Borough Council,* 1911[486] and see *AG* v. *Gastonia Coaches,* 1976.)[607]

Obstructions to the highway occur daily in our cities and towns, e.g. road repairs and scaffolding. However, these obstructions, being for reasonable purposes, are lawful unless they last for an excessive time. *Dangerous activities* carried on near to the highway may amount to a nuisance. Thus in *Castle* v. *St Augustine's Links,* 1922,[608] damages were awarded against a golf club to a taxi-driver who lost an eye when a golf ball was sliced from the course on to the highway; the hole being sufficiently close to the highway to constitute a public nuisance. With regard to *projections* on to the highway there is no liability for *things naturally on land,* e.g. trees, unless the person responsible for them knew, or ought to have known, that they were in a dangerous condition, as where a branch of a tree is rotten. However, liability appears to be strict in the case of *artificial projections.* (*Terry* v. *Ashton,* 1876.)[609] However, where an action is brought for damages for personal injuries arising out of other forms of obstruction on the highway, it appears that fault is essential to liability. (*Dymond* v.

Pearce, 1972.)[610] Thus in this respect the torts of nuisance and negligence are being drawn together.

Private nuisance

This is an unlawful interference with a man's use of his property or with his health, comfort or convenience, and such interference may vary according to the standard existing in his neighbourhood. It is a wrongful act causing material injury to property or sensible personal discomfort. In this connection injuries to *servitudes* may amount to private nuisance as where the defendant obstructs a right of way, or interferes with the plaintiff's water supply, access of air, light or support.

In considering whether an act or omission is a nuisance, the following points are relevant.

(i) There need be no direct injury to health. It is enough that a person has been prevented to an appreciable extent from enjoying the ordinary comforts of life.

(ii) The standard of comfort must be expected to vary with the district. There is no uniformity of standard between Park Lane and Poplar, although there may be common ground in some matters, e.g. light, since it requires the same amount of light to read in either place. However, where the alleged nuisance has caused *actual damage to property* it is no defence to show that the district concerned is of any particular type.

(iii) A person cannot take advantage of his peculiar sensitivity to noise and smells. There must be some give and take, and a man cannot expect the same amenities in an industrial town as he might enjoy in the country.

(iv) The utility of the alleged nuisance has no bearing on the question. Pigstyes and breweries may be regarded by the community as very necessary, but if they infringe a man's right to the ordinary comforts of life, they are nuisances. Consent cannot be implied from the fact that the plaintiff came to the premises knowing that the nuisance was in existence. (*Bliss* v. *Hall,* 1838.)[611] Nor is the fact that the nuisance arises out of the conferment of a public benefit a defence in the ordinary way. (*Adams* v. *Ursell,* 1913[612] and *Dunton* v. *Dover District Council,* 1977.)[613]

(v) The modes of annoyance are infinitely various, and may include such things as bell-ringing, circus performing, the excessive use of the radio, spreading tree roots and many others. (*Christie* v. *Davey,* 1893.)[614] It should also be noted that picketing a highway other than in pursuance of a trade dispute is unlawful and an injunction may be granted to prevent it. (*Hubbard* v. *Pitt.* 1975.)[615]

(vi) A nuisance may result from the acts of several wrongdoers. Any one of them may be proceeded against, and he cannot plead in excuse that the nuisance was a joint effort, although he has a right of contribution against joint tortfeasors for the damages which might be assessed against him.

(vii) Duration of the act. Although the acts complained of in nuisance are usually continuous, e.g. the constant emission of pungent smells from a factory, an act may constitute a nuisance even though it is temporary or instantaneous as in the case of an explosion. (*British Celanese* v. *Hunt,* 1969.)[616] The duration of the act complained of has a bearing upon the remedy which is appropriate and the court will not often grant an injunction in respect of a temporary nuisance because damages are an adequate remedy. Furthermore, a temporary nuisance may be too trivial to be actionable.

(viii) Sometimes malice or evil motive may become the gist of the offence, since it may be evidence that the defendant was not using his property in a lawful way. (*Hollywood Silver Fox Farm* v. *Emmett,* 1936.)[617]

(ix) It is possible to acquire the right to create a private nuisance by prescription, that is by twenty years' continuous operation since the act complained of first constituted a nuisance. There is no corresponding right in respect of a public nuisance. Since a public nuisance is a crime, no length of time will make it legitimate.

Nuisance is primarily a wrong to property, but even where there is no physical damage the court can award compensation for annoyance and discomfort. (*Bone* v. *Seale,* 1975.)[618] A claim in private nuisance cannot be based solely upon personal injury, where an action would be in negligence. Claims for personal injuries can be made in public nuisance, though as we have seen in *Dymond* v. *Pearce,* 1972,[610] *fault* in the defendant is generally required which makes the action in nuisance similar to that in negligence.

Furthermore, the tort of nuisance refers to the unreasonable use of property and is not a matter of reasonable care (compare negligence). Thus the defendant's use of his property may be offensive and constitute a nuisance no matter how careful he is.

Parties to sue or be sued

The occupant of the property affected by the nuisance is the person who should bring the action (*Malone* v. *Laskey,* 1907),[619] but a landlord may sue if the nuisance is effecting a permanent injury to his property, e.g. where the defendant is erecting a building which infringes the landlord's right to ancient lights.

Regarding liability, it is a general rule that the person who creates the nuisance is liable, and this will generally be the occupier. But a landlord may be liable, as a joint tortfeasor with his tenant, (*a*) if he created the nuisance and then leased the property (*Wilchick* v. *Marks,* 1934,[620] and *Mint* v. *Good,* 1951),[621] or (*b*) where the nuisance was due to the landlord's authorizing the tenant expressly or impliedly to create (*Harris* v. *James,* 1876[622] and *Smith* v. *Scott,* 1972)[623] or continue (*Brew Bros* v. *Snax (Ross),* 1969)[624] the nuisance; or (*c*) where the landlord knew or ought to have known of the nuisance before he let the premises. An occupier must abate a nuisance which was on the premises before he took them over, or is placed there afterwards, even by trespassers, provided that the occupier knows or ought to have known of the nuisance. (*Sedleigh-Denfield* v. *O'Callagan,* 1940.)[625] An occupier is also liable for nuisance arising out of the operations of an independent contractor engaged in work on the premises where there is a special danger of nuisance arising from the nature of the works being carried out, e.g. extensive tunnelling operations. (*Bower* v. *Peate,* 1876,[506] and *Padbury* v. *Holliday,* 1912.)[508]

Remedies

The remedies for nuisance are three in number—

(*a*) The injured party may abate the nuisance, that is, remove it, provided that no unnecessary damage is caused, that no injury arises to an innocent third party, e.g. a tenant, and that, where entry on the defendant's land is necessary, a notice requesting the removal of the nuisance has first been given.

(*b*) He may sue for damages.

(*c*) He may seek an injuction if (i) damages would be an insufficient remedy; and (ii) the nuisance is a continuing nuisance, e.g. smoke frequently emitted from a chimney.

Defences

Certain defences are available to a person who is charged with committing the nuisance—

(*a*) The injury is trivial. The legal maxim is: *De minimis non curat lex.* (The law does not concern itself with trifles.) Such a case would be an extremely short exposure to fumes from road repairs.

(*b*) The so-called nuisance arose from the lawful use of the land. (*Bradford Corporation* v. *Pickles,* 1895.)[471]

(*c*) The nuisance was covered by statutory authority, under the general principles elucidated under the defence of statutory authority.

(*d*) The person committing the alleged nuisance has acquired a prescriptive right through twenty years' user to do what is complained of. (*Sturges* v. *Bridgman,* 1879.)[626]

(*e*) The character of the neighbourhood is such that the act, while it might be a nuisance elsewhere, cannot be regarded as such in that particular district.

(*f*) Consent of the plaintiff is a possible defence but consent will not be implied simply because the plaintiff came to the premises knowing that the nuisance was in existence. (*Bliss* v. *Hall*, 1838.)[611]

Remoteness of damage

For the purpose of deciding problems of remoteness of damage the Privy Council held in *The Wagon Mound* (No. 2), [1966] 2 All E.R. 709 (see p. 324), that in a case of nuisance, as of negligence, it is not enough that the damage was a direct result of the nuisance if the injury was not *foreseeable*. (*British Celanese* v. *Hunt*, 1969.)[616]

We have been discussing the civil law of nuisance. However, there is also the Public Health (Recurring Nuisances) Act, 1969, which can be effective in suppressing noisy parties and the like. Under the Act a Public Health Inspector can be asked to visit the premises and issue a Prohibition Notice. If the situation is unchanged after two hours the local council may initiate a prosecution.

NEGLIGENCE

In ordinary language negligence may simply mean not done intentionally, e.g. the negligent publication of a libel. But while negligence may be one factor or ingredient in another tort, it is also a specific and independent tort with which we are now concerned.

The tort of negligence has three ingredients and to succeed in an action the plaintiff must show (i) the existence of a duty to take care which was owed to him by the defendant, (ii) breach of such duty by the defendant, and (iii) resulting damage to the plaintiff.

(i) The duty of care.   Whether a duty of care exists or not is a question law for the judge to decide, and it is necessary to know how this is done. The law of contract dominated the legal scene in the nineteenth century and this affected the law of torts. The judges, influenced by the doctrine of privity of contract, used it to establish the existence of a duty of care in negligence in those cases where a contract existed by laying down the principle that, if A is contractually liable to B, he cannot simultaneously be liable to C in tort for the same act or omission. (*Earl* v. *Lubbock*, 1905.)[627]

The House of Lords in *Donoghue* v. *Stevenson*, 1932,[468] dispelled the confusion caused by the application of the doctrine of privity of contract where physical injury is caused to the plaintiff by the defendant's negligent act. In this case Lord Atkin formulated what has now become the classic test for establishing a duty of care when he said—

> You must take reasonable care to avoid acts or omissions which you can reasonably foresee would be likely to injure your neighbour. Who then is my neighbour? The answer seems to be persons who are so

closely and directly affected by my act that I ought reasonably to have them in contemplation as being affected when I am directing my mind to the acts or omissions which are called in question.

It will be seen, therefore, that the duty of care is established by putting in the defendant's place a hypothetical 'reasonable man' and deciding whether the reasonable man would have foreseen the likelihood or probability of injury, not its mere possibility. The test is objective not subjective, and the effect of its application is that a person is not liable for every injury which results from his carelessness. There must be a duty of care. (*Bourhill* v. *Young,* 1943.)[564]

Although Lord Atkin's formula has been adopted as a broad general test, it has not been applied to all cases of carelessness. Thus English courts have refused to hold that a finance company is under a duty to register a hire purchase agreement. In *Moorgate Mercantile Co.* v. *Twitchings,* [1976] 2 All E.R. 641, the House of Lords held that a finance company which by negligence failed to register a hire purchase agreement in respect of a car with a central register of such agreements was not estopped from claiming damages for wrongful interference by conversion against a person who relied upon a negative response from the central agency, i.e. that the car was not on hire purchase before he bought it. Furthermore, there may be no liability for damage caused by a *careless omission* or failure to act. (*East Suffolk Rivers Catchment Board* v. *Kent,* 1941[628] and *Argy Trading Development Co. Ltd* v. *Lapid Developments Ltd,* 1977.)[629]

In addition there is, in general, no liability where the defendant's act causes mere *economic* or *monetary loss* to the plaintiff unless the economic or monetary loss arises out of and is accompanied by foreseeable physical injury to the plaintiff or damage to his property. (*The World Harmony,* 1965,[630] *Weller & Co.* v. *Foot and Mouth Disease Research Institute,* 1965,[631] *Electrochrome Ltd* v. *Welsh Plastics Ltd,* 1968,[470] *British Celanese* v. *Hunt,* 1969,[616] *S.C.M. (UK) Ltd* v. *Whittall & Son Ltd,* 1970[632] and *Spartan Steel & Alloys Ltd* v. *Martin & Co. Ltd,* 1972.)[633]

Occasionally, however, mere economic or monetary loss may not be too remote. This arises in the special case of imposition of liability for negligently uttered false statements. (See p. 353.) However, as Lord Macmillan said in *Donoghue* v. *Stevenson,* 1932,[468] 'the categories of negligence are never closed' and the courts do recognize extended forms of duties from time to time. (*Clay* v. *A. J. Crump & Sons Ltd,* 1963,[634] and *Home Office* v. *Dorset Yacht Club Ltd,* 1970.)[635]

Where the court does not recognize liability in the defendant, it will sometimes say that there is no duty of care. (*Weller & Co.* v. *Foot and Mouth Disease Research Institute,* 1965.)[631] On other occasions the court will find that the damage is too remote. (See Lord Denning, M.R., in *Spartan Steel & Alloys Ltd* v. *Martin & Co. Ltd,* 1972.)[633] However, the real reason for recognizing or not recognizing liability in a defendant appears to be public policy. (See Lord Denning, M.R., in *Spartan Steel.*)[633]

It is quite possible that this public policy test will take over from Lord Atkin's 'neighbour' test as a basis for deciding liability in negligence. In some cases it may be that the risk should be borne by the whole community who suffer the losses rather than rest on one pair of shoulders, i.e. upon one contractor who may or may not be insured against the risk.

(ii) Breach of the duty. If a duty of care is established as a matter of law, whether or not the defendant was in breach of that duty is a matter of fact to be decided by the judge.

Here we are concerned with how much care the defendant must take. It is obvious that if motorists did not take out their cars many lives would be saved, and yet it is not negligent to drive a car. Once again the test is to place the 'reasonable man' in the defendant's position. It is an objective test and was thus stated by Baron Alderson in *Blyth* v. *Birmingham Waterworks Co.* (1856), 11 Ex. 781

> Negligence is the omission to do something which a reasonable man guided upon those considerations which ordinarily regulate the conduct of human affairs would do, or doing something which a prudent and reasonable man would not do.

The standard required is not that of a particularly conscientious man but that of the average prudent man in the eyes of the jury. (*Daniels* v. *White and Sons*, 1938[636] but see *Hill* v. *J. Crowe*, 1977.)[637] It has been said that the reasonable man is the man on the Clapham omnibus, but it should not be thought that the average prudent man has a low standard of care. Most of us behave unreasonably from time to time, and if during one of these lapses a person suffers injury, it will be no good our pleading that we are usually reasonable men.

When a person has undertaken a duty which requires extraordinary skill, he will be expected to use a higher standard of care. For example, one would expect from a surgeon the degree of skill appropriate to a reasonably competent member of his profession. (*Greaves & Co.* v. *Baynham Meikle & Partners*, 1974.)[638] He may, therefore, be negligent even though he does his best. However, barristers provide an exception to this rule because no action lies against them for negligence in conducting a case (*Rondel* v. *Worsley, 1967*)[40] or possibly in preparatory work or advice. (*Saif Ali* v. *Sydney Mitchell & Co.*, 1977.)[39] In other cases public policy may also require a higher standard of care than the defendant possesses so that again he may be negligent even though he does his best. Thus in *Nettleship* v. *Weston*, 1971[524] the plaintiff, who was a non-professional driving instructor, was injured when he was a passenger in the defendant learner-driver's car which crashed into a lamp-standard. The Court of Appeal held that the defendant was liable to the plaintiff for negligence and both Lord Denning and Megaw, L.J. said that the standard of care in such circumstances was the same as that owed by the learner-driver to the injured non-passenger, i.e. the standard of the experienced and competent driver. This, apparently, was essential to avoid a doctrine of 'varying standards' per Megaw, L.J. at p. 592. According to Lord Denning, public policy was also involved. In the course of his judgment he said: 'The high standard thus imposed by the judges is, I believe, largely the result of the policy of the Road Traffic Acts. Parliament requires every driver to be insured against third party risks. The reason is so that a person injured by a motor car should not be left to bear the loss on his own, but should be compensated out of the insurance fund. . . . But the injured person is only able to recover if the driver is liable in law. So the judges see to it that he is liable, unless he can prove care and skill of a high standard. . . .' Lord Denning's word's have even more point now that passenger risk insurance is compulsory by law.

It should be noted that if precautions are taken which would have been reasonable in the case of persons possessed of the usual faculties of sight and hearing, this will be sufficient to absolve a person who does injury to those not possessed of such faculties, so long as he was not aware of their infirmity. (*Paris* v. *Stepney Borough Council,* 1951.)[639] However, persons engaged on operations on the *highway* must act reasonably so as not to cause damage to those who are using the highway, including blind people. (*Haley* v. *London Electricity Board,* 1964.)[640] Furthermore, the court will take into account the importance of the object which the defendant was trying to achieve (*Watt* v. *Hertfordshire County Council,* 1954)[641] and whether it was practicable and necessary for the defendant to have taken the precautions which the plaintiff alleged should have been taken. (*Latimer* v. *A.E.C. Ltd,* 1953.)[642]

(iii) Resulting damage to the plaintiff. It is necessary for the plaintiff to show that he has suffered some loss, since negligence is not actionable *per se* (in itself). The major problem arising here is the question of remoteness of damage which was dealt with earlier in the chapter. The judge decides the measure of general damages.

Res ipsa loquitur

Although the burden of proof in negligence normally lies on the plaintiff, there is a principle known as *res ipsa loquitur* (the thing speaks for itself), and where the principle applies the court is prepared to lighten his burden. The principle applies wherever it is so unlikely that such an accident would have happened without the negligence of the defendant that the court could find, without further evidence, that it was so caused. It seems also to be a commonsense rule in that there is no point in asking the plaintiff to prove negligence because he has no view of what happened. If two cars collide on a public road, at least the drivers have a view of what happened prior to the crash but when, for example, a barrel falls out of a warehouse onto A he has no view at all of the happenings leading to the impact.

However, two conditions must be satisfied—

(a) the thing or activity causing the harm must be wholly under the control of the defendant or his servants (*Easson* v. *L.N.E. Rly Co.,* 1944)[643] and

(b) the accident must be one which would not have happened if proper care had been exercised. (*Byrne* v. *Boadle,* 1863[644] and *Scott* v. *London & St Katherine Docks Co.,* 1865.)[645]

There is no value in the principle where there is no indication of who is the person likely to have been negligent, as where the events leading up to the accident were, or might well have been, under the control of others besides the defendant. (*Roe* v. *Minister of Health,* 1954.)[646]

It should be noted that just because the principle *res ipsa loquitur* applies, it is not certain that the plaintiff will succeed; the court is not bound to find the defendant negligent. The defendant may be able to prove how the accident happened and that he was not negligent. (*Pearson* v. *North Western Gas Board,* 1968.)[647] He may not know how the accident happened but he may be able to prove that it could not have arisen from his negligence. Finally, he may suggest ways in which the accident could have happened without his negligence, and the court may find his explanations convincing. If a tile falls off Y's roof and injures X who is lawfully on the highway below, this would probably be a situation in which *res ipsa loquitur* would apply. But if Y can show that at the time an explosion had occurred near by and this had probably dislodged the tile, and the court is impressed by this explanation of the event, the burden of proof reverts to X. However, it is not enough to offer purely hypothetical explanations (*Moore* v. *R. Fox and Sons,* [1956] 1 All E.R. 182), nor is it sufficient to explain how the accident happened unless the explanation also shows that the defendant was not negligent. (*Colville* v. *Devine,* [1969] 2 All E.R. 53.)

If the defendant successfully rebuts the presumption of *res ipsa loquitur* the plaintiff has to establish his case by positive evidence. He will probably be unable to do this by the very nature and cause of the accident and the chances are that he may lose his claim. If he had had such positive evidence he would probably have adduced it in the first place and not relied on the maxim at all.

Contributory negligence

Sometimes when an accident occurs, both parties have been negligent and this raises the doctrine of *contributory negligence*. At one time a plaintiff guilty of contributory negligence could not recover any damages unless the defendant could, with reasonable care, have avoided the consequences of the plaintiff's contributory want of care. Thus the courts were often concerned to find out who had the last chance of avoiding the accident, and this led to some unsatisfactory decisions.

Now, however, under the Law Reform (Contributory Negligence) Act, 1945, liability is apportionable between plaintiff and defendant. The claim is not defeated but damages may be reduced according to the degree of fault of the plaintiff. A person may contribute to the *damage* he suffers although he is not to *blame* for the accident. Thus failure by a plaintiff to wear a crash helmet on a motor cycle or scooter may reduce the damages he obtains on the ground of contributory negligence. (*O'Connell* v. *Jackson,* 1971.)[648] Similarly, failure by a plaintiff to wear a seat belt in a motor car may also reduce damages on the grounds of contributory negligence. (*Pasternack* v. *Poulton,* 1973.)[649] The defence of contributory negligence also applies to an action brought under the Fatal Accidents Act. Thus a wife whose husband failed to wear a seat belt and was thrown out of the van he was driving and killed had her damages reduced by one-fifth. (*Purnell* v. *Shields,* [1973] R.T.R. 414.)

Where the defendant is insured against the injury he has caused, which is often the case, the effect of a finding of contributory negligence is in a sense to punish the plaintiff. There have been suggestions that the rule should be abolished where the defendant is insured since the doctrine merely saves the insurance company money. Thus in *Smith* v. *Blackburn, The Times,* 18 May, 1974, O'Connor, J. distinguished the Court of Appeal decision in *O'Connell's* case[648] and *Pasternack*[649] because the leading case involved a crash helmet and proceeded to find that failure to wear a car seat belt does not amount to contributory negligence, at any rate if injury is suffered through the gross negligence of another. A grossly negligent driver's insurers should not be relieved from paying proper compensation when the injured person was doing nothing wrong. This view was also taken in *Chapman* v. *Ward, The Times,* 8 October, 1974 and *James* v. *Parsons, The Times,* 21 October, 1974. However, in *Froom* v. *Butcher,* [1975] 3 All E.R. 520, Lord Denning disapproved of these cases and held that where injuries resulting from a road accident would have been prevented or lessened if a fitted seat belt had been worn, the failure to wear a seat belt amounted to contributory negligence on the part of the plaintiff and damages awarded should therefore be reduced. In consequence Lord Denning has produced an additional definition of contributory negligence so that there are two, *viz.*—

(i) to contribute to the accident, which is the old view of contributory negligence; and

(ii) to contribute to the resulting damage, which is a new concept. Furthermore in *Froom* Lord Denning laid down a rather precise formula for contributory negligence by saying that if failure to wear a seat belt would have made no difference, then nothing should be taken off the damages. If it would have prevented the accident altogether the damages should be reduced by 25%, and if the accident would have been less severe the damages should be reduced by 15%, though exemptions would be made, said Lord Denning, for pregnant women and those who were very fat.

It should be mentioned that a young child will seldom, if ever, be guilty of contributory negligence (*Jones* v. *Lawrence,* 1969.)[650] Furthermore, the contributory negligence of an adult who happened to be with the child is no defence to an action brought by the child. (*Oliver* v. *Birmingham Bus Co.,* 1932.)[651]

The Doctrine of Alternative Danger or the 'Dilemma Principle'. It sometimes happens that a person is injured in anticipating negligence. If a passenger jumps off a bus which he believes to be out of control, and breaks his leg in so doing, he is not prejudiced by the fact that the driver later regains control and the anticipated accident is averted. He is not deprived of his remedy. This is sometimes referred to as the *doctrine of alternative danger,* and an act done in the agony of the moment cannot be treated as contributory negligence. Thus in *Jones* v. *Boyce,* (1816) 1 Starkie 493, in a coach accident, the plaintiff was placed by the negligence of the defendant in a perilous alternative either to jump or not to jump. He jumped off the coach and was injured and it transpired that had he kept his seat he would have escaped. However, he was able to recover from the defendant because he had acted reasonably and in the apprehension of danger.

Statutory Duties

Sometimes a particular duty of care is laid upon a person by statute, e.g. the duty laid on an employer as to guarding machinery under safety legislation. Such duties are high and very often absolute, though the employer can plead contributory negligence as a defence. In addition, where there is a breach of a statutory duty, it must be shown that the duty is owed to the plaintiff personally and not to the public as whole. (*Atkinson* v. *Newcastle Waterworks Co.,* 1877.)[652]

A conditional statutory power saying that the person upon whom it is conferred may act, cannot be converted into a statutory duty which says he must act. (*East Suffolk Rivers Catchment Board* v. *Kent,* 1941.)[628] However, where a statute prescribes provision to prevent damage, if an action is to be brought, the harm resulting from the breach of duty must be of the type contemplated by the statute. (*Gorris* v. *Scott,* 1874,[653] and *Lane* v. *London Electricity Board,* 1955.)[55]

LIABILITY FOR MIS-STATEMENTS

We have already considered the major principles of the *tort of deceit* in chapter 7 (p. 216) but it is perhaps worth repeating that deceit occurs where there is a false statement of fact made knowing it to be false, or believing it to be false, or recklessly not caring whether it be true or false. If it is made with the intention that it should be acted upon by another and is so acted upon there are grounds for an action. (*Derry* v. *Peek,* 1889.)[247]

It should also be noted that fraudulent misrepresentations as to a person's *credit* are not actionable unless they are in writing and signed by the defendant. (Lord Tenterden's Act, 1828.) However, the Act does not apply to negligent misstatements. (*Anderson (W.B.) & Sons* v. *Rhodes (Liverpool),* 1967.)[654]

Where monetary loss results from the defendant's negligent misstatements rather than his acts, it was, but is now no longer, necessary to prove the existence of a contract or fiduciary relationship in order to establish a duty of care (*Candler* v. *Crane, Christmas & Co.,* 1951,[655] *Hedley Byrne & Co. Ltd* v *Heller & Partners Ltd,* 1963[248] and *Anderson (W.B.) & Sons* v. *Rhodes (Liverpool),* 1967)[654] and the same is true if the plaintiff receives physical injuries as a result of the defendant's careless instructions. (*Clayton* v. *Woodman & Son (Builders) Ltd,* 1961.)[656] However, in the *Hedley Byrne*[248] case the House of Lords ruled that there must be a 'special relationship' between the person making the statement and the person relying upon it before a duty of care can arise. Since this aspect of the law of negligence is still being developed it is unwise to be too dogmatic with regard to what constitutes this 'special relationship'. However, Lord Morris said of it in the *Hedley Byrne* case—

> I consider that if follows and that it should now be regarded as settled that if someone possessed of a special skill undertakes, quite irrespective of contract, to apply that skill for the assistance of another person who relies on such skill, a duty of care will arise. . . . Furthermore, if, in a sphere in which a person is so placed that others could reasonably rely on his judgment or his skill or on his ability to make careful inquiry, a person takes it on himself to give information or advice to, or allows his information or advice to be passed on to, another person who, as he knows or should know, will place reliance on it, then a duty of care will arise.

Lord Hodson also agreed with that view. However, in *Mutual Life Assurance* v. *Evatt,* 1971,[657] the Privy Council took a somewhat narrower view of this form of liability, though Lord Morris's statement is wide enough to cover the facts of *Evatt's* case. The Privy Council seems to have restricted the decision in *Hedley Byrne* to cases where the advice is given by a person who is or purports to be an expert, whereas if Lord Morris's view is accepted a person who gives advice, at least on a topic with which he is familiar and competent to deal could be responsible for damage resulting from that advice if given erroneously. The fact that less-informed persons rely on the advice of better-informed persons is well known and where this happens, at least in a business context, there should be a duty of care. Decisions of the Privy Council are not, of course, binding on English Courts so that the decision in *Evatt's* case does not prevent the Court of Appeal or the House of Lords from reaching wider conclusions in a subsequent case. (See *Esso Petroleum* v. *Mardon,* 1976.)[658]

However, it is clear that professional men such as accountants and bankers are likely to be caught by the rule in the *Hedley Byrne*[248] case when they give a reference or advice. (*Dutton* v. *Bognor Regis* U.D.C., 1971.)[659] The rule also applies to render a local authority liable in damages when erroneous information is given to a person asking for search of the local land register. (*Coats Patons (Retail)* v. *Birmingham Corporation*, (1971) 69 L.G.R. 356.) An arbitrator is generally thought to enjoy the same immunity as a judge, at least when he is exercising the judicial function of deciding a dispute rather than merely answering a question. A valuer e.g. an auditor who on a sale values shares in a private company may also be immune if the parties who appoint him so agree, though otherwise he is liable in negligence. However, the House of Lords held in *Sutcliffe* v. *Thackrah*, (1974)[660], that when an architect issues an interim certificate stating that building work has been satisfactorily done, he does not act as an arbitrator and can therefore be made liable for negligence. Furthermore a statement will not be actionable under *Hedley Byrne* unless it amounts to advice. (*McInerny* v. *Lloyds Bank*, 1973.)[661]

As we have seen the maker of the statement can avoid liability by an express disclaimer. (*Hedley Byrne & Co. Ltd* v. *Heller and Partners Ltd*, 1963.)[248] As regards the measure of damages for negligent mis-statment, *Kenny* v. *Hall, Paine & Foster*, (1976) 239 E.G. 355, is of interest. In that case it was said that where, as in *Mardon*[658] the negligent mis-statement had caused the aggrieved party to enter into a contract, damages should be assesed on the principle that one should forecast what would have been likely to happen if he had never entered into the contract and contrast it with his position as it was now as a result of entering into it. Damages should then try to put the aggrieved party in the position he would have been in if he had never entered into the contract at all. This should ensure the recovery of capital losses at least.

We have already seen in Chapter 7 (p. 216) that damages for negligent mis-statements are also obtainable—

(i) under the Misrepresentation Act, 1967, provided the parties are in a pre-contractual relationship;

(ii) where the parties are in a fiduciary relationship, e.g. solicitor and client;

(iii) under Sect. 43 of the Companies Act, 1948, promoters and directors are liable for negligent mis-statements in prospectuses though they have certain defences.

Injurious falsehood, which is concerned with such matters as slander of goods, is briefly considered on p. 371.

OCCUPIER'S LIABILITY

The question of the liability of occupiers of premises to persons suffering injury thereon may be regarded as a further aspect of negligence. The occupier is the person who has *de facto* control of the premises or the possession of them; it is a question of fact in each case and does not depend entirely on title. It should also be noted that occupation may be *shared* between two or more persons, (*Wheat* v. *E. Lacon & Co. Ltd*, 1966)[662] and that an employer may be vicariously liable for the torts of an employee who is acting within the scope of his employment. Thus in *Stone* v. *Taffe*, [1974] 3 All E.R. 1016, the owner of an hotel was liable when the manager failed to ensure that there was adequate lighting on the premises so that a guest fell and was killed.

If a person, whilst on another's premises, suffers injury from some defect in the premises, the liability or otherwise of the occupier will vary according to the capacity in which such a person was there. This branch of the law has been affected by the Occupiers' Liability Act, 1957, but in order to understand the effect of the Act, it is necessary to consider in outline the former position at common law.

The common law divided entrants on to premises into three categories—

(a) Invitees. These were persons who entered premises on business which concerned themselves and the occupier, and at his express or implied invitation, e.g. workmen carrying out repairs on the premises, guests in an hotel, and the audience at a theatre or other place of entertainment. To an invitee the occupier owed a duty not to expose him to any unusual or unexpected dangers of which the occupier was aware, or would have been aware, if he had acted as a reasonable man.

(b) Licensees. These were persons entering premises by mere permission of the occupier granted gratuitously, e.g. guests in a private house or persons permitted to take a short cut across land or users of public parks. To licensees the occupier owed a duty to warn of any concealed danger of which he was aware, this liability being limited to dangers actually known to him.

It may be said then that the difference in the duty of care owed to an invitee and a licensee was that the occupier was liable to the former for dangers of which *he ought to have been aware,* and to the latter for dangers of which *he was in fact aware,* regardless of who created the danger.

The Occupiers' Liability Act, 1957

The Act was passed largely because of the anomalies which arose out of the attempts made by the courts to classify persons in the categories of invitees and licensees. Such persons are now called visitors, a term which includes anyone to whom the occupier has given, or is deemed to have given, an invitation or permission to use the premises. It includes some persons who enter the premises by right of law, such as inspectors, but not those who cross land in pursuance of a public or private right of way. Such rights of way must be taken as they are found. (*Greenhalgh* v. *British Railways Board*, [1969] 2 All E.R. 114.) Implied permission to enter premises is a matter of fact to be decided in the circumstances of each case, and the burden of proof is upon the person who claims implied permission.

However, persons who enter upon premises for purposes of business which they believe will be of interest to the occupier, as where they wish to sell him a product, have implied permission to enter even though their presence is distasteful to the occupier.

Under the Act, an occupier of premises owes to all visitors the duty to take such care as, in all the circumstances of the case, is necessary to see that the visitor will be reasonably safe in using the premises for the purpose for which he is invited permitted to be there. If the visitor uses the premises for some other purpose, the occupier does not owe him the same duty; such a person is in effect a trespasser, and liability to him falls to be decided on that basis. (See below.)

The occupier may restrict or exclude his liability, by giving adequate warning or by contract (but see preface). However, an occupier cannot exclude his liability to a person who has entered in the exercise of a right conferred by law, e.g. a factory inspector.

Where the accident has arisen through the defective work of an independent contractor, the occupier can avoid liability by showing that he behaved reasonably in the selection of the contractor and that, so far as he was able, he inspected the work done. (*Cook* v. *Broderip*, 1968.)[663]

The occupier may assume that persons who come on to his premises to exercise their calling will appreciate and guard against any special risks normally involved. The defence of *volenti non fit injuria* is available to the occupier, though he must show that the entrant assented to the risk, not that he merely knew of it: the entrant's knowledge is no longer a defence. (*Bunker* v. *Charles Brand & Son*, 1969.)[664]

The occupier may also raise the defence of *contributory negligence* by the entrant which, though not defeating his claim, may reduce damages.

Trespassers. Formerly, a trespasser took property as he found it in so far as his injuries were caused by the condition of the land or any structures erected on the land. However, an occupier was not allowed to set traps for trespassers and it appeared that in respect of injuries caused to trespassers by some *activity* carried out on the land by the occupier there was a duty of care towards a trespasser whose presence was reasonably foreseeable. (*Videan* v. *British Transport Commission*, 1963.)[521] The matter was fully considered by the House of Lords in *British Railways Board* v. *Herrington*, 1972[665] and more recently by the Privy Council in *Southern Portland Cement* v. *Cooper*, 1974.[666] As a result of these decisions it seems that while an occupier does not owe the same duty of care to a trespasser which he owes to a visitor, he owes a trespasser a duty to take such steps as common sense or common humanity would dictate to exclude or warn or otherwise within reasonable and practical limits to reduce or avert a danger. (*Herrington's* case.)[665] In addition, it appears that there is a financial constraint in that an occupier's duty towards potential trespassers is to do what a humane man with the occupier's *financial and other limitations* would do in the particular circumstances to prevent injury. This financial restriction is unfortunate in that an impecunious occupier presumably can get away with a lower standard of care. There seems no reason for such a financial restriction in view of the fact that most risks can be insured against these days. Furthermore, the test of foreseeability as advanced by Lord Denning, M.R. in *Videan*[521] contained no element of financial restriction and may well be a better test.

It is by no means certain whether it is possible to exclude the new duty of common humanity by exception clauses or other forms of consent. It may be that in creating the new duty of common humanity the courts have set minimum standards of conduct which are irreducible in terms of exception clauses (and see preface).

Children on premises.   Dealings with children always demand a high degree of care, whether a person is sued in the capacity of an occupier of premises or not (*Yachuk* v. *Oliver Blais & Co. Ltd,* 1949.)[667] However, in the case of an occupier of premises, the duty towards children was rather different from the corresponding duty to adults. If, with knowledge of the trespass of children on his land, the occupier made no reasonable attempt to prevent such trespass, e.g. by repairing fences, and a child was injured by something on the land which was especially alluring to children e.g. turntables, escalators, bright and poisonous berries, then the occupier in general was liable, even though the child was on the face of it a trespasser. (*Gough* v. *National Coal Board,* 1954.)[668] It should also be noted that what is adequate warning to an adult might not be so to a child. (*Mourton* v. *Poulter,* 1930[669] and *Pannett* v. *McGuinness & Co.,* 1972.)[670]

The difference owed to child trespassers and adult trespassers is no longer so great in view of the broader rules laid down in *Herrington*[665] and *Southern Portland Cement.*[666]

As regards landlord and tenant, Sect. 4 of the Occupiers Liability Act, 1957, provided that a landlord would be liable to his tenants' visitors who were injured or whose goods were damaged on the demised premises because of some defect which resulted from his failure to repair . However, Sect. 4 only applied where the landlord was under an obligation express, implied or statutory to repair, but the Defective Premises Act, 1972, which came into force on 1 January, 1974, also places liability on a landlord who has merely reserved a right to enter and repair. Thus, now that Sect. 4 of the 1957 Act is repealed, the landlord's liability is similar to his liability in nuisance. Of course, only an occupier can sue in nuisance but under the Defective Premises Act, 1972, the landlord is liable to all persons who might reasonably be expected to be affected by defects in the state of the premises. This covers not only the tenant, his family and his visitors, but also neighbours, passers-by and possibly trespassers. Furthermore, under the 1957 Act it became established that a landlord was only liable to his tenants' visitors if he had been notified of the defect by the tenant. However, Sect. 4(2) of the 1972 Act provides that the duty is owed where the landlord knew or ought to have known of the relevant defect, so notice given by the tenant is no longer essential. Where the lease or tenancy expressly imposes on the tenant a duty to inform the lessor of defects but the tenant fails to do so with the consequence that a third party is injured, then the landlord can still be sued provided it can be shown that he ought to have known of the defect but in this case he will have a right of indemnity against the tenant for what that may be worth.

Where the person injured is the tenant himself the 1972 Act allows a tenant to sue his landlord for breach of his statutory duty but then the lessor would be able to allege contributory negligence in that the tenant failed to notify him of the defect. Where, however, the defect was due to a tenant failing to carry out an obligation expressly imposed on him by the lease or tenancy, the landlord does not owe the tenant any duty, although he would still owe a duty to third parties if they were injured but in these circumstances could recover an indemnity or contribution from the tenant who would be a joint tortfeasor.

There is little a landlord can do to exclude or restrict his liability. Section 6(3) of the 1972 Act renders void any exclusion clause in a lease or tenancy agreement.

Reform. The Law Commission has published its provisional proposals for changing the liability of occupiers to trespassers in Working Paper No. 52. Two possible lines of action are suggested—

(*a*) to include trespassers in the Occupiers Liability Act and leave the fact that the entrant was a trespasser to be taken into account in deciding where the care taken was reasonable in the circumstances, or,

(*b*) to exclude the duty of care to trespassers in general but to include it in respect of those whom the occupier ought, as a reasonable man, to have contemplated as likely to be affected by his acts or omissions. All non-visitors should be treated in the same way, i.e. trespassers, or users of a public or private right of way and entrants on land by virtue of an access agreement or under the National Parks Act, 1949.

Clauses exempting the occupier from liability should not be banned but provisions limiting his right should apply to all entrants whether trespassers or not. In particular, an absolute prohibition on conditions in tickets of entry, programmes, etc., where death or personal injury is involved should be enacted and a reasonableness test should apply in other cases. The defence of *volenti* should also be abolished (and see preface).

HIGHWAY AUTHORITIES

A highway authority is liable for damage which is caused by its *active misfeasance* and, under the Highways (Miscellaneous Provisions) Act, 1961, Sect. 1(1) for damage which arises from its failure to repair.

In an action for damages against a highway authority based upon its failure to repair, it is a defence to prove that the authority has in all the circumstances taken reasonable care to ensure that the highway was not dangerous (Sect. 1(2)). (*Griffiths* v. *Liverpool Corporation*, 1966.)[671]

DEFECTIVE PREMISES ACT, 1972

This Act brings about three major changes. In the first place a landlords liability for defects in demised premises is increased. This has already been dealt with in occupiers liability (see p. 358). Secondly, much of the common law immunity of a vendor or landlord for negligence is abolished. Thirdly, there is a statutory duty on those concerned with providing dwellings to do the work properly. Section 1 places a duty on builders and developers, sub-contractors, architects and local authorities to see that building contracts are carried out in a workmanlike, of where appropriate, professional manner with proper materials so that the dwelling is fit for habitation. It should be noted that this statutory duty is owed not merely to the immediate client but to everyone who acquires a legal or equitable interest in the dwelling. The liability does not, of course, last for ever. It is subject to the Limitation Acts, though Sect. 1(5) or the 1972 Act provides that a cause of action accrues at the time when the dwelling was completed, but where further work has to be done to put right a fault then the cause of action accrues only when the further work is completed. This means that from that date a plaintiff has six years to start an action or three years where the defect has caused death or personal injury. Section 6(3) of the 1972 Act renders void any term of an agreement which purports to exclude or restrict this statutory duty.

Under Sect. 1(3) a mere agreement by a client to a particular design or specification being used does not discharge the builder or other persons involved from this statutory duty. Section 2 offers an alternative by providing that no action can be brought where a state approved scheme has conferred rights on the first sale or letting to those who have or will have an interest in the property in respect of defects in the state of the dwelling. Such schemes can be approved or withdrawn by the Secretary of State by statutory instrument.

The National Housebuilders Registration Council scheme is approved under these arrangements and where an N.H.R.C. scheme is in operation it applies rather than the Act. The advantage of an N.H.R.C. scheme over the Act is that if the builder becomes bankrupt the Council compensates the claimant. Section 3 of the Act sweeps away most of the old common law immunity from liability for negligence which was formerly enjoyed by sellers of property and lessors of property; they are now liable under the wider rule under *Donoghue* v. *Stevenson,* 1932.[468] Thus under the 1972 Act the maxim *caveat emptor* no longer provides a defence to a claim of negligence against a vendor or lessor in respect of defects in the premises sold or let and this liability extends beyond the immediate purchaser or lessee and can be brought by others who buy or rent the property within the constraints of the Limitation Acts, 1939 and 1954 and Sect. 1(5) of the 1972 Act.

EMPLOYER'S NEGLIGENCE

Where an employee's case is based on his employer's negligence *at common law,* he will have to prove that his injury was the result of the employer's breach of a duty of care. The employee is assisted in this task because certain specific duties of an employer were laid down by the House of Lords in the leading case of *Wilsons and Clyde Coal Co.* v. *English,* [1938] A.C. 57, and an employer must take reasonable care to provide—

(i) *proper and safe plant and appliances* for the work;
(ii) *a safe system of work* with adequate supervision and instruction;
(iii) *safe premises*; and
(iv) *a competent staff* of fellow employees.

The employer's duty is a personal one so that he remains liable even though he has delegated the performance of the duty to a competent independent contractor. Thus in *Paine* v. *Colne Valley Electricity Supply Co. Ltd,* [1938] 4 All E.R. 803, an employer was held liable for injuries to his employee caused by the failure of contractors to install sufficient insulation in an electrical kiosk.

However, in *Davie* v. *New Merton Board Mills,* [1958] 1 All E.R. 67, the House of Lords decided that an employer was not liable for damage caused by a defective implement purchased from a reputable manufacturer. The employee was thus left to sue the manufacturer and this could prove difficult where the manufacturer had left the country or gone out of business or could not for any other reason be identified. Now the Employer's Liability (Defective Equipment) Act, 1969, provides that an employee who is injured because of a defect in his employer's equipment can recover damages from the employer if he can show that the defect is due to the fault of some person, e.g. the manufacturer but if no one is at fault damages are not recoverable. Agreements by employees to contract out are void, and rights under the Act are *in addition* to common law rights. Thus, an injured employee can sue a third party such as a manufacturer if he wishes, e.g. as where the employer is insolvent, though the Employer's Liability (Compulsory Insurance) Act, 1969, requires employers to insure against their liability for personal injury to their employees. The injury must result from equipment provided for the employer's *business.* Thus, domestic servants injured by household equipment would not be covered.

There are numerous statutes which are designed to protect the health, and provide for the welfare and safety of employees. The relevance of such statutes for our present purposes is that where the breach of a statutory duty, e.g. failure to fence a dangerous machine, has caused injury to a worker, he may be able to sue his employer for damages by using the breach of statutory duty to establish the duty of care under the principles already discussed. (*Millard* v. *Serck Tubes Ltd,* 1969.)[672]

TORTS AGAINST BUSINESS INTERESTS

It is a tort knowingly to induce a person to *break his contract* with a third party whereby that party suffers damage. It is also an actionable wrong for two or more persons to combine together (*or conspire*) for the purpose of wilfully causing damage to the plaintiff. There is also an action for *passing off* which occurs where A represents his goods or services to be those of B.

Inducement of breach of contract

If A induces B to break his contract with C, C can sue A. (*Lumley* v. *Gye,* 1853[673] and *Daily Mirror Newspapers* v. *Gardner,* 1968.)[674]

Trade union activity often involves interference with contract and in this connection the Trade Union and Labour Relations Act, 1974, provides that an act done in contemplation or furtherance of a *trade dispute* is not actionable *simply because* it induces another person to break a contract of employment.

Furthermore, if A threatens to act unlawfully against B intending that B will act to the detriment of C, then A has committed the tort of intimidation, and if C suffers damage he will have a right of action against A. It is immaterial whether B's action in relation to C is or is not lawful. However, there is no action where A threatens a *lawful act* even though A's intention may be malicious. (*Allen* v. *Flood,* 1898.)[676]

An act done in contemplation or furtherance of a trade dispute is not actionable on the ground only that the intimidation involved consists in *threatening to break or to procure the breach of a contract.* (Trade Union and Labour Relations Act, 1974.) Threatening *other unlawful acts* is still actionable.

Conspiracy

Where two or more persons act without lawful justification for the purpose of wilfully causing damage to the plaintiff and actual damage results, they commit the tort of conspiracy. The tort was fully considered in *Crofter Hand Woven Harris Tweed Co. Ltd* v. *Veitch,* 1942,[677] where the following principles were laid down—

(i) the tort covers acts which would be *lawful if done by one person*;
(ii) the combination will be justified if the predominant motive is self-interest or protection of one's trade rather than injury to the plaintiff;
(iii) damage to the plaintiff must be proved.

It should be noted that under the Trade Union and Labour Relations Act, 1974, an act done in contemplation or furtherance of a trade dispute is not actionable simply because it was done in consequence of an agreement or combination.

Passing off

Any person, company or other organization which carries on or proposes to carry on business under a name calculated to deceive the public by confusion with the name of an existing concern, commits the civil wrong of *passing off* and will be restrained by injunction from doing so. Other examples of passing off are the use of similar wrappings, identification marks, and descriptions. Thus in *Bollinger* v. *Costa Brava Wine Co. Ltd*, [1959] 3 All E.R. 800, the champagne producers of France objected to the use of the name 'Spanish Champagne' to describe a sparkling wine which was made in Spain and they were granted an injunction to prevent the use of that term. The remedies other than an injunction are an action for damages or for an account of profits.

DEFAMATION

Defamation is the publication of a statement which tends to lower a person in the estimation of right-thinking members of society generally, or which tends to make them shun or avoid that person. (*Byrne* v. *Deane*, 1937.)[678] In order to constitute a tort the statement must be false and capable of bearing a defamatory meaning. Lord Reid in *Lewis* v. *Daily Telegraph Ltd*, [1964] A.C. 234 at p. 258 indicated how a trial judge might proceed in deciding whether words in their ordinary and natural meaning are capable of bearing a defamatory meaning. 'What the ordinary man would infer without special knowledge has generally been called the natural and ordinary meaning of the words. But the expression is rather misleading in that it conceals the fact that there are two elements in it. Sometimes it is not necessary to go beyond the words themselves, as where the plaintiff has been called a thief or a murderer. But more often the sting is not so much in the words themselves as in what the ordinary man will infer from them, and that is also regarded as part of their natural and ordinary meaning. . . . In this case it is, I think, sufficient to put the test in this way. Ordinary men and women have different temperaments and outlooks. Some are unusually suspicious, and some are unusually naive. One must try to envisage people between these two extremes and see what is the most damaging meaning they would put on the words in question.' In consequence the ordinary and natural meaning of words is to be gathered not only by considering a strictly literal interpretation but also from the inference which would be drawn by the ordinary person who heard or read the words.

The essence of the tort is the publication or communication of the falsehood to at least one person other than the person defamed, and other than the author's own husband or wife. Every successive repetition of the statement is a fresh commission of the tort. Hence a defamatory statement written upon a postcard is published by the sender not only to the ultimate recipient but also to the postal officials through whose hands it may pass, and to every individual who legitimately handles the message, e.g. the secretary of the sender or the receiver. Similarly a libel contained in a newspaper is published by the reporter or author, and by the editor, the printer, the publisher, the proprietor, the wholesaler and the retail seller of that newspaper.

The third person who receives the defamatory statement must be capable of appreciating its significance. A written defamatory statement cannot be published to a blind man except in Braille. It is not publication to repeat a defamatory statement in a foreign language in the presence only of persons who cannot understand the tongue. But if X writes a defamatory statement to Y in (say) German, knowing that Y cannot understand it, X will be responsible for the publication which results from Y's showing it to a linguist for the purpose of translation. In addition, to constitute publication, the person to whom the statement is communicated must understand that it refers to the plaintiff.

No action lies at civil law for defaming a dead person, no matter how much it may annoy or upset his relatives. There may possibly be a prosecution for criminal libel if the necessary or natural effect of the words used is to render a breach of the peace imminent or probable.

Libel and slander

The form of publication determines whether the tort committed is libel or slander. *Libel* is defamation in some permanent form; *slander* is a statement of a like kind in transient form. Pictures, effigies, writing and print are clearly libel. Speech is slander, and probably gestures and facial mimicry also. It has been held that a defamatory sound film was a libel (*Youssoupoff* v. *M.G.M. Pictures,* 1934),[679] and legislation states that the broadcasting of defamatory matter is libel, whether sound or visual images are transmitted. (Defamation Act, 1952, Sect. 1.) (See also Theatres Act, 1968, p. 370.)

It is necessary to determine whether a tort is libel or slander for two reasons—

(i) Libel may be a crime as well as a tort;
(ii) Libel is actionable without the plaintiff having to prove special damage, i.e. pecuniary loss, whereas the plaintiff in an action for slander must as a general rule prove such special damage.

Slander is actionable without proof of special damage in the following cases—

(*a*) Where there is an imputation that the plaintiff has been guilty of a criminal offence punishable with imprisonment.

(*b*) Where there is an imputation of unchastity to any woman or girl (Slander of Women Act, 1891). This probably includes the case where a woman is alleged to have been the victim of rape.

(*c*) Where there is an imputation that the plaintiff is suffering from venereal disease, and possibly other contagious diseases, e.g. leprosy or plague, which might cause him to be shunned and avoided.

(*d*) Where there have been words calculated to disparage the plaintiff in any office, profession, business or calling, by imputing dishonesty, unfitness or incompetence. (Defamation Act, 1952, Sect. 2.)

A suggestion, therefore, that a clergyman has been guilty of immoral conduct, or that a solicitor knows no law is actionable without proof of special damage. Spoken words in a broadcast are now actionable *per se* since they are regarded as libel. (Defamation Act, 1952, Sect. 1.)

It is not enough that the words are abusive. This say of A, a bricklayer, that he is a legal ignoramus is not defamatory, though the same words would be defamatory if said of B, a solicitor. Difficulties might arise if the words were said of a chartered accountant who is required to have a knowledge of certain branches of the law.

To resolve problems such as these, two questions must be answered—

(i) Are the alleged words capable of bearing a meaning which is defamatory of the plaintiff? (This is a matter of law and is decided by the judge.)

(ii) If so, in this particular case are the words in fact defamatory of the plaintiff? (This is a matter of fact to be decided by the jury.)

Innuendo

Cases may arise where the words are not at first sight defamatory, and only appear as such when the surrounding circumstances have been explained. Again a statement may be ironical, or accompanied by a wink or a gesture, or it may be ambiguous, e.g. the statement that 'X drinks'. In such a case the plaintiff must show that the words contain an innuendo or hidden meaning and that reasonable persons could, and in fact would, interpret the *words* used in a defamatory sense. (*Cassidy* v. *Daily Mirror Newspapers Ltd*, 1929.)[680] However, a newspaper article may be defamatory of a person whom readers only identify from their own knowledge of extrinsic facts. The defamation need not arise from words themselves. (*Morgan* v. *Odhams Press*, 1971.)[681] The judge decides as a matter of law whether the words are capable of bearing the innuendo alleged by the plaintiff, and the jury decides whether in fact the words do bear that meaning. (*Tolley* v. *Fry & Sons*, 1931.)[682] The meaning sought to be placed upon the words by the innuendo pleaded must be reasonable, and the court will not read into a statement a defamatory sense which is not there on a reasonable interpretation. (*Sim* v. *Stretch*, 1936.)[683] Furthermore, a plaintiff who claims that the innuendo to be drawn by those with special knowledge of the facts from a publication is libellous is bound to particularize those readers of the publication whom he alleges to have such special knowledge. (*Fulham* v. *Newcastle Chronicle and Journal*, 1977.)[684]

Reference to the plaintiff

If the judge decides that the words are capable of bearing a defamatory meaning, he must then consider whether the words are capable of referring to the plaintiff. This again is a question of law. If he finds the answer to be yes, he must leave to the jury the question: 'Do the words in fact refer to the plaintiff?' This is a simple matter where the plaintiff has been referred to by name, and until recently the rule was that an author used a name at his peril if it turned out that it could reasonably be taken to refer to the plaintiff. Indeed the more obscure the name selected, the greater the chance of success of a plaintiff who bore that name should he sue for libel. (*Hulton & Co.* v. *Jones,* 1910.)[685] It is not uncommon to attach a disclaimer at the beginning of a work of fiction: 'The persons and events described in this book are wholly imaginary,' but it is doubtful whether this affects the author's liability.

The practical restriction on so-called 'gold-digging' actions was the power of the jury to award contemptuous damages of a farthing, but the costs involved in defending an action might well lead a defendant to settle out of court for a substantial sum. The position has been modified by the Defamation Act, 1952, Sect. 4, which provides for an offer of amends which will be dealt with later.

It sometimes happens that a whole class of persons is the subject of a defamatory statement. Here a member of the class may only sue if he can show that he himself is the person pointed out by the defamatory statement. (*Knupffer* v. *London Express Newspaper Ltd*, 1944[686] and *Schloimovitz* v. *Clarendon Press*, 1973.)[687]

Words may, of course, be defamatory of the plaintiff without his being mentioned by name, if the statement can be shown to apply to him. (*Youssoupoff* v. *M.G.M.,* 1934.)[679]

The defendant's motives are generally immaterial. The most laudable motives will not by themselves prevent a defamatory statement from being actionable. But where the defendant puts his motives in issue, as where he pleads fair comment or qualified privilege, or relies on Sect. 4 of the Defamation Act, 1952 (unintentional defamation), the plaintiff may then prove the malice of the defendant, or improper motive, to rebut the defence.

Defences

There are certain special defences which are peculiar to an action for defamation, but these defences do not preclude a defendant from denying in addition that the words are defamatory, or asserting that they do not refer to the plaintiff, or that they were not published.

Justification. As the essence of defamation is a false statement, a defendant may always plead the truth of the statement as a defence in civil proceedings (but not in an action for criminal libel, where the rule is: 'The greater the truth, the greater the libel,' since true libels are more likely to influence passions). If the statement is true, no injury is done to the plaintiff's reputation; it is simply reduced to its true level.

In the defence of justification the defendant asserts that the statements are 'true both in substance and in fact'. He must show not merely that the words are literally true, but also that there are no significant omissions which would affect the truth of the statement taken as a whole. If, however, the statement is essentially true, an incidental inaccuracy will not deprive the defendant of his right to justify. (*Alexander* v. *N.E. Railway Co.*, 1865.)[688]

The defence of justification really amounts to a positive charge against the plaintiff, and if it fails the damages may be increased, since the original wrong has been aggravated. The defendant's honest belief that the statement is true is no justification, though it may reduce damages. Nor is it a justification to prove that a quoted statement was made, if the quotation cannot be proved to be true. Suppose a statement is made: 'Mrs A tells me that Dr B has been committing adultery with a woman patient.' It is no justification to show that Mrs A made the statement to the defendant; he must show that Dr B is actually guilty of the conduct alleged.

In connection with this defence, it is important to note Sect. 5 of the Defamation Act, 1952, which provides that in an action for libel and slander in respect of words containing two or more distinct charges against a plaintiff, a defence or justification shall not fail by reason only that the truth of every charge is not proved if the words not proved to be true do not materially injure the plaintiff's reputation having regard to the truth of the remaining charges.

In connection with justification it should be noted that under Sect. 8 of the Rehabilitation of Offenders Act, 1974 (see further p. 57) a plaintiff who proves that the defendant has maliciously published details of a spent conviction may recover damages. However, the section does not affect the defences of absolute or qualified privilege and fair comment. Thus an employer will, in the absence of malice, still be protected if he writes a reference which mentions a spent conviction.

Fair comment on a matter of public interest.   Here the defendant must show that the statement alleged to be defamatory is in fact legitimate comment. The statement must be comment, i.e. the speaker's opinion of a true state of affairs; it must not be an assertion of facts, but a comment on known facts. (*London Artists* v. *Littler*, 1969.)[689] The comment must be fair, that is, honestly believed in by the defendant, and made without any malicious or improper motive.

Comment is the individual reaction to facts, and the court and the jury require to be satisfied only of the defendant's honesty. The test is; 'Would any honest man, however prejudiced he may be, however exaggerated or obstinate his views, have said that which this criticism has said of what is criticized?' If the answer is, 'yes', the comment is fair for the purposes of raising this defence.

The matter upon which the comment is made must be one of legitimate public interest such as the conduct of Parliament, the Government, local authorities and other public authorities, or the behaviour of a trade union whose actions affect supplies and services to the public. Further, a matter may become the subject of public interest because the plaintiff has voluntarily submitted himself and his affairs to public criticism. A person who makes a public speech, or publishes a book, or presents a play thereby submits the subject matter of such thing for public comment, and cannot complain if the comment is adverse.

It should also be noted that the facts relied on to support a plea of fair comment must be facts existing at the time of the comment and not facts which have occurred some time before the comment was made. (*Cohen* v. *Daily Telegraph,* [1968] 2 All E.R. 407.)

Privilege. This defence protects statements made in circumstances where the public interest in securing a free expression of facts or opinion outweighs the private interests of the person about whom the statements are made. Privilege may be absolute—such a statement is never actionable—or qualified, when privilege may be defeated by proof of the defendant's malice.

Absolute privilege. The Bill of Rights, 1689, protects statements in either House of Parliament. The Parliamentary Papers Act, 1840, affords a similar protection to reports, papers, etc., published by order of either House, e.g. *Hansard* and Government White Papers. The Defamation Act, 1952, Sect. 9, protects verbatim broadcasts and newspaper reports of Parliamentary proceedings but Parliament itself can fine or imprison those who abuse this privilege.

With regard to the courts, statements by the judge, members of the jury, counsel, and the parties or witnesses are absolutely privileged, as are Orders of Court. Thus an Order of Court for divorce, including a finding of adultery against a woman, is not actionable even though reversed on appeal. A statement made by a witness is not actionable even though the judge finds it untrue and malicious. The abuse of the above privilege is checked by (*a*) the law of perjury (in the case of untrue statements by witnesses), (*b*) the power of the judge to report improper behaviour on the part of counsel to the Benchers of his Inn, and (*c*) the judge's general power to commit persons to prison for contempt of court.

Communications between senior and responsible public officers in the course of their duty are absolutely privileged.

Qualified privilege. Where such privilege exists, a person is entitled to communicate a defamatory statement so long as he does so honestly and reasonably with regard to the words used and the means of publication, and without malice. Qualified privilege has been held to arise in the following cases—

(i) Common interest, i.e. where a statement is made by a person who is under a legal or moral duty to communicate it to a person who has a similarly legitimate interest in receiving it. This covers testimonials or references to prospective employers, or to trade protection societies whose function it is to investigate the creditworthiness of persons who are the objects of their enquiry. (*London Association for the Protection of Trade* v. *Greenlands,* 1916.)[690]

(ii) Statements in protection of one's private interests are privileged. (*Osborn* v. *Thos Boulter and Son,* 1930.)[691]

(iii) Statements by way of complaint to a proper authority, e.g. petitions to Parliament and complaints to officials of local authorities and professional bodies. (*Beach* v. *Freeson,* 1971.)[692]

(iv) Professional confidential communications between solicitor and client on legal advice.

(v) Newspaper reports on various public matters. The Defamation Act, 1952, Sect. 7, confers qualified privilege upon fair and accurate newspaper reports of various matters of public interest and importance. These are of two classes—

(*a*) Those which are privileged without any explanation or contradiction being issued, e.g. reports of public proceedings of colonial or dominion legislatures, reports of public proceedings of the United Nations Organisation, of the International Court of Justice, or of British courts martial, and fair and accurate copies of and extracts from British public registers and notices.

(*b*) Those which are privileged only if the newspaper concerned is prepared, on the plaintiff's request, to publish a reasonable letter or statement in explanation or contradiction of the original report, e.g. semi-judicial findings of the governing bodies of learned societies, professional and trade associations, or authorities controlling games and sports. This also applies to fair and accurate reports of public meetings, meetings of local and public authorities, and the meetings of public companies.

(iv) Fair and accurate reports of Parliamentary proceedings are the subject of qualified privilege whether contained in a newspaper or not. (*Cook* v. *Alexander,* 1973.)[693]

(vii) Fair and accurate reports of public judicial proceedings are privileged. This does not protect reports of proceedings in domestic tribunals, e.g. The Law Society, unless the report is in a newspaper. Such reports will not be privileged if the court has forbidden publication, as is often done in cases affecting children, or if the matter reported is obscene or scandalous. It is also a criminal offence to report indecent matter relating to judicial proceedings. (Judicial Proceedings Act, 1926; Domestic and Appellate Proceedings etc. Act, 1968.)

Qualified privilege may be rebutted by proof of malice or some improper motive, and proof of actual spite or illwill in the publication will defeat it.

An improper motive may be inferred from the tone of the statement or from the circumstances attending its publication, and malice may also be inferred from abuse of the privilege, such as the giving of excessive publicity to statements protected by qualified privilege. However, the gross and unreasoning prejudice of the defendant will not defeat the defence of privilege if the defendant honestly believed that what he published was true. (*Horrocks* v. *Low,* 1972.)[694] But where a person without malice joins with a malicious person in publishing a libel in circumstances of qualified privilege, the person without malice is not liable to the person defamed. (*Egger* v. *Viscount Chelmsford,* 1964.)[695]

Offer of amends.   The Defamation Act, 1952, provides that the publisher of 'innocent defamation' may make an offer of amends as defined in the Act. (Sect. 4.) The words shall be treated as published innocently if the words were not defamatory on the face of them, and if the publisher did not know of circumstances by virtue of which they might be understood to be defamatory of the plaintiff, and if reasonable care was exercised in relation to the publication. Given that the above circumstances exist the defendant can apparently make an offer of amends, supported by an affidavit setting out the facts relied on to show that his publication was innocent.

An offer of amends requires the publication of a suitable apology to the party aggrieved and a suitable correction. The offeror must also take steps to notify persons to whom copies have been distributed that the words used are alleged to be defamatory of the party aggrieved. The High Court decides how the offer shall be carried into effect unless the parties have agreed on the matter.

It is a defence in any proceedings for defamation that the defendant's offer (i) has been accepted and performed, or (ii) that it has been refused, after having been made as soon as practicable after the defendant received notice that the words were or might be defamatory of the plaintiff, and that the offer has not been withdrawn.

If the plaintiff rejects the offer because he does not think the publication was innocent, or because the section of the Act has not been complied with, and fails to establish this at the trial, there seems no way of later enforcing the offer of amends.

Consent of the plaintiff to publication.   If the plaintiff has agreed to publication, he cannot subsequently sue in respect of that statement. (*Chapman* v. *Lord Ellesmere,* 1932.)[696] Consent may be given in respect of a particular publication, or it may be general.

Theatres Act, 1968

Section 4 of the Theatres Act, 1968, amends the law of defamation (including the law relating to criminal libel) by providing that the publication of words (including pictures, visual images, gestures, and the like) in the public performance of a play shall be treated as publication in permanent form, i.e. libel. Performances given on a domestic occasion in a private dwelling house are exempt (Sect. 7(1)) and so are rehearsals and performances for broadcast or recording purposes (Sect. 7(2)) provided such rehearsals and performances are attended only by the persons *directly* connected with the giving of them.

Section 5 of the Act creates an offence of incitement to racial hatred by presenting or directing the public performance of a play though again, rehearsals and performances attended only by persons directly concerned are exempt. Prosecution under Sect. 5 is with the consent of the Attorney General (Sect. 8).

It is of interest to note also that Sect. 1 of the Act abolishes the power of the Lord Chamberlain to censor plays.

Damages

Although many slanders are actionable only on proof of special damage to the plaintiff, actual damages awarded by the court will not be confined to the special damage so proved. For example, if as a result of defamation a man loses his employment, he can prove special damage in this connection, but the actual damages awarded may take in much more than this particular loss. Damages for defamation tend to be high. Juries are often used in such cases, and they are concerned with the *quantum* of damages. The damages awarded for loss of reputation may often be higher than damages awarded for the loss of life. However, damages should be compensatory and not punitive (*Rookes* v. *Barnard*, 1964,[675] and *Davis* v. *Rubin*, 1967),[697] though they may be *aggravated* by mental suffering arising from the defamation, or *mitigated* by a full apology, provocation by the plaintiff, or the plaintiff's bad reputation.

Injunctions

Apart from damages a defamed person may seek an injunction restraining further publication. Such injunctions are of two kinds—

(*a*) *A perpetual injunction,* which is usually granted at the trial, and

(*b*) *an interim injunction* (or interlocutory injunction), which is granted pending the trial, and may be *quia timet,* that is before the wrong is actually done.

However, publication of an article will not be restrained merely because it is defamatory where the defendant says he intends to justify it or make fair comment on a matter of public interest. (*Fraser* v. *Evans*, [1969] 1 All E.R. 8.)

Before concluding the tort of defamation we should notice also the separate tort of *injurious falsehood.* Just as defamation is an attack on a man's reputation, so injurious falsehood is an attack on his goods. To say that A's goods are inferior in quality to B's may be an injurious falsehood. To say that A sells inferior goods as goods of superior quality may, on the other hand, be a defamatory statement.

THE RULE IN *Rylands* v. *Fletcher*

This celebrated rule was stated in the case of *Rylands* v. *Fletcher*, 1868—

> Where a person for his own purposes brings and keeps on land in his occupation anything likely to do mischief if it escapes, he must keep it in at his peril, and if he fails to do so he is liable for all damage naturally accruing from the escape.

The rule has been held to apply whether the things brought on the land be 'beasts, water, filth or stenches'. The rule also applies to fire. (*Emanuel* v. *Greater London Council*, 1970.)[698] It does not apply to the pollution of beaches by oil because, *inter alia*, the oil does not escape from *land* but from the sea. (*Southport Corporation* v. *Esso Petroleum Co.*, 1954.)[584]

The duty is an absolute one and does not depend on negligence provided the use of the land is not natural use. (*British Celanese* v. *Hunt*, 1969.)[616] In the case which gave rise to the rule, the defendant had constructed a reservoir on his land, employing competent workmen for the purpose. Water escaped from the reservoir and percolated through certain old mine shafts, which had been filled with marl and earth, and eventually flooded the plaintiff's mine. The defendant was held liable in that he had collected water on his land, the water not being naturally there, and it had escaped and done damage. Since the defendant employed competent workmen, it follows that the liability is absolute and does not depend on negligence, and in any case the defendant's action was quite innocent as there was no reason why he should know of, or even suspect the existence of, the disused shafts.

In order for the rule to apply, there must be an escape of the thing which inflicts the injury from a place over which the defendant has occupation or control to a place which is outside his occupation or control. (*Read* v. *Lyons*, 1947.)[699]

The rule is not confined to wrongs between owners of adjacent land and does not depend on ownership of land (*Charing Cross Electricity Supply Co.* v. *Hydraulic Power Co.*, 1914),[700] but the plaintiff must have some interest in the land. (*Weller* v. *Foot and Mouth Disease Research Institute*, 1965.)[631] Neither is it confined to the escape of water, but may cover the escape of any offensive or dangerous matter arising out of abnormal use of land provided the defendant has control of it. (*Attorney-General* v. *Corke*, 1933[701] and *Smith* v. *Scott*, 1972.)[623] It seems doubtful at the moment whether the rule extends to personal injuries, and it may be that proof of negligence is always necessary in an action of this kind. (*Read* v. *Lyons*, 1947,[699] and *Perry* v. *Kendricks Transport*, 1956.)[702]

In general there is no liability under the rule for damage caused by the escape of things naturally on the land (*Giles* v. *Walker*, 1890),[703] though there may be an action in nuisance (*Davey* v. *Harrow Corporation*, 1957)[704] or in negligence.

Although *Rylands* v. *Fletcher* imposes strict liability, the following defences are still open to the defendant—

(*a*) That the escape was the plaintiff's fault. It should also be noted that there is no reason why the Law Reform (Contributory Negligence) Act, 1945, should not apply where the plaintiff is partly to blame.

(*b*) That it was an Act of God (*Nichols* v. *Marsland*, 1876),[527] though the defence is not often successfully pleaded. (*Greenock Corporation* v. *Caledonian Railway Co.*, 1917.)[705]

(*c*) That the escape was due to the wrongful act of a stranger. (*Rickards* v. *Lothian*, 1913,[706] and *Emanuel* v. *Greater London Council*, 1970.)[698]

(*d*) That the damage was caused by artificial works done for the common benefit of the plaintiff and the defendant. (*Peters* v. *Prince of Wales Theatre (Birmingham) Ltd*, 1943.)[707]

(*e*) That there was statutory authority for the act of the defendant, provided that the defendant was not negligent. It should be noted that the defence of statutory authority is not available in respect of reservoirs. (Reservoirs Act, 1975, Sect. 28 and Sched. 2.)

9 The Law of Property

English law divides property into real property and personal property. Real property includes only freehold interests in land, and personal property comprises all other proprietary rights, whether in land or chattels. This classification is not identical with the obvious distinction between immoveables and moveables, and this is the result of the attitude of early law to the nature of a lease.

THE NATURE OF PROPERTY

Actions in respect of property fall into two kinds: actions *in rem* or real actions, and actions *in personam* or personal actions. An action *in rem* in English law is an action in which a specific thing is recovered; an action *in personam* gives damages only.

It so happened that in early days the courts would allow a real action or *actio realis* only for the specific recovery of land. If an owner was dispossessed of other forms of property, the person who had taken the property had a choice; he could either restore the property taken or pay damages to the rightful owner. Hence land became known as real property or *realty,* and all other forms of property were called personal property or *personalty.* So far the distinction corresponds to that between moveables and immoveables, but this convenient classification was disturbed by the lease for a term of years.

Although a lease of land was an interest in immoveable property, the real action was not available to the dispossessed tenant. Leases did not fit into the feudal system of landholding by tenure but were regarded as personal business arrangements whereby one man allowed another the use of the land for a period in return for a rent.

These transactions were personal contracts and created rights *in personam* between the parties, and not rights *in rem* which could affect feudal status. It was not an uncommon form of investment to buy land and let it out on lease to obtain an income on capital invested, and such transactions were more akin to commercial dealings than to landholding as it was understood in early days. Moreover the system had its advantages, since a lease was immune from feudal burdens and could be bequeathed by will at a time when dispositions by will of other land were still not permitted.

Leaseholds, therefore, come under the heading of personal property or chattels, but because they partake so strongly of the character of land, they are often referred to as *chattels real* to distinguish them from pure personalty, e.g. a watch or a fountain pen. Since the property legislation of 1925 this distinction has lost much of its importance, but it is still true that if in his will a testator says 'All my personalty to P and all my realty to R,' P would get the leaseholds.

Pure personalty itself comprises two different kinds of property known as *choses in possession* and *choses in action*. Choses in possession denote chattels, such as jewellery and furniture, which are tangible objects and can be physically possessed and enjoyed by their owner. Choses in action are intangible forms of property which are incapable of physical possession, and their owner is usually compelled to bring an action if he wishes to enforce his rights over property of this kind. Examples of choses in action are debts, patents, copyrights, trade marks, shares, and negotiable instruments.

Up to now we have been considering in the main rights which one has in one's own things. However it is possible to have rights over the things of another. We have already mentioned the lease, which is the right to possess another's land for a term in return for a rent, but in addition it is possible to become the owner of a *servitude* over the land of another, e.g. a right of way, a right of light, or a right to the support of buildings. A servitude may also be a right to take something from the land of another, e.g. the right to fish or collect firewood. Rights of the first class are called *easements,* and of the second *profits à prendre*. Further, a person may raise a loan on the security of his property either real or personal, and the lender has certain rights over the property so used as a security if the loan is not repaid.

OWNERSHIP

Ownership is a term used to express the relationship which exists between a person and certain rights which are vested in him. Ownership is the greatest right or collection of rights—the ultimate right—which a person can have over or in a thing.

For example, X may own a fee simple in Blackacre and may lease the land to Y, so giving up possession. But however long the lease, the ultimate right of ownership is in X, and eventually the right to possess, which he has for the moment forfeited, will return to him or to his estate if he is dead. Z may have a right of way over Blackacre. This is not ownership of Blackacre, but is ownership of a right over it which limits X's enjoyment of the land. B may have lent money to X on the security of the land, so that B is a mortgagee and, therefore, the owner of a right in Blackacre, but this does not constitute ownership of the land; it is a mere encumbrance attached to it, limiting X's enjoyment to the extent of the rights given to B as mortgagee. Nevertheless the supreme right is vested in X, and this right is called ownership of Blackacre.

Ownership is a *de jure* relationship; there is no need to possess the thing. Possession tends to be *de facto,* i.e. evidenced by physical possession, although, as we shall see, physical possession is not necessary in order to have legal possession.

It may be said that in a general sense all rights are capable of ownership, which is of many kinds—

(a) Corporeal, i.e. the ownership of a thing or chose in possession such as a watch or a fountain pen.

(b) Incorporeal, i.e. the ownership of a right only, e.g the right to recover a debt of £20 from X by an action at law, or the ownership of a chose in action. A share certificate is a chose in action, and ownership of it is incorporeal, for it is ownership of certain rights: the right to dividends as and when declared, the right to vote at meetings, and so on.

(c) Sole ownership, as where X is the sole owner of Blackacre.

(d) Co-ownership, as where X and Y are simultaneously owners of Blackacre, as joint tenants or tenants in common.

(e) Legal or equitable ownership. Thus a grant giving X the fee simple absolute in possession of Blackacre constitutes him the legal owner. But a grant giving X a life interest only constitutes him as equitable owner, whose interest can exist only behind a trust, the legal estate being vested in trustees.

(f) Trust or beneficial ownership. In the grant set out above giving X a life interest, the trustees hold the legal estate but not beneficially; the beneficial interest is in X and Equity will protect it.

(g) Vested or contingent ownership. In a grant to X for life, with remainder to Y if he attains the age of eighteen years, X's interest is equitable and vested, Y's interest is equitable and contingent since he must satisfy the requirement of majority before his interest vests.

POSSESSION

The physical control of a thing by a person is what is normally known as possession, and if the idea of possession had remained wedded to physical control, the position would have been simple enough. But the widening sphere of legal activity made it necessary to attribute to persons who were not actually in physical control some or all of the advantages enjoyed by persons who were.

There are three possible situations at law—

(i) A person can have physical control without legal possession, as in the case of a porter carrying a traveller's suitcase in a station.

(ii) A person can have possession and its advantages without actual physical control, e.g. a person may have books at home which are still in his possession even when he is away on holiday.

(iii) A person can have both physical control and possession, e.g. a watch in his pocket or a pen in his hand.

Possession, therefore, has acquired a technical legal meaning, and the separation of possession from physical control has given the concept a high degree of flexibility.

The old theory of possession, derived from the Roman Law, relies upon (i) *corpus,* i.e. physical control, and (ii) *animus,* i.e. the intention to exclude others. But although these concepts help in deciding possession, they do not provide the complete answer. Indeed as Viscount Jowitt has said: 'In truth English law has never worked out a completely logical and exhaustive definition of possession.' The handing over of a key may be sufficient by itself to pass the possession of the contents of a room or box if it provides the effective means of control over the goods.

Wrongful Interference

In the law of torts, wrongful interference to property is an invasion of possession. The policy of this branch of the law is to compensate the party whose interests have been affected, and in order to enable such persons to recover, the court has contrived to attribute possession to them.

A *bailee* is a person who gets possession of a chattel from another with his consent. A bailment may be at will, i.e. revocable by the bailor at any time, or it may be for a term, i.e. for a fixed period of time. Where a bailment is at will, the bailee, who by definition has possession, can sue a third party for wrongful interference. Since the bailment is revocable at will, the bailor also has an interest worth protecting, and in order that he too may bring an action for wrongful interference, his right to possess is treated as possession itself. Where, on the other hand, the bailment is for a term, only the bailee can bring an action for wrongful interference and not the bailor, although, where the bailee brings the action, he will have to account to the bailor for any damages obtained.

Were an employer has temporarily handed a thing to his employee, possession remains with the employer and the employee takes only custody. Thus an employer can sue for wrongful interference for an injury to the goods by a third party.

A person who loses a thing retains his ownership in it, and for the purpose of suing for wrongful interference someone who has taken it, his right to regain possession will suffice. But for the purpose of claiming from an insurance company for loss, he will be regarded as having lost possession, within the terms of the contract, if the thing cannot in fact be found.

Trespass to land by relation is another example of the artificial manipulation of the concept of possession to provide a remedy in trespass to one who needs to be compensated. When a person, with a right to possess, enters in pursuance of that right, he is deemed to have been in possession from the time when his right originally accrued, e.g. from the time when he made the original contract for a purchase or a lease. He can, therefore, sue for any trespass that has been committed between the accrual of the right and the actual entry.

The owner of land possesses everything attached to or under the land, particularly if the place is one to which the public is not admitted. (*Elwes* v. *Brigg Gas Co.*, 1886,[599] *South Staffordshire Water Co.* v. *Sharman*, 1896),[600] and *Corporation of London* v. *Appleyard*, 1963.[601] Things lying loose on the land are not in the possession of the landowner but fall into the possession of the first finder, at any rate if he is lawfully on the land and the public is generally admitted thereto (*Bridges* v. *Hawkesworth*, 1851,[598] and *Hannah* v. *Peel*, 1945.)[602]

However, it should be noted that unless an owner of chattels can be shown to have *abandoned* or *sold* them he remains their owner and has a better title than a finder or a person on whose property they are found. (*Moffat* v. *Kazana*, 1968.)[708]

Adverse possession

A person may sometimes acquire the ownership of land by adverse possession. This arises from the occupation and use of land without the permission of, or any interference from, the true owner, as where a stranger encloses and cultivates a portion of a neighbour's land or occupies another's house. Adverse possession for a period of twelve years will give the possessor a title (*Hayward* v. *Challoner*, 1967),[709] but such adverse possession must take the form of overt acts which are inconsistent with the title of the owner, and in this case possession is viewed much more strictly than in the others we have been considering above. (*Littledale* v. *Liverpool College*, 1900.)[710] Whether adverse possession necessarily involves inconvenience to the true owner is not clear. In *Wallis's Caton Bay Holiday Camp* v. *Shell-Mex & B.P.*, [1974] 3 All E.R. 575, the defendants had purchased land for development, though they had no immediate use for it. The plaintiffs used it for 12 years for the purposes of grazing cattle on it and cultivating it. The Court of Appeal held that the plaintiffs had not established a good possessory title because what they had done was of no inconvenience to the defendants who had no immediate use for the land. However, in *Treloar* v. *Nute*, (1976) 120 S.J. 590, the plaintiff owned freehold land for which he had no immediate use and which was left derelict. The defendants bought land adjacent and occupied part of the derelict land for a period of 12 years. In holding that the defendants had a good possessory title to that land the Court of Appeal said it was not necessary to import into the definition of adverse possession a requirement that the owner must be inconvenienced or affected by that possession.

Where a tenant, during the currency of his tenancy, takes possession of other land belonging to the landlord, the land is presumed to have been taken as part of the holding comprised in the tenancy, and the tenant cannot acquire a good possessory title unless he communicates to his landlord some disclaimer of the landlord's title. (*Smirk* v. *Lyndale Developments Ltd,* 1974.)[711]

BAILMENT

Bailments are concerned with pure personalty and not with real property.

The bailment may or may not originate in a contract (*Fairline Shipping Corporation* v. *Adamson,* 1974)[99] and a minor may be a bailee of goods even though he obtained them under a void contract. (*Ballett* v. *Mingay,* 1943.)[476]

Possession

An essential feature of a bailment is the transfer of possession to the bailee. There is no precise definition of possession, but the basic features are *control* and *an intention to exclude others*. However, a person can have possession of chattels which he does not know exist (*South Staffordshire Water Co.* v. *Sharman,* 1896).[600] An employee who receives goods from his employer to take to a third party has mere *custody*; possession remains with the employer and the employee is not a bailee. If a third party hands goods to a employee for his employer the employee obtains possession and is the bailee.

In a bailment for a fixed term the bailee has possession to the exclusion of the bailor, and is, therefore, the only person who can sue a third party for wrongful interference. In a bailment at will, i.e. one which the bailor can terminate at will, the bailor retains either possession or an immediate right to possess and an action for wrongful interference is available to him as well as to the bailee. A bailee can sue a third party in tort for loss of or damage to the goods even though the bailee is not liable to the bailor for the loss or damage. (*The Winkfield,* 1902.)[712]

Bailment and licence

The problem of distinguishing between bailment and licence has arisen mainly in connection with the parking of vehicles. If a vehicle is parked on land, either gratuitously or even on payment of a change, the transaction may amount to a mere licence and not a bailment which gives rise to duties of care. (*Ashby* v. *Tolhurst,* 1937.)[713] The decisions in *Ultzen* v. *Nicols,* 1894,[714] and *Deyong* v. *Shenburn,* 1946,[715] are illustrative of the problems involved in distinguishing bailment and licence.

Finders and involuntary recipients

To constitute a bailment, the person who is given possession of goods must be entrusted with them for a particular purpose, e.g. to sue and return as in the case of loan or hire, or to take from one place to another as in carriage. A banker is not a bailee of money paid into a customer's account, for his obligation is to return an equivalent sum and not the identical notes and coins. However, a banker is a bailee of property deposited with him for safe custody.

A finder is not a true bailee because he is not entrusted with the goods for a particular purpose. However, if he takes them into his possession he will be liable for loss or damage resulting from his negligence. (*Newman* v. *Bourne and Hollingsworth*, 1915.)[716]

A person cannot be made a bailee against his will. (*Neuwirth* v. *Over Darwen Industrial Co-operative Society*, 1894.)[717] Where the receipt of the goods is involuntary it is unlikely that the recipient is under any higher duty than to refrain from intentional damage. However, he must not convert the goods, but although liability for conversion is usually strict, an involuntary recipient will only be liable if he acts intentionally or negligently. (*Elvin and Powell Ltd* v. *Plummer Roddis Ltd*, 1933.)[606]

The Unsolicited Goods and Services Act, 1971, is relevant in this connection. The Act is designed to deal with selling techniques involving the sending of unsolicited goods, thus rendering the recipient an involuntary bailee. The Act provides for fines to be made on persons making demands for payment for goods they know to be unsolicited. If the demand is accompanied by threats a higher scale of fines applies. Furthermore, unsolicited goods may be kept by the recipient without payment *after a period of thirty days* provided the recipient gives notice to the sender asking that they be collected, or *after six months* even if no notice has been given.

Obligations of the bailor

Where the bailment is gratuitous it has been said that the limit of the liability of the bailor is to communicate to the bailee defects in the article lent *of which he is aware*. However, the principle in *Donoghue* v. *Stevenson*, 1932,[468] may apply to gratuitous bailments so that the bailor would be liable if he had not taken reasonable care to ensure that the goods bailed were not dangerous, even though he had no actual knowledge of a defect in the chattels lent.

When the bailment is for reward there is an implied warranty on the part of the bailor that he has a title to the goods so that the bailee's possession will not be disturbed, and that the goods are fit and suitable for the bailee's purpose. This does not mean that the bailee is liable for all defects but only for those which skill and care can guard against. (*Hyman* v. *Nye*, 1881,[718] *Reed* v. *Dean*, 1949.)[719] However, the warranty as to fitness and suitability does not apply where the defect is apparent to the bailee and the does not rely on the skill or judgment of the bailor.

Obligations of the bailee

When Lord Holt, in *Coggs* v. *Bernard*, 1703,[134] established the liability of the bailee in negligence he laid down different duties of care for different kinds of bailments. Thus, in a bailment for the sole benefit of the bailee, such as a gratuitous loan, the bailee's duty of care was much higher than in a bailment for the benefit of both parties such as a hiring. However, in recent times there has been disapproval of Lord Holt's different standards of care (*Houghland* v. *R. Low (Luxury Coaches) Ltd*, 1962),[720] and it is now the better view that the standard of care required of a bailee is to take reasonable care in all the circumstances of the case, which equates his duty with that owed by any person in the law relating to negligence, though the burden of disproving negligence is on the bailee. (*Global Dress Co.* v. *Boase & Co.*, 1966.)[721]

The *main* circumstances which the court is likely to consider when deciding the question of negligence in a bailee are —

(a) The type of bailment. Although some current legal opinion is against a legal distinction between bailment for reward and gratuitous bailment, reward or lack of reward will continue to be an *important circumstance* in the matter of the bailee's negligence. A gratuitous bailee must take the same care of the property bailed as a reasonable man would take of his own property. It is no defence for a bailee to show that he kept the goods with as much care as his own because the test of reasonableness is objective. (*Doorman* v. *Jenkins* 1834.)[722] In a bailment for reward the duty of care tends to be somewhat higher. (*Brabant* v. *King*, 1895.)[723]

(b) The expertise of the bailee. If the bailee's profession or situation implies a certain expertise he will be liable if he fails to show it. (*Wilson* v. *Brett*, 1843.)[724]

(c) The property bailed. If the goods bailed are, to the knowledge of the bailee fragile or valuable, a high standard of care will be expected. (*Saunders (Mayfair) Furs* v. *Davies*, 1965.)[725]

A bailee may be liable in negligence if he does not give notice to the bailor of a loss or try to recover lost or stolen property. (*Coldman* v. *Hill*, 1919.)[726]

A bailee is vicariously liable for the torts of his servants, but a servant who became a thief was not regarded as acting within the scope of his employment. (*Cheshire* v. *Bailey*, 1905.)[727] However, in *Morris* v. *C. W. Martin & Sons Ltd*, 1965,[501] it was held that a bailee for reward cannot necessarily escape liability for loss of goods stolen by his servant because theft is not necessarily beyond the scope of employment.

A bailee may attempt to exclude his liability by an exemption clause in the contract of bailment. This matter must now be considered in the light of the *Suisse Case*[298] and subsequent decisions, the rules of construction of contracts and the Unfair Contract Terms Act, 1977 (p. 228).

Delegation by bailee

Whether a bailee can delegate performance of the contract to another depends upon the nature of the bailment and the particular contract which may authorize delegation. Contracts involving the carriage, storage, repair or cleaning of goods often assume personal performance by the bailee. (*Davies* v. *Collins*, 1945;[728] *Edwards* v. *Newland*, 1950.)[729] Where there is a delegation, even though unknown to the bailor, the delegate is a bailee and owes a duty of care directly to the bailor. (*Learoyd Bros* v. *Pope*, 1966.)[730]

Estoppel and interpleader

A bailee is estopped at common law from denying the title of his bailor and if the bailor demands the return of the goods it is no defence for the bailee to plead that the bailor is not the owner. However, a bailee may defend an action for non-delivery of the goods—

(*a*) by showing that he has delivered then under an authorization by the bailor;

(*b*) by showing that he has not got the goods because he has been dispossessed by a person with a better title, as in a bailment of stolen goods which are reclaimed by the owner;

(*c*) if he still retains possession he may allege that a third party has a better title but he must defend the action on behalf of, and with the authority of, the true owner. (*Rogers, Sons & Co.* v. *Lambert & Co.*, 1891.)[731]

Where adverse claims are made against the bailee by the bailor and a third party, the bailee should take interpleader proceedings under the Rules of the Supreme Court. The effect of this will be to bring the bailor and the third party together in an action which will decide the validity of their claims. The bailee can then hand over the goods to whichever party has established his claim and will not risk liability for wrongful interference.

Lien

A bailee may, in certain circumstances, have a lien on the goods and the general nature of a lien is described on p. 416.

LAND LAW

Estates in land

Since the Norman Conquest absolute ownership of land has been impossible. William the Conqueror considered himself owner of all land in
England and parcelled it out to his barons who became his tenants. In
return for this 'honour' the barons had to render to the Crown certain
services, either of a military or other public nature, but an exception was
made in the case of land held by the Church. The ecclesiatics were not able
to provide military services, and special spiritual tenures were introduced.

In order to assist themselves in supplying the services required by the
King, the barons began to subgrant part of the land, and a series of tenures
sprang up, all persons holding as tenants of the Crown in the last analysis.

It is outside our scope to pursue the rise and fall of the system of tenures,
but all land is now held on a single tenure called 'common socage', and all
obligations to the Crown have disappeared, except for certain ceremonials
preserved because of their antiquity. Even today, however, a person does
not own land; he holds an estate in land. The *tenure* answers the question
'How is the land held?' The term *estate* answers the question 'For how long
is the land held?'

Before 1926 there were the following estates in land—

Estates of freehold

These estates were divided as follows—

The estate in fee simple.   This was granted *to A and his heirs* or *to A in fee
simple*. The exact words used above were essential, and indeed only the
latter formula was valid after the Conveyancing Act, 1881. A grant in fee
simple confers full rights of possession, enjoyment and disposition during
life and by will. If the owner of the estate dies intestate, the land passes to
the relatives entitled under statute in that event. Only in the event of the
owner dying intestate and without relations will the estate come to an end
and the land pass to the Crown.

The estate tail.   (From the French 'tailler', to cut down.) This is an estate
less than a fee simple, e.g. granted *to A and the heirs of his body* or *to A in
tail*. The tenant in tail has full rights of possession and enjoyment and the
estate does not come to an end at his death; it passes to his heirs but only to
a limited class of heirs, the heirs of his body or his descendants. The line of
descent may be further restricted by making the estate *in tail male,* i.e.
descending only through males, or *in tail female,* descending through
females. There is also an *estate in special tail* inheritable only by the issue of
the tenant by a certain wife or husband.

Before 1926 a tenant in tail had no power to dispose of his estate by will,
but a tenant in tail in possession could in his lifetime, and still can, bar the

entail by deed. (The Law of Property Act, 1925, extending the Fines and Recoveries Act, 1833.) A disentailing deed operates to convert the entail into a fee simple estate. The tenant can now bar the entail by will by referring in the will to the entailed property or to entailed property generally. If the estate is not in possession, as where there is a grant to A for life and then to B in tail, A is the 'protector of the settlement' and B cannot wholly bar the entail without A's consent.

The estate for life.   This is granted *to A for life* or other period of uncertain duration, e.g. during widowhood. Such an estate was held only for the life of the grantee, so that it was not possible for him to leave it by will or to give rights to another *inter vivos* for longer than his own life.

The estate pur autre vie.   This is for the life of another, e.g. a grant *to A so long as B shall live.* This estate is similar to the life estate except that the duration of the estate depends on the life of a person other than the grantee.

Estates less than freehold

Such estates were of the nature of leaseholds and were divided as follows—

Estates for years, such as existed under leases, and including a tenancy from year to year.

Estates at will, where the tenancy is determinable at will by either the lessor or the lessee.

Estates by sufferance, where a person who had held a lawful title continued in possession after his title had ended.

Any of these estates might be either a legal estate or an equitable interest arising under a trust. Further these estates, whether legal or equitable, were either (i) in possession, thus carrying the right of present enjoyment, or (ii) in expectancy, being in reversion or remainder. Thus where there was a grant *to A for life and then to B,* B's interest was said to be *in remainder,* because his estate became effective only on the expiration of the estate of the previous owner. An example of a *reversion* is where A, who has a fee simple of Blackacre, grants B a life estate in the land but makes no further disposition of it. On B's death Blackacre will revert to A, and A is said to have a *reversionary interest* in Blackacre. A reversion is similar to a remainder in that the right to enjoy the land is postponed to a future date, but where there is a reversion the land eventually returns to the grantor, whereas with a remainder the land goes to some other person.

The legislation of 1925

The existence of so many estates in land made the transfer of land most complicated. There might be a large number of legal owners of the same piece of land, and before the land could be conveyed to a purchaser all the interests had to be got in. Other problems arose on intestacy, because the rules for intestate succession where not the same for realty and personalty. In 1925 a thorough reform of land law was undertaken and was eventually achieved by the following statutes: The Law of Property Act, 1925; The Settled Land Act, 1925; The Administration of Estates Act, 1925; The Land Charges Act, 1925; and the Land Registration Act, 1925.

The Law of Property Act, 1925, reduced the number of legal estates which can exist over land to two, and the number of legal interests or charges in or over land to five. All other estates, interests, and charges in or over land take effect as equitable interests, and can exist only behind a trust, the trustees having the legal fee simple estate.

The difference between a legal estate and a legal interest is that the owner of the legal estate is entitled to the enjoyment of the whole of the property, either in possession or receiving rents, whereas the owner of a legal interest has a limited right in or over the land of another.

The two legal estates possible today are—

(1) *A fee simple absolute in possession;* and
(2) *A term of years absolute.*

The word *fee* implies that the estate is an estate of inheritance, and the word *simple* shows that the fee is capable of descending to the general class of heirs, and is not restricted, as in an estate tail, to heirs of a particular class. The word *absolute* distinguishes a fee simple which will continue for ever, from a fee which may be determinable. The fee simple must be *in possession,* although this does not imply only physical possession but also the right to receive rents and profits. Even if a landlord has granted a lease he may still have a fee simple in possession because he is entitled to the rent reserved by the lease.

The *term of years absolute* is what is normally understood by a lease. But a term of years includes a term for less than a year, or for a year or years and a fraction of a year, or even a tenancy from year to year. The essential characteristic is that a term of years has a minimum period of certain duration. It seems, therefore, that a lease for life is no longer a legal estate; nor is a tenancy at will or sufferance since there is no certainty as to the period of their continuance. A term of years may be absolute notwithstanding that it may be determined by notice, re-entry, or operation of law or other event.

Types of fee simple.   The fee simple absolute in possession is the only fee simple which can exist as a legal estate. Any other form is necessarily an equitable interest only. Such may be—

(*a*) A fee simple absolute but not in possession, e.g. in expectancy.

(*b*) A fee simple not absolute which may be either a determinable fee, a conditional fee or a base fee.

A determinable fee is one limited to determine on the happening of some even which may never occur. If the event happens, the interest automatically reverts to the grantor, unless there is a gift over to someone. If the event becomes impossible, the fee becomes absolute, e.g. a grant to A in fee simple until B marries (and B dies a bachelor). If the event is one which must happen some time, the fee is not a determinable fee, e.g. a grant to A in fee simple until B dies (since B is bound to die); here A has an estate *pur autre vie*.

A conditional fee is a fee simple subject to either—

(i) *a condition precedent,* where the interest does not commence unless and until some even occurs, e.g. to A in fee simple when or if he attains the age of twenty-one years; or

(ii) *a condition subsequent,* where the interest is liable to determine on the happening of some event, e.g. to A in fee simple, provided he never sells out of the family.

The difference between a determinable fee and a conditional fee is primarily one of language. The words 'while, or until', or 'during', or 'so long as', usually create a determinable fee. A grant to a school in fee simple until it ceases to publish annual accounts would be a limitation creating a determinable fee; but a grant to a school in fee simple upon condition that it published annual accounts would create a conditional fee.

There is, however, one case where a fee simple upon a condition subsequent can exist as a legal estate. Before 1926 it was a common practice, more particularly in Lancashire, upon a sale of freeholds to reserve a perpetual rentcharge called a chief rent, instead of taking a lump sum of purchase money, with a right to re-enter and determine the fee simple for default of payment of rent. When the Law of Property Act, 1925, became law, the unfortunate purchasers of such property did not have a fee simple absolute and therefore no legal estate. The Law of Property (Amendment) Act, 1926, added to the 1925 Act a provision that a fee simple subject to a right of re-entry should be a fee simple absolute for the purposes of the Act.

The system of legal rentcharges was examined by the Law Commission, which noted that there was still some tendency towards the creation of new rentcharges in estate development. The Law Commission in working paper No. 49 found that the criticism that a rent charge makes a purchaser pay too much is not proved and that the unsatisfactory features of the rentcharges system are not inherently necessary. For raising money like a mortgage, rentcharges have the advantage of simplicity, are at fixed rates for longer terms but may be less beneficial from a tax point of view. They may be used as an alternative to the grant of long leaseholds.

The Rentcharges Act, 1977 now applies. Section 1 defines a rentcharge for the purpose of the Act as any annual or other periodic sum charged on or issuing out of land except to rent reserved by a lease or a sum payable by way of interest. Section 2 carries a general prohibition in regard to the creation of rentcharges, either at law or in equity. Section 3 provides that any rentcharge still in force shall be extinguished at the end of the period of 60 years starting on 22 July, 1977, or on the date the rentcharge first became payable, whichever is later, but without prejudice to the exercise of any right to recover rent which accrues during that period. Under Sect. 4 an owner of land affected by a rentcharge may apply to the Secretary of State for an order apportioning the rentcharge between different parts of the land, whether or not the applicant owns all the land affected by the rentcharge. The making of such orders is dealt with by Sects 5, 6 and 7. Under Sect. 8 an owner of land affected by a rentcharge may apply to the Secretary of State for a certificate certifying that the rent charge has been redeemed. Sections 9 and 10 provide for the issue of the redemption certificate and a formula for calculating the redemption price and the person to whom it is payable.

A *base fee* arises in the following circumstances. Suppose property is left to A for life with remainder to B in tail. It is possible for B to bar the entail, but if he wishes to do this during A's lifetime he must obtain A's consent. If this is not forthcoming, he can only bar the entail so as to defeat his own descendants, thus creating a base fee. He cannot prevent a reversion to the grantor without obtaining A's consent when the entail is barred. If then B's heirs fail at any time in the future, the land would revert to the grantor.

Legal Interests and charges. We have seen that there are, since 1926, only two possible legal estates: a fee simple absolute in possession and a term of years absolute, but the Law of Property Act, 1925, also lays down five possible legal interests in land—

(i) An easement, right or privilege for an interest equivalent to either of the above estates. Thus an easement for life would not be a legal interest.

(ii) A rentcharge in possession, either perpetual or for a term of years absolute. As we have seen, a rentcharge is a right which is independent of any lease or mortgage, and gives the owner a right to a periodical sum of money, e.g. where the fee simple owner of Blackacre charges the land with a payment of £500 per annum payable to R.

(iii) A charge by way of legal mortgage.

(iv) Land tax or other charge not created by any instrument, e.g. created by statute.

(v) Rights of entry over or in respect of a term of years absolute, and annexed for any purpose to a legal rentcharge.

EQUITABLE INTERESTS

All estates, interests or charges over land except those outlined above take effect as equitable interests only and must exist behind a trust. Life interests are equitable and so are entails. Reversions and remainders, together with conditional interests, are also equitable.

Settled land and trusts for sale

A settlement was designed to provide for successive interests in property. There are two methods of settling land: (*a*) the Strict Settlement and (*b*) the Trust for Sale.

The aim of a strict settlement was to keep the land in the family. On marriage a man would convey his property to trustees to carry out the terms of the settlement which were usually to give *a life interest* to the husband, *an entail* to his eldest son, a provision for the wife (called *a jointure*), other children being provided for by *portions* raised out of the property in the settlement.

By such a settlement the land became substantially inalienable, at least until the eldest son reached the age of twenty-one and was able to bar the entail. At twenty-one the son S usually barred the entail with the consent of his father F, and S's fee simple was resettled so that, after the death of F, S would receive a life interest with remainder to his own son in tail. This tied up the land for another generation when the process could be repeated. In this way, by means of settlement and resettlement, persons of full age never had more than a life estate.

A trust for sale had a somewhat different objective. Here the land was conveyed to trustees who were to sell it and invest the proceeds in order to provide the income for the beneficiaries under the trust. It was an essential characteristic of a trust for sale that the trustees had not merely a power but a binding duty to sell. However, it was usual to provide that the trustees should have power to postpone sale at their discretion, and manage the land until they deemed it prudent to sell.

Settlements

Where settlements are created after 1925 other than by will, the Settled Land Act, 1925, requires two deeds to be executed— the vesting deed and the trust instrument. The vesting deed must contain a description of the settled land, a statement that the settled land is vested in the tenant for life upon the trusts for the time being affecting the settled land, the names of the trustees of the settlement, and a statement of any larger powers granted to the tenant for life in addition of his statutory powers.

The trust instrument must contain the appointment of the trustees, the names of the persons entitled to appoint new trustees, a statement of any additional powers conferred by the settlement in extension of the statutory powers, and the trusts of the settlment. Where a settlement is created by will, the will is regarded as the trust instrument, and the personal representatives must execute a vesting instrument, vesting the legal estate in the tenant for life. Thus a purchaser of settled land is only concerned with the vesting deed or assent, since it is from such documents that he derives his title. The trusts can remain secret since the trust instrument need not be produced on sale.

Under the settlement the person obtaining the benefit from the estate is usually an adult with a life interest and he is called the *tenant for life*. It is his function to manage the estate and he has power to sell or exchange the settled land or any part of it with an adjustment of any difference in value in the case of exchange. He may grant leases subject to certain restrictions, but in the absence of a contrary provision in the settlement, he has no power to mortgage or charge the legal estate for his own benefit, although he can mortgage or assign his own beneficial life interest.

He has other powers which he can only exercise with the consent of the settlement trustees or the court, e.g. the power to sell or otherwise dispose of the principal mansion house, the power to cut and sell timber, the power to compromise claims and sell settled chattels. He has the power to make improvements at his own expense, or the cost may be borne by the capital money if he complies with the provisions of the Act. He has also power to select investments for capital money.

The tenant for life is in a strong position, for he is subject to no control in the exercise of his powers except that he must give notice to the trustees of his intention to exercise the most important ones, he must obtain the consent of the trustees or leave of the court in certain cases, and he is in fact himself a trustee for the other beneficiaries. There may be joint tenants for life under a settlement and, where this is so, they must usually agree as to the exercise of their joint powers. The court will exercise a power, e.g. by ordering a sale of property, but only if the joint tenant who does not agree to sell is acting in bad faith. (*Barker* v. *Addiscott*, [1969] 3 All E.R. 685.)

It is clear that under a settlement a proper balance must be preserved between the tenant for life and the persons who will be entitled to the land or the proceeds of the land after his death. He is not allowed, therefore, to run down the estate during his lifetime in order to increase his own income, but is only allowed to take from the land the current income and must pass on the estate substantially unimpaired.

Trusts for sale

A trust for sale is an immediate binding trust for sale whether or not exercisable at the request or with the consent of any person, and with or without a power at discretion to postpone the sale. Such a trust for sale may be either express or by operation of law. Trusts for sale are governed by the Law of Property Act, 1925, and not by the Settled Land Act, 1925.

An express trust for sale is almost always created by two documents— a conveyance on trust for sale and a trust instrument. But even where a trust for sale is embodied in a single document, a purchaser of the legal estate is not concerned with the trusts affecting the rents and profits of the land until sale, or with the proceeds of the sale.

There are cases where a trust for sale is imposed by statute. These are—

(a) where a person dies intestate,

(b) where two or more persons are entitled to land as joint tenants or tenants in common,

(c) where trustees lend money on mortgage and the property becomes vested in them free from the right of redemption.

It should, of course, be borne in mind that in addition to settlements deliberately created as such the setting up of an entailed or life interest *automatically creates a settlement*. Thus each of the following limitations will create a settlement—

(a) 'to A for life';

(b) 'to A in tail';

(c) 'to A for life, remainder to B in tail'.

In each of these cases A is the tenant for life as defined by Sects 19 and 20 of the Settled Land Act, 1925. (In effect these two sections provide that generally a person entitled to possession under the settlement is the tenant for life.) In each of the above cases the legal estate will be conveyed to A by a vesting deed and A will hold the legal estate on the limitations or trusts set out in the trust instrument, i.e. for himself for life or in tail, or for himself for life with remainder for B in tail.

CO-OWNERSHIP

Two persons may own land simultaneously. In such a case they are either joint tenants or tenants in common. Where they are joint tenants there is no question of a share of the property—each is the owner of the whole. Where there is a tenancy in common, each is regarded as owning an individual share in the property, but that share has not positively been marked out. Tenants in common hold property in undivided shares.

A joint tenancy arises where land is conveyed to two or more persons and no words of severance are used. A tenancy in common arises when there are words of severance. Thus a conveyance 'to A and B' would create a joint tenancy, whilst a conveyance 'to A and B equally' would create a tenancy in common. The right of survivorship or *jus accrescendi* is a distinguishing feature of joint tenancies, and upon the death of one joint tenant, his share in the property passes to the survivors until there is only one person left and he becomes the sole owner of the property. The *jus accrescendi* does not apply to tenancies in common and such a tenant may dispose of his share by will.

Both types of co-ownership have advantages and disadvantages. The *jus accrescendi* as applied to joint tenancies prevents too many interests being created in the land, because a joint tenant cannot leave any part of the property by will and so the number of interests decreases. When the land is sold the number of signatures on the conveyance will not be excessive. On the other hand joint tenancies are unfair in that eventual sole ownership depends merely on survival. Where there is a tenancy in common, each tenant can leave his interest by will possibly by dividing it between two or more persons, thus the number of interests increases and on sale many interests must be got in.

The common law preferred the joint tenancy, but Equity preferred the tenancy in common and would in certain circumstances treat persons as tenants in common rather than joint tenants regardless of words of severance. For instance where two persons lend money on mortgage, Equity regards them as tenants in common of the interest in the land subject to the mortgage; also where joint purchasers of land put up the purchase money in unequal shares; and in the case of partnership land, the partners are treated as tenants in common in Equity.

The Law of Property Act, 1925, has combined the best features of both types of co-ownership by providing that where land is owned by two or more persons they, or the first four of them if there are more than four, should be treated as holding the legal estate as trustees and joint tenants, for the benefit of themselves and other co-owners (if any) in Equity. Thus a purchaser of the property is never required to get more than four signatures on the conveyance, and the trusts attach to the purchase money for the benefit of the co-owners. The statutory trusts on which the property is held are: to sell the property with power to postpone the sale; and to hold the proceeds of sale, and the rents and profits until sale, for those benefically entitled under the trust.

It should be noted that although the provisions set out in the above paragraph deal with the problems which formerly arose in conveying land which was in joint ownership, it is still possible to create a joint tenancy in both the land and the proceeds of sale. Where such a joint tenancy exists the *jus accrescendi* will apply to the equitable interests of the joint tenants in the proceeds of sale, unless there has been a severance of the joint tenancy since the creation of the estate. Severance is possible under Sect. 36(2) of the Law of Property Act, 1925, which provides that—

. . . where a legal estate (not being settled land) is vested in joint tenants beneficially, and any tenant desires to sever the joint tenancy in Equity, he shall give to the other joint tenants a notice in writing of such desire or do such other acts or things as would, in the case of personal estate, have been effective to sever the tenancy in Equity, and thereupon under the trust for sale affecting the land the net proceeds of sale, and the net rents and profits until sale, shall be held upon the trusts which would have been requisite for giving effect to the beneficial interest if there had been an actual severance.

A notice of severance may be regarded as properly served if sent by post even if it is not received by the addressee. (*Re 88 Berkeley Road, London N.W.9; Rickwood* v. *Turnsek*, [1971] 1 All E.R. 254.)

The better view is that severance of a joint tenancy may be effected unilaterally by one party other than by giving notice. (*Re Draper's Conveyance*, 1967.)[732] Before leaving this topic it should be noted that one tenant in common is not entitled to rent from another tenant in common, even though that other occupies the whole of the property. (*Jones (A.E.)* v. *Jones (F.W.)*, [1977] 2 All E.R. 231.)

A LEASEHOLD OR A TERM OF YEARS

The major characteristics of a term of years are that the lessee is given exclusive possession of the land and that the period for which the term is to endure is fixed and definite. It is open to the parties to decide whether their agreement shall be a lease or licence, though the words used by the parties are not conclusive. If there is no right to exclusive possession then there is a mere licence and not a lease. (*Shell-Mex* v. *Manchester Garages*, 1971.)[733] For example, a guest in a hotel does not normally have a lease, because the proprietor retains general control over the room.

The duration of leases

Leases may be for a fixed period of time, and in this case the commencement and termination of the lease must be ascertainable before the lease takes effect. Thus a lease 'for the life of X' would not come under this heading. A lease may be for an indefinite period in the sense that it is to end when the lessor or lessee gives notice. Even so such an arrangement would operate as a valid lease, since the duration of the term can be made certain by the parties giving notice.

In the absence of agreement, the period of a lease may be determined by reference to the payment of rent. Thus if a person takes possession of the premises with the owner's consent for an indefinite period, but the owner accepts rent paid say weekly, monthly, quarterly or annually, then the term may be based on that period, though from early times there has been a presumption that the payment and acceptance of rent shows an intention to create a yearly tenancy but not if the rent is received by mistake. (*Legal and General Assurance Society* v. *General Metal Agencies*, 1969.)[213] A yearly tenancy requires half a year's notice to terminate it if there has been no agreement on the matter. Other periodical tenancies, in the absence of agreement, are determined by notice for the full period. Even where there has been a definite term, a periodical tenancy can arise. Where X is granted a lease of twenty-one years and stays on after the expiration of that term with the owner's consent, then there is a new implied term based on the period of payment of rent.

However, where the tenant is permitted to stay in possession on the understanding that there are to be negotiations for a new lease there is a tenancy at will.

THE LAW OF PROPERTY

A *tenancy at will* may also arise *by agreement* where a person takes possession of property with the owner's consent, the arrangement being that the term can be brought to an end by either party giving notice. However, the court will look at the transaction in order to ascertain its true nature and will not be put off by ambiguous or wrong terminology. (*Binions* v. *Evans,* 1972.)[734] If there is no agreement as to rent, the tenancy can become a periodical tenancy if the tenant pays and the owner accepts rent paid at given periods of time. A tenancy at will may also arise *by implication* from the conduct of the parties. For example, a prospective purchaser of land who is allowed to take possession before completion occupies the property as a tenant at will until completion

Where a tenant stays on after the expiration of his term without the consent of the owner, there is a *tenancy by sufferance.* No rent is payable under such a tenancy, but the tenant must compensate the owner by a payment in respect of the use and occupation of the land. This compensation is referred to as *mesne profits*. Such a tenancy can be brought to an end at any time, though it may become a periodical tenancy if the owner accepts a payment of rent at given intervals of time.

It should be noted that the law bases the duration of a periodic tenancy on the intervals of time at which the rent has been paid and accepted, on the ground that this is evidence on the parties' intention. If there is other evidence of intention, then the court will also take this into account, e.g. there may be a prior lease which negatives the intention to create the sort of periodic tenancy which the payment of rent suggests.

Creation of leases

Leases are normally created by a document under seal. However, where the lease is not to exceed three years, a written or oral lease will suffice, so long as the lease takes effect in possession at once at the best rent obtainable. Where a tenancy is in excess of three years then, if the agreement is not under seal, it will operate at common law as a yearly tenancy if the tenant enters into possession and pays rent on a yearly basis, i.e. by reference to a year, even if the rent is paid in quarterly instalments.

The position in Equity is rather different. In Equity, if a person has entered into an agreement for a lease but has no document under seal, then, if he has entered and paid rent or carried out repairs, i.e. if there is a sufficient act of part performance, Equity will insist that the owner of the property execute a formal lease under seal. The equitable maxim, 'Equity looks upon that as done which ought to be done,' applies. This principle is known as the Rule in *Walsh* v. *Lonsdale,* 1882.[735]

It may seem that this rule makes an agreement for a lease as effective as a lease under seal, and certainly, as between the parties to the agreement, absence of a seal is not vital.

However, the rights of the tenant under the rule are equitable and not legal rights, and the tenant can be turned out by a third party to whom the landlord sells the legal estate, if the third party purchases the property for value and without notice of the existence of the lease.

Nevertheless, since the property legislation of 1925, the tenant can register the agreement as an Estate Contract, and, once the agreement is so registered, all subsequent purchasers of the legal estate are deemed to have notice of the lease and are bound to honour it. (See further, p. 412.)

Rights and liabilities of landlord and tenant

The rights and liabilities of the parties depend largely upon the lease though a landlord has a special right at common law to distrain for rent, i.e. to move in on the tenant's personal property and remove it for sale to satisfy the amount owing for rent. Where the lease is by deed, the deed will usually fix the rights and liabilities by express clauses which are called convenants. Certain convenants are also implied by law where there is no provision in the lease. The most usual express covenants are covenants to pay rent, covenants regarding repairs and renewals, and a covenant that the tenant will not assign or sub-let.

The following covenants are implied where appropriate. The landlord covenants that he will not disturb the tenant's quiet enjoyment of the property, or make the use or enjoyment of the land difficult or impossible, i.e. the landlord undertakes not to *derogate from the grant*. As regards furnished houses, the landlord covenants that the property is fit for human habitation, and under the Housing Act, 1957, Sect. 6., where any house was let before 6 July, 1957, at a rent of £40 p.a. or less in London or £26 or less elsewhere, or where any house was let on or after 6 July, 1957, at a rent of £80 or less in London or £52 or less elsewhere, there is an implied condition that the premises are fit for human habitation at the time of letting, and will be maintained in that state. Tenants whose rent is in excess of the amounts laid down by the Act of 1957 may be able to take advantage of the implied covenants in Sect. 32 of the Housing Act, 1961, which requires the lessor to keep in repair the structure and exterior of the dwelling house, including drains, gutters and external pipes. A covenant to keep in repair, whether implied by Sect. 32 of the Housing Act, 1961 or express, does not impose any liability on a landlord to remedy a latent defect until he becomes aware of it. (*O'Brien* v. *Robinson*, 1973.)[736] The Act applies only to the lease of a dwelling house for a term of less than seven years granted on or after 24 October, 1961. The following tenant's convenants are implied by Law: a covenant to pay rent, rates and certain taxes, and to repair. The tenant must in general keep the premises wind- and water-tight, and must not commit waste, i.e. he must not do deliberate damage to the premises.

Breach of Covenant by the tenant can result in forfeiture of the lease. A landlord's covenant to repair can be enforced by specific performance. (*Jeune* v. *Queen's Cross Properties Ltd*, [1973] 3 All E.R. 97.) However, since specific performance is a discretionary remedy it is advisable for tenants to rely on doing their own repairs and recouping from the rent for relatively trivial breaches rather than to approach the courts for specific performance.

The Leasehold Reform Act, 1967

The main purpose of this legislation was to deal with the problems caused by the imminent expiration of the leases of many old houses, the problem being particularly acute in South Wales. Many leaseholders were faced with two alternatives—

(i) to be evicted; or
(ii) to buy the freehold, often at a price which they could not afford.

The Act has important commercial implications because—

(i) there are large leasehold estates in many English cities and towns and banks and other business organizations such as building societies and insurance companies are mortgagees of some of these properties;
(ii) banks and other business organizations may be approached with regard to lending money to a leaseholder to enable him to purchase the freehold of his property.

Under the provisions of the Act (as amended), occupants of leasehold houses are *offered the right either to buy the freehold or to have the lease extended by fifty years*, provided the following conditions are satisfied—

(i) the lease must be of the *whole house*, though the Act still applies where there has been sub-letting (it does not, however, apply to lease-holders of maisonettes or flats). However, the lessee of a house divided into flats will be entitled to buy the freehold of the whole house so long as he lives in one of the flats. The same applies if a leasehold house consists of a shop with a flat above so long as the lease includes the whole house and the lessee lives in the flat. It does not matter that part is used for business purposes. (*Lake* v. *Bennett*, [1970] 1 All E.R. 457.)
(ii) the rateable value of the house must not in general terms exceed £750 (£1500 in Greater London). (But see further Housing Act 1974, Sect. 118.)
(iii) the lease must have been granted for a term of more than twenty-one years (Sects 1(1) and 3(1)); (*Roberts* v. *Church Commissioners for England*, 1971.)[737]
(iv) the house must have been occupied by the leaseholder as his main or only residence for the last five years or for periods amounting to five years in the last ten years (Sect. 1(1) and (2));
(v) the yearly ground rent must not amount to more than two-thirds of the annual rateable value of the whole house. In London, this would be £1000 per annum and £500 per annum elsewhere.

Right to purchase freehold (i.e. enfranchise). A leaseholder who wishes to buy the freehold must give notice to the freeholder who will arrange for the property to be surveyed at the expense of the leaseholder. (Sect. 9(4).) Notice must be served before the existing lease comes to an end, otherwise the existing leaseholder loses his rights under the Act. The form of notice is somewhat complicated and has given rise to a number of cases in Court. The advice of a solicitor should be sought.

The price of the freehold depends solely upon the value of the land on which the house stands. The value of the house itself is not taken into account. The site value is also diminished because the freeholder has to wait for possession for the remainder of the existing lease and notionally for a further fifty years.

Where the leaseholder and freeholder cannot agree on a price ascertained on the above assumptions, the Lands Tribunal will settle the matter. (Sect. 21(1).)

Right to extend the lease.   A fifty-year extension of the lease involves the payment of a revised ground rent from the time when the extended term begins. (Sect. 14.) The revised ground rent must represent the letting value of the site for the uses to which the property has been put since the beginning of the existing tenancy, nothing being included for the value of buildings on the site. (Sect. 15.)

If the parties cannot reach agreement the rent will be fixed by the Lands Tribunal (Sect. 21(1)), and the new rent, whether fixed by agreement or otherwise, may be reviewed and revised after twenty-five years if the freehold owner so wishes. (Sect. 15(2).)

The effect of the above provisions is to produce a substantial increase in ground rent. It should also be noted that the right to buy the freehold is lost when the original lease expires and the right to purchase the freehold cannot be exercised at any time during the extension. (Sect. 16(1).)

Where the leaseholder has died before taking advantage of this Act, his widow or other member of his family who was living with the leaseholder for more than five years before his death need not wait a further five years but may buy the freehold as soon as he or she inherits the lease. Furthermore, it does not matter if one of two joint lessees does not live in the house. This is especially useful to a wife who is not living with her husband if the lease is in their joint names.

In practice it is better to buy the freehold than to seek an extension of the lease. A tenant can lose the extended lease if a landlord can prove that he wants to develop the property. The tenant would receive compensation for the loss of his lease but would lose his home.

SERVITUDES

Servitudes are rights over the property of another and may be either *easements* or *profits à prendre*.

Easements

An easement may be defined as a right to use or restrict the use of the land of another person in some way. There are various classes of easements and these include—

- (*a*) rights of way,
- (*b*) rights of light,
- (*c*) rights to abstract water,
- (*d*) rights to the support of buildings.

To be valid an easement must satisfy the following conditions—

There must be a dominant and servient tenement.   The land in respect of which, and for the benefit of which, the easement exists is called the dominant tenement, and the land over which the right is exercised is called the servient tenement. A valid easement cannot exist 'in gross', i.e. without reference to the holding of land (*Hill* v. *Tupper,* 1863),[738] and the grant of a right of way over his land by a landowner to be exercised by the grantee personally, and without reference to any land capable of deriving benefit from the right of way, is merely a licence and not an easement.

The easement must accommodate the dominant tenement.   The easement must confer some benefit on the land itself so as to make it a better and more convenient property; it is not enough that the owner obtains some personal advantage. A right of way over contiguous land generally benefits the dominant tenement, and an easement can exist even where two tenements do not actually adjoin, provided it is clear that the easement benefits the dominant tenement.

The dominant tenement and the servient tenement must not be both owned and occupied by the same person.   Thus, if P owns both Blackacre and Whiteacre and habitually walks over Blackacre to reach Whiteacre, he is not exercising a right of way in respect of Blackacre, but merely walking from one part of his land to another. For this rule to apply, P must have simultaneously both ownership and possession of the two properties concerned. It is not enough that he owns the two if they are leased to different tenants, or that he be tenant of both if they are owned by different owners.

The easement must be capable of forming the subject of a grant.   This means that the right must be sufficiently definite. (*Bass* v. *Gregory,* 1890.)[739] There must be a capable grantor and a capable grantee, and the right must be within the general nature of the rights capable of existing as easements. An easement is a right to use or restrict the use of a neighbour's land which should not normally involve him in doing any work or spending any money, though in *Crow* v. *Wood,* 1970,[740] the Court of Appeal recognized an easement of fencing.

The categories of easements are not closed and new rights have from time to time been recognized as easements (*Re Ellenborough Park*, 1956),[741] though in general the courts are still reluctant to extend the categories. (*Phipps* v. *Pears*, 1965.)[742] An easement of unlimited storage within a confined or defined space is probably not capable of existing as a matter of law. (*Grigsby* v. *Melville*, 1972.)[743]

Profits à prendre

A profit à prendre is the right to take something of legal value from the land of another, e.g. shooting, fishing, and grazing rights; the right to cut turf or take wood for fuel. The exception is a right to take water from a stream which is treated as an easement because running water cannot be privately owned and is not therefore a thing of legal value.

A profit necessarily involves a servient tenement but there may or may not be a dominant tenement, for a profit can exist *in gross*. A profit may be a several profit, where enjoyment is granted to an individual as is often the case with shooting and fishing rights; or a profit may be in common which may be enjoyed by more than one person, as is often the case with grazing rights and the right to take various materials for use as fuel.

Acquisition of servitudes

Servitudes may be acquired (*a*) by statute, (*b*) by express or implied grant, (*c*) by prescription, (*d*) by equitable estoppel. (See *Crabb* v. *Arun District Council*, 1975.)[165]

Easements created by statute are usually in connection with local Acts of Parliament.

When land is sold, a servitude may be expressly reserved in favour of another tenement of the seller, or may be expressly granted in similar circumstances by deed; and under the Law of Property Act, 1925, Sect. 62 a conveyance, if there is no contrary express intention operates to convey servitudes appertaining to the land conveyed. (*Crow* v. *Wood*, 1970.)[740]

Where an owner of two plots conveys one of them, then certain easements are implied. These are *easements of necessity,* as where the piece of land would be completely surrounded and inaccessible without a right of way; *intended easements,* which would be necessary to carry out the common intentions of the parties; *ancillary easements,* which would be necessary in view of the right granted, as the grant of the use of water implies the right of way to reach the water. Where part of a tenement is granted, then the grantee acquires easements over the land which are continuous and apparent, are necessary to the reasonable enjoyment of the land granted, and have been and are used by the grantor for the benefit of the part granted. (*Ward* v. *Kirkland*, 1966.)[744] An example of this is a window enjoying light.

Prescription

Prescription may be based on a presumed grant or alternatively may be established by user as of right.

Prescription at common law depended on user since time immemorial, which at law means since 1189. Clearly in most cases it is out of the question to show continuous user for this period, and so the courts were prepared to accept twenty years' continuous user as raising the presumption of a grant. This presumption may be rebutted by showing that at some time since 1189 the right could not have existed, and it follows that an easement of light cannot be claimed by prescription at common law in a building erected since 1189. This serious difficulty was met in part by the presumption of a lost modern grant, and juries were told that if there had been user during living memory or even for twenty years, they might presume a lost grant or deed, and this ultimately became mandatory, even though neither judge nor jury had any belief that such instrument had ever existed. (*Tehidy Minerals* v. *Norman,* 1971.)[745]

The position is now clear under the Prescription Act, 1832, which was passed to deal with the difficulties arising under the common law. Under this Act, which supplements the common law, we must distinguish easements other than light from easements of light and easements from profits.

Easements other than light. Twenty years' uninterrupted user as of right will establish an easement. User as of right means *nec vi, nec clam, nec precario,* i.e. without force, stealth or permission. The law of prescription rests upon the acquiescence of the owner of the servient tenement. Thus he must have knowledge of the exercise of the right claimed. (*Diment* v. *N. H. Foot,* 1974.)[746] If the owner of the so-called servient tenement can prove that he has given verbal permission, i.e. that the easement is *precario,* then it cannot be claimed. Nevertheless forty years' similar user will establish the easement, and in this case, if the owner of the servient tenement wishes to prove that the right was exercised by permission, he must produce a written agreement to that effect. To establish a right of way by prescription, periods of user of an original and a substituted way may be added together. (*Davis* v. *Whitby,* 1974.)[747]

Easements of light. These can be established by twenty years' user, the defences being that the owner of the servient tenement gave permission and that there is a deed or written agreement to this effect, or that the owner of the servient tenement interrupted the enjoyment of the right for a continous period of a year by erecting something which blocked the light. Under the Rights of Light Act, 1959, it is no longer necessary to erect something of this nature; the owner of the servient land may now register on the local land charges register a statutory notice indicating where he would have put up a screen, and this operates as if the access of light had been restricted for one year. User as of right is not necessary, and oral consent will not bar the claim even if the claimant has made regular money payments for the use of the right.

The right can only be claimed having regard to the type of room affected. A bedroom does not require the amount of light that other rooms do, and if the claimant has used the bedroom to repair watches for twenty years, he will still only be able to claim that amount of light appropriate to a bedroom. There is no right to receive unlimited light but in *Ough* v. *King*, [1967] 3 All E.R. 859, the Court of Appeal held that in determining whether there was an infringement of a right to light regard must be had to the nature of the locality and to the higher standard of lighting required in modern times. There is no claim to a view or a prospect which can be seen from a window.

Profits à prendre.   The general period for prescription here is thirty years under the Act of 1832, though twenty years is enough if the Court is presuming a lost modern grant. (*Tehidy Minerals* v. *Norman,* 1971.)[745]

If an easement is denied or threatened, it would be necessary to ask the court for an injunction to prevent the owner of the servient tenement from acting contrary to the easement, and its existence would have to be proved under one of the headings given above. The court may then—

(*a*) find the easement not proved; or

(*b*) grant an injunction to restrain the owner of the servient tenement from acting contrary to it; or

(*c*) if the infringement is not serious the court may award once for all damages, in which case the servient owner will have bought his right to act contrary to the easement.

Termination or extinguishment of servitudes

Servitudes may be extinguished by statute, or by express or implied release. At law a deed is necessary for express release, but in Equity an informal release will be effective if it would be inequitable for the dominant owner to claim that the right still exists.

If the dominant owner shows by his conduct an intention to release an easement, it will be extinguished. The demolition of a house to which an easement of light attaches may amount to an implied release, but not if it is intended to replace the house by another building. Mere non-user is not enough, although it may be some evidence of intention to abandon the right. (*Tehidy Minerals* v. *Norman,* 1971.)[745] There is no fixed time but twenty years' non-user usually constitutes abandonment.

We have already seen that an easement is extinguished when the dominant and servient tenements come into simultaneous ownership and possession of the same person, since a man cannot have an easement over his own land.

RESTRICTIVE COVENANTS

A restrictive convenant is essentially a contract between two owners of land whereby one agrees to restrict the use of his land for the benefit of the other. We are not concerned here with covenants in leases, which are governed by separate rules already outlined.

Such covenants where not adequately enforced by the common law because the doctrine of privity of contract applied, and as soon as one of the parties to the convenant transferred his land, the covenant was not enforceable by the transferee because he had not been a party to the original contract. However, the common law realized that this was rather too rigid and went so far as to allow a transferee to enforce the benefit of the covenant against the original party to it. Thus if A, the owner of Blackacre, agreed with B, the owner of Whiteacre, that he would not use Blackacre for the purposes of trade, then if B sold Whiteacre to C, C could enforce the covenant against A. However, if A sold Blackacre to D, C could not enforce the covenant against D, because the common law would not allow D to bear the burden of a covenant he did not make.

Equity takes a different view, and allows C to enforce the sort of covenant outlined above by injunction, if the following conditions are fulfilled—

(I) The covenant must be substantially negative.   Much depends upon the words used in the covenant, and an undertaking which seems *prima facie* to be positive may imply a negative undertaking and this may then be enforced. (*Tulk* v. *Moxhay*, 1848.)[153] A covenant to use a house as a dwelling house implies that it will not be used for other purposes, and would be enforceable in the negative sense. If the covenant requires the convenantor to spend money, it is not a negative covenant.

(ii) The covenant must benefit the land.   It is often said that the covenant must 'touch and concern' the land and must not be merely for the personal benefit of the claimant. Restrictive covenants usually endeavour to keep up the residential character of the district and benefit the land by preserving value and amenities as a residential property.

(iii) The person claiming the benefit must retain land which can benefit from the covenant taken.   (*Kelly* v. *Barrett*, 1924.)[748] If X owns a piece of land which he splits up into two plots, selling one plot to Y and taking a restrictive covenant in favour of the plot he has retained, then he can enforce the covenant so long as he retains the land to be benefited. If X now sells the plot he had retained, he will not be able to enforce the covenant for the future, although the purchaser from X will be able to do so.

There is an exception to this rule in the case of *building schemes* involving an estate of houses. Here the covenants are taken by the owner of the land from each person purchasing a house, and although the owner does not retain any of the land, the covenants may be enforced by the purchasers as between themselves. However, a building scheme will not be implied simply because there is a common vendor and the existence of common covenants. It was at one time thought that there must be a defined area and evidence of laying out in lots (*Re Wembley Park Estate Co. Ltd's Transfer*, [1968] 1 All E.R. 457). However, in *Re Dolphin's Conveyance*, [1970] 2 All E.R. 664, Stamp, J., held that so long as the covenants in the conveyances were, as a matter of construction, intended to give the purchasers of the parcels mutual rights, this was sufficient to make them enforceable and there was no need, in particular, to consider lotting.

Since restrictive covenants are in general enforceable only in Equity, the question of notice arises. So if X sells a piece of land which is subject to a covenant to a purchaser who has no notice of the covenant, the purchaser is not bound. However, it is possible to register a restrictive covenant as a land charge and this operates as notice to all purchasers. Under Sect. 84 of the Law of Property Act, 1925 (as amended by Sect. 28(6) of the Law of Property Act, 1969), the Lands Tribunal has power, on the application of any person interested, to discharge or modify a restrictive covenant.

THE TRANSFER OF LAND

It is usual, when a disposition of land is contemplated, to draw up a contract. For a contract of sale to be valid both parties must have contractual capacity, the contract must be legal, there must be clear agreement on all the essential terms, and acceptance of the offer must be unconditional. Where one accepts an offer to sell 'subject to contract', no contract is effected until a formal contract is approved.

Under Sect. 40 of the Law of Property Act, 1925, it is provided that no action may be brought upon any contract for the sale or other disposition of land, or any interest in land, unless the agreement upon which such action is brought, or some memorandum or note thereof, is in writing and signed by the party to be charged or some other person lawfully authorized. In the absence of a note or memorandum the contract is unenforceable, though the equitable doctrine of part performance may sometimes be invoked.

When a valid contract for sale exists, the purchaser acquires an equitable interest in the property and the vendor is in effect a qualified trustee for him. Thus if the property increases in value between contract and completion, the purchaser is entitled to the increase and similarly he must bear any loss. This is particularly important in cases where property is destroyed by fire between contract and completion, since the purchaser would still have to pay the purchase money, even although he only received a conveyance of the land with the useless buildings on it. It is now provided by Sect. 47 of the Law of Property Act, 1925, that in such a case the purchaser may become entitled to money payable on an insurance policy maintained by the vendor.

The vendor has a lien on the property sold to the extent of the unpaid purchase money and may enforce this by an order for sale; this lien may be registered as general equitable charge. The purchaser has a similar lien in respect of money paid under the contract prior to conveyance.

On a sale of land it is usual to use a standard form of contract prepared by The Law Society since this saves much trouble in drafting. In what is called an open contract for the sale of land the vendor must under Sect. 23 of the Law of Property Act, 1969, show a title for a least fifteen years, beginning with a good 'root or title', i.e. a document dealing with the whole legal and equitable interests in the land. It may be necessary to go back more than fifteen years in order to find such a document. The vendor prepares an abstract of title, listing all the relevant documents in connection with its establishment, and he must produce these documents in order to justify the abstract of title he has prepared. It should be noted that all the above matters are attended to by the parties' solicitors.

A contract for the sale of land will normally contain a completion date which is the time by which the transaction must be concluded. The transfer of land involves the following stages—

(*a*) The preparation of the contract.

(*b*) The exchange of contracts between the vendor's and purchaser's solicitors, when the purchaser pays a deposit, usually ten per cent of the purchase money.

(*c*) The delivery by the vendor's solicitors of an abstract of title.

(*d*) The examination of this title by the purchaser's solicitors and the checking of the abstract against the actual deeds to see that it is correct.

(*e*) After all outstanding queries have been solved, a conveyance is prepared by the purchaser's solicitors which is sent to the vendor's solicitors for approval. The draft conveyance may be exchanged a number of times before agreement is reached. Where the land is registered, a simpler form of transfer deed is used.

(*f*) Just before completion the purchaser's solicitors will make the necessary searches in the Land Charges Register and in the Register maintained by the appropriate local authority to see what encumbrances are registered in respect of the property.

(*g*) An appointment is then arranged for completion and the purchaser hands over the money, the vendor handing over the conveyance, which he has signed, together with the title deeds. This brings the transaction to a conclusion.

The above procedure refers to unregistered land where the need to examine title is to some extent cumbersome and expensive. The Land Registration Act, 1925, provides that the title to land can be examined by and registered with the state followed by the issue of a certificate guaranteeing ownership. Where there is a sale of registered land the certificate is handed over and the name of the new owner registered. This is a more simple procedure than the one outlined above for unregistered land and the legal fees for the transaction are less.

PERSONAL PROPERTY

We have already mentioned that personal property is divided into two classes—*choses in action* and *choses in possession,* the latter being divided into *chattels real* (i.e. leaseholds and *chattels personal*). We have already dealt with leaseholds, and the sale of chattels personal has been codified by the Sale of Goods Act, 1893, a study of which would not be appropriate to a book of this nature. The assignment of choses in action is considered on p. 419.

MORTGAGES OF LAND

Legal mortgage of freeholds

Under the 1925 legislation the mortgagor (the borrower) does not divest himself of his legal estate, but grants to the mortgagee (the lender) a demise for a term of years absolute. Thus, if X owns Blackacre and borrows money on mortgage from Y, he will grant Y a term of usually three thousand years in Blackacre, both agreeing that the term of years will end when the loan is repaid. X will also agree to pay interest on the loan at a stipulated rate.

Alternatively, under the provisions of Sect. 87 of the Law of Property Act, 1925, it is possible to create a legal mortgage of freeholds by means of a short deed stating that a charge on the land is created. Such a charge does not give a term of years, but the mortgagee has the same rights and powers as if he had received a term of years under a mortgage by demise.

Before 1926 mortgages were created by conveying the freehold to the mortgagee. Since 1925 an attempt to create a mortgage by this method operates as a grant of a mortgage lease of 3000 years, subject to cesser on redemption. (Section 85, Law of Property Act, 1925.)

Legal mortgages of leaseholds

If X, the owner of ninety-nine years lease of Blackacre, borrows money on mortgage from Y, he may grant Y a sub-lease of (say) ninety-nine years less ten days, both agreeing that when the loan is repaid the term shall cease. X also agrees to pay interest. Such a term is known as a *mortgage by demise.*

Alternatively a legal mortgage of leaseholds may be created by a charge by way of legal mortgage under Sect. 87 of the Law of Property Act, 1925, if made by deed. No sub-lease is created but the remedies of the mortgagee are the same as if it had been.

When a person has borrowed money by mortgaging property, he may still be able to borrow further sums, if the amount of the charge is not equal to the full value of the property and there seems to be adequate security for further loans. The owner of freehold land may grant a term of three thousand years plus one day to another mortgagee, whilst the owner of a lease may grant a second sub-lease of (say) ninety-nine years less nine days. Alternatively, a second charge by way of legal mortgage may created by a further deed.

The only limit to further borrowing on second and subsequent mortgages is that of finding a lender who is prepared to become a second, third, or fourth mortgagee.

Equitable mortgages

A mortgagee who receives a mere equitable interest in the land is said to have an equitable mortgage. Thus if the borrower's interest is equitable, e.g. a life interest, then any mortgage of it is necessarily equitable. Such an interest may be mortgaged by lease or charge, as in legal mortgages, or by a deposit of title deeds with the lender, usually accompanied by a memorandum explaining the transaction. Such mortgages must be in writing and signed by the borrower or his agent. (Section 53, Law of Property Act, 1925.)

An informal mortgage of a legal estate or interest creates an equitable mortgage, e.g. an attempt to create a legal mortgage otherwise than by deed.

Where there is a binding agreement to create a legal mortgage, but the formalities necessary to do so have not been carried out, Equity regards the agreement as an equitable mortgage. The agreement can be enforced by specific performance so that the mortgagee can obtain a legal mortgage from the borrower under the Rule in *Walsh* v. *Lonsdale,* 1882.[735] Before there is a binding agreement there must be either written evidence of the agreement, signed by the borrower or his agent, or a sufficient act of part performance by the lender.

Rights of the mortgagor or borrower

The main right of the mortgagor is the right to redeem (or recover) the land. Originally at common law the land became the property of the lender as soon as the date decided upon for repayment had passed, unless during that time the loan had been repaid. However, Equity regarded a mortgage as essentially a security, and gave the mortgagor the right to redeem the land at any time on payment of the principal sum, plus interest due to the date of payment. What is more important, this rule applied even though the common law date for repayment had passed. This right, which still exists, is called the *Equity of Redemption,* and there are two important rules connected with it—

(a) Once a mortgage always a mortgage. This means that Equity looks at the real purpose of the transaction and does not always have regard to its form. If Equity considers that the transaction is a mortgage, the rules appertaining to mortgages will apply, particularly the right to redeem the

property even though the contractual date for repayment has passed, or has not yet arrived. In the latter case, however, the mortgagor must generally give six months' notice of his intention to redeem, or pay six months' interest in lieu, so that the mortgagee may find another investment. However, if the parties contract at arm's length, and there is no evidence of oppression by the mortgagee, the court will endeavour to uphold the principle of sanctity of contract and will enforce any reasonable restriction on the right to redeem. (*Knightsbridge Estates Trust Ltd* v. *Byrne,* 1939.)[749]

(b) There must be no clog on the equity of redemption. This means—

(i) that the court will not allow postponement of the repayment period for an unreasonable time; and

(ii) the property mortgaged must, when the loan is repaid, be returned to the borrower in the same condition as when it was pledged. (*Noakes* v. *Rice,* 1902.)[750]

Nevertheless, particularly in modern times, so long as the parties are at arm's length when the loan is negotiated, Equity will allow a collateral transaction. (*Kreglinger* v. *New Patagonia Meat and Cold Storage Co.,* 1914,[751] and *Cityland and Property (Holdings) Ltd.* v. *Dabrah,* 1967.)[752]

It is worth noting that the mortgagor may, where he is in possession of the land, grant leases to third parties subject to any special agreement to the contrary.

Powers and remedies of the legal mortgagee

A legal mortgagee (the lender) has the following concurrent powers and remedies—

(a) To take possession. This right does not depend upon default by the mortgagor, but the mortgagee will normally only enter into possession of the property under the term of years granted to him, or under the charge by way of legal mortgage, when he is not being paid the sum due, and when he wishes to pay himself from the proceeds of the property. In addition, the court will grant a possession order where an insurance policy which is the security has been allowed to lapse by the borrower. (*Western Bank* v. *Schindler,* [1976] 2 All E.R. 393.) This is not a desirable remedy, however, because when the mortgagee takes possession he is strictly accountable to the mortgagor, not only for what he has received but for what he might have received with the exercise of due diligence and proper management. (*White* v. *City of London Brewery Co.,* 1889.)[752] If the mortgagee is simply concerned to intercept rents, where the mortgaged property is let and the mortgagor is a landlord, he will do better to appoint a receiver under the Law of Property Act, 1925, Sect. 109. Most mortgagees who ask for a possession order do so in order to sell with vacant possession. The

Administration of Justice Act, 1970, which is concerned, amongst other things, with mortgage possession actions, reinstates the old practice of the Chancery masters by allowing the Court to make an order adjourning the proceedings, or suspending or postponing a possession order provided it appears that the mortgagor is likely to be able to pay within a reasonable time any sums due under the mortgage (Sect. 36). However, the court cannot suspend the execution of an order for possession indefinitely and must specify the period of suspension. (*Royal Trust Co. of Canada* v. *Markham*, [1975] 3 All E.R. 433.)

The Act applies wherever a mortgage includes a dwelling house even though part may be used for business purposes. Unfortunately, it was held in *Halifax Building Society* v. *Clark,* [1973] 2 W.L.R. 1, that where, as is often the case, the mortgage provided that the whole sum should become payable on default by the mortgagor, the court's power to adjourn or stay execution under Sect. 36 could only be exercised if it appeared likely that the mortgagor could pay the whole sum within a reasonable period. This plainly defeated the intention of the 1970 Act in most cases as the period of the stay envisaged is short, and the likelihood of the mortgagor being able to repay the entire redemption figure, remote. Accordingly, Sect. 8 of the Administration of Justice Act, 1973, now provides that a court may treat as due under the mortgage only those instalments actually in arrear, but shall not exercise the power to postpone the order for possession unless the mortgagor will be able to catch up within a reasonable period. This means that not only must he be able to pay the instalments due month by month but also the arrears within a reasonable time.

(b) Foreclosure. The mortgagee may obtain a foreclosure order from the court if the mortgagor fails to pay for an unreasonable time. The first order is a *foreclosure order nisi* providing that the debt must be paid within a stated time. If it is not so paid, the order is made *absolute* and the property becomes that of the mortgagee, the mortgagor's equity of redemption being barred, and the property vesting in the mortgagee, free from any right of redemption either in law or Equity. Such orders are seldom used, for it is still open to the court to re-open the foreclosure, i.e. to give the mortgagor a further opportunity to redeem. Section 36 of the Administration of Justice Act, 1970, excluded the power to postpone a foreclosure order because it was considered that the court's power to give the mortgagor time to redeem when granting the decree *nisi* was an adequate remedy. The Payne Committee recommended including actions for foreclosure, and they are now included by the Administration of Justice Act, 1973, Sect. 8(3). Thus the courts now have power to postpone an order for foreclosure.

(c) Right of sale. Normally this is the most valuable right of the mortgagee. Subject to certain conditions he can, on the default of the mortgagor, sell and convey to a purchaser the whole of the mortgaged property, and recoup himself out of the proceeds. Unless the mortgagee is a building society (Building Societies Act, 1962, Sect. 36), he is not a trustee of the power of sale for the benefit of the mortgagor. However, he must not fraudulently, wilfully or recklessly sacrifice the property of the mortgagor (*Kennedy* v. *De Trafford,* [1897] A.C. 180) and in addition owes a duty to the mortgagor to take reasonable care to obtain the best price that can be had in the circumstances. (*Cuckmere Brick Co. Ltd* v. *Mutual Finance,* [1971] 2 All E.R. 633.) A mortgagee cannot sell to himself or to his nominee.

(d) To sue for the money owing. The mortgage is a pledge for the repayment of the money, but mortgagors almost invariably give a personal covenant to repay. This is of value should the property be destroyed or lose its value. When the date fixed for redemption is passed, the mortgage money is due and the mortgagee can sue for it. He will rarely do so, for in most cases the other remedies will be more satisfactory.

(e) The right to appoint a receiver. The Law of Property Act, 1925, Sect. 109, gives the mortgagee the right to appoint a receiver to receive the rents and profits on the mortgagee's behalf in order to pay the money due.The receiver is deemed to be the agent of the mortgagor, who is liable for his acts and defaults unless otherwise provided by the mortgage. The mortgagee thus avoids the disadvantage of strict accountability to which he would be subject if he entered himself.

Remedies of equitable mortgagees.

Where the mortgage is equitable and is created by deed, then the mortgagee has virtually the same remedies as have been set out above. Otherwise, if the mortgage is by a mere deposit of title deeds, then the mortgagee must ask the court—

(*a*) for an order to sell; or
(*b*) for an order appointing a receiver.

Other rights of mortgagees

A mortgagee has other rights and he may, where the mortgage is created by deed, insure the mortgaged property against loss by fire up to two-thirds of its value, and charge the premiums on the property in the same way as the mortgage money.

A mortgagee has a right to the title deeds of the property, and if the mortgage is redeemed by the mortgagor, the mortgagee must return the deeds to him in the absence of notice of a second or subsequent mortgage, in which case the deeds should be handed to the next mortgagee.

There are two other important rights which a mortgagee may exercise in appropriate circumstances—the right to consolidate and the right to tack.

Consolidation. Where a person has two or more mortgages, he may refuse to allow one mortgage to be redeemed unless the other or others are also redeemed. This right is particularly valuable where property might fluctuate in value, and where a mortgagor might redeem one mortgage where the security was more than adequate, leaving the mortgagee with a debt on the other property not properly secured.

Consolidation is only possible if the right to consolidate was reserved in one of the mortgage deeds, or if the mortgage was contracted prior to 1882. The contractual date for redemption must have passed on all mortgages and they must have been created by the same mortgagor, though not necessarily in favour of the same mortgagee. Nevertheless in such cases, where it is proposed to consolidate two mortgages, both the mortgages must have been vested in one person at the same time as both the equities or redemption were vested in another.

Tacking. The right to tack may bring about a modification of the priority of mortgages. It is now confined to the tacking of further advances. Thus, where a man has lent money on a first mortgage and there are second and third mortgages, if the first mortgagee agrees to advance a further sum, he may tack this to his first mortgage and thus get priority over the second and third, which would normally rank before the tacked mortgage. This can now only be done if the intervening mortgagees agree, or if the further advance is made without notice of an intervening mortgage, or if the prior mortgage imposed an obligation to make further advances.

Attornment clause. Many mortgages contain an attornment clause by which the borrower attorns or acknowledges himself as a tenant at will, or from year to year, of the lender at a nominal rent such as a peppercorn. The advantage of such a clause was that it entitled the lender to evict the borrower for failure to pay the mortgage instalments and so obtain possession more speedily. However, changes in the rules of court from 1933–37 made a speedy procedure available to mortgagees as such, and there is now no substantial advantage in an attornment clause.

Priority of mortgages

The Land Charges Act, 1925, introduced the principle of registering charges on land. The object of searching the Land Charges Register is to discover the rights, if any, of third parties which are enforceable against the land. It is a general principle that a purchaser or mortgagee of land is deemed to have actual notice of all third-party rights capable of registration and actually registered, whereas he acquires his interest in the land free from third-party rights capable of registration and not registered. There are five separate registers kept in the Land Charges Department of the Land Registry. Search is usually done by filling in an appropriate form and sending it to the Land Charges Superintendent. This results in an *official search certificate.*

Where there is a mortgage of a legal estate with deposit of title deeds, the mortgage ranks from the date of its creation and such a mortgage cannot be registered.

Where there is a mortgage of legal estate without deposit of title deeds, the mortgage ranks from its date of registration as a land charge.

Regarding mortgages of equitable interests, the question of priority is based on the rule in *Dearle* v. *Hall* (1828), 3 Russ. 1, and such mortgages rank from the date on which the mortgagee gave notice of his mortgage to the trustees of the equitable interest, though such notice will not postpone a previous mortgage of which the mortgagee giving notice was aware. Equitable mortgages of interests other than equitable interests rank in priority according to the date of creation. Thus, an equitable mortgage created in January, 1975, would take priority over one created in May, 1975. Legal mortgages take precedence over equitable mortgages, but an equitable mortgagee who obtains a legal interest does not thereby gain priority over an equitable interest of which he has constructive notice. Thus if A obtains an equitable interest in property, e.g. a contract to purchase land, in January, 1975, and fails to register it as an estate contract until May, 1975, and B in February, 1975, obtains an equitable mortgage over the land which is converted into a legal mortgage in April, 1975, at a time when B knows or ought to know that A has an interest, as where A is on the land and carrying out works, then B's mortgage, although legal will not rank over A's equitable interest. (*McCarthy and Stone* v. *Julian S. Hodge & Co.,* [1971] 2 All. E.R. 973.)

The Leasehold Reform Act, 1967

Where, under the provisions of this Act, a leaseholder buys the freehold, the conveyance automatically discharges the premises from any mortgage even though the lender is not a party to the conveyance. (Section 12(1).) However, the leaseholder must apply the money which he is using to buy the freehold, in the first instance, in or towards the payment (or redemption) of the mortgage. (Section 12(2).) If the lender raises difficulties the tenant may, in order to protect his interest, pay the money into court. (Section 13.) The lender (or mortgagee) must accept not less than three months' notice to pay off the whole or part of the principal secured by the mortgage, together with interest to the date of payment regardless of any provisions to the contrary in the mortgage. (Section 12(4).)

The court is also given power, under Sect. 36, to alter the rights of the parties to a mortgage in order to mitigate any financial hardship which may arise as a result of the purchase of a freehold under the provisions of the Act.

If it is desired that a mortgage of the former leasehold interest should be extended to cover the freehold, this may be done by requesting the borrower to execute a deed of substituted security. If a tenant acquires an extended lease a lender is entitled to possession of the documents of title relating to the new lease (Sect. 14(6)) and should ask for them when the borrower obtains an extended lease. The borrower should also be required to execute a mortgage of the extended lease.

REGISTRATION OF LAND CHARGES

The Land Charges Act, 1925, and the Land Registration Act, 1925, introduced the principle of registering charges on land. The object of searching the Land Charges Register is to discover the rights, if any, of third parties which are enforceable against the land. It is a general principle that a purchaser or mortgagee of land is deemed to have actual notice of all third-party rights capable of registration and actually registered, whereas he acquires his interest in the land free from third-party rights capable of registration and not registered.

The injustice to a purchaser of this rule lay in the fact that in practice there is no investigation of the title prior to the formation of the contract. In consequence, if a vendor did not actually disclose to a purchaser that there were charges over the land, then, if the charges were registered, the purchaser was unable to rescind the contract since he was deemed to know that they existed. In future, under Sect. 24 of The Law of Property Act, 1969, the purchaser will be affected *as against his vendor* only by land charges of which he had *actual* knowledge at the time of entering into the contract. If he completes the contract the purchaser remains bound by registered land charges *as against the holder of the charge* whether or not he has actual knowledge of them.

The present system of registration of land charges at the Land Registry is governed by the Land Charges Act, 1972, in the case of unregistered land and by the Land Registration Act, 1925, in the case of registered land. Prior registration of a land charge does not of itself confer priority; it merely gives notice to everyone dealing with the property so that they will take subject to the charge as purchasers with notice of it. Failure to register a land charge merely means that upon completion of a purchase the charge will be void against the purchaser. Right up to completion the person with the benefit of a land charge can preserve his rights by registering the charge.

The most important search is in the Registers of the Land Registry, though local land charges appear in registers kept by local authorities. A common example of a local land charge is road charges, i.e. charges against land which the local authority has in regard to the cost of making up a road which adjoins that land. Search may be in person at Plymouth or Croydon, or may be done by filling the details of the appropriate form and sending it to the Land Registry. This results in an official search certificate.

It is now possible to ask for search by telephone or telex, the applicant receiving a printed result of the search by post. The Land Charges Act,

1972, introduced a number of changes designed to simplify the procedure. These include changes made necessary by computerization.

The registers are basically registers of names, not properties. Thus a charge affecting Whiteacre, a property situated in Birmingham and owned by John Jones, will be indexed under John Jones, provided he was owner of Whiteacre when the charge was created. Sometimes charges are registered in the name of the property but now that search is by computer this does not give rise to difficulties.

There are five separate registers—

(1) A register of pending actions.   These are actions which are being pursued with regard to the land, e.g. a petition in bankruptcy.

(2) A register of annuities.   This Register contains annuities registered before 1926. Other annuities are registered as Class C Land Charges.

(3) A register of writs and orders affecting land.   These are various orders enforcing judgments, e.g. a receiving order in bankruptcy.

(4) A register of deeds of arrangement.   These are assignments of property for the benefit of creditors generally.

(5) A register of land charges.   The most important classes are as follows—
   Class A.   Charges created as a result of the application of some person under the provisions of an Act of Parliament, e.g. a charge under Sect. 72 of the Agricultural Holdings Act, 1948, by the provisions of which a tenant of agricultural land has a charge against the land in respect of the value of improvements he has carried out.
   Class C.   Such charges are subdivided as follows—

   (i) *Puisne mortgages.*   These are legal mortgages of a legal estate in land where the mortgagee does not obtain the title deeds. They are invariably second or third mortgages.

   (ii) *Limited owners' charges.*   These are equitable charges which a tenant for life acquires by discharging out of his own pocket liabilities due from the property. The commonest example is Capital Transfer Tax.

   (iii) *General equitable charges* (except those arising under a settlement or trust for sale. These are not registrable because the object of the law is to allow them to be over-reached). The most usual example is an equitable mortgage of a legal estate. Annuities created after 1925 are registrable here, but not if they arise under a settlement or trust for sale.

   (iv) *Estate contracts.*   These may be defined as 'any contract by an estate owner or by a person entitled at the date of the contract to have a legal estate conveyed to him, to convey or create a legal estate'. Thus if the owner of the legal estate in Whiteacre enters into an agreement for the sale thereof, this contract is registrable as an estate contract. However, the contract must be binding on the parties so that an agreement 'subject to contract' would not be capable of registration. (*Thomas* v. *Rose*, [1968] 3 All E.R. 765.) Nor would a contract unenforceable for want of a memorandum in writing sufficient to satisfy Sect. 40 of the Law of Property Act, 1925. (*Mens* v. *Wilson, The Times,* November 14, 1973.)

Class D. This class may be subdivided as follows—

(i) *Capital Transfer Tax.* The Commissioners of Inland Revenue may register a charge for Capital Transfer Tax.

(ii) *Restrictive covenants.* These are any covenants or agreements entered into after 1925 which restrict the use of land and are not between lessor and lessee.

(iii) *Equitable easements created after* 1925.

Class F. The Matrimonial Homes Act, 1967, created a new type of land charge registrable under this class. It was passed to restore the legal position to what it was before the decision of the House of Lords in *National Provincial Bank Ltd* v. *Ainsworth,* [1965] 2 All E.R. 472. In that case it was decided that a deserted wife had no special right or 'equity' to continue to occupy the matrimonial home though there had formerly been such a right. The effect of the decision in *Ainsworth's Case* was that a husband who was the owner of the matrimonial home could, having deserted his wife and children, sell or mortgage the house to a third party who would in most cases be able to get an order for possession in order to enforce his rights. In these circumstances the deserted wife and children would have to give up occupation of the matrimonial home and find other accommodation.

The Act provides that where one spouse owns or is the tenant of the matrimonial home, the other spouse has certain 'rights of occupation' (Sect. 1(1)) and cannot be evicted without an order of the court. Where a spouse is not in occupation of the matrimonial home he or she has a right, with the leave of the court, to enter and occupy the house. However, the court may order a spouse who is occupying the matrimonial home by reason of the Act to make periodical payments to the other spouse in respect of that occupation. It should be noted that the Act protects husbands as well as wives.

The Act provides that the rights of occupation provided for in Sect. 1(1) are a charge on the estate or interest of the other spouse (Sect. 2(1)), registrable as a new type of land charge (Class F) under the Land Charges Act, 1972. Where the land is registered land a notice or caution must be registered under the Land Registration Act, 1925. A purchaser or mortgagee is deemed to have notice of rights of occupation which have been properly registered. Rights of occupation may be registered on marriage though in most cases registration will not take place unless and until the marriage breaks down.

Where a spouse registers rights of occupation, the house is unlikely subsequently to be an acceptable security for a loan because the rights of occupation represent a prior charge on the property which cannot be sold with vacant possession. However, a spouse who is entitled to rights of occupation may, under Sect. 6(3) of the Act, agree in writing that any other charge shall rank in priority to his or her charge.

Searching applies to unregistered land, but in many parts of the country land registration is compulsory, e.g. in London, Middlesex and Surrey. The system of registration of title to land is similar to registration of title to shares. However, in place of the share register which a company keeps there is a register of land holdings which is maintained by the state and instead of a share certificate there is a land certificate. When the land is transferred the registered owner hands over the land certificate together with a deed of transfer signed by him to the purchaser who then registers these documents with the Registrar who amends the land register and the land certificate and returns the latter to the transferee. In general terms the state guarantees the accuracy of the register and if there is an error the register will be rectified and an indemnity paid to anyone who suffers loss, e.g. a person does not, in fact, get a good title to the land. The only interests in respect of which title may be registered are legal estates in land, i.e. a fee simple absolute in possession or a term of years absolute. As regards other interests in the land, all registered land is deemed to be subject to overriding interests listed in Sect. 70 of the Land Registration Act, 1925, whether these are on the register or not. Some of the more important overriding interests are easements and profits which exist over the land. Other interests may be protected by requiring an entry of, e.g. a caution on the register. This entitles the person who asks for the caution to be notified by the Registrar of any proposed dealings with the land and to object within a specified period of time. Thus a purchaser under an estate contract could protect himself against further sales of the property in a situation where he had purchased it but had not yet received the land certificate from the registered proprietor.

It is expected that the compulsory registration system will, broadly speaking, be extended to all areas of the country by 1980. However, registration only occurs when a particular property changes hands. This phases the work and means that a property which is not sold or leased stays unregistered.

MORTGAGES OF PERSONAL CHATTELS

Just as land can be used as a means of securing debts, so also can personal chattels. There are two principal ways in which this can be done—

(a) By mortgage. In this case the borrower retains possession of his goods but transfers their ownership to the lender to secure the loan.

This raises a problem because, since the borrower retains the chattels, he also retains an appearance of wealth, and this may mislead others into giving him credit. Accordingly the Bills of Sale Acts, 1878–91, were passed, and under the statutory provisions, where chattels are retained by the mortgagor, a bill of sale must be made out. Where ownership of the chattel passes to the mortgagee conditionally upon its being reconveyed to the mortgagor on repayment of the loan, the Bill of Sale is called a conditional bill. An absolute Bill of Sale is one which transfers completely the ownership in chattels by way of sale, gift or settlement.

All Bills of Sale must be attested and registered within seven days of execution. Registration is in the Central Office of the Supreme Court. Conditional Bills of Sale must be re-registered every five years if they are still operative.

A conditional Bill of Sale is totally void if it is not registered, whilst an unregistered absolute Bill of Sale is void against the trustee in bankruptcy and judgment creditors of the grantor so that the chattels represented by the Bill are available to pay the grantor's debts. However an absolute bill of sale will not be void for want of registration unless the chattels remain in the sole possession, or apparent possession, of the transferor (or grantor) of the bill. (*Koppel* v. *Koppel*, 1966.)[753]

(b) By pledge, or 'pawn'.   In this case the lender obtains possession of the goods, the borrower retaining ownership. Thus there is no danger that the borrower will obtain credit on the strength of his possession of the chattels, and the law relating to pledges is mainly concerned to protect the interests of the borrower (or pledger) against dishonest pawnbrokers.

MORTGAGES OF CHOSES IN ACTION

It is possible to use a chose in action as security for a loan, and mortgagees frequently take life assurance policies as security, e.g. a bank in the case of an overdraft. However, shares in companies are perhaps the commonest chose in action to be used as security.

Shares may be made subject to a legal mortgage, but here the shares must actually be transferred to the mortgagee so that his name is in fact on the company's share register. An agreement is made out in which the mortgagee agrees to re-transfer the shares to the mortgagor when the loan is repaid.

It is also possible to have an equitable mortgage of company shares, and this is in fact the usual method adopted. The share certificate is deposited with the mortgagee, together with a blank transfer signed by the registered holder, the name of the transferee being left blank. The shares are not actually transferred, but the agreement accompanying the transaction allows the mortgagee to sell the shares by completing the form of transfer and registering himself as the legal owner if the mortgagor fails to repay the loan.

OTHER FORMS OF SECURITY

A security is some right or interest in property given to a creditor so that, if the debt is not paid, the creditor can obtain the amount of the debt by exercising certain remedies against the property, rather than by suing the debtor by means of a personal action on his promise to pay. Securities, therefore, create rights over the property of another and since we have already discussed mortgages of land, chattels and choses in action it remains only to consider the lien.

LIEN

A lien is a right over the property of another which arises by operation of law and independently of any agreement. It gives a creditor the right (a) to retain possession of the debtor's property until he has paid or settled the debt, or (b) to sell the property in satisfaction of the debt in those cases where the lien is not possessory. Where the parties agree that a lien shall be created, such agreement will effectively create one.

Possessory or Common Law Lien

To exercise this type of lien the creditor must have actual possession of the debtor's property, in which case he can retain it until the debt is paid or settled. It should be noted that the creditor cannot ask for possession of the debtor's goods in order to exercise a lien.

A common law lien may be particular or general—

(a) Particular lien. This gives the possessor the right to retain goods until a debt arising in connection with those goods is paid.

(b) General lien. This gives the possessor the right to retain goods not only for debts specifically connected with them, but also for all debts due from the owner of the goods however arising.

The law favours particular rather than general liens.

If X sends a clock to R to be repaired at a cost of 50p, R may retain the clock under a particular lien until the 50p is paid. If, however, X owed R 75p for the earlier repair of a watch, R cannot retain the clock to enforce the payment of £1.25p unless, as is unlikely, he can claim a general lien.

The following are cases of *particular lien*—

(i) A carrier can retain goods entrusted to him for carriage until his charges are paid.

(ii) An innkeeper has a lien over the property brought into the inn by a guest and also over property sent to him while there, even if it does not belong to him. (*Robins* v. *Gray*, 1895.)[754] The lien does not extend to motor cars or other vehicles, or to horses or other animals.

(iii) A shipowner has a lien on the cargo for freight due.

(iv) In a sale of goods, the unpaid seller has a lien on the goods, if still in his possession, to recover the price.

(v) Where a chattel is bailed in order that work may be done on it or labour and skill expended in connection with it, it may be retained until the charge is paid. Such liens may arise in favour of a car repairer over the car repaired; by an arbitrator on the award; by an architect over plans he has prepared; and innumerable other instances of this character.

A *general lien* may arise out of contract or custom, and the following classes of persons have a general lien over the property of their customers or clients—factors, bankers, solicitors, stockbrokers, and in some cases insurance brokers. (*Caldwell* v. *Sumpters,* 1971.)[755] In the course of their professional work accountants have at least a particular lien for unpaid fees over any books, files and papers delivered to them by clients and also over any other documents which come into their possession while acting for clients. (See *Woodworth* v. *Conroy, The Times,* 12 November, 1975.)

Although a common law lien normally gives no power of sale, there are some exceptional cases in which a right of sale is given by statute. Such a right is given to innkeepers (Innkeepers Act, 1878), unpaid sellers of goods (Sale of Goods Act, 1893), and bailees who accept goods for repair or other treatment for reward (Torts (Interference with Goods) Act, 1977). Briefly, the latter Act provides for the sale of goods accepted for repair or other treatment or for valuation or appraisal or for storage and warehousing provided the bailee gives notice to the bailor specifying the date on or after which he proposes to sell the goods. The period between the notice and the date specifying sale must be such as will afford the bailor a reasonable opportunity of taking delivery of the goods. However, if he does not do so the bailee may sell them but must account to the bailor for the balance of the proceeds of sale after deduction of charges and expenses.

It should also be noted that the High Court has a discretion to order the sale of goods if it is just to do so, e.g. where the goods are perishable. (And see *Larner* v. *Fawcett,* 1950.)[756]

A common law lien is discharged—

(*a*) by payment of the sum owing;
(*b*) by parting with the possession of the goods or other property upon which the lien is being exercised (but see *Caldwell* v. *Sumpters,* 1971.)[755];
(*c*) by an agreement to give credit for the amount due;
(*d*) by accepting an alternative security for the debt owing.

Maritime lien

A maritime lien does not depend on possession. It is a right which attaches to a ship in connection with a maritime liability. It travels with the ship and may be enforced by the arrest and the sale of the ship through the medium of a court having Admiralty jurisdiction. Examples of such liens are—

(*a*) Liens of salvors.

(*b*) The lien of a master for his outgoings.

(*c*) Liens which arise from damage due to collision.

(*d*) Liens of bottomry bond holders.

The order of attachment of liens is important and depends on the circumstances.

Successive salvage liens attach in inverse order, later ones being preferred to earlier ones, since the earlier lien would be useless if the later salvage had not preserved the ship from loss. Claims for collision damage are treated as of equal rank. Liens for wages, in the absence of salvage liens, have priority over other liens; however, liens for wages earned before a salvage operation are postponed to the lien for salvage, since the value of such a lien has been preserved by the salvage operation.

If a ship which is subject to lien is sold, the purchaser takes it subject to the lien and is responsible for discharging it.

Equitable lien

An equitable lien is an equitable right, conferred by law, whereby one man acquires a charge on the property of another until certain claims have been met. It differs from a common law lien which is founded on possession and does not confer a power of sale. An equitable lien is independent of possession and may be enforced by a judicial sale.

An equitable lien may arise out of an express provision in a contract or from the relationship between parties. Thus a partner has an equitable lien upon the partnership assets for the purpose of ensuring that they are applied, on dissolution, to paying partnership debts. Furthermore, an *unpaid* vendor of land has an equitable lien on the property even after conveyance of ownership to the purchaser, or a third party who has taken it with notice of the lien, under which he may ask the court for an order to sell the property so that he may obtain the purchase money owing to him.

An equitable lien can, like all equitable rights, be extinguished by the owner selling the property to a *bona fide* purchaser for value who has no notice of the lien.

An equitable lien differs from a mortgage. A mortgage as we shall see is always created by the act of parties, and equitable lien may arise by operation of law.

Banker's lien

At common law a banker has a general possessory lien on all securities, and e.g. bills of exchange, promissory notes and bonds, deposited with him by customers in the ordinary course of business unless there is an agreement, express or implied, to the contrary. The lien does not extend to property or securities deposited for safe custody. However, a customer may deposit a security as collateral for a loan, in which case the banker has rights over it, but the transaction is an equitable mortgage rather than a lien.

A banker's lien gives a right of sale, at least of negotiable securities subject to the lien, because Sect. 27 of the Bills of Exchange Act, 1882, provides that a person having a possessory lien over a bill is deemed a holder for value to the extent of the lien, and can, therefore, sell and transfer the bill.

ASSIGNMENTS OF CHOSES IN ACTION

The common law does not recognize assignments of choses in action, but Equity does and so does statute.

Assignment by act of parties

There are four possible categories—

(a) A legal assignment of a legal chose under sect. 136 of the Law of Property Act, 1925.   (This provision was originally contained in the Judicature Act, 1873.) To be effective such an assignment, e.g. the goodwill of a business, must be absolute and not partial; must be in writing signed by the assignor; and must be notified in writing to the debtor, generally by the assignee. If the above requirements are complied with, the assignee can sue the debtor without making the assignor a party to the action. Failure to give notice to the debtor means that there is no legal assignment; the debtor can validly pay the assignor, and the assignee is liable to be postponed to a later assignee for value who notifies the debtor. However, it is not necessary for the date of the assignment to be given in the notice of assignment as long as the letter, or other form of written notice, states clearly that there has been an assignment and identifies the assignee. (*Van Lynn Developments Ltd* v. *Pelias Construction Co. Ltd, The Times,* 10 October, 1968.)

(b) Equitable assignments of legal choses.

(c) Equitable assignments of equitable choses.   The difference between a legal and an equitable chose is historical in that an equitable chose is a right which, before 1875, could only be enforced in the Court of Chancery, e.g. the interest of a beneficiary under a trust fund.

In equitable assignments of legal choses the assignor must be made a party in any action against the debtor, but if the chose is equitable this is not necessary. No particular form is required; all that is necessary is evidence of intention to assign. Notice should be given to the debtor or the trustees, as the case may be, in order to preserve priority as outlined above.

Thus the transfer of a debt by word of mouth, although invalid under statute, may nevertheless be good and enforceable in Equity.

(d) Equitable assignments of mere expectancies.   These are mere hopes of future entitlement, e.g. a legacy under the will of a living testator. The rules regarding such assignments are the same as those set out in (*b*) and (*c*) above, but no notice to the debtor can be given because there is none. Value is not needed for assignments within Sect. 136 of the Law of Property Act, 1925, or for equitable assignments of equitable choses in action. It is probably not needed for an equitable assignment of a legal chose, though the position is not clear. Value is needed for the assignment of mere expectancies; a document under seal is not enough. Value is also needed to support an agreement to assign an equitable chose, but if the assignee lawfully takes delivery of the property assigned, the assignor cannot recover it.

Assignments are said to be 'subject to equities'; the person to whom the right is assigned takes it subject to any right of set off which was available against the original assignor. So if X assigns to Z a debt of £10 due from Y, and X also owes Y £5, then in any action brought by Z for the money, Y can set off the debt of £5. But the assignee is not subject to purely personal claims which would have been available against the assignor, e.g. damages for fraud, though the remedy of rescission is available against the assignee where the assignor obtained the contract by fraud.

Assignments of certain choses in action are governed by special statutes so that the rules outlined above do not apply. In such cases the special statute must be complied with. Examples are—

(*a*)   Bills of exchange, cheques and promissory notes—Bills of Exchange Act, 1882.

(*b*)   Shares in companies registered under the Companies Act, 1948, and previous Acts—The Companies Act, 1948.

(*c*)   Policies of Life Assurance—Policies of Assurance Act, 1867.

Rights of a personal nature under a contract cannot be assigned. If X contracts to write newspaper articles for a certain newspaper, it cannot assign its rights under the contract to another. The right to recover damages in litigation cannot be assigned, for reasons of public policy. Liabilities under a contract cannot be assigned; the party to benefit cannot be compelled by mere notice to accept the performance of another, though a liability can be transferred by a novation (a new contract), if the party to benefit agrees.

Assignment by operation of law

The involuntary assignment of rights and liabilities arises in the case of death and bankruptcy.

(i) Death.   The personal representatives of the deceased acquire his rights and liabilities, the latter to the extent of the estate. Contracts of personal service are discharged.

(ii) Bankruptcy.   The trustee in bankruptcy has vested in him all the rights of the bankrupt, except for actions of a purely personal nature which in no way affect the value of the estate, e.g. actions for defamation. The trustee is liable to the extent of the estate for the bankrupt's liabilities, though the trustee has a right to disclaim onerous or unprofitable contracts.

10 Negotiable Instruments

The major characteristics of a negotiable instrument are as follows—

(*a*) The rights represented by the instrument are transferable merely by delivering it to another, though bills made payable to order require indorsement.

(*b*) Unlike the assignee of an ordinary contractual right, the transferee of a negotiable instrument does not take subject to equities, and he is not affected by defects in the title of his predecessor provided he is what is known as a *holder in due course.*

(*c*) The acceptor of a bill of exchange, or the banker in the case of a cheque, is under a duty to pay the *holder for the time being* of the instrument. So, upon transfer of the instrument, there is no need to notify the acceptor or the banker of a change of ownership, as there is on a legal assignment of other choses in action under the Law of Property Act, 1925.

(*d*) The holder of a bill of exchange can sue upon it in his own name. This can be done with a legal assignment, but not with an equitable one.

Types of instrument

The most important negotiable instruments are bills of exchange, promissory notes and cheques, and these three types are the subject-matter of the Bills of Exchange Act, 1882. Nevertheless, certain other instruments are negotiable namely—

(1) Treasury Bills, i.e. bills issued by the British Government.

(2) Share Warrants if they are to bearer but not otherwise.

(3) Dividend Warrants.

(4) Bonds issued by English companies are negotiable if payable to *bearer,* and bonds issued by a foreign government, or indeed by a foreign corporation, may be negotiable if they are negotiable in the country of issue and also negotiable by custom in England.

(5) Debentures payable to bearer.

(6) Bearer scrip, e.g. where debentures or debenture stock are allotted under terms that they shall be paid for by instalments provisional bearer scrip certificates may be issued to subscribers to be exchanged for proper debentures or stock certificates when all instalments have been paid.

Postal orders, money orders, IOUs, Share Certificates and Share Transfers are not negotiable instruments, nor is a bill of lading.

THE BILLS OF EXCHANGE ACT, 1882

The law relating to bills of exchange has been codified in the Bills of Exchange Act, 1882, and *all section references on this subject are to this Act unless otherwise indicated.*

The nature of a bill of exchange

A bill of exchange is an unconditional order in writing, addressed by one person to another, signed by the person giving it, requiring the person to whom it is addressed to pay on demand, or at a fixed or determinable future time, a sum certain in money to, or to the order of, a specified person or to bearer. (Bills of Exchange Act, 1882, Sect. 3.)

The example on p. 424 is a bill of exchange which is addressed by Richard Brown to G. Green, and requires him to pay £400 to J. White, or his order, six months after the date of the bill which is 1 January, 1978. Richard Brown is called the *drawer,* G. Green is called the *drawee,* and J. White is called the *payee.*

The advantages of a bill of exchange

Although bills of exchange are used mainly in overseas and not in UK transactions it is worth examining why they are used at all.

(1) A bill of exchange provides a creditor with a better remedy.   Once a bill of exchange has been accepted, it settles the amount of the debt owing, and makes a legal remedy easier to obtain than would be the case under an ordinary contract. For example, there is no need to prove in detail the terms of the contract giving rise to the debt.

(2) Bills of exchange may be discounted.   Thus anybody who holds the bill, and is entitled to claim the money on the due date, can discount the bill by taking it to a bank or discounting house. The bank will, in many cases, be willing to take the bill off the holder's hands, pay the holder the present value of the bill and collect the money when due.

(3) A bill may be negotiated.   Anyone who holds a bill of exchange can transfer it to a creditor in payment and White could, if he chose, use the bill in this manner to settle a debt with Gray.

THE PARTIES

The parties to the bill are Brown, the *drawer*; Green, the *drawee*; and White, the *payee*. If Green signs the bill he becomes the *acceptor*, and if White indorses the bill over to Gray, White becomes an *indorser* and Gray an *indorsee* and holder of the bill. Indorsement is effected by signing the bill on the back.

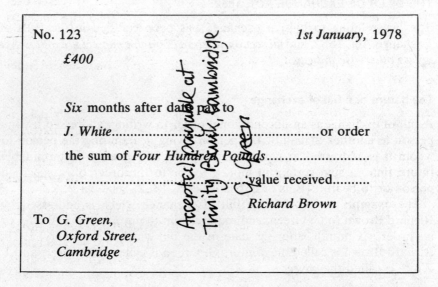

No. 123   *1st January*, 1978

£400

Six months after date pay to

J. White...or order

the sum of *Four Hundred Pounds*.............................

....value received..........

                                        Richard Brown

To G. Green,
    Oxford Street,
    Cambridge

Accepted payable at Trinity Bank, Cambridge. G. Green

Each of the parties to a bill makes certain promises which are implied by law. The drawer on signing the instrument promises that, if the bill is dishonoured, he will pay the amount thereof to the holder and that, if an indorser is called upon to pay the holder, he (the drawer) will indemnify that indorser.

The indorser on signing undertakes that, if the bill is dishonoured, he will pay the amount thereof to the holder and that, if a subsequent indorser is called upon to pay the holder, he (the prior indorser) will indemnify the subsequent indorser.

The acceptor on signing promises that he will pay the amount of the bill to the holder on maturity.

There are now three signatures on the specimen bill above: those of Brown as drawer, Green as acceptor, and White as indorser. The bill matures when six months have elapsed, i.e. on 1 July, 1978. (Banking and Financial Dealings Act, 1971.) On this date Gray, the holder, will present it to Green and demand payment. If Green pays, all parties are satisfied; but if Green dishonours the bill by non-payment, Gray has the following remedies—

(*a*) He can sue for the enforcement of Green's promise to pay when the bill matures;

(*b*) He can sue for the enforcement of Brown's promise to pay if the bill is dishonoured;

(*c*) He can sue for the enforcement of White's promise to pay if the bill is dishonoured.

Gray has thus three rights of action to obtain the money due to him. If he chooses to sue White, then White can recover from Brown on his promise to indemnify any indorser who has to pay the holder.

A bill may get into circulation without being accepted. If it is subsequently presented for acceptance and acceptance is refused, this amounts to dishonour, and the parties whose names appear on the bill can be sued on their implied promises. Since the drawee has not become the acceptor, his signature will not appear so there is no promise of his on which he could be sued.

Holders. A person is a *holder* for the purposes of the Act only if he is either a payee in possession, or an indorsee in possession, or a person in possession of a bearer bill.

A *holder for value* is a person in possession as above of a bill for which at any time value has been given. He is a holder for value as regards all parties prior to himself.

A *holder in due course* is a holder (as defined above) who has taken the bill complete and regular on the face of it (*Arab Bank Ltd* v. *Ross*, 1952);[757] before it was overdue; for value and in good faith; without notice of any defect in the title of his transferor; and if it has been dishonoured, then without notice of dishonour. Every one of these requirements must be satisfied if a holder is to be a holder in due course.

A bill is deemed overdue in the following circumstances—

(*a*) If it has been drawn so that it is payable a fixed number of days, weeks or months after date, the bill is overdue when the relevant period has expired. Days of grace are not now added. (Banking and Financial Dealings Act, 1971.)

(*b*) If the bill is payable a fixed number of days, weeks or months after sight, the period is calculated from the date on which the bill is presented for acceptance. The bill is overdue when the relevant period has expired, and no days of grace are now to be added.

(*c*) If the bill is payable at sight, or on demand, it is overdue when it has been in circulation for an unreasonable length of time. What is unreasonable has never been legally defined, but with regard to cheques it has been suggested that they are stale, from the point of view of taking free from equities, after ten days. With regard to payment by a banker, a cheque is usually held stale after six months, though the drawer is still liable to the holder for the limitation period of six years; the holder may in such a case have taken 'subject to equities'.

Consideration

A bill must be supported by consideration, and any consideration adequate to support an ordinary contract will support a bill (*Pollway Ltd* v. *Abdullah,* 1974)[758] in regard to an action by any person who is a *party* to it. The doctrine of privity of contract is not applicable as regards an action by a *party* to the instrument. Thus if A gives B a cheque for goods received and B indorses it over to C, his daughter, as a birthday present, C can sue A but not B because as between immediate parties the absence of consideration stops the claim. However, consideration passing between parties in other transactions cannot be used to support an action on a bill by a person who was not a *party* to those other transactions. (*Diamond* v. *Graham,* 1968[759] and *Oliver* v. *Davis and Another,* 1949.)[760]

ORDER IN WRITING

A bill of exchange is an unconditional order in writing addressed by one person to another. We will now consider these elements.

A bill of exchange is a written document and in this context writing includes print. (Sect. 2.) The person who originates it is called the *drawer,* and he must have capacity to incur liability and this is co-extensive with capacity to contract. (Sect. 22.)

The order must be unconditional, and an instrument which orders any act to be done in addition to the payment of money is not a bill of exchange. (Sect. 3(2).) An order to pay out of a particular fund is not unconditional, e.g. out of the money due to me from P when received. An unqualified order to pay, coupled with an indication of a particular fund out of which the drawee is to re-imburse himself, or a particular account to be debited with the amount, is regarded as unconditional, e.g. a cheque drawn on No. 2 A/c. (Sect. 3(3).) (And see *Bavins* v. *London and South Western Bank Ltd,* 1900[761] and *Nathan* v. *Ogdens Ltd,* 1905.)[762]

The bill of exchange must be signed, and no person is liable as drawer, indorser, or acceptor of a bill, who has not signed it as such. The following cases should be noted—

(1) Where a person signs a bill in a trade or assumed name, he is liable on it as if he had signed in his own name.

(2) The signature of the name of a firm is equivalent to the signature by the person so signing of the names of all the persons liable as partners in that firm. (Sect. 23.)

(3) A signature by procuration (e.g. per pro B. Brown, J. Jones), operates as notice that the agent has a limited authority to sign, and the principal is only bound by such signature if the agent so signing was acting within the actual limits of his authority. (Sect. 25.)

Where a person signs a bill as a drawer, indorser, or acceptor, and adds words to his signature indicating that he signs for or on behalf of a principal or in a representative character, he is not personally liable thereon; but the mere addition to his signature of words describing him as an agent, or as filling a representative character, does not exempt his from personal liability. (*Childs* v. *Monins and Bowles,* 1821.)[763]

(4) Section 108 of the Companies Act, 1948, has effect upon representative signatures on behalf of companies. The relevant law is illustrated by *Durham Fancy Goods Ltd* v. *Michael Jackson (Fancy Goods) Ltd,* 1968[164] and *Hendon* v. *Adelman,* 1973.[764]

Where a signature of a bill is forged or unauthorized, it is wholly inoperative and no rights can be acquired through or under that signature, unless the party against whom it is sought to retain or enforce payment of the bill is *precluded* from setting up the forgery or want of authority. However, an unauthorized signature not amounting to a forgery may be ratified. (Sect. 24.)

Nevertheless there are the following exceptions—

(1) *The acceptor of a bill,* by accepting it, is precluded from denying to a holder in due course the existence of the drawer, the genuineness of his signature, and his capacity and authority to draw the bill (Sect. 54(2));

(2) *The indorser of a bill,* by indorsing it, is precluded from denying to a holder in due course the genuineness and regularity in all respects of the drawer's signature and all previous indorsements (Sect. 55(2));

(3) If a signature on a bill has been forged and the party whose signature it purports to be gets to know of the forgery, he may, if he does not inform the holder within a reasonable time, be estopped from asserting it (*Greenwood* v. *Martins Bank Ltd,* 1933)[765];

(4) If an acceptor has admitted the authenticity of his signature, he cannot at a later date refuse to honour it on the ground that it is a forgery.

ACCEPTANCE

When the drawee signs the bill he becomes the acceptor, and promises to pay the holder the amount of the bill on maturity provided the acceptance is unqualified. *A general acceptance* assents without qualification to the order of the drawer.

An acceptance must not express that the drawee will perform his promise by any other means than the payment of money, and the acceptance must be written on the bill and signed by the drawee. The drawee's signature without additional words is sufficient and he need not sign with his own hand; the signature may be written by some other person by or under his authority.

A bill may be accepted before it has been signed by the drawer or while otherwise incomplete. (Sect. 18(1).) Incompleteness does not invalidate a bill and a bill is not invalid by reason (*a*) that it is not dated; (*b*) that it does not specify the value given, or that any value has been given therefor; (c) that it does not specify the place where it is drawn or the place where it is payable. (Sect. 3(4).)

When a bill lacks a material particular, the person in possession of it has *prima facie* authority to fill up the omission in any way he thinks fit.

Qualified acceptance. The acceptor may qualify his acceptance. In the case of a bill for £100 drawn six months after date, the acceptor may introduce a *qualification as to amount*: 'Accepted for fifty pounds only.' The acceptor can then only be sued for £50. He may also sign thus: 'Accepted nine months after date.' The acceptor cannot then be sued until nine months have expired, and this is known as a *qualification as to time.* An acceptance 'Payable at my office and there only' would amount to a *qualification as to place.* Finally, an acceptance 'subject to security being provided' would be a *general conditional acceptance.*

Qualified acceptance amounts to dishonour and gives a right of action against the parties immediately, but the person presenting the bill may agree to the qualification. In this case, if he wishes to retain his rights against the drawer and prior indorsers, he must obtain their assent, except in the case of qualification as to amount when he need only serve notice on them.

Accommodation bills. Sometimes a bill is what is called an *accommodation bill,* and an accommodation party to such a bill is one who has signed it as drawer, acceptor, or indorser, without receiving value for it. His object is to lend his name and credit to some other person.

An accommodation party is liable on the bill to a holder for value; and it is immaterial whether, when such a holder took the bill, he knew the party to be an accommodation party or not. (Sect. 28.) Thus, if A is in business and requires capital to purchase a new van but will not be able to pay for it out of the profits of the business for three months he may ask B to accept a bill drawn by A on B for, say, £2000 and payable 'three months after date'. If B is willing he will accept the bill but receives no value for it. However, A can now discount the bill at his bank and if B is a prosperous person the bank will probably give a good price for it. Where a drawee accepts a bill for the accommodation of the drawer, it is understood that the drawer will make available funds to meet the bill on maturity, and, if he does not do so, and the acceptor has to pay the bill, the drawer must indemnify the acceptor. This is, however, of no concern to the banker, who can sue B on his acceptance even though he knew that B was an accommodation party. However, B is not liable to A because no consideration was given by A to B.

Presentment for acceptance

Where a bill expressly stipulates that it shall be presented for acceptance, or where a bill is drawn payable elsewhere that at the residence or place of business of the drawee, it must be presented for acceptance before it can be presented for payment. When a bill is payable after sight presentment is clearly necessary in order to fix the maturity of the instrument. The presentment must be made *by or on behalf of the holder to the drawee, or to some person authorized to accept or refuse acceptance on his behalf,* at a reasonable hour on a business day and before the bill is overdue.

When a bill is duly presented for acceptance and is not accepted within the customary time (usually twenty-four hours), the person presenting it must treat it as dishonoured by non-acceptance.

In case of such dishonour, the holder has an immediate right of recourse against the drawer and indorsers, and no presentment for payment is necessary. He must, however, give them notice of dishonour without delay otherwise they are discharged not only from liability on the bill but also on the consideration given for it.

PAYMENT

Where a bill is not payable to bearer, *the payee* must be named or otherwise indicated therein with reasonable certainty. A bill may also be made payable to the holder of an office for the time being, e.g. the Treasurer of the Barchester Football Club. Where the payee is a fictitious or non-existent person, the bill may be treated as payable to bearer. (Sect. 7.) The payee is considered existing where the drawer knows of his existence and intends him to benefit. (*Vinden* v. *Hughes,* 1905.)[766] The payee is considered fictitious when his name is inserted by the drawer by way of a pretence and without any intention that the named payee should obtain payment. (*Bank of England* v. *Vagliano Bros,* 1891.)[767] The payee is considered non-existent where the drawer does not connect the payee's name with any person to whom he owes or might owe money, though there may very well be a person in existence with that name. (*Clutton* v. *Attenborough,* 1879.)[768] These concepts are somewhat artificial but are designed to ensure that those who carelessly allow employees or others to obtain by way of fraud signatures on cheques or bills, should not escape liability on the instruments.

The sum payable by a bill is a *sum certain* although it is required to be paid with interest, by stated instalments, or according to an indicated rate of exchange. (Sect. 9(1).)

Where the sum payable is expressed in words and also in figures, and there is a discrepancy between the two, the sum denoted by the words is the amount payable, though a bank will usually return such a cheque marked 'words and figures differ'. (Sect. 9(2).)

Presentment for payment

A bill must be duly presented for payment, otherwise the drawer and indorsers are discharged from liability.

(*a*) Where the bill is not payable on demand, presentment must be made on the day it falls due.

(*b*) Where the bill is payable on demand, presentment must be made within a reasonable time after its issue in order to render the drawer liable, and within a reasonable time after its indorsement to render the indorser liable.

The bill must be presented by the holder or by some person authorized to receive payment on his behalf, at a reasonable hour on a business day, at the proper place. Where it is authorized by agreement or usage, a presentment through the post office is sufficient. (Sect. 45.)

Presentment for payment is dispensed with—

(*a*) Where, after the exercise of reasonable diligence, it cannot be effected;

(*b*) Where the drawee is a fictitious person;

(*c*) Where the acceptor is an accommodation party;

(*d*) By waiver of presentment, express or implied.

Time of payment

A bill is payable on demand (*a*) which is expressed to be payable on demand, or at sight, or on presentation; or (*b*) in which no time for payment is expressed.

A bill is payable at a fixed or determinable future time when it is expressed to be payable (i) at a fixed period after date or sight; (ii) on or at a fixed period after the occurrence of a specified event which is certain to happen, though the time of happening may be uncertain. An instrument expressed to be payable on a contingency is not a bill, and the happening of the event does not cure the defect. (Sect. 11.) Suppose a bill runs 'Pay B. Brown or Order Five Hundred Pounds on the marriage of his daughter Jane to William Smith.' This would not be a valid bill, even though the wedding took place shortly afterwards. The words 'on or before' a given date import an element of contingency and an instrument ordering payment in this form is not a valid bill. (*Williamson* v. *Rider*, 1962.)[769]

A bill is not invalid by reason only of the fact that it is ante-dated, post-dated, or dated on a Sunday. (Sect. 13.)

Where a bill expressed to be payable at a fixed period after date is issued undated, or where the acceptance of a bill payable at a fixed period after sight is undated, any holder may insert therein the true date of issue or acceptance, and the bill will be payable accordingly.

Where the holder in good faith and by mistake inserts the wrong date, and in every case where a wrong date is inserted and the bill comes into the hands of a holder in due course, the bill is valid and the date so inserted is deemed to be the true one. (Sect. 12.)

In calculating the due date of a bill not payable on demand the period is determined by excluding the day from which time begins to run and including the day of payment. All bills whose payment falls due on non-business days, i.e. Saturdays, Sundays and Bank Holidays, are payable on the succeeding business day. (Banking and Financial Dealings Act, 1971.)

NEGOTIABILITY

When a bill contains words prohibiting transfer, or indicating an intention that it should not be transferable, it is valid as between the parties thereto, but is not negotiable. An example of this would be a bill made payable to *G. Green only.* Where a bill is negotiable, it may be payable either to order or to bearer, and a bill is payable to bearer which is expressed to be so payable, or on which the only or last indorsement is an indorsement in blank.

A bill is negotiated when it is transferred from one person to another in such a manner as to constitute the transferee the holder of the bill. *A bill payable to bearer is negotiated by delivery; a bill payable to order is negotiated by the indorsement of the holder completed by delivery.*

Where a bill is negotiable in its origin, it continues to be negotiable until it has been (*a*) restrictively indorsed; or (*b*) discharged by payment or otherwise. Where an *overdue bill* is negotiated, it can only be negotiated subject to any defects of title affecting it at maturity, and thenceforward no person who takes it can acquire or give a better title than that which the person from whom he took it had. *Future holders cannot be holders in due course.*

Valid indorsement

An indorsement, in order to operate as a negotiation, must comply with the following conditions, namely—

(1) *It must be written on the bill itself* and be signed by the indorser. The simple signature of the indorser on the bill, without additional words, is sufficient. An indorsement on a copy of the bill, in countries where copies are recognized, is valid.

(2) *It must be an indorsement of the entire bill.* A partial indorsement which purports to transfer to an indorsee a part only of the amount payable, or which purports to transfer the bill to two or more indorsees severally, does not operate as a negotiation of the bill.

(3) Where a bill is payable to the order of *two or more payees* or indorsees who are not partners, *all must indorse* unless the one indorsing has authority to indorse for the others.

(4) Where, in a bill payable to order, the *payee or indorsee is wrongly designated,* or his name is mis-spelt, he may indorse the bill as therein described adding, if he wishes, his proper signature.

(5) *Where there are two or more indorsements* on the bill, each indose-

ment is deemed to have been made in the order in which it appears on the bill until the contrary is proved.

(6) *An indorsement may be made in blank or special.* It may also contain terms making it restrictive. (Sect. 32.)

(a) Conditional indorsement. Where a bill purports to be indorsed conditionally, e.g. 'pay X when he delivers the bill of lading', the condition may be disregarded by the payer, and a payment made to the indorsee is valid whether the condition has been fulfilled or not. (Sect. 33.) Nevertheless the indorsee is bound by the condition and holds the money in trust for the indorser until the condition is fulfilled.

(b) Special indorsement. An indorsement in blank specifies no indorsee, and a bill so indorsed becomes payable to bearer. *A special indorsement* specifies the person to whom, or to whose order, the bill is to be payable. When a bill has been indorsed in blank, any holder may convert the blank indorsement into a special indorsement, by writing above the indorser's signature a direction to pay the bill to, or to the order of, himself or some other person. (Sect. 34.)

(c) Restrictive indorsement. An indorsement is restrictive which prohibits the further negotiation of the bill, or which expresses that it is a mere authority to deal with the bill as thereby directed and not a transfer of the ownership thereof, e.g. 'Pay D only.' or 'Pay D for the Account of Y.' or 'Pay D or order for collection.' A restrictive indorsement could be used where X, the payee of a cheque, owes a debt to an overseas supplier, P, and wishes to indorse the cheque over to P's agent A in England but wishes to make it clear that A is not the beneficial owner of the cheque, X can indorse 'Pay A for the account of P'. A can now obtain payment and must then account to P, though A cannot transfer the bill.

Delivery

Section 21(1) provides that every contract on a bill, whether it be a drawer's or an indorser's , is incomplete and revocable until delivery of the instrument. Thus, where an indorsement or other signature is required the mere fact that a signature is placed upon the instrument is not enough; there must also be delivery, which would not be the case where an order instrument was stolen after indorsement. The indorser must deliver it. However, there are certain presumptions of delivery as follows—

(*a*) under Sect. 21(2) valid delivery by all prior parties is *conclusively* presumed in favour of a holder in due course but not if the bill is inchoate (see below).

(*b*) under Sect. 21(3) valid delivery is presumed *until the contrary is proved* in the case of other holders.

This presumption of valid delivery cannot be disproved against a holder in due course but it may be as regards other holders.

Inchoate bills.   These are bills lacking in some material particular(s) such as the names of the parties other than the drawer and the amount of the bill. Problems may arise e.g. from completion of a cheque in excess of authority given by the drawer. Section 20 applies and requires 'delivery by the signer in order that it may be converted into a bill'. The law does not presume delivery under Sect. 21 because two elements are required—

    (*a*) delivery, and
    (*b*) the intention in the signer that the order be converted into a bill.

Thus, if A signs a cheque form and does not complete it and it is stolen from his desk and filled in, A is under no liability to anyone on his signature, not even to a holder in due course, because he did not deliver it *in order that it might be converted into a bill.*

However, if A signs a blank cheque and gives it to his gardener to buy a lawn mower and the gardener fills it in and pays a private debt, then A would be liable to a holder in due course because he did deliver it with the intention that it should be converted into a bill. The gardener's lack of authority is a 'defect' so far as a holder for value is concerned and A would not be liable to him. It should be noted, however, that a payee cannot be a holder in due course (*Jones Ltd* v. *Waring & Gillow,* 1926)[770] so that if the gardener made it payable to X to settle a private debt, X would not be able to sue A because as a payee he could not be a holder in due course and would take it subject to the defect, i.e. the gardener's lack of authority. Thus before anyone could sue A on the cheque there would have to be an indorsement by the first payee to an indorsee who might then be able to set up the fact that he was a holder in due course.

DISCHARGE

A bill of exchange is discharged in the following ways—

    (*a*) *By payment in due course* by or on behalf of the acceptor.
    (*b*) *By express waiver,* where the holder absolutely and unconditionally renounces his rights against the acceptor. The waiver must be in writing unless the bill is delivered up to the acceptor.
    (*c*) *By material alteration* except as against a party who has himself made, authorized, or assented thereto, and against subsequent indorsers.

The following alterations are material, namely (i) any alteration of the date, the sum payable, the time of payment, the place of payment; and (ii) the addition of a place of payment without the acceptor's assent, where a bill has been accepted generally. (Sect. 64(2).) An alteration may be material even if the change is beneficial. (*Gardner* v. *Walsh,* 1855.)[771]

Examples of immaterial alterations are (i) changing a bill payable to

Jones or Bearer into *Jones or Order*; (ii) striking out of the words *or Order*; (iii) the alteration of the drawee's name, when it is wrong, to agree with a name correctly signed by way of acceptance.

(*d*) *By intentional and apparent cancellation* by the holder or his agent.

(*e*) *By negotiation back to the acceptor,* sometimes called merger or discharge by circuity. Suppose A has accepted a bill for £100 and has sold goods worth £100 to H. If a subsequent indorser I negotiates the bill to H, and H negotiates it back to A in settlement, the bill is discharged.

(*f*) *By the bill becoming statute barred.* A bill of exchange is a simple contract and becomes statute barred six years from the cause of action, i.e. dishonour.

DISHONOUR

A bill may be dishonoured by non-acceptance or by non-payment, and the holder can sue prior parties on their implied promises. A bill is dishonoured by non-payment—

(*a*) When it is duly presented for payment and payment is refused or cannot be obtained; and

(*b*) When presentment is excused and the bill is overdue and unpaid. When a bill is dishonoured by non-payment, an immediate right of recourse against the drawer and indorsers accrues to the holder. (Sect. 47.)

Notice of dishonour

When a bill has been dishonoured by non-acceptance or by non-payment, notice of dishonour must be given to the drawer and each indorser, and any drawer or indorser to whom such notice is not given is discharged. Notice, in order to be valid and effectual, must be given in accordance with the rules laid down in the Bills of Exchange Act, 1882.

(*a*) Where the notice is given on behalf of the holder it operates for the benefit of subsequent holders, and all prior indorsers who have a right of recourse against the party to whom it is given.

If D is the drawer, P the payee, I_1, I_2, I_3, subsequent indorsers and H the holder, then if H gives notice to P, this would retain the liability of P, not only to H and subsequent holders, but also to I_1, I_2 and I_3, *although these latter three would not be liable to H.*

(*b*) Where notice is given by or on behalf of an indorser entitled to give notice, it operates for the benefit of the holder, and all indorsers subsequent to the party to whom notice is given.

If I_2 gives notice to P, then P is liable to I_1, I_2, I_3, H and subsequent holders.

(*c*) Actually if H gives notice to I_3, the chances are that I_3 will give notice to I_2, I_2 to I_1, I_1 to P, and P to D, since otherwise the person breaking the chain would lose his right of recourse though remaining liable himself. However, since one of these might fail to give notice and lose the right of recourse both for himself and for subsequent parties, the safest way is for H to notify all prior parties.

Notice must be given when the bill is dishonoured but not before. However, in *Eagleshill Ltd* v. *J. Needham Builders Ltd,* 1972[772] it was held by the House of Lords that provided that the notice is received after dishonour it is valid regardless of when it was sent off.

Noting and protesting

It is convenient at this point to mention that, when a bill is dishonoured, it is sometimes obligatory and often desirable to *note* and *protest* the bill for non-acceptance or non-payment. Many solicitors carry out the office of *notary public,* and this office is universally recognized throughout the world.

In order to *note* the bill, the notary makes a formal demand upon the drawee for acceptance, or upon the acceptor for payment, as the case may be, and if the demand is refused, he writes a minute on the face of the bill consisting of the date, the noting charges, a reference to his register, and his initials. He also attaches to the bill a ticket giving the answer received to the request for acceptance or payment. To evidence these transactions the notary makes in his register a full copy of the bill, and a note of the answer, if any, received to his request.

The *protest* is against any loss sustained by the non-acceptance or non-payment of the bill, and is embodied in a solemn declaration made on behalf of the holder by a *notary public* who signs it. Where it is necessary to protest a bill and no notary is available, the function can be performed by a householder or substantial resident who gives a certificate of dishonour attested by two witnesses.

A protest must contain a copy of the instrument and must state the person who has requested the protest, the place and date of the protest, the reason for the protest, the demand made and the answer received, if any. Alternatively it may state that the drawee or acceptor cannot be found, if this is the case. The protest must be signed by the notary.

It is not necessary to note or protest inland bills, but there are certain advantages derived from noting a bill, and the costs of noting are recoverable as damages. The notary knows clearly what measures must be taken when a bill is dishonoured; he is the best witness at a trial that proper steps were taken; and his minute on the bill is the best record of dishonour for the purpose of notifying parties to the bill that they have acquired liability.

PROMISSORY NOTES

Definition

A promissory note is an unconditional promise in writing, made by one person to another, signed by the maker, engaging to pay, on demand or at a fixed or determinable future time, a sum certain in money to, or to the order of, a specified person or to bearer. (Sect. 83(1).)

A promissory note is inchoate and incomplete until delivery is made to the payee or to bearer.

Such an instrument has only two parties—the maker and the payee—and does not require acceptance. The relevant rules governing bills of exchange are applicable to promissory notes.

CHEQUES

A cheque is defined in Sect. 73 of the Bills of Exchange Act, 1882, as 'A bill of exchange drawn on a banker payable on demand'. The relevant provisions of the Act applicable to bills of exchange payable on demand apply also to cheques. However, the provisions regarding acceptance have no application to cheques and the rules relating to crossings on cheques do not apply to other bills. Further, a delay in presenting a cheque for payment will not, in itself, discharge the drawer. (Sect. 74.) If a banker pays a cheque bearing a forged or unauthorized indorsement he is nevertheless discharged, although in a similar case the acceptor of a bill could not be. There are also certain special obligations which arise in the case of cheques because of the contract between banker and customer.

The words 'on demand' are not usually printed on cheques but under the provisions of Section 10(1)(b) they are implied.

A cheque need not take any particular form unless there is a contrary agreement between banker and customer. Normally it is an implied term of the contract between banker and customer that the bank's cheque forms will be used.

RELATIONSHIP OF BANKER AND CUSTOMER

The relationship between a banker and a customer is that of *debtor and creditor* and is not fiduciary. Where a customer deposits money in a bank, this money is under the control of the banker and is not held by the banker in the form of a trust although he has obligations in connection with it.

Banker's obligation to repay

The banker can invest the money and deal with it as he pleases, but he is answerable for the amount deposited by the customer, and is under an obligation to pay it on demand, or to pay it to third parties on the order of the customer. The banker is not an agent or a factor, he is a debtor who promises to repay the money or any part of it at the branch of the bank where the account is kept, during banking hours, against the written order of the customer presented at, or addressed to, the bank at that branch. The bank must honour a customer's cheques up to the amount of the customer's deposit or alternatively up to the amount of an agreed overdraft, but not without enquiry in unusual cases. (*Karak Rubber Co. Ltd* v. *Burden,* 1972.)[773]

The banker is under *no obligation to pay cheques in part,* and if a customer with a deposit or agreed overdraft of £400 draws against it a cheque for £500, the bank is not empowered to pay it as to £400, but should either pay it in full or refuse payment altogether.

Banker's obligation not to disclose

The bank has a further contractual obligation not to disclose information concerning the customer's affairs. (*Tournier* v. *National Provincial and Union Bank of England,* 1924.)[774] The obligation extends to all facts discovered by the banker while acting in that capacity and is not confined merely to the state of the account. Failure to comply with this obligation will render the banker liable to damages which will, however, be nominal unless actual loss can be proved.

The duty of non-disclosure is not absolute but qualified. On principle disclosure is excusable—

(*a*) *Under compulsion of law,* for example, under Sect. 7 of the Bankers' Books Evidence Act, 1879, the court may by order authorize a party to an action to inspect and copy entries in a banker's books, although the power is exercized with caution. (*Williams* v. *Summerfield,* 1972.)[775]

(*b*) *Where there is a duty to the public to disclose,* as where the account concerned is that of a person suspected of being a spy and receiving payments from a foreign government. In addition, information may be given to the police. The police are asked to address a letter to the bank saying that information is necessary for due administration of justice and undertaking that the information will not be given in evidence unless the bank is ordered to give it by the court.

(*c*) *Where the interests of the bank require disclosure,* as where the bank is in the process of enforcing an overdraft.

(*d*) Where the disclosure is made with the express or implied consent of the customer. (*Sunderland* v. *Barclays Bank Ltd,* 1938.)[776]

(*e*) Where enquiries are being made by sequestrators. (*Eckman* v. *Midland Bank,* 1972.)[777]

There is a growing practice of making credit enquiries, and banker's references are commonly given and asked for. If the customer gives the bank's name as a reference, the position is clear enough, but in the absence of the customer's express or implied consent the general practice may not be justifiable merely on the ground that it is an existing usage to supply such information to another bank. It should be noted that the Younger Committee on Privacy said that banks should tell their customers of a reference system in use and get a standing consent or ask for consent each time there was a disclosure. A misleading and negligent reference may render the banker liable in damages. (*Hedley Byrne & Co. Ltd* v. *Heller and Partners Ltd,* 1964.)[248]

Customer's obligation of care

The customer on his part undertakes to exercise reasonable care in drawing up his written orders so as not to mislead the bank or facilitate forgery. (*London Joint Stock Bank Ltd* v *Macmillan and Arthur,* 1918;[778] *C. H. Slingsby* v. *District Bank,* 1931.)[779]

Although a customer receives from time to time a bank statement he is not under a duty to check it and is not bound by any errors in it which he does not find. However, a bank may, by reason of estoppel, have to pay a cheque drawn by a customer who has relied upon an incorrect credit balance on his bank statement. (*United Overseas Bank* v. *Jiwani,* [1977] 1 All E.R. 733.)

Wrongful dishonour

A banker has a duty to honour a customer's cheques up to the amount of his credit balance or agreed overdraft. (But see *Karak Rubber Co. Ltd* v. *Burden,* 1972.)[773] This duty is owed to the customer only and not to any other party. If a banker wrongfully dishonours the cheque of a customer, and if the customer is a man of business, the harm to his credit might lead to the award of substantial sums in an action for damages. Where, however, the customer is not in business, he will only receive nominal damages unless he can prove special damage. (*Gibbons* v. *Westminster Bank Ltd,* 1940.)[780] In certain cases there may indeed be a possible action for libel against the bank. (*Davidson* v. *Barclays Bank Ltd,* 1940,[781] and *Jayson* v. *Midland Bank Ltd,* 1968.)[782]

Presentment of cheque for payment

Since a cheque is payable on demand against funds which are already provided, presentment for acceptance is quite unnecessary and would indeed have no significance. The cheque must, however, be presented for payment, and if not so presented within a reasonable time of its issue, and if the drawer or the person on whose account it is drawn had the right at the time of such presentment as between him and the banker to have the cheque paid, and suffers actual damage through the delay, he is discharged to the extent of such damage. In determining what is a reasonable time regard is had to the nature of the instrument, the usage of trade and of bankers, and the facts of the particular case.

The holder of such cheque as to which such drawer or person is discharged shall be a creditor, in lieu of such drawer or person, of such banker to the extent of such discharge, and is entitled to recover the amount from him. (Sect. 74.)

The effect of Sect. 74 is that the drawer of a cheque is liable on it for the usual limitation period of six years, but he will be discharged before then if the holder does not present it for payment within a reasonable time and the drawer suffers actual damage because of the delay.

For example, if D has £500 in his banking account and draws a cheque in favour of P for £300, and P is dilatory in presenting it so that before he does so D's bank goes into liquidation and is only able to pay fifty pence in the pound, D will be regarded as a creditor of the bank for £200 and P for £300. Thus D will receive £100 and P £150 in the liquidation. It is obviously, therefore, in the interest of payees to present cheques for payment without undue delay. Quite apart from the question of loss on liquidation a cheque may go *stale*. In some banks a cheque goes stale after six months; in others it is as long as twelve months, and a bank might be reluctant to pay a stale cheque since such a payment would not be in the usual course of business.

Revocation of banker's authority

The duty and authority of a banker to pay a cheque drawn on him by his customer are determined by—

(1) Countermand of payment;
(2) Notice of the customer's death. (Sect. 75.)

Countermand of payment must be brought to the notice of the banker in unambiguous terms if it is to be effective. (*Curtice* v. *London, City and Midland Bank Ltd*, 1908.)[783] Moreover, it must be clear to the bank that the order for taking such a serious step comes from the person entitled to give the order. In this sense a telegram countermanding payment of a cheque might be acted upon by the bank to the extent of postponing honouring the cheque until further enquiries could be made. To countermand a cheque by an unauthenticated telegram would involve the bank in a certain amount of risk.

If a bank were to cash a cheque within a few minutes after the three o'clock closing time, and were to receive a countermand of payment before the opening of business at ten a.m. next day, the payment would nevertheless be in order from the bank's point of view. The bank would not be able to dishonour a cheque after closing hours, but is entitled, within a reasonable business margin of its advertised time of closing, to deal with a cheque, not to dishonour it, but to do what it is asked to do, namely, to pay it. If the bank closes its doors at 3 p.m. there may still be customers in the bank whose wishes have not yet been attended to.

It should be noted that a countermand notice sent to one branch of a bank does not operate as notice to another branch. (*Burnett* v. *Westminster Bank*, 1965.)[784]

A banker's authority to pay a cheque is determined by notice of the customer's death, and to this may be added notice of the customer's mental disorder, notice of an act of bankruptcy on which a bankruptcy petition could be presented against him, or that a receiving order has been made, or that he is an undischarged bankrupt, or on service of a garnishee order nisi. Garnishee proceedings may be taken by a judgment creditor where the judgment debtor (in this case the customer) is himself owed money by a third party (in this case the bank). The order nisi binds the debt in the hands of the bank and cheques drawn by the customer cannot be paid. The bank will usually open a new account for subsequent receipts and payments. Where the customer is a limited company, notice of a petition for compulsory winding up or a resolution for voluntary winding up will terminate the banker's duty to honour cheques. The banker need not, as we have seen, pay cheques where a customer has an insufficient balance to cover the cheque, or has not previously arranged an adequate overdraft, and the banker should not pay if he has notice of any defect in the title of the person presenting the cheque.

Payment without authority

A banker is liable for wrongfully dishonouring the cheques of his customers but may also be liable if he pays a cheque when he should not have done so. Thus, a banker will not be able to debit the customer's account if he pays a countermanded cheque, a cheque void for material alteration, or a cheque on which the drawer's signature is forged.

However, where the customer has been *negligent* in drawing up his cheque so as to mislead the bank or facilitate forgery, the bank may debit his account. (*London Joint Stock Bank* v. *Macmillan and Arthur*, 1918.)[778] Further, if the drawer's signature has been forged and he gets to know of the forgery, he may, if he does not inform the bank promptly and the bank is put to loss, be *estopped* from asserting the forgery. (*Greenwood* v. *Martins Bank*, 1933.)[765]

Where the wrongful payment by the bank actually satisfies a debt due from a customer to his creditor, the customer would make a profit by reason of the restoration rule. For example, if the bank paid a countermanded cheque which A, a customer, had drawn in favour of B, to whom A owed money, the result of the restoration rule would be that A's debt to B would be satisfied and A's balance at the bank would have to be restored. To prevent this profit being made the bank, on restoring A's account, is *subrogated* to B's rights against A, and can recover from A by this means.

Limitation

The six-year limitation period applicable to simple contract debts does not run against the customer of a bank from the date of payment in, for there is no cause of action until the customer demands the money and the demand is not met. For example, if A deposited £100 with his bank in 1970 and did not draw cheques against the account until 1978, there would be no question of the bank pleading the Limitation Act as an excuse for not paying it. However, if the cheque was not paid by the bank time would then begin to run against A and he would have to sue the bank in respect of their failure to pay within six years.

Joint accounts

In *Brewer* v. *Westminster Bank,* 1952,[785] McNair, J., decided that in the case of a joint account, the bank's duties were owed to the account holders *jointly* and *not severally*. The result of this decision was that where one account-holder forged the other's signature on cheques drawn on the account and then added his own signature, the innocent account-holder had no action against the bank.

However, in *Jackson* v. *White and Midland Bank Ltd,* [1967] 2 Lloyd's Rep. 68, where one joint-account-holder forged the signature of the other, Park, J., declined to follow *Brewer's* case, holding that where there was a joint account with say, A and B, the bank in effect agreed with A and B *jointly* that it would honour cheques signed by them both and with A *separately* that it would not honour cheques unless signed by him, and with B *separately* that it would not honour cheques unless signed by him. Thus, where the bank honours a cheque on which B has forged A's signature, A should be able to sue the bank because it is in breach of the separate agreement with him.

It should be noted that *Jackson's* case cannot overrule *Brewer's* case because both are decisions at first instance. However, the decision in *Brewer's* case has received much criticism and it is likely that the reasoning in *Jackson's* case will be applied in future.

Generally

Banks often accept valuable property for safe custody and are liable as ordinary bailees in this respect, i.e. they must take reasonable care for the safety of the property. Should the banker misdeliver the goods to the wrong person, then he is liable for wrongful interference even though there was no negligence on his part.

Bankers nowadays often give advice on investment to customers and potential customers and, if the giving of such advice forms part of the banker's business, he will be liable in damages if his advice is negligent. (*Woods* v. *Martins Bank,* 1958.)[786] If such advice is not part of the business of a particular banker, the person who gave the advice might be personally liable for negligence. (*Hedley Byrne & Co. Ltd* v. *Heller & Partners Ltd,* 1963.)[248]

In the absence of express instuctions, it is not part of a banker's duty to consider a customer's tax liability when crediting an account with a dividend. (*Schioler* v. *Westminster Bank Ltd,* 1970.)[787]

CROSSED CHEQUES

Nature of crossing

The Act provides—

(1) Where a cheque bears across its face an addition of—

(*a*) The words 'and company' or any abbreviation thereof between two parallel transverse lines, either with or without the words 'not negotiable';
or
(*b*) Two parallel transverse lines simply, either with or without the words 'not negotiable', *that addition constitutes a crossing and the cheque is crossed generally.* (Sect.76(1).)

Where there is a general crossing the banker must pay the cheque to another banker and must not cash the cheque across the counter.

(2) Where a cheque bears across its face an addition of the name of a banker, either with or without the words 'not negotiable,' that addition constitutes a crossing, and *the cheque is crossed specially and to that banker.* (Sect. 76(2).) Where there is a special crossing the cheque must be paid to the banker named in the crossing.

General and special crossings give additional protection to holders in the case of theft, for the thief may not have a bank account and, even if he has, the extra time involved in clearing the crossed cheque may enable the drawer or holder to stop payment.

In addition to the crossings specified in the Act, it is not uncommon for the drawer to add the words 'Account payee', and this is regarded as an instruction to the collecting banker to collect only for the account of that payee, an instruction which he neglects at his peril.

Crossing procedure

Section 77 of the Act lays down the following rules—

(1) A cheque may be crossed generally or specially by the drawer.
(2) Where a cheque is uncrossed, the holder may cross it generally or specially.
(3) Where a cheque is crossed generally, the holder may cross it specially.

(4) Where a cheque is crossed generally or specially, the holder may add the words 'not negotiable'.

(5) Where a cheque is crossed specially, the banker to whom it is crossed may again cross it specially to another banker for collection.

(6) Where an uncrossed cheque, or a cheque crossed generally, is sent to a banker for collection, he may cross it specially to himself. (Sect. 77.)

There is no reason why the payee cannot also add 'Account payee'.

A crossing authorized by the Act is a material part of the cheque and its is not lawful for any person to obliterate or, except as authorized by the Act, to add to or alter the crossing. (Sect. 78.) A crossed cheque cannot be converted into an uncrossed one except by the drawer.

Duties of banker as to crossed cheques

Section 79 provides that if a paying banker receives a cheque—

(i) crossed specially to more than one banker he must not pay it; however, if one of the bankers named is acting as an agent for collection for the other, the cheque may be paid to the agent bank; collection through an agent is rare today, but was more frequent when there were a number of small banks using a major London bank as agents for collection;

Examples of Crossings on Cheques

(ii) crossed specially to a named banker, he must pay only the named banker (or the named banker's agent for collection, if any);

(iii) crossed generally, it cannot be paid except through a banker, though payment through any banker will suffice.

If a banker fails to observe the above rules he is liable to the true owner for loss incurred because the cheque was not paid as directed by the crossing. There are two possible sets of circumstances to consider.

(*a*) *The banker may, in fact, have paid the true owner* in which case there can be no claim against him. However, Lord Cairns once said of such a cheque '. . . the drawers might refuse to be debited with it as having been paid contrary to their mandate.' (*Smith* v. *Union Bank of London* (1875), 1 Q.B.D. 31 at p. 36.)

(*b*) *Payment may have been made to a person who is not the true owner.* In the case of an uncrossed cheque, the banker may be protected by Sect. 59 of the Act if the person he pays is the holder, and by Sect. 60 if the person to whom payment was made was in possession under a forged or unauthorized indorsement.

Thus, if a bearer cheque is stolen from its owner by T, and the drawee bank pays him, it has no liability to the true owner because T is the holder and Sect. 59 applies. Furthermore, if A draws a cheque on his bank payable to C and it is stolen by T who forges C's indorsement and negotiates it to E, who is paid by the bank in good faith and in the ordinary course of business, Sect. 60 will apply and the bank will not be liable to the true owner, C.

However, if, in the examples given above, the cheque had been crossed and the banker had not observed the instructions on the crossing, he would be liable to the true owner in each case and could not derive protection from Sects 59 and 60.

Protection against alterations and obliterations

Where a cheque is presented for payment which does not at the time of presentment *appear to be crossed,* or to have had a crossing which has been obliterated, or to have been added to or altered otherwise than as authorized by the Act, *the banker paying the cheque in good faith and without negligence shall not be responsible or incur any liability.* Nor shall the payment be questioned *even if the cheque had been crossed,* or if the crossing had been obliterated or been added to or altered otherwise than as authorized by the Act, or if payment had been made otherwise than to a banker or to the banker to whom the cheque was crossed, or to his agent for collection being a banker, as the case may be. (Sect. 79.)

Effect of crossing 'not negotiable'

Where a person takes a crossed cheque which bears on it the words 'not negotiable', he shall not have and shall not be capable of giving a better title to the cheque than that which the person from whom he took it had. (Sect. 81.)

While the words 'not negotiable' do not prevent the cheque from being transferred, they do have a serious effect on the title of subsequent holders.

(1) Order cheques. To negotiate an order cheque, an appropriate indorsement must be made. If such a cheque were lost or stolen, then any

such indorsement would be forged and no subsequent holder could obtain a title, *even a holder in due course*. A forged or unauthorized indorsement is wholly inoperative and anyone taking the bill after such an indorsement has no title to it, or right to sue on it, even though he may have no knowledge that the indorsement is forged or unauthorized. However, if the party against whom it is sought to retain or enforce the payment of the bill is precluded (i.e. estopped) from setting up the forgery or want of authority, he will be liable on the instrument (*Greenwood* v. *Martins Bank Ltd*, 1933.)[765] In addition, an unauthorized signature may be ratified unless it amounts to forged signature. Thus, if a cheque is made payable to a company and the clerk in the company's employment without authority indorses the cheque on behalf of the company to creditors of the company, on the face of it the creditors have no title to the cheque, but the company could ratify the unauthorized indorsement if not put on for a fraudulent purpose, and the creditors could then sue on the cheques. In this context one must also consider Sect. 55(2) of the Act of 1882 which provides that the indorser of a bill by indorsing it—(*a*) engages that on due presentment it should be accepted and paid according to its tenor, and that if it be dishonoured he will compensate the holder or subsequent indorser who is compelled to pay it, provided that the requisite proceedings on dishonour be duly taken; (*b*) is precluded from denying to a holder in due course the genuineness and regularity in all respects of the drawer's signature on all previous indorsements; (*c*) is precluded from denying to his immediate or subsequent indorsee that the bill was at the time of his indorsement a valid and subsisting bill and that he had a good title thereto. Thus, suppose that a cheque is drawn in favour of C and indorsed by C to D. It is then stolen from D by a thief who forges D's indorsement and negotiates the cheque to E, who indorses it to F, who indorses it to G. G has no knowledge of the forgery and in all respects complies with the definition of a holder in due course, i.e. he would be a holder in due course but for the forgery. It is clear that G has no title to the bill because it rests on a forgery. However, he will have rights against E or F by virtue of Sect. 55. When E indorsed the cheque to F he impliedly guaranteed that it was a valid bill and that the signatures on it of the drawer and the previous indorsers were valid signatures. F gave an undertaking to the same effect when he indorsed the cheque to G. Therefore, because one of the earlier indorsements (D's) was forged, E, is liable for the amount of the cheque to G or if G chooses to claim it from F, E is then liable to indemnify F. The addition of the words 'not negotiable' does not affect the position.

(2) Bearer cheques. A bearer cheque is negotiable by transfer without indorsement and a person taking such a cheque might have a title as a holder in due course even if a previous holder had none. The addition of the words 'not negotiable' to a bearer cheque protects the rights of the true holder against a subsequent holder, and if such a cheque were stolen and transferred to an innocent third party who obtained payment, the true owner could demand restitution within the limitation period of six years.

The words 'not negotiable' can be written on a crossed cheque when making the crossing or subsequently. A cheque crossed 'not negotiable' is still transferable subject to defects in title. A bill of exchange so crossed is not even transferable. This is because the meaning generally given to the word 'negotiable' is 'transferable free from equities' but in Sect. 8(1) the draughtsman has used it to mean 'transferable' and therefore a bill of exchange payable to 'G. Green only' or marked 'not negotiable' is not even transferable. Thus if A draws a bill on B payable 'to C only' or the bill is marked 'not negotiable' it is valid as between A, B and C but C cannot transfer it. (*Hibernian Bank* v. *Gysin & Hanson,* 1939.)[788] If the words 'not negotiable' appear on a cheque otherwise than as part of the crossing, the better view is that they are of no effect.

Account payee

We have seen that, although such a crossing is not authorized by the Act, it is not uncommon for the drawer of a cheque to include in the crossing the words 'A/c payee' or 'A/c payee only'. This is an *instruction to the collecting banker* and not to the paying banker. It will be in order for the paying banker to pay the amount of the cheque to the collecting banker, leaving it to the latter to ensure that this instruction on the cheque is carried out. It would, no doubt, be negligence in the banker if he collected the money for some other account, but the point is rather academic for bankers do not normally collect for any account except that of the payee. The words 'Account payee' or 'Account payee only' do not prevent a cheque from being negotiated. The holder of such a cheque, not being the payee, might find it difficult to persuade a bank to collect the cheque for him, but he could collect the money himself from the drawer who would certainly be liable on such a cheque to a holder in due course.

Application of crossings rules

The crossing rules apply not only to cheques but also—

(i) to the instruments other than cheques specified in Sect. 4 of the Cheques Act, 1957 (see below, p. 448); and

(ii) to dividend warrants. (Sect. 95, Bills of Exchange Act, 1882).

BANKER'S PROTECTION

Paying bankers

If a banker pays one of his customer's cheques to the wrong person then he is liable to the true owner for wrongful interference for the face value of the cheque and he cannot debit the customer's account. However, the following statutory provisions may provide the banker with a defence—

(a) Under Sect. 59 payment by the banker to the holder at or after maturity in good faith and without notice of any defect in his title discharges the bill, frees the banker from all liability and enables him to debit the customer's account. However, the person paid *must be the holder,* and a person holding an order bill by means of a forged or unauthorized indorsement is not a holder. Therefore payment to him would not discharge the bill or free the banker from liability. The Section would provide a defence where a banker paid the bearer of a bearer cheque.

(b) Under Sect. 60 if a banker on whom a cheque is drawn pays it, in good faith and in the ordinary course of business, he is deemed to have paid it in due course and is not prejudiced by the fact that the *indorsement* was forged or made without authority. The Section applies only to indorsements on cheques and does not apply where the drawer's signature has been forged, nor where the cheque is void for material alteration.

(c) Where a cheque is crossed. Where the banker, on whom a crossed cheque is drawn, in good faith and without negligence pays it, if crossed generally, to a banker, and if crossed specially, to the banker to whom it is crossed (or his agent for collection being a banker), *the banker* paying the cheque, *and,* if the cheque has come into the hands of the payee, *the drawer shall* respectively be entitled to the same rights and *be placed in the same position as if payment of the cheque had been made to the true owner* thereof. (Sect. 80.)

For example, A draws a cheque on the B Bank payable to C. C, on receipt of the cheque, crosses it generally. The cheque is then stolen by T who opens an account at the Z Bank in the name of C. The Z Bank presents the cheque to the B bank which pays in good faith and without negligence. The B Bank is protected by Sect. 80 from liability to C, and C cannot sue A.

(d) Cheques Act, 1957, Sect. 1. Although cheques are bills of exchange, most of them have a very short life, being sent by the drawers to the payees who promptly pay them straight into their banking accounts. Prior to the Act, although there was no transfer by the payee to an indorsee, such cheques required indorsement, a laborious and rather useless process.

Section 1 of the Cheques Act, 1957, provides—

Where a *paying banker* in good faith and in the ordinary course of business pays a cheque drawn on him which is not indorsed or is irregularly indorsed, he does not, in doing so, incur any liability by reason only of the absence of, or irregularity in, indorsement, and he is deemed to have paid it in due course.

The same protection is extended to him if he pays—

(i) A document issued by a customer of the bank which, though not a bill of exchange, is intended to enable a person to obtain from the bank the sum mentioned in the document; or

(ii) A draft payable on demand drawn by him on himself, whether payable at the head office or some other office of the bank.

The Committee of London Clearing Bankers announced, shortly after the Act was passed, that they would still require indorsement of cheques other than those paid into a banking account for the credit of the payee. Accordingly, if the payee pays a cheque into his own account there is no need for him to indorse it. However, if a payee or indorsee presents a cheque for payment over the counter (the cheque being uncrossed), the person receiving payment will have to indorse it. Where a crossed cheque is negotiated and paid into a bank by the last indorsee, the banker will require the indorsement of all indorsers but not that of the last indorsee who is paying in.

Whilst the decisions of the Committee of London Clearing Bankers are not law, it is thought that a banker who pays a cheque without obtaining an indorsement where the Committee says he should would not be acting in the ordinary course of business and would not, therefore, be protected by Sect. 1 of the Cheques Act, 1957, nor by Sect. 60 of the Bills of Exchange Act, 1882. He would probably also be negligent and be unable to claim the protection of Sect. 80.

Further, it is assumed that where the Committee requires an indorsement it must be a regular indorsement, and payment of a cheque with an irregular indorsement would be negligent and not in the ordinary course of business, so that there could be no statutory protection if there was a wrongful payment.

Bankers collecting cheques

The Cheques Act, 1957, Sect. 4, extends protection to *bankers who collect payment* on the following instruments—

(i) Cheques.

(ii) Any document issued by a customer of a banker which, though not a bill of exchange, is intended to enable a person to obtain payment from that banker of the sum mentioned in the document.

(iii) Any document issued by a public officer which is intended to enable a person to obtain payment from the Paymaster General or the Queen's and Lord Treasurer's Remembrancer of the sum mentioned in the document but which is not a bill of exchange.

(iv) Any draft payable on demand drawn by a banker upon himself, whether payable at the head office or some other office of the bank. (Sect. 4(2).)

Where a banker, *in good faith and without negligence*—

(*a*) receives payment for a customer of one of the above instruments; or (*b*) having credited a customer's account with the amount of such an instrument receives payment thereof for himself;

and the customer has no title, or a defective title, to the instrument, the banker does not incur any liability to the true owner of the instrument by reason only of having received payment thereof. (Sect. 4(1).)

A banker is not to be treated for the purposes of the section as having been negligent by reason only of his failure to concern himself with absence of, or irregularity in, indorsement of an instrument. (Sect. 4(3).)

This section repeals, replaces and extends Sect. 82 of the Bills of Exchange Act, 1882, and provides *protection for the collecting banker against an action for wrongful interference* if he collects for someone with no, or a defective, title. (For wrongful interference generally see page 339.)

Section 4 applies to all cheques, whether crossed or not, and also extends to a range of other instruments. However, an instrument on which the drawer's signature is forged is not a cheque nor is it an instrument which has become void for material alteration, and no protection is given in respect of the collection of such instruments.

The Section applies only where the banker collects payment for a *customer* and acts without negligence, and in the matter of negligence the onus of proof is on him. Thus there must be an account, but it seems to be enough that the customer has opened it with the cheque which is in dispute.

A banker may be negligent on many counts, for example where he has failed to obtain or follow up the references of a customer opening an account, if this failure was to some extent responsible for the wrongful collection. Failure to inquire as to a new customer's employer is negligence if the banker knows that the customer is in a position which might enable him to misappropriate his employer' cheques, as where he is a cashier. A banker should not collect, without inquiry, cheques for employees or partners or officials which are drawn on their firm or company, nor should he collect a cheque marked 'Account Payee' for another account. Finally, a banker will be held to have been negligent in any case where it appears to the court that inquiries should have been made. (*Lloyds Bank Ltd* v. *E. B. Savory & Co.,* 1933[789] and see *Lumsden & Co.* v. *London Trustee Savings Bank,* 1971.)[790]

It should be noted, however, that the above decisions represent the high-water mark of judicial severity in the matter of bankers' negligence and in two recent cases, *Orbit Mining and Trading Co.* v. *Westminster Bank,* 1962,[791] and *Marfani & Co.* v. *Midland Bank,* 1967[792] the judiciary seems to have accepted that bank employees cannot be highly inquisitive if they are to deal promptly with the large number of cheques which are cleared every day, and the standard of care required has been lowered, possibly too far.

Collecting banker as holder in due course

Where a banker collects payment of a cheque for a person who is not the true owner, he may be liable for wrongful interference although, as we have seen, he may derive protection from Sect. 4 of the Cheques Act, 1957. However, he may also escape liability if he can prove that he has become a holder in due course of the cheque. Where this is so the banker will obtain a good title to the cheque even if the title of the transferee was non-existent or defective, and in spite of his own negligence, if any.

A banker, like any other person, must give *value* before he can become a holder in due course, and this may happen in *three* ways—

(i) where the customer pays in a cheque to reduce his overdraft, if the banker forgoes interest;

(ii) where there is an express or implied agreement between banker and customer under which the customer can and does draw against the cheque before it has been cleared: where there is no prior agreement it seems that the banker does not give value; and

(iii) where the banker cashes a cheque for a person who is not a customer and therefore *buys* it from that person rather than *collecting* it for him.

A banker cannot become a holder in due course if an *essential* indorsement is forged but he can, by virtue of Sect. 2 of the Cheques Act, 1957, become the holder in due course of an order cheque, even though it is not indorsed to him. The banker will, therefore, have the right to sue the drawer if the cheque is dishonoured.

The Section provides that a *collecting banker* who gives value for, or has a lien on, a cheque payable to order which the holder delivers to him for collection without indorsing it, has such (if any) rights as he would have had if, upon delivery, the holder had indorsed in blank.

The Section provides an exception to Sect. 31 of the Bills of Exchange Act, 1882, in that it allows an order cheque to be negotiated without indorsement. It should also be noted that the Section applies only to cheques and not to analogous instruments, as do Sects 1 and 4, and that it does not deal with the case in which an indorsement exists and is irregular. Presumably, where this is so the cheque is not complete and regular on the face of it and the banker will not be a holder in due course. The cases of *Westminster Bank Ltd* v. *Zang*, 1965,[793] and *Barclay's Bank Ltd* v. *Astley Industrial Trust Ltd*, 1970,[794] are illustrative of some of the problems arising out of the operation of Sect. 2.

Unindorsed cheques as evidence of payment

Section 3 of the Cheques Act provides that an unindorsed cheque which appears to have been paid by the banker on whom it is drawn is evidence of the receipt by the payee of the sum payable by the cheque. Prior to the Act such an indorsed cheque was *prima facie* but not conclusive evidence that the payee had received the sum payable; the Act merely confirms that in future an unindorsed cheque can fulfil the same function. Nevertheless, by drawing attention to this virtue of a cheque, it has led to a widespread practice among business men of dispensing with the issue of receipts where payment is by cheque, with a consequent saving in effort, time and money.

11 The Nature of Crime

CRIME AND CIVIL WRONGS DISTINGUISHED

The distinction does not lie in the *nature of the act* itself. For example, if a railway porter is offered a reward to carry A's case and runs off with it, then the porter has committed one crime, that of theft, and two civil wrongs, i.e. the tort of wrongful interference and a breach of his contract with A. Again, a signalman who carelessly fails to operate the signals so that a fatal accident occurs will have committed one crime, i.e. manslaughter, if persons are killed, and two civil wrongs, the tort of negligence in respect of those who died and those who are merely injured, and a breach of his contract of service with British Rail in which there is an implied term to take due care. It should also be noted that in this case the right of action in tort and the right of action in contract are vested in different persons.

The distinction does depend on the *legal consequences* which follow the act. If the wrongful act is capable of being followed by what are called criminal proceedings that means that it is regarded as a crime. If it is capable of being followed by civil proceedings that means that it is regarded as a civil wrong. If it is capable of being followed by both it is both a crime and a civil wrong. Criminal and civil proceedings are usually easily distinguishable, they are generally brought in different courts, the procedure is different, the outcome is different and the terminology is different. A major consequence of classifying proceedings as criminal is that the burden of proof is on the Crown. (*Woolmington* v. *DPP*, 1935.)[795]

TERMINOLOGY AND OUTCOME OF CRIMINAL AND CIVIL PROCEEDINGS

In criminal proceedings a prosecutor prosecutes a defendant. If the prosecution is successful it results in the conviction of the defendant. After the conviction the court may deal with the defendant by giving him a custodial sentence, e.g. prison or detention centre; or a non-custodial sentence, e.g. probation, or community service order. In rare cases the court may discharge the defendant without sentence.

As regards *civil proceedings,* a plaintiff *sues* (brings an action against) a defendant. If the plaintiff is successful this leads to the court entering judgment ordering, for example, that the defendant pay a debt owed to the plaintiff or damages. Alternatively, it may require the defendant to transfer property to the plaintiff or to do or not to do something (injunction) or to perform a contract (specific performance). Some of these remedies are legal, others equitable. The matter of remedies for breach of contract and for torts has already been dealt with in detail in the chapters on those topics.

NULLA POENA SINE LEGE

This important maxim leads to the proposition that a person should not be made to suffer criminal penalties except for a clear breach of *existing* criminal law, that law being precise and well defined.

The maxim thus prohibits—

(i) the introduction of new crimes which operate retrospectively under which a person might be found guilty of a crime for doing an act which was not criminal when he did it;

(ii) wide interpretation of precedents to include by analogy crimes which do not directly fall within it. Thus the extension of the criminal law in the way, for example, in which the civil law of negligence has been extended (see p. 347) is undesirable;

(iii) the formulation of criminal laws in wide and vague terms.

The last rule has in general terms been observed in England with perhaps the major exception of the law of conspiracy under which there has been a tendency to charge persons with criminal conspiracy rather than with specific criminal offences. Thus a conviction might be obtained for conspiracy to do an act even though there were doubts as to whether the act was or ought to be criminal. (See *Shaw* v. *DPP,* 1961.)[796]

Under the Criminal Law Act, 1977, the offence of conspiracy at common law is abolished and the new statutory offence of conspiracy is restricted to agreements to commit criminal offences, though the common law offences of conspiracy to defraud and conspiracy to corrupt public morals are retained.

CRIMINAL ACTS

A criminal offence results from the action of a human being, or his failure to act, which is referred to as the *actus reus* of the crime. This act or omission must, at least at common law, be accompanied by an appropriate state of mind which is referred to as the *mens rea.*

Actus reus

The *actus reus* may consist of voluntary conduct or an omission and matters of causation arise.

Voluntary conduct. The defence of automatism may be raised as where, for example, the accused person pleads that he acted during a stroke or epileptic fit in order to show that there was no voluntary act. However, it must be said that in general terms the defence is difficult to establish. (*Hill* v. *Baxter*, 1958.)[797] This is particularly so where the state of automatism is induced by drink or drugs, though automatism induced in such a way may be a defence to a crime requiring a specific intent, such as murder, but not to manslaughter where a specific intent is not a requirement. (See *AG* v. *Gallagher*, 1963[798] and *R* v. *Lipman*, 1969.)[799] Automatism may be non-insane (*R* v. *Charlson*, 1955)[800] or insane (*R* v. *Kemp*, 1957).[60]

Omissions. Some modern statutes make failure to act criminal. For example, the Road Traffic Act, 1972, Sect. 25, imposes a duty to stop after an accident. The cases regarding liability for omissions *at common law* are concerned with manslaughter (see *R* v. *Instan*, 1893)[801] and it does not seem likely that any significant developments outside the field of manslaughter are likely at common law.

Causation. The act of the accused must be *the cause* of the crime, though it is a general rule that the accused must take his victim as he finds him (see *R* v. *Hayward*, 1908),[802] and that the accused must be regarded as having intended the natural consequences of his acts (see *R* v. *Martin*, 1881).[803] The matter of causation has given rise to difficulties some of which are illustrated by comparing *R* v. *Jordan*, 1956[804] and *R* v. *Smith*, 1959.[805]

THE MENTAL ELEMENT—GENERAL PRINCIPLES

The *actus reus* must be accompanied by an appropriate state of mind which is referred to as *mens rea*. The *mens rea* and the *actus reus* must coincide in order to constitute a crime. (*Thabo Meli* v. *The Queen*, 1954.)[806]

Motive. As in torts the motive, i.e. the reason why the accused did the act, is irrelevant in regard to his guilt or innocence if his direct intention was to commit the offence. (*Chandler* v. *DPP*, 1964.)[807]

Intention, recklessness and negligence. The *mens rea* of a crime may be the existence in the mind of the accused of an *intention* to commit the act as where A shoots at B foreseeing and desiring or wishing that B will be killed, or as where A deliberately fails to feed an aged parent, B, in the hope and expectation of bringing about B's death.

It may in some cases be sufficient that the accused was reckless, as where when late for work A drives his car at an excessive speed through a crowded street where there is a chance that someone may be injured but not desiring or wishing injury to occur.

Negligence is not a mental state and consists more in failure to foresee consequences which an ordinary person would be expected to foresee. Obviously, in negligence there is no wish or desire to injure.

Thus negligence is not generally regarded as *mens rea* at common law but if it is of a sufficiently high degree, as where lack of foresight reveals in a particular set of circumstances a very low standard of care so that it might be called *gross* negligence, then it may be enough to provide the necessary mental state for the crime of manslaughter.

Malice.   This may also be a necessary mental state in certain crimes. Malice may be an intention to bring about the harm done or recklessness as to whether it should happen or not, as where there is foresight of consequence but the risk is nevertheless taken. It does not require any animosity towards the person or persons affected. (See *R* v. *Martin, 1881.*)[803]

Mistake.   The way in which a normal, sane and sober person sees the facts of a situation may be affected by mistake and may have an effect upon liability for crime. (*R* v. *Levett,* 1638.)[808]

Mistake is not always relevent so that, for example, in sexual offences with young girls, the fact that the accused was mistaken as to the age of the girl, she being younger than he thought, may not as a matter of policy be a defence. As would be expected, mistake as to law is no defence. (*R* v. *Bailey,* 1800.)[809]

Mens rea in statutory offences

The principles applied in regard to *mens rea* where the offence is set out in a statute are somewhat different from those applied in common law offences. The topic may be considered under the headings which follow.

Mens rea implied.   As Lord Reid said in *Sweet* v. *Parsley,* 1969:[810] '. . . there has for centuries been a presumption that Parliament did not intend to make criminals of persons who were in no way blameworthy in what they did. This means that whenever a section of an Act is silent as to the requirement of *mens rea* there is a presumption that, in order to give effect to the will of Parliament, we must read in words appropriate to require *mens rea*.' (See also *R* v. *Tolson,* 1889.)[811]

However, statutes which regulate public conduct and which cannot be enforced effectively if *mens rea* is required, e.g. pollution of the environment, are sometimes excepted from the rule that statutory crimes require *mens rea* by implication. (See *Alphacell* v. *Woodward,* 1972[812] and *Cundy v. Le Cocq,* 1884.)[813]

Particular words connoting mens rea.   The use of words such as 'maliciously', 'knowingly', 'wilfully', 'permitting' and 'suffering' in a statute is usually an indication that *mens rea* is required to establish the offence.

However, the absence of such words does not necessarily mean that no *mens rea* is required as we have seen from cases recently considered. The construction put upon these words in cases coming before the courts can be seen in *R* v. *Cunningham*, 1957;[814] *Gaumont British Distributors Ltd* v. *Henry*, 1939;[815] *R* v. *Lowe*, 1973[816] and *Somerset* v. *Wade*, 1894.[817]

Vicarious Liability

If the offence is one which does not require *mens rea* so that it is an *absolute offence* an employer may be liable where an employee commits the offence in the course of his employment. It is no defence for the employer to say that he had no *mens rea* because none is required. (See *Griffiths* v. *Studebakers Ltd*, 1924.)[818]

However, if the offence requires *mens rea* as where, for example, it is one involving 'permitting' an employer will not be liable vicariously if it is the employee who does the permitting. (*James and Son Ltd* v. *Smee*, 1955.)[819]

If a person carries on a business which requires a licence which is issued subject to the observance of certain conditions, he cannot escape liability by delegating the duty of seeing that those conditions are observed to either an employee or a stranger. However, where the offence requires *knowledge* the holder of the licence will not be liable for the acts of his delegate unless the delegation is of the whole function of the licensee as where he leaves the premises to take a holiday so that the management of the business is in the hands of the delegate. (*Vane* v. *Yiannopoullos*, 1965.)[820]

An employer cannot, it would appear, be liable vicariously for *aiding and abetting* an offence unless he has knowledge of the offence. The knowledge of an employee in regard to such a charge is not imputed to the employer in order to make him liable. (*Ferguson* v. *Weaving*, 1951.)[821]

Appendix

THE DEVELOPMENT OF ENGLISH LAW

(1) *The Earl of Oxford's case* (1615). 1 Rep. Ch. 1

Merton College, Oxford, had been granted a lease of Covent Garden for 72 years at £9 a year, and some 50 years later sold the lease to the Earl for £15 a year. Later the college retook possession of part of it, on the ground that a statute of Elizabeth prevented the sale of ecclesiastical and college lands so that the conveyance to the Earl was void. The Earl brought an action to eject the college from the land, and the common law judges found in favour of the college, saying that they were bound by the statute. The Earl filed a Bill in Equity for relief, and Lord Ellesmere granted it, stating that the claim of the college was against all good conscience. This brought law and Equity into open conflict and resulted in the ruling of James I that, where common law and Equity are in conflict, Equity shall prevail.

(2) *Cheney* v. *Conn*, [1968] 1 All E.R. 779

Cheney objected to his tax assessments under the Finance Act, 1964, on the ground that the government was applying part of the tax collected to the making of nuclear weapons. Cheney alleged that this was contrary to the Geneva Conventions—which had been incorporated into the Geneva Conventions Act, 1957—and conflicted with international law. *Held*—that even if there was a conflict between the 1964 and 1957 Acts, the 1964 Act gave clear authority to collect the taxes in question and being later in time prevailed. 'It is not for the court to say that a parliamentary enactment, the highest law in this country, is illegal.' (*Per* Ungoed-Thomas, J.)

(3) *Prince of Hanover* v. *Attorney-General*, [1956] Ch. 188

A statute of Anne in 1705 provided for the naturalization of Princess Sophia, Electress of Hanover, and the issue of her body. The statute was repealed by the British Nationality Act, 1948, Sect. 34(3), but by Sect. 12 a person who was a British subject immediately before the commencement of the Act (1 January, 1949) became a citizen of the United Kingdom and

457

Colonies. The plaintiff was born in 1914 in Hanover and was lineally descended from the Electress. He now claimed a declaration that he was a British subject immediately before the commencement of the British Nationality Act. It was necessary for him to establish this in order to make a claim on a fund, put up by the Polish Government, to compensate Britons who had lost property in Poland because of nationalization. Vaisey, J., held at first instance that the statute had not lost its force merely because of its age, but thought that, although the statute was unqualified and plain in its meaning, its words taken alone produced an absurd result, since, under the statute, the Kaiser would have been a British subject. Parliament must, therefore, have intended some limitation on the operation of the words used. By referring to the preamble it seemed possible to draw the conclusion that the purpose of the Act was to be effected in the lifetime of Anne, and that after that time its purpose was spent and the plaintiff was not entitled to his declaration. On reaching the Court of Appeal, *it was held* that the appellant was a British subject under the statute of Anne which had remained law until repealed by the 1948 Act, the statute being so clear in its meaning that it was unnecessary to apply rules of interpretation to it. Rules of interpretation were to be used only in case of ambiguity or doubts as to meaning.

(4) *Vauxhall Estates Ltd* v. *Liverpool Corporation*, [1932] 1 K.B. 733

In 1928 the Minister of Health made a Street Improvement Scheme Order for a certain area of Liverpool. The Order required the compulsory purchase of property, and the question of compensation payable to owners arose. Under Sect. 2 of the Acquisition of Land (Assessment of Compensation) Act, 1919, the plaintiffs would receive £2370, but if Sect. 46 of the Housing Act, 1925, applied, the plaintiffs would receive £1133. A provision in the Act of 1919 stated that other statutes inconsistent with the 1919 Act were not to have effect. *Held*—The 1925 Act impliedly repealed the 1919 Act in so far as it was inconsistent with it. Compensation was to be assessed under the latest enactment.

(5) *Beckett* (*A. F.*) *Ltd* v. *Lyons*, [1967] 1 All E.R. 833

A foreshore between Seaham and West Hartlepool was held partly by the plaintiff company and partly by the local authority. The plaintiff company had a right to collect coal from the local authority's part of the beach in return for a rent of £3500 per annum. The plaintiffs sued the defendants for trespass because they had been removing sea coal from the foreshore, these coals having been washed by the tide on to the foreshore from submarine outcrops off the Durham coast. The defendants did not raise questions of title to the foreshore but set up an alleged lawful custom in favour of the inhabitants of the County Palatine. Their witnesses included two elderly persons who had been resident in a near-by village since 1886 who said that people had taken bags of coal from the foreshore for their own use and for sale during the last five years of the last century, and other witnesses gave evidence of coal being carried away from 1912 to 1914 and again in the 1920s. There was also evidence that after the closure of the beaches during the Second World War of 1939–45 commercial exploitation started, coal being removed in inhabitants of the Palatinate, including residents in neighbouring villages, with the aid of motor-lorries. *Held*—by the Court of Appeal—the defendants had no right to remove sea-borne coal from the foreshore because—

(i) the evidence was insufficient to establish the existence of a custom supporting a right in the inhabitants of so large an area, since the evidence of removal extended in substance only to inhabitants of villages near to the foreshore who could remove it in buckets and wheelbarrows, and not to the inland area of the country where transport by lorry was required;

(ii) the practice of taking the sea-borne coal was not necessarily of right and might be explained by tolerance on the part of the foreshore owner of what was, at least in earlier times, an unimportant and non-commercial activity;

(iii) the present commercial exploitation of the coal by motor lorries was quite different from the old practice;

(iv) the right was a profit-à-prendre and not an easement (see p. 400) and a fluctuating body of persons such as the inhabitants of a county could not acquire a right of that nature by custom.

(6) *Boys* v. *Blenkinsop, The Times*, 25 June, 1968

Mrs Nellie Blenkinsop was charged at Lewes with having 'permitted' her son Donald to drive a car without third-party insurance contrary to Sect. 201 of the Road Traffic Act, 1960. The registered owner of the car was the driver's father whose insurance policy did not cover driving by his son. However, it appeared that the son had asked his mother's permission to drive and she had given it and had said she was the owner when asked by a constable. The defence submitted that there was no case to answer because only the registered owner could permit use of the vehicle. The prosecution submitted that this was wrong because Mrs Blenkinsop might have been, if not joint owner, at any rate responsible for care, management or control of the car within *Lloyd* v. *Singleton*, [1953] 1 All E.R. 291. The prosecuting inspector had asked the justices to refer to *Wilkinson's Road Traffic Offences* (5th ed. 1965, p. 202) which in relation to that case stated 'A person may "permit" though he is not the owner.' Counsel for the defence objected that unless the justices were referred to the case itself they were not allowed to look at the textbook. The inspector did not have a report of the case with him. The justices dismissed the case and the prosecution appealed to the Divisional Court. The Court allowed the appeal and remitted the case to the justices to continue the hearing of it. Parker, L. C. J., said 'They are entitled to and should look at the textbook; and if they then feel in doubt they should, of their own motion, send for the authority, and if necessary, adjourn for it to be obtained.'

THE COURTS OF LAW

(7) *Stonehewer* v. *Farrar* (1845), 6 Q.B. 730

The plaintiff, Martha Stonehewer, conducted a bleaching and dyeing business and the defendant polluted the water supply obtained from an adjacent stream by discharging into the stream quantities of lime. The dispute was submitted to arbitration and the arbitrator said the defendant must filter the effluent from his premises 'by the ordinary and most approved process of filtering'. The action was brought to set aside the award on the grounds of uncertainty. *Held*—The description of the action the defendant must take referred only to the 'ordinary and most approved process'. It was, therefore, uncertain and the award was bad and unenforceable.

(8) *Stiffel* v. *Industrial Dwellings Society Ltd*, [1973] 1 W.L.R. 855

The plaintiff brought proceedings in the County Court claiming damages for personal injuries limited to £750. Following further and conflicting medical reports, she applied under Sect. 43 of the County Courts Act, 1959, for the action to be transferred to the High Court. Her application was dismissed, the judge saying he was entitled to use his discretion as to the value of the claim and that the plaintiff should not be allowed to change her chosen court. The plaintiff appealed and it was *held*—by the Court of Appeal—that the appeal should be allowed. All a plaintiff had to establish was that there was 'reasonable ground' to believe that the damages would exceed £750 if the action were transferred to the High Court. Despite conflicting medical reports, this had been established and an order for transfer should be made.

(*Note:* the limit of the county court's jurisdiction in contract and tort at the time of the case was £750.)

(9) *The Eastbourne Herald Case, The Times*, 12 June, 1973

The *Eastbourne Herald* published an article upon the committal proceedings of a case in which a man was charged with unlawful sexual intercourse. The prosecution of the editor and proprietors which followed was based on the following matters which appeared in the articles—

    (i) a headline reading 'New Year's Day Bridegroom Bailed';

    (ii) a description of the offence charged as being 'serious';

    (iii) a description of the alleged offender as 'bespectacled and dressed in a dark suit';

    (iv) a note to the effect that he had been 'married at St. Michael's Church on New Year's Day';

    (v) a reference to the way in which the prosecuting solicitor had handled the case.

The editor and proprietors were each found guilty by the Eastbourne Magistrates on the five counts relating to these different passages and were each fined a total of £2000 and ordered to pay £37.50 costs. This strange decision stems initially from the fact that liability may be incurred under the 1967 Act where a report of committal proceedings contains any details other than those permitted by Sect. 3(4) and quite irrespective of whether or not the details are potentially prejudicial in nature. All that the prosecution is required to show is—

(i) that the defendant published a report of committal proceedings to which the restrictions apply, and

(ii) that the report contained matters for which no specific provision is made in Sect. 3(4).

Thus in this case it was an offence under the Act to describe unlawful sexual intercourse as a 'serious' offence for Sect. 3(4) permits of no such qualifying adjective. Equally, it was an offence to describe the defendant as 'bespectacled and dressed in a dark suit' for Sect. 3(4) only provides for reference to his name, address, and occupation. Furthermore, it is not necessary for the prosecution to show that the offending item purported to be an account of what transpired in Court, provided only that it is contained within a report of committal proceedings. Thus, in this case the Magistrates held that it was an offence under the Act to refer to the fact that the defendant had been married at St Michael's Church on New Year's Day although this piece of background information does not appear to have been adduced as evidence in Court.

(10) *Attorney General* v. *Fulham Corporation*, [1921] 1 Ch. 440

The local authority was authorized by the Baths and Wash-houses Acts, 1846–1878 to establish a wash-house where people could come and wash their own clothes. The Corporation decided to run a municipal laundry where people could bring their clothes to be washed by employees of the Corporation. *Held*—that the statutory powers did not cover running a laundry. The action of the authority was, therefore, *ultra vires* and an injunction was granted to prevent the Corporation from running the laundry.

(11) *Attorney General* v. *Smethwick Corporation*, [1932] 1 Ch. 562

It was *held* in this case that the setting up of a municipal printing establishment to provide all printing and stationery required by the Corporation was incidental to the normal functions of a local authority and therefore *intra vires*.

(12) *Allingham* v. *Ministry of Agriculture and Fisheries*, [1948] 1 All E.R. 780

The Minister had properly delegated to the Bedfordshire War Agricultural Committee his powers to give directions on the use of agricultural land. The Committee decided that a certain farmer should grow eight acres of sugar beet but left it to its Executive Officer to select which areas. The officer concerned served a notice on the farmer telling him which acres he must use to grow sugar beet. It was *held* that this notice was invalid as the statutory powers should have been exercised by the Committee itself.

(13) *Bradbury* v. *London Borough of Enfield*, [1967] 1 W.L.R. 1311

The local authority decided to adopt a comprehensive system of secondary schooling but failed to give public notice of its proposals. Section 13 of the Education Act, 1944, required such notice whenever a local authority decided to cease to maintain a school or to establish a new school. A change in the fundamental character of a school was *held* by the Court of Appeal to come within Sect. 13 and an injunction was granted to prevent the local authority from acting on its proposals until such notice was given.

(14) *Sydney Municipal Council* v. *Campbell*, [1925] A.C. 338

The Council was empowered by statute to acquire land by compulsory purchase in order to make streets or to carry out improvements in or to remodel the city. The Council made a compulsory purchase order to acquire land ripe for development not for any of these authorized purposes but simply to realize later the increase in the land's value. It was *held* by the Privy Council that an injunction should be granted against the Council to prevent the compulsory purchase.

(15) *Roberts* v. *Hopwood*, [1925] A.C. 578

Statute empowered the Poplar Borough Council to pay its employees such wages 'as they think fit'. The Council granted a minimum wage of £4 a week to all employees without distinction of sex, which amount was in excess of the rate prevailing locally. The district auditor disallowed the excess and surcharged the members of the Council. The House of Lords upheld the surcharge. Fixing an arbitrary minimum without regard to labour conditions, the cost of living, rates paid by other public authorities and so on, was not a proper exercise of the local authority's discretion.

Lord Atkinson said that the council had been swayed by 'eccentric principles of socialistic philanthropy, or by a feminist ambition to secure the equality of the sexes in the matter of wages in the world of labour'. He then added that a local authority administering funds of ratepayers 'stands somewhat in the position of trustees or managers of the property of others'.

(*Note:* in view of statutory and other developments in the field of labour law, Lord Atkinson's comments are out of line with present day attitudes. However, the payment of wages by a local authority in excess of the rates prevailing locally for similar jobs may still be an *ultra vires* activity.)

(16) *R.* v. *Aston University Senate, ex parte Roffey*, [1969] 2 Q.B. 538

Two students, Roffey and Pantridge, failed their university examinations in June, 1967, and again in September, 1967. They were required to withdraw from the University. This decision was reached by the board of examiners who considered also personal matters relating to the students, such as family problems, but did not give them a hearing. The students applied in July, 1968, for an order of *certiorari* to quash the decision ordering them to withdraw. *Held*—the principles of natural justice required that the students should have been heard but because of the delay in applying for what was a discretionary order it would not be granted.

(17) *R.* v. *Brighton Justices, ex parte Robinson*, [1973] Crim. L.R. 53
The defendant was convicted and ordered to pay a fine in her absence for failing to give information about a driver's identity. She applied for *certiorari* on the grounds that she had not received the summons. *Held*—by Queen's Bench Divisional Court—that the application would be granted but the court would not be minded to grant *certiorari* in such cases in the future since a statutory procedure existed under Sect. 24(3) of the Criminal Justice Act, 1967.

(*Note:* Section 24(3) provides that the defendant may make a statutory declaration that he did not know of any summons or proceedings until after the trial commenced. The statutory declaration must be served on the clerk to the justices within 14 days of the date when the defendant came to know of the proceedings whereupon the summons and subsequent proceedings are void.)

(18) *R.* v. *Hillingdon London Borough Council, ex parte Royco Homes Ltd*, [1974] 2 All E.R. 643.

Royco Homes Ltd applied for an order of *certiorari* quashing planning permission for residential development at Ickenham granted to them by Hillingdon London Borough Council. It appeared that the purported planning permission was subject to a condition to the effect that the occupiers of the proposed houses should be persons on the local authority waiting list, an extremely serious restriction on the character of the occupier. The Divisional Court granted the application and quashed the planning permission on the grounds that the conditions imposed upon it were the equivalent of requiring the applicant to take on a significant part of the local authority's housing duties and were such a departure from the rights of ownership and so unreasonable that no local authority, appreciating its duty and properly applying itself to the facts, could have imposed them. The planning permission disclosed on the face of it an error in the application of planning law. It was immaterial that the planning authority was not a body which had the duty to act judicially. *Certiorari* would issue to anybody which had jurisdiction to determine the rights of subjects, whether or not it was required to act judicially.

(*Note:* the use of *certiorari* in this way appears to provide an alternative method of appeal to the more usual method which is an appeal to the Secretary of State for the Environment.)

(19) *Herring* v. *Templeman*, [1973] All E.R. 569
By the trust deed governing a teacher training college it was provided that

the Archbishop of Canterbury should be the Visitor of the college; that it should be conducted so as to comply with the Education Acts, 1944–1967 and regulations for training of teachers made thereunder; that the academic board of the college should make recommendations to the Principal for suspension or dismissal of students whose standard of work was unsatisfactory and that the Principal should have power to recommend dismissal of a student and such recommendation should require confirmation by the governing body after considering representations in writing or in person as the student might wish to make. The academic board recommended to the governing body that the plantiff should be required to withdraw on academic grounds. He was not heard by the academic board but was present when the matter came before the governing body and had a copy of the academic board's report. The governing body accepted the recommendation of the academic board. The plaintiff brought an action against members of the governing body alleging that the resolution was in breach of the rules of natural justice and claiming a declaration that it was *ultra vires* and an injunction. It was *held*—by the Court of Appeal—that the statement of claim should be struck out as disclosing no reasonable cause of action. No principle of law required the implication of an obligation upon the board or the Principal to accord the plaintiff a hearing before recommending dismissal. In addition, the board had not acted unfairly and had taken into account nothing which it was not entitled to do. Furthermore, the procedure laid down for dismissal had been followed in substance if not in form and the hearing by the governing body was not a legal trial and that body was not required to re-open the board's assessment of the plaintiff's fitness to be a teacher but only to allow the plaintiff to show reasons why it should not accept the recommendations before it.

(*Note: R.* v. *Aston University Senate, ex parte Roffey*, 1969[16] was explained and distinguished, mainly on the grounds that the academic board did not consider extraneous matters such as family or other problems but dealt only with academic achievement. *Roffey*[16] was also criticized on another main ground which was that the relationship of the students and Aston University was one of contract and if the university was in breach of the contract *certiorari* was not an appropriate remedy for such a wrong. In general, the Court threw some doubt upon the decision in *Roffey*, particularly perhaps in regard to whether the deliberations of educational establishments are in fact judicial or quasi-judicial and therefore attract the supervisory jurisdiction of the High Court, at least in regard to decisions relating to scholastic inability.)

(20) *R.* v. *West Sussex Quarter Sessions, ex parte Albert and Maud Johnson Trust Ltd*, [1972] 3 All E.R. 468

The applicants had applied to Quarter Sessions (as it was then called) under Sect. 31 of the National Parks and Access to the Countryside Act, 1949, for a declaration that a certain path which ran across their land was not a public footpath. Quarter Sessions refused to make the declaration.

The applicants now asked for an order of *certiorari* to quash the decision of Quarter Sessions on the ground that additional evidence was available. It was *held*—by the Divisional Court—the *certiorari* does not lie to quash a decision of an inferior court or tribunal merely on the ground that fresh evidence has come to light since the date of the hearing. 'Should *certiorari* go in such a case? I would answer emphatically not. The prerogative orders are the great residual jurisdiction whereby this court controls the activities of subordinate tribunals, and it controls them in three main categories, first against excessive jurisdiction, secondly against errors of law on the face of their judgments, and thirdly and perhaps most important, against a denial of natural justice. Within these three heads, this court can and will by *certiorari* control the errors of lower tribunals, but it is a total misconception of the function of the prerogative orders to think they can be used as a supplementary or additional ground of appeal in circumstances such as the present.' (*Per* Lord Widgery, C.J.)

(*Note:* this decision was affirmed by the Court of Appeal, see [1973] 3 W.L.R. 149.)

(21) *R.* v. *London County Council, ex parte The Entertainments Protection Association Ltd*, [1931] 2 K.B. 215

The county council granted a new licence, under Sect. 2 of the Cinematograph Act, 1909, in respect of a cinema called the Streatham Astoria. One of the conditions contained in the Act was that the premises were not to be opened on Sundays, Christmas Day or Good Friday. Subsequent to the grant of the licence, a committee of the council considered an application that the Streatham Astoria be allowed to open on the above-mentioned days. The committee resolved that 'no action be taken for the present in the event of the premises being opened . . . on Sundays, Christmas Day and Good Friday', subject to the applicants paying a sum of money to a selected charity. The Association challenged the ruling of the committee by *certiorari*. *Held*—The council was usurping its jurisdiction in breaking a condition of the licence, and that this was prohibited by the Act of 1909. *Certiorari* lay to quash the committee's ruling.

(22) *R.* v. *Deal Justices, ex parte Curling* (1881), 45 L.T. 439

Justices, who were subscribers to the Society for the Prevention of Cruelty to Animals, had taken part in the conviction of the appellant for the offence of cruelty to a horse, the prosecution having been brought by the society. The appellant sought to quash the conviction by *certiorari*. *Held*—*Certiorari* must be refused. Subscribers to the society had no authority over prosecutions which were instituted by Central Office in London, and the society never accepted penalties taken from offenders, so that there was no bias.

(23) *Dimes* v. *Grand Junction Canal* (1852), 3 H.L.C. 759

Dimes was the Lord of a manor through which the canal passed, and he had been concerned in a case with the proprietors of the canal in which he disputed their title to certain land. Dimes had obtained an order of ejectment, but the canal company approached the Lord Chancellor (Lord Cottenham) to prevent Dimes enforcing the order and to confirm the company's title. The Lord Chancellor granted the relief sought. Dimes now appealed to the House of Lords on the ground that the Lord Chancellor was a shareholder in the company and was therefore biased. *Held*—The Lord Chancellor's order granting the relief must be quashed because, although there was no evidence that his pecuniary interest had influenced him, yet it should not appear that any court had laboured under influences of this nature.

(24) *R.* v. *Bingham Justices, ex parte Jowitt, The Times*, 3 July, 1974

In announcing the conviction of the defendant for speeding the chairman of the justices said: 'Quite the most unpleasant cases that we have to decide are those where the evidence is a direct conflict between a police officer and a member of the public. My principle in such cases has always been to believe the evidence of the police officer, and therefore we find the case proved.' Mr Jowitt applied to the Divisional Court for *certiorari* and it was *held* that the attitude of the chairman clearly amounted to bias and the conviction was quashed.

(25) *R.* v. *Altringham Justices, ex parte Pennington, The Times*, 7 November, 1974

On the trial of Norman and Arthur Pennington, who were farmers and wholesalers in Stretford, Manchester and who were charged with delivering short weight of vegetables to schools in Cheshire, they were each fined £250. One of the magistrates, Mrs W. M. Phillips, was a co-opted member of the Cheshire County Council Education Committee. The Penningtons applied for an order of *certiorari* to quash their convictions and it was *held* that the magistrate should have disqualified herself on the ground of possible suspicion of bias and the defendants' convictions would be quashed. A magistrate who has a number of local responsibilities of this kind should search the court list in advance. (*per* Lord Widgery, C.J.)

(26) *R.* v. *Paddington Rent Tribunal, ex parte Bell Properties Ltd*, [1949] 1 K.B. 666

Before a rent tribunal hearing took place members of the tribunal inspected flats in Park West, Paddington, and saw that the ceilings were not more than eight feet from the floor. This fact was mentioned in the tribunal's decision and one of the grounds it gave for its decision was that this height was less than required by current standards. The Divisonal Court *held* that the tribunal's decision must be quashed because *inter alia*, it was not proper that such a factor should have been considered by the tribunal without any opportunity being given to the landowner of dealing with it.

(27) *R.* v. *Stratford-on-Avon Justices, ex parte Edmunds*, [1973] R.T.R. 356

After the justices had concluded the hearing of a prosecution under the Road Safety Act, 1967, they retired to their private room with their clerk to consider their verdict. The person who had laid the information against the accused, who was a Chief Inspector, took a copy of the 1967 Act to the door of the justices' room, knocked, and when the door opened proffered the copy to the clerk, who declined it, as he already had a copy. A few words were spoken. *Held*—by the Divisional Court—that as any onlooker might well have thought that the Chief Inspector had the aim of making a point, which the defence would not have been able to deal with, and the opportunity to make it, the conviction must be quashed.

(28) *R.* v. *Metropolitan Police Commissioner, ext parte Parker*, [1953] 1 W.L.R. 1150

The Commissioner had revoked Parker's cab licence under powers given to him in the London Cab Order, 1934, on the ground that the cab had been used for the purpose of prostitution. The Order gave the Commissioner power to revoke a licence if satisfied that the licensee was not a fit person to hold one. He was not bound to hold an inquiry or hear evidence. Having made up his mind to revoke the licence, the Commissioner directed that Parker should appear before the licensing committee, and that if the committee saw any reason why the Commissioner should change his mind on the matter of revocation, they should report to him. Parker denied the allegations of the police and wished to call evidence in support of his denial at the committee but was not allowed to do so. The committee reported to the Commissioner that he should not alter his decision, and the licence was revoked. Parker asked for *certiorari* to quash the order of revocation. *Held*—*Certiorari* did not lie. The Commissioner and the committee were exercising administrative, not judicial or quasi-judicial functions. Therefore they need not observe the rules of natural justice by granting Parker a full hearing. However, if the Commissioner had set up the committee to hear evidence and report its findings so that he could decide whether or not to revoke the licence, then the committee would have been exercising judicial functions and must observe the rules of natural justice.

(29) *Brighton Corporation* v. *Parry* (1972), 70 L.G.R. 576

The defendant was the president of the Students' Union at a College of Education controlled by the local authority. As president he was given a year free of ordinary academic work but was still required to undertake certain study. After several warnings the academic board in his absence, but with the aid of written representations from him, ordered that as he had neglected his work he should be excluded from the college. The appeal committee of the governors dismissed his appeal but varied the penalty to rustication. The defendant failed to obey the order and the plaintiffs sought an injunction to restrain him from entering the college. The defendant objected that the rules of natural justice had not been complied with. *Held*—by Willis, J. that the injunction should be granted. The requirements of natural justice could be complied with without an oral hearing.

(30) *Pett* v. *The Greyhound Racing Association Ltd*, [1968] 2 All E.R. 145

The plaintiff held a licence to train greyhounds, issued to him by the defendant organization, whose rules gave disciplinary powers to track stewards. But there were no rules relating to the procedure to be followed at inquiries. A greyhound owned by the plaintiff and entered for a race was found to have traces of barbiturates in its urine and the stewards ordered an inquiry and granted the plaintiff an adjournment so that he might be legally represented, but later told the plaintiff that they would not allow such representation because it would cause delay and frustration. The plaintiff sought a declaration from the Court that he was entitled to representation and an injunction to restrain the holding of the inquiry if he was not. An interlocutory injunction was granted and the defendants appealed against it. *Held*—by the Court of Appeal—that where a person has a right of audience before a tribunal on a matter concerning his reputation and livelihood, he is entitled to be represented by an agent, including a lawyer, unless the rules of the tribunal expressly exclude that right. The appeal was dismissed.

The view of the Court of Appeal was obiter and given in interlocutory proceedings. At the trial Lyell, J., did not follow the Court of Appeal saying that a domestic tribunal was not acting contrary to natural justice by refusing legal representation. The better view is that the decision of the Court of Appeal is the correct one.

(*Note:* in *Pett* v. *Greyhound Racing Association Ltd* (No. 2), [1970] 1 All E.R. 243, the Association told the Court that they had made new rules permitting trainers to be legally represented at inquiries. The plaintiff would therefore be permitted legal representation and no issue remained between the parties.)

(31) *Enderby Town Football Club Ltd* v. *The Football Association Ltd*, [1971] 1 All E.R. 215

The football club, which had been censured by a local county football association for negligent administration, appealed to the F.A. and asked for representation. Two rules of the F.A. were brought into question. One was rule 38(*b*) which excluded legal representation and the other was rule 40(*b*) which said that legal proceedings should only be taken as a last resort and then only with the consent of the Council of the Association. The football club asked for an injunction restraining the hearing of the appeal unless the club was allowed legal representation. It was *held*—by the Court of Appeal—

(*a*) the points of law raised in the appeal were difficult and could be brought before the ordinary courts of law for a declaration of rights. These courts were the most appropriate place for such matters to be litigated. Rule 40(*b*) did not prevent this course of action. It was invalid since it attempted to oust the jurisdiction of the courts, but;

(*b*) if the Club did not want to go to the ordinary courts but chose to raise the matter before the F.A., then it must abide by rule 38(*b*) and could not have legal representation.

(32) *Ridge* v. *Baldwin*, [1963] 2 All E.R. 66

Mr Ridge, who was the Chief Constable of Brighton, had been acquitted on a charge of conspiring with other police officers to obstruct the course of justice, though the trial judge, Donovan, J., said that Mr Ridge had not given the necessary professional or moral leadership to the Brighton Police Force. The Brighton Watch Committee subsequently dismissed Mr Ridge from his post as Chief Constable under a power in the Municipal Corporations Act, 1882, giving them a right to dismiss 'any constable whom they think negligent in the discharge of his duty or otherwise unfit for the same'. Ridge was not given a chance to answer the charges or appear before the Watch Committee. *Held*—by the House of Lords—the dismissal was void; Mr Ridge should have been heard.

(33) *R.* v. *Secretary of State for Home Department, ex parte Hosenball, The Times*, 30 March, 1977

Mr Hosenball was an American journalist working in London. He received a letter from the Home Department saying that the Home Secretary had decided to deport him in the interests of national security. The statement said that Mr Hosenball had tried to obtain and, indeed, had obtained, information harmful to the security of the United Kingdom and that that information had included information prejudicial to the safety of servants of the Crown. Mr Hosenball was given no further particulars and was told that he could not appeal but might make representations and appear before an independent advisory panel. Mr Hosenball did so but he did not see the panel's report, though the Home Secretary gave it his personal consideration. A deportation order was made under the Immigration Act, 1971, Sect. 5, and Mr Hosenball applied for an order of *certiorari* to quash the Home Secretary's decision. The Court of Appeal *held* unanimously that the application would be refused. Mr Hosenball had not been given enough information to enable him to meet the charge made against him. However, this was a case in which national security was involved and where the State was in danger so that the rules of natural justice must take second place.

In addition, there was no infringement of Article 6 of the Convention for the Protection of Human Rights and Fundamental Freedoms. The European Commission of Human Rights in the case of Mr Philip Agee, whose deportation had been ordered by the Home Secretary at the same time as Mr Hosenball, had considered his application against the United Kingdom under the Convention as manifestly illfounded. The Commission considered that where the public authorities of a state decided to deport an alien on grounds of security that constituted an act of state falling within the public sphere and did not constitute a determination of his civil rights or obligations within the meaning of Article 6.

(34) *R. v. Commissioner of Police of the Metropolis, ex parte Blackburn*, [1973] 1 All E.R. 324

Blackburn sought an order of *mandamus* requiring the Commissioner of Police to secure the enforcement of the law against pornography upon various publishers and booksellers, and to reverse his decision that no prosecution should be undertaken without the prior consent of the Director of Public Prosecutions. *Held*—by the Queen's Bench Divisional Court—that although the evidence showed that pornography was widely available, the Commissioner, because of an under-manned force, had to decide an order of priorities to deal with various offences. In these circumstances it was perfectly proper for the Commissioner to seek the Director's advice before embarking on a prosecution, so long as he did not consider himself bound to follow his advice, and, accordingly the situation in London was not attributable to any breach of legal duty by the Commissioner and the Court would not interfere with the legitimate exercise of his discretion in the matter of police powers.

(35) *R. v. Secretary of State for Social Services, ex parte Grabaskey, The Times*, 15 December, 1972

A dentist treating a patient with a broken tooth, claimed payment not only for crowning the tooth but also for an amalgam filling. The latter claim was disallowed by the Dental Estimates Board and the Minister dismissed the appeal as unarguable under the proviso to reg. 18 of the National Health Service (Service Committees and Tribunals) regulations, 1956. *Held*—by the Queen's Bench Divisional Court—that the dentist's case was reasonably arguable and accordingly the Minister had no jurisdiction to dismiss the appeal and *mandamus* would be granted requiring him to refer the matter to two dental referees.

(36) *Laker Airways* v. *Department of Trade*, [1977] 2 All E.R. 182

The Civil Aviation Authority granted Laker Airways a licence for ten years from 1973 for a cheap passenger service between the UK and the USA called 'Skytrain'. Laker Airways was then designated as an airline under the Bermuda Agreement of 1946 made between the UK and the USA. Such designation was essential to get 'Skytrain' across the Atlantic. The Civil Aviation Act, 1971, gives the Secretary of State for Trade wide powers to revoke licences without reference to anyone and subject only to questions being asked in Parliament. However, these powers are restricted to time of war or great national emergency or where international relations might be affected. This part of the Act could not, therefore, have been applicable in regard to the revocation of the licence granted to Laker

Airways. The Act also gives the Secretary of State power to give policy guidance in regard to civil aviation and it was under this power that the Secretary of State announced in 1976 by a White Paper that future policy would be to licence only one UK airline on any given long route. Paragraphs 7 and 8 of the White Paper contained an instruction to the Civil Aviation Authority to revoke the licence for 'Skytrain'. Laker Airways now claimed a declaratory judgment that paras 7 and 8 were *ultra vires* and that the Secretary of State was not entitled to withdraw their licence. Mocatta, J. granted the declaration sought, holding among other things that the power given to the Secretary of State to issue policy guidance did not extend to the revocation of licences in this way. On appeal to the Court of Appeal by the Department of Trade it was held, dismissing the appeal, the Laker Airways were entitled to the declaration sought. The Secretary of State could not lawfully use the procedure of 'guidance' for the revocation of licences.

(37) *Congreve* v. *Home Office*, [1976] 1 All E.R. 697

The plaintiff, on discovering that the price of the television licence was about to be increased, bought a new licence at the old rate before the expiry of his old licence, thus saving himself about £6. 25,000 other people did the same thing. The Home Secretary, in order to frustrate the scheme, threatened that unless the extra £6 was paid, the licences would be revoked under Sect. 1(4) of the Wireless Telegraphy Act, 1949. The plaintiff refused to pay the £6 and brought an action against the Home Office claiming a declaratory judgment that revocation of the licences would be unlawful, invalid and of no effect. It was *held*—by the Court of Appeal—that although the Home Secretary had an undoubted discretion under Sect. 1(4) of the 1949 Act to revoke a TV licence, that discretion was fettered to the extent that the courts would intervene if it was exercised arbitrarily or improperly. The Minister's action was unfair, unjust, and unlawful. It was an improper exercise of the discretionary power as a means of levying money which the executive had no authority to demand and the court could, and should, intervene to declare the proposed revocation unlawful, invalid and of no effect.

(38) *Secretary of State for Education and Science* v. *Tameside Metropolitan Borough Council*, [1976] 3 All E.R. 665

Tameside, a local education authority, submitted proposals for a comprehensive system of education to the Secretary of State in March, 1975. These proposals were approved and Tameside planned to implement them by September, 1976. In May, 1976, local elections were held and the membership of Tameside changed from a Labour to a Conservative authority. The Conservative council decided not to implement the scheme for comprehensive education fully and on 7 June, 1976, notified the Secretary of State of that intention. The Secretary of State is given a supervisory role by Sect. 68 of the Education Act, 1944. The section provides 'If the Secretary of State is satisfied, either on complaint by any person or otherwise, that any local education authority or the managers or the governors of any county or voluntary school have acted or are proposing to act unreasonably with respect to the exercise of any power conferred or the performance of any duty imposed by or under this Act, he may, notwithstanding any enactment rendering the exercise of the power or the performance of the duty contingent upon the opinion of the authority or of the managers or governors, give such directions as to the exercise of the power or the performance of the duty as appear to him to be expedient'. On 11 June the Secretary of State replied to Tameside saying that they had acted, or were proposing to act, unreasonably within Sect. 68 of the 1944 Act and accordingly directed Tameside to implement the 1975 scheme. Tameside refused, so the Secretary of State applied for *mandamus*. The Divisional Court of Queen's Bench granted the order but the Court of Appeal and the House of Lords reversed that decision. Before giving direction, under Sect. 68 the Secretary of State had to be satisfied that Tameside were acting unreasonably, i.e. that their conduct was such that no authority could reasonably engage in it. It had been alleged that there was insufficient time to carry out the necessary selection procedure for entry into grammer school. However, the House of Lords said that there were no grounds for concluding that the authority were acting unreasonably in taking the view that there was sufficient time available to carry out the necessary selection procedure. Although the Secretary of State might legitimately take the view that the authority's proposal to retain the grammar schools and to implement the selection procedure for the two schools where places were available was misguided or wrong, there were no grounds which could justify a conclusion that the proposal was such that no education authority, acting reasonably, would carry it out. It followed that the Secretary of State's direction was *ultra vires* and of no effect.

(39) *Saif Ali* v. *Sydney Mitchell & Co., The Times*, 14 May, 1977

The plaintiff, Mr Ali, sought damages for alleged professional negligence against Sydney Mitchell & Co., a firm of solicitors, and a barrister. His allegations against the barrister were that he had advised Mr Ali to bring an action against the husband of a woman driving the family car who, so Mr Ali said, had injured him by negligent driving. Subsequently it appeared that the wife was not driving as her husband's agent and so he was not the proper defendant. As a result Mr Ali's action had to be discontinued and before another action could be commenced the limitation period had expired and it was too late for Mr Ali to proceed against the wife. It was *held*—by the Court of Appeal—that the barrister was not liable. A barrister could not be sued for alleged professional negligence in respect of his conduct and management of a case in court and in respect of advising on litigation about a case out of court.

(40) *Rondel* v. *Worsley*, [1967] 3 All E.R. 993

The appellant was charged with causing grievous bodily harm and was tried and convicted. He was represented at the trial by the respondent barrister who had appeared on a 'dock brief'. The appellant later issued a writ and statement of claim against the respondent claiming damages for professional negligence in the respondent's presentation of the case and in his dealing with the evidence. The statement was ordered to be struck out by the Master as disclosing no cause of action and this order was upheld by Lawton, J., and the Court of Appeal. On further appeal to the House of Lords it was *held* that the appeal must be dismissed. A barrister's conduct and management of litigation either in court or at an earlier stage could not give rise to a claim for professional negligence. This ruling arose out of public policy in that—

(*a*) a barrister should be able to carry out *his duty to the court* independently and without fear;

(*b*) actions against barristers would amount in effect to a retrial of the case in which it was suggested negligence arose; this would prolong litigation contrary to the public interest; and

(*c*) barristers are obliged to accept any client if a proper fee is paid and cannot refuse clients on any other ground.

Lords Reid, Morris of Borth-y-Gest and Upjohn were of the opinion that public policy did not require the extension of this immunity to the non-litigious aspects of a barrister's work, and along with Lord Pearce thought that a solicitor should be given the same immunity in litigious work which could have been done by a barrister as the latter would have had if engaged.

(41) *Gouriet* v. *Union of Post Office Workers*, [1977] 1 All E.R. 696

Under Sects 58 and 68 of the Post Office Act, 1953, it is an offence punishable by fine and imprisonment for persons employed by the Post Office wilfully to delay or omit to deliver postal packets and messages in the course of transmission and for any person to solicit or endeavour to procure another to commit such an offence. The Council of the Union of Post Office Workers called on its members not to handle mail to South Africa for a week because they disapproved of South Africa's policies. The plaintiff, who was the Secretary of the National Association for Freedom, asked the Attorney-General for his consent to act as plaintiff in relator proceedings for an injunction to restrain the Union from soliciting or endeavouring to procure any person wilfully to detain or delay a postal packet in the course of transmission to South Africa. The Attorney-General refused. The plaintiff issued the writ of summons in his own name and applied to a judge in chambers for an injunction. The judge refused, saying he had no jurisdiction to grant relief where the Attorney-General had refused consent. The plaintiff appealed to the Court of Appeal who granted him an interim injunction against the Union. At a subsequent hearing the plaintiff amended his pleadings to claim permanent injunctions against the Union and a declaration that the Attorney-General, by refusing his consent, had acted improperly and wrongfully exercised his discretion. The Attorney-General stated that his discretion in relator proceedings was absolute and could not be reviewed by the courts. Furthermore, he did not have to give reasons and the courts could not enquire into them. He was answerable only to Parliament and he applied for the declaration claim to be struck out. It was *held*—by the Court of Appeal—that although the Attorney-General's refusal could not be reviewed or questioned, the Court was not without power to provide a remedy. It could grant a member of the public without any special interest in the matter a declaration and an interim injunction pending its final determination. The interim injunctions were in fact sufficient to stop the interference with mail to South Africa. Lord Denning, M.R., in a dissenting judgment, said that the Attorney-General had no prerogative, by which he alone could say whether or not the criminal law shall be enforced in the courts and if the court can grant a declaration, there is no reason why it should not be able to grant a permanent injunction.

(*Note:* the House of Lords decided [1977] 3 W.L.R. 300 that proceedings to prevent the infringement of public rights can only be instituted by consent of the Attorney-General unless any individual has a special interest as where his private rights are threatened. Mr Gouriet had no such interest and was not entitled to the relief sought.)

LAW IN ACTION

(42) *British Railways Board* v. *Pickin*, [1974] 1 All E.R. 609

Section 259 of the Bristol and Exeter Railway Act, 1836, provides that if the railway, which it set up, should at any time be abandoned, the land acquired for the track should vest in the adjoining landowners; the same provision was contained in the Act setting up the Yatton to Clevedon line. The British Railways Board, in whom the railways had become vested, closed the line in the early 1960s and took up the tracks in 1969. A private Act of Parliament, the British Railways Act, was passed in 1968 cancelling the effect of Sect. 259 and vesting the track in the Board; the Act's preamble recited that plans and books of reference had been deposited with Somerset County Council. Pickin, who objected to the closing of the line, purchased a few feet of land adjoining the track in 1969 and sought a declaration that he owned the land as far as the middle of the track, the railway having been abandoned within Sect. 259. In reply to the Board's defence that the land was vested in them by virtue of Sect. 18 of the Act of 1968, Pickin pleaded that that Act had contained a false recital in that the requisite documents had not been deposited, that the Board had misled Parliament in obtaining the Act *ex parte* (in effect without hearing other views) and that it was ineffective to deprive him of his land. It was *held*—by the House of Lords—that the courts had no power to disregard an Act of Parliament, whether public or private, nor had they any power to examine proceedings in Parliament in order to determine whether the passing of an Act was obtained by means of any irregularity or fraud, so that Mr Pickin failed.

(43) *Van Duyn* v. *The Home Office*, [1974] 3 All E.R. 178

Yvonne Van Duyn, a Dutch national, was a Scientologist who tried to enter the United Kingdom on 9 May, 1973. She was refused entry on the grounds that the Secretary of State considered it undesirable to give anyone leave to enter the United Kingdom on the business of, or in the employment of, the Church of Scientology because its activities were considered contrary to public policy. Miss Van Duyn did not appeal under the Immigration Act of 1971 but sought a declaration in the Chancery Division that she was entitled to enter the country. She claimed that Art. 48 of the Treaty which allowed nationals of Member States to accept offers of employment and to remain in a Member State for the purposes of employment applied in her case. She conceded that these rights were subject to 'limitation justified on grounds of public policy, public security or public health' (Art. 48(3)), but said that Art. 3 of Directive 64/221 of 25 February, 1964, provided that measures taken on grounds of public policy should be based exclusively on the personal conduct of the individual concerned and not merely on the basis of employment by a given organization. In the Chancery Division the Vice Chancellor (Sir John Pennycuick) made the first reference to the European Court (i.e. the Court of Justice of the European Communities) under the Rules of the Supreme Court Order 114. Among the matters referred was the question whether or not the directive of 1964 was 'directly applicable so as to confer on individuals rights enforceable by them in the courts of the United Kingdom'. The Court of Justice decided ([1975] 3 All E.R. 190)—(i) that obligations imposed on member states by Art. 48(1) and (2) of the Treaty to abolish discrimination based on nationality as regards employment were directly applicable so as to confer on individuals rights enforceable by them in the courts of member states, since those provisions imposed on member states precise obligations which did not require the adoption of any further measures by the Community or member states; (ii) although Art. 189 of the Treaty provided that regulations were to 'be directly applicable' in member states, it did not follow that directives could not be applicable also. In order to determine whether a directive was directly applicable it was necessary to examine whether the nature, general scheme and wording of the provision were capable of having a direct effect on the relations between member states and individuals. On that basis Art. 3(1) of Directive 64/221 was directly applicable since it laid down an obligation which was not subject to any exception or condition and which did not require any further act or measure for its implementation, and (iii) its function was to impose a limitation of the power on member states to implement a provision which delegated from one of the fundamental principles of the Treaty in favour of individuals, i.e. the freedom of movement for workers.

However, the Court of Justice decided that the Home Secretary had power to do what he had done because the voluntary act of an individual in associating with a particular organization which involved participation in its activities and identification with its aims, could properly be regarded as matter of 'personal conduct' within Art. 3(1) of directive 64/221. A member state was therefore permitted under Art. 48 of the Treaty and Art. 3(1) of the Directive to prohibit, on the grounds of public policy, an individual from entering its territory where the individual was associated with an organization which the member state considered to be socially harmful and the individual was proposing to enter the territory of the member state in order to take up employment with that organization. It was immaterial that the organization was not subject to any restrictions under the law of the member state and that nationals of that state were permitted to take up employment with the organization.

(44) *Amies* v. *Inner London Education Authority*, [1977] 2 All E.R. 100

In October, 1975 Mrs Amies applied for a post as head of department of a school but her application was rejected and a man was appointed to the post. The Sex Discrimination Act, 1975, came into force on 29 December, 1975, as regards all acts of discrimination committed on or after that date. Mrs Amies brought a complaint before an industrial tribunal arguing, amongst other things, that although the appointment had taken place before the Act came into force, she was entitled to relief under Article 119 of the Treaty of Rome which had direct effect in the English courts. Article 119 concerned itself mainly with equal pay for equal work and there was no other article which dealt with discrimination based on sex other than that relating to pay. It was *held*—by the Employment Appeal Tribunal—that Mrs Amies had no claim because—(i) the act of which she complained was one which had occurred before the 1975 Act came into force and therefore an industrial tribunal had no jurisdiction to entertain her application. (ii) As regards the Treaty of Rome, a major consideration in determining whether one of its provisions was intended to create an 'enforceable Community right' for the purposes of Sect. 2(1) of the European Communities Act, 1972, was that a municipal court of a member state should need nothing more precise than the terms of the Treaty itself in order to determine whether the right it created had been infringed. Since Article 119 did not define the right which Mrs Amies alleged had been infringed, it could not be construed as conferring on her any enforceable right in respect of discrimination based on sex, other than in relation to equal pay. (iii) Even if Article 119 did confer an enforceable right on Mrs Amies, an industrial tribunal had no jurisdiction to give effect to that right since industrial tribunals were the creatures of statute and therefore their jurisdiction was limited to the jurisdiction conferred on them by statute.

They had no statutory jurisdiction to give effect to rights directly conferred by the Treaty of Rome; such rights could only be enforced in the High Court.

(45) *Hotel and Catering Industry Training Board* v. *Automobile Pro-prietory Ltd*, [1969] 2 All E.R. 582

This was a test case brought by the Board to decide whether the Industrial Training (Hotel and Catering Board) Order 1966 made by the Minister of Labour pursuant to powers conferred upon him by the Industrial Training Act, 1964, was *ultra vires* in so far as it purported to extend to any members' clubs. If the order was *ultra vires*, the R.A.C. club in Pall Mall was not liable to pay a levy to the Board by reason of its activities in providing midday and evening meals and board and lodging for reward. The relevant order was made under Sect 1(1) of the Act of 1964, which provides that the Minister may 'for the purpose of making better provision for ... training ... for employment in any activities of industry or commerce' make an order specifying 'those activities', and establishing a board to exercise the functions of an industrial training board. The 1966 order specified 'the activities' as including the supply of main meals and lodging for reward by a members' club. *Held*—by the House of Lords—the general object of the Act of 1964 was to provide employers in industry and commerce with trained personnel and to finance the training by a levy on employers in the industry, and that it was not intended to allow a levy to be made on private institutions like members' clubs. Although such institutions might pursue activities not unlike those of an hotel keeper, they could not be regarded as within the phrase 'activities of industry or commerce'.

(46) *R.* v. *Immigration Appeal Tribunal, ex parte Joyles*, [1972] 3 All E.R. 213

In this case an applicant for *certiorari* alleged that certain regulations made under the Immigration Appeals Act, 1969 had not been properly laid before Parliament as required by Sect. 24(2) of the 1969 Act. A Divisional Court of the Queen's Bench relied on letters from the Clerks of the Journal to the Commons and Lords stating that the rules had been duly presented and laid. The Court was not prepared to go further and examine the internal proceedings of Parliament.

(*Note:* this ruling is similar to that in *British Railways Board* v. *Pickin*, 1974,[42] though Pickin's case applied to Acts of Parliament, whereas this one is concerned with delegated legislation.)

(47) *Denithorne* v. *Davies*, [1967] 2 Lloyd's Rep. 489

Fishermen were charged with using edible crab as bait in their lobster pots contrary to a by-law made by the Eastern Sea Fisheries Joint Committee under the Sea Fisheries Regulation Acts, 1888 to 1894. The by-law prohibited the use of any edible crab of whatever size for bait but under the general law only the taking of crabs under four-and-a-half inches in width is prohibited. However, the by-law was made because the breaking of the crab's shell before using it for bait made it impossible to tell what size it had been before being used as bait. The accused contended that the by-law was unreasonable and therefore unenforceable because only edible crab of less than four-and-a-half inches in width required protection. The justices accepted this contention. The prosecution appealed to the Divisional Court of Queen's Bench which allowed the appeal and directed the justices to convict. A court should only interfere with the by-laws of a public body if they were patently oppressive. The magistrate's finding that the difficulty in proving that edible crabs under four-and-a-half inches in width had been used as bait was an insufficient justification for the absolute prohibition could not be supported in the light of *Kruse* v. *Johnson*, [1898] 2 Q.B. 91, because although drastic it was not unreasonable. *N.B.* in *Kruse* v. *Johnson*, Lord Russell of Killowen laid it down that a court will not treat the by-laws of a public authority as unreasonable unless they are manifestly oppressive.

(48) *Schorsh Meier Gmbh* v. *Hennin*, [1975] 1 All E.R. 152

The plaintiffs, who carried on business in West Germany, had sold goods to the defendants in England. They had not been paid in full for the goods and DM 3756 remained owing. At the date of the invoice the sterling equivalent of this sum was £452 but between the invoice date and the date of the County Court summons sterling had been devalued so that the value of £452 was only £266. Consequently, the plaintiffs asked for judgment in deutschmarks. The difficulty facing the plaintiffs was that the House of Lords had decided in *Re United Railways of Havana*, [1961] A.C. 1007 that an English court could not give judgment for an amount in foreign currency. The plaintiffs challenged this on the grounds that the *Havana* case ran contrary to Article 106 of the EEC Treaty. The County Court judge held that he was bound by the *Havana* case and could only give judgment in sterling. On Appeal, however, the Court of Appeal with Lord Denning, M.R., came to a different decision and found for the plaintiffs on two grounds—(i) as an English court had since *Beswick* v. *Beswick*, 1967[147] the power to order specific performance of a contract to make a money payment of a specific kind there was no longer a justification for the rule in *Havana* that judgment could only be given for a sum of money in sterling; (ii) secondly, that the effect of Article 106 of the EEC Treaty was to require the English courts to give judgment in favour of a creditor of a member state in the currency of that state.

(49) *Miliangos* v. *George Frank (Textiles) Ltd*, [1975] 3 All E.R. 801

This case was concerned with a contract for the sale of polyester yarn and in particular the money of payment and the money of account in the contract were in Swiss francs. The Swiss seller, who was unpaid, was allowed in view of the decision in *Schorsch Meier*[48] to claim payment in

Swiss francs. Sterling had fallen in value against the Swiss franc and if the new rule in *Schorsch*[48] were to be applied the plaintiff stood to gain £60,000 as opposed to £42,000 under the *Havana* principle. At first instance Bristow, J., held that the decision in *Schorsch*[48] had been decided *per incuriam*, the Court of Appeal having been bound by the *Havana* case. Consequently, he felt able to give a judgment only in sterling. From his judgment an appeal was made to the Court of Appeal and his decision was reversed by a court presided over by Lord Denning, who had been in the majority in the Court of Appeal when *Schorsch* was decided. From the judgment of the Court of Appeal a further appeal was made to the House of Lords. Their Lordships quickly reached the conclusion that the *Havana* case had not been overruled, since the only means by which that could have been done was by the House of Lords itself under the declaration of 1966 and, accordingly, the Court of Appeal should have felt bound by the case. It was, however, now open for the House of Lords to re-examine its previous decision in *Havana*. The House of Lords concluded that as the situation regarding currency stability had substantially changed since 1961 when the *Havana* case was decided, there was justification for a departure from that decision under the 1966 declaration. Accordingly, the House refused to follow the *Havana* case and held that an English court may give judgment in a foreign currency. However, the majority of their Lordships were highly critical of the wide interpretation of Article 106 adopted by the Court of Appeal and it remains to be seen when the matter comes before the courts again whether that Article is adequate to sustain the view taken in *Schorsch*.[48]

(50) *R. v. Gould* (1968), 112 S.J. 69

The appellant was convicted of bigamy although when he remarried he believed on reasonable grounds that a decree nisi of divorce in respect of his previous marriage had been made absolute which it had not, so that he was still married at the time of the second ceremony. The Court of Criminal Appeal in *R. v. Wheat and Stocks*, [1921] 2 K.B. 119, had decided on similar facts that a reasonable belief in the dissolution of a previous marriage was no defence. In this appeal to the Court of Appeal (Criminal Division) the court quashed the conviction *holding* that in spite of the decision in *R. v. Wheat and Stocks*, a defendant's honest belief on reasonable grounds that at the time of his second marriage his former marriage had been dissolved was a good defence to a charge of bigamy. Diplock, L.J.,giving the judgment of the court, said that in its criminal jurisdiction the Court of Appeal does not apply the doctrine of *Stare decisis* as rigidily as in its civil jurisdiction, and if it is of the opinion that the law has been misapplied or misunderstood it will depart from a previous decision.

(*Note:* in this case a three-judge court expressly overruled *Wheat and Stocks* which was itself a decision of a five-judge Court of Criminal Appeal.)

(51) *Tiverton Estates Ltd* v. *Wearwell Ltd*, [1974] 1 All E.R. 209

Tiverton Estates Ltd was the registered proprietor of leasehold property. The company entered into an oral agreement on 4 July, 1973, to sell it to Wearwell Ltd. The same day Wearwell's solicitors wrote to Tiverton's solicitors saying 'We understand that you act for the vendor in respect of the proposed sale of (the property) to our clients . . . £190,000 subject to contract. We look forward to receiving the draft contract for approval.' On 9 July Tiverton's solicitors replied 'We refer to your letter dated July 4th upon which we have taken our client's instruction. We now send you a draft contract for approval . . . We await hearing from you.' Wearwell claimed that the oral contract was enforceable, sufficient note or memorandum for the purposes of Sect. 40(1) of the Law of Property Act, 1925, being the draft contract, read in conjunction with the letter from Wearwell's solicitors. *Held*—by the Court of Appeal—for the purposes of Sect. 40(1) the note or memorandum relied on must contain not only the terms of the contract but also express an implied recognition that a contract had in fact been entered into. Documents which are part of a correspondence expressed subject to contract could not, therefore, constitute a sufficient memorandum.

The earlier decision by the Court of Appeal in *Law* v. *Jones*, [1973] 2 All E.R. 437, to the effect that it was unnecessary for the memorandum to acknowledge the existence of the contract, was not binding on the Court because it was in conflict with earlier decisions of equal authority. Although in general the Court of Appeal was bound to follow its earlier decisions, it was not bound to do so where the decision was in conflict with another decision of the court.

(52) *Hutton* v. *Esher Urban District Council*, [1973] 2 W.L.R. 917

The Council proposed to construct a sewer to drain surface water from houses and roads and also to take flood water from a river. The most economical line of the sewer would take it straight through the plaintiff's bungalow which would have to be demolished but might be rebuilt after the sewer had been constructed. The Public Health Act of 1936 empowered the Council to construct a public sewer 'in, on, or over any land not forming part of a street'. The plaintiff argued that the expression 'land' did not include buildings and therefore the Council had no power to demolish his bungalow. However, Sect. 3 of the Interpretation Act of 1889 provides that unless a contrary intention appears the expression 'land' includes messuages, tenements and hereditaments, houses and buildings of any tenure. It was *held*—by the Court of Appeal—that the Interpretation Act was applicable and 'land' therefore included buildings. In consequence the Council had the power to demolish the plaintiff's bungalow.

(53) *Gardiner* v. *Sevenoaks R.D.C.* (1950), 66 T.L.R. 1091

The local authority served a notice under the Celluloid and Cinematograph Film Act, 1922, on the occupier of a cave where film was stored, requiring him to comply with certain safety regulations. The cave was described in the notice as 'premises'. Gardiner, who was the occupier, appealed against the notice on the ground that a cave could not be considered 'premises' for the purpose of the Act. *Held*—Whilst it was not possible to lay down that every cave would be 'premises' for all purposes, the Act was a safety Act and was designed to protect persons in the neighbourhood and those working in the place of storage. Therefore, under the 'Mischief Rule' this cave was 'premises' for the purposes of this Act.

(54) *Evans* v. *Cross*, [1938] 1 K.B. 694

The appellant was charged with having driven a car on the outside of a white line when overtaking on a bend in the road. He was charged under the Road Traffic Act, 1930, Sect. 49, with ignoring a traffic sign and was convicted by the justices. He now appealed on the ground that a white painted line on a road was not a traffic sign within the meaning of the Act. Section 48(1) of the Act defines a traffic sign as 'all signals, warning signposts, direction posts, signs or other devices'. *Held*—The last three words must be construed as something *ejusdem generis* with the preceding words and, therefore, a white painted line on a road was not a traffic sign. The appropriate charge would have been careless or dangerous driving.

(55) *Lane* v. *London Electricity Board*, [1955] 1 All E.R. 324

The plaintiff was an electrician employed by the defendants to instal additional lighting in one of their sub-stations. While inspecting the sub-station, he tripped on the edge of an open duct and fell, sustaining injuries. The plaintiff claimed that the defendants were in breach of their statutory duty under the Electricity (Factories Act) Special Regulations in that the part of the premises where the accident occurred was not adequately lighted to prevent 'danger'. *Held*—It appeared that the word 'danger' in the regulations meant 'danger from shock, burn or other injury'. Danger from tripping was not *ejusdem generis*, since the specific words related to forms of danger resulting from contact with electricity.

(56) *Muir* v. *Keay* (1875), L.R. 10 Q.B. 594

Section 6 of the Refreshment Houses Act, 1860, stated that all houses, rooms, shops or buildings, kept open for public refreshment, resort and entertainment during certain hours of the night, must be licensed. The defendant had premises called 'The Cafe', and certain persons were found there during the night when the cafe was open. They were being supplied with cigars, coffee and ginger beer which they were seen to consume. The justices convicted the defendant because the premises were not licensed. He appealed to the divisional court by case stated, suggesting that a licence was required only if music or dancing was going on. The divisional court, applying the *noscitur a sociis* rule, *held*—That 'entertainment' meant matters of bodily comfort, not matters of public enjoyment such as music and dancing, so that the justices were right to convict.

LAW OF PERSONS AND FUNDAMENTAL CONCEPTS

(57) *IRC* v. *Bullock*, [1976] 3 All E.R. 353

Mr Bullock was born in Nova Scotia in 1910 and had his domicil of origin there. In 1932 he came to England to join the RAF, intending to go back to Canada when his service was completed. In 1946 he married an Englishwoman and they went on a number of visits to Mr Bullock's father in Canada. In 1959 Mr Bullock retired from the RAF and took up civilian employment in England. In 1961 he was able to retire fully, having become entitled to money from his father's estate on the latter's death. Mr Bullock had always tried to persuade his wife to live in Canada but she would not do so. Even so, Mr Bullock always hoped she would change her mind. In 1966 he made a will subject to Nova Scotia law under which he said that his domicil was Nova Scotia and that he intended to return and remain there if his wife died before him. The Crown claimed that he had acquired a domicil of choice in England and that all his income from Canada was chargeable to Income Tax. If Mr Bullock was not domiciled in England then tax would be chargeable only on that part of the income from his father's estate which was actually sent to him in England. This was less than all the income. It was *held*—by the Court of Appeal—that the fact that Mr Bullock had established a matrimonial home in England was evidence of his intention; but was not conclusive. On the evidence of his retention of Canadian citizenship and of the terms of a declaration as to domicil in his will, it was impossible not to hold that Mr Bullock had always maintained a firm intention to return to Canada in the event of his surviving his wife, and there was a sufficiently substantial possibility of his surviving his wife to justify regarding the intention to return as a real determination to do so, in that event, rather than a vague hope or aspiration. Accordingly, Mr Bullock could not be said to have formed the intention to acquire an English domicil of choice. Thus he could be taxed only on that part of the Canadian estate which was remitted to England.

(58) *Tee* v. *Tee*, [1973] 3 All E.R. 1105

The parties were married in England in November, 1946 when the husband was a domiciled Englishman and the wife was an American citizen. In 1951 they went to the United States and in 1953 the husband became an American citizen and acquired a domicil of choice in that country. In 1960 the husband was posted to Germany by his employers, and in 1965 he left his wife and set up home with a German woman by whom he had two children. Some time during 1966/67 the husband decided to make his permanent home in England but it was not until November, 1972, that the husband with his mistress and children actually took up residence in the house he had bought in England in May, 1972. The husband had been granted a permit to work in England in 1969. In July, 1972, he presented a petition for divorce under the Divorce Reform Act, 1969 (see now Matrimonial Causes Act, 1973) based on five years' separation. The wife challenged the jurisdiction of the English Court to hear this petition and the question for the court was whether the husband was domiciled in England in July, 1972. *Held*—by the Court of Appeal—that the husband was domiciled in England. He had left the United States in 1960 and the intention not to return there was formed over the period 1966/67. In consequence the two elements necessary to establish the abandonment of a domicil of choice had been proved. When a domicil of choice was lost, the domicil of origin revives; the fact that the husband did not actually take up permanent residence in England until 1972 was immaterial since it is not necessary for the revival of a domicil of origin that residence should also be taken up in that country.

(59) *Steiner* v. *Inland Revenue Commissioners*, [1973] STC 547

Steiner was born in the former Austro/Hungarian Empire. He lived in Berlin from 1906 but was driven out of Germany by the Nazis in 1939 and came to England. He acquired a flat in London in 1941 and by the end of 1948 had established a business in England and was naturalized in 1948. From 1948 to 1963 he spent six months of each year in Berlin where he had a property. He was assessed to Income Tax for the years 1960/61 to 1966/67 on rents on properties in West Berlin, the Special Commissioners holding that he had acquired an English domicil of choice. He appealed. *Held*—by the Court of Appeal—that the appeal would be dismissed; there were no grounds for holding the Special Commissioners' decision to be erroneous in law. The Court refused to grant leave to appeal to the House of Lords.

(*Note:* if a person is domiciled and resident in England and Wales, tax is charged on the full amount of income arising within a given year wherever made or received. (Income and Corporation Taxes Act, 1970, Sect. 122(1).)

(60) *R.* v. *Kemp*, [1957] 1 Q.B. 399

The accused struck his wife with a hammer without, so he said, being conscious of doing so and was charged with causing grievous bodily harm. He was an elderly man of good character who suffered from arteriosclerosis. Medical opinions differed as to the precise effects of this disease on his mind. It was *held* that, whichever medical opinion was accepted, arteriosclerosis was a disease capable of affecting the mind, and was thus a disease of the mind within the M'Naghten Rules, whether or not it was recognized medically as a mental disease.

(61) *Salomon* v. *Salomon & Co.*, [1897] A.C. 22

Salomon carried on business as a leather merchant and boot manufacturer. In 1892 he formed a limited company to take over the business. The Memorandum of Association was signed by Salomon, his wife, daughter and four sons. Each subscribed for one share. The company paid £38,782 to Salomon for the business and the mode of payment was to give Salomon

£10,000 in debentures, secured by a floating charge, 20,000 shares of £1 each and £8782 in cash. The company fell on hard times and a liquidator was appointed. The debts of the unsecured creditors amounted to nearly £8000, and the company's assets were approximately £6000. The unsecured creditors claimed all the remaining assets on the ground that the company was a mere alias or agent for Salomon. *Held*—The company was a separate and distinct person. The debentures were perfectly valid and therefore Salomon was entitled to the remaining assets in part payment of the secured debentures held by him.

(62) *Jenkin* v. *Pharmaceutical Society*, [1921] 1 Ch. 392

The defendant society was incorporated by Royal Charter in 1843 for the purpose of advancing chemistry and pharmacy and promoting a uniform system of education of those who should practise the same, and also for the protection of those who carried on the business of chemists or druggists. *Held*—The expenditure of the funds of the society in the formation of an industrial committee, to attempt to regulate hours of work and wages and conditions of work between masters and employee members of the society, was *ultra vires* the charter, because it was a trade union activity which was not contemplated by the Charter of 1843. Further, the expenditure of money on an insurance scheme for members was also not within the powers given in the charter, for it amounted to converting the defendant society into an insurance company. The plaintiff, a member of the society, was entitled to an injunction to restrain the society from implementing the above schemes.

(63) *Norwich Pharmacal Co.* v. *Commissioners of Customs and Excise*, [1973] 2 All E.R. 943

The plaintiffs held the patent of a chemical compound used in animal foods, which they discovered was being infringed by unknown importers. The Commissioners of Customs and Excise were allowing the importation and charging duty thereon, and consequently knew the identity of the importers concerned. The plaintiffs brought proceedings against the Commissioners for infringement of their patent, and for an order that they disclose the identity of the importers. The order was granted by the judge but reversed by the Court of Appeal. On appeal to the House of Lords by the plaintiffs it was *held*—allowing the appeal—that the interests of justice outweighed any public interest in the confidential nature of such information. The Commissioners were under a duty to assist a person wronged by disclosing the identity of the wrongdoer.

(64) *Alfred Crompton Amusement Machines* v. *Customs and Excise Commissioners (No. 2)*, [1973] 2 All E.R. 1169

The appellants had paid Purchase Tax on the wholesale value of amusement machines for some years on the basis of a formula negotiated with the Commissioners of Customs and Excise. The appellants claimed that the

Assessments were too high and thereupon the Commissioners investigated the appellants' books and obtained from customers and other sources information bearing on the ascertainment of the wholesale value of the machines. The appellants did not agree with the opinion of the Commissioners as to the way in which the Tax should be computed and in subsequent arbitration proceedings Crown privilege was claimed in respect of documents received by the Commissioners from third parties. It was *held*—by the House of Lords—that the considerations for and against disclosure were evenly balanced. In these circumstances it was held that the Court ought to uphold the claim to privilege and trust the Executive to mitigate the ill-effects of non-disclosure. Thus it seems that where there is a doubt in regard to disclosure the benefit of the doubt is unfortunately to be allowed in favour of the Executive and against discovery. On considering the issue of Crown privilege their Lordships indicated by way of preface that the title is a misnomer; a more accurate term would be privilege on the ground of 'public interest'.

THE LAW OF CONTRACT

(65) *Vincent* v. *Premo Enterprises (Voucher Sales) Ltd and Others*, [1969] 2 All E.R. 941

The plaintiffs, Mr Vincent and his sister Miss Vincent, owned a freehold house in Central Road, Yeovil. They let four rooms on the first floor to Darch and Willcox Ltd who kept two of the rooms for themselves and sublet the other two rooms to the first defendants, Premo Enterprises. The tenancy of Darch and Willcox Ltd was due to end on 25 March, 1967, whereupon the subtenancy of Premo Enterprises would also end. However, negotiations took place whereby Premo Enterprises were to take a tenancy of the whole floor direct from the plaintiffs.

The terms of the agreement were set out in two letters from which it appeared that Premo Enterprises were to take a tenancy of the whole first floor for five years from 25 March, 1967, at a rent of £250 per annum subject to the lease being prepared and signed.

On 25 March, 1967, Darch and Willcox Ltd vacated their accommodation and moved into premises across the road, Mr Willcox taking the key saying to Premo's two girl employees that they could have the key whenever they required it. It was accepted by the court that the girls did not ask for the key until 1 May, 1967, which was regarded as the date when Premo's went into possession of the whole of the first floor.

The plaintiffs signed, sealed and delivered the lease and handed it to their solicitors. Premo's signed and sealed the counterpart on condition that the date when they took vacant possession should be agreed and that no rent should be payable in respect of the time before they took vacant possession, i.e. between 25 March, 1967, and 1 May, 1967. Before the solicitors exchanged the documents Premo's sought to withdraw from the transaction. The plaintiffs claimed that the lease was binding and sued in the Yeovil County Court for rent from 25 March, 1967. Premo's said in defence that the deed had not been delivered but was an escrow and that the conditions had not been fulfilled. At the hearing in the County Court the plaintiffs agreed to give credit for the period 25 March, 1967 to 1 May, 1967, but the judge held that the lease was not binding on Premo's, being an escrow, and that it was too late for the plaintiffs to say that the condition had been fulfilled at the hearing. He rejected the plaintiff's claim and they appealed. *Held*—by the Court of Appeal—since the first defendants intended to be bound subject only to the date of possession being agreed, the deed was delivered as an escrow. However, it was not too late to fulfil the condition at the hearing and the deed was therefore binding on the first defendants.

The question is whether this deed was 'delivered' at all, or whether it was delivered subject to a condition, i.e. as an 'escrow'. . . . The defendants did intend to be bound, but subject to the date of possession being agreed. That makes it, I think, an escrow. . . . This deed was signed, sealed and delivered by the first defendants, subject only to the condition that the date on which possession was given should be ascertained and the rent adjusted accordingly. The next question is whether the condition was fulfilled. I think it was fulfilled at the hearing before the county court when the date of possession was ascertained by the judge to be 1st May, 1967; and the plaintiffs agreed to adjust the rent accordingly. The judge thought it was too late. He did not think the condition could be fulfilled after the action was brought. I do not share his view. . . . I see nothing in this case to debar the plaintiffs from insisting on their legal rights. They did not know of this condition imposed by the defendants to their solicitors until the defence was pleaded; and they acted quite reasonably from that time onwards. The deed having been delivered, the condition having been fulfilled, the defendants are bound.

(*Per* Lord Denning, M.R.)

(66) *Wilson* v. *Wilson*, [1969] 3 All E.R. 945

In 1961 the defendant wished to buy a freehold property in Battersea but his income was not sufficient to qualify him for a building society loan. Accordingly his brother, the plaintiff, joined him in the application to the building society but paid no part of the purchase price, nor any of the costs and expenses, or the mortgage repayments. The transfer of the property declared that the plaintiff and defendant were joint owners and the title was registered in their joint names as was the charge in favour of the building society.

In March, 1967, the plaintiff commenced an action claiming a half share in the property. The defendant alleged that it was never intended that he and his brother should be beneficial joint owners but that the property was held on trust by the defendant and his brother for the sole benefit of the defendant. The defendant asked, amongst other things, for rectification of the deed of transfer. *Held*—by Buckley, J.—that the court would order rectification of the deed by striking out that part of it which declared beneficial interests so as to show the true intention of the parties, i.e. that the beneficial ownership of the property was in the defendant alone. In the course of his judgment Buckley, J., said '. . . where a deed is rectifiable (that is to say, ought to be rectified), the doctrine of estoppel by deed will not bind the parties to it. . . .'

(67) *Carlill* v. *Carbolic Smoke Ball Co.*, [1893] 1 Q.B. 256

The defendants were proprietors of a medical preparation called 'The Carbolic Smoke Ball'. They inserted advertisements in various newspapers in which they offered to pay £100 to any person who contracted influenza after using the ball three times a day for two weeks. They added that they had deposited £1000 at the Alliance Bank, Regent Street, 'to show our sincerity in the matter'. The plaintiff, a lady, used the ball as advertised, and was attacked by influenza during the course of treatment, which in her case extended from 20 November, 1891 to 17 January, 1892. She now sued for £100 and the following matters arose out of the various defences raised by the company. (*a*) It was suggested that the offer was too vague since no time limit was stipulated in which the user was to contract influenza. The court said that it must surely have been the intention that the ball would protect its user during the period of its use, and since this covered the present case it was not necessary to go further. (*b*) The suggestion was made that the matter was an advertising 'puff' and that there was no intention to create legal relations. Here the court took the view that the deposit of £1000 at the bank was clear evidence of an intention to pay claims. (*c*) It was further suggested that this was an attempt to contract with the whole world and that this was impossible in English law. The court took the view that the advertisement was an offer to the whole world and that, by analogy with the reward cases, it was possible to make an offer of this kind. (*d*) The company also claimed that the plaintiff had not supplied any consideration, but the court took the view that using this inhalant three times a day for two weeks or more was sufficient consideration. It was not necessary to consider its adequacy. (*e*) Finally the defendants suggested that there had been no communication of acceptance but here the court, looking at the reward cases, stated that in contracts of this kind acceptance may be by conduct.

(68) *Pharmaceutical Society of Great Britain* v. *Boots Cash Chemists (Southern) Ltd*, [1953] 1 Q.B. 401

The defendants' branch at Edgware was adapted to the 'self service' system. Customers selected their purchases from shelves on which the goods were displayed and put them into a wire basket supplied by the defendants. They then took them to the cash desk where they paid the price. One section of shelves was set out with drugs which were included in the Poisons List referred to in Sect. 17 of the Pharmacy and Poisons Act,

1933, though they were not dangerous drugs and did not require a doctor's prescription. Section 18 of the Act requires that the sale of such drugs shall take place in the presence of a qualified pharmacist. Every sale of the drugs on the Poison List was supervised at the cash desk by a qualified pharmacist, who had authority to prevent customers from taking goods out of the shop if he thought fit. One of the duties of the society was to enforce the provisions of the Act, and the action was brought because the plaintiffs claimed that the defendants were infringing Sect. 18. *Held*—The display of goods in this way did not constitute an offer. The contract of sale was not made when a customer selected goods from the shelves, but when the company's servant at the cash desk accepted the offer to buy what had been chosen. There was, therefore, supervision in the sense required by the Act at the appropriate moment of time.

(69) *Spencer* v. *Harding* (1870), L.R. 5 C.P. 561

The defendants had sent out a circular in the following terms: 'We are instructed to offer to the wholesale trade for sale by tender the stock-in-trade of Messrs Gilbeck and Co., amounting as per stock-book to £2503 13s. 1d. and which will be sold at a discount in one lot. Payment to be made in cash. The stock may be viewed on the premises up to Thursday the 20th instant, on which day, at 12 o'clock noon precisely, the tenders will be received and opened at our offices.' The plaintiffs suggested that the circular was an offer to sell the stock to the person who made the highest bid for cash, and that they had sent the highest bid which the defendants had refused to accept. *Held*—The circular was an invitation to treat and not an offer, and the defendants need not accept a tender unless they wished to do so. Willes, J., said of the circular: 'It is a mere attempt to ascertain whether an offer can be obtained within such a margin as the sellers are willing to accept.'

(70) *Partridge* v. *Crittenden*, [1968] 2 All E.R. 421

Mr Partridge inserted an advertisement in a publication called *Cage and Aviary Birds* containing the words 'Bramblefinch cocks, bramblefinch hens, 25s each'. The advertisement appeared under the general heading 'Classified Advertisements' and in no place was there any direct use of the words 'offer for sale'. A Mr Thompson answered the advertisement enclosing a cheque for 25s. and asking that a 'bramblefinch hen' be sent to him. Mr Partridge sent one in a box, the bird wearing a closed ring.

Mr Thompson opened the box in the presence of an RSPCA inspector, Mr Crittenden, and removed the ring without injury to the bird. Mr Crittenden brought a prosecution against Mr Partridge before the Chester magistrates alleging that Mr Partridge had offered for sale a brambling contrary to Sect. 6(1) of the Protection of Birds Act, 1954, the bird being other than a close-ringed specimen bred in captivity and being of a species which was resident in or visited the British Isles in a wild state.

The justices were satisfied that the bird has not been bred in captivity but had been caught and ringed. A close-ring meant a ring that was completely closed and incapable of being forced or broken except with the intention of damaging it; such a ring was forced over the claws of a bird when it was between three and ten days old, and at that time it was not possible to determine what the eventual girth of the leg would be so that the close-ring soon became difficult to remove. The ease with which the ring was removed in this case indicated that it had been put on at a much later stage and this, together with the fact that the bird had no perching sense, led the justices to convict Mr Partridge.

He appealed to the Divisional Court of the Queen's Bench Division where the conviction was quashed. The Court accepted that the bird was a wild bird, but since Mr Partridge had been charged with 'offering for sale', the conviction could not stand. The advertisement constituted in law an invitation to treat, not an offer for sale, and the offence was not, therefore, established. There was of course a completed sale for which Mr Partridge could have been successfully prosecuted but the prosecution in this case had relied on the offence of 'offering for sale' and failed to establish such an offer.

(71) *Harvey* v. *Facey*, [1893] A.C. 552

The plaintiffs sent the following telegram to the defendant: 'Will you sell us Bumper Hall Pen? Telegraph lowest cash price.' The defendant telegraphed in reply: 'Lowest price for Bumper Hall Pen £900.' The plaintiffs then telegraphed: 'We agree to buy Bumper Hall Pen for £900 asked by you. Please send us your title deeds in order that we may get early possession.' The defendant made no reply. The Supreme Court of Jamaica granted the plaintiffs a decree of specific performance of the contract. On appeal the Judicial Committee of the Privy Council *held* that there was no contract. The second telegram was not an offer, but was in the nature of an invitation to treat at a minimum price of £900. The third telegram could not therefore be an acceptance resulting in a contract.

(72) *Clifton* v. *Palumbo*, [1944] 2 All E.R. 497

The plaintiff who was the owner of a very large estate wrote to the defendant as follows: 'I am prepared to offer you or your nominee my Lytham estate for £600,000. I also agree that a reasonable and sufficient time shall be granted to you for the examination and consideration of all the data and details necessary for the preparation of the Schedule of Completion.' The defendant purported to accept this offer, but later the plaintiff thought the price too low and brought this action for a declaration that there was no binding contract between himself and the defendant. The defendant counterclaimed for specific performance. *Held*—The plaintiff's letter was an invitation to treat and not an offer, so that the defendant's purported acceptance did not give rise to a binding contract between the parties. Findlay, L.J. (following Lord Green, M.R.), said of the plaintiff's letter: 'It is quite possible for persons on a half sheet of notepaper, in the most informal and unorthodox language, to contract to sell the most extensive and most complicated estate that can be imagined. That is quite possible, but, having regard to the habits of the people in this country, it is very unlikely.'

(73) *Bigg* v. *Boyd Gibbins Ltd*, [1971] 2 All E.R. 183

The plaintiff and the defendants were negotiating for the sale of a freehold property called Shortgrove Hall at Newport, Essex. The following material correspondence passed between them—

(*a*) *on 22 December, 1969, from the plaintiffs to the defendants.*
'. . . As you are aware that I paid £25,000 for this property, your offer of £20,000 would appear to be at least a little optimistic. For a quick sale I would accept £26,000 so that my expenses may be covered. If you are not interested in this price, would you please let me know immediately as then I shall open negotiations with—(some other people).'

(*b*) *on 8 January, 1970, from the defendants to the plaintiffs.*
'*re*: Shortgrove Hall, Newport. Thank you for your letter of the 22 December. I have just recently returned from my winter holiday and, turning this matter over in my mind now, would advise you that I accept your offer. Perhaps you will be good enough to contact—(a firm of solicitors) who will be handling this for us.'

(*c*) *on 13 January, 1970, from the plaintiffs to the defendants.*
'Dear Mr. Gibbins, I thank you for your letter (i.e. the letter of 8 January, 1970) received this morning, accepting my price of £26,000 for the sale of Shortgrove Hall. I am putting the matter in the hands of my solicitors. . . . My wife and I are both pleased that you are purchasing the property. . . .'

The plaintiffs alleged that this exchange of letters constituted an agreement for the sale of the property and brought an action for specific performance. *Held*—by the Court of Appeal—that although an agreement on price did not necessarily mean an agreement for sale and purchase and the word 'offer' did not always mean offer in the sense of offer for actual sale, but might be related to a particular term of the agreement whilst other negotiations in respect of the agreement continued, in the present case it was clear from the terms of the letters that the plaintiff's first letter constituted an offer the acceptance of which by the defendants constituted a binding agreement; accordingly the plaintiffs were entitled to specific performance. *Harvey* v. *Facey*[71] and *Clifton* v. *Palumbo*[72] were distinguished on the facts. The following extract from the judgment of Russell, L. J. should also be noted—'We were finally invited to apply this passage in Fry on Specific Performance: 'A much more common question is whether negotiations have passed from that state (i.e. the state of negotiation) and resulted in actual contract. If it were only doubtful whether the contract was concluded or negotiation still remained open the Court of Chancery used to refuse specific performance, and leave the parties to their Common Law rights if any.' As to that I say, first, that I do not think that it is doubtful in this case. I say, secondly but with some temerity because we have not looked at the old authorities which are cited in support of that statement of law or practice, that I do not think that in these days a court dealing with the question of specific performance of a contract for the sale of land would take that sort of half and half course, saying 'We think the contract was concluded but it is a difficult case and therefore we will not order specific performance but will leave the plaintiff to his remedies at law'. I think nowadays the court would come to a conclusion and having come to a conclusion would, if the conclusion was that there was a formed contract whose terms were ascertained, order specific performance.'

(74) *Harris* v. *Nickerson* (1873), L.R. 8 Q.B. 286

The defendant, an auctioneer, advertised in London newspapers that a sale of office furniture would be held at Bury St Edmunds. A broker with a commission to buy furniture came from London to attend the sale. Several conditions were set out in the advertisement, one being: 'The highest bidder to be the buyer.' The lots described as office furniture were not put up for sale but were withdrawn, though the auction itself was held. The broker sued for loss of time in attending the sale. *Held*—He could not recover from the auctioneer. There was no offer since the lots were never put up for sale, and the advertisement was simply an invitation to treat.

(75) *British Car Auctions* v. *Wright*, [1972] 3 All E.R. 462

The company carried on the business of auctioneers of second-hand motor vehicles and conducted the auction sale of an unroadworthy car which was driven away. The company was convicted on an information which charged that it did 'offer for sale' the car for delivery contrary to what is now Sect. 60 of the Road Traffic Act, 1972. There was an appeal by way of case stated to the Queen's Bench Divisional Court contending that in the auction situation there was no 'offer to sell'. *Held*—allowing the appeal—that although colloquially an auctioneer offered to sell the goods auctioned, strictly in the law of contract he invited those present to make offers to buy, the offer came from the bidder and acceptance was communicated by the fall of the hammer, so that it was technically incorrect to describe an auctioneer as offering goods for sale. In the face of *Partridge* v. *Crittenden*, 1968,[70] the court regretfully was required to apply the strict and not the colloquial meaning to 'offer to sell' in the relevant section of the Road Traffic Act. Accordingly, the conviction was quashed.

(76) *Brogden* v. *Metropolitan Railway* (1877), 2 App. Cas. 666

The plaintiff had been a supplier of coal to the Railway Company for a number of years, though there was no formal agreement between them. Eventually the plaintiff suggested that there ought to be one, and the agents of the parties met and a draft agreement was drawn up by the

Railway Company's agent and sent to the plaintiff. The plaintiff inserted several new clauses into the draft, and in particular filled in the name of an arbitrator to settle the parties' differences under the agreement should any arise. He then wrote the word 'Approved' on the draft and returned it to the Railway Company's agent. There was no formal execution, the draft remaining in the agent's desk. However, coal was supplied according to the prices mentioned in the draft, though these were not the market prices, and prices were reviewed from time to time in accordance with the draft. The parties then had a disagreement and the plaintiff refused to supply coal to the Railway Company on the grounds that, since the Railway Company had not accepted the offer contained in the amended draft, there was no binding contract. *Held—*

(i) The draft was not a binding contract because the plaintiff had inserted new terms which the Railway Company had not accepted; but

(ii) the parties had indicated by their conduct that they had waived the execution of the formal document and agreed to act on the basis of the draft. There was, therefore, a binding contract arising out of conduct, and its terms were the terms of the draft.

(77) *Williams* v. *Carwardine* (1833), 5 C. & P. 566

The defendant published a handbill by the terms of which he promised to pay the sum of £20 to any person who should give information, leading to the discovery of the murderer of Walter Carwardine. Two persons were tried for the murder at Hereford Assizes and were acquitted. Shortly afterwards the plaintiff, who was living with one Williams, was severely beaten by him and, believing that she was going to die and to ease her conscience, she gave information leading to the conviction of the man Williams for the murder. In an action to recover the reward the jury found that the plaintiff was not induced to give the information by the reward offered, but by motives of spite and revenge. *Held—*She was nevertheless entitled to the reward, for she had seen the handbill and had given information. Patteson, J., said: 'We cannot go into the plaintiff's motives.'

(78) *Winn* v. *Bull* (1877), 7 Ch. D. 29

The defendant had entered into a written agreement with the plaintiff for the lease of a house, the term of the lease and the rent being agreed. However, the written agreement was expressly made 'subject to the preparation and approval of a formal contract'. It appeared that no other contract was made between the parties. The plaintiff now sued for specific performance of the agreement. *Held—*The written agreement provided a memorandum sufficient to satisfy Sect. 4 of the Statute of Frauds, 1677 (now Sect. 40 of the Law of Property Act, 1925), but there was no binding contract between the parties because, although certain covenants are normally implied into leases, it is also true that many and varied express covenants are often agreed between the parties. The words 'subject to contract' indicated that the parties were still in a state of negotiation, and until they entered into a formal contract there was no agreement which the Court could enforce.

(79) *Filby* v. *Hounsell*, [1896] 2 Ch. 737

Property had been offered for sale by auction but had not been sold. An offer was then made to buy the property, stating that if the offer was accepted the purchaser would sign a contract 'on the auction particulars'. This offer was accepted 'subject to contract as agreed'. *Held*—The parties were bound by a contract drafted on the auction particulars, although they had not signed a formal contract.

(80) *Michael Richards Properties* v. *Corporation of Wardens of St Saviour's Parish, Southwark*, [1975] 3 All E.R. 416

In this case the words 'subject to contract' were included by the defendants by mistake on a document accepting a full and complete tender for the purchase of a piece of land which had been submitted by the plaintiffs. It was *held* that the agreement was binding and the phrase 'subject to contract' could be ignored as meaningless (*Nicolene Ltd* v. *Simmonds*, 1953[89] applied). Mr Justice Goff said that he hoped that he was not sounding warning bells in solicitors' offices, and certainly the decision does not affect the general practise of heading standard correspondence before a draft contract is approved and exchanged with the words 'subject to contract'. The decision shows only that no protection can be achieved by using these words when a binding and evidenced agreement has been entered into. The case of a tender is a special one because the contract is normally constituted by the tender document itself when fully completed and the written acceptance.

(81) *Chillingworth and another* v. *Esche*, [1923] All E.R. Rep. 97

By a document, dated 10 July, 1922, Chillingworth and Cummings agreed to purchase the defendant's nursery gardens at Cheshunt, Herts., for £4800 'subject to a proper contract to be prepared by the vendor's solicitors'. The plaintiffs paid a deposit of £240. After the solicitors on both sides had agreed on the terms of a contract the plaintiffs refused, without reason, to go on and claimed a declaration that the document of 20 July, 1922, was not binding and that the deposit must be repaid. *Held*—by the Court of Appeal—that the document was nothing more than a conditional offer and a conditional acceptance and would only ripen into a binding agreement when a formal document was signed. Further, on the construction of the documents and in the circumstances, the plaintiffs were entitled to the repayment of the deposit. The plaintiffs' solicitors were not agents of their clients, so as to bind them, when they agreed with the defendant's solicitors on the terms of the contract.

(82) *Sorrel* v. *Finch*, [1976] 2 All E.R. 371

A Mr Levy, an undischarged bankrupt, was an estate agent. The plaintiff asked him to find a purchaser for his house. There was no agreement between the plaintiff and Mr Levy about deposits or commission. Mr Levy took deposits from five people and then disappeared. Mr Finch, one of those who had paid a deposit, sued the plaintiff for its return. It was *held*—by the House of Lords—that in the absence of express or implied agreement that he do so, an estate agent has no authority to receive a pre-contract deposit on behalf of the vendor, and the fact that the vendor knows a deposit has been received does not impose upon him an obligation to repay it.

(83) *Branca* v. *Cobarro*, [1947] 2 All E.R. 101

The defendant agreed to sell to the plaintiff the lease and goodwill of a mushroom farm. The contract ended with the words 'This is a provisional agreement until a full legalized agreement, drawn up by a solicitor and embodying all the conditions herewith stated is signed.' The defendant alleged that the agreement was not binding on him but it was *held*—by the Court of Appeal—that the words 'provisional' and 'until' were not appropriate words to indicate conditional assent. They indicated that the parties intended a binding agreement which would remain in force until superseded by a more formal contract between the parties.

(84) *Tomlin* v. *Standard Telephones and Cables Ltd*, [1969] 3 All E.R. 201

The plaintiff was a fitter employed to help on board H.M. telecommunications ship *Alert*. In the course of his duties he strained his back and claimed against the defendants, his employers, for damages in respect of that accident. The plaintiff's solicitor and the employers' insurers negotiated an agreement that liability would be accepted on a 50 per cent basis. In this action the defendants alleged that they were not bound by the agreement entered into by their representatives the insurers, because it appeared that the letters constituting the agreement were headed 'Without Prejudice'. *Held*—by the Court of Appeal—that on a proper construction of the letters written by the defendants' representatives there was a definite and binding agreement to pay half the damages though the actual amount was left for further negotiation.

A point that arises is that all the letters written by the agent of the insurance company bore the words, 'Without Prejudice'. The point is taken that, by reason of those words, there could not be any binding agreement between the parties . . . *Walker* v. *Wilsher* (1889), 23 Q.B.D. 335. . . . Lindley, L.J., said at p. 337 "What is the meaning of the words 'without prejudice'? I think they mean without prejudice to the position of the writer of the letter if the terms he proposes are not accepted. If the terms proposed in the letter are accepted a complete contract is established and the letter, although written without prejudice, operates to alter the old state of things and to establish a new one." That statement of Lindley, L.J., is of great authority and seems to me to apply exactly to the present case if in fact there was a binding agreement, or an agreement intended to be binding, reached between the parties; and, accordingly, it seems to me that not only was the court entitled to look at the letters although they were nearly all described as 'Without Prejudice', but it is quite possible (and in fact the intention of the parties was) that there was a binding agreement contained in that correspondence.

(*Per* Danckwerts, L.J.)

(85) *Hillas & Co. Ltd* v. *Arcos Ltd*, [1932] All E.R. Rep. 494

The plaintiffs had entered into a contract with the defendants under which the defendants were to supply the plaintiffs with '22,000 standards of soft wood (Russian) of fair specification over the season 1930'. The contract also contained an option allowing the plaintiffs to take up 100,000 standards as above during the season 1931. The parties managed to perform the contract throughout the 1930 season without any argument or serious difficulty in spite of the vague words used in connection with the specification of the wood. However, when the plaintiffs exercised their option for 100,000 standards during the season 1931, the defendants refused to supply the wood, saying that the specification was too vague to bind the parties, and the agreement was therefore inchoate as requiring a further agreement as to the precise specification. *Held*—by the House of Lords—that the option to supply 100,000 standards during the 1931 season was valid. There was a certain vagueness about the specification, but there was also a course of dealing between the parties which operated as a guide to the Court regarding the difficulties which this vagueness might produce. Since the parties had not experienced serious difficulty in carrying out the 1930 agreement, there was no reason to suppose that the option could not have been carried out without difficulty had the defendants been prepared to go on with it. Judgment was given for the plaintiffs.

(86) *Foley* v. *Classique Coaches Ltd*, [1934] 2 K.B. 1

F owned certain land, part of which he used for the business of supplying petrol. He also owned the adjoining land. The company wished to purchase the adjoining land for use as the headquarters of their charabanc business. F agreed to sell the land to the company on condition that the company would buy all their petrol from him. An agreement was made under which the company agreed to buy its petrol from F 'at a price to be agreed by the parties in writing and from time to time'. It was further agreed that any dispute arising under the agreement should be submitted 'to arbitration in the usual way'. The agreement was acted upon for three years. At this time the company felt it could get petrol at a better price, and the company's solicitor wrote to F repudiating the contract. *Held*—although the parties had not agreed upon a price, there was a contract to supply petrol at a reasonable price and of reasonable quality, and although the agreement did not stipulate the future price, but left this to the further agreement of the parties, a method was provided by which the price could be ascertained without such agreement, i.e. by arbitration. An injunction was therefore granted requiring the company to take petrol from F as agreed.

A similar problem arose in *F. & S. Sykes (Wessex)* v. *Fine-Fare*, [1967] 1 Lloyd's Rep. 53. In that case producers of broiler chickens agreed with certain retailers to supply between 30,000 and 80,000 chickens a week during the first year of the agreement and afterwards 'such other figures as might be agreed'. The agreement was to last for not less than five years, and it was agreed that any differences between the parties should be referred to arbitration. Eventually the retailers contended that the agreement was void for uncertainty. *Held*—by the Court of Appeal—it was not, because in default of the further agreement envisaged the number of chickens should be such reasonable number as might be decided by the arbitrator.

(87) *Brown* v. *Gould and Others*, [1971] 2 All E.R. 1505

A lease contained an option to renew 'at a rent to be fixed having regard to the market value of the premises at the time of exercising the option taking into account to the advantage of the tenant any increased value of such premises attributable to structural improvements made by the tenant'. The landlords maintained that the option was void for uncertainty. *Held*—by Megarry, J.—it was not. The parties had laid down a formula by which the rent might be ascertained. Although there was no machinery (e.g. arbitration) for resolving a dispute as to the application of the formula, the court could provide that machinery and determine the rent. The option was therefore valid and enforceable.

(88) *Scammell (G.) and Nephew Ltd* v. *Ouston*, [1941] A.C. 251

Ouston wished to acquire a new motor van for use in his furniture business. Discussions took place with the company's sales manager as a result of which the company sent a quotation for the supply of a suitable van. Eventually Ouston sent an official order making the following stipulation, 'This order is given on the understanding that the balance of the purchase price can be had on hire-purchase terms over a period of two years.' This was in accordance with the discussions between the sales manager and Ouston, which had taken place on the understanding that hire purchase would be available. The company seemed to be content with the arrangement and completed the van. Arrangements were made with a finance company to give hire-purchase facilities, but the actual terms were not agreed at that stage. The appellants also agreed to take Ouston's present van in part exchange, but later stated that they were not satisfied with its condition and asked him to sell it locally. He refused and after much correspondence he issued a writ against the appellants for damages for non-delivery of the van. The appellants' defence was that there was no contract until the hire-purchase terms had been ascertained. *Held*—The defence succeeded; it was not possible to construe a contract from the vague language used by the parties.

(*Note:* if there is evidence of a trade custom, business procedure or previous dealings between the parties, which assists the court in construing the vague parts of an agreement, then the agreement may be enforced. Here there was no such evidence.)

(89) *Nicolene Ltd* v. *Simmonds*, [1953] 1 All E.R. 882

The plaintiffs alleged that there was a contract for the sale to them of 3000 tons of steel reinforcing bars and that the defendant seller had broken his contract. When the plaintiffs claimed damages the seller set up the defence that, owing to one of the sentences in the letters which constituted the contract, there was no contract at all. The material words were 'We are in agreement that the usual conditions of acceptance apply'. In fact there were no usual conditions of acceptance so that the words were meaningless but the seller nevertheless suggested that the contract was unenforceable since it was not complete. *Held*—by the Court of Appeal—that the contract was enforceable and that the meaningless clause could be ignored.

> In my opinion a distinction must be drawn between a clause which is meaningless and a clause which is yet to be agreed. A clause which is meaningless can often be ignored, whilst still leaving the contract good; whereas a clause which has yet to be agreed may mean that there is no contract at all, because the parties have not agreed on all the essential terms. . . . In the present case there was nothing yet to be agreed. There was nothing left to further negotiation. All that happened was that the parties agreed that 'the usual conditions of acceptance apply'. That clause was so vague and uncertain as to be incapable of any precise meaning. It is clearly severable from the rest of the contract. It can be rejected without impairing the sense or reasonableness of the contract as a whole, and it should be so rejected. The contract should be held good and the clause ignored. The parties themselves treated the contract as subsisting. They regarded it as creating binding obligations between them; and it would be most unfortunate if the law should say otherwise. You would find defaulters all scanning their contracts to find some meaningless clause on which to ride free.

(*Per* Denning, L.J.)

(90) *Hyde* v. *Wrench* (1840), 3 Beav. 334

The defendant offered to sell his farm for £1000. The plaintiff's agent made an offer of £950 and the defendant asked for a few days for consideration, after which the defendant wrote saying he could not accept it, whereupon the plaintiff wrote purporting to accept the offer of £1000.

The defendant did not consider himself bound, and the plaintiff sued for specific performance. *Held*—The plaintiff could not enforce this 'acceptance' because his counter offer of £950 was an implied rejection of the original offer to sell at £1000.

(91) *Neale* v. *Merrett*, [1930] W.N. 189

The defendant offered to sell land to the plaintiff for £280. The plaintiff replied, purporting to accept the offer and enclosing £80, promising to pay the balance by monthly instalments of £50 each. *Held*—The plaintiff could not enforce the acceptance because it was not unqualified, since he had introduced a system of deferred payment.

(92) *Northland Airlines Ltd* v. *Dennis Ferranti Meters Ltd* (1970), 114 Sol. J. 845

Ferranti offered to sell Northland an aircraft by a telegram in the following terms—'Confirming sale to you—aircraft—£27,000 fob Winnipeg. Please remit £5000 for account of . . . (a bank account was named).'

Northland replied by telegram as follows—'This is to confirm your cable and my purchase—aircraft on terms set out in your cable. Price £27,000 delivered fob Winnipeg. £5000 forwarded your bank in trust for your account pending delivery. Balance payable on delivery. Please confirm delivery to be made 30 days within this date.' Ferranti did not regard this as an acceptance and disposed of the aircraft elsewhere. Northland sued for damages for breach of contract. *Held*—by the Court of Appeal—that the second telegram was not an acceptance because the deposit was not paid over outright as requested but left in trust pending delivery and Northland had inserted a delivery date whereas the offer did not mention one. These were new terms so that the second telegram was a counter offer and not an acceptance.

(93) *Butler Machine Tool Co.* v. *Ex-cell-O Corp. (England)*, (1977) 121 S.J. 406

In this case a sellers' quotation for machinery included a price variation clause. The buyers' order was on their terms and conditions which included no variation clause. The sellers acknowledged the order on the buyers' form and supplied the machinery. It was *held*—by the Court of Appeal—that the buyers had made a counter-offer which had been accepted and the contract contained no variation clause. (*Hyde* v. *Wrench*, 1840[90] applied.)

(94) *Stevenson* v. *McLean* (1880), 5 Q.B.D. 346

On Saturday the defendant offered to sell to the plaintiffs a quantity of iron at 40s. nett cash per ton open till Monday (close of business). On Monday the plaintiffs telegraphed asking whether the defendant would accept 40s. for delivery over two months, or if not what was the longest limit the defendant would give. The plaintiffs did not necessarily want to take delivery of the goods at once and pay for them. They would have liked to have been able to ask for delivery and pay from time to time over two months as they themselves found buyers for quantities of the iron. The defendant received the telegram at 10.1 a.m. but did not reply, so the plaintiffs, by telegram sent at 1.34 p.m., accepted the defendant's original offer. The defendant had already sold the iron to a third party, and informed the plaintiffs of this by a telegram despatched at 1.25 p.m. arriving at 1.46 p.m. The plaintiffs had therefore accepted the offer before the defendant's revocation had been communicated to them. If, however, the plaintiffs' first telegram constituted a counter offer, then it would amount to a rejection of the defendant's original offer. *Held*—The plaintiffs' first telegram was not a counter offer, but a mere inquiry for different terms which did not amount to a rejection of the defendant's original offer, so that the offer was still open when the plaintiffs accepted it.

(*Note:* the defendant's offer was not revoked merely by the sale of the iron to another person.)

(95) *Trollope & Colls Ltd* v. *Atomic Power Constructions Ltd*, [1962] 3 All E.R. 1035

The plaintiffs were sub-contractors for the civil engineering aspects of the building of a new power station. The defendants were the main contractors, the Central Electricity Board being the employing authority. The plaintiffs had submitted a tender in 1959 in which they had said that the price for their part of the work would be nine million pounds. Part A of this tender contained a price adjustment clause allowing the plaintiffs to adjust the price tendered according to variations, if any, in the cost of labour and materials during the course of completing the work. Numerous changes were made in this part of the tender and in the price adjustment clause by the Central Electricity Board, but at a meeting of the parties on 11 April, 1960, the tender as amended was agreed by the plaintiffs. The plaintiffs had by this time already done a considerable amount of work on the site.

Later the plaintiffs regretted the agreement of 11 April, 1960, and claimed that they were free to terminate operations at any time and asked for a *quantum meruit* for their services up to 11 April, 1960. The Board claimed that a binding contract existed between themselves and the plaintiffs on the terms of the agreement of 11 April, 1960, and that this agreement, when made, operated retrospectively to cover the work done by the plaintiffs up to 11 April and subsequently. The plaintiffs then alleged that the agreement of 11 April could only operate for the future, and that work done up to 11 April, 1960, should be assessed by the Court on a *quantum meruit*, or alternatively be based on an implied contract on the terms of the tender of 1959 before amendments. *Held*—The agreement of 11 April, 1960, operated retrospectively so that the plaintiffs were entitled to payment for work done prior to 11 April only on the basis of the amended tender and were also bound to operate for the future on the same basis.

(*Note:* the action was one in which many parties were joined, and the Central Electricity Board was in fact one of the defendants.)

(96) *Great Northern Railway* v. *Witham* (1873), L.R. 9 C.P. 16

The company advertised for tenders for the supply for one year of such stores as they might think fit to order. The defendant submitted a tender in these words: 'I undertake to supply the company for twelve months with such quantities of (certain specified goods) as the company may order from time to time.' The company accepted the tender, and gave orders under it which the defendant carried out. Eventually the defendant refused to carry out an order made by the company under the tender, and this action was brought. *Held*—The defendant was in breach of contract. A tender of this type was a standing offer which was converted into a series of contracts as the company made an order. The defendant might revoke his offer for the remainder of the period covered by the tender, but must supply the goods already ordered by the company.

(97) *Powell* v. *Lee* (1908), 99 L.T. 284

The defendants were managers of a school and wished to appoint a headmaster. Powell applied for the position and together with two other applicants was selected for the final choice of the managers. The managers passed a resolution appointing Powell but gave no instructions that this decision was to be communicated to him, although D (one of the managers) was instructed to inform one of the other candidates (Parker) that he had not been appointed. D, without authority, also informed Powell that he had been selected. The matter was then re-opened and Parker was properly appointed. Lee than informed the plaintiff that this appointment had been made. The plaintiff now sued the six managers for damages for breach of contract. *Held*—There was no contract because there was no authorized communication of the intention to contract by the managers.

(98) *Felthouse* v. *Bindley* (1862), 11 C.B.(N.S.) 869

The plaintiff had been engaged in negotiations with his nephew John regarding the purchase of John's horse, and there had been some misunderstanding as to the price. Eventually the plaintiff wrote to his nephew as follows: 'If I hear no more about him I consider the horse is mine at £30 15s.' The nephew did not reply but, wishing to sell the horse to his uncle, he told the defendant, an auctioneer who was selling farm stock for him, not to sell the horse as it had already been sold. The auctioneer inadvertently put the horse up with the rest of the stock and sold it. The plaintiff now sued the auctioneer in conversion, the basis of the claim being that he had made a contract with his nephew and the property in the animal was vested in him (the uncle) at the time of the sale. *Held*—The plaintiff's action failed. Although the nephew intended to sell the horse to his uncle, he had not communicated that intention. There was, therefore, no contract between the parties, and the property in the horse was not vested in the plaintiff at the time of the auction sale.

(99) *Fairline Shipping Corporation* v. *Adamson*, [1974] 2 All E.R. 967

Under an agreement made with Game and Meat Products Ltd, Fairline stored goods in a refrigerated store belonging to Mr Adamson, who was the managing director of Game and Meat. Game and Meat used the refrigerated store from time to time on an informal basis but never had a proper lease. Initially Fairline were doing business in regard to the storage of the goods with Game and Meat but prior to the arrival of the goods in the store Fairline received a letter and an invoice for the costs sent on behalf of Mr Adamson indicating that he regarded the storage as his own venture. As a result of Mr Adamson's negligence in that it was not discovered that there had been a breakdown in one of the fans distributing cold air into the store, Fairline's goods were damaged. Since Game and Meat was about to go into liquidation Fairline brought an action against Mr Adamson for breach of contract and negligence. As regards the claim for breach of contract, Kerr, J. decided that there was no contract between the plaintiffs and Mr Adamson. If the letter which he wrote could be regarded as an offer then there had been no acceptance of that offer by Fairline and the uncommunicated acceptance of an offer could not have the effect of binding the offeror. (*Felthouse* v. *Bindley*, 1862[98] applied.) As regards Mr Adamson's position as a bailee, one could be a bailee without the need for a contract. However, it was difficult to establish from the evidence whether at the time the goods were damaged Game and Meat were in exclusive possession of Mr Adamson, and the judge was not persuaded by the proposition of counsel for Fairline that the case might be regarded as one of joint bailment of Game and Meat and Mr Adamson. In any case the judge was of the opinion that the refinements of the concepts of legal possession and bailment were unnecessary in order to determine liability in the tort of negligence. The real answer to the plaintiffs' case was a straightforward action in negligence. There was evidence to show that whatever the contractual position or the bailment position might be Mr Adamson had, by his letter, assumed a duty of care in respect of the goods and he was in breach of that duty so that the plaintiffs succeeded and damages were awarded against Mr Adamson.

(100) *Eliason* v. *Henshaw* (1819), 4 Wheat. 225 (Supreme Court USA)

Eliason & Co. sent an offer to purchase 300 barrels of flour at $9.50 a barrel in a letter sent by wagon to Henshaw. In the letter they asked for an answer by return of the wagon which was to Harpers Ferry. Instead, Henshaw sent his acceptance by post to Georgetown, where Eliason also had an office. As it happened the letter arrived later than a reply by the waggoner would have done but this was immaterial. The Supreme Court of the United States *held* that there was no contract since not only had the letter not been sent by the method required, it had not been sent to the place required.

(*Note:* English law has never gone as far as the Supreme Court in *Eliason's* case. In *Tinn* v. *Hoffman* (1873), 29 L.T. 271, it was held that an acceptance 'by return of post' did not mean exclusively by letter by return of post. 'A telegram or verbal message or . . . any means not later than a letter written and sent by return of post' was sufficient.)

(101) *Manchester Diocesan Council for Education* v. *Commercial and General Investments Ltd*, [1969] 3 All E.R. 1593

The plaintiffs, a corporate body, were the owners of a freehold property known as Hesketh Fletcher Senior Church of England School. The property was vested in the plaintiffs on a condition that it could be sold subject 'to the approval of the purchase price' by the Secretary of State for Education and Science. Late in 1963 the plaintiffs decided to sell the property by tender, the conditions requiring that tenders be sent to the plaintiffs' surveyor by 27 August, 1964. Clause 4 of the form of tender stated 'The person whose tender is accepted shall be the purchaser and shall be informed of the acceptance of his tender by letter sent to him by post addressed to the address given in the tender. . . .' The following events then occurred—

(i) On 25 August, 1964, the defendants completed the form of tender and stated that they agreed to its conditions.

(ii) On 26 August, 1964, the completed tender was sent to the plaintiffs' surveyor.

(iii) On 1 September, 1964, the plaintiffs' surveyor informed the defendants' surveyor that he would recommend acceptance of the defendants' offer and would write again as soon as he had formal instructions.

(iv) On 14 September, 1964, the defendants' surveyor replied saying that he looked forward to receiving formal acceptance and naming the solicitors who would act for the defendants.

(v) On 15 September, 1964, the plaintiffs' solicitors acknowledged this letter by correspondence with the defendants' surveyor which also stated that the 'sale has now been approved', and that instructions had been given to obtain the approval of the Secretary of State.

(vi) On 18 November, 1964, the approval of the Secretary of State was obtained.

(vii) On 23 December, 1964, the plaintiffs' solicitors wrote to the defendants' solicitors stating that the contract was now binding on both parties.

(viii) The defendants' solicitors replied to the effect that they did not agree that there was any binding contract.

(ix) On 7 January, 1965, the plaintiffs' solicitors wrote to the defendants at the address given in the tender giving formal notice of acceptance.

The question in issue in this case was whether the offer contained in the tender lapsed before 7 January, 1965, by reason of lapse of time between 25 August, 1964, and 7 January, 1965. It was *held*—by Buckley, J.—

(i) That the letter of 15 September, 1964, looked at in the light of earlier correspondence, was communication to the defendants that their offer had been accepted. The failure to inform the defendants of the acceptance in the manner laid down in Clause 4 did not nullify acceptance of the offer since Clause 4 did not say that a letter addressed to the address given in the tender was the only mode of acceptance and acceptance by any other equally advantageous method was valid. (*Tinn* v. *Hoffman* (1873), 29 L.T. 271 applied.)

(ii) Alternatively, if the letter of 15 September, 1964, did not constitute an acceptance, the offer had not lapsed because the plaintiffs had not by any conduct refused the offer. In fact the letter of 15 September, 1964, showed a continuing intention to accept and there was no evidence of a change of mind before 7 January, 1965. Thus the offer was still open to be accepted on 7 January, 1965. (*Ramsgate Victoria Hotel Co.* v. *Montefiore*, 1866,[112] *distinguished.*)

(102) *Yates Building Co.* v. *R. J. Pulleyn & Sons (York)*, *The Times*, 26 February, 1975.

An option to purchase a certain plot of land was expressed to be exercisable by notice in writing by or an behalf of the intending purchaser to the intending vendor 'such notice to be sent by registered or Recorded Delivery post'. It was *held*—by the Court of Appeal—that the form of posting prescribed was directory rather than mandatory, or alternatively permissive rather than obligatory, and in consequence the option was validly exercised by a letter from the intending purchaser's solicitors to the intending vendor's solicitors sent by ordinary post.

(103) *Entores Ltd* v. *Miles Far Eastern Corporation*, [1955] 2 Q.B. 327

The plaintiffs, who conducted a business in London, made an offer to the defendants' agent in Amsterdam by means of a teleprinter service. The offer was accepted by a message received on the plaintiffs' teleprinter in London. Later the defendants were in breach of contract and the plaintiffs wished to sue them. The defendants had their place of business in New York and in order to commence an action the plaintiffs had to serve notice of writ on the defendants in New York. The Rules of Supreme Court allow service out of the jurisdiction when the contract was made within the jurisdiction. On this point the defendants argued that the contract was made in Holland when it was typed into the teleprinter there, stressing the rule relating to posting. *Held*—Where communication is instantaneous, as where the parties are face to face or speaking on the telephone, acceptance must be received by the offeror. The same rule applied to communications of this kind. Therefore the contract was made in London where the acceptance was received.

(*Note:* the suggestion was made that the doctrine of estoppel may operate in this sort of case so as to bind the offeror, e.g. suppose X telephones his acceptance to Y, and Y does not hear X's voice at the moment of acceptance, then Y should ask X to repeat the message, otherwise Y may be estopped from denying that he heard X's acceptance and will be bound in contract. It is thought that the conversation prior to the acceptance which is not heard must suggest the possibility of an impending acceptance.)

(104) *Household Fire Insurance Company* v. *Grant* (1879), 4 Ex.D. 216

The defendant handed a written application for shares in the company to the company's agent in Glamorgan. The application stated that the defendant had paid to the company's bankers the sum of £5, being a deposit of one shilling per share on an application for one hundred shares, and also agreed to pay nineteen shillings per share within twelve months of the allotment. The agent sent the application to the company in London. The company secretary made out a letter of allotment in favour of the defendant and posted it to him in Swansea. The letter never arrived. Nevertheless the company entered the defendant's name on the share register and credited him with dividends amounting to five shillings. The company then went into liquidation and the liquidator sued for £94 15s., the balance due on the shares allotted. It was *held* by the Court of Appeal that the defendant was liable. Acceptance was complete when the letter of allotment was posted on the ground that, in this sort of case, the Post Office must be deemed the common agent of the parties, and that delivery to the agent constituted acceptance. Bramwell, L.J., in a dissenting judgment, regarded actual communication as essential. If the letter of acceptance does not arrive, an unknown liability is imposed on the offeror. If actual communication is required the *status quo* is preserved, i.e. the parties have not made a contract.

(105) *Re London and Northern Bank, ex parte Jones*, [1900] 1 Ch. 220

Dr Jones, who lived in Sheffield, applied for shares in the bank. He then sent a letter of revocation which was received by the bank at 8.30 a.m. on 27 October. The bank's letter of allotment was taken to the GPO at St Martins-le-Grand at 7 a.m. on 27 October, but was handed to a postman. Evidence showed that the letter did not go straight into the system. The allotment letter to Jones was delivered at 7.30 p.m. on 27 October, the postmark showing that it was posted at a branch office, not at the GPO. If the letter had been posted at 7.30 a.m., it would have gone to Sheffield on the 10 a.m. train. Evidence showed that it went by the 12 o'clock train. *Held*—The letter was not posted when it was handed to the postman. The evidence did not show with any clarity when the letter was posted, but, since the burden of proof was on the company, it was possible to say that they had not shown the letter of acceptance was posted before 8.30, or even before 9.30 a.m., when the bank's secretary opened the letter of revocation.

An additional point is that evidence given for the Post Office showed that, under the terms of the Post Office Guide, a town postman is not allowed to take letters in this way, and would be disciplined if he did. The position may be different in the country where the custom of taking letters in this way is perhaps better established.

(106) *Holwell Securities Ltd* v. *Hughes*, [1974] 1 All E.R. 161

By an agreement of 19 October, 1971 Dr Hughes, a medical practitioner of Wembley, had granted to the plaintiffs an option to purchase his premises in Wembley for £45,000. The agreement provided that the option should be exercisable 'by notice in writing' to Dr Hughes at any time within six months of the date of the agreement. On 14 April, 1972, the plaintiffs' solicitors sent to Dr Hughes by ordinary post a written notice exercising the option. That notice was never delivered to Dr Hughes nor left at his address. *Held*—by the Court of Appeal—on a construction of the agreement—that notice in writing had to be given to Dr Hughes in the sense that he had either to have actually received it or to be deemed to have received it under Sect. 196 of the Law of Property Act, 1925, which provides for service of notices by registered post, or within the Recorded Delivery Service Act, 1962, which applies a similar rule to Recorded Delivery. This was not a case, said Russell, L.J., where the basic principle of the need for communication to the offeror was displaced by the artificial concept of communication by the act of posting: the language of the agreement 'notice ... to' was inconsistent with the theory that acceptance could be constituted by posting and Sect. 196 of the Law of Property Act, 1925 also impliedly excluded such a mode of acceptance.

(107) *Adams* v. *Lindsell* (1818), 1 B. & A. 681

The defendants were wool dealers in business at St Ives, Huntingdon. By letter dated 2 September they offered to sell wool to the plaintiffs who were wool manufacturers at Bromsgrove, Worcestershire. The defendants' letter asked for a reply 'in course of post' but was misdirected, being addressed to Bromsgrove, Leicestershire. The offer did not reach the plaintiffs until 7 p.m. on 5 September. The same evening the plaintiffs accepted the offer. This letter reached the defendants on 9 September. If the offer had not been misdirected, the defendants could have expected a reply on 7 September, and accordingly they sold the wool to a third party on 8 September. The plaintiffs now sued for breach of contract. *Held*—Where there is a misdirection of the offer, as in this case, the offer is made when it actually reaches the offeree, and not when it would have reached him in the ordinary course of post. The defendants' mistake must be taken against them and for the purposes of this contract the plaintiffs' letter was received 'in course of post'.

(*Note:* the position may be different if the fact of delay is obvious to the offeree so that he is put on notice that the offer has lapsed, e.g. A writes to B offering to sell him certain goods and saying that the offer is open until 30 June. If A misdirects the offer so that it does not reach B until 2 July, it is doubtful whether B could accept it.)

(108) *Byrne* v. *Van Tienhoven* (1880), 5 C.P.D. 344

On 1 October the defendants in Cardiff posted a letter to the plaintiffs in New York offering to sell them tin plate. On 8 October the defendants wrote revoking their offer. On 11 October the plaintiffs received the defendants' offer and immediately telegraphed their acceptance. On 15 October the plaintiffs confirmed their acceptance by letter. On 20 October the defendants' letter of revocation reached the plaintiffs who had by this time entered into a contract to resell the tin plate. *Held*—(*a*) that revocation of an offer is not effective until it is communicated to the offeree, (*b*) the mere posting of a letter of revocation is not communication to the person to whom it is sent. The rule is not, therefore, the same as that for acceptance of an offer. Thus the defendants were bound by a contract which came into being on 11 October.

(109) *Dunmore* (*Countess*) v. *Alexander* (1830), 9 Sh (Ct. of Sess.) 190

In this case a letter accepting an offer of employment was followed by a further letter withdrawing the acceptance. Both letters were received by the offerer by the same post. *Held*—The acceptance was validly cancelled.

(110) *Routledge* v. *Grant*, (1828) 4 Bing. 653

The defendant made an offer to take a lease of the plaintiff's premises: 'a definitive answer to be given within six weeks from 18 March, 1825'. On 9 April the defendant withdrew his offer and on 29 April the plaintiff purported to accept it. The Court of Common Pleas held that there was no contract. Best, C.J. *held* that the defendant could withdraw at any moment before acceptance, even though the time limit had expired. The plaintiff could only have held the defendant to his offer throughout the period, if he had bought the option, i.e. given consideration for it.

(111) *Dickinson* v. *Dodds* (1876), 2 Ch.D. 463

The defendant offered to sell certain houses by letter stating, 'This offer to be left over until Friday, 9 a.m.' On Thursday afternoon the plaintiff was informed by a Mr Berry that the defendant had been negotiating a sale of the property with one Allan. On Thursday evening the plaintiff left a letter of acceptance at the house where the defendant was staying. This letter was never delivered to the defendant. On Friday morning at 7 a.m. Berry, acting as the plaintiff's agent, handed the defendant a duplicate letter of acceptance explaining it to him. However, on the Thursday the defendant had entered into a contract to sell the property to Allan. *Held*—Since there was no consideration for the promise to keep the offer open, the defendant was free to revoke his offer at any time. Further Berry's communication of the dealings with Allan indicated that Dodds was no longer minded to sell the property to the plaintiff and was in effect a communication of Dodds' revocation. There was therefore no binding contract between the parties.

(112) *Ramsgate Victoria Hotel Co.* v. *Montefiore* (1866), L.R. 1 Exch. 109

The defendant offered by letter dated 8 June, 1864, to take shares in the company. No reply was made by the company, but on 23 November, 1864, they allotted shares to the defendant. The defendant refused to take up the shares. *Held*—His refusal was justified because his offer had lapsed by reason of the company's delay in notifying their acceptance.

(113) *Financings Ltd* v. *Stimson*, [1962] 3 All E.R. 386

On 16 March, 1961, the defendant saw a motor car on the premises of a dealer and signed a hire-purchase form provided by the plaintiffs (a finance company), this form being supplied by the dealer. The form was to the effect that the agreement was to become binding only when the finance company signed the form. It also carried a statement to the effect that the hirer (the defendant) acknowledged that before he signed the agreement he had examined the goods and had satisfied himself that they were in good order and condition, and that the goods were at the risk of the hirer from the time of purchase by the owners. On 18 March the defendant paid the first instalment and took possession of the car. However, on 20 March, the defendant being dissatisfied with the car, he returned it to the dealer though the finance company were not informed of this. On the night of 24–25 March the car was stolen from the dealer's premises and was recovered badly damaged. On 25 March the finance company signed the agreement accepting the defendant's offer to hire the car. The defendant did not regard himself as bound and refused to pay the instalments. The finance company sold the car, and now sued for damages for the defendant's breach of the hire-purchase agreement. *Held*—The hire purchase agreement was not binding on the defendant because—

(i) he had revoked his offer by returning the car, and the dealer was the agent of the finance company to receive notice;

(ii) there was an *implied* condition in the offer that the goods were in substantially the same condition when the offer was accepted as when it was made.

(114) *Bradbury* v. *Morgan* (1862), 1 H. & C. 249

The defendants were the executors of J. M. Leigh who had entered into a guarantee of his brother's account with the plaintiffs for credit up to £100. The plaintiffs, not knowing of the death of J. M. Leigh, continued to supply goods on credit to the brother, H. J. Leigh. The defendants now refused to pay the plaintiffs in respect of such credit after the death of J. M. Leigh. *Held*—The plaintiffs succeeded, the offer remaining open until the plaintiffs had *knowledge* of the death of J. M. Leigh.

(*Note:* this was a continuing guarantee which is in the nature of a standing offer accepted piecemeal whenever further goods are advanced on credit. Where the guarantee is not of this nature, it may be irrevocable. However, in *Lloyds* v. *Harper* (1880), 16 Ch.D. 290, the defendant, while living, guaranteed his son's dealings as a Lloyds underwriter in consideration of Lloyds admitting the son. It was *held* that, as Lloyds had admitted the son on the strength of the guarantee, the defendant's executors were still liable under it, because it was irrevocable and was not affected by the defendant's death. It continued to apply to defaults committed by the son after the father's death.)

(115) *Re Cheshire Banking Co., Duff's Executors' Case* (1886), 32 Ch.D. 301

In 1882 the Cheshire and Staffordshire Union Banking Companies amalgamated, and Duff received a circular asking whether he would exchange his shares in the S Bank for shares in the C Bank which took the S Bank over. Duff held 100 £20 shares on which £5 had been paid, but he did not reply to the circular and died shortly afterwards. The option was exercised on behalf of his executors. Muttlebury, Bridges and Watts, and a certificate was made out in their names and an entry made in the register in which they were entered as shareholders, described as 'executors of William Duff, deceased'. The executors objected to having the share certificate in their names, so the directors of the Cheshire Banking Co. cancelled the certificate and issued a fresh one in the name of William Duff. On 23 October, 1884, the company went into liquidation. *Held*—The liquidator acted rightly when he restored the executors' names to the register. The executors wished to enter into a new contract which had not previously existed. They could not make a dead man liable and so could only make themselves personally liable. Their names were improperly removed and must be restored. Although they had a right of indemnity against the estate, they were personally liable for the full amount outstanding on the shares, regardless as to whether the estate was adequate to indemnify them.

(116) *Clarke* v. *Dunraven*, [1897] A.C. 59

The owners of two yachts entered them for the Mudhook Yacht Club Regatta. The rules of the Club, which each owner undertook in a letter to the Club Secretary to obey, included an obligation to pay 'all damages' caused by fouling. While manoeuvring for the start the Satanita fouled the Valkyrie and sank her. The owner of the latter sued the owner of the former for damages. The defendant argued that his only liability was under the Merchant Shipping Act (Amendment) Act, 1862, Sect. 54(1) whereby his responsibility was limited to £8 per ton on the registered tonnage of his yacht. The plaintiff replied that the fact of entering the competition in accordance with the rules of the club created a contract between the respective competitors and that by these rules the defendant had bound himself 'to pay all damages'. The vital question therefore was whether any contract had been made between the two owners: their immediate relations were not with each other but with the Yacht Club. It was held both by the Court of Appeal and the House of Lords that a contract was created between them either when they entered their yachts for the race or at latest when they actually sailed. The competitors had accepted the rules as binding upon each other.

(117) *Rayfield* v. *Hands*, [1958] 2 All E.R. 194

The articles of a private company provided by Art. 11 that 'Every member who intends to transfer his shares shall inform the directors who will take the said shares . . . at a fair price'. The plaintiff held 725 full-paid shares of £1 each, and he asked the directors to buy them but they refused. *Held*—The directors were bound to take the shares. Having regard to Sect. 20(1) of the Companies Act, 1948, the provisions of Art. 11 constituted a binding contract between the directors, as members, and the plaintiff, as a member, in respect of his rights as a member. The word 'will' in the article did not import an option in the directors. Vaisey, J., did say that the conclusion he had reached in this case may not apply to all companies, but it did apply to a private company, because such a company was an intimate concern closely analogous with a partnership.

   (*Note:* although the articles placed the obligation to take shares of members on the directors, Vaisey, J., construed this as an obligation falling upon the directors in their capacity as members. Otherwise the contractual aspect of the provision in the articles would not have applied.)

(118) *Balfour* v. *Balfour*, [1919] 2 K.B. 571

The defendant was a civil servant stationed in Ceylon. In November, 1915, he came to England on leave with his wife, the plaintiff in the present action. In August, 1916, the defendant returned alone to Ceylon because his wife's doctor had advised her that her health would not stand up to a further period of service abroad. Later the husband wrote to his wife suggesting that they should remain apart, and in 1918 the plaintiff obtained a decree nisi. In this case the plaintiff alleged that before her husband sailed for Ceylon he had agreed, in consultation with her, that he would give her £30 per month as maintenance, and she now sued because of his failure to abide by the said agreement. The Court of Appeal *held* that there was no enforceable contract because the parties did not intend to create legal relations. The provision for a flat payment of £30 per month for an indefinite period with no attempt to take into account changes in the circumstances of the parties did not suggest a binding agreement. Duke, L.J., seems to have based his decision on the fact that the wife had not supplied any consideration.

(119) *Spellman* v. *Spellman*, [1961] 2 All E.R. 498

The parties were husband and wife and relations between them were very strained and the husband promised to buy a car for his wife in an effort to bring about a reconciliation. In May, 1960, the husband had a car delivered to the matrimonial home, saying that he had bought it for his wife. The registration book was put in the name of the wife, though the husband's reasons for doing this were not clear, although it had something to do with insurance. Relations between the parties continued to be strained, and eventually the husband left the matrimonial home taking the car with him, the wife keeping the registration book. The car was the subject of a hire-purchase agreement under which the husband was liable for the instalments. The Court of Appeal *held* that the husband was entitled to the car and that the wife should transfer the log book to him. The points of interest raised by the case are as follows—

(i) The wife claimed that the husband had made her a gift of the car. This was rejected by the court because, under the hire-purchase agreement, the title in the car was in the hire-purchase company. Therefore the car was not the husband's to give.

(ii) The wife also claimed that there had been an equitable assignment of the car to her. This was rejected because, although no formalities are required for an equitable assignment, intention to assign must be shown and there was insufficient evidence of this. Danckwerts, L.J., held the view that, although the hire-purchase agreement prohibited assignment, this would not have been fatal in the face of intention to assign by the husband. Willmer, L.J., thought it would.

(iii) A further claim by the wife was that, when the husband put the registration book in her name, he had declared a trust over it for her and held it on trust. The court rejected this view, stating that there was not sufficient evidence of declaration of trust.

(iv) The court applied the principle in *Balfour* v. *Balfour*[118] and held that there was no intention to create legal relations on the ground that domestic arrangements between spouses were not within the cognizance of the law.

(120) *Merritt* v. *Merritt*, [1970] 2 All E.R. 760

After a husband had formed an attachment for another woman and had left his wife, a meeting was held between the parties on 25 May, 1966, in the husband's car. The husband agreed to pay the wife £40 per month maintenance and also wrote out and signed a document stating that in consideration of the wife paying all charges in connexion with the matrimonial home until the mortgage repayments had been completed, he would agree to transfer the property to her sole ownership. The wife took the document away with her and had herself paid off the mortgage. The husband did not subsequently transfer the property to his wife and she claimed a declaration that she was the sole beneficial owner and asked for an order that her husband should transfer the property to her forthwith. The husband's defence was that the agreement was a family arrangement not intended to create legal relations. *Held*—by the Court of Appeal—

(i) That the agreement, having been made when the parties were not living together in amity, was enforceable. (*Balfour* v. *Balfour*, 1919,[118] *distinguished*.)

(ii) The contention that there was no consideration to support the husband's promise could not be sustained. The payment of the balance of the mortgage was a detriment to the wife and the husband had received the benefit of being relieved of liability to the building society.

Accordingly the wife was entitled to the relief she claimed.

(121) *Gould* v. *Gould*, [1969] 3 All E.R. 728

On 15 May, 1966, the appellant left his wife for the second time agreeing to pay her £15 per week as maintenance for herself and the two children of the marriage. The agreement was made orally and was subject to the qualification that the appellant would pay 'as long as I can manage it'. He kept to the agreement until October, 1967, when he began to fall behind with his payments. In February, 1968, he told the wife that he could not pay the full amount in the future. The wife then issued a writ claiming the balance outstanding for the period up to 17 February, 1968. She claimed 13 weeks at £15 per week but gave credit for payments made by the appellant in January and February of £60, making a total claim of £135. The appellant put in a defence denying that he had agreed to pay his wife maintenance as alleged or at all. The County Court judge at Exeter County Court found the agreement proved and enforceable, there being an intention to create legal relations. The husband appealed to the Court of Appeal where it was *held* that it had not been within the contemplation of the parties to make a legally binding agreement. The uncertainty of the terms and the absence of any consideration from the wife, such as an undertaking not to seek maintenance if the payments were kept up, precluded that result.

Lord Denning, M.R. dissented and would have held the agreement to be legally binding, saying with regard to the uncertainty of the agreement—

> I think a good meaning can be given to the husband's statement by implying a term that, if the husband found that he could not manage to keep up the payments, he could, on reasonable notice, determine the agreement. That is a perfectly intelligible term. If it were included in a written document, I have no doubt the court would enforce it. I should also do so when it is included in an oral agreement.

On the matter of consideration he said—

> There is ample consideration for such agreement. First, there is the consideration that neither is insisting on the matrimonial right to live together. Second, whilst the payments are being made, she cannot complain of wilful neglect to maintain. Third, the agreement means that she has no authority to pledge his credit at common law for necessaries. See now Matrimonial Proceedings and Property Act, 1970, Sect. 41,

under which a wife can no longer pledge her husband's credit for necessaries.

(122) *Simpkins* v. *Pays*, [1955] 3 All E.R. 10

The defendant and the defendant's granddaughter made an agreement with the plaintiff, who was a paying boarder, that they should submit in the defendant's name a weekly coupon, containing a forecast by each of them, to a Sunday newspaper fashion competition. On one occasion a forecast by the granddaughter was correct and the defendant received a prize of £750. The plaintiff sued for his share of that sum. The defence was that there was no intention to create legal relations but that the transaction was a friendly arrangement binding in honour only. *Held*—There was an intention to create legal relations. Far from being a friendly domestic arrangement, the evidence showed that it was a joint enterprise and that the parties expected to share any prize that was won.

(123) *Snelling* v. *John G. Snelling Ltd*, [1972] 1 All E.R. 79

The plaintiff and the second and third defendants were brothers and co-directors of John G. Snelling Ltd. Prior to 1967 the company had been financed by loans from each of them. In 1968 additional finance was required and a finance company agreed to provide it and the brothers agreed with the finance company not to reduce their loans to John G. Snelling Ltd until the loan from the finance company had been repaid. The brothers also made a separate agreement between themselves that if any of them voluntarily resigned before the loan from the finance company was repaid, the money due to him from John G. Snelling Ltd should be forfeited. The company John G. Snelling Ltd was not a party to this agreement. The plaintiff resigned voluntarily and sued the company for the return of his loan. His brothers were joined as co-defendants and counter-claimed for a declaration that the loans to the plaintiff had been forfeited. It was *held*—by Ormrod, J.—

(i) that the agreement between the brothers was intended to affect the legal rights of them all and was intended to create legal relations even though made by members of a family. This was not a 'family' situation like that in *Balfour* v. *Balfour*, 1919[118] because here the family relationship had already been destroyed by disagreements and nothing but the biological tie remained between them;

(ii) that the company could not rely directly on the agreement between the brothers since it was not a party to it;

(iii) that although the company could not rely on the agreement, the plaintiff brothers could enforce it being parties;

(iv) that their appropriate remedy was either to apply for an injunction before the plaintiff issued a writ (as had happened) or, after issue of the writ, to apply for a stay of proceedings under Sect. 41 of the Supreme Court of Judicature (Consolidation) Act, 1925, which allows the court, if it thinks fit, to direct a stay of proceedings in any matter before it;

(v) that since all the parties were before the court and also that the reality of the matter was that the plaintiff's case failed, the proper order to make was one dismissing the plaintiffs claim and not one which merely stopped his action.

(*Note:* this case does not affect the basic rule of privity but shows an additional method of avoiding the operation of the rule. It could, for example, have been used in cases such as *Adler* v. *Dickson*, 1955[500] since if A makes a contract with B under which B attempts to exclude the liability of his servants, it may be possible to enforce that clause because B could apply to the court which could stay any action by A against B's servants and in fact dismiss A's claim under Sect. 41 of the 1925 Act. The only qualification would seem to be that the promise not to sue should be clear and unambiguous (*Per* Ormrod, J.).)

(124) *Parker* v. *Clark*, [1960] 1 All E.R. 93

The plaintiffs, Mr & Mrs Parker, were a middle-aged couple and lived in their own cottage in Sussex. The defendants, Mr & Mrs Clark, who were aged 77 and 78 respectively, lived in a large house in Torquay. Mrs Parker was the niece of Mrs Clark. In 1955 the plaintiffs visited the defendants and, as a result of certain conversations held at that time, Mrs Clark wrote to Mrs Parker suggesting that the plaintiffs should come to live in the defendants' house in Torquay, setting out detailed financial terms as to the sharing of expenses. Mrs Clark also suggested that the plaintiffs' cottage might be sold and the proceeds invested, and that the defendants would leave the house in Torquay, and its major contents, to Mrs Parker, her sister and her daughter. Mrs Parker wrote accepting this offer and the cottage was sold. After the mortgage was paid off, £2000 of the remaining money was lent to their daughter to enable her to buy a flat. The plaintiffs then moved into the defendants' house in Torquay. For a time all went well and Mr Clark executed a will leaving the property as agreed. In 1957 differences between the parties arose, and after much unpleasantness Mr Clark told the plaintiffs to go and they left in December, 1957. The plaintiffs claimed damages for breach of contract. *Held*—There was an intention to create legal relations arising from the circumstances. In view of the fact that the plaintiffs had sold their home and lent £2000 to their daughter, it was obvious that, having 'burned their boats', they must have relied on the agreement. The letter from Mrs Clark was an offer sufficiently precise and detailed; it was not merely a statement of terms for a future agreement. Further it was a sufficient memorandum to satisfy Sect. 40 of the Law of Property Act, 1925. Finally, the fact that Mr Clark had altered his will indicated that he regarded the agreement as binding.

The damages awarded were divided as follows—

(i) Damages of £1200 plus costs, in favour of the parties jointly, based on the value per annum of living rent free in the house. (£300 multiplied by four because of the expectation of life of the defendants.)

(ii) Damages of £3400, in favour of Mrs Parker separately, in respect of the value to her of inheriting a share in the defendants' house on their death.

(125) *Jones* v. *Padavatton*, [1969] 2 All E.R. 616

In 1962 the plaintiff, Mrs Jones, who lived in Trinidad, made an offer to the defendant Mrs Padavatton, her daughter, to provide maintenance for her at the rate of £42 a month if she would leave her job in Washington in the United States and go to England and read for the Bar. Mrs Padavatton was at that time divorced from her husband having the custody of the child of that marriage. The agreement was an informal one and there was uncertainty as to its exact terms. Nevertheless the daughter came to England in November 1962, bringing the child with her, and began to read for the Bar, her fees and maintenance being paid for by Mrs Jones. In 1964 it appeared that the daughter was experiencing some discomfort in England occupying one room in Acton for which she had to pay £6 17s. 6d. per week. At this stage Mrs Jones offered to buy a large house in London to be occupied partly by the daughter and partly by tenants, the income from rents to go to the daughter in lieu of maintenance. Again there was no written agreement but the house was purchased for £6000 and conveyed to Mrs Jones. The daughter moved into the house in January, 1965, and tenants arrived, it still being uncertain what precisely was to happen to the surplus rent income (if any) and what rooms the daughter was to occupy. No money from the rents was received by Mrs Jones and no accounts were submitted to her. In 1967 Mrs Jones claimed possession of the house from her daughter, who had by that time married again, and the daughter counterclaimed for £1655 18s. 9d. said to have been paid in connection with running the house. At the hearing the daughter still had one subject to pass in Part I of the Bar examinations and also the whole of Part II remained to be taken.

Held—by the Court of Appeal—

(i) That the arrangements were throughout family agreements depending upon the good faith of the parties in keeping the promises made and not intended to be rigid binding agreements. Furthermore, the arrangements were far too vague and uncertain to be enforceable as contracts. (*Per* Danckwerts and Fenton Atkinson, L.J.)

(ii) That although the agreement to maintain while reading for the Bar might have been regarded as creating a legal obligation in the mother to pay (the terms being sufficiently stated and duration for a reasonable time being implied), the daughter could not claim anything in respect of that agreement which must be regarded as having terminated in 1967, five years being a reasonable time in which to complete studies for the Bar. The arrangements in relation to the home were very vague and must be regarded as made without contractual intent. (*Per* Salmon, L.J.)

The mother was therefore entitled to possession of the house and had no liability under the maintenance agreement. The counter-claim by the daughter was left to be settled by the parties, Salmon, L.J., saying—

If this reference is pursued, it will involve an account being meticulously taken of all receipts and expenditure from December, 1964, until the date on which the daughter yields up possession. This will certainly result in a great waste of time and money, and can only exacerbate ill-feeling between the mother and the daughter. With a little goodwill and good sense on both sides, this could and should be avoided by reaching a reasonable compromise on the figures. I can but express the hope that this may be done, for it would clearly be to the mutual benefit of both parties.

(126) *Peck* v. *Lateu, The Times*, January 18, 1973

Two ladies attended bingo sessions together and had an arrangement to pool their winnings. On one of them winning an additional 'bonanza' prize of £1107, and claiming that it was not covered by the sharing arrangements, it was *held*—by Pennycuick, V.C.—that—

(i) the arrangement was not void as a wager. As between the two ladies there was no question of one winning and the other losing, whether one looked at each bingo ticket in isolation or at the tickets as a whole. As between the ladies the position was simply whatever return either received should be shared between them. Clearly this did not fall within the mischief of Sect. 18 of the Gaming Act, 1845;

(ii) it was quite impossible to bring the arrangement between the two ladies within the definition of a lottery for the purposes of Sect. 41 of the Betting, Gaming and Lotteries Act, 1963. As between them no lot or chance of any kind was involved;

(iii) the contention that the arrangement was not legally binding must be rejected, and therefore the plaintiff was entitled to a share in the prize.

(127) *Jones* v. *Vernon's Pools Ltd* [1938] 2 All E.R. 626

The plaintiff said that he had sent to the defendants a football coupon on which the penny points pool was all correct. Defendants denied having received it and relied on a clause printed on every coupon. The said clause provided that the transaction should not 'give rise to any legal relationship . . . or be legally enforceable . . . but . . . binding in honour only'. The court *held* that this clause was a bar to any action in a court of law.

(*Note:* this case was followed by the Court of Appeal in *Appleson* v. *Littlewood Ltd*, [1939] 1 All E.R. 464, where the contract contained a similar clause.)

(128) *Rose and Frank Co.* v. *Crompton (J.R.) & Brothers Ltd*, [1925] A.C. 445

In 1913 the plaintiffs, an American firm, entered into an agreement with the defendants, an English company, whereby the plaintiffs were appointed sole agents for the sale in the USA of paper tissues supplied by the defendants. The contract was for a period of three years with an option to extend that time. The agreement was extended to March, 1920, but in 1919 the defendants terminated it without notice. The defendants had received a number of orders for tissues before the termination of the contract, and they refused to execute them. The plaintiffs sued for breach of contract and for non-delivery of the goods actually ordered. The agreement of 1913 contained an 'Honourable Pledge Clause' drafted as follows: 'This arrangement is not entered into nor is this memorandum written as a formal or legal agreement and shall not be subject to legal jurisdiction in the courts of the United States of America or England. . . .' It was *held* by the House of Lords that the 1913 agreement was not binding on the parties, but that in so far as the agreement had been acted upon by the defendants' acceptance of orders, the said orders were binding contracts of sale. Nevertheless the agreement was not binding for the future.

(129) *Dunlop* v. *Selfridge*, [1915] A.C. 847

The appellants were motor tyre manufacturers and sold tyres to Messrs Dew & Co. who were motor accessory dealers. Under the terms of the contract Dew & Co. agreed not to sell the tyres below Dunlop's list price, and as Dunlop's agents, to obtain from other traders a similar undertaking. In return for this undertaking Dew & Co., were to receive special discounts, some of which they could pass on to retailers who bought tyres. Selfridge & Co. accepted two orders from customers for Dunlop covers at a lower price. They obtained the covers through Dew & Co. and signed an agreement not to sell or offer the tyres below list price. It was further agreed that £5 per tyre so sold should be paid to Dunlop by way of liquidated damages. Selfridge's supplied one of the two tyres ordered below list price. They did not actually supply the other, but informed the customer that they could only supply it at list price. The appellants claimed an injunction and damages against the respondents for breach of the agreement made with Dew & Co., claiming that Dew & Co. were their agents in the matter. *Held*—There was no contract between the parties. Dunlop could not enforce the contract made between the respondents and Dew & Co. because they had not supplied consideration. Even if Dunlop were undisclosed principals, there was no consideration moving between them and the respondents. The discount received by Selfridge was part of that given by Dunlop to Dew & Co. Since Dew & Co. were not bound to give any part of their discount to retailers the discount received by Selfridge operated only as consideration between themselves and Dew & Co. and could not be claimed by Dunlop as consideration to support a promise not to sell below list price. (See now Resale Prices Act, 1976, Sect. 26.)

(130) *Thomas* v. *Thomas*, (1842) 2 Q.B. 851

The plaintiff's husband had expressed the wish that the plaintiff, if she survived him, should have the use of his house. After his death the defendant, his executor, agreed to allow her to occupy the house on payment of £1 per year. The defendant then refused to convey the house to the plaintiff, saying that there was no consideration for his promise. It was *held* that the plaintiff's promise to pay £1 a year was consideration and need not be adequate. The action for the conveyance of the house to the plaintiff succeeded.

(131) *White* v. *Bluett* (1853), 23 L.J. Ex. 36

This action was brought by White who was the executor of Bluett's father's estate. The plaintiff, White, alleged that Bluett had not paid a promissory note given to his father during his lifetime. Bluett admitted that he had given the note to his father, but said that his father had released him from it in return for a promise not to keep on complaining about the fact that he had been disinherited. *Held*—The defence failed and the defendant was liable on the note. The promise not to complain was not sufficient consideration to support his release from the note.

(*Note:* this case illustrates the general point that on formation of contract consideration must be capable of expression in terms of value. On its facts, of course, the case is concerned with consideration on discharge of contract, i.e. the promissory note, where the rule is the same.)

(132) *Chappell & Co. Ltd* v. *Nestlé Co. Ltd*, [1959] 2 All E.R. 701

The plaintiffs owned the copyright in a dance tune called 'Rockin' Shoes', and the defendants were using records of this tune as part of an advertising scheme. A record company made the records for Nestlés who advertised them to the public for 1s. 6d. each but required in addition three wrappers from their 6d. bars of chocolate. When they received the wrappers they threw them away. The plaintiffs sued the defendants for infringement of copyright. It appeared that under the Copyright Act of 1956 a person recording musical works for *retail* sale need not get the permission of the holder of the copyright, but had merely to serve him with notice and pay $6\frac{1}{4}$ per cent of the retail selling price as royalty. The plaintiffs asserted that the defendants were not retailing the goods in the sense of the Act and must therefore get permission to use the musical work. The basis of the plaintiff's case was that retailing meant selling entirely for money, and that as the defendants were selling for money plus wrappers, they needed the plaintiff's consent. The defence was that the sale was for cash because the wrappers were not part of the consideration. The House of Lords by a majority gave judgment for the plaintiffs. The wrappers were part of the consideration since the offer was to supply a record in return, not simply for money, but for the wrappers as well. On the question of adequacy Lord Somervell said: 'It is said that, when received, the wrappers are of no value to the respondents, the Nestlé Co. Ltd. This I would have thought to be irrelevant. A contracting party can stipulate for what consideration he chooses. A peppercorn does not cease to be good consideration if it is established that the promisee does not like pepper and will throw away the corn.'

(133) *Horton* v. *Horton*, [1961] 1 Q.B. 215

The parties were husband and wife. In March, 1954, by a separation agreement under seal the husband agreed to pay the wife £30 a month. On the true construction of the deed the husband should have deducted income tax before payment but for nine months he paid the money without deductions. In January, 1955, he signed a document, not under seal, agreeing that instead of 'the monthly sum of £30' he would pay such a monthly sum as 'after deduction of income tax should amount to the clear sum of £30'. For over three years he paid this clear sum but then stopped payment. To an action by his wife he pleaded that the later agreement was unsupported by consideration and that the wife could sue only on the earlier deed. The Court of Appeal held that there was consideration to support the later agreement. It was clear that the original deed did not implement the intention of the parties. The wife therefore might have sued to rectify the deed and the later agreement represented a compromise of this possible action. Whether such an action would have succeeded was irrelevant; it sufficed that it had some prospect of success and that the wife believed in it.

(134) *Coggs* v. *Bernard* (1703), 2 Ld. Ray. 909

The defendant had agreed to take several hogsheads of brandy, belonging to the plaintiff, from the cellar of one inn to another. One of the casks was broken and the brandy lost and the plaintiff alleged that this was due to the defendant's carelessness. The defendant denied liability on the grounds that there was no consideration to support the agreement to move the casks. *Held*—the plaintiff's claim succeeded. The court made an attempt to find consideration by saying that when the plaintiff entrusted the goods to the defendant this was sufficient consideration to oblige him to be careful with them. However, it is hard to see how such a 'trusting' can amount to consideration for it was not a benefit to the defendant, nor was it a detriment to the plaintiff because he wished his goods to be carried. It does not appear to have been the price of any promise and the case seems to have been decided on the ground that once the relationship of bailor and bailee is established certain duties fall upon the bailee independently of any contract.

(135) *Gilchrist Watt and Sanderson Pty* v. *York Products Pty*, [1970] 1 W.L.R. 1262

Two cases of German clocks were bought by the respondents and shipped to Sydney. The shipowners arranged for the appellant stevedores to unload the ship. The goods were put in the appellants' shed but when the respondents came to collect them one case of clocks was missing. It was admitted that this was due to the appellants' negligence. *Held*—by the Privy Council—that the appellants were liable. Although there was no contract between the parties an obligation to take due care of the goods was created by delivery and voluntary assumption of possession under the sub-bailment.

(136) *Collins* v. *Godefroy* (1831), 1 B. & Ad. 950

The plaintiff was subpoenaed to give evidence for the defendant in an action to which the defendant was a party. The plaintiff now sued for the sum of six guineas which he said the defendant had promised him for his attendance. *Held*—The plaintiff's action failed because there was no consideration for the promise. Lord Tenterden said: 'if it be a duty imposed by law upon a party regularly subpoenaed to attend from time to time to give his evidence, then a promise to give him any remuneration for loss of time incurred in such attendance is a promise without consideration'.

(137) *Vanbergen* v. *St Edmunds Properties Ltd*, [1933] 2 K.B. 223

The plaintiff owed the defendants £208 and the defendants had issued a bankruptcy notice to be served on 7 July. On 6 July the plaintiff told the defendants' solicitors that he hoped to raise the money at Eastbourne, but that he could not do so until 8 July. The solicitors agreed to put off the service of the notice until noon on 8 July, in return for the plaintiff's promise to pay the money into an Eastbourne bank by that time. The plaintiff paid the money in as directed on 7 July, but his letter advising the solicitors went astray. They thereupon served the bankruptcy notice. The plaintiff now sued for damages for breach of contract. *Held*—The action could not be sustained because the plaintiff was already bound to pay the sum of £208 long before 8 July and was not supplying consideration by paying it into the bank on 7 July. The solicitors were in order in serving the notice.

(138) *Stilk* v. *Myrick* (1809), 2 Camp. 317

A sea-captain, being unable to find any substitutes for two sailors who had deserted, promised to divide the wages of the deserters among the rest of the crew if they would work the ship home shorthanded. *Held*—The promise was not enforceable because of absence of consideration. In sailing the ship home the crew had done no more than they were already bound to do. Their original contract obliged them to meet the normal emergencies of the voyage of which minor desertions were one. *c/f. Hartley* v. *Ponsonby* (1857), 7 E. & B. 872, where a greater remuneration was promised to a seaman to work the ship home when the number of deserters was so great as to render the ship unseaworthy. *Held*—This was a binding promise because the sailor had gone beyond his duty in agreeing to sail an unseaworthy ship. In fact the number of desertions was so great as to discharge the remaining seamen from their original contract, leaving them free to enter into a new bargain.

(139) *Glasbrook Bros Ltd* v. *Glamorgan County Council*, [1925] A.C. 270

In 1921 the Glamorgan police were asked to provide 100 police officers to be billeted on the premises of Glasbrook's colliery near Swansea because it was feared that striking miners were going to prevent safety men going into the mine with the consequence that it would be flooded. The owners of the mine signed a document saying that they would not only pay for the services of the officers but also their travelling expenses. Glasbrook's also undertook to provide them with food and sleeping accommodation. Eventually a bill amounting to £2200 11s. 10d. was rendered by the police authority, the Glamorgan County Council, for the above services. Glasbrook's refused to pay the bill, alleging that the police were doing no more than was their duty and therefore there was no consideration for Glasbrook's written promise to pay for the protection which they had had. *Held*—by the House of Lords—that Glasbrook's promise was binding on them on the ground that the number of constables provided was in excess of what the local police superintendent thought was necessary and therefore provided consideration over and above the obligation resting on the police to take all steps necessary for protecting property from criminal injury. In the course of his judgment Viscount Cave, L.C. said—

'No doubt there is an absolute unconditional obligation binding the police authorities to take all steps which appear to them to be necessary for keeping the peace, preventing crime, or for protecting property from criminal injury; and the public, who pay for this protection through the rates and taxes, cannot lawfully be called upon to make a further payment for that which is their right. . . . But it has always been recognized that, where individuals desire that services of a special kind which, though not within the obligations of a police authority, can most effectively be rendered by them, should be performed by members of the police force, the police authorities may . . . "lend" the services of constables for that purpose in consideration of payment. Instances are the lending of constables on the occasions of large gatherings in and outside private premises, as on the occasions of weddings, athletic or boxing contests or race meetings, and the provision of constables at large railway stations.'

(140) *Ward* v. *Byham*, [1956] 2 All E.R. 318

An unmarried mother sued to recover a maintenance allowance by the father of the child. The defence was that, under Sect. 42 of the National Assistance Act, 1948, the mother of an illegitimate child was bound to maintain it. However, it appeared that in return for the promise of an allowance the mother had promised—

(a) to look after the child well and ensure that it was happy; and

(b) to allow it to decide whether it should live with her or the father.

Held—There was sufficient consideration to support the promise of an allowance because the promises given in (a) and (b) above were in excess of the statutory duty, which was merely to care for the child.

(*Note:* 'Is a promise to make a child happy adequate consideration?' (Compare *White* v. *Bluett*, 1853.)[131] This point is not taken in the case and shows the considerable power which judges have to find or not to find contractual obligations.)

(141) *Shadwell* v. *Shadwell* (1860), 9 C.B. (N.S.) 159

The plaintiff was engaged to marry a girl named Ellen Nicholl. In 1838 he received a letter from his uncle, Charles Shadwell, in the following terms: 'I am glad to hear of your intended marriage with Ellen Nicholl and, as I promised to assist you at starting, I am happy to tell you that I will pay you one hundred and fifty pounds yearly during my life and until your income derived from your profession of Chancery barrister shall amount to six hundred guineas, of which your own admission will be the only evidence that I shall receive or require.' The plaintiff duly married Ellen Nicholl and his income never exceeded six hundred guineas during the eighteen years his uncle lived after the marriage. The uncle paid twelve annual sums and part of the thirteenth but no more. On his death the plaintiff sued his uncle's executors for the balance of the eighteen instalments to which he suggested he was entitled. *Held*—The plaintiff succeeded even though he was already engaged to Ellen Nicholl when the promise was made. His marriage was sufficient consideration to support his uncle's promise, for, by marrying, the plaintiff had incurred responsibilities and changed his position in life. Further the uncle probably derived some benefit in that his desire to see his nephew settled had been satisfied.

(142) *Roscorla* v. *Thomas* (1842), 3 Q.B. 234

The plaintiff bought a horse from the defendant and, after the sale had been completed, gave an undertaking that the horse was sound and free from vice. The horse was in fact a vicious horse, and the plaintiff sued on the express warranty which he alleged had been given to him. *Held*—If the warranty had been given at the time of the sale it would have been supported by consideration and therefore actionable, but since it had been given after the sale had taken place, the consideration for the warranty was past, and no action could be brought upon it. There were no implied warranties in the contract of sale so that the plaintiff, having failed to show that the express warranty was enforceable, had no other cause of action.

(143) *Re McArdle*, [1951] Ch. 669

Certain children were entitled under their father's will to a house. However, their mother had a life interest in the property and during her lifetime one of the children and his wife came to live in the house with the mother. The wife carried out certain improvements to the property, and, after she had done so, the children signed a document addressed to her stating: 'In consideration of your carrying out certain alterations and improvements to the property ... at present occupied by you, the beneficiaries under the Will of William Edward McArdle hereby agree that the executors, the National Provincial Bank Ltd, ... shall repay to you from the said estate when so distributed the sum of £488 in settlement of the amount spent on such improvements. ...' On the death of the testator's widow the children refused to authorize payment of the sum of £488, and this action was brought to decide the validity of the claim. *Held*—Since the improvements had been carried out before the document was executed, the consideration was past and the promise could not be enforced.

(144) *Re Casey's Patents, Stewart* v. *Casey*, [1892] 1 Ch. 104

Patents were granted to Stewart and another in respect of an invention concerning appliances and vessels for transporting and storing inflammable liquids. Stewart entered into an arrangement with Casey whereby Casey was to introduce the patents. Casey spent two years 'pushing' the invention and then the joint owners of the patent rights wrote to him as follows: 'In consideration of your services as the practical manager in working both patents we hereby agree to give you one-third share of the patents.' Casey also received the letters patent. Some time later Stewart died and his executors claimed the letters patent from Casey, suggesting that he had no interest in them because the consideration for the promise to give him a one-third share was past. *Held*—The previous request to render the services raised an implied promise to pay. The subsequent promise could be regarded as fixing the value of the services so that Casey was entitled to a one-third share of the patent rights.

(145) *Dungate* v. *Dungate*, [1965] 3 All E.R. 818

The plaintiff lent £500 with interest at 5 per cent to his brother George and George's business partner, a Mr Elson. The loan was acknowledged in writing dated 12 October, 1953. The plaintiff also lent further sums of money to George in 1956 and 1957 although these loans were without interest.

George paid the interest of £25 per annum by quarterly instalments until 13 April, 1957. On 23 February, 1962, George wrote to the plaintiff saying, among other things, 'Keep a check on totals and amounts I owe you and we will have account now and then.' The letter did not say how much was owed. George died on 30 May, 1963, and on 16 October, 1964, the plaintiff sued George's widow and administratrix of his estate for the repayment of the loans. The defendant pleaded that the plaintiff's claim was statute barred. *Held*—The defence failed and the claim was not statute barred because the letter of 23 February, 1962, made it clear that George owed money to the plaintiff. Although no amount was stated it was sufficient acknowledgement of the plaintiff's claim to make time run again from 23 February, 1962, and not from the date of the loans.

(146) *Jackson* v. *Horizon Holidays*, [1975] 3 All E.R. 92

Mr Jackson had booked a four-week holiday in an hotel in Ceylon for himself and his family, everything to be 'of the highest standard'. The brochure issued by the defendants described the hotel as enjoying many facilities including a mini golf course, swimming pool, and beauty and hairdressing salons. None of these in fact materialized and the food was distasteful. It was *held* that Mr Jackson could sue on the contract not only for his own loss and disappointment but also for that of his family. The decision was not based on the fact that Mr Jackson was a trustee for the others but on the basis that he had entered into the contract partly for their benefit. On that basis an award of damages of £1100 was not excessive. In the course of his judgment Lord Denning, M.R. said: 'The case comes within the principle stated by Lush, L.J. in *Lloyd's* v. *Harper*, [1880] 16 Ch.D. 290 at p. 321: '. . . I consider it to be an established rule of law that where a contract is made with A for the benefit of B, A can sue on the contract for the benefit of B and recover all that B could have recovered if the contract had been made with B himself.' Speaking of these words, Lord Denning said: 'I think they should be accepted as correct, at any rate so long as the law forbids the third persons themselves to sue for damages. It is the only way in which a just result can be achieved.'

(147) *Beswick* v. *Beswick*, [1967] 2 All E.R. 1197

A coal merchant agreed to sell the business to his nephew in return for a weekly consultancy fee of £6 10s. payable during his lifetime, and after his death an annuity of £5 per week was to be payable to his widow for her lifetime. After the agreement was signed the nephew took over the business and paid his uncle the sum of £6 10s. as agreed. The uncle died on 3 November, 1963, and the nephew paid the widow one sum of £5 and then refused to pay her any more. On 30 June, 1964, the widow became the administratrix of her husband's estate, and on 15 July, 1964, she brought an action against the nephew for arrears of the weekly sums and for specific performance of the agreement for the future. She sued in her capacity as administratrix of the estate and also in her personal capacity. Her action failed at first instance and on appeal to the Court of Appeal, [1966] 3 All E.R. 1, it was decided amongst other things that—

(i) specific performance could in a proper case be ordered of a contract to pay money;

(ii) 'property' in Sect. 56(i) of the Law of Property Act, 1925, included a contractual claim not concerned with realty and that therefore a third party could sue on a contract to which he was a stranger. The widow's claim in her personal capacity was therefore good (*per* Denning, M.R., and Danckwerts, L.J.);

(iii) the widow's claim as administratrix was good because she was not suing in her personal capacity but on behalf of her deceased husband who had been a party to the agreement;

(iv) that no trust in her favour could be inferred.

There was a further appeal to the House of Lords, though not on the creation of a trust, and there it was *held* that the widow's claim as administratrix succeeded, and that specific performance of a contract to pay money could be granted in a proper case. However, having decided the appeal on these grounds their Lordships went on to say that the widow's personal claim would have failed because Sect. 56 of the Law of Property Act, 1925, was limited to cases involving realty. The 1925 Act was a consolidating not a codifying measure, so that if it contained words which were capable of more than one construction, effect should be given to the construction which did not alter the law. It was accepted that when the present provision was contained in the Real Property Act, 1845, it had applied only to realty. Although Sect. 205(i) of the 1925 Act appeared to have extended the provision to personal property, including things in action, it was expressly qualified by the words: 'unless the context otherwise requires', and it was felt that Parliament had not intended to sweep away the rule of privity by what was in effect a sidewind.

(148) *Tweddle* v. *Atkinson* (1861), 1 B. & S. 393

William Tweddle the plaintiff was married to the daughter of William Guy. In order to provide for the couple, Guy promised the plaintiff's father to pay the plaintiff £200 if the plaintiff's father would pay the plaintiff £100. An agreement was accordingly drawn up containing the above-mentioned promise, and giving William Tweddle the right to sue either promisor for the sums promised. Guy did not make the promised payment during his lifetime and the plaintiff now sued Guy's executor. *Held*—The plaintiff's action failed because he had not given any consideration to Guy in return for the promise to pay £200. The provision in the agreement allowing William Tweddle to sue was of no effect without consideration.

(149) *Dunlop* v. *New Garage & Motor Co. Ltd*, [1915] A.C. 79

The facts of this case are somewhat similar to case 129 mentioned above except that here the wholesalers obtained an undertaking from the respondents by means of a written agreement in which the wholesalers were clearly described as the agents of Dunlop. There was therefore a direct contractual relationship between the parties, and the appellants could enforce the agreement not to sell below the list price. The case is also concerned with the distinction between liquidated damages and a penalty, because it was suggested that the sum of £5 per tyre was not recoverable because it was not a genuine pre-estimate of loss, but it was inserted to compel performance by the respondents. There is, of course, a presumption that where a single sum is payable on the occurrence of one or more or all of several events then the sum stipulated is a penalty because it is unlikely that all the events can attract the same loss. The contract in this case listed five events on the occurrence of which the sum of £5 was payable. Even so the House of Lords *held* that the presumption need not always apply, and that it did not apply in this case. Where precise estimation is difficult as it was here, then any contractual provision is likely to represent the parties' honest attempt to provide for breach, and the court will follow it.

Certain points of interest arise out of cases 129 and 149—

(i) In neither case did the court regard a re-sale price maintenance agreement as illegal because it was in restraint of trade.

(ii) *Dunlop* v. *Selfridge*[129] illustrates that restrictive covenants do not run with chattels though they may with land. (Compare *Tulk* v. *Moxhay*.)[153]

(150) *Les Affréteurs Réunis Société Anonyme* v. *Walford*, [1919] A.C. 801

The respondent Walford was a broker and he had negotiated a charter party between the owners of a ship the S.S. *Flore* and a fuel oil company. One of the clauses in the charter party stated that the owners of the ship promised the charterers that they would pay the broker (Walford) a certain commission on a figure estimated to be the gross amount of hire. In an action for the commission it was *held*—Although Walford was not a party to the contract, which was between the owners and the charterers, there was nevertheless a trust created in his favour and the commission was recoverable.

(*Note:* the case was, with the agreement of the appellants, dealt with as if the charterers were co-plaintiffs though they had not in fact been joined.)

(151) *Shamia* v. *Joory*, [1958] 1 Q.B. 448

The defendant, an Iraqi merchant having a business in England, employed the plaintiff's brother as an agent in Baghdad. At the end of 1952 the defendant admitted that he owed his agent £1300, and was requested, and agreed, to pay £500 of this as a gift to the plaintiff, who was the agent's brother and a student in England. The agent informed his brother of the defendant's promise. The plaintiff then wrote to confirm this promise, and the defendant sent a cheque which was not paid because it was not properly drawn. The defendant asked for the return of the cheque to correct it, but shortly afterwards repudiated all liability to the plaintiff having, by this time, reason to doubt the account presented by the plaintiff's brother. The plaintiff now sued to recover the sum of £500 as money had and received to his use (an action in quasi-contract) and Barry, J., *held*—He must succeed.

(152) *Smith and Snipes Hall Farm Ltd* v. *River Douglas Catchment Board*, [1949] 2 K.B. 500

In 1938 the defendants entered into an agreement with eleven persons owning land adjoining a certain stream, that, on the landowners paying some part of the cost, the defendants would improve the banks of the stream and maintain the said banks for all time. In 1940 one landowner sold her land to Smith, and in 1944 Smith leased the land to Snipes Hall Farm Ltd. In 1946, because of the defendants' negligence, the banks burst and the adjoining land was flooded. *Held*—The plaintiffs could enforce the covenant given in the agreement of 1938 even though they were strangers to it. The covenants were for the benefit of the land and affected its use and value and could therefore be transferred with it.

(153) *Tulk* v. *Moxhay* (1848), 2 Ph. 774

The plaintiff was the owner of several plots of land in Leicester Square and in 1808 he sold one of them to a person called Elms. Elms agreed, for himself, his heirs and assigns, 'to keep the Square Garden open as a pleasure ground and uncovered with buildings'. After a number of conveyances, the land was sold to the defendant who claimed a right to build on it. The plaintiff sued for an injunction preventing the development of the land. The defendant, whilst admitting that he purchased the land with notice of the covenant, claimed that he was not bound by it because he had not himself entered into it. *Held*—An injunction to restrain building would be granted because there was a jurisdiction in Equity to prevent, by way of injunction, acts inconsistent with a restrictive covenant on land, so long as the land was acquired with notice of that covenant, and the plaintiff retains land which can benefit from the covenant.

(*Note:* such notice may now be constructive where the covenant is registered under the Land Charges Act, 1972.)

(154) *Edward Owen Engineering Ltd* v. *Barclays Bank International Ltd, The Times*, 1 July, 1977

In 1976 Edward Owen made a contract with the executive authority for Jabel El Akhaar to supply and erect glasshouses covering two hectares in Libya. The price of £502,030 was payable in Libyan dinars by instalments and payment of 20 per cent was guaranteed by the Umma Bank of Libya. The contract was governed by Libyan law and any disputes were to be brought before a Libyan court. The buyers agreed to open through the Umma Bank an irrevocable letter of credit in favour of Barclays International on behalf of Owens. Owens promised a performance guarantee and told their bankers, Barclays, to set it up to the value of £50,203. Barclays instructed Umma to issue a performance bond to the buyers for that sum, Barclays giving Umma a guarantee to pay it 'on demand' without proof or conditions. Owens gave Barclays a counter-guarantee. Owens did not receive what they regarded as a suitable letter of credit from Umma on behalf of the buyers and, perhaps understandably, did not go on with the contract. However, the Libyan buyers demanded payment from Umma on the performance bond and Umma in turn made a demand for payment on Barclays. Owens obtained an interim injunction to stop Barclays honouring their obligation (which they wished in good faith to do) to Umma. When the matter came to trial Mr Justice Kerr discharged the injunction against Barclays which would have allowed them to pay Umma but Owens appealed. The Court of Appeal decided that Barclays were right in seeking to honour their obligation to Umma. A performance bond was like the more common letter of credit given on behalf of the buyer to the seller and it was decided in *Malas* v. *British Imex*, [1958] 1 All E.R. 262, that banks must honour letters of credit even where there is a dispute between buyer and seller as to the performance of the contract. If banks were prevented from honouring obligations of this kind confidence would be lost and international trade would suffer. As regards disputes between buyer and seller, these were not the concern of the bank but must be dealt with by the parties themselves (in this case presumably by Libyan law in a Libyan court, which is in fact almost impossible because of the problem of getting visas). However, a bank ought not to honour a letter of credit or performance bond where there is fraud of which the bank is aware, as where one of the parties has to the bank's knowledge deliberately misled the other as to the quality of the goods. There was, however, no fraud in this case, the issues being in the nature of contractual disputes between the parties. Mr Justice Kerr had been right in discharging the injunction and the appeal by Owens was dismissed leaving Barclays free to honour the obligation to Umma.

(*Note:* although banks always honour obligations of the kind described above, there are technical difficulties if they ever had to be sued because there is no contract between them and the seller (letter of credit) or the buyer (performance bond). The issue is unlikely to arise but it might if a bank went into liquidation when the liquidator might be obliged to raise technical difficulties of this kind. If he did the court would hold the bank bound to the seller or buyer as the case may be on the basis of commercial custom, giving rise to an exception to the concept of privity of contract.)

(155) *Foakes* v. *Beer* (1884), 9 App. Cas. 605

Mrs Beer had obtained a judgment against Dr Foakes for debt and costs. Dr Foakes agreed to settle the judgment debt by paying £500 down and £150 per half-year until the whole was paid, and Mrs Beer agreed not to take further action on the judgment. Dr Foakes duly paid the amount of the judgment plus costs. However, judgment debts carry interest by statute, and while Dr Foakes had been paying off the debt, interest amounting to £360 had been accruing on the diminishing balance. In this action Mrs Beer claimed the £360. *Held*—She could do so. Her promise not to take further action on the judgment was not supported by any consideration moving from Dr Foakes.

(156) *D. & C. Builders Ltd* v. *Rees*, [1965] 3 All E.R. 837

D. & C. Builders, a small company, did work for Rees for which he owed

£482 13s. 1d. There was at first no dispute as to the work done but Rees did not pay. In August and October, 1964, the plaintiffs wrote for the money and received no reply. On 13 November, 1964, the wife of Rees (who was then ill) telephoned the plaintiffs, complained about the work, and said, 'My husband will offer you £300 in settlement. That is all you will get. It is to be in satisfaction.' D. & C. Builders, being in desperate straits and faced with bankruptcy without the money, offered to take the £300 and allow a year to Rees to find the balance. Mrs Rees replied: 'No, we will never have enough money to pay the balance. £300 is better than nothing.' The plaintiffs then said: 'We have no choice but to accept.' Mrs Rees gave the plaintiffs a cheque and insisted on a receipt 'in completion of the account'. The plaintiffs, being worried, brought an action for the balance. The defence was bad workmanship and also that there was a binding settlement. The question of settlement was tried as a preliminary issue and the judge, following *Goddard* v. *O'Brien*, [1880] 9 Q.B.D. 33, decided that a cheque for a smaller amount was a good discharge of the debt, this being the generally accepted view of the law since that date. On appeal it was *held* (*per* The Master of the Rolls, Lord Denning) that *Goddard* v. *O'Brien* was wrongly decided. A smaller sum in cash could be no settlement of a larger sum and 'no sensible distinction could be drawn between the payment of a lesser sum by cash and the payment of it by cheque'.

In the course of his judgment Lord Denning said of *Hightrees*: 'It is worth noting that the principle may be applied, not only so as to suspend strict legal rights, but also so as to preclude the enforcement of them'.

This principle has been applied to cases where a creditor agrees to accept a lesser sum in discharge of a greater. So much so that we can now say that, when a creditor and a debtor enter on a course of negotiation, which leads the debtor to suppose that, on payment of the lesser sum, the creditor will not enforce payment of the balance, and on the faith thereof the debtor pays the lesser sum and the creditor accepts it as satisfaction: then the creditor will not be allowed to enforce payment of the balance when it would be inequitable to do so. . . . But he is not bound unless there has been truly an accord between them.' In the present case there was no true accord. The debtor's wife had held the creditors to ransom, and there was no reason in law or Equity why the plaintiffs should not enforce the full amount of debt.

(157) *Good* v. *Cheesman* (1831), 2 B. & Ad. 328

The defendant had accepted two bills of exchange of which the plaintiff was the drawer. After the bills became due and before this action was brought, the plaintiff suggested that the defendant meet his creditors with a view perhaps to an agreement. The meeting was duly held and the defendant entered into an agreement with his creditors whereby the defendant was to pay one-third of his income to a trustee to be named by the creditors, and that this was to be the method by which the defendant's debts were to be paid. It was not clear from the evidence whether the plaintiff attended the meeting, though he certainly did not sign the agreement. There was, however, evidence that the agreement had been in his possession for some time and it was duly stamped before the trial. No trustee was in fact appointed, though the defendant was willing to go on with the agreement. *Held*—The agreement bound the plaintiff and the action on the bills could not be sustained. The consideration, though not supplied to the plaintiff direct, existed in the forbearance of the other creditors. Each was bound in consequence of the agreement of the rest.

The better view is that the basis of this decision is to be found not in the law of contract but in tort, in the sense that once an agreement of this kind has been made it would be a *fraud* on the other creditors for one of their number to sue the debtor separately.

(158) *Welby* v. *Drake* (1825), 1 C. & P. 557

The plaintiff sued the defendant for the sum of £9 on a debt which had originally been for £18. The defendant's father had paid the plaintiff £9 and the plaintiff had agreed to take that sum in full discharge of the debt. *Held*—The payment of £9 by the defendant's father operated to discharge the debt of £18.

(*Note:* here again the basis of the decision is that it would be a fraud on the third party to sue the original debtor. 'If the father did pay the smaller sum in satisfaction of this debt, it is a bar to the plaintiff's now recovering against the son; because by suing the son, he commits a fraud on the father, whom he induced to advance his money on the faith of such advance being a discharge of his son from further liability.' (*per* Lord Tenterden, C.J.)

(159) *Central London Property Trust Ltd* v. *High Trees House Ltd*, [1947] K.B. 130

In 1937 the plaintiffs granted to the defendants a lease of ninety-nine years of a new block of flats at a rent of £2500 per annum. The lease was under seal. During the period of the war the flats were by no means fully let owing to the absence of people from the London area. The defendant company, which was a subsidiary of the plaintiff company, realized that it could not meet the rent out of the profits then being made on the flats, and in 1940 the parties entered into an agreement which reduced the rent to £1250 per annum, this agreement being put into writing but not sealed. The defendants continued to pay the reduced rent from 1941 to the beginning of 1945, by which time the flats were fully let, and they continued to pay the reduced rent thereafter. In September, 1945, the receiver of the plaintiff company investigated the matter and asked for arears of £7916, suggesting that the liability created by the lease still existed, and that the agreement of 1940 was not supported by any consideration. The receiver then brought this friendly action to establish the legal position. He claimed £625, being the difference in rent for the two quarters ending 29 September and 25 December, 1945. *Held*—(i) A simple contract can in Equity vary a deed (i.e. the lease), though it had not done so here because the simple contract was not supported by consideration. (ii) As the agreement for the reduction of rent had been acted upon by the defendants, the plaintiffs were estopped in Equity from claiming the full rent from 1941 until early 1945 when the flats were fully let. After that time they were entitled to do so because the second agreement was only operative during the continuance of the conditions which gave rise to it. To this extent the limited claim of the receiver succeeded.

(160) *Tool Metal Manufacturing Co. Ltd* v. *Tungsten Electric Co. Ltd*, [1955] 2 All E.R. 657

The appellants were the registered proprietors of British letters patent. In April, 1938, they made a contract with the respondents whereby they gave the latter a license to manufacture 'hard metal alloys' in accordance with the inventions which were the subject of patent. By the contract the respondents agreed to pay 'compensation' to the appellants if in any one month they sold more than a stated quantity of metal alloys.

Compensation was duly paid by the respondents until the outbreak of war in 1939 but thereafter none was paid. It was found as a fact that in 1942 the appellants agreed to suspend the enforcement of compensation payments pending the making of a new contract. In 1944 negotiations for such new contracts were begun but broke down. In 1945 the respondents sued the appellants for breach of contract and the appellants counter-claimed for payment of compensation as from 1 June, 1945. As regards the arguments on the counter-claim, it was eventually *held* by the Court of Appeal that the agreement of 1942 operated in equity to prevent the appellants demanding compensation until they had given reasonable notice to the respondents of their intention to resume their strict legal rights and that such notice had not been given.

In September, 1950, the appellants themselves issued a writ against the respondents claiming compensation as from 1 January, 1947. The respondents pleaded the equity raised by the agreement of 1942 and argued that reasonable notice of its termination had not been given. When this action reached the House of Lords it was *held*—affirming *Hughes* v. *Metropolitan Railway Co*. and the *High Trees Case*, that the agreement of 1942 operated in equity to suspend the appellants legal rights to compensation until reasonable notice to resume them had been given. However, the counter-claim in the first action in 1945 amounted to such notice and since the appellants were not now claiming any compensation as due to them before 1 January, 1947, the appellants succeeded in this second action and were awarded £84,000 under the compensation clause.

(161) *Ajayi* v. *Briscoe (Nigeria) Ltd*, [1964] 3 All E.R. 556

The plaintiff claimed hire-purchase instalments due on Seddon Tipper lorries supplied to the defendant. The defendant claimed the equitable principle of promissory estoppel because, when the lorries could not be used by reason of servicing difficulties, the plaintiff had promised to service the vehicles and had also said, 'we are agreeable to you withholding instalments due on Seddon Tippers as long as they are withdrawn from active service'. The defendant could not establish that he had changed his position because of the promise. He was not using the lorries when they went for service and still did not use them after the plaintiffs had repaired them. He was not able to show that he had had to re-organize his business in any way, but in spite of this still did not pay the instalments. *Held*—by the Privy Council—that the plaintiff's action succeeded. The defence of promissory estoppel did not apply.

(162) *W. J. Alan & Co.* v. *El Nasr Export and Import Co.,* [1972] 2 All E.R. 127

A contract for the sale of coffee provided for the price expressed in Kenyan shillings to be paid by irrevocable letter of credit. The buyers procured a confirmed letter expressed in sterling and the sellers obtained part payment thereunder. While shipment was in progress sterling was devalued and the sellers claimed such additional sum as would bring the price up to the sterling equivalent of Kenyan shillings at the current rate. Orr, J. *held* that the buyers were liable to pay the additional sum as the currency of account was Kenyan shillings. On appeal by the buyers it was *held*—allowing the appeal—that the sellers by accepting payment in sterling had irrevocably waived their right to be paid in Kenyan currency or had accepted a variation of the sale contract, and that a party who has waived his rights cannot afterwards insist on them if the other party has acted on that belief differently from the way in which he would otherwise have acted; and the other party need not show that he has acted to his detriment. In the course of his judgment Lord Denning, M.R. said: '. . . if one party, by his conduct, leads another to believe that the strict rights arising under the contract will not be insisted on, intending that the other should act on that belief, and he does act on it, then the first party will not afterwards be allowed to insist on the strict legal rights when it would be inequitable for him to do so. . . . There may be no consideration moving from him who benefits by the waiver. There may be no detriment to him acting on it. There may be nothing in writing. Nevertheless, the one who waives his strict rights cannot afterwards insist on them. His strict rights are at any rate suspended so long as the waiver lasts. He may on occasion be able to revert to his strict legal rights for the future by giving reasonable notice in that behalf, or otherwise making it plain by his conduct that he will thereafter insist on them. . . . "I know that it has been suggested in some quarters that there must be a detriment. But I can find no support for it in the authorities cited by the judge. The nearest approach to it is the statement by Viscount Simonds in the *Tool Metal* case that the other must have been led "to alter his position" which was adopted by Lord Hodson in *Emmanuel Ayodeji Ajayi* v. *R. T. Briscoe (Nigeria) Ltd.*[161] But that only means that he must have been led to act differently from what he otherwise would have done. And, if you study the cases in which the doctrine has been applied, you will see that all that is required is that one should have "*acted* on the belief induced by the other party". That is how Lord Cohen put it in the *Tool Metal* case and it is how I would put it myself.'

(163) *Combe* v. *Combe*, [1951] 2 K.B. 215

The parties were married in 1915 and separated in 1939. In February, 1943, the wife obtained a decree *nisi* of divorce, and a few days later the husband entered into an agreement under which he was to pay his wife £100 per annum, free of income tax. The decree was made absolute in August, 1943. The husband did not make the agreed payments and the wife did not apply to the court for maintenance but chose to rely on the alleged contract. She brought this action for arrears under that contract. Evidence showed that her income was between £700 and £800 per annum and the defendant's was £650 per annum. Byrne, J., at first instance, held that, although the wife had not supplied consideration, the agreement was nevertheless enforceable, following the decision in the *High Trees*[159] case, as a promise made to be acted upon and in fact acted upon. *Held*—(i) That the *High Trees*[159] decision was not intended to create new actions where none existed before, and that it had not abolished the requirement of consideration in the formation of simple contracts. In such cases consideration was a cardinal necessity. (ii) In the words of Birkett, L.J., the doctrine was 'a shield not a sword', i.e. a defence to an action, not a cause of action. (iii) The doctrine applied to the modification of existing agreements by subsequent promises and had no relevance to the formation of a contract. (iv) It was not possible to find consideration in the fact that the wife forbore to claim maintenance from the court, since no such contractual undertaking by her could have been binding even if she had given it. Therefore this action by the wife must fail because the agreement was not supported by consideration.

(164) *Durham Fancy Goods Ltd* v. *Michael Jackson (Fancy Goods) Ltd*, [1968] 2 All E.R. 987

On 18 September, 1967, the plaintiffs drew a bill of exchange on the first defendants in the following form, 'M. Jackson (Fancy Goods) Co.' The bill was signed by Mr Jackson who was the director and company secretary. The bill was dishonoured and the plaintiffs brought an action against Mr Jackson contending that by signing the form of acceptance he had committed a criminal offence under Sect. 108 of the Companies Act, 1948, and had made himself personally liable on the bill because he should either have returned the bill with a request that it be re-addressed to Michael Jackson (Fancy Goods) Ltd, or he should have accepted it 'M. Jackson (Fancy Goods) Ltd p.p. Michael Jackson (Fancy Goods) Ltd, Michael Jackson'. It was *held*—by Donaldson, J.—that the misdescription was in breach of Sect. 108 of the Companies Act, 1948, and that Mr Jackson was personally liable, under the section, to pay the bill. However, since the error was really that of the plaintiffs they were estopped from enforcing Mr Jackson's personal liability. The principle of equity upon which the promissory estoppel cases were based was applicable and barred the plaintiff's claim. That principle was formulated by Lord Cairns in *Hughes* v. *Metropolitan Railway Co.* (1877), 2 App. Cas. 439, p. 448, and although in his enunciation Lord Cairns assumed a pre-existing contractual relationship between the parties, that was not essential provided that there was a pre-existing legal relationship which could in certain circumstances give rise to liabilities and penalties. Such a relationship was created by Sect. 108.

(*Note:* a holder other than the plaintiffs might have been able to bring an action against Mr Jackson under Sect. 108 since such a holder would not have been affected by the equity in that he would not have drawn the bill in an incorrect name.)

(*Note:* Section 108 provides: '(1) every company . . . (*c*) shall have its name mentioned in legible characters . . . in all bills or exchange . . . purporting to be signed by or on behalf of the company . . . (4) If an officer of the company or any person on his behalf . . . (*b*) signs . . . on behalf of the company any bill of exchange . . . wherein its name is not mentioned in manner aforesaid . . . he shall be liable to a fine not exceeding £50, and shall further be personally liable to the holder of the bill of exchange . . . for the amount thereof unless it is duly paid by the company.')

(165) *Crabb* v. *Arun District Council*, [1975] 3 All E.R. 865

The plaintiff and the defendants owned adjoining areas of land, the northern boundaries of which adjoined a public highway. The defendants were to build a road along the boundary with the plaintiff's land and the plaintiff was granted a right of access at a defined point from the northernmost position of his land to the roadway. The defendant desired to sell his land in two lots and in negotiations with the defendants was promised that a gap would be left in a proposed boundary fence adjoining the southern portion of the plaintiff's land and that there would be a right of access from such southern portion to the new road. Accordingly, when the fence was erected a gap was left at the agreed point and gates constructed. In reliance upon the defendants' assurance the plaintiff sold the northern portion of his land without reserving any right of way thereover to the public highway and in the result the only means of access from the southern portion to the public highway was *via* the agreed gap in the fence on to the road constructed by the defendants. Subsequently the defendants closed the gap in the fence and refused to allow the plaintiff access to the road unless he paid £3000 for such right. The plaintiff sought a declaration that he was entitled to such right of access and an injunction to enforce that right. It was *held*—by the Court of Appeal granting the declaration and injunction—that for over a year the defendants had not indicated their intention to go back on their promise that access would be allowed and that the plaintiff having acted to his detriment in reliance thereon the defendants were estopped from denying the right of access. The damage already suffered by the plaintiff as a result of his being denied access exceeded any sum he could reasonably be expected to pay towards the cost of providing access and consequently the plaintiff was not required to make any payment before the granting of the injunction.

(*Note:* this case is an illustration of a situation in which a plaintiff might use the principle of promissory estoppel and indeed base his action on it. Thus the expression of Birkett, L.J. in *Combe* v. *Combe*, 1951[163] that the doctrine is 'a shield not a sword' is not always applicable.)

(166) *Mountstephen* v. *Lakeman* (1871), L.R. 7 Q.B. 196

The defendant was chairman of the Brixham Local Board of Health. The plaintiff, who was a builder and contractor, was employed in 1866 by the board to construct certain main sewage works in the town. On 19 March, 1866, notice was given by the board to owners of certain homes to connect their house drains with the main sewer within twenty-one days. Before the expiration of the twenty-one days Robert Adams, the surveyor of the board, suggested to the plaintiff that he should make the connections. The plaintiff said he was willing to do the work if the board would see him paid. On the 5 April, 1866, i.e. before the expiration of the twenty-one days, the plaintiff commenced work on the connections. However, before work commenced it appeared that the plaintiff had had an interview with the defendant at which the following conversation took place—

Defendant: 'What objection have you to making the connections?'

Plaintiff: 'I have none, if you or the board will order the work or become responsible for the payment.'

Defendant: 'Go on Mountstephen and do the work and I will see you paid.'

The plaintiff completed the connections in April and May, 1866, and sent an account to the board on 5 December, 1866. The board disclaimed responsibility on the ground that they had never entered into any agreement with the plaintiff nor authorized any officer of the board to agree with him for the performance of the work in question. It was *held*—that Lakeman had undertaken a personal liability to pay the plaintiff and had not given a guarantee of the liability of a third party, i.e. the board. In consequence Lakeman had given an indemnity which did not need to be in writing under Sect. 4 of the Statute of Frauds, 1677. The plaintiff was therefore entitled to enforce the oral undertaking given by the defendant.

(167) *Carr* v. *Lynch*, [1900] 1 Ch. 613

The defendant was lessor of the Warden Arms, Kentish Town, which was leased to Charles Smith. In September, 1898, the premises were assigned to Arthur Jayne for the residue of the term. On the expiration of the lease Jayne applied to the defendant to grant him a further lease, and the defendant consented on condition that Jayne paid him £50. When Jayne paid the money he produced a memorandum which he had prepared and the defendant signed it. The memorandum read as follows: 'Dear Sir, In consideration of you having this day paid me the sum of £50, I hereby agree to grant you or your assigns a further lease of 24 years.' Before the new lease was to commence Jayne assigned the lease to the plaintiff, Arthur Carr, but the defendant refused to grant the new lease to Carr. This action was for specific performance of the agreement for a lease, and the defence was that the memorandum did not satisfy the Statute of Frauds because it did not sufficiently identify the parties. *Held*—The plaintiff succeeded. The memorandum was sufficient because the defendant had admitted that Jayne had paid him £50 on the day in question and the person who had paid was the person to get the lease according to the document. Therefore Jayne was adequately identified, and Carr, being Jayne's assignee, was entitled to a lease.

(168) *F. Goldsmith (Sicklesmere), Ltd* v. *Baxter*, [1969] 3 All E.R. 733

By an agreement dated 9 April, 1968, the defendant agreed to purchase a piece of land, cottage and buildings known as 'Shelley', Stanstead, Suffolk, from the plaintiff company. The memorandum of agreement was signed by a Mr Brewster, one of the company's directors, 'for and on behalf of Goldsmith Coaches (Sicklesmere) Limited'. Mr Brewster thought that this was the company's name and it did carry on business under that description. The property known as 'Shelley' was described in the particulars of sale and the memorandum of agreement stated that the vendor company, described as Goldsmith Coaches (Sicklesmere) Ltd, was the beneficial owner of it. The defendant's solicitors were subsequently unable to trace a company called Goldsmith Coaches (Sicklesmere) Ltd and the defendant refused to complete by conveying the property on the ground that since there was no vendor there was no contract. The company thereupon sued for specific performance. *Held*—by Stamp, J.—that specific performance would be granted. A contract was to be construed by reference to the surrounding circumstances or in the light of known facts. Accordingly it was clear that the name inserted in the memorandum of sale as being that of the vendor was merely an inaccurate description of the plaintiff company which was therefore a party to the contract and could easily be identified as such by reference to other characteristics.

Looking at the memorandum alone, and without regard to the surrounding circumstances, I find that the person—the persona ficta—said to be the vendor has the following characteristics:

(i) it is named Goldsmith Coaches (Sicklesmere), Ltd;
(ii) its registered office is said to be at Sicklesmere;
(iii) it has an agent called Brewster who claims to act for it;
(iv) it is the beneficial owner of 'Shelley'.

Then, applying the rule that a contract is to be construed by reference to the surrounding circumstances, or in the light of the known facts, I find first, that there is no limited company which in law has the name Goldsmith Coaches (Sicklesmere), Ltd, but that the plaintiff company is often known as 'Goldsmith Coaches' and carries on business as a bus and coach contractor, and does so at Sicklesmere. Then I find, secondly, that the plaintiff company's registered office is at Sicklesmere, in the very place at which it carries on the bus and coach business. Thirdly, I find that the plaintiff company has an agent called Brewster; and, fourthly, that it is the beneficial owner of 'Shelley'. I find in addition that there is no other company having those characteristics. Applying this process, if it be permissable, I conclude beyond peradventure that Goldsmith Coaches (Sicklesmere), Ltd, is no more, nor less than an inaccurate description of the plaintiff company, F. Goldsmith (Sicklesmere), Ltd. ... In the absence of authority constraining me to do so—and none has been cited—I would find it impossible to hold that a company incorporated under the Companies Acts has no identity but by reference to its correct name, or that, unless an agent acts on its behalf by that name, or a name so nearly resembling it that it is obviously an error for that name, he acts for nobody. A limited company has in my judgment characteristics other than its name by reference to which it can be identified: for example, a particular business, and a particular place or places where it carries on business, particular shareholders, and particular directors.

(169) *Tweddell* v. *Henderson*, [1975] 2 All E.R. 1096

Mr Henderson, a builder, agreed with Miss Tweddell, a potential purchaser, that she should buy a house when built on a plot of land at Tintagel for £8700. There was an oral agreement that Miss Tweddell should pay the purchase price in four instalments, the first when the footings of the house were built. Mr Henderson wrote to Miss Tweddell at a later stage saying that he had asked his solicitor to get a contract drawn up but this letter did not mention the system of payment. After a draft contract had been drawn up Mr Henderson said he could not go ahead with the sale unless Miss Tweddell could pay £9500 which she refused to do and Mr Henderson sold the house to somebody else. Miss Tweddell now claimed damages for breach of contract. It was *held*—by Plowman, V.C.—That the contract was not enforceable because there was not a sufficient memorandum in writing. In the course of his judgment Plowman, V.C. said: 'It seems to me that the provision that the purchase money was to be paid, not at the end of the day, when the bungalow had been completed and was ready for handing over, but by the four stages to which I have referred, is a material term in every relevant sense, and there is no reference to it anyway in the alleged memorandum.

'Accordingly, with some regret, because I think the plaintiff has been hardly treated, I have come to the conclusion that the defence of Sect. 40 must succeed.'

(170) *Hawkins* v. *Price*, [1947] Ch. 645

On 31 January, 1946, the plaintiff and defendant entered into a bargain for the sale of a freehold bungalow and land. The plaintiff paid a deposit of £100, and the defendant signed a deposit receipt thus: 'Received of H.H. the sum of £100 being deposit on bungalow named "Oakdene", Station Road, Stoke Mandeville, Bucks, sold for £1000.' The plaintiff now sued for specific performance of the agreement, and it was discovered that there was a term that vacant possession be given by 31 March, 1946. This term was not mentioned in the deposit receipt. Nevertheless the plaintiff claimed that the said receipt was a sufficient memorandum to satisfy Sect. 40 of the Law of Property Act, 1925. *Held*—It was not, because—

(i) The deposit receipt did not contain reference to the fact that the sale was with vacant possession. Although it is not necessary that the memorandum should contain every term, it must at least contain all material terms. In the view of the court the question of vacant possession was material and not collateral.

(ii) The plaintiff suggested that since the term was solely for his benefit he could waive it. The court decided that the term was not solely for his benefit because, although it governed the date on which he could take possession, it also informed Mrs Price of how long she might remain in possession.

(iii) It was difficult for the plaintiff to waive the term because he was suing for specific performance with vacant possession.

(171) *Scott* v. *Bradley*, [1971] 1 All E.R. 538

The plaintiff and defendant agreed that the defendant would sell her freehold property to the plaintiff for £5000. The plaintiff agreed to pay half the defendant's legal costs but this was not recorded on the receipt. The plaintiff sought to enforce the contract and offered to pay half the defendant's legal costs of the sale. *Held*—by Plowman, J.—that on making this offer the plaintiff could enforce the contract.

(172) *Caton* v. *Caton* (1867), L.R. 2 H.L. 127

A Mr Caton and a Mrs Henley proposed to marry, and decided to enter into a marriage settlement. A document was drafted as a basis for the marriage settlement and the names Caton and Henley appeared in it, but only for the purpose of showing what Mr Caton was to do and what Mrs Henley was to have under the agreement. The document was not signed by either of the parties. At the time when this action was brought a marriage settlement had to be evidenced in writing under the provisions of the Statute of Frauds, 1677, and this document was produced as a memorandum. *Held*—It was not a sufficient memorandum because, although the names of the parties appeared in the document, they did not appear as signatures intended to subscribe it.

(173) *Griffiths* v. *Young*, [1970] 3 W.L.R. 246

Following an agreement concerning the sale of land by the defendant to the plaintiff the plaintiff's solicitor wrote to the defendant's solicitor stating a price 'subject to contract'. A telephone conversation between the solicitors followed and later there was a letter from the defendant's solicitor confirming the defendant's instructions to sell for an agreed price. This letter was not 'subject to contract'. *Held*—by the Court of Appeal—the letters constituted a sufficient memorandum and the phrase 'subject to contract' did not render the first letter defective in view of later events.

(*Note:* in *Tiverton Estates Ltd* v. *Wearwell Ltd*, 1974[51] Lord Denning, M.R. was of the opinion that this case could be justified on other and better grounds, i.e. that after the initial contract there was a new and separate oral contract arising from the telephone conversation between the solicitors and that the letter which followed the telephone conversation was a sufficient memorandum.)

(174) *Pearce* v. *Gardner*, [1897] 1 Q.B. 688

The plaintiff brought this action to recover damages for breach of a contract by the defendant under the terms of which the defendant had agreed to sell the plaintiff certain gravel which was *in situ* on the land. At the trial the plaintiff put in evidence a letter signed by the defendant and commencing 'Dear Sir'. The letter did not contain the plaintiff's name. The plaintiff then put in evidence an envelope which had been used to post the letter, which showed the plaintiff's name and address. *Held*—The letter and the envelope together provided a memorandum sufficient to satisfy the Statute of Frauds.

(*Note:* before documents can be connected so as to provide a memorandum, they must be *prima facie* connected as in the case of a letter and an envelope. See *Williams* v. *Lake* (1860), 2 E. & E. 349. In this case the plaintiff put in evidence as a memorandum a letter similar to the one put forward in the above case. He was not able to produce an envelope, however, and the court *held* that the letter was not a memorandum sufficient to satisfy the Statute of Frauds.)

(175) *Timmins* v. *Moreland Street Property Ltd*, [1958] Ch. 110

The defendants agreed to buy certain property belonging to the plaintiff for £39,000 and gave him a cheque for £3900 as a deposit, the cheque being made payable to his solicitors. The plaintiff made out a signed deposit receipt which stated that the sum of £3900 was a deposit for the purchase of the property which was adequately described, and that the plaintiff agreed to sell for £39,000. Subsequently the defendants stopped the cheque and repudiated the contract. The plaintiff sued for breach of contract and the defendants pleaded absence of a memorandum under Sect. 40 of the Law of Property Act, 1925. The plaintiff claimed that a sufficient memorandum existed if the deposit receipt were read together with the cheque containing the defendants' signature. *Held*—The two documents could not be connected, because the cheque was made payable to the plaintiff's solicitors and there was no necessary connection between it and the deposit receipt.

(176) *Hardy* v. *Elphick*, [1973] 2 W.L.R. 824

In 1971 Hardy brought an action for specific performance of an oral contract for the sale of land, pleading a letter written by Elphick as a written memorandum within Sect. 40 of the Law of Property Act, 1925. Elphick denied the contract, and in the alternative pleaded that the letter did not contain all the contractual terms and was therefore insufficient as a memorandum. Following Hardy's request Elphick gave written particulars of two further terms which he alleged were missing in the original letter. In 1972 Hardy brought a further action for specific performance, pleading as a written memorandum both Elphick's letter and the particulars which he gave to Hardy in the 1971 action. It was *held*—by the Court of Appeal—that whether or not the particulars could constitute part of a memorandum within Sect. 40, it was at least not an abuse of the process of the court to plead them in a further action.

(*Note:* this case does not decide that details given as part of the pleadings in an action can constitute a memorandum. It does decide that it is not an abuse of the process of the court to suggest that they can but a further action is required to see what the court's view would be if it was asked specifically to accept statements made in pleadings as part of a written memorandum.)

(177) *Monnickendam* v. *Leanse* (1923), 39 T.L.R. 445

The plaintiff orally agreed to buy a house from the defendant and paid a deposit of £200. Later the plaintiff refused to go on with the contract and pleaded lack of memorandum in writing, though the defendant was always willing to complete. The plaintiff now sued to recover the deposit. *Held*—He could not recover the deposit.

(*Note:* the case illustrates that the difficulties arising out of the absence of a memorandum in writing are procedural rather than substantive. The contract, though unenforceable, is not wholly without effect, for in the above case the contract was raised as a defence to an action for the deposit. It is essential of course that the vendor be prepared to complete the bargain; he cannot deny the enforceability of the contract and yet claim its existence as a defence to the action for recovery of the deposit.

(178) *Rawlinson* v. *Ames*, [1925] 1 Ch. 96

The defendant orally agreed to take a lease of the plaintiff's flat. The plaintiff carried out alterations in the flat at the defendant's request and under her supervision. She then refused to take the lease and pleaded absence of memorandum required by the Statute of Frauds. The plaintiff claimed specific performance of the contract on the grounds that the alterations made in the flat were unequivocal acts of part-performance.

Held—The plaintiff succeeded. The Court, taking a strict view, decided the alterations were not in themselves unequivocal in that the plaintiff might have been altering the flat for some other purpose, but the fact that the defendant supervised and approved of the alterations indicated that she was then minded to take the lease.

(179) *Broughton* v. *Snook*, [1938] 1 Ch. 505

The plaintiff orally agreed to purchase an inn from X and gave an undertaking not to disturb the sitting tenant until the tenant's lease expired. Before the end of his term the tenant vacated the inn and let the plaintiff take possession with X's knowledge. The plaintiff thereupon effected substantial improvements. X died and his executors advertised the sale of the inn. The plaintiff claimed specific performance of the oral agreement. *Held*—Although the plaintiff had gone into possession, the Court, taking a strict view, decided that this did not constitute an act of part performance because it might have referred to an agreement with the tenant. However, the improvements he had made were unequivocal and constituted part performance. Specific performance was granted.

(180) *Daniels* v. *Trefusis*, [1914] 1 Ch. 788

The defendant orally agreed to buy land from the plaintiff. In the course of negotiations the plaintiff's solicitors, in accordance with the agreement, gave notice to two weekly tenants of the plaintiff so that the defendant might have vacant possession on completion. The tenants gave up possession and then the defendant refused to complete the contract, pleading absence of memorandum in writing. The plaintiff now claimed specific performance of the contract on the grounds of part performance. *Held*—Notice to the tenants was an act of part performance, and their subsequent eviction was an act referable to the contract. It would be a fraud on the plaintiff for the defendant to plead absence of memorandum, since the plaintiff had lost two good tenants. Specific performance was granted.

(181) *Wakeham* v. *MacKenzie*, [1968] 2 All E.R. 783

Some two years after his wife's death a widower aged 72 orally agreed with the plaintiff, a widow of 67, that if she would move into his house and look after him for the rest of his life she should have the house (of which he was the owner) together with the contents on his death. It was also agreed that the plaintiff should pay her own board and buy her own coal.

The plaintiff gave up her council flat and moved into the widower's house and looked after him as agreed, paying for her board and coal. He died in February, 1966, but did not leave the house or contents to her. The executor of the widower's estate contended that if there was a contract no action could be brought upon it at common law because there was no memorandum in writing as required by Sect. 40 of the Law of Property Act, 1925, which was accepted. However in respect of the plaintiff's claim for the equitable remedy of specific performance the adequacy of her acts of part performance was in question. On this matter Stamp, J., *held*—

I conclude from *Kingswood Estate Co. Ltd* v. *Anderson* first that it is not the law that the acts of part performance relied on must be not only referable to a contract such as that alleged, but referable to no other title, the doctrine to that effect laid down by Warrington, L.J., in *Chaproniere* v. *Lambert* having been exploded; and secondly that the true rule is that the operation of acts of part performance requires only that the acts in question be such as must be referred to some contract and may be referred to the alleged one; that they prove the existence of some contract and one consistent with the contract alleged.

His Lordship accordingly made an order for specific performance of the oral agreement on which the plaintiff relied.

(182) *Steadman* v. *Steadman*, [1973] 3 All E.R. 977

A husband and wife were married in 1962 and in 1963 bought a house which was conveyed into their joint names. Following proceedings in a magistrates' court in which the husband was ordered to pay maintenance, and a subsequent divorce, the wife applied under Sect. 17 of the Married Women's Property Act, 1882, for the house to be sold and that she should receive half the proceeds. Before the hearing, the parties made an oral agreement under which the wife would sell her interest in the house to the husband for £1500, that he would pay her £100 in respect of arrears of maintenance, the balance of the arrears being remitted and the maintenance order should be discharged except as to the payments in respect of the child. The magistrates varied the maintenance order and the husband paid the agreed £100 of the arrears. The Court of Appeal was asked to decide whether the husband could enforce the agreement for the transfer of the wife's interest in the house in consideration of his paying £1500. It was *held* that the husband's claim succeeded. (Edmund Davies, L.J. dissenting.) The agreement was one for the disposition of land within Sect. 40 of the Law of Property Act, 1925, but there had been a sufficient act of part performance by the husband in paying the agreed £100 off the maintenance arrears. That payment was unequivocally referable to some contract between the parties and evidence could be adduced to show what the contract was and that it included a term disposing of an interest in land. Dealing with the question of a payment of money as an act of part performance, Scarman, L.J. said—

Accepting, as I believe we must, that the payment of purchase money is on the authorities not a sufficient part performance to let in oral evidence of a contract for the sale of land, I think this payment of £100 is to be distinguished from a payment of purchase money. Unlike purchase money it is not certain to be recovered if the contract fails to go forward; for it is paid on account of arrears of maintenance and would be greatly at risk if in the absence of an agreement the justices should be required to consider the husband's application for the remission of arrears. The husband by undertaking to pay this money on account of arrears altered his position significantly on the faith of the oral agreement.

(*Note:* this decision was affirmed in the House of Lords [1974] 2 All E.R. 977, their Lordships saying in particular that there was no general rule that the payment of a sum of money could never constitute part performance.)

(183) *Maddison* v. *Alderson* (1883), 8 App. Cas. 467

The plaintiff had been employed as a housekeeper to Thomas Alderson for a number of years. At one period Alderson was pressed for money, and asked the plaintiff whether she would be willing to carry on working as housekeeper for the rest of his life without wages, in return for which he would leave her a life interest in a farm by his will. Alderson made a will in those terms but unfortunately it was not properly attested, and on his death it was declared void. The plaintiff brought this action against Alderson's executor who relied on absence of memorandum as required by the Statute of Frauds. The plaintiff claimed that the work she had carried out without payment constituted part performance, which entitled her to specific performance of the contract. *Held*—The work she had carried out was equivocal. There were many reasons why the plaintiff might have worked without wages. It did not follow that she was entitled to a life interest in the farm.

(*Note:* the above decision is difficult to reconcile with later cases such as *Wakenham*[181] and *Steadman*.[182] It is possible to say that the acts of the plaintiff were so equivocal that they did not even suggest a contract. Alternatively, it is possible to say that *Maddison* is irreconcilable with later decisions and that this arises from judicial development of the doctrine of part performance.)

(184) *Re Gonin (deceased)*, [1977] 2 All E.R. 720

In this case a daughter tried to claim a contract under which she was to have her mother's house. There was no memorandum in writing and she pleaded acts of part performance. These were that she had left her lodgings in Stroud to come to live with her mother in her mother's home at Bromley and to look after her on the basis (she said) of a contract for the property. Her mother died intestate and did not leave her the property by will so that the daughter's only method of getting the property was to establish a contract. It was *held*—by Walton, J.—that her acts of part performance did not necessarily suggest the existence of a contract. In the course of his judgment he said: 'Anyway, I do not think that there can be any doubt whatsoever but that the learned judges' alternative ground in *Wakeham* v. *Mackenzie*, 1968[181], namely that the conduct of a stranger in giving up a council tenancy and moving into the house of somebody else pointed irresistibly to the fact that there was some contract in relation to the secured occupation of that house by the stranger so moving in, is undeniably correct.

'Applying the law as I see it, therefore, to the present case, are the acts done by Miss Gonin such as in themselves must be referable to some contract concerning The Gables? I regret that in my opinion they are not. Here, . . . Miss Gonin had no home of her own to give up, she was simply billetted out at Stroud, and she did not move into the house of strangers, she went back to the house which had, down to 1940, been and doubtlessly still was in her mind's eye, home, back to her parents, back to the same kind of position and standing which she had had before she had left home because of the call of the war. This does not seem to me to indicate the likelihood of any contract at all, let alone one concerning land.'

(184) *Mighell* v. *Sultan of Johore*, [1894] 1 Q.B. 149

The Sultan, who was a foreign sovereign, was living in England as a private person under an assumed name. He made a promise of marriage to the plaintiff. *Held*—the promise was not actionable.

(185) *Coutts & Co.* v. *Browne-Lecky*, [1947] K.B. 104

The first defendant, an infant, had been permitted to overdraw his account with the plaintiffs, who were bankers. The overdraft was guaranteed by the second and third defendants, who were adults. The overdraft was not repaid and the plaintiffs now sued the adult guarantors. *Held*—Since the loan to the infant was void under the Infants Relief Act, 1874, the infant could not be in default because he was not liable to repay the loan. Since the essence of a guarantee is that the guarantor is liable for the default or miscarriage of the principal debtor, it followed that the adult guarantors could not be liable. The action therefore failed.

(*Note:* had the contract been one of indemnity the adult defendants would have been liable, because, under a contract of indemnity, the person giving the indemnity is in effect the principal debtor and his liability does not depend on the default of any other person. (See *Yeoman Credit Ltd* v. *Latter*, [1961] 1 W.L.R. 828.))

(186) *Nash* v. *Inman*, [1908] 2 K.B. 1

The plaintiff was a Savile Row tailor and the defendant was an infant undergraduate at Trinity College, Cambridge. The plaintiff sent his agent to Cambridge because he had heard that the defendant was spending money freely, and might be the sort of person who would be interested in high-class clothing. As a result of the agent's visit, the plaintiff supplied the defendant with various articles of clothing to the value of £145 0s. 3d. during the period October, 1902 to June, 1903. The clothes included eleven fancy waistcoats. The plaintiff now sued the infant for the price of the clothes. Evidence showed that the defendant's father was in a good position, being an architect with a town and country house, and it could be said that the clothes supplied were suitable to the defendant's position in life. However, his father proved that the defendant was amply supplied with such clothes when the plaintiff delivered the clothing now in question. *Held*—The plaintiff's claim failed because he had not established that the goods supplied were necessaries.

(187) *Elkington* v. *Amery*, [1936] 2 All E.R. 86

The defendant was an infant and the son of a former cabinet minister. He purchased from the plaintiffs an engagement ring and an eternity ring, the court treating the latter as a wedding ring. He also purchased a lady's gold vanity bag. The Court of Appeal treated the two rings as being necessaries, but did not accept that the vanity bag was a necessary because there was no evidence to show that it was purchased in respect of the engagement.

(188) *Roberts* v. *Gray*, [1913] 1 K.B. 520

The defendant wished to become a professional billiards player and entered into an agreement with the plaintiff, a leading professional, to go on a joint tour. The plaintiff went to some trouble in order to organize the tour, but a dispute arose between the parties and the defendant refused to go. The plaintiff now sued for damages of £6000. *Held*—The contract was for the infant's benefit, being in effect for his instruction as a billiards player. Therefore the plaintiff could sustain an action for damages for breach of contract, and damages of £1500 were awarded.

(189) *De Francesco* v. *Barnum* (1890), 45 Ch. D. 430

Two infants bound themselves in contract to the plaintiff for seven years to be taught stage dancing. The infants agreed that they would not accept any engagements without his consent. They later accepted an engagement with Barnum and the plaintiff sued Barnum for interfering with the contractual relationship between himself and the infants, and also to enforce the apprenticeship deed against the infants and to obtain damages for its breach. The contract was, of course, for the infants' benefit and was *prima facie* binding on them. However, when the court considered the deed in greater detail, it emerged that there were certain onerous terms in it. For example the infants bound themselves not to marry during the apprenticeship; the payment was hardly generous, the plaintiff agreeing to pay them 9d. per night and 6d. for matinee appearances for the first three years, and 1s. per night and 6d. for matinee performances during the remainder of the apprenticeship. The plaintiff did not undertake to maintain them whilst they were unemployed and did not undertake to find them engagements. The infants could also be engaged in performances abroad at a fee of 5s. per week. Further the plaintiff could terminate the contract if he felt that the infants were not suitable for the career of dancer. It appeared from the contract that the infants were at the absolute disposal of the plaintiff. *Held*—The deed was an unreasonable one and was therefore unenforceable against the infants. Barnum could not, therefore, be held liable, since the tort of interference with a contractual relationship presupposes the existence of an enforceable contract.

(190) *Clements* v. *L. & N.W. Railway,* [1894] 2 Q.B. 482

Clements became a porter with the railway company and agreed to join the company's insurance scheme and to forgo his rights under the Employers' Liability Act, 1880. He sustained an injury at work and claimed under the company's scheme. He now made a claim under the Act on the grounds that the contract was not for his benefit since it deprived him of an action under the Act. The company's scheme was on the whole a favourable one because it covered more injuries than the statute but the scale of compensation was lower. *Held*—The contract as a whole was for the infant's benefit and was binding on him. He had no claim under the Act.

(191) *Mercantile Union Guarantee Corporation* v. *Ball,* [1937] 2 K.B. 498

The purchase on hire-purchase terms of a motor lorry by an infant carrying on business as a haulage contractor was *held* not to be a contract for necessaries, but a trading contract by which the infant could not be bound.

(*Note:* it would be possible for the owner to recover the lorry because a hire-purchase contract is a contract of bailment not a sale. Thus, ownership does not pass when the goods are delivered.)

(192) *Chaplin* v. *Leslie Frewin (Publishers),* [1965] 3 All E.R. 764

The plaintiff, the infant son of a famous father, made a contract with the defendants under which they were to publish a book written for him and telling his life story. The plaintiff sought to avoid the contract on the ground that the book gave an inaccurate picture of his approach to life. *Held*—Amongst other things—that the contract was binding if it was for the infant's benefit. The time to determine that question was when the contract was made and at that time it was for the infant's benefit and could not be avoided.

(193) *Denmark Productions* v. *Boscobel Productions* (1967), 111 S.J. 715

Widgery, J., held that a contract by which an infant appoints managers and agents to look after his business affairs is, in modern conditions, necessary if he is to earn his living and rise to fame, and if it is for his benefit it will be upheld by analogy with a contract of service.

(194) *Steinberg* v. *Scala (Leeds) Ltd,* [1923] 2 Ch. 452

The plaintiff, Miss Steinberg, purchased shares in the defendant company and paid certain sums of money on application, on allotment and on one call. Being unable to meet future calls, she repudiated the contract whilst still an infant and claimed—

(*a*) rectification of the Register of Members to remove her name therefrom, thus relieving her from liability on future calls; and

(*b*) the recovery of the money already paid.

The company agreed to rectify the register and issue was joined on the claim to recover the money paid.

Held—The claim under (*b*) above failed because there had not been total failure of consideration. The shares had some value and gave some rights, even though the plaintiff had not received any dividends and the shares had always stood at a discount on the market.

(195) *Davies* v. *Beynon-Harris* (1931), 47 T.L.R. 424

An infant took a lease of a flat a fortnight before attaining his majority. Three years later he was sued for arrears of rent and claimed that he could avoid the contract. *Held*—He was liable to pay the rent because the lease was voidable not void, and was now binding on him because he had not repudiated it during minority or within a reasonable time thereafter.

(*Note:* an infant cannot take a legal estate in land (Sect. 1(6), Law of Property Act, 1925.) This prevents him from taking a lease at law. However, he does obtain an equitable interest and must observe the covenants in the lease so long as he retains a beneficial interest in the property.)

(196) *Goode* v. *Harrison* (1821), 5 B. & Ald. 147

An infant partner, who took no steps to avoid a partnership contract upon attaining his majority, was *held* liable for the debts of the firm incurred after he came of age.

(197) *Pearce* v. *Brain*, [1929] 2 K.B. 310

Pearce, an infant, exchanged his motor-cycle for a motor-car belonging to Brain. The infant had little use out of the car, and had in fact driven it only 70 miles in all when it broke down because of serious defects in the back axle. Pearce now sued to recover his motor-cycle, claiming that the consideration had wholly failed. *Held*—(*a*) That a contract for the exchange of goods, whilst not a sale of goods, is a contract for the supply of goods, and that if the goods are not necessaries, the contract is void if with an infant. (*b*) The car was not a necessary good and therefore the contract was void. (*c*) Even so the infant could only recover the motor-cycle in the same circumstances as he could recover money paid under a void contract, i.e. if the consideration had wholly failed. The court considered that the infant had received a benefit under the contract, albeit small, and that he could not recover the motor-cycle.

(198) *Corpe* v. *Overton* (1833), 10 Bing. 252

An infant agreed to enter into a partnership and deposited £100 with the defendant as security for the due performance of the contract. The infant rescinded the contract before the partnership came into being. *Held*—He could recover the £100 because he had received no benefit, having never been a partner.

(199) *Stocks* v. *Wilson*, [1913] 2 K.B. 235

An infant obtained furniture from the plaintiff by falsely stating that he was of full age. *Held*—The property in the furniture passed to the infant, under the Infants Relief Act, 1874. Even if he sold the property the infant could not be sued in conversion. The infant had sold part of the furniture to a third party for £30, and Lush, J., *held* that the plaintiff could recover this sum from the infant by applying the equitable principle of restitution.

(*Note: Pearce* v. *Brain*,[197] supports *Stocks* v. *Wilson* because, if the property in the car had not passed to the infant, there would have been total failure of consideration, thus enabling him to recover his motorcycle.)

(200) *Leslie (R) Ltd* v. *Sheill*, [1914] 3 K.B. 607

Sheill, an infant, borrowed £400 from R. Leslie, Ltd, moneylenders, by fraudulently representing that he was of full age. The contract was void under Sect. 1 of the Infants Relief Act, 1874, and the plaintiffs sued for the return of the money, either as damages for the tort of deceit, or as money had and received to the plaintiff's use, this latter being an action in quasi-contract. *Held*—Neither claim could succeed because they were attempts to circumvent the Act and the infant was entitled to retain the money advanced. With regard to the equitable doctrine of restitution, it was suggested that, since the money had been spent and could not be precisely traced, restitution was not possible; for to order restitution would mean that the infant would have to pay an equivalent sum out of his present or future resources, and this would be closer to enforcing a void contract than to granting equitable restitution. It was also suggested that *Stocks* v. *Wilson*,[199] was wrongly decided in so far as Lush, J., granted restitution of the £30 which the infant had received by selling the property to a third party. The court in this case suggested that 'Restitution ends where repayment begins', i.e. unless the actual property passing under the contract can be recovered, the remedy of restitution does not lie to recover money or property received in its stead.

(201) *Burnard* v. *Haggis* (1863), 14 C.B.N.S. 45

Haggis was an undergraduate and hired the plaintiff's mare for riding. The plaintiff warned the defendant that the mare was not to be used for 'jumping or larking'. The defendant allowed a friend to ride the mare and the latter put the mare at a fence, in consequence of which the mare was impaled on a stake and died. The plaintiff sued the defendant in trespass. *Held*—The infant was liable, though the trespass actually happened because there had been a contract, yet the act of jumping the mare was just as distinct from the contract as if the defendant had run a knife into her and killed her. Therefore the defendant's infancy, which might have been a defence in contract, did not apply in this action for pure tort.

(202) *Ashbury Railway Carriage & Iron Co.* v. *Riche* (1875), L.R. 7 H.L. 653

The company bought a concession for the construction of a railway system in Belgium, and entered into an agreement whereby Messrs Riche were to construct a railway line. Messrs Riche commenced the work, and the company paid over certain sums of money in connection with the contract. The company later ran into difficulties, and the shareholders wished the directors to take over the contract in a personal capacity, and indemnify the shareholders. The directors thereupon repudiated the contract on behalf of the company, and Messrs Riche sued for breach of contract. The case turned on whether the company was engaged in an *ultra vires* activity in building a complete railway system, because if so, the contract it had made with Messrs Riche would be *ultra vires* and void, and the claim against the company would fail. The objects clause of the company's memorandum stated that it was established—

'to make or sell or lend on hire railway carriages, wagons and all kinds of railway plant, fittings, machinery and rolling stock; to carry on the business of mechanical engineers and general contractors, to purchase and sell as merchants timber, coal, metal and other materials, and to buy and sell such materials on commission or as agents.'

The House of Lords *held* that the purchase of the concession to build a complete railway system from Antwerp to Tournai was *ultra vires* and void because it was not within the objects of the company. The words empowering the company to carry on the business of general contracting must be construed *ejusdem generis* with the preceding words, and must therefore be restricted to contracting in the field of plant, fittings and machinery only. The contract with Messrs Riche was therefore void, and the directors were entitled to repudiate it. It was also stated that even if all the shareholders had assented to the contract, it would still have been void because there can be no ratification of an *ultra vires* contract.

(*Note:* this strict interpretation of an objects clause contrasts sharply with the more modern approach seen in *Re New Finance and Mortgage Co. Ltd*, [1975] 1 All E.R. 684. In that case the memorandum of N Ltd stated its objects to be to carry on business as 'Financiers, capitalists, concessionaires, bankers, commercial agents, mortgage brokers, financial agents and advisers, exporters and importers of goods and merchandise of all kinds and merchants generally'. N Ltd carried on a petrol filling service station business which went into liquidation owing Total some £24,000 for petrol. The liquidator rejected T's proof as *ultra vires*. It was *held* that the words 'and merchants generally' were wide enough to cover the petrol filling service station business. T's claim was therefore good.)

(203) *Re Jon Beauforte*, [1953] Ch. 131

The company was authorized by its memorandum to carry on the business of costumiers, tailors, drapers, haberdashers, milliners and the like. It decided to manufacture veneered wall panels, and for this purpose had a factory erected, and ordered and was supplied with veneers. It was clear that the contracts for the erection of the factory and supply of veneers were *ultra vires* and void, but one of the questions before the court was whether the liquidator of the company had been correct in disallowing a claim made by a supplier of coke. The supplier argued that the coke might have been used in the good side of the business, and that he did not know that the coke was to be used for an *ultra vires* purpose. The court decided against him because the order for coke was given on headed paper describing the company as 'veneered panel manufacturers'. From this the coke supplier was deemed to know that the contract was *ultra vires*, because everyone is deemed to know the contents of the memorandum of association of a registered company, which is registered at the Companies' Registry, London, and can be inspected.

(*Note:* (i) this doctrine of constructive notice of a company's objects is now well established and yet it is based on the assumption that, because inspection is possible, it should always be made before contracts are entered into. However, business would grind to a halt if this sort of inquiry were made every time a contract was made; it does not accord, therefore, with normal business practice; (ii) where the transaction is decided on by the directors so that Sect. 9 of the European Communities Act, 1972 applies, there is no constructive notice of the contents of the memorandum and articles.)

(204) *Deuchar* v. *The Gas Light and Coke Co.*, [1925] A.C. 691

The plaintiff was a shareholder in the defendant company and was also the secretary of a company which supplied the defendants with caustic soda. The plaintiff sought a declaration from the court that the manufacture of caustic soda and chlorine by the defendants, and the erection of a factory for the purpose, was *ultra vires* the company. He also asked for an injunction to restrain the defendants from manufacturing caustic soda and chlorine. Astbury, J., at first instance, had found that the activities were fairly incidental to the powers given in the objects clause, and the Court of Appeal affirmed this decision. On appeal to the House of Lords it appeared that the defendants derived their powers from a special Act of Parliament, the Gas Light and Coke Companies Act, 1868, which gave them power to make and supply gas and deal with and sell by-products. The act authorized the conversion of the by-products into a marketable state. One of the residuals of gas-making was naphthalene which could be converted into beta-naphthol and profitably sold, conversion being by the use of caustic soda. The company had formerly purchased this from the company of which the plaintiff was secretary, but later erected a factory on their land and began to make it themselves, though they only made what they required for their own use and did not make caustic soda for resale. Chlorine was a by-product of the manufacture of caustic soda, and the chlorine, it was admitted, was converted into bleaching powder and sold. The House of Lords *held* that the manufacture of caustic soda was fairly incidental to the company's powers, and although the sale of the bleaching powder was not incidental, the matter was trivial and on the basis of the maxim *de minimis non curat lex* (the law takes no account of trifling matters) the court would not interfere.

(205) *Cotman* v. *Brougham*, [1918] A.C. 514

The parties to this action were liquidators. Cotman was liquidator of the Essequibo Rubber Estates Ltd, and Brougham was liquidator of Anglo-Cuban Oil Co. It appeared that E underwrote the shares in A-C although the main clause of E's objects clause was to develop rubber estates abroad. However, a sub-clause allowed E to promote companies and deal in the shares of other companies and gave numerous other powers. The final clause of E's objects clause said in effect that each sub-clause should be considered as an independent main object. The E Company, not having paid for the shares which it had agreed to underwrite, was put on the list of contributories of A-C, and E's liquidator asked that his company be removed from that list because the contract to underwrite was *ultra vires* and void. *Held*—by the House of Lords—that it was not, and that the E Company was liable to pay for the shares underwritten. The final clause of E's objects clause meant that each object could be pursued alone, because the Registrar had accepted the memorandum in this form and had registered the company. All the judges of the House of Lords deplored the idea of companies being registered with an objects clause in this wide form, and thought that the matter ought to have been raised by mandamus by the Registrar refusing to register the company. However, since the certificate of incorporation had been issued, it was conclusive; and matters concerning the company's registration could not be gone into.

(206) *Re Introductions Ltd: Introductions Ltd* v. *National Provincial Bank Ltd*, [1969] 1 All E.R. 887

Introductions Ltd was incorporated in 1951 and the objects of the company were to promote and provide entertainment and accommodation for overseas visitors. This business was not successful and in November, 1960, the company embarked on a new business, pig farming. The company ran short of cash and arranged to borrow money from the defendants. The company executed certain debentures in favour of the bank for its indebtedness, which at the time of the winding up order in November, 1965, was £29,571.

The bank now wished to enforce its security under the debentures and recover the loan. The liquidator of the company claimed that the loan was *ultra vires* and void, and the bank did not dispute that it was aware that the company's business was that of pig breeding and had notice of the company's objects. However, one of the sub-clauses of the memorandum related to borrowing and the bank said it was entitled to lend money on the strength of the sub-clause alone as it formed one of the objects of the company. There was a proviso to the memorandum which clearly stated that all sub-clauses of the memorandum were to be treated as separate and independent objects. *Held*—by the Court of Appeal—that the loan was *ultra vires* and void. The bare power to borrow contained in the sub-clause could not legitimately stand alone. The company must have had in view purposes to which the money was to be applied, i.e. for the purposes of the objects of the company. This being so the sub-clause did not authorize the raising or borrowing of money for something which was not an object of the company. However if the bank had not known the purpose for which the money was required the loan would have been valid because the bank was not bound to inquire as to its purpose, since there was a power to borrow.

(207) *Bell Houses Ltd* v. *City Wall Properties Ltd*, [1966] 2 All E.R. 674

The plaintiff company claimed £20,000 as commission under an alleged contract with the defendant company for the introduction of the latter to a financier who would lend the defendant company £1,000,000 for property development. As a preliminary issue the defendant company alleged that the contract was *ultra vires* and could not be enforced against them.

The principal business of the plaintiff company was the development of housing estates, and therefore the occasional raising of finance formed a necessary part of its activities. In consequence the company had obtained valuable knowledge of various sources of finance and because of this the company was able to arrange finance for the defendants. The defendants contended that the plaintiff company, in arranging finance for an outside organization, was, in effect, embarking on a new type of business, i.e. 'mortgage broking', and since this was not expressly included in the objects, nor reasonably incidental thereto, it was *ultra vires*. One of the sub-clauses in the objects clause of the plaintiff company was as follows: 'To carry on any other trade or business *whatsoever* which can *in the opinion of the board of directors* be *advantageously* carried on by (the company) in connection with, or as ancillary to, any of the above businesses or the general business of the (company).' *Held*—by the Court of Appeal—that the alleged contract was *intra vires* in particular because of the clause set out above. In the court's view the *bona fide* opinion of the board, in this case represented by the managing director who arranged the finance, that the contract could be advantageously carried on with the company's principal business, was enough no matter how unreasonable in the *objective* sense that opinion might seem to be.

(208) *Sharp Bros and Knight* v. *Chant*, [1917] 1 K.B. 771

Landlord and tenant agreed that the rent of a certain small house should be increased by the sum of 6d. per week. The tenant paid this increased rent for some time and it was then discovered that Rent Restriction legislation prevented the landlord from recovering any increase in rent he might make on certain properties of which the small house in question was one. *Held*—The tenant had paid the extra rent under a mistake of law, and could not sue for its return or deduct it from future payments of rent.

(*Note:* here the Court said that there was a mistake of law but see *Solle* below where the majority of the Court of Appeal held in somewhat similar circumstances that there was an actionable mistake of fact.)

(209) *Solle* v. *Butcher*, [1950] 1 K.B. 671

Butcher had agreed to lease a flat in Beckenham to Solle at a yearly rental of £250, the lease to run for seven years. Both parties had acted on the assumption that the flat, which had been substantially reconstructed so as to be virtually a new flat, was no longer controlled by the Rent Restriction legislation then in force. If it were so controlled, the maximum rent payable would be £140 per annum. Nevertheless Butcher would have been entitled to increase that rent by charging 8 per cent of the cost of repairs and improvements which would bring the figure up to about £250 per annum, the rent actually charged, if he had served a statutory notice on Solle before the new lease was executed. No such notice was in fact served. Actually they both for a time mistakenly thought that the flat was decontrolled when this was not the case. Solle realized the mistake after some two years, and sought to recover the rent he had overpaid and to continue as tenant for the balance of the seven years as a statutory tenant at £140 per annum. Butcher counterclaimed for rescission of the lease in Equity. It was *held* by a majority of the Court of Appeal that the mistake was one of *fact* and not of law, i.e. the fact that the flat was still within the provisions of the Rent Acts, and this was a bilateral mistake as to quality which would not invalidate the contract at common law. However, on the counterclaim for rescission, it was *held* that the lease could be rescinded even though it had been executed. In order not to dispossess Solle, the court offered him the following alternatives—

(*a*) to surrender the lease entirely; or

(*b*) to remain in possession as a mere licensee until a new lease could be drawn up after Butcher had had time to serve the statutory notice which would allow him to add a sum for repairs to the £140 which would bring the lawful rent up to £250 per annum.

(210) *Cooper* v. *Phibbs* (1867), L.R. 2 H.L. 149

Cooper agreed to take a lease of a fishery from Phibbs. Unknown to either party, because of a mix-up in family property, Cooper already had a life interest in the fishery and now brought the action to set aside the lease and for delivery up of the lease. *Held*—The agreement must be set aside on the grounds of common or identical bilateral mistake. However, since Equity has the power to give ancillary relief, Phibbs was given a lien on the fishery for the improvements he had made to it during the time be believed it to be his. This lien could be discharged by Cooper paying Phibbs the value of the improvements.

(211) *Saunders (Executrix of the Estate of Rose Maud Gallie)* v. *Anglia Building Society*, [1970] 3 All E.R. 961

Mrs Gallie, a widow aged 78 years, signed a document which a Mr Lee told her was a deed of gift of her house to her nephew. She did not read the document but believed what Lee had told her. In fact the document was an assignment of her leasehold interest in the house to Lee and Lee later mortgaged that interest to a building society. In an action by Mrs Gallie against Lee and the building society it was *held*—(i) that the assignment was void and did not confer a title on Lee, (ii) although the plaintiff had been negligent she was not estopped from denying the validity of the deed against the building society for she owed it no duty. The Court of Appeal, in allowing an appeal by the building society, *held* that the plea of *non est factum* was not available to the plaintiff. The transaction intended and carried out was the same, i.e. an assignment.

Mrs Gallie died and an appeal to the House of Lords was brought by the executrix of her estate. The House of Lords affirmed the decision of the Court of Appeal but took the opportunity to restate the law relating to the avoidance of documents on the ground of mistake as follows—

(*a*) The plea of *non est factum* will rarely be available to a person of full capacity who signs a document apparently having legal effect without troubling to read it.

(*b*) A mistake as to the identity of the person in whose favour the document is executed will not normally support a plea of *non est factum* though it may do if the court regards the mistake as fundamental (Lord Reid and Lord Hodson). Neither judge felt that the personality error made by Mrs Gallie was sufficient to support the plea.

(*c*) The distinction taken in *Howatson* v. *Webb*, [1908] 1 Ch. 1 that the mistake must be as to the class or character of the document and not merely as to its contents was regarded as confusing and illogical. A better test would be whether the document which was in fact signed was 'fundamentally different', 'radically different' or 'totally different'. This test is more flexible than the character/contents one and yet it still restricts the operation of the plea of *non est factum*.

(*d*) *Carlisle and Cumberland Banking Co.* v. *Bragg*, [1911] 1 K.B. 489, was overruled. Henceforth carelessness on the part of a person signing a document will prevent him from raising the plea. In addition the person claiming to have taken proper care bears the burden of proving that he did.

(212) *Foster* v. *Mackinnon* (1869), L.R. 4 C.P. 704

The plaintiff was a person entitled to receive payment on a bill of exchange for £3000; the defendant was an endorser of the bill and was *prima facie* liable on it. The evidence showed that the defendant was an old man of feeble sight, and that he had signed the bill under the mistaken impression that it was a guarantee. *Held*—The defendant was not in the circumstances negligent in signing the bill and his plea of mistake was successful so that he was not liable on it.

(213) *Legal and General Assurance Society* v. *General Metal Agencies*, (1969) 113 S.J. 876

Legal and General, who were the landlords of General Metal Agencies, served a statutory notice of termination of the tenancy. General Metal applied to the County Court for a new tenancy but Legal and General opposed the application on the grounds of persistent late payment of rent and it was dismissed. However, Legal and General subsequently sent by mistake a computerized demand for the next quarter's rent in advance over the signature of their general manager. General Metal sent a cheque for the rent and this was presented to the bank and paid. In this action Legal and General claimed possession of the premises and General Metal contended that Legal and General by demanding and accepting the next quarter's rent in advance had by implication created a new tenancy. It was *Held*—by Fisher, J.—

(i) that Legal and General were entitled to show that the demand was sent and the rent received by mistake. There was no intention to create a new tenancy, the use of a computer making no difference to the established common law principle;

(ii) that, in consequence, Legal and General were entitled to possession of the premises.

(214) *Higgins (W.) Ltd* v. *Northampton Corporation*, [1927] 1 Ch. 128

The plaintiff entered into a contract with the corporation for the erection of dwelling houses. The plaintiff made an arithmetical error in arriving at his price, having deducted a certain sum twice over. The corporation sealed the contract, assuming that the price arrived at by the plaintiff was correct. *Held*—The contract was binding on the parties. Rectification of such a contract was not possible because the power of the court to rectify agreements made under mistake is confined to common not unilateral mistake. Here, rectification would only have been granted if fraud or misrepresentation had been present.

(215) *Cundy* v. *Lindsay* (1878), 3 App. Cas. 459

The respondents were linen manufacturers with a business in Belfast. A fraudulent person named Blenkarn wrote to the respondents from 37 Wood Street, Cheapside, ordering a quantity of handkerchiefs but signed his letter in such a way that it appeared to some from Messrs Blenkiron, who were a well-known and solvent house doing business at 123 Wood Street. The respondents knew of the existence of Blenkiron but did not know the address. Accordingly the handkerchiefs were sent to 37 Wood Street. Blenkarn then sold them to the apppellants, and was later convicted and sentenced for the fraud. The respondents sued the appellants in conversion claiming that the contract they had made with Blenkarn was void for mistake, and that the property had not passed to Blenkarn or to the appellants. *Held*—The respondents succeeded; there was an operative mistake as to the party with whom they were contracting.

(216) *King's Norton Metal Co. Ltd* v. *Edridge, Merrett & Co. Ltd* (1897), 14 T.L.R. 98

The plaintiffs were metal manufacturers in Worcestershire, the defendants being metal manufacturers at Birmingham. In 1896 the plaintiffs received a letter from a firm called Hallam & Co., Soho Wire Works, Sheffield. The letter was written on headed paper, the heading depicting a large factory, and in one corner was a statement that the company had depots and agencies at Belfast, Lille and Ghent. The letter requested a quotation for the supply of brass rivet wire, and a quotation was sent and later an order was received and the goods dispatched. These goods were never paid for. It later emerged that a person named Wallis had set up in business at Hallam & Co. and had fraudulently obtained the goods by the above methods. Wallis sold the goods to the defendants who bought *bona fide* and for value. The plaintiffs had previously done business with Wallis's firm, Hallam & Co., and had been paid by cheque signed Hallam & Co. The plaintiffs sued the defendants in conversion, regarding this as a better action than the one for fraud against Wallis. In order to sustain the action in conversion, the plaintlffs had to establish that the contract with Hallam & Co. was void for mistake, and that because of this the defendants had no title to the wire. *Held*—The plaintiff's claim failed because the contract with Hallam & Co. was voidable for fraud but not void for mistake. The firm Hallam & Co. was a mere alias for Wallis, and since there was no other firm of Hallam & Co. with whom the plaintiffs had previously done business, they were really dealing with one person who from time to time used different names, i.e. Wallis or Hallam & Co. Although the contract was voidable for fraud, it had not been avoided when the goods were sold to the defendants; their title was good and they were not liable in conversion.

(217) *Phillips* v. *Brooks Ltd*, [1919] 2 K.B. 243

A fraudulent person named North went into the plaintiff's jeweller's shop and selected goods to the value of £3000. He then asked whether he could take away one of the items (a ring) which he said he wanted for his wife's birthday. He said, no doubt to reassure the jeweller, that he was Sir George Bullough of St James's Square. The plaintiff had heard of the name and, on referring to a directory and finding the address was correct, he allowed North to take away the ring in return for a cheque. Then North, using the name Firth, pledged the ring with the defendants, who were pawnbrokers. They took the ring in good faith and advanced £350 upon it. North was subsequently convicted of obtaining the ring by false pretences, and this action was brought by the plaintiff who claimed that he was mistaken in his contract with North, and that since the contract was void the property had not passed. He, therefore, asked that the ring be returned to him or that he be paid £450, its value. *Held*—The contract between Phillips and North was not void for mistake and Brooks obtained a good title to the ring. The representation by North that he was Sir George Bullough only affected the taking away of the ring and the acceptance by Phillips of the cheque. By that time the sale had taken place and so far as the sale was concerned the identity of the purchaser was not important to Phillips.

(218) *Ingram and others* v. *Little*, [1961] 1 Q.B. 31

The plaintiffs, three ladies, were the joint owners of a car. They wished to sell the car and advertised it for sale. A fraudulent person, introducing himself as Hutchinson, offered to buy it. He was taken for a drive in it and during conversation said that his home was at Caterham. Later the rogue offered £700 for the car but this was refused, though a subsequent offer of £717 was one which the plaintiffs were prepared to accept. At this point the rogue produced a cheque book and one of the plaintiffs, who was conducting the negotiations, said that the deal was off and that they would not accept a cheque. The rogue then said that he was P. G. M. Hutchinson, that he had business interests in Guildford, and that he lived at Stanstead House, Stanstead Road, Caterham. One of the plaintiffs checked this information in a telephone directory and, on finding it to be accurate, allowed him to take the car in return for a cheque. The cheque was dishonoured, and in the meantime the rogue had sold the car to the defendants and had disappeared without trace. The plaintiffs sued for the return of the car, or for its value as damages in conversion, claiming that the contract between themselves and the rogue was void for mistake, and that the property had not passed. At the trial judgment was given for the plaintiffs, Slade, J., finding the contract void. His judgment was affirmed by the Court of Appeal, though Devlin, L.J., dissented, saying that the mistake made was as to the credit-worthiness of the rogue, not as to his identity since he was before the plaintiffs when the contract was made. A mistake as to the substance of the rogue would be a mistake as to quality and would not avoid the contract. Devlin, L.J., also suggested that legislation should provide for an opportionment of the loss incurred by two innocent parties who suffer as a result of the fraud of a third.

(219) *Lewis* v. *Averay*, [1971] 3 All E.R. 907

Mr Lewis agreed to sell his car to a rogue who called on him after seeing an advertisement. Before the sale took place the rogue talked knowledgeably about the film world, giving the impression that he was the actor Richard Green in the 'Robin Hood' serial. He signed a dud cheque for £450 in the name of 'R. A. Green' and was allowed to have the log-book and drive the car away late the same night when he produced a film studio pass in the name of 'Green'. It was *held*—by the Court of Appeal—that Mr Lewis had effectively contracted to sell the car to the rogue and could not recover it or damages from Mr Averay, a student, who had bought it from the rogue for £200. The contract between Mr Lewis and the rogue was voidable for fraud but not void for unilateral mistake.

(*Note:* the distinctions drawn in some of these cases are fine ones. It is difficult to distinguish *Ingram*[218] from *Phillips*[217] and *Lewis*. The question for the court to answer in these cases is whether or not the offeror at the time of making the offer regarded the identity of the offeree as a matter of vital importance. The general rule seems to be that where the parties are face to face when the contract is made identity will not be vital and the contract voidable only. *Ingram* would appear to be the exceptional case.)

(220) *Webster* v. *Cecil* (1861), 30 Beav. 62

The parties had been negotiating for the sale of certain property. Later Cecil offered by letter to sell the property for £1250. Webster was aware that this offer was probably a slip because he knew that Cecil had already refused an offer of £2000, and in fact Cecil wished to offer the property at £2250. Webster accepted the offer and sued for specific performance of the contract. The court refused to grant the decree.

(221) *Amalgamated Investment & Property Co. Ltd* v. *John Walker & Sons Ltd*, [1976] All E.R. 509

The defendants sold a warehouse to the plaintiffs for £1,710,000 which the plaintiffs wanted, as the defendants knew, for redevelopment. Both parties knew that planning permission would be required. On 25 September, 1973, the parties signed a contract of sale and on 26 September, 1973, the Department of the Environment wrote informing the defendants that the warehouse has been placed on a list of buildings regarded as being of special architectural or historic interest. Development was not therefore possible without a listed building consent which would be difficult to obtain. If it was not obtained the value of the property would be £200,000. The plaintiffs claimed rescission of the contract on the ground of common mistake or that the contract had been frustrated. The Court of Appeal had no doubt that common mistake did not upset the contract. On this Buckley, L.J. said: 'So the alleged common mistake was that the property was property suitable for and capable of being developed. . . . For the application of the doctrine of mutual mistake as a ground for setting aside the contract it is of course necessary to show that the mistake existed at the date of the contract. . . . But at the date when the contract was entered into I cannot see that there is any ground for saying that the parties were then subject to some mutual mistake of facts relating to the circumstances surrounding the contract. . . .'

On the question of frustration the Court said that the obligation of the defendants was to sell the property at the contract price and to show a good title. The defendants had given no warranty that planning permission could be obtained. The subsequent listing of the property was not a frustrating event. It was a risk that the purchaser of property had to take and loss resulting from that risk would have to lie where it fell.

(*Note:* it is not certain whether the doctrine of frustration is capable of applying to contracts for the sale of land. (*Hillingdon Estate Co.* v. *Stonefield Estates Ltd*, 1952.)[418] The point was not argued in this case. Buckley, L.J. and Lawton, L.J. referred to it but did not pronounce upon it. However, they were prepared to assume for the sake of argument that such contracts were subject to the frustration principle.

(222) *Couturier* v. *Hastie* (1856), 5 H.L.C. 673

Messrs Hastie dispatched a cargo of corn from Salonica and sent the charter-party and bill of lading to their London agents so that the corn might be sold. The London agents employed Couturier to sell the corn and a person named Callander bought it. Unknown to the parties the cargo had become overheated, and had been landed at the nearest port and sold, so that when the contract was made the corn was not really in existence. Callander repudiated the contract and Couturier was sued because he was a *del credere* agent, i.e. an agent who, for an extra commission, undertakes to indemnify his principal against losses arising out of the repudiation of the contract by any third party introduced by him. *Held*—The claim against Couturier failed because the contract presupposed that the goods were in existence when they were sold to Callander.

(223) *McRae* v. *The Commonwealth Disposals Commission*, [1951] Argus L.R. 771

The defendants had invited tenders for the purchase of a tanker, said to be lying on the Jourmand Reef off Papua, together with the oil it was said to contain. The plaintiff submitted a tender of £285 which the defendants accepted. The plaintiff went to considerable trouble and expense to modify a ship which he owned for salvage work, and also bought equipment and engaged a crew. In fact there was no tanker anywhere near the latitude and longitude given by the defendants, and there was no such place as the Jourmand Reef. The plaintiff sued for damages for breach of contract. The High Court of Australia *held* that the plaintiff succeeded because the defendants had impliedly warranted that the goods existed. The court distinguished *Couturier* v. *Hastie* (1856)[222] on the ground that in that case the goods had existed but had perished whereas in the present case the goods had never existed at all.

The implied term solution is not too sound because when the court implies a term it generally does so on the ground that the parties would have included it had they addressed themselves to the matter. It is by no means certain in this case that the defendants would have agreed to such a term. However, there would now be a possible solution in tort if the plaintiff chose to sue in negligence because since the decision of the House of Lords in *Hedley Byrne* v. *Heller and Partners* (1963),[248] there is a liability for careless misstatements resulting in monetary loss if negligence can be proved.

(224) *Cochrane* v. *Willis* (1865), 1 Ch. App. 58

Cochrane was the trustee in bankruptcy of Joseph Willis who was the tenant for life of certain estates in Lancaster. Joseph Willis had been adjudicated bankrupt in Calcutta where he resided. The remainder of the estate was to go to Daniel Willis, the brother of Joseph, on the latter's death, with eventual remainder to Henry Willis, the son of Daniel. Joseph Willis had the right to cut the timber on the estates during his life interest, and the representative of Cochrane in England threatened to cut and sell it for the benefit of Joseph's creditors. Daniel and Henry wished to preserve the timber and so they agreed with Cochrane through his representatives to pay the value of the timber to Cochrane if he would refrain from cutting it. News then reached England that when the above agreement was made Joseph was dead, and therefore the life interest had vested in Daniel. In this action by the trustee to enforce the agreement it was *held* that Daniel was making a contract to preserve something which was already his and the Court found, applying the doctrine of *res sua*, that the agreement was void for an identical or common mistake.

'It would be contrary to all the rules of Equity and common law to give effect to such an agreement.' *per* Knight Bruce, L.J.

(225) *Bell* v. *Lever Bros Ltd*, [1932] A.C. 161

Lever Bros had a controlling interest in the Niger Company. Bell was the chairman, and a person called Snelling was the vice-chairman, of the Niger Company's Board. Both directors had service contracts which had some time to run. They became redundant as a result of amalgamations and Lever Bros contracted to pay Bell £30,000 and Snelling £20,000 as compensation. These sums were paid over and then it was discovered that Bell and Snelling had committed breaches of duty during their term of office by making small but secret profits on a cocoa pooling scheme. They could, therefore, have been dismissed without compensation. Lever Bros sought to set aside the payments on the ground of mistake. *Held*—The contract was not void because Lever Bros had got what they bargained for, i.e. the cancellation of two service contracts which, though they might have been terminated, were actually in existence when the cancellation agreement was made. The mistake was as to the quality of the two directors and such mistakes do not avoid contracts.

(*Note:* (i) the case also illustrates that the contract of service is not of utmost good faith. A servant is not bound to disclose his wrongdoing to his master, so that the silence of the two directors did not amount to a misrepresentation which could assist Lever Bros in the setting aside of the agreement. (ii) In order to regard the case as one of common mistake the Court had to accept (which it did) that Bell and Snelling thought they were entitled to compensation in spite of the taking of secret profits.)

(226) *Leaf* v. *International Galleries*, [1950] 2 K.B. 86

In 1944 the plaintiff bought from the defendants a picture of Salisbury Cathedral for £85. The defendants said that the picture was by Constable. Five years later the plaintiff tried to sell the picture and was told that this was not so. He now sued for rescission of the contract. The decision in the county court was that rescission could not be granted because the representation was innocent and the contract had been executed. The appeal to the Court of Appeal was concerned with the question of the right to rescind; no claim for damages was made. The following points of interest emerged: (i) it was possible to restore the *status quo* by the mere exchange of the picture and the purchase money so that rescission was not affected by inability to restore the previous position. (ii) The mistake made by the parties in assuming the drawing to be a Constable was a mistake as to quality and did not avoid the contract. (iii) The statement that the picture was by Constable could have been treated as a warranty giving rise to a claim for damages, but it was not possible to award damages because the appeal was based on the plaintiff's right to rescind. (iv) The court, therefore, treated the statement as a representation and, finding it to be innocent, refused to rescind the contract because of the passage of time since the purchase.

(*Note:* the plaintiff may now have had a successful action for damages for negligent misrepresentation under the Act of 1967.)

(227) *Jones* v. *Clifford* (1876), 3 Ch.D. 779

Clifford agreed to buy from Jones some freehold and leasehold land, thinking that Jones was the owner. Before Clifford actually completed the contract, he entered into an agreement with a sub-purchaser for the sale of the property. The sub-purchaser discovered, whilst searching the title, that Clifford was in fact the true owner of the property, having derived his title from a conveyance to one of his ancestors in 1781. Clifford, on learning this, refused to complete, and Jones now sued for specific performance. *Held*—Specific performance would not be granted because the contract was affected by an identical bilateral or common mistake. The court also ordered an investigation into the title.

(228) *Magee* v. *Pennine Insurance Co. Ltd*, [1969] 2 All E.R. 891

In 1961 the plaintiff, a man of 58, acquired an Austin car. He also signed a proposal form for insurance in which he said that the car belonged to him. He was asked to give details of his driving licence and of all other persons who, to his present knowledge, would drive the car. He gave the necessary details to a Mr Atkinson at the garage where he bought the car and it appeared that Mr Atkinson did not write them down correctly on the proposal form. However, the details given were that the vehicle would be driven by the plaintiff as a provisional licence holder, his elder son, who had an annual licence, and his younger son, John aged 18, who was shown as a provisional licence holder. In fact the plaintiff was buying the car for John and it transpired that the plaintiff had never held a licence, not even a provisional one. Thus, although the trial judge later found that the plaintiff was not fraudulent, a misrepresentation had been made and on the faith of it being true the defendants granted an insurance policy to the plaintiff. The plaintiff was also required by the defendants to sign the following declaration—

I do hereby declare that the Car described is and shall be kept in good condition and that the answers above given are in every respect true and correct and I hereby agree what this Declaration shall be the basis of the Contract of Insurance between the Company and myself.

This normally has the effect of making all the statements in the proposal form conditions of the contract. (See *Dawsons Ltd* v. *Bonnin*, 1922.[305])

The policy was renewed each year and the premiums paid and in 1964 the car was replaced by another. The policy was renewed for the new car without anything further being said about the drivers or the ownership. At 4 a.m. on 25 April, 1965, John Magee was driving the new car when he ran into a shop window. The plate glass was smashed and the car was a complete wreck. The insurance company sent an engineer to look at the car and he pronounced it a write-off, whereupon the insurers offered to pay the plaintiff £385 and this offer was accepted by him. Afterwards the insurance company made further enquiries and on discovering that the statements in the proposal form of 1961 were untrue refused to pay. The plaintiff then sued the insurers and was given judgment for £385 in the County Court. The insurers appealed to the Court of Appeal where it was *held* in allowing the appeal—

(i) (*Per* Lord Denning, M.R.) that although the acceptance by the plaintiff of the insurance company's offer constituted a contract of compromise that contract was made under circumstances of common mistake which rendered the contract voidable in equity. (*Solle* v. *Butcher*, 1950,[209] applied);

(ii) (*Per* Fenton Atkinson, L.J.—referring to the misapprehension as a mutual mistake) that on the basis of certain statements in *Bell* v. *Lever Bros*, 1932,[225] the contract could be avoided at common law, where, as in this case, the misapprehension was on a fundamental matter.

(*Note:* Lord Denning, M.R., and Winn, L.J., did not take this view of the decision in *Bell* v. *Lever Bros*, 1932[225]);

(iii) (*Per* Winn, L.J., dissenting) that following *Bell* v. *Lever Bros*,

1932,[225] the contract was binding on the insurers—no reference was made by Winn, L.J., to *Solle* v. *Butcher*, 1950.[209]

(229) *Grist* v. *Bailey*, [1966] 2 All E.R. 875

In September, 1954, the defendant agreed to sell to the plaintiff a freehold dwelling house for £850 'subject to the existing tenancy'. Both parties believed at that time that the property was occupied by a tenant who was protected by the Rent Acts. In fact both the tenant and her husband had died before the contract was made and since the rent had always been paid to the vendor's agent he was not aware of the true position. The house was occupied by the son of the former tenant, but he was not protected by the Rent Acts and gave up possession. The plaintiff sought specific performance of the contract of sale and the defendant asked for rescission. *Held*—by Goff, J.—applying the dictum of Denning, L.J., in *Solle* v. *Butcher*, 1950,[209]—there was a jurisdiction in Equity to set aside an agreement for common mistake of a fundamental fact. Had the defendant known the true state of affairs she would not have agreed to sell at such a low price. However, being a case of equitable relief it could be granted unconditionally or on terms, and a term offered by the defendant was imposed, i.e. that, if required, she would enter into a fresh contract with the plaintiff at a proper price for vacant possession.

(230) *Joscelyne* v. *Nissen*, [1970] 1 All E.R. 1213

The plaintiff, Mr Joscelyne, sought rectification of a written contract made on 18 June, 1964, under which he had made over his car-hire business to his daughter, Mrs Margaret Nissen. It had been well understood during negotiations that in return for the car-hire business Mrs Nissen would pay certain expenses including gas, electricity and coal bills but the agreement on these matters was not expressly incorporated into the written contract.

Mrs Nissen failed to pay the bills and the plaintiff brought an action in the Edmonton County Court claiming amongst other things a declaration that Mrs Nissen should pay the gas, electricity and coal bills and alternatively that the written agreement of 18 June, 1964, should be rectified to include a provision to that effect. The County Court judge allowed the claim for rectification and Mrs Nissen appealed to the Court of Appeal on the ground that the judge had misdirected himself, in ordering rectification, in view of his finding that there was no complete antecedent agreement in the sense of an oral contract between the parties on the issue of payment of the expenses. The Court of Appeal, after considering different expressions of judicial views upon what was required before a contractual instrument might be rectified by the court, *held* that the law did not require a complete antecedent concluded agreement provided there was some outward expression of agreement between the contracting parties, which there was in this case. Mrs Nissen's appeal was dismissed.

(231) *Frederick Rose (London) Ltd* v. *William Pim & Co. Ltd*, [1953] 2 Q.B. 450

The plaintiffs received an order from an Egyptian firm for feveroles (a type of horse bean). The plaintiffs did not know what was meant by feveroles and asked the defendants what they were and whether they could supply them. The defendants said that feveroles were horse beans and that they could supply them, so the plaintiffs entered into a written agreement to buy horse beans from the defendants which were then supplied to the Egyptian firm under the order. In fact there were three types of horse beans: feves, feveroles and fevettes, and the plaintiffs had been supplied with feves, which were less valuable than feveroles. The plaintiffs were sued by the Egyptian firm and now wished to recover the damages they had had to pay from the defendants. In order to do so they had to obtain rectification of the written contract with the defendants in which the goods were described as 'horsebeans'. The word 'horsebeans' had to be rectified to 'feveroles', otherwise the defendants were not in breach.

Held—

(i) Rectification was not possible because the contract expressed what the parties had agreed to, i.e. to buy and sell horsebeans. Thus the supply of any of the three varieties would have amounted to fulfilment of the contract.

(ii) The plaintiffs might have rescinded for misrepresentation but they could not restore the *status quo*, having sold the beans.

(iii) The plaintiffs might have recovered damages for breach of warranty, but the statement that 'feveroles are horsebeans and we can supply them' was oral, and warranties in a contract for the sale of goods of £10 and upwards had in 1953 to be evidenced in writing. (Sale of Goods Act, 1893, Sect. 4.) The plaintiff would now have a remedy because Sect. 4 was repealed by the Law Reform (Enforcement of Contracts) Act, 1954. (See p. 194.)

(iv) The defence of mistake was also raised, i.e. both buyer and seller thought that all horsebeans were feveroles. This was an identical bilateral or common mistake, but since it was not a case of *res extincta* or *res sua* it had no effect on the contract.

(232) *Henkel* v. *Pape* (1870), L.R. 6 Ex. 7

The parties to this action had been negotiating for the sale of certain rifles. No contract was made but later the purchaser ordered three rifles by telegram. Owing to the telegraph clerk's negligence the message was transmitted as 'the' rifles. From previous negotiations this was understood to mean fifty rifles and that number was dispatched. *Held*—there was no contract between the parties.

(233) *Wood* v. *Scarth* (1858), 1 F. & F. 293

The plaintiff was suing for damages for breach of contract alleging that the defendant had entered into an agreement to grant the plaintiff a lease of a public house, but had refused to convey the property. It was shown in evidence that the defendant intended to offer the lease at a rent, and also to include a premium on taking up the lease of £500. The defendant had told his agent to make this clear to the plaintiff, but the agent had not mentioned it. After discussions with the agent the plaintiff wrote to the defendant proposing to take the lease 'on the terms already agreed upon' to which the defendant replied accepting the proposal. There was a mutual or non-identical bilateral mistake. The defendant thought that he was agreeing to lease the premises for a rent plus a premium, and the plaintiff thought he was taking a lease for rental only because he did not know of the premium. The plaintiff had sued for specific performance in 1855, and the court in the exercise of its equitable jurisdiction had decided that specific performance could not be granted in view of the mistake, as to grant it would be unduly hard on the defendant. However, in this action the plaintiff sued at common law for damages, and damages were granted to him on the ground that in mutual or non-identical mistake the court may find the sense of the promise and regard a contract as having been made on these terms. Here it was quite reasonable for the plaintiff to suppose that there was no premium to be paid. Thus a contract came into being on the terms as understood by the plaintiff, and he was entitled to damages for breach of it.

(234) *Raffles* v. *Wichelaus* (1864), 2 H. & C. 906

The defendants agreed to buy from the plaintiffs 125 bales of cotton to arrive '*ex Peerless* from Bombay'. There were two ships called *Peerless* sailing from Bombay, one in October and one in December. The defendants thought they were buying the cotton on the ship sailing in October, and the plaintiffs meant to sell the cotton on the ship sailing in December. In fact the plaintiffs had no cotton on the ship sailing in October. The defendants refused to take delivery of the cotton when the second ship arrived and were now sued for breach of contract. *Held*—Since there was a mistake as to the subject matter of the contract there was in effect no contract between the parties. There were no circumstances which would clearly indicate to a disinterested bystander that the contract made more sense if the cotton in the October ship was the subject matter than if the contract in the December ship was. Consequently it was impossible to determine the sense of the promise.

(235) *Scriven Bros & Co.* v. *Hindley & Co.*, [1913] 3 K.B. 564

An auctioneer was selling bales of tow and hemp. Hindley's agent bid £17 per ton for certain bales which had been put up for sale. The bid was about right for hemp but extravagant for tow. The auctioneer knew that the bales were of tow but he accepted the bid. Hindley & Co. refused to take delivery of the tow and were sued for breach of contract. *Held*—There was no contract between the parties since there was no consensus; and there was no negligence on the part of the agent in mistaking the lot offered, because the markings in the catalogue were such that such a mistake might be made. In fact the ship which had brought the tow normally brought hemp, and buyers were given to assuming that all her cargo was hemp. The sense of the promise could not be determined. The circumstances were ambiguous and it could not be said with any certainty which commodity was the subject of the contract.

(236) *Tamplin* v. *James* (1880), 15 Ch.D. 215

James purchased a public house following an auction sale, at which it was not sold. The property was adequately described in the particulars of sale and by reference to a plan. James thought he knew the property and did not bother to refer to the particulars. In fact a field which had been occupied by the publican, and which James thought to be included in the sale, was held under a separate lease and was not part of the lot offered. Tamplin sued for specific performance and James raised this mistake as a defence. *Held*—Specific performance would be granted. Although the parties were not at one on the question of the subject matter, James had by his conduct raised an implication that he was prepared to buy the property offered.

(*Note:* the £750 paid by James was presumably regarded as a fair price for the public house alone otherwise specific performance would not have been granted on the grounds of undue hardship to the defendant. (See *Wood* v. *Scarth*, 1858.)[233]

(237) *Edgington* v. *Fitzmaurice* (1885), 29 Ch.D. 459

The plaintiff was induced to lend money to a company by representations made by its directors that the money would be used to improve the company's buildings and generally expand the business. In fact the directors intended to use the money to pay off the company's existing debts as the creditors were pressing hard for payment. When the plaintiff discovered that he had been misled, he sued the directors for damages for fraud. The defence was that the statement they had made was not a statement of a past or present fact but a mere statement of future intention which could not be the basis of an action for fraud. *Held*—The directors were liable in deceit. Bowen, L.J., said: 'There must be a misstatement of an existing fact; but the state of a man's mind is as much a fact as the state of his digestion. It is true that it is very difficult to prove what the state of a man's mind at a particular time is, but if it can be ascertained, it is as much a fact as anything else. A misrepresentation as to the state of a man's mind is, therefore, a mis-statement of fact.'

(238) *Smith* v. *Land and House Property Corporation* (1884), 28 Ch.D. 7

The plaintiffs put up for sale on 4 August, 1882, the Marine Hotel, Walton-on-the-Naze, stating in the particulars that it was let to 'Mr Frederick Fleck (a most desirable tenant) at a rental of £400 for an unexpired term of 27½ years'. The directors of the defendant company sent the Secretary, Mr Lewin, to inspect the property and he reported that Fleck was not doing much business and that the town seemed to be in the last stages of decay. The directors, on receiving this report, directed Mr Lewin to bid up to £5000, and in fact he bought the hotel for £4700. Before completion Fleck became bankrupt and the defendant company refused to complete the purchase, whereupon the plaintiffs sued for specific performance. It was proved that on 1 May, 1882, the March quarter's rent was wholly unpaid; that a distress was then threatened, and that Fleck paid £30 on 6 May, £40 on 13 June, and the remaining £30 shortly before the sale. No part of the June quarter's rent had been paid. The chairman of the defendant company said that the hotel would not have been purchased but for the statement in the particulars that Fleck was a most desirable tenant. *Held*—Specific performance would not be granted. The description of Fleck as a most desirable tenant was not a mere expression of opinion, but contained an implied assertion that the vendors knew of no facts leading to the conclusion that he was not. The circumstances relating to the unpaid rent showed that Fleck was not a desirable tenant and there was a misrepresentation. Bowen, L.J., said—

> It is material to observe that it is often fallaciously assumed that a statement of opinion cannot involve the statement of a fact. In a case where the facts are equally well known to both parties, what one of them says to the other is frequently nothing but an expression of opinion. The statement of such opinion is in a sense a statement of a fact about the condition of the man's own mind, but only of an irrelevant fact, for it is of no consequence what the opinion is. But if the facts are not equally known to both sides, then a statement of opinion by the one who knows the facts best involves very often a statement of a material fact, for he impliedly states that he knows facts which justify his opinion.

(239) *Curtis* v. *Chemical Cleaning and Dyeing Co.*, [1951] 1 K.B. 805

The plaintiff took a wedding dress, with beads and sequins, to the defendant's shop for cleaning. She was asked to sign a receipt which contained the following clause: 'The company is not liable for damage howsoever arising.' The plaintiff asked what the effect of the document was, and the assistant told her that it exempted the company from liability in certain ways, and particularly that in her case she would have to take the risk of damage to beads and sequins. Thereupon the plaintiff signed the document without reading it. The dress was returned stained, and the plaintiff sued for damages. The company relied on the clause. *Held*—The company could not rely on the clause because the assistant had misrepresented the effect of the document so that the plaintiff was merely running the risk of damage to the beads and sequins.

(240) *With* v. *O'Flanagan*, [1936] Ch. 575

The defendant was a medical practitioner who wished to sell his practice.

The plaintiff was interested and in January, 1934, the defendant represented to the plaintiff that the income from the practice was £2000 a year. The contract was not signed until May, 1934, and in the meantime the defendant had been ill and the practice had been run by various other doctors as *locum tenentes*. In consequence the receipts fell to £5 per week, and no mention of this fact was made when the contract was entered into. The plaintiff now claimed rescission of the contract. *Held*—He could do so. The representation made in January was of a continuing nature and induced the contract made in May. The plaintiff had a right to be informed of a change in circumstances, and the defendant's silence amounted to a misrepresentation.

(241) *Tate* v. *Williamson* (1866), 2 Ch. App. 55

An extravagant Oxford undergraduate who was being pressed for money by his creditors sought financial advice from Williamson who recommended the sale of the undergraduate's estate in Staffordshire. Williamson then offered to buy it himself for £7000 without disclosing the existence of minerals under the land which made the undergraduate's interest worth at least £14,000. The offer was accepted and a conveyance executed but some years later the sale was set aside by the Court at the instance of the undergraduate's heir. Williamson had been guilty of constructive fraud in that he had exploited to his own advantage the confidence placed in him.

(242) *Peek* v. *Gurney* (1873), L.R. 6 H.L. 377

Peek purchased shares in a company on the faith of statements appearing in a prospectus issued by the respondents who were directors of the company. Certain of the statements were false and Peek sued the directors. It appeared that Peek was not an original allottee, but had purchased the shares on the market, though he had relied on the prospectus. *Held*—Peek's action failed because the statements in the prospectus were only intended to mislead the original allottees. Once the statements had induced the public to be original subscribers, their force was spent.

(243) *Gross* v. *Lewis Hillman Ltd and Another*, [1969] 3 All E.R. 1476

Mrs Gross instructed property dealers Grace Rymer Investments to find a suitable shop for her to purchase as an investment. Lewis Hillman Ltd owned a shop which they had leased and Henry James and partners had been instructed to sell the shop. Lewis Hillman Ltd was controlled by a Mr Edward James who also controlled the firm of Henry James and Partners. Edward James had arranged to let the shop to a dormant wool company, H. G. Somers & Sons Ltd whose shares had recently been bought by two brothers planning to set up a chain of wool shops. Henry James and Partners introduced the shop to Grace Rymer by two letters the first of which said that the shop had been let to H. G. Somers and Sons Ltd on a twenty-one years' full repairing and insuring lease at £800 p.a. exclusively for the sale of wool and hosiery and that the company had branches in

Liverpool, Blackpool and Southport. Grace Rymer asked for tenants' references and in a second letter Henry James and Partners replied that H. G. Somers and Sons Ltd was incorporated in 1928, had a paid up capital of £5000 and enclosed a bankers reference relating to the letting of another shop to H. G. Somers & Sons Ltd at a rent of £3000 p.a.

Grace Rymer believing as a result of the letters that H. G. Somers was a going concern agreed to purchase the shop on its own behalf and recommended Mrs Gross to purchase it offering to let her have the benefit of Grace Rymer's contract for a commission of 2¼ per cent of the purchase price. Mrs Gross purchased the shop and it was conveyed directly by Lewis Hillman Ltd to whom she paid the purchase price at the request of Grace Rymer. Three months later H. G. Somers & Sons Ltd became insolvent and went into liquidation. In an action by Mrs Gross against Lewis Hillman Ltd to rescind the conveyance and against both Lewis Hillman Ltd and Henry James & Partners for damages for deceit on the ground of fraudulent misrepresentation Mrs Gross relied upon the representations in the two letters relating to the status of H. G. Somers & Sons Ltd. *Held*—by the Court of Appeal—that although the letters if read together might have amounted to fraudulent misrepresentation the trial judge had acquitted Edward James of any intention to deceive and the court would not interfere with that finding not having seen or heard James. Neither would the court order a new trial since even if there was fraudulent misrepresentation Mrs Gross could not rescind the contract on the strength of it. The right to rescind for misrepresentation was not an equity which ran with the land and any misrepresentation to Mrs Gross was spent when her agents, Grace Rymer, bought the property on their own behalf prior to selling it to her. Had Grace Rymer remained her agents throughout the misrepresentations made to them as agents would have been, in effect, made to Mrs Gross who could then have rescinded the contract.

(244) *Redgrave* v. *Hurd* (1881), 20 Ch.D. 1

The plaintiff was a solicitor who wished to take a partner into the business. During negotiations between the plaintiff and Hurd the plaintiff stated that the income of the business was £300 a year. The papers which the plaintiff produced showed that the income was not quite £200 a year, and Hurd asked about the balance. Redgrave then produced further papers which he said showed how the balance was made up, but which only showed a very small amount of income making the total income up to about £200. Hurd did not examine these papers in any detail, but agreed to become a partner. Later Hurd discovered the true position and refused to complete the contract. The plaintiff sued for breach and Hurd raised the misrepresentation as a defence, and also counterclaimed for rescission of the contract. *Held*—Hurd had relied on Redgrave's statements regarding the income, and not his own skill and judgment, so the contract could be rescinded. It did not matter that Hurd had the means of discovering their untruth; he was entitled to rely on Redgrave's statement.

(245) *Smith* v. *Chadwick* (1884), 9 App. Cas. 187

This action was brought by the plaintiff who was a steel manufacturer, against Messrs Chadwick, Adamson and Collier, who were accountants and promoters of a company called the Blochairn Iron Co. Ltd. The plaintiff claimed £5750 as damages sustained through taking shares in the company which were not worth the price he had paid for them because of certain misrepresentations in the prospectus issued by the defendants. The action was for fraud. Among the misrepresentations alleged by Smith was that the prospectus stated that a Mr J. J. Grieves, M.P., was a director of the company, whereas he had withdrawn his consent the day before the prospectus was issued. It was *held* that the statement regarding Mr Grieves was untrue but was not material to the plaintiff, because the evidence showed that he had never heard of Mr Grieves. His action for damages failed.

(246) *Horsfall* v. *Thomas* (1862), 1 H. & C. 90

Thomas asked Horsfall to make him a gun and agreed to pay for it by means of two bills of exchange. Horsfall made the gun, and at the third trial by Thomas the gun flew to pieces. Evidence showed that the breech was defective and that a plug of metal had been driven into the breech to conceal the defect. Horsfall sued on one of the bills and Thomas pleaded fraud. *Held*—Horsfall succeeded and the defence failed because it appeared that Thomas had never inspected the gun so that any attempt to conceal the defect could not have had any operation on his mind. Even if the plug had not been put into the breech the defendant's position would have been the same.

(247) *Derry* v. *Peek* (1889), 14 App. Cas. 337

The Plymouth, Devonport and District Tramways Company had power under a special Act of Parliament to run trams by animal power, and with the consent of the Board of Trade by mechanical or steam power. Derry and the other appellants were directors of the company and issued a prospectus, inviting the public to apply for shares in it, stating they had power to run trams by steam power, and claiming that considerable economies would result. The directors had assumed that the permission of the Board of Trade would be granted as a matter of course, but in the event the Board of Trade refused permission except for certain parts of the tramway. As a result the company was wound up and the directors were sued for fraud. The court *decided* that the directors were not fraudulent but honestly believed the statement in the prospectus to be true.

(*Note:* this case gave rise to the Directors' Liability Act, 1890, now Sect. 43 of the Companies Act, 1948, which makes directors liable to pay compensation for misrepresentation in a prospectus, subject to a number of defences.)

(248) *Hedley Byrne & Co. Ltd* v. *Heller & Partners Ltd*, [1963] 2 All E.R. 575

The appellants were advertising agents and the respondents were merchant bankers. The appellants had a client called Easipower Ltd who were customers of the respondents. The appellants had contracted to place orders for advertising Easipower's products on television and in newspapers, and since this involved giving Easipower credit, they asked the respondents, who were Easipower's bankers, for a reference as to the creditworthiness of Easipower. Heller's replied: 'without responsibility on the part of the bank or its officials' that Easipower was a 'respectably constituted company, considered good for its ordinary business engagements. Your figures are larger than we are accustomed to see'. In fact bankers normally use careful terms when giving these references, but Heller's language was so guarded that only a very suspicious person might have appreciated that he was being warned not to give credit to the extent of £100,000. In fact Heller's were trying to warn the plaintiffs off because Easipower had an overdraft with Heller's which Heller's knew they were about to call in and that Easipower might have difficulty in meeting the payment. One week after the reference was given Heller's began to press Easipower to reduce their overdraft. However, relying on this reply, the appellants placed orders for advertising time and space for Easipower Ltd, and the appellants assumed personal responsibility for payment to the television and newspaper companies concerned. Easipower Ltd went into liquidation, and the appellants lost over £17,000 on the advertising contracts. The appellants sued the respondents for the amount of the loss, alleging that the respondents had not informed themselves sufficiently about Easipower Ltd before writing the statement, and were therefore liable in negligence. *Held*—In the present case the respondents' disclaimer was adequate to exclude the assumption by them of the legal duty of care, but, in the absence of the disclaimer, the circumstances would have given rise to a duty of care in spite of the absence of a contract or fiduciary relationship. The dissenting judgment of Denning, L.J., in *Candler* v. *Crane, Christmas*, 1951,[655] was approved, and the majority judgment in that case was disapproved.

(249) *Doyle* v. *Olby (Ironmongers) Ltd and Others*, [1969] 2 All E.R. 119

In 1963 the plaintiff wished to buy a business. He saw an advertisement in *Dalton's Weekly* and obtained particulars of an ironmonger's business in Epsom belonging to the first defendants. The price asked for the lease, the business and goodwill was £4500, the stock to be taken at valuation. In 1964 after negotiations with various members of the Olby family the plaintiff purchased the business paying £4500 covering goodwill and fixtures and fittings, and £5000 for the stock. He also needed a longer lease and so surrendered the existing lease taking on a longer one at an increased rent. The owner of the shop who benefited from this transaction was another member of the Olby family. In order to pay the money the plaintiff put up all the cash he had, i.e. £7000 and borrowed £3000 on mortgage. When he went into occupation he discovered that the defendants had made a number of false statements relating to the business. In particular the plaintiff discovered that half the trade was wholesale which could only be obtained by employing a traveller to go round to the customers. The plaintiff could not afford to employ a traveller and all the wholesale trade was lost. The second defendant had told the plaintiff in the course of negotiations that all the trade was over the counter.

The plaintiff was most dissatisfied and in May, 1964, he brought an action for damages for fraud and conspiracy against Olby (Ironmongers) Ltd and several members of the Olby family who had been involved in the sale of the Epsom business. At the trial the judge awarded damages on a contractual basis as if the statement 'the trade is all over the counter. There is no need to employ a traveller' had been a term of the contract. In consequence the judge accepted that the proper measure of foreseeable damage was, in accordance with *Hadley* v. *Baxendale* 1854,[429] the reduction in the value of goodwill due to the mis-statement. The goodwill was valued at £4000 and since 50 per cent of the turnover was wholesale goodwill would have been reduced by 35 to 40 per cent giving £1500 as a round figure for damages.

In the Court of Appeal Lord Denning, M.R., said on this point:

On principle the distinction seems to be this: in contract, the defendant has made a promise and broken it. The object of damages is to put the plaintiff in as good a position, as far as money can do it, as if the promise had been performed. In fraud, the defendant has been guilty of a deliberate wrong by inducing the plaintiff to act to his detriment. The object of damages is to compensate the plaintiff for all the loss he has suffered, so far, again, as money can do it. In contract, the damages are limited to what may reasonably be supposed to have been in the contemplation of the parties. In fraud, they are not so limited. The defendant is bound to make reparation for all the actual damage directly flowing from the fraudulent inducement. The person who has been defrauded is entitled to say: 'I would not have entered into this bargain at all but for your representation. Owing to your fraud, I have not only lost all the money I have paid you, but, what is more, I have been put to a large amount of extra expense as well and suffered this or that extra damages.' All such damages can be recovered: and it does not lie in the mouth of the fraudulent person to say that they could not reasonably have been foreseen. For instance, in this very case the plaintiff has not only lost the money which he paid for the business, which he would never have done if there had been no fraud; he put all that money in and lost it; but also he has been put to expense and loss in trying to run a business which has turned out to be a disaster for him. He is entitled to damages for all his loss, subject, of course, to giving credit for any benefit that he has received. There is nothing to be taken off in mitigation: for there is nothing more that he could have done to reduce his loss. He did all that he could reasonably be expected to do.

Accordingly damages were assessed by the Court of Appeal at £5500 being made up as follows—

	£	£	
Cost of acquiring business		4500	
Cost of acquiring stock		5000	
		9500	
Less: Cash received by Doyle when business sold in 1967	3500		
Cash received on sale of stock	800		
Value of living accommodation during the three years	2500	7000	(as a round figure)
Loss		2500	
Additional damages for strain and worry and interest on loans and bank overdraft		3000	
Damages awarded		£5500	

(250) *Mafo* v. *Adams*, [1969] 3 All E.R. 1404

In July, 1965, the plaintiff, a Nigerian, was granted a weekly tenancy in Richmond by the defendant, a West Indian. On 10 December, 1965, the defendant gave the plaintiff notice to quit though the plaintiff appeared to have been a good tenant. The plaintiff then claimed the benefit of the Rent Acts and refused to leave. On 15 February, 1966, the plaintiff was invited to see alternative accommodation at Norbury and saw a lady who posed as Mrs Williams. The plaintiff arranged to move into the accommodation at Norbury and paid Mrs Williams £6 10s. representing two weeks' rent in advance, though the cheque was never cashed. The plaintiff and his pregnant wife then left the Richmond tenancy but were unable to obtain entry to the Norbury accommodation. It later emerged that Mrs Williams was in fact Adams' wife, from whom he was separated, and that he and she had combined in a piece of trickery to get the plaintiff out of the Richmond tenancy. The plaintiff was unable to resume possession of the Richmond accommodation and subsequently suffered physical inconvenience but no financial damage although it appeared that the accommodation he found was unlikely to be as securely protected by the Rent Acts as the Richmond flat had been. On appeal by the landlord from an award to the tenant of

£100 for breach of covenant of quiet enjoyment and £100 exemplary damages for deceit it was *held*—by the Court of Appeal—

    (i) £100 was a proper figure for compensatory damages;

    (ii) that Lord Devlin's statements in *Rookes* v. *Barnard*, [1964] 1 All E.R. 367, at p. 411, that 'Exemplary damages can properly be awarded whenever it is necessary to teach a wrongdoer that tort does not pay' might well have extended the number of cases in which exemplary damages could potentially be awarded. However, assuming that exemplary damages could be awarded in an action for deceit, the plaintiff was not entitled to them because there was no finding that the landlord had acted in such a way as to bring himself within Lord Devlin's statement. Exemplary damages are in the main to be awarded in cases where the defendant realises that he is breaking the law, and that damages may be awarded against him, but nevertheless makes what has been described as a cynical calculation of profit and loss and says that he will flout the powers of the court because on a purely cash basis he can show a profit. Where exemplary damages were claimed the court must be careful to see that the case for punishment was as well established as in other penal proceedings. The plaintiff was not therefore entitled to exemplary damages.

(251) *Gosling* v. *Anderson, The Times*, 6 February, 1972

Miss Gosling, a retired schoolmistress, entered into negotiations for the purchase of one of three flats in a house at Minehead owned by Mrs Anderson. Mr Tidbury, who was Mrs Anderson's agent in the negotiations, represented to Miss Gosling by letter that planning permission for a garage to go with the flat had been given. Mrs Anderson knew that this was not so. The purchase of the flat went through on the basis of a contract and a conveyance showing a parking area but not referring to planning permission which was later refused. Miss Gosling now sought damages for misrepresentation under Sect. 2(1) of the Misrepresentation Act, 1967. *Held*—the facts revealed an innocent misrepresentation by Mr Tidbury made without reasonable grounds for believing it to be true. Mrs Anderson was liable for the acts of her agent and must pay damages under the Act of 1967. The Court ordered an inquiry as to damages before the local county court judge.

    (Note: the effect of this case and the Misrepresentation Act, 1967, on *Armstrong* v. *Strain*, 1952.[252] Before the 1967 Act, where both agent and principal were innocent of actual fraud there was no cause of action in damages. Now there need not be any question of fraud. Where the statement is made negligently the agent may be made liable for his own negligence and the principal is liable also under the doctrine of vicarious liability.)

(252) *Armstrong* v. *Strain*, [1952] 1 K.B. 232

The plaintiffs purchased a bungalow from Strain and during the negotiations Strain's agent made certain statements about the property and in particular that it was in nice condition. The property was subject to subsidence of the clay foundations, and had been underpinned several times, but the agent was aware of one underpinning only. After the plaintiffs had purchased the bungalow, large cracks appeared in the walls and the plaintiffs sued Strain and the agent for fraudulent misrepresentation. *Held*—They were unable to prove fraud because the ingredients of deceit were split, Strain having knowledge of the defects but not having made the statement, and the agent having made the statement without full knowledge of the defects. Devlin, J., at first instance suggested that Strain might have been liable if the evidence had shown that he deliberately kept his agent in ignorance of the defects in the expectation and hope that he would mislead the plaintiff, but the evidence did not establish this. Regarding an action for breach of warranty, Devlin, J., held that no warranty could arise out of the rather casual conversations which preceded the sale. Regarding liability of the agent in negligence, there was no duty of care in respect of careless mis-statements of this sort, following *Candler* v. *Crane, Christmas*, 1951.[655]

(*Note*: in *Hedley Byrne* v. *Heller and Partners*, 1963,[248] the House of Lords decided that there was a duty of care in respect of careless mis-statements of this kind, and this decision may provide a remedy in negligence in a situation like that in *Armstrong* v. *Strain*. Furthermore, a principal is liable for the negligent mis-statements of his agent under the Misrepresentation Act, 1967. (See *Gosling* v. *Anderson*, 1972.)[251])

(253) *Car & Universal Finance Co. Ltd* v. *Caldwell*, [1963] 2 All E.R. 547

On 12 January, 1960, Mr Caldwell sold a motor car to a firm called Dunn's Transport, receiving a cheque signed 'for and on behalf of Dunn's Transport, W. Foster, F. Norris'. Caldwell presented the cheque to the bank but it was dishonoured, and so he went to see the police and asked them to recover the car. He also saw officials of the Automobile Association and asked them to trace the car by their patrols. The car was found on 20 January, 1960, in the possession of a director of a firm of car dealers called Motobella & Co. Ltd. The company claimed to have bought it on 15 January from Norris and to have a good title. On 29 January, the defendant's solicitors demanded the car from Motobella and at the same time Norris was arrested and pleaded guilty to obtaining the car by false pretences. The defendant sued Motobella & Co. Ltd for the return of the car and obtained judgment, but when he tried to repossess the car, a finance house, Car & Universal Finance Co. Ltd, claimed that it belonged to them. It appeared that Motobella had transferred the ownership to a finance house called G. & C. Finance on 15 January, 1960, and they had transferred it to the plaintiffs on 3 August, 1960, the latter company taking the vehicle in good faith. In this action the plaintiffs claimed the car. It was *held* that Caldwell was entitled to it because, amongst other things, he had avoided the contract of sale to Norris when he asked the police to get the car back for him so that later sales of the car to Motobella and to G. & C. Finance did not pass the property.

(*Note:* (i) this case is of little practical importance because a buyer in possession of goods will give a good title to a third party under Sect. 9 of the Factors Act, 1889. This section was not discussed in *Caldwell's* case; (ii) the Law Reform Committee (Cmnd 2958) recommends that an innocent purchaser should obtain a good title until notice of rescission is communicated to the other contracting party.)

(254) *Long* v. *Lloyd*, [1958] 2 All E.R. 402

The plaintiff and the defendant were haulage contractors. The plaintiff was induced to buy the defendant's lorry by the defendant's misrepresentation as to condition and performance. The defendant advertised the lorry for sale at £850, the advertisement describing the vehicle as being in 'exceptional condition'. The plaintiff saw the lorry at the defendant's premises at Hampton Court on a Saturday. During a trial run on the following Monday the plaintiff found that the speedometer was not working, a spring was missing from the accelerator pedal, and it was difficult to engage top gear. The defendant said there was nothing wrong with the vehicle except what the plaintiff had found. He also said at this stage that the lorry would do 11 miles to the gallon.

The plaintiff purchased the lorry for £750, paying £375 down and agreeing to pay the balance at a later date. He then drove the lorry from Hampton Court to his place of business at Sevenoaks. On the following Wednesday, the plaintiff drove from Sevenoaks to Rochester to pick up a load, and during that journey the dynamo ceased to function, an oil seal was leaking badly, there was a crack in one of the road wheels, and he used 8 gallons of petrol on a journey of 40 miles. That evening the plaintiff told the defendant of the defects, and the defendant offered to pay half the cost of a reconstructed dynamo, but denied any knowledge of the other defects. The plaintiff accepted the offer and the dynamo was fitted straight away. On Thursday the lorry was driven by the plaintiff's brother to Middlesbrough, and it broke down on the Friday night. The plaintiff, on learning of this, asked the defendant for his money back, but the defendant would not give it to him. The lorry was subsequently examined and an expert said that it was not roadworthy. The plaintiff sued for rescission. *Held*—at first instance, by Glyn-Jones, J.—that the defendant's statements about the lorry were innocent and not fraudulent because the evidence showed that the lorry had been laid up for a month and it might therefore have deteriorated without the defendant's precise knowledge. The Court of Appeal affirmed this finding of fact and made the following additional points—

(1) The journey to Rochester was not affirmation because the plaintiff was merely testing the vehicle in a working capacity.

(2) However, the acceptance by the plaintiff of the defendant's offer to

pay half the cost of the reconstructed dynamo, and the subsequent journey to Middlesbrough, did amount to affirmation, and rescission could not be granted to the plaintiff.

(*Note:* (i) presumably the Court would not treat the defendant's statements as warranties because he was not a dealer in lorries but merely a user. (ii) Damages could now be obtained for negligent misrepresentation under the Misrepresentation Act, 1967, Sect. 2(1), for how could the seller say he had reasonable grounds for believing that the lorry was in first-class condition?)

(255) *Clarke* v. *Dickson* (1858), E.B. & E. 148

In 1853 the plaintiff was induced by the misrepresentation of the three defendants, Dickson, Williams and Gibbs, to invest money in what was in effect a partnership to work lead mines in Wales. In 1857 the partnership was in financial difficulty and with the plaintiff's assent it was converted into a limited company and the partnership capital was converted into shares. Shortly afterwards the company commenced winding-up proceedings and the plaintiff, on discovery of the falsity of the representations, asked for rescission of the contract. *Held*—Rescission could not be granted because capital in a partnership is not the same as shares in a company. The firm was no longer in existence, having been replaced by the company, and it was not possible to restore the parties to their original positions.

(*Note:* it should be noted that in addition to the problem of restoration, third-party rights, i.e. creditors, had accrued on the winding up of the company and this is a further bar to rescission.)

(256) *Jarvis* v. *Swans Tours Ltd*, [1973] 1 All E.R. 71

The plaintiff booked a 15-day winter sports holiday with the defendants on the faith of their brochure which described the holiday in very attractive terms. He paid their charges of £63.45. The holiday was a great disappointment to him. For the first week it was to some extent inferior and for the second week much inferior to what he had been led to expect. The County Court judge awarded him £31.72 damages. On the plaintiff's appeal against the amount awarded it was *held*—by the Court of Appeal allowing the appeal—that he was entitled to be compensated for his disappointment and distress, because if the representation had been true he would not have been disappointed or distressed and it was not enough merely to give him half the charges as damages. The damages should be increased to £125. In the course of his judgment Lord Denning, .M.R. said (at p. 73) 'What is the legal position? I think that the statements in the brochure were representations or warranties. The breaches of them gave Mr Jarvis a right to damages. It is not necessary to decide whether they were representations or warranties; because, since the Misrepresentation Act, 1967, there is a remedy in damages for misrepresentation as well as for breach of warranty.'

(257) *Davies & Co. (Wines) Ltd* v. *Afa-Minerva (EMI) Ltd*, [1974] 2 Lloyd's Rep. 27

The defendants agreed to supply and instal a burglar alarm at the plaintiffs' business premises where they stored liquor and other stock. They were induced to enter into the contract for the alarm by the defendants' representation that once the alarm was set off the bell would ring until the batteries were run down. This representation was not true because the bell also stopped if the control panel was pulled off the wall to which it was attached. Some days after installation of the alarm the plaintiffs' premises were burgled and a quantity of liquor was taken. The control panel had been wrenched off the wall and the alarm bell, if it had rung at all, would only have done so for a few seconds. The plaintiffs were held to be entitled to damages under Sect. 2(1) of the Misrepresentation Act, 1967, and were awarded damages for the loss of stock on the basis that the removal of the quantity of stock which would have taken a great deal of time and effort would not have been carried out had a loud alarm bell been going off at the time. Judge Fay said little about the measure of damages. However, he said that he found Lord Denning's *dicta* in *Jarvis*[256] 'helpful' and seems to have taken the contractual view.

(258) *Henderson & Co.* v. *Williams*, [1895] 1 Q.B. 521

The plaintiffs were sugar merchants at Hull. The defendant was a warehouseman at Hull and Goole. On 3 June, 1894, a fraudulent person named Fletcher, posing as the agent of one Robinson, negotiated a purchase of sugar from Messrs Grey & Co., who were Liverpool merchants. The sugar was lying in the defendant's warehouse at Goole, and Messrs Grey & Co. sent a telegram and later a letter advising the defendant that the sugar was to be held to the order of Fletcher, and the defendant entered the order in his books. Robinson was a reputable dealer and a customer of Messrs Grey & Co., and of course Fletcher had no right to act on Robinson's behalf. Fletcher sold the goods to the plaintiffs who, before paying the price, got a statement from the defendant that the goods were held to the order of Fletcher. The defendant later discovered Fletcher's fraud and refused to release the sugar to the plaintiffs who now sued in conversion. *Held*—The defendant was estopped from denying Fletcher's title and was liable in damages based on the market price of the goods at the date of refusal to deliver. Further the true owners, Messrs Grey & Co., could not set up their title to the sugar against that of the plaintiffs, since they had allowed Fletcher to hold himself out as the true owner.

(259) *Whittington* v. *Seale-Hayne* (1900), 82 L.T. 49

The plaintiffs were breeders of prize poultry and they took a lease of the defendant's premises. The defendant innocently misrepresented that the premises were in a sanitary condition but in fact the water supply was poisoned, and this caused the illness of the plaintiff's manager. In addition, certain of their poultry died or became valueless for breeding purposes. The local authority required the plaintiffs to carry out certain work in order to render the premises sanitary, the plaintiffs having agreed in the lease to do such work if it became necessary. The plaintiffs now asked for rescission of the contract and for an indemnity against the following losses: Stock lost, £750; loss of profit on sales, £100; loss of breeding season, £500; removal of stores and rent, £75; medical expenses, £100. *Held*—The lease could be rescinded, but the plaintiffs' indemnity was restricted to the losses necessarily incurred by taking a lease of the premises, i.e. rent, rates and the cost of the repairs ordered by the local authority.

(*Note:* the reason for restricting the indemnity in this sort of case seems to be based on the fact that although Equity is prepared to rescind contracts for non-fraudulent misrepresentation, thus providing a remedy where the common law does not, Equity will not circumvent the law by making an indemnity (the object of which is to help restore the *status quo*) the equivalent of damages for fraud.)

(260) *Pym* v. *Campbell* (1856), 6 E. & G. 370

An agreement for the sale of a patent was drawn up and signed. It was also agreed at the time that the written agreement was not to be binding unless a third party approved of the invention. In an action on the written agreement evidence was admitted to show that the third party had not approved and therefore the agreement was not effective.

(261) *Quickmaid Rental Services Ltd* v. *Reece* (1970), *The Times*, 22 April, 1970

In 1967 a salesman named Burbridge persuaded Mr Reece to install on his service station premises in Ashton New Road, Manchester, a Quickmaid machine which supplied coffee, tea and other beverages to travellers by putting coins into a slot. Mr Reece was asked to sign two written agreements, one for the machine itself and the other for a canopy. It was to be for five years. Mr Reece paid £37 10s. deposit for the machine and was to pay monthly rentals thereafter. But before he agreed or signed anything Mr Burbridge made an important statement to him. He said that he would not install any other such machine on Ashton New Road. That stipulation induced Mr Reece to sign the documents. Mr Burbridge realized that any other machine would affect Mr Reece's business considerably. Later he made a memorandum saying he would not sell any more machines in that particular road.

However in May, 1968, Mr Reece discovered that in January the company, through another salesman, had installed another machine up the road. That was within two and a half months of the promise to him; and the second machine was in a more advantageous position for getting custom. On discovering that, Mr Reece, who had had trouble with his machine, stopped his banker's order for the rental. The company thereupon sued Mr Reece in the County Court for £73 15s., being the instalments from June to

October, 1968. *Held*—by the Court of Appeal—that the company's claim failed. The proper way to approach the case was to regard it as a contract made partly in writing by the signed documents and partly by word of mouth, by what was said at the time. The stipulation about no other machine being in the road was most important; it was a term which amounted to a condition; and when it was broken it was broken in a manner which went to the root of the contract. It destroyed the profitable basis of the contract. Breach of that condition gave Mr Reece the right to say he would no longer go on; nor on the evidence did he affirm the contract after discovering the breach. The appeal should be dismissed. (*Per* Lord Denning, M.R.)

(262) *Bannerman* v. *White* (1861), 10 C.B.(N.S.) 844

The defendant was intending to buy hops from the plaintiff and he asked the plaintiff whether sulphur had been used in the cultivation of the hops, adding that if it had he would not even bother to ask the price. The plaintiff said that no sulphur had been used, though in fact it had. It was *held* that the plaintiff's assurance that sulphur had not been used was a term of the contract and the defendant was justified in raising the matter as a defence to an action for the price.

(263) *D'Mello* v. *Loughborough College of Technology* (1970), *The Times*, 17 June, 1970

In 1961 the college advertised a one-year postgraduate course in economics and administration in the oil industry. The plaintiff, who was then working for an oil company in India saw the advertisement and wrote asking for further details. The college sent him a prospectus containing a syllabus of the course and a college calendar for 1961/62 and 1962/63 together with an application form. In due course the college accepted him for the course and in September, 1963, he joined four other students who had already begun their studies. All the other students completed the course but D'Mello gave up early in 1964 because he said that the course was different from the one in the prospectus and in particular did not have sufficient relevance to the oil industry. He now claimed damages for breach of contract. *Held*—by O'Connor, J.—that the prospectus was part of the contract but the plaintiff failed in that he had not shown that the college was in breach of it. It was a matter for the College authorities to decide as a matter of skill and judgment how to conduct the course and their was no evidence to show that they were in breach of their duty to the plaintiff in this regard.

(264) *Oscar Chess Ltd* v. *Williams*, [1957] 1 W.L.R. 370

In May, 1955, Williams bought a car from the plaintiffs on hire-purchase terms. The plaintiffs took Williams's Morris car in part exchange. Williams described the car as a 1948 model and produced the registration book, which showed that the car was first registered in April, 1948, and that there had been several owners since that time. Williams was allowed £290 on the Morris. Eight months later the plaintiffs discovered that the Morris car was a 1939 model, there being no change in appearance in the model between 1939 and 1948. The allowance for a 1939 model was £175 and the plaintiffs sued for £115 damages for breach of warranty that the car was a 1948 model. Evidence showed that some fraudulent person had altered the registration book but he could not be traced, and that Williams honestly believed that the car was a 1948 model. *Held*—The contract might have been set aside in Equity for misrepresentation but the delay of eight months defeated this remedy. The mistake was a mistake of quality which did not avoid the contract at common law and in order to obtain damages the plaintiffs must prove a breach of warranty. The court was unable to find that Williams was in a position to give such a warranty, and suggested that the plaintiffs should have taken the engine and chassis number and written to the manufacturers, so using their superior knowledge to protect themselves in the matter. The plaintiffs were not entitled to any redress. Morris, L.J., dissented, holding that the statement that the car was a 1948 model was a fundamental condition.

(265) *Poussard* v. *Spiers and Pond* (1876), 1 Q.B.D. 410

Madame Poussard had entered into an agreement to play a part in an opera, the first performance to take place on 28 November, 1874. On 23 November Madame Poussard was taken ill and was unable to appear until 4 December. The defendants had hired a substitute, and discovered that the only way in which they could secure a substitute to take Madame Poussard's place was to offer that person the complete engagement. This they had done, and they refused the services of Madame Poussard when she presented herself on 4 December. The plaintiff now sued for breach of contract. *Held*—The failure of Madame Poussard to perform the contract as from the first night was a breach of condition, and the defendants were within their rights in regarding the contract as discharged.

(266) *Bettini* v. *Gye* (1876), 1 Q.B.D. 183

The plaintiff was an opera singer. The defendant was the director of the Royal Italian Opera in London. The plaintiff had agreed to sing in Great Britain in theatres, halls and drawing rooms for a period of time commencing on 30 March, 1875, and to be in London for rehearsals six days before the engagement began. The plaintiff was taken ill and arrived on 28 March, 1873, but the defendant would not accept the plaintiff's services, treating the contract as discharged. *Held*—The rehearsal clause was subsidiary to the main purposes of the contract, and its breach constituted a breach of warranty only. The defendant had no right to treat the contract as discharged and must compensate the plaintiff, but he had a counterclaim for any damage he had suffered by the plaintiffs' late arrival.

(267) *Harling* v. *Eddy*, [1951] 2 K.B. 739

The plaintiff purchased a heifer at an auction sale. The auction sale was subject to certain conditions which were printed in the catalogue issued to potential buyers. One of the conditions stated that no warranties were given regarding animals purchased unless such warranties appeared on the purchaser's account. When the heifer was brought into the ring, potential buyers showed little interest, and no bids were made until the auctioneer, with the authority of the owner, said: 'There is nothing wrong with her. I will guarantee her in every respect and I will take her back if she is not what I say she is.' The plaintiff thereupon purchased the animal, no warranties being given on the account. The heifer gave little milk and died of tuberculosis four months after purchase. The plaintiff sued for damages and the defence was the exemption clause in the auctioneer's catalogue. *Held*—The plaintiff succeeded. The following points arise out of the judgment in the Court of Appeal—

(*a*) A statement that an animal is sound in every respect would *prima facie* have been no more than a warranty, but the auctioneer's statement that he would take the animal back implied a right in the purchaser to reject the animal, thus making the statement a condition and not a warranty so that the exemption clause was not effective to exclude it. However, since the plaintiff had sued for breach of warranty, it was necessary also to treat the statement of the auctioneer as a warranty in which case it was possible to take the view that the statement was not incorporated into the original contract but was a collateral contract. This conclusion could be reached by bearing in mind the initial silence which greeted the entry of the animal into the ring; and the fact that the bidding only began when the statement had been made suggested that the defendants were not contracting on the auction particulars but on the auctioneer's statement. (*per* Evershed, M.R.)

(*b*) Denning, L.J., proceeded on the assumption that the statement was a warranty and held that, even so, the exemption clause did not exclude it because 'the party who is liable in law cannot escape liability by simply putting up a printed notice or using a printed catalogue containing exempting conditions. He must go further and show affirmatively that it is a contractual document and accepted as such by the party affected'.

(268) *Behn* v. *Burness* (1863), 3 B. & S. 751

A ship, the *Martaban*, was chartered to carry coal from Newport to Hong Kong. The charter party described the ship as 'now in the port of Amsterdam' whereas in fact the ship was at Niewdiep about 62 miles from Amsterdam. She was late in arriving at Newport and the charterers refused to load her. *Held*—The charterers were justified in repudiating the contract. In a charter party the situation of the ship when the charter was made was a term of great commercial importance and must be treated as a condition.

(269) *L. Schuler A.G.* v. *Wickham Machine Tool Sales*, [1973] 2 All E.R. 39

Schuler, a German company, entered into a contract with Wickham, an English company, giving Wickham the sole rights to sell Schuler's panel presses in England. Clause 7(b) provided that 'it shall be a condition of this agreement' that Wickham's representatives should visit six named firms each week to solicit orders. Wickham's representatives failed on a few occasions to do so. Schuler claimed to be entitled to repudiate the agreement on the basis that a single failure was a breach of condition, giving them an absolute right to treat the contract as at an end. *Held*—by the House of Lords—that such a breach did not entitle Schuler to repudiate, since such a construction of the clause was so unreasonable that the parties could not have intended it. Furthermore, in construing a contract, whether to resolve an ambiguity or for any other purpose, a court is not entitled to take into account the conduct of the parties subsequent to the execution of the contract as throwing light on the meaning to be given to it.

(270) *Cehave NV* v. *Bremer Handelsgesellschaft, mbH*, [1975] 3 All E.R. 739

The defendants sold citrus pulp pellets to the plaintiffs. A term of the contract was 'shipment to be made in good condition'. The goods were not delivered all at once but in consignments, and when a particular consignment arrived at Rotterdam the market price of the goods had fallen and it was found that 1260 tons of the goods out of a total consignment of 3293 tons was damaged. The plaintiffs rejected the whole cargo on the grounds that the shipment was not made in good condition. They then claimed the recovery of the price which amounted to £100,000. In the event, a middle man bought the goods at the price of £33,720 and resold them to the plaintiffs at the same price. The plaintiffs then used the pellets for making cattle food as was the original intention. The total result of the transaction, if it had been left that way, was that the plaintiffs had received goods which they had bought for £100,000 for the reduced price of £33,720. The Court of Appeal decided in favour of the sellers. The court *held* that the contractual term 'shipment to be made in good condition' was not a condition within the meaning of the Sale of Goods Act, 1893, but was an intermediate term. As Lord Denning, M.R. said: 'If a small portion of the whole cargo was not in good condition and arrived a little unsound, it should be met by a price allowance. The buyers should not have the right to reject the whole cargo unless it was serious or substantial.'

Lord Denning also rejected the view that the goods were not of merchantable quality simply because they were not perfect in every way. He said that the definition contained in Sect. 7(2) of the Supply of Goods (Implied Terms) Act, 1973, was to be preferred because it was more flexible than some of the earlier judicial decisions on previous legislation.

In fact the definition delegates to the court the task of deciding what is merchantable in the circumstances of each particular case.

(271) *Heron Garage Properties Ltd* v. *Moss*, [1974] 1 All E.R. 421

Moss contracted to sell part of his land to Heron Garage Properties. Heron wanted to develop the property, and the contract was therefore made conditional upon Heron obtaining detailed planning permission. The contract further stipulated that if permission was not forthcoming within a six-month period either Moss or Heron might serve notice determining the contract. Shortly before the sixth-month period expired Heron wrote to Moss purporting to waive the benefit of these terms of the contract. Shortly after the expiry of the six-month period (no planning permission having been received) Moss gave notice purporting to determine the contract according to its terms. Heron now sued for specific performance. *Held*—by Brightman, J.—that since the planning permission was expressed to be a condition fundamental to the enforceability of the agreement as a whole, it could not be waived by Heron unilaterally. Heron could not show that the stipulation was exclusively for their benefit and therefore had no right to waive it without the consent of Mr Moss. The obtaining of planning permission was not expressed as a condition which was precedent only to the liability of the plaintiffs' as purchasers but was expressed to confer rights on both parties. The action was dismissed.

(272) *Hutton* v. *Warren* (1836), 150 E.R. 517

The plaintiff was the tenant of a farm and the defendant the landlord. At Michaelmas, 1833, the defendant gave the plaintiff notice to quit on the Lady Day following. The defendant insisted that the plaintiff should cultivate the land during the period of notice which he did. The plaintiff now asked for a fair allowance for seeds and labour of which he had no benefit having left the farm before harvest. It was proved that by custom a tenant was bound to farm for the whole of his tenancy and on quitting was entitled to a fair allowance for seeds and labour. *Held*—the plaintiff succeeded.

> We are of opinion that this custom was, by implication, imported into the lease. It has long been settled, that, in commercial transactions, extrinsic evidence of custom and usage is admissible to annex incidents to written contracts, in matters with respect to which they are silent. The same rule has also been applied to contracts in other transactions of life, in which known usages have been established and prevailed; and this has been done upon the principle of presumption that, in such transactions, the parties did not mean to express in writing the whole of the contract by which they intended to be bound, but to contract with reference to those known usages. (*Per* Parke, B.)

(273) *Rowland* v. *Divall*, [1923] 2 K.B. 500

In April, 1922, the defendant bought an 'Albert' motor car from a man who had stolen it from the true owner. One month later the plaintiff, a dealer, purchased the car from the defendant for £334, repainted it, and sold it for £400 to Colonel Railsdon. In September, 1922, the police seized the car from Colonel Railsdon and the plaintiff repaid him the £400. The plaintiff now sued the defendant for £334 on the grounds that there had been a total failure of consideration since the plaintiff had not obtained a title to the car. *Held*—The defendant was in breach of Sect. 12 of the Sale of Goods Act, 1893, which implies conditions and warranties into a sale of goods relating to the seller's right to sell, and there had been a total failure of consideration in spite of the fact that the car had been used by the plaintiff and his purchaser. The plaintiff contracted for the property in the car and not the mere right to possess it. Since he had not obtained the property, he was entitled to recover the sum of £334 and no deductions should be made for the period of user.

(*Note:* (i) although the court purported to deal with this case as a breach of Sect. 12(1) of the Act, it would appear that in fact they operated on common law principles and gave complete restitution of the purchase price because of total failure of consideration arising out of the seller's lack of title. The condition under Sect. 12(1) had by reason of the plaintiff's use of the car and the passage of time become a warranty when the action was brought and if the court had been awarding damages for breach of warranty it would have had to reduce the sum of £334 by a sum representing the value to the plaintiff of the use of the vehicle which he had had. (ii) The Law Reform Committee (1966 Cmnd 2958 para. 36) recommends that subject to further study of the law relating to restitution, an allowance in respect of use and enjoyment should be deducted from the purchase price and the balance returned to the plaintiff.)

(274) *Microbeads A.C.* v. *Vinhurst Road Markings*, [1975] 1 All E.R. 529

In this case A sold road marking machines to B. After the sale C obtained a patent on the machine so that their continued use by B was in breach of that patent and C was bringing an action against B in respect of this. In a claim by A against B for the purchase price, B wished to include in their defence breach of Sect. 12(2) of the Sale of Goods Act, 1893, which deals with quiet possession. It was *held*—by the Court of Appeal—that Sect. 12(2) applied but there was no breach of Sect. 12(1) which deals with the right to sell. There had been no breach of Sect. 12(1) at the time of sale because A had the right to sell and had not infringed that sub-section, but since B's quiet possession had been disturbed after sale A was in breach of Sect. 12(2). Therefore when the case came to trial it would be right for B to raise the breach as a defence in an action for the price of the goods.

(*Note:* since the passing of the Supply of Goods (Implied Terms) Act,

1973, the provisions of old Sect. 12(2) are contained in new Sect. 12(1)(b).)

(275) *Beale* v. *Taylor*, [1967] 1 W.L.R. 1193

The defendant advertised a car for sale as being a 1961 Triumph Herald 1200 and he believed this description to be correct. The plaintiff answered the advertisement and later visited the defendant to inspect the car. During his inspection he noticed, on the rear of the car, a metal disc with the figure 1200 on it. The plaintiff purchased the car, paying the agreed price. However, he later discovered that the car was made up of the rear of a 1961 Triumph Herald 1200 welded to the front of an earlier Triumph Herald 948. The welding was unsatisfactory and the car was unroadworthy. *Held*—by the Court of Appeal—that the plaintiff's claim for damages for breach of the condition implied in the contract by Sect. 13 of the Sale of Goods Act, 1893 (i.e. sale by description) succeeded. The plaintiff had relied on the advertisement and on the metal disc on the rear and the sale was one by description even though the plaintiff had seen and inspected the vehicle.

(276) *Godley* v. *Perry*, [1960] 1 All E.R. 36

The first defendant, Perry, was a newsagent who also sold toys and in particular displayed plastic toy catapults in his window. The plaintiff, who was a boy aged six, bought one for 6d. While using it to fire a stone, the catapult broke, and the plaintiff was struck in the eye, either by a piece of the catapult or the stone, and as a result he lost his left eye. The chemist's report given in evidence was that the catapults were made from cheap material unsuitable for the purpose and likely to fracture, and that the moulding of the plastic was poor, the catapults containing internal voids. Perry had purchased the catapults from a wholesaler with whom he had dealt for some time, and this sale was by sample, the defendant's wife examining the sample catapult by pulling the elastic. The wholesaler's supplier was another wholesaler who had imported the catapults from Hong Kong. This sale was also by sample and the sample catapult was again tested by pulling the elastic. In this action the plaintiff alleged that the first defendant was in breach of the conditions implied by Sect. 14(1) (now 14(3)) (i.e. fitness for purpose) and (2) (i.e. merchantable quality) of the Sale of Goods Act. The first defendant brought in his supplier as third party, alleging against him a breach of the conditions implied by Sect. 15(2)(c) (i.e. sale by sample), and the third party brought in his supplier as fourth party, alleging breach of Sect. 15(2)(c) against him. *Held*—

(i) The first defendant was in breach of Sect. 14(1) (now 14(3)) and (2) because—

(*a*) The catapult was not reasonably fit for the purpose for which it was required. The plaintiff relied on the seller's skill or judgment, this being readily inferred where the customer was of tender years. (Sect. 14(1) (now 14(3)).)

(b) The catapult, even though sold over the counter, was bought by description and was not merchantable. (Sect. 14(2).)

(ii) The third and fourth parties were both in breach of Sect. 15(2)(c) because the catapult had a defect which rendered it unmerchantable, and this defect was not apparent on reasonable examination of the sample. The test applied, i.e. the pulling of the elastic, was all that could be expected of a potential purchaser. The third and fourth parties had done business before, and the third party was entitled to regard without suspicion any sample shown to him and to rely on the fourth party's skill in selecting his goods.

(277) *The Moorcock* (1889), 14 P.D. 64

The appellants in this case were in possession of a wharf and a jetty extending into the River Thames, and the respondent was the owner of the steamship *Moorcock*. In November, 1887, the appellants and the respondent agreed that the ship should be discharged and loaded at the wharf and for that purpose should be moored alongside the jetty. Both parties realized that when the tide was out the ship would rest on the river bed. In the event the *Moorcock* sustained damage when she ceased to be waterborne owing to the centre of the vessel settling on a ridge of hard ground beneath the mud. There was no evidence that the appellants had given any warranty that the place was safe for the ship to lie in, but it was *held*—by the Court of Appeal—that there was an implied warranty by the appellants to this effect, for breach of which they were liable in damages.

Now, an implied warranty, or, as it is called, a covenant in law, as distinguished from an express contract or express warranty, really is in all cases founded on the presumed intention of the parties, and upon reason. The implication which the law draws from what must obviously have been the intention of the parties, the law draws with the object of giving efficacy to the transaction and preventing such a failure of consideration as cannot have been within the contemplation of either side; and I believe if one were to take all the cases, and they are many, of implied warranties or covenants in law, it will be found that in all of them the law is raising an implication from the presumed intention of the parties with the object of giving to the transaction such efficacy as both parties must have intended that at all events it should have. In business transactions such as this, what the law desires to effect by the implication is to give such business efficacy to the transaction as must have been intended at all events by both parties who are business men; not to impose on one side all the perils of the transaction, or to emancipate one side from all the chances of failure, but to make each party promise in law as much, at all events, as it must have been in the contemplation of both parties that he should be responsible for in respect of those perils or chances.

(*Per* Bowen, L.J.)

(278) *Lister* v. *Romford Ice and Cold Storage Co. Ltd*, [1957] 1 All E.R. 125

The defendants' lorry driver negligently reversed the company's vehicle into another servant of the company (his father) who received damages from the company under the doctrine of vicarious liability. The defendants were insured against this liability and the insurance company paid the damages and, under the doctrine of subrogation, sued the lorry driver in the name of the company to recover what they had paid. It was unanimously *held* by the House of Lords that the lorry-driver, as a servant of the company, owed them a duty to perform his work with reasonable care and skill, and that a servant who involves his master in vicarious liability by reason of negligence is liable in damages to the master for breach of contract. This liability arises out of an implied term in the contract of service to indemnify the master for loss caused to him by the servant's negligence. The damages will in such a case amount to a complete indemnity in respect of the amount which the employer has been held vicariously liable to pay the injured plaintiff.

(*Note:* although this case is an illustration of a judicial implied term, it should be noted that employers are not likely in ordinary circumstances to be required by their insurers to bring an action to enforce their right to an indemnity which was the position in *Lister's* case. A committee was set up to deal with the implications of the *Lister* case. As an outcome of its report all members of the British Insurance Association entered into an agreement to the effect that they would not enforce their rights of subrogation in an employer's liability policy, except where there was evidence of collusion or willful misconduct on the part of the employee. A number of other insurance organizations have also entered into similar agreements.)

(279) *Trollope & Colls Ltd* v. *North West Metropolitan Regional Hospital Board*, [1973] 2 All E.R. 260

The plaintiffs agreed to do some work for the defendants in three stages. The work on stage one was to be completed by April, 1969, subject to extensions caused by certain events. Work on stage three was to begin six months after stage one had been completed and was to be completed by April, 1972. There was the same provision for extending the completion date of stage three, but these events did not include any delay in the completion of stage one. Completion of stage one was delayed (mainly by events which under the terms of the contract, allowed for an extension of the completion date of stage one) and was not completed until June, 1970. Thus the plaintiffs were due to begin work on stage three in December. The House of Lords was asked by what date the plaintiffs were contractually bound to finish stage three. *Held*—that the plaintiffs were bound to complete by April, 1972. The contract expressly provided for what events would permit an extension to the completion date of stage three and these did not include any delay in the completion of stage one. A term could not be implied for allowing an extension of time in respect of such delays. 'The court will not ... improve the contract which the parties have made, however desirable the improvement might be. ... If the express terms are perfectly clear and free from ambiguity, there is no choice to be made between different possible meanings: the clear terms must be applied. ...' (per Lord Pearson at p. 267.)

(280) *L'Estrange* v. *Graucob (F.)*, [1934] 2 K.B. 394

The defendant sold to the plaintiff a slot machine, inserting in the order form the following clause: 'Any express or implied condition, statement or warranty, statutory or otherwise, is hereby excluded.' The plaintiff signed the order form but did not read the relevant clause, and she now sued in respect of the unsatisfactory nature of the machine supplied. *Held*—The clause was binding on her, although the defendants made no attempt to read the document to her nor call her attention to the clause.

(281) *Chapelton* v. *Barry Urban District Council*, [1940] 1 K.B. 532

The plaintiff Chapelton wished to hire deck chairs and went to a pile owned by the defendants, behind which was a notice stating: 'Hire of chairs 2d. per session of three hours.' The plaintiff took two chairs, paid for them, and received two tickets which he put into his pocket after merely glancing at them. One of the chairs collapsed and he was injured. A notice on the back of the ticket provided that 'The council will not be liable for any accident or damage arising from hire of chairs.' The plaintiff sued for damages and the council sought to rely on the clause in the ticket. *Held*—The clause was not binding on Chapelton. The board by the chairs made no attempt to limit the liability, and it was unreasonable to communicate conditions by means of a mere receipt.

(282) *Thompson* v. *L.M.S. Railway*, [1930] 1 K.B. 41

Thompson, who could not read, asked her niece to buy her an excursion ticket, on the front of which were printed the words, 'Excursion. For conditions see back.' On the back was a notice to the effect that the ticket was issued subject to the conditions in the company's timetables, which excluded liability for injury however caused. Thompson was injured and claimed damages. *Held*—Her action failed. She had constructive notice of the conditions which had, in the court's view, been properly communicated to the ordinary passenger.

(*Note:* the Transport Act, 1962, Sect. 43(7), provides that the British Railways Board as it is now called shall not carry passengers by rail on conditions which purport directly or indirectly to exclude the Board's liability in respect of death or bodily injury to passengers other than passengers travelling on a free pass. On its own facts, therefore, the above case is of historical interest only, though it is still relevant on the question of constructive notice.) (See now Unfair Contract Terms Act, 1977.)

283 *Richardson Steamship Company Ltd* v. *Rowntree*, [1894] A.C. 217

Rowntree booked a passage on the appellants' ship travelling from Philadelphia to Liverpool. The ticket was folded so that no writing was visible until it was opened. A clause printed on the ticket limited the appellants' liability for injury or damage to passengers or their luggage to $100. The clause was printed in rather small type and was rendered less obvious by a red ink stamp on the ticket. *Held*—Rowntree was not bound by the clause as she did not know of its existence, and there was no constructive notice because the shipowner had not given reasonable notice of the condition.

(284) *McCutcheon* v. *David MacBrayne*, [1964] 1 All E.R. 430

McCutcheon wished to have his motor car transported from Islay to the Scottish mainland, and McCutcheon's agent made a contract of carriage on behalf of McCutcheon with the respondent company. The ship sank owing to the respondents' negligent navigation and the appellant sued for damages. The respondents contended that they were not liable because of certain exemption clauses displayed on a notice in the booking office and also contained in a 'risk note' which was normally given to each customer, though one was not given to the appellant's agent in this case. However, on previous occasions when the parties had done business, 'risk notes' containing exemptions had sometimes been given either to the appellant or his agent. The appellant and his agent knew that some conditions were attached to the respondents' contracts, but did not know specifically what they were. *Held*—by the House of Lords—allowing the appellant's appeal, that since this was an oral contract, the conditions relied on were not incorporated into it so as to exempt the respondents from liability in negligence. Lord Devlin was of opinion that previous dealings are relevant only if they prove actual and not constructive knowledge of the terms and also prove assent to them.

(285) *Hollier* v. *Rambler Motors Ltd*, [1972] 1 All E.R. 399

Mr Hollier had telephoned Rambler Motors and asked if they would repair his car at their garage. The garage manager agreed, if Mr Hollier had it towed to the garage. While in the garage the car was damaged by a fire which started as a result of the garage's negligence, and Mr Hollier claimed damages from the proprietors, Rambler Motors. On three or four occasions in the previous five years Mr Hollier had had repairs carried out at the garage and on each of these occasions had signed a form which under the place for the signature stated 'the company is not responsible for damage caused by fires to customers' cars on the premises'. In the action brought by Mr Hollier claiming damages for negligence, Rambler Motors contended that although Mr Hollier had not signed the form on this occasions, the exemption clause, as set out on the form, had been incorporated into the unwritten contract between them by a 'course of dealing', and that the effect was to exclude liability for negligently causing a fire while Mr Hollier's car was in their garage. The Court of Appeal refused to accept this argument and *held* that Rambler Motors were liable to Mr Hollier for their negligence. They had not established a 'course of dealing' and so the clause set out in the printed form which had been the basis of their earlier dealings, was not incorporated into the oral contract which had been made over the telephone. Salmon, L.J. went on to say that in order to establish that a term has been implied into a contract by a course of dealing, it is necessary to show that the party concerned had actual and not merely constructive knowledge of the term, and with such actual knowledge he had in fact assented to it. Furthermore, the Court of Appeal took the view that even if the clause had been incorporated its wording was not sufficiently plain to exclude liability for negligence.

(286) *British Crane Hire Corporation* v. *Ipswich Plant Hire*, [1974] 1 All E.R. 1059

The plaintiff and defendant were both engaged in the business of hiring out earth moving equipment. The defendants were also involved in drainage work on marshy ground and urgently requiring a crane, agreed to hire such a crane from the plaintiffs, terms of payment being agreed but no mention being made of the plaintiffs conditions of hire. The plaintiffs sent the defendants a copy of such conditions which provided, *inter alia*, that the hirer would be responsible for all expenses arising out of the crane's use. Before the defendant signed the form containing the conditions the crane sank into a marsh through no fault of the defendants and the plaintiffs claimed from the defendants the cost of recovering the crane. *Held*—by the Court of Appeal allowing the plaintiffs' claim—that the plaintiffs conditions of hire applied since both parties were in the trade and of equal bargaining power and on the evidence the defendants and the plaintiffs both understood that the plaintiffs conditions of hire would apply.

(287) *Olley* v. *Marlborough Court Ltd*, [1949] 1 K.B. 532

Husband and wife arrived at an hotel as guests and paid for a room in advance. They went up to the room allotted to them; on one of the walls was the following notice: 'The proprietors will not hold themselves responsible for articles lost or stolen unless handed to the manageress for safe custody.' The wife closed the self-locking door of the bedroom and took the key downstairs to the reception desk. A third party took the key and stole certain of the wife's furs. In the ensuing action the defendants sought to rely on the notice as a term of contract. *Held*—The contract was completed at the reception desk and no subsequent notice could affect the plaintiff's rights.

(*Note:* it was said in *Spurling* v. *Bradshaw*, [1956] 1 W.L.R. 461, that if the husband and wife had seen the notice on a previous visit to the hotel it would have been binding on them, though this is by no means certain in view of cases such as *Hollier*[285] which suggest that in consumer transactions previous dealings are not incorporated.)

(288) *Thornton* v. *Shoe Lane Parking Ltd*, [1971] 1 All E.R. 686

The plaintiff suffered physical injuries when taking his car out of a multi-storey car park and sued the proprietors for these injuries. They claimed that they were not liable by reason of an exclusion clause on a ticket issued to the plaintiff. The sequence of relevant events was as follows—

(*a*) The plaintiff drove up to the automatic barrier where there was a notice saying 'All cars parked at owner's risk.' This did not cover physical injury. Most people would think it referred to the car or its contents.

(*b*) An automatic device issued a ticket at the barrier. This referred to further conditions which were displayed inside the premises. These conditions exempted the defendants from a number of possible liabilities including physical injury. The plaintiff did not read these and had not used the park before.

Held—by the Court of Appeal—the terms of the offer were those contained in the notice at the ticket machine. The plaintiff was not bound by the conditions inside the premises to which the ticket referred because the ticket came too late in the transaction to incorporate them.

(289) *The New Zealand Shipping Co. Ltd* v. *A. M. Satterthwaite & Co. Ltd*, [1974] 1 All E.R. 1015

In this case the makers of an expensive drilling machine entered into a contract for the carriage of the machine by sea to New Zealand. The contract of carriage (the bill of lading) exempted the carriers from full liability for any loss or damage to the machine during carriage and also purported to exempt any servant or agent of the carrier, including independent contractors employed from time to time by the carrier. The machine was damaged by the defendants, who were stevedores, in the course of unloading, and the question to be decided was whether the defendant stevedores, who had been employed by the carrier to unload the machine, could take advantage of the exemption clause in the bill of lading since they were not parties to the contract. It was decided by the Privy Council that they could. The stevedores provided consideration and so became parties to the contract when they actually unloaded the machine. (*Carlill* v. *Carbolic Smoke Ball Co.*, 1893[67] applied.) The performance of services by the stevedores in discharging the cargo was sufficient consideration to constitute a contract, even though they were already under an obligation to the carrier to perform those services because the actual performance of an outstanding contractual obligation was sufficient to support the promise of an exemption from liability given by the makers of the drill, i.e. the shippers, who were, in effect, third parties to the contract between the carrier and the stevedores. (*Shadwell* v. *Shadwell*, 1860[141] applied.)

(290) *Burnett* v. *British Waterways Board*, [1973] 1 W.L.R. 700

Burnett was a lighterman working on his employer's barge. Due to the defendants' negligence a capstan rope parted while the barge was docking, injuring Burnett. At the dock office was a notice stating that persons availed themselves of the dock facilities at their own risk. Burnett had read the notice when he was a young apprentice. The defendants admitted negligence but claimed that Burnett had voluntarily undertaken the risk of injury. *Held*—by the Court of Appeal—that Burnett was an employee sent by his employer and it could not be said that he had freely and voluntarily incurred the risk of negligence on the part of the defendant. In the course of his judgment Lord Denning, M.R. said: 'If there was a contract with Mr Burnett, of course, the Board could rely upon it. But there was no contract with him. He was just one of the men working on the barges. The contract was with the barge owners. . . .'

(*Note:* if the defence of *volenti* succeeds then of course the plaintiff's claim fails.)

(291) *Akerib* v. *Booth*, [1961] 1 All E.R. 380

The defendants were the owners of premises where they carried on business as packers and forwarders of goods. They made a contract with the plaintiff under which they agreed to pack the plaintiff's goods and also to lease to him six rooms in the premises to be used partly as an office and partly as a store by the plaintiff. Because of the defendants' negligence water escaped from a cistern on the top floor of the premises, and this damaged the plaintiff's goods and some office material in the rooms which he was leasing. The plaintiff sued for damages, and the defendants pleaded a paragraph in the schedule to the contract which said that the defendants were not in any circumstances to be responsible for damage caused by water to any goods whether in the possession of the defendants or not. The Court was concerned to decide the meaning and scope of these words. Taken as they stood and read in isolation, the words applied to all goods without any restriction. However, the plaintiff argued that if the words were read in the context of the whole contract, the *main* purpose of which was to cover the defendants in the process of packing, the words must be confined to goods which had been handed over to the defendants for this purpose. The Court of Appeal *held* that either interpretation was possible. However, since the words were ambiguous they must be construed against the defendants who had drafted the contract and put the term into it. The immunity must, therefore, be confined to goods handed over to the defendants for packing, and the plaintiff succeeded.

(*Note:* this is really an aspect of the *contra proferentem* rule which construes all ambiguous statements in written contracts against the draftsman and in favour of the other party.)

(292) *Pollock & Co.* v. *Macrae*, [1922] S.C. (H.L.) 192

The defendants entered into a contract to build and supply marine engines. The contract carried an exemption clause which was designed to protect the defendant from liability for defective materials and workmanship. The engines supplied under the contract had a great many defects and could not be used. *Held*—by the House of Lords—that on a true construction of the contract the exemption clause did not apply because it was repugnant to the main purpose of the contract. Lord Dunedin said: 'Now, when there is such a congeries of defects as to destroy the workable character of the machine I think this amounts to a total breach of contract, and that each defect cannot be taken by itself separately so as to apply the provisions of the conditions of guarantee and make it impossible to claim damages.'

(293) *Mendelssohn* v. *Normand Ltd*, [1969] 2 All E.R. 1215

The plaintiff left his car in the defendants' garage as he had done before. He was about to lock it as he had done on previous occasions when the attendant said that he could not do so. The plaintiff explained that there was a suitcase containing jewellery on the back seat and the attendant agreed to lock the car when he had moved it. He gave the plaintiff a ticket on the back of which was printed a statement that the proprietors would not 'accept responsibility for any loss sustained . . . no variation of these conditions will bind the (proprietors) unless made in writing signed by their duly authorized manager'. A conspicuous written notice at the reception desk exempted the defendants from loss or damage to the vehicle or its contents. When he returned the plaintiff found the car unlocked and the key in the ignition. It was later discovered that the suitcase had been stolen while the car was in the defendants' garage. In an action by the plaintiff for damages it was held—by the Court of Appeal—that

(*a*) The notice at the reception desk was of no effect. It was not seen by a driver until he came to collect his car. The plaintiff had seen it before but had not read it.

(*b*) The plaintiff must be taken to have agreed to the conditions on the ticket which were incorporated in the contract; but

(*c*) the defendants could not rely upon the ticket because—

(i) the attendant had ostensible authority to promise to lock the car and thus to see that the contents were safe. This promise was repugnant to and took priority over the printed condition; and

(ii) the defendants had through their employee agreed to keep the car locked and left it unlocked so performing the contract in an entirely different way from the manner agreed. The defendants were therefore liable.

(294) *J. Evans & Son (Portsmouth) Ltd* v. *Andrea Merzario Ltd*, [1976] 2 All E.R. 930

The plaintiffs imported machines from Italy. They had contracted with the defendants since about 1959 for the transport of these machines. Before the defendants went over to the use of containers the plaintiffs' machines had always been crated and carried under deck. When the defendants went over to containers they orally agreed with the plaintiffs that the plaintiffs' goods would still be carried under deck. However, on a particular occasion a machine being transported for the plaintiffs was carried in a container on deck. At the start of the voyage the ship met a swell which caused the container to fall off the deck and the machine was lost. The contract was expressed to be subject to the printed standard conditions of the forwarding trade which contained an exemption clause excusing the defendants from liability for loss or damage to the goods unless the damage occurred whilst the goods were in their actual custody and by reason of their wilful neglect or default, and even in those circumstances, the clause limited the defendants' liability for loss or damage to a fixed amount. The plaintiffs claimed damages against the defendants for loss of the machine alleging that the exemption clause did not apply. It was *held* by the Court of Appeal that it did not apply. The printed conditions were repugnant to the oral promise for, if they were applicable, they would render that promise illusory. Accordingly, the oral promise was to be treated as over-riding the printed conditions and the plaintiffs' claim succeeded, the exemption clause being inapplicable.

(295) *Thomas National Transport (Melbourne) Pty Ltd and Pay* v. *May and Baker (Australia) Pty Ltd*, [1966] 2 Lloyd's Rep. 347

The owners of certain packages made a contract with carriers under which the packages were to be carried from Melbourne to various places in Australia. The carriers employed a sub-contractor to collect the parcels and take them to the carriers' depot in Melbourne. When the sub-contractor arrived at the Melbourne depot it was locked and so he drove the lorry full of packages to his own house and left it in a garage there. There was a fire and some of the packages were destroyed. The owners sued the carriers who pleaded an exemption clause in the contract of carriage. *Held*—by the High Court of Australia—that the plaintiffs succeeded. There had been a fundamental breach of contract. The intention of the parties was that the goods would be taken to the carriers' depot and not to the sub-contractors' house, in which case the carriers could not rely on the clause. The decision in the *Suisse Case*[298] was applied.

(296) *Karsales (Harrow) Ltd* v. *Wallis*, [1956] 2 All E.R. 866

The defendant inspected a Buick car which a Mr Stanton wished to sell him. The defendant found it to be in excellent condition and agreed to pay £600 for it, effecting the purchase through a finance company. The car was badly damaged before it was delivered to Wallis; the new tyres which were on the car when Wallis saw it had been replaced by old ones; the radio had been removed; the cylinder head was off; all the valves were burnt; and the engine had two broken pistons. Wallis would not agree to take delivery of the car but it was towed to his place of business and left there. The finance company originally involved assigned its rights under the agreement with Wallis to Karsales, and in this action Karsales were trying to recover the instalments due under the agreement. In so doing they relied on the following clause in the agreement assigned to them: 'No condition or warranty that the vehicle is roadworthy, or as to its age condition or fitness for any purpose, is given by the owner or implied herein.' The county court judge decided that the exemption clause was effective and ordered Wallis to pay. Wallis now appealed. The Court of Appeal held that Wallis was not liable because exemption clauses, no matter how widely expressed, only avail the party who includes them when he is carrying out his contract in its essential respects. Here there was a breach of a fundamental term amounting to non-performance. As Birkett, L.J., said: 'A car that will not go is not a car at all.'

(297) *Alexander* v. *Railway Executive*, [1951] 2 All E.R. 422

Alexander was a magician who had been on a tour together with an assistant. He left three trunks at the parcels office at Launceston station, the trunks containing various properties which were used in an 'escape illusion'. The plaintiff paid 5d. for each trunk deposited and received a ticket for each one. He then left saying that he would send instructions for their dispatch. Some weeks after the deposit and before the plaintiff had sent instructions for the dispatch of the trunks, the plaintiff's assistant persuaded the clerk in the parcels office to give him access to the trunks, though he was not in possession of the ticket. The assistant took away several of the properties and was later convicted of larceny. The plaintiff sued the defendants for damages for breach of contract, and the defendants pleaded the following term which was contained in the ticket and which stated that the Railway Executive was 'not liable for loss misdelivery or damage to any articles where the value was in excess of £5 unless at the time of the deposit the true value and nature of the goods was declared by the depositor and an extra charge paid'. No such declaration or payment had been made. *Held*—The plaintiff succeeded because, although sufficient notice had been given constructively to the plaintiff of the term, the term did not protect the defendants because they were guilty of a breach of a fundamental obligation in allowing the trunks to be opened and things to be removed from them by an unauthorized person.

(Note: Devlin, J., said that a deliberate delivery to the wrong person did not fall within the meaning of 'misdelivery', and this may be regarded as the real reason for the decision, as it involves the application of the *contra proferentem* rule.)

(298) *Suisse Atlantique Société D'Armament Maritime S.A.* v. *N.V. Rotterdamsche Kolen Centrale*, [1966] 2 All E.R. 61

The plaintiffs were shipowners and the defendants chartered a ship from them for 'two years' continuous voyages'. Under the contract, demurrage of $1000 per day had to be paid by the charterers to the owners if the ship was detained in port longer than the loading time permitted and specified by the contract. There were substantial delays and the demurrage was paid, but the shipowner's loss of freight was greater than the demurrage they had received and they claimed general damages over and above the demurrage. It was suggested for the owners that the delay was deliberate and enabled them to regard the contract as *repudiated* so that the demurrage provisions did not apply and they could recover their full loss. The owners further argued that because of the cases relating to fundamental breach and exemption clauses the demurrage clause could not cover a breach as serious as this. The House of Lords, after consideration of the fundamental breach cases, *Held*—that—

(*a*) a fundamental breach no longer automatically nullifies an exemption clause. The matter is one of construction of the contract.

(*b*) The demurrage clause was not so much an exemption clause as a provision for liquidated damages, but was wide enough to cover the breaches complained of.

(*c*) Even if the charterer's conduct had given the owners the right to treat the contract as repudiated, they had not done so and the contract including the demurrage clause remained in force.

(299) *Harbutt's Plasticine Ltd* v. *Wayne Tank and Pump Co. Ltd*, [1970] 1 All E.R. 225

In 1961 the defendants agreed to install certain equipment in the plaintiff's factory for the purpose of storing, heating and dispensing wax for certain manufacturing processes. A clause of the contract provided that until the installation was taken over by the plaintiff the defendant would indemnify the plaintiff for any damage caused by the negligence of the defendant's servants, but that the total liability should not exceed £2330. Owing to the negligent switching on of the machine by the defendant's servants it became overheated, caught fire and destroyed the factory. *Held*—

(i) The defendants were liable for the full amount of loss (£146,581). There had been a fundamental breach of the contract and in the circumstances the exclusion clause limiting the damage to £2330 did not apply.

(ii) In order to determine whether a breach of contract was fundamental not only the breach itself but also the events resulting from the breach must be considered. In this case the breaches by the defendants and the consequences of them were so fundamental as to bring the contract to an end.

(iii) Where the defendant had been guilty of such a fundamental breach that the contract was automatically at an end so that the innocent party had no chance of an election whether to continue or not the guilty party could not rely on an exclusion or limitation clause when sued for damages for breach.

(iv) Where the innocent party with knowledge of a fundamental breach can and does treat the contract as continuing and sues for damages, the application of an exclusion clause exempting the defendant from liability depends upon the relevant rules of construction of contracts.

(v) The proper measure of damages was the cost of building a new factory, even though the new factory was in many ways better than the old one. However, the money received by the plaintiffs from their insurance company should go in relief of the damages paid by the defendants and reduce them by the relevant amount.

(300) *Farnworth Finance Facilities Ltd* v. *Attryde*, [1970] 2 All E.R. 774

Mr Attryde bought a motor-cycle on hire purchase. The contract which was not covered by the Hire Purchase Acts contained a clause to the effect that the vehicle was supplied 'subject to no conditions or warranties whatsoever express or implied'. The machine had many faults and although Mr Attryde always complained about them he did drive the machine for some 4000 miles before deciding to repudiate the contract. He was then sued by the finance company who claimed that the exemption clause applied to exclude liability for defects. *Held*—by the Court of Appeal—that it did not. There was a rule of construction which provided that in general terms an exclusion clause was not effective to exclude a fundamental breach which was what had occurred in this case. The defects taken together amounted to a fundamental breach. Mr Attryde had not affirmed the contract by using the machine. He had always complained about the defects and had indicated that he would only finally accept the machine if they were remedied. It should be noted that Lord Denning appears in his judgment to have tried to square the decision with both *Harbutt*[299] and *Suisse*[298] as follows—

We have in this case to apply the principles about fundamental breach, which were recently considered by this court in *Harbutt's Plasticine Ltd* v. *Wayne Tank and Pump Co. Ltd*. The first thing to do, is, no doubt, to construe the contract, remembering always the proposition of Pearson, L.J., which was approved by the House of Lords in *Suisse Atlantique Société d'Armament Maritime S.A.* v. *N.V. Rotterdamsche Kolen Centrale*: '. . . there is a rule of construction that normally an exception or exclusion clause or similar provision in a contract should be construed as not applying to a situation created by a fundamental breach of contract.' That rule of construction applies here. It means that we must see if there was a fundamental breach of contract. If there was, then the exempting condition should not be construed as applying to it. We look, therefore, to the terms of the contract, express or implied (apart from the exception clauses) and see which of them were broken. If they were broken in a fundamental respect, the finance company cannot rely on the exception clauses. (See also *Kenyon etc*. v. *Baxter Hoare Ltd*, 1971.[301])

(301) *Kenyon, Son and Craven Ltd* v. *Baxter Hoare & Co. Ltd*, [1971] 2 All E.R. 708

The defendants stored nuts for the plaintiffs. The contract included an exception clause under which the defendants were not liable for loss or damage unless due to their 'wilful neglect'. The nuts were seriously damaged by rats. The defendants' servant had made some effort to control the rats but had not, through ignorance, used appropriate measures. The plaintiffs sued for breach of the contract of bailment. *Held*—the defendants neglect could not be said to be 'wilful'. They were not, therefore, guilty of a fundamental breach and could rely on the exception clause (*Suisse Case* applied).[298] The plaintiff's claim failed.

(302) *Wathes (Western)* v. *Austins (Menswear) Ltd*, [1976] 1 Lloyds Rep. 14

The plaintiffs' contract to supply and install an air conditioning plant for the defendants contained a clause exempting the plaintiffs from all consequential liabilities. When the plant was installed the defendants found that they could not use it without the excessive noise of the external condensing unit creating a nuisance to their neighbours and proceedings were threatened. The plaintiffs offered to fit a screen to reduce the noise but this was rejected by Austins since it was conditional on this being the full extent of the plaintiffs' liability, whether effective or not, and on the defendants paying the contract price. The defendants continued to use the plant and eventually themselves took steps to prevent the nuisance. The plaintiffs brought this action for the price of the installation and the defendants counter-claimed for damages. It was *held* that the plaintiffs were guilty of a fundamental breach of contract and in their action for the price could not rely on the exemption clause in answer to the defendants' counterclaim for damages. The Court of Appeal stressed that an exclusion clause is not readily to be construed as exempting from liability for fundamental breach, and found that the clause in the contract relating to consequential loss or damage arising from any cause whatever did not on its true construction cover fundamental breach and even affirmation of the contract did not alter the matter.

(303) *Hunt and Winterbotham (West of England) Ltd* v. *B.R.S. (Parcels) Ltd*, [1962] 1 All E.R. 111

The defendants entered into a contract with the plaintiffs under the terms of which the defendants were to carry 15 parcels of woollen goods to Manchester. In fact only 12 parcels arrived and the plaintiffs now sued for damages for the value of the three parcels lost. The defendants pleaded an exemption clause excluding their liability for loss 'however sustained'. The plaintiffs based their claim on negligence and did not plead breach of a fundamental obligation. There was no evidence as to how the parcels had been lost, the defendants being unable to offer an explanation. In view of this the Court of Appeal gave judgment for the defendants saying that if they were negligent, the exemption clause would protect them. The plaintiffs had not alleged breach of a fundamental obligation and had produced no evidence to suggest that the defendants were in breach of a fundamental obligation which would have been essential if such a breach were alleged.

(*Note:* it is not clear why carriage should be differentiated from other forms of bailment.)

(304) *Levison* v. *Patent Steam Carpet Cleaning Co. Ltd*, [1977] 3 W.L.R. 90

In this case the value of a Chinese carpet sent to cleaners and not returned by them was recovered by the owners in spite of limiting conditions on the cleaners' printed form. The Court of Appeal *held* that the defendants' conditions of sale that 'all merchandise is expressly accepted at the owner's risk' were adequate to exclude liability for negligence but were not sufficiently clear or strong to exclude liability for fundamental breach. In addition, the burden was upon the defendants as bailees to show that the loss was due to negligence and not to some other cause and that as on the evidence they had failed to discharge such burden they could not rely upon the exemption clause. In his judgment Lord Denning, M.R., said that the Court should not give effect to an unreasonable exclusion clause and in particular exclusion of liability for fundamental breach should not be permitted where the party relying thereon enjoys superior bargaining power.

(305) *Dawsons Ltd* v. *Bonnin*, [1922] 2 A.C. 413

Dawsons Ltd insured their motor lorry against loss by fire with Bonnin and others, and signed a proposal form which contained the following as Condition 4: 'Material misstatement or concealment of any circumstance by the insured material to assessing the premium herein, or in connection with any claim, shall render the policy void.' The policy also contained a clause saying that the 'proposal shall be the basis of the contract and shall be held as incorporated therein'. Actually the proposal form was filled up by an insurance agent, and although he stated the proposer's address correctly as 46 Cadogan Street, Glasgow, he also stated that the vehicle would usually be garaged there, although there was no garage accommodation in the Cadogan Street address and the lorry was garaged elsewhere. Dawsons' secretary , who signed the proposal, overlooked this slip made by the agent. The lorry was destroyed by fire and Dawsons claimed under the policy. *Held*—on appeal, by the House of Lords—The statement was not material within the meaning of Condition 4. However, the basis clause was an independent provision, and since the statement, though not material, was untrue, the policy was void. Viscount Cave said: 'The meaning and effect of the basis clause, taken by itself, is that any untrue statement in the proposal, or any breach of its promissory clauses, shall avoid the policy, and if that be the contract of the parties, the question of materiality has not to be considered.'

(306) *Gordon* v. *Gordon*, (1819) 3 Swan. 400

Two brothers made an agreement for division of the family estates. The elder supposed he was born before the marriage of his parents and was therefore illegitimate. The younger knew that their parents had been married before the birth of the elder brother and the elder brother was therefore legitimate and his father's heir. He did not communicate this information to his elder brother; 19 years afterwards the elder brother discovered that he was legitimate and the agreement was set aside at his suit. He would have had no case if at the time of the agreement both brothers had been in honest error as to the date of their parents' marriage.

(307) *Welch* v. *Cheesman*, (1974) 229 Estates Gazette 99

Mrs Welch lived with Cheesman for many years in a house which she owned. Cheesman was a man given to violence and after threats from him Mrs Welch transferred her house to him for £300. Cheesman then died and his widow claimed the house which was worth about £3000. Mrs Welch sought to set aside the transfer on the grounds of duress and her claim succeeded.

(308) *Cumming* v. *Ince* (1847), 11 Q.B. 112

An old lady was induced to settle property on one of her relatives by the threat of unlawful confinement in a private mental home. *Held*—The settlement could be set aside on the ground of duress, i.e. the threat of false imprisonment.

(309) *Williams* v. *Bailey* (1866), L.R. 1 H.L. 200

A father agreed to make a mortgage of property to a bank in consideration of the return by the bank of certain promissory notes forged by his son. The banker concerned had suggested in conversation with the father that the son would be prosecuted if some agreement were not reached. The promise to make the mortgage was held invalid because of undue influence which, though not presumed in this case, had been proved.

(310) *Allcard* v. *Skinner* (1887), 36 Ch.D. 145

In 1868 the plaintiff joined a Protestant institution called the sisterhood of St Mary at the Cross, promising to devote her property to the service of the poor. The defendant Miss Skinner was the Lady Superior of the Sisterhood. In 1871 the plaintiff ceased to be a novice and became a sister in the order, taking her vows of poverty, chastity and obedience. By this time she had left her home and was residing with the sisterhood. The plaintiff remained a sister until 1879 and, in compliance with the vow of poverty, she had by then given property to the value of about £7000 to the defendant. The plaintiff left the order in 1879 and became a Roman Catholic. Of the property she had transferred, £1671 remained in 1885 and the plaintiff sought to recover this sum, claiming that it had been transferred in circumstances of undue influence. *Held*—The gifts had been made under pressure of an unusually persuasive nature, particularly since the plaintiff was prevented from seeking outside advice under a rule of the sisterhood which said, 'Let no sister seek the advice of any extern without the superior's leave.' However, the plaintiff's claim was barred by her delay because, although the influence was removed in 1879, she did not bring her action until 1885.

(311) *Mustafa* v. *Hudaverdi* (1972) 223 Estates Gazette 1751

The plaintiff had signed a deed by which he renounced his beneficial interest in certain property. The plaintiff had a son aged eight by the daughter of the defendant. The plaintiff alleged that the defendant told him he could have the child if he signed the deed. *Held*—by Goff, J.—that the plaintiff had made out a case of undue influence against the defendant who was a patriarchal dominating figure. The plaintiff had reason to believe also that if he did not sign the deed he would see little of the child; the deed of renunciation would be cancelled and the plaintiff should have a declaration that he was entitled to a beneficial interest in the property and an account of the rents and profits.

(312) *Lancashire Loans Ltd* v. *Black*, [1934] 1 K.B. 380

A daughter married at eighteen and went to live with her husband. Her mother was an extravagant woman and was in debt to a firm of moneylenders. When the daughter became of age, her mother persuaded her to raise £2000 on property in which the daughter had an interest, and this was used to pay off the mother's debts. Twelve months later mother and daughter signed a joint and several promissory note of £775 at eighty-five per cent interest in favour of the moneylenders, and the daughter created a further charge on her property in order that the mother might borrow more money. The daughter did not understand the nature of the transaction, and the only advice she received was from a solicitor acting for the mother and the moneylenders. The moneylenders brought this action against the mother and daughter on the note. *Held*—The daughter's defence that she was under the undue influence of her mother succeeded, in spite of the fact that she was of full age and married with her own home.

(313) *Hodgson* v. *Marks*, [1970] 3 All E.R. 513

Mrs Hodgson, who was a widow of 83, owned a freehold house in which she lived. In 1959 she took in a Mr Evans as a lodger. She soon came to trust Evans and allowed him to manage her financial affairs. In June, 1960, she transferred the house to Evans, her sole reason for so doing being to prevent her nephew from turning Evans out of the house. It was orally agreed between Mrs Hodgson and Evans that the house was to remain hers although held in the name of Evans. Evans later made arrangements to sell the house without the knowledge or consent of Mrs Hodgson. The house was bought by Mr Marks and Mrs Hodgson now asked for a declaration that he was bound to transfer the property back to her. The following questions arose—

(*a*) Whether Evans held the house in trust for Mrs Hodgson. It was *held* by Ungoed—Thomas, J., that he did. The absence of written evidence of the trust as required by Sect. 53 of the Law of Property Act, 1925, was not a bar to Mrs Hodgson's claim. The Act was not intended to assist a fraud.

(*b*) Whether Evans had exercised undue influence. It was *held* that he had and a presumption of undue influence was raised. Although the parties were not in the established categories Evans had a relationship of trust and confidence with Mrs Hodgson of a kind which raised a presumption of undue influence.

However, Mrs Hodgson lost the case at first instance because Mr Marks was protected by Sect. 70 of the Land Registration Act, 1925, which gives rights to a purchaser of property for value in respect of interests in that property of which the purchaser is not aware. However, Mrs Hodgson's appeal succeeded. To ensure a good title a purchaser must, in spite of Sect. 70, pay heed to the possibility of rights in all occupiers. ([1971] 2 All E.R. 684.)

(314) *Lloyds Bank* v. *Bundy*, [1974] 3 All E.R. 757

The defendant and his son' s company both banked with the plaintiffs, the defendant having been a customer for many years. The company's affairs deteriorated over a period of years and at the son's suggestion the bank's assistant manager visited the defendant and said that the bank could not continue to support an overdraft to the company unless the defendant entered into a guarantee of the account. The defendant received no independant advice, nor did the bank's assistant manager suggest that he should do so. The defendant charged his house as security for the overdraft and shortly afterwards the company went into receivership. The bank obtained possession of the house from the defendant in the county court where the assistant branch manager in evidence said that he thought that the defendant had relied upon him implicitly to advise him about the charge. The defendant appealed to the Court of Appeal in an attempt to set aside the guarantee and the security and it was *held*—allowing the defendant's appeal—that in the particular circumstances a special relationship existed between the defendant and the bank's assistant manager, as agent for the bank, and the bank was in breach of its duty of fiduciary care in procuring the charge which would be set aside for undue influence. The defendant, without any benefit to himself, had signed away his sole remaining asset without taking independent advice.

(*Note:* while the majority of the Court of Appeal (Cairns, L.J. and Sir Eric Sachs) were content to decide the appeal on the conventional ground that a fiduciary relationship existed between the bank and its customer, which is to suggest that a new fiduciary relationship has come into being, Lord Denning took the opportunity to break new ground by deciding that in addition to avoiding the contract on the grounds of a fiduciary relationship Mr Bundy could also have done so on the basis of 'inequality of bargaining power'. Although inequality of bargaining power obviously includes undue influence, Lord Denning made it clear that the principle does not depend on the will of one party being dominated or overcome by the other. This is clear from that part of the judgment where he says: 'One who is in extreme need may knowingly consent to a most improvident bargain, solely to relieve the straits in which he finds himself.' This approach is, of course, at variance with the traditional view of undue influence which was that it was based on dominance resulting in an inferior party being unable to exercise independent judgment.)

(315) *Kaufman* v. *Gerson*, [1904] 1 K.B. 591

The defendant's husband had misappropriated money entrusted to him by the plaintiff, his employer. The defendant made a contract in writing with the plaintiff under which she agreed to make good the loss, the plaintiff agreeing not to prosecute. The events took place in France and the agreement was governed by French law, which did not regard the element of coercion in the case of a vitiating element. Nevertheless, the action being brought on the contract in an English court, it was dismissed because it was contrary to public policy for an English court to enforce a contract obtained in this way.

(316) *Rother* v. *Colchester Corporation*, [1969] 2 All E.R. 600

The Corporation as landlords convenanted with Mr Rother as a tenant of a hardware shop on an estate in Colchester that they would not let any other shop on the estate for the purpose of a general hardware merchant and ironmonger. They let a shop to the local Co-operative Society as a food hall, the lease stating that they were not to sell any commodity or item which might cause the landlord to commit a breach of any of his covenants for the benefit of tenants of adjacent shops. The premises were used by the

Society mainly as a food hall but items usually sold by hardware merchants were on display for sale. In this action by Mr Rother for breach of the convenant it was *held* by Megarry, J., that a covenant not to let premises for a particular purpose could not be enlarged into a covenant not to permit the premises to be used for that purpose. A restrictive covenant must be construed strictly so as not to create a wider obligation than is imputed by the actual words.

(317) *Dann* v. *Curzon*, (1911), 104 L.T. 66

An agreement was made for advertising a play by means of collusive criminal proceedings brought as a result of a pre-arranged disturbance at the theatre. The plaintiffs, who agreed to create the disturbance and did in fact do so, sued for the remuneration due to them under the agreement. *Held*—The action failed because it was an agreement to commit a criminal offence and was therefore against public policy.

(318) *Pearce* v. *Brooks* (1866), L.R. I. Exch. 213

The plaintiffs hired a carriage to the defendant for a period of twelve months during which time the defendant was to pay the purchase price by instalments. The defendant was a prostitute and the carriage, which was of attractive design, was intended to assist her in obtaining clients. One of the plaintiffs knew that the defendant was a prostitute but he said that he did not know that she intended to use the carriage for purposes of prostitution. The evidence showed to the contrary. The jury found that the plaintiffs knew the purpose for which the carriage was to be used and thereupon the court held that the plaintiffs' claim for the sum due under the contract failed for illegality.

(319) *Foster* v. *Driscoll*, [1929] I K.B. 470

Several persons entered into what was in effect a partnership contract to equip a ship and load it with six different varieties of whisky. The ship was then to be sent to the USA and the whisky was to be sold either in the USA or on its borders to persons who would then dispose of it in violation of the USA's prohibition laws. This action was brought on a bill of exchange which had been accepted by members of the syndicate or partnership as a method of paying for the whisky. *Held*—The contract of partnership was void as against public policy because it had been formed to procure an act which was illegal by the law of a foreign but friendly country, and no action was possible in respect of any matter arising out of the scheme.

(320) *Regazzoni* v. *K. C. Sethia Ltd*, [1958] A.C. 301

The defendants agreed to sell and deliver jute bags to the plaintiff, both parties knowing and intending that the goods would be shipped from India to Genoa so that the plaintiff might then send them to South Africa. Both parties knew that the law of India prohibited the direct or indirect export of

---

goods from India to South Africa, this law being directed at the policy of apartheid adopted by South Africa. The defendants did not deliver the jute bags as agreed and the plaintiff brought this action in an English court, the contract being governed by English law. *Held*—Although the contract was not illegal in English law, it could not be enforced because it had as its object the violation of the law of a foreign and friendly country in which part of the contract was to be carried out.

(321) *John* v. *Mendoza*, [1939] I K.B. 141

The defendant owed the plaintiff some £852. The defendant was made bankrupt and the plaintiff was intending to prove for his debt in the bankruptcy. The defendant asked him not to do so, but to say that the £852 was a gift whereupon the defendant would pay the plaintiff in full regardless of the sum received by other creditors. In view of the defendant's promise the plaintiff withdrew his proof, but in the event all the other creditors were paid in full and the bankruptcy was annulled. The plaintiff now sued for the debt. *Held*—There was no claim, for the plaintiff abandoned all right to recover on failure to prove in the bankruptcy, and the defendant's promise to pay in full was unenforceable, being an agreement designed to defeat the bankrupty laws.

(322) *Parkinson* v. *The College of Ambulance Ltd and Harrison*, [1925] 2 K.B. I

The first defendants were a charitable institution and the second defendant was the secretary. Harrison fraudulently represented to the plaintiff, Colonel Parkinson, that the charity was in a position to obtain some honour (probably a knighthood) for him if he would make a suitable donation to the funds of the charity. The plaintiff paid over the sum of £3000 and said he would pay more if the honour was granted. No honour of any kind was received by the plaintiff and he brought this action to recover the money he had donated to the College. *Held*—The agreement was contrary to public policy and illegal. No relief could be granted to the plaintiff.

(323) *Alexander* v. *Rayson*, [1936] 1 K.B. 169

The plaintiff was the lessee of certain flats in Piccadilly. He let one of the flats to Mrs Rayson by granting her an underlease at £450 a year. Another agreement was made whereby Mrs Rayson was to pay £750 a year for certain services provided by the plaintiff. The defendant paid both sums for a time, but later paid a quarter's rent under the underlease, refusing to pay for services on the ground that they had not been rendered. The plaintiff sued in respect of the sum owing for services. The defendant alleged, amongst other things, that the contract for services was illegal since it was designed to defraud the Westminster City Council, the latter having assessed the rateable value of the flat on the basis of a rental of £450 a year, which was the income under the lease shown to the assessment committee. *Held*—The agreement for services could not be enforced because it was illegal. In any case there was no consideration moving from the plaintiff in respect of the services, for it emerged that he was already bound to carry out the services under his own lease.

(324) *Napier* v. *National Business Agency Ltd*, [1951] 2 All E.R. 264

The defendants engaged the plaintiff to act as their secretary and accountant at a salary of £13 per week plus £6 per week for expenses. Both parties were aware that the plaintiff's expenses could never amount to £6 a week and in fact they never exceeded £1 per week. Income Tax was deducted on £13 per week, and £6 per week was paid without deduction of tax as reimbursement of expenses. The plaintiff, having been summarily dismissed, claimed payment of £13 as wages in lieu of notice. *Held*—The agreement was contrary to public policy and illegal. The plaintiff's action failed.

(325) *Bowmakers Ltd* v. *Barnet Instruments Ltd*, [1944] 2 All E.R. 579

Bowmakers bought machine tools from a person named Smith. This contract was illegal because it contravened an Order made by the Minister of Supply under the Defence Regulations, Smith having no licence to sell machine tools. Bowmakers hired the machine tools to Barnet Instruments under hire-purchase agreements which were also illegal because Bowmakers did not have a licence to sell machine tools. Barnet Instruments failed to keep up the instalments, sold some of the machine tools and refused to give up the others. Bowmakers sued, not on the illegal hire-purchase contracts, but in conversion, and judgment was given for Bowmakers. The Court of Appeal declared the contracts illegal but, since Bowmakers were not suing under the contracts but as owners, their action succeeded. The wrongful sales by Barnet Instruments terminated the hire-purchase contracts.

(*Note:* although the contract between Smith and Bowmakers was illegal ownership passed to Bowmakers by reason of delivery. When goods are delivered the person receiving them has some evidence of title by reason of possession and need not necessarily plead a contract. Where, in an illegal situation, the goods have not been delivered there may be difficulty in establishing ownership without relying on the illegal contract. Nevertheless, ownership was established without delivery in *Belvoir Finance Co. Ltd* v. *Stapleton*, [1970] 3 W.L.R. 530. In this case A (a dealer) sold certain cars to B (a finance company) which let them on hire purchase to C (a car-hire firm). C did not pay the minimum deposit required by regulation to B; thus the hire-purchase contract was illegal. Later, C's manager, S, sold the cars to innocent purchasers. C did not pay the hire-purchase instalments and B sued S in conversion, the company C having gone into liquidation. It was *held* by the Court of Appeal that B succeeded. They were the owners of the cars and S had converted their property. The decision is of interest since B (the finance company) had never taken delivery of the cars; they were sent direct from A to C as is usual in these transactions. Nevertheless B was accepted as owner although the only means of proving ownership open to B seems to have been the illegal hire purchase contract with C. This was the only document which showed how B came to acquire ownership of the cars.)

(326) *Edler* v. *Auerbach*, [1950] 1 K.B. 359

The defendant leased premises to the plaintiff for use as offices. The lease was contrary to the provisions of the Defence Regulations of 1939, since the premises had previously been used as residential accommodation and should have been let as such. The local authority discovered the illegal use and would not allow it to continue. The plaintiff now sued for rescission of the lease together with rent paid under it. The defendant counterclaimed for rent due and for damage done to the premises, including the removal of a bath. *Held*—The landlord could not enforce the illegal lease but was entitled to damages for the plaintiff's failure to replace the bath.

(327) *Hughes* v. *Liverpool Victoria Legal Friendly Society*, [1916] 2 K.B. 482

John Henry Thomas, a grocer, had originally taken out five policies on customers who owed him money. It was agreed that Thomas had an insurable interest in the customers because they were his debtors. Thomas let the policies drop and an agent of the defendant company persuaded a Mrs Hughes to take them up, assuring her that she had an insurable interest which she had not. She now brought this action to recover the premiums paid. *Held*—The contract was illegal but the plaintiff could recover the premiums. She had been induced to take up the policies by the fraud of the defendants' agent.

(328) *Atkinson* v. *Denby* (1862), 7 H. & N. 934

The plaintiff was in financial difficulties and offered to pay his creditors the sum of 25p in the £ as it would now be, as a full settlement. All the creditors except the defendant agreed to this. The defendant said that he would agree only if the plaintiff paid him £50. Afraid that the scheme would not go through without the defendant's co-operation, the plaintiff made the payment. *Held*—He could recover it because he had been coerced into defrauding his creditors.

(329) *Bigos* v. *Bousted*, [1951] I All E.R. 92

The defendant was anxious to send his wife and daughter abroad for the sake of the daughter's health, but restrictions on currency were in force so that a long stay abroad was impossible. In August, 1947, the defendant, in contravention of the Exchange Control Act, 1947, made an agreement under which the plaintiff was to supply £150 of Italian money to be made available at Rapallo, the defendant undertaking to repay the plaintiff with English money in England. As security, the defendant deposited with the plaintiff a share certificate for 140 shares in a company. The wife and daughter went to Italy but were not supplied with currency, and had to return sooner than they would have done. The defendant, thereupon, asked for the return of his share certificate but the plaintiff refused to give it up. This action was brought by the plaintiff to recover the sum of £150 which she insisted she had lent to the defendant. He denied the loan, and counter-claimed for the return of his certificate. In the course of the action the plaintiff abandoned her claim, but the defendant proceeded with his counter-claim saying that, although the contract was illegal, it was still executory so that he might repent and ask the court's assistance. *Held*—The court would not assist him because the fact that the contract had not been carried out was due to frustration by the plaintiff and not the repentance of the defendant. In fact his repentance was really want of power to sin.

(330) *Taylor* v. *Bowers* (1876), I Q.B.D. 291

The plaintiff was under pressure from his creditors and in order to place some of his property out of their reach he assigned certain machinery to a person named Adcock. The plaintiff then called a meeting of his creditors and tried to get them to settle for less than the amount of their debts, representing his assets as not including the machinery. The creditors would not and did not agree to a settlement. The plaintiff now sued to recover his machinery from the defendants who had obtained it from Adcock. *Held*—The plaintiff succeeded because the illegal fraud on the creditors had not been carried out.

(331) *Kearley* v. *Thomson*, (1890), 24 Q.B.D. 742

The plaintiff had a friend who was bankrupt and wished to obtain his discharge. The defendant was likely to oppose the discharge and accordingly the plaintiff paid the defendant £40 in return for which the defendant promised to stay away from the public examination and not to oppose the discharge. The defendant did stay away from the public examination but before an application for discharge had been made the plaintiff brought his action claiming the £40. *Held*—The claim failed because the illegal scheme had been partially effected.

(332) *Fisher* v. *Bridges* (1854), 188 E.R. 713

The plaintiff agreed to sell the defendant certain land which the defendant intended to use as a prize in a lottery. The use of land for lotteries was forbidden by statute but the land was conveyed and the purchase price all but £630 was paid. Later the defendant entered into a deed with the plaintiff under the terms of which he agreed to pay the £630 and the plaintiff now sued upon that deed. *Held*—No action lay on the deed. Jervis,

C.J., said: 'It is clear that the covenant was given for the payment of the purchase money. As it springs from, and is the creature of the illegal agreement, and as the law would not enforce the original illegal contract, so neither will it allow the parties to enforce a security for the purchase money which, by the original bargain, was tainted with illegality.'

(333) *Southern Industrial Trust* v. *Brooke House Motors* (1968), 112 S.J. 798

A customer wished to buy a car from the defendants who were dealers. The dealers and the customer inserted incorrect figures relating to price and deposit in the hire-purchase agreement so that it became illegal under statutory provisions then applying to such agreements. The car was then sold to the plaintiff finance company which was unaware of the true position. The finance company hired it out to the customer under the falsified hire-purchase agreement. The dealers had represented both to the customer and the finance company that the car was a 1962 model whereas in fact it was registered in 1958. When the customer discovered this he refused to pay any further instalments to the finance company and the company sued the dealers for breach of a warranty in the contract of sale to them, i.e. that the car was a 1962 model. It was *held*—by the Court of Appeal—that damages were recoverable notwithstanding the illegality of the hire-purchase agreement between the plaintiffs and the customer. The sale by the dealers to the finance company was collateral to that and was not tainted by the illegality in the other agreement.

(334) *Spector* v. *Ageda* (1971), 115 Sol. Jo. 426

The plaintiff was a solicitor acting for the defendant. The defendant was indebted to the plaintiff's sister who was a moneylender. The moneylender was not licensed under the relevant legislation. The plaintiff did not know this. She knew that the moneylending contract between the defendant and her sister provided for compound interest, this being a further illegality under the provisions of the Moneylenders' Act, 1927. The plaintiff lent the defendant money on the security of certain property to enable him to repay the loan made by her sister. This second loan was not repaid and the plaintiff claimed possession of the mortgaged property. The Court had to decide whether the second loan was affected by the admitted illegality of the first. *Held*—by Megarry, J.—that it was. A loan knowingly made to discharge a loan which was wholly or partially illegal was itself illegal and could not be recovered.

(335) *Clay* v. *Yates* (1856), 1 H. & B. 73

The plaintiff agreed to print a book for the defendant not knowing that the book contained libellous matter. After printing part of it he discovered the true position. *Held*—he was justified in refusing to print the rest of the book and his refusal did not prevent him from suing for work and labour done in printing the part which he had printed in ignorance of the libellous matter.

(336) *Fielding and Platt Ltd* v. *Najjar*, [1969] 2 All E.R. 150

The plaintiffs entered into an agreement with a Lebanese company to make and deliver an aluminium press. Payment was to be made by six promissory notes given at stated intervals by the defendant personally. The defendant, who was the managing director of the Lebanese company, told the plaintiffs that they ought to invoice the goods as part of a rolling mill, his intention being to mislead the Lebanese import authorities into believing that the import of the press was authorized whereas in fact it was not. The first promissory note was dishonoured and the plaintiffs stopped work on the press and cabled a message to the Lebanese company to that effect. The second promissory note was then dishonoured and the plaintiffs sued upon the notes. The case eventually reached the Court of Appeal where it was *held*, that—

(i) since the first note covered work in progress there was no defence based on failure of consideration;

(ii) any illegality in connection with the importing of the press was not part of the contract or agreed to by the plaintiffs;

(iii) the plaintiffs' claim was not, therefore, affected by illegality;

(iv) since the plaintiffs had repudiated the contract before the second note was dishonoured they had no claim for the amount of the note as such but could only sue for damages—the defendant was not liable on the second note.

(337) *Cowan* v. *Milbourn* (1867), L.R. 2 Ex. 230

A person hired a hall to deliver blasphemous lectures and then was refused possession of it. His action claiming possession was refused on the grounds that no relief could be granted by the court where the purpose of the contract was illegal.

(338) *Ashmore, Benson, Pease & Co. Ltd* v. *A. V. Dawson Ltd*, [1973] 2 All E.R. 856

The defendant haulage company agreed to carry some equipment for the plaintiff company. As the plaintiff's transport manager and his assistant watched but did not assist, the defendant company loaded their vehicles to a laden weight of 35 tons without objection being made. The maximum permitted laden weight was 30 tons under the Motor Vehicles (Construction and Use) Regulations, 1966. One of the vehicles toppled over, and the vehicle and its load were damaged. The plaintiff company claimed damages for negligent driving and negligence in placing the load on an unsuitable lorry. *Held*—that the contract, though lawful in its inception, was illegal in its carrying out to the knowledge and with the concurrence of the plaintiff company's servants. Thus damages were not recoverable, *Dictum* of Atkin, L.J., in *Anderson Ltd* v. *Daniel*, 1924 (see p. 248) applied.

(339) *Berg* v. *Sadler and Moore*, [1937] 1 All E.R. 637

The plaintiff was a hairdresser and sold tobacco and cigarettes. He was a member of the Tobacco Trade Association, the Association having as its object the prevention of price cutting. Manufacturers would supply tobacco to traders who agreed not to sell at less than the fixed retail price. The plaintiff sold tobacco at cut prices and was put on the manufacturers' stop list which meant that he could not obtain supplies. The plaintiff made contact with a person named Reece who was a member of the Association and Reece agreed to obtain goods from manufacturers and hand them over to the plaintiff, in return for which Reece was to receive a commission from the plaintiff. One such transaction was carried out. On a later occasion the plaintiff's assistant and a representative of Reece went to the defendant's premises to obtain a supply of cigarettes. The plaintiff's assistant handed over some £72 to Moore, who had some doubt about the matter and said he would send the goods direct to Reece's shop. Thereupon the plaintiff's assistant demanded the return of the money, Moore refused to give it back, and this action was brought to recover it. *Held*—This was an attempt by the plaintiff to obtain goods by false pretences and, since no action arises out of a base cause, the plaintiff's action failed.

(340) *Goodinson* v. *Goodinson*, [1954] 2 All E.R. 255

A contract made between husband and wife, who had already separated, provided that the husband would pay his wife a weekly sum by way of maintenance in consideration that she would indemnify him against all debts incurred by her, would not pledge his credit, and would not take matrimonial proceedings against him in respect of maintenance. The wife now sued for arrears of maintenance under this agreement. The last promise was admittedly void since its object was to oust the jurisdiction of the courts, but it was *held* that this did not vitiate the rest of the contract; it was not the sole or even the main consideration, and the wife's action for arrears succeeded this promise being severable.

(341) *Re Davstone Estates Ltd*, [1969] 2 All E.R. 849

The plaintiffs were landlords of a block of flats in St Albans. The plaintiffs agreed with the tenants to keep the common parts of the block in good repair and the tenants agreed to pay £15 per year to the plaintiffs for this service. The tenants were also required to agree to a clause which provided that if the tenants' proportionate share of the actual cost of repairs incurred by the plaintiffs should exceed £15 in any year the tenants would pay the excess. A certificate by the plaintiffs' surveyor was to be conclusive as to the tenants' liability to pay any excess. The plaintiffs had to make good any structural defects as distinct from repairs and maintenance and the court was required as a matter of construction of the tenancy agreement to say whether any of these costs were recoverable from the tenants. In the course of his judgment, Ungoed-Thomas, J., said that the provision as to the finality of the plaintiffs' surveyor's certificate ousted the jurisdiction of the court and was void as contrary to public policy.

(342) *Morris & Co.* v. *Saxelby*, [1916] 1 A.C. 688

On leaving school Saxelby entered the drawing office of a company engaged in the manufacture of lifting machinery, pulley blocks and travelling cranes. The company had its head office and works in Loughborough and branch offices in eight large cities. Eventually Saxelby became head of one of the company's departments at a salary of £3 17s. 6d. a week. He had entered into a covenant not to engage in a similar business in the United Kingdom for a period of seven years from the date of leaving the company's service. In this action the company sought to enforce that covenant and it was *held* by the House of Lords that it was unreasonably wide, having regard to Saxelby's interests because it would 'deprive him for a lengthened period of employing, in any part of the United Kingdom, that mechanical and technical skill and knowledge which, as I have said, his own industry, observation, and intelligence have enabled him to acquire in the very specialized business of the appellants, thus forcing him to begin life afresh, as it were, and depriving him of the means of supporting himself and his family:' *per* Lord Atkinson.

Furthermore, their Lordships were unanimously of the opinion that the covenant was wider than was necessary to protect those interests which the company was entitled to protect, being aimed at securing the appellants against all competition from Saxelby.

(343) *Wyatt* v. *Kreglinger and Fernau*, [1933] 1 K.B. 793

In June, 1923, the defendants wrote to the plaintiff, who had been in their service for many years, intimating that upon his retirement they proposed to give him an annual pension of £200, subject to the condition that he did not compete against them in the wool trade. The plaintiff's reply was lost, but he retired in the following September and received the pension until June, 1932, when the defendants refused to make any further payments. The plaintiff sued them for breach of contract. The defendants denied any contract existed and also pleaded that if a contract did exist, it was void as being in restraint of trade. The Court of Appeal gave judgment for the defendants and although there was no unanimity with regard to the *ratio decidendi*, it appeared to two judges that the contract was injurious to the interests of the public, since to restrain the plaintiff from engaging in the wool trade was to deprive the community of services from which it might derive advantage.

(344) *Forster & Sons Ltd* v. *Suggett* (1918), 35 T.L.R. 87

The works manager of the plaintiffs who were mainly engaged in making glass and glass bottles was instructed in certain confidential methods concerning, amongst other things, the correct mixture of gas and air in the furnaces. He agreed that during the five years following the termination of his employment he would not carry on in the United Kingdom, or be interested in, glass bottle manufacture or any other business connected with glass making as conducted by the plaintiffs. It was *held* that the plaintiffs were entitled to protection in this respect and that the restraint was reasonable.

(345) *Fitch* v. *Dewes*, [1921] 2 A.C. 158

A solicitor at Tamworth employed a person who was successively his articled clerk and managing clerk. In his contract of service, the clerk agreed, if he left the solicitor's employment, never to practise as a solicitor within seven miles of Tamworth Town Hall. *Held*—The agreement was good because during his service the clerk had become acquainted with the details of his employer's clients, and could be restrained even for life from using that knowledge to the detriment of his employer.

(346) *Commercial Plastics* v. *Vincent*, [1964] 3 All E.R. 546

The plaintiffs employed Vincent, a plastics technologist, to co-ordinate research and development in the production of their PVC (Poly-vinyl-chloride) calendered sheeting, which was made up into adhesive tape. Vincent's contract forbade him to seek employment with any of the plaintiffs' competitors in the PVC calendering field for one year after leaving their employment. Vincent had access to secret material, including certain mixing specifications recorded in code and, although, he could not remember these, he could probably remember, in relation to any matter concerning adhesive tape, what was the problem and what was the solution, what experiments were made and whether the results were positive or negative. Vincent left his employment with the plaintiffs and proposed to take up employment with a competitor. The plaintiffs asked for an injunction to restrain Vincent from breaking the restraining term in his contract with them. *Held*—by the Court of Appeal—An injunction could not be granted. Although what Vincent could remember was sufficiently definite to be capable of protection by an appropriate condition or covenant, the term in the agreement was excessive. It was world-wide in scope, although the plaintiffs did not, on the facts of the case, require protection outside the United Kingdom. Furthermore, the term extended to the plaintiff's competitors in the whole field of PVC whereas they required protection, so far as Vincent was concerned, only in relation to calendered sheeting for adhesive tape.

(347) *Home Counties Dairies* v. *Skilton*, [1970] 1 All E.R. 1227

Skilton, a milk roundsman employed by the plaintiffs, agreed, amongst other things, not 'to serve or sell milk or dairy produce' to persons who within six months before leaving his employment were customers of his employers. Skilton left his employment with the plaintiffs in order to work as a roundsman for Westcott Dairies. He then took the same milk round as he had worked when he was with the plaintiffs. *Held*—By the Court of Appeal—This was a flagrant breach of agreement. The words 'dairy produce' were not too wide. On a proper construction they must be restricted to things normally dealt in by a milkman on his round. 'A further point was taken that the customer restriction would apply to anyone who had been a customer within the last six months of the employment and had during that period ceased so to be, and it was said that the employer could have no legitimate interest in such persons. I think this point is met in the judgment in *G. W. Plowman & Sons Ltd* v. *Ash*, 1964, where it was said that a customer might have left temporarily and that his return was not beyond hope and was therefore a matter of legitimate interest to the employer.' (*per* Harman, L.J.)

(348) *Scorer* v. *Seymour Jones*, [1966] 3 All E.R. 347

Under a contract dated 2 June, 1964, between an estate agent and one of his unqualified employees who was the estate agent's clerk and negotiator, the employee agreed that he would not, for three years after leaving his employment, carry on or be employed or interested in the business of an auctioneer, surveyor or estate agent within five miles of the employer's premises at Kingsbridge and Dartmouth. The employee was the manager of the branch office at Kingsbridge and there were recurring customers at this branch. The employee was unsatisfactory and was dismissed in November, 1964; thereafter he practised on his own account as an estate agent in Salcombe within five miles of Kingsbridge, but outside a five-mile radius of Dartmouth. The employer Scorer asked for an injunction restraining his former employee Seymour Jones from practising within five miles of the Kingsbridge office. The injunction was granted at Kingsbridge County Court, and on appeal by the employee against the granting of an injunction it was *held* by the Court of Appeal that the injunction was rightly granted because the employer had many recurring clients and the restraint on practising within five miles of the Kingsbridge office was reasonable. Further, the restriction on practising within five miles of the Dartmouth office was not reasonable restraint but was severable. *Per* Sellers, L.J., in considering whether the restriction was contrary to the public interest, it was proper to take into account the fact that the employee was unqualified and not controlled by professional rules.

(349) *White (Marion) Ltd* v. *Francis*, [1972] 3 All E.R. 857

In this case the Court of Appeal declared valid a covenant which restrained the defendant from being in any capacity whatsoever engaged, concerned or interested in ladies' hairdressing within one half-mile of the plaintiff's premises during the continuance of her employment or within 12 months of her employment ceasing.

(350) *T. Lucas & Co. Ltd* v. *Mitchell*, [1972] 3 All E.R. 689

In 1968 Mitchell entered into a service agreement as a sales representative with the plaintiffs, a subsidiary of Spillers Ltd. The plaintiffs' principal business was the manufacture and sale of articles, products and commodities used in the meat processing industry. Mitchell was allocated the Manchester district as his sales area and it was divided into six 'journeys' each of which normally took a week. In the course of each journey he visited all the plaintiff company's customers on the route so that each customer was normally visited once every six weeks. In clause 16 of the agreement the defendant undertook 'not for a period of one year after the determination of his employment either by effluxion of time or otherwise howsoever either directly or indirectly whether as principal, partner, agent, servant or assistant within the allocated districts as existing at the termination of his employment to deal in any goods similar to or capable of being used in place of any of the allocated articles or solicit orders for or supply any such goods to any person firm or company carrying on business within the allocated districts as existing at the termination of his employment hereunder to whom the (plaintiff) company has supplied any of the allocated articles during the twelve months preceding such a determination'. In February, 1972, the plaintiff company's head office became aware that the defendant, who had terminated his employment in December of the previous year had been active in canvassing a considerable number of their customers in the Manchester area on behalf of his new employers, a rival firm in the same business as the plaintiffs. A writ was issued claiming damages and an injunction restraining further breaches of clause 16 of the contract of service. At first instance Pennycuick, V.C., following *Attwood* v. *Lamont*, 1920, held that the clause in effect prohibited two things—(*a*) dealing in allocated articles in the Greater Manchester area; and (*b*) soliciting the company's customers in the area. It followed that as stipulation (*a*) was plainly wider than was necessary to protect the company's trade connection in that it prevented the defendant from visiting persons with whom he could have had no possible previous connection, the whole restraint was unreasonable and void, it being impossible to sever the two restraints. On the issue of severance Pennycuick, V.C., took the view that the type of goods covered in part (*b*) of the restraint, i.e. goods similar to or capable of being used in place of any of the allocated articles, could only be ascertained by reference to part (*a*) of the restraint. In these circumstances it was not possible to treat the restrictions as entirely separate. The Court of Appeal, however, took a different view of the question of severance. In a judgment of the Court read by Russell, L.J., it was found that the restraint was not a single restraint against dealing, soliciting or supplying, but in essence two separate obligations, one against dealing and the other against soliciting and supplying. This being so, the Court of Appeal, finding its own decision in *Scorer* v. *Seymour Jones*, 1966[348] to be inconsistent with *Attwood* v. *Lamont*, 1920[373] preferred to follow the former case and allowed severance granting an injunction in respect of breaches of the clause restraining soliciting and supplying. It is perhaps unfortunate that *Scorer* was followed because in that case the restraint was clearly an attempt to protect the employers' several businesses and not his business as a whole, and as such, was more readily severable. In addition, the employee in *Scorer's* case had prior to dismissal, apparently been guilty of a particularly culpable breach of fidelity in the course of his employment.

(351) *General Billposting Co. Ltd* v. *Atkinson*, [1909] A.C. 118

Atkinson was manager to a Newcastle billposting company for a number of years upon terms that he should hold office subject to termination at twelve months' notice by either party, and with a restriction on his right to trade after termination of his employment. The restriction on trade was that he should not, whilst in the employment of the company or within two years afterwards, carry on a similar business within a certain radius of Newcastle without the company's permission. In 1906 Atkinson was dismissed without notice and he successfully sued the company for wrongful dismissal. Having recovered damages he began to trade as a billposter on his own account within the prohibited area. The General Billposting Co. Ltd, having taken over the company with which Atkinson was employed, brought an action for an injunction and for damages for breach of contract. *Held*—by the House of Lords—Atkinson was entitled to treat the dismissal as a repudiation of the contract and to sue for damages for breach of contract, and was no longer bound by the restriction on trade.

(352) *Bromley* v. *Smith*, [1919] 2 K.B. 235

The plaintiff was a baker at Clacton and it was his practice to send carts containing bread on various rounds to visit boarding houses and shops. In 1895 the plaintiff required an assistant to undertake what was known as the town round and by means of an advertisement he came into communication with the defendant, a young man of eighteen years, who lived some miles away at a place called Great Baddow. The defendant had since the age of twelve been engaged in the bakery trade. On 18 November, 1895, the plaintiff and defendant entered into an agreement under which the defendant agreed that he would not at any time within the space of three years after the date of leaving the plaintiff's service engage or be engaged in the business of miller, baker, hay, straw or corn dealer, or restaurant keeper, or in the manufacture of flour meal. Eventually the defendant terminated his employment by giving notice to the plaintiff and then in partnership with a man named Green he took over premises in Clacton, three miles from the plaintiff's premises, and commenced business as a baker and confectioner. Both before and after he left the plaintiff's employment the defendant, on his own admission, canvassed the plaintiff's customers and some of these customers gave their custom to the defendant. At the time of the agreement the plaintiff did not carry on any business other than that of a baker and confectioner but he was contemplating an extension of his business and was considering opening a restaurant. *Held*—by Channell, J.—The restraint must coincide with what is necessary for the protection of the existing business of the employer and the restriction relating to the business of restaurant keeper went further than was necessary. However, the restraint was severable because each of the prohibited trades was stated separately and those relating to the business of baker or confectioner were enforceable. Furthermore, the contract as severed was enforceable, even though the defendant was a minor when he made it. It was a contract for his benefit even though it contained restraints. 'A contract which contains only terms on which an infant can reasonably expect employment must, I think, be for his benefit.'

(353) *Bull* v. *Pitney-Bowes*, [1956] 3 All E.R. 384

The plaintiff was employed by the defendants and it was a term of that employment that the plaintiff should belong to a non-contributory pension scheme. It was also provided that any retired member of the pension scheme who took employment in any activity in competition with, or detrimental to, the defendant's interests would forfeit his rights under the pension scheme unless he discontinued the activity when required to do so. The plaintiff retired and took up employment with one of the defendant's competitors. He was requested to discontinue this activity but refused to do so, and he sued his former employer and the committee and custodian trustee of the pension fund for declarations that the forfeiture provision was void and that he was entitled to a pension. *Held*—by Thesiger, J.—that the declarations should be made; the forfeiture clause was void as an unreasonable restraint of trade.

(354) *Printers and Finishers* v. *Holloway (No. 2)*, [1964] 3 All E.R. 731

The plaintiffs brought an action against Holloway, their former works manager, and others, including Vita-Tex Ltd, into whose employment Holloway had subsequently entered, claiming injunctions against Holloway and other defendants based, as regards Holloway, on an alleged breach of an implied term in his contract of service with the plaintiffs that he should not disclose or make improper use of confidential information relating to the plaintiff's trade secrets. Holloway's contract did not contain an express covenant relating to non-disclosure of trade secrets. The plaintiffs were flock-printers and had built up their own fund of 'know-how' in this field. The action against Vita-Tex arose because Holloway had, on one occasion, taken a Mr James, who was an employee of Vita-Tex Ltd, round the plaintiff's factory. Mr James's visit took place in the evening and followed a chance meeting between himself and Holloway. However, the plant was working and James did see a number of processes. It also appeared that Holloway had, during his employment made copies of certain of the plaintiff's documentary material and had taken these copies away with him when he left their employ. The plaintiffs sought an injunction to prevent the use or disclosure of the material contained in the copies of documents made by Holloway.

Held—by Cross, J.—

(*a*) The plaintiffs were entitled to an injunction against Holloway so far as the documentary material was concerned, although there was no express term in his contract regarding non-disclosure of trade secrets.

(*b*) No injunction would be granted restraining Holloway from putting at the disposal of Vita-Tex Ltd his memory of particular features of the plaintiffs' plant and processes. He was under no express contract not to do so and the Court would not extend its equitable jurisdiction to restrain breach of confidence in this instance. Holloway's knowledge of the plaintiffs' trade secrets was not readily separable from his general knowledge of flock printing.

(*c*) An injunction would be granted restraining Vita-Tex Ltd from making use of the information acquired by James on his visit.

(355) *United Sterling Corporation* v. *Felton and Mannion*, [1973] F.S.R. 409

Prospective licensees had approached the plaintiffs to operate a new process designed by the plaintiffs for producing polystyrene. Mannion, until suspended, was in charge of polystyrene production at the plaintiff's plant, though not on the design team or subject to any restrictive covenants. On a motion to restrain Mannion from misusing confidential information relating to the process by imparting it to others, it was *held*—by Brightman, J. dismissing the motion—that there was no evidence that anything disclosed to Mannion was expressly in confidence or such that it should be regarded as part of his 'stock of knowledge' which was the employers' property as opposed to general information forming part of Mannion's total experience gained from his employment. (*Printers & Finishers* v. *Holloway*, 1964[354] applied.)

(356) *Robb* v. *Green*, [1895] 2 Q.B. 315

The plaintiff was a dealer in live game and eggs. The major part of his business consisted of procuring the eggs, and the hatching, rearing and sale of game birds. For the purpose of carrying on this business, the plaintiff occupied game farms at Liphook in Hampshire, and at Elstead near Godalming. His customers were numerous and for the most part were country gentlemen and their gamekeepers. The plaintiff kept a list of these customers in his order book. The defendant, who was for three years the plaintiff's manager, copied these names and addresses, and after leaving the plaintiff's employ set up in a similar business on his own and sent circulars both to the plaintiff's customers and their gamekeepers inviting them to do business with them. The plaintiff sought damages and an injunction. *Held*—by the Court of Appeal (affirming the judgment of Hawkins, J.)—Although there was no express term in the defendant's contract to restrain him from such activities, it was an implied term of the contract of service that the defendant would observe good faith towards his master during the existence of the confidential relationship between them. The defendant's conduct was a breach of that contract in respect of which the plaintiff was entitled to damages of £150 and an injunction.

(357) *Sanders* v. *Parry*, [1967] 2 All E.R. 803

In January, 1964, the defendant was engaged by the plaintiff solicitor as assistant solicitor. The defendant had been told by the plaintiff that he was to undertake the legal work of an important client, Mr Tully. The defendant took up his employment on 16 March, 1964. During August or September, 1964, the defendant and Tully agreed that the defendant would set up in practice on his own account whereupon Tully would transfer all his legal business from the plaintiff to the defendant and this was done. In an action for damages for breach of an implied term of the contract that the defendant would serve the plaintiff faithfully, the defendant admitted the term but said that he was not in breach of it because the agreement between him and Tully had been initiated by Tully and he had merely accepted an offer which Tully had made. *Held*—That even if the agreement had not been initiated by the defendant, he had, in accepting the offer during the substance of his agreement with the plaintiff, acted contrary to the interests of the plaintiff and was in breach of the implied term of fidelity.

(358) *Hivac Ltd* v. *Park Royal Scientific Instruments Ltd*, [1946] 1 All E.R. 350

The plaintiffs were manufacturers of midget valves used in deaf aids, the work requiring a high degree of skill. The defendants were newcomers to the trade and concerned themselves mainly with the assembly of hearing aids. The plaintiffs' employees worked a five and a half day week, having Sunday free. Five such employees worked on Sundays for the defendants, assisting in the assembly of midget valves. The plaintiffs asked for an injunction to restrain their employees from carrying out such work. *Held*—In the special circumstances of the case an injunction would be granted, not because of any specific contractual restraint but because the conduct of the particular employees constituted a breach of the duty of fidelity which every servant owes to his master.

(359) *Initial Services* v. *Putterill*, [1967] 3 All E.R. 145

The first defendant was employed by the plaintiff launderers as their sales manager but he resigned and took a number of the plaintiff's documents which he handed to reporters of the *Daily Mail*, who were the second defendants. He also gave the reporters of the same newspaper information about the company's affairs. The newspapers published articles alleging a liaison system between launderers to keep up their prices, and that the plaintiffs had increased their prices after the imposition of the Selective Employment Tax ostensibly to offset that tax, when in fact they were getting substantial extra profit. On the plaintiff's action for breach of an implied term of the defendant's contract of service that he would not disclose to strangers confidential information obtained by him in the course of his employment, the defendant pleaded that the plaintiffs had agreements which ought to have been registered under the Restrictive Trade Practices Act, 1956 (see now Restrictive Trade Practices Act, 1976), that they ought to have been referred to the Monopolies Commission, and that they had issued misleading circulars about their reasons for raising their prices. *Held*—in interlocutory proceedings to strike out the defence—

(i) The servant was under no obligation not to disclose information which ought, in the public interest, to be disclosed to a person having a proper interest to receive it;

(ii) it was at least arguable that the information supplied by the defendant was in the above category;

(iii) the allegations in the defence could not be said to be so invalid that they ought to be struck out.

There was argument on the question as to whether the press was the proper authority for the receipt of confidential information but this doubt was not enough to invalidate the defence at this stage.

(360) *A. Schroeder Music Publishing Co. Ltd* v. *Macauley*, [1974] 3 All E.R. 616

The plaintiff was a young songwriter who had made an exclusive service contract with some music publishers for five years and assigned to them the full copyright in all his songs both existing and those which he might compose in the five-year period. The publishers could at any time terminate the contract by one month's notice, they could assign the benefit of the contract and were under no obligation to exploit any of the compositions during the five years. The plaintiff asked for a declaration that the agreement was not binding on him. It was *held*—by the House of Lords—that this particular restraint was contrary to the public interest. Two matters appear to have influenced the decision of the Court; the first was that the contract appeared to be almost totally one-sided: the second was that the particular contract did not appear to be in accordance with standard trade practice.

(*Note:* in the case of *Davis* v. *W.E.A. Records*, [1975] 1 All E.R. 237 the Court of Appeal followed the above case making the additional point that it was a restraint contrary to the public interest, as well as an example of inequality of bargaining power verging upon undue influence.)

(361) *Lyne-Pirkis* v. *Jones*, [1969] 3 All E.R. 738

The plaintiff and the defendant were medical practitioners in practice at Godalming. A clause in the partnership deed stated that if any partner retired he should not 'for a period of five years immediately following such retirement . . . engage in practice as a medical practitioner whether alone or jointly with any other person within a radius of ten miles of the Market House in Godalming'. The defendant terminated the partnership and the plaintiff asked for an injunction to prevent him from practising within the stated area. The patients of the partnership all lived within a radius of five miles. *Held*—by the Court of Appeal—that the covenant was not enforceable. It was wider than was reasonably necessary to restrict competition because it used the phrase 'medical practitioner' which could include medical consultant and was not limited to general practice. In these circumstances there was no need for the court to decide whether a radius of ten miles was too wide though Russell, L.J., thought it was.

(362) *British Concrete Co.* v. *Schelff*, [1921] 2 Ch. 563

The plaintiffs carried on a large business for the manufacture and sale of 'B.R.C.' Road Reinforcements. The defendant carried on a small business for the sale of 'Loop Road Reinforcements'. The defendant sold his business to the plaintiffs and agreed not to compete with them in the manufacture or sale of road reinforcements. It was held that the covenant was void. All that the defendants transferred was the business of selling the reinforcements called 'Loop'. It was therefore only with regard to that particular variety that it was justifiable to curb his future activities.

(363) *Nordenfelt* v. *Maxim Nordenfelt Guns and Ammunition Co.*, [1894] A.C. 535

Nordenfelt was a manufacturer of machine guns and other military weapons. He sold the business to a company, giving certain undertakings which restricted his business activities. This company was amalgamated with another company and Nordenfelt was employed by the new concern as managing director. In his contract Nordenfelt agreed that for twenty-five years he would not manufacture guns or ammunition in any part of the world, and would not compete with the company in any way. *Held*—The covenant regarding the business sold was valid and enforceable, even though it was world-wide, because the business connection was world-wide and it was possible in the circumstances to sever this undertaking from the rest of the agreement. However, the further undertaking not to compete in any way with the company was unreasonable and void.

(364) *Kores Manufacturing Co. Ltd* v. *Kolok Manufacturing Co. Ltd*, [1959] Ch. 108

The two companies occupied adjoining premises in Tottenham and both manufactured carbon papers, typewriter ribbons and the like. They made an agreement in which each company agreed that it would not, without the written consent of the other, 'at any time employ any person who during the past five years shall have been a servant of yours'. The plaintiffs' chief chemist sought employment with the defendants, and the plaintiffs were not prepared to consent to this and asked for an injunction to enforce the agreement. *Held*—by the Court of Appeal—

(a) A contract in restraint of trade cannot be enforced unless—
    (i) it is reasonable as between the parties, and
    (ii) it is consistent with the interests of the public.

(b) The mere fact that the parties are dealing on equal terms does not prevent the court from holding that the restraint is unreasonable in the interests of those parties.

(c) The restraint in this case was grossly in excess of what was required to protect the parties and accordingly was unreasonable in the interests of the parties.

(d) The agreement therefore failed to satisfy the first of the two conditions set out in (a) above and was void and unenforceable.

(365) *Esso Petroleum Co. Ltd* v. *Harper's Garage Garage (Stourport) Ltd*, [1967] I All E.R. 699

The defendant company owned two garages with attached filling stations, the Mustow Green Garage, Mustow Green, near Kidderminster, and the Corner Garage at Stourport-on-Severn. Each garage was tied to the plaintiff oil company, the one at Mustow Green by a solus supply agreement only with a tie clause binding the dealer to take the products of the plaintiff company at its scheduled prices from time to time. There was also a price-maintenance clause which was no longer enforceable and a 'continuity clause' under which the defendants, if they sold the garage, had to persuade the buyer to enter into another solus agreement with Esso. The defendants also agreed to keep the garage open at all reasonable hours and to give preference to the plaintiff company's oils. The agreement was to remain in force for four years and five months from 1 July, 1963, being the unexpired residue of the ten-year tie of a previous owner. At the Corner Garage there was a similar solus agreement for twenty-one years and a mortgage under which the plaintiffs lent Harpers £7000 to assist them in buying the garage and improving it. The mortgage contained a tie covenant and forbade redemption for twenty-one years. In August 1964, Harpers offered to pay off the loan but Esso refused to accept it. Harpers then turned over all four pumps at the Corner Garage to V.I.P. and later sold V.I.P. at Mustow Green. The plaintiff company now asked for an injunction to restrain the defendants from buying or selling fuels other than Esso at the two garages during the subsistance of the agreements. *Held*—by the House of Lords—that the rule of public policy against unreasonable restraints of trade applied to the solus agreements and the mortgage. The shorter period of four years and five months was reasonable so that the tie was valid but the other tie for twenty-one years in the solus agreement and the mortgage was invalid, so that the injunction asked for by the plaintiffs could not be granted.

(*Note:* it appears from this case that the doctrine of restraint of trade applies to solus agreements where the petrol company lends money on mortgage to the garage proprietor, but does not apply to restrictions where property is sold or leased. In *Harper* Lord Reid said that 'A person buying or leasing land had no previous right to be there at all, let alone to trade there, and when he takes possession of that land subject to a negative restrictive covenant he gives up no right or freedom which he previously had.')

(366) *Cleveland Petroleum Co. Ltd* v. *Dartstone Ltd*, [1969] 1 All E.R. 201

The owner of a garage and filling station at Crawley in Sussex leased the property to Cleveland and they in turn granted an underlease to the County Oak Service Station Ltd. The underlease contained a covenant under which all motor fuels sold were to be those of Cleveland. There was power to assign in the underlease and a number of assignments took place so that eventually Dartstone Ltd became the lessees, having agreed to observe the covenants in the underlease. They then challenged the covenant regarding motor fuels and Cleveland asked for an injunction to enforce it. The injunction was granted. Dealing in the Court of Appeal with *Harper's Case*[365] Lord Denning, M.R., said—

'. . . it seems plain to me that in three at least of the speeches of their Lordships a distinction is taken between a man who is already in possession of the land before he ties himself to an oil company and a man who is out of possession and is let into it by an oil company. If an owner in possession ties himself for more than five years to take all his supplies from one company, that is an unreasonable restraint of trade and is invalid. But if a man, who is out of possession, is let into possession by the oil company on the terms that he is to tie himself to that company, such a tie is good.'

(*Note:* the period of five years is based upon figures given for such ties in the Monopolies Commission Report on the Supply of Petrol (1965).)

(367) *Pharmaceutical Society of Great Britain* v. *Dickson*, [1968] 2 All E.R. 686

The Society passed a resolution to the effect that the opening of new pharmacies should be restricted and be limited to certain specified services, and that the range of services in existing pharmacies should not be extended except as approved by the Society's council. The purpose of the resolution was clearly to stop the development of new fields of trading in conjunction with pharmacy. Mr Dickson, who was a member of the Society and retail director of Boots Pure Drug Company Ltd, brought this action on the grounds that the proposed new rule was *ultra vires* as an unreasonable restraint of trade. A declaration that the resolution was *ultra vires* was made and the Society appealed to the House of Lords where the appeal was dismissed, the following points emerging from the judgment.

(i) Where a professional association passes a resolution regulating the conduct of its members the validity of the resolution is a matter for the courts even if binding in honour only, since failure to observe it is likely to be construed as misconduct and thus become a ground for disciplinary action.

(ii) A resolution by a professional association regulating the conduct of its members is *ultra vires* if not sufficiently related to the main objects of the association. The objects of the society in this case did not cover the resolution, being 'to maintain the honour and safeguard and promote the interests of the members in the exercise of the profession of pharmacy'.

(iii) A resolution by a professional association regulating the conduct of its members will be void if it is unreasonable restraint of trade.

(368) *Horwood* v. *Millar's Timber Co.*, [1917] 1 K.B. 305

The plaintiff was a moneylender and he had lent money to a person named Bunyon who was employed as a clerk by the defendants. Bunyon owed £42 together with a sum of £31 as interest. Bunyon assigned to the plaintiff a policy of assurance on his life worth £100, and all the salary or wages due or to become due to him with the defendants or any other employer. The plaintiff attached certain conditions to the agreement and under these Bunyon agreed not to leave his job without the plaintiff's permission; to do nothing to get himself dismissed; not to borrow; not to sell, pledge or otherwise dispose of his property, and not to obtain credit. If Bunyon was in breach of any of the conditions the whole sum was immediately payable. The plaintiff now sued Bunyon's employers in respect of the salary assigned. *Held*—The contract was illegal, being against public policy, and it was therefore unenforceable. That part of the contract which dealt with the assignment of salary was not severable from the rest and so the action failed.

(369) *Denny's Trustee* v. *Denny*, [1919] 1 K.B. 583

A young man with dissolute habits had fallen into the hands of moneylenders. A deed was entered into under the terms of which the son transferred all his property to the father, who agreed to pay all his debts and to make him a reasonable allowance. The deed provided that the son should not go within eighty miles of Piccadilly Circus without his father's consent, otherwise the annuity would be forfeited. The son became bankrupt and his trustee, wishing to set aside the deed and claim the property for the benefit of creditors, suggested that the deed constituted an illegal restraint. *Held*—The deed was good and could not be set aside; its purpose was to reform the son.

(370) *Neville* v. *Dominion of Canada News Co. Ltd*, [1915] 3 K.B. 556

The plaintiff was a director of a land company engaged in property deals in Canada and the defendants were newspaper proprietors who owed the plaintiff a certain sum of money. Other newspapers had made adverse comments on certain of the plaintiff's land deals and had refused to accept his advertisements. The plaintiff agreed with the defendants to accept less than the sum owed to him, if the defendants would undertake not to comment unfavourably on his dealings. The defendants did publish such comment in spite of the agreement and the plaintiff sought to enforce the contract. *Held*—His action failed because the restraint was against public policy. It was the ordinary and proper business of a newspaper to comment on fraudulent schemes.

(371) *Hermann* v. *Charlesworth*, [1905] 2 K.B. 123

C agreed that he would introduce gentlemen to Miss Hermann with a view to marriage. She agreed to make an immediate payment of £52 and a payment of £250 on the day of marriage. He introduced her to several gentlemen and corresponded with others on her behalf but no marriage took place. Miss Hermann now sued for the return of the £52 and succeeded. Although the claim succeeded at common law on the ground of total failure of consideration. Sir Richard Henn-Collins said in the course of his judgment that he could have granted the return of the money by the use of Equity even after a marriage had taken place.

(372) *Wallis* v. *Day* (1837), 2 M. & W. 273

The plaintiff was in business as a carrier and he sold that business to the defendant. The plaintiff agreed in return for a weekly salary of £2.19 to serve the defendant as assistant for life and further agreed that except as assistant he would not for the rest of his life exercise the trade of carrier. This action was brought by the plaintiff to recover eighteen weeks' arrears of salary. The defence was that the contract was void as being an unlawful restraint of trade and that no part of it was enforceable. It was unnecessary to decide this point because the court held, perhaps surprisingly in modern terms, that the restraint was reasonable but Lord Abinger, dealing with the defence, said: 'The defendants demurred on the ground that the covenant being in restraint of trade was illegal and therefore the whole contract was void. I cannot however accede to that conclusion. If a party enters into several covenants one of which cannot be enforced against him he is not therefore released from performing the others, and in the present case the defendants might have maintained an action against the plaintiff for not rendering them the services he covenanted to perform, there being nothing illegal in that part of the contract.'

(373) *Attwood* v. *Lamont*, [1920] 3 K.B. 571

Attwood carried on business as a draper, tailor and general outfitter in a shop at Kidderminster. The business was organized into different departments, each with a manager. Lamont was appointed as head cutter and manager of the tailoring department, and in his contract of service he agreed that he would not at any time, whether on his own account or on behalf of anybody else, carry on the trades of tailor, dressmaker, general draper, milliner, hatter, haberdasher, gentlemen's, ladies', or children's outfitter at any place within ten miles of Kidderminster. Some time later Lamont asked Attwood to release him from the covenant or to make him a partner, but Attwood refused to do this. Lamont left his employment and set up in business at Worcester, which was outside the ten-mile limit. However, he did do business with Attwood's customers and took orders in Kidderminster. Attwood now asked for an injunction to restrain Lamont in respect of his tailoring activities, claiming that that part of the covenant was severable, though admitting the covenant as a whole was too wide. *Held*—The part of the agreement concerning tailoring was not severable; and even if severable was invalid because it was a covenant against competition. Lamont was a rival largely because of his skill and not because of trade connection.

'The doctrine of severance has not, I think, gone further than to make it permissible in a case where the covenant is not really a single covenant but is in effect a combination of several distinct covenants. In that case and where the severance can be carried out without the addition or alteration of a word, it is permissible. But in that case only. Now here, I think, there is in truth but one covenant for the protection of the respondent's entire business, and not several covenants for the protection of his several businesses. The respondent is, on the evidence, not carrying on several businesses but one business, and in my opinion this covenant must stand or fall in its unaltered form.' (*per* Younger, L.J.)

(374) *Kenyon* v. *Darwin Cotton Manufacturing Co.*, [1936] 2 K.B. 193

The plaintiff was employed by the defendants and joined a scheme under which the employees were to finance the company by taking up shares in it. Payment for the shares was to be made by deductions from wages and the employees signed documents agreeing to take the shares and authorizing a sum of money to be deducted from their wages. This second document was illegal under the Truck Act, 1831. The plaintiff now sued to recover that part of her wages which had been applied in paying for shares, and the defendants counterclaimed for the amount due on the shares. The plaintiff succeeded because her action was a statutory one under the Truck Act of

1831. The defendants claimed that the agreement to take the shares was legal and should be severed from the part of the agreement dealing with the method of payment. *Held*—There could be no severance because that would leave a contract in which the employees agreed to pay for the shares not out of their wages but out of their assets generally, and this was an agreement which they did not intend to make.

(375) *Shaw* v. *Groom*, [1970] 1 All E.R. 702

Mrs Groom was the tenant of a room in North London and Mrs Shaw was her landlord. The tenancy was a controlled one and Mrs Groom had occupied the room for some twenty years at a rent of 39p per week plus 12½p for electricity. Mrs Groom fell into arrears with her rent and Mrs Shaw brought this action to recover the money owing to her. Unfortunately Mrs Shaw had failed, during the tenancy, to comply with Sect. 4 of the Landlord and Tenant Act, 1962, which required that the tenant be provided with a rent book. Mrs Groom now alleged that Mrs Shaw could not recover the arrears of rent because her failure to provide a rent book was illegal performance of the contract. *Held*—by the Court of Appeal—that Mrs Shaw succeeded. The intention of the legislature was not to preclude the landlord from recovering rent due or to impose on him any forfeiture beyond the fines stipulated in the Act of 1962. It was accepted that the requirement of a rent book was to protect a class of persons of whom Mrs Groom was one. This did not, however, automatically prevent Mrs Shaw's claim. The rule that an illegal contract cannot be enforced by the guilty party must be sensibly restricted in its operation.

(376) *Kiriri Cotton Co.* v. *Dawani*, [1960] A.C. 192

A tenant paid a premium to his landlord in order to get possession of a flat. The acceptance of the premium was an offence under Sect. 3(2) of the Uganda Rent Restriction Ordinance, and the Ordinance did not provide for recovery of the premium. Both parties were ignorant of the Ordinance. In this action to recover the premium the Judicial Committee of the Privy Council *held* that the premium paid by the tenant must be recoverable because the object of the statute was to protect tenants.

(377) *Ravenseft Properties Ltd* v. *Director-General of Fair Trading*, [1977] 1 All E.R. 47

In this case the High Court considered for the first time the application of restrictive trade legislation to services. In the case Ravenseft Properties Ltd were the leasehold owners of a shopping centre in Salford and sub-let the centre in units for use as business premises. The subleases also provided that Ravenseft should provide services for their tenants including maintenance, cleaning and porterage, and the tenants agreed to this and the payment of a service charge. Ravenseft were, in effect, asking the Court to declare that the agreements regarding services in the under-leases did not constitute agreements to which restrictive practices legislation applied. The case was obviously important to property companies because there could be thousands of leases with service provisions which might have to be registered or become void and unenforceable by property companies as landlords. It was *held*—by Mocatta, J.—that while all leases cannot be regarded as beyond the scope of restrictive practices legislation, these particular leases were because Ravenseft was not *in business* to supply services. Furthermore (following *Cleveland Petroleum Co. Ltd* v. *Dartstone Ltd*, 1969[366]) where, as in this case, a person takes possession of premises under a lease, not having been in possession before, and enters into a restrictive covenant tying him to take supplies or services from the lessor, the tie is normally valid and not a restriction for the purposes of restrictive practices legislation, though restrictions in the case of a sale and lease-back might be.

(378) *Re Chocolate and Sugar Confectionery Reference*, [1967] 3 All E.R. 261

The Restrictive Practices Court was asked to make an order exempting chocolate, sugar confectionery, and related types of goods from the general ban on resale price maintenance. The case for the suppliers, i.e. virtually all of the major manufacturers, was that without resale price maintenance there would be a major shift in trade from confectionery shops to supermarkets as a result of price cutting. This would lead to a loss of sales since chocolate and similar goods were often bought on impulse from small outlets. This would lead to loss of variety and higher prices in the longer term.

That price cutting by supermarkets would take place was accepted by the Court but the consequences were not regarded as inevitably those put forward by the suppliers. A normal shopper would not, for example, travel more than a short distance to buy a bar of chocolate for say, one new penny less than the recommended price. Some shops would go out of business, probably to the extent of 10 per cent of outlets, but in the view of the Court this reduction would not cause the public significant inconvenience. Accordingly the Court ruled that the suppliers had not established their case and that resale price maintenance for chocolates and sweets was unlawful.

A significant feature of the case was the acceptance by the Court of evidence of econonic principles and statistics. It marks the first real sign of co-operation between lawyers and economists; the arguments were economic and statistical rather than legal.

(379) *Esso Petroleum Co. Ltd* v. *Kingswood Motors (Addlestone) Ltd*, [1973] C.M.L.R. D.10

This case raised the validity under Art. 85 of a solus agreement operating in England under which the defendants had agreed with the plaintiffs to supply customers exclusively with Esso petrol for five years, the agreement having been made in December, 1969. Bridge, J., decided that since the agreement had not at the time of the hearing been notified to the European Commission which had not, therefore, had an opportunity to pronounce on it, an English judge was bound in the interim to regard it as valid under Community law. In addition, since five years was regarded by the House of Lords in *Esso Petroleum* v. *Harper's Garage (Stourport) Ltd*, 1967[365] as a reasonable period for a solus agreement, it should be allowed to operate.

(*Note:* solus agreements are only potentially within Art. 85 and in the case of old agreements, i.e. those in force prior to the UK entry into the EEC of which this was one, the national court can interpret Art. 85 provided the Commission had not initiated proceedings to determine its validity which it had not done in this case. Bridge, J., quite rightly in order to save time in applying for a ruling from the Court of Justice decided himself that there was no infringement of Art. 85. New agreements made after accession of the United Kingdom to the EEC are void automatically even if duly notified or not subject to notification unless specifically exempted by the Commission. It would appear that they do not enjoy even provisional validity while a decision is being made. (*Brasserie de Haecht* v. *Wilkin (2)(ECJ)*, [1973] CMLR 287. The *Kingswood* case shows at least how our courts must now take into account EEC law.)

(380) *Re German Ceramic Tiles Discount Agreement*, [1971] C.M.L.R. D.6

Interessengemeinschaft was a company constituted under German law having as its members twelve German concerns producing ceramic tiles. The membership represented nearly all German producers of ceramic tiles, though two were not involved. Interessengemeinschaft gave a discount to buyers based on their purchases in the preceding year of tiles from any of the 12 member companies. They would not include for discount purposes purchases from the two non-member organizations except at the request of the purchaser who did not receive a full discount even then. *Held*—by the Commissioners of the European Community—that

(i) the agreement limited the freedom of economic action of producers and so restricted competition within the Community under Art. 85(1);

(ii) it tended towards a concentration of orders upon the producers of one country and restricted competition within the Common Market under Art. 85(1);

(iii) the agreement violated Art. 85(1) and, since exemption under Art 85(1) could not be granted, must be terminated without delay.

(381) *Moore* v. *Marrable* (1866), 1 Ch. App. 217

Under an original written agreement of 12 August, 1856, a house was let by A to B for 21 years. There were covenants by B to keep the premises in repair, to repaint the outside every three years and redecorate the inside every seven years according to a specification. On 12 October, 1859 an oral agreement was made under which C replaced B as tenant on the same terms, though B undertook to guarantee payment of the rent. It was *held* that the effect of this oral agreement was to relieve B of his liability under the original lease.

(382) *Goss* v. *Nugent* (1833), 5 B. and Ad. 58

The plaintiff, who was a vendor, brought this action to recover the purchase money due under a written contract for the sale of land. The defendant, who was the purchaser, pleaded that the title to part of the land was defective. This plea, which was true, would normally have been enough to defeat the action. It was replied, however, that by a later parol contract the purchaser had waived the defect and agreed to accept the actual title. *Held*—that the vendor could not rely on this parol variation and that his action must fail since he was unable to deliver the title that he had agreed to deliver by the original contract. The contract was no longer the original contract but the original contract as varied and there was no written evidence of the true agreement as it was ultimately made. The whole, not a mere part of the agreement must be evidenced by writing.

(383) *Moore & Co.* v. *Landauer & Co.*, [1921] 2 K.B. 519

The plaintiffs entered into a contract to sell the defendants a certain quantity of Australian canned fruit, the goods to be packed in cases containing 30 tins each. The goods were to be shipped 'per S.S. *Toromeo*'. The ship was delayed by strikes at Melbourne and in South Africa, and was very late in arriving at London. When the goods were discharged about one half of the consignment was packed in cases containing 24 tins only, instead of 30, and the buyers refused to accept them. *Held*—Although the method of packing made no difference to the market value of the goods, the sale was by description under Sect. 13 of the Sale of Goods Act, 1893, and the description had not been complied with. Consequently the buyers were entitled to reject the whole consignment by virtue of the provisions of Sect. 30(3) of the Sale of Goods Act.

(384) *Cutter* v. *Powell* (1795), 6 Term Rep. 320

The defendant was the master of a ship called the *Governor Parry* and the plaintiff was the second mate on that ship. The ship sailed from Jamaica on 2 August, 1793, and Cutter sailed in her and carried out all his duties as second mate. However, he died on 20 September, 1793, i.e. before the ship completed her voyage to Liverpool on 9 October, 1793. The contract under which Cutter rendered the services was worded as follows—

'Ten days after the ship Governor Parry my self master arrives at Liverpool I promise to pay to Mr T. Cutter the sum of 30 guineas provided he proceeds, continues and does his duty as second mate in the said ship from hence to the port of Liverpool. Signed at Kingston, 31 July, 1793.'

Cutter's widow now sued to recover a proportionate part of his wages, but Lord Kenyon, C.J., held that the contract was entire and there could be no claim on a *quantum meruit* for partial performance.

(Note: the Merchant Shipping Act, 1970, now provides for the payment of wages for partial performance in such cases, and the Law Reform (Frustrated Contracts) Act, 1943, would also have assisted the widow to recover, because the sailor had conferred a benefit on the master of the ship prior to his death (which would now frustrate the contract) giving the widow the right to sue the master for the benefit of Cutter's work up to the time of his death.)

(385) *Heywood* v. *Wellers*, [1976] 1 All E.R. 300

In this case the plaintiff Sheila Heywood tried to bring an action for a debt owed to her by Mr Marrion and also to stop him from molesting her. As regards the latter, the defendant solicitors got an interim injunction but did not bring M to court under it when he molested H again. She then decided to sue the solicitors for negligence and the Court of Appeal awarded her a sum of damages representing her mental distress and upset on the analogy of the failed holiday cases such as *Jarvis* v. *Swan's Tours Ltd*, 1973.[256] What was more surprising about the case was the finding by the Court that the solicitor-client contract is an 'entire contract'. Wellers sought to set off their costs against the damages and at first instance the County Court judge allowed this. Lord Denning, however, thought that the judge was in error in thinking that the solicitors could recover any costs at all. The contract was an entire contract which they were bound to carry on to the end and as they had not done so they were not entitled to any costs. Lord Denning went on to say that the law as to entire contracts was put vividly by Jessel, M.R., in *re Hall and Barker*, (1878) 9 Ch. D. 538 at 545 when he said: 'If a man engages to carry a box of cigars from London to Birmingham, it is an entire contract, and he cannot throw the cigars out of the carriage halfway there, and ask for half the money; or if a shoemaker agrees to make a pair of shoes, he cannot offer you one shoe and ask you to pay half the price.' Thus applying those words to this case, if litigation is not carried through to the end the proceedings are as useless to the client as the single shoe. Success or failure in the action does not matter but unless concluded the strength or otherwise of the case cannot be put to the test.

(386) *Sumpter* v. *Hedges*, [1898] 1 Q.B. 673

The plaintiff entered into a contract with the defendant under the terms of which the plaintiff was to erect some buildings for the defendant on the defendant's land for a price of £565. The plaintiff did partially erect the buildings up to the value of £333, and the defendant paid him a part of that figure. The plaintiff then told the defendant that he could not finish the job because he had run out of funds. The defendant then completed the work by using material belonging to the plaintiff which had been left on the site. The plaintiff now sued for work done and materials supplied, and the

Court gave him judgment for materials supplied, but would not grant him a sum of money by way of *quantum meruit* for the value of the work done prior to his abandonment of the job. The reason was given that, before the plaintiff could sue successfully on a *quantum meruit*, he would have to show that the defendant had voluntarily accepted the work done, and this implied that the defendant must be in a position to refuse the benefit of the work as where a buyer of goods refuses to take delivery. This was not the case here; and defendant had no option but to accept the work done, so his acceptance could not be presumed from conduct. There being no other evidence of the defendant's acceptance of the work, the plaintiff's claim for the work done failed.

(387) *IBMAC* v. *Marshall* (*Homes*) (1968), 208 E.G. 851

The plaintiffs contracted to build a roadway having forwarded to the defendants, their clients, their bill of quantities and rates and their price. The plaintiffs failed to realize that there would be trouble with water and abandoned the work about halfway through, alleging that the defendants were in breach by failing to provide a proper site. The plaintiffs sued the defendants, who were given leave to defend on paying into Court the value of the difference between what the defendants had had to pay other contractors to complete the work and the contract price. On appeal it was *held*—by the Court of Appeal—(i) that this was an entire contract; (ii) that having failed to complete it the plaintiffs were not entitled to anything under the rule in *Sumpter* v. *Hedges* since the defendants had no option but to accept the work done. Therefore the plaintiffs had no claim in law and would have been well advised to accept the payment in.

(388) *De Barnardy* v. *Harding* (1853), 8 Exch. 822

The plaintiff agreed to act as the defendant's agent for the purpose of preparing and issuing certain advertisements and notices designed to encourage the sale of tickets to see the funeral procession of the Duke of Wellington. The plaintiff was to be paid a commission of 10 per cent upon the proceeds of the tickets actually sold. The plaintiff duly issued the advertisements and notices, but before he began to sell the tickets, the defendant withdrew the plaintiff's authority to sell them and in consequence the plaintiff did not sell any tickets and was prevented from earning his commission. The plaintiff now sued upon a *quantum meruit* and his action succeeded.

(389) *Hoenig* v. *Isaacs*, [1952] 2 All E.R. 176

The defendant employed the plaintiff who was an interior decorator and furniture designer to decorate a one-room flat owned by the defendant. The plaintiff was also to provide furniture, including a fitted bookcase, a wardrobe and a bedstead, for the total sum of £750. The terms of the contract regarding payment were as follows—'Net cash as the work proceeds and the balance on completion.' The defendant made two payments to the plaintiff of £150 each, one payment on the 12 April and the other on the 19 April. The plaintiff claimed that he had completed the work on 28 August, and asked for the balance, i.e. £450. The defendant asserted that the work done was bad and faulty, but sent the plaintiff a sum of £100 and moved into the flat and used the furniture. The plaintiff now sued for the balance of £350, the defence being that the plaintiff had not performed his contract, or in the alternative that he had done so negligently, unskilfully and in an unworkmanlike manner.

The Official Referee assessed the work that had been done, and found that generally it was properly done except that the wardrobe door required replacing and that a bookshelf was too short and this meant that the bookcase would have to be remade. The defendant claimed that the contract was entire and that it must be completely performed before the plaintiff could recover. The Official Referee was of the opinion that there had been substantial performance, and that the defendant was liable for £750 less the cost of putting right the above-mentioned defects, the cost of this being assessed at £55 18s. 2d. The Court accordingly gave the plaintiff judgment for the sum of £294 1s. 10d.

(390) *Bolton* v. *Mahadeva*, [1972] 2 All E.R. 1322

The plaintiff, a plumbing and heating contractor, agreed to install a combined heating and domestic hot water system in the defendant's house for £560. There was a defect in the finished work which caused the system not to heat adequately and to give off fumes, and which would cost £174 to repair. The defendant refused to pay and the plaintiff sued him. The County Court judge held that there had been substantial performance of the contract and gave judgment for the plaintiff, subject to an appropriate set-off in favour of the defendant. On appeal by the defendant it was *held*—by the Court of Appeal—allowing the appeal—that having regard to the nature of the defects and the cost of remedying them, the plaintiff could not be said substantially to have performed the contract and he was not entitled to recover anything. (*Hoenig* v. *Isaacs*, 1952[389] distinguished.)

(391) *Narbeth* v. *James: (the Lady Tahilla)*, [1967] 1 Lloyds' Rep. 591

The plaintiff sold his motor-yacht to the defendant in April, 1960, for a price of £8000. The defendant paid £5000 and it was agreed that the balance be met at the defendant's option in one of three ways—(i) by allowing the plaintiff free use of the yacht for one month during each of the years 1962, 1963 and 1964, subject to the plaintiff giving the defendant three months' notice of the month in which he required the yacht; (ii) by paying the plaintiff £1000 for any year in which the yacht was not available for use under method (i); (iii) by payment in cash if the vessel was disposed of by the defendant. In April, 1960, the defendant secured the balance due from him by executing a mortgage in favour of the plaintiff. In 1966 the plaintiff sued the defendant for the whole balance with interest under the mortgage. The defendant denied liability and contended that the yacht was made available for the plaintiff in 1962, 1963 and 1964, but the plaintiff had not given notice of the month he required her. *Held*—By Brandon, J.,—that the plaintiff was entitled to the £3000 plus interest. As a general proposition where A had an option to perform a contract in more than one way and the obligations of B depended on which way A chose and could only be effectively performed by B if he had notice beforehand, then A would be under an implied obligation to give B proper notice. Thus in the present case in order to give business efficacy to the contract it was necessary to imply a term that the defendant would give the plaintiff reasonable prior notice whether or not he was choosing method (i) in respect of any of the three relevant years. No notice had been given, therefore the mortgage remained undischarged and the plaintiff was entitled to the judgment.

(392) *Bowes* v. *Shand* (1877), 2 App. Cas. 455

The action was brought for damages for non-acceptance of 600 tons (or 8200 bags) of Madras rice. The sold note stated that the rice was to be shipped during 'the months of March and/or April, 1874'. 8150 bags were put on board ship on or before 28 February, 1874, and the remaining 50 bags on 2 March, 1874. The defendants refused to take delivery because the rice was not shipped in accordance with the terms of the contract. *Held*—The bulk of the cargo was shipped in February and therefore the rice did not answer the description in the contract and the defendants were not bound to accept it.

(393) *Chas. Rickards Ltd* v. *Oppenheim*, [1950] 1 K.B. 616

The defendant ordered a Rolls-Royce chassis from the plaintiffs, the chassis being delivered in July, 1947. The plaintiffs found a coachbuilder prepared to make a body within six or at the most seven months. The specification for the body was agreed in August, 1947, so that the work should have been completed in March, 1948. The work was not completed by then but the defendant still pressed for delivery. On 29 June, 1948, the defendant wrote to the coachbuilders saying that he would not accept delivery after 25 July, 1948. The body was not ready by then and the defendant bought another car. The body was completed in October, 1948, but the defendant refused to accept delivery and counterclaimed for the value of the chassis which he had purchased. *Held*—Time was of the essence of the original contract, but the defendant had waived the question of time by continuing to press for delivery after the due date. However, by his letter of 29 June he had again made time of the essence, and had given reasonable notice in the matter. Judgment was given for the defendant on the claim and counterclaim.

(394) *Elmdore Ltd* v. *Keech* (1969), 113 S.J. 871

The plaintiffs agreed to print an advertisement in their plastic telephone directory cover which they said would be distributed within 120 days. The covers were distributed eleven days late. It was *Held*—by the Court of Appeal—that since this was a mercantile contract the general rule that time was of the essence applied unless the circumstances showed otherwise. There were no special circumstances on the facts of the case and the plaintiffs' action for the price must be dismissed.

(395) *Deeley* v. *Lloyds Bank Ltd*, [1912] A.C. 756

A customer of the bank had mortgaged his property to the bank to secure an overdraft limited to £2500. He then mortgaged the same property to the appellant for £3500, subject to the bank's mortgage. It is the normal practice of bankers, on receiving notice of a second mortgage, to rule off the customer's account, and not to allow any further withdrawals, since these will rank after the second mortgage. In this case the bank did not open a new account but continued the old current account. The customer thereafter paid in moneys which at a particular date, if they had been appropriated in accordance with the rule in *Clayton's* case, would have extinguished the bank's mortgage. Even so the customer still owed the bank money, and they sold the property for a price which was enough to satisfy the bank's debt but not that of the appellant. *Held*—The evidence did not exclude the rule in *Clayton's* case, which applied, so that the bank's mortgage had been paid off and the appellant, as second mortgagee, was entitled to the proceeds of the sale.

(396) *Hochster* v. *De la Tour* (1853), 2 E. & B. 678

The defendant agreed in April, 1852, to engage the plaintiff as a courier for European travel, his duties to commence on 1 June, 1852. On 11 May, 1852, the defendant wrote to the plaintiff saying that he no longer required his services. The plaintiff commenced an action for breach of contract on 22 May, 1852, and the defence was that there was no cause of action until the date due for performance, i.e. 1 June, 1852. *Held*—The defendant's express repudiation constituted an actionable breach of contract.

(397) *Gorse* v. *Durham County Council*, [1971] 1 W.L.R. 775

The plaintiffs were school teachers employed by the defendants. Their contracts allowed suspension for misconduct without loss of salary if there was reinstatement. On the instructions of their union the plaintiffs refused to serve school meals whereupon the education office excluded them from the school and withheld their salaries. They were later reinstated and sued for the salary withheld. Cusack, J., *held* that supervizing meals was a normal part of a teacher's duties and refusal was an express repudiation of the contract. However, since the defendants had not accepted the repudiation but had reinstated the plaintiffs they must be regarded as having been suspended and were entitled under the terms of their contracts to the salary withheld.

(398) *Omnium D'Entreprises and Others* v. *Sutherland*, [1919] 1 K.B. 618

The defendant was the owner of a steamship and agreed to let her to the plaintiff for a period of time and to pay the second plaintiffs a commission on the hire payable under the agreement. The defendant later sold the ship to a purchaser, free of all liability under his agreement with the plaintiffs. *Held*—The sale by the defendant was a repudiation of the agreement and the plaintiffs were entitled to damages for breach of the contract.

(399) *The Angelia, Trade and Transport Inc.* v. *Iino Kaiun Kaisha Ltd*, [1973] 2 All E.R. 144

A ship was chartered to transport phosphate rock from Israel. Under the charter the ship was to be supplied with rock at 1000 tons per day. However, there was a shortage of transport in Israel and it would have been impossible to load the ship at that rate. The result would have been that instead of completing loading in June/July the *Angelia* would not have completed her loading until the end of August. When the owners of the ship realized that transport would not be available to load at the agreed rate they cancelled the charter, reserving their claim for damages for wrongful repudiation of the contract. A number of points were made by Kerr, J., in the course of a long judgment; matters which are relevant here are as follows—(*a*) in terms of breach, the consequences were not regarded as sufficiently serious as to justify termination; (*b*) in relation to the estimated period of delay the judge found that the consequences would have been purely financial. In terms of frustration increased cost is rarely sufficient reason for invoking the defence; (*c*) presumably those who chartered the ship were only in breach of warranty and the owners of the ship were themselves in breach and had wrongfully repudiated the charter-party by not presenting the vessel for loading.

For these and other reasons Kerr, J., *held* that the shipowners failed in their action.

(400) *Decro-Wall International S.A.* v. *Practitioners in Marketing*, [1971] 1 W.L.R. 361

In the case the Court of Appeal *held* that the defendants' failure to pay for goods at the time stipulated in the agreement, i.e. within 90 days of invoice, was not a breach which went to the root of the contract and the plaintiffs had no right to repudiate it. Payments had been on average between two and 20 days late and the plaintiffs had never had any reason to doubt the defendants' ability to pay.

(401) *Maredelanto Compania Naviera S.A.* v. *Bergbau-Handel GmbH. the Mihalis Angelos*, [1970] 3 All E.R. 125

The vessel *Mihalis Angelos*, which was owned by Maredelanto, was chartered by Bergbau-Handel under a charter party dated 25 May, 1965. The charter party provided—

(a) that the vessel should be ready to load about 1 July, 1965; and
(b) that if it was not ready to load on or before 20 July, 1965, the charterers should have the option of cancelling the contract.

The purpose of the charter party was for the charterers to load mineral ore (apatite) in Haiphong in North Vietnam and transport it to Hamburg or another port in Europe. Sometime before 12 July, 1965, the railway which was to bring the ore to Haiphong was allegedly destroyed by American bombing. However, the *Mihalis Angelos* was in Hong Kong on 23 July and could not have reached Haiphong before 27 July. Instead of waiting until 20 July when they could have cancelled the contract legitimately, the charterers decided to repudiate it on 17 July on the grounds of *force majeure* because they thought the railway had been destroyed so that the apatite ore could not be transported to Haiphong, thus rendering the charter party useless to them. The shipowners did not accept that *force majeure* applied and they sued for £4000 being damages for loss of the charter. At first instance Mocatta, J., held that the charterers were not entitled to repudiate on 17 July. The situation was not necessarily one of *force majeure* at that time. They were therefore in breach on 17 July and the owners were entitled to sue at that time. In addition they were entitled to damages of £4000 and it did not matter that they would have been unable to perform the contract at the due date, i.e. 20 July. In the Court of Appeal, however, it was decided that the owners were only entitled to nominal damages. The fact that the owners could not have performed the contract on 20 July was a contingency which had to be taken into account.

(402) *Avery* v. *Bowden* (1855), 5 E. & B. 714

The defendant chartered the plaintiff's ship and agreed to load her with a cargo at Odessa within forty-five days. The ship went to Odessa and remained there for most of the forty-five-day period. The defendant told the captain of the ship that he did not propose to load a cargo and that he would do well to leave, but the captain stayed on at Odessa, hoping that the defendant would change his mind. Before the end of the forty-five-day period the Crimean War broke out so that performance of the contract would have been illegal. *Held*—The plaintiff might have treated the defendant's refusal to load a cargo as an anticipatory breach of contract but his agent, the captain, had waived that right by staying on at Odessa, and now the contract had been discharged by something which was beyond the control of either party.

(403) *White and Carter (Councils) Ltd* v. *McGregor*, [1961] 2 W.L.R. 17

The respondent was a garage proprietor on Clydebank and on 26 June, 1957, his sales manager, without specific authority, entered into a contract with the appellants whereby the appellants agreed to advertise the respondent's business on litter bins which they supplied to local authorities. The contract was to last for three years from the date of the first advertisement display. Payment was to be by instalments annually in advance, the first instalment being due seven days after the first display. The contract contained a clause that, on failure to pay an instalment or other breach of contract, the whole sum of £196 4s. became due. The respondent was quick to repudiate the contract for on 26 June, 1957, he wrote to the appellants asking them to cancel the agreement, and at this stage the appellants had not taken any steps towards carrying it out. The appellants refused to cancel the agreement and prepared the advertisement plates which they exhibited on litter bins in November, 1957, and continued to display them during the following three years. Eventually the appellants demanded payment, the respondent refused to pay, and the appellants brought an action against him for the sum due under the contract. *Held*—The appellants were entitled to recover the contract price since, although the respondent had repudiated the contract, the appellants were not obliged to accept the repudiation. The contract survived and the appellants had now completed it.

(*Note:* (i) although the respondent's agent had no actual authority, he had made a similar contract with the appellants in 1954, and it was not disputed that he had apparent authority to bind his principal. (ii) The ruling of the House of Lords appears to conflict with the principle of mitigation of loss (see p. 270). In fact it does not, at least in law, because it has been laid down in a number of cases, e.g. *Shindler* v. *Northern Raincoat Co. Ltd*, [1960] 1 W.L.R. 1038, that there is no duty on a plaintiff to mitigate his damages before there has been any breach which he has accepted as a breach. In this case the plaintiffs did not accept the first breach but preferred to wait until the date of performance. During that time they were, according to the law, not obliged to mitigate loss. However, the case produces a most unfair result and the problem could probably have been dealt with differently by saying that although the plaintiffs were under no duty to mitigate their loss, they were surely bound not to aggravate the damage. If the House of Lords had taken the line that the plaintiffs' expense was self-imposed and not in fact caused by the breach of contract, then the defendants would not have been liable for it.)

(404) *Allen* v. *Robles (Compagnie Parisienne de Garantie, Third Party)*, [1969] 3 All E.R. 154

The defendant, Mr Robles, drove his car in a negligent fashion and ran into the plaintiff's house. In an action at Nottingham Assizes the judge awarded the plaintiff damages against Mr Robles and the question arose as to whether Mr Robles could claim on his insurance policy with the French insurance company which was joined as third party in this action. Mr Robles was in breach of his contract of insurance because that contract provided that he must notify the insurance company of any claim made against him within five days of the claim. This he had not done. In fact he failed to inform the insurance company of the claim by the plaintiff until two months after he knew it had been made. On the other hand the insurance company did not repudiate their liability until some four months after Mr Robles informed them of the claim. It was *held*—by the Court of Appeal—that the insurance company had not lost its right to repudiate the contract. The delay was not so long as to indicate that they had accepted liability and it had in no way changed the circumstances of the case. It had not, for example, increased Mr Allen's loss or altered Mr Robles liability. There was thus no prejudice to those concerned.

(405) *Total Oil Great Britain Ltd* v. *Thompson Garages (Biggin Hill) Ltd*, *The Times*, 8 October, 1971

The plaintiffs leased a garage to the defendants for 14 years on terms that the defendants would purchase all their fuel supplies from the plaintiffs and that payment was on delivery. Later the plaintiffs changed the method of payment to a banker's draft sent to the plaintiff's depot *before* delivery. This was a repudiation of the contract by the plaintiffs which was accepted by the defendants who went elsewhere for their fuel. The plaintiffs claimed, amongst other things, an injunction restraining the defendants from selling fuels other than those obtained from the plaintiffs. The plaintiffs also agreed to revert to the 'cash on delivery' system of payment. *Held*—by the Court of Appeal—that an injunction would be granted. A lease which conveys an interest in land does not come to an end like an ordinary contract by repudiation and acceptance of repudiation, and so was still in existence in the present case. The plaintiffs could insist upon the enforcement of the tie since they were now prepared to adhere to the terms of supply and payment.

(*Note:* the Court referred to *Cricklewood Property and Investment Trust Ltd* v. *Leighton's Investment Trust Ltd*, 1945[417] and stated, following Lord Russell and Lord Goddard, that the better view was that a lease cannot come to an end by frustration.) (But see now *Amalgamated Investment and Property Co.* v. *Walker*, 1975.)[221]

(406) *Davis Contractors Ltd* v. *Fareham UDC*, [1956] A.C. 696

In July, 1946, the plaintiff contracted with the defendants to build seventy-eight houses for £92,425 within a period of eight months. Owing to lack of adequate supplies of labour and building materials, it took the plaintiffs twenty-two months to complete the work. There was no provision in the contract regarding such eventualities. The extra expense incurred by the plaintiffs was £17,651, and they claimed that the original contract with the council was frustrated and that they were entitled to recover the total cost on a *quantum meruit*. *Held*—Events had made the contract more onerous to the plaintiffs but had not frustrated the contract. The eventuality should have been provided for. The only claim the plaintiffs had was for the sum agreed in the contract; *quantum meruit* was not available in the absence of frustration. 'It by no means follows that disappointed expectations lead to frustrated contracts.' *per* Viscount Simmonds, L.C.

(*Note:* this case was followed in *Amalgamated Investments and Property Co. Ltd* v. *Walker*, 1975.)[221]

(407) *Re Shipton, Anderson & Co. and Harrison Bros' Arbitration*, [1915] 3 K.B. 676

A contract was made for the sale of wheat lying in a warehouse in Liverpool. Before the seller could deliver the wheat, and before the property in it had passed to the buyer, the Government requisitioned the wheat under certain emergency powers available in time of war. *Held*—Delivery being impossible by reason of lawful requisition by the Government, the seller was excused from performance of the contract.

(408) *Storey* v. *Fulham Steel Works* (1907), 24 T.L.R. 89

The plaintiff was employed by the defendants as manager for a period of five years. After he had been working for two years he became ill, and had to have special treatment and a period of convalescence. Six months later he was recovered, but in the meantime the defendant had terminated his employment. The plaintiff now sued for breach of contract, and the defendants pleaded that the plaintiff's period of ill-health operated to discharge the contract. *Held*—The plaintiff's illness and absence from duty did not go to the root of the contract, and was not so serious as to allow the termination of the agreement.

(409) *Mount* v. *Oldham Corporation*, [1973] 1 All E.R. 26

The plaintiff owned and was the headmaster of a school for maladjusted children. In July, 1970, he was arrested on a charge of indecency. He was released on bail but only on condition that he did not reside at the school and had no contact with the children. The rest of the staff attempted to carry on the school in the plaintiff's absence but nevertheless the defendants, who had sent four boys to the school, removed them. In December the plaintiff was acquitted and his character vindicated. As a result the defendants sent the boys back to school and the plaintiff now claimed the school fees for the period from July to December. *Held*—by the Court of Appeal—that the plaintiff was entitled to the fees. It was a trade usage that a parent could not withdraw his child from school but if he did so he had to give a term's notice or pay a term's fees in lieu. Although the defendants had acted reasonably in the circumstances, they had still committed a breach of contract by removing the four boys from the school without giving sufficient notice. The defendants would have been justified if the plaintiff committed a breach which went to the root of the contract but the plaintiff had not committed any breach of contract at all. Neither was the contract frustrated. The position of the headmaster in this school was not so personal and important that the school could not continue in his absence.

(*Note:* Lord Denning did say in the course of his judgment that if Mr Mount had been found guilty of the charges he would, of course, have been guilty of a breach going to the root of the contract and he could not have recovered any fees. That would have been the way of solving the problem if he had been found guilty because even if he had been found guilty his sentence would have been short and would not have frustrated the contract.)

(410) *Hare* v. *Murphy Brothers*, [1975] 3 All E.R. 940

Hare, a foreman, after 25 years' service in Murphy's employment was sentenced to 12 months' imprisonment for unlawful wounding during an incident wholly unconnected with his work. Evidence was given at his trial that if Hare was not sent to prison he would get his job back; otherwise the question would have to be considered on his release. On his release he was told that his post had been filled and the company had no other vacancy for him. They did, however, make him an *ex gratia* payment of £150. Hare claimed redundancy payment. It was *held*—by the Court of Appeal dismissing the application—that the sentence was of such length and Hare's position of such importance that the sentence rendered it impossible for Hare to perform his part of the contract of employment and the contract was accordingly terminated as from the date of the sentence.

(411) *Taylor* v. *Caldwell* (1863), 3 B. & S. 826

The defendant agreed to let the plaintiff have the use of a music hall for the purpose of holding four concerts. Before the first concert was due to be held the hall was destroyed by fire, and the plaintiff now sued for damages because of the defendant's breach of contract in not having the premises ready for him. *Held*—The contract was impossible of performance and the defendant was not liable.

(412) *Krell* v. *Henry*, [1903] 2 K.B. 740

The plaintiff owned a room overlooking the proposed route of the Coronation procession of Edward VII, and had let it to the defendant for the purpose of viewing the procession. The procession did not take place because of the King's illness and the plaintiff now sued for the agreed fee. *Held*—The fact that the procession had been cancelled discharged the parties from their obligations, since it was no longer possible to achieve the real purpose of the agreement.

(413) *Herne Bay Steamboat Co.* v. *Hutton*, [1903] 2 K.B. 683

The plaintiffs agreed to hire a steamboat to the defendant for two days, in order that the defendant might take paying passengers to see the naval review at Spithead on the occasion of Edward VII's Coronation. An official announcement was made cancelling the review, but the fleet was assembled and the boat might have been used for the intended cruise. The defendant did not use the boat, and the plaintiffs employed her on ordinary business. This action was brought to recover the fee of £200 which the defendant had promised to pay for the hire of the boat. *Held*—The contract was not discharged, as the review of the fleet by the sovereign was not the foundation of the contract. The plaintiffs were awarded the difference between £200 and the profits derived from the use of the ship for ordinary business on the two days in question.

(414) *Joseph Constantine Steamship Line Ltd* v. *Imperial Smelting Corporation Ltd*, [1942] A.C. 154

The respondents chartered a steamship to proceed to Port Pirie, Australia, to load a cargo. On the day before the ship was due to load her cargo, and whilst she was lying in the roads off Port Pirie, there was an explosion in one of her boilers. She was therefore unable to perform the charter as agreed, although she could have done so after rather extensive repairs. The respondents claimed damages for breach of contract. *Held*—The explosion frustrated the contract and the appellants were not liable. The cause of the explosion was unknown, and negligence could not be proved against the appellants; otherwise they would have been liable on the ground that the frustrating event would have been self-induced.

(415) *Jackson* v. *Union Marine Insurance Co.* (1874), L.R. 10 C.P. 125

The plaintiff was the owner of a ship which had been chartered to go with all possible dispatch from Liverpool to Newport, and there load a cargo of iron rails for San Francisco. The plaintiff had entered into a contract of insurance with the defendants, in order that he might protect himself against the failure of the ship to carry out the charter. The vessel was stranded in Caernarvon Bay whilst on its way to Newport. It was not re-floated for over a month, and could not be fully repaired for some time. The charterers hired another ship and the plaintiff now claimed on the policy of insurance. The insurance company suggested that since the plaintiff might claim against the charterer for breach of contract there was no loss, and the court had to decide whether such a claim was possible. *Held*—The delay consequent upon the stranding of the vessel put an end, in the commercial sense, to the venture, so that the charterer was released from his obligations and was free to hire another ship. Therefore, the plaintiff had no claim against the charterer and could claim the loss of the charter from the defendants.

(416) *Maritime National Fish Ltd* v. *Ocean Trawlers Ltd*, [1935] A.C. 524

The respondents were the owners and the appellants the charterers of a steam trawler, the *St Cuthbert*. The *St Cuthbert* was fitted with, and could only operate with, an otter trawl. When the charter party was renewed on 25 October, 1932, both parties knew that it was illegal to operate with an otter trawl without a licence from the Minister. The appellants operated five trawlers and applied for five licences. The Minister granted only three and said that the appellants could choose the names of three trawlers for the licences. The appellants chose three but deliberately excluded the *St Cuthbert* though they could have included it. They were now sued by the owners for the charter fee, and their defence was that the charter party was frustrated because it would have been illegal to fish with the *St Cuthbert*. It was *held* that the contract was not frustrated, in the sense that the frustrating event was self-induced by the appellants and that therefore they were liable for the hire.

(417) *Cricklewood Property and Investment Trust Ltd* v. *Leighton's Investment Trust Ltd*, [1945] A.C. 221

In May, 1936, a building lease was granted between the parties for 99 years, but before any building had been erected war broke out in 1939 and government restrictions on building materials and labour meant that the lessees could not erect the buildings as they intended, these buildings being in fact shops. Leighton's sued originally for rent due under the lease and Cricklewood, the builders, said the lease was frustrated. The House of Lords *held* that the doctrine of frustration did not apply because the interruption from 1939 to 1945 was not sufficient in duration to frustrate the lease, and so they did not deal specifically with the general position regarding frustration of leases, basing their judgment on the question of the degree of interruption. In so far as they did deal with the general position this was *obiter*, but Lord Simon thought that there could be cases in which a lease would be frustrated, and the example that he quoted was a building lease where the land was declared a permanent open space before building took place; there he thought that the fundamental purpose of the transaction would be defeated. Lord Wright took much the same view on the same example. Lord Russell thought frustration could not apply to a lease of real property, and Lord Goddard, C.J., took the same view. Lord Porter expressed no opinion with regard to leases generally and so this case does not finally solve the problem.

(418) *Hillingdon Estates Co.* v. *Stonefield Estates Ltd*, [1952] Ch. 627

By a contract dated 13 January, 1938, the vendors, Stonefield, and the plaintiffs, Hillingdon, who were the purchasers, agreed to buy and sell a freehold. The purchasers were to take a conveyance on 31 January, 1939, and the use of the land was to be for building an estate only. The completion was delayed by the outbreak of war and on 11 October, 1948, the contract was still not completed by a conveyance, and at that time the Middlesex County Council compulsorily purchased the land, leaving the *owners* with the compensation which would, of course, be less than the market value in 1948. The plaintiffs said that the contract was discharged. They did not ask for rescission but for a declaratory judgment to this effect and the defendants claimed specific performance. It was *held* that the plaintiffs failed and the defendants succeeded and specific performance was granted, the plaintiffs' claim being refused. It would appear therefore that the doctrine of frustration does not apply to a contract for the sale of land once a legal or equitable estate has passed.

(419) *Chandler* v. *Webster*, [1904] 1 K.B. 493

The defendant agreed to let the plaintiff have a room for the purpose of viewing the Coronation procession on 26 June, 1902, for £141 15s. The contract provided that the money be payable immediately. The procession did not take place because of the illness of the King and the plaintiff, who had paid £100 on account, left the balance unpaid. The plaintiff sued to recover the £100 and the defendant counter-claimed for £41 15s. It was *held* by the Court of Appeal that the plaintiff's action failed and the defendant's counter-claim succeeded because the obligation to pay the rent had fallen due before the frustrating event.

(420) *The Fibrosa Clause*, [1942] 2 All E.R. 122

An English company (Fairburn) agreed to sell to a Polish firm (Fibrosa), machinery for £4800, one-third to be paid with the order. Delivery of the machinery was to be made within three or four months of the settlement of final details at a place called Gdynia in Poland. Only £1000 was paid with the order and on 3 September, 1939, Britain declared war on Germany. On 23 September, Gdynia was occupied by the Germans, the machinery was not delivered and the Polish company sued for the return of the £1000. It was *held* by Mr Justice Tucker and the Court of Appeal that the contract was frustrated under the rule in *Chandler* v. *Webster* (1904)[419] and that the action failed. The House of Lords, however, *held* that the money was recoverable, not because the contract was void *ab initio*, but in quasi contract on the grounds that there had been a total failure of consideration. Lord Simon said that under the law relating to the formation of contracts, a promise to do something provides consideration (thus a promise supports a promise), but under the law relating to failure of consideration, the promise is not enough, the performance of the promise is looked to. Here the money was paid to secure performance and there was no performance.

(421) *Lynn* v. *Bamber*, [1930] 2 K.B. 72

In 1921 the plaintiff purchased some plum trees from the defendant, and was given a warranty that the trees were 'Purple Pershores'. In 1928 the plaintiff discovered that the trees were not 'Purple Pershores' and sued for damages. The defendant pleaded that the claim was barred by the Statutes of Limitation. *Held*—The defendant's fraudulent misrepresentation and fraudulent concealment of the breach of warranty provided a good answer to this plea, so that the plaintiff could recover.

(422) *Applegate* v. *Moss* (1970), 114 S.J. 971

In 1951 the plaintiff bought houses from the defendant who was an estate developer. In 1965 it was discovered that the foundations were inadequate and not according to specification and that the houses would have to be pulled down. The plaintiffs sued for damages and the defendant pleaded that the claims were statute-barred. *Held*—by the Court of Appeal—that the plaintiffs' right of action had been concealed by the builder who had not followed the specification. The builder was the agent of the estate developer for this purpose. It followed that the plaintiffs' claim was not statute barred since they had only discovered that they had a cause of action in 1965.

(423) *King* v. *Victor Parsons & Co.*, [1973] 1 All E.R. 206

Until 1954 a piece of land had been used as a rubbish tip. In 1961 the defendant estate agents, who had recently bought the land, arranged for a house with ordinary foundations to be built, although they had been advised that this was inadequate, and their contractor knew that the land had been used as a tip. The plaintiff bought the land from the defendants in 1961 and the defendants completed the house having given an implied warranty that it would be reasonably fit for human habitation. More than six years later subsidence caused severe damage. The plaintiff sued the defendant for breach of an implied term that the bungalow would be reasonably fit for habitation. He also contended that he was not statute barred by the Limitation Act of 1939 because his right of action was concealed by the fraud. *Held*—by the Court of Appeal—that the defendants were in breach of an implied term that the bungalow would be reasonably fit for habitation. Furthermore, the plaintiff's claim was not statute barred for his right of action had been concealed by the fraud of the defendants within the meaning of Sect. 26(b) of the Limitation Act, 1939, and the plaintiff could not with due diligence have discovered the relevant facts earlier.

Speaking of the defendants' concealment, Lord Denning, M.R., said—'It may be that he has no dishonest motive; but that does not matter. He has kept the plaintiff out of the knowledge of his right of action; and that is enough.' (*Applegate* v. *Moss*, 1970[422] applied.)

(424) *Wilson* v. *United Counties Bank*, [1920] A.C. 102

A business man left his business affairs in the hands of the bank whilst he went to serve in the war of 1914–18. The bank mismanaged his affairs, and he was eventually adjudicated bankrupt. The trader and his trustee brought this action against the bank for breach of their contractual duty. Damages of £45,000 were awarded for loss of estate, and of £7500 for the injury caused to the trader's credit and business reputation. With regard to the damages the court *held* that the £45,000 belonged to the trustee for the benefit of creditors, and the £7500 went to the trader personally.

(425) *Sunley & Co. Ltd* v. *Cunard White Star Ltd*, [1940] 1 K.B. 740

The defendants agreed to carry a machine, belonging to the plaintiffs, to Guernsey, but because of delays for which the defendants were responsible, the machine was delivered a week late. The plaintiffs were not able to show that they had an immediate use for the machine, and could not prove loss of profit. However, it was *held* that, to compensate the plaintiffs for the defendant's breach of contract, they should recover £20 as one week's depreciation of the machine, and the sum of £10 as interest on the capital cost.

(426) *Beach* v. *Reed Corrugated Cases Ltd*, [1956] 2 All E.R. 652

This was an action brought by the plaintiff for wrongful dismissal by the defendants. The plaintiff was the managing director of the company and he had a fifteen-year contract from 21 December, 1950, at a salary of £5000 per annum. His contract was terminated in August, 1954, when he was fifty-four years old and the sum of money that he might have earned would have been £55,000, but the general damages awarded to him were £18,000 after the court had taken into account income tax, including tax on his private investments.

(*Note:* (i) the same principle has been applied to damages recoverable in tort for loss of earnings (*B.T.C.* v. *Gourley*, [1956] A.C. 185). (ii) The tax deducted does not go to the Revenue but merely reduces the defendant's liability. The same is true where the action is in tort.)

(427) *Cox* v. *Philips Industries Ltd*, [1976] 3 All E.R. 161

In this case an employee was demoted because of breach of contract by his employers, though he remained on the same salary for several months. The demotion upset him and he was eventually persuaded to leave with full salary in lieu of notice. Mr Justice Lawson decided that he could recover damages of £500 for the mental distress which he suffered as a result of his demotion and of his working conditions.

(428) *Chaplin* v. *Hicks*, [1911] 2 K.B. 786

The defendant organized a beauty contest inviting the readers of certain newspapers to select fifty girls from whom the defendant would select twelve. The twelve successful entrants were to be offered theatrical engagements. The plaintiff was one of the fifty girls selected by the newspaper readers, but the defendant did not invite her to the final selection. She now claimed damages for breach of contract, and the defendant pleaded that, even if he had invited her to the final selection, it was by no means certain that she would have been one of the successful twelve, and therefore, the damages should be nominal. *Held*—Although it was difficult to assess damages, yet the plaintiff was entitled to an assessment, whereupon the jury awarded her £100.

(429) *Hadley* v. *Baxendale* (1854), 9 Exch. 341

The plaintiff was a miller at Gloucester. The driving shaft of the mill being broken, the plaintiff engaged the defendant, a carrier, to take it to the makers at Greenwich so that they might use it in making a new one. The defendant delayed delivery of the shaft beyond a reasonable time, so that the mill was idle for much longer than should have been necessary. The plaintiff now sued in respect of loss of profits during the period of additional delay. The court decided that there were only two possible grounds on which the plaintiff could succeed—(i) That in the usual course of things the work of the mill would cease altogether for want of the shaft. This the court rejected because, to take only one reasonable possibility, the plaintiff might have had a spare. (ii) That the special circumstances were fully explained, so that the defendant was made aware of the possible loss. The evidence showed that there had been no such explanation. In fact the only information given to the defendant was that the article to be carried was the broken shaft of a mill, and that the plaintiff was the miller of that mill. *Held*—That the plaintiff's claim failed, the damage being too remote.

However, loss of profits for non-delivery or delayed delivery are recoverable if foreseeable as a consequence of the breach. Thus in *Victoria Laundry Ltd* v. *Newman Industries Ltd*, [1949] 1 All E.R. 997, the defendants agreed to deliver a new boiler to the plaintiffs by a certain date but failed to do so with the result that the plaintiffs lost (*a*) normal business profits during the period of delay, and (*b*) profits from dyeing contracts which were offered to them during the period. It was *held* that (*a*) but not (*b*) were recoverable as damages.

(430) *The Heron II (Czarnikow Ltd* v. *Koufos)*, [1967] 3 All E.R. 686

Shipowners carrying sugar from Constanza to Basrah delayed delivery at Basrah for nine days during which time the market in sugar there fell and the charterers lost more than £4000. It was held that they could recover that sum from the shipowners because the very existence of a 'market' for goods implied that prices might fluctuate and a fall in sugar prices was reasonably foreseeable by the shipowners. In this case the House of Lords *held* that the correct criterion of liability is not whether the loss is reasonably foreseeable by the parties but whether it should have been within their reasonable contemplation at the time of the contract, having regard to their knowledge at that time. The difference between the two is probably slight, but in the view of the House of Lords 'foreseeability' and 'contemplation' are different concepts and the former is wider than the latter and should be restricted to cases of tort.

(431) *Horne* v. *Midland Railway Co.* (1873), L.R. 8 C.P. 131

The plaintiff had entered into a contract to sell 4595 pairs of boots to the French Army at a price above the market price. The defendants were responsible for a delay in the delivery of the boots, and the purchasers refused to accept delivery, regarding time as the essence of the contract. The plaintiff's claim for damages was based on the contract price, namely 4s. per pair, but it was *held* that he could only recover the market price of 2s. 9d. per pair unless he could show that the defendants were aware of the exceptional profit involved, and that they had undertaken to be liable for its loss.

(432) *Pinnock Brothers* v. *Lewis and Peat Ltd*, [1923] 1 K.B. 690

The plaintiffs bought from the defendants some East African Copra Cake which, to the defendants' knowledge, was to be used for feeding cattle. The cake was adulterated with castor oil and was poisonous. The plaintiffs resold the cake to other dealers, who in turn sold it to farmers, who used it for feeding cattle. Cattle fed on the cake died, and claims were made by the various buyers against their sellers, the whole liability resting eventually on the plaintiffs. In this action the plaintiffs sued for the damages and costs which they had been required to pay. Two major defences were raised, the first being an exemption clause saying that the goods were not warranted free from defects, and the other that the damage was too remote. The court dismissed the exemption clause and *held* that, when a substance is quite different from that contracted for, it cannot merely be defective. Further the damage was not too remote, since it was in the implied contemplation of the defendants that the cake would at some time be fed to cattle.

(433) *H. Parsons (Livestock) Ltd* v. *Uttley Ingham & Co. Ltd, The Times*, 19 May, 1977

The defendants agreed to sell the plaintiffs a pig hopper and to erect it. In breach of contract, the ventilator on the hopper was left in the closed position. As a result nuts in the hopper became mouldy and the pigs which ate them contracted an *E Coli* infection and many of them died. The trial judge thought that the illness and death of the pigs was too remote and there was an appeal on that decision to the Court of Appeal. Lord Denning in dealing with *The Heron II*[430] said that the narrower test of contemplation should apply in contract where there was monetary loss only but where damages were claimed for injury to person or property as in this case the test of remoteness should be similar to that in tort, i.e. there should be liability for losses reasonably foreseeable. Accordingly, he found for the plaintiffs, holding that the illness and death of the pigs was not too remote. Lord Justice Scarman did not feel the need to divide decisions under *The Heron II*[430] in the above way, holding that since it was within the contemplation of the defendants that food stored in the hopper would be fed to pigs it needed no more than common sense to include in that contemplation an appreciation of the fact that food affected by bad storage conditions might well cause illness or death if the pigs fed on it. Accordingly, he also found for the plaintiffs, saying that the illness and death of the pigs was not too remote. Lord Justice Orr delivered a judgment concurring with that of Lord Justice Scarman.

(434) *Brace* v. *Calder*, [1895] 2 Q.B. 253

The defendants, a partnership consisting of four members, agreed to employ the plaintiff as manager of a branch of the business for two years. Five months later the partnership was dissolved by the retirement of two of the members and the business was transferred to the other two who offered to employ the plaintiff on the same terms as before but he refused the offer. The dissolution of the partnership constituted a wrongful dismissal of the plaintiff and he brought an action for breach of contract seeking to recover the salary that he would have received had he served the whole period of two years. It was *held* that he was entitled only to nominal damages since it was unreasonable to have rejected the offer of continued employment.

(435 ▪▪▪ *.E.R. Ltd*, [1971] 3 All E.R. 517

In this case, ▪▪▪ ntist who ordered a new Rover 2000 to replace one which became a total loss in an accident instead of buying a second-hand car was *held* by the Court of Appeal to have acted reasonably. He had a busy practice and needed to be certain that his car was reliable. He was also entitled to the cost of hiring alternative transport for the time it took to obtain the new car even though he could have acquired a second-hand car much sooner.

(436) *Charter* v. *Sullivan*, [1957] 2 Q.B. 117

The plaintiffs, who were motor dealers, agreed to sell a Hillman Minx car to the defendant for £773 17s., which was the retail price fixed by the manufacturers. The defendant refused to complete the purchase and the plaintiffs resold the car a few days later to another purchaser at the same price. The plaintiffs sued for breach of contract and the measure of damages claimed was £97 15s., the profit the plaintiffs would have made on the sale if it had gone through. Evidence showed that the plaintiffs could have sold to a second purchaser another Hillman Minx which could have been ordered from the manufacturers' stock had the defendant taken the first Hillman Minx as agreed. The plaintiff's sales manager said in his evidence 'we can sell all the Hillman Minx cars we can get'. This evidence was accepted by the trial judge. The plaintiffs were really suggesting that but for the defendant's refusal to complete they would have sold two cars and not one, and in so doing would have made double the profit. *Held*—An award of nominal damages (i.e. forty shillings) would be made. The plaintiff's sales manager said the plaintiffs could always find a purchaser for every Hillman Minx car they could get from the manufacturers, and so the plaintiffs must have sold the same number of cars and made the same number of fixed profits as they would have made if the defendant had duly carried out his promise.

(437) *Lazenby Garages* v. *Wright*, [1976] 2 All E.R. 770

Lazenby's were dealers in new and second-hand cars. They bought a second-hand BMW for £1325. Wright agreed in writing to buy it for £1670 but before taking delivery changed his mind and refused to purchase the car. Six weeks later Lazenby sold the same car for £1770 to someone else but still claimed damages from Wright in the sum of £345, being the loss of profit on the sale to him. It was *held*—by the Court of Appeal—that as Lazenby's had sold the car at a higher price they had suffered no loss on the transaction. The argument that Lazenby's might have sold a different car to the other purchaser was rejected.

(438) *Thompson (W. L.) Ltd* v. *Robinson (Gunmakers) Ltd*, [1955] Ch. 177

On 4 March, 1954, the defendants agreed in writing ▮▮▮▮▮▮▮▮▮▮ffs, who were motor car dealers, to purchase from them a Sta▮▮▮▮▮▮guard car. On 5 March, 1954, the defendants said that they were not prepared to take delivery. The plaintiffs returned the car to their suppliers who did not ask for any compensation. The plaintiffs now sued for damages for breach of contract. The selling price of a Standard Vanguard was fixed by the manufacturers and the plaintiff's profit would have been £61 1s. 9d. When the agreement was made there was not sufficient demand for Vanguards in the locality as would absorb all such cars available for sale in the area, but evidence did not show that there was no available market in the widest sense, i.e. in the sense of the country as a whole. It was *held* that the plaintiffs were entitled to compensation for the loss of their bargain, i.e. the profit they would have made (being £61 1s. 9d.) because they had sold one car less than they would have done.—The decision depends to a large extent on the fact that in Yorkshire, at the time the contract was made, the supply of Standard Vanguards did exceed the demand.

(439) *Hoffberger* v. *Ascot International Bloodstock Bureau, The Times*, 30 January, 1976

After the defendants had broken their contract to buy a horse the plaintiff, who was the vendor, incurred considerable expense in keeping the animal in the hope of selling advantageously. Eventually the horse was sold for a much reduced figure. It was *held*—by the Court of Appeal—that the plaintiff had acted reasonably and was entitled as part of damages to the expenses of attempting to mitigate his loss, notwithstanding that his final claim exceeded the original sale price.

(440) *Luker* v. *Chapman* (1970), 114 S.J. 788

The plaintiff lost his right leg below the knee as a result of a traffic accident in which his motor cycle was in collision with the defendant's sports car. The accident was partly caused by the defendant's negligence. After the accident the plaintiff was unable to continue with his employment as a telephone engineer and refused a clerical job, taking up teacher training instead. *Held*—by Browne, J.—that the plaintiff was required to mitigate damages and should have accepted the clerical job. The defendant was not liable for the loss of income involved in the period of teacher training.

(441) *Ansell* v. *Thomas, The Times*, 23 May, 1973

The plaintiff, the managing director of a company, was in dispute with his co-directors who alleged that he had resigned. When the plaintiff refused to leave the company's premises, the police were called and threatened to use force if the plaintiff did not leave. On the plaintiff's action against his co-directors for assault and conspiracy, the County Court judge awarded him £750 including aggravated damages. *Held*—by the Court of Appeal—that the plaintiff was, on the judge's findings of fact, entitled to aggravated damages in respect of indignity, mental suffering, disgrace and humiliation. In addition, the defendants were liable for the conduct of the constables who were acting on their behalf.

(442) *Ford Motor Co. (England) Ltd* v. *Armstrong* (1915), 31 T.L.R. 267

The defendant was a retailer who received supplies from the plaintiffs. As part of his agreement with the plaintiffs the defendant had undertaken—

(i) not to sell any of the plaintiffs' cars or spares below list price;
(ii) not to sell Ford cars to other dealers in the motor trade;
(iii) not to exhibit any car supplied by the company without their permission.

The defendant also agreed to pay £250 for every breach of the agreement as being the agreed damage which the manufacturer will 'sustain'. The defendant was in breach of the agreement and the plaintiffs sued. It was *held* by the Court of Appeal that the sum of £250 was in the nature of a penalty and not liquidated damages. The same sum was payable for different kinds of breach which were not likely to produce the same loss. Furthermore its size suggested that it was not a genuine pre-estimate of loss.

(443) *Cellulose Acetate Silk Co. Ltd* v. *Widnes Foundry Ltd*, [1933] A.C. 20

The Widnes Foundry entered into a contract to erect a plant for the Silk Co. by a certain date. It was also agreed that the Widnes Foundry would pay the Silk Co. £20 per week for every week they took in erecting the plant beyond the agreed date. In the event the erection was completed thirty weeks late, and the Silk Co. claimed for their actual loss which was £5850. *Held*—The Widnes Foundry were only liable to pay £20 per week as agreed.

(444) *Craven-Ellis* v. *Canons Ltd*, [1936] 2 K.B. 403

The plaintiff was employed as managing director by the company under a deed which provided for remuneration. The Articles provided that directors must have qualification shares, and must obtain these within two months of appointment. The plaintiff and other directors never obtained the required number of shares so that the deed was invalid. However, the plaintiff had rendered services, and he now sued on a *quantum meruit* for a reasonable sum by way of remuneration. *Held*—He succeeded on a *quantum meruit*, there being no valid contract.

(445) *Gilbert and Partners* v. *Knight*, [1968] 2 All E.R. 248

The respondent Knight, agreed, in August, 1965, to pay Gilbert, who was a member of the appellant firm of surveyors, a fee of £30 to supervise specified building work estimated to cost £600. In May, 1966, when the builder started work, the respondent ordered some additional work which brought the cost to £2238. Gilbert supervised this additional work but made no request for an additional payment until the work was completed. He then rendered an account for £135 being the agreed £30 plus a scale fee of 100 guineas for supervising the additional work. The respondent paid only the agreed £30 and would not pay more. Gilbert and Partners' action against Knight was dismissed and they appealed. It was *held* by the Court of Appeal, dismissing the appeal, that the firm was entitled to £30 only. No *quantum meruit* claim lay for supervising the additional work unless a new contract to pay for that work had been made because the parties never discharged the original contract for one lump-sum fee of £30.

(446) *Sky Petroleum Ltd* v. *VIP Petroleum Ltd*, [1974] 1 All E.R. 954

Under a contract made in March, 1970, the plaintiff company agreed with the defendant that, for a minimum period of 10 years, it would buy all the petrol and diesel fuel it needed for its filling stations from the defendant. In November, 1973, the defendant purported to terminate the contract for an alleged breach of its terms by the plaintiff company. The plaintiff company brought an action against the defendant and sought an interlocutory injunction to restrain the defendant from withholding supplies of petrol and diesel from the plaintiff company. There was evidence that in November, 1973, the petroleum market was in an unusual state and that the plaintiff company would have little prospect of finding an alternative source of supply. Goulding, J., held that an interlocutory injunction would be granted and in the course of his judgment said: 'Now I come to the most serious hurdle in the way of the plaintiff company which is the well-known doctrine that the Court refuses specific performance of a contract to sell

and purchase chattels not specific or ascertained. . . . I am entirely uncon-
vinced by counsel for the plaintiff company when he tells me that an
injunction in the form sought by him would not be specific enforcement at
all. . . . It is, in my judgment, quite plain that I am for the time being
specifically enforcing the contract if I grant an injunction. However, the
ratio behind the rule is, as I believe, that under the ordinary contract for
the sale of non-specific goods, damages are a sufficient remedy. . . . Here,
the defendant company appears for practical purposes to be the plaintiff
company's sole means of keeping its business going, and I am prepared so
far to depart from the general rule as to try to preserve the position under
the contract until a later date. I therefore propose to grant an injunction.'

(447) *Metropolitan Electric Supply Co.* v. *Ginder*, [1901] 2 Ch. 799

The defendant entered into a contract with the plaintiffs in which he agreed
to take all the electricity he required from them. The plaintiffs sued for an
injunction to prevent the defendant from obtaining energy elsewhere.
Held—The plaintiffs succeeded since the agreement was in essence an
undertaking not to take supplies of electricity from elsewhere, and could be
enforced by injunction.

(448) *Whitwood Chemical Co.* v. *Hardman*, [1891] 2 Ch. 416

The defendant entered into a contract of service with the plaintiffs and
agreed to give the whole of his time to them. In fact he occasionally worked
for others, and the plaintiffs tried to enforce the undertaking in the service
contract by injunction. *Held*—An injunction could not be granted because
there was no express negative stipulation. The defendant had merely stated
what he would do, and not what he would not do, and to read into the
undertaking an agreement not to work for anyone else required the court
to imply a negative stipulation from a positive one. No such implication
could be made.

(449) *Warner Brothers Pictures Incorporated* v. *Nelson*, [1937] 1 K.B. 209

The defendant, the film actress Bette Davis, had entered into a contract in
which she agreed to act exclusively for the plaintiffs for twelve months. She
was anxious to obtain more money and so she left America, and entered
into a contract with a person in England. The plaintiffs now asked for an
injunction restraining the defendant from carrying out the English contract. *Held*—An injunction would be granted. The contract contained a
negative stipulation not to work for anyone else, and this could be
enforced. However, since the contract was an American one, the court
limited the operation of the injunction to the area of the court's jurisdiction, and although the contract stipulated that the defendant would not
work in any other occupation, the injunction was confined to work on stage
or screen.

(450) *Desk Advertising Co. Ltd* v. *Société Civile De Participations Du Group S.T. Dupont and Others*, 1973, *The Times*, June 15.

Since 1953 the plaintiffs had acted as the exclusive distributors in Great Britain of cigarette lighters made by Dupont. The sole shareholder in Dupont had been SCP. In January, 1970, after negotiations for the purchase by Gillette of a substantial shareholding in Dupont, SCP agreed to procure the execution by Dupont before the shareholding control passed from SCP of a contract appointing the plaintiffs exclusive distributing agents in Great Britain on the existing terms for a term certain to December, 1976. Gillette acquired a substantial shareholding and SCP did not procure the promised contract for the plaintiffs, thus breaking their 1970 agreement. The plaintiffs sought injunctions to restrain the marketing of the lighters otherwise than through the plaintiffs' exclusive agency. It was *held*—by the Court of Appeal—that SCP's breach of contract was complete when control of Dupont passed from it; it was not, therefore, a continuing breach. Specific performance was based upon a continuing contractual obligation. A mandatory injunction was based on a continuing wrong. The Court was unaware of a remedy which in general terms required wrongdoers (other than by damages) to take steps to right a past wrong, and accordingly an injunction could not be granted.

(451) *Bower* v. *Bantam Investments Ltd*, [1972] 1 W.L.R. 1120

The plaintiff, who wanted some land, that he owned developed as a marina, sold the land to Bantam Investments Ltd. They formed a company to carry out the development and the land was bought by this company. The contract for sale to the defendants was conditional upon planning permission which would enable the marina 'to proceed as envisaged'. The marina was not built and the plaintiff, fearing that the land would be sold, brought an action for an injunction to prevent a further sale and so by implication require the marina to be built. It was *held* by Goff, J. that an injunction would not be granted. There was no express obligation in the contract to develop the land so the plaintiff could only rely on an implied term to this effect. An injunction would be given to restrain breach of an implied negative undertaking but it was necessary to indicate some specific thing which the defendant had impliedly agreed not to do and conduct inconsistent with contractual obligation does not suffice. The defendant's obligations were, at the most, to use their best endeavours to develop the site as a marina if this was practical, so that an injunction could not be granted.

(452) *Hooper* v. *Rogers*, [1974] 3 All E.R. 417

Mr Hooper and Mr Rogers were tenants in common near Bude in Cornwall of steeply sloping land. At the top of the steep slope was Mr Hooper's farmhouse. In December, 1971, Mr Rogers, without warning and in a most high-handed manner, levelled and deepened a track which was owned and occupied by the two tenants and which cut across the slope, its nearest point being 80 feet from Mr Hooper's farmhouse. A surveyor, Mr Borton, inspected the site on behalf of Mr Hooper in January, 1972, and observed that there was erosion from the west of the track. He considered that there was a long-term danger to Mr Hooper's farmhouse by erosion aided by the prevailing westerly gales and rain. The result of the erosion and the fact that the natural repose of the hillside had been disturbed was likely to be that trees between the track and the farmhouse would lose their roothold and would no longer bind the soil together, the process ending with the footings of the farmhouse being deprived of earth support and the building being damaged and collapsing. Judge Chope at first instance awarded judgment for £750 based on the cost of reinstating the track to its former condition and consolidating it. Mr Rogers appealed on the ground that no damages based on the threat to the support of the farmhouse could be awarded. It was *held*—by the Court of Appeal—that a mandatory injunction or damages in lieu could be ordered where there was a real probability that in time the action of deepening the track would result in actual damage to the house unless prevented by filling in and consolidation. Russell, L.J. said: 'The evidence of Mr Borton, which I accept, is that there is a real probability, not just a possibility, a real probability of prejudice to the plaintiff's house if nothing is done . . . and I find that there is a real risk.'

(*Note:* although damages were awarded the Court of Appeal said that in the circumstances an injunction could have been awarded although no damage had actually occurred.)

(453) *Mountford* v. *Scott*, [1974] 1 All E.R. 248

The defendant, an illiterate West Indian who had lived in England for 20 years, signed an agreement in consideration of £1 giving the plaintiff an option to purchase his house for £10,000 within six months. He sought to resile after some weeks because the value of the house had gone up but his solicitors wrote telling him that he could not do so and three months later the plaintiffs purported to exercise their option. They then issued a writ claiming specific performance. Brightman, J. *held* that an order for specific performance must be made and in the course of his judgment said: 'As the plaintiffs had made no more than a token payment for the defendant's promise, ·are the plaintiffs, so far as the equitable remedy of specific performance is concerned, in the position of volunteers who ought to be left to their remedy in damages? . . . An option to purchase land creates an equitable interest in the land. . . . Such equitable interest is an inevitable consequence of the existence of the option. It would seem immaterial to this concept that the option happened to be gratuitous. It is only necessary, as I see it, that the option should have been validly created. It is not the function of equity to protect only those equitable interests which have been created for valuable consideration. . . . In the result, therefore, I am of the opinion that the plaintiffs acquired an equitable interest in the defendant's land at the moment when the option agreement came to be signed and that such interest will be enforced subject only to the exercise of the option, as has been done in this case, and the payment of the purchase money due for the land. I therefore conclude that the plaintiffs are entitled to a decree for specific performance.'

(*Note:* this decision was affirmed by the Court of Appeal [1975] 1 All E.R. 198.)

(454) *Ryan* v. *Mutual Tontine Westminster Chambers Association*, [1893] 1 Ch. 116

The defendants leased a residential flat to the plaintiff and also agreed to employ a porter who would be resident on the premises. The porter was to clean the flats and deliver parcels, take in articles for safe custody, and take charge of keys. The defendants appointed a porter but the man concerned was also a chef at a club in Westminster and was absent from the flats each day from 11 a.m. to 3 p.m., carrying out his duties as a chef. While he was away his duties were carried out in a most indifferent fashion by a number of boys and a charlady. These persons were not resident. The plaintiff now sued for breach of contract and asked for specific performance of the promise to appoint a full time porter. *Held*—Specific performance could not be granted because the court could not supervise the day-to-day performance of such an obligation. The plaintiff's remedy was an action for damages.

(455) *Hill* v. *C. A. Parsons & Co. Ltd*, [1971] 3 All E.R. 1318

The defendants capitulated to demands from a trade union (DATA) that certain of their employees should be required to join that union. The plaintiff, a chartered engineer aged 63 with 35 years' service, was accordingly told to join and when he refused was given one month's notice. He then started proceedings for, *inter alia*, an injunction to prevent the company from terminating his employment. The Court of Appeal (Stamp, L.J. dissenting) felt that six months, would have been a proper period of notice and granted an injunction which in effect resulted in specific performance of the contract of service for that period of time.

(*Note:* the Court was obviously influenced by the fact that by the time six months had elapsed the Industrial Relations Act 1971, would be in force and give greater rights of compensation to the plaintiff. Nevertheless, Lord Denning, M.R., treated the decision as based on the principle *ubi jus ibi remedium* (where there is a right there is a remedy) and regarded Mr Hill's right to damages as inadequate, thus allowing the Court to grant an injunction.

(456) *Page One Records Ltd* v *Britton*, [1967] 3 All E.R. 822

By a written contract made in 1966 the defendants, a group of four musicians ('The Troggs'), appointed the plaintiffs to manage their professional careers for five years, they being persons of no business experience who were unlikely to survive as a 'pop' group without the services of a manager. The contract was world-wide. The plaintiffs agreed to use all their resources of knowledge and experience to advance the defendants' careers, and the contract further provided that the defendants would not engage any other person to act as manager or agent for them, and that they would not act themselves in such capacity. The plaintiffs were to receive twenty per cent of all moneys earned by the defendants during the period of the contract. The Troggs became an established group, earning as much as £400 per night. In 1967 the defendants signified their intention to repudiate the management contract, but the court held that there had been no breaches of duty by the plaintiffs to justify the repudiation. In fact the plaintiffs had supported the group in the fullest measure and were to a large extent responsible for the success of the group. The plaintiffs sued for damages for breach of contract and applied also for an interlocutory injunction restraining the defendants until trial from engaging any person, firm or corporation, other than the plaintiffs, as their manager. *Held*—by Stamp, J.—that the injunction must be refused because—

(i) The defendants had no business experience and had to have a manager. If an injunction was granted it would *compel* not merely *encourage* the defendants to carry out their contract with the plaintiffs. *Warner Bros* v. *Nelson*, 1937,[449] was distinguishable because Bette Davis was a person of intelligence, capacity and means and if she had chosen not to act at all rather than for Warner Bros, she would have been able to employ herself both usefully and remuneratively in other spheres of activity. Other similarly remunerative employment was not available to the 'Troggs'.

(ii) The injunction, if granted, would also have the effect of enforcing a contract for personal services of a fiduciary nature, because the plaintiffs were managers and it would be necessary for them to see, and be friendly with, the defendants for a further four years. In *Warner Bros* v. *Nelson*, 1937, the obligation of the plaintiffs was largely to pay money to Miss Davis; they were not involved in the much more intimate relationship of managing her career.

(457) *Wroth* v. *Tyler*, [1973] 1 All E.R. 897

A vendor entered into a contract for the sale of his house with vacant possession. After the contract and unknown to the vendor the vendor's wife registered notice of statutory right of occupation under Sect. 1 of the Matrimonial Homes Act, 1967. This meant that the vendor was unable to complete and the purchaser brought an action for specific performance. The wife refused to remove the notice from the register. It was *held* by Megarry, J., that specific performance must be refused. It was unreasonable to decree specific performance if it would result in litigation between the spouses. In these circumstances the plaintiffs were awarded damages of

£5,500 representing the difference between the original sale price and the value of the property at the date of hearing.

(458) *Warmington* v. *Miller*, [1973] 2 All E.R. 372

The defendant held a lease of premises, the lease containing an absolute prohibition against assignment, underletting or parting with possession. The defendant orally agreed with the plaintiff to grant him an under-lease of part of the premises. He did not do so and the plaintiff brought an action for specific performance. *Held*—by the Court of Appeal—the action for specific performance must be dismissed. Specific performance of the contract to grant an underlease would not be ordered since it would result in a breach of covenant by the defendant.

(459) *Horsler* v. *Zorro*, [1975] 1 All E.R. 584

In this case the vendor of a property refused to complete when he realized that the amount which he owed on his mortgage was so great that he would be left with virtually nothing out of the proceeds of sale. The purchaser's claim was originally for specific performance or damages but later he amended it to rescission and damages after writing through his solicitor to the vendor and saying that he intended to buy another house and wanted his deposit back. Megarry, J., *held* that it was not possible to combine a claim for rescission with a claim for damages and that the purchaser, having elected to rescind could only ask for the restoration of the status quo to the extent of recovering his deposit plus his conveyancing costs; he could not claim loss of bargain damages.

(460) *Greenwood* v. *Bennet*, [1972] 3 All E.R. 586

In this case a thief stole a car from a company and sold it to the appellant who, in good faith and without notice of the defect in title, carried out extensive repairs. The repairs cost him £226. He sold the car to a finance company who let it out on hire purchase for £450. The police traced the car to the hirer and took possession of it. The Chief Constable then took out an interpleader summons to determine to whom he should return it. The County Court judge held that the company was entitled to possession of the car and that they did not have to reimburse the appellant with the money he had expended on repairs. The appellant appealed contending that he should be paid £226 by the company. *Held*—by the Court of Appeal—the appeal would be allowed. The appellant was entitled to be paid £226 by the company in respect of the improvements he had made to the car. If the police had not taken possession of it and the company had brought an action for conversion or detinue or for specific delivery of the car, the court would have ordered that an allowance should be made for the cost of the repairs. (See *Munro* v. *Willmot*, 1948.)[539] In interpleader proceedings a similar course must be adopted in favour of an innocent claimant for otherwise the true owner would be unjustly enriched at his expense. It should be noted that the decision in this case applies only where the person who does the work honestly believes himself to be the owner of the property. Where the person who does the work knows or ought to know that the property does not belong to him then he will not normally be paid for his work on it.

(461) *Brook's Wharf and Bull Wharf Ltd* v. *Goodman Bros*, [1936] 3 All E.R. 696

The plaintiff company had agreed to store in its warehouse goods imported by the defendants. The defendants were liable by Act of Parliament to pay customs duties but the Act also allowed the authorities to recover these duties from the warehouseman. The goods were stolen before the defendants had paid the customs duties and they refused to do so. The authorities claimed the duties from the plaintiffs who paid them. *Held*—by the Court of Appeal—that the plaintiffs could recover the sums paid by way of duty from the defendants in quasi-contract.

(462) *Metropolitan Police District Receiver* v. *Croydon Corporation*, [1957] 1 All E.R. 78

A policeman had recovered damages for an accident resulting from the defendants' negligence. The injuries were received while the policeman was on duty and his wages were paid while he was unfit by the Police Receiver who was required by Act of Parliament to make these payments. In this action the Receiver was seeking to recover the amount paid in wages on the ground that the defendants would have had to pay more in damages to the policeman if he had not received his pay. *Held*—by the Court of Appeal—that the action failed. The defendants were not under a common and legal obligation to pay the policeman's wages so that quasi-contract did not apply.

(463) *Cox* v. *Prentice* (1815), 3 M. & S. 344

The defendant wished to sell a bar of silver to Cox but before the sale the bar was weighed by an assay master. Cox paid £88 for the bar on the basis of the weight ascribed to it by the assay master. It was later discovered that the weight was less than certified by the assay master who had made a mistake in the weighing. *Held*—Cox could recover the excess from Prentice since the money had been paid under a mistake of fact.

(464) *Lovell* v. *Lovell*, [1970] 1 W.L.R. 1451

In the course of an action based on a claim for money lent fourteen years before the issue of a writ, the plaintiff served interrogatories on the defendant. This is allowed as part of civil procedure in order to ascertain facts material to the claim. Two of the questions were—'On (a certain date) did you owe (the plaintiff) £2300?' and 'If not £2300 did you owe her any sum and if so, what sum?' *Held*—by the Court of Appeal—the questions need not be answered. To allow interrogatories of this kind would mean that no one could ever rely on the Limitation Act since he would be forced to give an acknowledgement of the debt on which an action could subsequently be brought.

LAW OF TORTS

(465) *Perera* v. *Vandiyar*, [1953] 1 All E.R. 1109

The plaintiff was the tenant of a flat in Tooting, and the defendant was the landlord. On 8 October, 1952, the landlord cut off the supply of gas and electricity to the flat in order to induce the plaintiff to leave. As a result, the plaintiff was forced to move out of the flat and lived elsewhere until the services were restored on 15 October, 1952. The plaintiff claimed damages for breach of implied covenant for quiet enjoyment, and also for eviction. *Held*—The plaintiff was entitled to damages for breach of the implied covenant, but punitive damages on the purported tort of eviction were not recoverable because the defendant had not committed a tort. It had not been necessary for the defendant to trespass on any part of the demised premises in order to cut off the services, and mere intention to evict was not a tort.

(466) *Hargreaves* v. *Bretherton*, [1958] 3 W.L.R. 463

The plaintiff pleaded that the defendant had falsely and maliciously and without just cause or excuse committed perjury as a witness at the plaintiff's trial for certain criminal offences, and that as a result the plaintiff had been convicted and sentenced to eight years' preventive detention. A point of law arose because the plaintiff's action was in effect based on the purported tort of perjury. *Held*—No action lay on this cause, since there was no tort of perjury, and therefore the plaintiff's claim must be struck out.

(467) *Roy* v *Prior*, [1969] 3 All E.R. 1153

The plaintiff, a doctor, sued the defendant, a solicitor, for damages alleging, amongst other things, that the defendant had caused his arrest and forcible attendance at court to give evidence in a criminal case by saying falsely in court that the plaintiff was evading a witness summons. The action failed. Lord Denning, M.R., saying the course of his judgment—

It is settled law that, if a witness knowingly and maliciously tells untruths in the witness box, and as a result an innocent person is imprisoned, nevertheless no action lies against that witness. ... The reason lies in public policy. Witnesses must be able to give their evidence without fear of the consequences. They might be deterred from doing so if they were at risk of being sued for what they said. So the law gives a witness the cloak of absolute immunity from suit. This applies not only to statements made by a witness in the box, but also to statements made whilst he is giving his proof to his solicitor beforehand. The reason is because the protection given to the witness in the box would be useless to him if it could be got round by an action against him in respect of his proof. . . .

(468) *Donoghue (or M'Alister)* v. *Stevenson*, [1932] A.C. 562

The appellant's friend purchased a bottle of ginger beer from a retailer in Paisley and gave it to her. The respondents were the manufacturers of the ginger beer. The appellant consumed some of the ginger beer and her friend was replenishing the glass, when, according to the appellant, the decomposed remains of a snail came out of the bottle. The bottle was made of dark glass so that the snail could not be seen until most of the contents had been consumed. The appellant became ill and served a writ on the manufacturers claiming damages. The question before the House of Lords was whether the facts outlined above constituted a cause of action in negligence. The House of Lords *held* by a majority of three to two that they did. It was stated that a manufacturer of products, which are sold in such a form that they are likely to reach the ultimate consumer in the form in which they left the manufacturer with no possibility of intermediate examination, owes a duty to the consumer to take reasonable care to prevent injury. This rule has been broadened in subsequent cases so that the manufacturer is liable more often where defective chattels cause injury. The following important points also arise out of the case.

(i) It was in this case that the House of Lords formulated the test that the duty of care in negligence is based on the foresight of the reasonable man.

(ii) Lord Macmillan's remark that the categories of negligence are never closed suggests that the tort of negligence is capable of further expansion.

(iii) The duty of care with regard to chattels as laid down in the case relates to chattels not dangerous in themselves. The duty of care in respect of chattels dangerous in themselves, e.g. explosives, is much higher.

(iv) The appellant had no cause of action against the retailer in contract because her friend bought the bottle, so that there was no privity of contract between the retailer and the appellant. Therefore terms relating to fitness for purpose and merchantable quality, implied into such contracts by the Sale of Goods Act, 1893, did not apply here.

(469) *Best* v. *Samuel Fox & Co. Ltd* [1952] 2 All E.R. 394

Best was a workman at the defendants' factory and because of an accident caused by the defendants' negligence he was emasculated. Best's claim for damages was successful but his wife also claimed damages for loss of her husband's *consortium* through the defendants' negligence. The House of Lords *held* that her claim failed because the *damnum* was not of a kind recognized by law. 'It is true that a husband is entitled to recover damages for loss of *consortium* against a person who negligently injures his wife, but this exceptional right is an anomaly at the present day. A wife . . . was never regarded as having any proprietary right in her husband. . . .' *per* Lord Morton of Henryton.

(*Note:* some American jurisdictions allow such a claim.)

(470) *Electrochrome Ltd* v. *Welsh Plastics Ltd*, [1968] 2 All E.R. 205

A lorry driver employed by the defendants drove the defendants' vehicle into a fire hydrant near to the plaintiff's factory. Water escaped from the damaged hydrant and the supply had to be cut off while repairs were carried out. The plaintiffs lost a day's work at their factory and sued for this loss. However, since they were not the owners of the hydrant it was *held* that no action lay. They had suffered loss but there had been no infringement of their legal rights.

(*Note:* the case is a good example of the reluctance of a court to allow the law of tort to be used to compensate for economic loss, i.e. the mere loss of an opportunity to make a profit, perhaps on the grounds that the law of contract is more concerned with the loss of expectations. Furthermore, the decision in this case can be reached by way of *damnum sine injuria* or by saying that there was no duty of care or, if there was, that the damage was too remote.)

(471) *The Mayor of Bradford* v. *Pickles*, [1895] A.C. 587

The corporation had statutory power to take water from certain springs. Water reached the springs by percolating (but not in a defined channel) through neighbouring land belonging to Pickles. In order to induce the corporation to buy his land at a high price, Pickles sank a shaft on it, with the result that the water reaching the corporation's reservoir was discoloured and its flow diminished. The corporation asked for an injunction to restrain Pickles from collecting the subterranean water. *Held*—An injunction could not be granted. Pickles had a right to drain from his land subterranean water not running in a defined channel. (This right of a landowner was established by the House of Lords in *Chasemore* v. *Richards* (1859), 7 H.L. Cas. 349). Any malice which he might have had in doing it did not affect that right, since English law knows no doctrine of abuse of rights. No use of property which would be legal if due to a proper motive can become illegal because it is prompted by an improper or malicious motive.

(472) *Langbrook Properties* v. *Surrey County Council*, [1969] 3 All E.R. 1424

The plaintiffs claimed that buildings on their land had suffered from subsidence caused by the defendants' conduct in pumping out excavations for the construction of a motorway near Sunbury-on-Thames. They claimed damages for nuisance and negligence. *Held*—by Plowman, J.—the claim disclosed no cause of action, a landowner being entitled to abstract underground percolating water as much as he wished regardless of resulting damage to his neighbour. (*Bradford Corporation* v. *Pickles*, 1895, *applied*.)

(473) *Wilkinson* v. *Downton*, [1897] 2 Q.B. 57

The defendant, 'as a practical joke', called on Mrs Wilkinson and told her that her husband had been seriously injured in an accident and had had both his legs broken. Mrs Wilkinson travelled to see her husband at Leytonstone, and believing the message to be true, sustained nervous shock and in consequence was seriously ill. This action was brought for damages for false and malicious representation. Damages were awarded. The court *held* that intentional physical harm is a tort even though it does not consist of a trespass to the person. Further, whether the act is malicious or by way of a joke is irrelevant.

(474) *Williams* v. *Humphrey*, *The Times*, 20 February, 1975

The defendant, a youth of nearly 16, accompanied his friend and the friend's parents to a swimming pool. As part of the general fun the defendant pushed the friend's father, the plaintiff, a middle-aged man, into the shallow end of the pool, merely intending to cause a big splash. The plaintiff's left foot struck the edge of the pool and he sustained severe injuries to his foot and ankle. He underwent five operations and ended up crippled. It was *held*—by Talbot, J.—that the plaintiff had not taken such part in the pool activities that he could be said to have willingly accepted the risk of personal injury and the defendant was guilty of both negligence and trespass to the person. The plaintiff succeeded.

(475) *Jennings* v. *Rundall* (1799), 8 Term. Rep. 335

An infant hired a horse to take a ride. The contract was not regarded as a necessary contract and was therefore not binding on him. He injured it by excessive riding. It was *held* that the injury was essentially a breach of the contract of hiring. Therefore the infant was not liable in tort.

(476) *Ballet* v. *Mingay*, [1943] K.B. 281

The appellant was an infant and he borrowed from the respondent an amplifier and a microphone. When the respondent demanded the return of the articles, the appellant failed to do so having lent them to another. The infant was sued in detinue (now wrongful interference). It was suggested that in this action the respondent was seeking to make the appellant liable in tort for an act which was really a breach of contract and for which, as an infant, he could not be liable. *Held*—The infant was properly sued in tort because his action in parting with possession of the articles was not allowed by the contract of bailment and was therefore outside the terms of the contract.

(477) *Donaldson* v. *McNiven*, [1952] 1 All E.R. 1213

The defendant lived in a densely populated area of Liverpool and allowed his thirteen-year-old son to have an air rifle on condition that he did not use it outside the house. The defendant's house had a large cellar and the boy was told to use the rifle there. Without the defendant's knowledge the boy fired the air rifle at some children playing near to the house, injuring the plaintiff, a child of five. *Held*—In the circumstances the precautions taken by the defendant were reasonable and would have been adequate but for the son's disobedience, which could not have been foreseen because the boy was usually obedient. The defendant was not guilty of negligence.

(478) *Bebee* v. *Sales* (1916), 32 T.L.R. 413

A father allowed his fifteen-year-old son to retain a shot gun with which he knew he had already caused damage. The father was *held* liable for an injury to another boy's eye.

(*Note:* Cases 477 and 478 were decided on the ordinary principles of negligence at common law. However, since the Air Guns and Shot Guns Act, 1962 (see now Firearms Act, 1968), an action may lie against the parent for breach of statutory duty. The Act makes it a criminal offence to give an air weapon to a person under fourteen years, and restricts the use or possession of air weapons by young persons in public places except under supervision. In any case breaches of these statutory duties could be relied upon as evidence of negligence. Furthermore a person injured might now claim compensation from the Criminal Injuries Compensation Board. The age of the child causing the injury is not a bar to a claim against the Board because payments will be made even though the child inflicting the injury is below the age of criminal responsibility. In *Gorely* v. *Codd*, [1966] 3 All E.R. 891, the plaintiff was injured by a pellet from Codd's air rifle when they were larking about in a field in open country. Codd was sixteen-and-a-half years of age and when the plaintiff sued Codd's father the Court found that he had given proper instruction to his son and was not liable at common law. Since the shooting did not occur in a public place there was no breach of the Air Guns and Shot Guns Act, 1962 (see now Firearms Act, 1968).

(479) *Carmarthenshire County Council* v. *Lewis*, [1955] 1 All E.R. 565

A boy aged four years was a pupil at a nursery school run by the appellants who were the local education authority. The boy and another were made ready to go out for a walk with the mistress in charge who left them for a moment in order to get ready herself. She did not return for ten minutes, having treated another child who had cut himself. During her absence the boy got out of the classroom and made his way through an unlocked gate, down a lane, and into a busy highway. He caused the driver of a lorry to swerve into a telegraph pole, as a result of which the driver was killed. His widow brought an action for damages for negligence. *Held*—In the circumstances of the case the mistress was not negligent so the liability of the local authority was not vicarious. However, they were negligent themselves because they had not taken reasonable precautions to keep the young children who used the premises from getting out into the highway.

(480) *Butt* v. *Cambridgeshire and Isle of Ely County Council* (1969), *The Times*, 27 November, 1969.

The plaintiff was a pupil in a class of 37 girls of nine and ten years of age. She lost an eye when another girl in her class waved pointed scissors which the children were using to cut out illustrations. The teacher was giving individual attention to another child. *Held*—by the Court of Appeal—that her claim for damages failed. The teacher was not under a duty to require all work to stop while she was giving individual attention to members of the class. She was not negligent so that there was no vicarious liability in the local authority. The local authority was not liable for its own negligence in that evidence of experienced teachers showed that there was no fault in the system of using pointed scissors.

(481) *Morriss* v. *Marsden*, [1952] All 1 E.R. 925

The defendant took a room at an hotel in Brighton, and whilst there he violently attacked the plaintiff who was the manager of the hotel. Evidence showed that at the time of the attack the defendant was suffering from a disease of the mind. He knew the nature and quality of his act, but did not know that what he was doing was wrong. The plaintiff sued for damages for assault and battery. *Held*—Since the defendant knew the nature and quality of his tortious act, it did not matter that he did not know that what he was doing was wrong, and he was liable in tort.

(482) *Law* v. *Llewellyn*, [1906] 1 K.B. 487

Law appeared at Bridgend magistrates' court to prosecute two persons for obtaining money by false pretences. He was advised by counsel that, in the absence of certain witnesses, it would not be possible to secure a conviction. Law agreed to withdraw the charges and, after he had done son, Llewellyn, who was a presiding magistrate, said words which meant that the plaintiff was a blackmailer and had brought unfounded criminal charges. He also added that a term of imprisonment would do the plaintiff good. Law brought this action against Llewellyn for defamation, and it was *held* that judicial immunity extended to Llewellyn and therefore Law's claim showed no reasonable cause of action.

(483) *Dickinson* v. *Del Solar*, [1930] 1 K.B. 376

The plaintiff had been knocked down by a car driven by the defendant's servant. The defendant was the First Secretary of the Peruvian Legation in London. The Head of the Legation directed the defendant not to plead diplomatic privilege, and the defendant entered an appearance in the action. The plaintiff succeeded and the defendant's insurance company refused to indemnify their client, saying, in effect, that his diplomatic immunity was immunity from liability. *Held*—The insurers were liable to indemnify the defendant. Diplomatic agents are not immune from liability for wrongful acts, but are merely immune from suit. This immunity can be waived with the sanction of the sovereign of the state in question, or an offical superior of the person concerned. The defendant's act in entering an appearance operated as a waiver of diplomatic privilege, and judgment was properly entered against him.

(484) *D. & L. Caterers Ltd and Jackson* v. *D'Anjou*, [1945] 1 All E.R. 563

The plaintiffs owned a West-End restaurant called the 'Bagatelle'. The defendant made certain statements alleging that the restaurant was operated illegally and obtained its supplies on the Black Market. *Held*—The statements were defamatory and a limited liability company could sue for slander without proof of special damage. Where the slander related to its trade or business, the law implied the existence of damage to found the action.

(485) *Poulton* v. *London and South Western Railway Co.* (1867), L.R. 2 Q.B. 534

The plaintiff was arrested by a station-master for non-payment of carriage in respect of his horse. The defendants, who were the employers of the station-master, had power to detain passengers for non-payment of their own fare, but for no other reason. *Held*—Since there was no express authorization of the arrest by the defendants, the station-master was acting outside the scope of his employment and the defendants were not liable.

(486) *Campbell* v. *Paddington Borough Council*, [1911] 1 K.B. 869

The defendants, in accordance with a resolution duly passed, erected a stand in Burwood Place in order that members of the council might view the funeral procession of King Edward the Seventh passing along the Edgware Road. The plaintiff, who occupied certain premises in Burwood Place, often let the premises for the purpose of viewing public processions passing along the Edgware Road. The stand obstructed the view of the funeral procession from the plaintiff's house and she was unable to let the premises for that purpose. *Held*—As the stand constituted a public nuisance, the plaintiff could maintain an action for the special damage which she had sustained through the loss of view. The corporation was properly sued, and the fact that the erection of the stand was probably *ultra vires* did not matter.

(487) *Garrard* v. *Southey (A. E.) and Co. and Standard Telephones and Cables Ltd*, [1952] 2 Q.B. 174

Two persons employed by electrical contractors were sent to work in a factory on electrical installations. The electrical contractors continued to employ the men, paying their wages, stamping their insurance cards, and retaining the sole right to dismiss them. The electricians worked exclusively at the factory and used the factory canteen. The occupiers of the factory supplied them with all materials, tools and plant, except for certain special tools belonging to the electricians themselves. They were supervised by a foreman employed by the occupiers and they followed the system laid down in the factory. One of the electricians was injured when he fell from a defective trestle owned by some building contractors who were also working in the factory. *Held*—The occupiers of the factory, and not the electrical contractors, owed the injured electrician the common law duty of a master to his servant (to provide proper plant and equipment) and they were liable to him for breach of that duty.

(488) *Mersey Docks and Harbour Board* v. *Coggins and Griffiths (Liverpool) Ltd and McFarlane*, [1947] A.C. 1.

A firm of stevedores had hired from the Harbour Board the use of a crane together with its driver to assist in loading a ship lying in the Liverpool docks. The contract of hire was subject to the Board's regulations, one of which contained the clause: 'The driver provided shall be the servant of the applicants.' The driver of the crane was a skilled man appointed and paid by the Board, and the Board alone had power to dismiss him. The stevedores told the driver what they wanted the crane to lift but had no authority to tell him how to work the crane. McFarlane, who was a checker employed by the forwarding agents, was noting the number and marks on a case which the crane had picked up when he was trapped because of the negligence of the crane driver in failing to keep the crane still.

The question to be determined was whether in applying the doctrine of vicarious liability the general employers of the crane driver or the hirers were liable for his negligence. The Board contended that, under the terms of the contract between the Board and the stevedores, the stevedores were liable. *Held*—by the House of Lords—

(i) The question of liability was not to be determined by any agreement between the general employers and the hirers, but depended on the circumstances of the case. The test to apply was that of control.

(ii) The Board, as the general employers of the crane driver, had not established that the hirers had such control of the crane driver at the time of the accident as to become liable as employers for his negligence. Although the hirers could tell the crane driver where to go and what to carry, they had no authority to tell him how to operate the crane. The Board were, therefore, liable for his negligence.

(489) *Wright* v. *Tyne Improvement Commissioners (Osbeck & Co. Ltd, Third Party)*, [1968] 1 All E.R. 807

Tyne Improvement Commissioners hired a crane to Osbeck & Co. Ltd, under a written contract whereby the hirers agreed 'to bear the risk of and be responsible for all damage, injury or loss whatsoever, howsoever and whensoever caused arising directly or indirectly out of or in connection with the hiring or use of the said crane'. The plaintiff, who was a docker employed by Osbeck & Co., was injured when a wagon, in which he was standing to receive timber, was negligently moved forward by the capstan driver causing the plaintiff to collide with timber being lowered into the wagon by the crane. The plaintiff and the crane driver did all they could to avoid the accident but failed to do so and it was accepted that the capstan driver, who was employed by the Commissioners, was wholly to blame. Under the doctrine of vicarious liability the Commissioners were also to blame. When the action was tried at Newcastle upon Tyne Assizes, Waller, J., awarded the plaintiff damages of some £2985 against the Commissioners but dismissed a claim by the Commissioners against Osbeck & Co., as hirers of the crane, for an indemnity against the plaintiff's claim by virtue of the clause quoted above. The Commissioners now appealed against the dismissal of the claim for indemnity. *Held*—by the Court of Appeal—that as the accident arose directly or at least indirectly, out of or in connection with the use of the crane, the indemnity clause entitled the Commissioners to an indemnity against Osbeck & Co. even though the use to which the crane was being put was not a blameworthy cause of the accident.

(490) *Cassidy* v. *Ministry of Health*, [1951] 2 K.B. 343

The plaintiff's left hand was operated on at the defendants' hospital by a whole-time assistant medical officer of the hospital. After the operation the plaintiff's hand and forearm were put in a splint for fourteen days. During this time the plaintiff complained of pain but was merely given sedatives by the doctors who attended him. When the splint was removed, it was found that all four fingers of the plaintiff's hand were stiff, and that his hand was virtually useless. The plaintiff sued the defendants for negligence. *Held*—The defendants were liable in spite of their absence of real control over the type of work done by the doctors employed by them. Denning, L.J., stated that only where the patient himself selects and employs the doctor will the hospital authorities escape liability for that doctor's negligence. If the person causing the harm is part of the organization, the employer is liable.

(491) *Ferguson* v. *John Dawson & Partners (Contractors)*, [1976] 3 All E.R. 817

The plaintiff, who was working on 'the lump' was injured whilst working for the defendants who were contractors. No deductions were made by the defendants for income tax or National Insurance contributions and the plaintiff had been told that he was working 'purely as a lump labour force'. The defendants' site agent was responsible for hiring and dismissing the workmen, including the plaintiff; he told them what to do and moved them from site to site. If tools were required for the work, the defendants provided them. The plaintiff was injured when he fell off a roof which had no guard rail and he brought this action against the defendants on the basis that they were liable as his employers for failing to provide a guard rail on the flat roof which was required by construction regulations. It was *held*—by the Court of Appeal—that whatever label was put on the parties' relationship, other factors should be considered, such as the fact that the defendants could dismiss the workmen, including the plaintiff, and tell them what to do and where to do it. Accordingly, the plaintiff was the employee of the defendants who were therefore liable under the construction regulations and must pay the plaintiff damages for breach of that statutory duty.

(492) *Lee (Catherine)* v. *Lee's Air Farming Ltd*, [1960] 3 All E.R. 420

In 1954 the appellant's husband formed the respondent company which carried on the business of crop spraying from the air. In March, 1956, Mr Lee was killed while piloting an aircraft during the course of top soil dressing, and Mrs Lee claimed compensation from the company, as the employer of her husband, under the New Zealand Workers' Compensation Act, 1922. Since Mr Lee owned 2,999 of the company's 3000 £1 shares and since he was its governing director, the question arose as to whether the relationship of master and servant could exist between the company and him. He was employed as the company's chief pilot under a provision in the articles at a salary to be arranged by himself. *Held*—Mrs Lee was entitled to compensation because her husband was employed by the company in the sense required by the Act of 1922, and the decision in *Salomon* v. *Salomon & Co.*[61] was applied.

(493) *Century Insurance Co. Ltd* v. *Northern Ireland Road Transport Board*, [1942] A.C. 509

A tanker belonging to the respondents, and driven by one of their employees, was delivering petrol to a garage in Belfast. While the tanker was discharging petrol at the garage, the driver lit a cigarette and threw away the lighted match. The resulting explosion caused considerable damage. The contract under which the petrol was being delivered said that the respondents' employees were to take their orders from a petrol company to which the tankers were hired, a firm named Holmes, Mullin and Dunn, though they were not by virtue of this to be deemed the hirers' employees. The appellants had insured the defendants against liability to third parties, and pleaded that no claim could be made on them because, although the driver was admittedly negligent, he was at the time the servant of the hirers. *Held*—The appellants must pay the third party claim because the terms of the contract as a whole did not involve a transfer of the employees to Holmes, Mullin and Dunn; therefore, the respondents were liable for the negligence of the driver and were entitled to claim under their insurance.

(494) *Limpus* v. *London General Omnibus Co.* (1862), 1 H. & C. 526

The plaintiff's omnibus was overturned when the driver of the defendants' omnibus drove across it so as to be first at a bus stop to take all the passengers who were waiting. The defendants' driver admitted that the act was intentional, and arose out of bad feeling between the two drivers. The defendants had issued strict instructions to their drivers that they were not to obstruct other omnibuses. *Held*—The defendants were liable. Their driver was acting within the scope of his employment at the time of the collision, and it did not matter that the defendants had expressly forbidden him to act as he did.

(495) *Rose* v. *Plenty*, [1976] 1 All E.R. 97

Leslie Rose, aged 13, was given to helping Mr Plenty, a milkman, to deliver milk. Co-operative Retail Services Ltd, who employed Mr Plenty, expressly forbade their milkmen to take boys on their floats or to get boys to help them deliver the milk. On one occasion, while helping Mr Plenty, Leslie was sitting in the front of the float when his leg caught under the wheel. The accident was caused partly by Mr Plenty's negligence. It was *held*—by the Court of Appeal (Lord Denning, M.R. and Scarman, L.J.)—that Mr Plenty had been acting in the course of his employment so that his employers were liable to compensate Leslie Rose for his injuries. Lawton, L.J. (dissenting) said that the cases of *Twine* v. *Bean's Express*, (1946) and *Conway* v. *Geo. Wimpey*, (1951) were indistinguishable and that in giving Leslie a lift Mr Plenty had acted outside the scope of his employment.

(*Note:* there is really very little difference in the facts of *Rose* v. *Plenty* and *Twine* and *Conway* other than the fact that Leslie Rose was more than a mere hitch-hiker. His presence on the milk float was connected with the delivery of the milk which was a reason connected with the employment and this is why Lord Denning and Scarman, L.J. felt able to distinguish *Twine* and *Conway*.)

(496) *Vandyke* v. *Fender*, [1970] 2 All E.R. 335

Mr Vandyke and Mr Fender were employed by the same firm and lived thirty miles from the business premises. The employer agreed to supply a car to Mr Fender and to pay him 50p a day for petrol for the journey. The journey could have been made by train but was more convenient by car. Two other employees who lived in the same area were also carried. On one occasion the car loaned to Mr Fender was not available and he was allowed to use a car belonging to the company secretary. While driving this car an accident occurred resulting in an injury to Mr Vandyke who claimed damages from the company. It was *held* that the company was liable because Mr Fender, though not a paid driver, was driving the car as the company's agent and they were liable for his negligence. The question then arose as to which of the insurance companies involved should indemnify the company. If the risk was to be borne by the employers' liability insurance it was necessary to show that the accident occurred during and in the course of Mr Vandyke's employment, otherwise the risk would be borne by a road traffic insurance policy of Mr Fender's which covered him while driving someone else's car. It was *held*—by the Court of Appeal—that a man going to or from work as a passenger in a vehicle provided by his employers for that purpose is not in the course of employment unless he is obliged by the terms of his employment to travel in that vehicle. If not then, as here, the liability must be borne by the road traffic insurers and not by the employers' liability insurers.

(497) *Nottingham* v. *Aldridge; Prudential Assurance Co.* (1971), *The Times*, 23 February, 1971

In this case a Post Office trainee was returning to his normal work in his father's van after spending the week-end at his home having attended a training course the previous week. He was carrying another trainee, Nottingham, as a passenger and was entitled to a mileage allowance from the Post Office for himself and his passenger. Nottingham was injured as a result of an accident caused by the defendant's negligent driving. *Held*—by Eveleigh, J.—that the Post Office was not liable because the two trainees were not in the course of employment while travelling to work; nor was Aldridge the agent of the Post Office for the purposes of the journey. The vehicle did not belong to the Post Office nor was it provided by them. They had not prescribed the method of travel; admittedly a mileage allowance was payable but travelling expenses of any other kind would have been paid, e.g. bus or train fare. The question of agency was one of fact and on the facts of this case Aldridge was not an agent. The company which had insured the van was therefore liable to indemnify Aldridge in respect of his own liability to Nottingham.

(498) *Elleanor* v. *Cavendish Woodhouse Ltd*, *The Times*, 26 October, 1972

A Mr Comerford was employed by the defendants as a salesman in Darlington. He had to be at the defendants' premises between 9 a.m. and 5.30 p.m. It was also part of his job to solicit prospective customers in the evenings at their homes. He had to cover an area of 30 miles around Darlington. He had his own car which he was expected to use for his evening canvassing work. He was rewarded for his canvassing by the weekly sum of £2 paid as expenses, allowed to draw petrol on his employers' account at the local garage, and given a commission on the orders. In order to improve efficiency and to save petrol salesmen paired off for the evening working. The system of pairing off could not have worked without an implied term in their contracts of employment that the salesman who took the car would bring the other back in it and the employers were fully aware of the practise of pairing off. The plaintiff was injured in an accident caused by Mr Comerford's negligence. The accident happened on a country road at 9.30 p.m. after Mr Comerford and a fellow salesman had made their last call on a customer at about 8 p.m. They had stopped for a drink in a public house and were returning to Darlington when the collision occurred. The defendants contended that the salesmen were no longer acting in the course of their employment after they had made their last call and that the journey home after that call was no part of Mr Comerford's course of employment. The Court of Appeal did not accept that view. Mr Comerford was under a legal duty to take his fellow salesman back in his vehicle and therefore the accident took place in the course of his employment.

(499) *Britt* v. *Galmoye and Nevill* (1928), 44 T.L.R. 294

The first defendant, who had the second defendant in his employment as a van-driver, lent him his private motor car, after the day's work was finished, to take a friend to a theatre. The second defendant by his negligence injured the plaintiff. *Held*—that as the journey was not on the master's business and the master was not in control, he was not liable for his servant's act.

(500) *Adler* v. *Dickson*, [1955] 1 Q.B. 158

The plaintiff was travelling as a first-class passenger on the Peninsular and Orient Company's liner *Himalaya*. The ticket contained the following term: 'Passengers are carried at passengers' risk . . . The company will not be responsible for any injury whatsoever to the person of any passenger arising from, or occasioned by, the negligence of the company's servants.' The plaintiff fell from the gangway on to the wharf and was injured. Since the exemption clause exempted the company from liability, the plaintiff brought an action for negligence against the master and boatswain of the ship. *Held*—The plaintiff succeeded. The master and boatswain were not parties to the contract and could not claim the benefit of the exemption clause.

(*Note:* the Carriage of Goods by Sea Act, 1971, provides that an employee or agent of a carrier by sea, but not an independent contractor, shall be entitled to avail himself of the same defences and limits of liability as the carrier. This provision overrules *Adler* v. *Dickson* on its own facts. However the principle will apply in other situations, e.g. to an employee of a carrier of goods by road. In such circumstances note the device for protecting the employee which was apparently sanctioned in *Snelling* v. *J. G. Snelling*, 1972.)[123]

(501) *Morris* v. *C. W. Martin & Sons Ltd*, [1965] 2 All E.R. 725

The plaintiff sent a mink stole to a furrier for the purpose of cleaning. The furrier later told the plaintiff by telephone that he did not clean furs himself but intended to send the stole to the defendants, one of the biggest cleaners of fur in the country. The plaintiff knew of Martin & Sons and agreed that the stole be sent to them. Martin & Sons did work only for the fur trade and had issued to the furrier printed conditions which provided that goods belonging to customers were at customer's risk when on the premises of Martin & Sons, and that they should not be responsible for loss or damage however caused, though they would compensate for loss or damage to the goods during the cleaning process by reason of their negligence, but not by reason of any other cause. The furrier knew of these conditions when he handed the stole to the defendants and the defendants knew that it belonged to a customer of the furrier but they did not know that it was Morris. While in the possession of Martin & Sons the fur was stolen by a youth named Morrisey who had been employed by them for a few weeks only, though they had no grounds to suspect that he was dishonest. The plaintiff sued the defendants for conversion or negligence but the County Court Judge felt bound by *Cheshire* v. *Bailey*, 1905,[727] and held that the act of Morrisey, who had removed the stole by wrapping it round his body, was beyond the scope of his employment. In the Court of Appeal it was *held* that *Cheshire* v. *Bailey*, 1905,[727] had been impliedly overruled by *Lloyd* v. *Grace, Smith & Co.*, [1921] A.C. 716 (where it was held that a solicitor was liable for the criminal frauds of his managing clerk so long as the clerk was acting in the apparent scope of his authority). The defendants, as sub-bailees, were liable to the plaintiff, and on the matter of the exemption clause the Court of Appeal said that the terms of such a clause must be strictly construed, and since they referred only to goods 'belonging to customers' this could be taken to mean goods belonging to furrier and not to the furrier's customer, and because of this ambiguity the clause was inapplicable.

(*Note:* the above decision applies only to bailees for reward and only in circumstances where the servant is entrusted with, or put in charge of, the bailor's goods by his master. The mere fact that the servant's employment gave him the opportunity to steal the bailor's goods is not enough.)

(502) *Ormrod* v. *Crossville Motor Services Ltd*, [1953] 2 All E.R. 753

By an arrangement between the owner of a motor car and his friend, the friend was to drive the car from Birkenhead to Monte Carlo in order that the owner, the friend and the friend's wife, might use the car during their holiday in Monte Carlo. The owner of the car was travelling to Monte Carlo in another car as a competitor in the Monte Carlo Rally. Owing to the friend's negligent driving, the car was involved in a collision in which a motor bus was damaged. The question of the liability of the owner of the car for the damage arose. *Held*—The friend was acting as the owner's agent in the matter. The owner had an interest in the arrival of the car at Monte Carlo, and the driving was done for his benefit. Accordingly the owner was vicariously liable for his friend's negligence.

(503) *Morgans* v. *Launchbury*, [1972] 2 All E.R. 606

In this case the family car was registered in the name of the wife though it was used mainly by the husband who worked seven miles from home. The wife had asked her husband not to drive the car home himself if he had been drinking. On one occasion the husband had been drinking heavily and asked a friend, C, to drive him home together with three other passengers. There was an accident caused by the negligent driving of C and the husband and he were killed. The three passengers were injured and sued the wife claiming that she was liable vicariously for the negligence of C, who had been appointed to drive on her behalf by her husband. If the wife was held liable then her insurance company would be liable to the plaintiffs. The House of Lords held that she was not liable. The concept of agency required more than mere permission to use. Use must be at the owner's request or on his instructions.

(*Note:* before 1971 it was not compulsory for road traffic insurance to cover passengers. In fact Mrs Launchbury had an insurance policy which covered passengers but only in respect of accidents which occurred while she was driving. Obviously, the plaintiffs would have preferred to get their money from the insurance company than to sue the estate of C.)

(504) *Rambarran* v. *Gurrucharren*, [197] 1 All E.R. 749

In this case Rambarran, a chicken farmer in Guyana, owned a car which was used by several of his sons, Rambarran himself being unable to drive. One of his sons, Leslie, damaged Gurrucharren's car by negligently driving the family car. The Privy Council found that Rambarran was not liable for Leslie's negligence because he did not know that Leslie had taken the car since he was away from home at his chicken farm at the time in question. Furthermore, there was no evidence to show what the purpose of Leslie's journey was, but it was clearly not for any business or family purpose. Ownership of the vehicle was not enough in itself to establish liability.

(505) *Klein* v. *Calnori* (1971), *The Times*, 19 February, 1971

The defendant, Calnori, was the manager of a public house at Sunbury-on-Thames. While he was busy at the bar a Mr Freshwater, who knew Calnori, took his car and drove it away without his permission. Later Freshwater telephoned Calnori and told him he had taken his car. Calnori told him to bring it back. On the way back to Sunbury Freshwater collided with Klein's stationary car severely damaging it. Klein alleged that Calnori was liable for this damage because Freshwater was his agent. By asking Freshwater to bring the car back Freshwater was driving it partly for Calnori's purposes. *Held*—by Lyell, J.—Calnori was not liable. If Freshwater had borrowed the car with Calnori's consent then the loan to Freshwater, for his own purposes, would have involved returning it. In these circumstances Calnori would not have been liable for an accident on the return journey. Therefore Calnori's liability could not be greater in circumstances in which the car had been taken without his consent and had been used solely for the taker's purpose.

(506) *Bower* v. *Peate* (1876), 1 Q.B.D. 321

The plaintiff and defendant were respective owners of two adjoining houses, the plaintiff being entitled to the support for his house of the defendant's land. The defendant employed a contractor to pull down his house and to rebuild it after excavating the foundations. The contractor undertook the risk of supporting the plaintiff's house during the work and to make good any damage caused. The plaintiff's house was damaged in the progress of the work because the contractor did not take appropriate steps to support it. *Held*—that the defendant was liable. The fact that the injury would have been prevented if the contractor had provided proper support did not take away the defendant's liability. A person employing a contractor to perform a duty cast upon himself, in this case a duty of support, is responsible for the contractor's negligence in performing it.

(507) *Salsbury* v. *Woodland*, [1969] 3 All E.R. 863

The defendant employed, as an independent contractor, an experienced tree-feller to fell a large tree in his front garden. The contractor was negligent and the tree fell towards the highway bringing down telephone wires on to the highway. A car came along too fast, and the plaintiff, who was a bystander watching the whole operation, was injured when he dived out of the way of the inevitable collision between the car and the wire. *Held*—by the Court of Appeal—the defendant was not liable though the contractor was. There was no special liability in the defendant merely because the contractor was employed to work near, as distinct from on, the highway.

(508) *Padbury* v. *Holliday and Greenwood Ltd and Another* (1912), 28 T.L.R. 494

The defendants were employed to erect certain premises in Fenchurch Street, and the contract involved the employment by the defendants of sub-contractors to carry out the special work of putting metallic casements into the windows. While this work was being carried out an iron tool was placed by a servant of the sub-contractors on the window sill. The casement was blown by the wind and the tool fell and struck the plaintiff who was walking in the street below. The placing of the tool on the window sill was not the normal practice adopted in the work involved. *Held*—that the injuries were caused to the plaintiff by an act of collateral negligence on the part of a workman who was a servant of the sub-contractors and not of the defendants and that the latter were not, therefore, liable for the consequences of that negligence.

(509) *Simms* v. *Leigh Rugby Football Club*, [1969] 2 All E.R. 923

The plaintiff was a member of a visiting team playing rugby football on the defendant club's ground when his leg was broken as he was tackled and thrown towards a concrete wall which ran at a distance of 7 ft 3 in from the touch line. The League's by-laws proscribed that the distance had to be at least 7 ft. *Held*—by Wrangham J.—that the plaintiff must be taken willingly to have accepted the risks involved in playing on that field. The ground complied with the by-laws of the Rugby Football League and the defendants were not, therefore, liable under the Occupiers' Liability Act, 1957, or in general negligence by reason of the plaintiff's consent.

(510) *Murray* v. *Harringay Arena Ltd*, [1951] 2 K.B. 529

David Charles Murray, aged six, was taken by his parents to the defendants' ice rink to watch a hockey match. They occupied front seats at the rink, and during the game the boy was hit in the eye by the puck. This action was brought against the defendants for negligence. *Held*—The risk was voluntarily undertaken by the plaintiffs. The defendants had provided protection by means of netting and a wooden barrier which, in the circumstances, was adequate, since further protection would have seriously interfered with the view of the spectators.

(511) *Hall* v. *Brooklands Auto-Racing Club*, [1933] 1 K.B. 205

The plaintiff paid for admission to the defendants' premises to watch motor car races. During one of the races a car left the track, as a result of a collision with another car, and crashed through the railings injuring the plaintiff. It was the first time that a car had gone through the railings, and in view of that the precautions taken by the defendants were adequate. In this action by the plaintiff for personal injuries, it was *held* that the danger was not one which the defendants ought to have anticipated, and that the plaintiff must be taken to have agreed to assume the risk of such an accident.

(512) *White* v. *Blackmore*, [1972] 3 All E.R. 158

The husband of the plaintiff widow was a member of a 'jalopy' racing club. He went to a meeting organized by the defendants as a competitor but stood outside the spectators' ropes close to a stake. The wheel of a car caught on one of the ropes some distance away so that the stake was pulled up sharply and the husband was killed when he was catapulted some 20 feet. The defendants displayed notices warning the public of the danger and stating as a condition of admission that they were absolved from all liabilities for accidents howsoever caused. The widow claimed damages for breach of Sect. 2 of the Occupiers' Liability Act, 1957 and/or general negligence. *Held*—by the Court of Appeal—(i) that even though the deceased had been negligent in standing where he did, the defence of *volenti* would not succeed as the deceased did not know of the risk that had caused his death; (ii) however, the claim would fail as the defendants were entitled to exclude their liability and this they had done by warning notices.

(*Note*: it is true that the defendants could effectively exclude their liability under the Occupiers' Liability Act, 1957, by warning notices and without a contract. Section 2(1) of the Act of 1957 provides that an occupier owes 'a common duty of care' to all his visitors but that this can be restricted or excluded 'by agreement or otherwise'. However, as regards the claim in general negligence, it ought not to be possible to exclude liability for negligence unless the plaintiff assents in a contract. But see now Unfair Contract Terms Act, 1977.)

(513) *Baker* v. *James Bros*, [1921] 2 K.B. 674

The defendants were wholesale grocers and they employed the plaintiff as a traveller. He was supplied by the defendants with a motor car, the starting gear of which was defective. The plaintiff repeatedly complained about this to the defendants, but nothing was done to remedy the defect. While the plaintiff was on his rounds, the car stopped, and he was injured whilst trying to re-start. *Held*—Notwithstanding the plaintiff's knowledge of the defect, he had never consented to take upon himself the risk of injury from the continued use of the car. He was not guilty of any contributory negligence and was entitled to recover damages.

(514) *Dann* v. *Hamilton*, [1939] 1 K.B. 509

The plaintiff had been with a party to see the coronation decorations in London. They made the journey in the defendant's car. During the day and evening the defendant had consumed a quantity of intoxicating liquor, but he drove the party back to Staines where they all got out. The plaintiff was at this point a 2d. bus ride from her home but she accepted the defendant's invitation to take her there. During this part of the journey there was an accident caused by the defendant's negligence, and the plaintiff was injured. She now sued in respect of these injuries and the defendant pleaded *volenti non fit injuria*. *Held*—That the defence did not apply and the plaintiff succeeded. She had knowledge of a potential danger, but that did not mean that she assented to it.

(*Note:* (i) The court left open the question where the driver was 'dead drunk' or 'very drunk'. In such a case the maxim might have applied.

(ii) It should be noted that the defence of contributory negligence was not pleaded in *Dann* although Asquith, J., encouraged counsel for the defence to raise it but he would not be drawn. However, it is now accepted that although *volenti* may not apply in a situation such as *Dann* a plaintiff may be guilty of contributory negligence if he travels as a passenger when he knows the driver has consumed enough alcohol to impair his ability to drive safely, or if he goes drinking with the driver knowing he will be a passenger later when the drink deprives him of his own capacity to appreciate the danger.) (So decided in *Owens* v. *Brimmell*, [1976] 3 All E.R. 765.)

(515) *Smith* v. *Baker and Sons*, [1891] A.C. 325

Smith was employed by Baker and Sons to drill holes in some rock in a railway cutting. A crane, operated by fellow employees, often swung heavy stones over Smith's head while he was working on the rock face. Both Smith and his employers realized that there was a risk the stones might fall, but the crane was nevertheless operated without any warning being given at the moment of jibbing or swinging. Smith was injured by a stone which fell from the crane because of negligent strapping of the load. The House of Lords *held* that Smith had not voluntarily undertaken the risk of his employers' negligence, and that his knowledge of the danger did not prevent his recovering damages.

(516) *Imperial Chemical Industries Ltd.* v. *Shatwell*, [1964] 2 All E.R. 999

George and James Shatwell were certificated and experienced shotfirers employed by ICI. Statutory rules imposed an obligation on them personally (not on their employers) to ensure that certain operations connected with shotfiring should not be done unless all persons in the vicinity had taken cover. They knew of the risks of premature explosion which had been explained to them; they knew of the prohibition; but on one occasion because a cable they had was too short to reach the shelter, they decided to test without taking cover rather than wait ten minutes for their companion Beswick who had gone to fetch a longer cable. James gave George two wires, and George applied them to the galvanometer terminals. An explosion occurred and both men were injured. At the trial it was found that James was guilty of negligence and breach of statutory duty for which the employers were held vicariously liable, damages being assessed at £1500 on a basis of 50 per cent contributory negligence. The Court of Appeal affirmed, but the House of Lords *reversed*, the decision and *held* that, although James's acts were a contributory cause of the accident to George, the employers were not liable.

(*a*) They were not themselves in breach of a statutory duty.

(*b*) They could plead *volenti non fit injuria* to a claim of vicarious liability.

(*c*) They had shown no negligence. They had instilled the need for caution, made proper provision, and even arranged a scale of remuneration in a way which removed a temptation to take short cuts.

(*d*) The Shatwell brothers were trained men well aware of the risk involved so the principle of *volenti non fit injuria* applied. Lord Pearce said: 'The defence (of *volenti non fit injuria*) should be available where the employer was not in himself in breach of a statutory duty and was not vicariously in breach of a statutory duty through the neglect of some person of superior rank to the plaintiff and whose commands the plaintiff was bound to obey or who has some special and different duty of care.'

(*Note:* if the employers had been compelled to rely on the defence of contributory negligence, they might have escaped liability if only one man were involved and treated as solely responsible, but where two men were involved, as here, they would have been vicariously liable for James's contribution to George's injury and for George's contribution to James's injury so they would have been compelled to partially compensate each man.)

(517) *Haynes* v. *Harwood and Son*, [1935] 1 K.B. 146

The defendants' servant left his van unattended in a street and the horses bolted with it. The plaintiff was a police constable on duty in a police station and seeing the horses bolting into a crowded street, and realizing that, unless the horses were stopped, people in the street, including many children, would be likely to be injured, he darted out of the police station and, at great risk to himself, seized one of the horses and managed to bring them to a standstill. He was injured in doing so. It was *held* by the Court of Appeal that the defendants had been negligent, that the plaintiff was not guilty of contributory negligence, and that the damage was not too remote. The defendants also alleged assumption of risk by the plaintiff, but the court decided that the plaintiff's knowledge of the risk was not a bar to his claim.

(518) *Baker* v. *T. E. Hopkins and Son Ltd*, [1959] 1 W.L.R. 966

The defendants were building contractors and were engaged to clean out a well. Various methods had been used in order to pump out the water, including hand-operated pumps, but eventually a petrol-driven pump was employed. The exhaust from the engine on the pump resulted in a lethal concentration of carbon monoxide forming inside the well. Two of the defendants' employees went down the well to carry on the work of cleaning it and were overcome by the fumes. Baker was a local doctor and, on being told what had happened, he went along to give what assistance he could. He was lowered down the well on a rope, and on reaching the two men, he realized that they were beyond help. He then gave a pre-arranged signal to those at the top of the well and started his journey to the surface. Unfortunately the rope became caught on a projection and Dr Baker was himself overcome by fumes and died. His executors claimed damages in respect of Dr Baker's death. *Held*—The defendants were negligent towards their employees in using the petrol-driven pump and the maxim *volenti non fit injuria* did not bar the claim of Dr Baker's executors. Although Dr Baker may have had knowledge of the risk he was running, he did not freely and voluntarily undertake it, but acted under the compulsion of his instincts as a brave man and a doctor.

(519) *Cutler* v. *United Dairies (London) Ltd*, [1933] 2 K.B. 297

The defendants' carman left the defendants' horse and van, two wheels being properly chained, while he delivered milk. The horse, being startled by the noise coming from a river steamer, bolted down the road and into a meadow. It stopped in the meadow and was followed there by the carman who, being in an excited state, began to shout for help. The plaintiff, a spectator, went to the carman's assistance and tried to hold the horse's head. The horse lunged and the plaintiff was injured. In this action by the plaintiff against the defendants for negligence it was *held* that in the circumstances the plaintiff voluntarily and freely assumed the risk. This was not an attempt to stop a runaway horse so that there was no sense of urgency to impel the plaintiff. He therefore knew of the risk and had had time to consider it, and by implication must have agreed to incur it.

(520) *Hyett* v. *Great Western Railway Co.*, [1948] 1 K.B. 345

The plaintiff was employed by a firm of wagon repairers and he was on the defendants' premises with their authority to carry out his duties. While repairing a wagon he saw smoke rising from one of the defendants' wagons in the same siding and went to investigate. The floor of the wagon, which contained paraffin oil, was in flames. The plaintiff was trying to get the drums of paraffin oil out, when one of them exploded and injured him. Evidence showed that the defendants knew that there was a paraffin leakage in the wagon, but had nevertheless allowed it to remain in the siding. *Held*—The plaintiff was entitled to recover damages from the defendants, and the maxim *volenti non fit injuria* did not apply. A man may take reasonable risks in trying to preserve property put in danger by another's negligence.

(521) *Videan* v. *British Transport Commission*, [1963] 2 All E.R. 860

A child managed to get on to a railway line and was injured by a trolley. The Court of Appeal *held* that the child's presence was not in the circumstances foreseeable and the defendants did not owe him a duty of care. However, a duty was owed to his father who was injured trying to rescue him.

(*Note:* it is difficult to follow the reasoning by which the Court of Appeal held that the defendants ought to have foreseen that a stationmaster would try to rescue a minor on the line (the minor being the son of the stationmaster) yet need not have foreseen the presence of that minor himself.)

(522) *Wooldridge* v. *Sumner*, [1962] 2 All E.R. 978

A competitor of great skill and experience was riding a horse at a horse show when it ran wide at a corner and injured a cameraman who was unfamiliar with horses and who had ignored a steward's request to move outside the competition area. The rider was thrown, but later rode the horse again and it was adjudged supreme champion of its class. The cameraman brought an action for damages, and at the trial was awarded damages on the ground of negligence. *Held*, on appeal, that no negligence had been established because (i) any excessive speed at the corner was not the cause of the accident, and was not negligence but merely an error of judgment; and (ii) the judge's finding that the horse would have gone on to a cinder track without harm to the plaintiff if the rider had allowed it to, was an inference from primary facts and unjustified, and in any event an attempt to control the horse did not amount to negligence.

Per Diplock, L.J., 'If, in the course of a game or competition, at a moment when he has not time to think, a participant by mistake takes a wrong measure, he is not to be held guilty of any negligence. ... A person attending a game or competition takes the risk of any damage caused to him by any act of a participant done in the course of and for the purposes of the game or competition, notwithstanding that such act may involve an error of judgment or a lapse of skill, unless the participant's conduct is such as to evince a reckless disregard of the spectator's safety. The spectator takes the risk because such an act involves *no breach of the duty of care* owed by the participant to him. He does not take the risk by virtue of the doctrine expressed or obscured by the maxim *volenti non fit injuria*. . . . The maxim in English law *presupposes a tortious act* by the defendant. The consent that is relevant is not consent to the risk of injury but consent to the lack of reasonable care that may produce that risk.'

(523) *Wilks* v. *Cheltenham Home Guard Motor Cycle and Light Car Club, The Times*, 25 March, 1971.

The plaintiffs were father and daughter and they sued in negligence for injuries received as spectators at a motor cycle scramble at Withybridge on 21 September, 1966. They were in an enclosure fenced off with stakes and ropes designed to keep spectators in. Some ten feet away from this fence was another rope designed to keep any motor cycle from intruding into the enclosure. A competitor, Mr Ward, left the course, crashed through the safety rope and struck the plaintiffs. It was *held*—by the Court of Appeal—that Mr Ward was not negligent. He was going at about ten miles per hour when he left the track and although he lost control this could be expected in a scramble of this kind. A competitor in a race must use reasonable care. But that meant reasonable care having regard to the fact that he was a competitor in a race in which he was expected to go 'all out' to win. A batsman was expected to hit a six if he could, even if it landed among the spectators. So in a race a competitor was expected to go as fast as he could, as long as he was not foolhardy. In a race a reasonable man should do all that he could do to win, but he should not be foolhardy.

(524) *Nettleship* v. *Weston*, [1971] 3 All E.R. 581

The plaintiff, a non-professional driving instructor, gave the defendant driving lessons after having first satisfed himself that the car was insured to cover injury to passengers. The defendant was a careful driver but on the third lesson she failed to straighten out after turning left and struck a lamp standard breaking the plaintiff's kneecap. The defendant was convicted of driving without due care and attention. *Held*—by the Court of Appeal—that since the plaintiff had checked on the insurance position he had expressly not consented to run the risk and there was no question of *volenti*. Furthermore, the duty of care owed by a learner-driver was the same as that owed by every driver and the defendant was liable for the damages. A learner-driver owes a duty to his instructor to drive with proper skill and care, the test being the objective one of the careful driver and it is no defence that he was doing his best.

(525) *Stanley* v. *Powell*, [1891] 1 Q.B. 86

The defendant was a member of a shooting party, and the plaintiff was employed to carry cartridges and also any game which was shot. The defendant fired at a pheasant, but a shot glanced off an oak tree and injured the plaintiff. *Held*—The plaintiff's claim failed. The defendant's action was neither intentional nor was it negligent.

(526) *National Coal Board* v. *Evans (J. E.) & Co. (Cardiff) Ltd and Another*, [1951] 2 K.B. 861

Evans & Co. were employed by Glamorgan County Council to carry out certain work on land belonging to the council. It was necessary to excavate a trench across the land, and Evans & Co. sub-contracted with the second defendants to do this work. An electric cable passed under the land, but the council, Evans & Co., and the sub-contractors had no knowledge of this and it was not marked on any available map. During the course of the excavation a mechanical digger damaged the cable so that water seeped into it causing an explosion. The electricity supply to the plaintiff's colliery was cut off, and they sued the defendants in trespass and negligence. Donovan, J., at first instance, found that the defendants were not negligent, but were liable in trespass. The Court of Appeal *held* the defendants were entirely free from fault and there was no trespass by them.

(527) *Nichols* v. *Marsland* (1876), 2 Ex.D. 1

For many years there had existed certain artificial ornamental lakes on the defendant's land, formed by damming up of a natural stream the source of which was at a point higher up. An extraordinary rainfall 'greater and more violent than any within the memory of witnesses' caused the stream and the lakes to swell to such an extent that the artificial banks burst, and the escaping water carried away four bridges belonging to the county council. Nichols, the county surveyor, sued under the rule in *Rylands* v. *Fletcher*. *Held*—The defendant was not liable for this extraordinary act of nature which she could not reasonably have anticipated. The escape of water was owing to the act of God, and while one is bound to provide against the ordinary operations of nature, one is not bound to provide against miracles.

(*Note:* although *Rylands* v. *Fletcher* liability is strict, act of God is a defence.)

(528) *Cresswell* v. *Sirl*, [1948] 1 K.B. 241

The defendant, a farmer's son, was awakened during the night by dogs barking, and on going out found certain ewe sheep in lamb, penned up by the dogs in a corner of a field. The dogs seemed about to attack the sheep and had been chasing them for an hour. A light was turned on the dogs, who then left the sheep and started for the defendant. When they were about 40 yards away, the defendant fired and killed one of the dogs. The owner of the dog sued the defendant for damages. In the county court, judgment was given for the owner of the dog on the ground that such a killing could be justified only if it took place while the dog was actually attacking the sheep. In the view of the Court of Appeal, however, the defendant could justify his act by showing that it was necessary to avert immediate danger to property. It was not necessary that the dog should actually be attacking the sheep. This decision is affirmed by Sect. 9 of the Animals Act, 1971, which now covers the situation.

(529) *Cope* v. *Sharpe (No. 2)*, [1912] 1 K.B. 486

The plaintiff was a landowner and he let the shooting rights over part of his land to a tenant. A heath fire broke out on part of the plaintiff's land and the defendant, who was the head gamekeeper of the tenant, set fire to patches of heather between the main fire and a covert in which his master's pheasants were sitting. His object was to prevent the fire spreading. In fact the fire was extinguished independently of what the defendant had done, and the plaintiff now sued the defendant for damages for trespass. *Held*—The defendant was not liable because when he carried out the act it seemed reasonably necessary, and it did not matter that in the event it turned out to be unnecessary.

(530) *Beckwith* v. *Philby* (1827), 6 B. & C. 635

In this case it was *held* that the mistaken arrest of an innocent man on suspicion of felony by an ordinary citizen is not actionable as false imprisonment, if the felony has been committed, and if there are reasonable grounds for believing that the person arrested is guilty of it.

(531) *Buron* v. *Denman* (1848), 2 Exch. 167

The captain of a British warship was *held* not liable for trespass when he set fire to the barracoon of a Spaniard slave trader on the West Coast of Africa and released the slaves. The captain had general instructions to suppress the slave trade, and in any case his conduct in this matter was afterwards approved by the Admiralty and the Foreign and Colonial Secretaries. It seems, therefore, that neither the official responsible nor the Crown can be sued for injuries inflicted upon others outside the territorial jurisdiction of the Crown, if these are authorized or subsequently ratified by the Crown.

(532) *Nissan* v. *Attorney-General*, [1967] 2 All E.R. 1238

The plaintiff, a British subject, was the tenant of an hotel in Cyprus. In December, 1963, the Government of Cyprus accepted an offer that British Forces stationed in Cyprus should give assistance in restoring peace to the island. The British troops occupied the plaintiff's hotel for some months and the plaintiff now sued the Crown for compensation. It was *held inter alia* that the Crown was obliged to pay compensation and that a plea by the Crown of 'act of state' was no defence as against a British subject.

(533) *Johnstone* v. *Pedlar*, [1921] 2 A.C. 262

Johnstone was the Chief Commissioner of the Dublin Metropolitan Police. He was the defendant in an action in which Pedlar sued for the detention of £124 in cash and a cheque for £4 15s. 6d. Pedlar was convicted of being engaged in the illegal drilling of troops in Ireland, and the above property was found on him at the time of his arrest. Pedlar, who was a naturalized citizen of the United States of America, sued for the return of his property, and the defence was 'Act of State'. A certificate given by the Chief Secretary for Ireland was put in at the trial, certifying that the detention of the property was formally ratified as an act of state. *Held*—Pedlar was entitled to claim his property, because the defence of 'Act of State' cannot be raised against an alien who is a subject of a friendly nation.

(534) *Vaughan* v. *Taff Vale Railway* (1860), 5 H. & N. 679

The defendants were *held* not liable for fires caused by sparks from engines which they were bound by statute to run and constructed with proper care.

   (*Note:* by the Railway Fires Acts, 1905 and 1923, British Rail is under a liability of up to £200 for damage to crops caused by fire resulting from sparks from engines run under statutory authority, though the advent of diesel and electric trains makes the statute somewhat out of date.)

(535) *Penny* v. *Wimbledon Urban Council*, [1899] 2 Q.B. 72

The defendants, acting under conditional powers conferred upon them by Sect. 150 of the Public Health Act, 1875, employed a contractor to make up a road in their district. The contractor removed the surface soil and placed it in heaps on the road. The plaintiff, while passing along the road in the dark, fell over one of the heaps, which had been left unlighted and unguarded, and was injured. She now sued for damages. *Held*—She succeeded. Although the council were operating under statutory powers they must, if they do acts likely to cause danger to the public, see that the work is properly carried out, and take reasonable measures to guard against danger. The council did not discharge this duty by delegating it to a contractor, and the local authority were liable for negligence.

(536) *Marriage* v. *East Norfolk Rivers Catchment Board*, [1950] 1 K.B. 284

In pursuance of their powers under Sect. 34 of the Land Drainage Act, 1930, the Catchment Board deposited dredgings taken from the river on the south bank of that river, so raising its height by one to two feet. When the river next flooded, the flood waters instead of escaping over the south bank, as they had always done, ran over the north bank and swept away a bridge leading to a mill owned by the plaintiff. Section 34(3) of the Land Drainage Act, 1930, provided that, in the event of injury to any person by reason of the exercise by a drainage board of any of its powers, the board concerned should make full compensation, disputes being settled by a system of arbitration. The plaintiff had issued a writ for nuisance against the board. *Held*—No action in nuisance lay; the plaintiff's only remedy was to claim compensation under Sect. 34(3).

(537) *Parry* v. *Cleaver*, [1969] 1 All E.R. 555

The plaintiff was injured by the defendant's motor car and and to retire from the police force. He was entitled to a pension of £3 18s. 6d. per week for life. The defendant had admitted liability and the court was asked to decide whether the pension should be ignored in arriving at an assessment of damages. *Held*—by the House of Lords—the pension was similar to private insurance arrangements and should be ignored in assessing damages. The principle of *British Transport Commission* v. *Gourley*, [1955] 3 All E.R. 796, was inapplicable.

(538) *Hewson* v. *Downes*, [1969] 3 All E.R. 193

The plaintiff, aged 66, suffered injuries when the defendant, by negligent driving, pinned him against the wall of a shop. The plaintiff was still employed at the time of the accident but retired as a result of it. *Held*—by Park, J.—that the State retirement pension which he was receiving should not be taken into account in assessing damages. (*Parry* v. *Cleaver*, 1969,[537] *applied*.)

(539) *Smith* v. *London and South Western Railway Co.* (1870), L.R. 6 C.P. 14

During a hot and dry summer the defendants' employees cut certain hedges and trimmed grass. They left the resultant clippings by the side of the railway track for a fortnight and the sparks from a passing engine set fire to them. This fire ran two hundred yards, crossed the roadway, and eventually damaged the plaintiff's cottage. *Held*—Although a reasonable man would have foreseen the possibility of fire, he would not have foreseen the danger to the cottage. Nevertheless, the defendants were liable because, although the damage was a freak, they were liable for all direct consequences of their act, foreseeable or not.

(540) *Re Polemis and Furness Withy and Co.*, [1921] 3 K.B. 560

Stevedores were unloading the hold of a vessel which contained drums of petrol. There was some leakage from certain of the drums and the hold was filled with highly inflammable vapour. Through the negligence of a stevedore a plank was knocked into the hold, where, in its fall, it struck a spark, setting the vapour alight. The ensuing fire destroyed the ship. It was *held* that the employers of the stevedores were liable for the total loss, even though the negligent stevedore could not have reasonably foreseen that his act would destroy the ship, though he might have foreseen some damage. The destruction of the ship was a direct consequence of the negligent act, and damages were recoverable.

(541) *Liesbosch, Dredger* v. *S.S. Edison*, [1933] A.C. 449

The dredger *Liesbosch* was lost after being dragged into open sea from her mooring in Patras harbour. This was the result of the negligence of the navigator of the S.S. *Edison*. The *Liesbosch* was engaged in dredging Patras harbour, and the contract provided for heavy penalties for delay. The dredger could have been replaced by the purchase of a new one, but the owners of the *Liesbosch* were poorly placed financially and could not afford to do so immediately. They had, therefore, to hire a dredger (the *Adria*) in the meantime at great expense. The plaintiffs included this additional hiring in their claim for damages for the loss of the *Liesbosch*. *Held*—Damages in respect of the hiring were not recoverable under the rule in *Re Polemis*. This damage was not caused by the defendants' negligence but by the plaintiffs' poverty. However, the plaintiffs were entitled to the value of the *Liesbosch* as a going concern, not simply her value as a rather old dredger, on the basis that you take your victim as you find him.

(542) *Overseas Tankship (UK) Ltd* v. *Morts Dock and Engineering Co. Ltd (the Wagon Mound)*, [1961] A.C. 388

The appellants were the charterers of a ship called the *Wagon Mound*. While the ship was taking on furnace oil in Sydney harbour, the appellants' servants negligently allowed oil to spill into the water. The action of the wind and tide carried this oil some 200 yards and over to the respondents' wharf where the business of shipbuilding and repairing was carried on. The servants of the respondents were at this time engaged in repairing a vessel, the *Corrimal*, which was moored alongside the wharf, and for this purpose they were using welding equipment. The manager of the respondents, seeing the oil on the water, suspended welding operations and consulted the wharf manager who told him it was safe to continue work—a decision which was justified, because previous knowledge showed that sparks were not likely to set fire to oil floating on water. Work, therefore, proceeded with safety precautions being taken. However, a piece of molten metal fell from the wharf and set on fire a piece of cotton waste which was floating on the oil. This set the oil alight and the respondents' wharf was badly damaged. The Supreme Court of New South Wales held the appellants liable for the extensive damage by fire, and in doing so followed *Re Polemis*.[540] The case then came before the Judicial Committee of the Privy Council on appeal. *Held*—the appellants were successful in their appeal, the Judicial Committee holding that *Re Polemis*[540] should no longer be considered good law, and that foreseeability of the actual harm resulting was the proper test. On this principle, they held that the damage caused by the fire was too remote, though they would have awarded damages for the fouling of the respondents' slipways by oil, if such a claim had been made, since this was foreseeable.

(*Note:* in *Overseas Tankship (UK) Ltd* v. *Miller Steamship Property Ltd (The Wagon Mound (No. 2))*, [1966] 2 All E.R. 709, the same blaze had caused damage to the respondents' ship (they were the owners of the *Corrimal*). However, the Privy Council changed its mind and found as a fact that the fire and ensuing damage were foreseeable and the respondents recovered in negligence and also nuisance. The Privy Council *held* that in the case of nuisance, as of negligence, it is not enough that the damage was a direct result of the nuisance if the injury was not foreseeable.)

(543) *Hughes* v. *Lord Advocate*, [1963] 1 All E.R. 705

Workmen opened a manhole in the street and later left it unattended having placed a tent above it and warning paraffin lamps around it. The plaintiff and another boy, who were aged 8 and 10 respectively, took one of the lamps and went down the manhole. As they came out the lamp was knocked into the hole and an explosion took place injuring the plaintiff. The explosion was caused in a unique fashion because the paraffin had vapourized (which was unusual) and been ignited by the naked flame of the wick. The defendants argued that although some injury by burning was foreseeable, burning by explosion was not. *Held*—by the House of Lords—that the defendants were liable. 'The cause of this accident was a known source of danger, the lamp, but it behaved in an unpredictable way. . . . This accident was caused by a known source of danger but caused in a way which could not have been foreseen and in my judgment that affords no defence.' (*Per* Lord Reid.) 'The accident was but a variant of the foreseeable. It was, to quote the words of Denning, L.J., in *Roe* v. *Minister of Health*,[646] 'within the risk created by the negligence'. . . . The children's entry into the tent with the ladder, the descent into the hole, the mishandling of the lamp, were all foreseeable. The greater part of the path to injury had thus been trodden, and the mishandled lamp was quite likely at that state to spill and cause a conflagration. Instead, by some curious chance of combustion, it exploded and no conflagration occurred, it would seem, until after the explosion. There was thus an unexpected manifestation of the apprehended physical dangers. But it would be, I think, too narrow a view to hold that those who created the risk of fire are excused from the liability for the damage by fire because it came by way of explosive combustion. The resulting damage, though severe, was not greater than or different in kind from that which might have produced had the lamp spilled and caused a more normal conflagration in the hole.' (*Per* Lord Pearce.)

(544) *Bradford* v. *Robinson Rentals*, [1967] 1 All E.R. 267

In January, 1963, the plaintiff, a television engineer aged 57, was told by his employer to drive an old van from Exeter to Bedford, exchange it there for a new one and drive back to Exeter, a round journey of some 500 miles involving about 20 hours' driving.

The plaintiff protested because the weather was severe but he undertook the journey. The radiator of the old van had to be refilled frequently and neither of the vans had a heater so that the windscreen had to be kept open to prevent the formation of ice. The plaintiff took all reasonable precautions to protect himself from the cold but even so he sustained permanent injury to his hands and feet from frostbite. *Held*—that the defendant had been negligent and judgment was given for the plaintiff. Liability in negligence does not depend upon the precise nature of the injury being foreseeable. It is enough if the injury was of a kind that was foreseeable even though the form that it took was unusual. *Some* injury from cold was foreseeable.

(545) *Weiland* v. *Cyril Lord Carpets*, [1969] 3 All E.R. 1006

The plaintiff was injured when the bus on which she was travelling had to brake suddenly as a result of the negligent driving of the defendant's vehicle by one of their employees. As part of her treatment she had to have a collar fitted to her neck and in consequence was unable to use her bi-focal spectacles with her usual skill. At a later stage this caused her to fall down some stairs sustaining further injuries. *Held*—by Eveleigh, J.—that the second injury was attributable to the original negligence of the defendants and they were liable in damages. If an injury affects a person's ability to cope with the vicissitudes of life and thereby is the cause of another injury, the latter injury is a foreseeable consequence of the former within the terms of *The Wagon Mound*, 1961,[542] and *Hughes* v. *Lord Advocate*, 1963.[543]

(546) *Doughty* v. *Turner Manufacturing Co.*, [1964] 1 All E.R. 98

Doughty, a workman, was injured in a factory where he worked. A workman accidentally knocked an asbestos cement cover into a cauldon of sodium cyanide which was rendered molten by being raised to 800°C., eight times the heat of boiling water. The cover fell some four to six inches, and one or two minutes afterwards the heat caused a chemical change in the asbestos cement whereby it released water, which turned into steam and caused an explosion of the hot liquid which injured Doughty. Such an eruption was not expected, and indeed its cause was only discovered by subsequent experiments carried out by Imperial Chemical Industries Ltd, which revealed that the immersion of such a cover, or indeed any other object containing actual moisture, and its subjection to a temperature of 500°C., would cause such an eruption. Such a phenomenon could not have been known to the defendants beforehand. The Court of Appeal allowed an appeal by the Turner Manufacturing Co. against an award by the lower court of £150 damages to Doughty. It was *held* that a splash, such as was caused by the falling cover, would be a foreseeable danger and should be guarded against, but this was not the cause of the accident, and in any case the lid fell only a few inches and the heavy liquid would not travel far. Although the eruption had the same effect as a splash, it was quite unrealistic to regard it as a variant of the perils of splashing. The cause was quite different, it would be wrong to make such an inroad into the doctrine of foreseeability.

(*Note:* it might be thought that the plaintiff should have recovered damages in this case on the principles laid down in *Hughes* v. *Lord Advocate*, 1963.[543] It was a negligent act to fail to take reasonable care to prevent the cover from being knocked into the liquid. This being so it should not have mattered whether the cover caused a splash or an eruption. Injury caused by either event should have resulted in an award of damages.)

(547) *Tremain* v. *Pike*, [1969] 3 All E.R. 1303

The plaintiff, who was a herdsman, contracted Weil's disease through handling hay and washing his hands in a water trough both of which were contaminated by the urine of rats with which the farm was badly infected. Weil's disease is rarely contracted by human beings, but when it is, it results from the skin coming into contact with the urine of rats. *Held*—by Payne, J.—that the plaintiff's employer was not liable. Although the defendant was negligent in that a prudent farmer would have called in a rodent officer to deal with the infestation, the resulting injury to the plaintiff was not foreseeable, though an injury arising from a rat-bite or food poisoning by consumption of food or drink contaminated by rats might have been.

(*Note:* this decision seems to be out of line with *Hughes* v. *Lord Advocate*, 1963,[543] and *Bradford* v. *Robinson Rentals*, 1967.[544] An infestation of rats is a known source of danger to man. The fact that they attacked in an unusual and unpredictable way should not have affected the right of the plaintiff to damages.)

(548) *Smith* v. *Leech Braine & Co. Ltd*, [1962] 2 W.L.R. 148

The plaintiff was the widow of a person employed by the defendants. Mr Smith's work consisted in lowering articles into a galvanizing tank containing molten zinc. On one occasion he was struck on the lip by a piece of molten metal which caused a burn. This resulted in a cancer from which he died three years later. Mr Smith's work had given him a pre-disposition to cancer and the question arose whether, since the *Wagon Mound*, the so-called 'thin skull rule' had disappeared, so that the plaintiff had to show that the cancer was foreseeable. The Lord Chief Justice, Lord Parker, finding for the plaintiff, said in the course of his judgment: 'I am satisfied that the Judicial Committee of the Privy Council did not have what are called "thin skull" cases in mind. It has always been the common law that a tortfeasor must take his victim as he finds him.'

(549) *Martindale* v. *Duncan*, [1973] 1 W.L.R. 674

The plaintiff's car was damaged in a collision with the defendant's car due to the negligence of the defendant. The plaintiff delayed repairs to his car pending the approval of the defendant's insurers and also of his own. The defendant's insurers wished to seek the advice of independent engineers and did so. About nine weeks after the accident, the defendant's insurers approved the estimate. A few days later the plaintiff's insurers did so and the repairs were started one week afterwards. The District Registrar awarded the plaintiff damages including £220 for loss of use of his vehicle for ten weeks at the rate of £22 per week for hire of a substitute vehicle to cover the period during which he had delayed repairs pending approval of the estimate by the insurers. The defendant had argued that the repairs were not commenced as early as they could have been since the plaintiff was not himself able to pay for the repairs but had to wait to see what the position was as regards payment from an insurance company. On appeal by the defendant it was *held*—by the Court of Appeal—dismissing the appeal—that the plaintiff was not in breach of his duty to mitigate his loss and had acted reasonably in the circumstances. (*Liesbosch* v. *Edison*, 1933[541] distinguished.)

(550) *Morgan* v. *T. Wallis*, [1974] 1 Lloyd's Rep. 165

Mr Morgan, a lighterman on the River Thames, sustained back injuries in trying to avoid a wire rope thrown by a stevedore onto a barge where Mr Morgan was working. Liability for his injuries was admitted by the defendants, his employers, because they should have had a better system of working, but the amount of damages was disputed because Mr Morgan unreasonably refused to undergo tests and an operation because he genuinely feared both of these things. The highest estimate by a surgeon of the chances of success of such an operation was 90%. It was *held*—by Browne, J.—that the defendants had proved that Mr Morgan's refusal was unreasonable as to the investigations and the operation would have been successful on a balance of probabilities. Where there was no prior disability, physical, mental or psychological, a defendant did not have to take a plaintiff as he found him.

(551) *Scott* v. *Shepherd* (1773), 2 Wm. Bl. 892

On the evening of a fair-day at Milborne Port, Shepherd threw a lighted squib on to the market stall of one Yates who sold gingerbread. Then one Willis, in order to protect the wares of Yates, threw it away and it landed on the stall of one Ryal. He threw it to another part of the market house where it struck the plaintiff in the face, exploded and put out his eye. *Held*—Shepherd was liable for the injuries to Scott because he intended the initial act and there was no break in the chain of causation. Shepherd should have anticipated that Willis and Ryal would act as they did.

(552) *Barnett* v. *Chelsea and Kensington Hospital Management Committee*, [1968] 1 All E.R. 1068

Mr Barnett drank tea which had, unknown to him, been contaminated with arsenic. He attended at the casualty department of a hospital saying that he had been vomiting for some three hours after drinking the tea. The casualty doctor failed to examine him but sent a message that he should report to his own doctor. Some five hours later Mr Barnett died and on his widow's action for damages, it was *held* that the hospital authority owed a duty of care and that the doctor was negligent in failing to examine and admit Mr Barnett and accordingly there had been a breach of that duty. However, on the facts the deceased's condition was such that he must have died despite any medical attention which the hospital could have given so that causation was not established and the widow's claim failed.

(553) *Robinson* v. *The Post Office, The Times*, 26 October, 1973

The plaintiff suffered a minor injury for which the defendants, his employers, admitted liability. As a result the plaintiff received an anti-tetanus injection which produced the rare complication of encephalitis, with grave consequences. Ashworth, J., held that the doctor had acted negligently in administering the injection in that he had failed to administer a test dose. However, it appeared that even if such a test had been made the plaintiff would have shown no reaction to it. Thus the doctor's negligence had had no causative effect, since even with proper precautions the encephalitis would not have been prevented. The defendants appealed and it was *held*—by the Court of Appeal—that the judge's conclusions on the question of the medical negligence were correct and that accordingly the defendant could not rely on that negligence as a *novus actus interveniens*. They were therefore liable for all the plaintiff's disabilities and the contention that these were too remote was to be rejected.

(544) *Davies* v. *Liverpool Corporation*, [1949] 2 All E.R. 175

The plaintiff was trying to board a tramcar belonging to the defendants at a request stopping place. An unauthorized person (a passenger) rang the bell, whereupon the car started, throwing the plaintiff off the platform and causing her injury. The conductor was on the upper deck collecting fares. Evidence showed that the car had been standing at the request stop for an appreciable time, and that the conductor had been upstairs for the whole of that time, though it was not a particularly busy period. In this action for negligence brought by the plaintiff, it was *held* that the defendants were liable for the negligent act of the conductor. He should have foreseen that if he was absent from the platform of the car for an appreciable time, some passenger might ring the bell. The act of the passenger did not, therefore, break the chain of causation because it was just that sort of act which the conductor was employed to prevent.

(555) *Cobb* v. *Great Western Railway*, [1894] A.C. 419

The railway company allowed a railway carriage to become overcrowded, and because of this the plaintiff was hustled and robbed of £89. He now sued the company in respect of his loss. *Held*—This was too remote a consequence of the defendant's negligence. The robbery was a *novus actus interveniens* breaking the chain of causation.

(556) *Sayers* v. *Harlow U.D.C.*, [1958] 2 All E.R. 342

The defendants owned and operated a public lavatory. The plaintiff having paid for admission entered a cubicle. Finding that there was no handle on the inside of the door, and no means of opening the cubicle, the plaintiff had tried for some ten to fifteen minutes to attract attention. Having failed to do so, and wishing to catch a bus to London in the next few minutes, she tried to see if there was a way of climbing out. She placed one foot on the seat of the lavatory and rested her other foot on the toilet roll and fixture, holding the pipe from the cistern with one hand, resting the other hand on the top of the door. She then realized it would be impossible to climb out, and she proceeded to come down, but, as she was doing so, the toilet roll rotated owing to her weight on it and she slipped and injured herself. She sued the defendants for negligence. In the county court the defendants were found negligent, but, as the plaintiff was in no danger on that account, and as she chose to embark on a dangerous act, she must bear the consequences. It was *held* by the Court of Appeal that her act was not a *novus actus interveniens*, and the damage was not too remote a consequence of the defendants' negligence. She was thirty-six years of age, and in her predicament her act was not unreasonable, though if she had been an old lady it might have been. However, the damages recoverable by the plaintiff would be reduced by one quarter in respect of her share of the responsibility for the damage.

(557) *McKew* v. *Holland and Hannen and Cubitts (Scotland) Ltd*, [1969] 2 All E.R. 1621

McKew sustained an injury during the course of his employment for which his employers were liable. The injury caused him occasionally and unexpectedly to lose the use of his left leg. On one occasion he left a flat and started to descend some stairs which had no handrail. His leg gave way and he sustained further injury. *Held*—by the House of Lords—that his conduct in trying to descend the stairs was unreasonable and thus broke the chain of causation. The subsequent injury was therefore too remote and the employers were not liable.

(558) *Philco Radio Corporation* v. *Spurling*, [1949] 2 All E.R. 882

Certain packing cases containing inflammable film scrap were delivered in error by the defendants to the plaintiffs' premises. No warning as to their contents was given on the cases. The cases were opened by the plaintiffs' servants, and a foreman recognized the contents as inflammable, and gave instructions that the scrap was to be replaced, and that there was to be no smoking in the vicinity. He telephoned the defendants and arranged to have the cases delivered to their proper destination, 150 yards away. Before the cases had been moved, a typist employed by the plaintiffs negligently set light to the scrap with a cigarette, and it exploded causing damage. The defendants pleaded that the proximate cause of the damage was the typist's act and that the chain of causation was broken. *Held*—The defendants were negligent in not ensuring that such dangerous material was properly delivered. The act of the typist did not break the chain of causation; she did not intend to injure her employer, and when she approached the scrap with a cigarette she did so as a joke. Her act was not such a conscious act of violation as to relieve the defendants from liability, and in any case the act formed part of the very risk that was envisaged.

(559) *Dulieu* v. *White*, [1901] 2 K.B. 669

The defendant, who was driving a van negligently, ran into a public house. The plaintiff, who was pregnant, was in the public house and because of the shock became ill and gave birth to a premature and mentally deficient child. It was *held* that she could recover damages.

(560) *Hambrook* v. *Stokes*, [1925] 1 K.B. 141

The defendant left his lorry unattended on a sloping street and because of his negligence in failing to brake the vehicle properly, it began to run away. The plaintiff's wife had just left her children further down the street though they were in fact round a bend and not within her view. However, she saw the lorry moving and suffered shock, which resulted in her death, because she feared for the safety of her children. Her husband brought this action for loss of her services and was *held* entitled to recover damages provided that the shock was brought about by his wife's own experience and not by the account of bystanders.

(561) *Hinz* v. *Berry*, [1970] 1 All E.R. 1074

Mrs Hinz witnessed a car accident in which her husband was killed and her children injured. The accident was caused by the negligent driving of the defendant. As a result of seeing the accident Mrs Hinz, who had been a vigorous and lively woman, became morbid and depressed for years afterwards. *Held*—by the Court of Appeal—she was entitled to damages of £4000 for nervous shock. She was a woman of robust character who would probably have stood up to the strain if she had not *seen* the accident.

> Somehow or other the court has to draw a line between sorrow and grief for which damages are not recoverable; and nervous shock and psychiatric illness for which damages are recoverable. The way to do this is to estimate how much the plaintiff would have suffered if, for instance, her husband had been killed in an accident when she was fifty miles away; and compare it with what she is now, having suffered all the shock due to being present at the accident. The evidence shows that she suffered much more by being present.

(*Per* Lord Denning, M.R.)

(562) *Chadwick* v. *British Railways Board*, [1967] 1 W.L.R. 912

A serious railway accident was caused by negligence for which the Board was liable. A volunteer rescue worker suffered nervous shock and became psychoneurotic as a result. The plaintiff, as administratrix of his estate, claimed damages for nervous shock. It was *held* that—

(i) damages were recoverable for nervous shock even though the shock was not caused by fear for one's own safety or that of one's children;
(ii) in the circumstances injury by shock was foreseeable;
(iii) the defendants ought to have foreseen that volunteers might attempt rescue and accordingly owed a duty of care to those who did.

(563) *Owens* v. *Liverpool Corporation*, [1939] 2 K.B. 394

A funeral procession was making its way to the cemetery when a negligently driven tram owned by the defendants collided with the hearse and overturned the coffin. Several mourners who were following in a carriage suffered shock and it was *held* by the Court of Appeal that they were entitled to damages.

(564) *Hay (or Bourhill)* v. *Young*, [1943] A.C. 92

The plaintiff, a pregnant Edinburgh fishwife, alighted from a tramcar. While she was removing her fish-basket from the tram, Young, a motor cyclist, driving carelessly but unseen by her, passed the tram and collided with a motor car some fifteen yards away. Young was killed. The plaintiff heard the collision, and after Young's body had been removed, she approached the scene of the accident and saw a pool of blood on the road. She suffered a nervous shock and later gave birth to a stillborn child. The House of Lords *held* that her action against Young's personal representative failed, because Young owed no duty of care to persons whom he could not reasonably anticipate would suffer injuries as a result of his conduct on the highway.

(565) *Baker* v. *Willoughby*, [1969] 3 All E.R. 1528

In September, 1964, the plaintiff was involved in an accident on the highway caused by the negligent driving of the defendant, but attributable as to one quarter to the plaintiff's contributory negligence. The plaintiff received serious injuries to his left leg, but after long hospital treatment he took up employment with a scrap metal merchant. On 29 November, 1967, while in the course of his employment, the plaintiff was the innocent victim of an armed robbery receiving gunshot wounds necessitating the immediate amputation of his left leg which was already defective because of the previous accident. The question of the amount of damages for the plaintiff's injuries in the road accident of September, 1964, came before the Court for assessment in February, 1968. *Held*—by the Court of Appeal—that no consequence of the accident of September 1964 survived the amputation of the plaintiff's left leg and the defendant was liable only for loss suffered by the plaintiff up to 29 November, 1967. Damages are compensation for loss arising from a tortious act and cease when by reason of recovery, supervening disease, or further injury there is no continuing loss attributable to that act.

The House of Lords reversed the Court of Appeal decision holding that damages are not merely compensation for physical injury but for the loss which the injured person suffers. This loss was not diminished by the supervening event and the second injury was irrelevant. '. . . The supervening event has not made the appellant less lame nor less disabled nor less deprived of amenities. It has not shortened the period over which he will be suffering. It has made him more lame, more disabled, more deprived of amenities. He should not have less damages through being worse off than he might have expected . . .' (*per* Lord Pearson)

(566) *Performance Cars Ltd* v. *Abraham*, [1961] 3 All E.R. 413

The plaintiffs owned a motor car which was damaged in a collision with a car driven by the defendant. The damage to the plaintiff's car was such that it would necessitate respraying the whole of the lower body. Two weeks before the accident the plaintiffs' car had been involved in another collision which had also made respraying of the lower body of the car necessary. The plaintiffs obtained judgment against the driver responsible for the first collision but that judgment was not satisfied and the car had not been resprayed at the time when the second collision took place. The Court was asked to decide whether the plaintiffs were entitled to recover as damages from the defendant the cost of respraying the lower body of their car. *Held*—by the Court of Appeal—that the plaintiffs were not entitled to recover the cost of respraying from the defendant because that damage was not the result of his wrongful act.

(567) *Cutler* v. *Vauxhall Motors Ltd*, [1970] 2 All E.R. 56

In 1965 the plaintiff grazed his right ankle as a result of an accident at work for which the defendants were responsible. In 1966 the plaintiff had an operation for varicose veins in both legs. He would have had to have the operation a few years later had the grazing not occurred. The trial judge awarded £10 for the graze and nothing for the operation. *Held*—by the Court of Appeal—the sum awarded was adequate. The defendant's liability for the operation had not been established.

(568) *United Australia Ltd* v. *Barclays Bank Ltd*, [1941] A.C.1.

In November, 1934, certain debtors of United Australia sent to them a crossed cheque for £1900 payable to their order. On 12 November that cheque, purporting to have been indorsed in the name of United Australia by one A. H. Emons, their Secretary, in favour of MFG Trust, was presented at a branch of the respondent bank for payment into the account of MFG at that branch, and the amount was shortly collected, received and paid by the bank. On 13 May, 1935, the appellants, who alleged that Emons had no authority to indorse the cheque, issued a writ against MFG claiming £1900 as a loan to MFG or as money had and received to the appellant's use (i.e. an action in quasi-contract). This action never came to final trial and MFG afterwards went into liquidation. On 8 November, 1937, the appellants brought this action against the respondents for conversion of the cheque. *Held*—by the House of Lords—that the appellants by merely initiating proceedings against MFG in quasi-contract had not thereby elected to waive the tort of conversion by the bank and were not precluded from bringing the present action. It is judgment and satisfaction in the first action which constitutes a bar to a second action.

(569) *Verschures Creameries Ltd* v. *Hull and Netherlands Steamship Co. Ltd*, [1921] 2 K.B. 608

Certain boxes of margarine were delivered by the plaintiffs to the defendants, who were carriers and forwarding agents, to be carried by sea to Hull and thence forwarded to two customers in Liverpool and Manchester, S. Beilin and R. Beilin respectively. When the goods arrived at Hull the plaintiffs instructed the defendants not to deliver to the Beilins but to deliver to a Mr Schneiderman of Manchester, but in the event the goods were delivered to R. Beilin. The plaintiffs, having heard of the misdelivery, nevertheless invoiced the goods to R. Beilin and sued him and recovered judgment for the price of goods sold and delivered. Failing to get satisfaction from Beilin, the plaintiffs took proceedings in bankruptcy against him. *Held* they could not afterwards sue the forwarding agents for negligence and breach of duty.

(570) *Letang* v. *Cooper*, [1964] 2 All E.R. 929

In July, 1957, the plaintiff was run over by a motor car negligently driven by the defendant. She issued a writ on 2 February, 1961 (that is after the three years' period of limitation then provided by Sect. 2(1) of the Law Reform (Limitation of Actions, etc.) Act, 1954, had expired), claiming damages for personal injuries in negligence and in the alternative trespass to the person. Since the claim in negligence was statute-barred, she hoped to succeed in trespass to the person, believing the six-year limitation period to apply in this case. The action failed. It was *held* by the Court of Appeal that where the injury was not intentional, the only action is negligence not trespass. In the course of his judgment Lord Denning, M.R., said: 'The truth is that *the distinction between trespass and case is obsolete*. We have a different sub-division altogether. Instead of dividing actions for personal injuries into *trespass* (direct damage) or *case* (consequential damage), we divide the causes of action according as the defendant did the injury intentionally or unintentionally. . . . If intentional, it is the tort of assault and battery (or trespass to the person). If negligent and causing damage, it is the tort of negligence.'

Elsewhere Lord Denning made a point of interpretation: 'It is legitimate to look at a report of such a committee (in this case the Tucker Committee on the Limitation of Actions), so as to see what was the mischief at which the Act was directed. You can get the facts and surrounding circumstances from the report, so as to see the background against which the legislation was enacted. This is always a great help in interpreting it. But you cannot look at what the committee recommended, or at least, if you do look at it, you should not be unduly influenced by it. It does not help much, for the simple reason that Parliament may, and often does, decide to do something different to cure the mischief.'

(571) *Beaman* v. *ARTS*, [1949] 1 All E.R. 465

In November, 1935, Mrs Beaman, before leaving for Istanbul, deposited with the defendants several packages to be sent to her as soon as she gave notice requesting it. In May, 1936, the defendants at her request dispatched one of the packages but afterwards regulations made by the Turkish authorities prevented the dispatching of the other packages and Mrs Beaman asked the defendants to keep them in store pending further instructions. Three years later the defendants, who had not received instructions, wrote and asked the plaintiff to insure the contents of the packages. She did not do so but replied saying that she was hoping to return to England. However, the outbreak of war while she was still in Turkey prevented this.

On the entry of Italy into the war in 1940 the defendants, being a company controlled by Italian nationals, had their business taken over by the Custodian of Enemy Property. Wishing to wind up the business as soon as possible, the manager of ARTS Ltd examined the packages, reported that they were of no value and gave them to the Salvation Army. No steps were taken to obtain the plaintiff's consent. The plaintiff returned to England in 1946 and commenced proceedings more than six years after the packages were disposed of, claiming damages for conversion. The defendants set up the defence that the action was barred by Sect. 3 of the Limitation Act, 1939. The plaintiff relied on Sect. 26 which provides that where '(*a*) the action is based on fraud of the defendant . . . or (*b*) the right of action is concealed by the fraud of any such person . . . the period of limitation shall not begin to run until the plaintiff has discovered the fraud. . . .'
Held—

(i) That the action for conversion was not 'based on fraud' so that Sect. 26 (*a*) had no application.

(ii) The conduct of the defendants constituted a reckless 'concealment by fraud' of the right of action within Sect. 26(*b*). Therefore the plaintiff's action was not barred.

(*Note:* it appears that it is not necessary to prove a degree of moral turpitude to establish fraud for the purposes of Sect. 26(*b*). Thus in *Kitchen* v. *Royal Air Force Association*, [1958] 1 W.L.R. 563, solicitors negligently concealed a payment of money on behalf of the plaintiff and this conduct was held to amount to 'fraud' for the purposes of Sect. 26(*b*) even though the court accepted that the solicitors were not dishonest.)

(572) *Eddis* v. *Chichester Constable*, [1969] 2 All E.R. 912

The plaintiffs were trustees of a settlement. The trust property included, among other heirlooms, a valuable painting. In 1951 the tenant for life under the settlement sold the painting to a consortium who resold it to an art gallery in America. The tenant for life had no authority or power to sell the painting and concealed the sale from the trustees. The tenant for life died on 26 May, 1963, and on 7 March, 1966, the trustees, having discovered that the painting had been sold, commenced an action for conversion against members of the consortium. The defence was that the claim was statute barred. *Held*—by the Court of Appeal—that it was not. The fact that the trustees had an action in 1951 had been concealed by the fraud of the tenant for life and the period of limitation of six years did not begin to run until the fraud was discovered by the trustees in 1963.

(573) *Turbervell* v. *Savage* (1669), 2 Keb. 545

In this old case a man laid his hand menacingly on his sword, but at the same time said, 'If it were not assize time I would not take such language from you.' *Held*—This was not an assault because it was assize time, and there was no reason to fear violence.

(574) *Fagan* v. *Metropolitan Police Commissioner*, [1968] 3 All E.R. 442

Fagan was driving his car when he was told by a constable to draw into the kerb. He stopped his car with one wheel on the constable's foot and was slow in restarting the engine and moving the vehicle off. He was convicted of assault on the constable and Quarter Sessions dismissed his appeal. He then appealed to the Queen's Bench Divisional Court where it was *held*—dismissing his appeal—that whether or not the mounting of the wheel on the constable's foot had been intentional the defendant had deliberately allowed it to remain there when asked to move it and that constituted an assault. The decision seems to extend the law because there was no act but merely an omission. Furthermore, there was no intentional application of force but only a failure to withdraw it. A more appropriate charge might have been false imprisonment because the constable could not presumably have moved while the wheel remained on his foot.

(575) *Fowler* v. *Lanning*, [1959] 1 All E.R. 290

By a writ the plaintiff claimed damages for trespass to the person. In his statement of claim he alleged that on 19 November, 1957, at Vineyard Farm, Corfe Castle, in the County of Dorset, the defendant shot the plaintiff. By reason of the premises, the plaintiff sustained personal injuries and suffered loss and damage; particulars of the plaintiff's injuries were then set out. The defendant denied the allegations of fact and objected that the statement of claim disclosed no cause of action, because the plaintiff had not alleged that the shooting was either intentional or negligent. *Held*—In an action for trespass to the person, onus of proof of the defendant's intention or negligence lay on the plaintiff and the plaintiff must allege that the shooting was intentional or that the defendant was negligent, stating the facts alleged to constitute the negligence. The plaintiff's statement of claim, therefore, disclosed no cause of action.

(576) *Bird* v. *Jones* (1845), 7 Q.B. 742

A bridge company enclosed part of the public footway on Hammersmith Bridge, put seats on it for the use of spectators at a regatta on the river, and charged admission. The plaintiff insisted on passing along this part of the footpath, and climbed over the fence without paying the charge. The defendant, who was the clerk of the Bridge Company, stationed two policemen to prevent, and they did prevent, the plaintiff from proceeding forwards along the footway in the direction he wished to go. The plaintiff was at the same time told that he might go back into the carriage way and proceed to the other side of the bridge if he wished. He declined to do so and remained in the enclosure for about half an hour. *Held*—There was no false imprisonment, for the plaintiff was free to go off another way.

(577) *Herd* v. *Weardale Steel, Coal and Coke Co. Ltd*, [1915] A.C. 67

The plaintiff was an employee of the defendant company and at 9.30 a.m. on 30 May, 1911, he descended the defendants' mine. In the ordinary way he would have been entitled to be raised at the end of his shift at 4 p.m. The plaintiff and two other men were given certain work to do which they believed to be unsafe, and they refused to do it. At about 11 a.m. they, and twenty-nine men acting in sympathy with them, asked the foreman to allow them to ascend the shaft. The foreman, acting on instructions from the management, refused this request. At about 1 p.m. the cage came down carrying men, and emptied at the bottom of the shaft. The twenty-nine men were refused permission to enter, but some got in and refused to leave the cage, which was left stationary for some twenty minutes. At 1.30 p.m. permission was given for the men to leave and the plaintiff was brought to the top. He now sued for false imprisonment. *Held*—There was no false imprisonment. There was a collective agreement regarding the use of the cage, and the plaintiff's right to be taken to the surface did not arise under the agreement until 4 p.m. The defendants were perfectly willing to let the plaintiff ascend, but were not required in the absence of any emergency to provide him with the means of doing so except in accordance with the agreement.

(578) *Meering* v. *Grahame White Aviation Co. Ltd* (1919), 122 L.T. 44

The plaintiff, being suspected of stealing a keg of varnish from the defendants, his employers, was asked by two works policemen to accompany them to the Works Office to answer questions. The plaintiff, not realizing that he was suspected, assented to the suggestion and even suggested a short cut. He remained in the office for some time during which the works policemen stayed outside the room without his knowledge. The plaintiff later sued for false imprisonment and the question arose as to whether the plaintiff must know that the defendant is restraining his freedom. *Held*—The plaintiff was imprisoned and his knowledge was irrelevant, though knowledge of imprisonment might increase the damages.

(579) *Christie* v. *Leachinsky*, [1947] A.C. 573

The appellants, without the necessary warrant, arrested the respondent for unlawful possession of a number of bales of cloth. They had reasonable grounds for thinking that the bales were stolen but did not disclose this until later. *Held*—by the House of Lords—that the arrest was unlawful.

(580) *R.* v. *Kulynycz*, [1970] 3 W.L.R. 1029

The defendant was convicted of possessing drugs contrary to the Drugs (Prevention of Misuse) Act, 1964. He resided in Cambridge and was suspected of supplying drugs to persons who 'pushed' them in King's Lynn. He was arrested in Cambridge by a police officer who told him that a warrant for his arrest had been issued at King's Lynn on suspicion of offences committed there. The offences were not specified and in fact no warrant had been issued. At the police station in Cambridge the full nature of the charge was made clear to the defendant. He was committed for trial to Norfolk Quarter Sessions on an indictment charging possession of drugs in Cambridge. Under Sect. 11(1) of the Criminal Justice Act, 1925, Norfolk Quarter Sessions had jurisdiction to try the case only if the defendant was 'in custody on a charge for the offence' in Norfolk. On that basis the question for decision was whether the defendant was in lawful custody when he appeared before Norfolk Quarter Sessions. It was *held* by the Court of Appeal (Criminal Division) that he was because although the original arrest was unlawful in that there was no specification of the offences (*Christie* v. *Leachinsky*, 1947),[579] the defendant was informed of these in sufficient detail at Cambridge police station. It was not necessary that he should be released and re-arrested. It did not matter that the police officer was wrong in saying that a warrant had been issued. An arrested person is not bound to know whether he is arrested on warrant or on reasonable suspicion.

(581) *Wheatley* v. *Lodge* [1971] 1 All E.R. 173

The defendant's car collided with a parked vehicle. A constable saw him about an hour later and smelling alcohol on his breath, cautioned him and said that he was arrested for driving under the influence of drink contrary to Sect. 1(c) of the Road Safety Act, 1967. The defendant was deaf and could not lip read though the constable did not know this. Nevertheless the defendant got into a police car which the constable pointed to and was taken to the police station where he indicated his deafness. From then on the charge and all relevant matters were made clear to him by written and printed matter. On the question of the lawfulness of his arrest it was *held* by the Queen's Bench Divisional Court that the original arrest was valid. A police officer arresting a deaf person had to do what a reasonable person would do in the circumstances and the magistrates were clearly of the opinion that the constable had done so.

(*Note:* presumably on the basis of this decision if a person is arresting someone who cannot speak English he is not obliged to find an interpreter.)

(582) *Alderson* v. *Booth*, [1969] 2 All E.R. 271

The defendant's car was involved in an accident and he was asked by a constable to take a breath test. This proved positive and the constable then said to the defendant, 'I shall have to ask you to come to the police station for further tests.' The defendant went with the constable to the police station and after a further test was charged with driving contrary to Sect. 1(1) of the Road Safety Act, 1967, in that the proportion of alcohol in his blood was beyond the permitted limit. The magistrates were not satisfied that the defendant knew he was under compulsion when he went to the police station with the constable and decided that he had not been arrested. Arrest being a necessary part of the procedure under the 1967 Act, the information laid against the defendant was dismissed. The prosecution appealed to the Queen's Bench Divisional Court where it was *held* that:

(*a*) it was no longer the law that there could be no lawful arrest without an actual seizing or touching;

(*b*) there might be an arrest by mere words provided the defendant submitted and realized he was under compulsion—however, constables should use very clear words; the best thing to say was 'I arrest you'.

The prosecution's appeal was dismissed because although the magistrates decision was surprising in the circumstances they had felt as a matter of fact that the defendant did not know he was under compulsion.

(583) *R.* v. *Brown, The Times*, 17 December, 1976

Brown, who was a motorist, was waved down by two police officers after they had seen him crossing traffic lights in a slightly dangerous fashion. He drove on and then abandoned his car and ran away. The police officers caught him about 50 to 60 yards away and brought him down with a rugby tackle. He was then placed in the back of a police van and at that stage the officers noticed that Brown smelled of alcohol and asked him to take a breath test. He tried to push his way out of the van but was restrained and was again asked to take a breath test. He made no response and continued to refuse. He was then told that the officer was arresting him for failing to provide a specimen of blood and was cautioned and taken to the police station. He there provided a specimen of blood and this showed that he had more than twice the permitted level of alcohol in the bloodstream. He was convicted of driving with more than the permitted limit of drink. On appeal his main argument was that the entire procedure was a nullity. The police had no legal power to arrest him for failing to provide a specimen of breath because he was already under arrest. The court therefore had to decide at what moment in time the arrest took place. By unanimous decision the Court of Appeal decided that the first state of being detained by the rugby tackle and being placed in the van did not amount to an arrest. The arrest occurred when the police officer first informed Brown that he was being placed under arrest. The case merely adds to the confusion in the law as to the distinction between detention and arrest.

(584) *Southport Corporation* v. *Esso Petroleum Co.*, [1954] 2 Q.B. 182

The Esso company's tanker became stranded in the estuary of the River Ribble. The master of the tanker discharged oil in order to re-float the ship. The action of the wind and tide took the oil on to the corporation's foreshore and caused damage. The corporation sued in trespass and negligence. Devlin, J., at first instance, thought that trespass would lie, but on appeal to the Court of Appeal, Denning, L.J., contended that there could be no trespass because the injury was not direct, but was caused by the tides and prevailing winds; in trespass the injury must be direct and not consequential. In the House of Lords, [1956] A.C. 218, Lord Tucker agreed with Denning, L.J., though in the House of Lords trespass was not pursued. The appeal was based on negligence and the defendants were *held* not liable.

(*Note:* this case illustrates the difficulties of trying to recover for oil pollution damage in negligence or trespass. The action for nuisance has similar difficulties. *Rylands* v. *Fletcher* does not apply because, among other things, the oil does not escape from the land but from the sea and the sea is the equivalent of a public highway. Oil pollution is now dealt with by the Merchant Shipping (Oil Pollution) Act, 1971, which provides a more straightforward method of making claims.)

(585) *Kelson* v. *Imperial Tobacco Co.*, [1957] 2 All E.R. 343

The plaintiff was the lessee of a one-storey tobacconist's shop and brought this action against the defendants, seeking an injunction requiring them to remove from the wall above the shop a large advertising sign showing the words 'Players Please'. The sign projected into the air space above the plaintiff's shop by a distance of some eight inches. The plaintiff claimed that the defendants, by fixing the sign in that position, had trespassed on his air space. *Held*—The invasion of an air space by a sign of this nature constituted a trespass and, although the plaintiff's injury was small, it was an appropriate case in which to grant an injunction for the removal of the sign.

(*Note:* the plaintiff seemed prepared for the sign to remain until he became involved in a dispute with the defendants regarding the quota of cigarettes supplied to him. It was after the dispute that he brought this action, but the court found that the plaintiff's claim was not affected by his acts.)

(586) *Woollerton and Wilson* v. *Richard Costain (Midlands) Ltd* (1969), 119 N.L.J. 1093

In this case the Court granted to the owners of a factory and warehouse in Leicester an injunction restraining the defendants from trespassing on and invading air space over their premises by means of a swinging crane. The injunction was suspended for twelve months to enable the defendants to finish their work, the defendants having offered to pay for the right to continue to trespass and to provide insurance cover for neighbouring properties. It was also *held* that it was no answer to a claim for an injunction for trespass that the trespass did no harm to the plaintiff.

(587) *Bernstein* v. *Skyviews & General, The Times*, 11 February, 1977

The plaintiff claimed damages for trespass against a firm which had taken an aerial photograph of his home from about 630 feet, crossing his land in order to do so. It was *held*—by Griffiths, J.—that an owner of land at common law had rights above his land to such height as was necessary for the ordinary use and enjoyment of the land and the structures upon it. The plane was therefore too high to be trespassing. In any case Sect. 40(1) of the Civil Aviation Act, 1949 provided a defence to such a claim where the height was reasonable. However, the judge did say that constant surveillance from the air with photographing might well be actionable nuisance.

(588) *The Six Carpenters' case* (1610), 8 Co. Rep. 146a

Six carpenters went into an inn in Cripplegate and, having consumed a meal of wine and bread, refused to pay for it. Their right to enter was conferred by law, the place being an inn. *Held*—They were not liable because their act was a non-feasance, not a misfeasance. The complaint related to something they had not done, i.e. they had not paid, and trespass *ab initio* depends upon misfeasance.

(589) *Elias and Others* v. *Pasmore and Others*, [1934] 2 K.B. 164

The plaintiffs were officials of the National Unemployed Workers' Movement, and certain of them were tenants of premises occupied by the movement. These premises were entered by the defendants who were inspectors of the Metropolitan Police. One of the plaintiffs was arrested on a warrant on a charge of sedition, but the police also seized at the same time a number of books and papers. Some of these were returned to the plaintiffs, though others were later used at the trial of one of them, a trial which resulted in his conviction. The police still retained certain of the documents after the trial. *Held*—The defendants were trespassers *ab initio* in respect of the documents which were not used and which were unlawfully seized, but this did not make them trespassers *ab initio* in respect of their entry on the premises, for there was justification for that. The plaintiffs were entitled to damages for the detention of certain documents after the trial, and for the seizure of the documents which were returned.

(590) *Chic Fashions (West Wales)* v. *Jones*, [1968] 1 All E.R. 229

Police had reasonable grounds for believing that certain garments in the plaintiff company's shop had been stolen. They obtained a search warrant in respect only of clothing made by 'Jan Peters' of Leicester. They did not find any garments of 'Jan Peters' make, but they found and seized sixty-five garments of other makes which they reasonably believed to be stolen property. The plaintiff company gave an explanation as to the possession of these garments which the police accepted and the garments were returned. The plaintiff company then alleged trespass against the police, saying that although their entry was lawful it was for the restricted purpose of seizing 'Jan Peters' garments and by taking others they had committed trespass *ab initio. Held*—by the Court of Appeal—that the police were not liable. Lord Denning said that when a constable entered premises by virtue of a search warrant for stolen goods he could seize not only the goods which he reasonably believed to be covered by the warrant but also any other goods which he honestly believed on reasonable grounds to have been stolen and to be material evidence on a charge of stealing or receiving. The lawfulness of this conduct must be judged at the time and not by what happened afterwards. At one time a man could be made a trespasser *ab initio* by the doctrine of relation back but that was no longer true.

Diplock, L.J., said that the common law was not static. It comprised those rules which governed men's conduct in contemporary society on matters not expressly regulated by legislation. Today stealing was more widespread than it had ever been since statistics of crime were available. In 1967 the question at issue should be answered by allowing the appeal. The decision in *The Six Carpenters' Case*, 1610[588] was doubted.

(591) *Jeffrey* v. *Black, The Times*, 15 July, 1977

Police officers arrested a man for stealing a sandwich from a public house. They then proceeded to search his premises without a warrant and without permission and found cannabis there and prosecuted. It was *held* that in entering the premises the police were acting outside their powers and that *Ghani* v. *Jones*, [1970] 1 Q.B. 693, did not allow the police to search premises when the contents of the house bore no relation to the offence charged. However, the evidence having been found, it was admissible despite the irregularity in obtaining it, subject to the discretion of the court. The evidence in this case was not obtained in such a way that it should be excluded.

(592) *Wood* v. *Leadbitter* (1845), 13 M. & W. 838

Wood purchased a ticket for one guinea which entitled him to come into the stand, and the enclosure surrounding it, at Doncaster race course. The ticket was valid for the period of the race meeting. Lord Eglington was the steward of the Doncaster races and, while the races were going on, the defendant, who was Lord Eglington's servant, asked the plaintiff to leave.

Wood refused to go and the defendant ejected him using no more than reasonable force. *Held*—It was lawful for Lord Eglington, without returning the guinea or giving any reason for his action, to order any holder of a ticket to leave the stand and enclosure, even though such holder had not misconducted himself. The plaintiff's licence to remain could, therefore, be revoked, so making him a trespasser. From then on he could be removed by the use of reasonable force.

(593) *Hurst* v. *Picture Theatres Ltd*, [1915] 1 K.B. 1

Hurst paid sixpence for an unreserved seat at the defendants' theatre. He was given a metal check, which he gave up at the door, and was then shown to a seat. Some time later he was asked if he had paid for admission and replied that he had. He was then asked to go and see the manager, but he refused to do so. Eventually the manager sent the doorkeeper to eject the plaintiff, the police having refused to do so. The doorkeeper lifted the plaintiff out of his seat, whereupon the plaintiff walked out quietly. He now sued for damages for assault and false imprisonment. The defendants contended that they were entitled, without giving reasons, to ask the plaintiff to leave, and if he did not do so, to remove him, using no more than reasonable force. *Held*—The plaintiff's claim succeeded. The defendants could not revoke the plaintiff's right in that way so as to make him a trespasser.

(594) *Winter Garden Theatre (London) Ltd* v. *Millenium Productions Ltd*, [1948] A.C. 173

The respondents were permitted by a contractual licence to use the Winter Garden Theatre, Drury Lane, which belonged to the appellants, for the purpose of producing plays, concerts or ballets in return for a weekly payment of £300 a week. There was no express term in the licence providing that the appellants could revoke it. However, the appellants did revoke it, giving the respondents one month in which to quit the premises, but stating that they were prepared to give fresh notice for a later date if the respondents required further time in which to make other arrangements. The respondents contended that the licence could not be revoked so long as the weekly payments were continued. The appellants claimed that it was recovable on giving reasonable notice. *Held*—On a proper construction of the contract the licence was not intended to be perpetual, but nevertheless could only be determined by reasonable notice. What was reasonable notice depended on the commitments of the licensees and the circumstances of the parties. In this case the notice given by the appellants was reasonable and valid to determine the licence.

(595) *Hounslow London Borough Council* v. *Twickenham Garden Developments* [1970] 3 W.L.R. 538

A building owner granted a licence under a building contract to a builder to enter on his land and do work there. The procedure for terminating the building contract involved an architect giving notice that the work was not being carried out properly. Such a notice was given but the building contractor refused to leave the land and carried on his work. The owner claimed an injunction and damages for trespass. *Held*—by Megarry, J.—in view of the fact that it was not certain whether the architect's notice had been given as a result of following proper procedures the contract had not necessarily been terminated and the builder was not, unless and until that was done, a trespasser. The owner's action failed.

(596) *Hemmings* v. *Stoke Poges Golf Club*, [1920] 1 K.B. 720

The plaintiff was employed by the defendants and occupied a cottage belonging to them. Later he left the defendants' service and was called upon to give up possession. On refusal, he and his property were ejected with no more force than was necessary. *Held*—The defendants were not liable for assault or trespass.

(597) *The Tubantia*, [1924] P. 78

The plaintiff, who was a marine salvor, was trying to salvage the cargo of the S.S. *Tubantia* which had been sunk in the North Sea. He had discovered the wreck and marked it with a marker buoy, and his divers were already working in the hold, when the defendant, a rival salvor, appeared on the scene and started to send divers down to salvage cargo from the wreck. *Held*—Whoever was the owner of the property salvaged, the plaintiff was sufficiently in possession of the wreck to found an action in trespass.

(598) *Bridges* v. *Hawkesworth* (1851), 21 L.J. Q.B. 75

The plaintiff was a traveller for a large firm with which the defendant, who was a shopkeeper, had dealings. One day when the plaintiff called at the defendant's shop on business, he noticed and picked up a parcel, which was lying on the floor of the shop and which contained bank notes to the value of £55. The plaintiff handed the notes to the defendant, asking him to give them to the owner. Three years later, the owner not having been found in spite of advertisements, the plaintiff asked for the notes and the defendant refused to deliver them up. The plaintiff sued in conversion. *Held*—The property in the notes belonged to the finder, except as against the true owner, and not to the owner of the shop.

(599) *Elwes* v. *Brigg Gas Co.* (1886), 33 Ch.D. 562

The plaintiff leased land to the defendants for ninety-nine years. The lessees were carrying out excavations for the erection of a gasometer when they discovered an ancient boat cut out of an oak. The boat was in a good state of preservation. The question of title to the boat arose. *Held*—The boat did not pass to the lessees by virtue of the lease and belonged to the plaintiff as lessor.

(600) *South Staffordshire Water Co.* v. *Sharman*, [1896] 2 Q.B. 44

The plaintiffs sued the defendant in detinue, claiming possession of two gold rings found by the defendant in the Minster Pool at Lichfield. The plaintiffs were owners of the pool and the defendant was a labourer employed by them to clean it. It was in the course of cleaning the pool that the defendant came across the rings. He refused to hand them to his employers, but gave them to the police for enquiries to be made to find the true owners. No owner was found and the police returned the rings to the defendant who retained them. *Held*—The rings must be given over to the plaintiffs. The plaintiffs were freeholders of the pool, and had the right to forbid anyone coming on the land; they had a right to clean the pool out in any way they chose. They possessed and exercised a practical control over the pool and they had a right to its contents.

(601) *Corporation of London and Others* v. *Appleyard and Another*, [1963] 2 All E.R. 834

Two workmen, in the course of their employment on a building site, found an old wall safe in the cellar of a demolished building. The safe contained banknotes to the value of £5728 and the owner of the notes was never found. The Corporation of London owned the freehold of the site which was subject to a building lease in favour of Yorkwin Investments. Clause 15 of the lease provided that every relic or article of antiquity or value which might be found in or under any part of the site belonged to the Corporation, and should be carefully and without avoidable damage removed and delivered to the Corporation. *Held*—The Corporation was entitled to the notes as against anyone except the true owner because—

(i) the wall safe formed part of the leased premises and its contents were *de facto* in the possession of Yorkwin who had a better title than the workmen; but

(ii) the Corporation was entitled to the notes under Clause 15 of the lease.

(602) *Hannah* v. *Peel*, [1945] K.B. 509

The defendant owned a house in Shropshire which he had never actually occupied. During the Second World War the house was requisitioned for Army purposes. The plaintiff was stationed in the house and found, in an upstairs room which he was occupying, a brooch whose condition indicated that it must have been lost for some considerable time. The plaintiff, thinking the brooch might be valuable, handed it to the police. The real owner was never traced, and the police handed the brooch to agents of the defendant, the chief constable being given an indemnity against any claim to the brooch. The defendant later sold the brooch for £66. The plaintiff now claimed the brooch as finder, and the defendant claimed it as the freeholder of the property. *Held*—The plaintiff was entitled to the brooch or its value because the defendant had never been in actual possession of the house, and had no knowledge of the brooch until the plaintiff found it.

(603) *Jarvis* v. *Williams*, [1955] 1 All E.R. 108

Jarvis agreed to sell some bathroom fittings to Peterson and at Peterson's request delivered them to Williams. Peterson refused to pay the price and Jarvis agreed to take them back if Peterson would pay for collection. Peterson accepted this offer and Jarvis sent his lorryman, with a letter of authority, to collect the fittings but he was told that he could not take them, so he returned empty-handed. Jarvis claimed against Williams in detinue for the return of the goods. *Held*—On the delivery to Williams the property in the goods passed to Peterson, and the arrangement for recollection did not re-vest the property in Jarvis. It follows that at the time of collection, Jarvis had no right of property in the goods to sustain an action in detinue.

(604) *Fouldes* v. *Willoughby* (1841), 8 M. & W. 540

The plaintiff had put his horses on the defendant's ferry boat and, a dispute having arisen, the defendant asked the plaintiff to take them off. The plaintiff refused so the defendant did so, and since the plaintiff refused to leave the boat, the defendant ferried him across the river. The plaintiff sued in conversion. Maule, J., directed the jury that the putting of the horses ashore was a conversion, but on appeal, the Court of Exchequer *reversed* the decision and found there was no conversion. Lord Abinger, C.B., said: 'In order to constitute a conversion it is necessary either that the party taking the goods should intend some use to be made of them by himself or by those for whom he acts, or that owing to his act, the goods are destroyed or consumed to the prejudice of the lawful owner. The removal of the horses involved not the least denial of the right of the plaintiff to enjoyment or possession of them and was thus no conversion.'

(605) *Oakley* v. *Lyster*, [1931] 1 K.B. 148

Oakley, a demolition contractor, agreed to pull down an aerodrome on Salisbury Plain and reinstate the land, a process which involved disposing of 8000 tons of hard core and tar macadam. He thereupon rented three and a half acres of a farm on the opposite side of the road on which to dump it. He sold 4000 tons, but in January, 1929, there was still 4000 tons undisposed of when Lyster bought the freehold of the farm. Shortly afterwards Oakley found that some of the hardcore was being removed on Lyster's instructions, and Oakley saw him and was told that Lyster had bought the land and all that was on it, and on 9 July, 1929, his solicitors wrote to Oakley to this effect and forbade Oakley to remove the hard core otherwise he would become a trespasser on Lyster's land. Correspondence followed but at the trial it was admitted that Oakley was a lawful tenant and owner of the hard core. While the correspondence was continuing, Oakley agreed to sell the 4000 tons to Mr Edney, but in view of Lyster's claim, Edney withdrew and the stuff was undisposed of. The conversion alleged was the removal by Lyster of some of the hard core and the denial of title in the correspondence. *Held*—The defendant was liable in damages for conversion. In the correspondence Lyster was asserting and exercising dominion over the goods inconsistent with the rights of the true owner, Oakley. Nor was it sufficient to allow Oakley to resume dominion over the hardcore and remove it. He was entitled to damages of £300 for the loss of the sale to Edney.

(606) *Elvin and Powell Ltd* v. *Plummer Roddis Ltd* (1933), 50 T.L.R. 158

A fraudulent person ordered a consignment of goods from the plaintiffs in the name of the defendants. He then telephoned the defendants in the plaintiff's name, saying that the goods had been dispatched to them in error and that they would be collected. The fraudulent person then himself collected the goods from the defendants and absconded with them. The plaintiffs now sued the defendants for conversion. *Held*—As involuntary bailees of goods, the defendants had acted reasonably in returning them, as they believed, to the plaintiffs, by a trustworthy messenger. They had not committed conversion.

(607) *Attorney-General* v. *Gastonia Coaches, The Times*, 12 November, 1976

G, who were coach operators, owned 22 coaches of which 16 were parked in residential roads adjoining the Gastonia offices. No matter how carefully these coaches were parked they inevitably interfered with the free passage of other traffic. It was *held*—on a public relator action by the Attorney-General—that Gastonia were guilty of a public nuisance and would be restrained from parking the vehicles on the highway. Damages would also be awarded to private litigants who had suffered from the emission of exhaust gasses, excessive noise and obstruction of drives.

(608) *Castle* v. *St Augustine's Links Ltd and Another* (1922), 38 T.L.R. 615

On 18 August, 1919, the plaintiff was driving a taxicab from Deal to Ramsgate when a ball played by the second defendant, a Mr Chapman, from the thirteenth tee on the golf course, which was parallel with the Sandwich Road, struck the windscreen of the taxicab. In consequence a piece of glass from the screen injured the plaintiff's eye and a few days later he had to have it removed. He then brought this action. *Held*—the plaintiff succeeded. Judgment for £450 damages was given by Sankey, J. The proximity of the hole to the road constituted a public nuisance. *c/f Bolton* v. *Stone*, [1951] A.C. 650, where cricket balls had been hit out of the ground and into the highway six to ten times in thirty-five years but had injured nobody. *Held*—no nuisance. See also *Miller* v. *Jackson*, [1977] 3 W.L.R. 20, where the Court of Appeal held that the public interest, which requires young people to have the benefit of outdoor games, may be held to out-weigh the private interest of neighbouring householders who are the victims of sixes landing in their gardens so that it would be impossible to use the garden when cricket was being played. Thus no injunction was granted even though the sportsmen were held to be guilty of both nuisance and negligence.

(609) *Terry* v. *Ashton* (1876), 1 Q.B.D. 314

A lamp projected from the defendant's premises over the highway. It fell and injured the plaintiff who then sued the defendant in respect of his injuries.

The defendant had previously employed an independent contractor, who was not alleged to be incompetent, to repair the lamp and it was because of the negligence of that contractor that the lamp fell. Even so the defendant was *held* liable and the decision suggests that there is strict liability in respect of injuries caused by artificial projections over the highway.

(610) *Dymond* v. *Pearce*, [1972] 1 All E.R. 1142

A lorry was left parked on a road subject to a 30 m.p.h. speed limit with its lights on beneath a street lamp. The plaintiff collided with the vehicle and suffered injury. He sued the defendants alleging negligence and nuisance. It was *held*—by the Court of Appeal—that the claim in negligence failed as there was no evidence to show that the driver had not acted reasonably in the circumstances. The claim in nuisance also failed, for although a nuisance had been created, the injury suffered resulted solely from the negligence of the motorcyclist himself. Of more importance than the actual decision are the comments made in the Court of Appeal regarding the relationship between negligence and nuisance in terms of fault. See in particular Edmund Davies, L.J., who said: 'But if an obstruction be created, here to, in my judgment, fault is essential to liability in the sense that it must appear that a reasonable man would be bound to realize the likelihood of risk to highway users resulting from the presence of the obstructing vehicle on the road.'

(611) *Bliss* v. *Hall* (1838), L.J. C.P. 122

The defendant carried on the trade of a candle-maker in certain premises near to the dwelling house of the plaintiff and his family. Certain 'noxious and foul smells' issued from the defendant's premises and the plaintiff sued him for nuisance. The defence was that, for three years before the plaintiff occupied the dwelling house in question, the defendant had exercised the trade complained of in this present establishment. *Held*—This was no answer to the complaint and judgment was given for the plaintiff.

(612) *Adams* v. *Ursell*, [1913] 1 Ch. 269

The plaintiff was a veterinary surgeon and he purchased a house in 1907 for £2370. In November, 1912, the defendant opened a fried fish shop at premises adjoining the plaintiff's house. Very soon after the commencement of the business, the plaintiff's house was permeated with the odour of fried fish, and the vapour from the stoves filled the rooms 'like fog or steam'. The plaintiff sued the defendant for nuisance, seeking an injunction. *Held*—An injunction would be granted because the defendant's activities materially interfered with the ordinary comfort of the plaintiff and his family; and it did not matter that the shop was in a large working-class district and therefore supplied a public need.

(613) *Dunton* v. *Dover District Council, The Times,* 31 March, 1977

The Council provided a play area for children of a housing estate on grazing land at the rear of the plaintiff's hotel. The playground was not fenced and there was no restriction on the age of the children using it. The plaintiff suffered noise and inconvenience and was awarded £200 damages and a continued injunction against the Council that the playground should only be open between 10 a.m. and 6.30 p.m. to children under 12.

(614) *Christie* v. *Davey,* [1893] 1 Ch. 316

The plaintiff was the occupier of a semi-detached house, and she and her daughter gave pianoforte, violin and singing lessons in the house, four days a week for seventeen hours in all. There was also practice of music and singing at other times, and occasional musical evenings. The defendant was a woodcarver who occupied the contiguous portion of the house, and he found the musical activities of the plaintiff and her family somewhat annoying. In addition to writing abusive letters, he retaliated by playing concertinas, horns, flutes, pianos and other musical instruments, blowing whistles, knocking on trays or boards, hammering, shrieking or shouting, so as to annoy the plaintiffs and injure their activities. *Held*—What the plaintiff and her family were doing was not an unreasonable use of the house, and could not be retrained by the adjoining tenant. However, the adjoining tenant was himself restrained from making noises to annoy the plaintiff, the court being satisfied that such noises had been made wilfully for the purpose of annoyance.

(615) *Hubbard* v. *Pitt,* [1975] 3 All E.R. 1

The defendants picketed in the road outside the offices of the plaintiff estate agents to protest against a particular property development. An interlocutory injunction was granted to restrain them from doing so. The Court of Appeal *held*—dismissing their appeal—(i) that the original ground for granting the injunction, namely, that street picketing other than in furtherance of a trade dispute was unlawful, was correct; (ii) that the balance of convenience required an injunction to be issued there being a serious issue to be tried. (*American Cyanamid Co.* case applied.)

(616) *British Celanese Ltd* v. *A. H. Hunt (Capacitors) Ltd,* [1969] 2 All E.R. 1252

The defendants allowed metal foil to escape from their land and foul the bus bars of overhead electric cables. The plaintiffs lost power and their machines were clogged up and time and material wasted. *Held*—by Lawton, J., that—

(*a*) the defendants were not liable under *Rylands* v. *Fletcher*, because there was no non-natural use of land;

(*b*) the defendants owed a duty of care to the plaintiffs and could be liable in negligence, the plaintiffs had a proprietory interest in the machines which were damaged and could recover loss flowing from that; pure economic loss was not involved;

(*c*) the defendants were liable in nuisance, an isolated happening such as this could create an actionable nuisance and the plaintiffs were directly and foreseeably affected.

(617) *Hollywood Silver Fox Farm Ltd.* v. *Emmett*, [1936] 2 K.B. 468

The plaintiffs were breeders of silver foxes, and erected a notice board on their land inscribed: 'Hollywood Silver Fox Farm'. The defendant owned a neighbouring field, which he was about to develop as a building estate, and he regarded the notice board as detrimental to such development. He asked the plaintiffs to remove it, and when this request was refused, he sent his son to discharge a 12-bore gun close to the plaintiff's land, with the object of frightening the vixens during breeding. The result of this activity was that certain of the vixens did not mate at all, and others, having whelped, devoured their young. The plaintiff brought this action alleging nuisance, and the defence was that Emmett had a right to shoot as he pleased on his own land. *Held*—An injunction would be granted to restrain Emmett. His evil motive made an otherwise innocent use of land a nuisance.

(*Note:* it seems at first sight difficult to reconcile the above case with *Mayor of Bradford* v. *Pickles* (1895).[471] The difference probably is in the fact that *Hollywood Silver Fox Farm* v. *Emmett* was an action for nuisance by noise, so that the defendant's motive was relevant in establishing the tort. In *Mayor of Bradford* v. *Pickles*, the action was really one for interference with a servitude or right over land, and motive was not relevant in establishing the rights of the parties.)

(618) *Bone* v. *Seale*, [1975] 1 All E.R. 787

Over a period of $12\frac{1}{2}$ years smells coming from a neighbouring pig farm owned by the defendant had caused a nuisance to properties owned by the plaintiff who claimed an injunction restraining the nuisance and damages. The judge found that no diminution in the value of the properties had resulted but granted an injunction and awarded over £6000 damages. The defendants appealed, saying, amongst other things, that the award was too high. It was *held*—by the Court of Appeal allowing the appeal against the award—that by drawing a parallel with loss of sense of smell as a result of personal injury the award was erroneous and £1000 for the plaintiff would be substituted.

(619) *Malone* v. *Laskey*, [1907] 2 K.B. 141

The defendants owned a house which they leased to a firm named Witherby & Co., who sub-let it to the Script Shorthand Company. The plaintiff's husband was employed by the latter company, and was allowed to occupy the house as an emolument of his employment. A flush cistern in the lavatory of the house was unsafe, the wall brackets having been loosened by the vibration of the defendants' electric generator next door. The plaintiff told Witherby & Co. of the situation, and they communicated with the defendants who sent two of their plumbers to repair the cistern gratuitously. The work was carried out in an improper and negligent manner, and four months later the plaintiff was injured when the cistern came loose. The plaintiff sued the defendants (i) in nuisance, and (ii) in negligence. *Held*—There was no claim in nuisance against the defendants. The plaintiff was not their tenant, and in nuisance the tenant is the person to sue, not other persons present on the premises, though such persons may have a claim where the nuisance is a public nuisance. Further, there was no claim in negligence, because the defendants owed no duty of care: firstly, because there was no contractual relationship; secondly, because the defendants did not undertake any duty towards the plaintiff. They were under no obligation to carry out repairs but sent their plumbers merely as a matter of grace. This was a voluntary act and was not in any sense the discharge of a duty. The defendants were not in occupation of the premises and had not invited the plaintiff to occupy them.

(*Note:* the case still represents the law regarding nuisance. Regarding the claim for negligence it was overruled in *Billings* v. *Riden*, [1958] A.C. 240, where it was held that there may be liability in negligence, where premises are left in a dangerous condition by workmen so that injury results, even though the injured person is not the occupier but is a visitor to the premises.)

(620) *Wilchick* v. *Marks and Silverstone*, [1934] 2 K.B. 56

Landlords who had let premises with a defective shutter, and had expressly reserved the right to enter the premises to do repairs, were *held* liable along with their tenant, to a passer-by injured by the shutter.

(621) *Mint* v. *Good*, [1951] 1 K.B. 517

Landlords were *held* liable to the infant plaintiff, who was injured when a wall on the premises, which they had let, collapsed on to the highway. They had not reserved the right to enter to do repairs, but the Court of Appeal stated that such a right must be implied, because the premises were let on weekly tenancies and it was usual to imply a right to enter to do repairs in such tenancies.

(622) *Harris* v. *James* (1876), 45 L.J.Q.B. 545

A landlord was *held* liable for the nuisance created by his tenant's blasting operations at a quarry because he had let the property for that purpose. The tenant, therefore, inevitably created a nuisance.

(623) *Smith* v. *Scott*, [1972] 3 All E.R. 645

The local authority had placed in an adjoining house to the plaintiff's a family which it knew was likely to cause a nuisance but on conditions of tenancy which expressly prohibited the commission of such. These tenants had a large and unruly family and their conduct was in the words of Pennycuick, V.C. 'Altogether intolerable both in respect of physical damage and noise.' The plaintiff and his wife, an elderly couple, found it impossible to live next door and moved away. Notwithstanding protests on the part of the plaintiff, the local authority took no effective steps to control the unruly family or to evict them. It was *held* by Pennycuick, V.C., that, whatever the precise tests might be, it was impossible to apply the exception rendering a landlord liable for his tenants' acts in the present case. The exception was not based on cause and probable result apart from express or implied authority. The property had been let on conditions of tenancy which expressly forbade the commission of a nuisance and it would not be legitimate to say that the local authority had authorized the nuisance.

It should also be noted that the court held that the rule in *Rylands* v. *Fletcher* could not be applied and that the rights and liabilities of landowners had already been determined by the law and it was not open to the court to reshape those rights and liabilities by reference to the concept of duty of care. Thus the defendants were not liable in negligence. On the matter of *Rylands* v. *Fletcher* liability Pennycuick, V.C., said: 'The rule in *Rylands* v. *Fletcher* was applied in *Attorney-General* v. *Corke*[701] against a defendant who brought caravan dwellers on to his land as licencees but so far as counsel has been able to ascertain the rule has never been sought to be applied against a landlord who lets his property to undesirable tenants and I do not think it can be properly applied in such a case. The person liable under the rule in *Rylands* v. *Fletcher* is the owner or controller of the dangerous "thing", and this is normally the occupier and not the owner of the land. . . . A landlord parts with possession of the demised property in favour of his tenant and could not in any sense known to the law be regarded as controlling the tenant on property still occupied by himself. I should respectfully have thought that *Attorney-General* v. *Corke*[701] could equally well have been decided on the basis that the landowner there was in possession of the property and was himself liable in nuisance for the acts of his licencees.'

(624) *Brew Brothers* v. *Snax (Ross)*, [1969] 3 W.L.R. 657

In June, 1965, the freehold owners of premises leased to them for a term of 14 years. The lease contained covenants by the tenants regarding repairs, payment of maintenance expenses and viewing by the landlords. In November, 1966, one of the walls of the premises tilted towards the neighbouring premises which belong to the plaintiff. It was shored up but caused an obstruction for 18 months. It appeared that the reason why the wall had tilted was the seeping of water from certain drains and the removal of a tree by the tenants. The plaintiffs sued the landlords and the tenants, and the landlords contended that the responsibility fell entirely on the tenants under the lease. *Held*—by the Court of Appeal—

(*a*) the tenants were responsible for repairing defects pointed out by the landlords but that the work required on the wall was not within the terms of the lease;

(*b*) the landlords must be presumed to know the state of the premises and were liable for nuisance in that they allowed the state of affairs to continue;

(*c*) the tenants were jointly liable in nuisance in that they failed to put the matter right, this liability was quite independent of their duties under the lease.

(625) *Sedleigh-Denfield* v. *O'Callagan and others*, [1940] A.C. 880

One of the respondents (a college for training foreign missioners) was the owner of property adjoining the appellant's premises in Mill Hill. On the boundary of the property owned by the College there was a ditch and it was admitted that the ditch also belonged to the college. About 1934, when a block of flats was erected on the western side of the appellant's premises, the county council had laid a pipe and grating in the ditch but no permission was obtained and no steps were taken to inform the college authorities of the laying of the pipe. However, the presence of the pipe became known to a member of the college who was responsible for cleaning out the ditch twice a year. The council had not put a guard at the entrance to the pipe to prevent its being blocked by debris. The pipe became blocked and the appellant's garden was flooded. He claimed damages from the college on the ground that the pipe was a nuisance. *Held*—by the House of Lords—the college was liable because it appeared that they should have known about the pipe and realized the risk. Furthermore they had adopted the nuisance by using the pipe to drain their land.

(626) *Sturges* v. *Bridgman* (1879), 11 Ch. D. 852

For more than twenty years the defendant, a confectioner, had used large pestles and mortars in his premises in Wigmore Street. Then the plaintiff, a physician in Wimpole Street, built a consulting room in his garden abutting on the confectioner's premises. The noise and vibration made by the confectioner's activities interfered materially with the plaintiff's practice. He sued for an injunction to prevent the offensive activities and the defence was that the defendant had acquired a prescriptive right to commit the nuisance. *Held*—Though it was possible to acquire a right, the defendant had not done so, because the nuisance only arose when the consulting room was built.

(627) *Earl* v. *Lubbock*, [1905] 1 K.B. 253

The plaintiff was employed by a firm of mineral water manufacturers, and the defendant, a wheelwright, had agreed with the plaintiff's employers that he would keep a certain number of their delivery vans in repair. The defendant failed to keep a certain van in repair, the result being that a wheel came off while the plaintiff was driving, and he suffered injuries. The plaintiff sued the defendant for negligence. *Held*—The plaintiff could not maintain an action against the defendant, since any duty the defendant had to repair the van properly was owed to the plaintiff's employer, with whom he had a contract, and not to the plaintiff.

(628) *East Suffolk Rivers Catchment Board* v. *Kent*, [1941] A.C. 74

The respondents were owners of land in Suffolk protected by a wall from inundation by a tidal river. As a result of spring floods and a northerly gale, the wall was breached and the respondents' land was flooded. The appellants, acting under Sect. 34 of the Land Drainage Act, 1930, attempted to repair the breach. However, their approach to the job was rather inefficient and the respondents' land was flooded for much longer than it need have been and they now sued for damages. *Held*—The damage was due to the forces of nature and the appellants, in trying to put the matter right, were acting under a mere power so that they were under no duty to the respondents. Section 30 of the Land Drainage Act did not place upon a Catchment Board an imperative duty to repair a breach of this kind, but gave the board permissive power to do so. They had exercised their discretion honestly, and could not be made liable for damage which would have been avoided had they exercised their discretion in a more reasonable way. Furthermore, the appellants were guilty of an omission rather than a positive act because they did not cause the harm but were merely slow in doing good.

(629) *Argy Trading Development Co. Ltd* v. *Lapid Developments Ltd*, [1977] 1 W.L.R. 444

In an underlease for six years from 19 October, 1971 the tenant agreed to insure against fire for the full value of the premises, including two years' rent, and in the event of loss or damage by fire to reinstate the premises. In fact the landlords insured the premises under a block policy covering other property as well and the tenant paid the landlords the appropriate proportion of the premium. In 1973 there was a change in the control of the landlords and the landlords did not renew the block policy but failed to notify the tenant of its cancellation. In 1973, some months after the policy had lapsed, the premises were gutted by fire. Neither party wanted the premises, which were scheduled for redevelopment, to be reinstated. The landlords undertook not to enforce the covenant to reinstate but the tenant wished to recover damages from the landlords on the ground that it had been deprived of the insurance monies, which it would otherwise have received, by the landlords failure to continue the insurance or to notify the tenant of its cancellation so that it had no opportunity to take out the policy. It was *held*—by Croom-Johnson, J.—that there was no implied term that the landlords would maintain their block policy or not cancel it without notifying the tenant. Nor was their any equitable estoppel such as was applied in the *High Trees* case[159] since there was no representation by the landlords intended to affect the legal relations of the parties. There was a special relationship between the parties which might have created a duty of care under the principle of *Hedley Byrne*[248] but that duty was not to *give* negligent information. The *failure* to give information which amounted to an omission was not within the principle of *Hedley Byrne*.[248]

(630) *The World Harmony*, [1965] 2 All E.R. 139

A collision occurred in the Bosphorus in December, 1960, between two ships, as a result of which one of the two ships drifted into a third and all three were wrecked. The *Tarsus*, the innocent third ship, was under charter to one of the plaintiffs and he suffered *pecuniary loss* by having to find another ship to carry goods for him. Hewson, J., *held* that the claim in negligence would have to be restricted to the physical loss of actual chattels on board the *Tarsus* at the time of the collision as damages could not be awarded in respect of mere pecuniary loss.

   (*Note:* in *Margarine Union GmbH* v. *Cambay Prince Steamship Co. Ltd.*, [1967] 3 All E.R. 775, a similar problem arose. The defendants had negligently failed to fumigate their ship so that a cargo of copra being carried on the ship was damaged by cockroaches. Part of the cargo was sold to the plaintiffs but it was agreed that they acquired no title to their part of the cargo until it was unloaded and separated from the bulk. Thus, the plaintiffs had no legal title to the goods at the time of the defendants' negligent act. Therefore, the plaintiff's were suing for economic loss arising from having to obtain other copra, and their action failed. Roskill, J., felt that this conclusion had not been affected by the *Hedley Byrne*[248] case.)

(631) *Weller & Co.* v. *Foot and Mouth Disease Research Institute*, [1965] 3
          All E.R. 560

The defendants carried out experiments on their land concerning foot and mouth disease. They imported an African virus which escaped and infected cattle in the vicinity. As a consequence two cattle markets in the area had to be closed and the plaintiffs, who were auctioneers, sued for damages for loss of business. *Held*—by Widgery, J.—that so far as negligence was concerned the defendants owed no duty of care to the plaintiffs who were not cattle owners, and had no proprietary interest in anything which could be damaged by the virus. Furthermore, the defendants owed no absolute duty to the plaintiffs under *Rylands* v. *Fletcher*, 1868, because the plaintiffs had no interest in any land to which the virus could have escaped.

(632) *SCM (United Kingdom) Ltd* v. *W. J. Whittall & Son Ltd*, [1970] 3
All E.R. 245

A workman employed by the defendants who were carrying out construction work near the plaintiffs' factory, cut into an underground electric cable
so that the power to the plaintiffs' factory failed. The plaintiffs made
typewriters and the lack of power caused molten materials to solidify in
their machines which were *physically* damaged. The machines had to be
stripped down and reassembled and production was brought to a halt for
seven and a half hours. In the Court of Appeal the plaintiffs limited their
claim to damages in respect of the physical damage to the machines and the
financial loss *directly* resulting from that damage. This enabled the court to
decide that the plaintiffs' property had foreseeably been damaged by the
defendants' act so that the plaintiffs could recover for damage to the
machines and the consequential financial loss flowing from it. Nevertheless
the Court went on to consider economic loss in the context of negligence
and dealt in effect with the position as it might have been if the power cut
had stopped production without damaging the machines. The following
aspects of the judgments are important: *Per* Lord Denning, M.R.—

> In actions of negligence, when the plaintiff has suffered no damage to
> his person or property, but has only sustained economic loss, the law
> does not usually permit him to recover that loss. Although the defen-
> dants owed the plaintiffs a duty of care, that did not mean that additional
> economic loss which was not consequent on the material damage
> suffered by the plaintiffs would also be recoverable; in cases such as
> *Weller & Co.* v. *Foot and Mouth Disease Research Institute*, 1965,[631] and
> *Electrochrome Ltd.* v. *Welsh Plastics Ltd*, 1968,[470] the plaintiffs did not
> recover for economic loss because it was too remote to be a head of
> damage, not because there was no duty owed to the plaintiffs or because
> the loss suffered in each case was not caused by the negligence of the
> defendants.

(*Per* Winn L.J.)

> Apart from the special case of imposition of liability for negligently
> uttered false statements, there is no liability for unintentional negligent
> infliction of any form of economic loss which is not itself consequential
> on foreseeable physical injury or damage to property.

(*Note:* the power shut-off lasted for some time and during that time the
plaintiffs would normally have processed four more 'melts'. Because they
had been unable to do so they had lost the profits they would have made on
them. However, this was regarded as economic loss not consequent upon
the physical damage and therefore what was recoverable was only the loss
of profit on the melt which was actually interrupted by the failure of
electrical supplies.)

(633) *Spartan Steel and Alloys Ltd* v. *Martin & Co. Ltd*, [1972] 3 All E.R. 557

While digging up a road the defendants' employees damaged a cable which the defendants knew supplied the plaintiffs' factory. The cable belonged to the local electricity board and the resulting electrical power failure meant that the plaintiffs' factory was deprived of electricity. The temperature of their furnace dropped and so metal that was in melt had to be poured away. Furthermore, while the cable was being repaired the factory received no electricity so it was unable to function for some 14 hours. The Court of Appeal, however, allowed only the plaintiffs' damages for the spoilt metal and the loss of profit on one 'melt'. They refused to allow the plaintiffs to recover their loss of profit which resulted in the factory being unable to function during the period when there was no electricity. Lord Denning, M.R., chose to base his decision of remoteness of damage rather than the absence of any duty of care to avoid causing economic loss. However, he did make it clear that public policy was involved. In the course of his judgment he said: 'At bottom I think the question of recovering economic loss is one of policy. Whenever the courts draw a line to mark out the bounds of duty, they do so as a matter of policy so as to limit the responsibility of the defendant. Whenever the courts set bounds to the damages recoverable—saying that they are, or are not, too remote—they do it as a matter of policy so as to limit the liability of the defendant.'

(634) *Clay* v. *A. J. Crump & Sons Ltd and Others*, [1963] 3 All E.R. 687

Garage owners employed demolition contractors to demolish an old building, and building contractors to erect an extension to a garage in Dudley. They also employed an architect to prepare plans and supervise both operations. The old building and the gable wall at the end of the existing garage were to be demolished to allow for an extension which would lengthen the existing building. Having demolished the old building, the demolition contractors were told to leave the gable wall for the time being. Before the demolition contractors left the site, two walls supporting the gable wall had been knocked down and the earth had been dug out from the foundations of the gable wall, thus exposing unsafe foundations. The architect inspected the site just before the demolition contractors left and could, if he had carried out a proper inspection, have seen that the wall was unsafe. However, he did advise the building owners that it was safe. The foreman of the demolition company also declared the wall safe. The building contractors did not examine the wall in any detail because they relied, as the architect and demolition contractors should have assumed they would, on the wall being left safe. The plaintiff was a labourer employed by the building contractors, and while he was on the site, the gable wall collapsed and injured him. He now sued the demolition contractors, the architect and the building contractors. *Held*—All three were liable being in breach of a duty of care owed to the plaintiff—the damages being apportioned 42% against the architect; 38% against the demolition contractors; and 20% against the building contractor. Regarding the architect's liability the Court of Appeal said that he owed a duty of care to the plaintiff because he gave an assurance of the safety of the wall. It was also argued for the architect that *Candler* v. *Crane, Christmas & Co.*, 1951,655 provided him with a defence because his contract was with the building owner only and he could not owe a duty of care to the plaintiff. Here the Court of Appeal said that *Hedley Byrne & Co. Ltd* v. *Heller & Partners Ltd*, 1963,248 had thrown doubt on the rule in *Candler's* case and the architect could not derive assistance from it. The building contractors were liable because they owed a duty to the plaintiff to see that the place where he had to work was safe. It should be noted that the architect was in effect liable for an omission because he should have foreseen the danger and carried out a proper inspection of the wall.

(635) *Home Office* v. *Dorset Yacht Co. Ltd*, [1970] 2 All E.R. 294

The respondents' yacht was damaged by a number of Borstal boys who had escaped at night from an island when they were left uncontrolled by their guards. The respondents sued the Home Office for the amount of damage. *Held*—by the House of Lords—

(i) The officers guarding the boys owed a duty of care to the respondents. The fact that the boys might take nearby yachts was foreseeable. The Home Office was therefore liable vicariously for the negligence of the officers.

(ii) The fact that the Borstal was conducted under statutory authority did not warrant unreasonable acts or justify negligent conduct.

(iii) There was no ground in public policy for granting *complete* immunity from liability in negligence to the Home Office or its officers in respect of the acts of prisoners or other detainees.

(636) *Daniels* v. *R. White and Sons Ltd*, [1938] 4 All E.R. 258

The plaintiffs, who were husband and wife, sued the first defendants, who were manufacturers of mineral waters, in negligence. The plaintiffs had been injured because a bottle of the first defendants' lemonade, which they had purchased from a public house in Battersea, contained carbolic acid. Evidence showed that the manufacturer took all possible care to see that no injurious matter got into the lemonade. It was *held* that the manufacturers were not liable in negligence because the duty was not one to ensure that the goods were in perfect condition but only to take reasonable care to see that no injury was caused to the eventual consumer. This duty had been fulfilled.

(637) *Hill* v. *J. Crowe (Cases), The Times*, 19 May, 1977

The plaintiff was injured when he stood on a packing case whose boards collapsed causing him to fall. It was *held*—by MacKenna, J.—that the case had been badly made and the manufacturers owed a duty of care to the plaintiff. They could not escape liability by showing that they had a good system of work and proper supervision. *Daniels* v. *White and Sons*, 1938[636] not followed.

(638) *Greaves & Co. (Contractors)* v. *Baynham Meikle & Partners*, [1974] 3 All E.R. 666

The plaintiff, a builder, was instructed to build a warehouse and subcontracted its structural design to the defendants who were a firm of consultant structural engineers. B knew, or by reason of the relevant British Standard Code of Practice, ought to have known that as the warehouse was to carry loaded trucks there was a danger of vibration. The design was competent but inadequate for the purpose of carrying the trucks and it was *held*—by Kilner Brown, J., allowing the plaintiff's claim for breach of duty of care and breach of an implied term of the contract—that the duty of the defendants was not simply to exercise the care and skill of a competent engineer which they had done, but to design a building fit for its purpose in the light of the knowledge which they had as to its proposed use.

(639) *Paris* v. *Stepney Borough Council*, [1951] A.C. 367

The plaintiff was employed by the defendants on vehicle maintenance. He had the use of only one eye and the defendants were aware of this. The plaintiff was endeavouring to remove a bolt from the chassis of a vehicle, and was using a hammer for the purpose, when a chip of metal flew into his good eye so that he became totally blind. The plaintiff claimed damages from his employers for negligence in that he had not been supplied with goggles. The defendants showed in evidence that it was not the usual practice in trades of this nature to supply goggles, at least where the employees were men with two good eyes. The trial judge found for the plaintiff, but the Court of Appeal reversed the decision on the grounds that the plaintiff's disability could be relevant only if it increased the risk, i.e. if a one-eyed man was more likely to get a splinter in his eye than a two-eyed man. Having found that the risk was not increased they allowed the appeal. The House of Lords reversed the judgment of the Court of Appeal, holding that the gravity of the harm likely to be caused would influence a reasonable employer, so that the duty of care to a one-eyed employee required the supply of goggles, and Paris therefore succeeded.

(640) *Haley* v. *London Electricity Board*, [1964] 3 All E.R. 185

The appellant, Haley, a blind man who was on his way to his work as a telephonist, tripped over an obstacle placed by servants of the London Electricity Board near the end of a trench excavated in the pavement of a street in Woolwich. He fell and suffered an injury which rendered him deaf, and brought about his premature retirement from his employment. The guard was sufficient warning for sighted people but was by its nature inadequate to protect or warn the blind. It consisted of a hammer hooked in the railings and resting on the pavement at an angle of thirty degrees, and Haley's white stick, which he was properly using as a guide, did not encounter the obstacle with the result that instead of warning him he fell over it. Evidence was given that about one in five hundred people were blind and there were 258 registered blind people in Woolwich, many of whom were capable of walking in the streets alone, taking the normal precautions such blind persons were accustomed to take. The House of Lords *held*, reversing the decision of the Court of Appeal, that the London Electricity Board were liable in negligence. Those engaged in operations on the pavement of a highway must act reasonably to danger to passers-by including blind people who must, however, also take reasonable care of themselves. The Board had not fulfilled this duty and were liable in damages for negligence which were assessed at £3000 general damages, and £2250 special damages, Haley's retirement being accelerated by four years.

(641) *Watt* v. *Hertfordshire County Council*, [1954] 2 All E.R. 368

A fireman was injured by a heavy jack which slipped while being carried in a lorry which was going to the scene of an accident. The lorry was not equipped to carry such a heavy jack but it was required to free a woman who had been trapped in the wreckage. No proper vehicle was available and it was *held* that the fire authority was not liable.

(642) *Latimer* v. *AEC Ltd*, [1953] 2 All E.R. 449

A heavy rainstorm flooded a factory and made the floor slippery. The occupiers of the factory did all they could to get rid of the water and make the factory safe, but the plaintiff fell and was injured. He alleged negligence in that the occupiers did not close down the factory. *Held*—the occupiers of the factory were not liable. The risk of injury did not justify the closing down of the factory.

(643) *Easson* v. *L.N.E. Railway Co.*, [1944] 1 All E.R. 246

The plaintiff, a boy aged four years, fell through the open door of a corridor train seven miles from its last stopping place. It was *held* that the defendants did not have sufficient control over the doors for *res ipsa loquitur* to apply. In the course of his judgment Goddard, L.J., said: 'It is impossible to say that the doors of an express corridor train travelling from Edinburgh to London are continuously under the sole control of the railway company . . . passengers are walking up and down the corridors during the journey and get in and out at stopping places. The fact that the door came open could as well have been due to interference by a passenger as to the negligence of the defendants' servants.'

(644) *Byrne* v. *Boadle* (1863), 2 H. & C. 722

The plaintiff brought an action in negligence alleging that, as he was walking past the defendant's shop, a barrel of flour fell from a window above the shop and injured him. The defendant was a dealer in flour, but there was no evidence that the defendant or any of his servants were engaged in lowering the barrel of flour at the time. The defendant submitted that there was no evidence of negligence to go to the jury, but it was *held* that the occurrence was of itself evidence of negligence sufficient to entitle the jury to find for the plaintiff, in the absence of an explanation by the defendant.

(645) *Scott* v. *London and St Katherine Docks Co.* (1865), 3 H. & C. 596

The plaintiff, a Customs officer, proved that when he was passing in front of the defendant's warehouse six bags of sugar fell upon him. It was *held* that the maxim *res ipsa loquitur* applied. In the course of his judgment Erle, C.J., said: '. . . where the thing is shewn to be under the management of the defendant, or his servants, and the accident is such as, in the ordinary course of things, does not happen if those who have the management use proper care, it affords reasonable evidence, in the absence of explanation by the defendant, that the accident arose from want of care.'

(*Note:* this case was followed in *Ward* v. *Tesco Stores*, [1976] All E.R. 219, where the Court of Appeal held that an accident which had occurred due to a spillage of yoghourt on a shop floor put an evidential burden upon the defendant shopowners to show that the accident did not occur through any want of care on their part. They were not able to satisfy that burden and the plaintiff succeeded.)

(646) *Roe* v. *Minister of Health*, [1954] 2 Q.B. 66

Two patients in a hospital had operations on the same day. Both operations were of a minor character and in each case nupercaine, a spinal anaesthetic, was injected by means of a lumbar puncture. The injections were given by a specialist anaesthetist, assisted by the theatre staff of the hospital. The nupercaine had been contained in sealed glass ampoules, stored in a solution of phenol. After the operations both patients developed symptoms of spastic pariplegia caused by the phenol, which had contaminated the nupercaine by penetrating almost invisible cracks in the ampoules. In the event, both patients became permanently paralysed from the waist down, and they now sued the defendants for negligence. *Held*—The defendants were vicariously liable for the negligence (if any) of those concerned with the operations, but on the standard of medical knowledge in 1947, when the operations took place, those concerned were not negligent. The cracks in the ampoules were not visible on ordinary examination, and could not be reproduced even by deliberate experiment. It was true that in 1954, when the case was brought, phenol used for disinfectant purposes was tinted so that it might be seen on examination, but the case must be decided on medical knowledge at the time when the operations were carried out. It was also suggested that once the accident has been explained, there is no question of *res ipsa loquitur* applying. Nor does the maxim apply when many persons might have been negligent. Denning, L.J., suggested that every surgical operation is attended by risks, and one cannot take the benefits of surgery without accepting the risks. Doctors, like the rest of us, have to learn by experience. Further, one must not condemn as negligence that which is only misadventure.

(647) *Pearson* v. *North-Western Gas Board*, [1968] 2 All E.R. 669

The plaintiff's husband was killed by an explosion of gas which also destroyed her house. It appeared from the evidence that a gas main had fractured due to a movement of earth caused by a severe frost. When the weather was very cold the defendants had men standing by ready to deal with reports of gas leaks, but unless they received reports there was no way of predicting or preventing a leak which might lead to an explosion. *Held*—by Rees, J.—that assuming the principle of *res ipsa loquitur* applied, the defendants had rebutted the presumption of negligence and the plaintiff's case failed.

(648) *O'Connell* v. *Jackson*, [1971] 3 All E.R. 129

The defendant, who was driving a car, came out of a minor road on to a major road and collided with the plaintiff who was riding a moped. The plaintiff was thrown on to the road and suffered severe head injuries. Medical evidence showed that if the plaintiff had been wearing a crash helmet his injuries would have been much reduced. *Held*—the plaintiff's damages would be reduced by 15 per cent. Although it was accepted and admitted that the defendant was solely responsible for the accident, one must always take into account the possibility of others being careless, and by not wearing a crash helment the plaintiff had contributed to the harm suffered.

(649) *Pasternack* v. *Poulton*, [1973] 2 All E.R. 74

The plaintiff, a front seat passenger in the defendant's car suffered facial injuries in a collision caused by the defendant's negligence. She was not wearing a seat belt and did not know that one was available but was familiar with seat belts generally. On the issue of liability it was *held*—by Judge Kenneth Jones—that she ought to have foreseen the possibility of an accident resulting in injury to herself and as a prudent passenger ought to have inquired about the availability of a safety device and worn the seat belt which was available. Thus she was guilty of contributory negligence but as the defendant had taken no steps to encourage her to wear the belt the plaintiff's damages would be reduced by only five per cent. (*O'Connell* v. *Jackson*, 1971[648] applied.)

(650) *Jones* v. *Lawrence*, [1969] 3 All E.R. 267

A boy aged seven years and three months ran out from behind a parked van across a road apparently without looking in order to get to a fun fair. He was knocked down by Lawrence who was travelling on his motorcycle at fifty miles per hour in a built-up area. The boy's injuries adversely affected his school work and he subsequently failed his eleven-plus examination. In action on his behalf for damages it was *held* by Cumming-Bruce, J.—that

(*a*) his conduct was only that to be expected of a seven-year-old child and could not amount to contributory negligence;

(*b*) the failure to obtain a grammar-school place and the permanent impairment of his powers of concentration affected his job attainment potential and were factors to be taken into account in assessing damages.

(651) *Oliver* v. *Birmingham Bus Co.*, [1932] 1 K.B. 35

A grandfather was walking with his grandchild aged four, when a bus approached quickly and without warning. The grandfather, being startled, let go the child's hand and the bus struck the child. It was *held* that the damages awarded to the child should not be reduced to take account of the grandfather's negligence.

(652) *Atkinson* v. *Newcastle and Gateshead Waterworks Co.* (1877), L.R.2 Ex. D. 441

The plaintiff's timber yard caught fire and was destroyed, there being insufficient water in the mains to put it out. The defendants were required by the Waterworks Clauses Act, 1874, to maintain a certain pressure of water in their water pipes, and the Act provided a penalty of £10 for failure to keep the required pressure and 40s. for each day during which the neglect continued, the sums being payable to aggrieved ratepayers. The plaintiff sued the defendants for loss caused by the fire on the ground that they were in breach of a statutory duty regarding the pressure in the pipes. *Held*—The defendants were not liable. The statute did not disclose a cause of action by individuals for damage of this kind. It was most improbable that the legislature intended the company to be gratuitous insurers against fire of all the buildings in Newcastle.

(653) *Gorris* v. *Scott* (1874), L.R. 9 Exch. 125

A statutory order placed a duty on the defendant to supply pens of a specified size in those parts of a ship's deck occupied by animals. The defendant did not supply the pens, and sheep belonging to the plaintiff were swept overboard. The plaintiff claimed damages from the defendant for breach of statutory duty. *Held*—The plaintiff could not recover for his loss under breach of statutory duty, because the object of the statutory order was to prevent the spread of disease, not to prevent animals from being drowned.

(654) *Anderson (W.B.) and Sons* v. *Rhodes (Liverpool)*, [1967] 2 All E.R. 850

The plaintiff and the first defendant were wholesalers in the Liverpool fruit and vegetable market. In April, 1965, the manager of a newly formed company bought some potatoes for cash from Rhodes & Co. and later purchased potatoes from them on credit. The manager of Rhodes & Co. made no credit inquiries about the new company. The market rule was that payment should be made within seven days of invoice but at all material times substantial amounts were overdue as between Rhodes & Co. and the new company, but the salesman and buyer of Rhodes & Co. were not informed of this fact. Rhodes & Co. also acted from time to time as commission agents and their buyer, a man called Reid, later arranged sales on a commission basis between the new company and the plaintiffs. Reid represented orally to the plaintiffs that the new company was credit-worthy and he acted throughout in good faith. The plaintiffs supplied goods on credit to the new company which then became insolvent and could not pay its debts. The plaintiffs sued Rhodes & Co. for negligence in representing that the new company was credit-worthy. *Held*—by Cairns, J.—that the plaintiffs were entitled to recover damages against Rhodes & Co. because—

(i) Rhodes & Co. owed a duty of care to the plaintiffs in respect of Reid's representations acting as their servant or agent (*Hedley Byrne*[248] applied);

(ii) Rhodes & Co. were vicariously liable for the negligence of their manager who knew that the new company was not credit-worthy even though Reid and not the manager made the representation;

(iii) Section 6 of the Statute of Frauds Amendment Act (Lord Tenterden's Act), was not a defence to a claim based on negligence as distinct from fraud.

(655) *Candler* v. *Crane, Christmas & Co.*, [1951] 2 K.B. 164

The defendants, a firm of accountants and auditors, prepared the accounts and balance sheet of a limited company at the request of its managing director, knowing that they were required to induce the plaintiff to invest money in the company. The plaintiff, relying on the accounts, invested £2000 in the company. The accounts were negligently prepared and failed to give an accurate picture of the company's financial state. The company was wound up within a year and the plaintiff lost his money. He now sued the accountants in negligence. The Court of Appeal *held* that, in the absence of a contractual or fiduciary relationship between the parties, the defendants owed no duty of care to the plaintiff in preparing the accounts. Denning, L.J., thought that the defendants might be held liable because they knew that the accounts were to be shown to the plaintiff, though he would not have found them liable to complete strangers.

(656) *Clayton* v. *Woodman & Son (Builders) Ltd and Others*, [1961] 3 All E.R. 249

The plaintiff was a bricklayer employed by the first defendants, Woodman & Son, a firm of builders. The builders had entered into a contract with the second defendants, a regional hospital board, to install a lift at a hospital.

The work was carried out in accordance with the instructions given by a firm of architects who were made third defendants. An architect employed by the third defendants allowed the plaintiff to cut a chase or wide groove in an unsupported gable. This had the effect of weakening the gable and the architect should have known that it would fall if not supported. The plaintiff cut the chase, and the gable collapsed and injured him. The question of the liability of each of the defendants arose. At first instance Salmon, J., *held*—(*a*) The first defendants (the builders) were liable for negligence at common law because they had failed to provide a safe system of work. They were also liable for breach of their statutory duty under the Building (Safety, Health and Welfare) Regulations, 1948. (*b*) The second defendants (the hospital authorities) were not liable. They were not in breach of their duty under the Occupiers' Liability Act, 1957. Further, they were not vicariously liable for the negligence of the architect since he was an independent contractor. (*c*) The architects were liable. The decision in *Candler* v. *Crane, Christmas & Co.* (1951)[655] did not apply, because the architect was not making careless misstatements, but was giving careless orders or instructions, and in any case the injury here was physical not financial.

(*Note:* in *Clayton* v. *Woodman & Sons (Builders) Ltd and Others*, [1962] 2 All E.R. 33, the Court of Appeal reversed the part of the above decision which found the architect liable, saying that the question of his liability did not arise for decision because. (*a*) The architect had not given orders to the bricklayer. All he had done was to refuse to allow the gable to be demolished, and he was bound to do this because he had instructions to preserve certain features of the building of which the gable was one. The cutting of the chase followed from that refusal. (*b*) From then on it was the duty of the plaintiff's employers to provide a safe system of doing the job, and they were solely responsible.)

(657) *Mutual Life Assurance* v. *Evatt*, [1971] 1 All E.R. 152

Evatt had made certain investments in P. Ltd and wished to know whether he should retain these investments or expand them. P. Ltd and the assurance company were both subsidiaries of the same holding company, the only relationship between Evatt and the assurance company being that Evatt was one of their policy holders. On the basis of that and the assurance company's personal knowledge of P. Ltd's affairs Evatt sought the assurance company's advice as to P. Ltd's financial prospects. The advice was given, without any disclaimer, and Evatt invested accordingly. Soon afterwards the investments fell in value and Evatt claimed that the advice was given negligently. It was *held*—by the Judicial Committee of the Privy Council (Lords Reid and Morris dissenting) that there was no cause of action. The liability in the *Hedley Byrne* case was limited to persons who held themselves out as being skilled in the subject matter of the inquiry and, since it was no part of the business of an insurance company to give advice on the financial position of other companies the appeal was allowed.

It would not in their Lordships' view be consonant with the principles hereto accepted in the common law that the duty to comply with that objective standard should be extended to an advisor who, at the time when his advice is sought, has not let it be known to the advisee that he claims to possess the standard of skill and competence and is prepared to exercise diligence which is generally shown by persons who carry on the business of giving advice of the kind sought. He has given the advisee no reason to suppose that he is acquainted with the standard or capable of complying with it, or that he has such appreciation of the nature and magnitude of the loss which the advisee may sustain by reason of any failure by that advisor to attain that standard as a reasonable man would require before assuming a liability to answer for the loss.

(*Per* Diplock, L.J.)

(658) *Esso Petroleum* v. *Mardon*, [1976] 2 All E.R. 5

In this case it was held that the principle in *Hedly Byrne*[248] could apply even where the parties concerned were in a pre-contractual relationship, and, in addition, that the person who made the statement need not necessarily be in business to give advice. Mr Mardon was awarded damages for a negligent mis-statement by a senior sales representative of Esso in regard to the amount of petrol he could expect to sell per year from a petrol station which he was leasing from Esso. The facts of *Mardon* pre-dated this Misrepresentation Act, 1967, and the judge could not use it. The decision is obviously important, but where the facts have occurred since 1967, the Misrepresentation Act is likely to prove more popular to plaintiffs since they can ask the representor to show that he is not negligent. In *Hedley Byrne*[248] claims the burden of proof is on the plaintiff to prove negligence. However, the fact that *Hedley Byrne* can be used in a precontractual relationship is of some importance because where there is a breach of contract time, under the Limitation Act, runs from the breach but in tort from the cause of action. Thus, for example, an accountant could be liable under *Mardon* even in retirement for accounts which were prepared in his first year of practise if the cause of action arose in tort from a person who relied upon them.

(659) *Dutton* v. *Bognor Regis Urban District Council*, [1972] 1 All E.R. 462

In 1958 a builder, Mr Holroyd, bought some land for development. One of the plots was on the site of a rubbish tip ·which had been filled in. A building inspector employed by the council inspected the foundations of a house to be built on the plot and passed them. The house in question was completed and sold to a purchaser in 1958 who resold to the plaintiff, Mrs Dutton, in 1960. In 1963 the house was examined by a surveyor after cracks had appeared in the walls and a staircase had slipped. The surveyor informed Mrs Dutton that the house had been built on a rubbish tip which was not a stable foundation. Mrs Dutton sued the local authority for damages. *Held*––by the Court of Appeal––

(i) a local authority had extensive legislative control over building operations and must exercise that control with reasonable care;

(ii) as a result of the decision in *Hedley Byrne*[248] a professional man who gave guidance to others owed a duty of care not merely to his client but also to others who might in the ordinary course of events rely on his skill;

(iii) a professional man who gave advice as to the safety of buildings, machinery or materials owed a duty to all those who might suffer injury as a result of their subsequent use;

(iv) the inspector should have realized that once the foundations were covered the defect would not be discovered until damage actually emerged;

(v) thus the inspector should have had later purchasers in mind when carrying out his inspection (Lord Atkin's 'neighbour' test in *Donoghue* v. *Stevenson*, 1932[468] applied);

(vi) the defendants were therefore vicariously liable for their servant's negligence.

(660) *Sutcliffe* v. *Thackrah*, [1974] 1 All E.R. 859

The plaintiff had acquired a site and wished to have a house built on it. The defendants, a firm of architects, were employed to prepare designs. There was no formal contract but the defendants knew that builders would be employed under the RIBA form of contract and that they would be the architects supervising construction. The plaintiff entered into a contract with builders for the construction of the house. Under a clause in that contract the parties agreed, amongst other things, that at intervals which were specified the architects should issue interim certificates stating how much was due to the builders in respect of work properly executed and that the plaintiff would within 14 days pay the amounts so stated. There were delays in completion of the house. A number of interim certificates were issued to the builders by the defendants and the plaintiff paid the sums certified. Later the plaintiff terminated the builders' contract for reasons which it was accepted were sufficient. The builders later became insolvent. The plaintiff brought an action against the defendants claiming damages for negligence and breach of duty in the following respects—

(i) in the course of supervising the building, and

(ii) in certifying, in two of the interim certificates, for work not done or improperly done by the builders.

The Court of Appeal held that in issuing interim certificates, the defendants were acting in an arbitral capacity and provided they acted honestly were not therefore under any duty to the plaintiff to exercise care or professional skill. The plaintiff appealed to the House of Lords where it was *held*—

(i) that although every case depended on its own facts and on the particular provisions of the relevant contract, in general any architect or valuer would be liable to the person who employed him if he caused loss by reason of his negligence, but as an exception to that rule, immunity would be accorded to the architect or valuer if he could show that, by agreement, he had been appointed to act as an arbitrator or quasi-arbitrator, i.e. that he had been appointed to determine a specific dispute submitted to him, or define differences that might arise in the future, and there was agreement that his decision would be binding. Where, however, a professional man was employed to make a valuation and, to his knowledge, that valuation was to be binding on his principal and another party under an agreement between them, it did not follow that, because he was under a duty to act fairly in making his valuation, he was acting in a judicial capacity and was therefore immune from liability to his principal for loss caused to him by a negligent valuation;

(ii) that the defendants were not immune from liability to the plaintiff for their negligent over-certification because (*a*) the giving of an interim certificate was not the decision of a dispute between the plaintiff and the builders, (*b*) there was no agreement to abide by the decision of the defendants as to the value of the work done, and (*c*) the defendants owed a duty to the plaintiff to exercise care and skill in the giving of certificates. The fact that the plaintiff became obliged to pay the amount certified by the defendants did not place them in the position of arbitrators: nor did the fact that the defendants could only properly perform their duties if they acted fairly as between the plaintiff and the builders.

Accordingly, the plaintiff's appeal would be allowed.

(661) *McInerny* v. *Lloyds Bank*; [1973] 2 Lloyd's Rep. 389

P wished to sell his business to M. Payment was to be made over a period of time by P drawing bills of exchange on M. M asked Lloyds Bank to guarantee payment of the bills but they wrote to him saying that English banking regulations precluded guarantees by the bank of the payment of trade debts. They went on to say that they would establish irrevocable credit by an alternative method and stating that 'I think . . . P ought to be satisfied with this and that the bank had 'agreed in principle' to the amended terms of credit which we will not finally establish, under the advice to P from Barclays Bank until we receive your confirmation of the exact amount due on 3 March, 1968'. M asked the bank to send a copy of this letter to P and on the basis of it P signed the contract with M relying, so he said, on the fact that the bank was to in some way back the bills drawn on M. Later M failed to honour some of the bills of exchange. *Held*—by Kerr, J., that—

(i) it was impossible to infer any contract between the bank and P from the circumstances or their conduct and in any event no consideration in respect of such a contract had moved from P;

(ii) since it was unlikely that P would consider the sentence indicating that he should be satisfied as advice to him and since the whole contents of the letter were merely to inform P of the action the bank were prepared to take, there was no misrepresentation for the purposes of the rule in *Hedley Byrne* v. *Heller & Partners*, 1963.[248] The Court should give great weight to the fact that the contents of the statement were primarily prepared for the purposes of and addressed to someone else; and

(iii) accordingly P's claim against the bank failed in contract and tort.

(662) *Wheat* v. *E. Lacon & Co. Ltd*, [1966] 1 All E.R. 582

The manager of a public house was permitted by the owners, Lacon & Co., to take paying visitors who were accommodated in a part of the premises labelled 'Private'. The plaintiff's husband, while a paying visitor, was killed by a fall from a staircase in the private part of the premises. Lacon & Co. denied liability on the ground that they were not occupiers of the private part of the premises. *Held*—by the House of Lords—

(i) that the defendants retained occupation and control together with the manager;

(ii) the deceased was a visitor to whom the defendants owed a common duty of care;

(iii) on the facts the staircase, though not lit, was not dangerous if used with proper care.

Wheat's claim therefore failed because there was no breach of the duty of care.

(663) *Cook* v. *Broderip, The Times*, 27 February, 1968

The owner of a flat employed an apparently competent contractor to put in a new socket. Mrs Cook, who was a cleaner, received an electric shock caused because the socket was faulty. It appeared that the contractor had negligently failed to test the socket for reversed polarity. *Held*—by O'Connor, J.—that Major Broderip, the owner of the flat, was not vicariously liable for the contractor's negligence and was not in breach of duty under the Occupiers' Liability Act, 1957. Damages of £3081 were awarded against the contractor who was the second defendant.

(664) *Bunker* v. *Charles Brand & Son*, [1969] 2 All E.R. 59

The plaintiff's employers were engaged as sub-contractors by the defendants who were the main contractors for tunnelling in connection with the Victoria Line. The plaintiff was required to carry out modifications to a digging machine. He had seen the machine *in situ* and was taken to have appreciated the danger in crossing its rollers when in operation. He was injured while attempting to cross the rollers in the course of his work and sued for damages. *Held*—by O'Connor, J.—that the defendants having retained control of the tunnel and the machine were the occupiers. They were not absolved from liability under the Act of 1957 merely because of the plaintiff's knowledge of the danger. Knowledge was not assent.

However, the plaintiff's damages were reduced by 50 per cent on the ground of his contributory negligence.

(665) *British Railways Board* v. *Herrington*, [1972] 1 All E.R. 749

An electrified railway line owned by the British Railways Board ran through National Trust Property which was open to the public. The fences on each side were in poor condition and in April, 1965, children had been seen on the line. A particular part of the fence had clearly been used as a route to cross the railway. In June, 1965, the plaintiff aged six, was injured when he stepped on to the line, having got through the broken part of the fence. He claimed damages for negligence, and the judge at first instance held that since the emergence of a child from the surrounding land on to the line was reasonably foreseeable, by allowing the fence to fall in to, and remain, in substantial disrepair, the defendants were guilty of negligence. The Court of Appeal further held that the defendants had acted in reckless disregard for the plaintiff's safety. The House of Lords *held* that the defendants were in breach of their duty and stated that the old rules relating to trespass did not necessarily apply. While an occupier does not owe the same duty of care to a trespasser which he owes to a visitor, he owes a trespasser a duty to take such steps as common sense or common humanity would dictate, to exclude or warn, or otherwise, within reasonable and practicable limits reduce or avert a danger.

(666) *South Portland Cement* v. *Cooper*, [1974] 1 All E.R. 87

A quarrying company tipped waste material on its land beside posts which carried a high tension electric cable and near which children often played. When they did so they were warned off, at least during working hours. One Sunday, the plaintiff, aged 13, was playing on the mound when his arm came in contact with the electric cable and he was injured. On the company's appeal to the Privy Council against an award of damages to Cooper for his injuries it was *held*—dismissing the appeal—that since it was to be expected that children would be attracted to play on the heap the company should have taken the steps necessary to prevent the dangerous situation from arising and so were liable to the plaintiff for their failure. An occupier's duty towards potential trespassers is to do what a humane man with the occupier's financial and other limitations would do in the particular circumstances to prevent injury.

(667) *Yachuk* v. *Oliver Blais & Co. Ltd*, [1949] A.C. 386

In this appeal from the Supreme Court of Canada to the Judicial Committee of the Privy Council the facts were as follows: a servant of Oliver Blais & Co. Ltd had supplied five cents' worth of gasoline in an open lard pail to certain boys, aged nine and seven, who told him that they needed it for their mother's car, which had run out of petrol down the road. In fact they wanted it for a game of Red Indians. The boys dipped a bullrush into the pail and lit it. This set fire to the petrol in the pail and the boy Yachuk was seriously injured. The Judicial Committee *held* that the company was liable for the negligence of its servant in allowing the boys to take away the gasoline. The question of contributory negligence did not arise, because there was no evidence that the infants appreciated the dangerous quality of gasoline. The company was fully responsible even though the boys had resorted to deceit to overcome the supplier's scruples.

(668) *Gough* v. *National Coal Board*, [1954] 1 Q.B. 191

The defendants were owners of a colliery which included a small railway which was constantly in use. The railway lines were not fenced or guarded, although there were houses on both sides. The public had for a long time been permitted to cross the lines, and children often played on the wagons, although the defendants' servants had been told to keep children off. The plaintiff, a boy aged six and a half, was seriously injured when he jumped off a wagon on which he had been riding. At the trial the boy admitted that he knew he was not supposed to ride on the wagons, and that this father had threatened to punish him if he did. Nevertheless it was *held* that the defendants were liable. The fact that children had for many years played near the railway made them licensees, and although the boy was strictly speaking a trespasser as regards the wagon, he was allured by the slow-moving wagons which the defendants knew were an attraction to children.

(669) *Mourton* v. *Poulter*, [1930] 2 K.B. 183

The owner of certain land wished to carry out building operations on it, but before he could so do, it was necessary to fell a large elm tree. The land was unfenced, and children of the locality were in the habit of using it as a playground. During the process of felling, a large number of children gathered near the tree, and Poulter, who had been employed to fell the tree, warned the children of the danger likely to arise when the tree came down. He failed to repeat the warning when the tree was about to fall, and the plaintiff, a boy of ten, was crushed by the falling tree. *Held*—The defendant was liable. Even though the children were trespassers, he owed them a duty to give adequate warning.

(670) *Pannett* v. *McGuinness & Co.*, [1972] 3 All E.R. 137

The defendants were demolishing a warehouse in a heavily populated area near a park where children played. Three workmen were specially appointed to make a bonfire of rubbish and to keep a lookout for children and to see that they came to no harm. The plaintiff, a boy of five, got in while the three men were away and was severely burned. The men had frequently chased children away in the past and in particular the plaintiff on a number of occasions. The contractors contended that the plaintiff was a trespasser, that he had been warned off and that they were under no duty. *Held*—the contractors were in breach of the duty of care owed to the child, their workmen had failed to keep a proper look out. (*British Railways Board* v. *Herrington*, 1972[665] applied.)

(*Note: Penny* v. *Northampton Borough Council, The Times*, 20 July, 1974, provides a contrast. In that case a child trespasser was not successful in recovering damages following injury from an aerosol can which exploded when it was thrown into a fire by another child. The accident took place in a discarded rubbish tip some 50 acres in area which resembled a rough field. The children had often been warned off the land by the council's workmen. The Court considered the authority had behaved with commonsense and humanity and could not have known of the danger on the land so that it had discharged its duty of care. However, in *Harris* v. *Birkenhead Corporation*, [1975] 1 All E.R. 1001, a local authority was not successful in showing that it had discharged its duty of care to a child trespasser who had entered a derelict house which the corporation had purchased under a compulsory purchase order. The child fell from an upstairs window and the authority was held to be the occupier since the previous owner had got out of the premises in view of the order. The authority was fixed with knowledge of the relevant facts and Kilner Brown, J., found for the plaintiff after applying the 'commonsense' and 'common humanity' test.)

(671) *Griffiths* v. *Liverpool Corporation*, [1966] 2 All E.R. 1015

The plaintiff tripped and fell on a flagstone which rocked on its centre. In this action against the highway authority for breach of Sect. 1(1) of the Highways (Miscellaneous Provisions) Act, 1961, it appeared that a regular system of inspection was desirable but was not carried out because the authority could not get tradesmen to put right faults discovered. The present fault could, however, have been put right by a labourer and no shortage of labourers was alleged. *Held*—by The Court of Appeal—the authority had not brought itself within the statutory defence in Sect. 1(2) and damages should be awarded.

(672) *Millard* v. *Serck Tubes Ltd*, [1969] 1 All E.R. 598

The plaintiff operated a power drill during the course of his employment. The drill was fenced, but the guard was not complete in that there was a gap in it through which the operator's hand could be drawn. While the plaintiff's hand was resting on the guard a piece of swarf thrown out from the drill wound itself around the plaintiff's hand and drew it into the drill causing injury to the plaintiff. The defendant employers conceded that the drill had not been properly fenced but contended that they were not liable because the accident itself was unforeseeable. This defence was rejected by the Court of Appeal and the plaintiff succeeded in his claim for damages. Where a defendant has failed to fence dangerous machinery, as here, in breach of Sect. 14 of the Factories Act, 1961, he cannot escape liability for injury on the grounds that such injury occurred in a way that was not reasonably foreseeable. Thus a plaintiff might succeed when suing on a statutory duty and fail if suing on a common law one.

(673) *Lumley* v. *Gye* (1853), 2 E. & Bl. 216

The plaintiff, who was the manager of an opera house, made a contract with a *prima donna* Johanna Wagner for her exclusive services for a period of time. Gye induced Johanna Wagner to break her operatic engagement with the plaintiff and sing for him. It was *held* that whatever might have been the origin of the right to sue in such cases as this, it was not now confined to actions by masters for the enticement of their servants but extended to wrongful interference with any contract of personal service.

(674) *Daily Mirror Newspapers* v. *Gardner*, [1968] 2 All E.R. 163

The executive committee of the retailers' federation recommended their member to boycott the *Daily Mirror* for one week after that newspaper had announced that the retailers' discount rate was to be reduced when the price of the newspaper was increased. The newspaper asked for interlocutory injunctions requiring the committee to communicate with their members and withdraw the recommendation on the grounds—

(i) that it was an unlawful interference with the newspaper's contracts with the wholesalers because the wholesalers would not want to take copies of the *Daily Mirror* if the retailers would not take it; and

(ii) that it was equivalent to an agreement contrary to the public interest within Sect. 21(1) of the Restrictive Trades Practices Act, 1956.

Held—by the Court of Appeal—that a sufficient *prima facie* case had been made out on both grounds and the injunctions would be granted.

(675) *Rookes* v. *Barnard*, [1964] 1 All E.R. 367

Rookes, who was employed in the design office of BOAC, resigned from membership of his trade union. Under an agreement made in 1949 between BOAC and its employees it was provided that no lockout or strike should take place and any disputes should be referred to arbitration. This agreement formed part of each contract of employment. Rookes' office was subject to a 'closed-shop' agreement and when he refused to re-join the union certain officials of the union served notice on BOAC that unless Rookes was removed they would withdraw the labour of their members, and would not go to arbitration. They were thus in breach of their contract. As a result BOAC lawfully terminated Rookes' contract of service after giving a much longer period of notice than the contract required. Rookes brought an action for damages against the defendants for using unlawful means to induce BOAC to terminate the contract of service with him and/or conspiring to have him dismissed by threatening BOAC with strike action if he were retained. A jury awarded Rookes £7500 damages on the basis of a direction in the summing up that any deliberate illegality might be punished by exemplary damages. The Court of Appeal reversed the decision holding that, although the tort of intimidation existed, it did not cover threats to break a contract. Rookes appealed to the House of Lords and the defendants cross-appealed on the question of damages. The House of Lords allowed the appeal and the cross-appeal and ordered a new trial on the question of damages, but observed—

> that exemplary damages can be awarded only in cases of (*a*) oppressive, arbitrary or unconstitutional acts by government servants; (*b*) where the defendants' conduct had been calculated by him to make a profit for himself which might exceed the compensation payable to the plaintiff; (*c*) where expressly authorized by statute.

(676) *Allen* v. *Flood*, [1898] A.C. 1

The plaintiffs were shipwrights engaged by the day by a concern called the Glengall Iron Company. The defendants, who were officials of a trade union, advised the manager of the company to discharge them, threatening to give proper notice of a strike if he did not. There was, however, no evidence of conspiracy, intimidation, coercion or breach of contract, though the defendants acted with malice. The plaintiffs were not engaged by the company and sued the defendants for damages. The House of Lords *held* that the plaintiffs' action failed, because the defendants had not been guilty of any wrong.

(677) *Crofter Hand Woven Harris Tweed Co. Ltd* v. *Veitch*, [1942] A.C. 435

Veitch and other defendants were officials of the Transport and General Workers Union. The dockers at Stornaway on the island of Lewis were all members of the union and so were most of the employees in the spinning mills on the island. The yarn when spun in the mills was woven into tweed cloth by crofters working at home, the woven cloth being finished in the mills. The tweed thus produced was sold by the owners of the mill as Harris Tweed. The Crofter Company also produced tweed cloth but their yarn was not spun on the island but was obtained more cheaply on the mainland. This cloth was sold as Harris Tweed but did not bear the trade mark in the form of a special stamp. The mill owners making the genuine Harris Tweed were being pressed by the union to increase wages but they said that they could not accede to union requests because of the damaging competition of the Crofter Company. Consequently Veitch and others acting in combination placed an embargo on the Crofter Company's imported yarn and exported tweed by instructing dockers at Stornaway to refuse to handle these goods. The dockers obeyed these instructions but were not on strike or in breach of contract. The Crofter Company sought an interdict (or injunction) against the embargo. The House of Lords *held* that the union officials were not liable in conspiracy because their purpose was to benefit the members of the union and the means employed were not unlawful.

(678) *Byrne* v. *Deane*, [1937] 1 K.B. 818

The plaintiff was a member of a golf club in which there had been some gaming machines. The defendants, Mr and Mrs Deane, were proprietors of the club. As a result of a complaint being made to the police the machines were removed. Shortly afterwards, the following typewritten lampoon was placed on the wall of the clubhouse near to the place where the machines had stood—

> For many years upon this spot
> You heard the sound of the merry bell
> Those who were rash and those who were not,
> Lost and made a spot of cash
> But he who gave the game away,
> May he Byrne in hell and rue the day.   Diddleramus.

The plaintiff brought this action for libel alleging that the defendants were responsible for exhibiting the lampoon, and that the lampoon was defamatory in that it suggested that he was disloyal to his fellow club members. *Held*—The words were not defamatory because the standard was the view which would be taken by right-thinking members of society, and, in the view of the court, right-thinking persons would not think less of a person who put the law into motion against wrongdoers.

(679) *Youssoupoff* v. *Metro-Goldwyn-Mayer Pictures Ltd* (1934), 50 T.L.R. 571

The plaintiff was a member of the Russian Royal House. The defendants produced in England a film dealing with the life of Rasputin who had been the adviser of the Tsarina of Russia. The film also dealt with the murder of Rasputin. In the course of the film, a lady (Princess Natasha), who was affectionate towards the murderer of Rasputin, was also represented as having been raped by Rasputin, a man of the worst possible character. The plaintiff was married to a man who was undoubtedly one of the persons concerned in the killing of Rasputin. The plaintiff alleged that because of her marriage reasonable people would think that she was the person who was so raped. The action was for libel. *Held*—The action was properly framed in libel and the plaintiff succeeded.

(*Note:* This case is generally accepted as authority for the view that a defamatory talking film is always libel. However the rape of Princess Natasha was in the pictorial part of the film and not on the sound track. It is also uncertain whether a plaintiff can sue for a slanderous imputation of rape without proving special damage. The Slander of Women Act, 1891, provides that the 'words spoken and published . . . which impute unchastity or adultery to any woman or girl shall not require special damage to render them actionable'. However lack of consent, which is essential in rape, may mean that there is no imputation of unchastity.)

(680) *Cassidy* v. *Daily Mirror Newspapers Ltd*, [1929] 2 K.B. 331

A man named Cassidy or Corrigan who was well known for his indiscriminate relations with women, allowed a racing photographer to take a photograph of himself and a lady, and said that she was his fiancée and that the photographer might announce his engagement. The photograph was published in the *Daily Mirror* with the following caption: 'Mr M. Corrigan, the race-horse owner, and Miss X whose engagement has been announced.' The plaintiff, Cassidy's lawful wife, who was also known as Mrs Corrigan, sued the newspaper for libel alleging as an innuendo that, if Mr Corrigan was unmarried and able to become engaged, she must have been co-habiting with him in circumstances of immorality. *Held*—Since there was evidence that certain of her friends thought this to be so, she was entitled to damages.

(681) *Morgan* v. *Odhams Press*, [1971] 2 All E.R. 1156

In 1965 *The Sun* reported that a kennel girl had been kidnapped by a dog-doping gang. In or about the relevant period various witnesses had seen her in the company of Mr Morgan whose friend she was. The newspaper article made no mention of Mr Morgan's name. Nevertheless he began an action against the newspaper pleading that he had been libelled by innuendo in that persons would think he was involved either in the kidnapping or the dog-doping, or both. *Held*—by the House of Lords—that—

(*a*) the newspaper article was not, by itself, capable of being so understood;

(*b*) an article to be defamatory of a person need not contain a 'key or pointer' showing it refers to him. Evidence is admissible to import a defamatory meaning to otherwise innocent words.

(682) *Tolley* v. *J. S. Fry & Sons Ltd*, [1931] A.C. 333

The plaintiff was a well-know amateur golfer. The defendants published an advertisement without the plaintiff's consent containing his picture and underneath the following words—

The caddy to Tolley said, 'Oh Sir,
Good shot, Sir! That ball, see it go, Sir.
My word, how it flies,
Like a cartet of Fry's,
They're handy, they're good, and priced low, Sir.'

The plaintiff brought an action for libel, alleging an innuendo. It was said that a person reading the advertisement would assume that the plaintiff had been paid for allowing the use of his name in it, and that in consequence he had prostituted his amateur status as a golfer. *Held*—The evidence showed that the advertisement was capable of this construction and the plaintiff was awarded damages.

(683) *Sim* v. *Stretch* (1936), 52 T.L.R. 669

The defendant had encouraged the plaintiff's housemaid to leave the plaintiff's employ and re-enter the defendant's. The defendant later sent the following telegram to the plaintiff: 'Edith has resumed her services with us to-day. Please send her possessions and the money you borrowed, also her wages.' The telegram was said to impute that the plaintiff was in financial difficulties and had in consequence borrowed from his house-maid, and that he had been unable to pay her wages, and was a person of no credit. The plaintiff succeeded at first instance and in the Court of Appeal, but the House of Lords reversed the judgment, *holding* that the telegram was incapable of bearing a defamatory meaning. In the words of Lord Atkin: 'It seems to me unreasonable that, when there are a number of good interpretations, the only bad one should be seized upon to give a defamatory sense to the statement.' It was also in this case that Lord Atkin suggested the following test of a 'defamatory' statement: 'Would the words tend to lower the plaintiff in the estimation of right-thinking members of society generally?'

(684) *Fulham* v. *Newcastle Chronicle and Journal*, [1977] 1 W.L.R. 651

In 1962 the plaintiff left the Catholic priesthood. He married in 1964, a child being born 14 months later. In 1973 he was appointed as deputy headmaster of a school in Teesside having previously lived in South Yorkshire. A Newcastle newspaper published by the defendant com-mented upon his appointment stating that he 'went off very suddenly' from Salford where he had been a priest 'about seven years ago' and had subsequently married. The plaintiff claimed that such statements contained a libellous imputation that he had married while still a priest and had fathered an illegitimate child. The particulars supplied by the plaintiff simply stated his date of marriage and the date of birth of his eldest child. The defendants sought to strike out his claim. It was *held*—by the Court of Appeal—that only those knowing of the dates of the plaintiff's marriage and/or the birth of his child could draw the imputation alleged and that since the defendants' newspaper did not circulate in the area where the plaintiff had been a priest or subsequently lived it was necessary for him to plead particulars of persons receiving the publication having the requisite knowledge and that unless he was able to do so his allegation of innuendo would be struck out.

(685) *E. Hulton & Co.* v. *Jones*, [1910] A.C. 20

A newspaper published an article descriptive of life in Dieppe in which one Artemus Jones, described as a churchwarden at Peckham, was accused of living with a mistress in France. All persons concerned contended that they were ignorant of the existence of any person of that name, and the writer of the article said that he had invented it. Unfortunately the name so chosen was that of an English barrister and journalist, and the evidence showed that those who knew him thought that the article referred to him. *Held*—The newspaper was responsible for the libel and the plaintiff was awarded damages.

   (*Note:* in cases of this kind the defence of offer of amends may be available under Sect. 4 of the Defamation Act, 1952. However, it is by no means certain that it would have been available on the actual facts of this case, because Sect. 4 applies only where the defendant can show that he and his servants or agents have taken all reasonable care with regard to the publication. On the facts of *Hulton* v. *Jones* it seems that the publication was attended by some carelessness.)

(686) *Knupffer* v. *London Express Newspaper Ltd*, [1944] A.C. 116

The plaintiff was head in the United Kingdom of a Russian Refugee organization, active in France and the United States of America, but having only twenty-four members in England. An article in the newspaper ascribed Fascism to this 'minute body established in France and the United States of America,' but without mentioning the English branch. *Held*—The article was not defamatory of the plaintiff since he was not marked out by it, even assuming that it was defamatory to call someone a Fascist.

(687) *Schloimovitz* v. *Clarendon Press, The Times*, 6 July, 1973

The plaintiff by statement of claim alleged that the definitions of the word 'Jew' contained in three dictionaries published by the defendants were derogatory, defamatory and deplorable and sought an injunction restraining the defendants from publishing such definitions, at least without qualification, in any future editions of such dictionaries. *Held*—by Goff, J., that what was before the Court was not whether the definitions were right or wrong or whether they were justly applied to any Jews, but whether in law the plaintiff had a cause of action to restrain the conduct of the defendant. No individual could maintain an action in respect of defamatory matter published about a body of persons unless in its terms, or by reason of the circumstances, it should and must be construed as a reference to him as an individual. There were two questions: (i) were the words defamatory? (ii) did they in fact apply to the plaintiff or were they capable in law of being so regarded? The plaintiff failed to satisfy the latter test and accordingly the defendants were entitled to have the writ and statement of claim struck out. (*Knupffer*[686] applied.)

(688) *Alexander* v. *The North Eastern Railway Co.* (1865), 6 B. & S. 340

The defendants published the following notice—

> North Eastern Railway. Caution. J. Alexander, manufacturer and general merchant, Trafalgar Street, Leeds, was charged before the magistrates of Darlington on 28th September, for riding on a train from Leeds, for which his ticket was not available, and refusing to pay the proper fare. He was convicted in the penalty of £9 1s., including costs, or three weeks' imprisonment.

In this action for libel, the plaintiff contended that the defence of justification could not lie because, although he had been convicted as stated, the alternative prison sentence was fourteen days not three weeks.

Held—The substitution of three weeks for a fortnight did not make the statement libellous. It could be justified, since the rest of it was true.

(689) *London Artists* v. *Littler*, [1969] 2 All E.R. 193

In 1965 four of the principal actors and actresses in a play called *The Right Honourable Gentleman* simultaneously wrote to the defendant, who was the producer of the play, terminating their engagement by four weeks' formal notice. This was, of course, highly unusual and the defendant wrote to the actors and actresses concerned wrongly accusing the plaintiffs, who were their agents, of conspiracy to close down the play. The defendant also communicated the letter to the press. The defendant was now sued for libel. It was *held*—by the Court of Appeal—that he had libelled the plaintiffs because although the subject matter of the allegations was of public interest, i.e. the fate of the play, the defence of fair comment did not apply to the allegation of a plot which was an allegation of fact. The allegation of a plot was defamatory and had not been justified. In fact it seemed that all the actors and actresses involved had their own good and different reasons for leaving the play. There was no evidence of combination.

(690) *London Association for the Protection of Trade* v. *Greenlands*, [1916] 2 A.C. 15

The respondents were a limited company carrying on business as drapers and general furnishers at Hereford. The appellants were an unincorporated association consisting of about 6300 traders and had, as one of their objects, the making of private inquiries as to the means, respectability and trustworthiness of individuals and firms. A member of the association was about to sell goods to the respondents and he asked the association to report on them, and particularly to say whether the respondents were a good risk for credit of between £20 and £30. In the report submitted, the association declared that the respondents were a fair trade risk for the sum mentioned, but said that they had heavy mortgages charged on their assets, and that the assets barely covered the loans. In fact the mortgages were secured by a charge upon the real and leasehold property only, and all other assets were entirely free from any mortgage whatever, and constituted a large and valuable fund. The respondents were originally the plaintiffs in an action for libel contained in the statement about the mortgages, and the statement that they were only good for credit of between £20 and £30. *Held*—The occasion was privileged and thus the respondents had no claim in the absence of malice, which they had not proved. Judgment was therefore given for the appellants.

(691) *Osborn* v. *Thomas Boulter & Son*, [1930] 2 K.B. 226

The plaintiff, a publican, wrote a letter to the defendants, his brewers, complaining of the quality of the beer. The defendants sent one of their employees to investigate and report. After receiving the report, Mr Boulter dictated a letter to his typist in which he suggested that the plaintiff had been adding water to the beer, and pointing out the penalties attaching to this if the plaintiff was caught. The plaintiff sued, alleging publication to the typist and certain clerks. *Held*—The occasion was privileged, and since the plaintiff could not prove malice in the defendants, his action failed.

(692) *Beach* v. *Freeson*, [1971] 2 W.L.R. 805

A member of Parliament wrote to the Law Society complaining of the conduct of a firm of solicitors reported to him by his constituents. He also sent a copy of the letter to the Lord Chancellor. *Held*—by Geoffrey Lane, J.—that both publications were protected by qualified privilege. The privilege arose out of a Member of Parliament's duty to his constituents and the responsibilities of the Law Society and the Lord Chancellor.

(693) *Cook* v. *Alexander,* [1973] 3 W.L.R. 617

The plaintiff sued the defendant for libel in respect of an account of a House of Lords debate which he had written for the *Daily Telegraph.* The debate had been about an approved school where the plaintiff had been a teacher and which had been closed partly because of the plaintiff's revelations as to the system of punishment there. The newspaper had published a precis of each speech on one of the inside pages, but the plaintiff objected to a report written by the defendant which appeared on the back page. In this report, known as 'Parliamentary Sketch', the writer gave his impression of the debate and emphasized the salient aspects of it, but there was a reference to the more detailed account on another page. The plaintiff alleged that the sketch was defamatory of him because it gave great prominence to a speech that was very critical of him and his conduct, while it dismissed in uncomplimentary terms a speech which defended his actions. It was *held*—by the Court of Appeal—that such a Parliamentary sketch was protected by qualified privilege. A reporter was entitled to select from a debate those parts which seemed to him to be of public interest and provided that the account as a whole was fair and honest, such a Parliamentary sketch was protected by qualified privilege.

(694) *Horrocks* v. *Low*, [1972] 1 W.L.R. 1625

At a local authority council meeting Low made a speech defamatory of Horrocks who in answer to Low's defence of justification, fair comment and qualified privilege, alleged that Low had been actuated by express malice. *Held*—by the Court of Appeal—that malice could not be inferred. Low held an honest and positive belief in the truth of his statement and had not abused the privileged occasion. '(The defendant) is not to be held malicious merely because he was angry or prejudiced even unreasonably prejudiced, against the plaintiff, so long as he honestly believed what he said to be true. Such is the law as I have always understood it to be.' (*per* Lord Denning, M.R.)

'What has to be proved is that the defendant was activated by malice in the popular meaning of the word: that is to say, in speaking as he did, he must have been actuated by spite or ill-will against the person defamed or by some indirect or improper motive.' (*per* Edmund Davis, L.J.)

'When there is . . . (gross and unreasoning) prejudice there will often, perhaps usually, be reckless indifference whether what is said is true or false. But if there is honest belief that it is true, there cannot in any judgment be recklessness whether it be true or false.' (*per* Stephenson, L.J.)

(695) *Egger* v. *Viscount Chelmsford*, [1964] 3 All E.R. 406

Mrs Egger, a judge of Alsatian dogs, was on the list of judges of the Kennel Club, and Miss Ross, the secretary of a dog club in Northern Ireland, wrote to the Kennel Club asking them to approve of Mrs Egger as a judge of Alsatians at a show. The assistant secretary of the Kennel Club, C. A. Burney, wrote to Miss Ross to say that the committee could not approve the appointment. Mrs Egger brought an action for libel against the ten members of the committee and the assistant secretary on the grounds that the letter reflected on her competence and integrity. There were two long trials at both of which the judge ruled that the occasion was privileged. The jury disagreed the first time, but at the second trial the jury found that the letter was defamatory and that five members of the committee were actuated by malice but three were not. The other two had meanwhile died. The judge gave judgment against all the defendants including the assistant secretary. *Held*—on appeal—The defence of qualified privilege is a defence for the individual who is sued, and not a defence for the publication. It is quite erroneous to say that it is attached to the publication. The three committee members innocent of malice were entitled to protection and were not liable. The assistant secretary also had an independent and individual privilege, and was not responsible or liable for the tort of those members of the committee who had acted with malice. Even in a joint tort, the tort is the separate act of each individual; each is severally answerable for it; and each is severally entitled to his own defence.

(696) *Chapman* v. *Lord Ellesmere and Others*, [1932] 2 K.B. 431

The plaintiff was a trainer and one of his horses, after winning a race, was found to be doped. An inquiry was held by the Stewards of the Jockey Club, as a result of which they decided to disqualify the horse for future racing, and to warn the plaintiff off Newmarket Heath. The decision was published in the *Racing Calendar*. The plaintiff contended that the words were defamatory because they implied that he had doped the horse. The defendants, who were the proprietors of the *Racing Calendar*, contended that the words were not defamatory, and meant simply that the plaintiff had been warned off for not protecting the horse against doping. Evidence showed that it was a condition of a trainer's licence that the withdrawal of that licence should appear in the *Racing Calendar*, which was also to be the recognized vehicle of communication for all matters concerning infringement of rules. *Held*—The plaintiff being bound by the terms of his licence, the doctrine of *volenti non fit injuria* applied as regards publication in the *Racing Calendar*, so that the plaintiff had no cause of action.

(697) *Davis* v. *Rubin*, [1967] 112 S.J. 51

The plaintiffs were chartered accountants of good reputation and they wished to buy the lease of business premises. The defendants, who were the landlords, wrote to the holder of the lease saying that they would not accept the plaintiffs if the lease was assigned and referred in a defamatory fashion to the plaintiff's business and references. The plaintiffs claimed damages in respect of the libel published in the letter, and were awarded £4000 each. The Court of Appeal, allowing the defendants' appeal, said that the damages were 'excessive, extravagant and exorbitant'. There had been publication to one person only and there was no evidence that the plaintiffs' reputation had been diminished in the minds of other persons. A reasonable sum would not have exceeded £1000 each and a new trial was ordered.

(698) *Emanuel* v. *Greater London Council* (1970), 114 S.J. 653

A contractor employed by the Ministry of Public Building and Works removed prefabricated bungalows from the Council's land. The contractor lit a fire and negligently allowed sparks to spread to the plaintiff's land where buildings and goods were damaged. The plaintiff claimed against the G.L.C. and it was *held*—by James, J.—that—

(*a*) on the facts the Council remained in occupation of the site;

(*b*) the contractor was not a 'stranger' to the Council since they retained a power of control over his activities; and

(*c*) although the Council had not been negligent and were not vicariously liable for the contractors' negligence since they did not employ him, they were strictly liable under *Rylands* v. *Fletcher* for the escape of fire.

(699) *Read* v. *J. Lyons & Co. Ltd*, [1947] A.C. 156

The appellant was employed by the Ministry of Supply as an Inspector of Munitions in the respondent's munitions factory. In the course of her employment there she was injured by the explosion of a shell which was in course of manufacture. She did not allege negligence on the part of the defendants, but based her claim on *Rylands* v. *Fletcher*. The trial judge found that there was liability under the rule, but the Court of Appeal and the House of Lords reversed this decision, *holding* that the rule did not apply since there had been no escape of the thing that inflicted the injury. In the words of Viscount Simon, L.C., 'Escape for the purpose of applying the proposition in *Rylands* v. *Fletcher* means escape from a place which the defendant has occupation of, or control over, to a place which is outside his occupation or control.' It was also suggested in this case that the rule in *Rylands* v. *Fletcher* does not extend to personal injuries, but only to injury to property.

(700) *Charing Cross Electricity Supply Co.* v. *Hydraulic Power Co.*,
[1914] 3 K.B. 772

The defendants' water mains under a public street burst and damaged the
plaintiffs' cables which were also laid under the street. *Held*—The defendants were liable under the rule in *Rylands* v. *Fletcher*, because the rule was
not confined to wrongs between owners of adjacent land and does not
depend on ownership of land. Here it could be applied to owners of
adjacent chattels.

(701) *Attorney-General* v. *Corke*, [1933] Ch. 89

The defendant was the owner of disused brickfields, and he permitted a
number of gypsies to occupy them and live in caravans and tents. The
gypsies threw slop water about in the neighbourhood of the fields and
accumulated all sorts of filth thereabouts. The court *held* that *Rylands* v.
Fletcher applied, and an injunction was granted against the defendant.
While it was not unlawful to license caravan dwellers, it was abnormal use
of land, since such persons often have habits of life which are offensive to
those persons with fixed homes.

(702) *Perry* v. *Kendricks Transport*, [1956] 1 W.L.R. 85

The defendants had placed on their parking ground a disused coach, having
drained off the petrol and screwed a cap over the entrance pipe. The
plaintiff, a boy of ten, was injured as he approached the parking ground by
an explosion of petrol fumes from the coach. The trial judge found that the
cap had been removed by some unknown person, and that a lighted match
had been thrown in the tank, probably by one of two boys who hurried
away as the plaintiff approached. The Court of Appeal *held* that the facts
were within the rule in *Rylands* v. *Fletcher*, but the defendants were not
liable because the escape was caused by the act of a stranger.

(703) *Giles* v. *Walker* (1890), 24 Q.B.D. 656

The defendant wished to redeem certain forest land and ploughed it up.
Thistles grew up on the land and thistle-seed was blown in large quantities
by the wind from the defendant's land to that of the plaintiff. *Held*—There
was no duty as between adjoining occupiers to cut things such as thistles
which are the natural growth of the soil; therefore the defendant was not
liable. Presumably if a person deliberately set thistles on his land he would
be liable under the rule in *Rylands* v. *Fletcher*, for it is not usual to cultivate
weeds on one's land.

(*Note:* an action for nuisance would probably have succeeded here,
because a person is liable for a nuisance on his land (even if he has not
caused it) if he lets it continue.)

(704) *Davey* v. *Harrow Corporation*, [1957] 2 All E.R. 305

The roots of the defendants' elm trees spread to the plaintiff's land and caused damage to the plaintiff's property. *Held*—The defendants were liable in nuisance, whether the trees were self-sown or not. It was no defence to an action for nuisance that the thing causing the nuisance was naturally on the defendants' land, though it might be a defence to liability under the rule in *Rylands* v. *Fletcher*.

(705) *Greenock Corporation* v. *Caledonian Railway Co.*, [1917] A.C. 556

The corporation, in laying out a park, constructed a concrete paddling pool for children in the bed of a stream, thereby altering its course and natural flow. Owing to rainfall of extraordinary violence, the stream overflowed and poured down the street, flooding the railway company's premises. The House of Lords *held* that this was not an act of God and the corporation was liable. The House of Lords indicated the restricted range of the defence of act of God and of the decision in *Nichols* v. *Marsland* (1876),[527] distinguishing that case on the grounds that whereas in *Nichols* v. *Marsland* the point at issue was the liability for storing water in artificial lakes, the point here was interference with the natural course of a stream, and anyone so interfering must provide even against exceptional rainfall.

(706) *Rickards* v. *Lothian*, [1913] A.C. 263

The defendant was the occupier of business premises and leased part of the second floor to the plaintiff. On the fourth floor was a men's cloakroom with a wash basin. The cloakroom was provided for the use of tenants and persons in their employ. The plaintiff's stock in trade was found one morning seriously damaged by water which had seeped through the ceiling from the wash basin on the fourth floor. Examination showed that the waste pipe had been plugged with various articles such as nails, penholders, string and soap, and the water tap had been turned full on. The defendant's caretaker found the cloakroom in proper order at 10.20 p.m. the previous evening. *Held*—The defendant was not liable under the rule in *Rylands* v. *Fletcher* because the damage had been caused by the act of a stranger.

(707) *Peters* v. *Prince of Wales Theatre (Birmingham) Ltd*, [1943] K.B. 73

The defendants leased to the plaintiff a shop in a building which contained a theatre. In the latter there was, to the plaintiff's knowledge, a sprinkler system installed as a precaution against fire and the system extended to the plaintiff's shop. In a thaw, following a severe frost, water poured from the sprinklers in the defendants' rehearsal room into the plaintiff's shop and damaged his stock. The plaintiff claimed damages for negligence, and under *Rylands* v. *Fletcher*. *Held*—There was no negligence on the part of the defendants and there was no liability under *Rylands* v. *Fletcher*, because the sprinkler had been installed for the common benefit of the plaintiff and defendants.

THE LAW OF PROPERTY

(708) *Moffat* v. *Kazana*, [1968] 3 All E.R. 271

The plaintiff hid banknotes in a biscuit tin in the roof of his house. He sold the house to the defendant, one of whose workmen discovered the money. In this action by the plaintiff to recover the money it was *held*—by Wrangham, J.—that the plaintiff succeeded. He had never evinced any intention to pass the title in the money to anyone. Therefore his title was good, not only against the finder, but also against the new owner of the house.

(709) *Hayward* v. *Challoner*, [1967] 3 All E.R. 122

The predecessors in title of the plaintiff landowner let land to the rector of a parish at a rent of 10s. a year. The rent was not collected after 1942 and the plaintiff now sued for possession. *Held*—by the Court of Appeal—that a right of action in respect of rent or possession must be held to have accrued when the rent due was first unpaid, and therefore was barred by the Limitation Act, 1939. The rector as a corporation sole had acquired a good squatter's title.

(710) *Littledale* v. *Liverpool College*, [1900] 1 Ch. 19

The plaintiffs had a right of way for agricultural purposes over a strip of grass land belonging to the defendants. The plaintiffs put up gates which they kept locked at each end of the strip, and used the grass for grazing, keeping the hedges of the strip clipped. They now claimed ownership of the land by virtue of adverse possession. *Held*—The plaintiff's acts could be construed as protecting the right of way, rather than excluding the owner, and were insufficient to establish the plaintiffs' title to the land.

(711) *Smirk* v. *Lyndale Developments Ltd*, [1974] 2 All E.R. 8

The plaintiff had a service tenancy of a house owned by the British Railways Board. In 1960 he took effective possession of an adjacent plot of land owned by the Board, though the Board was unaware of his action. The plaintiff did not communicate to the Board at any time that he disclaimed the Board's title. The Board sold the house and the plot to the defendants who granted a new tenancy of the house to Smirk on different terms not including the adjacent plot. The plaintiff claimed a possessory title to that plot. It was *held*—by Pennycuick, V.C.—that the plaintiff did not have a good possessory title to the plot.

(712) *The Winkfield*, [1902] P. 42

This was an Admiralty action arising because a ship called the *Mexican* was negligently struck and sunk by a ship called the *Winkfield*. The *Mexican* was carrying mail from South Africa to England during the Boer War. The Postmaster General made, among other things, a claim for damages in respect of the estimated value of parcels and letters for which no claim had been made or instructions received from the senders. The Postmaster General undertook to distribute the amount recovered when the senders were found. An objection was made that the Postmaster General represented the Crown and was not liable to the senders (see now Crown Proceedings Act, 1947). *Held*—As a bailee in possession the Postmaster General could recover damages for the loss of the goods irrespective of whether or not he was liable to the bailors.

(713) *Ashby* v. *Tolhurst*, [1937] 2 All E.R. 837

The plaintiff drove his car on to a piece of land at Southend owned by the defendants. He paid 1s. to an attendant who was the defendants' servant and was given a ticket. He left the car with the doors locked. When he returned his car had gone, the attendant having allowed a thief, who said he was a friend of the plaintiff, to drive it away. The ticket was called a 'car-park ticket' and contained the words 'The proprietors do not take any responsibility for the safe custody of any cars or articles therein, nor for any damage to the cars or articles however caused nor for any injuries to any persons, all cars being left in all respects entirely at their owner's risk. Owners are requested to show a ticket when required.' *Held*—

(i) The relationship between the parties was that of licensor and licensee, not that of bailor and bailee because there was in no sense a transfer of possession. There was, therefore, no obligation upon the defendants towards the plaintiff in respect of the car.

(ii) If there was a contract of bailment, the servant delivered possession of the car quite honestly under a mistake and the conditions on the tickets were wide enough to protect the defendants.

(iii) There could not be implied into the contract a term that the car should not be handed over without production of the ticket.

(*Note:* where the plaintiff hands over the key, the court may find a transfer of possession and a bailment, but the delivery of the key is not conclusive.)

(714) *Ultzen* v. *Nicols*, [1894] 1 Q.B. 92

A waiter took a customer's overcoat, without being asked to do so, and hung it on a peg behind the customer. The coat was stolen and it was *held* that the restaurant keeper was a bailee of the coat and that there was negligence in supervision on the part of the bailee.

(*Note:* in this case the servant seems to have been regarded as taking possession, but it is unlikely that a bailment will arise if a customer merely hangs his coat on a stand or other device provided by the establishment.)

(715) *Deyong* v. *Shenburn*, [1946] 1 All E.R. 226

An allegation that an actor who left his clothes in a dressing room had constituted the theatre owners bailees of the clothes was not sustained.

(716) *Newman* v. *Bourne & Hollingsworth* (1915), 31 T.L.R. 209

The plaintiff went into the defendant's shop on a Saturday in order to buy a coat. While trying on coats she took off a diamond brooch and put it on a show case. She left the shop having forgotten the brooch; an assistant found it and handed it to the shopwalker who put it in his desk. By the firm's rules the brooch ought to have been taken to their lost property office. The brooch could not be found on the following Monday. *Held*—There was evidence to support the trial judge's finding that the firm had become bailees and had not exercised proper care.

(717) *Neuwirth* v. *Over Darwen Industrial Co-operative Society* (1894), 70 T.L.R. 374

A concert hall was hired for an evening performance. No mention was made of rehearsal but the orchestra rehearsed in the hall during the afternoon without opposition from the proprietors or the keeper of the hall. After the rehearsal Neuwirth left his double-bass fiddle in an ante-room in such a position that when the hall keeper came to turn on the gas in the ante-room he could not do so without first moving the instrument. The fiddle fell and was badly damaged. *Held*—There was no contract of bailment between the parties. the care of musical instruments was outside the scope of the hall keeper's authority and there was no evidence that he had been guilty of negligence in the course of his employment.

(718) *Hyman* v. *Nye* (1881), 6 Q.B.D. 685

The plaintiff hired a landau with a pair of horses and a driver for a drive from Brighton to Shoreham and back. The plaintiff was involved in an accident owing to a broken bolt which caused the carriage to upset so that the plaintiff was thrown out of it. *Held*—The trial judge's direction to the jury that the plaintiff must prove negligence was wrong. There was an implied warranty that the carriage was as fit for the purpose for which it was hired as skill and care could make it.

(719) *Reed* v. *Dean*, [1949] 1 K.B. 188

The plaintiffs hired a motor launch called the *Golden Age* from the defendant for a family holiday on the Thames. The plaintiffs set sail at about 7 p.m. on 22 June, 1946, and at about 9 p.m., when they were near Sonning, they discovered that a liquid in the bilge by the engine was on fire. They attempted to extinguish the fire but were unable to do so, the fire-fighting equipment with which the launch was supplied being out of order. The plaintiffs had to abandon the launch and suffered personal injuries and loss of belongings. The plaintiffs admitted to a fireman after the accident that they might have spilt some petrol when the tank was refilled. *Held*—The plaintiffs succeeded because there was an implied undertaking by the defendant that the launch was as fit for the purpose for which it was hired as reasonable care and skill could make it. Further, as the launch had caught fire due to an unexplained cause, there was a presumption that it was not fit for this purpose. The defendant's failure to provide proper fire-fighting equipment was a breach of the implied warranty of fitness.

(720) *Houghland* v. *R. Low (Luxury Coaches) Ltd*, [1962] 2 All E.R. 159

The defendants supplied a coach for the purposes of an old people's outing to Southampton. On returning the passengers put their luggage into the boot of the coach. During a stop for tea the coach was found to be defective and another one was sent for and the luggage was transferred from the first coach to the relief coach. The removal of the luggage from the first coach was not supervised, but the restacking of the luggage into the new coach was supervised by one of the defendants' employees. When the passengers arrived home a suitcase belonging to the plaintiff was missing and he brought an action against the defendants for its loss. It was *held*, by the Court of Appeal, that whether the action was for negligence or in detinue, the defendants were liable unless they could show that they had not been negligent. On the facts they had failed to prove this and were therefore liable. It was in this case that Ormerod, L.J., made some observations on bailments in general. The County Court Judge had found that the bailment was gratuitous and that the defendants were liable only for gross negligence. Dealing with this question, Ormerod, L.J., said 'For my part I have always found some difficulty in understanding just what was gross negligence, because it appears to me that the standard of care required in a case of bailment or any other type of case is the standard demanded by the circumstances of the particular case. It seems to me to try and put bailment, for instance, into a water-tight compartment, such as gratuitous bailment on the one hand and bailment for reward on the other, is to overlook the fact that there might well be an infinite variety of cases which might come into one or other category.'

(721) *Global Dress Co.* v. *W. H. Boase & Co.*, [1966] 2 Ll. Rep. 72

B & Co. were master porters and had custody of thirty cases of goods belonging to G & Co. at a Liverpool dock shed. One case was stolen and G & Co. brought an action for damages against B & Co. B & Co. offered evidence of their system of safeguarding the goods and the County Court Judge at first instance found the system to be as good as any other in the Liverpool Docks, but notwithstanding this he found B & Co. liable. On appeal to the Court of Appeal it was *held* that if B & Co. could not affirmatively prove that their watchman was not negligent it was of no avail to show that they had an impeccable system, and the appeal should be dismissed. Thus the onus of proving that their servant was not negligent lay upon B & Co.

(722) *Doorman* v. *Jenkins* (1843), 2 Ad. & El. 256

The plaintiff left the sum of £32 10s. with the defendant, who was a coffeehouse keeper, for safe custody and without any reward. The defendant put the money in with his own in a cash box which he kept in the taproom. The taproom was open to the public on a Sunday but the rest of the house was not and the cash was, in fact, stolen on a Sunday. Lord Denman *held* that the loss of the defendant's own money was not enough to prove reasonable care and the court found for the plaintiff.

(723) *Brabant* v. *King*, [1895] A.C. 632

This action was brought against the government of Queensland for damage to certain explosives belonging to the plaintiff which the government as bailees for reward had stored in sheds situated near the water's edge on Brisbane River. The water rose to an exceptional height and the store was flooded. The question of inevitable accident was raised and also the degree of negligence required. The Privy Council *held* that because of the nature of the site the bailees were required to place the goods at such a level as would in all probability ensure their absolute immunity from flood water, and the defendants were held liable. The Privy Council went on to say that in a case of a deposit for reward the bailees were 'under a legal obligation to exercise the same degree of care, towards the preservation of the goods entrusted to them from injury, which might reasonably be expected from a skilled storekeeper, acquainted with the risks to be apprehended from the character either of the storehouse or of its locality; and the obligations included, not only the duty of taking all reasonable precautions to obviate these risks but the duty of taking all proper measures for the protection of the goods when such risks were imminent or had actually occurred'. Counsel for the government suggested that a bailee was not liable for damage caused by the defects in his warehouse where these defects were known to the bailor, in this case the proximity of the warehouse to the Brisbane River. The Privy Council dismissed this argument on the grounds that it was a dangerous one, not supported by any authority. They said that the bailor could rely on the skill of the bailee in this matter. It will be seen from this decision that a bailee for reward is liable even in the case of uncommon or unexpected danger, unless he uses efforts which are in proportion to the emergency to ward off that danger.

(724) *Wilson* v. *Brett* (1843), 11 M. & W. 113

Wilson was in process of selling his horse and Brett volunteered to ride the horse in order to show it off to a likely purchaser. Brett rode the horse on to wet and slippery turf and the horse fell and was injured. Brett pleaded that he was not negligent but the court *held* that he had not used the skill he professed to possess when he volunteered to ride the horse and that he was liable.

(725) *Saunders (Mayfair) Furs* v. *Davies* (1965), 109, S.J. 922

The plaintiffs delivered a valuable fur coat to a shop belonging to the defendants, on sale-or-return terms. The defendants displayed it in their shop window and at 2.30 a.m. one morning the coat was stolen in a smash-and-grab raid. *Held*—That in all the circumstances and because of the valuable nature of the property, the defendants had taken an unreasonable risk and were negligent in leaving the coat on display in the window all night.

(726) *Coldman* v. *Hill*, [1919] 1 K.B. 443

The defendant was a bailee of cows belonging to the plaintiff. Two of these cows were stolen through no fault of the defendant, though he failed to notify the plaintiff and did not inform the police or take any steps to find the cows. The plaintiff now sued him for negligence and it was *held* by the Court of Appeal that it was up to the defendant to prove that, even if notice had been given, the cows would not have been recovered. In the circumstances of this case that burden had not been discharged and the defendant was liable.

(727) *Cheshire* v. *Bailey*, [1905] 1 K.B. 237

In this case jewellery had been deposited in a carriage by the hirer and was stolen by thieves. It transpired that the coachman, who was the servant of the person who let out the carriage, was in league with the thieves, but it was *held* that the owner of the carriage was not liable for the loss because the dishonesty of his servant was beyond the scope of employment.

(728) *Davies* v. *Collins*, [1945] 1 All E.R. 247

An American Army officer sent his uniform to the defendants to be cleaned. It was accepted on the following conditions—'Whilst every care is exercised in cleaning and dyeing garments, all orders are accepted at owner's risk entirely and we are unable to hold ourselves responsible for damage.' The defendants did not clean the uniform but sub-contracted the work to another firm of cleaners. In the event the uniform was lost and the defendants were *held* liable in damages. The Court of Appeal took the view that the limitation clause operated to exclude the right to sub-contract because is used the words 'every care is exercised', which postulated personal service.

(729) *Edwards* v. *Newland*, [1950] 2 All E.R. 1072

The defendant agreed to store the plaintiff's furniture for reward. Later, without the plaintiff's knowledge, the defendant made arrangements with another company to store the plaintiff's furniture. The third party's warehouse was damaged by a bomb and they asked the defendant to remove the furniture but this was not done immediately because there was a dispute about charges. Eventually the plaintiff removed his furniture but some pieces were missing. *Held*—The plaintiff could recover from the defendant because he had departed from the terms of the contract of bailment by sub-contracting. However, the defendant was not entitled to damages against the third party because the latter, though a bailee, had not, in the circumstances, been negligent.

(730) *Learoyd Bros & Co.* v. *Pope & Sons*, [1966] 2 Ll. Rep. 142

The plaintiffs entered into an agreement with a carrier for the transport of their goods. The carrier sub-contracted the work to the defendants, who were also a firm of carriers, though the plaintiffs had no notice of this arrangement. The lorry was stolen while the defendants' driver was in the wharf office upon arrival at London Docks, and the carrier with whom the plaintiffs had contracted paid some of the plaintiffs' loss and the plaintiffs now sued the defendants for the balance. *Held*—That the defendants were bailees to the plaintiffs, notwithstanding the absence of any contract between them, and that the defendants' driver was negligent in leaving the lorry unattended and therefore the defendants were liable for the plaintiffs' loss.

(731) *Rogers Sons & Co.* v. *Lambert & Co.*, [1891] 1 Q.B. 318

The plaintiffs had purchased copper from the defendants but did not take delivery of it and left it with the defendants as warehousemen. The plaintiffs then resold the copper to a third person. Sometime later the plaintiffs asked for delivery of the copper from the defendants but the defendants refused to deliver on the grounds that the plaintiffs no longer had a title to it. *Held*—This was no defence to an action of detinue. The defendants must show that they were defending the action on behalf, and with the authority, of the true owner.

(732) *Re Draper's Conveyance,* [1967] 3 All E.R. 853

In 1951 a house was conveyed to a husband and wife in fee simple as joint tenants at law *and* of the proceeds of the trust for sale. In November, 1965, the wife was granted a decree *nisi* of divorce and this was made absolute in March, 1966. In February, 1966, she applied by summons under Sect. 17 of the Married Women's Property Act, 1882, for an order that the house be sold and in her affidavit asked that the proceeds of sale be distributed equally between her husband and herself. The court made such an order in May, 1966, and in August, 1966, a further order was made under the Act of 1882 that the former husband give up possession of the house. In spite of the order the former husband remained in possession until January, 1967, when a writ of possession was executed. Four days later he died without having made a will. The former wife now applied to the court to determine whether she held the proceeds of any sale absolutely (which would have been the case if she and her former husband had been joint tenants at his death) or for herself and the deceased's estate as tenants in common in equal shares (which would have been the case if there had been severance). *Held*—Severance of a joint tenancy in a matrimonial home may be effected by the wife's issue of a summons under Sect. 17 of the Married Women's Property Act, 1882, and her affidavit in support. The affidavit had stated the former wife's wish for severance and had operated accordingly. Therefore she held any proceeds of sale as trustee for herself and the estate of her former husband as tenants in common in equal shares.

(733) *Shell-Mex and B.P. Ltd* v. *Manchester Garages Ltd*, [1971] 1 All E.R. 841

The plaintiffs by an agreement contained in a document called a licence, let the defendants into occupation of a petrol filling station for one year. The parties had some disagreements during this time and at the end of the year the plaintiffs asked the defendants to leave. The defendants refused claiming that the agreement gave them a business tenancy protected by the Landlord and Tenant Act, 1954, Part II, which deals with the method of terminating business tenancies. This method had not been followed by the plaintiffs. *Held*—by the Court of Appeal—it was open to parties to an agreement to decide whether that agreement should constitute a lease or a licence but the fact that it was called a licence was not conclusive. However, in this case it was a licence because the plaintiffs retained, under the agreement, the right to visit the premises whenever they liked and to exercise general control over the layout, decoration and equipment of the filling station. These rights were inconsistent with the grant of a tenancy.

(734) *Binions* v. *Evans*, [1972] 2 All E.R. 70

Mr Evans was employed as a chauffeur by the Tredegar Estate which owned a number of houses. His father and grandfather had also worked for the estate. Mr Evans died in 1965 and the trustees of the estate allowed Mrs Evans to continue to reside in a cottage which belonged to the estate, free of rent and rates. In 1968 the trustees made a formal agreement with Mrs Evans, the defendant in this case, who was then aged 76. The agreement purported to create a tenancy at will in order to provide her with a temporary home for the rest of her life free of rent without any right to assign, sub-let or part with possession. Two years later the trustees sold the cottage and other properties to Mr and Mrs Binions, the plaintiffs, expressly subject to the tenancy of Mrs Evans and because of that tenancy the trustees accepted a lower price. A copy of the trustees' agreement with Mrs Evans was given to the purchasers. Shortly afterwards the purchasers tried to evict Mrs Evans on the ground that her tenancy, being at will, was liable to determination at any time. She refused to vacate and the Court was asked to decide whether her occupation was in the nature of a tenancy at will or a mere licence. *Held*—by the Court of Appeal—that the interest of the defendant was not a tenancy at will although it had been so described in the agreement. When the trustees created a right in her favour to live in the cottage for the rest of her life it could not be a tenancy at will liable to be terminated at any time. It was therefore a mere licence though equity would not permit the plaintiffs to revoke it as long as the defendant was not in breach of the licence. The plaintiffs held on a constructive trust to give effect to the agreement with Mrs Evans.

(735) *Walsh* v. *Lonsdale* (1882), 21 Ch.D. 9

The defendant agreed in writing to grant a seven years' lease of a mill to the plaintiff at a rent payable one year in advance. The plaintiff entered into possession without any formal lease having been granted, and he paid his rent quarterly and not in advance. Subsequently the defendant demanded a year's rent in advance, and as the plaintiff refused to pay, the defendant distrained on his property. At common law the plaintiff was a tenant from year to year because no formal lease had been granted, and as such his rent was not payable in advance. The plaintiff argued that the legal remedy of distress was not available to the defendant. *Held*—As the agreement was one of which the court could grant specific performance, and as equity regarded as done that which ought to be done, the plaintiff held on the same terms as if a lease had been granted. Therefore the distress was valid.

(736) *O'Brien* v. *Robinson,* [1973] 1 All E.R. 583

The plaintiff was the tenant of a flat to which Sect. 32 of the Housing Act, 1961 applied. In 1965 the plaintiff had complained about stamping on the ceiling above, but it was found that the landlord was not given notice that the ceiling was defective. In 1968 the ceiling fell and the plaintiff was injured. *Held*—by the House of Lords—that the defendant landlord was not liable for breach of covenant.

(*Note:* in *Sheldon* v. *West Bromwich Corporation*, (1973) 25 P & C.R. 360, the Court of Appeal held the defendant landlords liable where a water tank in a council house had remained discolored for some considerable time to the knowledge of the Council. The tank burst and the Council were in breach of their implied covenant under Sect. 32 of the Housing Act, 1961, to keep the installation for the supply of water in repair. The discoloration of the tank, which the Council knew about, meant that this was not a latent defect.)

(737) *Roberts* v. *Church Commissioners for England*, [1971] 3 All E.R. 703

In May, 1950, landlords granted a lease from 25 March, 1950, for $10\frac{3}{4}$ years to the tenant's predecessor at a ground rent of £10 per annum. Subsequently, by a lease dated 29 October, 1952, the landlord's granted a lease for 21 years from March 25th, 1950, at a yearly rent of £29, the first instalment being deemed to have become due on 24 June, 1950. On the tenant's application for a declaration that she was entitled to acquire the freehold under the Leasehold Reform Act, 1967, it was *held*—by the Court of Appeal—that the Act could not be construed as extending to a relationship which ultimately produced a continuous relationship of land-lord and tenant for over 21 years, not a case where the parties to a short tenancy subsequently agreed to enlarge it retrospectively. To fulfil the definition of a long tenancy within Sect. 3(1) of the Leasehold Reform Act, 1967, a tenant must at some point of time be, or have been, in a position to say that he is or was entitled to remain tenant for the next 21 years, whether at law or in equity.

(738) *Hill* v. *Tupper* (1863), 2 H. & C. 121

Hill was the lessee of land on the bank of a canal. The land and the canal were owned by the lessor, and Hill was granted the sole and exclusive right of putting pleasure boats on the canal. Later Tupper, without authority, put rival pleasure boats on the canal. Hill now sued Tupper for the breach of a so-called easement granted by the owner of the canal. *Held*—The right to put pleasure boats on the canal was not an interest in property which the law could recognize as attaching to land. It was in the nature of a contractual licence which could not be enforced against the whole world. Tupper could have been sued by the owner of the canal, or by Hill, as lessee, if he had also been granted a lease of the canal.

(739) *Bass* v. *Gregory* (1890), 25 Q.B.D. 481

The plaintiffs were the owners of a public house in Nottingham, and the defendant was the owner of some cottages and a yard adjoining the plaintiffs' premises. The plaintiffs claimed to be entitled, by user as of right, to have the cellar of their public house ventilated by means of a hole or shaft cut from the cellar to an old well situated in the yard occupied by the defendant. The plaintiffs claimed an injunction to prevent the defendant from continuing to block the passage of air from the well. *Held*—The right having been established, an injunction would be granted because the access of air to the premises came through a strictly defined channel, and it was possible to establish it as an easement.

(*Note:* in *Bryant* v. *Lefever* (1879), 4 C.P.D. 172, the plaintiff and defendant occupied adjoining premises, and the plaintiff's complaint was that the defendant, in rebuilding his house, carried up the building beyond its former height and so checked the access of the draught of air to the plaintiff's chimneys. The Court of Appeal held that the right claimed could not exist at law, because it was an attempt to claim special rights over the general current of air which is common to all mankind.)

(740) *Crow* v. *Wood*, [1970] 3 All E.R. 425

This case arose out of damage done on a farm in Yorkshire by sheep which strayed on to it from an adjoining moor. The owner of the sheep, who was the owner of another farm adjoining the moor, raised, as a defence against an action for trespass, an obligation on the plaintiff to fence her own property to keep the sheep out. It was *held*—by the Court of Appeal—that a duty to fence existed as an easement and that it had passed under Sect. 62 of the Law of Property Act, 1925, when the defendant purchased his farm, even though his conveyance and previous ones had made no reference to the obligation of other farmers to keep up their fences. However, the right was appurtenant to the land sold and therefore became an easement in favour of the purchaser and his successors in title.

(741) *Re Ellenborough Park*, [1956] Ch. 131

Ellenborough Park was a piece of open land near the seafront at Weston-super-Mare. The park and the surrounding land was jointly owned by two persons. The surrounding land was sold for building purposes, and the conveyances granted an easement over the park in favour of the owners of the houses. The owners of the houses undertook to be responsible for some of the maintenance, and the owners of the park agreed not to erect dwelling houses or buildings, other than ornamental buildings, on the park. The park was later sold, and the question of the rights of the owners or occupiers of the houses fronting on to the park to enforce their rights over the park arose. It was contended that the rights created by the conveyances were not enforceable, because they did not conform to the essential qualities of an easement, and that they gave a right of perambulation which was not a right legally capable of creation. *Held*—The rights granted to the owners of the houses were enforceable as a legal easement.

(742) *Phipps* v. *Pears*, [1964] 2 All E.R. 35

A Mr Field owned two houses, Nos 14 and 16 Market Street, Warwick, and in 1930 he demolished No. 16 and built a new house with a wall adjacent to the existing wall of No. 14. In 1962, 14 was demolished under an order of Warwick Corporation, leaving exposed the wall of No. 16. This wall had never been pointed; indeed it could not have been because it was built hard up against the wall of No. 14. It was not, therefore, weather-proof, the rain got in and froze during the winter causing cracks in the wall. The plaintiff claimed for damage done, claiming an *easement of protection*. It was *held* by the Court of Appeal that there is no such easement. There is a right of support in appropriate cases, but No. 16 did not depend on No. 14 for support; the walls, though adjoining, were independent. Lord Denning, M.R., said in the course of his judgment: 'A right to protection from the weather (if it exists) is entirely negative. It is a right to stop your neighbour pulling down his house. Seeing that it is a negative easement, it must be looked at with caution because the law has been very chary of creating any new negative easements. . . . If we were to stop a man pulling down his house, we would put a break on desirable improvement. If it exposes your house to the weather, that is your misfortune. It is not wrong on his part. . . . The only way for an owner to protect himself is by getting a covenant from his neighbour that he will not pull down his house. . . . Such a covenant would be binding in contract; and it would be enforceable on any successor who took with notice of it, but it would not be binding on one who took without notice.'

(743) *Grigsby* v. *Melville*, [1972] 1 W.L.R. 1355

A Mr Holroyd owned two adjoining properties, consisting of a cottage and a shop which had recently been occupied in single occupation by a butcher. Beneath the drawing room of the cottage there was a cellar, the only practical means of access to which was by way of steps from the shop and which the butcher had used for storing brine in connection with the business of the shop. In 1962, Holroyd conveyed the cottage to Natinvil Builders Ltd, the predecessor in title of the plaintiff in this case. The conveyance accepted 'such rights and easements or quasi-rights and quasi-easements as may be enjoyed in connection with the . . . adjoining property'. A month later Holroyd conveyed the shop to a Mrs Melville. Mrs Melville, who was a veterinary surgeon, began to use the cellar for storage. The plaintiff acquired the cottage in 1969 but did not realize the situation until 1971 when she heard hammering beneath her drawing room floor. She sought an injunction to prevent Mrs Melville from trespassing there. The defendants claimed that the cellar was excluded from the property conveyed, or alternatively that they enjoyed an easement of storage there equivalent to an estate in fee simple. *Held*—by Brightman, J.—(i) that the cellar, though not the steps leading to it, formed part of the property conveyed to Natinvil Builders Ltd; (ii) that the exclusive right of user claimed was so extensive as probably to be incapable of constituting an easement at law; (iii) that in any event on the facts use of the cellar for the purposes of the shop had ceased when the properties were divided, it had never been contemplated that such would be the case in the future and the defendants' claim to an easement failed. This decision was confirmed by the Court of Appeal [1973] 3 All E.R. 455.

(744) *Ward* v. *Kirkland*, [1966] 1 All E.R. 609

The wall of a cottage could only be repaired from the yard of the adjoining farm. Before 1928 both properties belonged to a rector and the tenant of the cottage repaired the wall without seeking the permission of the tenant of the farm. In that year the cottage was conveyed to a predecessor in the title of Ward and in 1942 Mrs Kirkland became the tenant of the farm. From 1942 to 1954 work to the wall was done with her permission as tenant and in 1958 she bought the farm. In October, 1958, Ward did not make entry on to the farmyard to maintain the wall because Mrs Kirkland would not let him enter as of right. In this action, which was brought to determine, amongst other things, whether Ward was entitled to enter the farmyard to maintain the wall and for an injunction to prevent interference with drains running from the cottage through the farmyard, it was *held* by Ungoed—Thomas, J.—

(i) assuming such a right could exist as an easement it would not be defeated on the ground that it would amount to possession or joint possession of the defendant's property;

(ii) that although such a right was not created by implication because it was not 'continuous and apparent' yet the advantage having in fact been enjoyed it was transformed into an easement by Sect. 62 of the Law of Property Act, 1925;

(iii) no easement had arisen by prescription because permission had been given between 1942 and 1958;

(iv) permission having been granted by the rector to Ward to lay drains from the cottage through the farmyard and Ward having incurred expense in so doing it was assumed that the permission was of indefinite duration and an injunction would be granted to prevent interference with the drains by Mrs Kirkland.

(745) *Tehidy Minerals* v. *Norman*, [1971] 2 W.L.R. 711

The owner of a number of farms adjoining a down claimed to be entitled to grazing rights over it. The facts of the case were as follows—

(*a*) the farms and the down had been owned by one person until 19 January, 1920;

(*b*) the down had been requisitioned by the Government on 6 October, 1941;

(*c*) during the period of requisition the owners of surrounding farms had grazed cattle on the down by arrangement with the Ministry concerned;

(*d*) on 31 December, 1960, the down was derequisitioned and the association of farms which had made the arrangements with the Ministry entered into a further arrangement with the owner of the down for the maintenance of certain fences erected by the Ministry and grazing continued but under the control of the association of farmers.

On appeal from a decision of the County Court judge that the farmers were entitled to grazing rights over the down it was *held* by the Court of Appeal—that

(*a*) as there had been no enjoyment of the grazing rights between 6 October, 1941, and 31 December, 1960, except by permission of the Ministry, the farmers could not claim thirty years prescription which the Act of 1832 required for a profit to be established by user as of right;

(*b*) despite the extreme unreality of such a presumption it must be presumed that a modern grant, since lost, had been made of grazing rights at some time between 19 January, 1920, and 6 October, 1921, i.e. twenty years before the requisition, this presumption could not be rebutted by evidence that no such grant had been made but only by evidence—of which there was none—that it could not have been made;

(*c*) the period of twenty years applied to profits as well as to easements for the purposes of the law of lost modern grant although the Act of 1832 provided for different periods in the two cases;

(*d*) only the demonstration of a fixed intention never at any time to assert the right or to attempt to transmit it to anyone else could amount to an abandonment of an easement or profit, thus the acquiescence by the farmers in the arrangement under which the association controlled the grazing for a period of time did not amount to abandonment.

(746) *Diment* v. *N. H. Foot, The Times*, 7 February 1974

A vehicular way across the plaintiff's field was claimed and had been used by the defendant from time to time without dispute between 1936 and 1967. The plaintiff, although the registered owner of the field throughout that period, had never farmed the land herself but had had tenants and during much of the time had lived far away or abroad. Until 1967 the plaintiff knew nothing of the way claimed. *Held*—by Pennycuick, V.C.—(i) the law of prescription rested upon acquiescence for which knowledge was essential; (ii) the plaintiff had no actual knowledge and knowledge was not to be imputed to her either (*a*) because there was a gateway from the field to a parcel of the defendant's land to which there was no vehicular access; there were a number of possible explanations for it; or (*b*) because the plaintiff had not shown that her agents did not have knowledge of the use of the way or the means of knowledge. The presumption that long user was known to the owner was rebuttable and in the present case had been rebutted. It did not extend to the knowledge of agents. The burden of proving such knowledge or means of knowledge lay on the defendant and there was no evidence of either in the present case.

(747) *Davis* v. *Whitby*, [1974] 1 All E.R. 806

The plaintiff and his predecessors in title had enjoyed a right of way over the defendant's land by a certain route for 15 years and then by another route, substituted by agreement, for a further 18 years. On appeal by the defendant to the Court of Appeal against the decision that a right of way over the substituted route had been established by prescription, it was *held*—by the Court of Appeal—that the appeal should be dismissed. '. . . When you have a way used for some time and then afterwards a substituted way is used for the same purpose, both users being as of right, with the apparent consent or acquiescence of those concerned, then the original way and the substituted way should be considered as one.' *per* Lord Denning, M.R.

(748) *Kelly* v. *Barrett*, [1924] 2 Ch. 379

The owner of an estate in Hamsptead developed it for building purposes. He made a new road through it, and sold plots of land along the road to a building firm who erected dwelling houses on the land. The purchasers undertook that the houses built should be used as private dwelling houses only. The owner of the estate did not retain any land except the road, which was afterwards taken over and vested in the local authority. A subsequent purchaser of two adjoining houses carried on a nursing and maternity home in them. The tenant for life under the former estate owner's will and one of the original purchasers claimed an injunction to restrain the defendant's activities. *Held*—No injunction could be granted because the agreement was not a valid building scheme, and the vendor's successor did not retain any interest capable of being affected by the restrictions.

(749) *Knightsbridge Estates Trust Ltd.* v. *Byrne*, [1939] Ch. 441

The plaintiffs were the owners of a large freehold estate close to Knightsbridge. This estate was mortgaged to a friendly society for a sum of money, which, together with interest, was to be repaid over a period of forty years in eighty half-yearly instalments. The company wished to redeem the mortgage before the expiration of the term, because it was possible for them to borrow elsewhere at a lower rate of interst. *Held*—The company was not entitled to redeem the mortgage before the end of the forty years because, in the circumstances, the postponement of the right was not unreasonable, since the parties were men of business and equal in bargaining power. A postponement of the right of redemption is not by itself a clog on the equity of redemption; much depends upon the circumstances. Further, the postponement did not offend the rule against perpetuities, which did not apply to mortgages.

(750) *Noakes* v. *Rice*, [1902] A.C. 24

The appellants were a brewery company and the respondent wished to become the purchaser of a public house owned by the company. The respondent borrowed money from the company in order to effect the purchase, and agreed that the company should have the exclusive right to supply the premises with malt liquors during the period of the mortgage and afterwards, whether any money was or was not owed. The respondent subsequently gave notice to the company that he was prepared to pay off the money secured by the mortgage, if the company would release him from the above-mentioned contract. This was refused and the respondent asked the court for relief. *Held*—The covenant was invalid as a clog on the equity of redemption in so far as it purported to tie the public house after payment of the principal money and interest due on the security.

(751) *Kreglinger* v. *New Patagonia Meat and Cold Storage Co.*, [1914] A.C. 25

The appellants were a firm of merchants and wool brokers. The respondents carried on the business of preserving and canning meant, and of boiling down carcasses of sheep and other animals. The appellants advanced money to the respondents, the loan being secured by a charge over all the respondents' property. The appellants agreed not to demand repayment for five years, but the respondents could repay the debt at an earlier period on giving notice. The agreement also contained a provision that the respondents should not sell sheepskins to anyone but the appellants for five years from the date of the agreement, so long as the appellants were willing to purchase the same at an agreed price. The loan was paid off before the expiration of the five years. *Held*—The option of purchasing the sheepskins was not terminated on repayment, but continued for the period of five years. The option was a collateral contract which was not a mortgage and in no way affected the right to redeem the property.

(752) *Cityland and Property (Holdings) Ltd* v. *Dabrah*, [1967] 2 All E.R. 639

A first mortgage of £2900 was granted by the seller of property to a purchaser and was expressed to be repayable in the sum of £4553 for which the property was charged. The £4553 was to be repaid over six years by equal monthly instalments and there was no mention in the mortgage of any interest. The whole of the balance of the £4553 became payable if the borrower defaulted and for this reason Goff, J., *held* that the premium amounting to £1653 was an unreasonable collateral advantage and there-fore void under the principle in *Kreglinger's Case*, 1914.[751] The Judge having disallowed the premium was prepared to allow interest at seven per cent on a day-to-day basis which he thought to be somewhat more than market rates, but in fact it was far below market rates. The premium was an interest computation of nine-and-a-half per cent, non-reducing over six years and if it had been expressed as such in the mortgage it would appear that the court could not have set it aside since the court can only set aside unreasonable collateral advantages. However, in regard to interest rates, it appears that 'equity does not reform mortgage transactions because they are unreasonable', Greene, M.R., in *Knightsbridge Estates Trust Ltd* v. *Byrne*, 1939.[749] But this case was not cited to Goff, J. It would seem that for the future interest in mortgages should be expressed as such and not disguised as premium.

(752) *White* v. *City of London Brewery Co.* (1889), 42 Ch.D. 237

The plaintiff had a lease of a public house in Canning Town, and he mortgaged it to the defendants to secure a loan of £900 with interest. One year later, no interest having been paid since the date of the mortgage, the defendants entered into possession of the public house. They later let the premises on a tenancy determinable at three months' notice under which the tenant was to take all his beer from the defendants. Eventually the lease was sold by the defendants, and the plaintiff asked the defendants to account and pay him what should be found due. *Held*—The defendants must account to the plaintiff for the increased rent they might have received if they had let the public-house without the restrictive condition regarding the sale of the defendants' beer, since a 'free house' would produce more rent than a 'tied house'.

(753) *Koppel* v. *Koppel*, [1966] 2 All E.R. 187

Mr Koppel, who was estranged from his wife, invited a Mrs Wide to come to his house and look after his children on a permanent basis. Mrs Wide agreed to do so provided that Mr Koppel transferred the contents of his house to her to compensate for giving up her own home and disposing of her furniture. The transfer was recorded in writing. Later Mrs Koppel sought to levy execution on the contents of the house for her unpaid maintenance which amounted to £114. In proceedings resulting from Mrs Wide's claim to the property, the Registrar of the County Court held that the written transfer of the property to Mrs Wide was void as an unregistered Bill of Sale. *Held*—by the Court of Appeal—that the contents of the house were not in Mr Koppel's 'possession or apparent possession' within Sect. 8 of the Bills of Sale Act, 1878, because —

(i) Mr Koppel had transferred possession to Mrs Wide under the document which was an absolute Bill of Sale;

(ii) the grantor of the Bill, Mr Koppel, had therefore neither possession nor apparent possession. He did not have apparent possession because Mrs Wide was living in the house with him and both had apparent possession of the property, not merely Mr Koppel;

(iii) Mrs Wide was therefore entitled to the property.

(754) *Robins & Co.* v. *Gray*, [1895] 2 Q.B. 501

The plaintiffs dealt in sewing machines and employed a traveller to sell the machines on commission. The plaintiff's traveller put up at the defendant's inn in April, 1894, and stayed there until the end of July, 1894. During this time the plaintiffs sent the traveller machines to sell in the neighbourhood. At the end of July, the traveller owed the defendant £4 for board and lodging, and he failed to pay. The defendant detained certain of the goods sent by the plaintiffs to their traveller, claiming he had a lien on them for the amount of the debt due to him although the defendant knew that the goods were the property of the plaintiffs. *Held*—The defendant was entitled to a lien on the plaintiffs' property for the travellers' debt.

(755) *Caldwell* v. *Sumpters, The Times,* 7 July, 1971

The defendants, who were a firm of solicitors, were holding the title deeds to property recently sold by a former client, Mrs Caldwell, who had not paid their charges. They voluntarily released the deeds to another firm which had been instructed to take their place to complete the sale, stating that they did so on the understanding that the deeds would be held to their order until Mrs Caldwell had paid. The second firm of solicitors kept the deeds and refused to accept that understanding. *Held*—by Megarry, J.—Sumpters' lien was lost when they voluntarily parted with possession of the deeds and could not be retained by a one-sided reservation of the kind made. If the agreement of the second firm of solicitors had been obtained the lien would have been preserved as it would also if Sumpters had lost possession by trickery or other wrongdoing. The second firm was under no obligation to accept the reservation or to return the deeds.

(*Note:* the decision of Megarry, J., was reversed by the Court of Appeal (*Caldwell* v. *Sumpters, The Times*, 20 December, 1971), the Court holding that Sumpters' lien was not lost when they parted with the deeds since—

(*a*) possession was given up on the clear and express understanding that the deeds were to be held to Sumpters' order; and

(*b*) solicitors as officers of the court could not be allowed to take advantage of this sort of situation even out of regard for any duty owed to a client.)

(756) *Larner* v. *Fawcett,* [1950] 2 All E.R. 727

The defendant owned a racehorse and made an agreement with a Mr Davis under which it was agreed that Davis would train and race the filly and receive half of any prize money she might win. Davis, unknown to the defendant, agreed to let Larner have the animal to train. Larner did so, and when his charges had reached £125, he discovered that Fawcett was the true owner. Larner, being unable to recover the cost of training and feeding the filly from Davis, who had no funds, now applied to the court for an order for sale. Fawcett was brought in as defendant. *Held*, by the Court of Appeal, that Larner had a common law lien for his charges, and although such a lien does not carry with it a power of sale, the power given in the Rules of the Supreme Court to make an order for sale was appropriate here, particularly since the filly was eating her head off. Fawcett had not made any attempt to get his property back but had clothed Davis with all the indicia of ownership. An order for sale would therefore be made unless Fawcett paid into court the amount of Larners' charges by a given date.

NEGOTIABLE INSTRUMENTS

(757) *Arab Bank Ltd* v. *Ross*, [1952] 2 Q.B. 216

The plaintiffs claimed to be holders in due course of two promissory notes made by Ross and payable to 'Fathi and Faysal Nabulsy Company', a firm of which the two men named were the only partners. Ross alleged that he had been induced to make the notes by the fraud of the payees, and attempted unsuccessfully to show that the plaintiffs had knowledge of this fraud and had not taken the notes in good faith. The plaintiffs claimed to be holders in due course, but the point was taken that the indorsement on the notes was simply 'Fathi and Faysal Nabulsy' with the omission of the word 'Company'. *Held*—By the Court of Appeal, that an indorsement could be valid to pass the property without being regular on the face of it. Regularity is different from validity. The Arab Bank were not holders in due course, because the indorsement was not regular, but were holders for value. Although the indorsers were in fact the only two partners, the word Company did not imply this, and therefore the indorsement was not manifestly regular by reference only to the instrument. The circumstances under which an indorsement gives rise to doubt is a practical matter and is best answered by the practice of bankers. This practice insists that the indorsement shall correspond exactly with the payee as named.

(758) *Pollway Ltd* v. *Abdullah*, [1974] 2 All E.R. 381

D contracted at an auction to purchase land from V. P, the auctioneer acting for V in the sale, signed the memorandum of the contract and, as agent for V, accepted D's cheque in payment of the ten cent deposit. The payee named in the cheque was P. D wrongfully stopped the cheque and refused to pay the deposit, whereupon V exercised his right to treat the contract as repudiated. Was P a holder for value and thus able to enforce the cheque against D?

Yes, said the Court of Appeal (Megaw, Buckley and Roskill, L.JJ.). P was the holder of the cheque within the Bills of Exchange Act, 1882, Sect. 2. The consideration for the cheque was sufficient to support a simple contract, viz. either (a) P's warranty of his authority to sign the memorandum on V's behalf and to receive the cheque or (b) P's acceptance of a cheque in place of legal tender. Valuable consideration within the Bills of Exchange Act, 1882, Sect. 27(1) having been given, P could enforce payment against D.

(*Note:* in this case the vendors had not supplied consideration to the defendant because they had not gone on with the sale. The defendant had forfeited his deposit and the plaintiffs were the only ones who might have been in a position to claim consideration sufficient to enforce the cheque, which, in the event, the Court held they had done. The cheque was, of course, also in the plaintiffs' name but if they had endorsed it over to the vendors this would not have enabled the vendors to sue because, as we have seen, they had not supplied consideration to the defendant.)

(759) *Diamond* v. *Graham*, [1968] 2 All E.R. 909

A Mr Herman was anxious to borrow the sum of £1650 for immediate commitments and he asked a Mr Diamond whether he would lend him that sum. Mr Diamond agreed provided Mr Herman could repay by the following Monday the sum of £1665. Mr Herman said that he would have a cheque from a Mr Graham by that time which he would ask to be made payable to Mr Diamond. Mr Diamond then drew a cheque for £1650 in favour of Mr Herman. Mr Herman could not get a cheque from Mr Graham on the following Monday because he was not available on that day. However, Mr Herman presented the cheque for payment but Mr Diamond countermanded payment and told the bank manager not to pay it until authorized by Mr Diamond. Some days later Mr Herman obtained a cheque from Mr Graham in favour of Mr Diamond. Mr Graham asked who was providing Mr Herman with temporary relief and was told it was the plaintiff. Mr Herman gave the cheque to Mr Diamond who paid it into his bank and authorized payment of his cheque to Mr Herman. However, the cheque drawn by Mr Graham was dishonoured. Mr Herman had also drawn a cheque in favour of Mr Graham and this was also dishonoured, Mr Diamond's cheque being the only one paid. Mr Diamond now sued Mr Graham on his unpaid cheque. The defendant argued that the plaintiff was not a holder for value within Sect. 27(2) of the Bills of Exchange Act, 1882, because no value had passed between him and Mr Graham. It was held by Danckwerts, L.J., that there was nothing in Sect. 27(2) which required value to be given by the holder of a cheque so long as value had been given by someone. Here value had been given as follows—

(i) by Mr Herman who gave his own cheque to Mr Graham in return for Mr Graham drawing a cheque in favour of Mr Diamond; and

(ii) by Mr Diamond when he released his cheque to Mr Herman.

Thus, Mr Diamond was a holder for value of the cheque and was entitled to judgment and the appeal must be dismissed. Diplock and Sachs, L.JJ., also dismissed the appeal.

(*Note:* the plaintiff in this case gave consideration after the defendant's cheque was issued, i.e. he released his cheque to Mr Herman.)

(760) *Oliver* v. *Davis and Another*, [1949] 2 K.B. 727

On 18 July, 1947, the plaintiff lent £350 to William Davis and received from him a cheque for £400, post-dated to 8 August, 1947. This was presented on 19 August, 1947, and Davis was not able to meet it. Davis persuaded a Miss Marjorie Woodcock (he was 'engaged' to her sister although he was married) to draw a cheque of £400 in favour of the plaintiff, and an envelope containing this cheque, but without any covering letter, was left at the plaintiff's house.

The plaintiff was away at the time and returned on 22 August when he received Miss Woodcock's cheque but did not know who had sent it. Miss Woodcock, however, had discovered that Davis was a rogue and she informed the plaintiff within an hour or two of his receiving the cheque why she had sent it and also that she had stopped payment of it. On 23 August, the plaintiff presented Davis's cheque which was dishonoured and later presented Miss Woodcock's cheque which was returned marked, 'Stopped by order of the drawer'. In an action by the plaintiff against Miss Woodcock, suing her on the cheque, the plaintiff relied, inter alia, on Sect. 27(1)(*b*) of the Bills of Exchange Act, 1882. Miss Woodcock contended that there was no consideration for the cheque. *Held*—An antecedent debt or liability within the meaning of Sect. 27(1)(*b*) was a debt or liability due from the maker or negotiator of the instrument and not from a third party. The plaintiff, therefore, could not rely on Sect. 27(1)(*b*) but must show consideration sufficient to satisfy a simple contract under Sect. 27(1)(*a*). This he could not do because he had not given her any promise, express or implied, to forbear in respect of any remedy he might have against Davis, nor had he changed his position for the worse in regard to his claim on Davis's cheque. There was no evidence of any consideration and the plaintiff's action failed.

(*Note:* in this case the plaintiff did nothing after Miss Woodcock's cheque was issued which could be regarded as amounting to consideration to Davis or Miss Woodcock. If, for example, he had said after receiving Miss Woodcock's cheque that he would not sue Davis, he might have provided consideration sufficient to enable him to enforce Miss Woodcock's cheque since forbearance to sue can amount to consideration.)

(761) *Bavins* v. *London and South Western Bank Ltd*, [1900] 1 Q.B. 270

In the course of this action, the Court of Appeal had to deal with an instrument given to the plaintiffs by the Great Northern Railway Co. for work done. The instrument read as follows: 'The Great Northern Railway Company No. 1 Accountants drawing account London, 7 July 1898. The Union Bank of London Limited. . . . Pay to J. Bavins, Jnr. and Sims the sum of Sixty-nine Pounds Seven Shillings. Provided the receipt form at the foot hereof is duly signed, stamped, and dated. £69.7s.' *Held*—That the instrument was not a cheque within the definition given by the Bills of Exchange Act, 1882, because it was not an unconditional order. The bank was not to pay the instrument unless the receipt was signed.

(762) *Nathan* v. *Ogdens Ltd* (1905), 94 L.T. 126

In the course of this action the Court of Appeal was dealing with an instrument on the face of which were printed the words 'The receipt at the back hereof must be signed, which signature will be taken as an indorsement of the cheque.' *Held*—The order to pay was unconditional and therefore the cheque was valid. The words could be taken as addressed to the payee and not to the bank.

(*Note:* it may now be settled that it is not a condition that a banker must obtain the payee's signature, on a receipt form, on a cheque before paying out. If the condition is regarded as addressed to the payee, the instrument is unconditional. However, bankers usually obtain an indemnity from customers having receipt forms on their cheques. This indemnity protects the bank if it incorrectly treats an instrument requiring a receipt as a cheque.)

(763) *Child* v. *Monins and Bowles* (1821), 2 Brod. and B. 460

The defendants were the executors of Thomas Taylor, and as such executors made a promissory note as follows: 'Ringwould, 28 December, 1816, as executors to the late Thomas Taylor, of Ringwould, we severally and jointly promise to pay to Mr Nathaniel Childs the sum of £200 on demand, together with lawful interest for the same. J. Monins, Phineas Bowles, executors.' *Held*—The executors were personally liable. The words 'on demand' implied that the executors had assets to satisfy the note. If they had meant to limit their liability, they should have added the words 'out of the estate of Thomas Taylor'. Burrough, J., said, 'The insertion of the words "as executors" cannot alter the case if, on the whole instrument, the parties appear liable.'

(764) *Hendon* v. *Adelman, The Times*, 16 June, 1973

A cheque signed on behalf of L. & R. Agencies omitted the ampersand in the company's name. *Held* by MacKenna, J., that the directors who had signed the cheque had not complied with Sect. 108(1)(c) of the Companies Act, 1948, and, accordingly, were personally liable under Sect. 108(4)(b).

(765) *Greenwood* v. *Martins Bank Ltd*, [1933] A.C. 51

The appellant, who was a dairy man in Blackpool, opened with the respondents a joint account in the name of himself and his wife. Cheques drawn on this account were to bear the signature of them both. Later on the appellant opened a further account with the respondents in his own name, though the wife kept the pass books and cheque books in respect of both accounts. In October, 1929, Greenwood asked his wife to give him a cheque, saying he wanted to draw £20 from his own account. His wife then told him that there was no money in the bank, and that she had used it to help her sister who was involved in legal proceedings over property. He asked her who had forged his signature but she would not say. However, she did ask him not to inform the respondents of the forgeries until her sister's case was over. Greenwood complied with this request until 5 June, 1930, when he discovered that there were no legal proceedings instituted by his wife's sister and that his wife had been deceiving him. He told his wife that he intended to go the bank and reveal her forgeries, but before he actually made the visit she shot herself. Greenwood now claimed £410 6s. 0d. from the Bank on the grounds that this sum had been paid out of his own account and the joint account by means of forged cheques. The Bank pleaded ratification, adoption or estoppel. *Held*—There could be no ratification or adoption in this sort of case, but the essential elements of estoppel were present. The appellant's failure to inform the Bank was a representation that the cheques were good. The Bank had suffered a detriment because, if Greenwood had told the Bank when his wife first confessed to forgery, they might have brought an action against her. Under the law *existing at that time* they could not bring such an action after her death. The Bank had, therefore, a legal right to debit Greenwood's account with the amount of the forged cheques.

(766) *Vinden* v. *Hughes*, [1950] 1 K.B. 795

A clerk persuaded the plaintiff, his employer, to draw cheques in favour of his actual customers by saying the employer owed money to them which he did not. The clerk then forged the customers' indorsements and kept the proceeds. *Held*—These were existing payees and therefore order cheques and the defendants had no title.

This case was followed in *North & South Wales Bank* v. *Macbeth*, [1908] A.C. 137. It may be that the principle in *Vagliano's* Case[767] can never apply to a cheque, since the drawer of a cheque usually intends the payee to receive payment.

(767) *Bank of England* v. *Vagliano Bros*, [1891] A.C. 107

Glyka, a clerk of Vagliano Bros, forged the signatures of Vucina and Petriai and Co. as drawer and payees of bills drawn on Vagliano Bros. The bills were accepted by Vagliano, since he knew the parties concerned and had done business with them. Glyka got possession of the bills and then forged indorsements in favour of fictitious persons whereby he was able to cash them with the Bank of England. Glyka was arrested and acknow-ledged the forgeries but the Bank had debited Vagliano Bros account with the sums paid out. Vagliano now sued the Bank for repayment. *Held*—by the House of Lords on appeal—Fictitious does not mean 'imaginary' but 'feigned' or 'counterfeit'. The bills were fictitious from beginning to end and all the persons were feigned or counterfeit persons put forward as real persons, and were not less fictitious because real persons did correspond to the names used. Since bills drawn payable to a fictitious payee can be treated as payable to bearer, the Bank of England was in order in paying them and Vagliano Bros failed in their action.

(768) *Clutton* v. *Attenborough & Son* (1879), A.C. 90

A clerk persuaded his employer to draw cheques in favour of one Brett by telling the employer that Brett had done work for the firm. The employer had never heard of Brett. The clerk then forged the indorsements. *Held*—Brett was a non-existing payee. Therefore the cheques were bearer cheques and the indorsee received a good title to them.

(769) *Williamson* v. *Rider*, [1962] 2 All E.R. 268

R signed a document in these terms 'In consideration of the loan of £100 from W., I, R, agree to repay W the sum of £100 on, or before, 31 December, 1956.' *Held*—This was not a promissory note because the option to pay at an earlier date created an uncertainty or contingency in the time of payment.

(770) *Jones (R.E.) Ltd* v. *Waring and Gillow*, [1926] A.C. 670

A fraudulent person named Bodenham was indebted to Waring and Gillow in the sum of £5000 which he could not pay. He went to the plaintiffs and said that he was an agent for International Motors' new car the Roma, but they would have to take 500 cars and pay a deposit of £5000. The plaintiffs were interested in the deal but did not wish to pay Bodenham or International Motors because they did not know these parties. Bodenham then said that Waring and Gillow were the real backers and asked the plaintiffs to make out a cheque for £5000 to them, which the plaintiffs did. Waring and Gillow received payment of the cheque and when the fraud was discovered the plaintiffs sought to recover their money from Waring and Gillow. The House of Lords held that the plaintiffs succeeded because the money was paid under a mistake of fact and that the original payee of a bill of exchange is not a holder in due course.

(771) *Gardner* v. *Walsh* (1855), 5 E. & B. 83

This was an action against the defendant and Elizabeth Burton and Alice Clarke on a promissory note now overdue. The defendant agreed to be jointly and severally liable to pay to the plaintiff or his order the sum of £500. Evidence showed that Elizabeth Burton was indebted to the plaintiff and she agreed to get two sureties, the defendant and Alice Clarke, to join her in a joint and several promissory note to the plaintiff. Burton and Walsh signed the note together and gave it to the plantiff. The plaintiff got Alice Clarke to sign it although the defendant did not know there was to be another party. In this action on the note Walsh alleged that the note was avoided by virtue of a material alteration after issue, namely the addition of another party without Walsh's knowledge. *Held*—The addition of Clarke's name was a material alteration and if made after the note was issued would avoid it.

(772) *Eagleshill Ltd* v. *J. Needham Builders Ltd*, [1972] 3 All E.R. 895

The plaintiffs were holders for value of a bill of exchange for £7660 drawn by the defendants and accepted by Fir View Furniture Co. payable at a certain bank. The bill became due and payable on 31 December, 1970, but prior to that date Fir View Furniture Co. went into liquidation. By mistake, the plaintiffs posted their notice of dishonour dated 1 January, 1971, on 30 December, 1970, and it arrived at Fir View Furniture Co's office on 31 December. The Court of Appeal held that the notice was not subsequent to the dishonour within the Bills of Exchange Act, 1882, and was therefore invalid. On appeal by the plaintiffs it was *held*—by the House of Lords allowing the appeal—that a notice of dishonour was given when it was received, i.e. when it was opened in the ordinary course of business or would have been if the ordinary course of business were followed. Provided that notice is received after dishonour it is valid regardless of when it is sent off. The notice was valid and the plaintiff's action succeeded.

(773) *Karak Rubber Co. Ltd.* v. *Burden (No. 2)*, [1972] 1 All E.R. 1210

A take-over transaction involved the purchase by a director of the company's issued share capital. The director used the company's assets to finance the purchase of the shares by borrowing money from a third party to buy them and repaying the third party by a cheque for £99,504 drawn on the company's account at Barclays Bank. The cheque was paid by the bank which was held liable to repay Karak for breach of their contractual duty because—

(*a*) although a bank was obliged to pay on demand a cheque which was in proper form and backed by adequate funds, it did not follow that a paying bank was under an absolute unqualified duty to pay without enquiry; it was, on the contrary, under a contractual duty to exercise such care and skill as would be exercised by a reasonable banker and that care and skill included, in appropriate circumstances, a duty to enquire before paying;

(*b*) in exercising its duty of care the paying bank was bound to make such enquiries as might, in given circumstances, be appropriate and practical, where it had, or a reasonable banker would have, grounds for believing that the authorized signatories were misusing their authority for the purpose of defrauding their principal or otherwise defeating his true intentions;

(*c*) the circumstances in which the Karak cheque came to be tendered to Barclays were so unusual and out of the ordinary course of banking business, the sum involved was so large, and the ground so solid for suspecting that someone was using Karak money to finance the takeover transaction, that a reasonable banker, in the interests of his customers, would have made further enquiries before inviting or allowing the customer's signatories to pay over £99,504 of the customer's money.

The bank was also liable as a constructive trustee. Although, in order to establish liability as a constructive trustee on the part of a third party who has assisted a trustee as his agent in a breach of trust, it was necessary to show that the third party had assisted with knowledge of a dishonest and fraudulent design on the part of the trustee, it was not necessary to show that the third party had actual knowledge; it was sufficient to show constructive knowledge, i.e. that the third party had knowledge of circumstances which would have indicated to an honest, reasonable man that such a design was being committed or would have put him on enquiry whether it was being committed.

(774) *Tournier* v. *National Provincial and Union Bank of England*, [1924] 1 K.B. 461

Tournier banked with the defendants and, being overdrawn by £9 6s. 8d., signed an agreement to pay this off at the rate of £1 a week, disclosing the name and address of his employers, Kenyon & Co., with whom he had a three months' contract as a traveller. The agreement to repay was not observed and the bank also discovered, through another banker, that Tournier had indorsed a cheque for £45 over to a bookmaker. The manager of the bank thereupon telephoned Kenyon & Co. to find out Tournier's private address and told them that Tournier was betting heavily. Kenyon & Co., as a result of this conversation, refused to renew Tournier's contract of employment. Tournier sued the bank for slander and for breach of an implied contract not to disclose the state of his account or his transactions. Judgment was entered for the defendants but the Court of Appeal allowed Tournier's appeal and ordered a new trial. Bankes, L.J., laid down four qualifications to the duty of non-disclosure: (*a*) where the disclosure is under compulsion of law; (*b*) where there is a duty to the public to disclose; (*c*) where the interests of the bank require disclosure; (*d*) where the disclosure is made by the express or implied consent of the customer. Atkin, L.J., said: 'I do not desire to express a final opinion on the practice of bankers to give one another information as to the affairs of their respective customers, except to say it appears to me that if it is justified it must be upon the basis of an implied consent of the customer.'

(775) *Williams* v. *Summerfield*, [1972] 3 W.L.R. 131

Police issued summonses against employees alleging theft of sums of money from their employer. The defendants handed back £19,000. The justices granted an application by police to inspect the defendants' accounts, there being a large sum outstanding which the police could not specify without sight of them. On appeal by the defendants to the Divisional Court it was held that the appeal must be dismissed. Police investigating charges of theft may be granted permission to inspect defendants' bank accounts when otherwise unable to specify the sum stolen. However, an application for an order under Sect. 7 of the 1879 Act should be rejected if legal proceedings were started with the sole object of investigating a suspect bank account. It would be proper for justices faced with a difficult case to decline to make such an order on the ground that they feel that the concurrent jurisdiction of a High Court judge may be invoked instead.

(776) *Sunderland* v. *Barclays Bank Ltd* (1938), *The Times*, 25 November

Mrs Sunderland had drawn a cheque in favour of her dressmaker on an account containing insufficient funds. The cheque was returned because the bank knew she indulged in gambling and thought it unwise to grant her an overdraft. Mrs Sunderland complained to her husband and the manager of the bank informed him, over the 'phone, of the wife's transactions with bookmakers. Mrs Sunderland regarded this as a breach of the bank's duty of secrecy, but in fact the husband's telephone conversation was a continuation of one of her own in which she requested the bank to give an explanation to the husband concerning the return of the cheque. The bank pleaded implied authority to disclose. du Parcq, L.J., gave judgment for the defendants and affirmed the criteria relating to disclosure laid down in *Tournier* v. *National Provincial and Union Bank of England*, 1924.[774] However, each case must depend on its own facts. The relationship of husband and wife was a special one. The demand by Dr Sunderland for an explanation required an account of why the bank had done what it had done. It might be said that the disclosure was with the implied consent of the customer and the interests of the bank required disclosure. Since the husband had taken over conduct of the matter, the manager was justified in thinking that the wife did not object to the offer of an explanation. If judgment had been for the plaintiff, the damages were assessed at forty shillings—nominal damages.

(777) *Eckman* v. *Midland Bank, The Times*, 9 December, 1972

A union was fined £5000 for contempt of court and writs of sequestration were issued. The union's bankers refused to disclose assets and make payment unless a court order was made on the basis that until then they were not compelled to do so, and their relationship with their client prevented them from doing so. *Held*—by the National Industrial Relations Court—that the bankers were not affected until they knew of the issue of the writ of sequestration but that thereafter their duty and their only duty was to refuse to take any action they knew to have as its object the frustration of the writ. A demand by sequestrators for disclosure of property must be complied with. However, since the bankers had not acted unreasonably in coming to court to clarify the position, no order would be made as to costs.

(778) *London Joint Stock Bank Ltd.* v. *Macmillan and Arthur*, [1918] A.C. 777

Macmillan and Arthur were customers of the bank and entrusted their clerk with the duty of filling in cheques for signature. The clerk presented a cheque to a partner for signature, drawn in favour of the firm or bearer, and made out for £2 0s. 0d. in figures but with no sum in words. The clerk then easily altered the figures to £120 0s. 0d. and wrote 'one hundred and twenty pounds' in words, presenting the cheque to the bank and obtaining £120 in cash. The firm contended that the bank could only debit them with £2; the bank alleged negligence on the part of the firm. *Held*—by the House of Lords—that the relationship of banker and customer imposes a special duty of care on the customer in drawing cheques. A cheque is a mandate to the banker to pay according to the tenor. The customer must exercise reasonable care to prevent the banker being misled. If he draws a cheque in a manner which facilitates fraud, he is guilty of a breach of duty as between himself and the banker, and he will be responsible to the banker for any loss sustained by the banker as a natural and direct consequence of this breach of duty. If the cheque is drawn in such a way as to facilitate or almost to invite an increase in the amount by forgery if the cheque should get into the hands of a dishonest person, forgery is not a remote but a very natural consequence of such negligence. The bank could, therefore, debit Macmillan and Arthur with the full £120 0s. 0d.

Cf. *Scholfield* v. *Earl of Londesborough*, [1896] A.C. 514, where it was held that the drawer of a bill of exchange owed no such duty to other parties.

(779) *Slingsby* v. *District Bank*, [1931] All E.R. Rep. 147

The executors of an estate drew a cheque payable to John Prust & Co. but left a space between the payee's name and the printed words 'or order'. A fraudulent solicitor named Cumberbirch wrote 'per Cumberbirch and Pott's after the payee's name. He then indorsed the cheque and received payment. *Held*—There was no negligence on the part of the executors; it was not a usual precaution to draw lines before or after the name of the payee and the executors were entitled to recover the amount of the cheque from the bank.

(*Note:* if the precaution of filling in the gap after the payees' name is more usual now than in 1931, then a present-day court may not follow *Slingsby* because the question of what is usual is purely one of evidence.)

(780) *Gibbons* v. *Westminster Bank Ltd*, [1939] 2 K.B. 882

The plaintiff drew a cheque for rent which she gave to her landlords and which was dishonoured in error. The bank had credited to another account funds paid in by the plaintiff sufficient to meet the cheque. The bank offered her £1 1s. 0d. in full satisfaction of her complaint, but the jury found that she did not accept this. As a result of the bank's action the plaintiff's landlords insisted thereafter that she pay her rent in cash. However, she did not claim special damage and was not allowed to amend her statement of claim during the trial. *Held*—The plaintiff was entitled to nominal damages of forty shillings. A trader is entitled to recover substantial damages for wrongful dishonour without pleading or proving actual damage, but a person who is not a trader is not entitled to recover substantial damages for the wrongful dishonour of a cheque, unless the damage he has suffered is alleged and proved as special damage.

(781) *Davidson* v. *Barclays Bank Ltd*, [1940] 1 All E.R. 316

Davidson was both a cash and credit bookmaker who drew a cheque for £2 15s. 8d. on his account. The bank had previously paid a cheque for £7 15s.9d. which Davidson had stopped by letter, and his wrongful payment made it appear that Davidson had not funds to meet the cheque for £2 15s. 8d. which was therefore returned marked 'Not sufficient' across its face. The plaintiff alleged libel in that the bank held him out to be a person who had drawn a cheque on an account without sufficient funds to meet it, and gave the impression that the plaintiff and his firm were unsafe to do business with or to deal with on credit. The bank pleaded that the words were published only to the payee to whom they owed an explanation as to why the cheque had not been met; that the words were published in the honest though mistaken belief that they were true; and that the occasion was privileged. *Held*—The bank had no duty to publish. There was no common interest requiring such a communication. The bank made a mistake in returning the cheque and this was the reason for the need for explanation. It was self-created. The case is essentially different from one where the bank might make an error in replying to a specific request for a reference, since then the occasion of privilege is already constituted. Judgment was given for the plaintiff for £250.

(782) *Jayson* v. *Midland Bank Ltd*, [1968] 1 Lloyd's Rep. 409

The plaintiff claimed damages for breach of contract and libel against the bank who had returned two cheques drawn by her marked 'refer to drawer'. She alleged that the bank had agreed to pay the cheques if she paid £100 into her account the following week (which she in fact did). The bank's contention was that they had agreed to pay the cheques only if the plaintiff's overdraft limit of £500 were not exceeded (which it would have been if the cheques concerned had been paid). The action was tried before Blain, J., and a jury and the jury *found* as follows—

    (i) the bank's contention was proved;

    (ii) the effect of the words 'refer to drawer' was to lower the plaintiff's reputation in the eyes of right-thinking people and was defamatory—however, this did not avail the plaintiff because the bank was quite justified in its action; and

(iii) the plaintiff would have exceeded the overdraft if the cheques had been met.

An appeal to the Court of Appeal against judgment for the bank was dismissed.

(*Note:* this case goes some way towards removing the doubts which had previously existed regarding the defamatory nature of the words 'refer to drawer'. This decision supports the view that they are defamatory and unless the bank can plead justification, it would seem to be liable.)

(783) *Curtice* v. *London, City & Midland Bank Ltd*, [1908] 1 K.B. 293

The plaintiff drew a cheque for £63 in favour of a Mr Jones to pay for some horses. When the horses were not delivered he stopped the cheque by a telegram to the bank which was delivered into the bank's letter box at 6.15 pm. The telegram was not noticed on the next day and the bank paid the cheque, only to find on the following day both the telegram which had been overlooked and a written confirmation of countermand which had been posted. The plaintiff was notified that the countermand was received too late to be effective, and he retorted by drawing a cheque on the bank for the whole of his funds, including the £63, which the bank naturally enough dishonoured. The plaintiff brought an action for money had and received. The county court gave judgment for the plaintiff; the Divisional Court dismissed the bank's appeal; but it was *held* by the Court of Appeal that there had been no effective countermand of payment and the bank were not liable for money had and received. They might have been held liable in negligence, but the damages would not then have been the same. Cozens-Hardy, M.R., said: 'There is no such thing as a constructive countermand in a commercial transaction of this kind.'

(784) *Burnett* v. *Westminster Bank*, [1965] 3 All E.R. 81

P had for a number of years had accounts at the X branch and the Y branch of the defendant bank. The bank then began to issue him with cheque books with a notice on the cover to this effect 'the cheques in this book will be applied to the account for which they have been prepared'. In the course of a transaction P used an X branch cheque but altered it as payable at Y branch and later stopped payment by giving notice to Y branch. The cheque was electronically sorted by a computer which was not equipped to read the alteration and the cheque went to X branch, which paid it. P sued the bank for the amount of the cheque. *Held*—The bank should not have debited P's account with the cheque and he succeeded.

(*Note:* P seems to have succeeded largely because he was an *existing* customer and the notice was on the cover. The court did say that if such a cheque book was in fact issued to a customer on opening an account, he might be bound by it, and any customer would have been bound by a notice printed on each cheque.)

(785) *Brewer* v. *Westminster Bank*, [1952] 2 All E.R. 650

Cheques drawn on an estate account required the signature of each of the two executors. One executor drew over £3000 by forging the signature of his co-executor. The latter brought an action for a declaratory judgment to the effect that the account should not have been debited. The declaration was refused by the court on the grounds that a joint contractor could not sue on a joint contract unless the other joint contractor could sue also, which in this case he could not. The decision has been criticized and in fact settlement was made, the bank paying the plaintiff the full amount claimed, and costs.

(See now *Jackson* v. *White and Midland Bank Ltd*, [1967] 2 Lloyd's Rep. 68.)

(786) *Woods* v. *Martins Bank Ltd*, [1958] 3 All E.R. 166

The plaintiff claimed, amongst other things, damages against the defendant bank and Mr Joseph Johnson, the manager of the defendants' Quayside branch at Newcastle upon Tyne, and the case is reported only on the liability of the bank. The bank had advertised investment advice, saying 'the very best advice is available through our managers', and as a result of a request for financial advice by the plaintiff, who was a customer, the manager arranged for the plaintiff to invest £14,800 in a private company called Brocks Refrigeration, although, to the manager's knowledge, the company had a considerable overdraft and was in need of funds. The whole of this sum was eventually lost. The bank's defence was that the giving of financial advice was not part of a banker's business, relying on earlier decisions that had suggested this, and that they were not therefore vicariously liable for the negligence of their manager, since he was not acting within the scope of his employment. *Held*—By Salmon, J., (i) The limits of a banker's business could not be laid down as a matter of law. In this case the advertisement showed that the giving of financial advice was part of the business and therefore the bank was vicariously liable for the act of its servant, the manager. (ii) The duty to give proper and not negligent advice extended to potential customers as well as existing customers.

(787) *Schioler* v. *Westminster Bank Ltd*, [1970] 3 All E.R. 177

Mrs Schioler was Danish, residing in England but domiciled in Denmark. She opened an account in 1962 with a bank in Guernsey. Dividends were forwarded in sterling to the Guernsey branch by a Malaysian company and Mrs Schioler's account was credited without deduction of UK income tax to which she was not liable unless the dividends were sent to a branch in the United Kingdom. In 1969 the Malaysian company converted its shares from sterling units into Malaysian dollars. They also sent the 1967 dividend voucher and warrant to the Guernsey branch expressed in Malaysian dollars. The Guernsey branch lacked the facilities to realize the warrant so it was sent to the bank's stock officer in England for realization. The dividends thus became liable to UK income tax. In this action by the plaintiff for breach of contractual duty by the bank it was *held*—by Mocatta, J.—that in the absence of special arrangements bankers could not in discharge of their contractual duties in crediting an account with a dividend be obliged to consider the tax implications to the customer or consult him before acting in accordance with their ordinary practice.

(788) *Hibernian Bank* v. *Gysin and Hanson*, [1939] 1 All E.R. 166

A bill of exchange was drawn by the Irish Casing Co. on the defendants in the terms 'Payable to the order of the Irish Casing Co. only—not negotiable'. The defendants accepted the bill and the Casing Co. indorsed it to the plaintiffs who presented it for payment and it was dishonoured because the defendants were owed a greater sum of money by the Casing Co. and wished to set off. *Held*—The bill was not a negotiable instrument and the defendants were not liable to anyone but the Casing Co. The words 'to order' did not negative the crossing 'not negotiable' and the latter covered the whole legal position of the bill.

(789) *Lloyds Bank Ltd* v. *E. B. Savory & Co.*, [1933] A.C. 201

Two clerks, Perkins and Smith, stole bearer cheques from Savory & Co., their employers, who were stockbrokers, and paid them into branches of Lloyds Bank—Perkins into an account at Wallington, and Smith into his wife's account at Redhill and subsequently at Weybridge. The clerks paid in the cheques at other branches, using the 'branch credit' system, with the result that branches in which the accounts were kept did not receive particulars of the cheques. Neither bank made inquiries concerning the employers of Smith and Perkins. The frauds were discovered and Savory & Co. brought an action against the bank for conversion. The bank pleaded Sect. 82 of the Bills of Exchange Act, and denied negligence, since the 'branch credit' system was in common use by bankers. At first instance judgment was given for the bank, but this was reversed on appeal and the bank then appealed to the House of Lords. *Held*—The appeal should be dismissed as the bank had not been able to rebut the charge of negligence. With regard to the defence under Sect. 82, the court held that, although the branch credit system had been in use for forty years, it had 'an inherent and obvious defect which no reasonable banker could fail to observe'. Lord Wright said: 'Where a new customer is employed in some position which involves his handling, and having the opportunity of stealing, his employer's cheques, the bankers fail in taking adequate precautions if they do not ask the name of his employers. ... Otherwise they cannot guard against the danger known to them of his paying in cheques stolen from his employers.' This is not the ordinary practice of bankers but that does not acquit them of negligence. Such inquiries should be made on the opening of an account even though they could turn out to be useless if the customer changed his employment immediately afterwards.

(790) *Lumsden & Co.* v. *London Trustee Savings Bank*, [1971] 1 Lloyd's Rep. 114

Stockbrokers employed a temporary accountant called Mr Blake. Blake opened an account with the bank in the fictitious name of 'Brown' and managed to divert to that account a sum of £5541 paid out by his employer ostensibly to other stockbrokers. When opening the account he gave the bank the name and address of a spurious referee and subsequently made up and submitted his own reference. The bank made no check on 'Brown's' business address nor did they obtain independent confirmation of his identity. The bank manager did ask for the address of the spurious referee's own bankers but drew no adverse conclusions when this information was not given to him. The stockbrokers claimed the value of the cheques from the bank. *Held*—by Donaldson, J.—that the bank was guilty of negligence and was not protected by Sect. 4(1) of the Cheques Act, 1957. However, the stockbrokers could only recover 90 per cent of the damages which would otherwise have been awarded because they had drawn their cheques in a negligent fashion, often omitting the initials of the payee; this had facilitated Blake's fraud.

(*Note:* this is the first reported case in which damages for conversion have been reduced by appointment under the Law Reform (Contributory Negligence) Act, 1945.)

(791) *Orbit Mining and Trading Co. Ltd* v. *Westminster Bank*, [1962] 3 All E.R. 565

The plaintiff company had an account with the Midland Bank, and cheques drawn on this account had to be signed by two directors. One of these directors, A, was often abroad and had been in the habit of signing cheque forms in blank before going abroad, assuming that the other director authorised to sign, B, would use the cheques only for trading purposes.

B added his signature to three cheque forms and inserted the word 'cash' between the printed words 'Pay' and 'or order' and passed the cheques for collection to the Westminster Bank Ltd, where he had a private account. The Westminster Bank collected the sums due on the cheques and B used the money for his private purposes. The Westminster Bank did not know that B was connected with the plaintiff company and his signature on the cheques was, in any case, illegible. Each cheque form was crossed generally and was stamped 'for and on behalf of' the company under which appeared the signatures of A and B. *Held*—The three instruments in this case were not cheques, but were documents issued by a customer of a banker intended to enable a person to obtain payment from the banker within Sect. 4(2) of the Cheques Act, 1957, and since the bank had acted without negligence it was entitled to the protection of the Act in respect of the collection of an instrument to which the customer had no title.

(792) *Marfani & Co.* v. *Midland Bank*, [1967] 3 All E.R. 967

The managing director of the plaintiff company signed a cheque for £3000 drawn by the office manager Kureshy payable to Eliaszade and gave it to Kureshy for despatch. However, Kureshy opened an account with the cheque at the Midland Bank by falsely representing that he was Eliaszade and that he was about to set up a restaurant business. The bank asked for references and Kureshy gave the names of two satisfactory customers of the bank, and one of these references indicated, while on a visit to the bank, that Kureshy, whom he knew as Eliaszade, would be a satisfactory customer. The second referee did not reply to the bank's inquiry. Kureshy then drew a cheque for £2950 on the account and absconded. It appeared that the bank did not ask to see Kureshy's passport and his spelling of Eliaszade was inconsistent with the spelling on the cheque. Further the bank officials did not notice the similarity in handwriting between the cheque and the indorsement. The plaintiff company sued the bank for conversion and it was held that the bank had not fallen short of the standard of ordinary practice of careful bankers and was protected by Sect. 4 of the Cheques Act, 1957.

(793) *Westminster Bank Ltd* v. *Zang*, [1965] 1 All E.R. 1023

Mr Zang, having lost heavily at seven-card rummy, drew a cheque for £1000 payable to 'J. Tilley or order', receiving from Mr Tilley £1000 in cash to pay part of his gambling debts. The £1000 cash belonged to Tilley's Autos Ltd, a company of which Mr Tilley was managing director. Tilley took Zang's cheque to his bank, asking them to credit the account of the company, which was overdrawn. Tilley did not indorse the cheque before paying it in. The cheque was dishonoured and the bank returned it to Tilley so that he could sue Zang. The action was commenced but discontinued and the cheque was returned to the bank who sued Zang as holder in due course or holder for value of the cheque. The bank failed in its claim. The reasons given in the Court of Appeal were—

(i) as the payee (Tilley) had asked the bank to credit the cheque to the account of a third party (Tilley's Autos), the cheque had not been received for collection within the meaning of the Cheques Act, 1957, Sect. 2, and as the cheque was not indorsed the bank were not 'holders' (*per* Denning, M.R.);

(ii) the cheque had been received for collection but the bank had not given value, so that Sect. 2 did not apply (*per* Salmon, L.J.);

(iii) the cheque had been received for collection but the bank in returning the cheque to Tilley lost their lien and consequently the protection of Sect. 2 (*per* Danckwerts, L.J.).

In the House of Lords their Lordships unanimously held that the cheque had been received for collection, but the bank had not given value.

The company's account was overdrawn, but it was hard to see how, by crediting the cheque to the account and reducing the overdraft, the bank gave value for it, because in fact interest had been charged on the original amount of the overdraft unreduced by the cheque. There was no agreement express or implied to honour the cheques of Tilley's Autos before they had been cleared, and consideration could not, therefore, be established in this way.

(794) *Barclays Bank Ltd* v. *Astley Industrial Trust, Ltd*, [1970] 1 All E.R. 719

Mabons Garage Ltd were motor dealers who banked with the plaintiffs and arranged hire-purchase transactions with the defendants. In November, 1964, the plaintiffs gave Mabons a temporary overdraft up to £2000 and on 18 November, when the account was £1910 overdrawn, cheques for £2673 drawn by Mabons were presented for payment. The bank manager agreed to pay them only after receiving an assurance from the directors of Mabons that cheques for £2850 in favour of Mabons and drawn by the defendants would be paid into the account the next day. On 19 November, when Mabons overdraft stood at £4673, two further cheques for £345 drawn by Mabons were presented for payment and the bank manager refused to pay these until he had received the defendants' cheques for £2850. On 20 November the defendants stopped their cheques which it appeared they had been induced to draw by the fraud of Mabons' directors. In an action by the bank claiming to be holders in due course of the cheques, the defendants alleged that the bank had not taken them for value. *Held*—by Milmo, J.—that the bank was holder in due cause since—

(*a*) a banker who takes a cheque as agent for collection can also be a holder in due course under Sect. 2 of the Cheques Act, 1957;

(*b*) the bank was a holder in due cause. They were holders because they had a lien on the cheques and were entitled to hold them pending payment of the overdraft. The value was the overdraft of £4673. An antecedent debt would support a bill of exchange.

The bank was entitled to recover the amount of the cheques from the defendants.

THE NATURE OF CRIME

(795) *Woolmington* v. *Director of Public Prosecutions*, [1935] A.C. 462

W had been charged with the murder of his wife. He had, on his own admission, shot her but said in his defence that the gun had gone off accidentally. The judge told the jury that so long as the prosecution had shown that the accused had caused the death malice was presumed and that the accused must prove that the killing was an accident. The jury convicted W who appealed to what was then the Court of Criminal Appeal where his conviction was upheld. However, on appeal to the House of Lords his conviction was quashed. 'Throughout the web of English Criminal Law one golden thread is always to be seen, that it is the duty of the prosecution to prove the prisoner's guilt subject to what I have already said as to the defence of insanity and subject also to any statutory exceptions. If, at the end of and on the whole of the case, there is a reasonable doubt created by the evidence given by either the prosecution or the prisoner, as to whether the prisoner killed the deceased with a malicious intention, the prosecution has not made out the case and the prisoner is entitled to an acquittal.' (*per* Viscount Sankey, L.C.)

(796) *Shaw* v. *Director of Public Prosecutions*, [1961] 2 All E.R. 446

S published a booklet called '*The Ladies' Directory*' which contained the names and addresses of prostitutes. The entries gave telephone numbers and indicated that they were offering their services for sexual intercourse and some of them for the practice of sexual perversions. S was convicted of conspiracy to corrupt public morals and his appeal eventually reached the House of Lords. His appeal was dismissed and his conviction affirmed. However, Lord Reid, in a strong dissenting judgment, said that in his view there was no such general offence known to the law as conspiracy to corrupt public morals and the court in convicting S of it was creating a new crime on the basis of public mischief which is the criminal law equivalent of public policy. He thought that if the courts had stopped creating new heads of public policy in, for example, the civil law of contract, then they certainly should refrain from doing so in criminal law.

(797) *Hill* v. *Baxter*, [1958] 1 All E.R. 42

The defendant had been charged with dangerous driving and failing to conform with a traffic sign under Sects 11 and 49(b) of the Road Traffic Act, 1930, respectively. He said in his defence that he had been unconscious at the time because a sudden illness had overtaken him. The magistrates accepted his defence and dismissed the charges and the prosecutor appealed. The appeal was allowed and the defendant therefore convicted. 'I agree that there may be cases where the circumstances are such that the accused could not really be said to be driving at all. Suppose he had a stroke or an epileptic fit, both instances of what may properly be called acts of God; he might well be in the driver's seat even with his hands on the wheel, but in such a state of unconsciousness that he could not be said to be driving. A blow from a stone or an attack by a swarm of bees I think introduces some conception akin to *novus actus interveniens*. In this case, however, I am content to say that the evidence falls far short of what would justify a court holding that this man was in some automatous state'. (*per* Lord Goddard, C.J.)

(798) *Attorney-General for Northern Ireland* v. *Gallagher*, [1963] A.C. 349

G was convicted of murdering his wife. In his defence he pleaded insanity under the M'Naghten Rules or, as an alternative, that he was too drunk at the time to form the necessary intent for murder so that he was only guilty of manslaughter. G had shown intention to kill his wife before taking the drink. The case eventually reached the House of Lords where Lord Denning gave a useful summary of the effect of drunkenness when he said: '1. If a man is charged with an offence in which a specific intention is essential (as in murder, though not in manslaughter), then evidence of drunkenness, which renders him incapable of forming that intention is an answer . . . 2. If a man by drinking brings on a distinct disease of the mind such as *delirium tremens*, so that he is temporarily insane within the M'Naghten Rules, that is to say, he does not at the time know what he is doing or that it is wrong, then he has a defence on the ground of insanity. . . .' However, G's original conviction for murder was upheld because he did not fit the above categories. As Lord Denning said: 'My Lords, I think the law on this point should take a clear stand. If a man, whilst sane and sober, forms an intention to kill and makes preparation for it, knowing it is a wrong thing to do, and then gets himself drunk so as to give himself Dutch courage to do the killing, and whilst drunk carries out his intention, he cannot rely on this self-induced drunkenness as a defence to a charge of murder, nor even as reducing it to manslaughter.'

(799) *R* v. *Lipman*, [1969] 3 All E.R. 410

L was charged with murder of a girl but convicted of manslaughter. Both he and the girl had taken LSD together in her room and L said that while under the influence of the drug he had an illusion of being attacked by snakes and that he must have killed the girl during this time. The girl had received two severe blows on the head but the immediate cause of her death was asphyxia as a result of having part of a sheet pushed down her mouth. The Court of Appeal affirmed the conviction, saying that when the killing results from the unlawful act of the accused, no specific intent was to be proved to convict of manslaughter and mental states which are self-induced by drink or drugs are no defence to a charge of manslaughter.

(800) *R* v. *Charlson*, [1955] 1 All E.R. 859

C had been charged with unlawfully and maliciously causing grievous bodily harm. He hit his small son with a mallett and then threw him out of a window. He could have been suffering from a cerebral tumour at the time and certainly there was no obvious motive or rage which would have caused him to do as he did. He said in defence that he was unconscious at the time. He was acquitted by the jury both on the charge mentioned above and on the more serious charges of causing grievous bodily harm with intent to do so and with intent to murder.

(801) *R* v. *Instan*, [1893] 1 Q.B. 450

Instan lived with her 73-year-old aunt. The aunt seemed to be in reasonable health until shortly before her death. During the 12 days prior to her death she had gangrene in her leg and could not look after herself or summon help. That she was in this condition was a matter known only to Instan. It appeared that she had not given her aunt any food nor had she tried to obtain medical or nursing aid. Following the death of her aunt she was accused of manslaughter and convicted. The Court for Crown Cases Reserved (as it then was) affirmed the conviction. 'The prisoner was under a moral obligation to the deceased from which arose a legal duty towards her; that legal duty the prisoner has wilfully and deliberately left unperformed, with the consequence that there has been an acceleration of the death of the deceased owing to the non-performance of that legal duty. It is unnecessary to say more than that upon the evidence this conviction was most properly arrived at'. (*per* Lord Coleridge, C.J.)

(802) *R* v. *Hayward*, (1908) 21 Cox 692

H came home one night in a violent state of excitement. He had said previously that he was going to 'give his wife something' when she returned home. When she arrived there were sounds of quarrelling and soon afterwards the wife ran out of the house followed by H. The wife fell onto the road and H kicked her on her left arm. She died and the medical examination showed that the kick was not the cause of her death. She was in good health apart from thymus gland trouble, on which the medical evidence was that a person with such a condition might die from the combined effects of fright, strong emotion and physical exertion. H was charged with manslaughter at Maidstone Assizes and found guilty. Ridley, J., said that the abnormal state of the deceased's health did not affect the question whether the prisoner knew or did not know of it, if it were proved to the satisfaction of the jury that the death was accelerated by the prisoner's illegal act.

(803) *R* v. *Martin*, (1881) 8 Q.B.D. 54

Just before a theatrical performance came to an end M, intending to terrify people leaving the theatre, put out lights on the staircase which he knew a large number of people would use when leaving the theatre. He then placed an iron bar across an exit door. As a result of his actions several people were hurt as they tried to leave the theatre. M was convicted on a charge of unlawfully and maliciously inflicting grievous bodily harm. 'The prisoner must be taken to have intended the natural consequences of that which he did. He acted "unlawfully and maliciously", not that he had any personal malice against the particular individuals injured, but in the sense of doing an unlawful act calculated to injure, and by which others were in fact injured. Just as in the case of a man who unlawfully fires a gun among a crowd, it is murder if one of the crowd is thereby killed. The prisoner was most properly convicted'. (*per* Lord Coleridge, C.J.)

(804) *R* v. *Jordan*, (1956) 40 Cr. App. R. 152

J stabbed his victim in the stomach; the victim was rushed to hospital where the wound was stitched, but he died a few days later. J was convicted of murder at Leeds Assizes. On his appeal he brought forward additional medical evidence which revealed that the stab wound had penetrated the intestine in two places but that these wounds were in the main healed at the time of death. A hospital doctor had administered terramycin to prevent infection but the victim was intolerant to it and its use was stopped. Two new witnesses said also that abnormal quantities of liquid had been given intravenously so that the victim's lungs became waterlogged and pulmonary oedema resulted. The Court of Criminal Appeal quashed J's conviction. 'It is sufficient to point out here that this was not normal treatment. Not only one feature, but two separate and independent features, of treatment were, in the opinion of the doctors, palpably wrong and these produced the symptoms discovered at the post-mortem examination which were the direct and immediate cause of death, namely, the pneumonia resulting from the condition of oedema which was found.' (*per* Hallett, J.)

(805) *R* v. *Smith*, [1959] 2 All E.R. 193

The facts were that the victim of a barrack room brawl who was stabbed twice with a bayonet was dropped twice by those trying to get him to hospital and given artificial respiration when he got there although he was wounded in the lungs so that this was not advisable. Nevertheless these events were held not to break the chain of causation. 'However, it must be said that the events in this case, including the death of Private Creed who was the victim, all occurred within a period of some two hours. . . . a man is stabbed in the back, his lung is pierced and haemorrhage results; two hours later he dies of haemorrhage from that wound; in the interval there is no time for a careful examination, and the treatment given turns in the light of subsequent knowledge to have been inappropriate and, indeed, harmful. In those circumstances no reasonable jury or court could, properly directed, in our view possibly come to any other conclusion that the death resulted from the original wound. Accordingly the court dismisses this appeal.' (*per* Lord Parker, C.J.)

(806) *Thabo-Meli* v. *The Queen*, [1954] 1 All E.R. 373

In this case the accused persons planned to kill the victim in a hut and thereafter to roll his body over a cliff so that it would appear that he had died an accidental death. The victim was made unconscious in the hut by the attack and thinking him to be dead, the accused persons rolled him over a cliff. There was evidence that the victim was not in fact killed in the hut but that he died on account of exposure at the bottom of the cliff. 'The point of law which was raised in this case can be simply stated. It is said that two acts were necessary and were separable; first, the attack in the hut; and, secondly, the placing of the body outside afterwards. It is said that, while the first act was accompanied by *mens rea*, it was not the cause of death; but that the second act, while it was the cause of death, was not accompanied by *mens rea*; and on that ground it is said that the accused are not guilty of any crime, except perhaps culpable homicide.

'It appears to their Lordships impossible to divide up what was really one transaction in this way. There is no doubt that the accused set out to do all these acts in order to achieve their plan and as part of their plan; and it is much too refined a ground of judgment to say that, because they were under a misapprehension at one stage and thought that their guilty purpose had been achieved before in fact it was achieved, therefore they are to escape the penalties of the law. . . .' (*per* Lord Reid.)

The appeal of the accused persons was therefore dismissed.

(807) *Chandler* v. *Director of Public Prosecutions*, [1964] 3 All E.R. 142

In this case the accused impeded the operation of an airfield at Wethersfield. Their object was to demonstrate against nuclear armament. 'In the result, I am of opinion that if a person's direct purpose in approaching or entering is to cause obstruction or interference, and such obstruction or interference is found to be a prejudice to the defence dispositions of the State, an offence is thereby committed, and his indirect purposes or his motives in bringing about the obstruction or interference do not alter the nature or content of his offence. . . . Is a man guilty of an offence, it was asked, if he rushes onto an airfield intending to stop an airplane taking off because he knows that a time-bomb has been concealed on board? I should say that he is not, for the reason that his direct purpose is not to bring about an obstruction but to prevent a disaster, the obstruction that he causes being merely a means of securing that end.' (*per* Lord Radcliffe.)

(808) *R* v. *Levett*, (1638) 79 E.R. 1064

L and his wife were in bed and asleep at night when their servant, having procured without their knowledge the services of a Frances Freeman to help her about the house, let Frances out at about midnight. She thought she heard thieves at the door offering to break in and in fear she ran to Mr and Mrs Levett and told them that she thought thieves were breaking down the door. On receiving this information Mr Levett arose and fetched a drawn rapier. At the same time the servant hid Frances Freeman in the buttery in case Mr Levett found her. Mrs Levett caught a glimpse of Frances Freeman in the buttery and turned to her husband in great fear and said: 'Here they be that would undo us'. Hearing this Mr Levett, not knowing that Frances was in the buttery, rushed in with a drawn rapier. It was dark and he thrust his rapier ahead giving Frances a mortal wound in the left breast from which she instantly died. It was resolved by the court that it was not manslaughter for what Mr Levett did he did ignorantly without intention of hurt to Frances.

(809) *R* v. *Bailey*, (1800) 168 E.R. 651

Bailey, who was the captain of a ship, fired at another ship on the high seas without any justification and wounded one of the sailors on that other ship. He was charged under an act of Parliament which made such a shooting on the high seas triable and punishable in this country. The following extract from the judgment of the court is relevant: 'It was then insisted that the prisoner could not be found guilty of the offence with which he was charged, because the Act of 39 Geo. 3, c.37 upon which . . . the prisoner was indicted at this Admiralty Sessions, . . . only received the Royal Assent on 10 May, 1799, and the fact charged in the indictment happened on 27 June in the same year when the prisoner could not know that any such Act existed (his ship the *Langley* being at the time upon the coast of Africa). Lord Eldon told the jury that he was of opinion that he was, in strict law, guilty within the statutes . . . though if the facts laid were proved, though he could not then know that the Act of 39 Geo. 3, c.37 had passed, and that ignorance of that fact, could in no otherwise affect the case, than that it might be the means of recommending him to a merciful consideration elsewhere should he be found guilty. . . .'

(*Note:* at the next Admiralty Sessions the prisoner was pardoned.)

(810) *Sweet* v. *Parsley*, [1969] 1 All E.R. 347

The magistrates had convicted Sweet of being concerned in the management of premises which were used for the purpose of smoking cannabis or cannabis resin, contrary to Sect. 5(b) of the Dangerous Drugs Act, 1965. The evidence showed that she had no knowledge whatever that the house was being used for the purpose of smoking cannabis or cannabis resin. She visited the premises only occasionally to collect letters and rent and though sometimes she stayed overnight, generally she did not. Section 5 of the 1965 Act provides 'if a person (*a*) being the occupier of any premises, permits those premises to be used for the purpose of smoking cannabis or cannabis resin or of dealing in cannabis or cannabis resin (whether by sale or otherwise); or (*b*) is concerned in the management of any premises used for any such purposes aforesaid; he shall be guilty of an offence under the Act'. The House of Lords, after holding that in spite of the wording of the Act *mens rea* must be implied, found that there was no *mens rea* in the accused in this case and that therefore her appeal should be allowed and her conviction quashed.

(811) *R* v. *Tolson*, (1889) 23 Q.B.D. 168

Martha Ann Tolson, who married in September, 1880, was deserted by her husband in December, 1881. She made enquiries and learned from his elder brother that he had been lost at sea in a ship bound for America which sank with all hands. Believing herself to be a widow, she went quite openly through a ceremony of marriage on 10 January, 1887, with Y who was fully aware of the circumstances. It was held that she could not be convicted of bigamy under Sect. 57 of the Offences Against the Person Act, 1861, even though the opening part of that section says: 'Whosoever, being married, shall marry any other person during the life of the former husband or wife . . . shall be guilty of a felony. . . .' She had no *mens rea*. The object of Parliament was not to treat the marriage of widows as an act to be if possible prevented as presumably immoral. Mrs Tolson's conduct was not immoral but perfectly natural and legitimate. A statute may relate to such subject matter and may be so framed as to make an act criminal whether there has been any intention to break the law or not. In other cases a more reasonable construction requires the implication into the statute that a guilty mind is required.

(812) *Alphacell* v. *Woodward*, [1972] 2 All E.R. 475

A Ltd was the owner of paper-making mills. In the course of manufacture effluent passed into two tanks on the banks of a river. Pumps were used to remove the effluent from the tanks but it was inevitable that if the pumps failed the effluent would enter the river and pollute it. As a result of foliage blocking the pump inlets such an overflow occurred and A Ltd was charged with 'causing' polluting matter to enter the river under Sect. 2(1) of the Rivers (Prevention of Pollution) Act, 1951. It was *held*—by the House of Lords—that they were guilty of that offence even though they had not been negligent. The intervening act of a trespass or act of God would have been a defence but there was no such trespass or act of God in this case.

(813) *Cundy* v. *Le Cocq*, (1884) 13 Q.B.D. 207

C, who was a licensed victualler, sold liquor to a person who was drunk though C did not know this. He was, however, convicted of unlawfully selling liquor to a drunken person contrary to Sect. 13 of the Licensing Act, 1872, which provided that: 'If any licensed person . . . sells any intoxicating liquor to a drunken person he shall be liable to a penalty. . . .' It was *held*—by Stephen, J.—that knowledge of the condition of the person to whom the liquor was sold was not necessary to constitute the offence. 'Against this view we have had quoted the maxim that in every criminal offence there must be a guilty mind; but I do not think that maxim has so wide an application as it is sometimes considered to have. In oldtime, and as applicable to the common law or to earlier statutes, the maxim may have been of general application; but a difference has arisen owing to the greater precision of modern statutes. It is impossible now, . . . to apply the maxim generally to all statutes, and the substance of all the reported cases is that it is necessary to look at the object of each Act that is under consideration to see whether and how far knowledge is of the essence of the offence created. Here, as I have already pointed out, the object of this part of the Act is to prevent the sale of intoxicating liquor to drunken persons, and it is perfectly natural to carry that out by throwing on the publican the responsibility of determining whether the person supplied comes within that category. I think, therefore, the conviction was right and must be affirmed.'

(814) *R* v. *Cunningham*, [1957] 2 All E.R. 412

C was convicted of unlawfully and maliciously causing to be taken by Sarah Wade a certain noxious thing, namely, coal gas, so as to endanger her life contrary to Sect. 23 of the Offences Against the Person Act, 1861. C had gone into an empty house and torn away the gas meter in the cellar in order to take the money it contained with the intention of stealing that money. However coal gas poured out of the pipe he had fractured and percolated into the house next door where it almost asphyxiated the occupant, Sarah Wade. C appealed and his appeal was allowed. '. . . we think it is incorrect to say that the word "malicious" in a statutory offence merely means wicked. We think the judge was, in effect, telling the jury that if they were satisfied that the appellant wickedly—and he had clearly acted wickedly in stealing the gas meter and its contents—they ought to find that he had acted maliciously in causing the gas to be taken by Mrs Wade so as thereby to endanger her life.

'In our view it should have been left to the jury to decide whether, even if the appellant did not intend to injure Mrs Wade, he foresaw that the removal of the gas meter might cause injury to someone but nevertheless removed it. We are unable to say that a reasonable jury, properly directed as to the meaning of the word "maliciously" in the context of Sect. 23, would without doubt have convicted.

'In these circumstances this court has no alternative but to allow the appeal and quash the conviction' (*per* Byrne, J.)

(815) *Gaumont British Distributors Ltd* v. *Henry*, [1939] 2 K.B. 717

Gaumont British were charged under Sect. 1(a) of the Dramatic and Musical Performers' Protection Act, 1925, with knowingly making a record of a musical work without the written consent of the performers. No consent had actually been given but GB said, and it was accepted, that they had never thought about the question of consent. Nevertheless GB was convicted and appealed. The appeal was allowed. 'I desire to add emphatically that no colour can be obtained from this case, or from the argument, or from any opinion which is present to my mind, that the wholesome and fundamental principle *ignorantia juris neminem excusat* is in any degree to be modified or departed from. . . . . I should be very sorry, directly or indirectly, even to appear to add any colour to the suggestion, if it were made—as I do not think it is—that in circumstances of this kind ignorance of the law might excuse. The way in which the topic of the appellants' knowledge came in was solely with reference to the words 'knowingly makes any record without the consent in writing of the performers', and the contention was a contention of fact. According to a true view of the evidence of fact in this case it was incorrect to say that the appellants did knowingly without the consent in writing of the performers that which was done'. (*per* Lord Hewart, C.J.)

(816) *R* v. *Lowe*, [1973] 1 All E.R. 805

Lowe was charged under Sect 1. of the Children and Young Persons Act of 1933 as being a person who had the charge of a child and wilfully neglected it in a manner likely to cause it unnecessary suffering or injury to health. L's case was that the child's critical condition arose after he had told the woman he was living with, who was the child's mother, to take the child to a doctor and that she later falsely told him that she had done so. He was convicted and appealed. 'It did not matter what he ought to have realized as the possible consequences of his failure to call a doctor; the sole question was whether his failure to do so was deliberate and thereby occasioned the results referred to in Sect. 1(1) of the Act of 1933. We are quite satisfied that the conviction on count 2 was justified both on the law and the facts . . .' (per Phillimore, L.J.)

(817) *Somerset* v. *Wade*, [1894] 1 Q.B. 574

Wade was charged with permitting drunkenness under Sect. 13 of the Licensing Act, 1872, which provides that if any licensed person permits drunkenness, or any violence, quarrelsome or riotous conduct to take place on his premises or sells any intoxicating liquor to any drunken person, he commits an offence. A drunken woman was actually found on Wade's premises but it was accepted that Wade did not know that she was drunk. The charge having been dismissed the prosecutor appealed. The appeal of the prosecutor failed and Wade was not convicted. '. . . but the word "suffers" is not distinguishable from "permits", which is the word used in Sect. 13, the section now before us. In a case where the defendant does not know that the person who was on his premises was in fact drunk, he cannot be said to permit drunkenness. In the present case the justices have found that the respondent did not know that the woman was drunk and there was evidence to support that finding.' (per Mathew, J.)

(*Note:* in this case Mathew, J. was prepared to say that the word 'suffers' was the same as 'permits', i.e. a word requiring *mens rea* in the accused.)

(818) *Griffiths* v. *Studebakers Ltd*, [1924] 1 K.B. 102

Studebakers were holders of a limited trade licence and were charged with having used on a public road a motor car carrying more than two persons in addition to the driver, which was an offence under the Road Vehicles (Trade Licences) Regulations, 1922. At the time of the alleged offence the car was being driven by a servant of the respondents. He was in the course of his employment because he was giving a trial run to prospective purchasers of the car but by carrying more than two passengers he was infringing the express orders of his employers. The employers were convicted and appealed to the Divisional Court. 'It would be fantastic to suppose that a manufacturer, whether a limited company, a firm, or an individual, would, even if he could, always show cars to prospective purchasers himself; and it would defeat the scheme of this legislation if it were open to an employer, whether a company, or a firm, or an individual, to say that although the car was being used under the limited licence in contravention of the conditions upon which it was granted: "My hand was not the hand that drove the car." On these facts there ought to have been a conviction of the respondents and also the driver as aider and abettor.' Thus the conviction of Studebakers was affirmed by the Divisional Court.

(819) *James and Son Ltd* v. *Smee*, [1955] 1 Q.B. 78

Under the Motor Vehicles (Construction and Use) Regulations in force at the time the alleged offence occurred the braking system of a vehicle or trailer used on the road had to be in efficient working order and further anyone who used or caused or permitted to be used on the road a motor vehicle or trailer where the braking system was not in efficient working order was liable to a fine. James and Son Ltd sent out in the charge of their employee a lorry and trailer the braking system of which was in efficient working order. However, during the course of his rounds the employee had to disconnect the braking system of the trailer and forgot to connect it up again. James and Son were convicted of 'permitting to be used' the trailer in contravention of the regulations then in force. However, their appeal was allowed by the Divisional Court. 'In other words, it is said that in committing the offence of the user in contravention he at the same time made his master guilty of the offence of permitting such user. In our opinion this contention is highly artificial and divorced from reality. We prefer the view that before the company can be held guilty of permitting a user in contravention of the regulations it must be proved that some person for whose criminal acts the company is responsible permitted as opposed to committed the offence. There was no such evidence in the present case.' (*per* Parker J.)

(820) *Vane* v. *Yiannopoullos*, [1965] A.C. 486

Section 22(1) of the Licensing Act, 1961, which was relevant in this case provided 'If—(a) the holder of a Justices' On-licence knowingly sells or supplies intoxicating liquor to persons to whom he is not permitted by the conditions of the licence to sell or supply it . . . he shall be guilty of an offence.' Y was the licensee of a restaurant and had been granted a justices on-licence subject to a condition that intoxicating liquor was to be sold only to those who ordered meals. He employed a waitress and he instructed her to serve drinks only to customers who ordered meals but on one occasion whilst Y was in another part of the restaurant the waitress did serve drinks to two youths who had not in fact ordered a meal. Y did not know of that sale. He was charged with knowingly selling intoxicating liquor on the premises to persons to whom he was not permitted to sell contrary to Sect. 22(1)(a) of the Act. The magistrates dismissed the information and the prosecutor appealed eventually to the House of Lords. The appeal of the prosecutor was dismissed and there was therefore no conviction of Y. 'So far, however, as the present case is concerned, I feel no doubt that the decision of the Divisional Court was right. There was clearly no "knowledge" in the strict sense proved against the licensee: I agree also with the Lord Chief Justice that there was no sufficient evidence of such "delegation" on his part of his powers, duties and responsibilities to render him liable on that ground. I would therefore without hesitation dismiss the appeal.' (*per* Lord Evershed.)

(821) *Ferguson* v. *Weaving*, [1951] 1 All E.R. 412

Section 4 of the Licensing Act, 1921, which was relevant in this case, made it an offence for any person, except during permitted hours, to consume intoxicating liquor on any licensed premises. In a large public house of which W was the manager customers were found consuming liquor outside permitted hours and were convicted of an offence under the section. The evidence did not show that W knew that the liquor was being consumed. It had in fact been supplied to customers by waiters employed by her who had neglected to collect the glasses in time. A charge against W of aiding and abetting the customers' offence was dismissed and the prosecutor appealed. The appeal was dismissed. 'There can be no doubt that this court has more than once laid it down in clear terms that before a person can be convicted of aiding and abetting the commission of an offence he must at least know the essential matters which constitute the offence. . . .' (*per* Lord Goddard, C.J.)

Index to Statutes

Index to Cases

General Index